ST/ESA/STAT/SER.R/38

Department of Economic and Social Affairs
Département des affaires économiques et sociales

2007
Demographic Yearbook
Annuaire démographique

Fifty-ninth issue/Cinquante-neuvième édition

United Nations/Nations Unies
New York, 2009

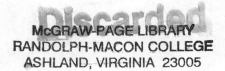

The Department of Economic and Social Affairs of the United Nations Secretariat is a vital interface between global policies in the economic, social and environmental spheres and national action. The Department works in three main interlinked areas: (i) it compiles, generates and analyses a wide range of economic, social and environmental data and information on which States Members of the United Nations draw to review common problems and to take stock of policy options; (ii) it facilitates the negotiations of Member States in many intergovernmental bodies on joint courses of action to address ongoing or emerging global challenges; and (iii) it advises interested Governments on the ways and means of translating policy frameworks developed in United Nations conferences and summits into programmes at the country level and, through technical assistance, helps build national capacities.

Le Département des affaires économiques et sociales du Secrétariat de l'Organisation des Nations Unies sert de relais entre les orientations arrêtées au niveau international dans les domaines économiques, sociaux et environnementaux et les politiques exécutées à l'échelon national. Il intervient dans trois grands domaines liés les uns aux autres : i) il compile, produit et analyse une vaste gamme de données et d'éléments d'information sur des questions économiques, sociales et environnementales dont les États Membres de l'Organisation se servent pour examiner des problèmes communs et évaluer les options qui s'offrent à eux; ii) il facilite les négociations entre les États Membres dans de nombreux organes intergouvernementaux sur les orientations à suivre de façon collective afin de faire face aux problèmes mondiaux existants ou en voie d'apparition; iii) il conseille les gouvernements intéressés sur la façon de transposer les orientations politiques arrêtées à l'occasion des conférences et sommets des Nations Unies en programmes exécutables au niveau national et aide à renforcer les capacités nationales au moyen de programmes d'assistance technique.

NOTE

Symbols of United Nations documents are composed of capital letters combined with figures. Mention of such a symbol indicates reference to a United Nations document.

The designations employed and the presentation of material in this publication do not imply the expression of any opinion whatsoever on the part of the Secretariat of the United Nations concerning the legal status of any country, territory, city or area, or of its authorities, or concerning the delimitation of its frontiers or boundaries.

Where the designation "country or area" appears in the headings of tables, it covers countries, territories, cities or areas. In prior issues of this publication, where the designation "country" appears in the headings of tables, it should be interpreted to cover countries, territories, cities or areas.

NOTE

Les cotes des documents de l'Organisation des Nations Unies se composent de lettres majuscules et de chiffres. La simple mention d'une cote dans un texte signifie qu'il s'agit d'un document de l'Organisation.

Les appellations employées dans cette publication et la présentation des données qui y figurent n'impliquent de la part du Secrétariat de l'Organisation des Nations Unies aucune prise de position quant au statut juridique des pays, territoires, villes ou zones, ou de leurs autorités, ni quant au tracé de leurs frontières ou limites.

L'appellation "pays ou zone" figurant dans les titres des rubriques des tableaux désigne des pays, des territoires, des villes ou des zones. L'appellation "pays" figurant dans certaines rubriques des tableaux de numéros antérieurs de cette publication doit être interprétée comme désignant des pays, des territoires, des villes ou des zones.

ST/ESA/STAT/SER.R/38

UNITED NATIONS PUBLICATION
Sales number: E/F.10.XIII.1

PUBLICATION DES NATIONS UNIES
Numéro de vente: E/F.10.XIII.1

ISBN 978-92-1-051102-5
ISSN 0082-8041

Topics of the Demographic Yearbook series: 1948 - 2007

Sujets des diverses éditions de l'Annuaire démographique: 1948 - 2007

Year Année	Sales No. - Numéro de vente	Issue - Edition	Special topic - Sujet spécial
1948	49.XIII.1	First-Première	General demography-Démographie générale
1949-50	51.XIII.1	Second-Deuxième	Natality statistics-Statistiques de la natalité
1951	52.XIII.1	Third-Trosième	Mortality statistics-Statistiques de la mortalité
1952	53.XIII.1	Fourth-Quatrième	Population distribution-Répartition de la population
1953	54.XIII.1	Fifth-Cinquième	General demography-Démographie générale
1954	55.XIII.1	Sixth-Sixième	Natality statistics -Statistiques de la natalité
1955	56.XIII.1	Seventh-Septième	Population censuses-Recensement de population
1956	57.XIII.1	Eighth-Huitième	Ethnic and economic characteristics of population-Caractéristiques ethniques et économiques de la population
1957	58.XIII.1	Ninth-Neuvième	Mortality statistics- Statistiques de la mortalité
1958	59.XIII.1	Tenth-Dixième	Marriage and divorce statistics- Statistiques de la nuptialité et de la divortialité
1959	60.XIII.1	Eleventh-Onzième	Natality statistics- Statistiques de la natalité
1960	61.XIII.1	Twelfth-Douzième	Population trends- l' évolution de la population
1961	62.XIII.1	Thirteenth-Treizième	Mortality Statistics- Statistiques de la mortalité
1962	63.XIII.1	Fourteenth-Quatorzième	Population census statistics I- Statistiques des recensements de population I
1963	64.XIII.1	Fifteenth-Quinzième	Population census statistics II- Statistiques des recensements de population II
1964	65.XIII.1	Sixteenth-Seizième	Population census statistics III- Statistiques des recensements de population III
1965	66.XIII.1	Seventeenth-Dix-septième	Natality statistics- Statistiques de la natalité
1966	67.XIII.1	Eighteenth-Dix-huitième	Mortality statistics I- Statistiques de la mortalité I
1967	E/F.68.XIII.1	Nineteenth-Dix-neuvième	Mortality statistics II - Statistiques de la mortalité II
1968	E/F.69.XIII.1	Twentieth-Vingtième	Marriage and divorce statistics-Statistiques de la nuptialité et de la divortialité
1969	E/F.70.XIII.1	Twenty-first-Vingt et unième	Natality statistics-Statistiques de la natalité
1970	E/F.71.XIII.1	Twenty-second-Vingt-deuxième	Population trends-l' évolution de la population
1971	E/F.72.XIII.1	Twenty-third-Vingt-troisième	Population census statistics I- Statistiques de recensements de population I
1972	E/F.73.XIII.1	Twenty-fourth-Vingt-quatrième	Population census statistics II- Statistiques des recensements de population II
1973	E/F.74.XIII.1	Twenty-fifth-Vingt-cinquième	Population census statistics III- Statistiques des recensements de population III
1974	E/F.75.XIII.1	Twenty-sixth-Vingt-sixième	Mortality statistics - Statistiques de la mortalité
1975	E/F.76.XIII.1	Twenty-seventh-Vingt-septième	Natality statistics- Statistiques de la natalité
1976	E/F.77.XIII.1	Twenty-eighth-Vingt-huitième	Marriage and divorce statistics- Statistiques de la nuptialité et de la divortialité
1977	E/F.78.XIII.1	Twenty-ninth-Vingt-neuvième	International Migration Statistics- internationales
1978	E/F.79.XIII.1	Thirtieth-Trentième	General tables- Tableaux de caractère général
1978	E/F.79.XIII.8	Special issue-Edition spéciale	Historical supplement-Supplément rétrospectif
1979	E/F.80.XIII.1	Thirty-first-Trente et unième	Population census statistics-Statistiques des recensements de population
1980	E/F.81.XIII.1	Thirty-second-Trente-deuxième	Mortality statistics- Statistiques de la mortalité
1981	E/F.82.XIII.1	Thirty-third-Trente-troisième	Natality statistics-Statistiques de la natalité

Topics of the Demographic Yearbook series: 1948 - 2007

Sujets des diverses éditions de l'Annuaire démographique: 1948 - 2007

Year Année	Sales No. - Numéro de vente	Issue - Edition	Special topic - Sujet spécial
1982	E/F.83.XIII.1	Thirty-fourth- Trente-quatrième	Marriage and divorce statistics- Statistiques de la nuptialité et de la divortialité
1983	E/F.84.XIII.1	Thirty fifth- Trente-cinquième	Population census statistics I- Statistiques des recensements de population I
1984	E/F.85.XIII.1	Thirty-sixth- Trente-sixième	Population census statistics II- Statistiques des recensements de population II
1985	E/F.86.XIII.1	Thirty-seventh- Trente-septième	Mortality statistics- Statistiques de la mortalité
1986	E/F.87.XIII.1	Thirty-eighth- Trente-huitième	Natality statistics- Statistiques de la natalité
1987	E/F.88.XIII.1	Thirty-ninth- Trente-neuvième	Household composition- Les éléments du ménage
1988	E/F.89.XIII.1	Fortieth- Quarantième	Population census statistics- Statistiques des recensements de population
1989	E/F.90.XIII.1	Forty-first- Quarante-et-unième	International Migration Statistics- Statistiques des migration internationales
1990	E/F.91.XIII.1	Forty-second- Quarante-deuxième	Marriage and divorce statistics- Statistiques de la nuptialité et de la divortialité
1991	E/F.92.XIII.1	Forty-third- Quarante-troisième	General tables- Tableaux de caractère général
1992	E/F.94.XIII.1	Forty-fourth- Quarante-quatrième	Fertility and mortality statistics- Statistiques de la fecondité et de la mortalité
1993	E/F.95.XIII.1	Forty-fifth- Quarante-cinquième	Population census statistics I- Statistiques des recensements de population I
1994	E/F.96.XIII.1	Forty-sixth- Quarante-sixième	Population census statistics II- Statistiques des recensements de population II
1995	E/F.97.XIII.1	Forty-seventh- Quarante-septième	Household composition-Les éléments du ménage
1996	E/F.98.XIII.1	Forty-eighth- Quarante-huitième	Mortality statistics- Statistiques de la mortalité
1997	E/F.99.XIII.1	Forty-ninth- Quarante-neuvième	General tables- Tableaux de caractère général
1997	E/F.99.XIII.12	Special issue- Edition spéciale (CD)	Historical supplement- Supplément rétrospectif
1998	E/F.00.XIII.1	Fiftieth- Cinquantième	General tables- Tableaux de caractère général
1999	E/F.01.XIII.1	Fifty-first- Cinquante-et-unième	General tables- Tableaux de caractère général
1999	E/F.02.XIII.6	Special issue- Edition spéciale (CD)	Natality Statistics- Statistiques de la natalité
2000	E/F.02.XIII.1	Fifty-second- Cinquante-deuxième	General tables- Tableaux de caractère général
2001	E/F.03.XIII.1	Fifty-third- Cinquante- troisième	General tables- Tableaux de caractère général
2002	E/F.05.XIII.1	Fifty-fourth- Cinquante-quatrième	General tables- Tableaux de caractère général
2003	E/F.06.XIII.1	Fifty-fifth- Cinquante-cinquième	General tables- Tableaux de caractère général
2004	E/F.07.XIII.1	Fifty-sixth- Cinquante-sixième	General tables- Tableaux de caractère général
2005	E/F.08.XIII.1	Fifty-seventh- Cinquante-septième	General tables- Tableaux de caractère général
2006	E/F.09.XIII.1	Fifty-eighth- Cinquante-huitième	General tables- Tableaux de caractère général
2007	E/F.10.XIII.1	Fifty-ninth- Cinquante-neuvième	General tables- Tableaux de caractère général

CONTENTS - TABLE DES MATIERES

EXPLANATIONS OF SYMBOLS

Category not applicable ....

Data not available.. ...

Magnitude zero or less than half of unit employed .... -

Provisional .... *

Data tabulated by year of registration rather than occurrence .... +

Based on less than specified minimum .... ◆

Relatively reliable data .... Roman type

Data of lesser reliability .... *Italics*

EXPLICATION DES SIGNES

Sans objet ....

Données non disponibles ....

Néant ou chiffre inférieur à la moitié de l'unité employée .... -

Données provisoires .... *

Donnée exploitées selon l'année de l'enregistrement et non l'année de l'événement .. +

Rapport fondé sur un nombre inférieur à celui spécifié............................... ◆

Données relativement sûres... Caractères romains

Données dont l'exactitude est moindre .... *Italiques*

INTRODUCTION

The *Demographic Yearbook* is an international compendium of national demographic statistics, provided by national statistical authorities to the Statistics Division of the United Nations Department of Economic and Social Affairs. The *Yearbook* is part of the set of coordinated and interrelated publications issued by the United Nations and its specialized agencies[1], designed to supply basic statistical data for such users as demographers, economists, public-health workers and sociologists. Through the co-operation of national statistical services, official demographic statistics are compiled in the *Yearbook*, as available, for more than 230 countries or areas throughout the world.

The *Demographic Yearbook 2007* is the fifty-ninth in a series published by the United Nations since 1948. It contains general tables including a world summary of selected demographic statistics, statistics on the size, distribution and trends in national populations, natality, foetal mortality, infant and maternal mortality, general mortality, nuptiality and divorce. Data are shown by urban/rural residence, as available. In addition, the volume provides Technical Notes, a synoptic table, a historical index and a listing of the issues of the *Yearbook* published to date.

The Technical Notes on the Statistical Tables are provided to assist the reader in using the tables. Table A, the synoptic table, provides a glance of the completeness of data coverage of the current *Yearbook*. The cumulative historical index is a guide on content and coverage of all fifty-ninth issues, and indicates for each of the topics that have been published, the issues in which they are presented and the years covered. A list of the *Demographic Yearbook* issues, with their corresponding sales number and the special topics featured in each issue are shown on pages iii and iv.

Until the 48th issue (1996), each issue consisted of two parts, the general tables and special topic tables, published in the same volume[2]. Beginning with the 49th issue (1997), the special topic tables were being disseminated on CD-ROMs as supplements to the regular issues. Two CD-ROMs have so far been issued: the *Demographic Yearbook Historical Supplement*, which presents a wide panorama of basic demographic statistics for the period 1948 to 1997, and the *Demographic Yearbook: Natality Statistics*, which contains a series of detailed tables dedicated to natality and covering the period from 1980 to 1998. Three volumes of a new Demographic Yearbook Special Census Topics have now been prepared and are presented at http://unstats.un.org/unsd/demographic/products/dyb/dybcens.htm.

Population statistics are not available for all countries or areas, for a variety of reasons. In an effort to provide estimates of mid-year population and of selected vital statistics for all countries and areas, two annexes have been introduced since the 53rd issue of the *Demographic Yearbook*. Annex 1 presents United Nations population estimates for the period 1998-2007 and the second presents the medium variant estimates of crude birth and death rates, infant mortality and total fertility rates, as well as expectation of life at birth over the period 2005-2010. These data were produced by the United Nations Population Division and are published in the *World Population Prospects - The 2008 Revision*[3].

Demographic statistics shown in this issue of the *Yearbook* are available online at the *Demographic Yearbook* website http://unstats.un.org/unsd/demographic/products/dyb/dyb2007.htm. Information about the Statistics Division's data collection and dissemination programme is also available on the same website. Additional information can be made available by contacting the Statistics Division of the United Nations Secretariat, at demostat@un.org.

TECHNICAL NOTES ON THE STATISTICAL TABLES

1. GENERAL REMARKS

1.1 Arrangement of Technical Notes

These Technical Notes are designed to provide the reader with relevant information for using the statistical tables. Information pertaining to the *Yearbook* in general is presented in the sections dealing with geographical aspects, population and vital statistics. In addition, preceding each table are notes describing the variables, remarks on the reliability and limitation of the data, countries and areas covered, and information on the presentation of earlier data. When appropriate, details on computation of rates, ratios or percentages are presented.

1.2 Arrangement of tables

This issue contains general tables only. Since the numbering of the tables does not correspond exactly to those in previous issues, the reader is advised to use the historical index that appears at the end of this book to find the reference to data in earlier issues.

1.3 Source of data

The statistics presented in the *Demographic Yearbook* are national data provided by official statistical authorities unless otherwise indicated. The primary source of data for the *Yearbook* is a set of questionnaires sent annually by the United Nations Statistics Division to over 230 national statistical services and other appropriate government offices. Data reported on these questionnaires are supplemented, to the extent possible, with data taken from official national publications, official websites and through correspondence with national statistical services. In the interest of comparability, rates, ratios and percentages have been calculated by the Statistics Division of the United Nations, except for the life table functions, the total fertility rate, and also crude birth rate and crude death rate for some countries or areas as appropriately noted. The methods used by the Statistics Division to calculate these rates and ratios are described in the Technical Notes for each table. The population figures used for these computations are those pertaining to the corresponding years published in this or previous issues of the *Yearbook*.

In cases when data in this issue of the *Demographic Yearbook* differ from those published in earlier issues or related publications, statistics in this issue may be assumed to reflect revisions to these data received by June 2008.

2. GEOGRAPHICAL ASPECTS

2.1 Coverage

Data are shown for all individual countries or areas that provided information. Table 3 is the most comprehensive in geographical coverage, presenting data on population and surface area for all countries or areas with a population of at least 50 persons. Not all of these countries or areas appear in subsequent tables. In many cases the data required for a particular table are not available. In general, the more detailed the data required for a table, the fewer the number of countries or areas that can provide them.

In addition, rates and ratios are presented only for countries or areas reporting at least a minimum number of relevant events. The minimums are stated in the Technical Notes to individual tables.

Except for summary data shown for the world and by major areas and regions in tables 1 and 2 and data shown for capital cities and cities with a population of 100 000 or more in table 8, all data are presented at the national level. The number of countries shown in each table is provided in table A, the synoptic table.

2.2 Territorial composition

To the extent possible, all data, including time series data, relate to the territory within 2007 boundaries, when the data were requested from the countries or areas. Exceptions are footnoted in individual tables. Relevant clarifications are specified below.

Data relating to the **People's Republic of China** generally do not include those for Taiwan Province except in tables 1 and 2.

Data relating to **France** exclude Overseas Departments, namely, French Guiana, Guadeloupe, Martinique and Réunion, which are shown separately.

Data relating to **Denmark** exclude Faeroe Islands and Greenland, which are shown separately.

Data relating to **Western Sahara** comprise the Northern Region (former Saguia el Hamra) and Southern Region (former Rio de Oro).

Data relating to **United Kingdom of Great Britain and Northern Ireland** exclude Guernsey, Isle of Man and Jersey which are shown separately.

Data relating to **Norway** exclude Svalbard and Jan Mayen Island shown separately, if available.

Data relating to **Finland** include Åland Islands.

Data relating to **Åland Islands** are also included in Finland.

2.3 Nomenclature

Because of space limitations, the country or area names listed in the tables are generally the commonly employed short titles in use in the United Nations as of June 2009[4], the full titles being used only when a short form is not available. The latest version of the *Standard Country or Area Codes for Statistics Use* can be accessed at http://unstats.un.org/unsd/methods/m49/m49alpha.htm.

2.3.1 Order of presentation

Countries or areas are listed in English alphabetical order within the following continents: Africa, North America, South America, Asia, Europe and Oceania.

The designations and presentation of the material in this publication were adopted solely for the purpose of providing a convenient geographical basis for the accompanying statistical series. The same qualification applies to all notes and explanations concerning the geographical units for which data are presented.

2.4 Surface area data

Surface area data, shown in tables 1 and 3, represent the total surface area, comprising land area and inland waters (assumed to consist of major rivers and lakes) and excluding only Polar Regions and uninhabited islands. The surface area given is the most recent estimate available. They are presented in square kilometres, a conversion factor of 2.589988 having been applied to surface areas originally reported in square miles.

2.4.1 Comparability over time

Comparability over time in surface area estimates for any given country or area may be affected by changes in the surface area estimation procedures, increases in actual land surface by reclamation, boundary changes, changes in the concept of "land surface area" used or a change in the unit of measurement used. In most cases it was possible to ascertain the reason for a revision; otherwise, the latest figures have generally been accepted as correct and substituted for those previously on file.

2.4.2 International comparability

Lack of international comparability between surface area estimates arises primarily from differences in definition. In particular, there is considerable variation in the treatment of coastal bays, inlets and gulfs, rivers and lakes. International comparability is also impaired by the variation in methods employed to estimate surface area. These range from surveys based on modern scientific methods to conjectures based on diverse types of information. Some estimates are recent while others may not be. Since neither the exact method of determining the surface area nor the precise definition of its composition and time reference is known for all countries or areas, the estimates in table 3 should not be considered strictly comparable from one country or area to another.

3. POPULATION

Population statistics, that is, those pertaining to the size, geographical distribution and demographic characteristics of the population, are presented in a number of tables of the *Demographic Yearbook*.

Data for countries or areas include population census figures, estimates based on results of sample surveys (in the absence of a census), postcensal or intercensal estimates and those derived from continuous population registers. In the present issue of the *Yearbook*, the latest available census figure of the total population of each country or area and mid-year estimates for 2005 and 2007 are presented in table 3. Mid-year estimates of total population for 10 years (1998-2007) are shown in table 5 and mid-year estimates of urban and total population by sex for 10 years (1998-2007) are shown in table 6. The latest available data on population by age, sex and urban/rural residence are given in table 7. The latest available figures on the population of capital cities and of cities or urban agglomerations of 100 000 or more inhabitants are presented in table 8.

Summary estimates of the mid-year population of the world, major areas and regions for selected years and of its age and sex distribution in 2007 are set forth in tables 1 and 2, respectively.

The statistics on total population, population by age, sex and urban/rural distribution are used in the calculation of rates in the *Yearbook*. Vital rates by age, sex and residence (urban/rural) were calculated using data that appear in table 7 in this issue or the corresponding tables of previous issues of the *Demographic Yearbook*.

3.1 Sources of variation of data

The comparability of data is affected by several factors, including (1) the definition of total population; (2) the definition used to classify the population into its urban/rural components; (3) the accuracy of age reporting; (4) the extent of over-enumeration or under-enumeration in the most recent census or other source of benchmark population statistics; and (5) the quality of population estimates. These five factors will be discussed in some detail in sections 3.1.1 to 3.2.2 below. Other relevant problems are discussed in the technical notes to the individual tables. Readers interested in more detail, relating in particular to the basic concepts of population size, distribution and characteristics as elaborated by the United Nations, should consult the *Principles and Recommendations for Population and Housing Censuses, Revision 2*[5].

3.1.1 Total population

The most important impediment to comparability of total populations is the difference between the concept of a de facto and de jure population. A de facto population should include all persons physically present in the country or area at the reference date. The de jure population, by contrast, should include all usual residents of the given country or area, whether or not they were physically present in the area at the reference date. By definition, therefore, a de facto total and a de jure total are not entirely comparable.

Comparability of even two de facto or de jure totals is often affected by the fact that strict conformity to either of these concepts is rare. For example, some so-called de facto counts do not include foreign military, naval and diplomatic personnel present in the country or area on official duty, and their accompanying family members and servants; some do not include foreign visitors in transit through the country or area or transients on ships in the harbour. On the other hand, they may include such persons as merchant seamen and fishermen who are temporarily out of the country or area working at their trade.

The de jure population figure presents even greater variations in comparability, in part because it depends in the first place on the concept of "usual residence", which varies from one country or area to another and is difficult to apply consistently in a census or survey enumeration. For example, non-national civilians temporarily in a country or area as short-term workers may officially be considered residents after a stay of a specified period of time or they may be considered as non-residents throughout the duration of their stay; at the same time, these individuals may be officially considered as residents or non-residents of the country or area from which they came, depending on the duration and/or purpose of their absence. Furthermore, regardless of the official treatment, individual respondents may apply their own interpretation of residence in responding to the inquiry. In addition, there may be considerable differences in the accuracy with which countries or areas are informed about the number of their residents temporarily out of the country or area.

As far as possible, the population statistics presented in the tables of the *Yearbook* refer to the de facto population. Those reported to have been based on the de jure concept are identified as such. Figures not otherwise qualified may, therefore, be assumed to have been reported by countries or areas as being based on a de facto definition of the population. In an effort to overcome, to the extent possible, the effect of the lack of strict conformity to either the de facto or the de jure concept given above, significant exceptions with respect to inclusions and exclusions of specific population groups, are footnoted when they are known.

It should be remembered, however, that the necessary detailed information has not been available in many cases. It cannot, therefore, be assumed that figures not thus qualified reflect strict de facto or de jure definitions.

A possible source of variation within the statistics of a single country or area may arise from the fact that some countries or areas collect information on both the de facto and the de jure population in, for example, a census, but prepare detailed tabulations for only the de jure population. Hence, even though the total population shown in table 3 is de facto, the figures shown in the tables presenting various characteristics of the population, for example, urban/rural distribution, age and sex distribution, may be de jure.

3.1.2 Urban/rural classification

International comparability of urban/rural distributions is seriously impaired by the wide variation among national definitions of the concept of "urban". The definitions used by individual countries or areas and their implications are shown at the end of technical notes for table 6.

3.1.3 Age distribution

The classification of population by age is a core element of most analyses, estimation and projection of population statistics. Unfortunately, age data are subject to a number of sources of error and non-comparability. Accordingly, the reliability of age data should be of concern to users of these statistics.

3.1.3.1 Collection and compilation of age data

Age is the estimated or calculated interval of time between the date of birth and the date of the census or survey, expressed in completed solar years[6]. There are two methods of collecting information on age. The first is to obtain the date of birth for each member of the population in a census or survey and then to calculate the completed age of the individual by subtracting the date of birth from the date of enumeration[7]. The second method is to record the individual's completed age at the time of the census or survey, that is to say, age at last birthday.

The recommended method is to calculate age at last birthday by subtracting the exact date of birth from the date of the census. Some practices, however, do not use this method but instead calculate the difference between the year of birth and the year of the census. Classifications of this type are footnoted whenever possible. They can be identified to a certain extent by a smaller than expected population under one year of age. However, an irregular number of births from one year to the next or age selective omission of infants may also obscure the expected population under one year of age.

3.1.3.2 Errors in age data

Errors in age data may be due to a variety of causes, including ignorance of the correct age; reporting years of age in terms of a calendar concept other than completed solar years since birth[8]; carelessness in reporting and recording age; a general tendency to state age in figures ending in certain digits (such as zero, two, five and eight); a tendency to exaggerate length of life at advanced ages; a subconscious aversion to certain numbers; and wilful misrepresentations.

These reasons for errors in reported age data are common to most investigations of age and to most countries or areas, and they may significantly impair comparability of the data.

As a result of the above-mentioned difficulties, the age-sex distribution of population in many countries or areas shows irregularities which may be summarized as follows: (1) a deficiency in the number of infants and young children; (2) a concentration at ages ending with zero and five (that is, 5, 10, 15, 20, ...); (3) heaping at even ages (for example, 10, 12, 14, ...) relative to odd ages (for example, 11, 13, 15, ...); (4) unexpectedly large differences between the frequency of males and females at certain ages; and (5) unaccountably large differences between the frequencies in adjacent age groups. Comparing of identical age-sex cohorts from successive censuses, as well as studying the age-sex composition of each census, may reveal these and other inconsistencies, some of which in varying degree are characteristic of even the most modern censuses.

3.1.3.3 Evaluation of accuracy

To measure the accuracy of data by age, based on the evidence of irregularities in 5-year groups, an index was devised for presentation in the *Demographic Yearbook 1949-1950*[9]. Although this index was sensitive to various sources of inaccuracy in the data, it could also be affected considerably by real fluctuations in past demographic processes. It could not, therefore, be applied indiscriminately to all types of statistics, unless certain adjustments were made and caution used in the interpretation of results.

The publication of population statistics by single years of age in the *Demographic Yearbook 1955* made it possible to apply a simple, yet highly sensitive, index known as Whipple's Index, or the Index of Concentration[10], the interpretation of which is relatively free from consideration of factors not connected with the accuracy of age reporting. More refined methods for the measurement of accuracy of distributions by single year of age have been devised, but this particular index was selected for presentation in the *Demographic Yearbook* for its simplicity and the wide use it has already found in other sources.

Whipple's Index is obtained by summing the age returns between 23 and 62 years inclusive and finding what percentage is borne by the sum of the returns of years ending with 5 and 0 to one-fifth of the total sum.

The results would vary between a minimum of 0, if no returns were recorded ending with 0 or 5, and a maximum of 500, if no returns were recorded ending with any digits other than 0 or 5. If there is no age heaping at ages ending 0 or 5, the Whipple's index is 100.[11]

The index is applicable to all age distributions for which single years are given at least to the age of 62, with the following exceptions: (1) where the data presented are the result of graduation, no irregularity is scored by Whipple's Index, even though the graduated data may still be affected by inaccuracies of a different type; and (2) where statistics on age have been derived by reference to the year of birth, and tendencies to round off the birth year would result in an excessive number of ages ending in odd numbers, the frequency of age reporting with terminal digits 5 and 0 is not an adequate measure of their accuracy.

Most recently, the index has been computed for all the single-year age distributions from censuses held between 1985 and 2003, with the exception of those excluded on the criteria set forth above. Such data are published in the special issue of the *Demographic Yearbook* special topic on population censuses, Volume 1, which is available online at http://unstats.un.org/unsd/demographic/products/dyb/dybcens.htm.

Although Whipple's Index measures only the effects of preferences for ages ending in 5 and 0, it can be assumed that such digit preference is usually connected with other sources of inaccuracy in age statements and the index can be accepted as a fair measure of the general reliability of the age distribution.

3.2 Methods used to indicate quality of published statistics

To the extent possible, efforts have been made to give the reader an indication of reliability of the statistics published in the *Demographic Yearbook*. This has been approached in several ways. Any information regarding a possible under-enumeration or over-enumeration, coming from a postcensal survey, for example, has been noted in the footnotes to table 3. Any deviation from full national coverage, as explained in section 2.1 under Geographical Aspects, has also been noted. In addition, national statistical offices have been asked to evaluate the estimates of total population they submit to the Statistics Division of the United Nations.

3.2.1 Treatment of time series of population estimates

When a series of mid-year population estimates are presented, the same indication of quality is shown for the entire series as was determined for the latest estimate. The quality is indicated by the type face employed.

No attempt has been made to split the series even though it is evident that in cases where the data are now considered reliable, in earlier years, many may have been considerably less reliable than the current classification implies. Thus it will be evident that this method overstates the probable reliability of the time series in many cases. It may also understate the reliability of estimates for years immediately preceding or following a census enumeration.

3.2.2 Treatment of estimated distributions by age and other demographic characteristics

Estimates of the age-sex distribution of population may be constructed by two major methods: (1) by applying the specific components of population change to each age-sex group of the population as enumerated at the time of the census, and (2) by distributing the total estimated for a postcensal year proportionately according to the age-sex structure at the time of the census. Estimates constructed by the latter method are not published in the *Demographic Yearbook*.

Estimated age-sex distributions are categorized as "reliable" or otherwise, according to the method of construction established for the latest estimate of total mid-year population. Hence, the quality designation of the total figure, as indicated by the code, is considered to apply also to the whole distribution by age and sex, and the data are set in *italic* or roman type, as appropriate, on this basis alone. Further evaluation of detailed age structure data has not been undertaken to date.

4. VITAL STATISTICS

For purposes of the *Demographic Yearbook*, vital statistics have been defined as statistics of live birth, death, foetal death, marriage and divorce.

This volume of the *Yearbook* presents general tables on natality, nuptiality and divorce as well as tables on mortality referring to: foetal mortality, infant and maternal mortality and general mortality.

4.1 Sources of variation of data

Most of the vital statistics data published in this *Yearbook* come from national civil registration systems. The completeness and the accuracy of the data that these systems produce vary from one country or area to another.

The provision for a national civil registration system is not universal, and in some cases, the registration system covers only certain vital events. For example, in some countries or areas only births and deaths are registered. There are also differences in the effectiveness with which national laws pertaining to civil registration operate in the various countries or areas. The manner in which the law is implemented and the degree to which the public complies with the legislation determine the reliability of the vital statistics obtained from the civil registers.

It should be noted that some statistics on marriage and divorce are obtained from sources other than civil registers. For example, in some countries or areas, the only source for data on marriages is church registers. Divorce statistics, on the other hand, are obtained from court records and/or civil registers according to national practice. The actual compilation of these statistics may be the responsibility of the civil registrar, the national statistical office or other government offices.

Other factors affecting international comparability of vital statistics are much the same as those that must be considered in evaluating the variations in other population statistics. Differences in statistical definitions of vital events, differences in geographical and ethnic coverage of the data and diverse tabulation procedures may also influence comparability.

In addition to vital statistics from civil registers, some vital statistics published in the *Yearbook* are official estimates. These estimates are frequently from population censuses and sample surveys. As such, their comparability may be affected by the national completeness of reporting in population censuses and household surveys, whether a de facto or de jure based census, non-sampling and sampling errors and other sources of bias.

Readers interested in more detailed information on standards for vital statistics should consult the *Principles and Recommendations for a Vital Statistics System Revision 2*[12]; *Handbook on Civil Registration and Vital Statistics Systems: Preparation of a Legal Framework*[13]; *Handbook on Civil Registration and Vital*

Statistics Systems: Management, Operation and Maintenance[14]; *Handbook on Civil Registration and Vital Statistics Systems: Developing Information, Education and Communication*[15]; *Handbook on Civil Registration and Vital Statistics Systems: Policies and Protocols for the Release and Archiving of Individual Records*[16]; and *Handbook on Civil Registration and Vital Statistics Systems: Computerization*[17]. The *Handbook on the Collection of Fertility and Mortality Data*[18] provides information in collection and evaluation of data on fertility and mortality collected in population censuses and household surveys. These publications are also available on the website at http://unstats.un.org/unsd/demographic/standmeth/handbooks/default.htm.

4.1.1 Statistical definition of events

An important source of variation lies in the statistical definition of each vital event. The *Demographic Yearbook* attempts to collect data on vital events, using the standard definitions put forth in paragraph 57 of *Principles and Recommendations for a Vital Statistics System Revision 2*[12]. These are as follows:

LIVE BIRTH is the complete expulsion or extraction from its mother of a product of conception, irrespective of the duration of pregnancy, which after such separation breathes or shows any other evidence of life such as beating of the heart, pulsation of the umbilical cord, or definite movement of voluntary muscles, whether or not the umbilical cord has been cut or the placenta is attached; each product of such a birth is considered live-born regardless of gestational age.

DEATH is the permanent disappearance of all evidence of life at any time after live birth has taken place (postnatal cessation of vital functions without capability of resuscitation). This definition therefore excludes foetal deaths.

FOETAL DEATH is death prior to the complete expulsion or extraction from its mother of a product of conception, irrespective of the duration of pregnancy; the death is indicated by the fact that after such separation the foetus does not breathe or show any other evidence of life, such as beating of the heart, pulsation of the umbilical cord, or definite movement of voluntary muscles. Late foetal deaths are those of twenty-eight or more completed weeks of gestation. These are synonymous with the events reported under the pre-1950 term stillbirth[19].

MARRIAGE is an act, ceremony or process by which the legal relationship of husband and wife is constituted. The legality of the union may be established by civil, religious or other means as recognized by the laws of each country or area.

DIVORCE is a final legal dissolution of a marriage, that is, that separation of husband and wife which confers on the parties the right to remarriage under civil, religious and/or other provisions, according to the laws of each country.

In addition to these recommended definitions, the *Demographic Yearbook* collects and presents data on abortions, defined as:

ABORTION is defined, with reference to the woman, as any interruption of pregnancy before 28 weeks of gestation with a dead foetus. There are two major categories of abortion: spontaneous and induced. Induced abortions are those initiated by deliberate action undertaken with the intention of terminating pregnancy; all other abortions are considered spontaneous.

4.1.2 Problems relating to standard definitions

A basic problem affecting international comparability of vital statistics is deviations from the standard definitions of vital events. An example of this can be seen in the cases of live births and foetal deaths[20]. In some countries or areas, an infant must survive for at least 24 hours, to be inscribed in the live-birth register. Infants who die before the expiration of the 24-hour period are classified as late foetal deaths and, barring special tabulation procedures, they would not be counted either as live births or as deaths. Similarly, in several other countries or areas, those infants who are born alive but die before registration of their birth, are also considered late foetal deaths.

Unless special tabulation procedures are adopted in such cases, the live-birth and death statistics will both be deficient by the number of these infants, while the incidence of late foetal deaths will be increased by the same amount. Hence the infant mortality rate is underestimated. Although both components (infant deaths and live births) are deficient by the same absolute amount, the deficiency is proportionately greater in relation to the infant deaths, causing greater errors in the infant mortality rate than in the birth rate.

Moreover, the practice exaggerates the late foetal death ratios. Some countries or areas make provision for correcting this deficiency (at least in the total frequencies) at the tabulation stage. Data for which the correction has not been made are indicated by footnote whenever possible.

The definitions used for marriage and divorce also present problems for international comparability. Unlike birth and death, which are biological events, marriage and divorce are defined only in terms of law and custom and as such are less amenable to universally applicable statistical definitions. They have therefore been defined for statistical purposes in general terms referring to the laws of individual countries or areas. Laws pertaining to marriage and particularly to divorce, vary from one country or area to another. With respect to marriage, the most widespread requirement relates to the minimum age at which persons may marry but frequently other requirements are specified.

When known the minimum legal age of men and women at which marriage can occur with (or in some cases without) parental consent is presented in table 22-1. Laws and regulations relating to the dissolution of marriage by divorce range from total prohibition, through a wide range of grounds upon which divorces may be granted, to the granting of divorce in response to a simple statement of desire or intention by husbands.

4.1.3 Fragmentary geographical or ethnic coverage

Ideally, vital statistics for any given country or area should cover the entire geographical area and include all ethnic groups. Fragmentary coverage is, however, not uncommon. In some countries or areas, registration is compulsory for only a small part of the population, limited to certain ethnic groups, for example. In other places there is no national provision for compulsory registration, but only municipal or state ordinances that do not cover the entire geographical area. Still others have developed a registration area that comprises only a part of the country or area, the remainder being excluded because of inaccessibility or for economic and cultural considerations that make regular registration practically impossible.

4.1.4 Tabulation procedures

4.1.4.1 By place of occurrence

Vital statistics presented at the national level relate to the de facto, that is, the present-in-area population. Thus, unless otherwise noted, vital statistics for a given country or area cover all the events that occur within its present boundaries and among all segments of the population therein. They may be presumed to include events among nomadic tribes and indigenous peoples, and among nationals and foreigners. When known, deviations from the de facto concept are footnoted.

Urban/rural differentials in vital rates for some countries may vary considerably depending on whether the relevant vital events were tabulated on the basis of place of occurrence or place of usual residence. For example, if a substantial number of women residing in rural areas near major urban centres travel to hospitals or maternity homes located in a city to give birth, urban fertility and neo-natal and infant mortality rates will usually be higher (and the corresponding rural rates will usually be lower) if the events are tabulated on the basis of place of occurrence rather than on the basis of place of usual residence. A similar process will affect general mortality differentials if substantial numbers of persons residing in rural areas use urban health facilities when seriously ill.

4.1.4.2 By date of occurrence versus by date of registration

To the extent possible, the vital statistics presented in the *Demographic Yearbook* refer to events that occurred during the specified year, rather than to those that were registered during that period. However, a considerable number of countries or areas tabulate their vital statistics not by date of occurrence, but by date of registration. Because such statistics can be very misleading, the countries or areas known to tabulate vital statistics by date of registration are identified in the tables by a plus sign "+". Since information on the method of tabulating vital statistics is not available for all countries and areas, tabulation by date of registration may be more prevalent than the symbols on the vital statistics tables would indicate.

Because quality of data is inextricably related to the timeliness of registration, this must always be considered in conjunction with the quality code description in section 4.2.1 below. If registration of births is complete and timely (code "C"), the ill effects of tabulating by date of registration, are, for all practical purposes, nullified. Similarly, with respect to death statistics, the effect of tabulating events by date of registration may be minimized in many countries or areas in which the sanitary code requires that a death must be registered before a burial permit can be issued, and this regulation tends to make registration prompt. With respect to foetal death, registration is usually done right away or not at all. Therefore, if registration is prompt, the difference between statistics tabulated by date of occurrence and those tabulated by date of registration may be negligible. In many cases, the length of the statutory time period allowed for registering various vital events plays an important part in determining the effects of tabulation by date of registration on comparability of data.

With respect to marriage and divorce, the practice of tabulating data by date of registration does not generally pose serious problems. In many countries or areas marriage is a civil legal contract which, to establish its legality, must be celebrated before a civil officer. It follows that for these countries or areas registration would tend to be almost automatic at the time of, or immediately following, the marriage ceremony. Because the registration of a divorce in many countries or areas is the responsibility solely of the court or the authority which granted it, and since the registration record in such cases is part of the records of the court proceedings, it follows that divorces are likely to be registered soon after the decree is granted.

On the other hand, if registration is not prompt, vital statistics by date of registration will not produce internationally comparable data. Under the best circumstances, statistics by date of registration will include primarily events that occurred in the immediately preceding year; in countries or areas with less developed systems, tabulations will include some events that occurred many years in the past. Examination of available information reveals that delays of many years are not uncommon for birth registration, though the majority is recorded between two to four years after birth.

As long as registration is not prompt, statistics by date of registration will not be internationally comparable either among themselves or with statistics by date of occurrence.

It should also be mentioned that lack of international comparability is not the only limitation introduced by date-of-registration tabulation. Even within the same country or area, comparability over time may be lost by the practice of counting registrations rather than occurrences. If the number of events registered from year to year fluctuates because of ad hoc incentives to stimulate registration, or to the sudden need, for example, for proof of (unregistered) birth or death to meet certain requirements, vital statistics tabulated by date of registration are not useful in measuring and analyzing demographic levels and trends. All they can give is an indication of the fluctuations in the need for a birth, death or marriage certificate and the work-load of the registrars. Therefore, statistics tabulated by date of registration may be of very limited use for either national or international studies.

4.2 Methods used to indicate quality of published vital statistics

The quality of vital statistics can be assessed in terms of a number of factors. Most fundamental is the completeness of the civil registration system on which the statistics are based. In some cases, the incompleteness of the data obtained from civil registration systems is revealed when these events are used to compute rates. However, this technique applies only where the data are markedly deficient, where they are tabulated by date of occurrence and where the population base is correctly estimated. Tabulation by date of registration will often produce rates which appear correct, simply because the numerator is artificially inflated by the inclusion of delayed registrations and, conversely, rates may be of credible magnitude because the population at risk has been underestimated. Moreover, it should be remembered that knowledge of what is credible in regard to levels of fertility, mortality and nuptiality is extremely scanty for many parts of the world, and borderline cases, which are the most difficult to appraise, are frequent.

4.2.1 Quality code for vital statistics from registers.

In the *Demographic Yearbook* annual "Questionnaire on Vital Statistics" national statistical offices are asked to provide their own estimates of the completeness of the births, deaths, late foetal deaths, marriages and divorces recorded in their civil registers.

On the basis of information from the questionnaires, from direct correspondence and from relevant official publications, it has been possible to classify current national statistics from civil registers of birth, death, infant death, late foetal death, marriage and divorce into three broad quality categories, as follows:

C: Data estimated to be virtually complete, that is, representing at least 90 per cent of the events occurring each year.

U: Data estimated to be incomplete, that is representing less than 90 per cent of the events occurring each year.

|: Data not derived from civil registration systems but considered reliable, such as estimates derived from projections, other estimation techniques or population and housing census.

...: Data for which no specific information is available regarding completeness.

These quality codes appear in the first column of the tables which show total frequencies and crude rates (or ratios) over a period of years for all tables on live births, late foetal deaths, infant deaths, deaths, marriages, and divorces. Reliability of maternal mortality statistics is provided by the World Health Organisation and instead of indicating data quality in the first column, reliable data are shown in roman type while unreliable data are shown in italics.

The classification of countries and areas in terms of these quality codes may not be uniform. Nevertheless, it was felt that national statistical offices were in the best position to judge the quality of their data. It was considered that even the very broad categories that could be established on the basis of the available information would provide useful indicators of the quality of the vital statistics presented in this *Yearbook*.

In the past, the bases of the national estimates of completeness were usually not available. In connection with the *Demographic Yearbook 1977*, countries were asked, for the first time, to provide some indication of the basis of their completeness estimates. They were requested to indicate whether the completeness estimates reported for registered live births, deaths, and infant deaths were prepared on the basis of demographic analysis, dual record checks or some other specified method. Relatively few countries or areas have responded to this new question; therefore, no attempt has been made to revise the system of quality codes used in connection with the vital statistics data presented in the *Yearbook*. It is hoped that, in the future, more countries will be able to provide this information so that the system of quality codes used in connection with the vital statistics data presented in the *Yearbook* may be revised.

Among the countries or areas indicating that the registration of live births was estimated to be 90 per cent or more complete (and hence classified as "C" in table 9), the following countries or areas provided information on the basis of this completeness estimate:

(a) Demographic analysis -- Andorra, Argentina, Austria, Bulgaria, Croatia, Cuba, Czech Republic, Estonia, Iceland, Israel, Italy, Latvia, Lithuania, Malta, Mauritius, Mexico, Monaco, Occupied Palestinian Territory, Poland, Puerto Rico, Republic of Korea, Republic of Moldova, Romania and Singapore.

(b) Dual record check -- Bahamas, Bulgaria, Cuba, Estonia, Greece, Hungary, Iceland, Italy, Jamaica, Kyrgyzstan, Malta, Norway, Puerto Rico, Qatar, Republic of Korea, Romania, Saint Lucia and Switzerland.

(c) Other specified methods -- Aruba, Austria, Costa Rica, Cuba, Cyprus, Denmark, Estonia, Finland, Germany, Gibraltar, Greenland, Guam, Islamic Republic of Iran, Ireland, Jamaica, Latvia, Liechtenstein, Luxembourg, Netherlands Antilles, Occupied Palestinian Territory, Puerto Rico, Réunion, Slovenia, Sri Lanka and Sweden.

Among the countries or areas indicating that the registration of deaths was estimated to be 90 per cent or more complete (and hence classified as "C" in table 18), the following countries or areas provided information on the basis of this completeness estimate:

(a) Demographic analysis -- Argentina, Austria, Bulgaria, Croatia, Cuba, Czech Republic, Estonia, Iceland, Israel, Italy, Latvia, Lithuania, Malta, Mauritius, Mexico, Monaco, Poland, Puerto Rico, Republic of Korea, Republic of Moldova, Romania and Singapore.

(b) Dual record check -- Bulgaria, Cuba, Cyprus, Estonia, Greece, Hungary, Iceland, Israel, Italy, Kyrgyzstan, Lithuania, Malta, Mexico, Norway, Puerto Rico, Qatar, Republic of Korea, Romania, Saint Lucia and Switzerland.

(c) Other specified methods -- Aruba, Austria, Costa Rica, Cuba, Denmark, Estonia, Finland, Germany, Gibraltar, Greenland, Guam, Liechtenstein, Luxembourg, Netherlands Antilles, Puerto Rico, Réunion, Slovenia, Sri Lanka and Sweden.

Among the countries or areas indicating that the registration of infant deaths was estimated to be 90 per cent or more complete (and hence classified as "C" in table 15), the following countries or areas provided information on the basis of this completeness estimate:

(a) Demographic analysis -- Andorra, Argentina, Austria, Bulgaria, Croatia, Cuba, Czech Republic, Estonia, Iceland, Israel, Italy, Latvia, Lithuania, Malta, Mauritius, Mexico, Poland, Puerto Rico, Republic of Korea, Republic of Moldova, Romania and Singapore.

(b) Dual record check -- Bulgaria, Cuba, Cyprus, Estonia, Greece, Hungary, Iceland, Ireland, Israel, Italy, Kyrgyzstan, Lithuania, Malta, Norway, Puerto Rico, Qatar, Republic of Korea, Romania, Saint Lucia, and Switzerland.

(c) Other specified methods -- Aruba, Austria, Cayman Islands, Costa Rica, Cuba, Denmark, Estonia, Finland, Germany, Greenland, Guam, Liechtenstein, Luxembourg, Netherlands Antilles, Puerto Rico, Réunion, Slovenia and Sweden.

4.2.2 Treatment of vital statistics from registers

On the basis of the quality code described above, the vital statistics shown in all tables of the *Yearbook* are treated as either reliable or unreliable. Data coded "C" are considered reliable and appear in roman type. Data coded "U" or "..." are considered unreliable and appear in *italics*. Although the quality code itself appears only in certain tables, the indication of reliability (that is, the use of *italics* to indicate unreliable data) is shown in all tables presenting vital statistics data.

In general, the quality code for deaths shown in table 18 is used to determine whether data on deaths in other tables appear in roman or *italic* type. However, for some of the maternal deaths data shown in *italics* in table 17, the known quality code differs from that ascribed on the basis of the completeness of registration of the total number of deaths. In cases where the quality code in table 18 does not correspond with the quality level implied by the typeface used in table 17, relevant information regarding the completeness of maternal mortality is given in a footnote.

The same indication of reliability used in connection with tables showing the frequencies of vital events is also used in connection with tables showing the corresponding vital rates. For example, death rates computed using deaths from a register that is incomplete or of unknown completeness are considered unreliable and appear in *italics*. Strictly speaking, to evaluate vital rates more precisely, one would have to also take into account the accuracy of population data used in the denominator of these rates. The quality of population data is discussed in section 3.2 of the Technical Notes.

It should be noted that the indications of reliability used for infant mortality rates, maternal mortality rates and late foetal death ratios (all of which are calculated using the number of live births in the denominator) are determined on the basis of the quality codes for infant deaths, deaths and late foetal deaths respectively. To evaluate these rates and ratios more precisely, one would have to take into account the quality of the live-birth data used in the denominator of these rates and ratios. The quality codes for live births are shown in table 9 and described more fully in the text of the technical notes for that table.

4.2.3 Treatment of time series of vital statistics from registers

The quality of a time series of vital statistics is more difficult to determine than the quality of data for a single year. Since a time series of vital statistics is usually generated only by a system of continuous civil registration, it was assumed that the quality of the entire series was the same as that for the latest year's data obtained from the civil register. The entire series is treated as described in section 4.2.2 above. That is, if the quality code for the latest registered data is "C", the frequencies and rates for earlier years are also considered reliable and appear in roman type. Conversely, if the latest registered data are coded as "U" or "..." then data for earlier years are considered unreliable and appear in *italics*. It is recognized that this method is not entirely satisfactory because it is known that data from earlier years in many of the series were considerably less reliable than the current code implies.

4.2.4 Treatment of estimated vital statistics

In addition to data from vital registration systems, estimated frequencies and rates of the events, usually ad hoc official estimates that have been derived either from the results of a sample survey or by demographic analyses, also appear in the *Demographic Yearbook*. Estimated frequencies and rates have been included in the tables because it is assumed that they provide information that is more accurate than that from existing civil registration systems. By implication, they are assumed to be reliable and as such they are set in roman type. Estimated frequencies and rates continue to be treated in this manner even when they are interspersed in a time series with data from civil registers.

In tables showing the quality code, the code applies only to data from civil registers. If a series of data for a country or area contains both data from a civil register and estimated data, the code applies only to the registered data; if only estimated data are shown, the symbol "|" is shown.

4.3 Cause of death

World Health Organization (WHO) Member States are bound by the International Nomenclature Regulations to provide the Organization with cause of death data coded in accordance with the current revision of the International Statistical Classification of Diseases and Related Health Problems (ICD) as adopted from time to time by the World Health Assembly[21]. The data are collected by the WHO using the ICD. In order to promote international comparability of cause of death statistics, the World Health Organization organizes and conducts an international Conference for the revision of the ICD on a regular basis in order to ensure that the Classification is kept current with the most recent clinical and statistical concepts. The data are now usually submitted to WHO at the full four-character level of detail provided by the ICD and are stored in the WHO Mortality Database at the level of detail as provided by the country. For earlier versions, however, the data are only available according to the ICD's list of 150 causes. Data from the WHO Mortality Database are available in electronic format at http://www3.who.int/whosis/menu.cfm.

Although revisions provide an up-to-date version of the ICD, such revisions create several problems related to the comparability of cause of death statistics. The first is the lack of comparability over time that inevitably accompanies the use of a new classification. The second problem affects comparability between countries and areas because they may adopt a new classification at different times. The more refined the classification becomes the greater is the need for expert clinical diagnosis of cause of death. In many countries or areas, few of the deaths occur in the presence of an attendant, who is medically trained, i.e., most deaths are certified by a lay attendant. Because the ICD contains many diagnoses that cannot be identified by a non-medical person, the ICD does not always promote international comparability particularly between countries and areas where the level of medical services differ widely.

The chapters of the tenth revision[22], the latest revision of the ICD, consist of an alphanumeric coding scheme of one letter followed by three numbers at the four-character level. Chapter one contains infectious and parasitic diseases, chapter two refers to all neoplasms, chapter three to disorders of the immune mechanism including diseases of the blood and blood-forming organs; and chapter four to endocrine, nutritional and metabolic diseases. The remaining chapters group diseases according to the anatomical site affected, except for chapters that refer to mental disorders; complications of pregnancy, childbirth and the puerperium; congenital malformations; and conditions originating in the perinatal period. Finally, an entire chapter is devoted to symptoms, signs, and abnormal findings.

4.3.1 Maternal mortality

According to the tenth revision of the ICD, "Maternal death" is defined as the death of a woman while pregnant or within 42 days of termination of pregnancy, irrespective of the duration and the site of the pregnancy, from any cause related to or aggravated by the pregnancy or its management but not from accidental or incidental causes.

"Maternal deaths" should be subdivided into direct and indirect obstetric deaths. Direct obstetric deaths are those resulting from obstetric complications of the pregnant state (pregnancy, labour and puerperium), from interventions, omissions, incorrect treatment, or from a chain of events resulting from any of the above. Indirect obstetric deaths are those resulting from previous existing disease or disease that developed during pregnancy and which was not due to direct obstetric causes, but which was aggravated by physiologic effects of pregnancy.

While the denominator maternal rate should be the number of pregnant women, it is impossible to determine the number of pregnant women. A further recommendation by the tenth revision conference is therefore that maternal mortality rates be expressed per 100,000 live births or per 100,000 total births (live births and foetal deaths)[23]. The maternal mortality rate calculated here is expressed per 100,000 live births. Although live births do not represent an unbiased estimate of pregnant women, this figure is more reliable than other estimates in particular, live births are more accurately registered than live births plus foetal deaths.

NOTES

[1] The data on maternal mortality are from the World Health Organization, and are available at http://www3.who.int/whosis/menu.cfm, as one cause of death.

[2] There are two exceptions – the 1978 and 1991 issues, which were disseminated in separate volumes from the respective regular issues.

[3] *United Nations, Department of Economic and Social Affairs, Population Division (2009). World Population Prospects: The 2008 Revision, CD-ROM Edition..* Highlights and selected output are available by following links at www.unpopulation.org.

[4] ST/ESA/STAT/SER.M/49/Rev.4/WWW ; http://unstats.un.org/unsd/methods/m49/m49.htm; see also Standard Country or Area Codes for Statistical Use, Sales No. M.98.XVII.9, United Nations, New York, 1999.

[5] Sales No. E.07.XVII.8, United Nations, New York, 2007. The publication is available online at : http://unstats.un.org/unsd/demographic/standmeth/principles/Series_M67Rev2en.pdf

[6] Ibid, para. 2.135.

[7] Alternatively, if a population register is used, completed ages are calculated by subtracting the date of birth of individuals listed in the register from a reference date to which the age data pertain.

[8] A source of non-comparability may result from differences in the method of reckoning age, for example, the Western versus the Eastern or, as it is usually known, the English versus the Chinese system. By the latter, a child is considered one year old at birth and advances an additional year at each Chinese New Year. The effect of this system is most obvious at the beginning of the age span, where the frequencies in the under-one-year category are markedly understated. The effect on higher age groups is not so apparent. Distributions constructed on this basis are often adjusted before publication, but the possibility of such aberrations should not be excluded when census data by age are compared.

[9] In this index, differences were scored from expected values of ratios between numbers of either sex in the same age group, and numbers of the same sex in adjoining age group. In compounding the score, allowance had to be made for certain factors such as the effects of past fluctuations in birth rates, of heavy war casualties, and of the smallness of the population itself. A detailed description of the index, with results from its application to the data presented in the 1949-1950 and 1951 issues of the *Demographic Yearbook*, is furnished in *Population Bulletin, No. 2* (United Nations publication, Sales No. 52.XIII.4), pp. 59-79. The scores obtained from statistics presented in *Demographic Yearbook 1952* are presented in that issue, and the index has also been briefly explained in that issue, as well as those of 1953 and 1954.

[10] United States, Bureau of the Census, Thirteenth Census, Vol. I (Washington, D.C., U.S. Government Printing Office, 1913; Reprint: New York, N.Y., Norman Ross Pub., 1999), pp. 291-292.

[11] Sales No. E.83.XIII.2, United Nations, New York, 1983.

[12] Sales No. E.01.XVII.10, United Nations, New York, 2001.

[13] Sales No. E.98.XVII.7, United Nations, New York, 1998.

[14] Sales No. E.98.XVII.11, United Nations, New York, 1998.

[15] Sales No. E.98.XVII.4, United Nations, New York, 1998.

[16] Sales No. E.98.XVII.6, United Nations, New York, 1998;

[17] Sales No. E.98.XVII.10, United Nations, New York, 1998.

[18] Sales No. E.03.XVII.11, United Nations, New York, 2004.

[19] For more detailed discussion on this issue, refer to *Principles and Recommendations for a Vital Statistics System Revision 2*, Sales No. E. 01.XVII.10, United Nations, New York, 2001, para 57.

[20] For more information on historical and legal background on the use of differing definitions of live births and foetal deaths, comparisons of definitions used as of 1 January 1950, and evaluation of the effects of these differences on the calculation of various rates, see *Handbook of Vital Statistics Systems and Methods Volume 2, Review of National Practices*, Sales No. E.84.XVII.11, United Nations, New York, 1985, Chapter IV.

[21] The World Health Assembly is the annual meeting of the Member States of the World Health Organization and its highest governing body.

[22] *International Statistical Classification of Diseases and Related Health Problems*, Tenth Revision, Volume 2, World Health Organization, Geneva, 1992.

[23] *Ibid*, pp. 129-136.

INTRODUCTION

L'Annuaire démographique est un recueil de statistiques démographiques internationales qui est établi par la Division de statistique du Département des affaires économiques et sociales de l'Organisation des Nations Unies. Il fait partie d'un ensemble de publications complémentaires publiées par l'Organisation des Nations Unies et les institutions spécialisées[1], qui ont pour objet de fournir des statistiques de base aux démographes, aux économistes, aux spécialistes de la santé publique et aux sociologues. Grâce à la coopération des services nationaux de statistique, il a été possible de faire figurer dans la présente édition des statistiques démographiques officielles pour plus de 230 pays ou zones du monde entier.

L'Annuaire démographique 2007 est le cinquante-neuvième d'une série que publie l'ONU depuis 1948. Le présent volume contient des tableaux à caractère général, y compris un aperçu mondial des statistiques démographiques de base et des tableaux qui regroupent des statistiques sur la dimension, la répartition et les tendances de la population, la natalité, la mortalité fœtale, la mortalité infantile et la mortalité liée à la maternité, la mortalité générale, la nuptialité et la divortialité. Des données classées selon le lieu de résidence (zone urbaine ou rurale) sont présentées dans un grand nombre de tableaux. En outre, l'*Annuaire* contient des notes techniques, un tableau synoptique, un index historique et une liste des éditions de l'*Annuaire* publiées jusqu'à présent.

Les notes techniques sur les tableaux statistiques sont destinées à aider le lecteur. Le tableau A, qui correspond au tableau synoptique, permet de se rendre compte en un coup d'oeil du niveau d'exhaustivité des données publiées dans le présent *Annuaire* et l'index thématique facilite le repérage des sujets abordés. Un index cumulatif donne des renseignements sur les matières traitées dans chacune des 59 éditions et sur les années sur lesquelles portent les données. Les numéros de vente des éditions antérieures et une liste des sujets spéciaux traités dans les différentes éditions sont indiqués aux pages iii et iv.

Jusqu'à la 48ème édition (1996), chaque édition se composait de deux parties : les tableaux de caractère général et ceux sur des sujets spéciaux[2]. À partir de 49ème édition (1997), les tableaux sur les sujets spéciaux ont été publiés sur CD-ROM sous forme de suppléments à l'*Annuaire*. Deux CD-ROM ont été produits jusqu'à présent : l'*Annuaire démographique : Supplément historique*, qui présente un grand nombre de statistiques démographiques pour la période allant de 1948 à 1997, et l'*Annuaire démographique : Statistiques de la natalité*, qui contient des tableaux détaillés sur la natalité pour la période allant de 1980 à 1998. Trois volumes concernant un nouvel Annuaire démographique consacré à des thèmes de recensement spéciaux ont été produits et sont présentés à l'adresse suivante : http://unstats.un.org/unsd/demographic/products/dyb/dybcens.htm.

Les statistiques sur la population ne sont pas disponibles pour tous les pays et zones pour plusieurs raisons. Deux annexes ont été ajoutées à partir de la 53ème édition afin d'offrir des estimations sur la population en milieu d'année et un aperçu des statistiques de l'état civil. La première porte sur des estimations concernant la population pour chaque pays ou zone pour la période 1998-2007. La seconde présente les estimations des variantes moyennes concernant les taux bruts de natalité et de mortalité, la mortalité infantile, les indicateurs synthétiques de fécondité et l'espérance de vie à la naissance pour la période 2005-2010. Ces données ont été établies par la Division de la population de l'ONU et publiées dans *World Population Prospects - The 2008 Revision*[3].

Les statistiques démographiques figurant dans la présente édition de l'*Annuaire* sont disponibles en ligne sur les pages Web consacrées à l'Annuaire : http://unstats.un.org/unsd/demographic/products/dyb/dyb2007.htm. On trouvera également des renseignements sur le programme de collecte et de diffusion des données de la Division de statistique sur le même site. Il est possible de se procurer d'autres données en contactant la Division de statistique de l'Organisation des Nations Unies à l'adresse suivante : demostat@un.org.

NOTES TECHNIQUES SUR LES TABLEAUX STATISTIQUES

1. REMARQUES D'ORDRE GÉNÉRAL

1.1 Notes techniques

Les notes techniques ont pour but de donner au lecteur tous les renseignements dont il a besoin pour se servir des tableaux statistiques. Les renseignements qui concernent l'*Annuaire* en général sont présentés dans des sections portant sur diverses considérations géographiques, sur la population et sur les statistiques de natalité et de mortalité. Les tableaux sont ensuite commentés séparément et l'on trouvera pour chacun une description des variables et des observations sur la fiabilité et les lacunes des données ainsi que sur les pays et zones visés et sur les données publiées antérieurement. Des détails sont également donnés, le cas échéant, sur le mode de calcul des taux, quotients et pourcentages.

1.2 Tableaux

La présente édition contient seulement des tableaux de caractère général. Comme la numérotation des tableaux ne correspond pas exactement à celle des éditions précédentes, il est recommandé de se reporter à l'index qui figure à la fin du présent ouvrage pour trouver les données publiées dans les précédentes éditions.

1.3 Origine des données

Sauf indication contraire, les statistiques présentées dans l'*Annuaire démographique* sont des données nationales fournies par les organismes de statistique officiels. Elles sont recueillies essentiellement au moyen de questionnaires qui sont envoyés tous les ans à plus de 230 services nationaux de statistique et autres services gouvernementaux compétents. Les données communiquées en réponse à ces questionnaires sont complétées, dans toute la mesure possible, par des données tirées de publications nationales officielles et des sites web d'organismes officiels et des renseignements communiqués par les services nationaux de statistique à la demande de l'ONU. Pour que les données soient comparables, les taux, rapports et pourcentages ont été calculés par la Division de statistique de l'ONU, à l'exception des paramètres des tables de mortalité et des indicateurs synthétiques de fécondité ainsi que des taux bruts de natalité et de mortalité pour certains pays et zones, qui ont été dûment signalés en note. Les méthodes suivies par la Division pour le calcul des taux et rapports sont décrites dans les notes techniques relatives à chaque tableau. Les chiffres de population utilisés pour ces calculs sont ceux qui figurent dans la présente édition de l'*Annuaire* ou qui ont paru dans des éditions antérieures.

Chaque fois que l'on constatera des différences entre les données du présent volume et celles des éditions antérieures de l'*Annuaire démographique*, ou de certaines publications apparentées, on pourra en conclure que les statistiques publiées cette année sont des chiffres révisés communiqués à la Division de statistique avant juin 2008.

2. CONSIDÉRATIONS GÉOGRAPHIQUES

2.1 Portée

La portée géographique des tableaux du présent *Annuaire* est aussi complète que possible. Des données sont présentées sur tous les pays ou zones qui en ont communiquées. Le tableau 3, le plus complet, contient des données sur la population et la superficie de chaque pays ou zone ayant une population d'au moins 50 habitants. Ces pays ou zones ne figurent pas tous dans les tableaux qui suivent. Dans bien des cas, les données requises pour un tableau particulier n'étaient pas disponibles. En général, les pays ou zones qui peuvent fournir des données sont d'autant moins nombreux que les données demandées sont plus détaillées.

De plus les taux et rapports ne sont présentés que pour les pays ou zones ayant communiqué des chiffres correspondant à un nombre minimal de faits considérés. Les minimums sont indiqués dans les notes techniques relatives à chacun des tableaux.

À l'exception des données récapitulatives présentées dans les tableaux 1 et 2 pour l'ensemble du monde et les grandes zones et régions et des données relatives aux capitales et aux villes de

100 000 habitants ou plus dans le tableau 8, toutes les données se rapportent aux pays. Le nombre de pays sur lequel porte chacun des tableaux est indiqué dans le tableau A.

2.2 Composition territoriale

Autant que possible, toutes les données, y compris les séries chronologiques, se rapportent au territoire de 2007. Les exceptions à cette règle sont signalées en note à la fin des tableaux. On trouve dans le tableau 3 des renseignements concernant les changements intervenus récemment et d'autres précisions intéressantes. Des clarifications importantes sont présentées ci-dessous.

Les données relatives à la République populaire de Chine ne comprennent généralement pas celles de la province de Taiwan ; à l'exception de celles des tableaux 1 et 2.

Les données relatives à la France ne comprennent pas les départements d'outre mer, c'est-à-dire la Guyane française, la Martinique et La Réunion, qui font l'objet de rubriques distinctes.

Les données relatives au Danemark ne comprennent pas les Iles Féroé et le Gröenland, qui font l'objet de rubriques distinctes.

Les données relatives au Sahara Occidental comprennent la région septentrionale (ancien Saguia-el-Hamra) et la région méridionale (ancien Rio de Oro).

Les données relatives au Royaume-Uni de Grande-Bretagne et d'Irlande du Nord ne comprennent pas la Guernesey, l'île de Man et Jersey, qui font l'objet de rubriques distinctes.

Les données relatives à la Norvège ne comprennent pas Svalbard et Jan Mayen qui font l'objet de rubriques distinctes, si disponible.

Les données relatives à la Finlande comprennent les Îles d'Åland.

Les données relatives aux Îles d'Åland sont aussi comprises dans celles relatives à la Finlande.

2.3 Nomenclature

En règle générale, pour gagner de la place, on a jugé commode de désigner dans les tableaux les pays ou zones par les noms abrégés couramment utilisés par l'Organisation des Nations Unies en juin 2009[4], les désignations complètes n'étant utilisées que lorsqu'il n'existait pas de forme abrégée. La liste des désignations des pays ou zones est disponible à l'adresse suivante : http://unstats.un.org/unsd/methods/m49/m49alphaf.htm.

2.3.1 Ordre de présentation

Les pays ou zones sont classés dans l'ordre alphabétique anglais et regroupés par continent comme ci-après : Afrique, Amérique du Nord, Amérique du Sud, Asie, Europe et Océanie.

Les appellations employées dans la présente édition et la présentation des données qui y figurent n'ont d'autre objet que de donner un cadre géographique commode aux séries statistiques. La même observation vaut pour toutes les notes et précisions concernant les unités géographiques pour lesquelles des données sont présentées.

2.4 Superficie

Les données relatives à la superficie qui figurent dans les tableaux 1 et 3 représentent la superficie totale, c'est-à-dire qu'elles englobent les terres émergées et les eaux intérieures (qui sont censées comprendre les principaux lacs et cours d'eau) mais excluent les régions polaires et les îles inhabitées. Les données relatives à la superficie correspondent aux chiffres estimatifs les plus récents. Les superficies sont toutes exprimées en kilomètres carrés ; les chiffres qui avaient été communiqués en miles carrés ont été convertis au moyen d'un coefficient de 2,589988.

2.4.1 Comparabilité dans le temps

La révision des estimations antérieures de la superficie, des augmentations effectives de la superficie terrestre due par exemple à des travaux d'assèchement, à des rectifications de frontières, à des changements d'interprétation du concept de « terres émergées » ou à l'utilisation de nouvelles unités de mesure peut avoir des incidences sur la comparabilité dans le temps des estimations relatives à la superficie d'un pays ou d'une zone donnés. Dans la plupart des cas, il a été possible de déterminer la raison de ces révisions; toutefois, même lorsque la raison n'était pas connue, on a remplacé les anciens chiffres par les nouveaux et on a généralement admis que ce sont ces derniers qui sont exacts.

2.4.2 Comparabilité internationale

Le manque de comparabilité internationale entre les données relatives à la superficie est dû principalement à des différences de définition. En particulier, la définition des golfes, baies et criques, lacs et cours d'eau varie sensiblement d'un pays à l'autre. La diversité des méthodes employées pour estimer les superficies nuit elle aussi à la comparabilité internationale. Certaines données proviennent de levés effectués selon des méthodes scientifiques modernes ; d'autres ne représentent que des conjectures reposant sur diverses catégories de renseignements. Certains chiffres sont récents, d'autres pas. Étant donné que ni la méthode de calcul de la superficie ni la composition du territoire et la date à laquelle se rapportent les données ne sont connues avec précision pour tous les pays ou zones, les estimations figurant dans le tableau 3 ne doivent pas être considérées comme rigoureusement comparables d'un pays ou d'une zone à une autre.

3. POPULATION

Les statistiques de la population, c'est-à-dire celles qui se rapportent à la dimension, à la répartition géographique et aux caractéristiques démographiques de la population, sont présentées dans un certain nombre de tableaux de *l'Annuaire démographique*.

Les données concernant les pays ou les zones représentent les résultats de recensements de population, des estimations fondées sur les résultats d'enquêtes par sondage (s'il n'y a pas eu recensement), des estimations postcensitaires ou intercensitaires, ou des estimations établies à partir de données provenant des registres permanents de population. Dans la présente édition, le tableau 3 indique pour chaque pays ou zone le chiffre le plus récent de la population totale issu du dernier recensement et des estimations établies au milieu de l'année 2005 et de l'année 2007. Le tableau 5 contient des estimations de la population totale au milieu de chaque année pendant 10 ans (1998-2007), et le tableau 6 des estimations de la population urbaine et de la population totale, par sexe, au milieu de chaque année pendant 10 ans (1998-2007). Les dernières données disponibles sur la répartition de la population selon l'âge, le sexe et le lieu de résidence (zone urbaine ou rurale) sont présentées dans le tableau 7. Les derniers chiffres disponibles sur la population des capitales et des villes de 100 000 habitants ou plus sont regroupés dans le tableau 8.

Les tableaux 1 et 2 présentent respectivement des estimations récapitulatives de la population du monde, des grandes zones et des régions en milieu d'année, pour certaines années, ainsi que des estimations récapitulatives pour 2007, concernant la population répartie selon l'âge et le sexe.

On a utilisé pour le calcul des taux les statistiques de la population totale et de la population répartie selon l'âge, le sexe et le lieu de résidence (zone urbaine ou rurale). Les taux démographiques selon l'âge, le sexe et la résidence (urbaine/rurale) ont été calculés à partir des données qui figurent dans le tableau 7 de la présente édition ou dans les tableaux correspondants d'éditions précédentes de *l'Annuaire démographique*.

3.1 Sources de variation des données

Plusieurs facteurs influent sur la comparabilité des données : 1) la définition de la population totale ; 2) les définitions utilisées pour faire la distinction entre population urbaine et population rurale ; 3) les difficultés liées aux déclarations d'âge ; 4) l'étendue du sur-dénombrement ou du sous-dénombrement dans le recensement le plus récent ou dans une autre source de statistiques de référence sur la population ; 5) la qualité des estimations relatives à la population. Ces cinq facteurs sont analysés en détail aux sections 3.1.1 à 3.2.2 ci-après. D'autres questions seront traitées dans les notes techniques relatives à chaque tableau. Pour plus de précisions concernant, notamment, les notions fondamentales de dimension, de répartition et de caractéristiques de la population qui ont été élaborées par l'Organisation des Nations Unies, le lecteur est invité à se reporter aux *Principes et recommandations concernant les recensements de la population et de l'habitat. Révision 2*[5].

3.1.1 Population totale

Le principal obstacle à la comparabilité des données relatives à la population totale est la différence qui existe entre population de fait et population de droit. La population de fait comprend toutes les personnes présentes dans le pays ou la zone à la date de référence, tandis que la population de droit comprend toutes celles qui résident habituellement dans le pays ou la zone, qu'elles y aient été ou non présentes à la date de référence. Par définition, la population totale de fait et la population totale de droit ne sont donc pas rigoureusement comparables entre elles.

Même lorsque l'on veut comparer deux totaux qui se rapportent à des populations de fait ou deux totaux qui se rapportent à des populations de droit, on risque souvent de faire des erreurs pour cette raison qu'il est rare que l'une et l'autre notions soient appliquées strictement. Pour citer quelques exemples, certains chiffres qui sont censés porter sur la population de fait ne tiennent pas compte du personnel militaire, naval et diplomatique étranger en fonction dans le pays ou la zone, ni des membres de leurs familles et de leurs domestiques les accompagnant; d'autres ne comprennent pas les visiteurs étrangers de passage dans le pays ou la zone ni les personnes à bord de navires ancrés dans les ports. En revanche, il arrive que l'on compte des personnes, inscrits maritimes et marins pêcheurs par exemple, qui, en raison de leur activité professionnelle, se trouvent hors du pays ou de la zone de recensement.

Les risques de disparités sont encore plus grands quand il s'agit de comparer des populations de droit, car les comparaisons dépendent au premier chef de la définition que l'on donne à l'expression « lieu de résidence habituel », qui varie d'un pays ou d'une zone à l'autre et qu'il est, de toute façon, difficile d'appliquer uniformément pour le dénombrement lors d'un recensement ou d'une enquête. Par exemple, les civils étrangers qui se trouvent temporairement dans un pays ou une zone comme travailleurs à court terme peuvent officiellement être considérés comme résidents après un séjour d'une durée déterminée, mais ils peuvent aussi être considérés comme non-résidents pendant toute la durée de leur séjour ; ailleurs, ces mêmes personnes peuvent être considérées officiellement comme résidents ou comme non-résidents du pays ou de la zone d'où elles viennent, selon la durée et, éventuellement, la raison de leur absence. Qui plus est, quel que soit son statut officiel, chacun des recensés peut, au moment de l'enquête, interpréter à sa façon la notion de résidence. De plus, les autorités nationales ou les entités responsables des zones ne savent pas toutes avec la même précision combien de leurs résidents se trouvent temporairement à l'étranger.

Les chiffres de population présentés dans les tableaux de l'*Annuaire* représentent, autant qu'il a été possible, la population de fait. Sauf indication contraire, on peut supposer que les chiffres présentés ont été communiqués par les pays ou les zones comme se rapportant à la population de fait. Les chiffres qui ont été communiqués comme se rapportant à la population de droit sont indiqués comme tels. Lorsque l'on savait que les données avaient été recueillies selon une définition de la population de fait ou de la population de droit qui s'écartait sensiblement de celle exposée plus haut, on l'a signalé en note, de manière à compenser dans toute la mesure possible les conséquences des divergences.

Il ne faut pas oublier néanmoins que l'on ne disposait pas toujours de renseignements détaillés à ce sujet. On ne peut donc partir du principe que les chiffres qui ne sont pas accompagnés d'une note signalant une divergence correspondent exactement aux définitions de la population de fait ou de la population de droit.

Il peut y avoir hétérogénéité dans les statistiques d'un même pays ou d'une même zone dans le cas des pays ou zones qui ne font une exploitation statistique détaillée des données que pour la population de droit alors qu'ils recueillent des données sur la population de droit et sur la population de fait à l'occasion d'un recensement, par exemple. Ainsi, tandis que les chiffres relatifs à la population totale qui figurent au tableau 3 se rapportent à la population de fait, ceux des tableaux qui présentent des données sur diverses caractéristiques de la population, par exemple le lieu de résidence (zone urbaine ou rurale), l'âge et le sexe, peuvent n'avoir trait qu'à la population de droit.

3.1.2 Lieu de résidence (zone urbaine ou rurale)

L'hétérogénéité des définitions nationales du terme « urbain » nuit considérablement à la comparabilité internationale des données concernant la répartition selon le lieu de résidence. Les définitions utilisées par les différents pays ou zones et leurs implications sont exposées à la fin des notes techniques correspondant au tableau 6.

3.1.3 Répartition par âge

La répartition de la population selon l'âge est un paramètre fondamental de la plupart des analyses, estimations et projections relatives aux statistiques de la population. Malheureusement, ces données sont sujettes à un certain nombre d'erreurs et difficilement comparables. C'est pourquoi pratiquement tous les utilisateurs de ces statistiques doivent considérer ces répartitions avec la plus grande circonspection.

3.1.3.1 Collecte et exploitation des données sur l'âge

L'âge est l'intervalle de temps déterminé par calcul ou par estimation qui sépare la date de naissance de la date du recensement et qui est exprimé en années solaires révolues.[6] Les données sur l'âge peuvent être recueillies selon deux méthodes : la première consiste à obtenir la date de naissance de chaque personne à l'occasion d'un recensement ou d'un sondage, puis à calculer l'âge en années révolues en soustrayant la date de naissance de celle du dénombrement[7]. La seconde consiste à enregistrer l'âge en années révolues au moment du recensement, c'est-à-dire l'âge au dernier anniversaire.

La méthode recommandée consiste à calculer l'âge au dernier anniversaire en soustrayant la date exacte de la naissance de la date du recensement. Toutefois, on n'a pas toujours recours à cette méthode ; certains pays ou zones calculent l'âge en faisant la différence entre l'année du recensement et l'année de la naissance. Lorsque les données sur l'âge ont été établies de cette façon, on l'a signalé chaque fois que possible par une note. On peut d'ailleurs s'en rendre compte dans une certaine mesure, car les chiffres dans la catégorie des moins d'un an sont plus faibles qu'ils ne devraient l'être. Cependant, un nombre irrégulier de naissances d'une année à l'autre ou l'omission de certains âges parmi les moins d'un an peut aussi fausser les chiffres de la population de moins d'un an.

3.1.3.2 Erreurs dans les données sur l'âge

Les causes d'erreurs dans les données sur l'âge sont diverses : on peut citer notamment l'ignorance de l'âge exact, la déclaration d'années d'âge correspondant à un calendrier différent de celui des années solaires révolues depuis la naissance[8], la négligence dans les déclarations et dans la façon dont elles sont consignées, la tendance générale à déclarer des âges se terminant par certains chiffres tels que 0, 2, 5 ou 8, la tendance pour les personnes âgées à exagérer leur âge, une aversion subconsciente pour certains nombres, et les fausses déclarations faites délibérément.

Les causes d'erreurs mentionnées ci-dessus, communes à la plupart des enquêtes sur l'âge et à la plupart des pays ou zones, peuvent nuire sensiblement à la comparabilité.

À cause des difficultés indiquées ci-dessus, les répartitions par âge et par sexe de la population d'un grand nombre de pays ou de zones font apparaître les irrégularités suivantes : 1) sous-estimation des groupes d'âge correspondant aux enfants de moins d'un an et aux jeunes enfants ; 2) polarisation des déclarations sur les âges se terminant par les chiffres 0 ou 5 (c'est-à-dire 5, 10, 15, 20...) ; 3) prépondérance des âges pairs (par exemple 10, 12, 14...) au détriment des âges impairs (par exemple 11, 13, 15...) ; 4) écart considérable et surprenant entre le rapport masculin/féminin à certains âges ; 5) différences importantes et difficilement explicables entre les données concernant des groupes d'âge voisins. En comparant les statistiques provenant de recensements successifs pour des cohortes identiques sur le plan de l'âge et de la répartition par sexe et en étudiant la répartition par âge et par sexe de la population à chaque recensement, on peut déceler l'existence de ces incohérences et de quelques autres, un certain nombre d'entre elles se retrouvant à des degrés divers même dans les recensements les plus modernes.

3.1.3.3 Évaluation de l'exactitude

Pour déterminer, sur la base des anomalies relevées dans les groupes d'âge quinquennaux, le degré d'exactitude des statistiques par âge, on avait mis au point un indice spécial[9] pour l'Annuaire démographique 1949-1950. Cet indice était sensible à l'influence des différents facteurs qui limitent l'exactitude des données et il n'échappait pas non plus à celle des véritables fluctuations démographiques du passé. On ne pouvait donc l'appliquer indistinctement à tous les types de données à moins d'effectuer les ajustements nécessaires et de faire preuve de prudence dans l'interprétation des résultats.

La publication dans l'*Annuaire démographique 1955* de statistiques de la population par année d'âge a permis d'utiliser un indice simple, mais très sensible, connu sous le nom d'indice de Whipple ou indice de concentration[10], dont l'interprétation échappe pratiquement à l'influence des facteurs sans rapport avec l'exactitude des déclarations d'âge. Il existe des méthodes plus perfectionnées pour évaluer l'exactitude des répartitions de population par année d'âge, mais on a décidé de se servir ici de l'indice de Whipple à cause de sa simplicité et de la large utilisation dont il a déjà fait l'objet dans d'autres publications.

L'indice de Whipple s'obtient en additionnant les déclarations d'âge comprises entre 23 et 62 ans inclusivement et en calculant le pourcentage des âges déclarés se terminant par 0 ou 5 par rapport au cinquième du nombre total de déclarations.

Les résultats varient entre 0, si aucun âge déclaré ne se termine par 0 ou 5, et un maximum de 500, si aucun âge déclaré ne se termine par un chiffre autre que 0 ou 5. S'il n'y a pas de concentration sur les âges se terminant par 0 et 5, l'indice de Whipple est de 100[11].

Cet indice est applicable à toutes les répartitions par âge pour lesquelles les années d'âge sont données au moins jusqu'à 62 ans, sauf dans les cas suivants : 1) lorsque les données présentées ont déjà fait l'objet d'un ajustement, l'indice de Whipple ne révèle aucune irrégularité bien que des inexactitudes d'un type différent puissent fausser ces données ; 2) lorsque les statistiques relatives à l'âge sont établies sur la base de l'année de naissance et que la tendance à arrondir l'année de naissance se traduit par une fréquence excessive des âges impairs, on ne peut utiliser la méthode reposant sur les déclarations d'âge se terminant par 5 et 0 pour évaluer l'exactitude des données recueillies.

L'indice a dernièrement été calculé pour toutes les distributions par année d'âge des recensements effectués entre 1985 et 2003, à l'exception de celles que l'on a écartées pour les motifs indiqués plus haut. Ces données sont publiées dans l'édition spéciale de l'*Annuaire démographique* consacrée aux recensements de la population, volume I , que l'on peut consulter en ligne à l'adresse http://unstats.un.org/unsd/demographic/products/dyb/dybcens.htm .

Bien que l'indice de Whipple ne mesure que les effets de la préférence pour les âges se terminant par 5 et 0, il semble que l'on puisse admettre qu'il existe généralement certains liens entre cette préférence et d'autres sources d'inexactitudes dans les déclarations d'âge, de telle sorte que l'on peut dire qu'il donne une assez bonne idée de l'exactitude de la répartition par âge en général.

3.2 Méthodes utilisées pour indiquer la qualité des statistiques publiées

On a cherché dans toute la mesure possible à donner au lecteur une indication du degré de fiabilité des statistiques publiées dans l'*Annuaire démographique*. Pour ce faire, on a procédé de diverses façons. Chaque fois que l'on savait, grâce par exemple à une enquête post censitaire, qu'il y avait eu sous-dénombrement ou surdénombrement, on l'a signalé dans les notes qui accompagnent le tableau 3. Comme on l'a indiqué à la section 2.1 sous la rubrique « Considérations géographiques », chaque fois que les données ne portaient pas sur la totalité du pays, on l'a également signalé en note. De plus, les services nationaux de statistique ont été invités à fournir une évaluation des estimations de la population totale qu'ils communiquaient à la Division de statistique de l'ONU.

3.2.1 Traitement des séries chronologiques d'estimations de la population

En ce qui concerne les séries d'estimations de la population en milieu d'année, on considère que la qualité de la série tout entière est la même que celle de la dernière estimation. La qualité de la série est indiquée par le caractère d'imprimerie utilisé.

On n'a pas cherché à subdiviser les séries, mais il est évident que les données qui sont jugées sûres actuellement n'ont pas toutes le même degré de fiabilité et que, pour les premières années, nombre d'entre elles étaient peut-être bien moins sûres que la classification actuelle ne le laisse supposer. Ainsi, il apparaît clairement que cette méthode tend, dans bien des cas, à surestimer la fiabilité probable des séries chronologiques. Elle peut aussi inciter à sous-estimer la fiabilité des estimations pour les années qui précèdent ou qui suivent immédiatement un recensement.

3.2.2 Traitement des séries estimatives selon l'âge et d'autres caractéristiques démographiques

Des estimations de la répartition de la population par âge et par sexe peuvent être obtenues selon deux grandes méthodes : 1) en appliquant les composantes spécifiques du mouvement de la population, pour chaque groupe d'âge et pour chaque sexe, à la population dénombrée lors du recensement ; 2) en répartissant proportionnellement le chiffre total estimé pour une année postcensitaire d'après la composition par âge et par sexe au moment du recensement. Les estimations obtenues par la seconde méthode ne sont pas publiées dans l'*Annuaire démographique*.

Les séries estimatives selon l'âge et le sexe qui sont publiées sont classées en deux catégories, « sûres » ou « moins sûres », selon la méthode retenue pour le plus récent calcul estimatif de la population totale en milieu d'année. Ainsi, l'appréciation de la qualité du chiffre total, telle qu'elle ressort des signes de code, est censée s'appliquer aussi à l'ensemble de la répartition par âge et par sexe, et c'est sur cette seule base que l'on décide si les données figureront en caractères italiques ou romains. On n'a pas encore procédé à une évaluation plus poussée des données détaillées concernant la composition par âge.

4. STATISTIQUES DE L'ÉTAT CIVIL

Aux fins de l'*Annuaire démographique*, on entend par statistiques de l'état civil les statistiques des naissances vivantes.

Dans le présent volume de l'*Annuaire*, on n'a présenté que les tableaux de caractère général sur la natalité, la mortalité, la nuptialité et la divortialité. Les tableaux consacrés à la mortalité sont groupés sous les rubriques suivantes : mortalité fœtale, mortalité infantile, mortalité liée à la maternité et mortalité générale, y compris des tableaux portant sur la cause des décès.

4.1 Sources de variations des données

La plupart des statistiques de l'état civil publiées dans le présent *Annuaire* émanent des systèmes nationaux d'enregistrement des faits d'état civil. Le degré d'exhaustivité et d'exactitude de ces données varie d'un pays ou d'une zone à l'autre.

Il n'existe pas partout de système national d'enregistrement des faits d'état civil et, dans quelques cas, seuls certains faits sont enregistrés. Par exemple, dans certains pays ou zones, seuls les naissances et les décès sont enregistrés. Il existe également des différences quant au degré d'efficacité avec lequel les lois relatives à l'enregistrement des faits d'état civil sont appliquées dans les divers pays ou zones. La fiabilité des statistiques provenant des registres d'état civil dépend des modalités d'application de la loi et de la mesure dans laquelle le public s'y soumet.

Il est à signaler que dans certains cas les statistiques de la nuptialité et de la divortialité sont tirées d'autres sources que les registres d'état civil. Dans certains pays ou zones, par exemple, les seules données disponibles sur la nuptialité proviennent des registres des églises. Selon la pratique suivie par chaque pays, les statistiques de la divortialité sont tirées des actes des tribunaux et/ou des registres d'état civil. L'officier de l'état civil, le service national de statistique ou d'autres services administratifs peuvent être chargés d'établir ces statistiques.

Les autres facteurs qui influent sur la comparabilité internationale des statistiques de l'état civil sont à peu près les mêmes que ceux qu'il convient de prendre en considération pour interpréter les variations observées dans les statistiques de la population. La définition des faits d'état civil aux fins de statistique, la portée des données du point de vue géographique et ethnique ainsi que les méthodes d'exploitation des données sont autant d'éléments qui peuvent influer sur la comparabilité.

En plus des statistiques tirées des registres d'état civil, l'*Annuaire* présente des statistiques de l'état civil qui sont des estimations officielles nationales, fondées souvent sur les résultats de sondages. Aussi leur comparabilité varie-t-elle en fonction du degré d'exhaustivité des déclarations recueillies lors d'enquêtes sur les ménages, des erreurs d'échantillonnage ou autres, et des distorsions d'origines diverses.

Pour plus de détails au sujet des pratiques nationales relatives au rassemblement des statistiques d'état civil, le lecteur pourra se reporter aux : *Principes et recommandations pour un système de statistiques de l'état civil, deuxième révision*[12] ; *Manuel des systèmes d'enregistrement des faits d'état civil et de statistiques de l'état civil : Élaboration d'un cadre juridique*[13] ; *Manuel des systèmes d'enregistrement des faits d'état civil et de statistiques de l'état civil : Gestion, fonctionnement et tenue*[14] ; *Manuel des systèmes d'enregistrement des faits d'état civil et de statistiques de l'état civil : Élaboration de programmes d'information, d'éducation et de communication*[15] ; *Manuel des systèmes d'enregistrement des faits d'état civil et de statistiques de l'état civil : Principes et protocoles concernant la communication et l'archivage des* documents individuels[16]; *Manuel des systèmes d'enregistrement des faits d'état civil et de statistiques de l'état civil : Informatisation*[17]. Le *Manuel de collecte de données sur la fécondité et la mortalité*[18] fournit des informations ayant trait à la collecte et à l'évaluation des données sur la fécondité, sur la mortalité et sur d'autres faits d'état civil, qui ont été recueillies au cours des enquêtes sur les ménages. Ces publications sont également disponibles sur le Web à partir de l'adresse suivante : http://unstats.un.org/unsd/demographic/sources/civilreg/default.htm.

4.1.1 Définition des faits d'état civil aux fins de la statistique

Une cause importante d'hétérogénéité dans les données est le manque d'uniformité des définitions des différents faits d'état civil. Aux fins de *l'Annuaire démographique*, il est recommandé de recueillir les données relatives aux faits d'état civil en utilisant les définitions établies au paragraphe 57 des *Principes et recommandations pour un système de statistiques de l'état civil, deuxième révision*[12]. Ces définitions sont les suivantes :

La NAISSANCE VIVANTE est l'expulsion ou l'extraction complète du corps de la mère, indépendamment de la durée de la gestation, d'un produit de la conception qui, après cette séparation, respire ou manifeste tout autre signe de vie, tel que battement de cœur, pulsation du cordon ombilical ou contraction effective d'un muscle soumis à l'action de la volonté, que le cordon ombilical ait été coupé ou non et que le placenta soit ou non demeuré attaché; tout produit d'une telle naissance est considéré comme « enfant né vivant ».

Le DÉCÈS est la disparition permanente de tout signe de vie à un moment quelconque postérieur à la naissance vivante (cessation des fonctions vitales après la naissance sans possibilité de réanimation). Cette définition ne comprend donc pas les morts fœtales.

La MORT FŒTALE est le décès d'un produit de la conception lorsque ce décès est survenu avant l'expulsion ou l'extraction complète du corps de la mère, indépendamment de la durée de la gestation; le décès est indiqué par le fait qu'après cette séparation le fœtus ne respire ni ne manifeste aucun signe de vie, tel que battement de cœur, pulsation du cordon ombilical ou contraction effective d'un muscle soumis à l'action de la volonté. Les morts fœtales tardives sont celles qui sont survenues après 28 semaines de gestation ou plus. Il n'y a aucune différence entre ces « morts fœtales tardives » et les faits désignés, avant 1950, par le terme « mortinatalité[19] *».*

Le MARIAGE est l'acte, la cérémonie ou la procédure qui établit un rapport légal entre mari et femme. L'union peut être rendue légale par une procédure civile ou religieuse, ou par toute autre procédure, conformément à la législation du pays.

Le DIVORCE est la dissolution légale et définitive des liens du mariage, c'est-à-dire la séparation de l'époux et de l'épouse qui confère aux parties le droit de se remarier civilement ou religieusement, ou selon toute autre procédure, conformément à la législation du pays.

Des données concernant les avortements sont également recueillies et présentées dans *l'Annuaire démographique*, la définition retenue étant la suivante :

Par référence à la femme, l'AVORTEMENT se définit comme toute interruption de grossesse qui est survenue avant 28 semaines de gestation et dont le produit est un fœtus mort. Il existe deux grandes catégories d'avortement : l'avortement spontané et l'avortement provoqué. L'avortement provoqué a pour origine une action délibérée entreprise en vue d'interrompre une grossesse. Tout autre avortement est considéré comme spontané.

4.1.2 Problèmes posés par les définitions établies

Les variations par rapport aux définitions établies des faits d'état civil sont le principal obstacle à la comparabilité internationale des statistiques de l'état civil. Un exemple en est fourni par le cas des naissances vivantes et celui des morts fœtales[20]. Dans certains pays ou zones, il faut que le nouveau-né ait vécu 24 heures pour pouvoir être inscrit sur le registre des naissances vivantes. Les décès d'enfants qui surviennent avant l'expiration du délai de 24 heures sont classés parmi les morts fœtales tardives et, en l'absence de méthodes spéciales d'exploitation des données, ne sont comptés ni dans les naissances vivantes ni dans les décès. De même, dans plusieurs autres pays ou zones, les décès d'enfants nés vivants et décédés avant l'enregistrement de leur naissance sont également comptés parmi les morts fœtales tardives.

À moins que des méthodes spéciales n'aient été adoptées pour l'exploitation de ces données, les statistiques des naissances vivantes et des décès ne tiendront pas compte de ces cas, qui viendront en revanche accroître d'autant le nombre des morts fœtales tardives. Le taux de mortalité infantile sera donc sous-estimé. Bien que les éléments constitutifs du taux (décès d'enfants de moins d'un an et naissances vivantes) accusent exactement la même insuffisance en valeur absolue, les lacunes sont proportionnellement plus fortes pour les décès de moins d'un an, ce qui cause des erreurs plus importantes dans les taux de mortalité infantile.

De plus, cette pratique augmente les rapports de mortinatalité. Quelques pays ou zones effectuent les ajustements nécessaires pour corriger cette anomalie (du moins dans les fréquences totales) au moment de l'établissement des tableaux. Si aucun ajustement n'a été effectué, cela est indiqué dans les notes chaque fois que possible.

Les définitions du mariage et du divorce posent aussi un problème du point de vue de la comparabilité internationale. Contrairement à la naissance et au décès, qui sont des faits biologiques, le mariage et le divorce sont uniquement déterminés par la législation et la coutume et, de ce fait, il est moins facile d'en donner une définition statistique qui ait une application universelle. À des fins statistiques, ces notions ont donc été définies de manière générale par référence à la législation de chaque pays ou zone. La législation relative au mariage et plus particulièrement au divorce varie d'un pays ou d'une zone à l'autre. En ce qui concerne le mariage, l'âge de nubilité est la condition la plus fréquemment requise mais il arrive souvent que d'autres conditions soient exigées.

Lorsqu'il est connu, l'âge minimum auquel le mariage peut avoir lieu avec le consentement des parents (et dans certains cas sans le consentement des parents) est indiqué au tableau 22-1. Les lois et règlements relatifs à la dissolution du mariage par le divorce vont de l'interdiction absolue, en passant par diverses conditions requises pour l'obtention du divorce, jusqu'à la simple déclaration, par l'époux, de son désir ou de son intention de divorcer.

4.1.3 Portée géographique ou ethnique restreinte

En principe, les statistiques de l'état civil devraient s'étendre à l'ensemble du pays ou de la zone auxquels elles se rapportent et englober tous les groupes ethniques. En fait, il n'est pas rare que les données soient fragmentaires. Dans certains pays ou zones, l'enregistrement n'est obligatoire que pour une petite partie de la population, par exemple pour certains groupes ethniques. Dans d'autres, il n'existe pas de disposition qui prescrive l'enregistrement obligatoire sur le plan national, mais seulement des règlements ou décrets des municipalités ou des États, qui ne s'appliquent pas à l'ensemble du territoire. Il en est encore autrement dans d'autres pays ou zones où les autorités ont institué une zone d'enregistrement comprenant seulement une partie du territoire, le reste étant exclu en raison des difficultés d'accès ou parce qu'il est pratiquement impossible, pour des raisons d'ordre économique ou culturel, d'y procéder à un enregistrement régulier.

4.1.4 Exploitation des données

4.1.4.1 Selon le lieu de l'événement

Les statistiques de l'état civil qui sont présentées pour l'ensemble du territoire national se rapportent à la population de fait ou population présente. En conséquence, sauf indication contraire, les statistiques de l'état civil relatives à une zone ou à un pays donné portent sur tous les faits survenus dans l'ensemble de la population, à l'intérieur des frontières actuelles de la zone ou du pays considéré. On peut donc estimer qu'elles englobent les faits d'état civil survenus dans les tribus nomades et parmi les populations autochtones ainsi que parmi les ressortissants du pays et les étrangers. Des notes signalent les exceptions lorsque celles-ci sont connues.

Pour certains pays, les écarts entre les taux démographiques pour les zones urbaines et pour les zones rurales peuvent varier notablement selon que les faits d'état civil ont été exploités sur la base du lieu de l'événement ou du lieu de résidence habituel. Par exemple, si un nombre appréciable de femmes résidant dans des zones rurales proches de grands centres urbains accouchent dans les hôpitaux ou maternités d'une ville, les taux de fécondité ainsi que les taux de mortalité néo-natale et infantile seront généralement plus élevés dans les zones urbaines (et par conséquent plus faibles dans les zones rurales) si les faits sont exploités en se fondant sur le lieu de l'événement et non sur le lieu de résidence habituel. Le phénomène sera le même dans le cas de la mortalité générale si un bon nombre de personnes résidant dans des zones rurales font appel aux services de santé des villes lorsqu'elles sont gravement malades.

4.1.4.2 Selon la date de l'événement ou la date de l'enregistrement

Autant que possible, les statistiques de l'état civil figurant dans *l'Annuaire démographique* se rapportent aux faits survenus pendant l'année considérée et non aux faits enregistrés au cours de ladite année. Bon nombre de pays ou zones, toutefois, exploitent leurs statistiques de l'état civil selon la date de l'enregistrement et non selon la date de l'événement. Comme ces statistiques risquent d'induire gravement en erreur, les pays ou zones dont on sait qu'ils établissent leurs statistiques d'après la date de l'enregistrement sont signalés dans les tableaux par un signe plus "+". On ne dispose toutefois pas pour tous les pays ou zones de renseignements complets sur la méthode d'exploitation des statistiques de l'état civil et les données sont peut-être exploitées selon la date de l'enregistrement plus souvent que ne le laisserait supposer l'emploi des signes.

Étant donné que la qualité des données est inextricablement liée aux retards dans l'enregistrement, il faudra toujours considérer en même temps le code de qualité qui est décrit à la section 4.2.1 ci-après. Évidemment, si l'enregistrement des naissances est complet et effectué en temps voulu (code "C"), les effets perturbateurs de la méthode consistant à exploiter les données selon la date de l'enregistrement seront pratiquement annulés. De même, s'agissant des statistiques des décès, les effets pourront bien souvent être réduits au minimum dans les pays ou zones où le code sanitaire subordonne la délivrance du permis d'inhumer à l'enregistrement du décès, ce qui tend à hâter l'enregistrement. Quant aux morts fœtales, elles sont généralement déclarées immédiatement ou ne sont pas déclarées du tout. En conséquence, si l'enregistrement se fait dans un délai très court, la différence entre les statistiques établies selon la date de l'événement et celles qui sont établies selon la date de l'enregistrement peut être négligeable. Dans bien des cas, la durée des délais légaux accordés pour l'enregistrement des faits d'état civil est un facteur dont dépend dans une large mesure l'incidence sur la comparabilité de l'exploitation des données selon la date de l'enregistrement.

En ce qui concerne le mariage et le divorce, la pratique consistant à exploiter les statistiques selon la date de l'enregistrement ne pose généralement pas de graves problèmes. Le mariage étant, dans de nombreux pays ou zones, un contrat juridique civil qui, pour être légal, doit être conclu devant un officier de l'état civil, il s'ensuit que dans ces pays ou zones l'enregistrement a lieu presque systématiquement au moment de la cérémonie ou immédiatement après. De même, dans de nombreux pays ou zones, le tribunal ou l'autorité qui a prononcé le divorce est seul habilité à enregistrer cet acte, et comme l'acte d'enregistrement figure alors sur les registres du tribunal l'enregistrement suit généralement de peu le jugement.

En revanche, si l'enregistrement n'a lieu qu'avec un certain retard, les statistiques de l'état civil établies selon la date de l'enregistrement ne sont pas comparables sur le plan international. Au mieux, les statistiques par date de l'enregistrement prendront surtout en considération des faits survenus au cours de l'année précédente ; dans les pays ou zones où le système d'enregistrement n'est pas très développé, il y entrera des faits datant de plusieurs années. Il ressort des documents dont on dispose que des retards de plusieurs années dans l'enregistrement des naissances ne sont pas rares, encore que, dans la majorité des cas, les retards ne dépassent pas deux à quatre ans.

Tant que l'enregistrement se fera avec retard, les statistiques fondées sur la date d'enregistrement ne seront comparables sur le plan international ni entre elles ni avec les statistiques établies selon la date de fait d'état civil.

Il convient également de noter que l'exploitation des données selon la date de l'enregistrement ne nuit pas seulement à la comparabilité internationale des statistiques. Même à l'intérieur d'un pays ou d'une zone, le procédé qui consiste à compter les enregistrements et non les faits peut compromettre la comparabilité des chiffres sur une longue période. Si le nombre des faits d'état civil enregistrés varie d'une année à l'autre (par suite de l'application de mesures visant tout particulièrement à encourager l'enregistrement ou parce qu'il est subitement devenu nécessaire de produire le certificat d'une naissance ou d'un décès non enregistré pour l'accomplissement de certaines formalités), les statistiques de l'état civil établies d'après la date de l'enregistrement ne permettent pas de quantifier ni d'analyser l'état et l'évolution de la population. Tout au plus peuvent-elles révéler l'évolution des conditions d'exigibilité du certificat de naissance, de décès ou de mariage et les fluctuations du volume de travail des bureaux d'état civil. Les statistiques établies selon la date de l'enregistrement peuvent donc ne présenter qu'une utilité très réduite pour des études nationales ou internationales.

4.2 Méthodes utilisées pour indiquer la qualité des statistiques de l'état civil qui sont publiées

La qualité des statistiques de l'état civil peut être évaluée en se fondant sur plusieurs facteurs. Le facteur essentiel est la complétude du système d'enregistrement des faits d'état civil d'après lequel les statistiques sont établies. Dans certains cas, on constate que les données tirées de l'enregistrement ne sont pas complètes lorsque l'on les utilise pour le calcul des taux. Toutefois, cette observation est valable uniquement lorsque les statistiques présentent des lacunes évidentes, qu'elles sont exploitées d'après la date de l'événement et que l'estimation du chiffre de population pris pour base est exacte. L'exploitation des données d'après la date de l'enregistrement donne souvent des taux qui paraissent exacts, tout simplement parce que le numérateur est artificiellement gonflé par suite de l'inclusion d'un grand nombre d'enregistrements tardifs ; inversement, il arrive que des taux paraissent vraisemblables parce que l'on a sous-évalué la population étudiée. Il ne faut pas non plus oublier que les renseignements dont on dispose sur les taux de fécondité, de mortalité et de nuptialité considérés comme normaux sont extrêmement sommaires dans un grand nombre de régions du monde et que les cas limites, qui sont les plus difficiles à évaluer, sont fréquents.

4.2.1 Codage qualitatif des statistiques provenant des registres de l'état civil

Dans le questionnaire relatif au mouvement de la population qui leur est envoyé chaque année dans le cadre de l'établissement de *l'Annuaire démographique*, les services nationaux de statistique sont invités à donner leur propre évaluation du degré de complétude des données sur les naissances, les décès, les décès d'enfants de moins d'un an, les morts fœtales tardives, les mariages et les divorces figurant dans leurs registres d'état civil.

D'après les renseignements directement communiqués par les gouvernements ou extraits des questionnaires ou de publications officielles pertinentes, il a été possible de classer les statistiques de l'enregistrement des faits d'état civil (naissances, décès, décès d'enfants de moins d'un an, morts fœtales tardives, mariages et divorces) en trois grandes catégories, selon leur qualité :

C : Données jugées pratiquement complètes, c'est-à-dire représentant au moins 90 p. 100 des faits d'état civil survenant chaque année.

U : Données jugées incomplètes, c'est-à-dire représentant moins de 90 p. 100 des faits survenant chaque année.

| : Données ne provenant pas des systèmes nationaux d'enregistrement des faits d'état civil mais jugées fiables, telles que les estimations dérivées des projections, d'autres techniques d'estimation ou recensements de population ou du logement.

... : Données dont le degré de complétude ne fait pas l'objet de renseignements précis.

Ces codes de qualité figurent dans la deuxième colonne des tableaux qui présentent, pour un nombre d'années déterminé les chiffres absolus et les taux (ou rapports) bruts concernant les naissances vivantes (tableau 9), les morts fœtales tardives (tableau 12), les décès d'enfants de moins d'un an (tableau 15), les décès (tableau 18), les mariages (tableau 23) et les divorces (tableau 25).

La classification des pays ou zones selon ces codes de qualité peut ne pas être uniforme. On a estimé néanmoins que les services nationaux de statistique étaient les mieux placés pour juger de la qualité de leurs données. On a pensé que les catégories que l'on pouvait distinguer sur la base des renseignements disponibles, bien que très larges, permettaient cependant de se faire une idée de la qualité des statistiques de l'état civil publiées dans l'*Annuaire*.

Par le passé, les bases sur lesquelles les pays évaluaient l'exhaustivité de leurs données n'étaient généralement pas connues. À l'occasion de l'établissement de l'*Annuaire démographique 1977*, les pays ont été invités, pour la première fois, à donner des indications à ce sujet. On leur a demandé de préciser si leurs estimations du degré d'exhaustivité des données d'enregistrement des naissances vivantes, des décès et de la mortalité infantile reposaient sur une analyse démographique, un double contrôle des registres ou d'autres méthodes qu'ils devaient spécifier. Relativement peu de pays ou zones ont jusqu'à présent répondu à cette nouvelle question ; on n'a donc pas cherché à réviser le système de codage qualitatif utilisé pour les statistiques de l'état civil présentées dans l'*Annuaire*. Il faut espérer qu'à l'avenir davantage de pays pourront fournir ces renseignements afin que l'on puisse adapter le système de codage qualitatif.

Sur les pays ou zones qui ont estimé à 90 p. 100 ou plus le degré d'exhaustivité de leur enregistrement des naissances vivantes (classé "C" dans le tableau 9), les pays ou zones suivants ont communiqué des renseignements concernant les bases sur lesquelles leur estimation reposait :

a) Analyse démographique : Andorre, Argentine, Autriche, Bulgarie, Croatie, Cuba, Estonie, Islande, Israël, Italie, Lettonie, Lituanie, Malte, Maurice, Mexique, Monaco, Territoire palestinien occupé, Pologne, Porto Rico, République de Corée, République de Moldova, République tchèque, Roumanie et Singapour.

b) Double contrôle des registres : Bahamas, Bulgarie, Cuba, Estonie, Grèce, Hongrie, Islande, Italie, Jamaïque, Kirghizstan, Malte, Norvège, Porto Rico, Qatar, République de Corée, Roumanie, Sainte-Lucie et Suisse..

c) Autre méthode : Allemagne, Antilles néerlandaises, Aruba, Autriche, Costa Rica, Cuba, Chypre, Danemark, Estonie, Finlande, Gibraltar, Groenland, Guam, Irlande, Jamaïque, Lettonie, Liechtenstein, Luxembourg, Porto Rico, République islamique d'Iran, Réunion, Slovénie, Sri Lanka, Suède et Territoire palestinien occupé.

Sur les pays ou zones qui ont estimé à 90 p. 100 ou plus le degré d'exhaustivité de leur enregistrement des décès (classé "C" dans le tableau 18), les pays ou zones suivants ont donné des indications touchant la base de cette estimation :

a) Analyse démographique : Argentine, Autriche, Bulgarie, Croatie, Cuba, Estonie, Islande, Israël, Italie, Lettonie, Lituanie, Malte, Maurice, Mexique, Monaco, Pologne, Porto Rico, République de Corée, République de Moldova, République tchèque, Roumanie et Singapour.

b) Double contrôle des registres : Bulgarie, Cuba, Chypre, Estonie, Grèce, Hongrie, Islande, Israël, Italie, Kirghizstan, Lituanie, Malte, Mexique, Norvège, Porto Rico, Qatar, République de Corée, Roumanie, Sainte-Lucie et Suisse.

c) Autre méthode : Allemagne, Antilles néerlandaises, Aruba, Autriche, Costa Rica, Cuba, Danemark, Estonie, Finlande, Gibraltar, Groenland, Guam, Liechtenstein, Luxembourg, Porto Rico, Réunion, Slovénie, Sri Lanka et Suède.

Sur les pays ou zones qui ont estimé à 90 p. 100 ou plus le degré d'exhaustivité de leur enregistrement des décès à moins d'un an (classé "C" dans le tableau 15), les pays ou zones suivants ont donné des indications touchant la base de cette estimation :

a) Analyse démographique : Andorre, Argentine, Autriche, Bulgarie, Croatie, Cuba, Estonie, Islande, Israël, Italie, Lettonie, Lituanie, Malte, Maurice, Mexique, Pologne, Porto Rico, République de Corée, République de Moldova, République tchèque, Roumanie et Singapour.

b) Double contrôle des registres : Bulgarie, Cuba, Chypre, Estonie, Grèce, Hongrie, Islande, Irlande, Israël, Italie, Kirghizstan, Lituanie, Malte, Norvège, Porto Rico, Qatar, République de Corée, Roumanie, Sainte-Lucie et Suisse.

c) Autre méthode : Allemagne, Antilles néerlandaises, Aruba, Autriche, Costa Rica, Cuba, Danemark, Estonie, Finlande, Groenland, Guam, Îles Caïmanes, Liechtenstein, Luxembourg, Porto Rico, Réunion, Slovénie et Suède.

4.2.2 Traitement des statistiques tirées des registres d'état civil

Dans tous les tableaux de l'*Annuaire*, on a indiqué le degré de fiabilité des statistiques de l'état civil en se fondant sur le codage qualitatif décrit ci-dessus. Les statistiques codées "C", jugées sûres, sont imprimées en caractères romains. Celles qui sont codées "U" ou "...", jugées douteuses, sont reproduites en *italique*. Bien que le codage qualitatif proprement dit n'apparaisse que dans certains tableaux, l'indication du degré de fiabilité (c'est-à-dire l'emploi des caractères italiques pour désigner les données douteuses) se retrouve dans tous les tableaux présentant des statistiques de l'état civil.

En général, le code de qualité pour les décès utilisé au tableau 18 sert à déterminer si, dans les autres tableaux, les données relatives aux décès apparaissent en caractères romains ou en italique. Toutefois, le code associé à certaines données sur les décès liés à la maternité dans le tableau 17 diffère de celui employé dans le tableau 18 lorsque l'on sait que le degré d'exhaustivité des données diffère grandement de celui du nombre total des décès. Dans les cas où le code de qualité du tableau 18 ne correspond pas aux caractères utilisés dans le tableau 17, les renseignements concernant l'exhaustivité des statistiques des décès selon la cause sont indiqués en note à la fin du tableau.

On a utilisé la même indication de fiabilité dans les tableaux des taux démographiques et dans ceux des fréquences correspondantes. Par exemple, les taux de mortalité calculés d'après les décès figurant sur un registre incomplet ou d'exhaustivité indéterminée sont jugés douteux et apparaissent en italique. Au sens strict, pour évaluer de façon plus précise les taux démographiques, il faudrait tenir compte de la précision des données sur la population figurant au dénominateur dans les taux. La qualité des données sur la population est étudiée à la section 3.2 des notes techniques.

Il convient de noter que, pour les taux de mortalité infantile, les taux de mortalité liée à la maternité et les rapports de morts fœtales tardives (calculées en utilisant au dénominateur le nombre de naissances vivantes), les indications relatives à la fiabilité sont déterminées sur la base des codes de qualité utilisés pour les décès d'enfants de moins d'un an, les décès totaux et les morts fœtales tardives, respectivement. Pour évaluer ces taux et rapports de façon plus précise, il faudrait tenir compte de la qualité des données relatives aux naissances vivantes, utilisées au dénominateur dans leur calcul. Les codes de qualité pour les naissances vivantes figurent au tableau 9 et sont décrits plus en détail dans les notes techniques se rapportant à ce tableau.

4.2.3 Traitement des séries chronologiques de statistiques tirées des registres d'état civil

Il est plus difficile de déterminer la qualité des séries chronologiques de statistiques de l'état civil que celle des données pour une seule année. Étant donné qu'une série chronologique de statistiques de l'état civil ne peut généralement avoir pour source qu'un système permanent d'enregistrement des faits d'état civil, on a arbitrairement supposé que le degré d'exactitude de la série tout entière était le même que celui de la dernière tranche annuelle de données tirées du registre d'état civil. La série tout entière est traitée de la manière décrite à la section 4.2.2 ci-dessus : lorsque le code de qualité relatif aux données d'enregistrement les plus récentes est "C", les fréquences et les taux relatifs aux années antérieures sont eux aussi considérés comme sûrs et figurent en caractères romains. Inversement, si les données d'enregistrement les plus récentes sont codées "U" ou "...", les données des années antérieures sont jugées douteuses et figurent en italique. Cette méthode n'est certes pas entièrement satisfaisante, car les données des premières années de la série sont souvent beaucoup moins sûres que le code actuel ne le laisse supposer.

4.2.4 Traitement des estimations fondées sur les statistiques de l'état civil

En plus des données provenant des systèmes d'enregistrement des faits d'état civil, l'Annuaire démographique contient aussi des estimations relatives aux fréquences et aux taux. Il s'agit d'estimations officielles, généralement calculées à partir des résultats d'un sondage ou par analyse démographique. Si des estimations concernant les fréquences et les taux figurent dans les tableaux, c'est parce que l'on considère qu'elles fournissent des renseignements plus exacts que les systèmes existants d'enregistrement des faits d'état civil. En conséquence, elles sont également jugées sûres et sont donc imprimées en caractères romains, même si elles sont entrecoupées dans une série chronologique de données tirées des registres d'état civil.

Dans les tableaux qui indiquent le code de qualité, ce code ne s'applique qu'aux données tirées des registres d'état civil. Si une série pour un pays ou une zone comprend à la fois des données tirées d'un registre d'état civil et des données estimatives, le code ne s'applique qu'aux données d'enregistrement. Si seules des données estimatives apparaissent, le symbole "|" est utilisé.

4.3 Causes de décès

Les États membres de l'Organisation mondiale de la santé (OMS) sont tenus de communiquer à celle-ci les données sur les causes de décès codifiées selon la révision en vigueur de la Classification internationale des maladies et des problèmes de santé connexes (CIM) adoptée par l'Assemblé mondiale de la santé[21]. Les données sont collectées par l'OMS sur la base de la CIM. Pour assurer la comparabilité internationale des statistiques des causes de décès, l'OMS organise régulièrement des conférences internationales de révision de la Classification internationale des maladies afin de suivre, au fur et à mesure, les progrès les plus récents de la médecine clinique et de la statistique. Les données sont généralement envoyées à l'OMS selon la classification à 4 caractères prévue par la CIM et sont archivées dans la base de données sur la mortalité de l'OMS telles qu'elles ont été présentées par le pays. Pour les versions antérieures, par contre, les données sont disponibles seulement selon la liste A de 150 causes de la CIM. Les données de l'OMS sont disponibles sur le site Internet suivant: http://www3.who.int/whosis/menu.cfm.

Les révisions de la CIM permettent certes de disposer d'une version actualisée, mais elles posent plusieurs problèmes de comparabilité des statistiques des causes de décès. Le premier tient au manque de comparabilité dans le temps, qui accompagne inévitablement la mise en oeuvre d'une classification nouvelle. Le deuxième est celui de la comparabilité entre pays ou zones, car les différents pays peuvent adopter la nouvelle classification à des époques différentes. Établir la cause des décès exige des compétences de plus en plus poussées à mesure que la classification devient plus précise. Or, dans beaucoup de pays ou zones, il est rare que les décès se produisent en présence d'un témoin possédant une formation médicale et le certificat de décès est le plus souvent établi par quelqu'un qui n'est pas qualifié sur le plan médical. Étant donné que la CIM répertorie de nombreux diagnostics qu'il est impossible d'établir si l'on n'a pas de formation en médecine, elle ne favorise pas toujours la comparabilité internationale, notamment entre pays ou zones où la qualité des services médicaux est très disparate.

La dixième révision[22] est la dernière qu'ait connue la CIM. Les chapitres de la dixième révision se fondent sur un système de codification alphanumérique à une lettre suivie de trois chiffres pour les catégories à quatre caractères. Le chapitre 1 concerne les maladies infectieuses et parasitaires et le chapitre 2 l'ensemble des néoplasmes. Le chapitre 3 a trait aux troubles du système immunitaire, aux maladies du sang et aux organes hématopoïétiques. Le chapitre 4 porte sur les maladies du système endocrinien, de la nutrition et du métabolisme. Les autres chapitres groupent les maladies selon leur site anatomique, à l'exception de ceux qui concernent les affections mentales, les complications de la grossesse, de l'accouchement et des suites de couches, les malformations congénitales et les affections de la période périnatale. Enfin, un chapitre entier est consacré aux symptômes, manifestations et résultats anormaux.

4.3.1 Mortalité liée à la maternité

D'après la dixième révision de la CIM, la « mortalité liée à la maternité » est définie comme le décès d'une femme survenu au cours de la grossesse ou dans un délai de 42 jours après sa terminaison, quelle qu'en soit la durée et la localisation, pour une cause quelconque déterminée ou aggravée par la grossesse ou les soins qu'elle a motivés, mais ni accidentelle ni fortuite.

Les décès liés à la maternité se répartissent en deux groupes :

1) Décès par cause obstétricale directe qui résultent de complications obstétricales (grossesse, travail et suites de couches), d'interventions, d'omissions, d'un traitement incorrect ou d'un enchaînement d'événements de l'un quelconque des facteurs ci-dessus ;
2) Décès par cause obstétricale indirecte qui résultent d'une maladie préexistante ou d'une affection apparue au cours de la grossesse, sans qu'elle soit due à des causes obstétricales directes, mais qui a été aggravée par les effets physiologiques de la grossesse.

Il est recommandé dans la dixième révision d'exprimer les taux de mortalité liée à la maternité sur la base de 100 000 naissances vivantes ou 100 000 naissances totales (naissances vivantes et morts fœtales)[23]. Le nombre de femmes enceintes aurait dû être pris comme dénominateur, mais étant donné qu'il est impossible de le déterminer, le taux de mortalité liée à la maternité est ici calculé par 100 000 naissances vivantes. Bien que les naissances vivantes ne permettent pas d'évaluer sans distorsion le nombre des femmes enceintes, leur nombre est plus fiable que d'autres estimations car le nombre des naissances vivantes est plus exactement enregistré que celui des naissances vivantes et des morts fœtales.

NOTES

[1] Les données relatives à la mortalité liée à la maternité et aux taux de mortalité selon la cause émanent de l'Organisation mondiale de la santé et sont disponibles à l'adresse suivante : http://www3.who.int/whosis/menu.cfm.

[2] Les éditions de 1978 et de 1991 font exception à la règle, puisque les tableaux sur des sujets spéciaux ont été publiés séparément.

[3] *Nations Unies, Département de Questions Economiques et Sociales, Division de Population (2009). World Population Prospects, The 2008 Revision, CD Rom Edition.* Dans l'intervalle, on peut consulter des extraits et certaines données sur le site www.unpopulation.org.

[4] ST/ESA/STAT/SER.M/49/Rev.4/WWW ; http://unstats.un.org/unsd/methods/m49/m49frnch.htm; voir également *Code standard des pays et des zones à usage statistique*, numéro de vente : M.98.XVII.9, Nations Unies, New York, 1999.

[5] Numéro de vente : F.07.XVII.8, Nations Unies, New York, 2007. Avant d'être publiée, cette publication est disponible en ligne à l'adresse suivante : http://unstats.un.org/unsd/demographic/standmeth/principles/Series_M67Rev2en.pdf

[6] Ibid., par. 2.135.

[7] Lorsque l'on utilise un registre de la population, on peut également calculer l'âge en années révolues en soustrayant la date de naissance de chaque personne inscrite sur le registre de la date de référence à laquelle se rapportent les données sur l'âge.

[8] L'emploi de méthodes différentes de calcul de l'âge, par exemple la méthode occidentale et la méthode orientale, ou, comme on les désigne plus communément, la méthode anglaise et la méthode chinoise, représente une cause de non-comparabilité. Selon la méthode chinoise, on considère que l'enfant est âgé d'un an à sa naissance et qu'il avance d'un an à chaque nouvelle année chinoise. Les répercussions de cette méthode sont particulièrement apparentes dans les données pour le premier âge : les données concernant les enfants de moins d'un an sont nettement inférieures à la réalité. Les effets sur les chiffres relatifs aux groupes d'âge suivants sont moins visibles. Les séries ainsi établies sont souvent ajustées avant d'être publiées, mais il ne faut pas exclure la possibilité d'aberrations de ce genre lorsque l'on compare des données censitaires sur l'âge.

[9] Dans cet indice, on déterminait les différences à partir des rapports prévus de masculinité dans un groupe d'âge et dans les groupes d'âge adjacents. Il fallait pour cela tenir compte de l'influence de facteurs tels que les mouvements passés des taux de natalité, les pertes de guerre élevées et, le cas échéant, le faible effectif de la population. On trouvera dans le *Bulletin démographique*, no 2 (publication des Nations Unies, numéro de vente : 52.XIII.4), p. 64 à 87, un exposé détaillé sur cet indice ainsi que les résultats de son application aux données présentées dans les éditions de 1949-1950 et de 1951 de l'*Annuaire démographique*. On a fait les mêmes calculs sur les statistiques publiées dans l'*Annuaire démographique 1952* et les résultats obtenus sont indiqués dans l'édition correspondante de l'*Annuaire*, qui, comme celles de 1953 et de 1954, donne de brèves explications sur l'indice en question.

[10] United States Bureau of the Census, Thirteenth Census, vol. I (Washington, D.C., U.S. Government Printing Office, 1913; Reprint: New York, N.Y., Norman Ross Pub., 1999), p. 291 et 292.

[11] Numéro de vente : F.83.XIII.2, publication des Nations Unies, New York, 1984.

[12] Numéro de vente : F.01.XVII.10, publication des Nations Unies, New York, 2003.

[13] Numéro de vente : F. 98.XVII.7, publication des Nations Unies, New York, 1998.

[14] Numéro de vente : F.98.XVII.11, publication des Nations Unies, New York, 1998.

[15] Numéro de vente : F.98.XVII.4, publication des Nations Unies, New York, 1998.

[16] Numéro de vente : F.98.XVII.6, publication des Nations Unies, New York, 1998.

[17] Numéro de vente : F.98.XVII.10, publication des Nations Unies, New York, 1998.

[18] Numéro de vente : F.03.XVII.11, United Nations, New York, 2004.

[19] Pour plus de précisions, voir *Principes et recommandations pour un système de statistiques de l'état civil, deuxième révision*, numéro de vente : F.01.XVII.10, publication des Nations Unies, New York, 2001, par. 57.

[20] Pour plus de précisions au sujet des considérations historiques et juridiques auxquelles se rattachent les différentes définitions correspondant aux naissances vivantes et aux morts fœtales, pour une comparaison des définitions utilisées depuis le 1er janvier 1950 et pour une évaluation des effets de ces différences de définition sur le calcul de divers taux, voir le *Manuel de statistique de l'état civil, Volume II, Étude des pratiques nationales*, numéro de vente : F.84.XVII.11, publication des Nations Unies, New York, 1985, chap. IV.

[21] Les États membres de l'Organisation mondiale de la santé se réunissent annuellement dans le cadre de l'Assemblée mondiale de la santé, qui est l'organe directeur de l'Organisation.

[22] Organisation mondiale de la santé, *Classification statistique internationale des maladies et problèmes de santé connexes*, dixième révision, vol. 2, Genève, 1992.

[23] Ibid., pp. 129-136.

Table A. *Demographic Yearbook 2007* synoptic table: Availability of data by country/area, table and sex, where applicable

Tableau A. Tableau synoptique de l'*Annuaire démographique 2007*: Disponibilité des données par pays ou zone, tableau et le sexe , si disponible

General topic and table number- Sujet général et numéro de tableau

Continent, country or area / Continent, pays ou zone	Table totals	Summary - Apercu 3 Total	3 M/F	4	5	Population 6 Total	6 M/F	7 Total	7 M/F	8 Total	8 M/F	Natality 9	10 Total	10 M/F	11	Foetal mortality 12	13	14
Total number of countries or areas - Total des pays ou zones	..	236	225	180	217	223	220	203	202	216	136	170	141	118	83	99	64	50
AFRICA — AFRIQUE																		
Algeria - Algérie	14	•	...	•	...	•	...	•	•	•	...	•	...	...	...	...	...	...
Angola	4	•	•	...	...	•	...	•	•	•	•	...	...	...	...	...	...	...
Benin - Bénin	9	•	•	...	•	•	...	•	•	•	...	...	...	...	...	...	...	...
Botswana	12	•	•	...	•	•	...	•	•	•	•	...	...	...	...	...	...	...
Burkina Faso	14	•	•	•	•	•	...	•	•	•	...	•	...	...	...	...	...	...
Burundi	7	•	•	...	•	•	...	•	...	•	...	•	...	...	...	...	...	...
Cameroon - Cameroun	4	•	...	...	•	•	...	•	...	•	...	...	...	...	...	...	...	...
Cape Verde - Cap-Vert	10	•	•	...	•	•	...	•	•	•	...	•	...	...	...	...	...	...
Central African Republic - République centrafricaine	6	•	•	...	•	•	...	•	...	•	...	...	...	...	...	...	...	...
Chad - Tchad	4	•	•	...	•	•	...	•	...	•	...	...	...	...	...	...	...	...
Comoros - Comores	3	•	...	...	•	•	...	•	...	•	...	...	...	...	...	...	...	...
Congo	7	•	•	...	•	•	...	•	...	...	...	•	...	...	...	...	...	...
Côte d'Ivoire	6	•	•	...	•	•	...	•	...	•	...	...	...	...	...	...	...	...
Democratic Republic of the Congo - République démocratique du Congo	2	•	...	...	•	...	...	...	...	...	...	...	...	...	...	...	...	...
Djibouti	4	•	...	...	•	•	...	•	...	•	...	...	...	...	...	...	...	...
Egypt - Égypte	28	•	•	•	•	•	...	•	...	•	...	•	...	•	...	•	...	...
Equatorial Guinea - Guinée équatoriale	4	•	•	...	•	•	...	•	...	•	...	...	...	...	...	...	...	...
Eritrea - Érythrée	3	•	•	...	•	•	...	•	...	•	...	...	...	...	...	...	...	...
Ethiopia - Éthiopie	9	•	•	...	•	•	...	•	...	•	...	...	...	...	...	...	...	...
Gabon	6	•	...	...	•	•	...	•	...	•	...	...	...	...	...	...	...	...
Gambia - Gambie	7	•	•	...	•	•	...	•	...	•	•	...	...	...	...	...	...	...
Ghana	10	•	•	...	•	•	...	•	•	•	...	...	...	...	...	...	...	...
Guinea - Guinée	4	•	•	...	•	•	...	•	...	•	...	...	...	...	...	...	...	...
Guinea-Bissau - Guinée-Bissau	4	•	•	...	•	•	...	•	...	•	...	...	...	...	...	...	...	...
Kenya	16	•	•	...	•	•	...	•	•	•	...	•	•	...	...	...	...	...
Lesotho	8	•	•	...	•	•	...	•	•	...	...	...	...	...	...	...	...	...
Liberia - Libéria	2	•	•	...	...	...	...	...	...	...	...	...	...	...	...	...	...	...
Libyan Arab Jamahiriya - Jamahiriya arabe libyenne	10	•	•	...	•	•	...	•	...	•	...	•	•	...	...	...	...	...
Madagascar	8	•	•	...	•	•	...	•	...	•	...	•	...	...	...	...	...	...
Malawi	15	•	•	...	•	•	...	•	...	•	...	•	...	...	...	...	...	...
Mali	7	•	•	...	•	•	...	•	...	•	...	...	...	...	...	...	...	...
Mauritania - Mauritanie	8	•	•	...	•	•	...	•	...	•	...	...	...	...	...	...	...	...
Mauritius - Maurice	28	•	•	•	•	•	...	•	•	•	...	•	•	•	...	•	•	...
Mayotte	9	•	•	...	•	•	...	•	...	•	...	...	...	...	...	...	...	...
Morocco - Maroc	14	•	•	...	•	•	...	•	...	•	...	•	...	...	...	...	...	...
Mozambique	8	•	•	...	•	•	...	•	...	•	...	...	...	...	...	...	...	...
Namibia - Namibie	16	•	•	...	•	•	...	•	...	•	...	...	...	...	...	...	...	...
Niger	9	•	•	...	•	•	...	•	...	•	...	•	...	...	...	...	...	...
Nigeria - Nigéria	8	•	•	...	•	•	...	•	...	•	...	...	...	...	...	...	...	...
Réunion	27	•	•	...	•	•	...	•	...	•	...	•	•	...	•	•	•	...
Rwanda	8	•	•	...	•	•	...	•	...	•	...	...	...	...	...	...	...	...
Saint Helena ex. dep. - Sainte-Hélène sans dép.	22	•	•	...	•	•	...	•	...	•	...	9	•	...	...	...	...	...
Saint Helena: Ascension - Sainte-Hélène: Ascension	6	•	•	...	...	•	...	...	...	...	...	...	...	...	...	...	...	...
Saint Helena: Tristan da Cunha - Sainte-Hélène: Tristan da Cunha	3	•	•	...	...	•	...	...	...	...	...	...	...	...	...	...	...	...
Sao Tome and Principe - Sao Tomé-et-Principe	9	•	•	...	•	•	...	•	...	•	...	...	...	...	...	...	...	...
Senegal - Sénégal	8	•	•	...	•	•	...	•	...	•	...	...	...	...	...	...	...	...
Seychelles	25	•	•	...	•	•	...	•	...	•	...	•	•	...	•	•	•	...
Sierra Leone	6	•	•	...	•	•	...	•	...	•	...	...	...	...	...	...	...	...
Somalia - Somalie	7	•	•	...	•	•	...	•	...	•	...	...	...	...	...	...	...	...

Table A. *Demographic Yearbook 2007* synoptic table: Availability of data by country/area, table and sex, where applicable

Tableau A. Tableau synoptique de l'*Annuaire démographique 2007*: Disponibilité des données par pays ou zone, tableau et le sexe , si disponible (continued — suite)

Continent, country or area / Continent, pays ou zone	Infant and maternal mortality - Mortalité infantile et mortalité liée à la maternité				General mortality - Mortalité générale				Nuptiality and divorces - Nuptialité et divortialité				
	15	16 Total	16 M/F	17	18	19 Total	19 M/F	20	21	22	23	24	25
Total number of countries or areas - Total des pays ou zones	142	110	106	111	171	155	153	143	136	109	120	81	68
AFRICA — AFRIQUE													
Algeria - Algérie	...	...	...	...	•	•	•	•	•	...	...	...	...
Angola	...	...	...	...	...	...	...	...	...	...	...	...	...
Benin - Bénin	...	...	...	...	...	...	...	...	...	...	...	...	...
Botswana	...	...	...	...	•	•	•	•	...	...	...	...	...
Burkina Faso	•	...	...	...	•	...	...	•	...	...	...	...	...
Burundi	...	...	...	...	...	...	...	...	...	...	...	...	...
Cameroon - Cameroun	...	...	...	...	...	...	...	...	...	...	...	...	...
Cape Verde - Cap-Vert	...	...	...	...	...	...	...	...	...	...	...	...	...
Central African Republic - République centrafricaine	...	...	...	...	...	...	...	...	...	...	...	...	...
Chad - Tchad	...	...	...	...	...	...	...	...	...	...	...	...	...
Comoros - Comores	...	...	...	...	...	...	...	...	...	...	...	...	...
Congo	...	...	...	...	...	...	...	...	...	...	...	...	...
Côte d'Ivoire	...	...	...	...	...	...	...	...	...	...	...	...	...
Democratic Republic of the Congo - République démocratique du Congo	...	...	...	...	...	...	...	...	...	...	...	...	...
Djibouti	...	...	...	...	...	...	...	•	...	...	...	...	...
Egypt - Égypte	•	•	•	•	•	•	•	•	•	•	•	•	•
Equatorial Guinea - Guinée équatoriale	...	...	...	...	...	...	...	...	...	...	...	...	...
Eritrea - Érythrée	...	...	...	...	...	...	...	...	...	...	...	...	...
Ethiopia - Éthiopie	...	...	...	...	...	...	...	...	...	...	...	...	...
Gabon	...	...	...	...	...	...	...	...	...	...	...	...	...
Gambia - Gambie	...	...	...	...	...	...	...	...	...	...	...	...	...
Ghana	...	...	...	...	...	...	...	...	...	...	...	...	...
Guinea - Guinée	...	...	...	...	...	...	...	...	...	...	...	...	...
Guinea-Bissau - Guinée-Bissau	...	...	...	...	...	...	...	...	...	...	...	...	...
Kenya	•	...	...	...	•	•	•	•	...	...	...	...	...
Lesotho	...	...	...	...	...	...	...	•	...	...	...	...	...
Liberia - Libéria	...	...	...	...	...	...	...	...	...	...	...	...	...
Libyan Arab Jamahiriya - Jamahiriya arabe libyenne	...	...	...	...	...	...	...	...	...	...	...	...	...
Madagascar	...	...	...	...	...	...	...	...	...	...	...	...	...
Malawi	...	...	...	...	•	•	•	•	...	...	...	...	...
Mali	...	...	...	...	...	...	...	...	...	...	...	...	...
Mauritania - Mauritanie	...	...	...	...	...	...	...	...	...	...	...	...	...
Mauritius - Maurice	•	•	•	•	•	•	•	•	•	•	•	•	...
Mayotte	...	...	...	...	•	...	...	...	...	...	...	...	...
Morocco - Maroc	...	•	•	...	•	•	...	•	...	...	...	...	...
Mozambique	...	...	...	...	...	...	...	...	...	...	...	...	...
Namibia - Namibie	...	...	...	...	•	•	...	...	...	...	...	...	...
Niger	...	...	...	...	...	...	...	...	...	...	...	...	...
Nigeria - Nigéria	...	...	...	...	...	...	...	...	...	...	...	...	...
Réunion	•	•	•	•	•	•	•	•	•	•	•	•	...
Rwanda	...	...	...	...	...	...	...	...	...	...	...	...	...
Saint Helena ex. dep. - Sainte-Hélène sans dép.	•	•	•	•	...	...	...	...	...	...	...	...	...
Saint Helena: Ascension - Sainte-Hélène: Ascension	...	...	...	...	...	...	...	...	...	...	...	...	...
Saint Helena: Tristan da Cunha - Sainte-Hélène: Tristan da Cunha	...	...	...	...	...	...	...	...	...	...	...	...	...
Sao Tome and Principe - Sao Tomé-et-Principe	...	...	...	...	...	...	...	...	...	...	...	...	...
Senegal - Sénégal	...	...	...	...	...	...	...	...	...	...	...	...	...
Seychelles	•	•	•	•	•	•	•	•	•	•	•	...	...
Sierra Leone	...	...	...	...	...	...	...	...	...	...	...	...	...
Somalia - Somalie	...	...	...	...	...	...	...	...	...	...	...	...	...

Table A. *Demographic Yearbook 2007* synoptic table: Availability of data by country/area, table and sex,
where applicable
Tableau A. Tableau synoptique de l'*Annuaire démographique 2007*: Disponibilité des données par pays ou zone, tableau et le
sexe , si disponible (continued — suite)

General topic and table number- Sujet général et numéro de tableau

Continent, country or area / Continent, pays ou zone	Table totals	Summary - Apercu 3 Total	3 M/F	4	5	Population 6 Total	6 M/F	7 Total	7 M/F	8 Total	8 M/F	Natality 9	10 Total	10 M/F	11	Foetal mortality 12	13	14
AFRICA — AFRIQUE																		
South Africa - Afrique du Sud	28	•	•	•	•	•	•	•	•	•	•	•	...	•	...	•	•	...
Sudan - Soudan	6	•	•	...	•	•	•	...	...	•	...	...	•	...	...	...	...	...
Swaziland	5	•	•	...	•	•	•	...	•	...	...	...	...	...	...	...	...	...
Togo	4	•	•	...	•	•	...	...	...	...	...	...	...	...	...	...	...	...
Tunisia - Tunisie	21	•	•	•	•	•	•	•	•	•	•	•	•	...	...	...	...	...
Uganda - Ouganda	9	•	•	...	•	•	•	...	•	...	...	...	...	...	...	...	...	...
United Republic of Tanzania - République Unie de Tanzanie	9	•	•	...	•	•	•	...	•	...	...	...	...	...	...	...	...	...
Western Sahara - Sahara occidental	3	•	•	...	...	•	...	...	...	...	...	...	...	...	...	...	...	...
Zambia - Zambie	12	•	•	•	•	•	•	•	•	•	...	...	...	...	...	...	...	...
Zimbabwe	13	•	•	•	•	•	•	•	•	•	...	...	...	...	...	...	...	...
AMERICA, NORTH — AMERIQUE DU NORD																		
Anguilla	21	•	•	•	•	•	•	•	•	•	•	•	...	...	...	•	...	...
Antigua and Barbuda - Antigua-et-Barbuda	11	•	•	•	•	•	•	•	•	...	...	...	...	...	...	...	...	...
Aruba	25	•	•	•	•	•	•	•	•	•	•	•	•	...	...	...	...	...
Bahamas	28	•	•	•	•	•	•	•	•	•	•	•	•	...	•	•	•	...
Barbados - Barbade	14	•	•	•	•	•	•	•	•	...	...	•	...	...	•	...	...	...
Belize	19	•	•	•	•	•	•	•	•	•	•	•	...	...	•	•	...	...
Bermuda - Bermudes	23	•	•	•	•	•	•	•	•	•	•	•	...	...	•	•	...	...
British Virgin Islands - Îles Vierges britanniques	17	•	•	•	•	•	•	•	•	•	•	•	...	...	...	...	...	•
Canada	30	•	•	•	•	•	•	•	•	•	•	•	•	...	•	...	•	•
Cayman Islands - Îles Caïmanes	19	•	...	•	•	•	•	•	•	•	•	...	...	...	...	...	...	...
Costa Rica	26	•	•	•	•	•	•	•	•	•	•	•	•	...	•	...	•	•
Cuba	29	•	•	•	•	•	•	•	•	•	•	•	•	...	•	•	•	•
Dominica - Dominique	19	•	•	•	•	•	•	•	•	•	•	•	...	...	•	...	...	...
Dominican Republic - République dominicaine	24	•	•	•	•	•	•	•	•	•	•	•	...	...	•	...	...	...
El Salvador	27	•	•	•	•	•	•	•	•	•	•	...	•	...	•	...	...	...
Greenland - Groenland	23	•	•	•	•	•	•	•	•	•	•	...	...	...	...	...	...	...
Grenada - Grenade	12	•	•	...	•	•	•	...	•	...	...	...	...	...	...	...	...	...
Guadeloupe	25	•	•	•	•	•	•	•	•	•	•	•	...	...	...	•	•	...
Guatemala	26	•	•	•	•	•	•	•	•	•	•	•	•	...	...	...	...	...
Haiti - Haïti	14	•	•	•	•	•	•	•	•	...	...	...	...	...	...	...	...	...
Honduras	13	•	•	•	•	•	•	•	•	...	...	...	...	...	...	...	...	...
Jamaica - Jamaïque	24	•	•	•	•	•	•	•	•	•	•	•	...	...	•	...	...	...
Martinique	26	•	•	•	•	•	•	•	•	•	•	•	...	...	•	•	•	...
Mexico - Mexique	29	•	•	•	•	•	•	•	•	•	...	•	•	...	•	•	•	•
Montserrat	15	•	•	•	•	•	•	•	•	•	•	•	...	...	...	...	...	...
Netherlands Antilles - Antilles néerlandaises	21	•	•	•	•	•	•	•	•	•	•	•	...	...	...	...	...	...
Nicaragua	23	•	•	•	•	•	•	•	•	•	•	•	...	...	•	...	...	...
Panama	30	•	•	•	•	•	•	•	•	•	•	•	•	...	•	•	•	•
Puerto Rico - Porto Rico	28	•	•	•	•	•	•	•	•	•	•	•	•	...	•	•	•	•
Saint Kitts and Nevis - Saint-Kitts-et-Nevis	13	•	•	...	•	•	•	•	•	...	...	•	...	...	•	...	...	...
Saint Lucia - Sainte-Lucie	27	•	•	•	•	•	•	•	•	•	•	•	...	...	•	•	...	...
Saint Pierre and Miquelon - Saint Pierre-et-Miquelon	5	•	...	...	•	•	...	...	•	...	...	...	...	...	...	...	...	...
Saint Vincent and the Grenadines - Saint-Vincent-et-les Grenadines	22	•	•	•	•	•	•	•	•	•	•	•	...	...	•	...	...	...
Trinidad and Tobago - Trinité-et-Tobago	28	•	•	•	•	•	•	•	•	•	•	•	...	...	•	•	...	...
Turks and Caicos Islands - Îles Turques et Caïques	27	•	•	•	•	•	•	•	•	•	•	•	...	...	•	•	•	•
United States of America - États-Unis d'Amérique	22	•	•	•	•	•	•	•	•	•	...	•	...	...	•	•	•	...
United States Virgin Islands - Îles Vierges américaines	18	•	•	•	•	•	•	•	•	•	...	•	...	...	...	...	...	...

Table A. *Demographic Yearbook 2007* synoptic table: Availability of data by country/area, table and sex, where applicable
Tableau A. Tableau synoptique de l'*Annuaire démographique 2007*: Disponibilité des données par pays ou zone, tableau et le sexe , si disponible (continued — suite)

Continent, country or area / Continent, pays ou zone	General topic and table number- Sujet général et numéro de tableau												
	Infant and maternal mortality - Mortalité infantile et mortalité liée à la maternité				General mortality - Mortalité générale				Nuptiality and divorces - Nuptialité et divortialité				
	15	16 Total	16 M/F	17	18	19 Total	19 M/F	20	21	22	23	24	25
AFRICA — AFRIQUE													
South Africa - Afrique du Sud	•	•	•	•	•	•	•	•	•	•	•	•	•
Sudan - Soudan	...	...	...	...	...	...	...	...	...	...	...	...	...
Swaziland	...	...	...	...	...	...	...	...	...	...	...	...	...
Togo	...	...	...	...	...	...	...	...	...	...	...	...	...
Tunisia - Tunisie	...	•	•	...	•	•	•	•	•	•	•	...	...
Uganda - Ouganda	...	...	...	...	...	...	...	...	...	...	...	...	...
United Republic of Tanzania - République Unie de Tanzanie	...	...	...	...	...	...	...	...	...	...	...	...	...
Western Sahara - Sahara occidental	...	...	...	...	...	...	...	...	...	...	...	...	...
Zambia - Zambie	...	...	...	...	•	...	...	...	...	...	...	...	...
Zimbabwe	...	...	...	...	•	•	•	...	...	...	...	...	...
AMERICA, NORTH — AMERIQUE DU NORD													
Anguilla	•	...	...	•	•	•	•	•	•	•	•	...	...
Antigua and Barbuda - Antigua-et-Barbuda	...	...	...	•	•	•	•	•	•	•	...	...	...
Aruba	•	•	•	•	•	•	•	•	•	•	•	•	•
Bahamas	•	•	•	•	•	•	•	•	•	•	•	•	•
Barbados - Barbade	•	...	...	•	•	•	•	•	•	•	...	...	...
Belize	•	...	...	•	•	•	•	•	•	•	...	...	...
Bermuda - Bermudes	•	...	...	•	•	•	•	•	•	•	...	...	...
British Virgin Islands - Îles Vierges britanniques	...	...	...	•	•	•	•	•	•	•	...	...	...
Canada	•	•	•	•	•	•	•	•	•	•	•	•	•
Cayman Islands - Îles Caïmanes	•	•	•	•	•	•	•	•	•	•	•	...	...
Costa Rica	•	•	•	•	•	•	•	•	•	•	•	•	•
Cuba	•	•	•	•	•	•	•	•	•	•	•	•	•
Dominica - Dominique	•	...	...	•	•	•	•	•	•	•	•	...	...
Dominican Republic - République dominicaine	•	...	...	•	•	•	•	•	•	•	•	•	•
El Salvador	•	...	...	•	•	•	•	•	•	•	•	•	•
Greenland - Groenland	•	•	•	...	•	•	•	•	...	...	...	...	...
Grenada - Grenade	...	...	•	...	•	•	•	•	...	...	...	...	...
Guadeloupe	•	•	•	•	•	•	•	•	...	...	...	...	...
Guatemala	•	•	•	•	•	•	•	•	•	•	•	•	•
Haiti - Haïti	•	...	...	•	•	...	...	...	...	...	...	...	...
Honduras	•	...	...	...	•	...	...	...	...	...	...	...	...
Jamaica - Jamaïque	•	...	...	...	•	•	•	•	•	•	•	•	•
Martinique	•	•	•	•	•	•	•	•	•	•	•	•	•
Mexico - Mexique	•	•	•	•	•	•	•	•	•	•	•	•	•
Montserrat	...	...	...	•	•	•	•	•	•	•	...	...	...
Netherlands Antilles - Antilles néerlandaises	•	•	•	•	•	•	•	•	•	•	•	...	...
Nicaragua	•	•	•	•	•	•	•	•	•	•	•	•	...
Panama	•	•	•	•	•	•	•	•	•	•	•	•	•
Puerto Rico - Porto Rico	•	•	•	•	•	•	•	•	•	•	•	•	•
Saint Kitts and Nevis - Saint-Kitts-et-Nevis	...	...	...	•	•	•	•	•	•	•	•	•	•
Saint Lucia - Sainte-Lucie	•	...	...	•	•	•	•	•	•	•	•	•	•
Saint Pierre and Miquelon - Saint Pierre-et-Miquelon	...	...	...	•	...	...	...	...	...	...	...	...	...
Saint Vincent and the Grenadines - Saint-Vincent-et-les Grenadines	•	•	•	•	•	•	•	•	•	•	•	...	...
Trinidad and Tobago - Trinité-et-Tobago	•	•	•	•	•	•	•	•	•	•	•	•	•
Turks and Caicos Islands - Îles Turques et Caïques	•	...	...	•	•	•	•	•	•	•	•	...	...
United States of America - États-Unis d'Amérique	•	•	•	•	•	•	•	•	•	•	•	•	•
United States Virgin Islands - Îles Vierges américaines	•	...	...	•	•	•	•	•	•	•	•	...	...

Table A. *Demographic Yearbook 2007* synoptic table: Availability of data by country/area, table and sex, where applicable
Tableau A. Tableau synoptique de l'*Annuaire démographique 2007*: Disponibilité des données par pays ou zone, tableau et le sexe , si disponible (continued — suite)

Continent, country or area / Continent, pays ou zone	Table totals	Summary - Apercu				Population						Natality - Natalité				Foetal mortality - Mortalité foetale		
		3 Total	3 M/F	4	5	6 Total	6 M/F	7 Total	7 M/F	8 Total	8 M/F	9	10 Total	10 M/F	11	12	13	14
AMERICA, SOUTH — AMERIQUE DU SUD																		
Argentina - Argentine	21	•	•	•	•	•	•	•	•	•	...	•	•	...	...	•	...	...
Bolivia - Bolivie	14	•	•	•	•	•	•	•	•	•	...	•	•	...	...	•	...	...
Brazil - Brésil	26	•	•	•	•	•	•	•	•	•	•	•	•	...	...	•	...	...
Chile - Chili	27	•	•	•	•	•	•	•	•	•	•	•	•	•	...	•	...	...
Colombia - Colombie	22	•	•	•	•	•	•	•	•	•	...	•	•	•	...	•	...	...
Ecuador - Équateur	26	•	•	•	•	•	•	•	•	•	...	•	•	...	...	•	...	...
Falkland Islands (Malvinas) - Îles Falkland (Malvinas)	10	•	•	•	...	•	•	•	•	•	...	•	•	...	...	...	...	...
French Guiana - Guyane française	26	•	•	•	•	•	•	•	•	•	...	•	•	•	...	•	...	...
Guyana	13	•	•	•	•	•	•	•	•	•	...	•	•	...	...	•	...	...
Paraguay	19	•	•	•	•	•	•	•	•	•	...	•	•	...	...	•	...	...
Peru - Pérou	21	•	•	•	•	•	•	•	•	•	...	•	•	...	...	•	...	...
Suriname	23	•	•	•	•	•	•	•	•	•	...	•	•	•	...	•	...	...
Uruguay	27	•	•	•	•	•	•	•	•	•	•	•	•	•	...	•	•	...
Venezuela (Bolivarian Republic of) - Venezuela (République bolivarienne du)	25	•	•	•	•	•	•	•	•	•	•	•	•	•	...	•	...	...
ASIA — ASIE																		
Afghanistan	7	•	•	...	•	•	...	•	...	•	...	•	...	...	...	...	...	...
Armenia - Arménie	30	•	•	•	•	•	•	•	•	•	•	•	•	•	...	•	•	•
Azerbaijan - Azerbaïdjan	30	•	•	•	•	•	•	•	•	•	•	•	•	•	...	•	•	•
Bahrain - Bahreïn	29	•	•	•	•	•	•	•	•	•	•	•	•	•	...	•	•	•
Bangladesh	12	•	•	•	•	•	•	•	•	•	...	•	•	...	...	...	...	...
Bhutan - Bhoutan	18	•	•	•	•	•	•	•	•	•	•	•	•	...	...	...	...	...
Brunei Darussalam - Brunéi Darussalam	25	•	•	•	•	•	•	•	•	•	•	•	•	•	...	...	...	...
Cambodia - Cambodge	15	•	•	•	•	•	•	•	•	•	•	•	•	...	...	...	...	...
China - Chine[1]	17	•	•	•	•	•	•	•	•	•	...	•	•	...	...	...	...	...
China, Hong Kong SAR - Chine, Hong Kong RAS	27	•	•	•	•	•	•	•	•	•	•	•	•	•	...	•	•	•
China, Macao SAR - Chine, Macao RAS	27	•	•	•	•	•	•	•	•	•	•	•	•	•	...	•	•	...
Cyprus - Chypre	26	•	•	•	•	•	•	•	•	•	•	•	•	•	...	•	...	...
Democratic People's Republic of Korea - République populaire démocratique de Corée	4	•	•	...	•	•	...	...	...	...	...	...	...	...	...	...	...	...
Georgia - Géorgie	28	•	•	•	•	•	•	•	•	•	•	•	•	•	...	•	•	...
India - Inde[2]	14	•	•	•	•	•	•	•	•	•	...	•	•	...	...	...	...	...
Indonesia - Indonésie	10	•	•	•	•	•	•	•	•	...	...	...	•	...	...	...	...	...
Iran (Islamic Republic of) - Iran (République islamique d')	14	•	•	•	•	•	•	•	•	•	...	•	•	...	...	...	...	...
Iraq	13	•	•	•	•	•	•	•	•	•	...	•	•	...	...	...	...	...
Israel - Israël[3]	29	•	•	•	•	•	•	•	•	•	•	•	•	•	...	•	•	•
Japan - Japon	30	•	•	•	•	•	•	•	•	•	•	•	•	•	...	•	•	•
Jordan - Jordanie	15	•	•	•	•	•	•	•	•	•	...	•	•	...	...	•	...	•
Kazakhstan	30	•	•	•	•	•	•	•	•	•	•	•	•	•	...	•	•	•
Kuwait - Koweït	25	•	•	•	•	•	•	•	•	•	•	•	•	•	...	•	...	...
Kyrgyzstan - Kirghizistan	30	•	•	•	•	•	•	•	•	•	•	•	•	•	...	•	•	•
Lao People's Democratic Republic - République démocratique populaire lao	10	•	•	•	•	•	•	•	•	•	...	...	•	...	...	...	...	...
Lebanon - Liban	13	•	•	...	•	•	•	•	•	•	...	•	•	...	...	...	...	...
Malaysia - Malaisie	20	•	•	•	•	•	•	•	•	•	•	•	•	...	...	•	...	...
Maldives	24	•	•	•	•	•	•	•	•	•	•	•	•	...	...	•	...	...
Mongolia - Mongolie	23	•	•	•	•	•	•	•	•	•	•	•	•	...	...	•	...	...
Myanmar	14	•	•	•	•	•	•	•	•	...	...	•	•	...	...	...	...	...
Nepal - Népal	13	•	•	•	•	•	•	•	•	•	...	•	•	...	...	...	...	...
Occupied Palestinian Territory - Territoire palestinien occupé	21	•	•	•	•	•	•	•	•	•	...	•	•	...	...	...	...	...

Table A. *Demographic Yearbook 2007* synoptic table: Availability of data by country/area, table and sex, where applicable
Tableau A. Tableau synoptique de l'*Annuaire démographique 2007*: Disponibilité des données par pays ou zone, tableau et le sexe, si disponible (continued — suite)

Continent, country or area / Continent, pays ou zone	Infant and maternal mortality - Mortalité infantile et mortalité liée à la maternité				General mortality - Mortalité générale				Nuptiality and divorces - Nuptialité et divortialité				
	15	16 Total	16 M/F	17	18	19 Total	19 M/F	20	21	22	23	24	25
AMERICA, SOUTH — AMERIQUE DU SUD													
Argentina - Argentine	•	•	•	•	•	•	•	•	•	...	...	...	...
Bolivia - Bolivie	...	...	...	•	•	•	•	•	•	...	...	...	...
Brazil - Brésil	•	...	...	•	•	•	•	•	•	•	•	•	•
Chile - Chili	•	•	•	•	•	•	•	•	•	•	•	•	•
Colombia - Colombie	•	•	•	•	•	•	•	•	•	...	...	...	...
Ecuador - Équateur	•	•	•	•	•	•	•	•	•	•	•	•	•
Falkland Islands (Malvinas) - Îles Falkland (Malvinas)	...	...	...	...	...	...	...	...	...	...	...	...	...
French Guiana - Guyane française	•	•	•	•	•	•	•	•	...	...	...	...	...
Guyana	•	•	...	•	•	•	•	•	...	...	...	...	...
Paraguay	•	•	...	•	•	•	•	•	•	•	•	•	•
Peru - Pérou	•	•	...	•	•	•	•	•	•	•	•	•	•
Suriname	•	•	...	•	•	•	•	•	•	•	•	•	•
Uruguay	•	•	•	•	•	•	•	•	•	•	•	•	•
Venezuela (Bolivarian Republic of) - Venezuela (République bolivarienne du)	...	•	•	•	•	•	•	•	•	•	•	•	•
ASIA — ASIE													
Afghanistan	...	...	...	...	...	...	...	•	...	...	...	...	...
Armenia - Arménie	•	•	•	•	•	•	•	•	•	•	•	•	•
Azerbaijan - Azerbaïdjan	•	•	•	•	•	•	•	•	•	•	•	•	•
Bahrain - Bahreïn	•	•	•	•	•	•	•	•	•	•	•	•	•
Bangladesh	•	...	...	...	•	•	...	•	...	...	...	...	...
Bhutan - Bhoutan	•	...	...	...	•	•	...	•	...	...	...	...	...
Brunei Darussalam - Brunéi Darussalam	•	...	...	•	•	•	•	•	•	•	•	•	•
Cambodia - Cambodge	•	...	...	...	•	•	...	•	...	•	...	...	...
China - Chine[1]	...	...	...	...	•	•	...	•	...	...	...	...	...
China, Hong Kong SAR - Chine, Hong Kong RAS	•	•	•	•	•	•	•	•	•	•	•	•	•
China, Macao SAR - Chine, Macao RAS	•	•	•	•	•	•	•	•	•	•	•	•	•
Cyprus - Chypre	•	•	•	•	•	•	•	•	•	•	•	•	•
Democratic People's Republic of Korea - République populaire démocratique de Corée	...	...	...	...	...	...	...	...	...	...	...	...	...
Georgia - Géorgie	•	•	•	•	•	•	•	•	•	•	•	•	•
India - Inde[2]	•	...	...	...	•	•	...	•	•	•	•	•	•
Indonesia - Indonésie	...	...	...	...	...	...	...	...	...	...	...	...	...
Iran (Islamic Republic of) - Iran (République islamique d')	•	...	...	...	•	•	•	•	...	...	...	...	...
Iraq	•	...	...	...	•	•	...	•	•	...	...	...	...
Israel - Israël[3]	•	•	•	•	•	•	•	•	•	•	•	•	•
Japan - Japon	•	•	•	•	•	•	•	•	•	•	•	•	•
Jordan - Jordanie	•	...	...	...	•	•	•	•	•	•	•	•	•
Kazakhstan	•	•	•	•	•	•	•	•	•	•	•	•	•
Kuwait - Koweït	•	•	•	•	•	•	•	•	•	•	•	•	•
Kyrgyzstan - Kirghizistan	•	•	•	•	•	•	•	•	•	•	•	•	•
Lao People's Democratic Republic - République démocratique populaire lao	...	...	...	...	...	...	...	...	...	...	•	...	...
Lebanon - Liban	•	...	...	...	•	•	...	•	...	...	•	...	...
Malaysia - Malaisie	•	•	•	•	•	•	•	•	•	•	•	•	•
Maldives	•	•	•	•	•	•	•	•	•	•	•	•	•
Mongolia - Mongolie	•	...	...	...	•	•	•	•	•	•	•	•	•
Myanmar	•	...	...	...	•	•	...	•	...	...	...	...	...
Nepal - Népal	...	...	...	...	...	•	...	•	...	...	...	...	...
Occupied Palestinian Territory - Territoire palestinien occupé	•	•	•	•	•	•	•	•	•	•	•	•	...

Table A. *Demographic Yearbook 2007* synoptic table: Availability of data by country/area, table and sex, where applicable

Tableau A. Tableau synoptique de l'*Annuaire démographique 2007*: Disponibilité des données par pays ou zone, tableau et le sexe , si disponible (continued — suite)

Continent, country or area / Continent, pays ou zone	Table totals	Summary - Aperçu 3 Total	3 M/F	4	5	Population 6 Total	6 M/F	7 Total	7 M/F	8 Total	8 M/F	Natality - Natalité 9	10 Total	10 M/F	11	Foetal mortality - Mortalité foetale 12	13	14
ASIA — ASIE																		
Oman	21	•	•	•	•	•	•	•	•	•	•	•	•	•	...	•	...	...
Pakistan[4]	20	•	•	•	•	•	•	•	•	•	•	•	•	•	...	•	...	...
Philippines	24	•	•	•	•	•	•	•	•	•	•	•	•	•	...	•	•	...
Qatar	27	•	•	•	•	•	•	•	•	•	•	•	•	•	•	•	•	•
Republic of Korea - République de Corée	27	•	•	•	•	•	•	•	•	•	•	•	•	•	•	•	•	•
Saudi Arabia - Arabie saoudite	19	•	•	•	•	•	•	•	•	•	•	...	•	•	•	•	•	•
Singapore - Singapour	29	•	•	•	•	•	•	•	•	•	•	•	•	•	•	•	•	•
Sri Lanka	18	•	•	•	•	•	•	•	•	•	•	•	•	•	...	•	...	...
Syrian Arab Republic - République arabe syrienne	14	•	•	•	•	•	•	•	•	•	•	...	•	•	•	•	•	•
Tajikistan - Tadjikistan	30	•	•	•	•	•	•	•	•	•	•	•	•	•	•	•	•	•
Thailand - Thaïlande	21	•	•	•	...	•	•	•	•	•	•	...	•	•	...	•	...	...
Timor-Leste	5	•	•	...	...	•	•	•	...	•	...	...	•	...	...	...	...	...
Turkey - Turquie	20	•	•	•	...	•	•	•	•	•	•	...	•	•	...	•	...	...
Turkmenistan - Turkménistan	9	•	•	•	...	•	•	•	...	•	...	...	•	...	...	•	...	...
United Arab Emirates - Émirats arabes unis	21	•	•	•	...	•	•	•	•	•	•	•	•	•	...	•	...	...
Uzbekistan - Ouzbékistan	17	•	•	•	...	•	•	•	•	•	•	...	•	•	...	...	...	...
Viet Nam	14	•	•	•	•	•	•	•	•	•	•	•	•	...	...	...	...	...
Yemen - Yémen	13	•	•	•	•	•	•	•	•	•	•	...	•	...	...	...	...	...
EUROPE																		
Åland Islands - Îles d'Åland	25	•	•	•	•	•	•	•	•	•	•	•	•	•	...	•	•	•
Albania - Albanie	26	•	•	•	•	•	•	•	•	•	•	•	•	•	...	•	•	...
Andorra - Andorre	21	•	•	•	•	•	•	•	•	•	•	•	•	•	...	•	...	...
Austria - Autriche	28	•	•	•	•	•	•	•	•	•	•	•	•	•	•	•	•	•
Belarus - Bélarus	30	•	•	•	•	•	•	•	•	•	•	•	•	•	...	•	•	•
Belgium - Belgique	26	•	•	•	•	•	•	•	•	•	•	•	...	•	...	•	•	•
Bosnia and Herzegovina - Bosnie-Herzégovine	23	•	•	•	•	•	•	...	•	•	•	•	•	•	•	•	•	•
Bulgaria - Bulgarie	30	•	•	•	•	•	•	•	•	•	•	•	•	•	•	•	•	•
Croatia - Croatie	29	•	•	•	•	•	•	•	•	•	•	•	•	•	•	•	•	•
Czech Republic - République tchèque	30	•	•	•	•	•	•	•	•	•	•	•	•	•	•	•	•	•
Denmark - Danemark	29	•	•	•	•	•	•	•	•	•	•	•	•	•	•	•	•	•
Estonia - Estonie	30	•	•	•	•	•	•	•	•	•	•	•	•	•	•	•	•	•
Faeroe Islands - Îles Féroé	16	•	•	•	•	•	•	•	•	•	•	•	•	•	...	•	•	•
Finland - Finlande	30	•	•	•	•	•	•	•	•	•	•	•	•	•	•	•	•	•
France	30	•	•	•	•	•	•	•	•	•	•	•	•	•	•	•	•	•
Germany - Allemagne	30	•	•	•	•	•	•	•	•	•	•	•	•	•	...	•	...	...
Gibraltar	18	•	•	•	•	•	•	•	•	•	•	...	•	•	...	•	...	...
Greece - Grèce	30	•	•	•	•	•	•	•	•	•	•	•	•	•	•	•	•	•
Guernsey - Guernesey	17	•	•	•	•	•	•	•	•	•	•	•	•	•	...	•	...	•
Holy See - Saint-Siège	7	•	•	•	•	•	•	•	•	•	•	•	...	...	...	...	...	...
Hungary - Hongrie	30	•	•	•	•	•	•	•	•	•	•	•	•	•	•	•	•	•
Iceland - Islande	30	•	•	•	•	•	•	•	•	•	•	•	•	•	•	•	•	•
Ireland - Irlande	26	•	•	•	•	•	•	•	•	•	•	•	•	...	...	•	•	•
Isle of Man - Îles de Man	20	•	•	•	•	•	•	•	•	•	•	•	•	•	...	•	...	•
Italy - Italie	30	•	•	•	•	•	•	•	•	•	•	•	•	•	•	•	•	•
Jersey	15	•	•	•	•	•	•	•	•	•	•	•	•	•	...	•	...	•
Latvia - Lettonie	30	•	•	•	•	•	•	•	•	•	•	•	•	•	•	•	•	•
Liechtenstein	21	•	•	•	•	•	•	•	•	•	•	•	•	•	...	•	•	•
Lithuania - Lituanie	30	•	•	•	•	•	•	•	•	•	•	•	•	•	•	•	•	•
Luxembourg	27	•	•	•	•	•	•	•	•	•	•	...	•	•	...	•	•	•
Malta - Malte	25	•	•	•	•	•	•	•	•	•	•	•	•	•	...	•	•	•
Monaco	16	•	•	•	•	•	•	•	•	•	•	...	...	•	...	•	...	...
Montenegro - Monténégro	26	•	•	•	•	•	•	•	•	•	•	•	•	•	...	•	•	...

Table A. *Demographic Yearbook 2007* synoptic table: Availability of data by country/area, table and sex,
where applicable
Tableau A. Tableau synoptique de l'*Annuaire démographique 2007:* Disponibilité des données par pays ou zone, tableau et le sexe , si disponible (continued — suite)

Continent, country or area / Continent, pays ou zone	General topic and table number- Sujet général et numéro de tableau											
	Infant and maternal mortality - Mortalité infantile et mortalité liée à la maternité				General mortality - Mortalité générale			Nuptiality and divorces - Nuptialité et divortialité				
	15	16 Total	16 M/F	17	18	19 Total	19 M/F	20	21	22	23	24	25
ASIA — ASIE												
Oman	•	•	•	...	•	•	•	•	...	...	...	...	...
Pakistan[4]	•	•	•	...	•	•	•	•	...	...	...	...	...
Philippines	•	•	•	•	•	•	...	•	•	•	...	•	...
Qatar	•	•	•	•	•	•	•	•	...	•	...	•	...
Republic of Korea - République de Corée	•	•	•	•	•	•	•	•	•	•	•	•	•
Saudi Arabia - Arabie saoudite	•	...	...	•	•	•	•	•	•	•	•	•	•
Singapore - Singapour	•	•	•	•	•	•	•	•	•	•	•	•	•
Sri Lanka	...	...	...	...	•	•	...	•	...	...	...	...	...
Syrian Arab Republic - République arabe syrienne	...	...	...	...	•	•	...	•	...	...	•	...	...
Tajikistan - Tadjikistan	•	•	•	•	•	•	•	•	•	•	•	...	...
Thailand - Thaïlande	•	•	•	•	•	•	•	•	•	•	•	...	...
Timor-Leste	...	...	...	...	•	...	...	•	...	...	...	...	...
Turkey - Turquie	•	•	•	...	•	...	•	...	•	•	•	•	•
Turkmenistan - Turkménistan	...	...	...	...	•	...	...	•	•	•	...	...	...
United Arab Emirates - Émirats arabes unis	•	...	...	•	•	•	•	•	•	•	•	...	...
Uzbekistan - Ouzbékistan	•	•	•	...	•	•	•	•	•	•	...	...	...
Viet Nam	•	...	...	...	•	...	...	•	•	...	...	...	...
Yemen - Yémen	...	...	...	•	...	...	...	•	...	•	...	...	...
EUROPE												
Åland Islands - Îles d'Åland	•	...	...	...	•	•	•	•	•	•	•	...	...
Albania - Albanie	•	•	•	...	•	•	•	•	•	•	•	...	•
Andorra - Andorre	•	•	•	...	•	•	•	•	•	•	•	...	...
Austria - Autriche	•	•	•	•	•	•	•	•	•	•	•	•	•
Belarus - Bélarus	•	•	•	•	•	•	•	•	•	•	•	•	•
Belgium - Belgique	•	•	•	•	•	•	•	•	•	•	•	...	•
Bosnia and Herzegovina - Bosnie-Herzégovine	•	•	•	...	•	•	•	•	•	•	•	...	•
Bulgaria - Bulgarie	•	•	•	•	•	•	•	•	•	•	•	•	•
Croatia - Croatie	•	•	•	•	•	•	•	•	•	•	•	•	•
Czech Republic - République tchèque	•	•	•	•	•	•	•	•	•	•	•	•	•
Denmark - Danemark	•	•	•	•	•	•	•	•	•	•	•	•	•
Estonia - Estonie	•	•	•	•	•	•	•	•	•	•	•	•	•
Faeroe Islands - Îles Féroé	...	...	...	•	•	•	•	•	•	•	•	...	...
Finland - Finlande	•	•	•	•	•	•	•	•	•	•	•	•	•
France	•	•	•	•	•	•	•	•	•	•	•	•	•
Germany - Allemagne	•	•	•	•	•	•	•	•	•	•	•	•	•
Gibraltar	•	•	•	...	•	•	•	•	•	•	•	...	...
Greece - Grèce	•	•	•	•	•	•	•	•	•	•	•	•	•
Guernsey - Guernesey	...	...	...	•	•	...	...	•	...	...	...	...	...
Holy See - Saint-Siège	...	...	...	...	...	...	...	...	...	...	...	...	...
Hungary - Hongrie	•	•	•	•	•	•	•	•	•	•	•	•	•
Iceland - Islande	•	•	•	•	•	•	•	•	•	•	•	•	•
Ireland - Irlande	•	•	•	•	•	•	•	•	•	•	•	•	•
Isle of Man - Îles de Man	•	•	•	...	•	•	•	•	•	•	•	...	...
Italy - Italie	•	•	•	•	•	•	•	•	•	•	•	•	•
Jersey	...	...	...	...	•	•	...	•	...	...	...	...	...
Latvia - Lettonie	•	•	•	•	•	•	•	•	•	•	•	•	•
Liechtenstein	•	...	...	•	•	•	•	•	•	•	•	•	•
Lithuania - Lituanie	•	•	•	•	•	•	•	•	•	•	•	•	•
Luxembourg	•	•	•	•	•	•	•	•	•	•	•	•	•
Malta - Malte	•	•	•	•	•	•	•	•	•	•	•	•	•
Monaco	...	...	...	...	•	•	•	•	•	•	•	...	...
Montenegro - Monténégro	•	•	•	...	•	•	•	•	•	•	•	•	•

Table A. *Demographic Yearbook 2007* synoptic table: Availability of data by country/area, table and sex, where applicable

Tableau A. Tableau synoptique de l'*Annuaire démographique 2007*: Disponibilité des données par pays ou zone, tableau et le sexe , si disponible (continued — suite)

Continent, country or area / Continent, pays ou zone	Table totals	Summary - Apercu 3 Total	3 M/F	4	5	Population 6 Total	6 M/F	7 Total	7 M/F	8 Total	8 M/F	Natality 9	10 Total	10 M/F	11	Foetal mortality 12	13	14
EUROPE																		
Netherlands - Pays-Bas	28	•	•	•	•	•	•	•	•	•	•	•	•	•	...	•	•	...
Norway - Norvège	30	•	•	•	•	•	•	•	•	•	•	•	•	•	•	•	•	•
Poland - Pologne	30	•	•	•	•	•	•	•	•	•	•	•	•	•	•	•	•	•
Portugal	28	•	•	•	•	•	•	•	•	•	•	•	•	•	...	•	•	•
Republic of Moldova - République de Moldova	29	•	•	•	•	•	•	•	•	•	•	•	•	•	•	•	•	•
Romania - Roumanie	30	•	•	•	•	•	•	•	•	•	•	•	•	•	...	•	•	•
Russian Federation - Fédération de Russie	27	•	•	•	•	•	•	•	•	•	•	•	•	•	...	•	•	•
San Marino - Saint-Marin	27	•	•	•	•	•	•	•	•	•	•	•	•	•	...	•	•	•
Serbia	30	•	•	•	•	•	•	•	•	•	•	•	•	•	•	•	•	•
Slovakia - Slovaquie	30	•	•	•	•	•	•	•	•	•	•	•	•	•	•	•	•	•
Slovenia - Slovénie	30	•	•	•	•	•	•	•	•	•	•	•	•	•	•	•	•	•
Spain - Espagne	30	•	•	•	•	•	•	•	•	•	•	•	•	•	•	•	•	•
Svalbard and Jan Mayen Islands - Îles Svalbard et Jan-Mayen	3	•	•	...	•	•	...	...	...	...	...	...	...	...	...	...	...	...
Sweden - Suède	30	•	•	•	•	•	•	•	•	•	•	•	•	•	•	•	•	•
Switzerland - Suisse	30	•	•	•	•	•	•	•	•	•	•	•	•	•	•	•	•	•
The Former Yugoslav Republic of Macedonia - L'ex-République yougoslave de Macédoine	27	•	•	•	•	•	•	•	•	•	•	•	•	•	...	•	•	•
Ukraine	29	•	•	•	•	•	•	•	•	•	•	•	•	•	•	•	•	•
United Kingdom of Great Britain and Northern Ireland - Royaume-Uni de Grande-Bretagne et d'Irlande du Nord	30	•	•	•	•	•	•	•	•	•	•	•	•	•	•	•	•	•
OCEANIA — OCEANIE																		
American Samoa - Samoas américaines	17	•	•	•	•	•	•	•	•	•	•	•	•	•	...	...	•	...
Australia - Australie	27	•	•	•	•	•	•	•	•	•	•	•	•	•	•	•	•	...
Cook Islands - Îles Cook	13	•	•	•	•	•	•	•	•	•	•	•	•	•	•	...	...	...
Fiji - Fidji	20	•	•	•	•	•	•	•	•	•	•	•	•	•	...	•	...	...
French Polynesia - Polynésie française	15	•	...	•	•	•	•	•	•	•	•	•	•	•	•	...	...	...
Guam	23	•	•	•	•	•	•	•	•	•	•	•	•	•	...	...	...	...
Kiribati	10	•	•	...	•	•	•	•	•	•	•	•	...	•	...	...	...	...
Marshall Islands - Îles Marshall	16	•	•	•	•	•	•	•	•	•	•	•	•	•	...	...	...	...
Micronesia (Federated States of) - Micronésie (États fédérés de)	14	•	•	•	•	•	•	•	•	•	•	•	...	•	...	...	...	...
Nauru	9	•	•	...	•	•	•	•	•	•	•	•	...	•	...	...	...	...
New Caledonia - Nouvelle-Calédonie	26	•	•	•	•	•	•	•	•	•	•	•	•	•	...	•	•	•
New Zealand - Nouvelle-Zélande	30	•	•	•	•	•	•	•	•	•	•	•	•	•	...	•	•	•
Niue - Nioué	12	•	•	•	•	•	•	•	•	•	•	•	...	•	...	...	...	...
Norfolk Island - Île Norfolk	7	•	•	...	•	•	...	...	...	...	•	•	...	...	...	...	...	...
Northern Mariana Islands - Îles Mariannes septentrionales	18	•	•	•	•	•	•	•	•	•	•	•	•	•	...	...	...	...
Palau - Palaos	19	•	•	•	•	•	•	•	•	•	•	•	•	•	•	•	...	...
Papua New Guinea - Papouasie-Nouvelle-Guinée	15	•	...	•	•	•	•	•	•	•	•	•	•	•	...	...	...	...
Pitcairn	13	•	...	•	•	•	•	•	•	•	•	•	...	•	...	...	...	...
Samoa	14	•	•	•	•	•	•	•	•	•	•	•	...	•	...	...	...	...
Solomon Islands - Îles Salomon	6	•	•	...	•	•	•	•	...	...	•	•	...	...	...	...	...	...
Tokelau - Tokélaou	6	•	•	...	•	•	•	•	...	...	...	...	...	...	...	...	...	...
Tonga	20	•	•	•	•	•	•	•	•	•	•	•	•	•	...	...	...	...
Tuvalu	17	•	•	•	•	•	•	•	•	•	•	•	•	•	...	...	...	...
Vanuatu	9	•	•	...	•	•	•	•	•	•	•	•	...	•	...	...	...	...
Wallis and Futuna Islands - Îles Wallis et Futuna	10	•	...	•	•	•	•	...	...	...	•	•	...	•	...	...	...	...

Table A. *Demographic Yearbook 2007* synoptic table: Availability of data by country/area, table and sex, where applicable

Tableau A. Tableau synoptique de l'*Annuaire démographique 2007*: Disponibilité des données par pays ou zone, tableau et le sexe , si disponible (continued — suite)

Continent, country or area / Continent, pays ou zone	Infant and maternal mortality - Mortalité infantile et mortalité liée à la maternité				General mortality - Mortalité générale				Nuptiality and divorces - Nuptialité et divortialité				
	15	16 Total	16 M/F	17	18	19 Total	19 M/F	20	21	22	23	24	25
EUROPE													
Netherlands - Pays-Bas	•	•	•	•	•	•	•	•	•	•	•	•	•
Norway - Norvège	•	•	•	•	•	•	•	•	•	•	•	•	•
Poland - Pologne	•	•	•	•	•	•	•	•	•	•	•	•	•
Portugal	•	•	•	•	•	•	•	•	•	•	•	•	•
Republic of Moldova - République de Moldova	•	•	•	•	•	•	•	•	•	•	•	•	•
Romania - Roumanie	•	•	•	•	•	•	•	•	•	•	•	•	•
Russian Federation - Fédération de Russie	•	•	•	•	•	•	•	•	•	•	•	...	...
San Marino - Saint-Marin	•	•	•	•	•	•	•	•	•	•	•	•	...
Serbia	•	•	•	•	•	•	•	•	•	•	•	•	•
Slovakia - Slovaquie	•	•	•	•	•	•	•	•	•	•	•	•	•
Slovenia - Slovénie	•	•	•	•	•	•	•	•	•	•	•	•	•
Spain - Espagne	•	•	•	•	•	•	•	•	•	•	•	•	•
Svalbard and Jan Mayen Islands - Îles Svalbard et Jan-Mayen	...	...	...	...	...	...	...	...	...	...	...	...	...
Sweden - Suède	•	•	•	•	•	•	•	•	•	•	•	•	•
Switzerland - Suisse	•	•	•	•	•	•	•	•	•	•	•	•	•
The Former Yugoslav Republic of Macedonia - L'ex-République yougoslave de Macédoine	•	•	•	•	•	•	•	•	•	•	•	•	•
Ukraine	•	•	•	•	•	•	•	•	•	•	•	•	•
United Kingdom of Great Britain and Northern Ireland - Royaume-Uni de Grande-Bretagne et d'Irlande du Nord	•	•	•	•	•	•	•	•	•	•	•	•	•
OCEANIA — OCEANIE													
American Samoa - Samoas américaines	•	...	...	...	•	•	•	...	•	...	...	...	...
Australia - Australie	•	...	•	•	•	•	•	•	•	•	•	•	•
Cook Islands - Îles Cook	•	...	...	...	•	...	...	...	•	...	...	...	...
Fiji - Fidji	•	...	...	...	•	...	...	...	•	•	...	...	...
French Polynesia - Polynésie française	•	•	...	...	•	...	...	...	•	•	...	...	...
Guam	•	...	...	...	•	...	...	...	•	•	•	...	...
Kiribati	...	...	...	•	...	...	...	•	...	...	...	...	...
Marshall Islands - Îles Marshall	...	...	...	...	•	...	•	...	•	...	...	...	...
Micronesia (Federated States of) - Micronésie (États fédérés de)	...	...	...	...	•	...	•	...	...	...	...	...	...
Nauru	...	...	...	...	...	...	•	...	...	...	...	...	...
New Caledonia - Nouvelle-Calédonie	•	...	•	•	•	•	•	•	•	...	...	...	...
New Zealand - Nouvelle-Zélande	•	•	•	•	•	•	•	•	•	•	•	•	•
Niue - Nioué	...	...	...	...	•	...	...	...	•	...	...	...	...
Norfolk Island - Île Norfolk	...	...	...	...	...	...	...	...	...	...	...	...	...
Northern Mariana Islands - Îles Mariannes septentrionales	•	...	...	...	•	...	...	...	...	•	...	•	•
Palau - Palaos	•	...	...	...	•	...	...	...	•	...	...	...	...
Papua New Guinea - Papouasie-Nouvelle-Guinée	•	...	...	...	•	...	...	...	•	...	...	...	...
Pitcairn	•	...	...	...	•	•	...	...	...	...	...	...	...
Samoa	...	...	...	...	...	...	...	...	...	•	•	...	...
Solomon Islands - Îles Salomon	•	...	...	...	•	...	...	...	...	...	...	...	...
Tokelau - Tokélaou	...	...	...	...	...	...	...	...	...	...	...	...	...
Tonga	•	...	...	...	•	...	•	...	•	•	•	...	...
Tuvalu	•	...	...	...	•	...	•	•	...	...	...	...	...
Vanuatu	...	...	...	...	...	...	•	...	...	...	...	...	...
Wallis and Futuna Islands - Îles Wallis et Futuna	...	...	...	•	•	•	...	...	...	...	...	...	...

FOOTNOTES - NOTES

• Data presented in the table - Les données présentées dans le tableau.

··· Data not available - Données non disponibles.

¹ For statistical purposes, the data for China do not include those for the Hong Kong Special Administrative Region (Hong Kong SAR), Macao special Administrative Region (Macao SAR) and Taiwan province of China. - Pour la présentation des statistiques, les données pour Chine ne comprennent pas la Région Administrative Spéciale de Hong Kong (Hong Kong RAS), la Région Administrative Spéciale de Macao (Macao RAS) et Taïwan province de Chine.
² Including data for the Indian-held part of Jammu and Kashmir, the final status of which has not yet been determined. - Y compris les données pour la partie du Jammu et du Cachemire occupée par l'Inde dont le statut définitif n'a pas encore été déterminé.
³ Including data for East Jerusalem and Israeli residents in certain other territories under occupation by Israeli military forces since June 1967. - Y compris les données pour Jérusalem-Est et les résidents israéliens dans certains autres territoires occupés depuis 1967 par les forces armées israéliennes.
⁴ Excluding data for the Pakistan-held part of Jammu and Kashmir, the final status of which has not yet been determined. - Non compris les données concernant la partie du Jammu et Cachemire occupée par le Pakistan dont le statut définitif n'a pas été déterminé.

Table 1

Table 1 presents for the world, major areas and regions estimates of the order of magnitude of population size, rates of population increase, crude birth and death rates, surface area as well as population density.

Description of variables: Estimates of world population by major areas and by regions are presented for 1950, 1960, 1970, 1980, 1990, 2000 and 2007. Average annual percentage rates of population growth, crude birth and crude death rates are shown for the period from 2005 to 2010. Surface area in square kilometers and population density estimates relate to 2007.

All population estimates and rates presented in this table were prepared by the Population Division of the United Nations, Department of Economic and Social Affairs, and have been published in *World Population Prospects: The 2008 Revision, CD Rom Edition – Extended Dataset*[1].

The scheme of regionalization used for these estimates is described below. Although some continental totals are given, and all can be derived, the basic scheme presents six major areas that are so drawn as to obtain greater homogeneity in sizes of population, types of demographic circumstances and accuracy of demographic statistics. Five of the major areas are subdivided into a total of 20 regions, which are arranged within the major areas; these regions together with Northern America, which is not subdivided, make a total of 21 regions.

The major areas of Northern America and Latin America are distinguished, rather than the conventional continents of North America and South America, because population trends in the middle American mainland and the Caribbean region more closely resemble those of South America than those of America north of Mexico. Data for the traditional continents of North and South America can be obtained by adding Central America and Caribbean region to Northern America and deducting from Latin America. Latin America, as defined here, has somewhat wider limits than it would be if defined only to include the Spanish-speaking, French-speaking and Portuguese-speaking countries.

The average annual percentage rates of population growth are calculated by the Population Division, United Nations Department of Economic and Social Affairs, using an exponential rate of increase.

Crude birth and crude death rates are expressed in terms of the average annual number of births and deaths, respectively, per 1 000 mid-year population. These rates are estimated.

Surface area totals are estimated by Population Division, United Nations Department of Economic and Social Affairs.

Computation: Density, calculated by the Statistics Division of the United Nations Department of Social and Economic Affairs, is the number of persons in the 2007 total population per square kilometer of total surface area.

Reliability of data: With the exception of surface area, all data are set in *italic* type to indicate their conjectural quality.

Limitations: The estimated orders of magnitude of population and surface area are subject to all the basic limitations set forth in connection with table 3, and to the same qualifications set forth for population and surface area statistics in sections 3 and 2.4 of the Technical Notes, respectively.

Likewise, rates of population increase and density index are affected by the limitations of the original figures. However, it may be noted that, in compiling data for regional and major areas totals, errors in the components may tend to compensate each other and the resulting aggregates may be more reliable than the quality of the individual components would imply.

Because of their estimated character, many of the birth and death rates shown should also be considered only as orders of magnitude, and not as measures of the true level of natality or mortality.

In interpreting the population densities, one should consider that some of the regions include large segments of land that are uninhabitable or barely habitable, and density values calculated as described make no allowance for this, nor for differences in patterns of land settlement.

Composition of macro geographical regions and sub-regions

AFRICA

Eastern Africa
Burundi
Comoros
Djibouti
Eritrea
Ethiopia
Kenya
Madagascar
Malawi
Mauritius
Mayotte
Mozambique
Réunion
Rwanda
Seychelles
Somalia
Uganda
United Republic of Tanzania
Zambia
Zimbabwe

Middle Africa
Angola
Cameroon
Central African Republic
Chad
Congo
Democratic Republic of the
  Congo
Equatorial Guinea
Gabon
Sao Tome and Principe

Northern Africa
Algeria
Egypt
Libyan Arab Jamahiriya
Morocco
Sudan
Tunisia
Western Sahara

Southern Africa
Botswana
Lesotho
Namibia
South Africa
Swaziland

Western Africa
Benin
Burkina Faso
Cape Verde
Côte d'Ivoire
Gambia
Ghana

Guinea
Guinea-Bissau
Liberia
Mali
Mauritania
Niger
Nigeria
Saint Helena
Senegal
Sierra Leone
Togo

ASIA

Eastern Asia
China
China, Hong Kong SAR
China, Macao SAR
Democratic People's
  Republic of Korea
Japan
Mongolia
Republic of Korea

South-central Asia
Afghanistan
Bangladesh
Bhutan
India
Iran (Islamic Republic of)
Kazakhstan
Kyrgyzstan
Maldives
Nepal
Pakistan
Sri Lanka
Tajikistan
Turkmenistan
Uzbekistan

South-eastern Asia
Brunei Darussalam
Cambodia
Indonesia
Lao People's Democratic
  Republic
Malaysia
Myanmar
Philippines
Singapore
Thailand
Timor Leste
Viet Nam

Western Asia
Armenia
Azerbaijan
Bahrain

Cyprus
Georgia
Iraq
Israel
Jordan
Kuwait
Lebanon
Occupied Palestinian Territory
Oman
Qatar
Saudi Arabia
Syrian Arab Republic
Turkey
United Arab Emirates
Yemen

EUROPE

Eastern Europe
Åland Islands
Belarus
Bulgaria
Czech Republic
Hungary
Poland
Republic of Moldova
Romania
Russian Federation
Slovakia
Ukraine

Northern Europe
Denmark
Estonia
Faeroe Islands
Finland
Guernsey
Iceland
Ireland
Isle of Man
Jersey
Latvia
Lithuania
Norway
Sweden
United Kingdom of Great Britain
  and Northern Ireland

Southern Europe
Albania
Andorra
Bosnia and Herzegovina
Croatia
Gibraltar
Greece
Holy See
Italy

Malta
Montenegro
Portugal
San Marino
Serbia
Slovenia
Spain
The Former Yugoslav Republic
  of Macedonia

Western Europe
Austria
Belgium
France
Germany
Liechtenstein
Luxembourg
Monaco
Netherlands
Switzerland

**LATIN AMERICA
  and the CARIBBEAN**

Caribbean
Anguilla
Antigua and Barbuda
Aruba
Bahamas
Barbados
British Virgin Islands
Cayman Islands
Cuba
Dominica
Dominican Republic
Grenada
Guadaloupe
Haiti
Jamaica
Martinique
Montserrat

Netherlands Antilles
Puerto Rico
Saint Kitts and Nevis
Saint Lucia
Saint Vincent and the
  Grenadines
Trinidad and Tobago
Turks and Caicos Islands
United States Virgin
  Islands

Central America
Belize
Costa Rica
El Salvador
Guatemala
Honduras
Mexico
Nicaragua
Panama

South America
Argentina
Bolivia (Plurinational State of)
Brazil
Chile
Colombia
Ecuador
Falkland Islands (Malvinas)
French Guiana
Guyana
Paraguay
Peru
Suriname
Uruguay
Venezuela (Bolivarian Republic of)

NORTHERN AMERICA

Bermuda
Canada

Greenland
Saint Pierre and Miquelon
United States of America

OCEANIA

Australia and New Zealand
Australia
New Zealand
Norfolk Island

Melanesia
Fiji
New Caledonia
Papua New Guinea
Solomon Islands
Vanuatu

Micronesia
Guam
Kiribati
Marshall Islands
Micronesia (Federated States of)
Nauru
Northern Mariana Islands
Palau

Polynesia
American Samoa
Cook Islands
French Polynesia
Niue
Pitcairn
Samoa
Tokelau
Tonga
Tuvalu
Wallis and Futuna Islands

NOTES

[1] United Nations, Department of Economic and Social Affairs, Population Division (2009). *World Population Prospects: The 2008 Revision,* CD-ROM Edition.

Tableau 1

Le tableau 1 présente, pour l'ensemble du monde et les grandes zones et régions, des estimations concernant l'ordre de grandeur de la population, les taux d'accroissement démographique, les taux bruts de natalité et de mortalité, la superficie et la densité de peuplement.

Description des variables : des estimations de la population mondiale par grandes zones et régions sont présentées pour 1950, 1960, 1970, 1980, 1990 et 2000 ainsi que pour 2007. Les taux annuels moyens d'accroissement de la population et les taux bruts de natalité et de mortalité portent sur la période allant de 2005 à 2010. Les indications concernant la superficie exprimée en kilomètres carrés et les estimations de la densité de population se rapportent à 2007.

Toutes les estimations de population et les taux de natalité, taux de mortalité et taux annuels d'accroissement de la population qui sont présentés dans le tableau 1 ont été établis par la Division de la population du Département des affaires économiques et sociales (Secrétariat de l'Organisation des Nations Unies), et ont été publiés dans *World Population Prospects: The 2008 Revision, CD Rom Edition – Extended Dataset*[1].

Bien que l'on ait donné certains totaux pour les continents (tous les autres pouvant être calculés), on a réparti le monde en huit grandes zones qui ont été découpées de manière à obtenir une plus grande homogénéité du point de vue des dimensions de population, des types de situations démographiques et de l'exactitude des statistiques démographiques.

Cinq de ces huit grandes zones ont été subdivisées en 20 régions. Avec l'Amérique septentrionale, qui n'est pas subdivisée, on arrive à un total de 21 régions.

Au lieu de faire la distinction classique entre l'Amérique du Nord et l'Amérique du Sud, on a choisi d'opérer une comparaison entre l'Amérique septentrionale et l'Amérique latine, parce que les tendances démographiques dans la partie continentale de l'Amérique centrale et dans la région des Caraïbes se rapprochent davantage de celles de l'Amérique du Sud que de celles de l'Amérique au nord du Mexique. On obtient les données pour les continents traditionnels de l'Amérique du Nord et de l'Amérique du Sud en extrayant les données concernant l'Amérique centrale et les Caraïbes de celles relatives à l'Amérique latine et en les regroupant avec celles relatives à l'Amérique septentrionale. L'Amérique latine ainsi définie a par conséquent des limites plus larges que celles des pays ou zones de langues espagnole, portugaise et française qui constituent l'Amérique latine au sens le plus strict du terme.

La Division de la population a calculé les taux annuels moyens d'accroissement de la population en appliquant un taux d'accroissement exponentiel.

Les taux bruts de natalité et de mortalité représentent respectivement le nombre annuel moyen de naissances et de décès par millier d'habitants en milieu d'année. Ces taux sont estimatifs.

La superficie totale a été estimée par la Division de la population du Département des affaires économiques et sociales.

Calculs : la densité, calculée par la Division de statistique du Département des affaires économiques et sociales, est égale au rapport entre l'effectif total de la population en 2007 et la superficie totale exprimée en kilomètres carrés.

Fiabilité des données : á l'exception des données concernant la superficie, toutes les données sont reproduites en *italique* pour en faire ressortir le caractère conjectural.

Insuffisance des données : les estimations concernant l'ordre de grandeur de la population et la superficie reposent en partie sur les données du tableau 3 ; elles appellent donc toutes les réserves fondamentales formulées à propos de ce tableau, et celles qui ont été respectivement formulées aux sections 3 et 2.4 des Notes techniques en ce qui concerne les statistiques relatives à la population et à la superficie.

Les taux d'accroissement et les indices de densité de la population se ressentent eux aussi des insuffisances inhérentes aux données de base. Toutefois, il est à noter que, lorsque l'on additionne des données par territoire pour obtenir des totaux régionaux et par grandes zones, les erreurs qu'elles comportent arrivent parfois à s'équilibrer, de sorte que les agrégats obtenus peuvent être un peu plus exacts que chacun des éléments dont on est parti.

Vu leur caractère estimatif, nombre des taux de natalité et de mortalité du tableau 1 doivent être considérés uniquement comme des ordres de grandeur et ne sont pas censés mesurer exactement le niveau de la natalité ou de la mortalité.

Parce que les totaux des superficies ont été obtenus en additionnant les chiffres pour chaque pays ou zones, qui apparaissent dans le tableau 3, ils ne comprennent pas les lieux où la population est inférieure à 50 personnes, tels que les régions polaires inhabitées.

Pour interpréter les valeurs de la densité de population, on se souviendra qu'il existe dans certaines des régions de vastes étendues de terres inhabitables ou à peine habitables et que les chiffres calculés selon la méthode indiquée ne tiennent compte ni de ce fait ni des différences de dispersion de la population selon le mode d'habitat.

Composition des grandes zones et régions

AFRIQUE

Afrique orientale
Burundi
Comores
Djibouti
Érythrée
Éthiopie
Kenya
Madagascar
Malawi
Maurice
Mayotte
Mozambique
Ouganda
République-Unie de Tanzanie
Réunion
Rwanda
Seychelles
Somalie
Zambie
Zimbabwe

Afrique centrale
Angola
Cameroun
Congo
Gabon
Guinée équatoriale
République centrafricaine
République démocratique du Congo
Sao Tomé-et-Principe
Tchad

Afrique septentrionale
Algérie
Égypte
Jamahiriya arabe libyenne
Maroc
Sahara occidental
Soudan
Tunisie

Afrique australe
Afrique du Sud
Botswana
Lesotho
Namibie
Swaziland

Afrique occidentale
Bénin
Burkina Faso
Cap-Vert
Côte d'Ivoire
Gambie
Ghana
Guinée
Guinée-Bissau
Libéria
Mali
Mauritanie
Niger
Nigéria
Sainte-Hélène
Sénégal
Sierra Leone
Togo

AMÉRIQUE LATINE ET CARAÏBES

Caraïbes
Anguilla
Antigua-et-Barbuda
Antilles néerlandaises
Aruba
Bahamas
Barbade
Cuba
Dominique
Grenade
Guadeloupe
Haïti

Îles Caïmanes
Îles Turques et Caïques
Îles Vierges américaines
Îles Vierges britanniques
Jamaïque
Martinique
Montserrat
Porto Rico
République dominicaine
Saint-Kitts-et-Nevis
Sainte-Lucie
Saint-Vincent-et-les Grenadines
Trinité-et-Tobago

Amérique centrale
Belize
Costa Rica
El Salvador
Guatemala
Honduras
Mexique
Nicaragua
Panama

Amérique du Sud
Argentine
Bolivie (État plurinational de)
Brésil
Chili
Colombie
Équateur
Guyana
Guyane française
Îles Falkland (Malvinas)
Paraguay
Pérou
Suriname
Uruguay
Venezuela (République bolivarienne du)

AMÉRIQUE SEPTENTRIONALE

Bermudes
Canada
États-Unis d'Amérique
Groenland
Saint-Pierre-et-Miquelon

ASIE

Asie orientale
Chine
Chine, Région administrative
spéciale de Hong Kong
Chine, Région administrative
spéciale de Macao
Japon
Mongolie
République de Corée
République populaire démocratique
de Corée

Asie centrale et Asie du Sud
Afghanistan
Bangladesh
Bhoutan
Inde
Iran (République Islamique d')
Kazakhstan
Kirghizistan
Maldives
Népal
Ouzbékistan
Pakistan
Sri Lanka
Tadjikistan
Turkménistan

Asie du Sud-Est
Brunéi Darussalam
Cambodge
Indonésie
Malaisie
Myanmar
Philippines
République démocratique populaire
lao
Singapour
Thaïlande
Timor-Leste
Viet Nam

Asie occidentale
Arabie saoudite
Arménie
Azerbaïdjan
Bahreïn

Chypre
Émirats arabes unis
Géorgie
Iraq
Israël
Jordanie
Koweït
Liban
Oman
Qatar
République arabe syrienne
Territoire palestinien occupé
Turquie
Yémen

EUROPE

Europe orientale
Bélarus
Bulgarie
Fédération de Russie
Hongrie
Pologne
République de Moldova
République tchèque
Roumanie
Slovaquie
Ukraine

Europe septentrionale
Danemark
Estonie
Finlande
Guernesey
Île de Man
Îles d'Åland
Îles Féroé
Îles Svalbard et Jan Mayen
Irlande
Islande
Jersey
Lettonie
Lituanie
Norvège
Royaume-Uni de Grande-
Bretagne et d'Irlande du
Nord
Suède

Europe méridionale
Albanie
Andorre
Bosnie-Herzégovine
Croatie
Espagne
Gibraltar
Grèce

Italie
L'ex-République yougoslave de
Macédoine
Malte
Monténégro
Portugal
Saint-Marin
Saint-Siège
Serbie
Slovénie

Europe occidentale
Allemagne
Autriche
Belgique
France
Liechtenstein
Luxembourg
Monaco
Pays-Bas
Suisse

OCÉANIE

Australie et Nouvelle-Zélande
Australie
Île Norfolk
Nouvelle-Zélande

Mélanésie
Fidji
Îles Salomon
Nouvelle-Calédonie
Papouasie-Nouvelle-Guinée
Vanuatu

Micronésie
Guam
Îles Mariannes septentrionales
Îles Marshall
Kiribati
Micronésie (États fédérés de)
Nauru
Palaos

Polynésie
Îles Cook
Îles Wallis et Futuna
Nioué
Pitcairn
Polynésie française
Samoa
Samoa américaines
Tokélaou
Tonga
Tuvalu

---

[1] *Nations Unies, Département de Questions Economiques et Sociales, Division de Population (2009). World Population Prospects, The 2008 Revision, CD Rom Edition.*

1. Population, rate of increase, birth and death rates, surface area and density for the world, major areas and regions: selected years
Population, taux d'accroissement, taux de natalité et taux de mortalité, superficie et densité pour l'ensemble du monde, les régions macro géographiques et les composantes géographiques: diverses années

Major areas and regions / Régions macro géographiques et composantes	Mid-year population estimates - Estimations de population au milieu de l'année (millions)							Annual rate of increase - Taux d'accroissement annuel (%)	Crude birth rate - Taux bruts de natalité	Crude death rate - Taux bruts de mortalité	Surface area (km2) - Superficie (km2) (000s)	Density - Densité[1]
	1950	1960	1970	1980	1990	2000	2007	2005 - 2010			2007	
WORLD TOTAL - ENSEMBLE DU MONDE	2 520	3 024	3 697	4 442	5 280	6 086	6 671	1.2	20	9	136 127	49
AFRICA - AFRIQUE	224	282	364	479	636	812	965	2.2	39	13	30 312	32
Eastern Africa - Afrique orientale	65	82	109	146	198	256	303	2.5	39	14	6 361	48
Middle Africa - Afrique centrale	26	32	41	54	73	96	119	2.8	45	17	6 613	18
Northern Africa - Afrique septentrionale	53	67	86	112	144	175	202	1.7	24	6	8 525	24
Southern Africa - Afrique méridionale	16	20	26	33	42	52	56	0.6	23	17	2 675	21
Western Africa - Afrique occidentale	64	80	102	134	178	234	284	2.4	40	15	6 138	46
LATIN AMERICA AND CARIBBEAN - AMERIQUE LATINE ET CARAIBES	167	219	285	362	444	523	570	1.2	20	6	20 546	28
Caribbean - Caraïbes	17	20	25	29	34	38	41	0.9	19	8	234	176
Central America - Amérique centrale	37	50	68	91	113	136	148	1.3	21	5	2 480	60
South America - Amérique du Sud	113	148	192	242	297	349	381	1.2	19	6	17 832	21
NORTHERN AMERICA - AMERIQUE SEPTENTRIONALE[2]	172	204	232	256	283	315	342	1.0	14	8	21 776	16
ASIA - ASIE[3]	1 396	1 699	2 140	2 630	3 169	3 676	4 029	1.1	19	7	31 880	126
Eastern Asia - Asie orientale	671	792	987	1 178	1 350	1 479	1 538	0.5	13	7	11 763	131
South Central Asia - Asie centrale méridionale	496	617	780	978	1 226	1 485	1 703	1.5	24	8	10 791	158
South Eastern Asia - Asie méridionale orientale	178	223	286	358	440	519	568	1.2	20	6	4 495	126
Western Asia - Asie occidentale[3]	51	67	88	116	154	193	220	1.8	24	6	4 831	45
EUROPE[3]	547	604	656	692	721	728	731	0.0	10	12	23 049	32
Eastern Europe - Europe orientale	220	254	276	295	311	305	294	-0.5	10	15	18 814	16
Northern Europe - Europe septentrionale	77	81	86	89	92	94	97	0.4	12	10	1 810	54
Southern Europe - Europe méridionale	109	118	127	138	143	146	152	0.3	10	10	1 317	115
Western Europe - Europe occidentale	141	152	166	170	176	184	187	0.2	10	10	1 108	169
OCEANIA - OCEANIE[2]	12.8	15.9	19.6	22.9	26.7	30.9	34.5	1.2	17	7	8 564	4
Australia and New Zealand - Australie et Nouvelle-Zélande	10.1	12.6	15.5	17.8	20.3	22.9	25.0	1.0	13	7	8 012	3
Melanesia - Melanésie	2.3	2.7	3.4	4.4	5.5	6.9	8.2	1.9	28	9	541	15
Micronesia - Micronésie	0.1	0.2	0.2	0.3	0.4	0.5	0.6	1.3	22	5	3	200
Polynesia - Polynésie	0.2	0.3	0.4	0.5	0.5	0.6	0.7	1.0	22	5	8	88

FOOTNOTES - NOTES

[1] Population per square kilometre of surface area. Figures are estimates of population divided by surface area and are not to be considered as either reflecting density in the urban sense or as indicating the supporting power of a territory's land and resources. — Habitants par kilomètre carré. Il s'agit simplement du quotient calculé en divisant la population par la superficie et n'est par considéré comme indiquant la densité au sens urbain du terme ni l'effectif de population que les terres et les ressources du territoire sont capables de nourrir.

[2] Hawaii, a state of the United States of America, is included in Northern America rather than in Oceania. — Hawaii, un Etat des Etats-Unis d'Amérique, est compris en Amérique septentrionale plutôt qu'en Océanie.

[3] The European part of Turkey is included in Western Asia rather than Europe. — La partie européenne de la Turquie est comprise en Asie Occidentale plutôt qu'en Europe.

Table 2

Table 2 presents estimates of population and the percentage distribution by age and sex as well as the sex ratio for all ages; data are presented for the world, the six major areas and the 20 regions for 2007.

Description of variables: All population estimates presented in this table are prepared by the Population Division of the United Nations Department of Economic and Social Affairs. These estimates were published (using more detailed age groups) in the *World Population Prospects: The 2008 Revision, CD Rom Edition – Extended Dataset*[1].

The scheme of regionalization used for these estimates is discussed in detail in the technical notes for table 1. Age groups presented in this table are: under 15 years, 15-64 years and 65 years and over. Sex ratio refers to the number of males per 100 females of all ages.

The percentage distributions and the sex ratios that appear in this table were calculated by the Statistics Division of the United Nations Department of Economic and Social Affairs using the Population Division estimates.

Reliability of data: All data are set in *italic* type to indicate their conjectural quality.

Limitations: The data presented in this table are from the same series of estimates, prepared by the Population Division, presented in table 1. The estimated orders of magnitude of population are subject to all the basic limitations set forth for population statistics in section 3 of the Technical Notes. In brief, because they are estimates, these distributions by broad age groups and sex should be considered only as orders of magnitude. However, in compiling data for regional and macro region totals, errors in the components tend to compensate each other and the resulting aggregates may be somewhat more reliable than the quality of the individual components would imply.

In addition, data in this table are limited by factors affecting data by age. These factors are described in the technical notes for table 7. Because the age groups presented in this table are so broad, these problems are minimized.

NOTES

[1] *World Population Prospects: The 2008 Revision, CD-ROM Edition (United Nations, Department of Economic and Social Affairs, Population Division (2009)).*

Tableau 2

Le tableau 2 présente, pour l'ensemble du monde, les six grandes zones et les 20 régions, des estimations concernant la population en 2007 ainsi que sa répartition en pourcentage selon l'âge et le sexe, et le rapport de masculinité pour tous les âges.

Description des variables : toutes les données figurant dans le tableau 2 ont été établies par la Division de la population du Département des affaires économiques et sociales (Secrétariat de l'Organisation des Nations Unies) et ont été publiées dans l'ouvrage intitulé *World Population Prospects: The 2008 Revision, CD Rom Edition – Extended Dataset* [1].

La classification géographique utilisée pour établir ces estimations est exposée en détail dans les notes techniques relatives au tableau 1. Les groupes d'âge présentés dans ce tableau sont définis comme suit : moins de 15 ans, de 15 à 64 ans et 65 ans et plus. Le rapport de masculinité correspond au nombre d'individus de sexe masculin pour 100 individus de sexe féminin sans considération d'âge.

Les pourcentages et les rapports de masculinité qui sont présentés dans le tableau 2 ont été calculés par la Division de statistique de l'ONU à partir des estimations établies par la Division de la population.

Fiabilité des données : toutes les données figurant dans ce tableau sont reproduites en *italique* pour en faire ressortir le caractère conjectural.

Insuffisance des données : les données de ce tableau appartiennent à la même série d'estimations, établie par la Division de la population, que celles qui figurent au tableau 1. Les estimations concernant l'ordre de grandeur de la population appellent donc toutes les réserves fondamentales qui ont été formulées à la section 3 des Notes techniques à propos des statistiques relatives à la population. Sans entrer dans le détail, il convient de préciser que les données relatives à la répartition par grand groupe d'âge et par sexe doivent être considérées uniquement comme des ordres de grandeur en raison de leur caractère estimatif. Toutefois, il est à noter que, lorsque l'on additionne des données par territoire pour obtenir des totaux régionaux et par grandes zones, les erreurs qu'elles comportent arrivent parfois à s'équilibrer, de sorte que les agrégats obtenus peuvent être un peu plus exacts que chacun des éléments dont on est parti.

En outre, les donnés figurant dans le tableau 2 comportent certaines imprécisions en raison des facteurs influant sur les données par âge (voir à ce propos les notes techniques relatives au tableau 7). Ces imprécisions sont cependant atténuées du fait de l'étendue des groupes d'âge présentés dans le tableau 2.

NOTE

[1] *Perspectives de la population mondiale: La Révision de 2008, CD-ROM (Nations Unies, Département des affaires économiques et sociales, Division de la population (2009)).*

2. Estimates of population and its percentage distribution, by age and sex and sex ratio for all ages for the world, major areas and regions: 2007

Estimations de la population et pourcentage de répartition selon l'âge et le sexe et rapport de masculinité pour l'ensemble du monde, les grandes régions et les régions géographiques: 2007

Major areas and regions / Grandes régions et régions	Population (millions)												Sex ratio - Rapport de masculinité[1]
	Both sexes - Les deux sexes				Male - Masculin				Female - Féminin				
	All ages - Tous âges	-15	15-64	65+	All ages - Tous âges	-15	15-64	65+	All ages - Tous âges	-15	15-64	65+	
WORLD TOTAL - ENSEMBLE DU MONDE													
Number - Nombre	6 671	1 849	4 329	492	3 363	956	2 190	217	3 308	893	2 140	275	
Percent - Pourcentage	100.0	27.7	64.9	7.4	100.0	28.4	65.1	6.4	100.0	27.0	64.7	8.3	101.7
AFRICA - AFRIQUE													
Number - Nombre	965	393	539	33	481	199	268	15	484	195	271	18	
Percent - Pourcentage	100.0	40.8	55.8	3.4	100.0	41.3	55.6	3.1	100.0	40.2	56.1	3.7	99.4
Eastern Africa - Afrique orientale													
Number - Nombre	303	134	160	9	150	67	79	4	153	67	81	5	
Percent - Pourcentage	100.0	44.2	52.8	3.0	100.0	44.8	52.5	2.7	100.0	43.6	53.1	3.3	98.3
Middle Africa - Afrique centrale													
Number - Nombre	119	54	62	3	59	27	31	2	60	27	31	2	
Percent - Pourcentage	100.0	45.4	51.7	2.9	100.0	45.9	51.6	2.6	100.0	44.9	51.9	3.2	98.3
Northern Africa - Afrique septentrionale													
Number - Nombre	202	65	128	9	102	33	64	4	101	32	64	5	
Percent - Pourcentage	100.0	32.4	63.1	4.5	100.0	32.9	63.0	4.1	100.0	31.8	63.2	4.9	100.9
Southern Africa - Afrique méridionale													
Number - Nombre	56	18	36	2	28	9	18	1	29	9	18	1	
Percent - Pourcentage	100.0	31.9	63.9	4.2	100.0	32.6	64.0	3.4	100.0	31.2	63.8	5.0	96.8
Western Africa - Afrique occidentale													
Number - Nombre	284	122	154	8	142	62	77	4	142	60	77	5	
Percent - Pourcentage	100.0	42.9	54.1	3.0	100.0	43.4	53.8	2.8	100.0	42.4	54.3	3.2	100.4
LATIN AMERICA AND CARIBBEAN - AMÉRIQUE LATIN ET CARAÏBES													
Number - Nombre	570	165	368	37	282	84	181	16	288	81	186	21	
Percent - Pourcentage	100.0	28.9	64.6	6.5	100.0	29.8	64.4	5.8	100.0	28.1	64.7	7.2	97.7
Caribbean - Caraïbes													
Number - Nombre	41	11	27	3	20	6	13	2	21	6	13	2	
Percent - Pourcentage	100.0	27.6	64.4	8.0	100.0	28.4	64.2	7.4	100.0	26.8	64.6	8.6	98.2
Central America - Amérique centrale													
Number - Nombre	148	47	93	9	73	24	45	4	75	23	47	5	
Percent - Pourcentage	100.0	31.6	62.6	5.8	100.0	32.6	62.1	5.3	100.0	30.6	63.1	6.2	97.1
South America - Amérique méridionale													
Number - Nombre	381	107	249	25	188	54	123	11	192	52	126	14	
Percent - Pourcentage	100.0	28.0	65.3	6.6	100.0	28.9	65.3	5.8	100.0	27.2	65.3	7.4	97.8
NORTHERN AMERICA - AMÉRIQUE SEPTENTRIONALE[2]													
Number - Nombre	342	69	230	43	169	35	115	18	173	34	115	25	
Percent - Pourcentage	100.0	20.2	67.2	12.6	100.0	21.0	68.1	10.9	100.0	19.5	66.3	14.2	97.3
ASIA - ASIE[3]													
Number - Nombre	4 029	1 100	2 671	258	2 063	576	1 368	120	1 966	524	1 304	139	
Percent - Pourcentage	100.0	27.3	66.3	6.4	100.0	27.9	66.3	5.8	100.0	26.7	66.3	7.0	104.9
Eastern Asia - Asie orientale													
Number - Nombre	1 538	311	1 089	138	792	169	559	64	746	143	530	74	
Percent - Pourcentage	100.0	20.2	70.8	9.0	100.0	21.3	70.6	8.1	100.0	19.1	71.0	9.9	106.1
South Central Asia - Asie centrale méridionale													
Number - Nombre	1 703	555	1 070	78	875	288	550	37	828	267	519	41	
Percent - Pourcentage	100.0	32.6	62.8	4.6	100.0	32.9	62.9	4.2	100.0	32.3	62.8	4.9	105.8
South Eastern Asia - Asie méridionale orientale													
Number - Nombre	569	162	375	32	283	83	186	14	286	79	189	18	
Percent - Pourcentage	100.0	28.5	65.9	5.6	100.0	29.2	65.9	4.9	100.0	27.7	66.0	6.3	99.0
Western Asia - Asie occidentale													
Number - Nombre	220	71	138	10	113	37	72	5	107	35	66	6	
Percent - Pourcentage	100.0	32.5	62.8	4.7	100.0	32.3	63.6	4.0	100.0	32.7	61.9	5.4	105.8
EUROPE[3]													
Number - Nombre	731	114	500	117	352	58	247	46	379	55	252	71	
Percent - Pourcentage	100.0	15.6	68.4	16.1	100.0	16.6	70.3	13.1	100.0	14.6	66.6	18.8	92.8
Eastern Europe - Europe orientale													
Number - Nombre	295	44	209	42	138	22	102	14	156	21	108	27	
Percent - Pourcentage	100.0	14.8	71.0	14.2	100.0	16.2	73.4	10.4	100.0	13.6	68.9	17.5	88.5
Northern Europe - Europe septentrionale													
Number - Nombre	97	17	65	16	48	9	32	7	50	8	32	9	
Percent - Pourcentage	100.0	17.6	66.4	16.0	100.0	18.5	67.7	13.8	100.0	16.8	65.1	18.1	96.0
Southern Europe - Europe méridionale													
Number - Nombre	152	23	102	27	74	12	51	11	77	11	51	16	
Percent - Pourcentage	100.0	15.1	67.2	17.7	100.0	15.8	69.0	15.2	100.0	14.3	65.6	20.1	95.8

2. Estimates of population and its percentage distribution, by age and sex and sex ratio for all ages for the world, major areas and regions: 2007
Estimations de la population et pourcentage de répartition selon l'âge et le sexe et rapport de masculinité pour l'ensemble du monde, les grandes régions et les régions géographiques: 2007 (continued - suite)

Major areas and regions / Grandes régions et régions	Population (millions)												Sex ratio - Rapport de masculinité[1]
	Both sexes - Les deux sexes				Male - Masculin				Female - Féminin				
	All ages - Tous âges	-15	15-64	65+	All ages - Tous âges	-15	15-64	65+	All ages - Tous âges	-15	15-64	65+	
Western Europe - Europe occidentale													
Number - Nombre	187	30	124	33	92	15	62	14	96	15	62	19	
Percent - Pourcentage	100.0	16.1	66.2	17.8	100.0	16.8	68.1	15.1	100.0	15.3	64.4	20.3	95.6
OCEANIA - OCÉANIA[2]													
Number - Nombre	34.49	8.52	22.40	3.57	17.23	4.38	11.23	1.62	17.26	4.13	11.17	1.95	
Percent - Pourcentage	100.0	24.7	64.9	10.4	100.0	25.4	65.2	9.4	100.0	24.0	64.7	11.3	99.9
Australia and New Zealand - Australie et Nouvelle Zélande													
Number - Nombre	25.05	4.92	16.85	3.28	12.43	2.52	8.43	1.48	12.61	2.39	8.42	1.80	
Percent - Pourcentage	100.0	19.6	67.3	13.1	100.0	20.3	67.8	11.9	100.0	19.0	66.8	14.3	98.6
Melanesia - Melanésie													
Number - Nombre	8.23	3.21	4.79	0.23	4.19	1.66	2.42	0.11	4.04	1.55	2.37	0.12	
Percent - Pourcentage	100.0	39.0	58.2	2.8	100.0	39.6	57.7	2.7	100.0	38.4	58.6	3.0	103.6
Micronesia													
Number - Nombre	0.55	0.17	0.36	0.02	0.27	0.09	0.17	0.01	0.28	0.08	0.18	0.01	
Percent - Pourcentage	100.0	31.3	64.3	4.3	100.0	32.5	63.5	4.0	100.0	30.1	65.1	4.7	98.3
Polynesia - Polynésie													
Number - Nombre	0.66	0.22	0.40	0.04	0.34	0.11	0.21	0.02	0.32	0.11	0.20	0.02	
Percent - Pourcentage	100.0	33.4	61.3	5.3	100.0	33.6	61.6	4.8	100.0	33.1	61.0	5.9	105.0

FOOTNOTES - NOTES

[1] Males per 100 females of all ages - Hommes pour 100 femmes de tous âges

[2] Hawaii, a state of the United States of America, is included in Northern America rather than in Oceania. - Hawaii, un Etat des Etats-Unis d'Amérique, est compris en Amérique septentrionale plutôt qu'en Océanie.

[3] The European part of Turkey is included in Western Asia rather than Europe. - La partie européenne de la Turquie est comprise en Asie Occidentale plutôt qu'en Europe.

Table 3

Table 3 presents for each country or area of the world the total, male and female population enumerated at the latest population census, estimates of the mid-year total population for 2005 and 2007, the average annual exponential rate of increase (or decrease) for the period 2005 to 2007, the surface area and the population density for 2007.

Description of variables: The total, male and female population is, unless otherwise indicated, the *de facto* (present-in-area) population enumerated at the most recent census for which data are available. The date of this census is given. Population census data are usually the results of a nation-wide enumeration (traditional census). Alternatively other approaches for generating reliable statistics on population and housing can be used by countries, such as the use of population registers. Data that are the result of such an alternative approach are also coded as census and are footnoted accordingly. Also, the results of sample surveys, essentially national in character, may be presented showing the appropriate code. However, results of surveys referring to less than 50 percent of the total territory or population are not included.

Mid-year population estimates refer to the population on 1 July. Otherwise, a footnote is appended. Mid-year estimates of the total population are those provided by national statistical offices.

Surface area, expressed in square kilometres, refers to the total surface area, comprising land area and inland waters (assumed to consist of major rivers and lakes) and excluding Polar Regions as well as uninhabited islands. Exceptions to this are noted. Surface areas, originally reported in square miles by the country or area, have been converted to square kilometres using a conversion factor of 2.589988.

Computation: The annual rate of increase is the average annual percentage rate of population growth between 2005 and 2007, computed by the Statistics Division of the United Nations Department of Economic and Social Affairs using the unrounded mid-year estimates as presented in this table.

Density is the number of persons in the 2007 total population per square kilometre of total surface area.

Reliability of data: Reliable mid-year population estimates are those that are based on a complete census (or a sample survey) and have been adjusted by a continuous population register or on the basis of the calculated balance of births, deaths and migration. Mid-year estimates of this type are considered reliable and appear in roman type. Mid-year estimates not calculated on this basis are considered less reliable and are shown in italics. Estimates for years prior to 2007 are considered reliable or less reliable on the basis of the 2007 code and appear in roman type or in *italics*, accordingly.

Census data and sample survey results are considered reliable and, therefore, appear in roman type.

Rates of population increase that were calculated using population estimates considered less reliable, as described above, are set in italics rather than roman type.

All surface area data are assumed to be reliable and therefore appear in roman type.

Population density data, however, are considered reliable or less reliable on the basis of the reliability of the 2007 population estimates used as the numerator.

Limitations: Statistics on the total population enumerated at the time of the census, estimates of the mid-year total population and surface area data are subject to the same qualifications as have been set forth for population and surface area statistics in sections 3 and 2.4 of the Technical Notes, respectively.

Regarding the limitations of census data, it should be noted that although census data are considered reliable, and therefore appear in roman type, the actual quality of census data varies widely from one country or area to another. When known, an estimate of the extent of over-enumeration or under-enumeration is given in footnotes. In the case of sample surveys, a description of the population covered is provided.

Because the reliability of the population estimates for any given country or area is based on the quality of the 2007 estimate, the reliability of estimates prior to 2007 may be overstated.

Rates of population increase are subject to all the qualifications of the population estimates mentioned above. In some cases, they simply reflect the rate calculated or assumed in constructing the estimates themselves when adequate measures of natural increase and net migration were not available. Despite their shortcomings, these rates provide a useful index for studying population change and can be also useful in evaluating the accuracy of vital and migration statistics.

Population density data as shown in this table give only an indication of actual population density as they do not take account of the dispersion or concentration of population within countries or areas nor the proportion of habitable land. They should not be interpreted as reflecting density in the urban sense or as indicating the supporting power of a territory's land and resources.

Tableau 3

Le tableau 3 indique pour chaque pays ou zone du monde la population totale selon le sexe d'après les derniers recensements effectués, les estimations concernant la population totale au milieu de l'année 2005 et de l'année 2007, le taux moyen d'accroissement annuel exponentiel positif ou négatif pour la période allant de 2005 à 2007, ainsi que la superficie et la densité de population en 2007.

Description des variables : la population masculine et féminine totale est, sauf indication contraire, la population de fait (c'est-à-dire présente) enregistrée lors du recensement le plus récent sur lequel on dispose de données. La date de ce recensement est indiquée. Les données des recensements de la population sont habituellement obtenues au moyen d'un enregistrement à l'échelle nationale (recensement traditionnel). Les pays peuvent recourir à d'autres moyens pour établir des statistiques fiables sur la population et le logement, tels que des registres de la population. Les données obtenues par ce moyen sont présentées comme celles d'un recensement et sont annotées en conséquence. Par ailleurs, les résultats des enquêtes par sondage, réalisées habituellement à l'échelle nationale, peuvent être présentés à l'aide du code correspondant. En revanche, les résultats des enquêtes portant sur moins de 50 % du territoire total ou de la population ne sont pas indiqués.

Les estimations de la population en milieu d'année sont celles de la population au 1er juillet. Lorsque la date est différente, cela est signalé par une note. Les estimations de la population totale en milieu d'année sont celles qui ont été communiquées par les services nationaux de statistique.

La superficie - exprimée en kilomètres carrés - représente la superficie totale, c'est-à-dire qu'elle englobe les terres émergées et les eaux intérieures (qui sont censées comprendre les principaux lacs et cours d'eau) mais exclut les régions polaires et certaines îles inhabitées. Les exceptions à cette règle sont signalées en note. Les superficies initialement exprimées en miles carrés par les pays ou les zones ont été transformées en kilomètres carrés au moyen d'un coefficient de conversion de 2,589988.

Calculs : le taux d'accroissement annuel est le taux annuel moyen de variation (en pourcentage) de la population entre 2005 et 2007, calculé par la Division de statistique du Département des affaires économiques et sociales (Secrétariat de l'Organisation des Nations Unies) à partir des estimations en milieu d'année non arrondies qui figurent dans le tableau.

La densité est égale au rapport de l'effectif total de la population en 2007 à la superficie totale, exprimée en kilomètres carrés.

Fiabilité des données : les estimations en milieu d'année qui sont considérées sûres sont fondées sur un recensement complet (ou sur une enquête par sondage) et ont été ajustées en fonction des données provenant d'un registre permanent de population ou en fonction de la balance établie par le calcul des naissances, des décès et des migrations. Les estimations de ce type sont considérées comme sûres et apparaissent en caractères romains. Les estimations en milieu d'année dont le calcul n'a pas été effectué sur cette base sont considérées comme moins sûres et apparaissent en italique. Les estimations relatives aux années antérieures à 2007 sont jugées plus ou moins sûres en fonction du codage de 2007 et indiquées, selon le cas, en caractères romains ou en italique.

Les données de recensements ou les résultats d'enquêtes par sondage sont considérés comme sûrs et apparaissent par conséquent en caractères romains.

Les taux d'accroissement de la population, calculés à partir d'estimations jugées moins sûres d'après les normes décrites ci-dessus, sont indiqués en italique plutôt qu'en caractères romains.

Toutes les données de superficie sont présumées sûres et apparaissent par conséquent en caractères romains. En revanche, les données relatives à la densité de la population sont considérées plus ou moins sûres en fonction de la fiabilité des estimations de la population en 2007 ayant servi de numérateur.

Insuffisance des données : les statistiques portant sur la population totale dénombrée lors d'un recensement, les estimations de la population totale en milieu d'année et les données de superficie appellent les mêmes réserves que celles formulées aux sections 3 et 2.4 des Notes techniques à propos des statistiques relatives à la population et à la superficie.

S'agissant de l'insuffisance des données obtenues par recensement, il convient d'indiquer que, bien que ces données soient considérées comme sûres et apparaissent par conséquent en caractères romains, leur qualité réelle varie considérablement d'un pays ou d'une région à l'autre. Lorsque l'on possédait les renseignements voulus, on a donné une estimation du degré de sur-dénombrement ou de sous-dénombrement. Dans le cas des enquêtes par sondage, une description de la population considérée est fournie.

La fiabilité des estimations de la population d'un pays ou zone quelconque reposant sur la qualité des estimations de 2007, il se peut que la fiabilité des estimations antérieures à 2007 soit surévaluée.

Les taux d'accroissement appellent toutes les réserves formulées plus haut à propos des estimations concernant la population. Dans certains cas, ils représentent seulement le taux calculé ou que l'on a pris pour base pour établir les estimations elles-mêmes lorsque l'on ne disposait pas de mesures appropriées de l'accroissement naturel et des migrations nettes. Malgré leurs imperfections, ces taux fournissent des indications intéressantes pour l'étude du mouvement de la population et, utilisés avec les précautions nécessaires, ils peuvent également servir à évaluer l'exactitude des statistiques de l'état civil et des migrations.

Les données relatives à la densité de population figurant dans le tableau 3 n'ont qu'une valeur indicative en ce qui concerne la densité de population effective, car elles ne tiennent compte ni de la dispersion ou de la concentration de la population à l'intérieur des pays ou zones, ni de la proportion du territoire qui est habitable. Il ne faut donc y voir d'indication ni de la densité au sens urbain du terme ni du nombre d'habitants qui pourraient vivre sur les terres et avec les ressources naturelles du territoire considéré.

3. Population by sex, rate of population increase, surface area and density
Population selon le sexe, taux d'accroissement de la population, superficie et densité

Continent, country or area and census date / Continent, pays ou zone et date du recensement	Census type[a]	Latest available census / Dernier recensement disponible (in units — en unités)			Estimate type[a]	Mid-year estimates / Estimations au milieu de l'année (in thousands — en milliers)		Annual rate of increase Taux d' accrois sement annuel 2005-07	Surface area Superficie (km²) 2007	Density Densité 2007[b]
		Both sexes Les deux sexes	Male Masculin	Female Feminin		2005	2007			
AFRICA - AFRIQUE										
Algeria - Algérie 16 IV 2008	DJ	*34 760 000	...	...	DJ	32 906	34 096	1.8	2 381 741	14
Angola 15 XII 1970	DF	5 646 166	2 943 974	2 702 192		...	...	...	1 246 700	...
Benin - Bénin 11 II 2002	DJ	6 769 914	3 284 119	3 485 795	DF	*7 395[1]	*8 054[1]	4.3	112 622	72
Botswana 17 VIII 2001	DF	1 680 863	813 488	867 375	DF	1 708	1 736	0.8	582 000	3
Burkina Faso 9 XII 2006	DJ	14 017 262	6 768 739	7 248 523	DJ	12 802	14 252[1]	5.4	274 222	52
Burundi 16 VIII 1990	DF	5 139 073	2 473 599	2 665 474		...	...	...	27 834	...
Cameroon - Cameroun 10 IV 1987	DF	10 493 655	...	...		...	...	...	475 442	...
Cape Verde - Cap-Vert 16 VI 2000	DF	436 863	211 479	225 384	DF	475	491	1.7	4 033	122
Central African Republic - République centrafricaine 8 XII 2003	DF	3 151 072	1 569 446	1 581 626		...	...	...	622 984	...
Chad - Tchad 8 IV 1993	DF	6 158 992	2 950 415	3 208 577		...	...	...	1 284 000	...
Comoros - Comores 1 IX 2003	DF	575 660[2]	...	...		...	...	...	2 235	...
Congo 6 VI 1996	DF	*2 600 000	...	...	DF	...	*3 695	...	342 000	11
Côte d'Ivoire 21 XI 1998	DF	15 366 672	7 844 621	7 522 050	DF	19 097	20 228	2.9	322 463	63
Democratic Republic of the Congo - République démocratique du Congo 1 VII 1984	DF	29 916 800	14 543 800	15 373 000		...	...	...	2 344 858	...
Djibouti 11 XII 1960	DF	81 200	...	...		...	...	...	23 200	...
Egypt - Égypte 11 XI 2006	DF	72 798 031[3]	37 219 056[3]	35 578 975[3]	DF	70 653	73 644	2.1	1 002 000	73
Equatorial Guinea - Guinée équatoriale 1 II 2002	DF	1 014 999	501 387	513 612		...	...	...	28 051	...
Eritrea - Érythrée 9 V 1984	DF	2 748 304	1 374 452	1 373 852		...	...	...	117 600	...
Ethiopia - Éthiopie 28 V 2007	DF	73 918 505[4]	37 296 657[4]	36 621 848[4]	DF	73 044	...	...	1 104 300	...
Gabon 1 XII 2003	DF	*1 269 000	...	...	DF	1 313[5]	...	...	267 668	...
Gambia - Gambie 15 IV 2003	DF	*1 364 507	*676 726	*687 781	DF	1 436	...	...	11 295	...
Ghana 26 III 2000	DF	18 912 079	9 357 382	9 554 697	DF	21 343[1]	...	...	238 539	...
Guinea - Guinée 1 XII 1996	DF	7 156 406	3 497 979	3 658 427		...	...	...	245 857	...
Guinea-Bissau - Guinée-Bissau 1 XII 1991	DF	983 367	476 210	507 157	DF	1 326[1]	1 389[1]	2.3	36 125	38
Kenya 24 VIII 1999	DF	28 686 607	14 205 589	14 481 018	DF	35 267	37 184	2.6	580 367	64
Lesotho 9 IV 2006	DJ	*1 880 661	*916 281	*964 380		...	...	...	30 355	...
Liberia - Libéria 21 III 2008	DF	*3 489 072	*1 764 555	*1 724 517		...	...	...	111 369	...
Libyan Arab Jamahiriya - Jamahiriya arabe libyenne 11 VIII 1995	DF	4 404 986[6]	2 236 943[6]	2 168 043[6]		...	...	...	1 759 540	...
Madagascar 1 VIII 1993	DF	12 238 914	6 088 116	6 150 798	DF	17 730	18 820	3.0	587 041	32

3. Population by sex, rate of population increase, surface area and density
Population selon le sexe, taux d'accroissement de la population, superficie et densité (continued - suite)

Continent, country or area and census date / Continent, pays ou zone et date du recensement	Census type[a]	Latest available census — Dernier recensement disponible (in units — en unités)			Estimate type[a]	Mid-year estimates — Estimations au milieu de l'année (in thousands — en milliers)		Annual rate of increase Taux d'accrois sement annuel 2005-07	Surface area Superficie (km²) 2007	Density Densité 2007[b]
		Both sexes Les deux sexes	Male Masculin	Female Feminin		2005	2007			
AFRICA - AFRIQUE										
Malawi										
8 VI 2008 .... DF	DF	*13 066 320	*6 365 771	*6 700 549	DF	12 341[1]	13 188[1]	3.3	118 484	111
Mali										
1 IV 1998 .... DF	DF	9 926 219[7]	4 905 510[7]	5 020 709[7]	DF	11 732[8]	12 378[8]	2.7	1 240 192	10
Mauritania - Mauritanie										
1 XI 2000 .... DF	DF	2 548 157	1 240 414	1 307 743	DF	2 906	3 075	2.8	1 025 520	3
Mauritius - Maurice										
2 VII 2000 .... DJ	DJ	1 178 848	583 756	595 092	DJ	1 243	1 260	0.7	2 040	618
Mayotte										
31 VII 2007 .... DJ	DJ	186 387	91 405	94 982		...	...	...	...	...
Morocco - Maroc										
1 IX 2004 .... DF	DF	29 680 069	14 640 662	15 039 407	DF	30 172	*30 841	1.1	446 550	69
Mozambique										
1 VIII 2007 .... DF	DF	*20 530 714	*9 787 135	*10 743 579	DF	19 420[1]	20 367[1]	2.4	801 590	25
Namibia - Namibie										
27 VIII 2001 .... DF	DF	1 830 330	887 721[9]	942 572[9]	DF	1 957[1]	2 028[1]	1.8	824 116	2
Niger										
20 V 2001 .... DF	DF	*10 790 352	*5 380 287	*5 410 065	DJ	12 628	13 475	3.2	1 267 000	11
Nigeria - Nigéria										
21 III 2006 .... DF	DF	*140 003 542	*71 709 859	*68 293 683	DF	133 767[1]	...	...	923 768	...
Réunion										
1 I 2006 .... DJ	DJ	781 962	379 176	402 786	DJ	777	*798	1.3	2 513	317
Rwanda										
16 VIII 2002 .... DJ	DJ	8 128 553	3 879 448	4 249 105		...	...	...	26 338	...
Saint Helena ex. dep. - Sainte-Hélène sans dép.										
10 II 2008 .... DF	DF	*4 255	*2 166	*2 089	DF	...	4	...	122	33
Saint Helena: Ascension - Sainte-Hélène: Ascension										
8 III 1998 .... DJ	DJ	712	458	254		...	...	...	88	...
Saint Helena: Tristan da Cunha - Sainte-Hélène: Tristan da Cunha										
31 XII 1988 .... DF	DF	296	139	157	DF	...	0[10]	...	98	3
Sao Tome and Principe - Sao Tomé-et-Principe										
25 VIII 2001 .... DF	DF	136 554	67 422	69 132	DF	149	155	1.9	964	161
Senegal - Sénégal										
8 XII 2002 .... DF	DF	9 552 442	4 665 730	4 886 712	DJ	10 848	...	...	196 722	...
Seychelles										
26 VIII 2002 .... DJ	DJ	81 755[11]	40 751[11]	41 004[11]	DF	83	85	1.3	455	187
Sierra Leone										
4 XII 2004 .... DF	DF	4 976 871	2 420 218	2 556 653		...	...	...	71 740	...
Somalia - Somalie										
15 II 1987 .... DF	DF	7 114 431	3 741 664	3 372 767		...	...	...	637 657	...
South Africa - Afrique du Sud										
10 X 2001 .... DF	DF	44 819 778	21 434 041	23 385 737	DF	47 335[12]	48 287[12]	1.0	1 221 037	40
Sudan - Soudan										
22 IV 2008 .... DF	DF	*39 154 490	*20 073 977	*19 080 513	DF	35 397	...	...	2 505 813	...
Swaziland										
11 V 2007 .... DF	DF	*953 524	*460 498	*493 026	DF	1 126	...	...	17 364	...
Togo										
22 XI 1981 .... DF	DF	2 719 567	1 325 641	1 393 926	DF	5 337	5 465	1.2	56 785	96
Tunisia - Tunisie										
28 IV 2004 .... DF	DF	9 910 872	4 965 435	4 945 437	DF	10 029	10 225	1.0	163 610	62
Uganda - Ouganda										
12 IX 2002 .... DF	DF	24 442 084	11 929 803	12 512 281	DF	26 495	28 247	3.2	241 038	117
United Republic of Tanzania - République Unie de Tanzanie										
24 VIII 2002 .... DF	DF	*34 443 603	*16 829 861	*17 613 742	DF	37 379	39 446	2.7	945 087	42
Western Sahara - Sahara occidental[13]										
31 XII 1970 .... DF	DF	76 425	43 981	32 444		...	...	...	266 000	...

3. Population by sex, rate of population increase, surface area and density
Population selon le sexe, taux d'accroissement de la population, superficie et densité (continued - suite)

Continent, country or area and census date / Continent, pays ou zone et date du recensement	Census type[a]	Latest available census Dernier recensement disponible (in units — en unités)			Estimate type[a]	Mid-year estimates Estimations au milieu de l'année (in thousands — en milliers)		Annual rate of increase Taux d'accrois sement annuel 2005-07	Surface area Superficie (km²) 2007	Density Densité 2007[b]
		Both sexes Les deux sexes	Male Masculin	Female Feminin		2005	2007			
AFRICA - AFRIQUE										
Zambia - Zambie										
25 X 2000	DF	9 337 425	4 594 290	4 743 135	DF	*11 441*[1]	**12 161*[1]	3.0	752 612	*16*
Zimbabwe										
17 VIII 2002	DF	11 631 657	5 634 180	5 997 477		...	...	...	390 757	...
AMERICA, NORTH - AMÉRIQUE DU NORD										
Anguilla										
9 V 2001	DF	11 430	5 628	5 802	DF	14	15	4.4	91	164
Antigua and Barbuda - Antigua-et-Barbuda										
28 V 2001	DF	77 426	37 002	40 424	DF	83	...	...	442	...
Aruba										
14 X 2000	DJ	90 508	43 435	47 073	DJ	101	104	1.6	180	578
Bahamas										
1 V 2000	DF	303 611	147 715	155 896	DF	325	334	1.3	13 943	24
Barbados - Barbade										
1 V 2000	DF	250 010	119 926	130 084	DF	273	274	0.2	430	638
Belize										
12 V 2000	DF	240 204	121 278	118 926	DF	*292*	*311*	3.3	22 966	*14*
Bermuda - Bermudes										
20 V 2000	DJ	62 059[14]	29 802[14]	32 257[14]	DJ	64	64	0.3	54	1 178
British Virgin Islands - Îles Vierges britanniques										
21 V 2001	DF	20 647	10 627	10 020		...	...	...	151	...
Canada										
16 V 2006	DJ	31 612 895[15]	15 475 970[15]	16 136 930[15]	DJ	32 312[16]	*32 976[17]	1.0	9 984 670	3
Cayman Islands - Îles Caïmanes										
10 X 1999	DF	40 786	...	...	DJ	48	...	...	264	...
Costa Rica										
26 VI 2000	DJ	3 810 179	1 902 614	1 907 565	DJ	4 266	4 443	2.0	51 100	87
Cuba										
6 IX 2002	DJ	11 177 743	5 597 233	5 580 510	DJ	11 243	11 238	0.0	109 886	102
Dominica - Dominique										
12 V 2001	DF	69 625[14]	35 073[14]	34 552[14]	DF	71	...	...	751	...
Dominican Republic - République dominicaine										
18 X 2002	DJ	8 562 541	4 265 215	4 297 326	DF	*9 226*[1]	*9 493*[1]	1.4	48 671	*195*
El Salvador										
12 V 2007	DJ	5 744 113	2 719 371	3 024 742	DF	6 875	7 105	1.6	21 041	338
Greenland - Groenland										
1 I 2008	DJ	56 462[18]	29 885[18]	26 577[18]	DJ	57[18]	57[18]	-0.3	2 166 086	0
Grenada - Grenade										
25 V 2001	DF	102 632	50 481	52 151	DF	...	107	...	344	312
Guadeloupe										
1 I 2006	DJ	400 736	188 720	212 016	DJ	*446	*403[8]	-5.0	1 705	236
Guatemala										
24 XI 2002	DJ	11 237 196	5 496 839	5 740 357	DF	12 701[12]	13 345[12]	2.5	108 889	123
Haiti - Haïti										
11 I 2003	DJ	8 373 750	4 039 272	4 334 478		...	...	...	27 750	...
Honduras										
28 VII 2001	DF	6 071 200	3 000 530	3 070 670	DF	*7 197*	**7 537*	2.3	112 492	67
Jamaica - Jamaïque										
10 IX 2001	DJ	2 607 632	1 283 548	1 324 084	DJ	2 650	2 676	0.5	10 991	243
Martinique										
1 I 2006	DJ	397 732	185 604	212 128	DJ	398	*400[8]	0.3	1 128	355
Mexico - Mexique										
17 X 2005	DJ	103 263 388	50 249 955	53 013 433	DJ	*103 947*[1]	*105 791*[1]	0.9	1 964 375	*54*
Montserrat										
12 V 2001	DF	4 491	2 418	2 073	DF	5	5	0.4	102	47

Continent, country or area and census date / Continent, pays ou zone et date du recensement	Census type[a]	Latest available census / Dernier recensement disponible (in units — en unités)			Estimate type[a]	Mid-year estimates / Estimations au milieu de l'année (in thousands — en milliers)		Annual rate of increase / Taux d' accrois sement annuel 2005-07	Surface area / Superficie (km²) 2007	Density / Densité 2007[b]
		Both sexes / Les deux sexes	Male / Masculin	Female / Feminin		2005	2007			
AMERICA, NORTH - AMÉRIQUE DU NORD										
Netherlands Antilles - Antilles néerlandaises										
29 I 2001 .... DJ		175 653	82 521	93 132	DJ	184[8]	*194[8]	2.7	800	242
Nicaragua										
4 VI 2005 .... DJ		5 144 553	2 535 461	2 609 092	DJ	5 450	5 596	1.3	130 373	43
Panama										
14 V 2000 .... DF		2 839 177	1 432 566	1 406 611	DF	3 228	3 340	1.7	75 517	44
Puerto Rico - Porto Rico										
1 IV 2000 .... DJ		3 808 610[19]	1 833 577[19]	1 975 033[19]	DJ	3 912[19]	3 942[19]	0.4	8 870	444
Saint Kitts and Nevis - Saint-Kitts-et-Nevis										
14 V 2001 .... DF		45 841	22 784	23 057	DF	*39	...	...	261	...
Saint Lucia - Sainte-Lucie										
22 V 2001 .... DF		157 164	76 741	80 423	DF	164	168	1.2	539	312
Saint Pierre and Miquelon - Saint-Pierre-et-Miquelon										
19 I 2006 .... DF		6 125	...	...		...	...	...	242	
Saint Vincent and the Grenadines - Saint-Vincent-et-les Grenadines										
14 V 2001 .... DF		109 022[14]	55 456[14]	53 566[14]	DF	104	...	...	389	...
Trinidad and Tobago - Trinité-et-Tobago										
15 V 2000 .... DF		1 262 366	633 051	629 315	DF	1 294[20]	1 303[20]	0.3	5 130	254
Turks and Caicos Islands - Îles Turques et Caïques										
10 IX 2001 .... DF		19 886	9 897	9 989	DJ	31	35	6.5	948[21]	37
United States of America - États-Unis d'Amérique										
1 IV 2000 .... DJ		281 421 906[22]	138 053 563[22]	143 368 343[22]	DJ	295 896[22]	301 621[22]	1.0	9 629 091	31
United States Virgin Islands - Îles Vierges américaines										
1 IV 2000 .... DJ		108 612[19]	51 864[19]	56 748[19]	DJ	110[19]	110[19]	0.1	347	316
AMERICA, SOUTH - AMÉRIQUE DU SUD										
Argentina - Argentine										
18 XI 2001 .... DF		36 260 130	17 659 072	18 601 058	DF	38 592	39 356	1.0	2 780 400	14
Bolivia (Plurinational State of) - Bolivie (État plurinational de)										
5 IX 2001 .... DF		8 274 325	4 123 850	4 150 475	DF	9 427	9 828	2.1	1 098 581	9
Brazil - Brésil										
1 VIII 2000 .... DJ		169 799 170[23]	83 576 015[23]	86 223 155[23]	DF	183 383[23]	187 642[23]	1.1	8 514 877[24]	22
Chile - Chili										
24 IV 2002 .... DF		15 116 435	7 447 695	7 668 740	DF	16 267	16 598	1.0	756 102	22
Colombia - Colombie										
22 V 2005 .... DF		41 468 384	20 336 117	21 132 267	DF	42 889[25]	43 926[25]	1.2	1 141 748	38
Ecuador - Équateur										
25 XI 2001 .... DF		12 156 608[26]	6 018 353[26]	6 138 255[26]	DF	13 215[27]	13 605[27]	1.5	256 369	53
Falkland Islands (Malvinas) - Îles Falkland (Malvinas)[28]										
8 X 2006 .... DF		2 955	1 569	1 386		...	...	...	12 173	...
French Guiana - Guyane française										
1 I 2006 .... DJ		205 954	101 930	104 023	DJ	*200	214[8]	3.3	83 534	3
Guyana										
15 IX 2002 .... DF		751 223	376 034	375 189	DF	758	763	0.3	214 969	4
Paraguay										
28 VIII 2002 .... DF		5 163 198	2 603 242	2 559 956	DF	5 899	6 120	1.8	406 752	15

3. Population by sex, rate of population increase, surface area and density
Population selon le sexe, taux d'accroissement de la population, superficie et densité (continued - suite)

Continent, country or area and census date / Continent, pays ou zone et date du recensement	Census type[a]	Latest available census — Dernier recensement disponible (in units — en unités)			Estimate type[a]	Mid-year estimates — Estimations au milieu de l'année (in thousands — en milliers)		Annual rate of increase — Taux d'accrois-sement annuel 2005-07	Surface area — Superficie (km²) 2007	Density — Densité 2007[b]
		Both sexes Les deux sexes	Male Masculin	Female Feminin		2005	2007			
AMERICA, SOUTH - AMÉRIQUE DU SUD										
Peru - Pérou										
21 X 2007 .... DF		27 412 157	13 622 640	13 789 517	DF	27 811[12]	28 482[12]	1.2	1 285 216	22
Suriname										
2 VIII 2004 .... DJ		492 829[29]	247 846[30]	244 618[30]	DJ	499	510	1.1	163 820	3
Uruguay										
1 VI 2004 .... DF		3 241 003[31]	1 565 533[31]	1 675 470[31]	DF	3 306[12]	3 324[1]	0.3	176 215	19
Venezuela (Bolivarian Republic of) - Venezuela (République bolivarienne du)										
30 X 2001 .... DF		23 054 210[32]	11 402 869[32]	11 651 341[32]	DF	26 577[32]	27 483[32]	1.7	912 050	30
ASIA - ASIE										
Afghanistan										
23 VI 1979 .... DF		13 051 358[33]	6 712 377[33]	6 338 981[33]		...	...	...	652 090	...
Armenia - Arménie										
10 X 2001 .... DF		3 002 594[34]	1 407 220[34]	1 595 374[34]	DJ	3 218	3 227	0.1	29 743	108
Azerbaijan - Azerbaïdjan										
27 I 1999 .... DJ		7 953 438	3 883 155	4 070 283	DF	8 392	8 581	1.1	86 600	99
Bahrain - Bahreïn										
7 IV 2001 .... DJ		650 604	373 649	276 955	DF	889	1 039	7.8	750	1 386
Bangladesh										
22 I 2001 .... DF		130 522 598[35]	67 731 320[35]	62 791 278[35]	DF	138 600	142 600	1.4	143 998	990
Bhutan - Bhoutan										
30 V 2005 .... DF		634 982	333 595	301 387	DF	...	659[36]	...	38 394	17
Brunei Darussalam - Brunéi Darussalam										
21 VIII 2001 .... DF		*332 844	*168 974	*163 870	DF	370	390	2.6	5 765	68
Cambodia - Cambodge										
3 III 2008 .... DF		*13 388 910	*6 495 512	*6 893 398	DF	*13 661[37]	...	...	181 035	...
China - Chine										
1 XI 2000 .... DJ		1 242 612 226[38]	640 275 969[38]	602 336 257[38]	DF	1 303 720[39]	1 324 655[40]	0.8	9 596 961	138
China, Hong Kong SAR - Chine, Hong Kong RAS										
14 VII 2006 .... DJ		6 864 346	3 272 956	3 591 390	DJ	6 813	6 926	0.8	1 104	6 273
China, Macao SAR - Chine, Macao RAS										
19 VIII 2006 .... DJ		502 113[41]	245 167[41]	256 946[41]	DJ	473	526	5.2	29	18 131
Cyprus - Chypre										
1 X 2001 .... DJ		689 565[42]	338 497[42]	351 068[42]	DJ	758[43]	784[43]	1.7	9 251	85
Democratic People's Republic of Korea - République populaire démocratique de Corée										
1 X 2008 .... DF		*24 051 218	*11 722 403	*12 328 815		...	...	...	120 538	...
Georgia - Géorgie										
17 I 2002 .... DJ		4 371 535	2 061 753	2 309 782	DF	4 361	4 388	0.3	69 700	63
India - Inde										
1 III 2001 .... DF		1 028 610 328[44]	532 156 772[44]	496 453 556[44]	DF	1 101 318[45]	1 134 023[45]	1.5	3 287 263	345
Indonesia - Indonésie										
30 VI 2000 .... DF		206 264 595[46]	103 417 180[46]	102 847 415[46]	DJ	219 852	225 642	1.3	1 860 360	121
Iran (Islamic Republic of) - Iran (République islamique d')										
28 X 2006 .... DJ		70 495 782	35 866 362	34 629 420	DJ	69 390[47]	71 532[47]	1.5	1 628 750	44
Iraq										
16 X 1997 .... DF		19 184 543[48]	9 536 570[48]	9 647 973[48]	DF	27 963	29 682	3.0	438 317	68
Israel - Israël										
4 XI 1995 .... DJ		5 548 523[49]	2 738 175[49]	2 810 348[49]	DJ	6 930[49]	7 180[49]	1.8	22 072	325
Japan - Japon										
1 X 2005 .... DJ		127 767 994	62 348 977	65 419 017	DF	127 773[50]	127 772[50]	0.0	377 930[51]	338

3. Population by sex, rate of population increase, surface area and density
Population selon le sexe, taux d'accroissement de la population, superficie et densité (continued - suite)

Continent, country or area and census date / Continent, pays ou zone et date du recensement	Census type[a]	Latest available census / Dernier recensement disponible (in units — en unités)			Estimate type[a]	Mid-year estimates / Estimations au milieu de l'année (in thousands — en milliers)		Annual rate of increase / Taux d' accrois sement annuel 2005-07	Surface area / Superficie (km²) 2007	Density / Densité 2007[b]
		Both sexes / Les deux sexes	Male / Masculin	Female / Feminin		2005	2007			
ASIA - ASIE										
Jordan - Jordanie										
1 X 2004	DF	5 103 639[52]	2 626 287[52]	2 477 352[52]	DF	5 473[53]	5 723[53]	2.2	89 342	64
Kazakhstan										
26 II 1999	DJ	14 953 126	7 201 785	7 751 341	DF	15 147	15 484	1.1	2 724 900	6
Kuwait - Koweït										
20 IV 2005	DF	*2 213 403	*1 310 067	*903 336	DF	2 245	2 411	3.6	17 818	135
Kyrgyzstan - Kirghizstan										
24 III 1999	DF	4 850 734	2 392 579	2 458 155	DF	5 144	5 235	0.9	199 951	26
Lao People's Democratic Republic - République démocratique populaire lao										
1 III 2005	DJ	5 621 982	2 800 551	2 821 431	DF	5 679[54]	5 874[54]	1.7	236 800	25
Lebanon - Liban										
3 III 2007	SDF	3 759 134[55]	1 857 659[55]	1 901 475[55]		...	...	...	10 452	...
Malaysia - Malaisie										
5 VII 2000	DJ	23 274 690[56]	11 853 432[56]	11 421 258[56]	DF	26 128[57]	27 174[57]	2.0	330 803	82
Maldives										
21 III 2006	DF	298 968	151 459	147 509	DF	294	305	1.9	300	1 016
Mongolia - Mongolie										
5 I 2000	DF	2 373 493	1 177 981	1 195 512	DF	2 548	2 615	1.3	1 564 100	2
Myanmar										
31 III 1983	DF	35 307 913	17 518 255	17 789 658		...	...	...	676 578	...
Nepal - Népal										
22 VI 2001	DJ	23 151 423[58]	11 563 921[58]	11 587 502[58]	DJ	25 343	*26 427	2.1	147 181	180
Occupied Palestinian Territory - Territoire palestinien occupé										
1 XII 2007	DF	*3 761 646[59]	*1 908 432[59]	*1 853 214[59]	DF	3 508	3 719	2.9	6 020	618
Oman										
7 XII 2003	DF	2 340 815	1 313 239	1 027 576	DF	2 514	2 743	4.4	309 500	9
Pakistan										
2 III 1998	DF	130 579 571[60]	67 840 137[60]	62 739 434[60]	DF	153 960[60]	159 570[60]	1.8	796 095	200
Philippines										
1 VIII 2007	DJ	*88 574 614	...	...	DJ	84 241	*88 706	2.6	300 000	296
Qatar										
16 III 2004	DF	744 029	496 382	247 647	DF	888	1 226	16.1	11 586	106
Republic of Korea - République de Corée										
1 XI 2005	DJ	47 278 951[61]	23 623 954[61]	23 654 997[61]	DJ	48 138	48 456	0.3	99 678	486
Saudi Arabia - Arabie saoudite										
15 IX 2004	DF	22 678 262	12 557 240	10 121 022	DF	23 119	*24 243	2.4	2 149 690	11
Singapore - Singapour										
30 VI 2000	DF	4 017 700[62]	2 061 800[62]	1 955 900[62]	DF	4 266	4 589	3.6	705	6 508
Sri Lanka										
17 VII 2001	DF	16 929 689[63]	8 425 607[63]	8 504 082[63]	DF	19 668	20 010	0.9	65 610	305
Syrian Arab Republic - République arabe syrienne										
3 IX 1994	DF	13 782 315[64]	7 048 906[64]	6 733 409[64]	DF	18 138[64]	19 172[64]	2.8	185 180	104
Tajikistan - Tadjikistan										
20 I 2000	DF	6 127 493	3 069 100	3 058 393	DF	6 850	7 140	2.1	143 100	50
Thailand - Thaïlande										
1 IV 2000	DJ	60 617 200	29 850 100	30 767 100	DJ	64 839[1]	66 042[1]	0.9	513 120	129
Timor-Leste										
11 VII 2004	DF	*924 642	*467 757	*456 885		...	...	...	14 874	...
Turkey - Turquie										
22 X 2000	DF	67 803 927	34 346 735	33 457 192	DF	72 065	73 875	1.2	783 562	94
Turkmenistan - Turkménistan										
10 I 1995	DF	4 483 251	2 225 331	2 257 920		...	...	...	488 100	...
United Arab Emirates - Émirats arabes unis										
5 XII 2005	DF	4 106 427	2 806 141	1 300 286	DF	...	4 488	...	83 600	54

3. Population by sex, rate of population increase, surface area and density
Population selon le sexe, taux d'accroissement de la population, superficie et densité (continued - suite)

Continent, country or area and census date / Continent, pays ou zone et date du recensement	Census type[a]	Latest available census Dernier recensement disponible (in units — en unités)			Estimate type[a]	Mid-year estimates Estimations au milieu de l'année (in thousands — en milliers)		Annual rate of increase Taux d' accrois sement annuel 2005-07	Surface area Superficie (km²) 2007	Density Densité 2007[b]
		Both sexes Les deux sexes	Male Masculin	Female Feminin		2005	2007			
ASIA - ASIE										
Uzbekistan - Ouzbékistan										
12 I 1989	DJ	19 810 077	9 784 156	10 025 921		...	...	...	447 400	...
Viet Nam										
1 IV 1999	DF	76 323 173	37 469 117	38 854 056	DF	*83 106*	*85 172*	1.2	331 212	257
Yemen - Yémen										
16 XII 2004	DF	19 685 161	10 036 953	9 648 208	DF	*20 283*[65]	*21 539*[65]	3.0	527 968	41
EUROPE										
Åland Islands - Îles d'Åland[66]										
31 XII 2000	DJ	25 776[18]	12 700[18]	13 076[18]	DJ	27[18]	27[18]	0.7	1 552	17
Albania - Albanie										
1 IV 2001	DF	3 069 300	1 530 500	1 538 800	DF	3 142	3 161	0.3	28 748	110
Andorra - Andorre										
1 VII 2000	DF	66 089[18]	34 344[18]	31 745[18]	DF	79[18]	82[18]	2.4	468	176
Austria - Autriche										
15 V 2001	DJ	8 032 926	3 889 189	4 143 737	DJ	8 233	8 315	0.5	83 871	99
Belarus - Bélarus										
16 II 1999	DJ	10 045 237	4 717 621	5 327 616	DF	9 775	9 702	-0.4	207 600	47
Belgium - Belgique										
1 X 2001	DJ	10 296 350	5 035 446	5 260 904	DJ	10 473	10 623	0.7	30 528	348
Bosnia and Herzegovina - Bosnie-Herzégovine										
31 III 1991	DJ	4 377 033	2 183 795	2 193 238	DF	3 843	...	...	51 209	...
Bulgaria - Bulgarie										
1 III 2001	DF	7 928 901	3 862 465	4 066 436	DF	7 740	7 660	-0.5	110 879	69
Croatia - Croatie										
31 III 2001	DJ	4 437 460	2 135 900	2 301 560	DJ	4 442	4 436	-0.1	56 594	78
Czech Republic - République tchèque.										
1 III 2001	DJ	10 230 060	4 982 071	5 247 989	DJ	10 234	10 334	0.5	78 867	131
Denmark - Danemark[67]										
1 I 2001	DJ	5 349 212[18]	2 644 319[18]	2 704 893[18]	DJ	5 416[18]	5 457[18]	0.4	43 094	127
Estonia - Estonie										
31 III 2000	DJ	1 370 052	631 851	738 201	DF	1 346	1 342	-0.2	45 227	30
Faeroe Islands - Îles Féroé										
1 I 2008	DJ	48 433[18]	25 174[18]	23 259[18]	DJ	48	48	0.0	1 393	35
Finland - Finlande[68]										
31 XII 2000	DJ	5 181 115[18]	2 529 341[18]	2 651 774[18]	DJ	5 246[18]	5 289[18]	0.4	338 419	16
France[69]										
1 I 2006	DJ	61 399 541[70]	29 714 539[70]	31 685 002[70]	DJ	60 996[70]	*61 707[70]	0.6	551 500	112
Germany - Allemagne										
28 III 2004	SDJ	82 491 000[71]	40 330 000[71]	42 161 000[71]	DJ	82 464	82 263	-0.1	357 114	230
Gibraltar										
12 XI 2001	DF	27 495[72]	13 644[72]	13 851[72]	DF	29[72]	29[73]	0.7	6	4 876
Greece - Grèce										
18 III 2001	DF	10 964 020[74]	5 427 682[74]	5 536 338[74]	DF	11 104[75]	11 193[75]	0.4	131 957	85
Guernsey - Guernesey										
29 IV 2001	DJ	59 807	29 138	30 669	DF	...	62[76]	...	78	792
Holy See - Saint-Siège[77]										
1 VII 2000	DF	*798[18]	*529[18]	*269[18]		...	...	...	0[78]	...
Hungary - Hongrie										
1 II 2001	DF	10 198 315	4 850 650	5 347 665	DF	10 087	10 056	-0.2	93 028	108
Iceland - Islande										
1 VII 2000	DJ	281 154[18]	140 718[18]	140 436[18]	DJ	296[18]	311[18]	2.6	103 000	3
Ireland - Irlande										
23 IV 2006	DF	4 239 848	2 121 171	2 118 677	DF	4 131[79]	4 339[79]	2.5	70 273	62
Isle of Man - Île de Man										
23 IV 2006	DJ	80 058	39 523	40 535	DJ	79[80]	81[80]	1.3	572	141
Italy - Italie										
21 X 2001	DF	57 110 144	27 617 335	29 492 809	DJ	58 607	59 375	0.7	301 336	197

3. Population by sex, rate of population increase, surface area and density
Population selon le sexe, taux d'accroissement de la population, superficie et densité (continued - suite)

Continent, country or area and census date / Continent, pays ou zone et date du recensement	Census type[a]	Latest available census / Dernier recensement disponible (in units — en unités)			Estimate type[a]	Mid-year estimates / Estimations au milieu de l'année (in thousands — en milliers)		Annual rate of increase / Taux d' accrois sement annuel 2005-07	Surface area / Superficie (km²) 2007	Density / Densité 2007[b]
		Both sexes Les deux sexes	Male Masculin	Female Feminin		2005	2007			
EUROPE										
Jersey										
11 III 2001 .... DJ	DJ	87 186	42 484	44 702	DF	88	90	1.1	116	776
Latvia - Lettonie										
31 III 2000 .... DJ	DJ	2 377 383	1 094 964	1 282 419	DJ	2 301	2 276	-0.5	64 559	35
Liechtenstein										
5 XII 2000 .... DF	DF	33 307	16 420	16 887	DF	35	35	0.8	160	221
Lithuania - Lituanie										
6 IV 2001 .... DJ	DJ	3 483 972	1 629 148	1 854 824	DJ	3 414	3 376	-0.6	65 300	52
Luxembourg										
15 II 2001 .... DJ	DJ	439 539	216 541	222 998	DJ	465	480	1.6	2 586	186
Malta - Malte										
27 XI 2005 .... DJ	DJ	404 962	200 819	204 143	DJ	404	*409	0.7	316	1 295
Monaco										
9 VI 2008 .... DJ	DJ	31 109	15 076[81]	15 914[81]		...	...	...	2	...
Montenegro - Monténégro										
31 X 2003 .... DJ	DJ	620 145	305 225	314 920	DJ	623	626	0.2	13 812	45
Netherlands - Pays-Bas										
1 I 2002 .... DJ	DJ	16 105 285[82]	7 971 967[82]	8 133 318[82]	DJ	16 320	16 382	0.2	37 354	439
Norway - Norvège[83]										
3 XI 2001 .... DJ	DJ	4 520 947[84]	2 240 281[84]	2 280 666[84]	DJ	4 623[85]	4 709[85]	0.9	323 802	15
Poland - Pologne										
20 V 2002 .... DF	DF	38 230 080[86]	18 516 403[86]	19 713 677[86]	DF	38 161[86]	38 116[86]	-0.1	312 685[87]	122
Portugal										
12 III 2001 .... DF	DF	10 356 117	5 000 141	5 355 976	DJ	10 549	10 608	0.3	92 090	115
Republic of Moldova - République de Moldova										
5 X 2004 .... DF	DF	*3 388 071[88]	*1 632 519[88]	*1 755 549[88]	DJ	3 595[88]	3 577[88]	-0.3	33 846	106
Romania - Roumanie										
18 III 2002 .... DJ	DJ	21 680 974	10 568 741	11 112 233	DJ	21 624	21 538	-0.2	238 391	90
Russian Federation - Fédération de Russie										
9 X 2002 .... DJ	DJ	145 166 731[89]	67 605 133[89]	77 561 598[89]	DJ	143 114[89]	142 115[89]	-0.4	17 098 242	8
San Marino - Saint-Marin										
1 VII 2000 .... DF	DF	26 941[18]	13 185[18]	13 756[18]	DF	31[18]	32[18]	1.5	61	522
Serbia - Serbie										
31 III 2002 .... DJ	DJ	7 498 001[90]	3 645 930[90]	3 852 071[90]	DJ	7 441[90]	7 382[90]	-0.4	88 361	84
Slovakia - Slovaquie										
25 V 2001 .... DJ	DJ	5 379 455	2 612 515	2 766 940	DJ	5 387	5 398	0.1	49 035	110
Slovenia - Slovénie										
31 III 2002 .... DJ	DJ	1 964 036	958 576	1 005 460	DJ	2 001	2 019	0.5	20 273	100
Spain - Espagne										
1 XI 2001 .... DF	DF	40 847 371	20 012 882	20 834 489	DJ	43 398	44 874	1.7	505 992	89
Svalbard and Jan Mayen Islands - Îles Svalbard et Jan Mayen										
1 XI 1960 .... DF	DF	3 431[91]	2 545[91]	886[91]	DF	2[92]	...	...	62 422	...
Sweden - Suède										
31 XII 2003 .... DJ	DJ	8 975 670[18]	4 446 656[18]	4 529 014[18]	DJ	9 030[18]	9 148[18]	0.7	441 370	21
Switzerland - Suisse										
5 XII 2000 .... DJ	DJ	7 204 055	3 519 698	3 684 357	DJ	7 437	7 551	0.8	41 277[93]	183
The Former Yugoslav Republic of Macedonia - L'ex-République yougoslave de Macédoine										
1 XI 2002 .... DJ	DJ	2 022 547	1 015 377	1 007 170	DF	2 037	2 044	0.2	25 713	79
Ukraine										
5 XII 2001 .... DF	DF	48 240 902	22 316 317	25 924 585	...	*47 075	46 646[8]	...	603 500	77
United Kingdom of Great Britain and Northern Ireland - Royaume-Uni de Grande-Bretagne et d'Irlande du Nord[94]										
29 IV 2001 .... DF	DF	58 789 187	28 579 867	30 209 320	DF	60 238	60 975	0.6	242 900	251

3. Population by sex, rate of population increase, surface area and density
Population selon le sexe, taux d'accroissement de la population, superficie et densité (continued - suite)

Continent, country or area and census date / Continent, pays ou zone et date du recensement	Census type[a]	Latest available census Dernier recensement disponible (in units — en unités)			Estimate type[a]	Mid-year estimates Estimations au milieu de l'année (in thousands — en milliers)		Annual rate of increase Taux d' accrois sement annuel 2005-07	Surface area Superficie (km²) 2007	Density Densité 2007[b]
		Both sexes Les deux sexes	Male Masculin	Female Feminin		2005	2007			

OCEANIA - OCÉANIE

American Samoa - Samoas américaines										
1 IV 2000	DJ	57 291[19]	29 264[19]	28 027[19]	DJ	66[19]	68[19]	2.0	199	343
Australia - Australie										
8 VIII 2006	DF	20 061 646	9 896 500	10 165 146	DJ	20 395[12]	21 072[12]	1.6	7 692 024	3
Cook Islands - Îles Cook[95]										
1 XII 2006	DF	*19 569	*9 932	*9 637	DF	20	*21	2.2	236	89
Fiji - Fidji										
16 IX 2007	DF	837 271	427 176	410 095	DF	825	834	0.5	18 272	46
French Polynesia - Polynésie française										
20 VIII 2007	DJ	*259 596	...	...	DF	253	259	1.2	4 000	65
Guam										
1 IV 2000	DJ	154 805[19]	79 181[19]	75 624[19]	DJ	*169[19]	*173[19]	1.4	541	320
Kiribati										
7 XII 2005	DF	92 533	45 612	46 921		...	...	...	726	...
Marshall Islands - Îles Marshall										
1 VI 1999	DF	50 848	26 034	24 814	DF		53	...	181	291
Micronesia (Federated States of) - Micronésie (États fédérés de)										
1 IV 2000	DJ	107 008	54 191	52 817		...	...	...	702	...
Nauru										
23 IX 2002	DF	10 065	5 136	4 929		...	...	...	21	...
New Caledonia - Nouvelle-Calédonie										
31 VIII 2004	DF	*230 789	*116 485	*114 304	DF	234	242	1.7	18 575	13
New Zealand - Nouvelle-Zélande										
7 III 2006	DF	4 143 282	2 021 277	2 122 005	DJ	4 134	4 228	1.1	270 467	16
Niue - Nioué										
9 IX 2006	DF	1 625	802	823	DJ	2	...	...	260	...
Norfolk Island - Île Norfolk										
8 VIII 2006	DF	2 523	1 218	1 305		...	...	...	36	...
Northern Mariana Islands - Îles Mariannes septentrionales										
1 IV 2000	DF	69 221	31 984	37 237	DF	80	85	2.5	464	182
Palau - Palaos										
1 IV 2005	DJ	19 907	10 699	9 208	DF		21		459	46
Papua New Guinea - Papouasie-Nouvelle-Guinée										
9 VII 2000	DF	5 190 786	2 691 744	2 499 042		...	...	...	462 840	...
Pitcairn										
31 XII 1991	DF	66	...	...	DF		0[65]	...	5	13
Samoa										
5 XI 2006	DF	*179 186	*92 961	*86 225	DF	183	187	0.9	2 831	66
Solomon Islands - Îles Salomon										
21 XI 1999	DF	409 042	211 381	197 661	DF	471	495	2.5	28 896	17
Tokelau - Tokélaou										
19 X 2006	DF	1 151	583	568		...	...	...	12	...
Tonga										
30 XI 2006	DF	101 991	51 772	50 219	DF	102[96]	103[96]	0.4	747	138
Tuvalu										
1 XI 2002	DF	9 561	4 729	4 832	DF	10	...	...	26	...
Vanuatu										
16 XI 1999	DJ	186 678	95 682	90 996		...	...	...	12 189	...
Wallis and Futuna Islands - Îles Wallis et Futuna										
21 VII 2008	DF	*13 484	...	...		...	...	...	142	...

FOOTNOTES - NOTES

Italics: estimates which are less reliable. - Italiques: estimations moins sûres.

* Provisional. - Données provisoires.

a 'Code' indicates the source of data, as follows:
DF - De facto
DJ - De jure
SDF - Sample survey, de facto
SDJ - Sample survey, de jure

Le 'Code' indique la source des données, comme suit:
DF - Population de fait
DJ - Population de droit
SDF - Enquête par sondage, population de fait
SDJ - Enquête par sondage, Population de droit

b Population per square kilometre of surface area. Figures are estimates of population divided by surface area and are not to be considered either as reflecting density in the urban sense or as indicating the supporting power of a territory's land and resources. - Nombre d'habitants au kilomètre carré. Il s'agit simplement d'éstimations de la population divisé par celui de la superficie: il ne faut pas y voir d'indication de la densité au sens urbain du terme ni de l'effectif de population que les terres et les ressources du territoire sont capables de nourrir.

1 Data refer to national projections. - Les données se réfèrent aux projections nationales.
2 Excluding Mayotte. - Non compris Mayotte.
3 Excluding border population. - À l'exception de la population frontalière.
4 Total includes the estimated population of eight rural kebeles (21,410) in Elidar wereda (Affar Region). - Le total comprend l'effectif estimé de la population de huit kebele ruraux (21 410 habitants) du woreda d'Elidar (région Afar).
5 Based on the results of the Gabonese Survey for the Evaluation and Tracking of Poverty. - Sur base des résultats de l'enquête gabonaise sur l'évaluation et le suivi de la pauvreté.
6 Data refer to Libyan nationals only. - Les données se raportent aux nationaux libyens seulement.
7 Including residents outside the country. - Y compris les résidents hors du pays.
8 Data refer to 1 January. - Données se raportent au 1 janvier.
9 The number of males and/or females excludes persons whose sex is not stated (18 urban, 19 rural). - Il n'est pas tenu compte dans le nombre d'hommes et de femmes des personnes dont le sexe n'est pas indiqué (18 en zone urbaine et 19 en zone rurale).
10 Data refer to 31 December. Based on the results of a population count. - Données se raportent au 31 décembre. D'après les rêsultats d'un comptage de la population.
11 Data have not been adjusted for underenumeration, estimated at 2.4 per cent. - Les données n'ont pas été ajustées pour compenser les lacunes du dénombrement, estimées à 2,4 p. 100.
12 Mid-year estimates have been adjusted for underenumeration, at latest census. - Les estimations au milieu de l'année tiennent compte d'un ajustement destiné à compenser les lacunes du dénombrement lors du dernier recensement.
13 Comprising the Northern Region (former Saguia el Hamra) and Southern Region (former Rio de Oro). - Comprend la région septentrionale (ancien Saguia-el-Hamra) et la région méridionale (ancien Rio de Oro).
14 Excluding the institutional population. - Non compris la population dans les institutions.
15 Because of rounding, totals are not in all cases the sum of the parts. - Les chiffres étant arrondis, les totaux ne correspondent pas toujours rigoureusement à la somme des chiffres partiels.
16 Updated postcensal estimates. - Estimations post censitaires mises à jour.
17 Preliminary postcensal estimates. - Estimations postcensitaires préliminaires.
18 Population statistics are compiled from registers. - Les statistiques de la population sont compilées à partir des registres.
19 Including armed forces stationed in the area. - Y compris les militaires en garnison sur le territoire.
20 Based on the results of the population census. - D'après le résultats du recensement de la population.
21 Including low water level for all islands (area to shoreline). - Incluent le niveau de basses eaux pour toutes les îles.
22 Excluding armed forces overseas and civilian citizens absent from country for an extended period of time. - Non compris les militaires à l'étranger, et les civils hors du pays pendant une période prolongée.

23 Data include persons in remote areas, military personnel outside the country, merchant seamen at sea, civilian seasonal workers outside the country, and other civilians outside the country, and exclude nomads, foreign military, civilian aliens temporarily in the country, transients on ships and Indian jungle population. - Y compris les personnes vivant dans des régions éloignées, le personel militaire en dehors du pays, les marins marchands, les ouvriers saisonniers en dehors du pays, et autres civils en dehors du pays, et non compris les nomades, les militaires étrangers, les étrangers civils temporairement dans le pays, les transiteurs sur des bateaux et les Indiens de la jungle.
24 Exact reference date unknown. - La date de référence exacte n'est pas connue.
25 Data have been adjusted on the basis of the Population Census of 2005. - Données ajustées sur la base du recensement de la population de 2005.
26 Excluding nomadic Indian tribes. - Non compris les tribus d'Indiens nomades.
27 Excluding nomadic Indian tribes. Data refer to national projections. - Non compris les tribus d'Indiens nomades. Les données se réfèrent aux projections nationales.
28 A dispute exists between the governments of Argentina and the United Kingdom of Great Britain and Northern Ireland concerning sovereignty over the Falkland Islands (Malvinas). - La souveraineté sur les îles Falkland (Malvinas) fait l'objet d'un différend entre le Gouvernement argentin et le Gouvernement du Royaume-Uni de Grande-Bretagne et d'Irlande du Nord.
29 The previous census was conducted only 16 months earlier (on 31 Mar 2003) but it was repeated because all of its data were destroyed in a fire before they could be fully processed, analyzed, and reported. - Le recensement précédent a eu lieu seulement 16 mois auparavant (le 31 mars 2003), mais a dû être refait parce que toutes les données ont été détruites dans un incendie avant que l'on n'ait pu les traiter et les analyser.
30 The previous census was conducted only 16 months earlier (on 31 Mar 2003) but it was repeated because all of its data were destroyed in a fire before they could be fully processed, analyzed, and reported. Figures for male and female population do not add up to the figure for total population, because they exclude 365 persons of unknown sex. - Le recensement précédent a eu lieu seulement 16 mois auparavant (le 31 mars 2003), mais a dû être refait parce que toutes les données ont été détruites dans un incendie avant que l'on n'ait pu les traiter et les analyser. Les chiffres relatifs à la population masculine et féminine ne correspondent pas au chiffre de la population totale, parce que l'on en a exclu 365 personnes de sexe inconnu.
31 Data refer to resident population in Uruguay according to Census Phase 1, carried out between the months of June and July 2004. - Les données se rapportent à la population résidente en Uruguay d'après la phase 1 du recensement, qui a eu lieu entre juin et juillet 2004.
32 Excluding Indian jungle population. - Non compris les Indiens de la jungle.
33 Excluding nomad population. - Non compris les nomades.
34 The methodology used for calculating the number of the de facto and de jure population in the 2001 census data differs as follows from the methodology used in previous censuses: the duration that defines a person as being ' temporary present ' or 'temporary absent' is now 'under one year'. The previously applied definition was for '6 months'. - La méthode utilisée pour dénombrer la population de fait et la population de droit dans le contexte du recensement de 2001 diffère de celle qui a été appliquée lors des recensements antérieurs en ce que la durée considérée pour définir une ' présence temporaire 'ou' l'absence temporaire' était dorénavant fixée à 'moins d'un an' alors qu'elle était de '6 mois' auparavant.
35 Data have been adjusted for underenumeration, estimated at 4.96 per cent. - Les données ont été ajustées pour compenser les lacunes du dénombrement, estimées à 4,96 p.100.
36 Data refer to projections based on the 2005 population census. - Les données se réfèrent aux projections basées sur le recensement de la population de 2005.
37 From 1998 based on census result. Excluding foreign diplomatic personnel and their dependants. - Depuis 1998, à partir des résultats de recensement. Non compris le personnel diplomatique étranger et les membres de leur famille les accompagnant.
38 Data refer to the civilian population of 31 provinces, municipalities and autonomous regions. For statistical purposes, the data for China do not include those for the Hong Kong Special Administrative Region (Hong Kong SAR), Macao Special Administrative Region (Macao SAR) and Taiwan province of China. - Pour la population civile seulement de 31 provinces, municipalités et régions autonomes. Pour la présentation des statistiques, les données pour la Chine ne comprennent pas la Région Administrative Spéciale de Hong Kong (Hong Kong RAS), la Région Administrative Spéciale de Macao (Macao RAS) et Taïwan province de Chine.
39 For statistical purposes, the data for China do not include those for the Hong Kong Special Administrative Region (Hong Kong SAR), Macao Special Administrative Region (Macao SAR) and Taiwan province of China. Data for 2005 are estimated from the National Sample Survey of 1 per cent population. -

Pour la présentation des statistiques, les données pour la Chine ne comprennent pas la Région Administrative Spéciale de Hong Kong (Hong Kong RAS), la Région Administrative Spéciale de Macao (Macao RAS) et Taïwan province de Chine. Les données pour 2005 ont été estimées à partir de l'enquête nationale qui a porté sur un échantillon de 1 % de la population.

[40] For statistical purposes, the data for China do not include those for the Hong Kong Special Administrative Region (Hong Kong SAR), Macao Special Administrative Region (Macao SAR) and Taiwan province of China. Data have been estimated on the basis of the annual National Sample Surveys on Population Changes. - Pour la présentation des statistiques, les données pour la Chine ne comprennent pas la Région Administrative Spéciale de Hong Kong (Hong Kong RAS), la Région Administrative Spéciale de Macao (Macao RAS) et Taïwan province de Chine. Les données ont été estimées sur la base de l'enquête annuelle "National Sample Survey on Population Changes".

[41] Based on the results of the By-Census 2006, held during 19 to 31 of August 2006. - Donnes dérivées du recensement partiel de 2006 organisé entre les 19 et 31 août 2006.

[42] Including all persons irrespective of citizenship, who at the time of the census resided in the country or intended to reside for a period of at least one year. It does not distinguish between those present or absent at the time of census. Data refer to government controlled areas. - Les chiffres comprennent toute la population, quelle que soit la nationalité, qui à l'époque de recensement avait résidé dans le pays, ou avait l'intention de résider, pendant une période d'au moins un an. Il n'y a pas de distinction entre les personnes présentes ou absentes au moment du recensement. Les données se rapportent aux zones contrôlées par le Gouvernement.

[43] Data refer to government controlled areas. - Les données se rapportent aux zones contrôlées par le Gouvernement.

[44] Including data for the Indian-held part of Jammu and Kashmir, the final status of which has not yet been determined. Excluding Mao-Maram, Paomata and Purul sub-divisions of Senapati district of Manipur. The population of Manipur including the estimated population of the three sub-divisions of Senapati district is 2,291,125 (Males 1,161,173 and females 1,129,952). - Y compris les données pour la partie du Jammu et du Cachemire occupée par l'Inde dont le statut définitif n'a pas encore été déterminé. Non compris les subdivisions Mao-Maram Paomata et Purul du district de Senapati dans l'État du Manipur. Cet État compte 2 291 125 habitants (1 161 173 hommes et 1 129 952 femmes), y compris la population estimative des trois subdivisions du district de Senapati.

[45] Including data for the Indian-held part of Jammu and Kashmir, the final status of which has not yet been determined. Data refer to national projections. - Y compris les données pour la partie du Jammu et du Cachemire occupée par l'Inde dont le statut définitif n'a pas encore été déterminé. Les données se réfèrent aux projections nationales.

[46] The figure includes an estimated population of 459 557 persons in urban and 1 857 659 persons in rural areas that were not directly enumerated, and a population of 566 403 persons in urban and 1 717 578 persons in rural areas that decline the participation. Also included are 421 399 non permanent residents (the homeless, the crew of ships carrying national flag, boat/floating house people, remote located tribesmen and refugees.) - Y compris la population estimée a 459 557 personnes dans les zones urbaines et de 1 857 659 personnes dans les zones rurales qui n'ont pas été énumérées directement, aussi que 566 403 personnes qui non pas répondu dans les zones urbaines et de 1 717 578 personnes dans les zones rurales. Y compris 421 399 résidants non permanents (les sans abri, l'équipage des bateaux portant le pavillon national, les habitants des embarcations ou des maisons flottantes, les habitants des tribus isolées et les réfugiés.)

[47] Data refer to the Iranian Year which begins on 21 March and ends on 20 March of the following year. - Les données concernent l'année iranienne, qui commence le 21 mars et se termine le 20 mars de l'année suivante.

[48] Excluding the population in three autonomous provinces in the north of the country. - La population des trois provinces autonomes dans le nord du pays est exclue.

[49] Including data for East Jerusalem and Israeli residents in certain other territories under occupation by Israeli military forces since June 1967. - Y compris les données pour Jérusalem-Est et les résidents israéliens dans certains autres territoires occupés depuis 1967 par les forces armées israéliennes.

[50] Excluding diplomatic personnel outside the country and foreign military and civilian personnel and their dependants stationed in the area. - Non compris le personnel diplomatique hors du pays ni les militaires et agents civils étrangers en poste sur le territoire et les membres de leur famille les accompagnant.

[51] Data refer to 1 October 2007. - Les données se réfèrent au 1er octobre 2007.

[52] Excluding data for Jordanian territory under occupation since June 1967 by Israeli military forces. Excluding foreigners, including registered Palestinian refugees. - Non compris les données pour le territoire jordanien occupé depuis juin 1967 par les forces armées israéliennes. Non compris les étrangers, mais y compris les réfugiés de Palestine enregistrés.

[53] Excluding data for Jordanian territory under occupation since June 1967 by Israeli military forces. Excluding foreigners, including registered Palestinian refugees. Data refer to 31 December. - Non compris les données pour le territoire jordanien occupé depuis juin 1967 par les forces armées israéliennes. Non compris les étrangers, mais y compris les réfugiés de Palestine enregistrés. Données se raportent au 31 décembre.

[54] Based on the results of the 2005 Population and Housing Census. - Données fondées sur les résultats du recensement de la population et de l'habitat de 2005.

[55] Based on the results of a household survey. - D'après les résultats d'une enquête des ménages.

[56] Data have been adjusted for underenumeration. Excluding Malaysian citizens and permanent residents who were away or intended to be away from the country for more than six months. Excluding Malaysian military, naval and diplomatic personnel and their families outside the country, and tourists, businessman who intended to be in Malaysia for less than six months. - Les données ont été ajustées pour compenser les lacunes du dénombrement. Non compris les citoyens malaisiens et les résidents permanents qui étaient ou qui ont prévu d'être hors du pays pour six mois ou plus. Non compris le personnel militaire Malaisien, le personnel naval ou diplomatique et leurs familles hors du pays, et les touristes et les hommes d'affaires qui avaient l'intention de rester en Malaisie moins de six mois.

[57] Data refer to projections based on the 2000 population census. - Les données se réfèrent aux projections basées sur le recensement de la population de 2000.

[58] Data including estimated population from household listing from Village Development Committees and Wards which could not be enumerated at the time of census. - Les données incluent la population estimée par les listes des ménages des comités de développement des villages et des circonscriptions qui n'ont pas pu être énumérée au moment du recensement.

[59] Data have been adjusted for underenumeration, estimated at 2.70 per cent. - Les données ont été ajustées pour compenser les lacunes du dénombrement, estimées à 2,70 p. 100.

[60] Excluding data for the Pakistan-held part of Jammu and Kashmir, the final status of which has not yet been determined. - Non compris les données concernant la partie du Jammu et Cachemire occupée par le Pakistan dont le statut définitif n'a pas été déterminé.

[61] Excluding usual residents not in country at time of census. - À l'exclusion des résidents habituels qui ne sont pas dans le pays au moment du recensement.

[62] Excluding transients afloat and non-locally domiciled military and civilian service personnel and their dependants. - Non compris les personnes de passage à bord de navires, ni les militaires et agents civils domiciliés hors du territoire et les membres de leur famille les accompagnant.

[63] The Population and Housing Census 2001 did not cover the whole area of the country due to the security problems; data refer to the 18 districts for which the census was completed only (in three districts it was not possible to conduct the census at all and in four districts it was partially conducted). - Le recensement de la population et du logement de 2001 n'a pas été réalisé sur la superficie totale du pays à cause de problèmes de sécurité; les données ne concernent que les 18 districts entièrement recensés (3 districts n'ont pas été recensés du tout, et 4 ont été recensés en partie).

[64] Including Palestinian refugees. - Y compris les réfugiés de Palestine.

[65] Data refer to 31 December. - Données se raportent au 31 décembre.

[66] Also included in Finland. - Comprise aussi dans Finlande.

[67] Excluding Faeroe Islands and Greenland shown separately, if available. - Non compris les Iles Féroé et le Gröenland, qui font l'objet de rubriques distinctes, si disponible.

[68] Including Aland Islands. - Y compris les Îles d'Åland.

[69] Excluding Overseas Departments, namely, French Guiana, Guadeloupe, Martinique and Reunion, shown separately, if available. - Non compris les départements d'outre mer, c'est-à-dire la Guyane française, la Guadeloupe, la Martinique et la Réunion, qui font l'objet de rubriques distinctes, si disponible.

[70] Excluding diplomatic personnel outside the country and including members of alien armed forces not living in military camps and foreign diplomatic personnel not living in embassies or consulates. - Non compris le personnel diplomatique hors du pays et y compris les militaires étrangers ne vivant pas dans des camps militaires et le personnel diplomatique étranger ne vivant pas dans les ambassades ou les consulats.

[71] Data of the microcensus - a 1% household sample survey - refer to a single reference week in spring (usually last week in April). Excluding homeless persons. Excluding foreign military personnel and foreign diplomatic and consular personnel and their family members in the country. - Les données du microrecensement (enquête sur les ménages, réalisée sur un échantillon de 1 %) concernent une seule semaine de référence au printemps (habituellement la dernière semaine d'avril). Non compris les personnes sans domicile fixe. Non compris le personnel militaire étranger, le personnel diplomatique et consulaire étranger et les membres de leur famille se trouvant dans le pays.

[72] Excluding families of military personnel, visitors and transients. - Non compris les familles des militaires, ni les visiteurs et transients.

[73] Excluding families of military personnel, visitors and transients. Data refer to 31 December. - Non compris les familles des militaires, ni les visiteurs et transients. Données se raportent au 31 décembre.

[74] Including armed forces stationed outside the country, but excluding alien armed forces stationed in the area. - Y compris les militaires nationaux hors du pays, mais non compris les militaires étrangers en garnison sur le territoire.

[75] Excluding armed forces stationed outside the country, but including alien armed forces stationed in the area. - Non compris les militaires en garnison hors du pays, mais y compris les militaires étrangers en garnison sur le territoire.

[76] Data refer to 1 March. - Données se raportent au 1 mars.

[77] Data refer to the Vatican City State. - Les données se rapportent à l'Etat de la Cité du Vatican.

[78] Surface area is 0.44 Km2. - Superficie: 0,44 Km2.

[79] Data refer to 15 April. - Données se raportent au 15 avril.

[80] Data refer to 30 April. - Données se raportent au 30 avril.

[81] Figures for male and female population do not add up to the figure for total population, because they exclude 119 persons of unknown sex. - Les chiffres relatifs à la population masculine et féminine ne correspondent pas au chiffre de la population totale, parce que l'on en a exclu 119 personnes de sexe inconnu.

[82] Census results based on compilation of continuous accounting and sample surveys. - Les résultat du recensement, d'après les résultats des dénombrements et enquêtes par sondage continue.

[83] Excluding Svalbard and Jan Mayen Island shown separately, if available. - Non compris Svalbard et Jan Mayen qui font l'objet de rubriques distinctes, si disponible.

[84] Population statistics are compiled from registers. Including residents temporarily outside the country. - Les statistiques de la population sont compilées à partir des registres. Y compris les résidents se trouvant temporairement hors du pays.

[85] Including residents temporarily outside the country. - Y compris les résidents se trouvant temporairement hors du pays.

[86] Excluding civilian aliens within country, but including civilian nationals temporarily outside country. - Non compris les civils étrangers dans le pays, mais y compris les civils nationaux temporairement hors du pays.

[87] Includes inland waters as well as part of internal waters. - Comprend les eaux intérieures et une partie des eaux situées en deçà de la ligne de base de la mer territoriale.

[88] Excluding Transnistria and the municipality of Bender. - Les données ne tiennent pas compte de l'information sur la Transnistria et la municipalité de Bender.

[89] Data refer to resident population only. - Pour la population résidante seulement.

[90] Excluding data for Kosovo and Metohia. - Sans les données pour le Kosovo et Metohie.

[91] Inhabited only during the winter season. Census data are for total population while estimates refer to Norwegian population only. Included also in the de jure population of Norway. - N'est habitée pendant la saison d'hiver. Les données de recensement se rapportent à la population totale, mais les estimations ne concernent que la population norvégienne, comprise également dans la population de droit de la Norvège.

[92] Data refer to 1 January. Data refer to Svalbard only. - Données se raportent au 1 janvier. Données ne concernant que le Svalbard.

[93] Excluding state forests and communanzas (7.15 km2). - Non comprises les forêts domaniales et communanzas (7,15 km2).

[94] Excluding Channel Islands (Guernsey and Jersey) and Isle of Man, shown separately, if available. - Non compris les îles Anglo-Normandes (Guernesey et Jersey) et l'île de Man, qui font l'objet de rubriques distinctes, si disponible.

[95] Excluding Niue, shown separately, which is part of Cook Islands, but because of remoteness is administered separately. - Non compris Nioué, qui fait l'objet d'une rubrique distincte et qui fait partie des îles Cook, mais qui, en raison de son éloignement, est administrée séparément.

[96] Data refer to national projections. Based on the results of the 1996 population census not necessarily mid year estimated. - Les données se réfèrent aux projections nationales. À partir des résultats du recensement de la population de 1996, pas nécessairement des estimations en milieu d'année.

Table 4

Table 4 presents, for each country or area of the world, basic vital statistics including: live births, crude birth rate, deaths, crude death rate, rate of natural increase, infant deaths, infant death rate, expectation of life at birth by sex and total fertility rate.

Description of variables: The vital events and rates shown in this table are defined as follows[1]:

Live birth is the complete expulsion or extraction from its mother of a product of conception, irrespective of the duration of pregnancy, which after such separation breathes or shows any other evidence of life such as beating of the heart, pulsation of the umbilical cord, of definite movement of voluntary muscles, whether or not the umbilical cord has been cut or the placenta is attached. Each product of such a birth is considered live-born regardless of gestational age.

Death is the permanent disappearance of all evidence of life at any time after live birth has taken place (post-natal cessation of vital functions without capability of resuscitation).

Infant deaths are deaths of live-born infants under one year of age.

Expectation of life at birth is defined as the average number of years of life for males and females if they continued to be subject to the same mortality experienced in the year(s) to which these life expectancies refer.

The total fertility rate is the average number of children that would be born alive to a hypothetical cohort of women if, throughout their reproductive years, the age-specific fertility rates remained unchanged. The standard method of calculating the total fertility rate is the sum of the age-specific fertility rates.

Crude birth rates and crude death rates presented in this table are calculated using the number of live births and the number of deaths obtained from civil registers. These civil registration data are used only if they are considered reliable (estimated completeness of 90 per cent or more).

Similarly, infant mortality rates presented in this table are calculated using the number of live births and the number of infant deaths obtained from civil registers. If, however, the registration of births or infant deaths for any given country or area is estimated to be less than 90 per cent complete, the rates are not calculated.

Rate computation: The crude birth and death rates are the annual number of each of these vital events per 1 000 mid-year population.

Infant mortality rate is the annual number of deaths of infants under one year of age per 1 000 live births in the same year.

Rates of natural increase are the difference between the crude birth rate and the crude death rate. It should be noted that the rates of natural increase presented here may differ from the population growth rates presented in table 3 as rates of natural increase do not take net international migration into account while the population growth rates do.

Rates that appear in this table have been calculated by the Statistics Division of the United Nations Department of Economic and Social Affairs, unless otherwise noted. Exceptions include official estimated rates for Bangladesh and India, which were based on sample registration systems in these countries.

Rates calculated by the Statistics Division of the United Nations presented in this table have been limited to those countries or areas having a minimum number of 30 events (for life births and deaths) or 100 events (for infant deaths) in a given year.

Reliability of data: Rates calculated on the basis of registered vital statistics which are considered unreliable (estimated to be less than 90 per cent complete) are not calculated. Estimated rates, prepared by individual countries or areas, are presented whenever applicable.

The designation of vital statistics as being either reliable or unreliable is discussed in general in section 4.2 of the Technical Notes. The technical notes for tables 9, 15 and 18 provide specific information on reliability of statistics on live births, infant deaths and deaths, respectively.

The values shown for life expectancy in this table come from official life tables. It is assumed that, if necessary, the basic data (population and deaths classified by age and sex) have been adjusted for deficiencies before their use in constructing the life tables.

Limitations: Statistics on births, deaths and infant deaths are subject to the same qualifications as have been set forth for vital statistics, in general, in section 4 of the Technical Notes and in the technical notes for individual tables presenting detailed data on these events (table 9, live births; table 15, infant deaths; table 18, deaths).

In assessing comparability it is important to take into account the reliability of the data used to calculate the rates, as discussed above.

The problem of obtaining precise correspondence between numerator (births and deaths) and denominator (population for crude birth and death rates) as regards the inclusion or exclusion of armed forces, refugees, displaced persons and other special groups is particularly difficult where vital rates are concerned. This is the case for Japan, where births and deaths refer to Japanese nationals only while the population include foreigners except foreign military and civilian personnel and their dependants stationed in the area.

It should also be noted that crude rates are particularly affected by the age-sex structure of the population. Infant mortality rates, and to a much lesser extent crude birth rates and crude death rates, are affected by the variation in the definition of a live birth and tabulation procedures.

NOTES

[1] *Principles and Recommendations for a Vital Statistics System, Revision 2,* United Nations publication, Sales No. E.01.XVII.10, United Nations, New York, 2001.

Tableau 4

Le tableau 4 présente, pour chaque pays ou zone du monde, des statistiques de base de l'état civil comprenant, dans l'ordre, les naissances vivantes, le taux brut de natalité, les décès, le taux brut de mortalité et le taux d'accroissement naturel de la population, les décès d'enfants de moins d'un an et le taux de mortalité infantile, l'espérance de vie à la naissance par sexe et l'indice synthétique de fécondité.

Description des variables : les faits d'état civil utilisés aux fins du calcul des taux présentés dans le tableau 4 sont définis comme suit[1] :

La naissance vivante est l'expulsion ou l'extraction complète du corps de la mère, indépendamment de la duré de la gestation, d'un produit de la conception qui après cette séparation, respire ou manifeste tout autre signe de vie, tel que battement de cœur, pulsation du cordon ombilical ou contraction effective d'un muscle soumis à l'action de la volonté, que le cordon ombilical ait été coupé ou non et que le placenta soit ou non demeuré attaché ; tout produit d'une telle naissance est considéré comme « enfant né vivant ».

Le décès est la disparition permanente de tout signe de vie à un moment quelconque postérieur à la naissance vivante (cessation des fonctions vitales après la naissance sans possibilité de réanimation).

Il convient de préciser que les chiffres relatifs aux décès d'enfants de moins d'un an se rapportent aux naissances vivantes.

L'espérance de vie à la naissance est le nombre moyen d'années que vivraient les individus de sexe masculin et de sexe féminin s'ils continuaient d'être soumis aux mêmes conditions de mortalité que celles qui existaient pendant les années auxquelles se rapportent les valeurs indiquées.

L'indice synthétique de fécondité représente le nombre moyen d'enfants que mettrait au monde une cohorte hypothétique de femmes qui seraient soumises, tout au long de leur vie, aux mêmes conditions de fécondité par âge que celles auxquelles sont soumises les femmes, dans chaque groupe d'âge, au cours d'une année ou d'une période donnée. La méthode standard pour calculer l'indice synthétique de fécondité consiste à additionner les taux de fécondité par âge simple.

Les taux bruts de natalité et de mortalité ont été établis sur la base du nombre de naissances vivantes et du nombre de décès inscrits sur les registres de l'état civil. Ces données n'ont été utilisées que lorsqu'elles étaient considérées comme sûres (degré estimatif de complétude égal ou supérieur à 90 p. 100).

De même, les taux de mortalité infantile présentés dans le tableau 4 ont été établis à partir du nombre de naissances vivantes et du nombre de décès d'enfants de moins d'un an inscrits sur les registres de l'état civil. Toutefois, lorsque les données relatives aux naissances ou aux décès d'enfants de moins d'un an pour un pays ou zone quelconque n'étaient pas considérées complètes à 90 p. 100 au moins, les indices n'ont pas été calculés.

Calcul des taux : les taux bruts de natalité et de mortalité, représentent le nombre annuel de chacun de ces faits d'état civil pour 1 000 habitants au milieu de l'année considérée.

Les taux de mortalité infantile correspondent au nombre annuel de décès d'enfants de moins d'un an pour 1 000 naissances vivantes survenues pendant la même année.

Le taux d'accroissement naturel est égal à la différence entre le taux brut de natalité et le taux brut de mortalité. Il y a lieu de noter que les taux d'accroissement naturel indiqués dans le tableau 4 peuvent différer des taux d'accroissement de la population figurant dans le tableau 3, les taux d'accroissement naturel ne tenant pas compte des taux nets de migration internationale, alors que ceux-ci sont inclus dans les taux d'accroissement de la population.

Sauf indication contraire, les taux figurant dans le tableau 4 ont été calculés par la Division de statistique du Département des affaires économiques et sociales (Secrétariat de l'Organisation des Nations Unies). Les exceptions comprennent le Bangladesh et l'Inde, pour lesquels les taux estimatifs officiels ont été fournis sur la base d'un système d'enregistrement par échantillonnage.

Les taux calculés par la Division de statistique de l'ONU qui sont présentés dans le tableau 4 se rapportent aux seuls pays ou zones où l'on a enregistré au moins 30 événements (pour les naissances vivantes et les décès) ou 100 événements (pour les décès d'enfants de moins d'un an) au cours d'une année donnée.

Fiabilité des données : les taux n'ont pas été calculés lorsque les statistiques de l'état civil issues de systèmes d'enregistrement d'état civil étaient jugées douteuses (degré estimatif de complétude inférieur à 90 p.100) et des taux estimatifs, calculés par les pays ou zones, ont été présentés lorsqu'ils étaient disponibles.

On trouve à la section 4.2 des Notes techniques des explications générales concernant la façon dont les statistiques de l'état civil ont été classées selon leur degré de fiabilité. Les notes techniques relatives aux tableaux 9, 15 et 18 ont trait respectivement à la fiabilité des statistiques des naissances vivantes, des décès d'enfants de moins d'un an et des décès.

Les valeurs relatives à l'espérance de vie figurant dans le tableau 4 proviennent de tables officielles de mortalité. On présume que les données de base (population t décès par sexe et âge) ont été rectifiées d'éventuelles insuffisances avant d'être utilisées pour construire les tables de mortalité.

Insuffisance des données : les statistiques des naissances, décès et décès d'enfants de moins d'un an appellent toutes les réserves qui ont été formulées à propos des statistiques de l'état civil en général à la section 4 des Notes techniques et dans les notes techniques relatives aux différents tableaux présentant des données détaillées sur ces événements [tableau 9 (naissances vivantes), tableau 15 (décès d'enfants de moins d'un an) et tableau 18 (décès)].

Pour évaluer la comparabilité des divers taux, il importe de tenir compte de la fiabilité des données utilisées pour calculer ces taux, comme il a été indiqué précédemment.

Le calcul des taux est particulièrement affecté par la difficulté à obtenir une correspondance parfaite entre le numérateur (naissances et décès) et le dénominateur (population, pour les taux bruts de natalité et de mortalité) en raison de l'inclusion ou non dans la population des forces armées, des réfugiés, des personnes déplacées ou d'autres groupes sociaux. C'est le cas pour le Japon, où les naissances et les décès se réfèrent aux seuls nationaux japonais tandis que la population inclus les étrangers, à l'exception toutefois des militaires étrangers ainsi que des personnels civils et leurs familles stationnés sur le territoire.

Il y a lieu de noter que la structure par âge et par sexe de la population influe de façon particulière sur les taux bruts. Le manque d'uniformité dans la définition des naissances vivantes et dans les procédures de mise en tableaux a une incidence sur les taux de mortalité infantile et, à un moindre degré, sur les taux bruts de natalité et les taux bruts de mortalité.

NOTE

[1] *Principes et recommandations pour un système de statistiques de l'état civil, deuxième révision,* numéro de vente : F.01.XVII.10, publication des Nations Unies, New York, 2001.

4. Vital statistics summary and expectation of life at birth: 2003 - 2007
Aperçu des statistiques de l'état civil et espérance de vie à la naissance: 2003 - 2007

Continent, country or area and year / Continent, pays ou zone et année	Code[a]	Live births Naissances vivantes — Number Nombre	Live births — Crude birth rate Taux brut de natalité	Code[a]	Deaths Décès — Number Nombre	Deaths — Crude death rate Taux brut de mortalité	Rate of natural increase Taux d'accrois-sement naturel	Code[a]	Infant deaths Décès d'enfants de moins d'un an — Number Nombre	Infant deaths — Rate (per 1000 births) Taux (par 1000 naiss-ances)	Expectation of life at birth Espérance de vie à la naissance — Male[b] Masculin[b]	Female[b] Féminin[b]	Total fertility rate L'indice synthétique de fécondité
AFRICA - AFRIQUE													
Algeria - Algérie[1]													
2003	C	649 000	20.4	U	145 000	...	...		...	...	...	...	...
2004	C	669 000	20.7	U	141 000	...	...		...	...	...	...	...
2005	C	703 000	21.4	U	147 000	...	...		...	...	...	...	...
2006	C	739 000	22.1	U	144 000	...	...		...	...	...	...	...
2007	C	783 000	23.0	U	149 000	...	...		...	...	...	...	...
Burkina Faso													
2006	I	612 840[2]	46.7	I	116 199[3]	8.9	37.9	I	16 259[3]	26.5	55.8	57.5	6.200
Cape Verde - Cap-Vert													
2003	C	13 334	28.9		...	...	...		...	...	...	...	...
Congo[4]													
2003	+U	44 132	...		...	...	...		...	...	...	...	...
2004	+U	44 473	...		...	...	...		...	...	...	...	...
Egypt - Égypte													
2003	C	1 777 418	26.2	C	440 149	6.5	19.7	C	38 859	21.9	67.9	72.3	3.200
2004	C	1 779 500	25.7	C	440 790	6.4	19.3	C	40 177	22.6	...	...	...
2005	C	1 800 972	25.5	C	450 646	6.4	19.1	C	36 146	20.1	...	...	3.100
2006	C	1 853 746	25.7	C	451 863	6.3	19.5	C	35 952	19.4	...	...	...
2007	C	1 949 569	26.5	C	450 596	6.1	20.4	C	34 612	17.8	...	...	...
Ghana													
2003		...	...		...	...	...		...	...	...	...	4.400
Kenya													
2003	U	495 433	...	U	174 950	...	...	U	35 515	...	...	...	4.900
2004		...	...	U	178 051	...	...	U	35 321	...	...	...	...
2005		...	...	U	168 919	...	...	U	35 252	...	...	...	...
2006		...	...	U	174 856	...	...	U	35 786	...	...	...	...
Madagascar													
2003		...	...		...	...	...		...	...	...	...	5.200
2004		...	...		...	...	...		...	...	...	...	5.200
Malawi													
2003	U	578 978[5]	...	U	213 705[5]	...	...		...	...	43.4[6]	46.0[6]	...
2004	U	590 774[5]	...	U	210 936[5]	...	...		...	...	...	...	...
2005	U	602 590[5]	...	U	209 019[5]	...	...		...	...	...	...	...
2006	U	614 410[5]	...	U	207 641[5]	...	...		...	...	...	...	...
2007	U	626 181[5]	...	U	206 527[5]	...	...		...	...	45.7[5]	48.3[5]	...
Mauritius - Maurice													
2003	+C	19 343	15.8	+C	8 520	7.0	8.9	+C	250	12.9	68.6	75.3	1.870
2004	+C	19 230	15.6	+C	8 475	6.9	8.7	+C	277	14.4	III68.4	75.3	1.870
2005	+C	18 820	15.1	+C	8 646	7.0	8.2	+C	248	13.2	68.9	75.6	1.820
2006	+C	17 604	14.1	+C	9 162	7.3	6.7	+C	249	14.1	69.1	75.9	1.700
2007	+C	17 034	13.5	+C	8 498	6.7	6.8	+C	261	15.3	...	...	1.662
Mayotte													
2003	C	7 197	...		...	...	...		...	...	...	...	...
2004	C	7 452	...	C	513	...	...		...	...	...	...	...
Namibia - Namibie[5]													
2003		...	...	U	29 425	...	...		...	...	...	...	...
2004		...	...	U	29 262	...	...		...	...	...	...	...
2005		...	...	U	29 073	...	...		...	...	...	...	...
2006		...	...	U	28 879	...	...		...	...	...	...	...
2007		...	...	U	28 673	...	...		...	...	...	...	...
Réunion													
2003	C	14 427[7]	19.1	C*	4 022[7]	5.3	13.8	C	107[7]	7.4	71.3	79.8	2.430
2004	C	14 545[7]	19.0	C	3 958[7]	5.2	13.8	C	104[7]	7.2	...	...	2.450
2005	C	14 610[7]	18.8	C	4 357[7]	5.6	13.2	C	117[7]	8.0	...	...	2.490
2006	C	14 495[7]	18.4	C	4 323[7]	5.5	12.9	C	96[7]	...	73.2	80.9	2.440
2007	C	14 808[7]	18.6	C	4 045[7]	5.1	13.5	C	91[7]	...	...	...	...
Saint Helena ex. dep. - Sainte-Hélène sans dép.													
2003	C	37	...	C	44	...	...	C	1	...	...	...	...
2004	C	34	...	C	33	...	...	C	-	...	X71.9	79.1	...

Continent, country or area and year Continent, pays ou zone et année	Live births Naissances vivantes			Deaths Décès			Rate of natural increase Taux d'accrois-sement naturel	Infant deaths Décès d'enfants de moins d'un an			Expectation of life at birth Espérance de vie à la naissance		Total fertility rate L'indice synthétique de fécondité
	Code[a]	Number Nombre	Crude birth rate Taux brut de natalité	Code[a]	Number Nombre	Crude death rate Taux brut de mortalité		Code[a]	Number Nombre	Rate (per 1000 births) Taux (par 1000 naiss-ances)	Male[b] Masculin[b]	Female[b] Féminin[b]	
AFRICA - AFRIQUE													
Saint Helena ex. dep. - Sainte-Hélène sans dép.													
2005	C	34	...	C	39	...	...	C	1	...	...	...	...
2006	C	35	...	C	52	...	...	C	-	...	...	...	...
2007	C	42	10.6	C	59	14.9	-4.3	C	-	...	[x]70.8	77.3	...
Seychelles													
2003	+C	1 498	18.1	+C	668	8.1	10.0	+C	24	...	...	...	...
2004	+C	1 435	17.4	+C	611	7.4	10.0	+C	17	...	...	...	2.200
2005	+C	1 536	18.5	+C	673	8.1	10.4	+C	16	...	...	...	2.200
2006	+C	1 467	17.3	+C	664	7.8	9.5	+C	14	...	68.3	77.1	2.200
2007	+C	1 499	17.6	+C	630	7.4	10.2	+C	16	...	68.9	77.7	...
South Africa - Afrique du Sud													
2003	U	926 592	...	U	554 199	...	...		38 306	...	...	...	2.820
2004	U	971 142	...	U	572 620	...	...		41 132	...	49.9	52.9	2.800
2005	U	998 257	...	U	593 341	...	...		46 122	...	...	...	2.780
2006	U	999 874	...	U	607 184	...	...		47 703	...	...	...	...
2007	U	911 494	...			...	...		...	...	...	...	...
Tunisia - Tunisie													
2003	C	168 022	17.1	U	59 781	...			...	...	71.1	75.1	...
2004	C	166 551	16.8	U	59 269	...			...	...	71.4	75.3	...
2005	C	170 999	17.1	U	58 673	...			...	...	71.6	75.5	...
2006	C	173 390	17.1	U	57 000	...			...	...	71.9	76.0	...
2007	C	177 503	17.4	U	56 741	...			...	...	72.3	76.2	...
Zambia - Zambie[5]													
2006	U	509 766	...	U	152 549	...			...	...	...	...	...
Zimbabwe													
2005		...	...		...	...			...	...	...	...	3.800
AMERICA, NORTH - **AMÉRIQUE DU NORD**													
Anguilla													
2003	+C	139	11.4	+C	65	5.3	6.1	+C	2	...	...	...	...
2004	+C	164	13.1	+C	52	4.2	8.9	+C	-	...	...	...	2.910
2005	+C	167	12.2	+C	60	4.4	7.8	+C	3	...	...	...	1.840
2006	+C	183	12.8	+C	58	4.1	8.8	+C*	1	...	...	...	2.000
2007	+C	148	9.9	+C	70	4.7	5.2	+C	-	...	...	...	...
Aruba													
2003	C	1 244	13.1	C	501	5.3	7.8	+U	3	...	...	...	1.627
2004	C	1 193	12.2	C	502	5.1	7.1	+U	3	...	...	...	1.749
2005	C	1 263	12.5	C	482	4.8	7.8	+U	6	...	...	...	1.778
2006	C	1 227	11.9	C	537	5.2	6.7	+U	8	...	...	...	1.713
2007	C	1 239	11.9	C	521	5.0	6.9	+U	4	...	...	...	1.739
Bahamas													
2003	U	5 054	...	C	1 649	5.2	...	C	54	...	...	...	1.875
2004	U	5 154	...	C	1 655	5.2	...	C	57	...	...	...	1.900
2005	U	5 548	...	C	1 824	5.6	...	C	100	...	...	...	2.050
2006	U	5 296	...	C	1 730	5.3	...	C	79	...	...	...	1.925
2007	U	5 854	...	C	1 798	5.4	...	C	69	...	...	...	2.295
Barbados - Barbade													
2003	+C*	3 748	13.8	+C*	2 274	8.4	5.4	+C*	37	...	...	...	...
2004	+C*	3 473	12.7	+C*	2 424	8.9	3.9	+C*	64	...	...	...	...
2005	+C*	3 508	12.8	+C*	2 162	7.9	4.9	+C*	29	...	...	...	...
2006	+C*	3 414	12.5	+C*	2 317	8.5	4.0	+C*	38	...	...	...	...
2007	+C*	3 537	12.9	+C*	2 213	8.1	4.8	+C*	46	...	...	...	...

4. Vital statistics summary and expectation of life at birth: 2003 - 2007
Aperçu des statistiques de l'état civil et espérance de vie à la naissance: 2003 - 2007 (continued - suite)

Continent, country or area and year / Continent, pays ou zone et année	Code[a]	Live births Number Nombre	Crude birth rate Taux brut de natalité	Code[a]	Deaths Number Nombre	Crude death rate Taux brut de mortalité	Rate of natural increase Taux d'accroissement naturel	Code[a]	Infant deaths Number Nombre	Rate (per 1000 births) Taux (par 1000 naissances)	Male[b] Masculin[b]	Female[b] Féminin[b]	Total fertility rate L'indice synthétique de fécondité
AMERICA, NORTH - AMÉRIQUE DU NORD													
Belize													
2003	U	7 440	...	U	1 277	...	...		...	...	...	...	...
2004	U	8 083	...	U	1 298	...	...	U	112	...	...	...	...
2005	U	8 396	...	U	1 369	...	...	U	137	...	...	...	...
Bermuda - Bermudes													
2003	C	834[8]	13.2	C	434[8]	6.9	6.3	C	2	...	...	...	...
2004	C	831[8]	13.1	C	406[8]	6.4	6.7	C	-	...	...	...	...
2005	C	835[8]	13.1	C	437[8]	6.9	6.3	C	2	...	...	...	...
2006	C	798[8]	12.5	C	461[8]	7.2	5.3	C	6	...	...	...	...
British Virgin Islands - Îles Vierges britanniques													
2003	C	269	12.6	C	104	4.9	7.7		...	...	73.8	78.9	1.700
2004	C	318	14.7	C	120	5.5	9.1		...	...	69.9	78.5	1.990
Canada													
2003	C	335 202[9]	10.6	C	226 169[9]	7.1	3.4	C	1 765[9]	5.3	77.4	82.4	1.525
2004	C	337 422[9]	10.5	C	226 584[9]	7.1	3.5	C	1 775[9]	5.3	77.8	82.6	1.526
2005	C	342 176[9]	10.6	C	230 132[9]	7.1	3.5	C	1 863[9]	5.4	...	...	1.543
2006	C*	350 181[9]	10.7	C*	233 415[9]	7.1	3.6		...	...	...	...	...
Cayman Islands - Îles Caïmanes													
2003	C	623[10]	14.3	C	153[11]	3.5	10.8	C	6	...	...	...	...
2004	C	611[10]	13.8	C	165[11]	3.7	10.1	C	3	...	...	...	...
2005	C	699[10]	14.5	C	170[11]	3.5	10.9	C	4	...	...	...	...
2006	C	710[10]	13.7	C	181[11]	3.5	10.2	C	8	...	76.3[12]	83.8[12]	...
2007	C	744[10]	13.8	C	159[11]	2.9	10.8	C	5	...	...	...	...
Costa Rica													
2003	C	72 938	17.8	C	15 800	3.9	14.0	C	737	10.1	...	...	2.100
2004	C	72 247	17.3	C	15 949	3.8	13.5	C	668	9.2	...	...	2.000
2005	C	71 548	16.8	C	16 139	3.8	13.0	C	700	9.8	...	...	2.000
2006	C	71 291	16.4	C	16 766	3.9	12.5	C	692	9.7	...	...	1.900
2007	C	73 144	16.5	C	17 070	3.8	12.6	C	735	10.0	76.8	81.7	2.000
Cuba													
2003	C	136 795	12.2	C	78 434	7.0	5.2	C	859	6.3	III75.1	79.0	1.628
2004	C	127 192	11.3	C	81 110	7.2	4.1	C	736	5.8	...	...	1.543
2005	C	120 716	10.7	C	84 824	7.5	3.2	C	746	6.2	...	...	1.493
2006	C	111 323	9.9	C	80 831	7.2	2.7	C	589	5.3	...	...	1.393
2007	C	112 472	10.0	C	81 927	7.3	2.7	C	592	5.3	III76.0	80.0	1.432
Dominica - Dominique													
2003	+C	1 056	15.0	+C	557	7.9	7.1	+C	20	...	...	...	...
2004	+C	1 066	15.1	+C	557	7.9	7.2	+C	14	...	...	...	...
2005	+C	1 009	14.3	+C	489	6.9	7.4	+C	22	...	...	...	...
2006	+C	1 058	14.9	+C	536	7.5	7.4	+C	13	...	...	...	...
Dominican Republic - République dominicaine													
2003	U	151 466	...	U	28 950	...	...	U	451	...	...	...	2.830
2004	U	139 215	...	U	33 370	...	...	U	359	...	...	...	2.798
2005	U	131 101	...	U	33 035	...	...	U	369	...	...	...	2.766
2006	U	121 038	...	U	30 759	...	...	U	158	...	...	...	2.734
2007	U	106 405	...	U	31 204	...	...	U	60	...	...	...	2.703[13]
El Salvador													
2003	C	124 476	18.8	C	29 377	4.4	14.3	C	1 322	10.6	...	...	...
2004	C	119 710	17.7	C	30 058	4.4	13.3	C	1 255	10.5	...	...	...
2005	C	112 769	16.4	C	30 933	4.5	11.9	C	1 097	9.7	VI67.7[14]	73.7[14]	...
2006	C	107 111	15.3	C	31 453	4.5	10.8	C	1 013	9.5	...	...	...
2007	C	106 471	15.0	C	31 349	4.4	10.6	C	981	9.2	...	...	...
Greenland - Groenland													
2003	C	895	15.8	C	412	7.3	8.5	C	8	...	V64.1	69.5	2.361
2004	C	893	15.7	C	475	8.3	7.3	C	10	...	...	...	2.380
2005	C	887	15.6	C	466	8.2	7.4	C	7	...	...	...	2.330

Continent, country or area and year / Continent, pays ou zone et année	Live births / Naissances vivantes			Deaths / Décès			Rate of natural increase / Taux d'accrois-sement naturel	Infant deaths / Décès d'enfants de moins d'un an			Expectation of life at birth / Espérance de vie à la naissance		Total fertility rate / L'indice synthétique de fécondité
	Code[a]	Number Nombre	Crude birth rate Taux brut de natalité	Code[a]	Number Nombre	Crude death rate Taux brut de mortalité		Code[a]	Number Nombre	Rate (per 1000 births) Taux (par 1000 naiss-ances)	Male[b] Masculin[b]	Female[b] Féminin[b]	
AMERICA, NORTH - AMÉRIQUE DU NORD													
Greenland - Groenland													
2006	C	842	14.8	C	440	7.7	7.1	C	13	...	V65.7	71.0	2.222
2007	C	853	15.1	C	451	8.0	7.1	C	7	...	V66.3	71.3	2.278
Guadeloupe[7]													
2003	C	7 047	16.1	C	2 636	6.0	10.1	C	56	...	...	...	...
2004	C	7 273	16.4	C	2 676	6.0	10.3	C	50	...	...	...	...
2005	C	7 551	16.9	C	2 904	6.5	10.4	C	...	...	...	...	...
2006	C	7 193	15.7	C	2 902	6.3	9.4	C	...	...	...	...	...
2007	C	6 862	17.0	C	2 769	6.9	10.2	C	...	...	...	...	...
Guatemala													
2003	C	375 092	31.0	C	66 695	5.5	25.5	C	11 022	29.4	...	...	...
2004	C	383 704	31.0	C	66 991	5.4	25.6	C	10 038	26.2	...	...	3.959
2005	C	374 066	29.5	C	71 039	5.6	23.9	C	9 947	26.6	...	...	3.738
2006	C	368 399	28.3	C	69 756	5.4	22.9	C	9 042	24.5	...	...	3.570
Haiti - Haïti[15]													
2003		...	...	U	8 011	...							
Honduras													
2003	+U	218 173	...	+U	34 754	...	...	+U	6 902	...	...	...	...
2004	+U	220 040	...	+U	35 075	...	...	+U	6 740	...	...	...	...
2005	+U	221 759	...	+U	35 356	...	...	+U	6 566	...	...	...	...
2006	+U	222 512	...	+U	35 682	...	...	+U	6 400	...	...	...	...
Jamaica - Jamaïque													
2003	C	47 110[16]	17.9	U	16 699[17]	...	...	U	1 004[16]	...	71.3	77.1	2.420
2004	C	47 127[16]	17.9	U	16 905[17]	...	...	U	1 004[16]	...	...	...	2.350
2005	C	47 255[16]	17.8	U	17 552[17]	...	...	U	1 007[16]	...	...	...	2.290
2006	C	46 277[16]	17.4	U	16 317[17]	...	...		...	...	69.7	75.2	2.220
2007	C	45 590[16]	17.0	U	17 048[17]	...	...		...	...	...	...	2.220
Martinique													
2003	C	5 430[7]	13.9	C	2 727[7]	7.0	6.9	C	34	...	...	...	1.920
2004	C	5 255[7]	13.3	C	2 647[7]	6.7	6.6	C	27	...	...	...	1.910
2005	C	5 032[7]	12.7	C	2 610[7]	6.6	6.1	C	47	...	...	...	1.850
2006	C	5 370[7]	13.4	C	2 663[7]	6.7	6.8	C	44	...	...	...	2.030
2007	C	5 317[7]	13.3	C	2 830[7]	7.1	6.2	C	47	...	76.5	82.9	...
Mexico - Mexique													
2003	+U	2 165 318[18]	...	+C	470 692[19]	4.6	...	+U	33 331[19]	...	...	...	2.333
2004	+U	2 154 927[18]	...	+C	472 273[19]	4.6	...	+U	32 758[19]	...	...	...	2.247
2005	+U	2 141 083[18]	...	+C	493 957[19]	4.8	...	+U	32 590[19]	...	71.9	77.4	2.203
2006		...	...	+C	493 296[19]	4.7	...	+U	30 890[19]	...	...	...	2.167
2007		...	...	+C	513 122[19]	4.9	...	+U	30 412[19]	...	72.6	77.4	2.134
Montserrat													
2003	+C	40	8.9	+C	55	12.3	-3.3		...	...	...	...	...
2004	+C	47	10.0	+C	56	12.0	-1.9		...	...	...	...	...
2005	+C	63	13.2	+C	59	12.3	0.8		...	...	...	...	...
2006	+C	49	10.5	+C	47	10.1	0.4		...	...	...	...	...
2007	+C	43	8.9	+C	44	9.1	-0.2		...	...	...	...	...
Netherlands Antilles - Antilles néerlandaises													
2003	C	2 488[19]	14.1	C	1 374[19]	7.8	6.3	C	19	...	...	...	2.060
2004	C	2 388[19]	13.4	C	1 413[19]	7.9	5.5	C	20	...	III70.6	79.0	1.931
2005	C	2 553[19]	13.9	C	1 304[19]	7.1	6.8	C	26	...	...	...	2.009
2006	C	2 578[19]	13.6	C	1 327[19]	7.0	6.6	C	40	...	...	...	1.987
2007	C*	2 558[19]	13.2	C	1 339[19]	6.9	6.3	C	33	...	V72.0	79.3	1.887
Nicaragua													
2003	+U	120 784	...	+U	15 379	...	...	+U	2 008	...	...	...	...
2004	+U	121 402	...	+U	15 821	...	...	+U	1 827	...	...	...	...
2005	+U	121 380	...	+U	16 770	...	...	+U	1 970	...	...	...	...
2006	+U	123 886	...	+U	16 595	...	...	+U	1 925	...	...	...	2.690
2007	+U	128 171	...	+U	17 288	...	...	+U	1 955	...	...	...	...

4. Vital statistics summary and expectation of life at birth: 2003 - 2007
Aperçu des statistiques de l'état civil et espérance de vie à la naissance: 2003 - 2007 (continued - suite)

Continent, country or area and year / Continent, pays ou zone et année	Code[a]	Live births / Naissances vivantes — Number / Nombre	Crude birth rate / Taux brut de natalité	Code[a]	Deaths / Décès — Number / Nombre	Crude death rate / Taux brut de mortalité	Rate of natural increase / Taux d'accroissement naturel	Code[a]	Infant deaths / Décès d'enfants de moins d'un an — Number / Nombre	Rate (per 1000 births) / Taux (par 1000 naissances)	Male[b] / Masculin[b]	Female[b] / Féminin[b]	Total fertility rate / L'indice synthétique de fécondité
AMERICA, NORTH - AMÉRIQUE DU NORD													
Panama													
2003	C	61 753	19.8	U	13 248	...	...	U	940	...	...	...	2.400
2004	C	62 743	19.8	U	13 475	...	...	U	932	...	...	...	2.400
2005	C	63 645	19.7	U	14 180	...	...	U	980	...	...	...	2.400
2006	C	65 764	20.0	U	14 358	...	...	U	971	...	...	...	2.400
2007	C	67 364	20.2	U	14 775	...	...	U	992	...	...	...	2.500
Puerto Rico - Porto Rico													
2003	C	50 803	13.1	C	28 356	7.3	5.8	C	498	9.8	...	...	1.760
2004	C	51 239	13.2	C	29 066	7.5	5.7	C	416	8.1	III73.7	81.1	1.776
2005	C	50 687	13.0	C	29 702	7.6	5.4	C	472	9.3	III73.7	80.9	1.755
2006	C	48 744	12.4	C	28 589	7.3	5.1	C	442	9.1	III74.1	81.5	1.696
Saint Lucia - Sainte-Lucie													
2003	C	2 486	15.5	C	1 046	6.5	9.0	C	37	...	...	...	...
2004	C	2 322	14.3	C	1 114	6.9	7.4	C	45	...	...	...	...
2005	C*	2 298	14.0	C*	1 107	6.7	7.2	C*	46	...	69.9	75.7	...
Saint Vincent and the Grenadines - Saint-Vincent-et-les Grenadines													
2003	+C	1 923	18.3	+C	790	7.5	10.8	+C	35	...	...	...	...
2004	+C	1 804	17.3	+C	812	7.8	9.5	+C	33	...	...	...	...
2005	+C	1 779	17.1	+C	813	7.8	9.3	+C	29	...	...	...	...
Trinidad and Tobago - Trinité-et-Tobago													
2003	C	17 989	14.0	C	10 206	8.0	6.1	C	431	24.0	...	...	...
2004	C	17 235	13.4	C	9 872	7.6	5.7	C	284	16.5	...	...	...
2005		...	...	C	9 885	7.6	...	C	266	...	...	...	...
Turks and Caicos Islands - Îles Turques et Caïques													
2003	C	213	8.5	C	61	2.4	6.0	C	2	...	...	...	...
2004	C	300	10.9	C	46	1.7	9.2	C	-	...	...	...	...
2005	C	318	10.4	C	53	1.7	8.7	C	1	...	...	...	...
2006	C	409	12.3	C	73	2.2	10.1	C	4	...	...	...	...
2007	C	512	14.7	C	114	3.3	11.4	C	2	...	...	...	...
United States of America - États-Unis d'Amérique													
2003	C	4 089 950	14.1	C	2 448 288	8.4	5.7	C	28 025	6.9	74.8	80.1	2.043
2004	C	4 112 052	14.0	C	2 397 615	8.2	5.8	C	27 936	6.8	75.2	80.4	2.050
2005	C	4 138 349	14.0	C	2 448 017	8.3	5.7	C	28 440	6.9	74.9	79.9	2.054
2006	C	4 265 555	14.3	C	2 426 264	8.1	6.2	C	28 527	6.7	...	...	2.100
2007	C	4 317 119	14.3		...	...	...		...	...	...	...	...
United States Virgin Islands - Îles Vierges américaines													
2003	C	1 610	14.8	C	615	5.6	9.1	C	8	...	...	...	...
2004	C	1 672	15.3	C	628	5.7	9.5	C	8	...	...	...	...
2005	C	1 686	15.4	C	674	6.1	9.2	C	9	...	...	...	...
2006	C	1 763	16.1	C	629	5.7	10.3	C	8	...	...	...	...
2007	C	1 771	16.1	C	727	6.6	9.5	C	12	...	...	...	...
AMERICA, SOUTH - AMÉRIQUE DU SUD													
Argentina - Argentine													
2003	C	697 952	18.4	C	302 064	8.0	10.5	C	11 494	16.5	...	...	2.406
2004	C	736 261	19.3	C	294 051	7.7	11.6	C	10 576	14.4	...	...	2.501
2005	C	712 220	18.5	C	293 529	7.6	10.8	C	9 507	13.3	...	...	2.389
2006	+C	696 451	17.9	C	292 313	7.5	10.4	C	8 986	12.9	...	...	2.304
2007	C	700 792	17.8	C	315 852	8.0	9.8	C	9 300	13.3	...	...	2.288

4. Vital statistics summary and expectation of life at birth: 2003 - 2007
Aperçu des statistiques de l'état civil et espérance de vie à la naissance: 2003 - 2007 (continued - suite)

Continent, country or area and year / Continent, pays ou zone et année	Code[a]	Live births / Naissances vivantes Number Nombre	Crude birth rate Taux brut de natalité	Code[a]	Deaths / Décès Number Nombre	Crude death rate Taux brut de mortalité	Rate of natural increase Taux d'accrois-sement naturel	Code[a]	Infant deaths / Décès d'enfants de moins d'un an Number Nombre	Rate (per 1000 births) Taux (par 1000 naiss-ances)	Expectation of life at birth / Espérance de vie à la naissance Male[b] Masculin[b]	Female[b] Féminin[b]	Total fertility rate / L'indice synthétique de fécondité
AMERICA, SOUTH - AMÉRIQUE DU SUD													
Bolivia (Plurinational State of) - Bolivie (État plurinational de)													
2003	U	204 683	...	U	27 589[20]	...	...		...	...	...	...	...
2004	U	177 306	...	U	27 942[20]	...	...		...	...	...	...	...
2005	U	160 052	...	U	27 129[20]	...	...		...	...	...	...	...
2006	U	135 069	...	U*	25 954[20]	...	...		...	...	...	...	...
2007	U*	96 856	...	U*	21 846[20]	...	...		...	...	...	...	...
Brazil - Brésil													
2003	U	2 822 462[21]	...	U	977 717[21]	...	...	U	48 039[21]	...	...	...	2.205
2004	U	2 813 704[21]	...	U	998 725[21]	...	...	U	41 851[21]	...	...	...	2.134
2005	U	2 874 542[21]	...	U	979 854[21]	...	...	U	39 259[21]	...	68.1[21]	75.8[21]	2.062
2006	U	2 798 964[21]	...	U	1 023 545[21]	...	...	U	37 677[21]	...	...	...	1.992
2007	U	2 750 667[21]	...	U	1 032 450[21]	...	...	U	35 159[22]	...	68.8[21]	76.4[21]	1.925
Chile - Chili													
2003	C	234 486	14.7	C	83 672	5.3	9.5	C	1 935	8.3	...	...	1.900
2004	C	230 352	14.3	C	86 138	5.4	9.0	C	2 034	8.8	...	...	1.910
2005	C	230 831	14.2	C	86 102	5.3	8.9	C	1 911	8.3	VI74.8	81.1	1.930
2006	C	231 383	14.1	C	85 639	5.2	8.9	C	1 839	7.9	...	...	1.910
Colombia - Colombie													
2003	U	710 702	...	U	192 121	...	...	U	12 210	...	...	...	...
2004	U	723 099	...	U	188 933	...	...	U	11 772	...	...	...	...
2005	U	719 968	...	U	189 022	...	...	U	11 456	...	VI69.2	75.3	2.446
2006	U	714 450	...	U	192 814	...	...	U	11 049	...	VI69.4	75.5	...
2007	U*	685 609	...	U*	184 530	...	...	U*	9 997	...	VI69.6	75.7	...
Ecuador - Équateur[23]													
2003	U	262 004	...	U	53 521	...	...	U	3 985	...	...	...	...
2004	U	254 362	...	U	54 729	...	...	U	3 942	...	...	...	...
2005	U	252 725	...	U	56 825	...	...	U	3 717	...	VI71.3	77.2	...
2006	U	278 591	...	U	57 940	...	...	U	3 715	...	...	...	...
2007	U	195 051[24]	...	U	58 016	...	...	U	3 529	...	...	...	...
Falkland Islands (Malvinas) - Îles Falkland (Malvinas)													
2003	+C	34	...	+C	20	...	...		...	...	...	...	...
2004	+C	44	...	+C	15	...	...		...	...	...	...	...
2005	+C	18	...	+C	19	...	...		...	...	...	...	...
2006	+C	27	...	+C	20	...	...		...	...	...	...	...
French Guiana - Guyane française													
2003	C	5 553[7]	30.7	C	721[7]	4.0	26.7	C	61[7]	...	71.3	79.7	3.770
2004	C	5 312[7]	28.4	C	719[7]	3.8	24.5	C	55[7]	...	...	...	3.470
2005	C	5 998[7]	30.0	C	705[7]	3.5	26.5	C	64[7]	...	...	...	3.780
2006	C	6 276[7]	31.9	C	711[7]	3.6	28.2	C	79[7]	...	74.4	81.0	3.810
2007	C	6 386[7]	29.9	C	690[7]	3.2	26.7	C	77[7]	...	75.1	80.8	...
Guyana													
2003		...	...	+C	4 986	6.6	...		...	...	...	...	...
2004		...	...	+C	5 141	6.8	...		...	...	...	...	...
2005		...	...	+C	5 259	6.9	...		...	...	...	...	...
2006		...	...	+C	5 031	6.6	...		...	...	...	...	...
2007		...	...	+C	5 066	6.6	...		...	...	...	...	...
Paraguay													
2003	U	45 669	...	U	19 593	...	...	U	674	...	...	...	...
2004	U	49 857	...	U	20 283	...	...	U	647	...	...	...	...
2005	U	51 444	...	U	17 360	...	...	U	539	...	VI68.6	73.1	...
2006		...	...	U	19 298	...	...	U	549	...	...	...	...
Peru - Pérou													
2003	+U	383 919[20]	...	+U	84 265[20]	...	...	I	14 015[5]	...	...	...	2.830
2004	+U	344 804[20]	...	+U	87 189[20]	...	...	I	13 135[5]	...	...	...	...

Continent, country or area and year — Continent, pays ou zone et année	Code[a]	Live births — Naissances vivantes Number Nombre	Crude birth rate Taux brut de natalité	Code[a]	Deaths — Décès Number Nombre	Crude death rate Taux brut de mortalité	Rate of natural increase Taux d'accrois-sement naturel	Code[a]	Infant deaths — Décès d'enfants de moins d'un an Number Nombre	Rate (per 1000 births) Taux (par 1000 naiss-ances)	Expectation of life at birth — Espérance de vie à la naissance Male[b] Masculin[b]	Female[b] Féminin[b]	Total fertility rate L'indice synthétique de fécondité
AMERICA, SOUTH - AMÉRIQUE DU SUD													
Peru - Pérou													
2005	+U*	310 611[20]	...	+U	88 704[20]	...	...		12 343[5]	...	...	...	...
2006	+U*	307 779[20]	...	+U	82 620[20]	...	...		11 584[5]	...	...	...	...
2007	+U*	508 384[20]	...		...	...	...		...	...	...	...	...
Suriname													
2003	C	9 634[25]	20.0	C	3 154[26]	6.5	13.4	C	109[26]	11.3	...	...	...
2004	C	9 062[25]	18.6	C	3 319[26]	6.8	11.8	C	120[26]	13.2	67.0[27]	73.3[27]	2.244
2005	C	8 657[25]	17.4	C	3 392[26]	6.8	10.6	C	136[26]	15.7	...	...	2.120
2006	C	9 311[25]	18.5	C	3 247[26]	6.4	12.0	C	129[26]	13.9	68.0[27]	73.7[27]	2.292
2007	C	9 769[25]	19.2	C	3 374[26]	6.6	12.5	C	134[26]	13.7	...	...	2.387
Uruguay													
2003	C	50 631	15.3	C	32 587	9.9	5.5	C*	757	15.0	71.3	79.2	2.178
2004	C	50 052	15.2	C	32 222	9.8	5.4	C*	659	13.2	71.7	78.9	2.075
2005	C	47 150	14.3	C	32 319	9.8	4.5	C*	601	12.7	72.0	79.4	2.045
2006	C	47 231	14.2	C	31 056	9.4	4.9	C*	497	10.5	72.1	79.5	2.019
2007	C	47 372	14.3	C	33 706	10.1	4.1	C	573	12.1	72.3	79.6	2.008
Venezuela (Bolivarian Republic of) - Venezuela (République bolivarienne du)[21]													
2003	C	555 614	21.6	C	118 562	4.6	17.0		...	...	...	...	2.720
2004	C	637 799	24.4	C	110 946	4.2	20.2		...	...	...	...	2.690
2005	C	665 997	25.1	C	110 301	4.2	20.9		...	...	...	...	2.650
2006	C	646 225	23.9	C	115 348	4.3	19.6		...	...	...	...	2.620
2007	C	615 371	22.4	C	118 594	4.3	18.1		...	...	...	...	2.580
ASIA - ASIE													
Armenia - Arménie													
2003	C	35 793[28]	11.1	C	26 014[28]	8.1	3.0	C	422[28]	11.8	69.9	75.8	1.349
2004	C	37 520[28]	11.7	C	25 679[28]	8.0	3.7	C	430[28]	11.5	70.3	76.4	1.383
2005	C	37 499[28]	11.7	C	26 379[28]	8.2	3.5	C	460[28]	12.3	70.3	76.5	1.365
2006	C	37 639[29]	11.7	C	27 202[28]	8.4	3.2	C	523[28]	13.9	...	...	1.348
2007	C	40 105	12.4	C	26 830[28]	8.3	4.1	C	433[28]	10.8	‖70.2	76.6	1.417
Azerbaijan - Azerbaïdjan													
2003	+C	113 467[28]	13.8	+C	49 001[28]	6.0	7.8	+C	1 649[28]	14.5	69.5	75.1	1.910
2004	+C	131 609[28]	15.8	+C	49 568[28]	6.0	9.9	+C	1 892[28]	14.4	69.6	75.2	2.050
2005	+C	141 901[28]	16.9	+C	51 962[28]	6.2	10.7	+C	1 580[28]	11.1	69.6	75.2	...
2006	+C	148 946[28]	17.6	+C	52 248[28]	6.2	11.4	+C	1 882[28]	12.6	69.6	75.1	...
2007	+C	151 963[28]	17.7	+C	53 655[28]	6.3	11.5	+C	1 756[28]	11.6	69.7	75.1	2.329
Bahrain - Bahreïn													
2003	C	14 560	19.0	C	2 114	2.8	16.3	C	107	7.3	...	...	1.940
2004	C	14 968	18.2	C	2 215	2.7	15.5	C	141	9.4	...	...	2.000
2005	C	15 198	17.1	C	2 222	2.5	14.6	C	134	8.8	73.1	77.3	2.020
2006	C	15 053	15.7	C	2 317	2.4	13.3	C	115	7.6	...	...	2.000
2007	C	16 062	15.5	C	2 270	2.2	13.3	C	133	8.3	...	...	1.960
Bangladesh													
2003	I	...	20.9[30]	I	...	5.9[30]	...	I	...	53.0[30]	64.3	65.4	2.570
2004	I	...	20.8[30]	I	...	5.8[30]	...	I	...	52.0[30]	64.4	65.7	2.510
2005	I	...	20.7[30]	I	...	5.8[30]	...	I	...	49.0[30]	64.6	65.8	2.470
2006	I	...	20.6[30]	I	...	5.6[30]	...	I	...	45.0[30]	65.2	68.2	2.410
2007	I	...	20.9[30]	I	...	6.2[30]	...	I	...	43.0[30]	65.4	67.9	2.390

Continent, country or area and year / Continent, pays ou zone et année	Code[a]	Live births Number Nombre	Crude birth rate Taux brut de natalité	Code[a]	Deaths Number Nombre	Crude death rate Taux brut de mortalité	Rate of natural increase Taux d'accroissement naturel	Code[a]	Infant deaths Number Nombre	Rate (per 1000 births) Taux (par 1000 naissances)	Male[b] Masculin[b]	Female[b] Féminin[b]	Total fertility rate L'indice synthétique de fécondité
ASIA - ASIE													
Bhutan - Bhoutan													
2005	I	12 538[31]	19.7	I	4 498[31]	7.1	12.7	I	503[31]	40.1	65.7	66.9	3.590
Brunei Darussalam - Brunéi Darussalam													
2003	+C	7 047	20.2	+C	1 010	2.9	17.3	+C	67	...	74.4	77.4	2.100
2004	+C	7 163	19.9	+C	1 010	2.8	17.1	+C	63	...	74.6	77.5	2.100
2005	+C	6 933	18.7	+C	1 072	2.9	15.8	+C*	51	...	75.2	77.8	2.000
2006	+C	6 526	17.0	+C	1 095	2.9	14.2		...	...	75.9	77.5	1.800
2007	+C	6 314	16.2	+C	1 174	3.0	13.2		...	...	75.2	77.8	1.700
Cambodia - Cambodge													
2003	U	375 799	...	U	124 981	...	...	...	80	...	...	...	3.780
2004	U	384 267	...	U	124 391	...	...	...	76	...	...	...	3.680
China - Chine[32]													
2003	I	15 990 000[33]	12.4	I	8 250 000[33]	6.4	6.0		...	...	...	...	...
2004	I	15 930 000[33]	12.3	I	8 320 000[33]	6.4	5.9		...	...	...	...	...
2005	I	16 170 000[34]	12.4	I	8 490 000[34]	6.5	5.9		...	...	...	...	...
2006	I	15 840 000[33]	12.1	I	8 920 000[33]	6.8	5.3		...	...	...	...	...
2007	I	15 940 000[33]	12.0	I	9 130 000[33]	6.9	5.1		...	...	...	...	...
China, Hong Kong SAR - Chine, Hong Kong RAS													
2003	C	46 965	7.0	C	36 971	5.5	1.5	C	109	2.3	78.5	84.4	0.901[35]
2004	C	49 796	7.3	C	36 918	5.4	1.9	C	132	2.7	79.0	84.8	0.922[35]
2005	C	57 098	8.4	C	38 830	5.7	2.7	C	131	2.3	78.8	84.6	0.959[35]
2006	C	65 626	9.6	C*	37 457	5.5	4.1	C*	118	1.8	79.4	85.5	0.984[35]
2007	C*	70 875	10.2	C*	39 476	5.7	4.5	C*	125	1.8	...	...	...
China, Macao SAR - Chine, Macao RAS													
2003	C	3 212	7.2	C	1 474	3.3	3.9	C	2	...	...	...	0.837
2004	C	3 308	7.3	C	1 533	3.4	3.9	C	10	...	IV77.5	82.1	0.855
2005	C	3 671	7.8	C	1 615	3.4	4.3	C	12	...	IV77.6	82.3	0.912
2006	C	4 058	8.1	C	1 566	3.1	5.0	C	11	...	...	...	0.954
2007	C	4 537	8.6	C	1 545	2.9	5.7	C	9	...	...	...	...
Cyprus - Chypre[36]													
2003	C	8 088	11.2	C	5 200	7.2	4.0	C	33	...	II77.0	81.4	1.498
2004	C	8 309	11.3	C	5 225	7.1	4.2	C	29	...	...	...	1.487
2005	C	8 243	10.9	C	5 425	7.2	3.7	C	38	...	II77.0	81.7	1.420
2006	C	8 731	11.3	C	5 127	6.7	4.7	C	27	...	...	...	1.437
2007	C	8 575	10.9	C	5 391	6.9	4.1	C	32	...	...	...	1.390
Georgia - Géorgie													
2003	C	46 194[28]	10.7	C	46 055[28]	10.6	0.0	C	1 144[28]	24.8	69.1	74.7	1.370
2004	C	49 572[28]	11.5	C	48 793[28]	11.3	0.2	C	1 178[28]	23.8	67.8	74.9	1.440
2005	C	46 512[28]	10.7	C	40 721[28]	9.3	1.3	C	916[28]	19.7	69.3	76.7	1.350
2006	C	47 795[28]	10.9	C	42 255[28]	9.6	1.3	C	753[28]	15.8	69.8	78.5	1.400
2007	C	49 287[28]	11.2	C	41 178[28]	9.4	1.8	C	656[28]	13.3	70.5	79.4	1.450
India - Inde[37]													
2003	I	...	24.8[38]	I	...	8.0[38]	...	I	...	60.0[38]	V61.8	63.5	2.959
2004	I	...	24.1[38]	I	...	7.5[38]	...	I	...	58.0[38]	V62.1	63.7	2.900
2005	I	...	23.8[38]	I	...	7.6[38]	...	I	...	58.0[38]	V62.3	63.9	2.900
2006	I	...	23.5[38]	I	...	7.5[38]	...	I	...	57.0[38]	V62.6	64.2	2.785
2007	I	...	23.1[38]	I	...	7.4[38]	...	I	...	55.0[38]	...	...	2.683
Indonesia - Indonésie													
2007		...	...		...	...	...		...	...	...	...	2.173
Iran (Islamic Republic of) - Iran (République islamique d')													
2003	C	1 171 573[39]	17.4	C	368 518[39]	5.5	11.9		...	...	...	...	...
2004	C	1 154 368[39]	16.9	C	355 213[39]	5.2	11.7		...	...	...	...	...
2005	C	1 233 873[39]	17.8	C	361 326[39]	5.2	12.6		...	...	...	...	...

Continent, country or area and year / Continent, pays ou zone et année	Code[a]	Live births Naissances vivantes — Number Nombre	Crude birth rate Taux brut de natalité	Code[a]	Deaths Décès — Number Nombre	Crude death rate Taux brut de mortalité	Rate of natural increase Taux d'accrois-sement naturel	Code[a]	Infant deaths Décès d'enfants de moins d'un an — Number Nombre	Rate (per 1000 births) Taux (par 1000 naiss-ances)	Expectation of life at birth — Male[b] Masculin[b]	Female[b] Féminin[b]	Total fertility rate L'indice synthétique de fécondité
ASIA - ASIE													
Iran (Islamic Republic of) - Iran (République islamique d')													
2006	C	1 253 506[39]	17.8	C	408 566[39]	5.8	12.0		...	...	71.1	73.1	1.780
2007	C	1 286 716[39]	18.0	C	412 735[39]	5.8	12.2		...	...	...	...	...
Iraq													
2003	U*	691 269	...	U*	95 935	...	...		...	...	...	...	...
2004	U*	840 257	...	U*	101 820	...	...	U*	10 972	...	...	...	...
2005	U*	896 340	...	U*	115 775	...	...	U*	12 460	...	...	...	...
2006	U*	902 934	...	U*	211 757	...	...	U*	48 078	...	...	...	...
Israel - Israël[40]													
2003	C	144 936	21.7	C	38 499[41]	5.8	15.9	C	717[42]	4.9	77.7	81.9	2.945
2004	C	145 207	21.3	C	37 938[43]	5.6	15.8	C	670[42]	4.6	78.1	82.4	2.904
2005	C	143 913	20.8	C	39 047	5.6	15.1	C	629[42]	4.4	78.3	82.3	2.836
2006	C	148 170	21.0	C	38 776	5.5	15.5	C	598[42]	4.0	ᵛ78.0	82.0	2.879
2007	C	151 679	21.1	C	39 836	5.5	15.6	C	591[42]	3.9	78.8	82.5	2.905
Japan - Japon[44]													
2003	C	1 123 610	8.9	C	1 014 951	8.0	0.9	C	3 364	3.0	78.4	85.3	1.290
2004	C	1 110 721	8.8	C	1 028 602	8.1	0.7	C	3 122	2.8	78.6	85.6	1.289
2005	C	1 062 530	8.4	C	1 083 796	8.6	-0.2	C	2 958	2.8	78.5	85.5	1.260
2006	C	1 092 674	8.7	C	1 084 450	8.6	0.1	C	2 864	2.6	79.0	85.8	1.317
2007	C	1 089 818	8.6	C	1 108 334	8.8	-0.1	C	2 828	2.6	79.2	86.0	1.337
Jordan - Jordanie[45]													
2003	C	148 294	27.1	U	16 937	...	...		...	...	70.6	72.4	3.700
2004	C	150 248	28.1	U	17 011	...	...		...	...	70.6	72.4	3.700
2005	C	152 276	27.8	U	17 883	...	...		...	...	70.6	72.4	3.700
2006	C	162 972	29.1	U	20 397	...	...		...	...	70.8	72.5	3.700
2007	C	185 011	32.3	U	20 924	...	...		...	...	71.6	74.4	3.600
Kazakhstan													
2003	C	247 946[28]	16.6	C	155 277[28]	10.4	6.2	C	3 806[28]	15.4	60.5	71.5	2.030
2004	C	273 028[28]	18.2	C	152 250[28]	10.1	8.0	C	3 901[28]	14.3	60.6	72.0	2.210
2005	C	278 977[28]	18.4	C	157 121[28]	10.4	8.0	C	4 213[28]	15.1	60.3	71.8	2.220
2006	C	301 756[28]	19.7	C	157 210[28]	10.3	9.4	C	4 154[28]	13.8	60.7	72.2	2.350
2007	C	321 963[28]	20.8	C	158 297[28]	10.2	10.6	C	4 646[28]	14.4	60.7	72.6	2.490
Kuwait - Koweït													
2003	C	43 982	21.0	C	4 424	2.1	18.9	C	412	9.4	...	...	4.540
2004	C	47 274	21.8	C	4 793	2.2	19.6	C	422	8.9	...	...	4.538
2005	C	50 941	22.7	C	4 784	2.1	20.6	C	420	8.2	...	...	4.634
2006	C	52 759	22.7	C	5 247	2.3	20.4	C	456	8.6	...	...	4.568
2007	C	53 587	22.2	C	5 293	2.2	20.0	C	449	8.4	...	...	4.447
Kyrgyzstan - Kirghizstan													
2003	C	105 490	20.9	C	35 941	7.1	13.8	C	2 186	20.7	...	...	2.521
2004	C	109 939[46]	21.6	C	35 061	6.9	14.7	C	2 812[46]	25.6	64.4	72.3	2.582
2005	C	109 839	21.4	C	36 992	7.2	14.2	C	3 258	29.7	64.2	71.9	2.531
2006	C	120 737	23.3	C	38 566	7.4	15.8	C	3 526	29.2	63.5	72.1	2.735
2007	C	123 251	23.5	C	38 180	7.3	16.3	C	3 771	30.6	63.7	72.3	2.750
Lao People's Democratic Republic - République démocratique populaire lao[47]													
2005		...	...		...	...	...		...	...	55.0	63.0	4.500
Lebanon - Liban													
2003	C	71 702	...	C	17 187	...	...		...	...	...	...	...
2004	C	73 900	19.7	C	17 774	4.7	14.9		...	...	...	...	...
2005	C	73 973	...	C	18 012	...	...		...	...	...	...	...
2006	C	72 790	...	C	18 787	...	...		...	...	...	...	...
2007	C	80 896	21.5	C	21 092	5.6	15.9		...	...	...	...	...
Malaysia - Malaisie													
2003	C	480 083	19.2	C	111 644	4.5	14.7	C	3 148	6.6	70.9	75.6	2.488
2004	C	477 768	18.7	C	112 700	4.4	14.3	C	3 105	6.5	71.7	76.1	2.438

Continent, country or area and year / Continent, pays ou zone et année	Live births / Naissances vivantes			Deaths / Décès			Rate of natural increase / Taux d'accrois-sement naturel	Infant deaths / Décès d'enfants de moins d'un an			Expectation of life at birth / Espérance de vie à la naissance		Total fertility rate / L'indice synthétique de fécondité
	Code[a]	Number / Nombre	Crude birth rate / Taux brut de natalité	Code[a]	Number / Nombre	Crude death rate / Taux brut de mortalité		Code[a]	Number / Nombre	Rate (per 1000 births) / Taux (par 1000 naissances)	Male[b] / Masculin[b]	Female[b] / Féminin[b]	
ASIA - ASIE													
Malaysia - Malaisie													
2005	C	469 204	18.0	C	113 714	4.4	13.6	C	3 112	6.6	70.6	76.4	2.355
2006	C	465 112	17.5	C	115 084	4.3	13.1	C	2 877	6.2	71.5	76.2	2.295
2007	C*	456 443	16.8	C*	116 672	4.3	12.5	C*	2 878	6.3	...	...	2.216*
Maldives													
2003	C	5 157	18.1	C	1 030	3.6	14.5	C	72	...	70.4	71.3	...
2004	C	5 220	18.0	C	1 015	3.5	14.5	C	76	...	71.1	72.1	...
2005	C	5 543	18.9	C	1 027	3.5	15.4	C	67	...	71.7	72.7	...
2006	C	5 829	19.5	C	1 084	3.6	15.9	C	92	...	...	...	...
2007	C	6 569	21.5	C	1 119	3.7	17.9	C	66	...	...	...	...
Mongolia - Mongolie													
2003	C	45 723	18.4	C	16 006	6.4	11.9	C	1 051	23.0	...	...	2.000
2004	C	45 501	18.1	C	16 404	6.5	11.6	C	1 016	22.3	...	...	2.000
2005	C	45 326	17.8	C	16 480	6.5	11.3	C	938	20.7	...	...	1.948
2006	C	49 092	19.0	C	16 682	6.5	12.6	C	937	19.1	X62.6	69.4	2.067
2007	C	56 636	21.7	C	16 259	6.2	15.4	C	994	17.6	X63.1	70.2	2.340
Myanmar													
2003	U	*685 443*	...	U	*197 716*	...	...	U	*31 873*	...	...	...	...
2004	U	*791 600*	...	U	*230 683*	...	...	U	*36 812*	...	...	...	2.150[48]
2005	U	*836 124*	...	U	*242 549*	...	...	U	*38 872*	...	62.5[48]	66.6[48]	2.110[48]
Nepal - Népal													
2005		...			...				...		62.3	63.1	3.600
2006		...			...				...		62.9	63.7	3.500
Occupied Palestinian Territory - Territoire palestinien occupé													
2003	C	106 355	32.1	U	*10 207*	...	...	U	*1 150*	...	...	...	4.600
2004	C	111 245	32.6	U	*10 029*	...	...	U	*1 103*	...	...	...	...
2005	C	109 439	31.2	U	*9 645*	...	...	U	*1 057*	...	...	...	4.600
2006	C	108 874	30.1	U	*9 938*	...	...	U	906	...	...	...	...
2007	C	108 674	29.2	U	*9 887*	...	...	U	794	...	70.0	72.6	4.600
Oman													
2003	U	*40 062*[49]	...	U	*2 701*[49]	...	...	U	*335*[49]	...	73.1	75.4	3.560
2004	U	*40 584*[49]	...	U	*2 743*[49]	...	...	U	*336*[49]	...	73.2	75.4	3.190
2005	U	*42 065*[49]	...	U	*2 849*[49]	...	...	U	*315*[49]	...	73.2	74.4	3.130
2006	U	*44 116*[49]	...	U	*3 027*[49]	...	...	U	*381*[49]	...	73.2	75.4	3.190
2007	U	*48 041*[50]	...	U	*6 449*[50]	...	...	...	...	...	...	...	...
Pakistan[51]													
2003	I	3 683 290[52]	24.9	I	970 428[52]	6.5	18.3	I	280 729[52]	76.2	64.7[52]	65.6[52]	3.900[52]
2005	I	3 772 494[53]	24.5	I	1 019 467[53]	6.6	17.9	I	289 169[53]	76.7	64.0[53]	65.0[53]	3.800[53]
Philippines													
2003	C	1 669 442	20.6	C	396 331	4.9	15.7	C	22 844	13.7	...	...	2.600
2004	C	1 710 994	20.7	C	403 191	4.9	15.8	C	22 557	13.2	...	...	2.600
2005	C	1 688 918	20.0	C	426 054	5.1	15.0	C	21 674	12.8	...	...	2.500
Qatar													
2003	C	12 856	17.9	C	1 311	1.8	16.1	C	137	10.7	...	...	2.864
2004	C	13 190	17.4	C	1 341	1.8	15.7	C	113	8.6	76.1	75.6	2.780
2005	C	13 401	15.1	C	1 545	1.7	13.3	C	110	8.2	III75.1	75.6	2.600
2006	C	14 120	13.6	C	1 750	1.7	11.9	C	114	8.1	76.7	76.7	2.710
2007	C	15 681	12.8	C	1 776	1.4	11.3	C	117	7.5	81.0	79.2	2.400
Republic of Korea - République de Corée													
2003	C	493 471[54]	10.2	C	245 817[54]	5.1	5.1	C	2 470[54]	5.0	73.9	80.8	1.190
2004	C	476 052[54]	9.8	C	245 771[54]	5.1	4.7	C	2 209[54]	4.6	74.5	81.4	1.160
2005	C	438 062[54]	9.0	C	245 511[54]	5.0	4.0	C	1 822[54]	4.2	75.1	81.9	1.080
2006	C	451 514[54]	9.2	C	243 934[54]	5.0	4.2	C	1 709[54]	3.8	75.7	82.4	1.130
2007	C*	496 710[54]	10.3	C*	244 874[54]	5.1	5.2	C*	1 703[54]	3.4	76.1	82.7	1.260

4. Vital statistics summary and expectation of life at birth: 2003 - 2007
Aperçu des statistiques de l'état civil et espérance de vie à la naissance: 2003 - 2007 (continued - suite)

Continent, country or area and year / Continent, pays ou zone et année	Live births / Naissances vivantes			Deaths / Décès			Rate of natural increase / Taux d'accrois-sement naturel	Infant deaths / Décès d'enfants de moins d'un an			Expectation of life at birth / Espérance de vie à la naissance		Total fertility rate / L'indice synthétique de fécondité
	Code[a]	Number Nombre	Crude birth rate Taux brut de natalité	Code[a]	Number Nombre	Crude death rate Taux brut de mortalité		Code[a]	Number Nombre	Rate (per 1000 births) Taux (par 1000 naiss-ances)	Male[b] Masculin[b]	Female[b] Féminin[b]	
ASIA - ASIE													
Saudi Arabia - Arabie saoudite													
2003	...	567 433	...	...	89 976	...	...	...	11 297	...	...	...	...
2004	...	574 211	...	...	91 243	...	...	...	11 165	...	...	...	3.320
2005	...	582 582	...	...	92 487	...	...	...	11 078	...	...	...	3.280
2006	...	589 223	...	...	93 752	...	...	...	10 954	...	...	...	3.220
Singapore - Singapour													
2003	C	37 485	9.1	+C	16 036	3.9	5.2	+C	100	2.7	77.0	80.9	1.270
2004	C	37 174	8.9	+C	15 860	3.8	5.1	+C	82	...	77.4	81.3	1.260
2005	C	37 492	8.8	+C	16 215	3.8	5.0	+C	95	...	77.9	81.6	1.260
2006	C	38 317	8.7	+C	16 393	3.7	5.0	+C	117	3.1	77.8	82.6	1.280
2007	C	39 490	8.6	+C	17 140	3.7	4.9	+C	94	...	78.1	82.9	1.290
Sri Lanka													
2003	+C	370 642	19.3	+C	114 310	5.9	13.3		...	...	...	...	...
2004	+C	360 220	18.5	+C	112 568	5.8	12.7		...	...	...	...	...
2005	+C	370 424	18.8	+C	129 822	6.6	12.2		...	...	...	...	...
2006	+C	371 264	18.7	+C	115 424	5.8	12.9		...	...	...	...	...
2007	+C	380 069	19.0	+C	116 883	5.8	13.2		...	...	...	...	...
Syrian Arab Republic - République arabe syrienne[55]													
2003	U	609 774	...	U	62 880	...	...		...	...	...	...	...
2004	U	598 221	...	U	68 551	...	...		...	...	...	...	...
2005	U	634 170	...	U	73 928	...	...		...	...	...	...	...
2006	U	656 599	...	U	72 534	...	...		...	...	...	...	...
2007	U	727 439	...	U	76 064	...	...		...	...	...	...	...
Tajikistan - Tadjikistan													
2003	U	177 938[56]	...	U	26 785[28]	...	...	U	1 944[28]	...	...	...	3.420
2004	U	179 563[56]	...	U	26 770[28]	...	...	U	2 071[28]	...	...	...	3.354
2005	U	180 790[56]	...	U	28 913[28]	...	...	U	2 129[28]	...	68.1	73.2	3.274
2006	U	186 463[56]	...	U	29 366[28]	...	...	U	2 160[28]	...	...	...	3.266
2007	U	200 010[56]	...	U	30 332[28]	...	...	U	2 168[28]	...	...	...	...
Thailand - Thaïlande													
2003	+U	742 183	...	+U	384 131	...	...	+U	5 349	...	...	...	...
2004	+U	813 069	...	+U	393 592	...	...	+U	6 061	...	...	...	...
2005	+U	809 485	...	+U	395 374	...	...	+U	6 183	...	...	...	...
2006	+U	793 623	...	+U	391 126	...	...	+U	5 855	...	‖69.9	77.6	...
2007	+U	797 588	...	+U	393 255	...	...	+U	5 781	...	...	...	...
Turkey - Turquie													
2003	I	1 291 000[57]	18.4 [57]	I	430 000[57]	6.1 [57]	12.3	I	29 822[57]	23.1 [57]	...	...	2.220
2004	I	1 286 000[57]	18.1 [57]	I	433 000[57]	6.1 [57]	12.0	I	26 877[57]	20.9 [57]	68.8[58]	73.6[58]	2.210
2005	I	1 281 000[57]	17.8 [57]	I	436 000[57]	6.1 [57]	11.7	I	24 211[57]	18.9 [57]	...	...	2.190
2006	I	1 277 000[57]	17.5 [57]	I	440 000[57]	6.0 [57]	11.5	I	22 348[57]	17.5 [57]	69.1[58]	74.0[58]	2.180
2007	I	1 275 000[57]	17.3 [57]	I	447 000[57]	6.1 [57]	11.2	I	21 293[57]	16.7 [57]	...	...	2.150
United Arab Emirates - Émirats arabes unis													
2003	...	61 165	...	...	6 002	...	...	...	488	...	...	...	...
2004	...	63 113	...	...	6 123	...	...	...	550	...	...	...	...
2005	...	64 623	...	...	6 361	...	...	...	500	...	...	...	...
2006	...	62 969	...	...	6 563	...	...	...	455	...	76.7	78.8	...
Viet Nam													
2003	C	1 292 086	16.0	C	372 721	4.6	11.4	C	27 134	21.0	...	...	2.120
2004	C	1 249 191	15.2	C	351 801	4.3	10.9	C	22 610	18.1	...	...	2.230
2005	C	1 252 882	15.1	C	336 405	4.0	11.0	C	22 301	17.8	...	...	2.110
2006	C	1 243 463	14.8	C	334 432	4.0	10.8	C	19 895	16.0	...	...	2.090
2007	C	1 326 464	15.6	C	382 624	4.5	11.1	C	21 223	16.0	...	...	2.070
Yemen - Yémen													
2003	U	130 112	...	U	20 346	...	...		...	...	...	...	6.200
2004	U	153 945	...	U	22 255	...	...		...	...	60.2	62.0	6.100
2005	U	167 830	...	U	20 451	...	...		...	...	...	...	...

Continent, country or area and year / Continent, pays ou zone et année	Code[a]	Live births Naissances vivantes — Number Nombre	Crude birth rate Taux brut de natalité	Code[a]	Deaths Décès — Number Nombre	Crude death rate Taux brut de mortalité	Rate of natural increase Taux d'accroissement naturel	Code[a]	Infant deaths Décès d'enfants de moins d'un an — Number Nombre	Rate (per 1000 births) Taux (par 1000 naissances)	Expectation of life at birth Espérance de vie à la naissance — Male[b] Masculin[b]	Female[b] Féminin[b]	Total fertility rate L'indice synthétique de fécondité
ASIA - ASIE													
Yemen - Yémen													
2006	U	298 437	...	U	21 456	...	...		...	...	...	...	...
2007	U	256 288	...	U	24 449	...	...		...	...	...	...	...
EUROPE													
Åland Islands - Îles d'Åland[59]													
2003	C	262	10.0	C	268	10.2	-0.2	C	2	...	77.3	84.1	1.640
2004	C	281	10.6	C	262	9.9	0.7	C	1	...	76.1	84.0	1.752
2005	C	268	10.1	C	259	9.7	0.3	C	-	...	78.8	81.1	1.717
2006	C	295	11.0	C	257	9.6	1.4	C	-	...	...	...	1.717
2007	C	286	10.6	C	249	9.2	1.4	C	-	...	...	...	1.867
Albania - Albanie													
2003	C	47 012	15.1	C	17 967	5.8	9.3	C	395	8.4	...	...	1.980
2004	C	43 022	13.8	C	17 749	5.7	8.1	C	336	7.8	72.5	77.3	1.800
2005	C	39 612	12.6	C	17 427	5.5	7.1	C	303	7.6	...	...	1.600
2006	C	34 229	10.9	C	16 935	5.4	5.5	C	253	7.4	...	...	1.400
2007	C	33 163	10.5	C	14 528	4.6	5.9	C	205	6.2	...	...	...
Andorra - Andorre													
2003	C	721	10.3	C	221	3.2	7.2	C	-	...	...	...	1.190
2004	C	814	10.9	C	281	3.8	7.1	C	2	...	...	...	1.210
2005	C	828	10.5	C	276	3.5	7.0	C	5	...	...	...	1.231
2006	C	843	10.5	C	260	3.2	7.3	C	3	...	...	...	1.226
2007	C	826	10.0	C	230	2.8	7.2	C	1	...	...	...	1.170
Austria - Autriche													
2003	C	76 944	9.5	C	77 209	9.5	0.0	C	343	4.5	75.9	81.6	1.378
2004	C	78 968	9.7	C	74 292	9.1	0.6	C	353	4.5	76.4	82.1	1.419
2005	C	78 190	9.5	C	75 189	9.1	0.4	C	327	4.2	75.5	81.5	1.407
2006	C	77 914	9.4	C	74 295	9.0	0.4	C	281	3.6	75.5	81.5	1.405
2007	C	76 250	9.2	C	74 625	9.0	0.2	C	280	3.7	...	...	1.379
Belarus - Bélarus													
2003	C	88 512[28]	9.0	C	143 200[28]	14.5	-5.5	C	685[28]	7.7	62.7	74.7	1.206
2004	C	88 943[28]	9.1	C	140 064[28]	14.3	-5.2	C	614[28]	6.9	63.2	75.0	1.201
2005	C	90 508[28]	9.3	C	141 857[28]	14.5	-5.3	C	640[28]	7.1	...	...	1.210
2006	C	96 721[28]	9.9	C	138 426[28]	14.2	-4.3	C	587[28]	6.1	63.6	75.5	1.287
2007	C	103 626[28]	10.7	C	132 993[28]	13.7	-3.0	C	534[28]	5.2	64.5	76.2	1.373
Belgium - Belgique													
2003	C	112 149[60]	10.8	C	107 039[60]	10.3	0.5	C	462[60]	4.1	...	...	...
2004	C	115 618[60]	11.1	C	101 946[60]	9.8	1.3	C	437[60]	3.8	76.5	82.4	...
2005	C	118 002[60]	11.3	C	103 278[60]	9.9	1.4	C	441[60]	3.7	...	...	...
2006	C	121 382[60]	11.5	C	101 587[60]	9.6	1.9	C	489[60]	4.0	77.0	82.7	...
2007	C	120 663[60]	11.4	C	100 658[60]	9.5	1.9	C	487[60]	4.0	...	...	1.805
Bosnia and Herzegovina - Bosnie-Herzégovine													
2003	C	35 234	9.2	C	31 757	8.3	0.9	C	268	7.6	71.3	76.7	1.215
2004	C	35 151	9.1	C	32 616	8.5	0.7	C	253	7.2	...	...	1.217
2005	C	34 627	9.0	C	34 402	9.0	0.1	C	233	6.7	...	...	1.214
2006	C	34 033	8.9	C	33 221	8.6	0.2	C	255	7.5	...	...	1.176
2007	C	33 835	...	C	35 044	...	...	C	231	6.8	...	...	1.174
Bulgaria - Bulgarie													
2003	C	67 359	8.6	C	111 927	14.3	-5.7	C	831	12.3	[III]68.7	75.6	1.232
2004	C	69 886	9.0	C	110 110	14.2	-5.2	C	814	11.6	[III]69.1	76.2	1.285
2005	C	71 075	9.2	C	113 374	14.6	-5.5	C	739	10.4	[III]69.0	76.3	1.310
2006	C	73 978	9.6	C	113 438	14.7	-5.1	C	720	9.7	[III]69.1	76.3	1.377
2007	C	75 349	9.8	C	113 004	14.8	-4.9	C	690	9.2	[III]69.2	76.3	1.416

85

4. Vital statistics summary and expectation of life at birth: 2003 - 2007
Aperçu des statistiques de l'état civil et espérance de vie à la naissance: 2003 - 2007 (continued - suite)

Continent, country or area and year / Continent, pays ou zone et année	Code[a] / Code[a]	Live births / Naissances vivantes Number / Nombre	Crude birth rate Taux brut de natalité	Code[a] / Code[a]	Deaths / Décès Number / Nombre	Crude death rate Taux brut de mortalité	Rate of natural increase Taux d'accrois-sement naturel	Code[a] / Code[a]	Infant deaths / Décès d'enfants de moins d'un an Number / Nombre	Rate (per 1000 births) Taux (par 1000 naiss-ances)	Expectation of life at birth / Espérance de vie à la naissance Male[b] / Masculin[b]	Female[b] / Féminin[b]	Total fertility rate L'indice synthétique de fécondité
EUROPE													
Croatia - Croatie													
2003	C	39 668	8.9	C	52 575	11.8	-2.9	C	251	6.3	...	...	1.327
2004	C	40 307	9.1	C	49 756	11.2	-2.1	C	245	6.1	...	...	1.346
2005	C	42 492	9.6	C	51 790	11.7	-2.1	C	242	5.7	...	...	1.420
2006	C	41 446	9.3	C	50 378	11.3	-2.0	C	215	5.2	...	...	1.381
2007	C	41 910	9.4	C	52 367	11.8	-2.4	C	234	5.6	...	...	1.401
Czech Republic - République tchèque													
2003	C	93 685	9.2	C	111 288	10.9	-1.7	C	365	3.9	72.0	78.5	1.179
2004	C	97 664	9.6	C	107 177	10.5	-0.9	C	366	3.7	72.5	79.0	1.226
2005	C	102 211	10.0	C	107 938	10.5	-0.6	C	347	3.4	72.9	79.1	1.282
2006	C	105 831	10.3	C	104 441	10.2	0.1	C	352	3.3	73.4	79.7	1.328
2007	C	114 632	11.1	C	104 636	10.1	1.0	C	360	3.1	73.7	79.9	1.438
Denmark - Danemark[61]													
2003	C	64 599	12.0	C	57 574	10.7	1.3	C	286	4.4	‖74.9	79.5	1.758
2004	C	64 609	12.0	C	55 806	10.3	1.6	C	283	4.4	‖75.2	79.9	1.784
2005	C	64 282	11.9	C	54 962	10.1	1.7	C	280	4.4	‖75.6	80.2	1.799
2006	C	64 984	12.0	C	55 477	10.2	1.7	C	250	3.8	‖75.9	80.4	1.850
2007	C	64 082	11.7	C	55 604	10.2	1.6	C	256	4.0	‖75.9	80.5	1.846
Estonia - Estonie													
2003	C	13 036	9.6	C	18 152	13.4	-3.8	C	91	...	66.1	77.1	1.371
2004	C	13 992	10.4	C	17 685	13.1	-2.7	C	90	...	66.4	77.8	1.465
2005	C	14 350	10.7	C	17 316	12.9	-2.2	C	78	...	67.2	78.1	1.497
2006	C	14 877	11.1	C	17 316	12.9	-1.8	C	66	...	67.4	78.5	1.545
2007	C	15 775	11.8	C	17 409	13.0	-1.2	C	79	...	...	...	1.638
Faeroe Islands - Îles Féroé													
2003	C	705	14.7	C	404	8.4	6.3		...	...	...	...	2.524
2004	C	713	14.8	C	379	7.9	6.9		...	...	...	...	2.584
2005	C	712	14.8	C	419	8.7	6.1		...	...	...	...	2.622
2006	C	661	13.7	C	416	8.6	5.1		...	...	...	...	2.480
2007	C	674	14.0	C	383	7.9	6.0		...	...	...	...	2.533
Finland - Finlande[62]													
2003	C	56 630[63]	10.9	C	48 996[63]	9.4	1.5	C	176[63]	3.1	75.1	81.8	1.760
2004	C	57 758[63]	11.0	C	47 600[63]	9.1	1.9	C	191[63]	3.3	75.3	82.3	1.800
2005	C	57 745[63]	11.0	C	47 928[63]	9.1	1.9	C	174[63]	3.0	75.5	82.3	1.803
2006	C	58 840[63]	11.2	C	48 065[63]	9.1	2.0	C	167[63]	2.8	75.8	82.8	1.837
2007	C	58 729[63]	11.1	C	49 077[63]	9.3	1.8	C	161[63]	2.7	75.8	82.9	1.829
France[64]													
2003	C	761 464[65]	12.6	C	552 339[65]	9.2	3.5	C	3 053[65]	4.0	75.9	82.9	1.875
2004	C	767 816[65]	12.7	C	509 429[65]	8.4	4.3	C	2 988[65]	3.9	76.7	83.8	1.897
2005	C	774 355[65]	12.7	C	527 533[65]	8.6	4.0	C	2 775[65]	3.6	76.8	83.8	1.921
2006	C	796 896[65]	13.0	C	516 416[65]	8.4	4.6	C	2 906[65]	3.6	77.2	84.2	1.983
2007	C	785 985[65]	12.7	C*	516 000[65]	8.4	4.4		...	...	...	...	1.956
Germany - Allemagne													
2003	C	706 721	8.6	C	853 946	10.3	-1.8	C	2 990	4.2	75.8	81.3	1.340
2004	C	705 622	8.6	C	818 271	9.9	-1.4	C	2 918	4.1	‖‖75.9	81.5	1.355
2005	C	685 795	8.3	C	830 227	10.1	-1.8	C	2 696	3.9	‖‖76.2	81.8	1.340
2006	C	672 724	8.2	C	821 627	10.0	-1.8	C	2 579	3.8	‖‖76.6	82.1	1.331
2007	C	684 862	8.3	C	827 155	10.1	-1.7	C	2 656	3.9	‖‖76.9	82.3	1.370
Gibraltar													
2003	+C	372[66]	13.0	C	234[66]	8.2	4.8	C	2	...	...	...	...
2004	+C	421[66]	14.7	C	242[66]	8.4	6.2	C	...	...	...	...	...
2005	+C	418[66]	14.5	C	249[66]	8.6	5.9	C	1	...	...	...	...
2006	+C	373[66]	12.8	C	230[66]	7.9	4.9	C	1	...	...	...	...
2007	+C	400[66]	13.7		...	...	...		...	...	...	...	...
Greece - Grèce													
2003	C	104 420	9.5	C	105 529	9.6	-0.1	C	420	4.0	76.5	81.3	1.288
2004	C	105 655	9.6	C	104 942	9.5	0.1	C	429	4.1	76.6	81.3	1.300
2005	C	107 545	9.7	C	105 091	9.5	0.2	C	409	3.8	76.8	81.7	1.338

86

Continent, country or area and year / Continent, pays ou zone et année	Code[a]	Live births / Naissances vivantes Number / Nombre	Crude birth rate Taux brut de natalité	Code[a]	Deaths / Décès Number / Nombre	Crude death rate Taux brut de mortalité	Rate of natural increase Taux d'accroissement naturel	Code[a]	Infant deaths / Décès d'enfants de moins d'un an Number / Nombre	Rate (per 1000 births) Taux (par 1000 naissances)	Expectation of life at birth / Espérance de vie à la naissance Male[b] / Masculin[b]	Female[b] / Féminin[b]	Total fertility rate L'indice synthétique de fécondité
EUROPE													
Greece - Grèce													
2006	C	112 042	10.0	C	105 476	9.5	0.6	C	415	3.7	77.1	82.0	1.410
2007	C	111 926	10.0	C	109 895	9.8	0.2	C	397	3.5	77.0	82.0	1.417
Guernsey - Guernesey													
2003	C	650	...	C	564	...	...		...	...	...	...	...
2004	C	586	9.7	C	537	8.9	0.8		...	...	...	...	...
2005	C	638	...	C	525	...	...		...	...	...	...	...
2006	C	598	9.8	C	498	8.2	1.6		...	...	...	...	...
2007	C	645	10.4	C	513	8.3	2.1		...	...	...	...	...
Hungary - Hongrie													
2003	C	94 647	9.3	C	135 823	13.4	-4.1	C	690	7.3	68.3	76.5	1.276[67]
2004	C	95 137	9.4	C	132 492	13.1	-3.7	C	628	6.6	68.6	76.9	1.285[67]
2005	C	97 496	9.7	C	135 732	13.5	-3.8	C	607	6.2	68.6	76.9	1.317[67]
2006	C	99 871	9.9	C	131 603	13.1	-3.2	C	571	5.7	69.0	77.4	1.350[67]
2007	C	97 613	9.7	C	132 938	13.2	-3.5	C	577	5.9	69.2	77.3	1.323[67]
Iceland - Islande													
2003	C	4 143	14.3	C	1 827	6.3	8.0	C	10	...	II79.0	82.4	1.990
2004	C	4 234	14.5	C	1 824	6.2	8.2	C	12	...	78.9	83.2	2.033
2005	C	4 280	14.5	C	1 838	6.2	8.3	C	10	...	II79.2	83.3	2.052
2006	C	4 415	14.5	C	1 903	6.3	8.3	C	6	...	II79.4	83.0	2.074
2007	C	4 560	14.6	C	1 942	6.2	8.4	C	9	...	II79.4	82.9	2.102
Ireland - Irlande													
2003	C	61 529[68]	15.5[68]	C	29 074[68]	7.3[68]	8.2	C	326[68]	5.3[68]	...	...	1.980
2004	C	61 972[68]	15.3[68]	C	28 665[68]	7.1[68]	8.2	C	287[68]	4.6[68]	...	...	1.950
2005	C	61 372[68]	14.9[68]	C	28 260[68]	6.8[68]	8.0	+C*	244	4.0	...	...	1.882
2006	+C*	64 237	15.2	+C*	27 479	6.5	8.7	+C*	237	3.7	...	...	1.905
2007	+C*	70 620	16.3	+C*	28 050	6.5	9.8		...	...	...	...	2.030
Isle of Man - Île de Man													
2003	+C	860	11.1	+C	852	11.0	0.1	+C	6	...	...	...	...
2004	+C	862	11.1	+C	798	10.3	0.8	+C	2	...	...	...	...
2005	+C	901	11.4	+C	775	9.8	1.6	+C	1	...	...	...	...
2006	+C	905	11.3	+C	768	9.6	1.7		...	...	...	...	...
2007	+C	919	11.4	+C	789	9.8	1.6		...	...	...	...	...
Italy - Italie													
2003	C	544 063	9.4	C	588 897	10.2	-0.8	C	2 134	3.9	77.2	82.8	1.285
2004	C	562 599	9.7	C	545 050	9.4	0.3	C	2 168	3.9	77.9	83.7	1.334
2005	C	554 022	9.5	C	568 328	9.7	-0.2	C	2 108	3.8	78.1	83.7	1.319
2006	C	560 010	9.5	C*	560 875	9.5	0.0	C*	2 112	3.8	...	...	1.352
2007	C	563 933	9.5	C*	573 026	9.7	-0.2	C*	2 085	3.7	...	...	1.374
Jersey													
2003	+C	1 009[18]	11.5	+C	768	8.8	2.8		...	...	...	...	1.508
2004	+C	973[18]	11.1	+C	745	8.5	2.6		...	...	...	...	1.497
2005	+C	970[18]	11.0	+C	761	8.6	2.4		...	...	...	...	1.522
2006	+C	962[18]	10.8	+C	758	8.5	2.3		...	...	...	...	1.553
2007	+C	1 031[18]	11.4	+C	708	7.9	3.6		...	...	...	...	1.679
Latvia - Lettonie													
2003	C	21 006	9.0	C	32 437	13.9	-4.9	C	198	9.4	65.9	76.9	1.290
2004	C	20 334	8.8	C	32 024	13.8	-5.1	C	191	9.4	67.1	77.2	1.240
2005	C	21 497	9.3	C	32 777	14.2	-4.9	C	168	7.8	65.6	77.4	1.309
2006	C	22 264	9.7	C	33 098	14.5	-4.7	C	170	7.6	65.9	76.8	1.353
2007	C	23 273	10.2	C	33 042	14.5	-4.3	C	203	8.7	65.8	76.5	1.412
Liechtenstein													
2003	C	347	10.2	C	217	6.4	3.8	C	1	...	...	...	1.357
2004	C	372	10.8	C	198	5.7	5.0	C	1	...	...	...	1.458
2005	C	381	11.0	C	215	6.2	4.8	C	1	...	...	...	1.510
2006	C	361	10.3	C	220	6.3	4.0	C	2	...	...	...	1.400
2007	C*	351	9.9	C*	227	6.4	3.5	C*	-	...	...	...	1.400
Lithuania - Lituanie													
2003	C	30 598	8.9	C	40 990	11.9	-3.0	C	206[28]	6.7	66.5	77.8	1.262
2004	C	30 419	8.9	C	41 340	12.0	-3.2	C	240[28]	7.9	66.4	77.7	1.260

87

4. Vital statistics summary and expectation of life at birth: 2003 - 2007
Aperçu des statistiques de l'état civil et espérance de vie à la naissance: 2003 - 2007 (continued - suite)

Continent, country or area and year / Continent, pays ou zone et année	Code[a]	Live births Number Nombre	Live births Crude birth rate Taux brut de natalité	Code[a]	Deaths Number Nombre	Deaths Crude death rate Taux brut de mortalité	Rate of natural increase Taux d'accrois-sement naturel	Code[a]	Infant deaths Number Nombre	Infant deaths Rate (per 1000 births) Taux (par 1000 naiss-ances)	Expectation of life at birth Male[b] Masculin[b]	Expectation of life at birth Female[b] Féminin[b]	Total fertility rate L'indice synthétique de fécondité
EUROPE													
Lithuania - Lituanie													
2005	C	30 541	8.9	C	43 799	12.8	-3.9	C	209[28]	6.8	65.4	77.4	1.272
2006	C	31 265	9.2	C	44 813	13.2	-4.0	C	213[28]	6.8	65.3	77.1	1.306
2007	C	32 346	9.6	C	45 624	13.5	-3.9	C	190[28]	5.9	64.9	77.2	1.353
Luxembourg													
2003	C	5 303	11.7	C	4 053	9.0	2.8	C	26	...	...	...	1.634
2004	C	5 452	11.9	C	3 578	7.8	4.1	C	21	...	...	...	1.656
2005	C	5 371	11.5	C	3 621	7.8	3.8	C	14	...	...	...	1.624
2006	C	5 514	11.7	C	3 766	8.0	3.7	C	14	...	...	...	1.644
2007	C	5 477	11.4	C	3 866	8.1	3.4	C	10	...	[III]77.6	82.7	1.607
Malta - Malte													
2003	C	4 050	10.2	C	3 164	7.9	2.2	C	23	...	76.4	80.4	1.480
2004	C	3 887	9.7	C	2 999	7.5	2.2	C	23	...	76.7	80.5	1.370
2005	C	3 858	9.6	C	3 130	7.8	1.8	C	23	...	77.7	81.4	1.370
2006	C	3 885	9.6	C	3 216	7.9	1.6	C	14	...	76.8	81.2	1.410
2007	C	3 871	9.5	C	3 111	7.6	1.9	C	25	...	77.2	81.7	1.370
Monaco													
2003	C	842	...	C	617	...	...		...	...	...	...	...
2004	C	825	...	C	525	...	...		...	...	...	...	...
2005	C	894	...	C	601	...	...		...	...	...	...	...
2006	C	880[69]	...	C	535[69]	...	...		...	...	...	...	...
Montenegro - Monténégro													
2003	C	8 342	13.4	C	5 704	9.2	4.3	C	92	...	...	...	1.830
2004	C	7 848	12.6	C	5 707	9.2	3.4	C	61	...	...	...	1.710
2005	C	7 352	11.8	C	5 839	9.4	2.4	C	70	...	...	...	1.600
2006	C	7 531	12.1	C	5 968	9.6	2.5	C	83	...	...	...	1.640
2007	C	7 834	12.5	C	5 979	9.5	3.0	C	58	...	...	...	1.690
Netherlands - Pays-Bas													
2003	C	200 297[70]	12.3	C	141 936[70]	8.7	3.6	C	962[70]	4.8	76.2	80.9	1.747
2004	C	194 007[70]	11.9	C	136 553[70]	8.4	3.5	C	852[70]	4.4	76.9	81.4	1.726
2005	C	187 910[70]	11.5	C	136 402[70]	8.4	3.2	C	928[70]	4.9	77.2	81.6	1.708
2006	C	185 057[70]	11.3	C	135 372[70]	8.3	3.0	C	820[70]	4.4	77.4	81.7	1.720
2007	C	181 336[70]	11.1	C	133 022[70]	8.1	2.9	C	736[70]	4.1	78.0	82.3	1.718
Norway - Norvège[71]													
2003	C	56 458	12.4	C	42 478[72]	9.3	3.1	C	190[72]	3.4	77.0	81.9	1.797
2004	C	56 951	12.4	C	41 200[72]	9.0	3.4	C	185[72]	3.2	77.5	82.3	1.828
2005	C	56 756	12.3	C	41 232[72]	8.9	3.4	C	175[72]	3.1	77.7	82.5	1.836
2006	C	58 545	12.6	C	41 253[72]	8.9	3.7	C	185[72]	3.2	78.1	82.7	1.904
2007	C	58 459	12.4	C	41 954[72]	8.9	3.5	C	180[72]	3.1	78.2	82.7	1.900
Poland - Pologne													
2003	C	351 072	9.2	C	365 230	9.6	-0.4	C	2 470	7.0	70.5	78.9	1.222
2004	C	356 131	9.3	C	363 522	9.5	-0.2	C	2 423	6.8	70.7	79.2	1.227
2005	C	364 383	9.5	C	368 285	9.7	-0.1	C	2 340	6.4	70.8	79.4	1.243
2006	C	374 244	9.8	C	369 686	9.7	0.1	C	2 238	6.0	70.4	79.0	1.267
2007	C	387 873	10.2	C	377 226	9.9	0.3	C	2 322	6.0	71.0	79.7	1.306
Portugal													
2003	C	112 515[18]	10.8	C	108 795[19]	10.4	0.4	C	466[19]	4.1	[II]73.7	80.6	1.444
2004	C	109 298[18]	10.4	C	102 010[19]	9.7	0.7	C	418[19]	3.8	[II]74.5	81.0	1.403
2005	C	109 399[18]	10.4	C	107 462[19]	10.2	0.2	C	382[19]	3.5	[II]74.9	81.4	1.408
2006	C	105 449[18]	10.0	C	101 990[19]	9.6	0.3	C	349[19]	3.3	[II]75.2	81.8	1.362
2007	C	102 492[18]	9.7	C	103 512[19]	9.8	-0.1	C	353[19]	3.4	[III]75.2	81.6	1.335
Republic of Moldova - République de Moldova													
2003	C	36 471[73]	10.1	C	43 079[73]	11.9	-1.8	C	522[73]	14.3	64.5	71.6	1.219
2004	C	38 272[73]	10.6	C	41 668[73]	11.6	-0.9	C	464[73]	12.1	64.5	72.2	1.257
2005	C	37 695[73]	10.5	C	44 689[73]	12.4	-1.9	C	468[73]	12.4	...	...	1.219
2006	C	37 587[73]	10.5	C	43 137[73]	12.0	-1.5	C	442[73]	11.8	64.6	72.2	1.229
2007	C	37 973[73]	10.6	C	43 050[73]	12.0	-1.4	C	428[73]	11.3	65.0	72.6	1.256

4. Vital statistics summary and expectation of life at birth: 2003 - 2007
Aperçu des statistiques de l'état civil et espérance de vie à la naissance: 2003 - 2007 (continued - suite)

Continent, country or area and year / Continent, pays ou zone et année	Code[a]	Live births Naissances vivantes — Number Nombre	Crude birth rate Taux brut de natalité	Code[a]	Deaths Décès — Number Nombre	Crude death rate Taux brut de mortalité	Rate of natural increase Taux d'accrois-sement naturel	Code[a]	Infant deaths Décès d'enfants de moins d'un an — Number Nombre	Rate (per 1000 births) Taux (par 1000 naiss-ances)	Expectation of life at birth — Male[b] Masculin[b]	Female[b] Féminin[b]	Total fertility rate L'indice synthétique de fécondité
EUROPE													
Romania - Roumanie													
2003	C	212 459	9.8	C	266 575	12.3	-2.5	C	3 546	16.7	67.4	74.8	1.270
2004	C	216 261	10.0	C	258 890	11.9	-2.0	C	3 641	16.8	...	...	1.291
2005	C	221 020	10.2	C	262 101	12.1	-1.9	C	3 310	15.0	68.2	75.5	1.319
2006	C	219 483	10.2	C	258 094	12.0	-1.8	C	3 052	13.9	[III]68.7	75.8	1.313
2007	C	214 728	10.0	C	251 965	11.7	-1.7	C	2 574	12.0	[III]69.2	76.1	1.293
Russian Federation - Fédération de Russie													
2003	C	1 477 301[28]	10.2	C	2 365 826[28]	16.4	-6.1	C	18 142[28]	12.3	58.6	71.8	1.319
2004	C	1 502 477[28]	10.4	C	2 295 402[28]	16.0	-5.5	C	17 339[28]	11.5	58.9	72.3	1.340
2005	C	1 457 376[28]	10.2	C	2 303 935[28]	16.1	-5.9	C	16 073[28]	11.0	58.9	72.4	1.287
2006	C	1 479 637[28]	10.4	C	2 166 703[28]	15.2	-4.8	C	15 079[28]	10.2	60.4	73.2	1.296
2007	C	1 610 122[28]	11.3	C	2 080 445[28]	14.6	-3.3	C	14 858[28]	9.2	61.4	73.9	1.406
San Marino - Saint-Marin													
2003	+C	300	10.3	+C	216	7.5	2.9	+C	2	...	...	...	1.250
2004	+C	306	10.4	+C	185	6.3	4.1	+C	1	...	...	...	1.255
2005	+C	284	9.2	+C	219	7.1	2.1	+C	-	...	...	...	...
2006	+C	302	9.6	+C	225	7.2	2.5	+C	-	...	...	...	...
2007	+C	292	9.2	+C	225	7.1	2.1	+C	...	...	...	...	...
Serbia - Serbie													
2003	+C	79 025[74]	10.6	+C	103 946[74]	13.9	-3.3	+C	711[74]	9.0	[III]69.6	75.0	1.591
2004	+C	78 186[74]	10.5	+C	104 320[74]	14.0	-3.5	+C	633[74]	8.1	...	...	1.575
2005	+C	72 180[74]	9.7	+C	106 771[74]	14.3	-4.6	+C	579[74]	8.0	69.9	75.4	1.453
2006	+C	70 997[74]	9.6	+C	102 884[74]	13.9	-4.3	+C	525[74]	7.4	70.6	75.9	1.432
2007	+C	68 102[74]	9.2	+C	102 805[74]	13.9	-4.7	+C	484[74]	7.1	70.7	76.2	1.379
Slovakia - Slovaquie													
2003	C	51 713	9.6	C	52 230	9.7	-0.1	C	406	7.9	69.8	77.6	1.199
2004	C	53 747	10.0	C	51 852	9.6	0.4	C	365	6.8	70.3	77.8	1.241
2005	C	54 430	10.1	C	53 475	9.9	0.2	C	392	7.2	70.1	77.9	1.253
2006	C	53 904	10.0	C	53 301	9.9	0.1	C	355	6.6	70.4	78.2	1.239
2007	C	54 424	10.1	C	53 856	10.0	0.1	C	334	6.1	70.5	78.1	1.251
Slovenia - Slovénie													
2003	C	17 321	8.7	C	19 451	9.7	-1.1	C	69	...	72.5	80.3	1.202
2004	C	17 961	9.0	C	18 523	9.3	-0.3	C	66	...	[II]73.5	81.1	1.247
2005	C	18 157	9.1	C	18 825	9.4	-0.3	C	75	...	[II]74.1	81.3	1.262
2006	C	18 932	9.4	C	18 180	9.1	0.4	C	64	...	[II]74.8	81.9	1.314
2007	C	19 823	9.8	C	18 584	9.2	0.6	C	55	...	[II]75.0	82.3	1.380
Spain - Espagne													
2003	C	441 881	10.5	C	384 828	9.2	1.4	C	1 733	3.9	...	...	1.310
2004	C	454 591	10.6	C	371 934	8.7	1.9	C	1 813	4.0	[II]76.7	83.2	1.329
2005	C	466 371	10.7	C	387 355	8.9	1.8	C	1 765	3.8	[II]77.0	83.5	1.346
2006	C	481 102	10.9	C	371 267	8.4	2.5	C	1 812	3.8	...	...	1.373
2007	C	493 702	11.0	C	385 122	8.6	2.4	C	1 704	3.5	...	...	1.400
Sweden - Suède													
2003	C	99 157	11.1	C	92 961	10.4	0.7	C	308	3.1	77.9	82.4	1.720
2004	C	100 928	11.2	C	90 532	10.1	1.2	C	314	3.1	78.4	82.7	1.752
2005	C	101 346	11.2	C	91 710	10.2	1.1	C	246	2.4	78.4	82.8	1.769
2006	C	105 913	11.7	C	91 177	10.0	1.6	C	297	2.8	78.7	82.9	1.853
2007	C	107 421	11.7	C	91 729	10.0	1.7	C	268	2.5	78.9	83.0	1.879
Switzerland - Suisse													
2003	C	71 848	9.8	C	63 070	8.6	1.2	C	311	4.3	77.9	83.0	1.385
2004	C	73 082	9.9	C	60 180	8.1	1.7	C	309	4.2	78.2	83.3	1.416
2005	C	72 903	9.8	C	61 124	8.2	1.6	C	308	4.2	[II]78.6	83.7	1.420
2006	C	73 371	9.8	C	60 283	8.1	1.7	C	325	4.4	[II]78.9	83.9	1.437
2007	C	74 494	9.9	C	61 089	8.1	1.8	C	293	3.9	79.2	84.1	1.460

Continent, country or area and year / Continent, pays ou zone et année	Live births / Naissances vivantes			Deaths / Décès			Rate of natural increase / Taux d'accroissement naturel	Infant deaths / Décès d'enfants de moins d'un an			Expectation of life at birth / Espérance de vie à la naissance		Total fertility rate / L'indice synthétique de fécondité
	Code[a]	Number Nombre	Crude birth rate Taux brut de natalité	Code[a]	Number Nombre	Crude death rate Taux brut de mortalité		Code[a]	Number Nombre	Rate (per 1000 births) Taux (par 1000 naissances)	Male[b] Masculin[b]	Female[b] Féminin[b]	
EUROPE													
The Former Yugoslav Republic of Macedonia - L'ex-République yougoslave de Macédoine													
2003	C	27 011	13.3	C	18 006	8.9	4.4	C	305	11.3	71.1	75.7	1.540
2004	C	23 361	11.5	C	17 944	8.8	2.7	C	308	13.2	71.4	75.9	1.520
2005	C	22 482	11.0	C	18 406	9.0	2.0	C	287	12.8	71.6	75.9	1.457
2006	C	22 585	11.1	C	18 630	9.1	1.9	C	260	11.5	71.7	75.9	1.460
2007	C	22 688	11.1	C	19 594	9.6	1.5	C	234	10.3	...	...	1.458
Ukraine													
2003	C	408 589[28]	8.5	C	765 408[28]	16.0	-7.5	C	3 882[28]	9.5	II62.6	74.1	1.147
2004	C	427 259[28]	9.0	C	761 261[28]	16.1	-7.1	C	4 024[28]	9.4	II62.6	74.1	1.192[75]
2005	C	426 086[28]	9.1	C	781 961[28]	16.6	-7.6	C	4 259[28]	10.0	...	...	1.211[75]
2006	C	460 368[76]	9.8	C	758 092[77]	16.2	-6.4	C	4 433[77]	9.6	II62.4	74.1	1.254[75]
2007	C	472 657[76]	10.1	C	762 877[77]	16.4	-6.2	C	5 188[77]	11.0	II62.5	74.2	1.300
United Kingdom of Great Britain and Northern Ireland - Royaume-Uni de Grande-Bretagne et d'Irlande du Nord[78]													
2003	C	695 549[79]	11.7	C*	611 188	10.3	1.4	C*	3 686	5.3	...	...	1.710
2004	C	715 996[80]	12.0	C*	584 600	9.8	2.2	C*	3 606	5.0	...	...	1.780
2005	C	722 549[80]	12.0	C*	582 900	9.7	2.3	C*	3 670	5.1	...	...	1.790
2006	C	748 563[80]	12.4	C*	572 200	9.4	2.9	C*	3 740	5.0	...	...	1.840
2007	C	772 245[80]	12.7		...	...	...		...	...	...	...	1.900
OCEANIA - OCÉANIE													
American Samoa - Samoas américaines													
2003	C	1 608	25.7	C	257	4.1	21.6	C	20	...	...	...	...
2004	C	1 713	26.7	C	289	4.5	22.2	C	26	...	...	...	...
2005	C	1 720	26.3	C	279	4.3	22.0	C	12	...	...	...	...
2006	C	1 442	21.6	C	267	4.0	17.6	C	17	...	...	...	...
Australia - Australie													
2003	+C	250 518[81]	12.6	+C	131 848[81]	6.6	6.0	+C	1 195[81]	4.8	III77.8	82.8	1.748
2004	+C	253 652[81]	12.6	+C	132 051[81]	6.6	6.0	+C	1 178[81]	4.6	III78.1	83.0	1.763
2005	+C	259 177[81]	12.7	+C	130 274[81]	6.4	6.3	+C	1 296[81]	5.0	III78.5	83.3	1.791
2006	+C	265 423[81]	12.8	+C	133 273[81]	6.4	6.4	+C	1 247[81]	4.7	...	...	1.817
2007	+C	284 466[81]	13.5	+C	137 372[81]	6.5	7.0	+C	1 171[81]	4.1	III79.0	83.7	1.931
Cook Islands - Îles Cook[82]													
2003	+C	298	16.2	+C	87	4.7	11.5	+C	5	...	...	...	...
2004	+C	295	14.5	+C	99	4.9	9.7	+C	5	...	...	...	...
2005	+C	280	13.9	+C	91	4.5	9.4	+C	6	...	...	...	...
2006	+C*	278	13.4	+C*	85	4.1	9.3	+C*	3	...	...	...	...
2007	+C*	287	13.6	+C*	82	3.9	9.7	+C*	3	...	...	...	...
Fiji - Fidji													
2003	+C	17 701	21.7	+C	5 068	6.2	15.5	+C	304	17.2	...	...	2.600
2004	+C	17 189	20.9	+C	5 628	6.9	14.1	+C	338	19.7	...	...	...
2005	+C	17 826	21.6	+C	...	...	...		...	...	...	...	...
2006	+C	18 394	22.2	+C	...	...	...		...	...	...	...	...
2007	+C	19 298	23.1		...	...	...		...	...	...	...	...
French Polynesia - Polynésie française													
2003	C	4 501	18.2	C	1 122	4.5	13.7	C	31	...	70.9	76.3	...
2004	C	4 431	17.7	C	1 131	4.5	13.2	C	20	...	71.5	76.7	...
2005	C	4 467	17.7	C	1 239	4.9	12.8	C	28	...	71.4	76.4	...

Continent, country or area and year / Continent, pays ou zone et année	Live births / Naissances vivantes			Code[a]	Deaths / Décès		Rate of natural increase / Taux d'accrois-sement naturel	Code[a]	Infant deaths / Décès d'enfants de moins d'un an		Expectation of life at birth / Espérance de vie à la naissance		Total fertility rate / L'indice synthétique de fécondité
	Code[a]	Number / Nombre	Crude birth rate / Taux brut de natalité		Number / Nombre	Crude death rate / Taux brut de mortalité			Number / Nombre	Rate (per 1000 births) / Taux (par 1000 naiss-ances)	Male[b] / Masculin[b]	Female[b] / Féminin[b]	
OCEANIA - OCÉANIE													
French Polynesia - Polynésie française													
2006	C	4 592	17.9	C	1 152	4.5	13.4	C	31	...	73.0	76.9	...
2007	C	4 434	17.1	C	1 215	4.7	12.4	C	30	...	...	...	...
Guam													
2003	C	3 298[83]	19.8	C	700[83]	4.2	15.6	C	37[83]	...	74.8	81.0	2.700
2004	C	3 427[83]	20.6	C	691[83]	4.2	16.5	C	42[83]	...	75.1	81.3	...
2005	C*	3 203[83]	19.0	C*	697[83]	4.1	14.9		...	...	...	...	...
2006	C*	3 414[83]	20.0	C*	682[83]	4.0	16.0		...	...	...	...	...
2007	C*	3 501[83]	20.2	C*	786[83]	4.5	15.7		...	...	...	...	...
Kiribati													
2005		...	...		...	...	...		...	...	58.9	63.1	...
Marshall Islands - Îles Marshall													
2003	+U	1 565[84]	...	+U	306	...	...		...	...	...	...	...
2004	+U	1 512[84]	...	+U	263	...	...		...	...	66.8	70.4	...
2005	+U	1 589[84]	...	+U	302	...	...		...	...	67.0	70.6	...
2006	+U	1 576[84]	...	+U	318	...	...		...	...	...	...	...
Micronesia (Federated States of) - Micronésie (États fédérés de)													
2003	U	2 483	...	U	427	...	...		...	...	...	...	...
New Caledonia - Nouvelle-Calédonie													
2003	C	4 102	18.2	C	1 121	5.0	13.2	C	24	...	71.3	77.3	2.270
2004	C	4 006	17.4	C	1 100	4.8	12.6	C	25	...	72.1	79.1	2.180
2005	C	4 035	17.2	C	1 139	4.9	12.4		...	...	71.9	78.6	2.200
2006	C	4 224	17.7	C	1 115	4.7	13.0		...	...	72.9	80.2	2.290
2007	C	4 093	16.9	C	1 207	5.0	11.9	C	25	...	71.8	80.3	2.200
New Zealand - Nouvelle-Zélande													
2003	+C	56 134	13.9	+C	28 010[19]	7.0	7.0	+C	277[19]	4.9	III76.7	81.2	1.932
2004	+C	58 073	14.2	+C	28 419[19]	7.0	7.3	+C	324[19]	5.6	III77.0	81.3	1.983
2005	+C	57 745	14.0	+C	27 034[19]	6.5	7.4	+C	295[19]	5.1	III77.5	81.7	1.965
2006	+C	59 193	14.1	+C	28 245[19]	6.7	7.4	+C	300[19]	5.1	III77.9	81.9	2.007
2007	+C	64 044	15.1	+C	28 522[19]	6.7	8.4	+C	317[19]	4.9	III78.0	82.2	2.172
Niue - Nioué													
2003	C	33[85]	19.2	C	16[86]	...	...		...	...	...	...	...
2004	C	18[85]	...	C	18[86]	...	...		...	...	...	...	...
2005	C	23[85]	...	C	15[86]	...	...		...	...	...	...	...
2006	C	35[85]	20.8	C	19[86]	...	...		...	...	...	...	...
2007	C	28[85]	...	C	9[86]	...	...		...	...	...	...	...
Northern Mariana Islands - Îles Mariannes septentrionales													
2003	U	1 355	...	U	144	...	...	U	7	...	...	...	...
2004	U	1 350	...	U	165	...	...	U	12	...	...	...	...
2005	U	1 335	...	U	189	...	...	U	6	...	...	...	...
2006	U	1 422	...	U	174	...	...	U	9	...	...	...	...
2007	U	1 385	...	U	140	...	...	U	6	...	...	...	...
Palau - Palaos													
2003	C	312	15.4	C	136	6.7	8.7	C	2	...	...	...	...
2004	C	259	12.6	C	142	6.9	5.7	C	7	...	...	...	...
2005	C	279	14.0	C	134	6.7	7.3	C	6	...	...	...	...
2006	C	259	12.0	C	144	6.6	5.3	C	2	...	...	...	...

4. Vital statistics summary and expectation of life at birth: 2003 - 2007
Aperçu des statistiques de l'état civil et espérance de vie à la naissance: 2003 - 2007 (continued - suite)

Continent, country or area and year / Continent, pays ou zone et année	Live births - Naissances vivantes Code[a]	Number Nombre	Crude birth rate Taux brut de natalité	Deaths - Décès Code[a]	Number Nombre	Crude death rate Taux brut de mortalité	Rate of natural increase Taux d'accroissement naturel	Infant deaths - Décès d'enfants de moins d'un an Code[a]	Number Nombre	Rate (per 1000 births) Taux (par 1000 naissances)	Expectation of life at birth - Espérance de vie à la naissance Male[b] Masculin[b]	Female[b] Féminin[b]	Total fertility rate L'indice synthétique de fécondité
OCEANIA - OCÉANIE													
Papua New Guinea - Papouasie-Nouvelle-Guinée													
2003	U	*192 817*	...	U	*7 054*	...	...	U	*2 082*	...	...	...	...
Pitcairn													
2007	C	1	...	C	1	...	...	C	-	...	...	...	...
Samoa													
2003	C*	2 070	11.5	U*	*551*	...	...		...	...	...	...	...
2004	C*	1 679	9.2	U*	*547*	...	...		...	...	...	...	...
Tonga													
2003	+C*	2 781	27.4	+C	617	6.1	21.3	+C	34	...	...	...	3.900
2004	+C*	2 628	25.8	+C	559	5.5	20.3	+C*	35	...	...	...	3.400
2005		...	...	+C	543	5.3	...		...	...	67.3	73.0	4.100
2006	+C	2 945	28.6	I	709[8][7]	6.9	21.7		...	...	...	...	3.700
2007		...	...		...	...	...		...	...	...	...	...
Tuvalu													
2003	U	*185*	...	U	*83*	...	...	U	4	...	...	...	...
2004	U	*190*	...	U	*89*	...	...	U	5	...	...	...	...
2005	U	*231*	...	U	*64*	...	...	U	6	...	...	...	...
2006	U	*184*	...	U	*31*	...	...		...	...	...	...	...
Wallis and Futuna Islands - Îles Wallis et Futuna													
2003	C	290	19.4	C	88	5.9	13.5		...	...	...	...	...
2004	C	241	...	C	72	...	...		...	...	...	...	...
2005	C	223	...	C	65	...	...		...	...	...	...	...
2006	C	220	...	C	77	...	...		...	...	...	...	...

FOOTNOTES - NOTES

Italics: data from civil registers which are incomplete or of unknown completeness. -
Italiques: données incomplètes ou dont le degré d'exactitude n'est pas connu, provenant des registres de l'état civil.

* Provisional. -
Données provisoires.

[a]
'Code' indicates the source of data, as follows:
C - Civil registration, estimated over 90% complete
U - Civil registration, estimated less than 90% complete
| - Other source, estimated reliable
+ - Data tabulated by date of registration rather than occurence.
... - Information not available

Le 'Code' indique la source des données, comme suit:
C - Registres de l'état civil considérés complets à 90 p. 100 au moins.
U - Registres de l'état civil qui ne sont pas considérés complets à 90 p. 100 au moins.
| - Autre source, considérée fiable.
+ - Données exploitées selon la date de l'enregistrement et non la date de l'événement.
... - Information non disponible.

[b]
A Roman number in front of the data for males specifiies the range of the reference period of life expectancy for males and females presented on the row. For example, a reference year of 2005 and a range of V years means that the reference period for the life expectancy is 2001 - 2005. The absence of a Roman number means the reference period is one year and the reference period therefore coincides with the reference year.

Un chiffre romain devant la donnée relative aux hommes indique l'étendue de la période de référence concernant l'espérance de vie des hommes et des femmes présentées dans la ligne. Par exemple, une année de référence 2005 et une étendue de V signifie que la période de référence pour l'espérance de vie est 2001-2005. L'absence de chiffre romain signifie que la période de référence est d'un an et donc coïncide avec l'année de référence.

[1] Excluding live-born infants who died before their birth was registered. Data refer to Algerian population only. - Non compris les enfants nés vivants décédés avant l'enregistrement de leur naissance. Les données ne concernent que la population algérienne.
[2] Data refer to the twelve months preceding the census in December. Data refer to mothers aged 15-49. - Les données se rapportent aux douze mois précédant le recensement de décembre. Les données se réfèrent aux mères âgées de 15 à 49 ans.
[3] Data refer to the twelve months preceding the census in December. - Les données se rapportent aux douze mois précédant le recensement de décembre.
[4] Data from civil registration centers of Brazzaville, Pointe-Noire, Dolisie, Nkayi, Mossendijo and Ouesso communes. - Données issues des centres d'enregistrement des faits d'état-civil des communes de Brazzaville, Pointe-Noire, Dolisie, Nkayi, Mossendijo et Ouesso.
[5] Data refer to national projections. - Les données se réfèrent aux projections nationales.
[6] Data refer to projections based on the 1998 population census. - Les données se réfèrent aux projections basées sur le recensement de la population de 1998.
[7] Excluding live-born infants who died before their birth was registered. - Non compris les enfants nés vivants décédés avant l'enregistrement de leur naissance.
[8] Excluding non-residents and foreign service personnel and their dependants. - À l'exclusion des non-résidents et du personnel diplomatique et de leurs charges de famille.
[9] Including Canadian residents temporarily in the United States, but excluding United States residents temporarily in Canada. - Y compris les résidents

canadiens se trouvant temporairement aux Etats-Unis, mais ne comprenant pas les résidents des Etats-Unis se trouvant temporairement au Canada.

[10] Resident births outside the islands are excluded. - Non compris les naissances de résidents hors des îles.

[11] Resident deaths outside the islands are excluded if they are not buried in the islands. - Les décès de résidents hors des îles ne sont pas compris s'ils ne sont pas inhumés dans les îles.

[12] Data are based on a small number of deaths and therefore vary from year to year. - Les données sont basées sur un nombre limité de décès et par conséquent varient d'année en année.

[13] Data refer to national projections for 2005 - 2010. - Les données se rapportent aux prévisions nationales pour 2005-2010.

[14] Data refer to projections based on the 1992 population census. - Les données se réfèrent aux projections basées sur le recensement de la population de 1992.

[15] Source: World Health Organization. - Source : Organisation mondiale de la santé.

[16] Data have been adjusted for underenumeration. - Les données ont été ajustées pour compenser les lacunes du dénombrement.

[17] Data have been adjusted for undercoverage of infant deaths and sudden and violent deaths. - Ajusté pour la sous-estimation de la mortalité infantile, du nombre de morts soudaines et de morts violentes.

[18] Data refer to resident mothers. - Données concernant les mères résidentes.

[19] Data refer to resident population only. - Pour la population résidante seulement.

[20] Data refer to registered events only. - Les données ne concernent que les événements enregistrés.

[21] Excluding Indian jungle population. - Non compris les Indiens de la jungle.

[22] Excluding Indian jungle population. Data as reported by national statistical authorities; they may differ from data presented in other tables. - Non compris les Indiens de la jungle. Les données comme elles ont été déclarées par l'institut national de la statistique; elles peuvent être différentes de celles présentées dans d'autres tableaux.

[23] Excluding nomadic Indian tribes. - Non compris les tribus d'Indiens nomades.

[24] Excluding events registered late. - Non compris les enregistrements tardifs.

[25] Including births to non-resident mothers. - Y compris les naissances chez des mères non résidentes.

[26] Including non-residents. - Y compris les résidents.

[27] Provisional - Données provisoires.

[28] Excluding infants born alive of less than 28 weeks' gestation, of less than 1 000 grams in weight and 35 centimeters in length, who die within seven days of birth. - Non compris les enfants nés vivants après moins de 28 semaines de gestations, pesant moins de 1 000 grammes, mesurant moins de 35 centimètres et décédés dans les sept jours qui ont suivi leur naissance.

[29] Since 16 October 2005 the definition of WHO on livebirths has been put into force in accordance with the 10th revision of the International Classification of Diseases. - Depuis le 16 octobre 2005, la définition de l'OMS concernant les naissances vivantes est en vigueur conformément à la dixième révision de la Classification internationale des maladies.

[30] Rates were obtained by the Sample Vital Registration System of Bangladesh. - Taux obtenus au moyen du Sample Vital Registration System du Bangladesh.

[31] Data refer to the twelve months preceding the census in May. - Les données se rapportent aux douze mois précédant le recensement de mai.

[32] For statistical purposes, the data for China do not include those for the Hong Kong Special Administrative Region (Hong Kong SAR), Macao Special Administrative Region (Macao SAR) and Taiwan province of China. - Pour la présentation des statistiques, les données pour la Chine ne comprennent pas la Région Administrative Spéciale de Hong Kong (Hong Kong RAS), la Région Administrative Spéciale de Macao (Macao RAS) et Taïwan province de Chine.

[33] Data have been estimated on the basis of the annual National Sample Surveys on Population Changes. - Les données ont été estimées sur la base de l'enquête annuelle "National Sample Survey on Population Changes".

[34] Data for 2005 are estimated from the National Sample Survey of 1 per cent population. - Les données pour 2005 ont été estimées à partir de l'enquête nationale qui a porté sur un échantillon de 1 % de la population.

[35] The fertility rates have been compiled using a population denominator which has excluded female foreign domestic helpers. - Les taux de fécondité ont été compilés pour une population (en dénominateur) ne comprenant pas les domestiques étrangères.

[36] Data refer to government controlled areas. - Les données se rapportent aux zones contrôlées par le Gouvernement.

[37] Including data for the Indian-held part of Jammu and Kashmir, the final status of which has not yet been determined. - Y compris les données pour la partie du Jammu et du Cachemire occupée par l'Inde dont le statut définitif n'a pas encore été déterminé.

[38] Rates were obtained by the Sample Registration System of India, actually a large demographic survey. - Les taux ont été obtenus par le Système de l'enregistrement par échantillon de l'Inde qui est une large enquête démographique.

[39] Data refer to the Iranian Year which begins on 21 March and ends on 20 March of the following year. - Les données concernent l'année iranienne, qui commence le 21 mars et se termine le 20 mars de l'année suivante.

[40] Including data for East Jerusalem and Israeli residents in certain other territories under occupation by Israeli military forces since June 1967. - Y compris les données pour Jérusalem-Est et les résidents israéliens dans certains autres territoires occupés depuis 1967 par les forces armées israéliennes.

[41] Including 182 deaths abroad of Israeli residents who were out of the country for less than a year. - Y compris les décès à l'étranger de 182 résidents israéliens qui ont quitté le pays depuis moins d'un an.

[42] Including deaths abroad of Israeli residents who were out of the country for less than a year. - Y compris les décès à l'étranger de résidents israéliens qui ont quitté le pays depuis moins d'un an.

[43] Including 183 deaths abroad of Israeli residents who were out of the country for less than a year. - Y compris les décès à l'étranger de 183 résidents israéliens qui ont quitté le pays depuis moins d'un an.

[44] Data refer to Japanese nationals in Japan only. - Les données se raportent aux nationaux japonais au Japon seulement.

[45] Excluding data for Jordanian territory under occupation since June 1967 by Israeli military forces. Excluding foreigners, including registered Palestinian refugees. - Non compris les données pour le territoire jordanien occupé depuis juin 1967 par les forces armées israéliennes. Non compris les étrangers, mais y compris les réfugiés de Palestine enregistrés.

[46] Since 2004, WHO criteria have been adopted in the country. - Depuis 2004, le pays a adopté les critères de l'OMS.

[47] Based on the results of the 2005 Population and Housing Census. - Données fondées sur les résultats du recensement de la population et de l'habitat de 2005.

[48] Data refer to urban areas only. - Données ne concernant que les zones urbaines.

[49] Data refer to the recorded events in Ministry of Health hospitals and health centres only. - Les données se rapportent aux faits d'état civil enregistrés dans les hôpitaux et les dispensaires du Ministère de la santé seulement.

[50] Data from Births and Deaths Notification System (Ministry of Health institutions and all other health care providers). - Les données proviennent du système de notification des naissances et des décès (établissements du Ministère de la santé et tous autres prestataires de soins de santé).

[51] Excluding data for the Pakistan-held part of Jammu and Kashmir, the final status of which has not yet been determined. - Non compris les données concernant la partie du Jammu et Cachemire occupée par le Pakistan dont le statut définitif n'a pas été déterminé.

[52] Based on the results of the Pakistan Demographic Survey (PDS 2003) . - Données extraites de l'enquête démographique effectuée par le Pakistan en 2003.

[53] Based on the results of the Pakistan Demographic Survey (PDS 2005). - Données extraites de l'enquête démographique effectuée par le Pakistan en 2005.

[54] Excluding alien armed forces, civilian aliens employed by armed forces, and foreign diplomatic personnel and their dependants. Including nationals outside the country. - Non compris les militaires étrangers, les civils étrangers employés par les forces armées ni le personnel diplomatique étranger et les membres de leur famille les accompagnant. Y compris les nationaux hors du pays.

[55] Excluding live-born infants who died before their birth was registered. Excluding nomad population and Palestinian refugees. - Non compris les enfants nés vivants décédés avant l'enregistrement de leur naissance. Non compris la population nomade et les réfugiés de Palestine.

[56] Excluding infants born alive of less than 28 weeks' gestation, of less than 1 000 grams in weight and 35 centimeters in length, who die within seven days of birth. Data have been adjusted for under-registration. - Non compris les enfants nés vivants après moins de 28 semaines de gestations, pesant moins de 1 000 grammes, mesurant moins de 35 centimètres et décédés dans les sept jours qui ont suivi leur naissance. Y compris un ajustement pour sous-enregistrement.

[57] Data are estimates based on Address Based Population Registration System and other survey. - Les données sont des estimations basées sur le registre national de la population basé sur l'adresse et d'autres enquêtes.

[58] Based on the results of the Population Demographic Survey. - D'après les résultats de la Population Demographic Survey.

[59] Also included in Finland. - Comprise aussi dans Finlande.

[60] Including armed forces stationed outside the country, but excluding alien armed forces stationed in the area. - Y compris les militaires nationaux hors du pays, mais non compris les militaires étrangers en garnison sur le territoire.

61 Excluding Faeroe Islands and Greenland shown separately, if available. - Non compris les Iles Féroé et le Gröenland, qui font l'objet de rubriques distinctes, si disponible.

62 Including Aland Islands. - Y compris les Îles d'Åland.

63 Including nationals temporarily outside the country. - Y compris les nationaux se trouvant temporairement hors du pays.

64 Excluding Overseas Departments, namely, French Guiana, Guadeloupe, Martinique and Reunion, shown separately, if available. - Non compris les départements d'outre mer, c'est-à-dire la Guyane française, la Guadeloupe, la Martinique et la Réunion, qui font l'objet de rubriques distinctes, si disponible.

65 Including armed forces stationed outside the country. - Y compris les militaires nationaux hors du pays.

66 Excluding armed forces. - Non compris les militaires en garnison.

67 Computations are based on five-year age-specific fertility rates by age completed. - Calcul basé sur les taux de fécondité par âge sur cinq ans.

68 Data refer to events registered within one year of occurrence. - Evénements enregistrés dans l'année qui suit l'événement.

69 Including residents outside the country. - Y compris les résidents hors du pays.

70 Including residents outside the country if listed in a Netherlands population register. - Y compris les résidents hors du pays, s'ils sont inscrits sur un registre de population néerlandais.

71 Excluding Svalbard and Jan Mayen Island shown separately, if available. - Non compris Svalbard et Jan Mayen qui font l'objet de rubriques distinctes, si disponible.

72 Including residents temporarily outside the country. - Y compris les résidents se trouvant temporairement hors du pays.

73 Excluding infants born alive of less than 28 weeks' gestation, of less than 1 000 grams in weight and 35 centimeters in length, who die within seven days of birth. Excluding Transnistria and the municipality of Bender. - Non compris les enfants nés vivants après moins de 28 semaines de gestations, pesant moins de 1 000 grammes, mesurant moins de 35 centimètres et décédés dans les sept jours qui ont suivi leur naissance. Les données ne tiennent pas compte de l'information sur la Transnistria et la municipalité de Bender.

74 Excluding data for Kosovo and Metohia. - Sans les données pour le Kosovo et Metohie.

75 Data based on fertility for range of two years shown under the year ending. - Données fournies sur la base de la fécondité pour une période de deux années consécutives ; les données qui apparaissent sont celles de l'année finale de cette période.

76 Data refer to births with weight 500g and more (if weight is unknown - with length 25 centimeters and more, or with gestation during 22 weeks or more). - Données concernant les nouveau-nés de 500 grammes ou plus (si le poids est inconnu – de 25 centimètres de long ou plus, ou après une grossesse de 22 semaines ou plus).

77 Excluding infants born living with birth weight of less than 500grams (or if birth weight is unknown - with length of less than 25 centimeters, or with gestation period of less than 22 weeks). - Non compris les données concernant les nouveau-nés pesant moins de 500 grammes (si le pods est inconnu – mesurant moins de 25 centimètres ou après moins de 22 semaines de gestations).

78 Excluding Channel Islands (Guernsey and Jersey) and Isle of Man, shown separately, if available. - Non compris les îles Anglo-Normandes (Guernesey et Jersey) et l'île de Man, qui font l'objet de rubriques distinctes, si disponible.

79 Excluding births to non-resident mothers of Northern Ireland. Data tabulated by date of occurrence for England and Wales, and by date of registration for Northern Ireland and Scotland. - Les données ne tiennent pas compte des enfants nés de mères non résidentes en Irlande du Nord. Données exploitées selon la date de l'événement pour l'Angleterre et le pays de Galles, et selon la date de l'enregistrement pour l'Irlande du Nord et l'Ecosse.

80 Data tabulated by date of occurrence for England and Wales, and by date of registration for Northern Ireland and Scotland. - Données exploitées selon la date de l'événement pour l'Angleterre et le pays de Galles, et selon la date de l'enregistrement pour l'Irlande du Nord et l'Ecosse.

81 Excluding data where usual residence was undefined, offshore or migratory and unknown. - En excluant les données lorsque le lieu du domicile n'est pas précisé, est à l'étranger, est mouvant ou inconnu.

82 Excluding Niue, shown separately, which is part of Cook Islands, but because of remoteness is administered separately. - Non compris Nioué, qui fait l'objet d'une rubrique distincte et qui fait partie des îles Cook, mais qui, en raison de son éloignement, est administrée séparément.

83 Including United States military personnel, their dependants and contract employees. - Y compris les militaires des Etats-Unis, les membres de leur famille les accompagnant et les agents contractuels des Etats-Unis.

84 Excluding United States military personnel, their dependants and contract employees. - Non compris les militaires des Etats-Unis, les membres de leur famille les accompagnant et les agents contractuels des Etats-Unis.

85 Includes children born in New Zealand to women resident in Niue who chose to travel to New Zealand to give birth. - Y compris les enfants nés en Nouvelle-Zélande de femmes résidant à Nioué qui ont choisi de se rendre en Nouvelle-Zélande pour accoucher.

86 Includes deaths occurred in New Zealand but buried in Niue and deaths occurred in Niue but buried elsewhere. - Y compris les personnes décédées en Nouvelle-Zélande qui sont enterrées à Nioué et les personnes décédées à Nioué qui sont enterrées ailleurs.

87 Estimate based on results of the population census. - Estimation fondée sur les résultats du recensement de la population.

Table 5

Table 5 presents national estimates of mid-year population for all available years between 1998 and 2007.

Description of variables: Mid-year estimates of the total population are those provided by national statistical offices. They refer to the *de facto* or *de jure* population on 1 July. Exceptions to this are footnoted accordingly. The data are presented in thousands, rounded by the Statistics Division.

For certain countries or areas, there is a discrepancy between the mid-year population estimates shown in this table and those shown in subsequent tables for the same year. Usually this discrepancy arises because the estimates for a given year are revised and the more detailed tabulations are not.

For some countries or areas the figures presented in this table and the figures used to calculate rates in subsequent tables are not the same, as these countries have provided a reference population for vital events that is different than the total population.

Unless otherwise indicated, all estimates relate to the population within present geographical boundaries. Major exceptions to this principle are explained in footnotes.

Reliability of data: Reliable mid-year population estimates are those that are based on a complete census (or on a sample survey) and have been adjusted on a basis of a continuous population register or on the balance of births, deaths and migration. Reliable mid-year estimates appear in roman type. Mid-year estimates that are not calculated on this basis are considered less reliable and are shown in *italics*.

Limitations: Statistics on estimates of the mid-year total population are subject to the same qualifications as have been set forth for population statistics in general in section 3 of the Technical Notes.

International comparability of mid-year population estimates is also affected by the fact that some of these estimates refer to the *de jure*, and not the *de facto*, population. These are indicated in the column titled "Code". The difference between the *de facto* and the *de jure* population is discussed in section 3.1.1 of the Technical Notes.

Earlier data: Estimates of mid-year population have been shown in previous issues of the *Demographic Yearbook*. Information on the years and specific topics covered is presented in the Historical Index.

Tableau 5

Le tableau 5 présente des estimations nationales de la population en milieu d'année pour le plus grand nombre possible d'années entre 1998 et 2007.

Description des variables : les estimations de la population totale en milieu d'année sont celles qui ont été communiquées par les services nationaux de statistique. Elles correspondent à la population de fait ou se réfèrent à la population de droit, au 1er juillet. Lorsque la date est différente, cela est signalé par une note. Sauf indication contraire, tous les chiffres sont exprimés en milliers. Les données ont été arrondies par la Division de statistique de l'ONU.

Pour certains pays ou territoires, il existe une différence entre les estimations de la population en milieu d'année et celles présentées dans les tableaux suivants pour la même année. Généralement, les différences apparaissent parce que les estimations de l'année ont été révisées mais que les autres tabulations ne l'ont pas été.

Pour certains pays ou territoires, les données présentées dans ce tableau sont différentes des données utilisées pour calculer les taux dans les tableaux suivants, parce que ces pays ont fourni une population de référence pour les événements démographiques différente de la population totale.

Sauf indication contraire, toutes les estimations se rapportent à la population présente sur le territoire actuel des pays ou zones considérés. Les principales exceptions à cette règle sont expliquées en note.

Fiabilité des données : les estimations de la population en milieu d'année sont considérées sûres quand elles sont fondées sur un recensement complet (ou sur une enquête par sondage) et ont été ajustées en fonction des données provenant d'un registre permanent de population ou en fonction des naissances, décès et mouvements migratoires qui ont eu lieu pendant la période. Les estimations considérées comme sûres apparaissent en caractères romains. Les estimations dont le calcul n'a pas été effectué sur cette base sont considérées comme moins sûres et apparaissent en italique.

Insuffisance des données : les statistiques concernant les estimations de la population totale en milieu d'année appellent toutes les réserves qui ont été formulées à la section 3 des Notes techniques à propos des statistiques de la population en général.

Le fait que certaines des estimations concernant la population en milieu d'année se réfèrent à la population de droit et non à la population de fait influe sur la comparabilité internationale. Ces cas ont été signalés dans la colonne « Code ». La différence entre la population de fait et la population de droit est expliquée à la section 3.1.1 des Notes techniques.

Données publiées antérieurement : des estimations de la population en milieu d'année ont été publiées dans des éditions antérieures de l'*Annuaire démographique*. Pour plus de précisions concernant les années et les sujets pour lesquels des données ont été publiées, se reporter à l'index.

5. Estimates of mid-year population: 1998 - 2007
Estimations de la population au milieu de l'année: 1998 - 2007

Continent and country or area / Continent et pays ou zone	Code[a]	Population estimates (in thousands) - Estimations (en milliers)									
		1998	1999	2000	2001	2002	2003	2004	2005	2006	2007
AFRICA - AFRIQUE											
Algeria - Algérie	DJ	29 507	29 965	30 416	30 872	31 332	31 848	32 364	32 906	33 481	34 096
Benin - Bénin	DF	6 044	5 990	6 169	*6 417	...	*6 974[1]	...	*7 395[1]	*7 612[1]	*8 054[1]
Botswana	DF	1 572	1 611	1 653	...	1 650	1 673	1 693	1 708	1 720	1 736
Burkina Faso	DJ	10 816	11 078	11 347	11 623	11 906	12 197	12 496	12 802	13 117[1]	14 252[1]
Burundi	DF	6 300	6 483	6 665	6 847	7 032	7 211	7 384	...	...	...
Cameroon - Cameroun[1]	DF	14 439	...	15 292	15 731	16 170	16 626	17 000	...	...	...
Cape Verde - Cap-Vert	DF	417	428	435	445	453	461	468	475	483	491
Central African Republic - République centrafricaine	DF	...	...	...	...	...	3 151	...	...	...	...
Chad - Tchad[1]	DF	7 105	7 283	...	8 322	...	...	...	...	...	...
Congo	DF	2 738	2 815	2 893	2 974	3 058	3 143	3 231	...	3 580	*3 695
Côte d'Ivoire	DF	15 366	15 881	16 402	16 928	17 461	18 001	18 546	19 097	19 658	20 228
Djibouti	DF	795	840	...	...	...	...	...	...	...	...
Egypt - Égypte	DF	61 341	62 639	63 975	65 298	66 628	67 965	69 304	70 653	72 009	73 644
Ethiopia - Éthiopie	DF	59 882	61 672	63 495	65 374	67 220	69 127	71 066	73 044	75 067[1]	...
Gabon	DF	1 148	1 177	1 206	*1 237	*1 268	*1 300	...	1 313[2]	...	...
Gambia - Gambie	DF	...	1 385	1 393	1 420	...	...	...	1 436	1 510	...
Ghana	DF	18 885	19 484	19 046[1]	19 396[1]	19 878[1]	20 359[1]	20 842[1]	21 343[1]	...	...
Guinea - Guinée	DF	...	...	...	...	...	...	9 214	...	...	...
Guinea-Bissau - Guinée-Bissau[1]	DF	...	...	...	1 211	1 238	1 267	1 296	1 326	1 357	1 389
Kenya	DF	28 611	29 453	30 150	31 121	32 118	33 142	34 191	35 267	36 433	37 184
Lesotho	DF	2 055	2 100	2 144	...	...	...	...	...	...	...
Libyan Arab Jamahiriya - Jamahiriya arabe libyenne[3]	DF	4 772	4 958	5 125	5 300	5 484	...	...	...	...	...
Madagascar	DF	14 222	14 650	15 085	15 529	15 981	16 441	17 206	17 730	...	18 820
Malawi[1]	DF	...	10 153	10 475	10 816	11 175	11 549	11 938	12 341	12 758	13 188
Mali[4]	DF	...	9 969	10 243	10 525	10 813	11 111	11 419	11 732	12 051	12 378
Mauritania - Mauritanie	DF	2 493	2 568	2 645	2 724	...	...	...	2 906	...	3 075
Mauritius - Maurice	DJ	1 160	1 175	1 187	1 200	1 210	1 223	1 233	1 243	1 253	1 260
Morocco - Maroc	DF	27 775	28 238	28 705	29 170	29 631	30 088	30 540	30 172	*30 506	*30 841
Mozambique[1]	DF	16 451	16 840	17 241	17 653	18 078	18 514	18 962	19 420	19 889	20 367
Namibia - Namibie[1]	DF	1 723	1 769	1 817	...	1 860	1 891	1 923	1 957	1 992	2 028
Niger	DJ	9 871	10 177	10 493	11 090	11 456	11 834	12 225	12 628	13 045	13 475
Nigeria - Nigéria[1]	DF	...	...	115 224	118 801	122 444	126 153	129 175	133 767	...	...
Réunion	DJ	698	710	723	735	746	756	767	777	786	*798
Saint Helena ex. dep. - Sainte-Hélène sans dép	DF	...	...	...	...	...	...	...	...	...	4
Saint Helena: Tristan da Cunha - Sainte-Hélène: Tristan da Cunha[5]	DF	...	...	...	...	...	...	...	...	...	0
Sao Tome and Principe - Sao Tomé-et-Principe	DF	131	133	135	...	140	143	146	149	152	155
Senegal - Sénégal	DJ	8 964	9 193	9 427	9 667	9 913	10 165	10 564	10 848	*11 000	...
Seychelles	DF	79	80	81	81	84	83	82	83	85	85
Sierra Leone	DF	4 730	4 836	4 944	5 054	5 167	5 280	...	...	...	...
South Africa - Afrique du Sud[6]	DF	42 131	43 054	43 686	44 929	45 587	46 206	46 787	47 335	46 787	48 287
Sudan - Soudan	DF	29 266	30 326	31 081	31 627	32 468	33 334	34 512	35 397	36 297	...
Swaziland	DF	952	977	1 003	1 030	1 056	1 081	1 105	1 126	1 146	...
Togo	DF	4 406	4 506	4 629	4 740	4 854	4 970	5 090	5 337	5 337	5 465
Tunisia - Tunisie	DF	9 333	9 456	9 564	9 674	9 749	9 840	9 932	10 029	10 128	10 225
Uganda - Ouganda	DF	21 175	21 864	22 575	23 310	24 069	24 851	25 660	26 495	27 357	28 247
United Republic of Tanzania - République Unie de Tanzanie	DF	...	...	...	...	...	...	36 308	37 379	38 251	39 446
Zambia - Zambie	DF	10 096	10 407	...	10 089[1]	10 409[1]	10 744[1]	11 090[1]	11 441[1]	11 799[1]	*12 161[1]
Zimbabwe	DF	12 685	13 079	...	12 960	...	...	...	...	12 225[7]	...
AMERICA, NORTH - AMÉRIQUE DU NORD											
Anguilla	DF	11	11	11	12	12	12	13	14	14	15
Antigua and Barbuda - Antigua-et-Barbuda	DF	70	71	72	77	78	80	81	83	...	...
Aruba	DJ	88	90	91	92	93	95	98	101	103	104
Bahamas	DF	293	298	...	308	312	317	321	325	330	334
Barbados - Barbade	DF	265	267	269	270	271	272	272	273	273	274
Belize	DF	239	243	250	257	265	274	283	292	301	311

5. Estimates of mid-year population: 1998 - 2007
Estimations de la population au milieu de l'année: 1998 - 2007 (continued - suite)

Continent and country or area / Continent et pays ou zone	Code[a]	Population estimates (in thousands) - Estimations (en milliers)									
		1998	1999	2000	2001	2002	2003	2004	2005	2006	2007
AMERICA, NORTH - AMÉRIQUE DU NORD											
Bermuda - Bermudes..........	DJ	62	63	62	62	63	63	63	64	64	64
British Virgin Islands - Îles Vierges britanniques.........	DF	19	20	20	21	21	21	22	...	...	...
Canada	DJ	30 157[8]	30 404[8]	30 689[8]	31 021[9]	31 373[9]	31 676[9]	31 995[9]	32 312[10]	32 649[10]	*32 976[11]
Cayman Islands - Îles Caïmanes	DJ	38	39	40	41	42	44	44	48	52	...
Costa Rica	DJ	3 341	3 413	3 810	3 907	3 998	4 089	4 179	4 266	4 354	4 443
Cuba.........................	DJ	11 055	11 095	11 130	11 157	11 184	11 215	11 236	11 243	11 241	11 238
Dominica - Dominique	DF	72	72	72	71	70	70	70	71	71	...
Dominican Republic - République dominicaine	DF	*8 288*	*8 420*	*8 554[1]*	*8 688[1]*	*8 823[1]*	*8 958[1]*	*9 093[1]*	*9 226[1]*	*9 360[1]*	*9 493[1]*
El Salvador..................	DF	6 031	6 154	6 276	6 397	6 518	6 638	6 757	6 875	6 991	7 105
Greenland - Groenland[12]	DJ	56	56	56	56	57	57	57	57	57	57
Grenada - Grenade...........	DF	100	101	101	101	...	...	...	...	...	107
Guadeloupe	DJ	419	424	428	432	437	439	445	*446	*458	*403[4]
Guatemala[6]	DF	10 799	11 088	11 385	11 678	11 987	12 084	12 390	12 701	13 019	13 345
Haiti - Haïti.................	DJ	*7 647*	*7 803*	*7 959*	*8 132*	...	...	...	...	...	...
Honduras	DF	*6 057*	*6 211*	*6 369*	*6 530*	*6 695*	*6 861*	*7 028*	*7 197*	*7 367*	*7 537
Jamaica - Jamaïque...........	DJ	2 557	2 574	2 589	2 604	2 615	2 626	2 638	2 650	2 663	2 676
Martinique...................	DJ	379	382	385	387	389	391	394	398	400	*400[4]
Mexico - Mexique	DJ	*95 790*	*97 115*	*98 439*	*99 716*	*100 909*	*102 000*	*103 002*	*103 947[1]*	*104 874[1]*	*105 791[1]*
Montserrat	DF	4	5	5	5	5	4	5	5	5	5
Netherlands Antilles - Antilles néerlandaises[4]	DJ	*194*	*190*	*183*	*176*	*173*	*177*	*179*	*184*	*189*	*194*
Nicaragua...................	DJ	*4 932*	*5 017*	*5 098*	*5 174*	*5 245*	*5 313*	*5 381*	*5 450*	*5 523*	*5 596*
Panama......................	DF	*2 764*	*2 809*	*2 856*	*2 897*	*3 060*	*3 116*	*3 172*	*3 228*	*3 284*	*3 340*
Puerto Rico - Porto Rico[13]	DJ	3 748	3 782	3 816	3 840	3 859	3 879	3 895	3 912	3 928	3 942
Saint Kitts and Nevis - Saint-Kitts-et-Nevis	DF	40	42	40	*46	...	...	...	*39	...	...
Saint Lucia - Sainte-Lucie	DF	152	154	156	158	159	161	162	164	166	168
Saint Vincent and the Grenadines - Saint-Vincent-et-les Grenadines..................	DF	112	112	110	...	108	105	105	104	...	...
Trinidad and Tobago - Trinité-et-Tobago...........	DF	1 282	1 290	...	1 267	1 276[7]	1 282[7]	1 291[7]	1 294[7]	1 298[7]	1 303[7]
Turks and Caicos Islands - Îles Turques et Caïques..........	DJ	*17*	*17*	*18*	*20*	*21*	*25*	*27*	*31*	*33*	*35*
United States of America - États-Unis d'Amérique[14]	DJ	275 854	279 040	282 194	285 112	287 888	290 448	293 192	295 896	298 755	301 621
United States Virgin Islands - Îles Vierges américaines[13] ...	DJ	109	109	109	109	109	109	109	110	110	110
AMERICA, SOUTH - AMÉRIQUE DU SUD											
Argentina - Argentine.........	DF	*36 005*	*36 399*	*36 784*	*37 156*	*37 516*	*37 870*	*38 226*	*38 592*	*38 971*	*39 356*
Bolivia (Plurinational State of) - Bolivie (État plurinational de).	DF	*8 035*	*8 229*	*8 428*	*8 624*	*8 824*	*9 025*	*9 227*	*9 427*	*9 627*	*9 828*
Brazil - Brésil[15]	DF	*166 252*	*168 754*	*171 280*	*173 808*	*176 304*	*178 741*	*181 106*	*183 383*	*185 564*	*187 642*
Chile - Chili.................	DF	14 997	15 197	15 398	15 572	15 746	15 919	16 093	16 267	16 433	16 598
Colombia - Colombie[16]	DF	*39 201*	*39 746*	*40 282*	*40 806*	*41 327*	*41 847*	*42 368*	*42 889*	*43 405*	*43 926*
Ecuador - Équateur[17]	DF	*11 948*	*12 121*	*12 299*	*12 480*	*12 661*	*12 843*	*13 027*	*13 215*	*13 408*	*13 605*
French Guiana - Guyane française	DJ	153	158	164	170	175	181	*187	*200	*197	214[4]
Guyana	DF	773	771	742	744	748	753	756	758	761	763
Paraguay	DF	*5 127*	*5 237*	*5 346*	*5 456*	*5 567*	*5 677*	*5 788*	*5 899*	*6 009*	*6 120*
Peru - Pérou[6]	DF	*25 182*	*25 589*	*25 984*	*26 367*	*26 739*	*27 103*	*27 460*	*27 811*	*28 151*	*28 482*
Suriname....................	DJ	452	458	464	470	476	483	487	499	504	510
Uruguay.....................	DF	3 274[6]	3 289[6]	3 301[6]	3 308[6]	3 309[6]	3 304[6]	3 302[6]	3 306[6]	3 314[6]	3 324[1]
Venezuela (Bolivarian Republic of) - Venezuela (République bolivarienne du)[18]	DF	23 413	23 867	24 311	24 766	25 220	25 674	26 127	26 577	27 031	27 483

5. Estimates of mid-year population: 1998 - 2007
Estimations de la population au milieu de l'année: 1998 - 2007 (continued - suite)

Continent and country or area / Continent et pays ou zone	Code[a]	Population estimates (in thousands) - Estimations (en milliers)									
		1998	1999	2000	2001	2002	2003	2004	2005	2006	2007
ASIA - ASIE											
Afghanistan	DF	20 760	21 200	21 770	22 080	22 930	...	...	...	22 576[19]	...
Armenia - Arménie	DJ	3 235	3 229	3 221	3 214	3 212	3 211	3 214	3 218	3 221	3 227
Azerbaijan - Azerbaïdjan	DF	7 913	7 983	8 049	8 111	8 172	8 234	8 307	8 392	8 485	8 581
Bahrain - Bahreïn	DF	605	621	638	661	711	765	824	889	960	1 039
Bangladesh	DF	126 200	*128 100	129 300	131 000	132 900	134 800	136 700	138 600	140 600	142 600
Bhutan - Bhoutan	DF	560	570	580	591	602	613	624	...	647[20]	659[20]
Brunei Darussalam - Brunéi Darussalam	DF	310	317	325	333	344	350	360	370	383	390
Cambodia - Cambodge[21]	DF	12 242	12 462	12 688	12 922	13 164	13 415	13 091	*13 661	...	...
China - Chine[22]	DF	1 241 935[23]	1 252 735[23]	1 262 645[23]	1 271 850[24]	1 280 400[24]	1 288 400[24]	1 296 075[24]	1 303 720[25]	1 311 020[24]	1 324 655[24]
China, Hong Kong SAR - Chine, Hong Kong RAS	DJ	6 544	6 607	6 665	6 714	6 744	6 731	6 784	6 813	6 857	6 926
China, Macao SAR - Chine, Macao RAS	DJ	422	427	431	434	438	444	455	473	499	526
Cyprus - Chypre[26]	DJ	679	686	694	701	710	721	737	758	771	784
Democratic People's Republic of Korea - République populaire démocratique de Corée	DF	22 554	22 754	22 963	23 149	23 313	23 464	23 612	...	...	...
Georgia - Géorgie	DF	4 487	4 453	4 418	4 386	4 357	4 329	4 318	4 361	4 398	4 388
India - Inde[27]	DF	978 981	997 556	1 016 210	1 034 931	1 051 258[1]	1 068 065[1]	1 084 757[1]	1 101 318[1]	1 117 734[1]	1 134 023[1]
Indonesia - Indonésie	DJ	204 393	207 437	...	208 643	211 439	214 251	217 077	219 852	222 747	225 642
Iran (Islamic Republic of) - Iran (République islamique d')[28]	DJ	62 103	63 152	64 219	65 301	66 300	67 315	68 345	69 390	70 603	71 532
Iraq	DF	22 702	23 382	24 086	24 813	25 565	26 340	27 139	27 963	28 810	29 682
Israel - Israël[29]	DJ	5 971	6 125	6 289	6 439	6 570	6 690	6 809	6 930	7 054	7 180
Japan - Japon[30]	DF	126 400	126 631	126 843	127 149	127 445	127 718	127 761	127 773	127 756	127 772
Jordan - Jordanie[31]	DF	4 623	4 738	4 857	4 978	5 098	5 230	5 350	5 473	5 600	5 723
Kazakhstan	DF	15 073	14 928	14 884	14 858	14 859	14 909	15 013	15 147	15 308	15 484
Kuwait - Koweït	DF	1 760	1 822	1 886	1 953	2 022	2 093	2 167	2 245	2 328	2 411
Kyrgyzstan - Kirghizstan	DF	4 797	4 865	4 915	4 955	4 993	5 039	5 093	5 144	5 192	5 235
Lao People's Democratic Republic - République démocratique populaire lao	DF	...	5 091[32]	5 218[32]	5 377[32]	5 526[32]	5 679[32]	5 836[32]	5 679[33]	5 747[33]	5 874[33]
Malaysia - Malaisie	DF	22 334[8]	22 909[8]	23 495[34]	24 013[34]	24 527[34]	25 048[34]	25 581[34]	26 128[34]	26 640[34]	27 174[34]
Maldives	DF	267	278	271	276	281	285	289	294	298	305
Mongolia - Mongolie	DF	2 281	2 332	2 390	2 425	2 459	2 490	2 519	2 548	2 579	2 615
Myanmar	DF	48 160	49 133	50 125	51 138	52 171	53 224	54 299	...	...	...
Nepal - Népal	DJ	21 843	22 367	*22 904	...	23 701	24 250	24 797	25 343	25 887	*26 427
Occupied Palestinian Territory - Territoire palestinien occupé	DF	2 872	2 962	3 053	3 138	3 225	3 315	3 407	3 508	3 612	3 719
Oman	DF	2 288	2 325	2 401	2 478	2 538	...	2 416	2 514	2 577	2 743
Pakistan[35]	DF	133 320	136 410	139 410	142 350	145 280	148 210	151 090	153 960	156 770	159 570
Philippines	DJ	73 148	74 746	76 348	77 926	79 504	81 081	82 664	84 241	*86 973	*88 706
Qatar	DF	557	586	617	649	682	718	756	888	1 042	1 226
Republic of Korea - République de Corée	DJ	46 287	46 617	47 008	47 357	47 622	47 859	48 039	48 138	48 297	48 456
Saudi Arabia - Arabie saoudite	DF	19 506	19 985	20 476	20 979	21 495	22 023	22 564	23 119	23 679	*24 243
Singapore - Singapour	DF	3 927	3 959	4 028	4 138	4 176	4 115	4 167	4 266	4 401	4 589
Sri Lanka	DF	18 802	19 043	19 359	18 732	19 007	19 252	19 462	19 668	19 886	20 010
Syrian Arab Republic - République arabe syrienne[36]	DF	15 473	15 891	16 320	16 720	17 130	17 550	17 829	18 138	18 717	19 172
Tajikistan - Tadjikistan	DF	5 939	6 064	6 188	6 313	6 441	6 573	6 710	6 850	6 992	7 140
Thailand - Thaïlande[1]	DJ	61 201	61 806	62 406	62 914	63 482	64 019	64 177	64 839	65 306	66 042
Turkey - Turquie	DF	65 215	66 350	67 420	68 365	69 302	70 231	71 152	72 065	72 974	73 875
Turkmenistan - Turkménistan	DF	4 859	...	4 892	4 974	5 052	5 124[37]	...	...	...	...
United Arab Emirates - Émirats arabes unis	DF	2 717	2 855	2 995	3 167	3 349	3 551	3 761	...	4 229	4 488
Uzbekistan - Ouzbékistan	DF	24 051	23 954	24 650	24 964	25 272	25 568	...	...	...	...
Viet Nam	DF	75 456	76 597	77 635	78 686	79 727	80 902	82 032	83 106	84 137	85 172
Yemen - Yémen	DF	17 072	17 671	17 461[38]	17 993[38]	18 540[38]	19 104[38]	...	20 283[38]	20 901[38]	21 539[38]
EUROPE											
Åland Islands - Îles d'Åland[39]	DJ	26	26	26	26	26	26	26	27	27	27
Albania - Albanie	DF	3 055	3 054	3 061	3 074	3 093	3 111	3 127	3 142	3 151	3 161
Andorra - Andorre[12]	DF	66	66	66	66	66	70	75	79	80	82

5. Estimates of mid-year population: 1998 - 2007
Estimations de la population au milieu de l'année: 1998 - 2007 (continued - suite)

Continent and country or area / Continent et pays ou zone	Code[a]	Population estimates (in thousands) - Estimations (en milliers)									
		1998	1999	2000	2001	2002	2003	2004	2005	2006	2007
EUROPE											
Austria - Autriche	DJ	7 977	7 992	8 012	8 043	8 084	8 118	8 175	8 233	8 282	8 315
Belarus - Bélarus	DF	10 072	10 035	10 005	9 971	9 925	9 874	9 825	9 775	9 733	9 702
Belgium - Belgique	DJ	10 203	10 226	10 251	10 287	10 333	10 372	10 417	10 473	10 542	10 623
Bosnia and Herzegovina - Bosnie-Herzégovine	DF	3 653	3 725	3 781	3 798	3 828	3 832	3 843	3 843	3 843	...
Bulgaria - Bulgarie	DF	8 257	8 211	8 170	7 913	7 869	7 824	7 781	7 740	7 699	7 660
Croatia - Croatie	DJ	4 501	4 554	4 426	4 440	4 440	4 440	4 439	4 442	4 440	4 436
Czech Republic - République tchèque	DJ	10 295	10 283	10 273	10 224	10 201	10 202	10 207	10 234	10 287	10 334
Denmark - Danemark[40]	DJ	5 301	5 327	5 337	5 359	5 374	5 387	5 401	5 416	5 435	5 457
Estonia - Estonie	DF	1 386	1 376	1 370	1 364	1 359	1 354	1 349	1 346	1 344	1 342
Faeroe Islands - Îles Féroé	DJ	45	45	46	47	47	48	48	48	48	48
Finland - Finlande[41]	DJ	5 153	5 165	5 176	5 188	5 201	5 213	5 228	5 246	5 266	5 289
France[42]	DJ	58 398	58 673	59 049	59 454	59 863	60 264	60 643	60 996	61 353	61 707
Germany - Allemagne	DJ	82 029	82 087	82 188	82 340	82 482	82 520	82 501	82 464	82 366	82 263
Gibraltar[43]	DF	27	27	27	...	29	29	29	29	29	29[38]
Greece - Grèce[44]	DF	10 835	10 883	10 917	10 950	10 988	11 024	11 062	11 104	11 149	11 193
Guernsey - Guernesey	DF	59	60	60	...	...	...	60	...	61[45]	62[45]
Holy See - Saint-Siège[46]	DJ	1									
Hungary - Hongrie	DF	10 114	10 068	10 024	10 188	10 159	10 130	10 107	10 087	10 071	10 056
Iceland - Islande[12]	DJ	274	277	281	285	288	289	293	296	304	311
Ireland - Irlande[47]	DF	3 703	3 742	3 790	3 847	...	3 979	4 044	4 131	4 235	4 339
Isle of Man - Île de Man[48]	DJ	73	74	75	...	77	77	78	79	80	81
Italy - Italie	DJ	56 907	56 916	56 942	56 977	57 157	57 605	58 175	58 607	58 941	59 375
Jersey	DF	...	...	...	87	88	88	88	88	89	90
Latvia - Lettonie	DJ	2 410	2 390	2 373	2 355	2 339	2 325	2 313	2 301	2 288	2 276
Liechtenstein	DF	32[38]	32[38]	33	33	34	34	34	35	35	35
Lithuania - Lituanie	DJ	3 549	3 524	3 500	3 481	3 469	3 454	3 436	3 414	3 394	3 376
Luxembourg	DJ	425	430	436	442	446	452	458	465	473	480
Malta - Malte	DJ	379	380	383	385	387	399	401	404	406	409
Monaco	DJ	...	33	...	...	...	...	...	...	...	...
Montenegro - Monténégro	DF	647	651	654	658	...	...	...	...	...	...
	DJ	...	...	...	...	618	620	622	623	624	626
Netherlands - Pays-Bas	DJ	15 707	15 812	15 926	16 046	16 149	16 225	16 282	16 320	16 346	16 382
Norway - Norvège[49]	DJ	4 431	4 462	4 491	4 514	4 538	4 565	4 592	4 623	4 661	4 709
Poland - Pologne[50]	DF	38 283	38 270	38 256	38 251	38 232	38 195	38 180	38 161	38 132	38 116
Portugal	DJ	10 129	10 172	10 226	10 293	10 368	10 441	10 502	10 549	10 584	10 608
Republic of Moldova - République de Moldova[51]	DJ	3 653	3 647	3 640	3 631	3 623	3 613	3 604	3 595	3 585	3 577
Romania - Roumanie	DJ	22 503	22 458	22 435	22 408	21 795	21 734	21 673	21 624	21 584	21 538
Russian Federation - Fédération de Russie[52]	DJ	147 671[53]	147 215[53]	146 597[53]	145 976[53]	145 306[53]	144 566[53]	143 821[53]	143 114	142 487	142 115
San Marino - Saint-Marin[12]	DF	28	28	27	28	28	29	29	31	31	32
Serbia - Serbie[54]	DJ	7 568	7 540	7 516	7 503	7 500	7 481	7 463	7 441	7 412	7 382
Slovakia - Slovaquie	DJ	5 391	5 395	5 401	5 380	5 379	5 379	5 383	5 387	5 391	5 398
Slovenia - Slovénie	DJ	1 983	1 986	1 990	1 992	1 996	1 997	1 997	2 001	2 009	2 019
Spain - Espagne	DJ	39 722	39 927	40 264	40 721	41 314	42 005	42 692	43 398	44 068	44 874
Svalbard and Jan Mayen Islands - Îles Svalbard et Jan Mayen[55]	DF	3	2	2	2	3	2	2	2	...	...
Sweden - Suède[12]	DJ	8 851	8 858	8 872	8 896	8 925	8 958	8 994	9 030	9 081	9 148
Switzerland - Suisse	DJ	7 110	7 144	7 184	7 227	7 285	7 339	7 390	7 437	7 484	7 551
The Former Yugoslav Republic of Macedonia - L'ex-République yougoslave de Macédoine	DF	2 008	2 017	2 024	2 035	2 031	2 027	2 033	2 037	2 040	2 044
Ukraine[4]	DF	50 371	49 918	49 430	48 923	48 457	48 003	47 622	47 281	46 930	46 646
United Kingdom of Great Britain and Northern Ireland - Royaume-Uni de Grande-Bretagne et d'Irlande du Nord[56]	DF	58 475[57]	58 684[57]	58 886[57]	59 113[57]	59 323[57]	59 557	59 846	60 238	60 587	60 975

5. Estimates of mid-year population: 1998 - 2007
Estimations de la population au milieu de l'année: 1998 - 2007 (continued - suite)

Continent and country or area / Continent et pays ou zone	Code[a]	Population estimates (in thousands) - Estimations (en milliers)									
		1998	1999	2000	2001	2002	2003	2004	2005	2006	2007
OCEANIA - OCÉANIE											
American Samoa - Samoas américaines[13]	DJ	56[58]	57[58]	58	59	61	63	64	66	67	68
Australia - Australie[6]	DJ	18 711	18 926	19 153	19 413	19 651	19 895	20 127	20 395	20 698	21 072
Cook Islands - Îles Cook[59]	DF	17	16	18	18	18	18	20	20	*21	*21
Fiji - Fidji	DF	795	802	807	810	811	816	822	825	830	834
French Polynesia - Polynésie française	DF	227	231	235	239	243	247	250	253	256	259
Guam[13]	DJ	150	153	...	158	161	167	166	*169	*171	*173
Marshall Islands - Îles Marshall	DF	63	51	53	55	...	...	55	...	52	53
Micronesia (Federated States of) - Micronésie (États fédérés de)	DJ	112	113	119	117	120	...	...	...	...	...
Nauru	DF	11	11	12	12	...	...	...	...	...	...
New Caledonia - Nouvelle-Calédonie	DF	204	208	213	217	221	226	230	234	238	242
New Zealand - Nouvelle-Zélande	DJ	3 815	3 835	3 858	3 881	3 949	4 027	4 088	4 134	4 185	4 228
Niue - Nioué	DJ	...	...	...	...	2	2	2	2	2	...
Northern Mariana Islands - Îles Mariannes septentrionales	DF	67	69	70	72	74	76	78	80	82	85
Palau - Palaos	DF	18	19	19	20	20	20	21	...	22	21
Papua New Guinea - Papouasie-Nouvelle-Guinée	DF	4 600	...	5 100	...	5 462	...	...	...	...	...
Pitcairn[38]	DF	...	...	...	...	...	...	...	...	...	0
Samoa	DF	168	169	171	...	178	180	182	183	185	187
Solomon Islands - Îles Salomon	DF	...	405	415	426	437	448	460	471	483	495
Tonga[60]	DF	99	100	100	101	101	101	102[1]	102[1]	103[1]	103[1]
Tuvalu	DF	9	9	9	9	9	9	10	10		
Vanuatu[1]	DF	...	...	...	...	...	...	216	...	221	...

FOOTNOTES - NOTES

Italics: estimates which are less reliable. - Italiques: estimations moins sûres.

* Provisional. - Données provisoires.

[a] 'Code' indicates source of data, as follows:
DF Estimates of population de facto - Population de fait
DJ Estimates of population de jure. - Population de droit

[1] Data refer to national projections. - Les données se réfèrent aux projections nationales.

[2] Based on the results of the Gabonese Survey for the Evaluation and Tracking of Poverty. - Sur base des résultats de l'enquête gabonaise sur l'évaluation et le suivi de la pauvreté.

[3] Data refer to Libyan nationals only. - Les données se raportent aux nationaux libyens seulement.

[4] Data refer to 1 January. - Données se raportent au 1 janvier.

[5] Data refer to 31 December. Based on the results of a population count. - Données se raportent au 31 décembre. D'après les résultats d'un comptage de la population.

[6] Mid-year estimates have been adjusted for underenumeration, at latest census. - Les estimations au millieu de l'année tiennent compte d'un ajustement destiné à compenser les lacunes du dénombrement lors du dernier recensement.

[7] Based on the results of the population census. - D'après le résultats du recensement de la population.

[8] Final intercensal estimates. - Estimations inter censitaires definitives.

[9] Final postcensal estimates. - Estimations postcensitaires definitives.

[10] Updated postcensal estimates. - Estimations post censitaires mises à jour.

[11] Preliminary postcensal estimates. - Estimations postcensitaires préiiminaires.

[12] Population statistics are compiled from registers. - Les statistiques de la population sont compilées à partir des registres.

[13] Including armed forces stationed in the area. - Y compris les militaires en garnison sur le territoire.

[14] Excluding armed forces overseas and civilian citizens absent from country for an extended period of time. - Non compris les militaires à l'étranger, et les civils hors du pays pendant une période prolongée.

[15] Data include persons in remote areas, military personnel outside the country, merchant seamen at sea, civilian seasonal workers outside the country, and other civilians outside the country, and exclude nomads, foreign military, civilian aliens temporarily in the country, transients on ships and Indian jungle population. - Y compris les personnes vivant dans des régions éloignées, le personel militaire en dehors du pays, les marins marchands, les ouvriers saisonniers en dehors du pays, et autres civils en dehors du pays, et non compris les nomades, les militaires étrangers, les étrangers civils temporairement dans le pays, les transiteurs sur des bateaux et les Indiens de la jungle.

[16] Data have been adjusted on the basis of the Population Census of 2005. - Données ajustées sur la base du recensement de la population de 2005.

[17] Excluding nomadic Indian tribes. Data refer to national projections. - Non compris les tribus d'Indiens nomades. Les données se réfèrent aux projections nationales.

[18] Excluding Indian jungle population. - Non compris les Indiens de la jungle.

[19] Data refer to the settled population based on the 1979 Population Census and the latest household prelisting. The refugees of Afghanistan in Iran, Pakistan and estimated 1.5 million nomads are not included. The so adjusted total population of the country for 2006 is 24.1 million of which 12.3 million males and 11.8 million females. - Les données se rapportent à la population stationnaire sur la base du recensement de 1979 et du recensement préliminaire des logements le plus récent. Sont exclus les réfugiés d'Afghanistan en Iran et au Pakistan et les nomades estimés à 1,5 million. La population totale du pays ainsi ajustée pour 2006 comprend 24,1 millions de personnes (12,3 millions d'hommes et 11,8 millions de femmes).

[20] Data refer to projections based on the 2005 population census. - Les données se réfèrent aux projections basées sur le recensement de la population de 2005.

[21] Excluding foreign diplomatic personnel and their dependants. From 1998 based on census result. - Non compris le personnel diplomatique étranger et les membres de leur famille les accompagnant. Depuis 1998, à partir des résultats de recensement.

[22] For statistical purposes, the data for China do not include those for the Hong Kong Special Administrative Region (Hong Kong SAR), Macao Special Administrative Region (Macao SAR) and Taiwan province of China. - Pour la

présentation des statistiques, les données pour la Chine ne comprennent pas la Région Administrative Spéciale de Hong Kong (Hong Kong RAS), la Région Administrative Spéciale de Macao (Macao RAS) et Taïwan province de Chine.

[23] Data have been adjusted on the basis of the Population Census of 2000. - Les données ont été ajustées à partir des résultats du recensement de la population de 2000.

[24] Data have been estimated on the basis of the annual National Sample Surveys on Population Changes. - Les données ont été estimées sur la base de l'enquête annuelle "National Sample Survey on Population Changes".

[25] Data for 2005 are estimated from the National Sample Survey of 1 per cent population. - Les données pour 2005 ont été estimées à partir de l'enquête nationale qui a porté sur un échantillon de 1 % de la population.

[26] Data refer to government controlled areas. - Les données se rapportent aux zones contrôlées par le Gouvernement.

[27] Including data for the Indian-held part of Jammu and Kashmir, the final status of which has not yet been determined. - Y compris les données pour la partie du Jammu et du Cachemire occupée par l'Inde dont le statut définitif n'a pas encore été déterminé.

[28] Data refer to the Iranian Year which begins on 21 March and ends on 20 March of the following year. - Les données concernent l'année iranienne, qui commence le 21 mars et se termine le 20 mars de l'année suivante.

[29] Including data for East Jerusalem and Israeli residents in certain other territories under occupation by Israeli military forces since June 1967. - Y compris les données pour Jérusalem-Est et les résidents israéliens dans certains autres territoires occupés depuis 1967 par les forces armées israéliennes.

[30] Excluding diplomatic personnel outside the country and foreign military and civilian personnel and their dependants stationed in the area. - Non compris le personnel diplomatique hors du pays ni les militaires et agents civils étrangers en poste sur le territoire et les membres de leur famille les accompagnant.

[31] Data refer to 31 December. Excluding data for Jordanian territory under occupation since June 1967 by Israeli military forces. Excluding foreigners, including registered Palestinian refugees. - Données se raportent au 31 décembre. Non compris les données pour le territoire jordanien occupé depuis juin 1967 par les forces armées israéliennes. Non compris les étrangers, mais y compris les réfugiés de Palestine enregistrés.

[32] Estimated based on the population census 1995 structure and growth rate at year 2000. - Pour les années 2000 à 2004, on a pris pour base la structure issue du recensement de population de 1995 et le taux de croissance de 2000.

[33] Based on the results of the 2005 Population and Housing Census. - Données fondées sur les résultats du recensement de la population et de l'habitat de 2005.

[34] Data refer to projections based on the 2000 population census. - Les données se réfèrent aux projections basées sur le recensement de la population de 2000.

[35] Excluding data for the Pakistan-held part of Jammu and Kashmir, the final status of which has not yet been determined. - Non compris les données concernant la partie du Jammu et Cachemire occupée par le Pakistan dont le statut définitif n'a pas été déterminé.

[36] Including Palestinian refugees. - Y compris les réfugiés de Palestine.

[37] Because of rounding, totals are not in all cases the sum of the parts. - Les chiffres étant arrondis, les totaux ne correspondent pas toujours rigoureusement à la somme des chiffres partiels.

[38] Data refer to 31 December. - Données se raportent au 31 décembre.

[39] Population statistics are compiled from registers. Also included in Finland. - Les statistiques de la population sont compilées à partir des registres. Comprise aussi dans Finlande.

[40] Excluding Faeroe Islands and Greenland shown separately, if available. Population statistics are compiled from registers. - Non compris les Îles Féroé et le Gröenland, qui font l'objet de rubriques distinctes, si disponible. Les statistiques de la population sont compilées à partir des registres.

[41] Population statistics are compiled from registers. Including Aland Islands. - Les statistiques de la population sont compilées à partir des registres. Y compris les Îles d'Åland.

[42] Excluding diplomatic personnel outside the country and including members of alien armed forces not living in military camps and foreign diplomatic personnel not living in embassies or consulates. Excluding Overseas Departments, namely, French Guiana, Guadeloupe, Martinique and Reunion, shown separately, if available. - Non compris le personnel diplomatique hors du pays et y compris les militaires étrangers ne vivant pas dans des camps militaires et le personnel diplomatique étranger ne vivant pas dans les ambassades ou les consulats. Non compris les départements d'outre mer, c'est-à-dire la Guyane française, la Guadeloupe, la Martinique et la Réunion, qui font l'objet de rubriques distinctes, si disponible.

[43] Excluding families of military personnel, visitors and transients. - Non compris les familles des militaires, ni les visiteurs et transients.

[44] Excluding armed forces stationed outside the country, but including alien armed forces stationed in the area. - Non compris les militaires en garnison hors du pays, mais y compris les militaires étrangers en garnison sur le territoire.

[45] Data refer to 1 March. - Données se raportent au 1 mars.

[46] Data refer to the Vatican City State. Population statistics are compiled from registers. Including nationals outside the country. - Les données se rapportent à l'Etat de la Cité du Vatican. Les statistiques de la population sont compilées à partir des registres. Y compris les nationaux hors du pays.

[47] Data refer to 15 April. - Données se raportent au 15 avril.

[48] Data refer to 30 April. - Données se raportent au 30 avril.

[49] Including residents temporarily outside the country. Excluding Svalbard and Jan Mayen Island shown separately, if available. - Y compris les résidents se trouvant temporairement hors du pays. Non compris Svalbard et Jan Mayen qui font l'objet de rubriques distinctes, si disponible.

[50] Excluding civilian aliens within country, but including civilian nationals temporarily outside country. - Non compris les civils étrangers dans le pays, mais y compris les civils nationaux temporairement hors du pays.

[51] Excluding Transnistria and the municipality of Bender. - Les données ne tiennent pas compte de l'information sur la Transnistria et la municipalité de Bender.

[52] Data refer to resident population only. - Pour la population résidante seulement.

[53] Figures were updated taking into account the results of the 2002 All-Russian population census. - Les chiffres ont été calculés compte tenu des résultats du recensement de la population de la Fédération de Russie de 2002.

[54] Excluding data for Kosovo and Metohia. - Sans les données pour le Kosovo et Metohie.

[55] Data refer to 1 January. Data refer to Svalbard only. - Données se raportent au 1 janvier. Données ne concernant que le Svalbard.

[56] Excluding Channel Islands (Guernsey and Jersey) and Isle of Man, shown separately, if available. - Non compris les îles Anglo-Normandes (Guernesey et Jersey) et l'île de Man, qui font l'objet de rubriques distinctes, si disponible.

[57] Population estimates for 1994 to 2002 were revised in light of the local studies. - Les estimations de la population pour les années 1994 à 2002 ont été révisées en fonction d'études locales.

[58] Population estimates for the years 1991 to 1999 have been smoothed using the 1995 mid-decade household survey and the year 2000 census. - L'estimation de la population a été lissée pour les années entre 1991 et 1999 en utilisant l'enquête des ménages de 1995 et le recensement de l'année 2000.

[59] Excluding Niue, shown separately, which is part of Cook Islands, but because of remoteness is administered separately. - Non compris Nioué, qui fait l'objet d'une rubrique distincte et qui fait partie des îles Cook, mais qui, en raison de son éloignement, est administrée séparément.

[60] Based on the results of the 1996 population census not necessarily mid year estimated. - À partir des résultats du recensement de la population de 1996, pas nécessairement des estimations en milieu d'année.

Table 6

Table 6 presents urban and total population by sex for as many years as possible between 1998 and 2007.

Description of variables: Data are from nation-wide population censuses or are estimates, some of which are based on sample surveys of population carried out among all segments of the population. The results of censuses are identified by a code following the date in the stub; sample surveys are further identified by footnotes; other data are generally estimates, the characteristics of which (*de jure* or *de facto*) are also indicated with a code.

Estimates of urban population presented in this table have been limited to countries or areas for which estimates have been based on the results of sample surveys or have been constructed by the component method from the results of a population census or sample survey. Distributions that result from the estimated total population being distributed by urban/rural residence according to percentages in each group at the time of a census or sample survey have not been included in this table.

Urban is defined according to the national census definition. The definition for each country is set forth at the end of the technical notes to this table.

Percentage computation: Percentages urban are the number of persons residing in an area defined as "urban" per 100 total population. They are calculated by the United Nations Statistics Division. In very few cases the data for total population has been revised but the data for the urban and rural population has not been. These data are footnoted accordingly. In these cases, particular caution should be used in interpreting the figures for percentage urban.

Reliability of data: Estimates that are believed to be less reliable are set in *italics* rather than in roman type. Classification in terms of reliability is based on the method of construction of the total population estimate discussed in the technical notes for table 3.

Limitations: Statistics on urban population by sex are subject to the same qualifications as have been set forth for population statistics in general, as discussed in section 3 of the Technical Notes.

The basic limitations imposed by variations in the definition of the total population and in the degree of under-enumeration are perhaps more important in relation to urban/rural than to any other distributions. The classification by urban and rural is affected by variations in defining usual residence for purposes of sub-national tabulations. Likewise, the geographical differentials in the degree of under-enumeration in censuses affect the comparability of these categories throughout the table. The distinction between *de facto* and *de jure* population is also very important with respect to urban/rural distributions. The difference between the *de facto* and the *de jure* population is discussed at length in section 3.1.1 of the Technical Notes.

A most important and specific limitation, however, lies in the national differences in the definition of urban. Because the distinction between urban and rural areas is made in so many different ways, the definitions have been included at the end of this table. The definitions are necessarily brief and, where the classification as urban involves administrative civil divisions, they are often given in the terminology of the particular country or area. As a result of variations in terminology, it may appear that differences between countries or areas are greater than they actually are. On the other hand, similar or identical terms (for example, town, village, district) as used in different countries or areas may have quite different meanings.

It will be seen from an examination of the definitions that they fall roughly into three major types: (1) classification of localities as urban based on size; (2) classification of administrative centres of minor civil divisions as urban and the remainder of the division as rural; and (3) classification of minor civil divisions on a set of criteria, which may include type of local government, number of inhabitants or proportion of population engaged in agriculture.

The designation of areas as urban or rural is so closely bound to historical, political, cultural, and administrative considerations that the process of developing uniform definitions and procedures moves very slowly. Not only do the definitions differ from one country or area to the other, but, they may also no longer reflect the original intention for distinguishing urban from rural. The criteria once established on the basis of administrative subdivisions (as most of these are) become fixed and resistant to change. For this reason, comparisons of time-series data may be severely affected because the definitions used become outdated. Special care must be taken in comparing data from censuses with those from sample surveys because the definitions of urban used may differ.

Despite their shortcomings, however, statistics on urban and rural population are useful in describing the diversity within the population of a country or area.

103

The definition of urban/rural areas is based on both qualitative and quantitative criteria that may include any combination of the following: size of population, population density, distance between built-up areas, predominant type of economic activity, conformity to legal or administrative status and urban characteristics such as specific services and facilities[1]. Although statistics classified by urban/rural areas are widely available, no international standard definition appears to be possible at this time since the meaning differs from one country or area to another. The urban/rural classification of population used here is reported according to the national definition.

Earlier data: Urban and total population by sex have been shown in previous issues of the Demographic Yearbook. For information on specific years covered, readers should consult the Historical Index.

DEFINITION OF "URBAN"

AFRICA

Botswana: Agglomeration of 5 000 or more inhabitants where 75 per cent of the economic activity is non-agricultural.
Burundi: Commune of Bujumbura.
Comoros: Administrative centres of prefectures and localities of 5 000 or more inhabitants.
Egypt: Governorates of Cairo, Alexandria, Port Said, Ismailia, Suez, frontier governorates and capitals of other governorates, as well as district capitals (Markaz).
Equatorial Guinea: District centres and localities with 300 dwellings and/or 1 500 inhabitants or more.
Ethiopia: Localities of 2 000 or more inhabitants.
Liberia: Localities of 2 000 or more inhabitants.
Malawi: All townships and town planning areas and all district centres.
Mauritius: Towns with proclaimed legal limits.
Niger: Capital city, capitals of the departments and districts
Senegal: Agglomerations of 10 000 or more inhabitants.
South Africa: Places with some form of local authority.
Sudan: Localities of administrative and/or commercial importance or with population of 5 000 or more inhabitants.
Swaziland: Localities proclaimed as urban.
Tunisia: Population living in communes.
United Republic of Tanzania: 16 gazetted townships.
Zambia: Localities of 5 000 or more inhabitants, the majority of whom all depend on non-agricultural activities.

AMERICA, NORTH

Canada: Places of 1 000 or more inhabitants, having a population density of 400 or more per square kilometre.
Costa Rica: Administrative centres of cantons.
Cuba: Population living in a nucleus of 2 000 or more inhabitants.
Dominican Republic: Administrative centres of municipalities and municipal districts, some of which include suburban zones of rural character.
El Salvador: Administrative centres of municipalities.
Greenland: Localities of 200 or more inhabitants.
Guatemala: Municipality of Guatemala Department and officially recognized centres of other departments and municipalities.
Haiti: Administrative centres of communes.
Honduras: Localities of 2 000 or more inhabitants, having essentially urban characteristics.
Mexico: Localities of 2 500 or more inhabitants.
Nicaragua: Administrative centres of municipalities and localities of 1 000 or more inhabitants with streets and electric light.
Panama: Localities of 1 500 or more inhabitants having essentially urban characteristics. Beginning 1970, localities of 1 500 or more inhabitants with such urban characteristics as streets, water supply systems, sewerage systems and electric light.
Puerto Rico: Agglomerations of 2 500 or more inhabitants, generally having population densities of 1 000 persons per square mile or more. Two types of urban areas: urbanized areas of 50 000 or more inhabitants and urban clusters of at least 2 500 and less than 50 000 inhabitants.
United States of America: Agglomerations of 2 500 or more inhabitants, generally having population densities of 1 000 persons per square mile or more. Two types of urban areas: urbanized areas of 50 000 or more inhabitants and urban clusters of at least 2 500 and less than 50 000 inhabitants.
United States Virgin Islands: Agglomerations of 2 500 or more inhabitants, generally having population densities of 1 000 persons per square mile or more. Two types of urban areas: urbanized areas of 50 000 or more inhabitants and

urban clusters of at least 2 500 and less than 50 000 inhabitants. (As of Census 2000, no urbanized areas are identified in the United States Virgin Islands.)

AMERICA, SOUTH

Argentina: Populated centres with 2 000 or more inhabitants.
Bolivia: Localities of 2 000 or more inhabitants.
Brazil: Urban and suburban zones of administrative centres of municipalities and districts.
Chile: Populated centres which have definite urban characteristics such as certain public and municipal services.
Ecuador: Capitals of provinces and cantons.
Falkland Islands (Malvinas): Town of Stanley.
Paraguay: Cities, towns and administrative centres of departments and districts.
Peru: Populated centres with 100 or more dwellings.
Suriname: The districts of Paramaribo and Wanica.
Uruguay: Cities.
Venezuela (Bolivarian Republic of): Centres with a population of 1 000 or more inhabitants.

ASIA

Armenia: Cities and urban-type localities, officially designated as such, usually according to the criteria of number of inhabitants and predominance of agricultural, or number of non-agricultural workers and their families.
Azerbaijan: Cities and urban-type localities, officially designated as such, usually according to the criteria of number of inhabitants and predominance of agricultural, or number of non-agricultural workers and their families.
Bahrain: Communes or villages of 2 500 or more inhabitants.
Cambodia: Towns.
China: Cities only refer to the cities proper of those designated by the State Council. In the case of cities with district establishment, the city proper refers to the whole administrative area of the district if its population density is 1 500 people per kilometre or higher; or the seat of the district government and other areas of streets under the administration of the district if the population density is less than 1 500 people per kilometre. In the case of cities without district establishment, the city proper refers to the seat of the city government and other areas of streets under the administration of the city. For the city district with the population density below 1 500 people per kilometre and the city without district establishment, if the urban construction of the district or city government seat has extended to some part of the neighboring designated town(s) or township(s), the city proper does include the whole administrative area of the town(s) or township(s).
Cyprus: Urban areas are those defined by local town plans.
Georgia: Cities and urban-type localities, officially designated as such, usually according to the criteria of number of inhabitants and predominance of agricultural, or number of non-agricultural workers and their families.
India: Towns (places with municipal corporation, municipal area committee, town committee, notified area committee or cantonment board); also, all places having 5 000 or more inhabitants, a density of not less than 1 000 persons per square mile or 400 per square kilometre, pronounced urban characteristics and at least three fourths of the adult male population employed in pursuits other than agriculture.
Indonesia: Places with urban characteristics.
Iran (Islamic Republic of): Every district with a municipality.
Israel: All settlements of more than 2 000 inhabitants, except those where at least one third of households, participating in the civilian labour force, earn their living from agriculture.
Japan: City (shi) having 50 000 or more inhabitants with 60 per cent or more of the houses located in the main built-up areas and 60 per cent or more of the population (including their dependants) engaged in manufacturing, trade or other urban type of business. Alternatively, a shi having urban facilities and conditions as defined by the prefectural order is considered as urban.
Kazakhstan: Cities and urban-type localities, officially designated as such, usually according to the criteria of number of inhabitants and predominance of agricultural, or number of non-agricultural workers and their families.
Kyrgyzstan: Cities and urban-type localities, officially designated as such, usually according to the criteria of number of inhabitants and predominance of agricultural, or number of non-agricultural workers and their families.
Malaysia: Gazetted areas with population of 10 000 and more.
Maldives: Malé, the capital.
Mongolia: Capital and district centres.
Pakistan: Places with municipal corporation, town committee or cantonment.
Republic of Korea: For estimates: Places with 50 000 or more inhabitants. For census: the figures are composed in the basis of the minor administrative divisions such as Dongs (mostly urban areas) and Eups or Myeons (rural areas).
Sri Lanka: Urban sector comprises of all municipal and urban council areas.
Syrian Arab Republic: Cities, Mohafaza centres and Mantika centres, and communities with 20 000 or more inhabitants.
Tajikistan: Cities and urban-type localities, officially designated as such, usually according to the criteria of number of inhabitants and predominance of agricultural, or number of non-agricultural workers and their families.

Thailand: Municipal areas.

Turkey: Population of settlement places, 20 001 and over.

Turkmenistan: Cities and urban-type localities, officially designated as such, usually according to the criteria of number of inhabitants and predominance of agricultural, or number of non-agricultural workers and their families.

Uzbekistan: Cities and urban-type localities, officially designated as such, usually according to the criteria of number of inhabitants and predominance of agricultural, or number of non-agricultural workers and their families.

Viet Nam: Urban areas include inside urban districts of cities, urban quarters and towns. All other local administrative units (communes) belong to rural areas.

EUROPE

Albania: Towns and other industrial centres of more than 400 inhabitants.

Austria: Communes of more than 5 000 inhabitants.

Belarus: Cities and urban-type localities, officially designated as such, usually according to the criteria of number of inhabitants and predominance of agricultural, or number of non-agricultural workers and their families.

Bulgaria: Towns, that is, localities legally established as urban.

Czech Republic: Localities with 2 000 or more inhabitants.

Estonia: Cities and urban-type localities, officially designated as such, usually according to the criteria of number of inhabitants and predominance of agricultural, or number of non-agricultural workers and their families.

Finland: Urban communes.

France: Communes containing an agglomeration of more than 2 000 inhabitants living in contiguous houses or with not more than 200 metres between houses, also communes of which the major portion of the population is part of a multicommunal agglomeration of this nature.

Greece: Population of municipalities and communes in which the largest population centre has 10 000 or more inhabitants. Including also the population of the 18 urban agglomerations, as these were defined at the census of 1991, namely: Greater Athens, Thessaloniki, Patra, Iraklio, Volos, Chania, Irannina, Chalkida, Agrinio, Kalamata, Katerini, Kerkyra, Salamina, Chios, Egio, Rethymno, Ermoupolis, and Sparti.

Hungary: Budapest and all legally designated towns.

Iceland: Localities of 200 or more inhabitants.

Ireland: Cities and towns including suburbs of 1 500 or more inhabitants.

Latvia: Cities and urban-type localities, officially designated as such, usually according to the criteria of number of inhabitants and predominance of agricultural, or number of non-agricultural workers and their families.

Lithuania: Urban population refers to persons who live in cities and towns, i.e., the population areas with closely built permanent dwellings and with the resident population of more than 3 000 of which 2/3 of employees work in industry, social infrastructure and business. In a number of towns the population may be less than 3 000 since these areas had already the states of "town" before the law was enforced (July 1994)

Netherlands: Urban: Municipalities with a population of 2 000 and more inhabitants. Semi-urban: Municipalities with a population of less than 2 000 but with not more than 20 per cent of their economically active male population engaged in agriculture, and specific residential municipalities of commuters.

Norway: Localities of 200 or more inhabitants.

Poland: Towns and settlements of urban type, e.g. workers' settlements, fishermen's settlements, health resorts.

Portugal: Agglomeration of 10 000 or more inhabitants.

Republic of Moldova: Cities and urban-type localities, officially designated as such, usually according to the criteria of number of inhabitants and predominance of agricultural, or number of non-agricultural workers and their families.

Romania: Cities, municipalities and other towns.

Russian Federation: Cities and urban-type localities, officially designated as such, usually according to the criteria of number of inhabitants and predominance of agricultural, or number of non-agricultural workers and their families.

Slovakia: 138 cities with 5 000 inhabitants or more.

Spain: Localities of 2 000 or more inhabitants.

Switzerland: Communes of 10 000 or more inhabitants, including suburbs.

Ukraine: Cities and urban-type localities, officially designated as such, usually according to the criteria of number of inhabitants and predominance of agricultural, or number of non-agricultural workers and their families.

United Kingdom of Great Britain and Northern Ireland: Settlements where the population is 10 000 or above.

OCEANIA

American Samoa: Agglomerations of 2 500 or more inhabitants, generally having population densities of 1 000 persons per square mile or more. Two types of urban areas: urbanized areas of 50 000 or more inhabitants and urban clusters of at least 2 500 and less than 50 000 inhabitants. (As of Census 2000, no urbanized areas are identified in American Samoa.)

Guam: Agglomerations of 2 500 or more inhabitants, generally having population densities of 1 000 persons per square mile or more, referred to as "urban clusters".

New Caledonia: Nouméa and communes of Païta, Nouvel Dumbéa and Mont-Dore.

New Zealand: All cities, plus boroughs, town districts, townships and country towns with a population of 1 000 or more.

Northern Mariana Islands: Agglomerations of 2 500 or more inhabitants, generally having population densities of 1 000 persons per square mile or more. Two types of urban areas: urbanized areas of 50 000 or more inhabitants and urban clusters of at least 2 500 and less than 50 000 inhabitants.

Vanuatu: Luganville centre and Vila urban.

NOTES

[1] For further information, see *Social and Demographic Statistics: Classifications of Size and Type of Locality and Urban/Rural Areas.* E/CN.3/551, United Nations, New York, 1980.

Tableau 6

Le tableau 6 présente des données sur la population urbaine et la population totale selon le sexe pour le plus grand nombre possible d'années entre 1998 et 2007.

Description des variables : les données proviennent de recensements de la population ou sont des estimations fondées, dans certains cas, sur des enquêtes par sondage portant sur toute la population. Le code qui figure dans la deuxième colonne du tableau indique comment les données ont été obtenues ; les enquêtes par sondage sont en outre signalées par une note en fin de tableau ; toutes les autres données sont en général des estimations et la colonne « Code » indique si elles portent sur la population de fait ou la population de droit.

Les estimations de la population urbaine qui figurent dans le tableau 6 ne concernent que les pays ou zones pour lesquels les estimations se fondent sur les résultats d'une enquête par sondage ou ont été établies par la méthode des composantes à partir des résultats d'un recensement de la population ou d'une enquête par sondage. Les répartitions selon le lieu de résidence (zone urbaine ou rurale) obtenues en appliquant à l'estimation de la population totale les pourcentages enregistrés pour chaque groupe lors d'un recensement ou d'une enquête par sondage n'ont pas été reproduites dans le tableau 6.

Le sens donné au terme « urbain » est conforme aux définitions utilisées dans les recensements nationaux. La définition pour chaque pays figure à la fin des présentes notes technique.

Calcul des pourcentages : les pourcentages de la population urbaine sont calculés par la Division de statistique de l'Organisation des Nations Unies et représentent le nombre de personnes qui vivent dans des régions considérées comme urbaines pour 100 personnes de la population totale. Dans de très rares cas, les données pour la population totale ont été révisées mais les données pour la population urbaine et la population rurale ne l'ont pas été. Ces données sont indiquées en note. Dans ces cas, les proportions de population urbaine ou rurale sont à interpréter avec précaution.

Fiabilité des données : les estimations considérées comme moins sûres sont indiquées en italique plutôt qu'en caractères romains. Le classement du point de vue de la fiabilité est fondé sur la méthode utilisée pour établir l'estimation de la population totale qui figure au tableau 3 (voir les explications dans les notes techniques relatives à ce même tableau).

Insuffisance des données : les statistiques de la population urbaine selon le sexe appellent toutes les réserves qui ont été formulées à la section 3 des Notes techniques à propos des statistiques de la population en général.

Les limitations fondamentales imposées par les variations de la définition de la population totale et par les lacunes du recensement se font peut-être sentir davantage dans la répartition de la population en population urbaine et population rurale que dans sa répartition suivant toute autre caractéristique. De fait, des différences dans la définition du lieu de résidence habituel utilisée pour l'exploitation des données à l'échelon sous-national influent sur la classification en population urbaine et en population rurale. De même, les différences de degré de sous-dénombrement suivant la zone, à l'occasion des recensements, ont une incidence sur la comparabilité de ces deux catégories dans l'ensemble du tableau. La distinction entre population de fait et population de droit est également très importante du point de vue de la répartition de la population en population urbaine et en population rurale. Cette distinction est expliquée en détail à la section 3.1.1 des Notes techniques.

Toutefois, la difficulté la plus importante tient aux différences de définition du terme « urbain » selon le pays. Les distinctions faites entre « zone urbaine » et « zone rurale » varient tellement que les définitions utilisées ont été reproduites à la fin des notes techniques du tableau 6. Les définitions sont forcément brèves et, lorsque le classement en « zone urbaine » repose sur des divisions administratives, on a souvent désigné celles-ci par le nom qu'elles portent dans la zone ou le pays considéré. Par suite des variations dans la terminologie, les différences entre pays ou zones peuvent sembler plus grandes qu'elles ne le sont réellement. Il se peut aussi que des termes similaires ou identiques, tels que ville, village ou district, aient des significations très différentes selon les pays ou zones.

On constatera, en examinant les définitions adoptées par les différents pays ou zones, qu'elles peuvent être ramenées à trois types principaux : 1) les localités dépassant certaines dimensions sont classées parmi les zones urbaines ; 2) les centres administratifs de petites circonscriptions administratives sont classées parmi les zones urbaines, le reste de la circonscription étant considéré comme zone rurale ; 3) les petites divisions administratives sont classées parmi les zones urbaines selon un critère déterminé, qui peut être soit le type d'administration locale, soit le nombre d'habitants, soit le pourcentage de la population exerçant une activité agricole.

La distinction entre régions urbaines et régions rurales est si étroitement liée à des considérations d'ordre historique, politique, culturel et administratif que l'on ne peut progresser que très lentement vers des définitions et des méthodes uniformes. Non seulement les définitions sont différentes d'une zone ou d'un pays à un autre, mais on n'y retrouve parfois même plus l'intention originale de distinguer les régions rurales des régions urbaines. Lorsque la classification est fondée, en particulier, sur le critère des circonscriptions administratives (comme la plupart le sont), elle a tendance à devenir rigide avec le temps et à décourager toute modification. Pour cette raison, la comparaison des données appartenant à des séries chronologiques risque d'être gravement faussée du fait que les définitions employées sont désormais périmées. Il faut être particulièrement prudent lorsque l'on compare des données issues de recensements avec des données provenant d'enquêtes par sondage, car il se peut que les définitions du terme « urbain » auxquelles ces données se réfèrent respectivement soient différentes.

Malgré leurs insuffisances, les statistiques sur la population urbaine et rurale permettent de mettre en évidence la diversité de la population d'un pays ou d'une zone.

La distinction entre « zone urbaine » et « zone rurale » repose sur une série de critères qualitatifs aussi bien que quantitatifs, notamment l'effectif de la population, la densité de peuplement, la distance entre îlots d'habitations, le type prédominant d'activité économique, le statut juridique ou administratif, et les caractéristiques d'une agglomération urbaine, c'est-à-dire l'existence de services publics et d'équipements collectifs[1]. Bien que les statistiques différenciant les zones urbaines des zones rurales soient très répandues, il ne paraît pas possible pour le moment d'adopter une classification internationale type de ces zones, vu la diversité des interprétations nationales. La classification de la population en population urbaine et population rurale retenue ici est celle qui correspond aux définitions nationales.

Données publiées antérieurement : des statistiques concernant la population urbaine et la population totale selon le sexe ont été publiées dans des éditions antérieures de l'*Annuaire démographique*. Pour plus de précisions concernant les années pour lesquelles ces données ont été publiées, se reporter à l'index historique.

DÉFINITIONS DU TERME « URBAIN »

AFRIQUE

Afrique du Sud : Zones dotées d'une administration locale.

Botswana : Agglomération de 5 000 habitants ou plus dont 75 p. 100 de l'activité économique n'est pas de type agricole.

Burundi : Commune de Bujumbura.

Comores : Chefs-lieux de préfectures et localités de 5 000 habitants ou plus.

Égypte : Chefs-lieux des gouvernorats du Caire, d'Alexandrie, de Port Saïd, d'Ismaïlia, de Suez ; chefs-lieux des gouvernorats frontaliers, autres chefs-lieux de gouvernorat et chefs-lieux de district (Markaz).

Éthiopie : Localités de 2 000 habitants ou plus.

Guinée équatoriale : Chefs-lieux de district et localités comprenant 300 habitations et/ou 1 500 habitants ou plus.

Libéria : Localités de 2 000 habitants ou plus.

Malawi : Toutes les villes et zones urbanisées et tous les chefs-lieux de district.

Maurice : Villes ayant des limites officiellement définies.

Niger : Ville capital, villes capitales de départements ou de districts.

République-Unie de Tanzanie : 16 townships érigées en communes.

Sénégal : Agglomérations de 10 000 habitants ou plus.

Soudan : Centres administratifs et/ou commerciaux ou localités ayant une population de 5 000 habitants ou plus.

Swaziland : Localités déclarées urbaines.

Tunisie : Population vivant dans les communes.

Zambie : Localités de 5 000 habitants ou plus dont l'activité économique prédominante n'est pas de type agricole.

AMÉRIQUE DU NORD

Canada : Agglomérations de 1 000 habitants ou plus ayant une densité de population d'au moins 400 habitants au kilomètre carré.

Costa Rica : Chefs-lieux de canton.

Cuba : Population vivant dans des agglomérations de 2 000 habitants ou plus.

El Salvador : Chefs-lieux de municipios.

États-Unis d'Amérique : Agglomérations de 2 500 habitants ou plus ayant généralement une densité de population d'au moins 1 000 habitants au mile carré. Deux types de zones urbaines : zones urbanisées de 50 000 habitants ou plus et groupements urbains comptant au moins 2 500 habitants mais moins de 50 000.

Groenland : Localités d'au moins 200 habitants.

Guatemala : Municipio du département de Guatemala et centres administratifs officiels d'autres départements et municipios.

Haïti : Chefs-lieux de communes.

Honduras : Localités d'au moins 2 000 habitants ayant des caractéristiques essentiellement urbaines.

Îles Vierges américaines : Agglomérations de 2 500 habitants ou plus ayant généralement une densité de population d'au moins 1 000 habitants au mile carré. Deux types de zones urbaines : zones urbanisées de 50 000 habitants ou plus et groupements urbains comptant au moins 2 500 habitants mais moins de 50 000. (D'après les résultats du recensement de 2000, les Îles Vierges américaines ne comptent aucune zone urbanisée.)

Mexique : Localités d'au moins 2 500 habitants.

Nicaragua : Chefs-lieux de municipios et agglomérations d'au moins 1 000 habitants dotées de rues et de l'éclairage électrique.

Panama : Localités d'au moins 1 500 habitants ayant des caractéristiques essentiellement urbaines. À partir de 1970, localités de 1 500 habitants ou plus présentant des caractéristiques urbaines, telles que rues, éclairage électrique, systèmes d'approvisionnement en eau et réseaux d'égouts.

Porto Rico : Agglomérations de 2 500 habitants ou plus ayant généralement une densité de population d'au moins 1 000 habitants au mile carré. Deux types de zones urbaines : zones urbanisées de 50 000 habitants ou plus et groupements urbains comptant au moins 2 500 habitants mais moins de 50 000.

République dominicaine : Chefs-lieux de municipios et districts municipaux, dont certains comprennent des zones suburbaines ayant des caractéristiques rurales.

AMÉRIQUE DU SUD

Argentine : Centres comptant au moins 2 000 habitants.

Bolivie : Localités de 2 000 habitants ou plus.

Brésil : Zones urbaines et suburbaines des chefs lieux de municipalités et de districts.

Chili : Centres de peuplement ayant des caractéristiques nettement urbaines (présence de certains services publics et municipaux).

Équateur : Capitales des provinces et chefs-lieux de canton.

Îles Falkland (Malvinas) : Ville de Stanley.

Paraguay : Grandes villes, villes et chefs-lieux des départements et des districts.

Pérou : Centres de peuplement comptant plus de 100 logements.

Suriname : Les districts de Paramaribo et de Wanica.

Uruguay : Villes.

Venezuela (République bolivarienne du) : Centres de 1 000 habitants ou plus.

ASIE

Arménie : Grandes villes et localités de type urbain, officiellement désignées comme telles, généralement sur la base du nombre d'habitants et de la prédominance des travailleurs agricoles ou non agricoles avec leur famille.

Azerbaïdjan : Grandes villes et localités de type urbain, officiellement désignées comme telles, généralement sur la base du nombre d'habitants et de la prédominance des travailleurs agricoles ou non agricoles avec leur famille.

Bahreïn : Communes ou villages comptant au moins 2 500 habitants.

Cambodge : Villes.

Chine : Villes désignées comme telles par le Conseil d'État. Dans le cas de villes ayant rang de district, la ville s'entend comme l'ensemble de la zone administrative qui relève du district si sa densité est d'au moins 1 500 habitants au kilomètre carré ou comme le siège des autorités du district et les rues qui relèvent du district si sa densité est inférieure à 1 500 habitants au kilomètre carré. Dans le cas des villes qui n'ont pas rang de district, la ville s'entend comme le siège des autorités de la commune et les rues qui relèvent des autorités de la commune. Dans le cas des villes ayant rang de district qui comptent moins de 1 500 habitants au kilomètre carré et des villes n'ayant pas rang de district, si l'urbanisation du siège du district ou du siège des autorités de la commune a empiété sur une partie de la ou des localités voisines, la ville inclut alors l'ensemble de la zone administrative desdites localités.

Chypre : Zones désignées comme urbaines dans les plans d'urbanisme locaux.

Géorgie : Grandes villes et localités de type urbain, officiellement désignées comme telles, généralement sur la base du nombre d'habitants et de la prédominance des travailleurs agricoles ou non agricoles avec leur famille.

Inde : Villes [localités dotées d'une charte municipale, d'un comité de zone municipale, d'un comité de zone déclarée urbaine ou d'un comité de zone de regroupement (cantonnement)] ; également toutes les localités qui ont une population de 5 000 habitants au moins, une densité de population d'au moins 1 000 habitants au mile carré ou 400 au kilomètre carré, des caractéristiques urbaines prononcées et où les trois quarts au moins des adultes de sexe masculin ont une occupation non agricole.

Indonésie : Localités présentant des caractéristiques urbaines.

Iran (République islamique d') : Tous les districts comptant une municipalité.

Israël : Tous les lieux comptant au moins 2 000 habitants, à l'exception de ceux où le tiers au moins des chefs de ménage faisant partie de la population civile active vivent de l'agriculture.

Japon : Villes (shi), comptant au moins 50 000 habitants, où 60 p. 100 au moins des logements sont situés dans les principales zones bâties, et dont 60 p. 100 au moins de population (y compris les personnes à charge) exercent un métier dans l'industrie, le commerce et d'autres branches d'activités essentiellement urbaines. Tout shi possédant les équipements et présentant les caractéristiques définies comme urbaines par l'administration préfectorale est également considéré comme zone urbaine.

Kazakhstan : Grandes villes et localités de type urbain, officiellement désignées comme telles, généralement sur la base du nombre d'habitants et de la prédominance des travailleurs agricoles ou non agricoles avec leur famille.

Kirghizistan : Grandes villes et localités de type urbain, officiellement désignées comme telles, généralement sur la base du nombre d'habitants et de la prédominance des travailleurs agricoles ou non agricoles avec leur famille.

Malaisie : Zones déclarées « zones urbaines » et comptant au moins 10 000 habitants.

Maldives : Malé (capitale).

Mongolie : Capitale et chefs-lieux de district.

Ouzbékistan : Grandes villes et localités de type urbain, officiellement désignées comme telles, généralement sur la base du nombre d'habitants et de la prédominance des travailleurs agricoles ou non agricoles avec leur famille.

Pakistan : Localités dotées d'une charte municipale ou d'un comité municipal et regroupements (cantonments).

République arabe syrienne : Villes, chefs-lieux de district (Mohafaza) et chefs-lieux de sous district (Mantika), et communes d'au moins 20 000 habitants.

République de Corée : Pour les estimations : localités de 50 000 habitants ou plus. Pour recensements, les données sont établies sont la base des divisions administratives mineures comme les Dongs (principalement en zone urbaines) et des Eups ou Myeons (en zones rurales).

Sri Lanka : Secteur urbain composé de toutes les zones municipales et zones dotées d'un conseil urbain.

Tadjikistan : Grandes villes et localités de type urbain, officiellement désignées comme telles, généralement sur la base du nombre d'habitants et de la prédominance des travailleurs agricoles ou non agricoles avec leur famille.

Thaïlande : Zones municipales.

Turkménistan : Grandes villes et localités de type urbain, officiellement désignées comme telles, généralement sur la base du nombre d'habitants et de la prédominance des travailleurs agricoles ou non agricoles avec leur famille.

Turquie : Population d'établissements humains s'établissant à plus de 20 000 personnes.

Viet Nam : Zones urbaines comprises à l'intérieur des districts urbains des villes ainsi que des quartiers urbains et des localités. Toutes les autres unités administratives locales (communes) sont considérées comme zones rurales.

Yémen : Définition non communiquée.

EUROPE

Albanie : Villes et autres centres industriels de plus de 400 habitants.

Autriche : Communes de plus de 5 000 habitants.

Bélarus : Grandes villes et localités de type urbain, officiellement désignées comme telles, généralement sur la base du nombre d'habitants et de la prédominance des travailleurs agricoles ou non agricoles avec leur famille.

Bulgarie : Villes, c'est-à-dire localités reconnues comme urbaines.

Espagne : Localités de 2 000 habitants et plus.

Estonie : Grandes villes et localités de type urbain, officiellement désignées comme telles, généralement sur la base du nombre d'habitants et de la prédominance des travailleurs agricoles ou non agricoles avec leur famille.

Fédération de Russie : Grandes villes et localités de type urbain, officiellement désignées comme telles, généralement sur la base du nombre d'habitants et de la prédominance des travailleurs agricoles ou non agricoles avec leur famille.

Finlande : Communes urbaines.

France : Communes comprenant une agglomération de plus de 2 000 habitants vivant dans des habitations contiguës ou qui ne sont pas distantes les unes des autres de plus de 200 mètres et communes où la majeure partie de la population vit dans une agglomération regroupant plusieurs communes de cette nature.

Grèce : Municipalités et communes de 10 000 habitants ou plus pour l'agglomération. Y compris également 18 agglomérations urbaines, selon la définition qui en a été donnée lors du recensement de 1991, à savoir : Athènes et sa banlieue, Thessalonique, Patras, Héraklion, Volos, Chania, Ioannina, Chalkida, Agrinio, Kalamata, Katerini, Kerkyra, Salamine, Chios, Egio, Rethymno, Ermoupolis et Sparte.

Hongrie : Budapest et toutes les autres localités reconnues officiellement comme urbaines.

Irlande : Localités, y compris leur banlieues, comptant 1 500 habitants ou plus.

Islande : Localités de 200 habitants ou plus.

Lettonie : Grandes villes et localités de type urbain, officiellement désignées comme telles, généralement sur la base du nombre d'habitants et de la prédominance des travailleurs agricoles ou non agricoles avec leur famille.

Lituanie : Par population urbaine, on entend les personnes qui vivent dans des villes ou des localités, à savoir les zones habitées comportant des logements permanents proches les uns des autres et dont la population est d'au moins 3 000 habitants, les deux tiers desquels étant employés dans le secteur industriel, l'infrastructure sociale ou le commerce. Un certain nombre de villes peuvent compter moins de 3 000 habitants dans la mesure où elles avaient acquis le statut de ville avant l'entrée en vigueur de la nouvelle loi en juillet 1994.

Norvège : Localités de 200 habitants ou plus.

Pays Bas : Zones urbaines : municipalités comptant au moins 2 000 habitants. Zones semi-urbaines : municipalités comptant moins de 2 000 habitants, mais où 20 p. 100 au maximum de la population active de sexe masculin pratiquent l'agriculture, et certaines municipalités de caractère résidentiel dont les habitants travaillent ailleurs.

Pologne : Villes et zones de type urbain, par exemple groupements de travailleurs ou de pêcheurs et stations climatiques.

Portugal : Agglomérations d'au moins 10 000 habitants.

République de Moldova : Grandes villes et localités de type urbain, officiellement désignées comme telles, généralement sur la base du nombre d'habitants et de la prédominance des travailleurs agricoles ou non agricoles avec leur famille.

République tchèque : Localités d'au moins 2 000 habitants.

Roumanie : Grandes villes, municipalités et autres villes.

Royaume-Uni de Grande-Bretagne et d'Irlande du Nord : Agglomérations de population de 10 000 habitants ou plus.

Slovaquie : 138 localités comptant 5 000 habitants ou plus.

Suisse : Communes de 10 000 habitants ou plus, et leurs banlieues.

Ukraine : Grandes villes et localités de type urbain, officiellement désignées comme telles, généralement sur la base du nombre d'habitants et de la prédominance des travailleurs agricoles ou non agricoles avec leur famille.

OCÉANIE

Guam : Agglomérations de 2 500 habitants ou plus ayant généralement une densité de population d'au moins 1 000 habitants au mile carré et considérées comme étant des groupements urbains.

Îles Mariannes septentrionales : Agglomérations de 2 500 habitants ou plus ayant généralement une densité de population d'au moins 1 000 habitants au mile carré. Deux types de zones urbaines : zones urbanisées de 50 000 habitants ou plus et groupements urbains comptant au moins 2 500 habitants mais moins de 50 000.

Nouvelle-Calédonie : Nouméa et communes de Païta, Dumbéa et Mont-Dore.

Nouvelle-Zélande : Grandes villes, boroughs, chefs-lieux, municipalités et chefs-lieux de comté d'au moins 1 000 habitants.

Samoa américaines : Agglomérations de 2 500 habitants ou plus ayant généralement une densité de population d'au moins 1 000 habitants au mile carré. Deux types de zones urbaines : zones urbanisées de 50 000 habitants ou plus et groupements urbains comptant au moins 2 500 habitants mais moins de 50 000. (D'après les résultats du recensement de 2000, les Samoa américaines ne comptent aucune zone urbanisée.)

Vanuatu : Centre de Luganville et Port-Vila.

NOTES

[1] Pour plus de précisions, voir *Social and Demographic Statistics: Classifications of Size and Type of Locality and Urban/Rural Areas*, E/CN.3/551, publication des Nations Unies, New York, 1980.

Continent, country or area, and date / Continent, pays ou zone et date	Code[a]	Both sexes - Les deux sexes			Male - Masculin			Female - Féminin		
			Urban - Urbaine			Urban - Urbaine			Urban - Urbaine	
		Total	Number Nombre	Percent P.100	Total	Number Nombre	Percent P.100	Total	Number Nombre	Percent P.100
AFRICA - AFRIQUE										
Algeria - Algérie										
25 VI 1998	CDJC	29 100 867	16 966 939	58.3	14 698 589	8 563 287	58.3	14 402 278	8 403 652	58.3
1 VII 1998	ESDJ	29 507 000	...	...	14 957 049	...	...	14 550 451	...	...
1 VII 1999	ESDJ	29 965 000	...	...	15 132 000	...	...	14 833 000	...	...
1 VII 2000	ESDJ	30 416 000	...	...	15 357 000	...	...	15 059 000	...	...
1 VII 2001	ESDJ	30 871 734	...	...	15 598 261	...	...	15 273 473	...	...
1 VII 2002	ESDJ	31 332 033	...	...	15 830 343	...	...	15 501 690	...	...
1 VII 2003	ESDJ	31 847 995	...	...	16 090 568	...	...	15 757 427	...	...
Benin - Bénin										
1 VII 1998	ESDF	6 044 223	2 324 608	38.5	2 943 619	1 132 116	38.5	3 100 604	1 192 492	38.5
1 VII 1999	ESDF	5 990 396	2 383 244	39.8	...	...	...	3 155 379	...	...
1 VII 2000	ESDF	6 169 084	2 492 967	40.4	3 013 705	1 220 905	40.5	3 155 379	1 272 062	40.3
1 VII 2001*	ESDF	6 416 692	...	...	3 136 516	...	...	3 280 176	...	...
11 II 2002	CDJC	6 769 914	2 630 133	38.9	3 284 119	1 280 418	39.0	3 485 795	1 349 715	38.7
1 VII 2003*[1]	ESDF	6 973 905	...	...	3 387 190	...	...	3 586 715	...	...
1 VII 2005*[1]	ESDF	7 395 040	...	...	3 599 824	...	...	3 795 216	...	...
1 VII 2006*[1]	ESDF	7 612 145	...	...	3 708 365	...	...	3 903 780	...	...
1 VII 2007*[1]	ESDF	8 053 690	...	...	3 934 723	...	...	4 118 967	...	...
Botswana										
1 VII 1998	ESDF	1 571 728	...	...	757 669	...	...	814 059	...	...
1 VII 1999	ESDF	1 611 021	...	...	779 010	...	...	832 011	...	...
1 VII 2000	ESDF	1 653 061	...	...	799 735	...	...	853 326	...	...
17 VIII 2001	CDFC	1 680 863	910 480[2]	54.2	813 488	428 856	52.7	867 375	481 624	55.5
1 VII 2002	ESDF	1 649 659	375 461	22.8	795 938	...	...	853 721	...	...
1 VII 2003	ESDF	1 673 184	384 940	23.0	809 278	...	...	863 906	...	...
1 VII 2004	ESDF	1 692 731	393 528	23.2	820 577	191 287	23.3	872 155	202 241	23.2
1 VII 2005	ESDF	1 708 327	...	...	829 850	...	...	878 477	...	...
1 VII 2006	ESDF	1 719 996	...	...	837 114	...	...	882 882	...	...
1 VII 2007	ESDF	1 736 396	...	...	847 539	...	...	888 857	...	...
Burkina Faso										
1 VII 1998	ESDJ	10 816 222	1 695 441	15.7	5 215 231	858 953	16.5	5 600 991	836 487	14.9
1 VII 1999	ESDJ	11 078 076	1 744 784	15.7	5 342 307	884 033	16.5	5 874 104	860 751	15.0
1 VII 2000	ESDJ	11 346 880	1 795 663	15.8	5 472 776	909 895	16.6	5 874 104	885 767	15.1
1 VII 2001	ESDJ	11 622 833	1 848 126	15.9	5 606 733	936 565	16.7	6 016 100	911 561	15.2
1 VII 2002	ESDJ	11 906 137	1 902 225	16.0	5 744 279	964 067	16.8	6 161 858	938 158	15.2
1 VII 2003	ESDJ	12 197 002	1 958 013	16.1	5 885 516	992 431	16.9	6 311 486	965 582	15.3
1 VII 2004	ESDJ	12 495 643	2 015 546	16.1	6 030 550	1 021 683	16.9	6 465 093	993 863	15.4
1 VII 2005	ESDJ	12 802 282	2 074 879	16.2	6 179 489	1 051 853	17.0	6 622 793	1 023 026	15.4
1 VII 2006[1]	ESDJ	13 117 147	2 136 071	16.3	...	...	...	...	...	...
9 XII 2006	CDJC	14 017 262	3 181 967	22.7	6 768 739	1 588 895	23.5	7 248 523	1 593 072	22.0
1 VII 2007[1]	ESDJ	14 252 012	3 322 360	23.3	6 880 824	1 629 956	23.7	7 371 188	1 692 404	23.0
Burundi										
1 VII 1998	ESDF	6 300 489	493 297	7.8	3 064 211	...	...	3 236 278	...	...
1 VII 1999	ESDF	6 482 662	...	...	3 152 810	...	...	3 329 852	...	...
1 VII 2000	ESDF	6 664 835	...	...	3 239 532	...	...	3 425 303	...	...
1 VII 2001	ESDF	6 847 007	...	...	3 336 727	...	...	3 510 280	...	...
1 VII 2002	ESDF	7 032 178	...	...	3 428 453	...	...	3 603 725	...	...
1 VII 2003	ESDF	7 211 356	...	...	3 515 469	...	...	3 695 887	...	...
1 VII 2004	ESDF	7 384 423	...	...	3 599 838	...	...	3 784 585	...	...
Cameroon - Cameroun[1]										
1 VII 1998	ESDF	14 439 000	6 960 000	48.2	...	...	...	...	...	...
1 VII 2001	ESDF	15 731 000	8 023 000	51.0	...	...	...	...	...	...
1 VII 2002	ESDF	16 170 000	8 392 000	51.9	...	...	...	...	...	...
1 VII 2003	ESDF	16 626 000	8 779 000	52.8	...	...	...	...	...	...
1 VII 2004	ESDF	17 000 000	9 086 000	53.4	...	...	...	...	...	...
Cape Verde - Cap-Vert										
1 VII 1998	ESDF	417 200	...	...	198 946	...	...	218 254	...	...
1 VII 1999	ESDF	428 230	...	...	204 433	...	...	223 797	...	...
16 VI 2000	CDFC	436 863	235 470	53.9	211 479	114 928	54.3	225 384	120 542	53.5
1 VII 2001	ESDF	444 921	248 557	55.9	215 352	118 350[3]	55.0	229 569	124 133[3]	54.1
1 VII 2002	ESDF	452 835	256 172	56.6	219 177	121 924[3]	55.6	233 658	127 870[3]	54.7
1 VII 2003	ESDF	460 601	263 791	57.3	222 911	125 652[3]	56.4	237 690	131 759[3]	55.4
1 VII 2004	ESDF	468 164	271 415	58.0	226 560	...	...	241 604	...	...
1 VII 2005	ESDF	475 465	278 947	58.7	230 063	...	...	245 402	...	...

Continent, country or area, and date / Continent, pays ou zone et date	Code[a]	Both sexes - Les deux sexes			Male - Masculin			Female - Féminin		
		Total	Urban - Urbaine		Total	Urban - Urbaine		Total	Urban - Urbaine	
			Number Nombre	Percent P.100		Number Nombre	Percent P.100		Number Nombre	Percent P.100
AFRICA - AFRIQUE										
Cape Verde - Cap-Vert										
1 VII 2006 ....ESDF		483 090	286 687	59.3	233 729	...	...	249 361	...	...
1 VII 2007 ....ESDF		491 419	295 046	60.0	237 842	...	...	253 577	...	...
Central African Republic - République centrafricaine										
8 XII 2003 ....CDFC		3 151 072	1 194 851	37.9	1 569 446	598 880	38.2	1 581 626	595 969	37.7
Comoros - Comores										
1 IX 2003...........CDFC		575 660[4]	160 865	27.9	...	...	...	...	...	...
Congo										
1 VII 1998 ....ESDF		2 737 928	...	...	1 333 371	...	...	1 404 557	...	...
1 VII 1999 ....ESDF		2 814 590	...	...	1 370 705	...	...	1 443 885	...	...
1 VII 2000 ....ESDF		2 893 398	...	...	1 409 085	...	...	1 484 313	...	...
1 VII 2001 ....ESDF		2 974 413	...	...	1 448 539	...	...	1 525 874	...	...
1 VII 2002 ....ESDF		3 057 697	...	...	1 489 098	...	...	1 568 599	...	...
1 VII 2003 ....ESDF		3 143 313	...	...	1 530 793	...	...	1 612 520	...	...
1 VII 2004 ....ESDF		3 231 326	...	...	1 573 656	...	...	1 657 670	...	...
Côte d'Ivoire										
21 XI 1998...........CDFC		15 366 672	6 529 138	42.5	7 844 621	...	...	7 522 050	...	...
1 VII 1999 ....ESDF		15 881 066	...	...	8 107 236	...	...	7 773 828	...	...
1 VII 2000 ....ESDF		16 401 514	...	...	8 372 518	...	...	8 028 996	...	...
1 VII 2001 ....ESDF		16 928 324	...	...	8 640 647	...	...	8 287 679	...	...
1 VII 2002 ....ESDF		17 461 446	...	...	8 911 589	...	...	8 549 848	...	...
1 VII 2003 ....ESDF		18 000 876	...	...	9 185 374	...	...	8 815 505	...	...
1 VII 2004 ....ESDF		18 545 968	...	...	9 461 591	...	...	9 084 374	...	...
1 VII 2005 ....ESDF		19 096 988	...	...	9 740 427	...	...	9 356 561	...	...
1 VII 2006 ....ESDF		19 657 738	...	...	10 023 964	...	...	9 633 774	...	...
1 VII 2007 ....ESDF		20 227 876	...	...	10 312 061	...	...	9 915 815	...	...
Egypt - Égypte										
1 VII 1998 ....ESDF		61 340 882	26 123 481	42.6	31 379 023	13 363 507	42.6	29 961 859	12 759 974	42.6
1 VII 1999 ....ESDF		62 638 849	26 589 809	42.4	32 034 553	13 632 299	42.6	30 604 296	13 008 893	42.5
1 VII 2000 ....ESDF		63 974 724	27 144 976	42.4	32 714 157	...	...	31 260 567	...	...
1 VII 2001 ....ESDF		65 298 293	28 168 172	43.1	33 378 636	...	...	31 919 657	...	...
1 VII 2002 ....ESDF		66 627 610	28 553 755	42.9	34 052 407	...	...	32 575 203	...	...
1 VII 2003 ....ESDF		67 965 096	29 130 214	42.9	34 720 973	...	...	33 244 123	...	...
1 VII 2004 ....ESDF		69 303 902	29 652 904	42.8	35 379 626	...	...	33 924 276	...	...
1 VII 2005 ....ESDF		70 653 326	30 187 331	42.7	36 037 030	...	...	34 616 296	...	...
1 VII 2006 ....ESDF		72 008 900	30 699 375	42.6	36 725 501	...	...	35 283 399	...	...
11 XI 2006[5] ....CDFC		72 798 031	...	...	37 219 056	...	...	35 578 975	...	...
1 VII 2007 ....ESDF		73 643 587	31 719 927	43.1	37 643 353	16 186 484	43.0	36 000 234	15 533 443	43.1
Equatorial Guinea - Guinée équatoriale										
1 II 2002...........CDFC		1 014 999	...	...	501 387	...	...	513 612	...	...
Ethiopia - Éthiopie										
1 VII 1998 ....ESDF		59 882 000	8 691 000	14.5	30 071 000	4 299 000	14.3	29 811 000	4 392 000	14.7
1 VII 1999 ....ESDF		61 672 000	9 074 000	14.7	30 956 000	4 504 000	14.5	30 716 000	4 570 000	14.9
1 VII 2000 ....ESDF		63 494 702	9 472 971	14.9	...	...	...	...	...	...
1 VII 2001 ....ESDF		65 374 320	9 883 138	15.1	32 815 082	4 938 725	15.1	32 559 238	4 944 413	15.2
1 VII 2002 ....ESDF		67 220 000	10 307 000	15.3	33 707 000	5 134 000	15.2	33 513 000	5 173 000	15.4
1 VII 2003 ....ESDF		69 127 000	10 745 000	15.5	34 653 000	5 347 000	15.4	34 474 000	5 398 000	15.7
1 VII 2004 ....ESDF		71 066 000	11 199 000	15.8	35 618 000	5 568 000	15.6	35 448 000	5 631 000	15.9
1 VII 2005 ....ESDF		73 043 510	11 674 521	16.0	36 604 591	5 802 931	15.9	36 438 919	5 871 590	16.1
1 VII 2006[1] ....ESDF		75 067 000	12 172 000	16.2	37 615 000	6 050 000	16.1	37 452 000	6 122 000	16.3
28 V 2007[6] ....CDFC		73 918 505	11 956 170	16.2	37 296 657	5 942 170	15.9	36 621 848	6 014 000	16.4
Gabon[7]										
1 VII 2005 ....ESDF		1 312 500	...	...	645 700	...	...	666 700	...	...
Gambia - Gambie										
15 IV 2003* ....CDFC		1 364 507	...	...	676 726	...	...	687 781	...	...
Ghana										
26 III 2000...........CDFC		18 912 079	8 274 270	43.8	9 357 382	4 043 830	43.2	9 554 697	4 230 440	44.3
1 VII 2000[1] ....ESDF		19 046 050	...	...	9 423 669	...	...	9 622 381	...	...
1 VII 2001[1] ....ESDF		19 395 730	...	...	9 595 836	...	...	9 799 894	...	...
1 VII 2002[1] ....ESDF		19 877 534	...	...	9 833 408	...	...	10 044 126	...	...
1 VII 2003[1] ....ESDF		20 359 380	...	...	10 071 077	...	...	10 288 303	...	...

Continent, country or area, and date / Continent, pays ou zone et date	Code[a]	Both sexes - Les deux sexes			Male - Masculin			Female - Féminin		
		Total	Urban - Urbaine		Total	Urban - Urbaine		Total	Urban - Urbaine	
			Number Nombre	Percent P.100		Number Nombre	Percent P.100		Number Nombre	Percent P.100

AFRICA - AFRIQUE

Ghana										
1 VII 2004[1] ....ESDF		20 841 844	...	...	10 309 156	...	...	10 532 728	...	...
1 VII 2005[1] ....ESDF		21 343 208	...	...	10 557 429	...	...	10 785 781	...	...
Kenya										
1 VII 1998 ....ESDF		28 611 152	...	...	14 772 000	...	...	14 858 000	...	...
1 VII 1999 ....ESDF		29 453 024	5 429 790	18.4	14 342 209	...	...	15 110 815	...	...
24 VIII 1999 ....CDFC		28 686 607	3 539 888	12.3	14 205 589	1 933 437	13.6	14 481 018	1 606 451	11.1
1 VII 2000 ....ESDF		30 149 656	5 234 577	17.4	14 846 350	3 096 394	20.9	15 303 306	2 138 183	14.0
1 VII 2001 ....ESDF		31 120 677	5 421 964	17.4	15 341 600	3 209 419	20.9	15 779 077	2 212 546	14.0
1 VII 2002 ....ESDF		32 117 987	5 613 669	17.5	15 850 411	3 325 186	21.0	16 267 576	2 288 483	14.1
1 VII 2003 ....ESDF		33 141 617	5 809 612	17.5	16 372 798	3 443 644	21.0	16 768 819	2 365 968	14.1
1 VII 2004 ....ESDF		34 191 382	6 009 718	17.6	16 908 648	3 564 746	21.1	17 282 734	2 444 972	14.1
1 VII 2005 ....ESDF		35 267 222	6 213 505	17.6	17 457 906	3 688 113	21.1	17 809 316	2 525 392	14.2
1 VII 2006 ....ESDF		36 432 866	...	...	18 052 944	...	...	18 379 922	...	...
1 VII 2007 ....ESDF		37 183 923	...	...	18 440 822	...	...	18 743 102	...	...
Lesotho										
1 VII 1998 ....ESDF		2 055 449	...	...	1 013 911	...	...	1 041 504	...	...
1 VII 1999 ....ESDF		2 099 646	...	...	1 036 504	...	...	1 063 142	...	...
1 VII 2000 ....ESDF		2 144 146	...	...	1 059 014	...	...	1 085 132	...	...
1 VII 2001 ....SSDJ		2 157 537	288 895	13.4	1 065 484	131 861	12.4	1 092 053	157 034	14.4
9 IV 2006* ....CDJC		1 880 661	447 970	23.8	916 281	207 848	22.7	964 380	240 122	24.9
Libyan Arab Jamahiriya - Jamahiriya arabe libyenne[8]										
1 VII 1998 ....ESDF		4 772 430	...	...	2 350 628	...	...	2 421 802	...	...
1 VII 1999 ....ESDF		4 957 663	...	...	2 444 706	...	...	2 512 957	...	...
1 VII 2000 ....ESDF		5 124 519	...	...	2 528 980	...	...	2 595 539	...	...
1 VII 2001 ....ESDF		5 299 943	...	...	2 682 254	...	...	2 617 689	...	...
1 VII 2002 ....ESDF		5 484 426	...	...	2 773 333	...	...	2 711 093	...	...
Madagascar										
1 VII 1998 ....ESDF		14 222 000	3 562 000	25.0	7 091 000[9]	1 745 000	24.6	7 132 000[9]	1 817 000	25.5
1 VII 1999 ....ESDF		14 650 000	3 741 000	25.5	7 306 000[9]	1 834 000	25.1	7 343 000[9]	1 907 000	26.0
1 VII 2000 ....ESDF		15 085 000	3 927 000	26.0	7 526 000	1 926 000	25.6	7 559 000	2 001 000	26.5
1 VII 2001 ....ESDF		15 529 000	4 122 000	26.5	...	...	...	...	...	...
1 VII 2002 ....ESDF		15 981 000	4 327 000	27.1	...	...	...	...	...	...
1 VII 2003 ....ESDF		16 441 000	4 544 000	27.6	...	...	...	...	...	...
1 VII 2004 ....ESDF		17 206 280	4 232 745	24.6	...	...	...	...	...	...
Malawi										
1 IX 1998...........CDFC		9 933 868	1 435 436	14.4	4 867 563	742 839	15.3	5 066 305	692 597	13.7
1 VII 1999[1] ....ESDF		10 152 753	1 155 924	11.4	4 978 411	603 406	12.1	5 174 342	552 518	10.7
1 VII 2000[1] ....ESDF		10 475 257	1 226 773	11.7	5 138 486	638 896	12.4	5 336 771	587 877	11.0
1 VII 2001[1] ....ESDF		10 816 294	1 300 093	12.0	5 307 972	675 613	12.7	5 508 322	624 480	11.3
1 VII 2002[1] ....ESDF		11 174 648	1 375 794	12.3	5 486 254	713 513	13.0	5 688 394	662 281	11.6
1 VII 2003[1] ....ESDF		11 548 841	1 453 771	12.6	5 672 569	752 544	13.3	5 876 272	701 227	11.9
1 VII 2004[1] ....ESDF		11 937 934	1 533 930	12.8	5 866 462	792 661	13.5	6 071 472	741 269	12.2
1 VII 2005[1] ....ESDF		12 341 170	1 616 169	13.1	6 067 563	833 812	13.7	6 273 607	782 357	12.5
1 VII 2006[1] ....ESDF		12 757 883	1 700 379	13.3	6 275 533	875 943	14.0	6 482 350	824 436	12.7
1 VII 2007[1] ....ESDF		13 187 632	1 786 434	13.5	6 490 146	918 991	14.2	6 697 486	867 443	13.0
Mali										
1 IV 1998[10] ....CDFC		9 926 219	2 691 782	27.1	4 905 510	1 344 623	27.4	5 020 709	1 347 159	26.8
1 I 1999 ....ESDF		9 968 933	2 726 550	27.4	4 934 237	1 365 851	27.7	5 034 696	1 360 699	27.0
1 I 2000 ....ESDF		10 243 339	2 868 329	28.0	5 069 994	1 436 707	28.3	5 173 346	1 431 622	27.7
1 I 2001 ....ESDF		10 524 600	3 018 079	28.7	5 209 227	1 511 556	29.0	5 315 375	1 506 523	28.3
1 I 2002 ....ESDF		10 813 478	3 176 399	29.4	5 352 318	1 590 701	29.7	5 461 160	1 585 697	29.0
1 I 2003 ....ESDF		11 111 219	3 344 066	30.1	5 499 912	1 674 538	30.4	5 611 305	1 669 528	29.8
1 I 2004 ....ESDF		11 419 483	3 522 033	30.8	5 652 867	1 763 554	31.2	5 766 615	1 758 478	30.5
1 I 2005 ....ESDF		11 732 416	3 707 315	31.6	5 808 166	1 856 224	32.0	5 924 252	1 851 091	31.2
1 I 2006 ....ESDF		12 051 021	3 900 404	32.4	5 966 339	1 952 802	32.7	6 084 681	1 947 601	32.0
1 I 2007 ....ESDF		12 377 542	4 102 223	33.1	6 128 544	2 053 767	33.5	6 248 999	2 048 456	32.8
Mauritania - Mauritanie										
1 XI 2000 ....CDFC		2 548 157	...	...	1 240 414	...	...	1 307 743	...	...
1 VII 2005 ....ESDF		2 905 727	...	...	1 450 418	...	...	1 455 309	...	...

6. Total and urban population by sex: 1998 - 2007
Population totale et population urbaine selon le sexe: 1998 - 2007 (continued - suite)

Continent, country or area, and date / Continent, pays ou zone et date	Code[a]	Both sexes - Les deux sexes			Male - Masculin			Female - Féminin		
		Total	Urban - Urbaine		Total	Urban - Urbaine		Total	Urban - Urbaine	
			Number Nombre	Percent P.100		Number Nombre	Percent P.100		Number Nombre	Percent P.100
AFRICA - AFRIQUE										
Mauritius - Maurice										
1 VII 1998	ESDJ	1 160 421	498 138	42.9	576 620	246 388	42.7	583 801	251 750	43.1
1 VII 1999	ESDJ	1 175 267	502 958	42.8	583 169	248 362	42.6	592 098	254 596	43.0
1 VII 2000	ESDJ	1 186 873	506 357	42.7	588 212	249 678	42.4	598 661	256 679	42.9
2 VII 2000	CDJC	1 178 848	503 045	42.7	583 756	247 844	42.5	595 092	255 201	42.9
1 VII 2001	ESDJ	1 199 881	510 822	42.6	594 490	251 721	42.3	605 391	259 101	42.8
1 VII 2002	ESDJ	1 210 203	513 761	42.5	599 165	252 848	42.2	611 038	260 913	42.7
1 VII 2003	ESDJ	1 222 811	518 368	42.4	605 084	255 077	42.2	617 727	263 291	42.6
1 VII 2004	ESDJ	1 233 386	521 588	42.3	610 108	256 542	42.0	623 278	265 046	42.5
1 VII 2005	ESDJ	1 243 253	524 318	42.2	614 786	257 785	41.9	628 467	266 533	42.4
1 VII 2006	ESDJ	1 252 698	527 138	42.1	619 243	259 028	41.8	633 455	268 110	42.3
1 VII 2007	ESDJ	1 260 403	528 961	42.0	622 926	259 800	41.7	637 477	269 161	42.2
Mayotte										
30 VII 2002	CDJC	160 301	...	...	80 281	...	...	80 020	...	...
31 VII 2007	CDJC	186 387	...	...	91 405	...	...	94 982	...	...
Morocco - Maroc										
1 VII 1998	ESDF	27 775 000	14 957 000	53.9	13 819 000	7 373 000	53.4	13 956 000	7 584 000	54.3
1 VII 1999	ESDF	28 238 000	15 401 000	54.5	14 049 000	7 580 000	54.0	14 189 000	7 821 000	55.1
1 VII 2000	ESDF	28 705 000	15 849 000	55.2	14 281 000	7 787 000	54.5	14 424 000	8 062 000	55.9
1 VII 2001	ESDF	29 170 000	16 307 000	55.9	14 512 000	8 000 000	55.1	14 658 000	8 307 000	56.7
1 VII 2002	ESDF	29 631 000	16 772 000	56.6	14 742 000	8 217 000	55.7	14 889 000	8 555 000	57.5
1 VII 2003	ESDF	30 088 000	17 244 000	57.3	14 972 000	8 438 000	56.4	15 116 000	8 806 000	58.3
1 VII 2004	ESDF	30 540 000	17 723 000	58.0	...	...	...	...	...	...
1 IX 2004	CDFC	29 680 069	16 339 561	55.1	14 640 662	8 022 273	54.8	15 039 407	8 317 288	55.3
1 VII 2007*	ESDF	30 841 000	17 404 000	56.4	15 246 000	8 572 000	56.2	15 595 000	8 832 000	56.6
Mozambique										
1 VII 1998[1]	ESDF	16 451 355	...	...	7 889 320	...	...	8 562 035	...	...
1 VII 1999[1]	ESDF	16 839 882	...	...	8 082 137	...	...	8 757 745	...	...
1 VII 2000[1]	ESDF	17 240 665	...	...	8 281 305	...	...	8 959 360	...	...
1 VII 2001[1]	ESDF	17 653 239	...	...	8 486 603	...	...	9 166 636	...	...
1 VII 2002[1]	ESDF	18 077 570	...	...	8 698 020	...	...	9 379 550	...	...
1 VII 2003[1]	ESDF	18 513 826	...	...	8 915 639	...	...	9 598 187	...	...
1 VII 2004[1]	ESDF	18 961 503	5 828 150	30.7	9 139 205	2 909 903	31.8	9 822 298	2 918 247	29.7
1 VII 2005[1]	ESDF	19 420 036	6 022 319	31.0	9 368 425	3 009 531	32.1	10 051 611	3 012 788	30.0
1 VII 2006[1]	ESDF	19 888 701	...	...	9 603 031	...	...	10 285 670	...	...
1 VII 2007[1]	ESDF	20 366 795	...	...	9 842 760	...	...	10 524 035	...	...
1 VIII 2007*	CDFC	20 530 714	...	...	9 787 135	...	...	10 743 579	...	...
Namibia - Namibie										
1 VII 1998[1]	ESDF	1 722 800	...	...	841 100	...	...	881 700	...	...
1 VII 1999[1]	ESDF	1 769 200	...	...	863 800	...	...	905 400	...	...
1 VII 2000[1]	ESDF	1 816 600	...	...	886 900	...	...	929 600	...	...
27 VIII 2001	CDFC	1 830 330	603 612	33.0	887 721[11]	300 358[11]	33.8	942 572[11]	303 236[11]	32.2
1 VII 2002[1]	ESDF	1 860 145	...	...	903 107	...	...	957 038	...	...
1 VII 2003[1]	ESDF	1 891 098	...	...	919 031	...	...	972 067	...	...
1 VII 2004[1]	ESDF	1 923 346	...	...	935 590	...	...	987 756	...	...
1 VII 2005[1]	ESDF	1 956 900	...	...	952 788	...	...	1 004 112	...	...
1 VII 2006[1]	ESDF	1 991 747	...	...	970 617	...	...	1 021 130	...	...
1 VII 2007[1]	ESDF	2 027 871	...	...	989 067	...	...	1 038 804	...	...
Niger										
1 VII 1998	ESDJ	9 871 076	1 576 639	16.0	4 918 547	790 858	16.1	4 952 529	785 781	15.9
1 VII 1999	ESDJ	10 177 080	1 633 578	16.1	5 072 184	818 138	16.1	5 104 896	815 440	16.0
1 VII 2000	ESDJ	10 492 569	1 692 532	16.1	5 230 620	846 331	16.2	5 261 949	846 201	16.1
20 V 2001*	CDFC	10 790 352	...	...	5 380 287	...	...	5 410 065	...	...
1 VII 2001	ESDJ	11 090 256	1 804 243	16.3	5 531 534	902 637	16.3	5 558 722	901 606	16.2
1 VII 2002	ESDJ	11 456 235	1 863 783	16.3	5 714 075	932 424	16.3	5 742 160	931 359	16.2
1 VII 2003	ESDJ	11 834 290	1 925 288	16.3	5 902 639	963 194	16.3	5 931 651	962 094	16.2
1 VII 2004	ESDJ	12 224 822	1 988 822	16.3	6 097 426	994 979	16.3	6 127 396	993 843	16.2
1 VII 2005	ESDJ	12 628 241	2 054 453	16.3	6 298 641	1 027 814	16.3	6 329 600	1 026 640	16.2
1 VII 2006	ESDJ	13 044 973	2 184 605	16.7	6 506 496	1 092 927	16.8	6 538 477	1 091 678	16.7
1 VII 2007	ESDJ	13 475 457	2 269 805	16.8	6 721 211	1 135 551	16.9	6 754 247	1 134 254	16.8
Nigeria - Nigéria										
1 VII 2000[1]	ESDF	115 224 312	...	...	57 750 754	...	...	57 473 558	...	...
1 VII 2001[1]	ESDF	118 800 696	...	...	59 538 640	...	...	59 262 056	...	...
1 VII 2002[1]	ESDF	122 443 748	...	...	61 369 212	...	...	61 074 536	...	...

Continent, country or area, and date / Continent, pays ou zone et date	Code[a]	Both sexes - Les deux sexes			Male - Masculin			Female - Féminin		
		Total	Urban - Urbaine		Total	Urban - Urbaine		Total	Urban - Urbaine	
			Number Nombre	Percent P.100		Number Nombre	Percent P.100		Number Nombre	Percent P.100
AFRICA - AFRIQUE										
Nigeria - Nigéria										
1 VII 2003[1] . . . . .ESDF	ESDF	126 152 844	...	...	63 241 808	...	...	62 911 036	...	...
1 VII 2004[1] . . . . .ESDF	ESDF	129 175 000	...	...	64 459 000	...	...	64 716 000	...	...
1 VII 2005[1] . . . . .ESDF	ESDF	133 767 000	...	...	67 111 000	...	...	66 656 000	...	...
21 III 2006* . . . . .CDFC	CDFC	140 003 542	...	...	71 709 859	...	...	68 293 683	...	...
Réunion										
1 VII 1998 . . . . .ESDJ	ESDJ	698 002	...	...	343 304	...	...	354 699	...	...
8 III 1999 . . . . .CDJC	CDJC	706 180	...	...	347 076	...	...	359 104	...	...
1 VII 1999 . . . . .ESDJ	ESDJ	710 067	...	...	348 863	...	...	361 204	...	...
1 VII 2000 . . . . .ESDJ	ESDJ	722 662	...	...	354 363	...	...	368 299	...	...
1 VII 2001 . . . . .ESDJ	ESDJ	734 609	...	...	359 576	...	...	375 033	...	...
1 VII 2002 . . . . .ESDJ	ESDJ	745 524	...	...	364 178	...	...	381 346	...	...
1 VII 2003 . . . . .ESDJ	ESDJ	756 235	...	...	368 715	...	...	387 521	...	...
1 VII 2004 . . . . .ESDJ	ESDJ	767 269	...	...	373 532	...	...	393 737	...	...
1 VII 2005 . . . . .ESDJ	ESDJ	777 435	...	...	377 593	...	...	399 842	...	...
1 I 2006 . . . . .CDJC	CDJC	781 962	...	...	379 176	...	...	402 786	...	...
1 VII 2006 . . . . .ESDJ	ESDJ	786 231	...	...	381 030	...	...	405 202	...	...
1 I 2007* . . . . .ESDJ	ESDJ	790 500	...	...	382 883	...	...	407 617	...	...
Rwanda										
16 VIII 2002 . . . . .CDJC	CDJC	8 128 553	1 372 604	16.9	3 879 448	727 172	18.7	4 249 105	645 432	15.2
Saint Helena ex. dep. - Sainte-Hélène sans dép.										
8 III 1998 . . . . .CDFC	CDFC	5 157	884	17.1	2 612	452	17.3	2 545	432	17.0
Saint Helena: Ascension - Sainte-Hélène: Ascension										
8 III 1998 . . . . .CDJC	CDJC	712	...	...	458	...	...	254	...	...
Sao Tome and Principe - Sao Tomé-et-Principe										
1 VII 1998 . . . . .ESDF	ESDF	131 234	...	...	65 002	...	...	66 232	...	...
1 VII 1999 . . . . .ESDF	ESDF	133 323	...	...	66 063	...	...	67 260	...	...
1 VII 2000 . . . . .ESDF	ESDF	135 445	...	...	67 141	...	...	68 304	...	...
25 VIII 2001 . . . . .CDFC	CDFC	136 554	73 907	54.1	67 422	35 679	52.9	69 132	38 228	55.3
1 VII 2002 . . . . .ESDF	ESDF	140 365	...	...	69 515	...	...	70 850	...	...
1 VII 2003 . . . . .ESDF	ESDF	143 186	...	...	70 821	...	...	72 365	...	...
1 VII 2004 . . . . .ESDF	ESDF	146 056	...	...	72 153	...	...	73 903	...	...
1 VII 2005 . . . . .ESDF	ESDF	148 968	...	...	73 506	...	...	75 462	...	...
1 VII 2006 . . . . .ESDF	ESDF	151 912	...	...	74 876	...	...	77 036	...	...
1 VII 2007 . . . . .ESDF	ESDF	154 875	...	...	76 256	...	...	78 619	...	...
Senegal - Sénégal										
1 VII 1998 . . . . .ESDJ	ESDJ	8 964 295	...	...	4 305 771	...	...	4 658 524	...	...
1 VII 1999 . . . . .ESDJ	ESDJ	9 192 572	...	...	4 415 174	...	...	4 777 398	...	...
1 VII 2000 . . . . .ESDJ	ESDJ	9 426 663	...	...	4 619 065	...	...	4 807 598	...	...
1 VII 2001 . . . . .ESDJ	ESDJ	9 666 715	...	...	4 740 557	...	...	4 926 158	...	...
1 VII 2002 . . . . .ESDJ	ESDJ	9 912 880	...	...	4 865 222	...	...	5 047 658	...	...
8 XII 2002 . . . . .CDFC	CDFC	9 552 442	3 938 299	41.2	4 665 730	1 939 894	41.6	4 886 712	1 998 405	40.9
1 VII 2003 . . . . .ESDJ	ESDJ	10 165 314	...	...	5 000 053	...	...	5 165 260	...	...
1 VII 2004 . . . . .ESDJ	ESDJ	10 564 303	...	...	5 069 869	...	...	5 494 434	...	...
1 VII 2005 . . . . .ESDJ	ESDJ	10 848 051	...	...	5 315 545	...	...	5 532 506	...	...
Seychelles										
1 VII 1998 . . . . .ESDF	ESDF	78 846	...	...	39 359	...	...	39 487	...	...
1 VII 1999 . . . . .ESDF	ESDF	80 410	...	...	40 199	...	...	40 211	...	...
1 VII 2000 . . . . .ESDF	ESDF	81 131	...	...	40 249	...	...	40 882	...	...
1 VII 2001 . . . . .ESDF	ESDF	81 202	...	...	39 973	...	...	41 229	...	...
1 VII 2002 . . . . .ESDF	ESDF	83 723	...	...	41 990	...	...	41 733	...	...
26 VIII 2002[12] . . . . . . .CDJC	CDJC	81 755	...	...	40 751	...	...	41 004	...	...
1 VII 2003 . . . . .ESDF	ESDF	82 781	...	...	40 859	...	...	41 922	...	...
1 VII 2004* . . . . .ESDF	ESDF	82 475	...	...	40 652	...	...	41 823	...	...
1 VII 2005 . . . . .ESDF	ESDF	82 852	...	...	41 233	...	...	41 619	...	...
1 VII 2006 . . . . .ESDF	ESDF	84 600	...	...	42 875	...	...	41 725	...	...
1 VII 2007 . . . . .ESDF	ESDF	85 032	...	...	43 160	...	...	41 872	...	...

6. Total and urban population by sex: 1998 - 2007
Population totale et population urbaine selon le sexe: 1998 - 2007 (continued - suite)

Continent, country or area, and date / Continent, pays ou zone et date	Code[a]	Both sexes - Les deux sexes			Male - Masculin			Female - Féminin		
		Total	Urban - Urbaine		Total	Urban - Urbaine		Total	Urban - Urbaine	
			Number Nombre	Percent P.100		Number Nombre	Percent P.100		Number Nombre	Percent P.100
AFRICA - AFRIQUE										
Sierra Leone										
1 VII 1998 . . . . ESDF		4 729 579	1 682 456	35.6	...	...	...	...	...	...
1 VII 1999 . . . . ESDF		4 836 011	1 727 184	35.7	...	...	...	...	...	...
1 VII 2000 . . . . ESDF		4 944 310	1 772 379	35.8	...	...	...	...	...	...
1 VII 2001 . . . . ESDF		5 054 476	1 818 044	36.0	...	...	...	...	...	...
1 VII 2002 . . . . ESDF		5 166 508	1 864 177	36.1	...	...	...	...	...	...
1 VII 2003 . . . . ESDF		5 280 406	1 910 779	36.2	...	...	...	...	...	...
4 XII 2004 . . . . CDFC		4 976 871	...	...	2 420 218	...	...	2 556 653	...	...
Somalia - Somalie[13]										
1 VII 2002 . . . . SSDF		6 799 079	2 310 817	34.0	3 499 523	1 168 410	33.4	3 299 556	1 142 407	34.6
South Africa - Afrique du Sud										
1 VII 1998[14] . . . . ESDF		42 130 500	22 565 300	53.6	20 330 100	11 073 800	54.5	21 800 400	11 491 500	52.7
1 VII 1999[14] . . . . ESDF		43 054 306	23 032 381	53.5	20 814 425	11 316 037	54.4	22 239 881	11 716 344	52.7
1 VII 2000[14] . . . . ESDF		43 685 699	23 125 194	52.9	21 016 530	11 273 108	53.6	22 669 169	11 852 086	52.3
1 VII 2001[14] . . . . ESDF		44 928 796	23 501 443[3]	52.3	21 537 608	11 439 101[3]	53.1	23 391 188	12 062 342[3]	51.6
10 X 2001 . . . . CDFC		44 819 778			21 434 041	...	...	23 385 737	...	...
1 VII 2002[14] . . . . ESDF		45 587 115	23 888 278[3]	52.4	21 863 840	11 612 775[3]	53.1	23 723 275	12 275 503[3]	51.7
1 VII 2003[14] . . . . ESDF		46 205 956	...	...	22 171 021	...	...	24 034 935	...	...
1 VII 2004[14] . . . . ESDF		46 787 089	...	...	22 461 706	...	...	24 325 383	...	...
1 VII 2005[14] . . . . ESDF		47 335 091	...	...	22 738 921	...	...	24 596 170	...	...
1 VII 2006[14] . . . . ESDF		46 787 089	...	...	22 461 706	...	...	24 325 383	...	...
1 VII 2007[14] . . . . ESDF		48 287 320	...	...	23 231 447	...	...	25 055 873	...	...
Sudan - Soudan										
1 VII 1998 . . . . ESDF		29 266 405	...	...	14 738 449	...	...	14 527 956	...	...
1 VII 1999 . . . . ESDF		30 326 000	...	...	15 276 000	...	...	15 050 000	...	...
1 VII 2000 . . . . ESDF		31 081 000	...	...	15 602 227	...	...	15 478 773	...	...
1 VII 2001 . . . . ESDF		31 626 526	...	...	16 014 575	...	...	15 611 951	...	...
1 VII 2002 . . . . ESDF		32 468 401	...	...	16 440 837	...	...	16 027 564	...	...
1 VII 2003 . . . . ESDF		33 333 648	...	...	16 793 306	...	...	16 540 342	...	...
1 VII 2004 . . . . ESDF		34 512 000	...	...	17 390 000	...	...	17 122 000	...	...
Swaziland										
11 V 2007* . . . . CDFC		953 524	206 459	21.7	460 498	102 171	22.2	493 026	104 288	21.2
Tunisia - Tunisie										
1 VII 1998 . . . . ESDF		9 333 300	...	...	4 709 000	...	...	4 624 300	...	...
1 VII 2002 . . . . ESDF		9 748 900	...	...	4 907 100	...	...	4 841 800	...	...
1 VII 2003 . . . . ESDF		9 839 800	...	...	4 933 600	...	...	4 906 200	...	...
28 IV 2004. . . . . CDFC		9 910 872	...	...	4 965 435	...	...	4 945 437	...	...
1 VII 2004 . . . . ESDF		9 932 400	...	...	4 976 200	...	...	4 956 200	...	...
1 VII 2005 . . . . ESDF		10 029 000	...	...	5 020 000	...	...	5 009 000	...	...
1 VII 2006 . . . . ESDF		10 127 900	...	...	5 062 100	...	...	5 065 800	...	...
1 VII 2007 . . . . ESDF		10 225 100	...	...	5 105 100	...	...	5 120 000	...	...
Uganda - Ouganda										
1 VII 1998 . . . . ESDF		21 174 700	2 418 400	11.4	...	...	...	...	...	...
1 VII 1999 . . . . ESDF		21 863 900	2 540 100	11.6	...	...	...	...	...	...
1 VII 2000 . . . . ESDF		22 575 400	2 668 000	11.8	...	...	...	...	...	...
1 VII 2001 . . . . ESDF		23 310 100	2 802 400	12.0	...	...	...	...	...	...
1 VII 2002 . . . . ESDF		24 068 800	2 943 500	12.2	...	...	...	...	...	...
12 IX 2002. . . . . CDFC		24 442 084	2 999 387	12.3	11 929 803	1 449 684	12.2	12 512 281	1 549 703	12.4
1 VII 2003 . . . . ESDF		24 850 700	3 091 400	12.4	...	...	...	...	...	...
1 VII 2004 . . . . ESDF		25 659 500	3 247 000	12.7	...	...	...	...	...	...
1 VII 2005 . . . . ESDF		26 494 600	3 410 500	12.9	...	...	...	...	...	...
1 VII 2006 . . . . ESDF		27 356 900	3 582 200	13.1	...	...	...	...	...	...
1 VII 2007 . . . . ESDF		28 247 300	3 762 600	13.3	...	...	...	...	...	...
United Republic of Tanzania - République Unie de Tanzanie										
24 VIII 2002* . . . . CDFC		34 443 603	...	...	16 829 861	...	...	17 613 742	...	...
Zambia - Zambie										
1 VII 1999 . . . . ESDF		10 406 681	...	...	5 198 440	...	...	5 208 241	...	...
25 X 2000 . . . . CDFC		9 337 425	3 347 069	35.8	4 594 290	1 662 739	36.2	4 743 135	1 684 330	35.5

Continent, country or area, and date / Continent, pays ou zone et date	Code[a]	Both sexes - Les deux sexes			Male - Masculin			Female - Féminin		
			Urban - Urbaine			Urban - Urbaine			Urban - Urbaine	
		Total	Number Nombre	Percent P.100	Total	Number Nombre	Percent P.100	Total	Number Nombre	Percent P.100
AFRICA - AFRIQUE										
Zimbabwe										
18 VIII 1998 ....ESDF		*12 684 679*	...	...	*6 190 176*	...	...	*6 494 503*	...	...
1 VII 1999 ....ESDF		*13 079 127*	...	...	*6 382 092*	...	...	*6 697 035*	...	...
17 VIII 2002 ....CDFC		11 631 657	4 029 707	34.6	5 634 180	1 988 176	35.3	5 997 477	2 041 531	34.0
AMERICA, NORTH - AMÉRIQUE DU NORD										
Anguilla										
9 V 2001 ....CDFC		11 430	...	...	5 628	...	...	5 802	...	...
1 VII 2001 ....ESDF		11 561	...	...	5 701	...	...	5 860	...	...
Antigua and Barbuda - Antigua-et-Barbuda										
1 VII 2000 ....ESDF		72 310	...	...	34 858	...	...	37 452	...	...
28 V 2001 ....CDFC		77 426	...	...	37 002	...	...	40 424	...	...
1 VII 2001 ....ESDF		76 886	...	...	36 107	...	...	40 779	...	...
1 VII 2002 ....ESDF		78 320	...	...	36 780	...	...	41 540	...	...
1 VII 2003 ....ESDF		79 781	...	...	37 467	...	...	42 314	...	...
1 VII 2004 ....ESDF		81 270	...	...	38 166	...	...	43 104	...	...
1 VII 2005 ....ESDF		82 786	...	...	38 878	...	...	43 908	...	...
Aruba										
1 VII 1998 ....ESDJ		88 452	...	...	43 027	...	...	45 425	...	...
1 VII 1999 ....ESDJ		89 659	...	...	43 362	...	...	46 297	...	...
1 VII 2000 ....ESDJ		90 600	...	...	43 594	...	...	47 005	...	...
14 X 2000 ....CDJC		90 508	...	...	43 435	...	...	47 073	...	...
1 VII 2001 ....ESDJ		91 870	...	...	44 042	...	...	47 828	...	...
1 VII 2002 ....ESDJ		93 310	...	...	44 651	...	...	48 659	...	...
1 VII 2003 ....ESDJ		95 076	...	...	45 461	...	...	49 615	...	...
1 VII 2004 ....ESDJ		97 658	...	...	46 657	...	...	51 001	...	...
1 VII 2005 ....ESDJ		100 644	...	...	48 038	...	...	52 606	...	...
1 VII 2006 ....ESDJ		102 833	...	...	49 063	...	...	53 770	...	...
1 VII 2007 ....ESDJ		104 005	...	...	49 614	...	...	54 391	...	...
Bahamas										
1 VII 1998 ....ESDF		293 261	...	...	144 786	...	...	148 475	...	...
1 VII 1999 ....ESDF		298 050	...	...	147 241	...	...	150 809	...	...
1 V 2000 ....CDFC		303 611	257 826	84.9	147 715	124 582	84.3	155 896	133 244	85.5
1 VII 2001 ....ESDF		307 800	...	...	149 600	...	...	158 200	...	...
1 VII 2002 ....ESDF		312 100	...	...	151 700	...	...	160 400	...	...
1 VII 2003 ....ESDF		316 900	...	...	154 100	...	...	162 800	...	...
1 VII 2004 ....ESDF		320 800	...	...	155 900	...	...	164 900	...	...
1 VII 2005 ....ESDF		325 200	...	...	158 000	...	...	167 200	...	...
1 VII 2006 ....ESDF		329 500	...	...	160 100	...	...	169 400	...	...
1 VII 2007 ....ESDF		334 000	...	...	162 300	...	...	171 700	...	...
Barbados - Barbade										
1 V 2000 ....CDFC		250 010	...	...	119 926	...	...	130 084	...	...
1 VII 2000 ....ESDF		268 750	...	...	129 222	...	...	139 528	...	...
1 VII 2001 ....ESDF		269 874	...	...	129 871	...	...	140 003	...	...
1 VII 2002 ....ESDF		270 750	...	...	130 390	...	...	140 360	...	...
1 VII 2003 ....ESDF		271 646	...	...	130 887	...	...	140 759	...	...
1 VII 2004 ....ESDF		272 436	...	...	131 418	...	...	141 018	...	...
1 VII 2005 ....ESDF		273 018	...	...	131 721	...	...	141 297	...	...
1 VII 2006 ....ESDF		273 428	...	...	131 916	...	...	141 512	...	...
1 VII 2007 ....ESDF		274 197	...	...	132 413	...	...	141 784	...	...
Belize										
1 VII 1998 ....ESDF		*238 500*	*120 110*	*50.4*	*118 500*	*57 095*	*48.2*	*120 000*	*63 015*	*52.5*
1 VII 1999 ....ESDF		*243 055*	*118 125*	*48.6*	*122 745*	*58 750*	*47.9*	*120 310*	*59 750*	*49.7*
12 V 2000 ....CDFC		240 204	114 541	47.7	121 278	56 565	46.6	118 926	57 976	48.7
1 VII 2000 ....ESDF		*249 800*	*121 455*	*48.6*	*126 080*	*59 985*	*47.6*	*123 720*	*61 470*	*49.7*
1 VII 2001 ....ESDF		*257 310*	*125 830*	*48.9*	*129 890*	*62 160*	*47.9*	*127 420*	*63 370*	*49.7*
1 VII 2002 ....ESDF		*265 200*	*130 500*	*49.2*	*133 900*	*64 400*	*48.1*	*131 300*	*66 100*	*50.3*
1 VII 2003 ....ESDF		*273 700*	*135 600*	*49.5*	*138 300*	*67 000*	*48.4*	*135 400*	*68 600*	*50.7*
1 VII 2004 ....ESDF		*282 600*	*141 000*	*49.9*	*142 700*	*69 500*	*48.7*	*139 900*	*71 500*	*51.1*

Continent, country or area, and date / Continent, pays ou zone et date	Code[a]	Both sexes - Les deux sexes			Male - Masculin			Female - Féminin		
		Total	Urban - Urbaine Number Nombre	Urban - Urbaine Percent P.100	Total	Urban - Urbaine Number Nombre	Urban - Urbaine Percent P.100	Total	Urban - Urbaine Number Nombre	Urban - Urbaine Percent P.100
AMERICA, NORTH - AMÉRIQUE DU NORD										
Belize										
1 VII 2005 .... ESDF		291 800	146 600	50.2	147 400	72 200	49.0	144 400	74 400	51.5
1 VII 2006 .... ESDF		301 386	152 583	50.6	149 676	73 495	49.1	151 710	79 089	52.1
Bermuda - Bermudes										
1 VII 1998 .... ESDJ		62 277	...	...	31 258	...	...	31 019	...	...
1 VII 1999 .... ESDJ		62 656	...	...	30 433	...	...	32 223	...	...
20 V 2000[15] .... CDJC		62 059	...	...	29 802	...	...	32 257	...	...
1 VII 2000 .... ESDJ		62 131	...	...	29 834	...	...	32 297	...	...
1 VII 2001 .... ESDJ		62 455	...	...	29 969	...	...	32 486	...	...
1 VII 2002 .... ESDJ		62 754	...	...	30 092	...	...	32 662	...	...
1 VII 2003 .... ESDJ		63 042	...	...	30 205	...	...	32 837	...	...
1 VII 2004 .... ESDJ		63 320	...	...	30 323	...	...	32 997	...	...
1 VII 2005 .... ESDJ		63 571	...	...	30 424	...	...	33 147	...	...
1 VII 2006 .... ESDJ		63 797	...	...	30 504	...	...	33 293	...	...
1 VII 2007 .... ESDJ		64 009	...	...	30 577	...	...	33 432	...	...
British Virgin Islands - Îles Vierges britanniques										
21 V 2001 .... CDFC		20 647	...	...	10 627	...	...	10 020	...	...
Canada										
1 VII 1998[16] .... ESDJ		30 157 082	23 704 015[3]	78.6	14 927 226	...	...	15 229 856	...	...
1 VII 1999[16] .... ESDJ		30 403 878	...	...	15 052 451	...	...	15 351 427	...	...
1 VII 2000[16] .... ESDJ		30 689 035	...	...	15 196 709	...	...	15 492 326	...	...
15 V 2001 .... CDJC		30 007 095[17]	23 908 105	79.7	14 706 850	11 594 915	78.8	15 300 245	12 313 190	80.5
1 VII 2001[18] .... ESDJ		31 021 251	...	...	15 364 404	...	...	15 656 847	...	...
1 VII 2002[18] .... ESDJ		31 372 587	...	...	15 538 572	...	...	15 834 015	...	...
1 VII 2003[18] .... ESDJ		31 676 077	...	...	15 688 977	...	...	15 987 100	...	...
1 VII 2004[18] .... ESDJ		31 995 199	...	...	15 846 832	...	...	16 148 367	...	...
1 VII 2005[19] .... ESDJ		32 312 077	...	...	16 003 804	...	...	16 308 273	...	...
16 V 2006[9] .... CDJC		31 612 895	25 350 585	80.2	15 475 970	12 289 025	79.4	16 136 930	13 061 560	80.9
1 VII 2006[19] .... ESDJ		32 649 482	...	...	16 170 723	...	...	16 478 759	...	...
1 VII 2007*[20] .... ESDJ		32 976 026	...	...	16 332 277	...	...	16 643 749	...	...
Cayman Islands - Îles Caïmanes										
1 VII 1999 .... ESDJ		39 000	...	...	19 023	...	...	19 977	...	...
10 X 1999[21] .... CDJC		39 020	...	...	19 033	...	...	19 987	...	...
1 VII 2004 .... ESDJ		44 240	...	...	21 235	...	...	23 005	...	...
1 VII 2006 .... ESDJ		51 992	...	...	26 340	...	...	25 652	...	...
1 IV 2007 .... SSDJ		54 100	...	...	27 281[3]	...	...	26 011[3]	...	...
Costa Rica										
1 VII 1998 .... ESDJ		3 340 909	1 440 272	43.1	1 662 735	693 376	41.7	1 678 174	746 896	44.5
1 VII 1999 .... ESDJ		3 412 613	1 576 288	46.2	1 688 946	757 345	44.8	1 723 667	818 943	47.5
26 VI 2000 .... CDJC		3 810 179	2 249 296	59.0	1 902 614	1 096 138	57.6	1 907 565	1 153 158	60.5
1 VII 2000 .... ESDJ		3 810 187	2 249 301	59.0	1 890 808	1 100 259	58.2	1 919 379	1 149 042	59.9
1 VII 2001 .... ESDJ		3 906 742	2 305 723	59.0	1 935 168	1 119 394	57.8	1 971 574	1 186 329	60.2
1 VII 2002 .... ESDJ		3 997 883	2 359 158	59.0	1 983 715	1 147 227	57.8	2 014 168	1 211 931	60.2
1 VII 2003 .... ESDJ		4 088 773	2 412 542	59.0	2 017 467	1 167 617	57.9	2 071 306	1 244 925	60.1
1 VII 2004 .... ESDJ		4 178 755	2 465 255	59.0	2 062 468	1 191 560	57.8	2 116 287	1 273 695	60.2
1 VII 2005 .... ESDJ		4 266 185	2 516 602	59.0	2 116 648	1 231 912	58.2	2 149 537	1 284 690	59.8
1 VII 2006 .... ESDJ		4 353 843	2 567 797	59.0	2 146 610	1 243 202	57.9	2 207 233	1 324 595	60.0
1 VII 2007 .... ESDJ		4 443 100	2 619 591	59.0	2 195 652	1 273 998	58.0	2 247 448	1 345 593	59.9
Cuba										
1 VII 1998 .... ESDJ		11 055 405	8 325 827	75.3	...	...	...	...	...	...
1 VII 1999 .... ESDJ		11 094 972	8 363 577	75.4	5 509 823	4 059 126	73.7	5 585 149	4 304 451	77.1
1 VII 2000 .... ESDJ		11 129 665	8 417 965	75.6	5 548 671	4 111 545	74.1	5 580 994	4 306 420	77.2
1 VII 2001 .... ESDJ		11 157 364	8 467 052	75.9	5 586 835	4 163 395	74.5	5 570 529	4 303 657	77.3
1 VII 2002 .... ESDJ		11 184 457	8 483 688	75.9	5 601 052	4 172 285	74.5	5 583 405	4 311 403	77.2
6 IX 2002 .... CDJC		11 177 743	8 479 329	75.9	5 597 233	4 169 722	74.5	5 580 510	4 309 607	77.2
1 VII 2003 .... ESDJ		11 215 229	8 501 628	75.8	5 616 275	4 181 234	74.4	5 598 954	4 320 394	77.2
1 VII 2004 .... ESDJ		11 235 687	8 503 738	75.7	5 626 690	4 183 047	74.3	5 608 997	4 320 691	77.0
1 VII 2005 .... ESDJ		11 242 519	8 497 885	75.6	5 629 843	4 180 296	74.3	5 612 676	4 317 589	76.9
1 VII 2006 .... ESDJ		11 241 440	8 490 101	75.5	5 629 168	4 176 538	74.2	5 612 272	4 313 563	76.9
1 VII 2007 .... ESDJ		11 237 916	8 478 510	75.4	5 627 694	4 171 388	74.1	5 610 222	4 307 122	76.8

Continent, country or area, and date / Continent, pays ou zone et date	Code[a]	Both sexes - Les deux sexes			Male - Masculin			Female - Féminin		
		Total	Urban - Urbaine		Total	Urban - Urbaine		Total	Urban - Urbaine	
			Number Nombre	Percent P.100		Number Nombre	Percent P.100		Number Nombre	Percent P.100
AMERICA, NORTH - AMÉRIQUE DU NORD										
Dominica - Dominique										
1 VII 1998 ....ESDF	ESDF	72 042	...	...	36 678	...	...	35 364	...	...
1 VII 1999 ....ESDF	ESDF	71 814	...	...	36 561	...	...	35 253	...	...
1 VII 2000 ....ESDF	ESDF	71 544	...	...	35 744	...	...	35 800	...	...
12 V 2001[15] ....CDFC	CDFC	69 625	...	...	35 073	...	...	34 552	...	...
1 VII 2001 ....ESDF	ESDF	70 922	...	...	35 241	...	...	35 681	...	...
1 VII 2002 ....ESDF	ESDF	70 382	...	...	35 472	...	...	34 910	...	...
1 VII 2003 ....ESDF	ESDF	70 352	...	...	35 442	...	...	34 910	...	...
1 VII 2004 ....ESDF	ESDF	70 417	...	...	35 645	...	...	34 772	...	...
1 VII 2005 ....ESDF	ESDF	70 665	...	...	35 991	...	...	34 675	...	...
1 VII 2006 ....ESDF	ESDF	71 008	...	...	36 169	...	...	34 839	...	...
Dominican Republic - République dominicaine										
1 VII 1998 ....ESDF	ESDF	8 288 051	4 788 653	57.8	4 157 798	2 369 337	57.0	4 130 253	2 419 316	58.6
1 VII 1999 ....ESDF	ESDF	8 420 461	4 927 197	58.5	4 222 459	2 438 508	57.8	4 198 002	2 488 689	59.3
1 VII 2000[1] ....ESDF	ESDF	8 553 739	5 068 203	59.3	4 287 520	2 508 903	58.5	4 266 219	2 559 300	60.0
1 VII 2001[1] ....ESDF	ESDF	8 688 212	5 213 919	60.0	4 353 126	2 581 510	59.3	4 335 086	2 632 409	60.7
1 VII 2002[1] ....ESDF	ESDF	8 823 188	5 361 983	60.8	4 418 914	2 655 257	60.1	4 404 274	2 706 726	61.5
18 X 2002 ....CDJC	CDJC	8 562 541	5 446 704	63.6	4 265 215	2 648 064	62.1	4 297 326	2 798 640	65.1
1 VII 2003[1] ....ESDF	ESDF	8 958 206	5 512 122	61.5	4 484 683	2 730 026	60.9	4 473 523	2 782 096	62.2
1 VII 2004[1] ....ESDF	ESDF	9 092 778	5 664 034	62.3	4 550 204	2 805 677	61.7	4 542 574	2 858 357	62.9
1 VII 2005[1] ....ESDF	ESDF	9 226 449	5 817 420	63.1	4 615 274	2 882 076	62.4	4 611 175	2 935 344	63.7
1 VII 2006[1] ....ESDF	ESDF	9 359 706	5 965 956	63.7	4 680 145	2 955 948	63.2	4 679 561	3 010 008	64.3
1 VII 2007[1] ....ESDF	ESDF	9 492 876	6 116 271	64.4	4 744 960	3 030 709	63.9	4 747 916	3 085 562	65.0
El Salvador										
1 VII 1998 ....ESDF	ESDF	6 031 326	3 485 465	57.8	2 957 835	1 673 250	56.6	3 073 491	1 812 215	59.0
1 VII 1999 ....ESDF	ESDF	6 154 311	3 575 957	58.1	3 019 645	1 717 489	56.9	3 134 666	1 858 468	59.3
1 VII 2000 ....ESDF	ESDF	6 276 037	3 665 747	58.4	3 080 704	1 761 327	57.2	3 195 333	1 904 420	59.6
1 VII 2001 ....ESDF	ESDF	6 396 890	3 754 903	58.7	3 141 208	1 804 804	57.5	3 255 682	1 950 099	59.9
1 VII 2002 ....ESDF	ESDF	6 517 798	3 843 878	59.0	3 201 720	1 848 194	57.7	3 316 078	1 995 684	60.2
1 VII 2003 ....ESDF	ESDF	6 638 168	3 932 569	59.2	3 261 938	1 891 429	58.0	3 376 230	2 041 140	60.5
1 VII 2004 ....ESDF	ESDF	6 757 408	4 020 878	59.5	3 321 564	1 934 445	58.2	3 435 844	2 086 433	60.7
1 VII 2005 ....ESDF	ESDF	6 874 926	4 108 703	59.8	3 380 300	1 977 177	58.5	3 494 626	2 131 526	61.0
1 VII 2006 ....ESDF	ESDF	6 990 658	4 195 925	60.0	3 438 107	2 019 556	58.7	3 552 551	2 176 369	61.3
12 V 2007 ....CDJC	CDJC	5 744 113	3 598 836	62.7	2 719 371	1 676 313	61.6	3 024 742	1 922 523	63.6
1 VII 2007 ....ESDF	ESDF	7 104 999	4 282 608	60.3	3 495 190	2 061 628	59.0	3 609 809	2 220 980	61.5
Greenland - Groenland[22]										
1 VII 1998 ....ESDJ	ESDJ	56 076	45 489	81.1	29 904	24 092	80.6	26 172	21 397	81.8
1 VII 1999 ....ESDJ	ESDJ	56 087	45 523	81.2	29 941	24 189	80.8	26 146	21 334	81.6
1 VII 2000 ....CDJC	CDJC	56 124	45 714	81.5	29 989	24 257	80.9	26 135	21 457	82.1
1 VII 2000 ....ESDJ	ESDJ	56 185	45 821	81.6	30 007	24 310	81.0	26 178	21 511	82.2
1 VII 2001 ....ESDJ	ESDJ	56 394	46 125	81.8	30 102	24 454	81.2	26 292	21 671	82.4
1 VII 2002 ....ESDJ	ESDJ	56 609	46 462	82.1	30 215	24 626	81.5	26 394	21 836	82.7
1 VII 2003 ....ESDJ	ESDJ	56 766	46 746	82.3	30 292	24 771	81.8	26 474	21 975	83.0
1 VII 2004 ....ESDJ	ESDJ	56 912	46 989	82.6	30 327	24 860	82.0	26 585	22 129	83.2
1 VII 2005 ....ESDJ	ESDJ	56 935	47 080	82.7	30 251	24 837	82.1	26 685	22 243	83.4
1 VII 2006 ....ESDJ	ESDJ	56 775	47 037	82.8	30 094	24 763	82.3	26 681	22 274	83.5
1 VII 2007 ....ESDJ	ESDJ	56 555	47 056	83.2	29 945	24 746	82.6	26 610	22 310	83.8
Grenada - Grenade										
1 VII 1998 ....ESDF	ESDF	100 100	...	...	49 600	...	...	50 500	...	...
1 VII 1999 ....ESDF	ESDF	100 700	...	...	49 800	...	...	50 900	...	...
1 VII 2000 ....ESDF	ESDF	101 400	...	...	50 100	...	...	51 300	...	...
25 V 2001 ....CDFC	CDFC	102 632	...	...	50 481	...	...	52 151	...	...
Guadeloupe										
1 VII 1998 ....ESDJ	ESDJ	418 876	...	...	201 713	...	...	217 163	...	...
8 III 1999 ....CDJC	CDJC	422 222	...	...	203 146	...	...	219 076	...	...
1 VII 1999 ....ESDJ	ESDJ	423 570	...	...	203 607	...	...	219 963	...	...
1 VII 2000 ....ESDJ	ESDJ	427 928	...	...	205 433	...	...	222 495	...	...
1 VII 2001 ....ESDJ	ESDJ	432 453	...	...	207 453	...	...	225 000	...	...
1 I 2002 ....ESDJ	ESDJ	393 024	...	...	186 827	...	...	206 197	...	...
1 VII 2003 ....ESDJ	ESDJ	438 820	...	...	210 130	...	...	228 690	...	...
1 I 2004 ....ESDJ	ESDJ	396 992	...	...	187 603	...	...	209 389	...	...

Continent, country or area, and date / Continent, pays ou zone et date	Code[a]	Both sexes - Les deux sexes Total	Urban - Urbaine Number Nombre	Urban - Urbaine Percent P.100	Male - Masculin Total	Urban - Urbaine Number Nombre	Urban - Urbaine Percent P.100	Female - Féminin Total	Urban - Urbaine Number Nombre	Urban - Urbaine Percent P.100
AMERICA, NORTH - AMÉRIQUE DU NORD										
Guadeloupe										
1 I 2005	ESDJ	399 178	...	...	188 158	...	...	211 020	...	...
1 I 2006	CDJC	400 736	...	...	188 720	...	...	212 016	...	...
1 I 2006	ESDJ	400 736	...	...	188 720	...	...	212 016	...	...
1 I 2007*	ESDJ	403 000	...	...	189 420	...	...	213 580	...	...
Guatemala										
1 VII 1998[14]	ESDF	10 799 133	...	...	5 447 743	...	...	5 351 390	...	...
1 VII 1999[14]	ESDF	11 088 362	...	...	5 592 313	...	...	5 496 049	...	...
1 VII 2000[14]	ESDF	11 385 338	...	...	5 740 720	...	...	5 644 618	...	...
1 VII 2001[14]	ESDF	11 678 411	...	...	5 888 426	...	...	5 789 985	...	...
24 XI 2002	CDJC	11 237 196	...	...	5 496 839	...	...	5 740 357	...	...
Haiti - Haïti										
1 VII 1998	ESDJ	7 647 496	2 630 383	34.4	...	...	...	...	...	...
1 VII 1999	ESDJ	7 803 230	2 731 843	35.0	...	...	...	...	...	...
1 VII 2000	ESDJ	7 958 964	2 835 433	35.6	...	...	...	...	...	...
11 I 2003	CDJC	8 373 750	...	...	4 039 272	...	...	4 334 478	...	...
Honduras										
1 VII 1998	ESDF	6 056 942	2 689 721	44.4	...	...	...	...	...	...
1 VII 1999	ESDF	6 211 412	2 796 156	45.0	...	...	...	...	...	...
1 VII 2000	ESDF	6 369 188	2 907 091	45.6	...	...	...	...	...	...
1 VII 2001	ESDF	6 530 331	3 022 150	46.3	3 228 483	1 439 896	44.6	3 301 848	1 582 254	47.9
28 VII 2001	CDFC	6 071 200	...	...	3 000 530	...	...	3 070 670	...	...
1 VII 2002	ESDF	6 694 761	3 140 880	46.9	3 308 253	1 497 291	45.3	3 386 508	1 643 589	48.5
1 VII 2003	ESDF	6 860 842	3 260 934	47.5	3 388 874	1 555 369	45.9	3 471 968	1 705 565	49.1
1 VII 2004	ESDF	7 028 389	3 382 254	48.1	3 470 259	1 614 104	46.5	3 558 130	1 768 150	49.7
1 VII 2005	ESDF	7 197 303	3 504 730	48.7	3 552 360	1 673 434	47.1	3 644 943	1 831 296	50.2
1 VII 2006*	ESDF	7 367 021	3 628 228	49.2	3 634 900	1 733 290	47.7	3 732 121	1 894 938	50.8
1 VII 2007*	ESDF	7 536 952	3 752 579	49.8	3 717 577	1 793 588	48.2	3 819 375	1 958 991	51.3
Jamaica - Jamaïque										
1 VII 1998	ESDJ	2 556 821	...	...	1 257 205	...	...	1 299 616	...	...
1 VII 1999	ESDJ	2 574 313	...	...	1 266 232	...	...	1 308 081	...	...
1 VII 2000	ESDJ	2 589 393	1 345 867	52.0	1 274 076	641 652	50.4	1 315 317	704 231	53.5
1 VII 2001	ESDJ	2 604 098	1 353 511	52.0	1 281 752	645 517	50.4	1 322 346	707 993	53.5
10 IX 2001	CDJC	2 607 632	1 355 347	52.0	1 283 548	646 422	50.4	1 324 084	708 925	53.5
1 VII 2002	ESDJ	2 615 248	1 359 292	52.0	1 287 663	648 494	50.4	1 327 585	710 798	53.5
1 VII 2003	ESDJ	2 625 708	1 364 719	52.0	1 293 121	651 243	50.4	1 332 587	713 476	53.5
1 VII 2004	ESDJ	2 638 074	1 371 144	52.0	1 299 406	654 407	50.4	1 338 668	716 736	53.5
1 VII 2005	ESDJ	2 650 402	1 377 546	52.0	1 305 639	657 546	50.4	1 344 763	720 000	53.5
1 VII 2006	ESDJ	2 663 106	1 384 145	52.0	1 312 025	660 763	50.4	1 351 081	723 383	53.5
1 VII 2007	ESDJ	2 675 831	1 390 754	52.0	1 318 444	663 995	50.4	1 357 387	726 759	53.5
Martinique										
1 VII 1998	ESDJ	379 042	...	...	180 005	...	...	199 038	...	...
8 III 1999[23]	CDJC	380 863	342 049	89.8	180 692	161 687	89.5	200 171	180 362	90.1
1 VII 1999	ESDJ	382 090	...	...	181 140	...	...	200 951	...	...
1 VII 2000	ESDJ	384 615	...	...	182 044	...	...	202 571	...	...
1 VII 2001	ESDJ	387 135	...	...	182 935	...	...	204 200	...	...
1 VII 2002	ESDJ	389 455	...	...	183 727	...	...	205 729	...	...
1 VII 2003	ESDJ	390 552	...	...	184 084	...	...	206 468	...	...
1 I 2004	ESDJ	393 852	...	...	184 303	...	...	209 549	...	...
1 I 2005	ESDJ	395 982	...	...	184 841	...	...	211 141	...	...
1 I 2006	CDJC	397 732	355 189	89.3	185 604	165 012	88.9	212 128	190 177	89.7
1 I 2007*	ESDJ	400 000	...	...	186 357	...	...	213 643	...	...
Mexico - Mexique										
1 VII 1998	ESDJ	95 790 135	76 083 002	79.4	47 502 593	...	...	48 287 542	...	...
1 VII 1999	ESDJ	97 114 831	77 348 051	79.6	48 111 343	...	...	49 003 488	...	...
14 II 2000	CDJC	97 483 412	72 759 822	74.6	47 592 253	35 317 569	74.2	49 891 159	37 442 253	75.0
1 VII 2000	ESDJ	98 438 557	73 515 485	74.7	48 722 412	...	...	49 716 145	...	...
1 VII 2001	ESDJ	99 715 527	74 840 402	75.1	49 312 382	...	...	50 403 145	...	...
1 VII 2002	ESDJ	100 909 374	76 108 582	75.4	49 862 638	...	...	51 046 736	...	...
1 VII 2003	ESDJ	101 999 555	77 303 384	75.8	50 361 179	...	...	51 638 376	...	...
1 VII 2004	ESDJ	103 001 867	78 436 582	76.2	50 814 580	...	...	52 187 287	...	...
1 VII 2005[1]	ESDJ	103 946 866	79 528 445	76.5	51 238 427	...	...	52 708 439	...	...
17 X 2005	CDJC	103 263 388	78 986 852	76.5	50 249 955	38 300 417	76.2	53 013 433	40 686 435	76.7

Continent, country or area, and date / Continent, pays ou zone et date	Code[a]	Both sexes - Les deux sexes Total	Urban - Urbaine Number Nombre	Urban - Urbaine Percent P.100	Male - Masculin Total	Urban - Urbaine Number Nombre	Urban - Urbaine Percent P.100	Female - Féminin Total	Urban - Urbaine Number Nombre	Urban - Urbaine Percent P.100
AMERICA, NORTH - AMÉRIQUE DU NORD										
Mexico - Mexique										
1 VII 2006[1] ....ESDJ		104 874 282	80 609 788	76.9	51 654 642	...	...	53 219 640	...	...
1 VII 2007[1] ....ESDJ		105 790 725	81 685 414	77.2	52 066 743	...	...	53 723 982	...	...
Montserrat										
1 VII 1998 ....ESDF		3 595	...	...	1 944	...	...	1 651	...	...
1 VII 1999 ....ESDF		4 771	...	...	2 536	...	...	2 235	...	...
1 VII 2000 ....ESDF		5 274	...	...	2 793	...	...	2 481	...	...
12 V 2001 ....CDFC		4 491	...	...	2 418	...	...	2 073	...	...
Netherlands Antilles - Antilles néerlandaises										
1 I 1998 ....ESDJ		194 499	...	...	92 489	...	...	102 010	...	...
1 I 1999 ....ESDJ		189 606	...	...	90 017	...	...	99 589	...	...
1 I 2000 ....ESDJ		182 746	...	...	86 308	...	...	96 438	...	...
1 I 2001 ....ESDJ		175 704	...	...	82 610	...	...	93 094	...	...
29 I 2001 ....CDJC		175 653	...	...	82 521	...	...	93 132	...	...
1 I 2002 ....ESDJ		172 586	...	...	80 884	...	...	91 702	...	...
1 I 2003 ....ESDJ		176 635	...	...	82 752	...	...	93 883	...	...
1 I 2004 ....ESDJ		178 719	...	...	83 303	...	...	95 416	...	...
1 I 2005 ....ESDJ		183 536	...	...	85 504	...	...	98 032	...	...
1 I 2006* ....ESDJ		188 923	...	...	87 896	...	...	101 027	...	...
1 I 2007* ....ESDJ		193 549	...	...	90 140	...	...	103 410	...	...
Nicaragua										
1 VII 1998 ....ESDJ		4 932 118	...	...	2 456 373	...	...	2 475 745	...	...
1 VII 1999 ....ESDJ		5 016 890	...	...	2 498 359	...	...	2 518 531	...	...
1 VII 2000 ....ESDJ		5 098 030	...	...	2 538 219	...	...	2 559 811	...	...
1 VII 2001 ....ESDJ		5 173 927	...	...	2 575 135	...	...	2 598 792	...	...
1 VII 2002 ....ESDJ		5 244 694	...	...	2 609 277	...	...	2 635 418	...	...
1 VII 2003 ....ESDJ		5 312 750	...	...	2 641 869	...	...	2 670 881	...	...
1 VII 2004 ....ESDJ		5 380 510	...	...	2 674 138	...	...	2 706 372	...	...
4 VI 2005 ....CDJC		5 144 553	2 877 002	55.9	2 535 461	1 369 108	54.0	2 609 092	1 507 894	57.8
1 VII 2005 ....ESDJ		5 450 387	3 047 740	55.9	2 707 309	1 462 218	54.0	2 743 078	1 585 522	57.8
1 VII 2006 ....ESDJ		5 522 605	3 099 917	56.1	2 741 416	1 488 694	54.3	2 781 189	1 611 223	57.9
1 VII 2007 ....ESDJ		5 595 543	3 152 811	56.3	2 775 634	1 515 433	54.6	2 819 909	1 637 378	58.1
Panama										
1 VII 1998 ....ESDF		2 763 612	1 540 742	55.8	1 395 475	751 450	53.8	1 368 137	789 292	57.7
1 VII 1999 ....ESDF		2 809 280	1 572 780	56.0	1 417 957	767 186	54.1	1 391 323	805 594	57.9
14 V 2000 ....CDFC		2 839 177	...	...	1 432 566	...	...	1 406 611	...	...
1 VII 2000 ....ESDF		2 855 703	1 604 823	56.2	1 440 801	782 928	54.3	1 414 902	821 895	58.1
1 VII 2004 ....ESDF		3 172 360	...	...	1 600 879	...	...	1 571 481	...	...
1 VII 2005 ....ESDF		3 228 186	2 050 965	63.5	1 628 720	1 011 700	62.1	1 599 466	1 039 265	65.0
1 VII 2006 ....ESDF		3 283 959	2 093 871	63.8	1 656 469	1 033 634	62.4	1 627 490	1 060 237	65.1
Puerto Rico - Porto Rico[24]										
1 VII 1998 ....ESDJ		3 748 150	...	...	1 806 604	...	...	1 941 546	...	...
1 VII 1999 ....ESDJ		3 782 143	...	...	1 821 772	...	...	1 960 371	...	...
1 IV 2000 ....CDJC		3 808 610	3 594 948[25]	94.4	1 833 577	1 723 589[25]	94.0	1 975 033	1 871 359[25]	94.8
1 VII 2000 ....ESDJ		3 815 893	3 604 039[25]	94.4	1 836 799	...	...	1 979 094	...	...
1 VII 2001 ....ESDJ		3 839 810	...	...	1 847 559	...	...	1 992 251	...	...
1 VII 2002 ....ESDJ		3 858 806	...	...	1 855 781	...	...	2 003 025	...	...
1 VII 2003 ....ESDJ		3 878 532	...	...	1 865 170	...	...	2 013 362	...	...
1 VII 2004 ....ESDJ		3 894 855	...	...	1 871 657	...	...	2 023 198	...	...
1 VII 2005 ....ESDJ		3 912 054	...	...	1 879 236	...	...	2 032 818	...	...
1 VII 2006 ....ESDJ		3 927 776	...	...	1 886 031	...	...	2 041 745	...	...
1 VII 2007 ....ESDJ		3 942 375	...	...	1 892 503	...	...	2 049 872	...	...
Saint Kitts and Nevis - Saint-Kitts-et-Nevis										
1 VII 1998 ....ESDF		40 130	...	...	20 230	...	...	19 900	...	...
1 VII 1999 ....ESDF		42 460	...	...	21 360	...	...	21 100	...	...
1 VII 2000 ....ESDF		40 410	...	...	20 400	...	...	20 010	...	...
14 V 2001 ....CDFC		45 841	...	...	22 784	...	...	23 057	...	...
1 VII 2001* ....ESDF		46 111	...	...	22 919	...	...	23 192	...	...

Continent, country or area, and date / Continent, pays ou zone et date	Code[a]	Both sexes - Les deux sexes			Male - Masculin			Female - Féminin		
		Total	Urban - Urbaine		Total	Urban - Urbaine		Total	Urban - Urbaine	
			Number Nombre	Percent P.100		Number Nombre	Percent P.100		Number Nombre	Percent P.100
AMERICA, NORTH - AMÉRIQUE DU NORD										
Saint Lucia - Sainte-Lucie										
1 VII 1998 ....ESDF		151 972	44 932	29.6	74 320	21 976	29.6	77 632	22 956	29.6
1 VII 1999 ....ESDF		153 703	...	...	75 266	...	...	78 437	...	...
1 VII 2000 ....ESDF		155 996	...	...	76 494	...	...	79 502	...	...
22 V 2001 ....CDFC		157 164	43 316	27.6	76 741	20 711	27.0	80 423	22 605	28.1
1 VII 2002 ....ESDF		159 133	...	...	77 868	...	...	81 265	...	...
1 VII 2003 ....ESDF		160 673	...	...	78 618	...	...	82 055	...	...
1 VII 2004 ....ESDF		162 434	...	...	79 407	...	...	83 027	...	...
1 VII 2005 ....ESDF		164 330	...	...	80 440	...	...	83 890	...	...
1 VII 2006 ....ESDF		166 387	...	...	81 558	...	...	84 829	...	...
1 VII 2007 ....ESDF		168 338	...	...	82 426	...	...	85 912	...	...
Saint Pierre and Miquelon - Saint Pierre-et-Miquelon										
8 III 1999 ....CDFC		6 316	...	...	3 147	...	...	3 169	...	...
Saint Vincent and the Grenadines - Saint-Vincent-et-les Grenadines										
1 VII 1998 ....ESDF		111 810	48 839	43.7	55 378	...	...	56 432	...	...
1 VII 1999 ....ESDF		112 030	...	...	55 925	...	...	56 105	...	...
1 VII 2000 ....ESDF		109 790	...	...	54 774	...	...	55 016	...	...
14 V 2001[15] ....CDFC		109 022	49 590	45.5	55 456	24 809	44.7	53 566	24 781	46.3
1 VII 2002 ....ESDF		107 854	48 535	45.0	54 434	...	...	53 420	...	...
1 VII 2003 ....ESDF		105 158	42 063	40.0	53 494	...	...	51 664	...	...
1 VII 2004 ....ESDF		104 555	41 822	40.0	53 187	...	...	51 368	...	...
1 VII 2005 ....ESDF		103 751	...	...	52 778	...	...	50 973	...	...
Trinidad and Tobago - Trinité-et-Tobago										
1 VII 1998 ....ESDF		1 281 825	...	...	638 096[3]	...	...	639 579[3]	...	...
1 VII 1999 ....ESDF		1 290 413	...	...	640 914[3]	...	...	642 949[3]	...	...
15 V 2000 ....CDFC		1 262 366	...	...	633 051	...	...	629 315	...	...
1 VII 2001 ....ESDF		1 266 797	...	...	635 299	...	...	631 498	...	...
1 VII 2002[26] ....ESDF		1 275 705	...	...	639 766	...	...	635 939	...	...
1 VII 2003[26] ....ESDF		1 282 447	...	...	642 037	...	...	640 410	...	...
1 VII 2004[26] ....ESDF		1 290 646	...	...	647 259	...	...	643 387	...	...
1 VII 2005[26] ....ESDF		1 294 494	...	...	649 189	...	...	645 305	...	...
1 VII 2006[26] ....ESDF		1 297 944	...	...	650 919	...	...	647 025	...	...
1 VII 2007[26] ....ESDF		1 303 188	...	...	653 549	...	...	649 639	...	...
Turks and Caicos Islands - Îles Turques et Caïques										
10 IX 2001 ....CDFC		19 886	...	...	9 897	...	...	9 989	...	...
1 VII 2002 ....ESDJ		20 900	...	...	10 402	...	...	10 498	...	...
1 VII 2003 ....ESDJ		25 143	...	...	12 513	...	...	12 630	...	...
1 VII 2004 ....ESDJ		27 496	...	...	13 684	...	...	13 812	...	...
1 VII 2005 ....ESDJ		30 602	...	...	15 230	...	...	15 372	...	...
1 VII 2006 ....ESDJ		33 202	...	...	16 524	...	...	16 678	...	...
1 VII 2007 ....ESDJ		34 862	...	...	18 023	...	...	16 839	...	...
United States of America - États-Unis d'Amérique[27]										
1 VII 1998 ....ESDJ		275 854 104	...	...	135 129 904	...	...	140 724 200	...	...
1 VII 1999 ....ESDJ		279 040 168	...	...	136 802 873	...	...	142 237 295	...	...
1 IV 2000 ....CDJC		281 421 906	222 360 539	79.0	138 053 563	108 375 797	78.5	143 368 343	113 984 742	79.5
1 VII 2000 ....ESDJ		282 194 308	...	...	138 469 840	...	...	143 724 468	...	...
1 VII 2001 ....ESDJ		285 112 030	...	...	140 016 603	...	...	145 095 427	...	...
1 VII 2002 ....ESDJ		287 888 021	...	...	141 462 599	...	...	146 425 422	...	...
1 VII 2003 ....ESDJ		290 447 644	...	...	142 748 033	...	...	147 699 611	...	...
1 VII 2004 ....ESDJ		293 191 511	...	...	144 224 452	...	...	148 967 059	...	...
1 VII 2005 ....ESDJ		295 895 897	...	...	145 648 705	...	...	150 247 192	...	...

6. Total and urban population by sex: 1998 - 2007
Population totale et population urbaine selon le sexe: 1998 - 2007 (continued - suite)

Continent, country or area, and date / Continent, pays ou zone et date	Code[a]	Both sexes - Les deux sexes			Male - Masculin			Female - Féminin		
		Total	Urban - Urbaine		Total	Urban - Urbaine		Total	Urban - Urbaine	
			Number Nombre	Percent P.100		Number Nombre	Percent P.100		Number Nombre	Percent P.100
AMERICA, NORTH - AMÉRIQUE DU NORD										
United States of America - États-Unis d'Amérique[27]										
1 VII 2006	ESDJ	298 754 819	...	...	147 160 189	...	...	151 594 630	...	...
1 VII 2007	ESDJ	301 621 157	...	...	148 658 898	...	...	152 962 259	...	...
United States Virgin Islands - Îles Vierges américaines[24]										
1 IV 2000	CDJC	108 612	...	...	51 864	...	...	56 748	...	...
1 VII 2000	ESDJ	108 637	...	...	51 876	...	...	56 761	...	...
1 VII 2001	ESDJ	108 749	...	...	51 920	...	...	56 829	...	...
1 VII 2002	ESDJ	108 923	...	...	51 893	...	...	57 030	...	...
1 VII 2003	ESDJ	109 148	...	...	51 954	...	...	57 194	...	...
1 VII 2004	ESDJ	109 354	...	...	52 007	...	...	57 347	...	...
1 VII 2005	ESDJ	109 600	...	...	52 081	...	...	57 519	...	...
1 VII 2006	ESDJ	109 764	...	...	52 113	...	...	57 651	...	...
1 VII 2007	ESDJ	109 821	...	...	52 089	...	...	57 732	...	...
AMERICA, SOUTH - AMÉRIQUE DU SUD										
Argentina - Argentine										
1 VII 1998	ESDF	36 005 387	...	...	17 650 012	...	...	18 355 375	...	...
1 VII 1999	ESDF	36 398 577	...	...	17 837 342	...	...	18 561 235	...	...
1 VII 2000	ESDF	36 783 859	32 902 070	89.4	18 021 900	15 957 354	88.5	18 761 959	16 944 716	90.3
1 VII 2001	ESDF	37 156 195	33 312 347	89.7	18 201 249	16 161 696	88.8	18 954 946	17 150 651	90.5
18 XI 2001	CDFC	36 260 130	32 431 950	89.4	17 659 072	15 629 299	88.5	18 601 058	16 802 651	90.3
1 VII 2002	ESDF	37 515 632	33 709 927	89.9	18 374 920	16 361 823	89.0	19 140 712	17 348 104	90.6
1 VII 2003	ESDF	37 869 730	34 101 536	90.0	18 546 570	16 559 682	89.3	19 323 160	17 541 854	90.8
1 VII 2004	ESDF	38 226 051	34 493 965	90.2	18 719 869	16 758 540	89.5	19 506 182	17 735 425	90.9
1 VII 2005	ESDF	38 592 150	34 894 057	90.4	18 898 472	16 961 698	89.8	19 693 678	17 932 359	91.1
1 VII 2006	ESDF	38 970 611	35 304 205	90.6	19 083 828	17 170 659	90.0	19 886 783	18 133 546	91.2
1 VII 2007	ESDF	39 356 383	35 719 891	90.8	19 273 494	17 383 239	90.2	20 082 889	18 336 652	91.3
Bolivia (Plurinational State of) - Bolivie (État plurinational de)										
1 VII 1998	ESDF	8 035 143	4 888 033	60.8	3 996 143	2 380 830	59.6	4 039 000	2 507 204	62.1
1 VII 1999	ESDF	8 229 487	5 047 016	61.3	4 094 229	2 457 763	60.0	4 135 259	2 589 253	62.6
1 VII 2000	ESDF	8 427 789	5 208 601	61.8	4 194 195	2 536 032	60.5	4 233 594	2 672 569	63.1
1 VII 2001	ESDF	8 624 268	5 373 504	62.3	4 293 345	2 615 967	60.9	4 330 924	2 757 537	63.7
5 IX 2001	CDFC	8 274 325	5 165 230	62.4	4 123 850	2 517 106	61.0	4 150 475	2 648 124	63.8
1 VII 2002	ESDF	8 823 743	5 541 707	62.8	4 393 968	2 697 501	61.4	4 429 776	2 844 206	64.2
1 VII 2003	ESDF	9 024 922	5 712 138	63.3	4 495 426	2 780 137	61.8	4 529 495	2 932 001	64.7
1 VII 2004	ESDF	9 226 511	5 883 724	63.8	4 597 081	2 863 378	62.3	4 629 430	3 020 347	65.2
1 VII 2005	ESDF	9 427 219	6 055 392	64.2	4 698 293	2 946 725	62.7	4 728 926	3 108 667	65.7
1 VII 2006	ESDF	9 627 269	6 227 367	64.7	4 799 178	3 030 290	63.1	4 828 091	3 197 077	66.2
1 VII 2007	ESDF	9 827 522	6 400 366	65.1	4 900 162	3 114 403	63.6	4 927 360	3 285 963	66.7
Brazil - Brésil[28]										
1 VII 1998	ESDF	166 252 088	...	...	81 940 241	...	...	84 311 847	...	...
1 VII 1999	ESDF	168 753 552	...	...	83 139 277	...	...	85 614 275	...	...
1 VII 2000	ESDF	171 279 882	...	...	84 350 720	...	...	86 929 162	...	...
1 VIII 2000	CDJC	169 799 170	137 953 959	81.2	83 576 015	66 882 993	80.0	86 223 155	71 070 966	82.4
1 VII 2001	ESDF	173 808 010	...	...	85 562 804	...	...	88 245 206	...	...
1 VII 2002	ESDF	176 303 919	...	...	86 758 217	...	...	89 545 702	...	...
1 VII 2003	ESDF	178 741 412	...	...	87 923 721	...	...	90 817 691	...	...
1 VII 2004	ESDF	181 105 601	...	...	89 051 847	...	...	92 053 754	...	...
1 VII 2005	ESDF	183 383 216	...	...	90 135 967	...	...	93 247 249	...	...
1 VII 2006	ESDF	185 564 212	...	...	91 171 295	...	...	94 392 917	...	...
1 VII 2007	ESDF	187 641 714	...	...	92 154 636	...	...	95 487 078	...	...
Chile - Chili										
1 VII 1998	ESDF	14 996 647	12 876 051	85.9	7 420 612	6 287 197	84.7	7 576 035	6 588 854	87.0
1 VII 1999	ESDF	15 197 213	13 106 477	86.2	7 520 454	6 403 647	85.1	7 676 759	6 702 830	87.3

Continent, country or area, and date / Continent, pays ou zone et date	Code[a]	Both sexes - Les deux sexes			Male - Masculin			Female - Féminin		
		Total	Urban - Urbaine		Total	Urban - Urbaine		Total	Urban - Urbaine	
			Number Nombre	Percent P.100		Number Nombre	Percent P.100		Number Nombre	Percent P.100
AMERICA, SOUTH - AMÉRIQUE DU SUD										
Chile - Chili										
1 VII 2000 ....ESDF		15 397 784	13 336 913	86.6	7 620 300	6 520 105	85.6	7 777 484	6 816 808	87.6
1 VII 2001 ....ESDF		15 571 679	13 494 230	86.7	7 706 752	6 598 130	85.6	7 864 927	6 896 100	87.7
24 IV 2002...........CDFC		15 116 435	13 090 113	86.6	7 447 695	6 366 311	85.5	7 668 740	6 723 802	87.7
1 VII 2002 ....ESDF		15 745 583	13 651 558	86.7	7 793 208	6 676 157	85.7	7 952 375	6 975 401	87.7
1 VII 2003 ....ESDF		15 919 479	13 808 880	86.7	7 879 658	6 754 181	85.7	8 039 821	7 054 699	87.7
1 VII 2004 ....ESDF		16 093 378	13 966 203	86.8	7 966 110	6 832 205	85.8	8 127 268	7 133 998	87.8
1 VII 2005 ....ESDF		16 267 278	14 123 527	86.8	8 052 564	6 910 230	85.8	8 214 714	7 213 297	87.8
1 VII 2006 ....ESDF		16 432 674	14 272 454	86.9	8 134 314	6 983 850	85.9	8 298 360	7 288 604	87.8
1 VII 2007 ....ESDF		16 598 074	14 421 386	86.9	8 216 068	7 057 476	85.9	8 382 006	7 363 910	87.9
Colombia - Colombie										
1 VII 1998 ....ESDF		39 201 321[29]	28 734 719[3]	73.3	19 343 246[29]	...	...	19 858 075[29]	...	...
1 VII 1999 ....ESDF		39 745 714[29]	29 435 181[3]	74.1	19 612 492[29]	...	...	20 133 222[29]	...	...
1 VII 2000 ....ESDF		40 282 217[29]	30 125 776[3]	74.8	19 877 987[29]	...	...	20 404 230[29]	...	...
1 VII 2001 ....ESDF		40 806 313[29]	30 772 485[3]	75.4	20 137 593[29]	...	...	20 668 720[29]	...	...
1 VII 2002 ....ESDF		41 327 459[29]	31 428 374[3]	76.0	20 395 870[29]	...	...	20 931 589[29]	...	...
1 VII 2003 ....ESDF		41 847 421[29]	32 101 585[3]	76.7	20 653 652[29]	...	...	21 193 769[29]	...	...
1 VII 2004 ....ESDF		42 367 528[29]	32 787 008[3]	77.4	20 911 536[29]	...	...	21 455 992[29]	...	...
22 V 2005 ....CDFC		41 468 384	31 510 379	76.0	20 336 117	15 086 536	74.2	21 132 267	16 423 843	77.7
1 VII 2005 ....ESDF		42 888 592[29]	31 890 892	74.4	21 169 835[29]	...	...	21 718 757[29]	...	...
1 VII 2006 ....ESDF		43 405 387[29]	32 399 518	74.6	21 425 328[29]	...	...	21 980 059[29]	...	...
1 VII 2007 ....ESDF		43 926 034[29]	32 902 074	74.9	21 682 836[29]	...	...	22 243 198[29]	...	...
Ecuador - Équateur[30]										
1 VII 1998[1] ....ESDF		11 947 586	7 118 271	59.6	6 001 552	3 517 425	58.6	5 946 036	3 600 846	60.6
1 VII 1999[1] ....ESDF		12 120 981	7 282 105	60.1	6 087 690	3 600 349	59.1	6 033 294	3 681 756	61.0
1 VII 2000[1] ....ESDF		12 298 745	7 450 308	60.6	6 175 859	3 685 298	59.7	6 122 886	3 765 010	61.5
1 VII 2001[1] ....ESDF		12 479 924	7 633 850	61.2	6 265 558	3 778 158	60.3	6 214 366	3 855 692	62.0
25 XI 2001...........CDFC		12 156 608	7 431 355	61.1	6 018 353	3 625 962	60.2	6 138 255	3 805 393	62.0
1 VII 2002[1] ....ESDF		12 660 728	7 817 018	61.7	6 354 906	3 870 667	60.9	6 305 821	3 946 351	62.6
1 VII 2003[1] ....ESDF		12 842 578	8 001 231	62.3	6 444 656	3 963 574	61.5	6 397 920	4 037 657	63.1
1 VII 2004[1] ....ESDF		13 026 891	8 187 908	62.9	6 535 564	4 057 642	62.1	6 491 327	4 130 266	63.6
1 VII 2005[1] ....ESDF		13 215 089	8 378 469	63.4	6 628 368	4 153 605	62.7	6 586 721	4 224 864	64.1
1 VII 2006[1] ....ESDF		13 408 270	8 580 090	64.0	6 723 629	4 254 974	63.3	6 684 641	4 325 116	64.7
1 VII 2007[1] ....ESDF		13 605 486	8 785 745	64.6	6 820 842	4 358 292	63.9	6 784 644	4 427 453	65.3
Falkland Islands (Malvinas) - Îles Falkland (Malvinas)[31]										
8 IV 2001 ....CDFC		2 913	...	...	1 598	...	...	1 315	...	...
8 X 2006 ....CDFC		2 955	...	...	1 569	...	...	1 386	...	...
French Guiana - Guyane française										
1 VII 1998 ....ESDJ		153 001	...	...	77 177	...	...	75 825	...	...
8 III 1999 ....CDJC		156 790	128 297	81.8	78 963	64 024	81.1	77 827	64 273	82.6
1 VII 1999 ....ESDJ		158 444	...	...	79 670	...	...	78 774	...	...
1 VII 2000 ....ESDJ		163 979	...	...	82 200	...	...	81 779	...	...
1 VII 2001 ....ESDJ		169 667	...	...	84 782	...	...	84 885	...	...
1 VII 2002 ....ESDJ		175 426	...	...	87 387	...	...	88 039	...	...
1 I 2003 ....ESDJ		184 792	...	...	92 273	...	...	92 519	...	...
1 I 2004 ....ESDJ		193 167	...	...	96 300	...	...	96 867	...	...
1 I 2005 ....ESDJ		199 206	...	...	99 223	...	...	99 983	...	...
1 I 2006 ....CDJC		205 954	167 454	81.3	101 930	81 888	80.3	104 023	85 565	82.3
1 I 2007 ....ESDJ		213 500	...	...	105 549	...	...	107 951	...	...
Guyana										
1 VII 1998 ....ESDF		773 432	...	...	381 070	...	...	392 362	...	...
1 VII 1999 ....ESDF		770 584	...	...	379 667	...	...	390 917	...	...
1 VII 2000 ....ESDF		742 000	...	...	365 583	...	...	376 417	...	...
1 VII 2001 ....ESDF		743 600	...	...	366 372	...	...	377 228	...	...
1 VII 2002 ....ESDF		747 712	...	...	371 351	...	...	376 361	...	...
15 IX 2002...........CDFC		751 223	...	...	376 034	...	...	375 189	...	...
1 VII 2003 ....ESDF		753 196	...	...	377 019	...	...	376 177	...	...
1 VII 2004 ....ESDF		755 685	...	...	378 265	...	...	377 420	...	...
1 VII 2005 ....ESDF		758 183	...	...	379 515	...	...	378 668	...	...

127

Continent, country or area, and date / Continent, pays ou zone et date — Code[a]	Both sexes - Les deux sexes Total	Urban - Urbaine Number Nombre	Urban - Urbaine Percent P.100	Male - Masculin Total	Urban - Urbaine Number Nombre	Urban - Urbaine Percent P.100	Female - Féminin Total	Urban - Urbaine Number Nombre	Urban - Urbaine Percent P.100
AMERICA, SOUTH - AMÉRIQUE DU SUD									
Guyana									
1 VII 2006 ....ESDF	760 689	...	...	380 770	...	...	379 919	...	...
1 VII 2007 ....ESDF	763 203	...	...	382 028	...	...	381 175	...	...
Paraguay									
1 VII 1998 ....ESDF	5 127 167	...	...	2 594 065	...	...	2 533 102	...	...
1 VII 1999 ....ESDF	5 236 543	...	...	2 649 827	...	...	2 586 716	...	...
1 VII 2000 ....ESDF	5 346 267	2 939 944	55.0	2 705 524	1 433 399	53.0	2 640 743	1 506 545	57.1
1 VII 2001 ....ESDF	5 456 418	3 020 281	55.4	2 761 141	1 473 081	53.4	2 695 278	1 547 200	57.4
1 VII 2002 ....ESDF	5 566 852	3 101 412	55.7	2 816 687	1 513 168	53.7	2 750 164	1 588 244	57.8
28 VIII 2002 ....CDFC	5 163 198	2 928 437	56.7	2 603 242	1 422 339	54.6	2 559 956	1 506 098	58.8
1 VII 2003 ....ESDF	5 677 448	3 183 160	56.1	2 872 186	1 553 561	54.1	2 805 262	1 629 599	58.1
1 VII 2004 ....ESDF	5 788 088	3 265 346	56.4	2 927 657	1 594 161	54.5	2 860 430	1 671 185	58.4
1 VII 2005 ....ESDF	5 898 651	3 347 793	56.8	2 983 123	1 634 869	54.8	2 915 528	1 712 924	58.8
1 VII 2006 ....ESDF	6 009 143	3 430 619	57.1	3 038 590	1 675 752	55.1	2 970 553	1 754 868	59.1
1 VII 2007 ....ESDF	6 119 642	3 513 944	57.4	3 094 044	1 716 874	55.5	3 025 598	1 797 070	59.4
Peru - Pérou									
1 VII 1998 ....ESDF	25 182 269[14]	17 978 819[3]	71.4	12 639 465[14]	9 017 356[3]	71.3	12 542 804[14]	8 961 463[3]	71.4
1 VII 1999 ....ESDF	25 588 546[14]	18 312 557[3]	71.6	12 842 387[14]	9 182 458[3]	71.5	12 746 159[14]	9 130 099[3]	71.6
1 VII 2000 ....ESDF	25 983 588[14]	18 647 242[3]	71.8	13 039 529[14]	9 348 264[3]	71.7	12 944 059[14]	9 298 978[3]	71.8
1 VII 2001 ....ESDF	26 366 533[14]	18 980 589[3]	72.0	13 230 410[14]	9 513 198[3]	71.9	13 136 123[14]	9 467 391[3]	72.1
1 VII 2002 ....ESDF	26 739 379[14]	19 310 309[3]	72.2	13 416 024[14]	9 676 260[3]	72.1	13 323 355[14]	9 634 049[3]	72.3
1 VII 2003 ....ESDF	27 103 457[14]	19 638 160[3]	72.5	13 597 121[14]	9 838 166[3]	72.4	13 506 336[14]	9 799 994[3]	72.6
1 VII 2004 ....ESDF	27 460 073[14]	19 966 180[3]	72.7	13 774 414[14]	9 999 924[3]	72.6	13 685 659[14]	9 966 256[3]	72.8
1 VII 2005[14] ....ESDF	27 810 538	...	...	13 948 639	...	...	13 861 899	...	...
18 VII 2005*[32] ......CDFC	26 152 265			13 061 026			13 091 239		
1 VII 2006 ....ESDF	28 151 443[14]	20 371 596[3]	72.4	14 118 112[14]	10 067 586[3]	71.3	14 033 331[14]	10 304 010[3]	73.4
1 VII 2007[14] ....ESDF	28 481 901	...	...	14 282 346			14 199 555	...	...
21 X 2007 ....CDFC	27 412 157	20 810 288	75.9	13 622 640	10 226 205	75.1	13 789 517	10 584 083	76.8
Suriname									
1 VII 1998 ....ESDJ	451 629	...	...	226 621	...	...	225 008	...	...
1 VII 1999 ....ESDJ	457 692	...	...	229 664	...	...	228 028	...	...
1 VII 2000 ....ESDJ	463 837	...	...	232 747	...	...	231 090	...	...
1 VII 2001 ....ESDJ	470 064	...	...	236 276	...	...	233 788	...	...
1 VII 2002 ....ESDJ	476 374	...	...	239 447	...	...	236 927	...	...
31 III 2003* ....CDJC	481 146[33]			241 837			239 292		
1 VII 2003 ....ESDJ	482 769			242 662	...	...	240 107	...	...
2 VIII 2004[34] ....CDJC	492 829	328 932	66.7	247 846[35]	164 297[35]	66.3	244 618[35]	164 370[35]	67.2
1 VII 2005 ....ESDJ	498 543	...	...	251 101	...	...	247 442	...	...
1 VII 2006 ....ESDJ	504 257	...	...	254 147	...	...	250 110	...	...
1 VII 2007 ....ESDJ	509 970	...	...	257 181	...	...	252 789	...	...
Uruguay									
1 VII 1998[14] ....ESDF	3 273 777	3 019 947	92.2	1 586 775	1 441 116	90.8	1 687 002	1 578 831	93.6
1 VII 1999[14] ....ESDF	3 288 819	3 040 697	92.5	1 593 452	1 451 298	91.1	1 695 368	1 589 399	93.7
1 VII 2000[14] ....ESDF	3 300 847	3 058 437	92.7	1 598 685	1 460 013	91.3	1 702 162	1 598 424	93.9
1 VII 2001[14] ....ESDF	3 308 356	3 071 727	92.8	1 601 593	1 466 408	91.6	1 706 763	1 605 319	94.1
1 VII 2002[14] ....ESDF	3 308 527	3 077 804	93.0	1 600 814	1 469 148	91.8	1 707 713	1 608 656	94.2
1 VII 2003[14] ....ESDF	3 303 540	3 078 812	93.2	1 597 362	1 469 246	92.0	1 706 177	1 609 565	94.3
1 VI 2004[36] ....CDFC	3 241 003	2 974 714	91.8	1 565 533	1 415 362	90.4	1 675 470	1 559 352	93.1
1 VII 2004[14] ....ESDF	3 301 732	3 083 096	93.4	1 595 635	1 471 098	92.2	1 706 097	1 611 998	94.5
1 VII 2005[14] ....ESDF	3 305 723	3 089 988	93.5	1 597 040	1 474 638	92.3	1 708 683	1 615 350	94.5
1 VII 2006[14] ....ESDF	3 314 466	3 101 685	93.6	1 601 024	1 480 779	92.5	1 713 442	1 620 906	94.6
1 VII 2007[1] ....ESDF	3 323 906	3 114 125	93.7	1 605 466	1 487 391	92.6	1 718 440	1 626 734	94.7
Venezuela (Bolivarian Republic of) - Venezuela (République bolivarienne du)[37]									
1 VII 1998 ....ESDF	23 412 742	20 534 451	87.7	11 784 967	10 222 629	86.7	11 627 775	10 311 822	88.7
1 VII 1999 ....ESDF	23 867 393	20 945 043	87.8	12 010 280	10 423 959	86.8	11 857 113	10 521 084	88.7
1 VII 2000 ....ESDF	24 310 896	21 345 288	87.8	12 229 953	10 620 092	86.8	12 080 943	10 725 196	88.8
1 VII 2001 ....ESDF	24 765 581	21 754 766	87.8	12 454 204	10 820 038	86.9	12 311 377	10 934 728	88.8
30 X 2001 ....CDFC	23 054 210	...	...	11 402 869			11 651 341		
1 VII 2002 ....ESDF	25 219 910	22 163 339	87.9	12 678 275	11 021 146	86.9	12 541 635	11 142 193	88.8
1 VII 2003 ....ESDF	25 673 550	...	...	12 901 999	...	...	12 771 551	...	...

Continent, country or area, and date / Continent, pays ou zone et date	Code[a]	Both sexes - Les deux sexes Total	Urban - Urbaine Number Nombre	Urban - Urbaine Percent P.100	Male - Masculin Total	Urban - Urbaine Number Nombre	Urban - Urbaine Percent P.100	Female - Féminin Total	Urban - Urbaine Number Nombre	Urban - Urbaine Percent P.100
Venezuela (Bolivarian Republic of) - Venezuela (République bolivarienne du)[37]										
1 VII 2004	ESDF	26 127 351	...	...	13 125 804	...	...	13 001 547	...	...
1 VII 2005	ESDF	26 577 423	...	...	13 347 732	...	...	13 229 691	...	...
1 VII 2006	ESDF	27 030 656	...	...	13 570 418·	...	...	13 460 238	...	...
1 VII 2007	ESDF	27 483 208	...	...	13 792 761	...	...	13 690 447	...	...
ASIA - ASIE										
Afghanistan										
1 VII 2002	ESDF	22 930 000	4 463 000[38]	19.5	10 453 500[38]	2 332 600[38]	22.3	9 844 300[38]	2 130 400[38]	21.6
1 VII 2006[39]	ESDF	22 575 900	4 862 100	21.5	11 545 800	2 503 100	21.7	11 030 100	2 359 000	21.4
Armenia - Arménie										
1 VII 1998	ESDJ	3 235 151	2 117 251	65.4	1 553 260	1 011 028	65.1	1 681 891	1 106 223	65.8
1 VII 1999	ESDJ	3 229 499	2 103 700	65.1	1 552 362	1 002 727	64.6	1 677 138	1 100 974	65.6
1 VII 2000	ESDJ	3 221 106	2 086 054	64.8	1 544 397	988 741	64.0	1 676 709	1 097 313	65.4
1 VII 2001	ESDJ	3 214 095	2 070 947	64.4	1 542 728	977 820	63.4	1 671 367	1 093 127	65.4
10 X 2001[40]	CDFC	3 002 594	1 945 514	64.8	1 407 220	898 977	63.9	1 595 374	1 046 537	65.6
1 VII 2002	ESDJ	3 211 593	2 063 913	64.3	1 542 974	974 775	63.2	1 668 619	1 089 138	65.3
1 VII 2003	ESDJ	3 211 267	2 061 952	64.2	1 545 168	975 356	63.1	1 666 099	1 086 596	65.2
1 VII 2004	ESDJ	3 214 030	2 061 984	64.2	1 548 713	976 728	63.1	1 665 317	1 085 256	65.2
1 VII 2005	ESDJ	3 217 535	2 062 472	64.1	1 552 382	978 396	63.0	1 665 153	1 084 076	65.1
1 VII 2006	ESDJ	3 221 094	2 064 268	64.1	1 555 755	980 272	63.0	1 665 339	1 083 996	65.1
1 VII 2007	ESDJ	3 226 520	2 067 650	64.1	1 559 978	982 632	63.0	1 666 542	1 085 018	65.1
Azerbaijan - Azerbaïdjan										
1 VII 1998	ESDF	7 913 000	4 072 600	51.5	3 882 100	1 993 500	51.4	4 030 900	2 079 100	51.6
27 I 1999	CDJC	7 953 438	4 053 584	51.0	3 883 155	1 970 022	50.7	4 070 283	2 083 562	51.2
1 VII 1999	ESDF	7 982 800	4 074 600	51.0	3 899 600	1 981 300	50.8	4 083 200	2 093 300	51.3
1 VII 2000	ESDF	8 048 600	4 096 900	50.9	3 936 400	1 994 300	50.7	4 112 200	2 102 600	51.1
1 VII 2001	ESDF	8 111 200	4 118 800	50.8	3 971 600	2 006 800	50.5	4 139 600	2 112 000	51.0
1 VII 2002	ESDF	8 172 000	4 142 200	50.7	4 005 900	2 020 200	50.4	4 166 100	2 122 000	50.9
1 VII 2003	ESDF	8 234 100	4 242 000	51.5	4 040 800	2 070 800	51.2	4 193 300	2 171 200	51.8
1 VII 2004	ESDF	8 306 500	4 276 300	51.5	4 081 100	2 089 500	51.2	4 225 400	2 186 800	51.8
1 VII 2005	ESDF	8 391 900	4 327 500	51.6	4 128 000	2 116 700	51.3	4 263 900	2 210 800	51.8
1 VII 2006	ESDF	8 484 500	4 377 100	51.6	4 178 600	2 143 000	51.3	4 305 900	2 234 100	51.9
1 VII 2007	ESDF	8 581 300	4 431 200	51.6	4 231 500	2 171 600	51.3	4 349 800	2 259 600	51.9
Bahrain - Bahreïn										
1 VII 1998	ESDF	604 842	...	...	348 100	...	...	256 742	...	...
1 VII 1999	ESDF	620 989	...	...	357 056	...	...	263 933	...	...
1 VII 2000	ESDF	637 582	...	...	366 247	...	...	271 335	...	...
7 IV 2001	CDJC	650 604	571 385[41]	87.8	373 649	328 817[41]	88.0	276 955	242 568[41]	87.6
1 VII 2001	ESDF	661 317	...	...	386 712	...	...	274 605	...	...
1 VII 2002	ESDF	710 554	...	...	418 196	...	...	292 358	...	...
1 VII 2003	ESDF	764 519	...	...	452 900	...	...	311 619	...	...
1 VII 2004	ESDF	823 744	...	...	491 195	...	...	332 549	...	...
1 VII 2005	ESDF	888 824	...	...	533 501	...	...	355 323	...	...
1 VII 2006	ESDF	960 425	...	...	580 285	...	...	380 141	...	...
1 VII 2007	ESDF	1 039 297	...	...	632 074	...	...	407 223	...	...
Bangladesh										
1 VII 1998	ESDF	126 200 000	...	...	64 800 000	...	...	61 400 000	...	...
1 VII 1999*	ESDF	128 100 000	...	...	65 900 000	...	...	62 200 000	...	...
1 VII 2000	ESDF	129 300 000	...	...	66 300 000	...	...	63 000 000	...	...
22 I 2001[42]	CDFC	130 522 598	31 077 952	23.8	67 731 320	16 844 256	24.9	62 791 278	14 233 696	22.7
1 VII 2002	ESDF	132 900 000	30 600 000	23.0	68 200 000	...	...	64 700 000	...	...
1 VII 2003	ESDF	134 800 000	31 300 000	23.2	69 100 000	...	...	65 700 000	...	...
1 VII 2004	ESDF	136 700 000	32 400 000	23.7	70 100 000	...	...	66 600 000	...	...
1 VII 2005	ESDF	138 600 000	33 600 000	24.2	71 000 000	...	...	67 600 000	...	...
1 VII 2006	ESDF	140 600 000	34 600 000	24.6	72 000 000	...	...	68 600 000	...	...
1 VII 2007	ESDF	142 600 000	35 700 000	25.0	73 100 000	...	...	69 500 000	...	...
Bhutan - Bhoutan										
1 VII 2000	ESDF	580 297	...	...	342 324[3]	...	...	335 610[3]	...	...
1 VII 2001	ESDF	590 543	...	...	352 935[3]	...	...	346 014[3]	...	...
1 VII 2002	ESDF	601 582	...	...	361 759[3]	...	...	354 665[3]	...	...
1 VII 2003	ESDF	612 515	...	...	370 805[3]	...	...	363 535[3]	...	...
1 VII 2004	ESDF	623 647	...	...	380 090[3]	...	...	372 610[3]	...	...

Continent, country or area, and date / Continent, pays ou zone et date	Code[a]	Both sexes - Les deux sexes			Male - Masculin			Female - Féminin		
			Urban - Urbaine			Urban - Urbaine			Urban - Urbaine	
		Total	Number Nombre	Percent P.100	Total	Number Nombre	Percent P.100	Total	Number Nombre	Percent P.100
ASIA - ASIE										
Bhutan - Bhoutan										
30 V 2005 ....CDFC		634 982	...	...	333 595	...	...	301 387	...	...
1 VII 2006[43] ....ESDF		646 851	204 691	31.6	339 403	109 920	32.4	307 448	94 771	30.8
1 VII 2007[43] ....ESDF		658 887	213 571	32.4	345 297	114 592	33.2	313 590	98 978	31.6
Brunei Darussalam - Brunéi Darussalam										
1 VII 1998 ....ESDF		309 500	...	...	159 000	...	...	150 500	...	...
1 VII 1999 ....ESDF		316 900	...	...	162 200	...	...	154 700	...	...
1 VII 2000 ....ESDF		324 800	...	...	165 500	...	...	159 300	...	...
1 VII 2001 ....ESDF		332 800	...	...	168 900	...	...	163 900	...	...
21 VIII 2001* ....CDFC		332 844	238 699	71.7	168 974	120 046	71.0	163 870	118 653	72.4
1 VII 2002 ....ESDF		344 200	...	...	180 600	...	...	163 600	...	...
1 VII 2003 ....ESDF		349 600	...	...	182 500	...	...	167 100	...	...
1 VII 2004 ....ESDF		359 700	...	...	189 400	...	...	170 300	...	...
1 VII 2005 ....ESDF		370 100	...	...	195 300	...	...	174 800	...	...
1 VII 2006 ....ESDF		383 000	...	...	203 300	...	...	179 700	...	...
1 VII 2007 ....ESDF		390 000	...	...	206 900	...	...	183 100	...	...
Cambodia - Cambodge[44]										
3 III 1998 ....CDFC		11 437 656	1 795 575	15.7	5 511 408	878 186	15.9	5 926 248	917 389	15.5
1 I 2002 ....ESDF		13 040 668	...	...	6 313 131	...	...	6 727 537		
1 I 2003 ....ESDF		13 287 053		...	6 437 037	...	...	6 850 016		
1 VII 2004[45] ....SSDF		12 824 170	1 920 752	15.0	6 197 128	932 126	15.0	6 627 042	988 626	14.9
China - Chine[46]										
1 VII 1998[47] ....ESDF		1 241 935 000	405 285 000[48]	32.6	635 355 000	...	...	606 580 000	...	...
1 VII 1999[47] ....ESDF		1 252 735 000	426 780 000[48]	34.1	643 160 000	...	...	609 575 000		
1 VII 2000[47] ....ESDF		1 262 645 000	448 270 000[48]	35.5	650 645 000	...	...	612 000 000		
1 XI 2000[49] ....CDJC		1 242 612 226	458 770 983	36.9	640 275 969	235 264 707	36.7	602 336 257	223 506 276	37.1
1 VII 2001[50] ....ESDF		1 271 850 000	469 850 000[48]	36.9	655 545 000	...	...	616 305 000		
1 VII 2002[50] ....ESDF		1 280 400 000	491 380 000[48]	38.4	658 935 000	...	...	621 465 000		
1 VII 2003[50] ....ESDF		1 288 400 000	512 940 000[48]	39.8	663 355 000	...	...	625 045 000		
1 VII 2004[50] ....ESDF		1 296 075 000	533 295 000[48]	41.1	667 660 000	...	...	628 415 000		
1 VII 2005[51] ....ESDF		1 303 720 000	552 475 000[48]	42.4	671 755 000	...	...	631 965 000		
1 VII 2006[50] ....ESDF		1 311 020 000	569 590 000[48]	43.4	675 515 000	...	...	635 505 000		
1 VII 2007[50] ....ESDF		1 324 655 000	600 230 000[48]	45.3	682 025 000	...	...	642 630 000		
China, Hong Kong SAR - Chine, Hong Kong RAS										
1 VII 1998 ....ESDJ		6 543 700	...	...	3 249 900	...	...	3 293 800	...	...
1 VII 1999 ....ESDJ		6 606 500	...	...	3 264 700	...	...	3 341 800	...	...
1 VII 2000 ....ESDJ		6 665 000	...	...	3 276 500	...	...	3 388 500	...	...
14 III 2001[52] ....CDJC		6 708 389	...	...	3 285 344	...	...	3 423 045	...	...
1 VII 2001 ....ESDJ		6 714 300	...	...	3 282 000	...	...	3 432 300	...	...
1 VII 2002 ....ESDJ		6 744 100	...	...	3 279 600	...	...	3 464 500	...	...
1 VII 2003 ....ESDJ		6 730 800	...	...	3 259 100	...	...	3 471 700	...	...
1 VII 2004 ....ESDJ		6 783 500	...	...	3 266 800	...	...	3 516 700	...	...
1 VII 2005 ....ESDJ		6 813 200	...	...	3 264 000	...	...	3 549 200	...	...
1 VII 2006 ....ESDJ		6 857 100	...	...	3 270 100	...	...	3 587 000	...	...
14 VII 2006 ....CDJC		6 864 346	...	...	3 272 956	...	...	3 591 390	...	...
China, Macao SAR - Chine, Macao RAS										
1 VII 1998 ....ESDJ		422 304	...	...	203 535	...	...	218 769	...	...
1 VII 1999 ....ESDJ		427 411	...	...	205 322	...	...	222 089	...	...
1 VII 2000 ....ESDJ		430 569	...	...	206 686	...	...	223 883	...	...
1 VII 2001 ....ESDJ		433 903	...	...	208 235	...	...	225 668	...	...
23 VIII 2001 ....CDJC		435 235	...	...	208 865	...	...	226 370	...	...
1 VII 2002 ....ESDJ		438 408	...	...	210 218	...	...	228 190	...	...
1 VII 2003 ....ESDJ		443 600	...	...	212 866	...	...	230 734	...	...
1 VII 2004 ....ESDJ		454 661	...	...	218 122	...	...	236 539	...	...
1 VII 2005 ....ESDJ		473 457	...	...	227 600	...	...	245 857	...	...
1 VII 2006 ....ESDJ		498 852	...	...	243 009	...	...	255 843	...	...
19 VIII 2006[53] ....CDJC		502 113	...	...	245 167	...	...	256 946	...	...
1 VII 2007 ....ESDJ		525 800	...	...	259 100	...	...	266 700	...	...
Cyprus - Chypre[54]										
1 VII 1998 ....ESDJ		678 900	...	...	334 600	...	...	344 300	...	...
1 VII 1999 ....ESDJ		686 400	...	...	337 800	...	...	348 600	...	...

Continent, country or area, and date / Continent, pays ou zone et date	Code[a]	Both sexes - Les deux sexes			Male - Masculin			Female - Féminin		
		Total	Urban - Urbaine		Total	Urban - Urbaine		Total	Urban - Urbaine	
			Number Nombre	Percent P.100		Number Nombre	Percent P.100		Number Nombre	Percent P.100
ASIA - ASIE										
Cyprus - Chypre[54]										
1 VII 2000 ....ESDJ		693 600	...	...	341 000	...	...	352 600	...	...
1 VII 2001 ....ESDJ		701 300	...	...	344 300	...	...	357 000	...	...
1 X 2001[55]..........CDJC		689 565	474 450	68.8	338 497	231 128	68.3	351 068	243 322	69.3
1 VII 2002 ....ESDJ		709 600	...	...	347 900	...	...	361 700	...	...
1 VII 2003 ....ESDJ		720 600	...	...	353 700	...	...	366 900	...	...
1 VII 2004 ....ESDJ		737 100	...	...	363 000	...	...	374 100	...	...
1 VII 2005 ....ESDJ		758 000	...	...	373 600	...	...	384 400	...	...
1 VII 2006 ....ESDJ		770 900	...	...	380 100	...	...	390 800	...	...
1 VII 2007 ....ESDJ		783 971	...	...	386 457	...	...	397 514	...	...
Georgia - Géorgie										
1 VII 1998 .....ESDF		4 487 400	2 352 000	52.4	2 119 100	...	...	2 368 300	...	...
1 VII 1999 .....ESDF		4 452 500	2 323 200	52.2	2 101 500	...	...	2 351 000	...	...
1 VII 2000 .....ESDF		4 418 300	2 294 500	51.9	2 084 300	...	...	2 334 000	...	...
1 VII 2001 .....ESDF		4 385 800	2 283 200	52.1	2 068 400	...	...	2 317 400	...	...
17 I 2002 .....CDJC		4 371 535	2 284 796	52.3	2 061 753	1 048 593	50.9	2 309 782	1 236 203	53.5
1 VII 2002 .....ESDF		4 357 100	2 275 800	52.2	2 054 200	...	...	2 302 900	...	...
1 VII 2003 .....ESDF		4 328 900	2 259 700	52.2	2 039 300	...	...	2 289 600	...	...
1 VII 2004 .....ESDF		4 318 300	2 255 000	52.2	2 034 400	...	...	2 283 900	...	...
1 VII 2005 .....ESDF		4 361 400	2 284 000	52.4	2 060 300	...	...	2 301 100	...	...
1 VII 2006 .....ESDF		4 398 000	2 309 700	52.5	2 081 700	...	...	2 316 300	...	...
1 VII 2007 .....ESDF		4 388 400	2 306 400	52.6	2 079 000	...	...	2 309 400	...	...
India - Inde[56]										
1 VII 1998 ....ESDF		978 980 920	266 283 953	27.2	507 668 333	140 183 037	27.6	471 312 587	126 100 916	26.8
1 VII 1999 ....ESDF		997 556 080	273 525 428	27.4	516 933 647	143 962 574	27.8	480 622 433	129 562 854	27.0
1 VII 2000 ....ESDF		1 016 209 642	280 992 154	27.7	526 131 774	147 866 984	28.1	490 077 868	133 125 170	27.2
1 III 2001[57] ....CDFC		1 028 610 328	286 119 689	27.8	532 156 772	150 554 098	28.3	496 453 556	135 565 591	27.3
1 VII 2001 ....ESDF		1 034 930 863	288 732 422[58]	27.9	535 244 661[58]	151 922 010[58]	28.4	499 686 202[58]	136 810 412[58]	27.4
1 VII 2002[1] ....ESDF		1 051 258 250	295 388 359	28.1	543 896 774	155 423 847	28.6	507 361 477	139 964 511	27.6
1 VII 2003[1] ....ESDF		1 068 065 117	302 416 034	28.3	552 616 508	159 117 861	28.8	515 448 609	143 298 173	27.8
1 VII 2004[1] ....ESDF		1 084 756 558	309 506 730	28.5	561 281 181	162 846 812	29.0	523 475 376	146 659 918	28.0
1 VII 2005[1] ....ESDF		1 101 317 709	316 648 000	28.8	569 882 367	166 604 533	29.2	531 435 342	150 043 467	28.2
1 VII 2006[1] ....ESDF		1 117 733 826	323 827 490	29.0	578 411 677	170 384 885	29.5	539 322 149	153 442 605	28.5
1 VII 2007[1] ....ESDF		1 134 023 232	331 060 644	29.2	586 879 523	174 195 527	29.7	547 143 709	156 865 117	28.7
Indonesia - Indonésie										
1 VII 1998 ....ESDJ		204 392 500	80 275 300[3]	39.3	101 719 200	...	...	102 673 300	...	...
1 VII 1999 ....ESDJ		207 437 100	83 718 400[3]	40.4	103 234 400	...	...	104 202 700	...	...
30 VI 2000[59]..........CDFC		206 264 595	86 601 850	42.0	103 417 180	43 368 496	41.9	102 847 415	43 233 354	42.0
1 VII 2001 ....ESDJ		208 643 100	...	...	104 465 300	...	...	103 971 500	...	...
1 VII 2003 ....ESDJ		214 251 300	...	...	107 335 600	...	...	106 915 700	...	...
1 VII 2005 ....ESDJ		219 852 000	...	...	110 092 400	...	...	109 759 600	...	...
31 X 2005[60] ....SSDF		213 375 287	92 005 069	43.1	107 274 528	46 055 993	42.9	106 100 759	45 949 076	43.3
1 VII 2006 ....ESDJ		222 746 900	...	...	111 528 600	...	...	111 218 300	...	...
1 VII 2007 ....ESDJ		225 642 000	...	...	112 966 900	...	...	112 675 100	...	...
Iran (Islamic Republic of) - Iran (République islamique d')										
1 VII 1998[61] ....ESDJ		62 102 515	39 065 737	62.9	31 565 637	19 938 581	63.2	30 536 877	19 127 155	62.6
1 VII 1999[61] ....ESDJ		63 152 048	40 234 013	63.7	32 102 088	20 528 071	63.9	31 049 960	19 705 943	63.5
1 VII 2000[61] ....ESDJ		64 219 318	41 407 340	64.5	32 647 964	21 120 123	64.7	31 571 354	20 287 217	64.3
1 VII 2001[61] ....ESDJ		65 301 308	42 587 465	65.2	33 201 477	21 715 641	65.4	32 099 830	20 871 824	65.0
1 VII 2002[61] ....ESDJ		66 300 418	43 709 980	65.9	33 713 360	22 281 715	66.1	32 587 058	21 428 265	65.8
1 VII 2003[61] ....ESDJ		67 314 814	44 834 988	66.6	34 233 497	22 849 043	66.7	33 081 317	21 985 945	66.5
1 VII 2004[61] ....ESDJ		68 344 730	45 966 432	67.3	34 761 738	23 419 649	67.4	33 582 992	22 546 783	67.1
1 VII 2005[61] ....ESDJ		69 390 405	47 095 882	67.9	35 298 812	23 989 204	68.0	34 091 593	23 106 678	67.8
28 X 2006 ....CDJC		70 495 782	48 259 964[62]	68.5	35 866 362	24 576 442[62]	68.5	34 629 420	23 683 522[62]	68.4
1 VII 2007[61] ....ESDJ		71 532 062	49 571 928	69.3	36 377 302	25 239 067	69.4	35 154 760	24 332 861	69.2
Iraq										
1 VII 1998 ....ESDF		22 702 000	...	...	11 328 000	...	...	11 374 000	...	...
1 VII 1999 ....ESDF		23 382 000	...	...	11 682 000	...	...	11 700 000	...	...
1 VII 2000 ....ESDF		24 086 000	...	...	12 047 000	...	...	12 039 000	...	...
1 VII 2001 ....ESDF		24 813 000	...	...	12 424 000	...	...	12 389 000	...	...
1 VII 2002 ....ESDF		25 565 000	...	...	12 814 000	...	...	12 751 000	...	...
1 VII 2003 ....ESDF		26 340 000	...	...	13 216 000	...	...	13 124 000	...	...

Continent, country or area, and date / Continent, pays ou zone et date	Code[a]	Both sexes - Les deux sexes			Male - Masculin			Female - Féminin		
		Total	Urban - Urbaine		Total	Urban - Urbaine		Total	Urban - Urbaine	
			Number Nombre	Percent P.100		Number Nombre	Percent P.100		Number Nombre	Percent P.100

ASIA - ASIE

Iraq

1 VII 2004 ....ESDF		27 139 000	...	...	13 629 000	...	...	13 510 000	...	...
1 VII 2005 ....ESDF		27 963 000	...	...	14 055 000	...	...	13 908 000	...	...
1 VII 2006 ....ESDF		28 810 441	19 226 476	66.7	14 493 207	9 698 293	66.9	14 317 234	9 528 183	66.6
1 VII 2007 ....ESDF		29 682 081	19 752 833	66.5	14 943 516	9 970 074	66.7	14 738 565	9 782 759	66.4

Israel - Israël[63]

1 VII 1998 ....ESDJ		5 970 700	5 418 400	90.7	...	...	...	...	...	...
1 VII 1999 ....ESDJ		6 125 300	5 554 200	90.7	3 021 743	...	...	3 103 533	...	...
1 VII 2000 ....ESDJ		6 289 200	5 696 100	90.6	3 102 400	2 797 800	90.2	3 186 800	2 898 300	90.9
1 VII 2001 ....ESDJ		6 439 000	5 900 700	91.6	3 176 600	2 900 200	91.3	3 262 500	3 000 500	92.0
1 VII 2002 ....ESDJ		6 569 900	6 017 300	91.6	3 241 700	2 958 200	91.3	3 328 200	3 059 100	91.9
1 VII 2003 ....ESDJ		6 689 700	6 122 400	91.5	3 301 800	3 010 900	91.2	3 387 900	3 111 600	91.8
1 VII 2004 ....ESDJ		6 809 000	6 226 900	91.5	3 362 000	3 063 600	91.1	3 447 000	3 163 300	91.8
1 VII 2005 ....ESDJ		6 930 128	6 359 940	91.8	3 423 132	3 131 229	91.5	3 506 996	3 228 711	92.1
1 VII 2006 ....ESDJ		7 053 707	6 475 600[64]	91.8	3 485 501	3 189 511[64]	91.5	3 568 206	3 286 089[64]	92.1
1 VII 2007 ....ESDJ		7 180 115	6 589 632[64]	91.8	3 549 216	3 247 280[64]	91.5	3 630 899	3 342 352[64]	92.1

Japan - Japon

1 VII 1998[65] ....ESDF		126 400 000	...	...	61 910 000	...	...	64 490 000	...	...
1 VII 1999[65] ....ESDF		126 631 000	...	...	61 996 000	...	...	64 635 000	...	...
1 VII 2000[65] ....ESDF		126 843 000	...	...	62 063 000	...	...	64 780 000	...	...
1 X 2000[65] ....CDFC		126 925 843	99 865 289	78.7	62 110 764	49 005 691	78.9	64 815 079	50 859 598	78.5
1 VII 2001[65] ....ESDF		127 149 000	...	...	62 178 000	...	...	64 971 000	...	...
1 VII 2002[65] ....ESDF		127 445 000	...	...	62 278 000	...	...	65 167 000	...	...
1 VII 2003[65] ....ESDF		127 718 000	...	...	62 370 000	...	...	65 348 000	...	...
1 VII 2004[65] ....ESDF		127 761 000	...	...	62 355 000	...	...	65 406 000	...	...
1 VII 2005[65] ....ESDF		127 773 000	...	...	62 332 000	...	...	65 441 000	...	...
1 X 2005 ....CDJC		127 767 994	110 264 324	86.3	62 348 977	53 886 000	86.4	65 419 017	56 378 324	86.2
1 VII 2006[65] ....ESDF		127 756 000	...	...	62 314 000	...	...	65 442 000	...	...
1 VII 2007[65] ....ESDF		127 772 000	...	...	62 301 000	...	...	65 471 000	...	...

Jordan - Jordanie[66]

31 XII 1998 ....ESDF		4 623 000	3 640 800	78.8	2 413 200	...	...	2 209 800	...	...
31 XII 1999 ....ESDF		4 738 000	3 730 300	78.7	2 473 200	...	...	2 264 800	...	...
31 XII 2000 ....ESDF		4 857 000	4 012 600	82.6	2 501 400	...	...	2 355 600	...	...
31 XII 2001 ....ESDF		4 978 000	4 112 600	82.6	2 563 700	...	...	2 414 300	...	...
31 XII 2002 ....ESDF		5 098 000	4 211 700	82.6	2 625 500	...	...	2 472 500	...	...
31 XII 2003 ....ESDF		5 230 000	4 320 600	82.6	2 693 500	...	...	2 536 500	...	...
1 X 2004 ....CDFC		5 103 639	3 997 383	78.3	2 626 287	2 055 431	78.3	2 477 352	1 941 952	78.4
31 XII 2004 ....ESDF		5 350 000	4 419 000	82.6	2 757 700	...	...	2 592 300	...	...
31 XII 2005 ....ESDF		5 473 000	4 520 600	82.6	2 821 100	...	...	2 651 900	...	...
31 XII 2006 ....ESDF		5 600 000	4 625 600	82.6	2 886 600	...	...	2 713 400	...	...
31 XII 2007 ....ESDF		5 723 000	4 727 100	82.6	2 950 000	...	...	2 773 000	...	...

Kazakhstan

1 VII 1998 ....ESDF		15 072 983	8 434 080	56.0	7 263 077	3 945 189	54.3	7 809 906	4 488 891	57.5
26 II 1999 ....CDJC		14 953 126	8 377 300	56.0	7 201 785	3 918 556	54.4	7 751 341	4 458 747	57.5
1 VII 1999 ....ESDF		14 928 373	8 406 019	56.3	7 190 238	3 933 622	54.7	7 738 135	4 472 397	57.8
1 VII 2000 ....ESDF		14 883 626	8 405 483	56.5	7 168 613	3 933 997	54.9	7 715 013	4 471 486	58.0
1 VII 2001 ....ESDF		14 858 335	8 421 366	56.7	7 156 582	3 942 353	55.1	7 701 753	4 479 013	58.2
1 VII 2002 ....ESDF		14 858 948	8 443 242	56.8	7 156 816	3 952 649	55.2	7 702 132	4 490 593	58.3
1 VII 2003 ....ESDF		14 909 018	8 487 697	56.9	7 179 583	3 971 520	55.3	7 729 435	4 516 177	58.4
1 VII 2004 ....ESDF		15 012 985	8 566 447	57.1	7 227 960	4 005 199	55.4	7 785 025	4 561 248	58.6
1 VII 2005 ....ESDF		15 147 029	8 655 586	57.1	7 290 852	4 044 092	55.5	7 856 177	4 611 494	58.7
1 VII 2006 ....ESDF		15 308 084	8 764 884	57.3	7 367 032	4 094 572	55.6	7 941 052	4 670 312	58.8
1 VII 2007 ....ESDF		15 484 192	8 195 389	52.9	7 450 418	3 815 422	51.2	8 033 774	4 379 967	54.5

Kuwait - Koweït

1 VII 1998 ....ESDF		1 759 799	...	...	1 026 429	...	...	733 370	...	...
1 VII 1999 ....ESDF		1 821 905	...	...	1 064 689	...	...	757 216	...	...
1 VII 2000 ....ESDF		1 886 234	...	...	1 104 396	...	...	781 838	...	...
1 VII 2001 ....ESDF		1 952 870	...	...	1 145 609	...	...	807 261	...	...
1 VII 2002 ....ESDF		2 021 895	...	...	1 188 384	...	...	833 511	...	...
1 VII 2003 ....ESDF		2 093 396	...	...	1 232 781	...	...	860 615	...	...
1 VII 2004 ....ESDF		2 167 467	...	...	1 278 865	...	...	888 602	...	...
20 IV 2005* ....CDFC		2 213 403	...	...	1 310 067	...	...	903 336	...	...
1 VII 2005 ....ESDF		2 244 995	...	...	1 326 871	...	...	918 124	...	...

Continent, country or area, and date / Continent, pays ou zone et date	Code[a]	Both sexes - Les deux sexes			Male - Masculin			Female - Féminin		
		Total	Urban - Urbaine		Total	Urban - Urbaine		Total	Urban - Urbaine	
			Number Nombre	Percent P.100		Number Nombre	Percent P.100		Number Nombre	Percent P.100
ASIA - ASIE										
Kuwait - Koweït										
1 VII 2006 ....ESDF		2 328 116	...	...	1 378 341	...	...	949 775	...	...
1 VII 2007 ....ESDF		2 410 829	...	...	1 430 584	...	...	980 245	...	...
Kyrgyzstan - Kirghizstan										
1 VII 1998 ....ESDF		4 797 000	1 696 900	35.4	2 365 200	811 200	34.3	2 431 800	885 700	36.4
24 III 1999 ....CDFC		4 850 734	1 713 836	35.3	2 392 579	819 550	34.3	2 458 155	894 286	36.4
1 VII 1999 ....ESDF		4 864 600	1 717 100	35.3	2 399 900	821 100	34.2	2 464 700	896 000	36.4
1 VII 2000 ....ESDF		4 915 300	1 738 800	35.4	2 425 800	831 300	34.3	2 489 500	907 500	36.5
1 VII 2001 ....ESDF		4 954 800	1 760 600	35.5	2 445 900	841 900	34.4	2 508 900	918 700	36.6
1 VII 2002 ....ESDF		4 993 200	1 763 600	35.3	2 465 500	843 400	34.2	2 527 700	920 200	36.4
1 VII 2003 ....ESDF		5 038 600	1 785 700	35.4	2 488 900	854 000	34.3	2 549 700	931 700	36.5
1 VII 2004 ....ESDF		5 092 800	1 816 400	35.7	2 516 400	868 300	34.5	2 576 400	948 100	36.8
1 VII 2005 ....ESDF		5 143 500	1 830 400	35.6	2 542 300	875 100	34.4	2 601 200	955 300	36.7
1 VII 2006 ....ESDF		5 192 000	1 839 000	35.4	2 566 700	879 700	34.3	2 625 300	959 300	36.5
1 VII 2007 ....ESDF		5 234 800	1 846 400	35.3	2 587 500	883 300	34.1	2 647 300	963 100	36.4
Lao People's Democratic Republic - République démocratique populaire lao										
1 VII 1999[67] ....ESDF		5 091 100	...	...	2 516 100	...	...	2 575 000	...	...
1 VII 2000[67] ....ESDF		5 218 300	...	...	2 579 000	...	...	2 639 300	...	...
1 VII 2001[67] ....ESDF		5 377 000	...	...	2 657 000	...	...	2 720 000	...	...
1 VII 2002[67] ....ESDF		5 526 000	...	...	2 731 000	...	...	2 795 000	...	...
1 VII 2003[67] ....ESDF		5 679 000	...	...	2 807 000	...	...	2 872 000	...	...
1 VII 2004[67] ....ESDF		5 836 000	...	...	2 884 000	...	...	2 952 000	...	...
1 III 2005 ....CDJC		5 621 982	...	...	2 800 551	...	...	2 821 431	...	...
1 VII 2005[68] ....ESDF		5 679 000	...	...	2 806 400	...	...	2 872 600	...	...
1 VII 2006[68] ....ESDF		5 747 000	...	...	2 864 000	...	...	2 883 000	...	...
1 VII 2007[68] ....ESDF		5 874 000	...	...	2 929 000	...	...	2 945 000	...	...
Lebanon - Liban[69]										
3 III 2004 ....SSDF		3 755 034	...	...	1 868 322	...	...	1 886 712	...	...
3 III 2007 ....SSDF		3 759 134	...	...	1 857 659	...	...	1 901 475	...	...
Malaysia - Malaisie										
1 VII 1998[16] ....ESDF		22 333 506	13 302 789	59.6	11 372 093	6 737 645	59.2	10 961 413	6 565 144	59.9
1 VII 1999[16] ....ESDF		22 909 452	13 928 555	60.8	11 666 584	7 058 558	60.5	11 242 868	6 869 997	61.1
1 VII 2000[70] ....ESDF		23 494 891	14 567 024	62.0	11 965 620	7 393 294	61.8	11 529 271	7 173 730	62.2
5 VII 2000[71] ....CDJC		23 274 690	14 426 871	62.0	11 853 432	7 318 396	61.7	11 421 258	7 108 475	62.2
1 VII 2001[70] ....ESDF		24 012 883	14 940 078	62.2	12 227 407	7 579 629	62.0	11 785 476	7 360 449	62.5
1 VII 2002[70] ....ESDF		24 526 549	15 310 727	62.4	12 487 060	7 765 266	62.2	12 039 489	7 545 461	62.7
1 VII 2003[70] ....ESDF		25 048 257	15 686 996	62.6	12 751 898	7 954 578	62.4	12 296 359	7 732 418	62.9
1 VII 2004[70] ....ESDF		25 580 942	16 071 044	62.8	13 023 276	8 148 552	62.6	12 557 666	7 922 492	63.1
1 VII 2005[70] ....ESDF		26 127 666	16 465 229	63.0	13 302 753	8 348 371	62.8	12 824 913	8 116 858	63.3
1 VII 2006[70] ....ESDF		26 640 197	16 838 500	63.2	13 562 596	8 535 275	62.9	13 077 601	8 303 225	63.5
1 VII 2007[70] ....ESDF		27 173 580	17 221 551	63.4	13 832 952	8 726 982	63.1	13 340 628	8 494 569	63.7
Maldives										
1 VII 1998 ....ESDF		267 464	...	...	135 986	...	...	131 478	...	...
1 VII 1999 ....ESDF		277 579	...	...	141 073	...	...	136 506	...	...
31 III 2000 ....CDFC		270 101	74 069	27.4	137 200	38 559	28.1	132 901	35 510	26.7
1 VII 2000 ....ESDF		271 410	...	...	137 697	...	...	133 713	...	...
1 VII 2001 ....ESDF		275 975	75 680	27.4	140 100	39 398[3]	28.1	135 875	36 282[3]	26.7
1 VII 2002 ....ESDF		280 549	76 934	27.4	142 357	40 051[3]	28.1	138 192	36 884[3]	26.7
1 VII 2003 ....ESDF		285 066	78 173	27.4	144 599	40 695[3]	28.1	140 467	37 477[3]	26.7
1 VII 2004 ....ESDF		289 480	79 383	27.4	146 799	41 326[3]	28.2	142 681	38 058[3]	26.7
1 VII 2005 ....ESDF		293 746	...	...	148 929	...	...	144 817	...	...
21 III 2006 ....CDFC		298 968	103 693	34.7	151 459	51 992	34.3	147 509	51 701	35.0
1 VII 2006 ....ESDF		298 333	...	...	151 201	...	...	147 132	...	...
1 VII 2007 ....ESDF		304 869	...	...	154 391	...	...	150 478	...	...
Mongolia - Mongolie										
1 VII 1998 ....ESDF		2 280 751	1 176 278	51.6	1 121 068	568 895	50.7	1 159 683	607 383	52.4
1 VII 1999 ....ESDF		2 332 394	1 264 012	54.2	1 151 535	613 955	53.3	1 180 859	650 057	55.0
5 I 2000 ....CDFC		2 373 493	1 344 516	56.6	1 177 981	657 081	55.8	1 195 512	687 435	57.5
1 VII 2000 ....ESDF		2 390 491	1 360 747	56.9	1 186 258	664 991	56.1	1 204 233	695 756	57.8
1 VII 2001 ....ESDF		2 425 017	1 387 045	57.2	1 202 132	677 838	56.4	1 222 885	709 207	58.0
1 VII 2002 ....ESDF		2 458 963	1 409 034	57.3	1 218 894	688 417	56.5	1 240 069	720 617	58.1

Continent, country or area, and date / Continent, pays ou zone et date	Code[a]	Both sexes - Les deux sexes			Male - Masculin			Female - Féminin		
		Total	Urban - Urbaine		Total	Urban - Urbaine		Total	Urban - Urbaine	
			Number Nombre	Percent P.100		Number Nombre	Percent P.100		Number Nombre	Percent P.100
ASIA - ASIE										
Mongolia - Mongolie										
1 VII 2003 . . . . .ESDF		2 489 702	1 442 589	57.9	1 235 164	705 367	57.1	1 254 538	737 222	58.8
1 VII 2004 . . . . .ESDF		2 518 573	1 481 205	58.8	1 249 487	723 856	57.9	1 269 086	757 349	59.7
1 VII 2005 . . . . .ESDF		2 547 751	1 520 763	59.7	1 263 962	741 689	58.7	1 283 789	779 074	60.7
1 VII 2006 . . . . .ESDF		2 578 587	1 561 417	60.6	1 268 249	756 004	59.6	1 310 338	805 413	61.5
1 VII 2007 . . . . .ESDF		2 614 981	1 590 253	60.8	1 274 852	764 608	60.0	1 340 128	825 645	61.6
Myanmar										
1 VII 1998 . . . . .ESDF		48 160 000	...	...	23 914 000	...	...	24 246 000	...	...
1 VII 1999 . . . . .ESDF		49 133 000	...	...	24 404 000	...	...	24 729 000	...	...
1 VII 2000 . . . . .ESDF		50 125 000	...	...	24 907 000	...	...	25 218 000	...	...
1 VII 2001 . . . . .ESDF		51 138 000	...	...	25 421 000	...	...	25 717 000	...	...
1 VII 2002 . . . . .ESDF		52 171 000	...	...	25 941 000	...	...	26 230 000	...	...
1 VII 2003 . . . . .ESDF		53 224 000	...	...	26 467 000	...	...	26 757 000	...	...
1 VII 2004 . . . . .ESDF		54 299 000	...	...	27 000 000	...	...	27 299 000	...	...
Nepal - Népal										
1 VII 1999 . . . . .ESDJ		22 367 048	...	...	11 167 503	...	...	11 199 545	...	...
22 VI 2001[72] . . . . .CDJC		23 151 423			11 563 921			11 587 502	...	...
1 VII 2002 . . . . .ESDJ		23 701 451	...	...	11 845 495	...	...	11 855 956	...	...
1 VII 2003 . . . . .ESDJ		24 249 996	...	...	12 126 262	...	...	12 123 734	...	...
1 VII 2004 . . . . .ESDJ		24 797 059	...	...	12 406 222	...	...	12 390 837	...	...
1 VII 2005 . . . . .ESDJ		25 342 638	...	...	12 685 375	...	...	12 657 263	...	...
1 VII 2006 . . . . .ESDJ		25 886 736	...	...	12 963 722	...	...	12 923 014	...	...
1 VII 2007* . . . . .ESDJ		26 427 399	...	...	13 187 166	...	...	13 240 233	...	...
Occupied Palestinian Territory - Territoire palestinien occupé										
1 VII 1998 . . . . .ESDF		2 871 568	2 053 171	71.5	1 457 429	...	...	1 414 139	...	...
1 VII 1999 . . . . .ESDF		2 962 226	2 117 992[73]	71.5	1 503 441	...	...	1 458 785	...	...
1 VII 2000 . . . . .ESDF		3 053 335	2 183 135[73]	71.5	1 549 682	...	...	1 503 653	...	...
1 VII 2001 . . . . .ESDF		3 138 471	2 244 007[73]	71.5	1 592 892	...	...	1 545 579	...	...
1 VII 2002 . . . . .ESDF		3 225 214	2 306 028[73]	71.5	1 636 917	...	...	1 588 297	...	...
1 VII 2003 . . . . .ESDF		3 314 509	2 369 874[73]	71.5	1 682 238	...	...	1 632 271	...	...
1 VII 2004 . . . . .ESDF		3 407 417	2 436 303[73]	71.5	1 729 392	...	...	1 678 025	...	...
1 VII 2005 . . . . .ESDF		3 508 126	2 508 310[73]	71.5	1 780 506	...	...	1 727 620	...	...
1 VII 2006 . . . . .ESDF		3 611 998	2 582 579[73]	71.5	1 833 225	...	...	1 778 773	...	...
1 VII 2007 . . . . .ESDF		3 719 189	3 086 102[73]	83.0	1 887 628	...	...	1 831 561	...	...
1 XII 2007*[74] . . . . .CDFC		3 761 646	...	...	1 908 432	...	...	1 853 214	...	...
Oman										
1 VII 1998 . . . . .ESDF		2 287 642	...	...	1 333 557	...	...	954 085	...	...
1 VII 1999 . . . . .ESDF		2 325 438	...	...	1 365 775	...	...	959 663	...	...
1 VII 2000 . . . . .ESDF		2 401 256	...	...	1 401 589	...	...	999 667	...	...
1 VII 2001 . . . . .ESDF		2 477 687	...	...	1 451 041	...	...	1 026 646	...	...
1 VII 2002 . . . . .ESDF		2 537 742	...	...	1 443 316	...	...	1 094 426	...	...
7 XII 2003 . . . . .CDFC		2 340 815	1 673 480	71.5	1 313 239	950 471	72.4	1 027 576	723 009	70.4
1 VII 2004 . . . . .ESDF		2 415 576	...	...	1 360 891	...	...	1 054 685	...	...
1 VII 2005 . . . . .ESDF		2 513 530	...	...	1 458 845	...	...	1 054 685	...	...
1 VII 2006 . . . . .ESDF		2 577 062	1 842 376	71.5	1 498 143	1 084 297	72.4	1 078 919	759 134	70.4
1 VII 2007 . . . . .ESDF		2 743 499	1 984 191	72.3	1 622 119	1 188 568	73.3	1 121 380	795 623	71.0
Pakistan[75]										
2 III 1998 . . . . .CDFC		130 579 571	42 458 339	32.5	67 840 137	22 419 286[3]	33.0	62 739 434	20 039 053[3]	31.9
1 VII 1998 . . . . .ESDF		133 320 000	43 320 000	32.5	69 170 000	22 100 000[3]	32.0	64 160 000	20 810 000[3]	32.4
1 VII 1999 . . . . .ESDF		136 410 000	44 470 000	32.6	70 780 000	...	...	65 640 000	...	...
1 VII 2000 . . . . .ESDF		139 410 000	45 660 000	32.8	72 340 000	...	...	67 080 000	...	...
1 VII 2001[76] . . . . .SSDF		133 652 121	47 739 853[77]	35.7	68 769 178	24 707 762[77]	35.9	64 882 943	23 032 091[77]	35.5
1 VII 2001 . . . . .ESDF		142 350 000	46 830 000	32.9	73 870 000	...	...	68 490 000	...	...
1 VII 2002 . . . . .ESDF		145 280 000	48 020 000	33.1	75 390 000	...	...	69 900 000	...	...
1 VII 2003[78] . . . . .SSDJ		138 979 270	49 640 104	35.7	71 741 403	25 819 279	36.0	67 237 867	23 820 825	35.4
1 VII 2003 . . . . .ESDF		148 210 000	49 210 000	33.2	76 910 000	...	...	71 300 000	...	...
1 VII 2004 . . . . .ESDF		151 090 000	50 800 000	33.6	78 410 000	...	...	72 690 000	...	...
1 VII 2005[79] . . . . .SSDJ		144 367 294	51 408 193	35.6	74 247 400	26 556 848	35.8	70 119 892	24 851 345	35.4
1 VII 2005 . . . . .ESDF		153 960 000	52 410 000	34.0	79 900 000	...	...	74 060 000	...	...
1 VII 2006 . . . . .ESDF		156 770 000	54 020 000	34.5	81 360 000	...	...	75 410 000	...	...
1 VII 2007 . . . . .ESDF		159 570 000	55 660 000	34.9	82 810 000	...	...	76 760 000	...	...

Continent, country or area, and date / Continent, pays ou zone et date	Code[a]	Both sexes - Les deux sexes			Male - Masculin			Female - Féminin		
		Total	Urban - Urbaine		Total	Urban - Urbaine		Total	Urban - Urbaine	
			Number Nombre	Percent P.100		Number Nombre	Percent P.100		Number Nombre	Percent P.100
ASIA - ASIE										
Philippines										
1 VII 1998	ESDJ	73 147 776	...	...	36 851 141	...	...	36 296 635	...	...
1 VII 1999	ESDJ	74 745 756	...	...	37 650 939	...	...	37 094 817	...	...
1 V 2000	CDJC	76 504 077	...	...	38 524 267	...	...	37 979 810	...	...
1 VII 2000	ESDJ	76 348 114	...	...	38 452 927	...	...	37 895 187	...	...
1 VII 2001	ESDJ	77 925 894	...	...	39 242 185	...	...	38 683 709	...	...
1 VII 2002	ESDJ	79 503 675	...	...	40 031 449	...	...	39 472 226	...	...
1 VII 2003	ESDJ	81 081 457	...	...	40 820 706	...	...	40 260 751	...	...
1 VII 2004	ESDJ	82 663 561	...	...	41 612 133	...	...	41 051 428	...	...
1 VII 2005	ESDJ	84 241 341	...	...	42 401 391	...	...	41 839 950	...	...
Qatar										
1 VII 1998	ESDF	557 335	...	...	371 829	...	...	185 506	...	...
1 VII 1999	ESDF	586 275	...	...	391 136	...	...	195 139	...	...
1 VII 2000	ESDF	616 719	...	...	411 447	...	...	205 272	...	...
1 VII 2001	ESDF	648 744	...	...	432 812	...	...	215 932	...	...
1 VII 2002	ESDF	682 434	...	...	455 289	...	...	227 145	...	...
1 VII 2003	ESDF	717 766	...	...	478 860	...	...	238 906	...	...
16 III 2004	CDFC	744 029	...	...	496 382	...	...	247 647	...	...
1 VII 2004	ESDF	756 486	...	...	504 693	...	...	251 793	...	...
1 VII 2005	ESDF	888 451	...	...	653 232	...	...	235 219	...	...
1 VII 2006	ESDF	1 041 733	...	...	774 312	...	...	267 421	...	...
1 VII 2007	ESDF	1 226 210	...	...	920 415	...	...	305 795	...	...
Republic of Korea - République de Corée										
1 VII 1998	ESDJ	46 286 503	...	...	23 295 727	...	...	22 990 776	...	...
1 VII 1999	ESDJ	46 616 677	...	...	23 457 837	...	...	23 158 840	...	...
1 VII 2000	ESDJ	47 008 111	...	...	23 666 769	...	...	23 341 342	...	...
1 XI 2000[80]	CDFC	46 136 101	36 755 144	79.7	23 158 582	18 484 139	79.8	22 977 519	18 271 005	79.5
1 VII 2001	ESDJ	47 357 362	...	...	23 843 136	...	...	23 514 226	...	...
1 VII 2002	ESDJ	47 622 179	...	...	23 970 035	...	...	23 652 144	...	...
1 VII 2003	ESDJ	47 859 311	...	...	24 089 703	...	...	23 769 608	...	...
1 VII 2004	ESDJ	48 039 415	...	...	24 165 488	...	...	23 873 927	...	...
1 VII 2005	ESDJ	48 138 077	...	...	24 190 906	...	...	23 947 171	...	...
1 XI 2005[81]	CDJC	47 278 951	38 514 753	81.5	23 623 954	19 258 840	81.5	23 654 997	19 255 913	81.4
1 VII 2006	ESDJ	48 297 184	...	...	24 267 609	...	...	24 029 575	...	...
1 VII 2007	ESDJ	48 456 369	...	...	24 344 276	...	...	24 112 093	...	...
Saudi Arabia - Arabie saoudite										
1 VII 1998	ESDF	19 506 225	...	...	10 857 670	...	...	8 648 555	...	...
1 VII 1999	ESDF	19 985 423	...	...	11 115 026	...	...	8 870 397	...	...
1 VII 2000	ESDF	20 476 393	...	...	11 378 473	...	...	9 097 920	...	...
1 VII 2001	ESDF	20 979 424	...	...	11 648 157	...	...	9 331 268	...	...
1 VII 2002	ESDF	21 494 814	...	...	11 924 224	...	...	9 570 590	...	...
1 VII 2003	ESDF	22 022 864	...	...	12 206 825	...	...	9 816 039	...	...
1 VII 2004	ESDF	22 563 886	...	...	12 493 910	...	...	10 069 976	...	...
15 IX 2004	CDFC	22 678 262	...	...	12 557 240	...	...	10 121 022	...	...
1 VII 2005	ESDF	23 118 994	...	...	12 791 330	...	...	10 327 664	...	...
1 VII 2006	ESDF	23 678 849	...	...	13 090 840	...	...	10 588 009	...	...
Singapore - Singapour										
1 VII 1998	ESDJ	3 180 000	...	...	1 591 800	...	...	1 588 200	...	...
1 VII 1999	ESDJ	3 229 700	...	...	1 614 800	...	...	1 614 900	...	...
30 VI 2000[82]	CDFC	4 017 700	...	...	2 061 800	...	...	1 955 900	...	...
1 VII 2000	ESDJ	3 273 400	...	...	1 634 700	...	...	1 638 700	...	...
1 VII 2001	ESDJ	3 325 900	...	...	1 658 600	...	...	1 667 300	...	...
1 VII 2002	ESDJ	3 382 900	...	...	1 684 300	...	...	1 698 600	...	...
1 VII 2003	ESDJ	3 366 900	...	...	1 673 400	...	...	1 693 500	...	...
1 VII 2004	ESDJ	3 413 300	...	...	1 695 000[9]	...	...	1 718 200[9]	...	...
1 VII 2005	ESDJ	3 467 800	...	...	1 721 100	...	...	1 746 700	...	...
1 VII 2006	ESDJ	3 525 900	...	...	1 748 200	...	...	1 777 700	...	...
1 VII 2007	ESDJ	3 583 100	...	...	1 775 500	...	...	1 807 600	...	...
Sri Lanka										
1 VII 1998	ESDF	18 802 000	...	...	9 570 000	...	...	9 204 000	...	...
1 VII 1999	ESDF	19 043 000	...	...	9 707 000	...	...	9 336 000	...	...
1 VII 2001	ESDF	18 732 000	...	...	9 267 000	...	...	9 465 000	...	...

Continent, country or area, and date / Continent, pays ou zone et date	Code[a]	Both sexes - Les deux sexes			Male - Masculin			Female - Féminin		
		Total	Urban - Urbaine		Total	Urban - Urbaine		Total	Urban - Urbaine	
			Number Nombre	Percent P.100		Number Nombre	Percent P.100		Number Nombre	Percent P.100

ASIA - ASIE

Sri Lanka

17 VII 2001[83] ....CDFC		16 929 689	2 467 301	14.6	8 425 607	1 252 173	14.9	8 504 082	1 215 128	14.3
1 VII 2002 ....ESDF		19 007 000	...	...	9 392 000	...	...	9 615 000	...	...
1 VII 2003 ....ESDF		19 252 000	...	...	9 510 000	...	...	9 742 000	...	...
1 VII 2004 ....ESDF		19 462 000	...	...	9 615 000	...	...	9 847 000	...	...
1 VII 2005 ....ESDF		19 668 000	...	...	9 718 000	...	...	9 950 000	...	...
1 VII 2006 ....ESDF		19 886 000	...	...	9 826 000	...	...	10 060 000	...	...
1 VII 2007 ....ESDF		20 010 000	...	...	9 888 000	...	...	10 122 000	...	...

Syrian Arab Republic - République arabe syrienne[84]

1 VII 1998 ....ESDF		15 473 000	...	...	7 914 000	...	...	7 559 000	...	...
1 VII 1999 ....ESDF		15 891 000	...	...	8 128 000	...	...	7 763 000	...	...
1 VII 2000 ....ESDF		16 320 000	...	...	8 343 000	...	...	7 977 000	...	...
1 VII 2001 ....ESDF		16 720 000	8 376 000	50.1	8 552 000	4 319 000	50.5	8 168 000	4 057 000	49.7
1 VII 2002 ....ESDF		17 130 000	8 599 000	50.2	8 763 000	4 439 000	50.7	8 367 000	4 160 000	49.7
1 VII 2003 ....ESDF		17 550 000	8 806 000	50.2	8 979 000	4 541 000	50.6	8 571 000	4 265 000	49.8
1 VII 2004 ....ESDF		17 829 000	9 539 000	53.5	9 150 000	4 916 000	53.7	8 679 000	4 623 000	53.3
1 VII 2005 ....ESDF		18 138 000	9 705 000	53.5	9 268 000	4 977 000	53.7	8 870 000	4 728 000	53.3
1 VII 2006 ....ESDF		18 717 000	10 013 000	53.5	9 563 000	5 139 000	53.7	9 154 000	4 874 000	53.2
1 VII 2007 ....ESDF		19 172 000	10 257 000	53.5	9 798 000	5 265 000	53.7	9 374 000	4 992 000	53.3

Tajikistan - Tadjikistan

1 VII 1998 ....ESDF		5 938 609	1 580 247	26.6	2 972 780	784 493	26.4	2 965 829	795 754	26.8
1 VII 1999 ....ESDF		6 064 048	1 609 723	26.5	3 036 700	800 021	26.3	3 027 348	809 702	26.7
20 I 2000 ....CDFC		6 127 493	1 626 027	26.5	3 069 100	808 650	26.3	3 058 393	817 377	26.7
1 VII 2000 ....ESDF		6 188 366	1 642 401	26.5	3 099 854	817 233	26.4	3 088 512	825 168	26.7
1 VII 2001 ....ESDF		6 312 756	1 675 211	26.5	3 163 111	834 679	26.4	3 149 645	840 532	26.7
1 VII 2002 ....ESDF		6 441 009	1 705 240	26.5	3 228 657	850 897	26.4	3 212 352	854 343	26.6
1 VII 2003 ....ESDF		6 573 224	1 738 838	26.5	3 296 211	868 890	26.4	3 277 013	869 948	26.5
1 VII 2004 ....ESDF		6 710 161	1 774 799	26.4	3 365 832	888 087	26.4	3 344 329	886 712	26.5
1 VII 2005 ....ESDF		6 850 324	1 808 339	26.4	3 436 922	906 229	26.4	3 413 402	902 110	26.4
1 VII 2006 ....ESDF		6 992 066	1 841 258	26.3	3 508 345	923 963	26.3	3 483 721	917 295	26.3
1 VII 2007 ....ESDF		7 139 772	1 877 203	26.3	3 581 930	943 032	26.3	3 557 842	934 171	26.3

Thailand - Thaïlande

1 VII 1998[1] ....ESDJ		61 201 000	...	...	30 531 000	...	...	30 670 000	...	...
1 VII 1999[1] ....ESDJ		61 806 000	...	...	30 819 000	...	...	30 987 000	...	...
1 IV 2000.............CDJC		60 617 200	18 833 700	31.1	29 850 100	9 085 400	30.4	30 767 100	9 748 300	31.7
1 VII 2000[1] ....ESDJ		62 406 000	...	...	31 105 000	...	...	31 301 000	...	...
1 VII 2001[1] ....ESDJ		62 914 000	...	...	31 348 000	...	...	31 566 000	...	...
1 VII 2002[1] ....ESDJ		63 482 287	20 731 494	32.7	31 623 509	10 072 055	31.8	31 858 778	10 659 439	33.5
1 VII 2003[1] ....ESDJ		64 018 857	20 990 626	32.8	31 883 154	10 188 273	32.0	32 135 703	10 802 353	33.6
1 VII 2004[1] ....ESDJ		64 177 484	19 300 414	30.1	31 574 765	9 261 252	29.3	32 602 719	10 039 162	30.8
1 VII 2005[1] ....ESDJ		64 838 628	19 538 420	30.1	31 848 905	9 360 642	29.4	32 989 723	10 177 778	30.9
1 VII 2006[1] ....ESDJ		65 305 736	19 792 296	30.3	32 060 034	9 474 510	29.6	33 245 702	10 317 786	31.0
1 VII 2007[1] ....ESDJ		66 041 512	20 117 497	30.5	32 467 223	9 733 251	30.0	33 574 289	10 384 246	30.9

Timor-Leste

11 VII 2004* ....CDFC		924 642	...	...	467 757	...	...	456 885	...	...

Turkey - Turquie

1 VII 1998 ....ESDF		65 215 000	37 724 702	57.8	32 956 000	...	...	32 259 000	...	...
1 VII 1999 ....ESDF		66 350 000	38 783 705	58.5	33 521 000	...	...	32 829 000	...	...
1 VII 2000 ....ESDF		67 420 000	39 818 088	59.1	34 053 000	...	...	33 367 000	...	...
22 X 2000 ....CDFC		67 803 927	44 006 274	64.9	34 346 735	22 427 603	65.3	33 457 192	21 578 671	64.5
1 VII 2001 ....ESDF		68 365 000	40 790 867	59.7	34 519 000	...	...	33 846 000	...	...
1 VII 2002 ....ESDF		69 302 000	41 770 289	60.3	34 981 000	...	...	34 320 000	...	...
1 VII 2003 ....ESDF		70 231 000	42 756 206	60.9	35 441 000	...	...	34 790 000	...	...
1 VII 2004 ....ESDF		71 152 000	43 748 475	61.5	35 897 000	...	...	35 255 000	...	...
1 VII 2005 ....ESDF		72 065 000	44 746 949	62.1	36 349 000	...	...	35 716 000	...	...
1 VII 2006 ....ESDF		72 974 000	45 753 990	62.7	36 797 000	...	...	36 177 000	...	...
1 VII 2007 ....ESDF		73 875 000	46 766 994	63.3	37 241 000	...	...	36 635 000	...	...

Continent, country or area, and date / Continent, pays ou zone et date	Code[a]	Both sexes - Les deux sexes			Male - Masculin			Female - Féminin		
		Total	Urban - Urbaine		Total	Urban - Urbaine		Total	Urban - Urbaine	
			Number Nombre	Percent P.100		Number Nombre	Percent P.100		Number Nombre	Percent P.100
ASIA - ASIE										
Turkmenistan - Turkménistan										
1 VII 2003 ....ESDF		5 123 940[9]	...	...	2 571 866	...	...	2 552 073	...	...
United Arab Emirates - Émirats arabes unis										
1 VII 1998 ....ESDF		2 717 000	...	...	1 861 000	...	...	915 000	...	...
1 VII 1999 ....ESDF		2 855 000	...	...	1 975 000	...	...	963 000	...	...
5 XII 2005 ....CDFC		4 106 427	3 384 839	82.4	2 806 141	...	...	1 300 286	...	...
1 VII 2006 ....ESDF		4 229 000	...	...	2 895 000	...	...	1 334 000	...	...
1 VII 2007 ....ESDF		4 488 000	...	...	3 084 000	...	...	1 404 000	...	...
Uzbekistan - Ouzbékistan										
1 VII 1998 ....ESDF		24 051 000	9 109 700	37.9	...	...	...	...	...	...
1 VII 1999 ....ESDF		23 953 922	9 037 904	37.7	11 913 994	4 450 641	37.4	12 039 928	4 587 263	38.1
1 VII 2000 ....ESDF		24 650 415	9 195 435	37.3	12 278 626	4 538 871	37.0	12 371 789	4 656 564	37.6
1 VII 2001 ....ESDF		24 964 433	9 256 101	37.1	12 442 510	4 573 055	36.8	12 521 923	4 683 046	37.4
Viet Nam										
1 VII 1998 ....ESDF		75 456 300	17 464 600	23.1	37 089 700	...	...	38 366 600	...	...
1 IV 1999 ....CDFC		76 323 173	18 076 823	23.7	37 469 117	8 825 112	23.6	38 854 056	9 251 711	23.8
1 VII 1999 ....ESDF		76 596 700	18 081 600	23.6	37 662 100	...	...	38 934 600	...	...
1 VII 2000 ....ESDF		77 635 424	18 771 943	24.2	38 166 447	...	...	39 468 977	...	...
1 VII 2001 ....ESDF		78 685 826	19 469 256	24.7	38 684 224	...	...	40 001 602	...	...
1 VII 2002 ....ESDF		79 727 379	20 022 142	25.1	39 197 378	...	...	40 530 001	...	...
1 VII 2003 ....ESDF		80 902 365	20 869 487	25.8	39 755 434	...	...	41 146 931	...	...
1 VII 2004 ....ESDF		82 031 670	21 737 225	26.5	40 310 514	...	...	41 721 156	...	...
1 VII 2005 ....ESDF		83 106 285	22 336 813	26.9	40 846 207	...	...	42 260 078	...	...
1 VII 2006 ....ESDF		84 136 803	22 792 577	27.1	41 354 889	...	...	42 781 914	...	...
1 VII 2007 ....ESDF		85 171 686	23 398 874	27.5	41 867 980	...	...	43 303 706	...	...
Yemen - Yémen										
1 VII 1998 ....ESDF		17 072 000	...	...	8 532 000	...	...	8 540 000	...	...
1 VII 1999 ....ESDF		17 671 000	...	...	8 837 000	...	...	8 834 000	...	...
16 XII 2004 ....CDFC		19 685 161	5 637 756	28.6	10 036 953	3 012 256	30.0	9 648 208	2 625 500	27.2
31 XII 2005 ....ESDF		20 282 944	5 849 749	28.8	...	...	...	...	...	...
31 XII 2006 ....ESDF		20 900 532	6 070 613	29.0	...	...	...	...	...	...
31 XII 2007 ....ESDF		21 538 995	6 256 462	29.0	...	...	...	...	...	...
EUROPE										
Åland Islands - Îles d'Åland[85]										
1 VII 1998 ....ESDJ		25 509	10 471	41.0	12 510	4 923	39.4	12 999	5 549	42.7
1 VII 1999 ....ESDJ		25 666	10 513	41.0	12 609	4 959	39.3	13 057	5 555	42.5
1 VII 2000 ....ESDJ		25 741	10 490	40.8	12 670	4 946	39.0	13 072	5 544	42.4
31 XII 2000 ....CDJC		25 776	...	...	12 700	...	...	13 076	...	...
1 VII 2001 ....ESDJ		25 892	10 549	40.7	12 750	4 967	39.0	13 142	5 582	42.5
1 VII 2002 ....ESDJ		26 133	10 621	40.6	12 866	5 004	38.9	13 267	5 617	42.3
1 VII 2003 ....ESDJ		26 302	10 629	40.4	12 945	5 011	38.7	13 358	5 619	42.1
1 VII 2004 ....ESDJ		26 439	10 669	40.4	13 030	5 036	38.7	13 409	5 633	42.0
1 VII 2005 ....ESDJ		26 648	10 746	40.3	13 174	5 087	38.6	13 475	5 660	42.0
1 VII 2006 ....ESDJ		26 845	10 802	40.2	13 299	5 123	38.5	13 546	5 680	41.9
1 VII 2007 ....ESDJ		27 038	10 863	40.2	13 407	5 151	38.4	13 631	5 712	41.9
Albania - Albanie										
1 VII 1998 ....ESDF		3 055 331	1 227 208	40.2	...	...	...	...	...	...
1 VII 1999 ....ESDF		3 053 831	1 234 975	40.4	...	...	...	...	...	...
1 VII 2000 ....ESDF		3 060 908	1 249 919	40.8	...	...	...	...	...	...
1 IV 2001 ....CDFC		3 069 300	1 292 800	42.1	1 530 500	...	...	1 538 800	...	...
1 VII 2001 ....ESDF		3 073 733	1 312 963	42.7	1 532 598	648 278	42.3	1 541 135	664 685	43.1
1 VII 2002 ....ESDF		3 093 465	1 347 871	43.6	1 542 211	625 060	40.5	1 551 254	722 811	46.6
1 VII 2003 ....ESDF		3 111 163	1 375 367	44.2	1 550 728	636 985	41.1	1 560 435	738 382	47.3
1 VII 2004 ....ESDF		3 127 263	1 406 443	45.0	1 558 376	661 335	42.4	1 568 887	745 108	47.5
1 VII 2005 ....ESDF		3 142 065	1 468 522	46.7	1 565 316	671 848	42.9	1 576 749	796 864	50.5
1 VII 2006 ....ESDF		3 150 886	1 528 877	48.5	1 580 446	711 123	45.0	1 570 440	817 754	52.1
1 VII 2007 ....ESDF		3 161 337	...	...	1 587 496	...	...	1 573 841	...	...

Continent, country or area, and date / Continent, pays ou zone et date	Code[a]	Both sexes - Les deux sexes			Male - Masculin			Female - Féminin		
		Total	Urban - Urbaine		Total	Urban - Urbaine		Total	Urban - Urbaine	
			Number Nombre	Percent P.100		Number Nombre	Percent P.100		Number Nombre	Percent P.100
EUROPE										
Andorra - Andorre[22]										
1 VII 1998 ....ESDF		65 592	...	...	34 387	...	...	31 205	...	...
1 VII 1999 ....ESDF		65 924	...	...	34 463	...	...	31 461	...	...
1 VII 2000 ....CDFC		66 089	...	...	34 344	...	...	31 745	...	...
1 VII 2000 ....ESDF		65 908	...	...	34 351	...	...	31 557	...	...
1 VII 2001 ....ESDF		66 089	...	...	34 344	...	...	31 746	...	...
1 VII 2002 ....ESDF		66 094	...	...	34 244	...	...	31 850	...	...
1 VII 2003 ....ESDF		69 840	...	...	36 258	...	...	33 582	...	...
1 VII 2004 ....ESDF		74 885	...	...	38 990	...	...	35 895	...	...
1 VII 2005 ....ESDF		78 607	...	...	41 097	...	...	37 510	...	...
1 VII 2006 ....ESDF		80 104	...	...	41 876	...	...	38 228	...	...
1 VII 2007 ....ESDF		82 392	...	...	43 100	...	...	39 292	...	...
Austria - Autriche										
1 VII 1998 ....ESDJ		7 976 789	...	...	3 852 166	...	...	4 124 623	...	...
1 VII 1999 ....ESDJ		7 992 323	...	...	3 862 180	...	...	4 130 143	...	...
1 VII 2000 ....ESDJ		8 011 566	...	...	3 874 717	...	...	4 136 849	...	...
15 V 2001 ....CDJC		8 032 926	5 368 693	66.8	3 889 189	2 564 828	65.9	4 143 737	2 803 865	67.7
1 VII 2001 ....ESDJ		8 043 046	...	...	3 894 129	...	...	4 148 917	...	...
1 VII 2002 ....ESDJ		8 083 797	...	...	3 918 990	...	...	4 164 807	...	...
1 VII 2003 ....ESDJ		8 117 754	...	...	3 938 582	...	...	4 179 172	...	...
1 VII 2004 ....ESDJ		8 174 733	...	...	3 969 190	...	...	4 205 543	...	...
1 VII 2005 ....ESDJ		8 233 306	...	...	4 001 861	...	...	4 231 445	...	...
1 VII 2006 ....ESDJ		8 281 948	...	...	4 028 658	...	...	4 253 290	...	...
1 VII 2007 ....ESDJ		8 315 379	...	...	4 046 289	...	...	4 269 090	...	...
Belarus - Bélarus										
1 VII 1998 ....ESDF		10 071 963	6 952 014	69.0	4 728 026	3 274 360	69.3	5 343 937	3 677 654	68.8
16 II 1999 ....CDJC		10 045 237	6 961 516	69.3	4 717 621	3 279 196	69.5	5 327 616	3 682 320	69.1
1 VII 1999 ....ESDF		10 035 210	6 971 629	69.5	4 711 688	3 282 317	69.7	5 323 522	3 689 312	69.3
1 VII 2000 ....ESDF		10 004 958	6 999 510	70.0	4 695 465	3 291 885	70.1	5 309 493	3 707 625	69.8
1 VII 2001 ....ESDF		9 970 688	7 022 386	70.4	4 677 096	3 298 787	70.5	5 293 592	3 723 599	70.3
1 VII 2002 ....ESDF		9 924 766	7 034 721	70.9	4 652 109	3 299 920	70.9	5 272 657	3 734 801	70.8
1 VII 2003 ....ESDF		9 873 826	7 040 950	71.3	4 623 963	3 297 535	71.3	5 249 863	3 743 415	71.3
1 VII 2004 ....ESDF		9 824 568	7 050 685	71.8	4 596 633	3 296 800	71.7	5 227 935	3 753 885	71.8
1 VII 2005 ....ESDF		9 775 307	7 057 463	72.2	4 569 189	3 294 851	72.1	5 206 118	3 762 612	72.3
1 VII 2006 ....ESDF		9 732 501	7 066 903	72.6	4 545 164	3 294 559	72.5	5 187 337	3 772 344	72.7
1 VII 2007 ....ESDF		9 702 116	7 091 407	73.1	4 528 222	3 302 285	72.9	5 173 894	3 789 122	73.2
Belgium - Belgique										
1 VII 1998 ....ESDJ		10 203 008	10 057 567	98.6	4 988 195	4 915 372	98.5	5 214 813	5 142 195	98.6
1 VII 1999 ....ESDJ		10 226 419	10 080 170	98.6	4 999 866	4 926 662	98.5	5 226 553	5 153 508	98.6
1 VII 2000 ....ESDJ		10 251 250	10 104 126	98.6	5 012 017	4 938 401	98.5	5 239 233	5 165 725	98.6
1 VII 2001 ....ESDJ		10 286 570	10 138 703	98.6	5 030 154	4 956 176	98.5	5 256 416	5 182 527	98.6
1 X 2001 ....CDJC		10 296 350	...	...	5 035 446	...	...	5 260 904	...	...
1 VII 2002 ....ESDJ		10 332 785	10 184 150	98.6	5 054 587	4 980 148	98.5	5 278 198	5 204 003	98.6
1 VII 2003 ....ESDJ		10 372 469	10 223 221	98.6	5 075 268	5 000 466	98.5	5 297 201	5 222 755	98.6
1 VII 2004 ....ESDJ		10 417 122	10 267 298	98.6	5 097 709	5 022 559	98.5	5 319 413	5 244 739	98.6
1 VII 2005 ....ESDJ		10 472 842	10 322 099	98.6	5 125 387	5 049 822	98.5	5 347 455	5 272 277	98.6
1 VII 2006 ....ESDJ		10 541 893	10 389 801	98.6	5 159 947	5 083 829	98.5	5 381 946	5 305 972	98.6
1 VII 2007 ....ESDJ		10 622 604	10 469 341	98.6	5 201 670	5 125 007	98.5	5 420 934	5 344 334	98.6
Bosnia and Herzegovina - Bosnie-Herzégovine										
1 VII 1998 ....ESDF		3 653 364	...	...	1 790 148	...	...	1 863 216	...	...
1 VII 1999 ....ESDF		3 724 672	...	...	1 825 089	...	...	1 899 583	...	...
1 VII 2000 ....ESDF		3 781 497	...	...	1 852 934	...	...	1 928 563	...	...
1 VII 2001 ....ESDF		3 797 937	...	...	1 860 989	...	...	1 936 948	...	...
1 VII 2002 ....ESDF		3 828 397	...	...	1 875 915	...	...	1 952 482	...	...
1 VII 2003 ....ESDF		3 832 301	...	...	1 877 827	...	...	1 954 474	...	...
1 VII 2004 ....ESDF		3 842 527	...	...	1 882 838	...	...	1 959 689	...	...
1 VII 2005 ....ESDF		3 842 537	...	...	1 882 843	...	...	1 959 694	...	...
1 VII 2006 ....ESDF		3 842 762	...	...	1 882 953	...	...	1 959 809	...	...
Bulgaria - Bulgarie										
1 VII 1998 ....ESDF		8 256 786	5 603 501	67.9	4 029 518	2 720 430	67.5	4 227 268	2 883 071	68.2
1 VII 1999 ....ESDF		8 210 624	5 587 165	68.0	4 002 616	2 708 093	67.7	4 208 008	2 879 072	68.4
1 VII 2000 ....ESDF		8 170 172	5 577 216	68.3	3 979 292	2 700 131	67.9	4 190 880	2 877 085	68.7
1 III 2001 ....CDFC		7 928 901	5 474 534	69.0	3 862 465	2 651 312	68.6	4 066 436	2 823 222	69.4
1 VII 2001 ....ESDF		7 913 301	5 477 604	69.2	3 853 710	2 652 367	68.8	4 059 591	2 825 237	69.6

Continent, country or area, and date / Continent, pays ou zone et date	Code[a]	Both sexes - Les deux sexes			Male - Masculin			Female - Féminin		
		Total	Urban - Urbaine		Total	Urban - Urbaine		Total	Urban - Urbaine	
			Number Nombre	Percent P.100		Number Nombre	Percent P.100		Number Nombre	Percent P.100
EUROPE										
Bulgaria - Bulgarie										
1 VII 2002	ESDF	7 868 900	5 467 777	69.5	3 828 882	2 644 285	69.1	4 040 018	2 823 492	69.9
1 VII 2003	ESDF	7 823 557	5 459 344	69.8	3 803 501	2 636 908	69.3	4 020 056	2 822 436	70.2
1 VII 2004	ESDF	7 781 161	5 440 536	69.9	3 779 224	2 624 031	69.4	4 001 937	2 816 505	70.4
1 VII 2005	ESDF	7 739 900	5 424 661	70.1	3 755 469	2 613 346	69.6	3 984 431	2 811 315	70.6
1 VII 2006	ESDF	7 699 020	5 428 388	70.5	3 732 130	2 613 030	70.0	3 966 890	2 815 358	71.0
1 VII 2007	ESDF	7 659 764	5 414 260	70.7	3 710 315	2 604 175	70.2	3 949 449	2 810 085	71.2
Croatia - Croatie										
1 VII 1998	ESDJ	4 501 149	...	...	2 163 164	...	...	2 337 985	...	...
1 VII 1999	ESDJ	4 553 769	...	...	2 188 455	...	...	2 365 314	...	...
1 VII 2000	ESDJ	4 426 233	...	...	2 130 747	...	...	2 295 486	...	...
31 III 2001	CDJC	4 437 460	2 471 328	55.7	2 135 900	1 171 950	54.9	2 301 560	1 299 378	56.5
1 VII 2001	ESDJ	4 439 635	...	...	2 137 014	...	...	2 302 621	...	...
1 VII 2002	ESDJ	4 440 385	...	...	2 136 831	...	...	2 303 554	...	...
1 VII 2003	ESDJ	4 440 290	...	...	2 137 037	...	...	2 303 253	...	...
1 VII 2004	ESDJ	4 439 353	...	...	2 136 887	...	...	2 302 466	...	...
1 VII 2005	ESDJ	4 441 989	...	...	2 138 663	...	...	2 303 326	...	...
1 VII 2006	ESDJ	4 440 022	...	...	2 138 934	...	...	2 301 088	...	...
1 VII 2007	ESDJ	4 435 982	...	...	2 137 984	...	...	2 297 998	...	...
Czech Republic - République tchèque										
1 VII 1998	ESDJ	10 294 943	7 675 220	74.6	5 007 480	...	...	5 287 463	...	...
1 VII 1999	ESDJ	10 282 784	7 659 954	74.5	5 002 823	...	...	5 279 961	...	...
1 VII 2000	ESDJ	10 272 503	7 641 415	74.4	4 999 326	3 694 433	73.9	5 273 177	3 946 982	74.9
1 III 2001	CDJC	10 230 060	7 564 200	73.9	4 982 071	3 657 775	73.4	5 247 989	3 906 425	74.4
1 VII 2001	ESDJ	10 224 192	7 559 732	73.9	4 978 951	3 655 116	73.4	5 245 241	3 904 616	74.4
1 VII 2002	ESDJ	10 200 774	7 536 154	73.9	4 964 598	3 640 572	73.3	5 236 176	3 895 582	74.4
1 VII 2003	ESDJ	10 201 651	7 533 782	73.8	4 968 189	3 640 805	73.3	5 233 462	3 892 977	74.4
1 VII 2004	ESDJ	10 206 923	7 526 698	73.7	4 971 730	3 637 603	73.2	5 235 193	3 889 095	74.3
1 VII 2005	ESDJ	10 234 092	7 552 515	73.8	4 991 439	3 655 100	73.2	5 242 653	3 897 415	74.3
1 VII 2006	ESDJ	10 287 189	7 574 397	73.6	5 026 184	3 671 881	73.1	5 261 005	3 902 516	74.2
1 VII 2007	ESDJ	10 334 160	7 609 077	73.6	5 054 559	3 692 988	73.1	5 279 601	3 916 089	74.2
Denmark - Danemark[86]										
1 VII 1998	ESDJ	5 301 304	...	...	2 618 854	...	...	2 682 450	...	...
1 VII 1999	ESDJ	5 327 358	...	...	2 632 641	...	...	2 694 717	...	...
1 VII 2000	ESDJ	5 337 344	...	...	2 637 878	...	...	2 699 466	...	...
1 I 2001	CDJC	5 349 212	...	...	2 644 319	...	...	2 704 893	...	...
1 VII 2001	ESDJ	5 358 783	...	...	2 649 233	...	...	2 709 551	...	...
1 VII 2002	ESDJ	5 374 255	...	...	2 657 341	...	...	2 716 914	...	...
1 VII 2003	ESDJ	5 387 174	...	...	2 664 526	...	...	2 722 648	...	...
1 VII 2004	ESDJ	5 401 177	...	...	2 671 907	...	...	2 729 270	...	...
1 VII 2005	ESDJ	5 415 978	...	...	2 679 857	...	...	2 736 121	...	...
1 VII 2006	ESDJ	5 434 567	...	...	2 690 179	...	...	2 744 388	...	...
1 VII 2007	ESDJ	5 457 415	...	...	2 702 894	...	...	2 754 521	...	...
Estonia - Estonie										
1 VII 1998	ESDF	1 386 156	1 003 119[3]	72.4	639 629	457 641[3]	71.5	746 527	545 478[3]	73.1
1 VII 1999	ESDF	1 375 654	997 188[3]	72.5	634 484	454 363[3]	71.6	741 170	542 825[3]	73.2
31 III 2000	CDJC	1 370 052	923 211	67.4	631 851	415 515	65.8	738 201	507 696	68.8
1 VII 2000	ESDF	1 369 515	947 308	69.2	631 579	426 593	67.5	737 936	520 715	70.6
1 VII 2001	ESDF	1 364 101	943 944	69.2	629 020	424 985	67.6	735 081	518 959	70.6
1 VII 2002	ESDF	1 358 644	940 465	69.2	626 276	423 224	67.6	732 368	517 241	70.6
1 VII 2003	ESDF	1 353 557	937 201	69.2	623 705	421 604	67.6	729 852	515 597	70.6
1 VII 2004	ESDF	1 349 290	934 665	69.3	621 525	420 309	67.6	727 765	514 356	70.7
1 VII 2005	ESDF	1 346 097	932 985	69.3	619 949	419 513	67.7	726 148	513 472	70.7
1 VII 2006	ESDF	1 343 547	931 855	69.4	618 772	419 103	67.7	724 775	512 752	70.7
1 VII 2007	ESDF	1 341 672	931 163	69.4	617 828	418 873	67.8	723 844	512 290	70.8
Faeroe Islands - Îles Féroé										
1 VII 1998	ESDJ	44 504	...	...	22 983	...	...	21 521	...	...
1 VII 1999	ESDJ	45 063	...	...	23 305	...	...	21 758	...	...
1 VII 2000	ESDJ	45 749	...	...	23 676	...	...	22 073	...	...
1 VII 2001	ESDJ	46 553	...	...	24 116	...	...	22 437	...	...
1 VII 2002	ESDJ	47 315	...	...	24 534	...	...	22 781	...	...
1 VII 2003	ESDJ	47 923	...	...	24 873	...	...	23 051	...	...

Continent, country or area, and date / Continent, pays ou zone et date	Code[a]	Both sexes - Les deux sexes			Male - Masculin			Female - Féminin		
			Urban - Urbaine			Urban - Urbaine			Urban - Urbaine	
		Total	Number Nombre	Percent P.100	Total	Number Nombre	Percent P.100	Total	Number Nombre	Percent P.100
EUROPE										
Faeroe Islands - Îles Féroé										
1 VII 2004 ....ESDJ		48 258	...	...	25 070	...	...	23 188	...	...
1 VII 2005 ....ESDJ		48 260	...	...	25 074	...	...	23 187	...	...
1 VII 2006 ....ESDJ		48 267	...	...	25 083	...	...	23 184	...	...
1 VII 2007 ....ESDJ		48 278	...	...	25 090	...	...	23 188	...	...
Finland - Finlande[87]										
1 VII 1998 ....ESDJ		5 153 498	3 089 077	59.9	2 512 587	1 476 277	58.8	2 640 911	1 612 800	61.1
1 VII 1999 ....ESDJ		5 165 474	3 112 147	60.2	2 519 551	1 488 063	59.1	2 645 924	1 624 084	61.4
1 VII 2000 ....ESDJ		5 176 209	3 157 401	61.0	2 526 184	1 511 406	59.8	2 650 025	1 645 995	62.1
31 XII 2000 ....CDJC		5 181 115	3 167 668	61.1	2 529 341	1 516 812	60.0	2 651 774	1 650 856	62.3
1 VII 2001 ....ESDJ		5 188 008	3 179 283	61.3	2 533 469	1 523 008	60.1	2 654 539	1 656 275	62.4
1 VII 2002 ....ESDJ		5 200 598	3 217 447	61.9	2 541 257	1 543 243	60.7	2 659 342	1 674 204	63.0
1 VII 2003 ....ESDJ		5 213 014	3 234 178	62.0	2 548 905	1 552 734	60.9	2 664 109	1 681 445	63.1
1 VII 2004 ....ESDJ		5 228 172	3 245 435	62.1	2 557 485	1 559 747	61.0	2 670 687	1 685 689	63.1
1 VII 2005 ....ESDJ		5 246 096	3 285 197	62.6	2 567 214	1 580 650	61.6	2 678 882	1 704 547	63.6
1 VII 2006 ....ESDJ		5 266 268	3 316 388	63.0	2 578 046	1 597 209	62.0	2 688 222	1 719 179	64.0
1 VII 2007 ....ESDJ		5 288 720	3 431 735	64.9	2 590 265	1 656 013	63.9	2 698 455	1 775 722	65.8
France[88]										
1 VII 1998 ....ESDJ		58 397 788	...	...	28 361 163	...	...	30 036 625	...	...
8 III 1999 ....CDJC		58 520 688	...	...	28 419 419	...	...	30 101 269	...	...
1 VII 1999 ....ESDJ		58 673 079	...	...	28 492 821	...	...	30 180 258	...	...
1 VII 2000 ....ESDJ		59 049 357	...	...	28 677 892	...	...	30 371 465	...	...
1 VII 2001 ....ESDJ		59 454 461	...	...	28 877 376	...	...	30 577 085	...	...
1 VII 2002 ....ESDJ		59 863 266	...	...	29 079 470	...	...	30 783 796	...	...
1 VII 2003 ....ESDJ		60 264 196	...	...	29 279 506	...	...	30 984 690	...	...
1 VII 2004 ....ESDJ		60 643 307	...	...	29 466 783	...	...	31 176 524	...	...
1 VII 2005 ....ESDJ		60 995 911	...	...	29 638 708	...	...	31 357 203	...	...
1 I 2006 ....CDJC		61 399 541	...	...	29 714 539	...	...	31 685 002	...	...
1 VII 2006 ....ESDJ		61 352 572	...	...	29 814 775	...	...	31 537 797	...	...
1 I 2007* ....ESDJ		61 538 322	...	...	29 907 166	...	...	31 631 156	...	...
Germany - Allemagne										
1 VII 1998 ....ESDJ		82 028 947	...	...	39 992 272	...	...	42 036 675	...	...
1 VII 1999 ....ESDJ		82 086 582	...	...	40 047 972	...	...	42 038 610	...	...
1 VII 2000 ....ESDJ		82 187 614	...	...	40 115 959	...	...	42 071 655	...	...
1 VII 2001 ....ESDJ		82 339 777	...	...	40 214 370	...	...	42 125 407	...	...
1 VII 2002 ....ESDJ		82 482 309	...	...	40 310 430	...	...	42 171 879	...	...
1 VII 2003 ....ESDJ		82 520 176	...	...	40 349 200	...	...	42 170 976	...	...
28 III 2004[89] ....SSDJ		82 491 000	...	...	40 330 000	...	...	42 161 000	...	...
1 VII 2004 ....ESDJ		82 501 274	...	...	40 350 091	...	...	42 151 183	...	...
1 VII 2005 ....ESDJ		82 464 344	...	...	40 348 986	...	...	42 115 358	...	...
1 VII 2006 ....ESDJ		82 365 810	...	...	40 317 807	...	...	42 048 003	...	...
1 VII 2007 ....ESDJ		82 262 643	...	...	40 287 823	...	...	41 974 820	...	...
Gibraltar[90]										
1 VII 1998 ....ESDF		27 025	...	...	13 419	...	...	13 606	...	...
1 VII 1999 ....ESDF		27 114	...	...	13 460	...	...	13 654	...	...
1 VII 2000 ....ESDF		27 118	...	...	13 453	...	...	13 665	...	...
12 XI 2001 ....CDFC		27 495			13 644			13 851		
1 VII 2002 ....ESDF		28 520	...	...	14 300	...	...	14 220	...	...
1 VII 2003 ....ESDF		28 562	...	...	14 342	...	...	14 220	...	...
1 VII 2004 ....ESDF		28 704	...	...	14 410	...	...	14 294	...	...
1 VII 2005 ....ESDF		28 827	...	...	14 422	...	...	14 406	...	...
1 VII 2006 ....ESDF		29 066	...	...	14 545	...	...	14 521	...	...
31 XII 2007 ....ESDF		29 257	...	...	14 655	...	...	14 602	...	...
Greece - Grèce										
1 VII 1998[91] ....ESDF		10 834 910	...	...	5 366 820	...	...	5 468 090	...	...
1 VII 1999[91] ....ESDF		10 882 607	...	...	5 389 881	...	...	5 492 726	...	...
1 VII 2000[91] ....ESDF		10 917 457	...	...	5 406 043	...	...	5 511 414	...	...
18 III 2001[92] ....CDFC		10 964 020	7 980 414	72.8	5 427 682	3 892 266	71.7	5 536 338	4 088 148	73.8
1 VII 2001[91] ....ESDF		10 949 953	...	...	5 421 043	...	...	5 528 910	...	...
1 VII 2002[91] ....ESDF		10 987 559	...	...	5 439 332	...	...	5 548 227	...	...
1 VII 2003[91] ....ESDF		11 023 532	...	...	5 456 496	...	...	5 567 036	...	...
1 VII 2004[91] ....ESDF		11 061 735	...	...	5 475 529	...	...	5 586 206	...	...
1 VII 2005[91] ....ESDF		11 103 929	...	...	5 497 372	...	...	5 606 557	...	...

Continent, country or area, and date / Continent, pays ou zone et date	Code[a]	Both sexes - Les deux sexes			Male - Masculin			Female - Féminin		
		Total	Urban - Urbaine		Total	Urban - Urbaine		Total	Urban - Urbaine	
			Number Nombre	Percent P.100		Number Nombre	Percent P.100		Number Nombre	Percent P.100
EUROPE										
Greece - Grèce										
1 VII 2006[91] ....ESDF		11 148 533	...	...	5 520 164	...	...	5 628 369	...	...
1 VII 2007[91] ....ESDF		11 192 849	...	...	5 543 018	...	...	5 649 831	...	...
Guernsey - Guernesey										
1 VII 1998 ....ESDF		59 050	...	...	28 434	...	...	30 616	...	...
1 VII 1999 ....ESDF		60 268	...	...	29 042	...	...	31 226	...	...
29 IV 2001...........CDJC		59 807	...	...	29 138	...	...	30 669	...	...
1 VII 2004 ....ESDF		60 382	...	...	29 841	...	...	30 541	...	...
1 III 2006 ....ESDF		61 029	...	...	30 034	...	...	30 995	...	...
1 III 2007 ....ESDF		61 811	...	...	30 345	...	...	31 466	...	...
Holy See - Saint-Siège[93]										
1 VII 1998[94] ....ESDJ		786	...	...	604	...	...	182	...	...
1 VII 2000* ....CDFC		798	...	...	529	...	...	269	...	...
Hungary - Hongrie										
1 VII 1998 ....ESDF		10 113 574	6 431 702[95]	63.6	4 829 734	3 028 148[95]	62.7	5 283 840	3 403 554[95]	64.4
1 VII 1999 ....ESDF		10 067 507	6 385 626[95]	63.4	4 804 690	3 003 675[95]	62.5	5 262 817	3 381 951[95]	64.3
1 VII 2000 ....ESDF		10 024 222	6 364 276[95]	63.5	4 781 701	2 991 619[95]	62.6	5 242 522	3 372 657[95]	64.3
1 II 2001 ....CDFC		10 198 315	6 572 880	64.5	4 850 650	3 091 857	63.7	5 347 665	3 481 023	65.1
1 VII 2001 ....ESDF		10 187 576	6 544 089[95]	64.2	4 843 996	3 073 458[95]	63.4	5 343 580	3 470 631[95]	64.9
1 VII 2002 ....ESDF		10 158 608	6 607 159[95]	65.0	4 827 718	3 101 463[95]	64.2	5 330 890	3 505 696[95]	65.8
1 VII 2003 ....ESDF		10 129 552	6 568 539[95]	64.8	4 811 285	3 079 592[95]	64.0	5 318 268	3 488 947[95]	65.6
1 VII 2004 ....ESDF		10 107 146	6 571 923[95]	65.0	4 798 614	3 078 582[95]	64.2	5 308 532	3 493 342[95]	65.8
1 VII 2005 ....ESDF		10 087 065	6 670 187	66.1	4 788 847	3 125 833	65.3	5 298 218	3 544 354	66.9
1 VII 2006 ....ESDF		10 071 370	6 749 388	67.0	4 781 829	3 163 716	66.2	5 289 541	3 585 673	67.8
1 VII 2007 ....ESDF		10 055 780	6 737 792	67.0	4 774 320	3 156 954	66.1	5 281 460	3 580 839	67.8
Iceland - Islande[22]										
1 VII 1998 ....ESDJ		273 794	252 356	92.2	137 092	125 634	91.6	136 702	126 722	92.7
1 VII 1999 ....ESDJ		277 184	255 910	92.3	138 783	127 433	91.8	138 401	128 477	92.8
1 VII 2000...........CDJC		281 154	259 661	92.4	140 718	129 258	91.9	140 436	130 403	92.9
1 VII 2000 ....ESDJ		281 154	259 661	92.4	140 718	129 258	91.9	140 436	130 403	92.9
1 VII 2001 ....ESDJ		285 054	263 409	92.4	142 660	131 217	92.0	142 308	132 192	92.9
1 VII 2002 ....ESDJ		287 559	266 010	92.5	143 860	132 371	92.0	143 699	133 639	93.0
1 VII 2003 ....ESDJ		289 272	267 957	92.6	144 713	133 340	92.1	144 559	134 617	93.1
1 VII 2004 ....ESDJ		292 587	270 931	92.6	146 697	134 827	91.9	145 890	136 104	93.3
1 VII 2005 ....ESDJ		295 864	275 017	93.0	148 449	137 003	92.3	147 415	138 014	93.6
1 VII 2006 ....ESDJ		304 334	281 961	92.6	154 287	141 673	91.8	150 047	140 288	93.5
1 VII 2007 ....ESDJ		311 396	289 119	92.8	158 866	146 168	92.0	152 530	142 951	93.7
Ireland - Irlande										
15 IV 1998..........ESDF		3 703 082	...	...	1 838 859	...	...	1 864 223	...	...
15 IV 1999..........ESDF		3 741 647	...	...	1 858 613	...	...	1 883 034	...	...
15 IV 2000..........ESDF		3 789 536	...	...	1 882 946	...	...	1 906 590	...	...
15 IV 2001..........ESDF		3 847 198	...	...	1 913 128	...	...	1 934 070	...	...
28 IV 2002..........CDFC		3 917 203	2 334 300	59.6	1 946 164	1 133 500	58.2	1 971 039	1 200 800	60.9
15 IV 2003..........ESDF		3 978 862	...	...	1 977 208	...	...	2 001 654	...	...
15 IV 2004..........ESDF		4 043 763	...	...	2 011 159	...	...	2 032 604	...	...
15 IV 2005..........ESDF		4 130 722	...	...	2 058 952	...	...	2 071 770	...	...
15 IV 2006..........ESDF		4 234 872	...	...	2 116 062	...	...	2 118 810	...	...
23 IV 2006..........CDFC		4 239 848	...	...	2 121 171	...	...	2 118 677	...	...
Isle of Man - Île de Man										
30 IV 1998..........ESDJ		73 274	...	...	35 656	...	...	37 619	...	...
30 IV 1999..........ESDJ		74 060	...	...	36 089	...	...	37 971	...	...
30 IV 2000..........ESDJ		74 911	...	...	36 560	...	...	38 351	...	...
29 IV 2001..........CDJC		76 315	...	...	37 372	...	...	38 943	...	...
30 IV 2002..........ESDJ		77 156	...	...	37 827	...	...	39 330	...	...
30 IV 2003..........ESDJ		77 464	...	...	38 019	...	...	39 444	...	...
30 IV 2004..........ESDJ		77 581	...	...	38 111	...	...	39 470	...	...
30 IV 2005..........ESDJ		78 800	...	...	38 775	...	...	40 025	...	...
23 IV 2006..........CDJC		80 058	...	...	39 523	...	...	40 535	...	...
30 IV 2006..........ESDJ		80 058	...	...	39 523	...	...	40 535	...	...
30 IV 2007..........ESDJ		80 885	...	...	39 995	...	...	40 889	...	...
Italy - Italie										
1 VII 1998 ....ESDJ		56 906 744	...	...	27 567 663	...	...	29 339 081	...	...
1 VII 1999 ....ESDJ		56 916 317	...	...	27 563 368	...	...	29 352 949	...	...
1 VII 2000 ....ESDJ		56 942 108	...	...	27 569 657	...	...	29 372 451	...	...

Continent, country or area, and date / Continent, pays ou zone et date	Code[a]	Both sexes - Les deux sexes			Male - Masculin			Female - Féminin		
		Total	Urban - Urbaine		Total	Urban - Urbaine		Total	Urban - Urbaine	
			Number Nombre	Percent P.100		Number Nombre	Percent P.100		Number Nombre	Percent P.100

EUROPE

Italy - Italie

1 VII 2001 ....ESDJ		56 977 217	...	...	27 581 784	...	...	29 395 433	...	...
21 X 2001 ....CDFC		57 110 144	...	...	27 617 335	...	...	29 492 809	...	...
1 VII 2002 ....ESDJ		57 157 406	...	...	27 676 733	...	...	29 480 674	...	...
1 VII 2003 ....ESDJ		57 604 658	...	...	27 917 416	...	...	29 687 242	...	...
1 VII 2004 ....ESDJ		58 175 310	...	...	28 222 706	...	...	29 952 604	...	...
1 VII 2005 ....ESDJ		58 607 043	...	...	28 451 846	...	...	30 155 197	...	...
1 VII 2006 ....ESDJ		58 941 499	...	...	28 622 665	...	...	30 318 835	...	...
1 VII 2007 ....ESDJ		59 375 289	...	...	28 834 094	...	...	30 541 195	...	...

Jersey

11 III 2001 ....CDJC		87 186	...	...	42 484	...	...	44 702	...	...

Latvia - Lettonie

1 VII 1998 ....ESDJ		2 410 019	1 649 491	68.4	1 110 461	746 363	67.2	1 299 558	903 128	69.5
1 VII 1999 ....ESDJ		2 390 482	1 630 335	68.2	1 101 163	735 684	66.8	1 289 319	894 651	69.4
31 III 2000 ....CDJC		2 377 383	1 618 144	68.1	1 094 964	729 745	66.6	1 282 419	888 399	69.3
1 VII 2000 ....ESDJ		2 372 985	1 614 159	68.0	1 092 871	727 722	66.6	1 280 114	886 437	69.2
1 VII 2001 ....ESDJ		2 355 011	1 599 272	67.9	1 084 484	720 359	66.4	1 270 527	878 913	69.2
1 VII 2002 ....ESDJ		2 338 624	1 586 220	67.8	1 076 587	713 616	66.3	1 262 037	872 604	69.1
1 VII 2003 ....ESDJ		2 325 342	1 576 965	67.8	1 070 697	709 024	66.2	1 254 645	867 941	69.2
1 VII 2004 ....ESDJ		2 312 819	1 570 406	67.9	1 065 627	706 082	66.3	1 247 192	864 324	69.3
1 VII 2005 ....ESDJ		2 300 512	1 563 372	68.0	1 060 101	702 490	66.3	1 240 411	860 882	69.4
1 VII 2006 ....ESDJ		2 287 948	1 554 766	68.0	1 054 159	697 812	66.2	1 233 789	856 954	69.5
1 VII 2007 ....ESDJ		2 276 100	1 545 560	67.9	1 048 969	693 369	66.1	1 227 131	852 191	69.4

Liechtenstein

31 XII 1998 ....ESDF		32 015	...	...	15 628	...	...	16 387	...	...
31 XII 1999 ....ESDF		32 426	...	...	15 776	...	...	16 650	...	...
1 VII 2000 ....ESDF		32 673	...	...	15 912	...	...	16 761	...	...
5 XII 2000 ....CDFC		33 307	...	...	16 420	...	...	16 887	...	...
1 VII 2001 ....ESDF		33 104	...	...	16 195	...	...	16 909	...	...
1 VII 2002 ....ESDF		33 678	...	...	16 514	...	...	17 164	...	...
1 VII 2003 ....ESDF		34 022	...	...	16 725	...	...	17 297	...	...
1 VII 2004 ....ESDF		34 477	...	...	16 974	...	...	17 503	...	...
1 VII 2005 ....ESDF		34 734	...	...	17 100	...	...	17 634	...	...
1 VII 2006 ....ESDF		35 010	...	...	17 256	...	...	17 754	...	...
1 VII 2007 ....ESDF		35 322	...	...	17 426	...	...	17 896	...	...

Lithuania - Lituanie

1 VII 1998 ....ESDJ		3 549 331	2 387 853	67.3	1 664 607	1 105 127	66.4	1 884 724	1 282 726	68.1
1 VII 1999 ....ESDJ		3 524 238	2 367 146	67.2	1 650 931	1 092 628	66.2	1 873 307	1 274 518	68.0
1 VII 2000 ....ESDJ		3 499 536	2 345 640	67.0	1 637 616	1 079 945	65.9	1 861 920	1 265 695	68.0
6 IV 2001 ....CDJC		3 483 972	2 332 098	66.9	1 629 148	1 071 986	65.8	1 854 824	1 260 112	67.9
1 VII 2001 ....ESDJ		3 481 292	2 330 184	66.9	1 627 704	1 070 901	65.8	1 853 588	1 259 283	67.9
1 VII 2002 ....ESDJ		3 469 070	2 321 713	66.9	1 620 891	1 065 912	65.8	1 848 179	1 255 801	67.9
1 VII 2003 ....ESDJ		3 454 205	2 307 326	66.8	1 612 996	1 058 108	65.6	1 841 209	1 249 218	67.8
1 VII 2004 ....ESDJ		3 435 591	2 289 399	66.6	1 603 421	1 048 397	65.4	1 832 170	1 241 002	67.7
1 VII 2005 ....ESDJ		3 414 304	2 275 118	66.6	1 592 402	1 040 296	65.3	1 821 902	1 234 822	67.8
1 VII 2006 ....ESDJ		3 394 082	2 264 535	66.7	1 581 807	1 034 128	65.4	1 812 275	1 230 407	67.9
1 VII 2007 ....ESDJ		3 375 618	2 255 508	66.8	1 571 979	1 028 619	65.4	1 803 639	1 226 889	68.0

Luxembourg

1 VII 1998 ....ESDJ		424 700	...	...	209 716	...	...	216 734	...	...
1 VII 1999 ....ESDJ		430 475	...	...	211 978	...	...	218 497	...	...
1 VII 2000 ....ESDJ		436 300	...	...	214 958	...	...	221 343	...	...
15 II 2001 ....CDJC		439 539	...	...	216 541	...	...	222 998	...	...
1 VII 2001 ....ESDJ		441 525	...	...	217 562	...	...	223 963	...	...
1 VII 2002 ....ESDJ		446 175	...	...	219 916	...	...	226 259	...	...
1 VII 2003 ....ESDJ		451 631	...	...	222 859	...	...	228 772	...	...
1 VII 2004 ....ESDJ		458 095	...	...	226 432	...	...	231 663	...	...
1 VII 2005 ....ESDJ		465 158	...	...	230 128	...	...	235 030	...	...
1 VII 2006 ....ESDJ		472 637	...	...	233 946	...	...	238 691	...	...
1 VII 2007 ....ESDJ		479 993	...	...	237 700	...	...	242 293	...	...

Malta - Malte

1 VII 1998 ....ESDJ		378 518	...	...	187 689	...	...	190 829	...	...
1 VII 1999 ....ESDJ		380 201	...	...	188 589	...	...	191 612	...	...
1 VII 2000 ....ESDJ		382 525	...	...	189 720	...	...	192 805	...	...
31 XII 2001 ....ESDJ		394 641	...	...	195 363	...	...	199 278	...	...
31 XII 2002 ....ESDJ		397 296	...	...	196 836	...	...	200 460	...	...

Continent, country or area, and date / Continent, pays ou zone et date	Code[a]	Both sexes - Les deux sexes			Male - Masculin			Female - Féminin		
		Total	Urban - Urbaine		Total	Urban - Urbaine		Total	Urban - Urbaine	
			Number Nombre	Percent P.100		Number Nombre	Percent P.100		Number Nombre	Percent P.100
EUROPE										
Malta - Malte										
1 VII 2003	ESDJ	398 582	...	...	197 468	...	...	201 114	...	...
1 VII 2004	ESDJ	401 306	...	...	198 860	...	...	202 446	...	...
1 VII 2005	ESDJ	403 509	...	...	200 104	...	...	203 405	...	...
27 XI 2005	CDJC	404 962	...	...	200 819	...	...	204 143	...	...
1 VII 2006	ESDJ	406 453	...	...	201 747	...	...	204 706	...	...
1 VII 2007*	ESDJ	409 092	...	...	203 381	...	...	205 711	...	...
Monaco										
21 VI 2000	CDJC	32 020	...	...	15 544	...	...	16 476	...	...
Montenegro - Monténégro										
1 VII 1998	ESDF	647 118	...	...	321 841	...	...	325 277	...	...
1 VII 1999	ESDF	650 758	...	...	323 686	...	...	327 072	...	...
1 VII 2000	ESDF	654 274	...	...	325 458	...	...	328 816	...	...
1 VII 2001	ESDF	658 223	...	...	327 538	...	...	330 685	...	...
1 VII 2002	ESDJ	617 511	...	...	304 814	...	...	312 697	...	...
1 VII 2003	ESDJ	620 279	385 205	62.1	305 745	187 299	61.3	314 534	197 906	62.9
31 X 2003	CDJC	620 145	...	...	305 225	...	...	314 920	...	...
1 VII 2004	ESDJ	622 118	387 501	62.3	306 428	188 266	61.4	315 690	199 235	63.1
1 VII 2005	ESDJ	623 277	389 678	62.5	306 839	189 222	61.7	316 439	200 456	63.3
1 VII 2006	ESDJ	624 241	391 884	62.8	307 271	190 286	61.9	316 970	201 598	63.6
1 VII 2007	ESDJ	626 104	394 653	63.0	308 267	191 692	62.2	317 836	202 961	63.9
Netherlands - Pays-Bas										
1 VII 1998	ESDJ	15 707 209	9 755 092	62.1	7 766 673	4 785 289	61.6	7 940 536	4 969 803	62.6
1 VII 1999	ESDJ	15 812 088	9 974 948	63.1	7 819 794	4 895 568	62.6	7 992 294	5 079 381	63.6
1 VII 2000	ESDJ	15 925 513	10 052 552	63.1	7 878 086	4 936 601	62.7	8 047 427	5 115 951	63.6
1 VII 2001	ESDJ	16 046 180	10 371 945	64.6	7 940 911	5 098 272	64.2	8 105 269	5 273 673	65.1
1 I 2002[96]	CDJC	16 105 285	10 447 684	64.9	7 971 967	5 137 422	64.4	8 133 318	5 310 262	65.3
1 VII 2002	ESDJ	16 148 929	10 482 679	64.9	7 993 719	5 155 143	64.5	8 155 210	5 327 536	65.3
1 VII 2003	ESDJ	16 225 302	10 556 424	65.1	8 030 693	5 191 871	64.7	8 194 610	5 364 553	65.5
1 VII 2004	ESDJ	16 281 779	10 687 028	65.6	8 055 947	5 255 716	65.2	8 225 833	5 431 312	66.0
1 VII 2005	ESDJ	16 319 868	10 764 171	66.0	8 071 693	5 292 532	65.6	8 248 175	5 471 640	66.3
1 VII 2006	ESDJ	16 346 101	10 803 902	66.1	8 082 961	5 311 812	65.7	8 263 141	5 492 090	66.5
1 VII 2007	ESDJ	16 381 696	10 825 307	66.1	8 100 294	5 322 596	65.7	8 281 402	5 502 712	66.4
Norway - Norvège[97]										
1 VII 1998	ESDJ	4 431 464	...	...	2 192 333	...	...	2 239 132	...	...
1 VII 1999	ESDJ	4 461 913	...	...	2 208 350	...	...	2 253 564	...	...
1 VII 2000	ESDJ	4 490 967	...	...	2 224 221	...	...	2 266 746	...	...
1 VII 2001	ESDJ	4 513 751	...	...	2 236 618	...	...	2 277 134	...	...
3 XI 2001[22]	CDJC	4 520 947	3 458 699	76.5	2 240 281	1 694 153	75.6	2 280 666	1 764 546	77.4
1 VII 2002	ESDJ	4 538 159	...	...	2 249 021	...	...	2 289 139	...	...
1 VII 2003	ESDJ	4 564 855	...	...	2 262 578	...	...	2 302 277	...	...
1 VII 2004	ESDJ	4 591 910	...	...	2 276 560	...	...	2 315 351	...	...
1 VII 2005	ESDJ	4 623 291	...	...	2 293 026	...	...	2 330 266	...	...
1 VII 2006	ESDJ	4 660 677	...	...	2 313 885	...	...	2 346 792	...	...
1 VII 2007	ESDJ	4 709 153	...	...	2 342 739	...	...	2 366 414	...	...
Poland - Pologne[98]										
1 VII 1998	ESDF	38 283 000	23 689 000	61.9	18 590 000	11 303 000	60.8	19 693 000	12 386 000	62.9
1 VII 1999	ESDF	38 270 000	23 668 000	61.8	18 566 000	11 281 000	60.8	19 704 000	12 387 000	62.9
1 VII 2000	ESDF	38 255 945	23 691 220	61.9	18 541 844	11 284 476	60.9	19 714 101	12 406 744	62.9
1 VII 2001	ESDF	38 250 790	23 656 606	61.8	18 532 945	11 261 781	60.8	19 717 845	12 394 825	62.9
20 V 2002	CDFC	38 230 080	23 610 365	61.8	18 516 403	11 234 165	60.7	19 713 677	12 376 200	62.8
1 VII 2002	ESDF	38 232 301	23 607 932	61.7	18 517 179	11 232 736	60.7	19 715 122	12 375 196	62.8
1 VII 2003	ESDF	38 195 177	23 543 325	61.6	18 492 950	11 195 269	60.5	19 702 227	12 348 056	62.7
1 VII 2004	ESDF	38 180 249	23 490 202	61.5	18 478 368	11 162 807	60.4	19 701 881	12 327 395	62.6
1 VII 2005	ESDF	38 161 313	23 450 597	61.5	18 460 730	11 135 706	60.3	19 700 583	12 314 891	62.5
1 VII 2006	ESDF	38 132 277	23 400 565	61.4	18 436 101	11 103 869	60.2	19 696 176	12 296 696	62.4
1 VII 2007	ESDF	38 115 967	23 350 920	61.3	18 417 074	11 070 886	60.1	19 698 893	12 280 034	62.3
Portugal										
1 VII 1998	ESDJ	10 129 290	...	...	4 884 189	...	...	5 245 102	...	...
1 VII 1999	ESDJ	10 171 949	...	...	4 906 235	...	...	5 265 714	...	...
1 VII 2000	ESDJ	10 225 836	...	...	4 934 469	...	...	5 291 367	...	...
12 III 2001	CDFC	10 356 117	5 680 711	54.9	5 000 141	2 713 204	54.3	5 355 976	2 967 507	55.4
1 VII 2001	ESDJ	10 292 999	...	...	4 969 817	...	...	5 323 183	...	...

Continent, country or area, and date / Continent, pays ou zone et date	Code[a]	Both sexes - Les deux sexes			Male - Masculin			Female - Féminin		
		Total	Urban - Urbaine		Total	Urban - Urbaine		Total	Urban - Urbaine	
			Number Nombre	Percent P.100		Number Nombre	Percent P.100		Number Nombre	Percent P.100
EUROPE										
Portugal										
1 VII 2002 .... ESDJ		10 368 403	...	...	5 009 592	...	...	5 358 811	...	...
1 VII 2003 .... ESDJ		10 441 075	...	...	5 048 278	...	...	5 392 798	...	...
1 VII 2004 .... ESDJ		10 501 970	...	...	5 080 324	...	...	5 421 647	...	...
1 VII 2005 .... ESDJ		10 549 424	...	...	5 105 041	...	...	5 444 383	...	...
1 VII 2006 .... ESDJ		10 584 344	...	...	5 122 840	...	...	5 461 504	...	...
1 VII 2007 .... ESDJ		10 608 335	...	...	5 134 372	...	...	5 473 963	...	...
Republic of Moldova - République de Moldova[99]										
1 VII 1998 .... ESDJ		3 652 741	1 519 851	41.6	1 748 683	732 340	41.9	1 904 058	787 511	41.4
1 VII 1999 .... ESDJ		3 647 001	1 515 473	41.6	1 745 826	731 531	41.9	1 901 175	783 942	41.2
1 VII 2000 .... ESDJ		3 639 592	1 500 283	41.2	1 742 535	724 447	41.6	1 897 057	775 836	40.9
1 VII 2001 .... ESDJ		3 631 462	1 485 810	40.9	1 739 081	717 661	41.3	1 892 381	768 149	40.6
1 VII 2002 .... ESDJ		3 623 062	1 484 676	41.0	1 735 430	716 822	41.3	1 887 632	767 854	40.7
1 VII 2003 .... ESDJ		3 612 874	1 481 035	41.0	1 730 861	714 970	41.3	1 882 013	766 065	40.7
1 VII 2004* .... ESDJ		3 603 940	1 476 980	41.0	1 726 630	712 971	41.3	1 877 310	764 009	40.7
5 X 2004* .... CDFC		3 388 071	1 308 911	38.6	1 632 519	615 387	37.7	1 755 549	693 521	39.5
1 VII 2005 .... ESDJ		3 595 187	1 472 929	41.0	1 722 105	710 796	41.3	1 873 082	762 133	40.7
1 VII 2006 .... ESDJ		3 585 209	1 481 398	41.3	1 720 139	706 649	41.1	1 865 070	774 749	41.5
1 VII 2007 .... ESDJ		3 576 910	1 477 062	41.3	1 719 246	694 308	40.4	1 857 664	782 754	42.1
Romania - Roumanie										
1 VII 1998 .... ESDJ		22 502 803	12 347 886	54.9	11 012 110	5 971 134	54.2	11 490 693	6 376 752	55.5
1 VII 1999 .... ESDJ		22 458 022	12 302 729	54.8	10 984 529	5 943 708	54.1	11 473 493	6 359 021	55.4
1 VII 2000 .... ESDJ		22 435 205	12 244 598	54.6	10 968 854	5 907 848	53.9	11 466 351	6 336 750	55.3
1 VII 2001 .... ESDJ		22 408 393	12 243 748	54.6	10 949 490	5 903 537	53.9	11 458 903	6 340 211	55.3
18 III 2002 .... CDJC		21 680 974	...	...	10 568 741	...	...	11 112 233	...	...
1 VII 2002 .... ESDJ		21 794 793	11 608 735	53.3	10 642 538	5 579 042	52.4	11 152 255	6 029 693	54.1
1 VII 2003 .... ESDJ		21 733 556	11 600 157	53.4	10 606 245	5 566 401	52.5	11 127 311	6 033 756	54.2
1 VII 2004 .... ESDJ		21 673 328	11 895 598	54.9	10 571 606	5 704 297	54.0	11 101 722	6 191 301	55.8
1 VII 2005 .... ESDJ		21 623 849	11 879 897	54.9	10 543 518	5 692 516	54.0	11 080 331	6 187 381	55.8
1 VII 2006 .... ESDJ		21 584 365	11 913 938	55.2	10 521 189	5 704 872	54.2	11 063 176	6 209 066	56.1
1 VII 2007 .... ESDJ		21 537 563	11 877 659	55.1	10 496 720	5 683 983	54.2	11 040 843	6 193 676	56.1
Russian Federation - Fédération de Russie[100]										
1 VII 1998[101] .... ESDJ		147 670 784	108 082 033	73.2	69 134 739	50 292 483	72.7	78 536 045	57 789 550	73.6
1 VII 1999[101] .... ESDJ		147 214 776	107 736 374	73.2	68 878 518	50 071 789	72.7	78 336 258	57 664 585	73.6
1 VII 2000[101] .... ESDJ		146 596 869	107 245 610	73.2	68 518 623	49 763 462	72.6	78 078 246	57 482 148	73.6
1 VII 2001[101] .... ESDJ		145 976 482	106 898 541	73.2	68 130 474	49 504 491	72.7	77 846 008	57 394 050	73.7
1 VII 2002[101] .... ESDJ		145 306 497	106 523 307	73.3	67 706 316	49 224 967	72.7	77 600 181	57 298 340	73.8
9 X 2002 .... CDJC		145 166 731	106 429 049	73.3	67 605 133	49 149 510	72.7	77 561 598	57 279 539	73.9
1 VII 2003[101] .... ESDJ		144 565 934	106 069 837	73.4	67 257 276	48 917 406	72.7	77 308 658	57 152 431	73.9
1 VII 2004[101] .... ESDJ		143 821 215	105 268 883	73.2	66 813 322	48 452 954	72.5	77 007 893	56 815 929	73.8
1 VII 2005 .... ESDJ		143 113 876	104 412 086	73.0	66 383 146	47 962 554	72.3	76 730 730	56 449 532	73.6
1 VII 2006 .... ESDJ		142 487 259	103 941 621	72.9	66 006 266	47 667 046	72.2	76 480 993	56 274 575	73.6
1 VII 2007 .... ESDJ		142 114 903	103 775 726	73.0	65 783 031	47 538 667	72.3	76 331 872	56 237 059	73.7
San Marino - Saint-Marin[22]										
1 VII 1998 .... ESDF		27 685	...	...	13 557	...	...	14 128	...	...
1 VII 1999 .... ESDF		28 106	...	...	13 733	...	...	14 373	...	...
1 VII 2000 .... CDFC		26 941	22 738	84.4	13 185	11 787	89.4	13 756	10 951	79.6
1 VII 2000 .... ESDF		26 941	22 738	84.4	13 185	11 787	89.4	13 756	10 951	79.6
1 VII 2001 .... ESDF		27 634	...	...	13 548	...	...	14 086	...	...
1 VII 2002 .... ESDF		28 486	...	...	13 946	...	...	14 540	...	...
1 VII 2003 .... ESDF		28 992	...	...	14 207	...	...	14 785	...	...
1 VII 2004 .... ESDF		29 421	...	...	14 422	...	...	14 999	...	...
1 VII 2005 .... ESDF		30 913	...	...	15 058	...	...	15 855	...	...
1 VII 2006 .... ESDF		31 359	...	...	15 309	...	...	16 050	...	...
1 I 2007 .... ESDF		31 614	...	...	15 453	...	...	16 161	...	...
Serbia - Serbie[102]										
1 VII 1998 .... ESDJ		7 567 745	4 206 039	55.6	3 686 518	2 017 237	54.7	3 881 227	2 188 802	56.4
1 VII 1999 .... ESDJ		7 540 401	4 204 900	55.8	3 669 187	2 013 781	54.9	3 871 214	2 191 119	56.6
1 VII 2000 .... ESDJ		7 516 346	4 206 307	56.0	3 655 777	2 012 848	55.1	3 860 569	2 193 459	56.8

Continent, country or area, and date Continent, pays ou zone et date	Code[a]	Both sexes - Les deux sexes			Male - Masculin			Female - Féminin		
		Total	Urban - Urbaine		Total	Urban - Urbaine		Total	Urban - Urbaine	
			Number Nombre	Percent P.100		Number Nombre	Percent P.100		Number Nombre	Percent P.100
EUROPE										
Serbia - Serbie[102]										
1 VII 2001 .... ESDJ		7 503 433	4 206 307	56.1	3 648 533	2 012 848	55.2	3 854 900	2 193 459	56.9
31 III 2002 .... CDJC		7 498 001	...	...	3 645 930	...	...	3 852 071		
1 VII 2002 .... ESDJ		7 500 031	4 241 006	56.5	3 647 190	2 027 187	55.6	3 852 841	2 213 819	57.5
1 VII 2003 .... ESDJ		7 480 591	4 239 980	56.7	3 637 789	2 026 423	55.7	3 842 802	2 213 557	57.6
1 VII 2004 .... ESDJ		7 463 157	4 249 544	56.9	3 629 194	2 030 310	55.9	3 833 963	2 219 234	57.9
1 VII 2005 .... ESDJ		7 440 769	4 257 880	57.2	3 618 040	2 033 179	56.2	3 822 729	2 224 701	58.2
1 VII 2006 .... ESDJ		7 411 569	4 263 386	57.5	3 603 698	2 034 616	56.5	3 807 871	2 228 770	58.5
1 VII 2007 .... ESDJ		7 381 579	4 270 400	57.9	3 588 957	2 037 012	56.8	3 792 622	2 233 388	58.9
Slovakia - Slovaquie										
1 VII 1998 .... ESDJ		5 390 866	3 066 457	56.9	...	...	...	...	...	...
1 VII 1999 .... ESDJ		5 395 324	3 061 062	56.7	...	...	...	...	...	...
1 VII 2000 .... ESDJ		5 400 679	3 059 010	56.6	...	...	...	...	...	...
25 V 2001 .... CDJC		5 379 455	3 022 106	56.2	2 612 515	1 453 638	55.6	2 766 940	1 568 468	56.7
1 VII 2001 .... ESDJ		5 379 780	3 017 527	56.1	...	...	...	...	...	...
1 VII 2002 .... ESDJ		5 378 809	3 011 737	56.0	2 611 452	1 447 959	55.4	2 767 357	1 563 778	56.5
1 VII 2003 .... ESDJ		5 378 950	3 001 776	55.8	2 610 872	1 442 174	55.2	2 768 078	1 559 602	56.3
1 VII 2004 .... ESDJ		5 382 574	2 994 284	55.6	2 612 313	1 438 019	55.0	2 770 261	1 556 265	56.2
1 VII 2005 .... ESDJ		5 387 285	2 989 291	55.5	2 614 912	1 435 469	54.9	2 772 373	1 553 822	56.0
1 VII 2006 .... ESDJ		5 391 184	2 989 769	55.5	2 616 924	1 435 472	54.9	2 774 260	1 554 297	56.0
1 VII 2007 .... ESDJ		5 397 766	2 985 680	55.3	2 621 095	1 433 808	54.7	2 776 671	1 551 872	55.9
Slovenia - Slovénie										
1 VII 1998 .... ESDJ		1 982 603	...	...	966 513	...	...	1 016 090	...	...
1 VII 1999 .... ESDJ		1 985 557	...	...	968 463	...	...	1 017 094	...	...
1 VII 2000 .... ESDJ		1 990 272	...	...	972 581	...	...	1 017 691	...	...
1 VII 2001 .... ESDJ		1 992 035	...	...	973 711	...	...	1 018 324		
31 III 2002 .... CDJC		1 964 036	997 772[103]	50.8	958 576	479 356[103]	50.0	1 005 460	518 416[103]	51.6
1 VII 2002 .... ESDJ		1 995 718	975 163[103]	48.9	976 111[103]	462 513[103]	47.4	1 019 607[103]	512 650[103]	50.3
1 VII 2003 .... ESDJ		1 996 773	971 513[103]	48.7	977 436[103]	460 811[103]	47.1	1 019 337[103]	510 702[103]	50.1
1 VII 2004 .... ESDJ		1 997 004	968 989[103]	48.5	977 092[103]	459 504[103]	47.0	1 019 912[103]	509 485[103]	50.0
1 VII 2005 .... ESDJ		2 001 114	965 538[103]	48.3	980 070[103]	457 869[103]	46.7	1 021 044[103]	507 669[103]	49.7
1 VII 2006 .... ESDJ		2 008 516	962 740[103]	47.9	985 876[103]	456 764[103]	46.3	1 022 640[103]	505 976[103]	49.5
1 VII 2007 .... ESDJ		2 019 406	1 006 767	49.9	995 125	490 610	49.3	1 024 281	516 157	50.4
Spain - Espagne										
1 VII 1998 .... ESDJ		39 722 075	...	...	19 448 294	...	...	20 273 781	...	...
1 VII 1999 .... ESDJ		39 927 224	...	...	19 547 393	...	...	20 379 831	...	...
1 VII 2000 .... ESDJ		40 264 162	...	...	19 719 334[3]	...	...	20 544 828[3]	...	...
1 VII 2001 .... ESDJ		40 721 447	...	...	19 956 780[3]	...	...	20 764 667[3]	...	...
1 XI 2001 .... CDFC		40 847 371	...	...	20 012 882	...	...	20 834 489	...	...
1 VII 2002 .... ESDJ		41 314 019	...	...	20 266 005	...	...	21 048 014	...	...
1 VII 2003 .... ESDJ		42 004 575	...	...	20 626 192	...	...	21 378 383	...	...
1 VII 2004 .... ESDJ		42 691 751	...	...	20 987 670	...	...	21 704 081	...	...
1 VII 2005 .... ESDJ		43 398 190	...	...	21 367 297	...	...	22 030 893	...	...
1 VII 2006 .... ESDJ		44 068 244	...	...	21 725 232	...	...	22 343 012	...	...
1 VII 2007 .... ESDJ		44 873 567	...	...	22 155 286	...	...	22 718 281	...	...
Sweden - Suède[22]										
1 VII 1998 .... ESDJ		8 850 974	...	...	4 373 766	...	...	4 477 208	...	...
1 VII 1999 .... ESDJ		8 857 874	...	...	4 377 869	...	...	4 480 006	...	...
1 VII 2000 .... ESDJ		8 872 110	...	...	4 386 436	...	...	4 485 674	...	...
1 VII 2001 .... ESDJ		8 895 960	...	...	4 400 599	...	...	4 495 361	...	...
1 VII 2002 .... ESDJ		8 924 958	...	...	4 417 776	...	...	4 507 182	...	...
1 VII 2003 .... ESDJ		8 958 229	...	...	4 436 882	...	...	4 521 348	...	...
31 XII 2003 .... CDJC		8 975 670	...	...	4 446 656	...	...	4 529 014	...	...
1 VII 2004 .... ESDJ		8 993 531	...	...	4 456 484	...	...	4 537 048	...	...
1 VII 2005 .... ESDJ		9 029 572	...	...	4 476 431	...	...	4 553 142	...	...
1 VII 2006 .... ESDJ		9 080 505	...	...	4 505 037	...	...	4 575 468	...	...
1 VII 2007 .... ESDJ		9 148 092	...	...	4 543 722	...	...	4 604 370	...	...
Switzerland - Suisse										
1 VII 1998 .... ESDJ		7 110 002	5 177 539	72.8	3 471 966	2 507 740	72.2	3 638 036	2 669 799	73.4
1 VII 1999 .... ESDJ		7 143 991	5 205 470	72.9	3 489 699	2 522 742	72.3	3 654 292	2 682 728	73.4
1 VII 2000 .... ESDJ		7 184 250	5 241 276	73.0	3 510 203	2 541 235	72.4	3 674 047	2 700 041	73.5
5 XII 2000 .... CDJC		7 204 055	4 871 989	67.6	3 519 698	2 357 890	67.0	3 684 357	2 514 099	68.2
1 VII 2001 .... ESDJ		7 226 647	5 279 814	73.1	3 529 342	2 559 297	72.5	3 697 305	2 720 517	73.6
1 VII 2002 .... ESDJ		7 284 754	5 329 197	73.2	3 559 690	2 585 292	72.6	3 725 064	2 743 905	73.7

6. Total and urban population by sex: 1998 - 2007
Population totale et population urbaine selon le sexe: 1998 - 2007 (continued - suite)

Continent, country or area, and date / Continent, pays ou zone et date	Code[a]	Both sexes - Les deux sexes			Male - Masculin			Female - Féminin		
		Total	Urban - Urbaine		Total	Urban - Urbaine		Total	Urban - Urbaine	
			Number Nombre	Percent P.100		Number Nombre	Percent P.100		Number Nombre	Percent P.100
EUROPE										
Switzerland - Suisse										
1 VII 2003 ....ESDJ		7 339 002	5 372 785	73.2	3 588 285	2 608 318	72.7	3 750 717	2 764 467	73.7
1 VII 2004 ....ESDJ		7 389 626	5 412 574	73.2	3 615 118	2 629 384	72.7	3 774 508	2 783 190	73.7
1 VII 2005 ....ESDJ		7 437 116	5 450 033	73.3	3 640 600	2 649 755	72.8	3 796 516	2 800 278	73.8
1 VII 2006 ....ESDJ		7 483 935	5 487 270	73.3	3 665 931	2 670 092	72.8	3 818 004	2 817 178	73.8
1 VII 2007 ....ESDJ		7 551 117	5 541 513	73.4	3 703 187	2 700 079	72.9	3 847 930	2 841 434	73.8
The Former Yugoslav Republic of Macedonia - L'ex-République yougoslave de Macédoine										
1 VII 1998 ....ESDF		2 007 523	...	...	1 004 771	...	...	1 002 752	...	...
1 VII 1999 ....ESDF		2 017 142	...	...	1 009 369	...	...	1 007 773	...	...
1 VII 2001 ....ESDF		2 034 882	...	...	1 017 927	...	...	1 016 955	...	...
1 VII 2002 ....ESDF		2 031 153	...	...	1 019 616	...	...	1 019 035	...	...
1 XI 2002 ....CDJC		2 022 547	...	...	1 015 377	...	...	1 007 170	...	...
1 VII 2003 ....ESDF		2 026 773	...	...	1 017 274	...	...	1 009 499	...	...
1 VII 2004 ....ESDF		2 032 544	...	...	1 019 903	...	...	1 012 641	...	...
1 VII 2005 ....ESDF		2 036 855	...	...	1 021 772	...	...	1 015 083	...	...
1 VII 2006 ....ESDF		2 040 228	...	...	1 023 069	...	...	1 017 159	...	...
1 VII 2007 ....ESDF		2 043 559	...	...	1 024 489	...	...	1 019 070	...	...
Ukraine										
1 I 1998 ....ESDF		50 370 800	34 048 200	67.6	23 341 968	15 868 721	68.0	26 903 240	18 112 429	67.3
1 I 1999 ....ESDF		49 918 100	33 702 100	67.5	23 164 347	15 738 141	67.9	26 686 579	17 988 760	67.4
1 I 2000 ....ESDF		49 429 800	33 338 600	67.4	22 978 364	15 617 268	68.0	26 477 724	17 888 594	67.6
1 I 2001 ....ESDF		48 923 200	32 951 700	67.4	22 775 737	...	...	26 260 782	...	...
5 XII 2001 ....CDFC		48 240 902	32 290 729	66.9	22 316 317	14 903 592	66.8	25 924 585	17 387 137	67.1
1 I 2002 ....ESDF		48 457 102	32 574 371	67.2	22 441 344	15 056 675	67.1	26 015 758	17 517 696	67.3
1 I 2003 ....ESDF		48 003 463	32 328 351	67.3	22 218 508	14 921 144	67.2	25 784 955	17 407 207	67.5
1 I 2004 ....ESDF		47 622 434	32 146 466	67.5	22 032 783	14 819 651	67.3	25 589 651	17 326 815	67.7
1 I 2005 ....ESDF		47 280 817	32 009 320	67.7	21 859 967	14 738 206	67.4	25 420 850	17 271 114	67.9
1 I 2006 ....ESDF		46 929 525	31 877 710	67.9	21 680 641	14 657 938	67.6	25 248 884	17 219 772	68.2
1 I 2007 ....ESDF		46 646 046	31 777 367	68.1	21 540 654	14 599 052	67.8	25 105 392	17 178 315	68.4
United Kingdom of Great Britain and Northern Ireland - Royaume-Uni de Grande-Bretagne et d'Irlande du Nord[104]										
1 VII 1998[105] ....ESDF		58 474 943	...	...	28 458 360	...	...	30 016 583	...	...
1 VII 1999[105] ....ESDF		58 684 427	...	...	28 578 474	...	...	30 105 953	...	...
1 VII 2000[105] ....ESDF		58 886 065	...	...	28 690 450	...	...	30 195 615	...	...
29 IV 2001 ....CDFC		58 789 187	47 007 427	80.0	28 579 867	22 769 606	79.7	30 209 320	24 237 821	80.2
1 VII 2001[105] ....ESDF		59 113 497	...	...	28 832 420	...	...	30 281 077	...	...
1 VII 2002[105] ....ESDF		59 323 498	...	...	28 964 375	...	...	30 359 123	...	...
1 VII 2003 ....ESDF		59 557 337	...	...	29 108 774	...	...	30 448 563	...	...
1 VII 2004 ....ESDF		59 845 842	...	...	29 277 960	...	...	30 567 882	...	...
1 VII 2005 ....ESDF		60 238 383	...	...	29 497 036	...	...	30 741 347	...	...
1 VII 2006 ....ESDF		60 587 349	...	...	29 693 967	...	...	30 893 382	...	...
1 VII 2007 ....ESDF		60 975 355	...	...	29 916 107	...	...	31 059 248	...	...
OCEANIA - OCÉANIE										
American Samoa - Samoas américaines[24]										
1 IV 2000 ....CDJC		57 291	...	...	29 264	...	...	28 027	...	...
Australia - Australie										
1 VII 1998[14] ....ESDJ		18 711 271	...	...	9 294 674	...	...	9 416 597	...	...
1 VII 1999[14] ....ESDJ		18 925 855	...	...	9 396 548	...	...	9 529 307	...	...
1 VII 2000[14] ....ESDJ		19 153 380	...	...	9 505 331	...	...	9 648 049	...	...
1 VII 2001[14] ....ESDJ		19 413 240	15 741 902	81.1	9 630 652	7 762 855	80.6	9 782 588	7 979 047	81.6
7 VIII 2001[14] ....CDJC		18 769 249	16 344 412	87.1	9 270 466	8 003 865	86.3	9 498 783	8 340 547	87.8
1 VII 2002[14] ....ESDJ		19 651 438	15 958 923	81.2	9 753 065	7 874 721	80.7	9 898 373	8 084 202	81.7
1 VII 2003[14] ....ESDJ		19 895 435	16 183 448	81.3	9 874 412	7 987 391	80.9	10 021 023	8 196 057	81.8

Continent, country or area, and date / Continent, pays ou zone et date	Code[a]	Both sexes - Les deux sexes Total	Urban - Urbaine Number Nombre	Urban - Urbaine Percent P.100	Male - Masculin Total	Urban - Urbaine Number Nombre	Urban - Urbaine Percent P.100	Female - Féminin Total	Urban - Urbaine Number Nombre	Urban - Urbaine Percent P.100
OCEANIA - OCÉANIE										
Australia - Australie										
1 VII 2004[14]	ESDJ	20 127 363	16 395 358	81.5	9 992 728	8 096 009	81.0	10 134 635	8 299 349	81.9
1 VII 2005[14]	ESDJ	20 394 791	16 626 325	81.5	10 128 064	8 213 288	81.1	10 266 727	8 413 037	81.9
1 VII 2006[14]	ESDJ	20 697 880	16 890 471	81.6	10 282 433	8 348 198	81.2	10 415 447	8 542 273	82.0
8 VIII 2006	CDFC	20 061 646	...	...	9 896 500	...	...	10 165 146	...	...
1 VII 2007[14]	ESDJ	21 072 452	17 219 832	81.7	10 475 527	8 518 406	81.3	10 596 925	8 701 426	82.1
Cook Islands - Îles Cook[106]										
1 XII 2001	CDFC	18 027	...	...	9 303	...	...	8 724	...	...
1 XII 2006*	CDFC	19 569	...	...	9 932	...	...	9 637	...	...
Fiji - Fidji										
16 IX 2007	CDFC	837 271	424 846	50.7	427 176	212 454	49.7	410 095	212 392	51.8
French Polynesia - Polynésie française										
1 I 1998	ESDF	224 332	...	...	116 225	...	...	108 107	...	...
1 I 1999	ESDF	227 525	...	...	117 738	...	...	109 787	...	...
Guam[24]										
1 VII 1998	ESDJ	149 724	57 124	38.2	...	...	...	...	...	...
1 VII 1999	ESDJ	152 590	58 217	38.2	...	...	...	...	...	...
1 IV 2000	CDJC	154 805	144 129[25]	93.1	79 181	...	...	75 624	...	...
1 VII 2001	ESDJ	158 330	147 411[25]	93.1	...	...	...	...	...	...
1 VII 2002	ESDJ	161 057	149 950[25]	93.1	...	...	...	...	...	...
1 VII 2003	ESDJ	166 593	152 311[25]	91.4	...	...	...	...	...	...
1 VII 2004	ESDJ	166 090	154 636[25]	93.1	...	...	...	...	...	...
Kiribati										
7 XI 2000*	CDFC	84 494	36 717	43.5	41 646	17 822	42.8	42 848	18 895	44.1
7 XII 2005	CDFC	92 533	40 311	43.6	45 612	19 435	42.6	46 921	20 876	44.5
Marshall Islands - Îles Marshall										
1 VII 1998	ESDF	63 301	...	...	32 235	...	...	31 066	...	...
1 VI 1999	CDFC	50 848	...	...	26 034	...	...	24 814	...	...
1 VII 1999	ESDF	50 840	...	...	26 026	...	...	24 814	...	...
1 VII 2000	ESDF	52 671	...	...	26 976	...	...	25 695	...	...
1 VII 2001	ESDF	54 584	...	...	27 960	...	...	26 624	...	...
1 VII 2004	ESDF	55 366	...	...	28 232	...	...	27 134	...	...
1 VII 2006	ESDF	52 163	...	...	26 746	...	...	25 417	...	...
1 VII 2007	ESDF	52 701	...	...	27 022	...	...	25 679	...	...
Micronesia (Federated States of) - Micronésie (États fédérés de)										
1 IV 2000	CDJC	107 008	...	...	54 191	...	...	52 817	...	...
Nauru										
23 IX 2002	CDFC	10 065	...	...	5 136	...	...	4 929	...	...
New Caledonia - Nouvelle-Calédonie										
1 VII 1998	ESDF	204 316	...	...	104 413	...	...	99 939	...	...
1 VII 1999	ESDF	207 612	...	...	105 996	...	...	101 662	...	...
1 I 2000	ESDF	211 200	...	...	107 769	...	...	103 431	...	...
1 I 2001	ESDF	215 260	...	...	109 580	...	...	105 680	...	...
1 I 2002	ESDF	219 387	...	...	111 465	...	...	107 922	...	...
1 I 2003	ESDF	223 592	...	...	113 320	...	...	110 272	...	...
1 VII 2004	ESDF	230 068	133 815	58.2	112 716	...	...	109 242	...	...
31 VIII 2004*	CDFC	230 789	...	...	116 485	...	...	114 304	...	...
1 I 2005	ESDF	232 258	...	...	117 221	...	...	115 037	...	...
1 I 2006	ESDF	236 528	...	...	119 415	...	...	117 113	...	...
1 VII 2007	ESDF	242 400	...	...	122 261	...	...	120 139	...	...
New Zealand - Nouvelle-Zélande										
1 VII 1998	ESDJ	3 815 000	3 269 700	85.7	1 877 800	...	...	1 937 200	...	...
1 VII 1999	ESDJ	3 835 100	3 289 300	85.8	1 884 900	...	...	1 950 200	...	...
1 VII 2000	ESDJ	3 857 800	3 310 100	85.8	1 893 800	...	...	1 964 000	...	...
6 III 2001	CDJC	3 820 749	...	...	1 863 309	...	...	1 957 440	...	...
1 VII 2001	ESDJ	3 880 500	3 331 400	85.8	1 903 200	...	...	1 977 300	...	...
1 VII 2002	ESDJ	3 948 500	3 393 200[9]	85.9	1 936 500[9]	1 649 500[9]	85.2	2 012 000[9]	1 743 700[9]	86.7

Continent, country or area, and date / Continent, pays ou zone et date	Code[a]	Both sexes - Les deux sexes Total	Urban - Urbaine Number Nombre	Urban - Urbaine Percent P.100	Male - Masculin Total	Urban - Urbaine Number Nombre	Urban - Urbaine Percent P.100	Female - Féminin Total	Urban - Urbaine Number Nombre	Urban - Urbaine Percent P.100
OCEANIA - OCÉANIE										
New Zealand - Nouvelle-Zélande										
1 VII 2003 ....ESDJ		4 027 200	3 464 600[9]	86.0	1 975 600[9]	1 685 300[9]	85.3	2 051 700[9]	1 779 300[9]	86.7
1 VII 2004 ....ESDJ		4 087 500	3 518 800[9]	86.1	2 003 800[9]	1 710 800[9]	85.4	2 083 800[9]	1 808 000[9]	86.8
1 VII 2005 ....ESDJ		4 133 900	3 559 400[9]	86.1	2 025 200[9]	1 729 600[9]	85.4	2 108 700[9]	1 829 800[9]	86.8
7 III 2006 ....CDFC		4 143 282	...	...	2 021 277	...	...	2 122 005	...	...
1 VII 2006 ....ESDJ		4 184 600	3 603 600[9]	86.1	2 048 300[9]	1 749 800[9]	85.4	2 136 200[9]	1 853 800[9]	86.8
1 VII 2007 ....ESDJ		4 228 300	3 642 600[9]	86.1	2 070 800[9]	1 770 000[9]	85.5	2 157 600[9]	1 872 600[9]	86.8
Niue - Nioué										
7 IX 2001 ....CDFC		1 788	...	...	897	...	...	891		
1 VII 2004 ....ESDJ		1 761	...	...	866	...	...	895		
1 VII 2005 ....ESDJ		1 746	...	...	849	...	...	896		
1 VII 2006 ....ESDJ		1 679	...	...	815	...	...	864		
9 IX 2006 ....CDFC		1 625	...	...	802	...	...	823		
Norfolk Island - Île Norfolk										
7 VIII 2001 ....CDFC		2 037	...	...	1 017	...	...	1 020	...	...
8 VIII 2006 ....CDFC		2 523	...	...	1 218	...	...	1 305	...	...
Northern Mariana Islands - Îles Mariannes septentrionales										
1 VII 1998 ....ESDF		*66 559*	...	...	*32 475*	...	...	*34 084*	...	...
1 VII 1999 ....ESDF		*69 341*	...	...	*33 636*	...	...	*35 705*	...	...
1 IV 2000 ....CDFC		69 221	...	...	31 984	...	...	37 237	...	...
1 VII 2000 ....ESDF		*69 706*	...	...	*32 090*	...	...	*37 616*	...	...
1 VII 2001 ....ESDF		*71 868*	...	...	*32 669*	...	...	*39 199*	...	...
1 VII 2002 ....ESDF		*74 003*	...	...	*33 256*	...	...	*40 747*	...	...
1 VII 2003 ....ESDF		*76 129*	...	...	*33 852*	...	...	*42 277*	...	...
1 VII 2004 ....ESDF		*78 252*	...	...	*34 468*	...	...	*43 784*	...	...
1 VII 2005 ....ESDF		*80 362*	...	...	*35 099*	...	...	*45 263*	...	...
1 VII 2006 ....ESDF		*82 459*	...	...	*35 744*	...	...	*46 715*	...	...
1 VII 2007 ....ESDF		*84 546*	...	...	*36 405*	...	...	*48 141*	...	...
Palau - Palaos										
1 VII 1998 ....ESDF		18 494	...	...	9 842	...	...	8 652		
1 VII 1999 ....ESDF		18 882	...	...	10 039	...	...	8 843		
15 IV 2000 ....CDFC		19 129	13 303	69.5	10 450	...	...	8 679		
1 VII 2000 ....ESDF		19 257	...	...	10 229	...	...	9 028		
1 VII 2001 ....ESDF		19 626	...	...	10 415	...	...	9 211		
1 VII 2002 ....ESDF		19 976	...	...	10 590	...	...	9 386		
1 IV 2005 ....CDJC		19 907	15 399	77.4	10 699	...	...	9 208	...	...
Papua New Guinea - Papouasie-Nouvelle-Guinée										
9 VII 2000 ....CDFC		5 190 786	686 301	13.2	2 691 744	372 453	13.8	2 499 042	313 848	12.6
1 VII 2002 ....ESDF		*5 461 940*	...	...	*2 826 212*	...	...	*2 635 722*	...	...
Pitcairn										
31 XII 2007 ....ESDF		64	...	...	37	...	...	27	...	...
Samoa										
5 XI 2001 ....CDFC		176 710	38 836	22.0	92 050	19 837	21.6	84 660	18 999	22.4
1 VII 2002 ....ESDF		*178 329*	*39 192*	22.0	*92 893*	*20 019*	21.6	*85 436*	*19 173*	22.4
1 VII 2003 ....ESDF		*179 962*	*39 551*	22.0	*93 744*	*20 202*	21.6	*86 218*	*19 349*	22.4
1 VII 2004 ....ESDF		*181 611*	*39 913*	22.0	*94 603*	*20 387*	21.6	*87 008*	*19 526*	22.4
1 VII 2005 ....ESDF		*183 275*	*40 279*	22.0	*95 470*	*20 574*	21.6	*87 805*	*19 705*	22.4
1 VII 2006 ....ESDF		*184 955*	*40 648*	22.0	*96 345*	*20 763*	21.6	*88 610*	*19 885*	22.4
5 XI 2006* ....CDFC		179 186	...	...	92 961	...	...	86 225	...	...
1 VII 2007 ....ESDF		*186 649*	...	...	*97 227*	...	...	*89 422*	...	...
Solomon Islands - Îles Salomon										
21 XI 1999 ....CDFC		409 042	...	...	211 381	...	...	197 661	...	...
1 VII 2003 ....ESDF		*448 286*	...	...	*231 267*	...	...	*217 019*	...	...
1 VII 2004 ....ESDF		*460 110*	...	...	*237 626*	...	...	*222 484*	...	...
1 VII 2005 ....ESDF		*471 266*	...	...	*242 927*	...	...	*228 339*	...	...
1 VII 2006 ....ESDF		*483 083*	...	...	*248 944*	...	...	*234 139*	...	...
1 VII 2007 ....ESDF		*495 026*	...	...	*255 063*	...	...	*239 963*	...	...

Continent, country or area, and date Continent, pays ou zone et date	Code[a]	Both sexes - Les deux sexes			Male - Masculin			Female - Féminin		
		Total	Urban - Urbaine		Total	Urban - Urbaine		Total	Urban - Urbaine	
			Number Nombre	Percent P.100		Number Nombre	Percent P.100		Number Nombre	Percent P.100
OCEANIA - OCÉANIE										
Tokelau - Tokélaou										
11 X 2001 . . . . CDFC		1 537	...	...	761	...	...	776	...	...
19 X 2006 . . . . CDFC		1 151	...	...	583	...	...	568	...	...
Tonga										
1 VII 1998[107] . . . . ESDF		*99 264*	...	...	*50 406*	...	...	*48 856*	...	...
1 VII 1999[107] . . . . ESDF		*99 821*	...	...	*50 731*	...	...	*49 088*	...	...
1 VII 2000[107] . . . . ESDF		*100 283*	...	...	*51 017*	...	...	*49 264*	...	...
1 VII 2001[107] . . . . ESDF		*100 673*	...	...	*51 272*	...	...	*49 400*	...	...
1 VII 2002[107] . . . . ESDF		*101 002*	...	...	*51 473*	...	...	*49 528*	...	...
1 VII 2003[107] . . . . ESDF		*101 405*	...	...	*51 710*	...	...	*49 694*	...	...
1 VII 2004[108] . . . . ESDF		*101 866*	...	...	*51 975*	...	...	*49 890*	...	...
1 VII 2005[108] . . . . ESDF		*102 371*	...	...	*52 261*	...	...	*50 109*	...	...
1 VII 2006[108] . . . . ESDF		*102 907*	...	...	*52 561*	...	...	*50 346*	...	...
30 XI 2006 . . . . CDFC		101 991	23 658	23.2	51 772	11 860	22.9	50 219	11 798	23.5
1 VII 2007[108] . . . . ESDF		*103 289*	...	...	*52 771*	...	...	*50 518*	...	...
Tuvalu										
1 XI 2002 . . . . CDFC		9 561	...	...	4 729	2 281	48.2	4 832	2 211	45.8
Vanuatu										
16 XI 1999 . . . . CDJC		186 678	40 094	21.5	95 682	20 726	21.7	90 996	19 368	21.3
1 VII 2004[1] . . . . ESDF		*215 541*	...	...	*110 441*[109]	...	...	*105 399*[109]	...	...
1 VII 2006[1] . . . . ESDF		*221 417*	...	...	*113 034*	...	...	*108 383*	...	...
Wallis and Futuna Islands - Îles Wallis et Futuna										
22 VII 2003 . . . . CDFC		14 944	...	...	7 494	...	...	7 450	...	...

FOOTNOTES - NOTES

Italics: estimates which are less reliable. - Italiques: estimations moins sûres.

* Provisional. - Données provisoires.

[a] 'Code' indicates the source of data, as follows:
CDFC - Census, de facto, complete tabulation
CDFS - Census, de facto, sample tabulation
CDJC - Census, de jure, complete tabulation
CDJS - Census, de jure, sample tabulation
SSDF - Sample survey, de facto
SSDJ - Sample survey, de jure
ESDF - Estimates, de facto
ESDJ - Estimates, de jure

Le 'Code' indique la source des données, comme suit:
CDFC - Recensement, population de fait, tabulation complète
CDFS - Recensement, population de fait, tabulation par sondage
CDJC - Recensement, population de droit, tabulation complète
CDJS - Recensement, population de droit, tabulation par sondage
SSDF - Enquête par sondage, population de fait
SSDJ - Enquête par sondage, population de droit
ESDF - Données estimées, population de fait
ESDJ - Données estimées, population de droit

[1] Data refer to national projections. - Les données se réfèrent aux projections nationales.
[2] Series not strictly comparable due to differences of definitions of "urban". - Les séries ne sont pas strictement comparables en raison de différences existant dans la définition des "regions urbaines".
[3] Unrevised data. - Les données n'ont pas été révisées.
[4] Excluding Mayotte. - Non compris Mayotte.
[5] Excluding border population. - À l'exception de la population frontalière.
[6] Total includes the estimated population of eight rural kebeles (21,410) in Elidar wereda (Affar Region). - Le total comprend l'effectif estimé de la population de huit kebele ruraux (21 410 habitants) du woreda d'Elidar (région Afar).

[7] Based on the results of the Gabonese Survey for the Evaluation and Tracking of Poverty. - Sur base des résultats de l'enquête gabonaise sur l'évaluation et le suivi de la pauvreté.
[8] Data refer to Libyan nationals only. - Les données se raportent aux nationaux libyens seulement.
[9] Because of rounding, totals are not in all cases the sum of the parts. - Les chiffres étant arrondis, les totaux ne correspondent pas toujours rigoureusement à la somme des chiffres partiels.
[10] Including residents outside the country. - Y compris les résidents hors du pays.
[11] The number of males and/or females excludes persons whose sex is not stated (18 urban, 19 rural). - Il n'est pas tenu compte dans le nombre d'hommes et de femmes des personnes dont le sexe n'est pas indiqué (18 en zone urbaine et 19 en zone rurale).
[12] Data have not been adjusted for underenumeration, estimated at 2.4 per cent. - Les données n'ont pas été ajustées pour compenser les lacunes du dénombrement, estimées à 2,4 p. 100.
[13] Based on the results of a Socio Economic Survey. - Basé sur les résultats d'une enquête Socio-Economique.
[14] Mid-year estimates have been adjusted for underenumeration, at latest census. - Les estimations au millieu de l'année tiennent compte d'un ajustement destiné à compenser les lacunes du dénombrement lors du dernier recensement.
[15] Excluding the institutional population. - Non compris la population dans les institutions.
[16] Final intercensal estimates. - Estimations inter censitaires definitives.
[17] Data have not been adjusted for underenumeration. - Les données n'ont pas été ajustées pour compenser les lacunes du dénombrement.
[18] Final postcensal estimates. - Estimations postcensitaires definitives.
[19] Updated postcensal estimates. - Estimations post censitaires mises à jour.
[20] Preliminary postcensal estimates. - Estimations postcensitaires préliminaires.
[21] Excluding 390 residents of institutions. - À l'exclusion de 390 personnes en établissements de soins.
[22] Population statistics are compiled from registers. - Les statistiques de la population sont compilées à partir des registres.

23 Data for urban and rural do not add up to the total; reason for discrepancy not ascertained. - La somme des données pour la résidence urbaine et rurale n'est pas égale au total; on ne sait pas comment s'explique la divergence.

24 Including armed forces stationed in the area. - Y compris les militaires en garnison sur le territoire.

25 Definition of urban and rural distribution changed from the year 2000. - La définition des régions urbaines et rurales a changée depuis 2000.

26 Based on the results of the population census. - D'après le résultats du recensement de la population.

27 Excluding armed forces overseas and civilian citizens absent from country for an extended period of time. - Non compris les militaires à l'étranger, et les civils hors du pays pendant une période prolongée.

28 Data include persons in remote areas, military personnel outside the country, merchant seamen at sea, civilian seasonal workers outside the country, and other civilians outside the country, and exclude nomads, foreign military, civilian aliens temporarily in the country, transients on ships and Indian jungle population. - Y compris les personnes vivant dans des régions éloignées, le personel militaire en dehors du pays, les marins marchands, les ouvriers saisonniers en dehors du pays, et autres civils en dehors du pays, et non compris les nomades, les militaires étrangers, les étrangers civils temporairement dans le pays, les transiteurs sur des bateaux et les Indiens de la jungle.

29 Data have been adjusted on the basis of the Population Census of 2005. - Données ajustées sur la base du recensement de la population de 2005.

30 Excluding nomadic Indian tribes. - Non compris les tribus d'Indiens nomades.

31 A dispute exists between the governments of Argentina and the United Kingdom of Great Britain and Northern Ireland concerning sovereignty over the Falkland Islands (Malvinas). - La souveraineté sur les îles Falkland (Malvinas) fait l'objet d'un différend entre le Gouvernement argentin et le Gouvernement du Royaume-Uni de Grande-Bretagne et d'Irlande du Nord.

32 The population for the year 2005 corresponds to the population actually enumerated in the census conducted between 18 July and 20 August 2005. The total (adjusted) population is 27 219 264 inhabitants. - La population pour 2005 correspond à la population effectivement dénombrée lors du recensement réalisé entre le 18 juillet et le 20 août 2005. La population totale (après ajustement) compte 27 219 264 habitants.

33 Including 17 diplomats. - La population totale indiquée comprend 17 diplomates.

34 The previous census was conducted only 16 months earlier (on 31 Mar 2003) but it was repeated because all of its data were destroyed in a fire before they could be fully processed, analyzed, and reported. - Le recensement précédent a eu lieu seulement 16 mois auparavant (le 31 mars 2003), mais a dû être refait parce que toutes les données ont été détruites dans un incendie avant que l'on n'ait pu les traiter et les analyser.

35 Figures for male and female population do not add up to the figure for total population, because they exclude 365 persons of unknown sex. - Les chiffres relatifs à la population masculine et féminine ne correspondent pas au chiffre de la population totale, parce que l'on en a exclu 365 personnes de sexe inconnu.

36 Data refer to resident population in Uruguay according to Census Phase 1, carried out between the months of June and July 2004. - Les données se rapportent à la population résidente en Uruguay d'après la phase 1 du recensement, qui a eu lieu entre juin et juillet 2004.

37 Excluding Indian jungle population. - Non compris les Indiens de la jungle.

38 For urban/rural distribution, data refer to the settled population based on the 1979 Population Census; an estimated 1.5 million nomads are not included. Unrevised data. - Pour la distribution urbaine/rurale, les données se rapportent à la population sédentaire sur la base du recensement de 1979; les nomades, estimées à 1.5 million, ne sont pas inclus. Les données n'ont pas été révisées.

39 Data refer to the settled population based on the 1979 Population Census and the latest household prelisting. The refugees of Afghanistan in Iran, Pakistan and estimated 1.5 million nomads are not included. The so adjusted total population of the country for 2006 is 24.1 million of which 12.3 million males and 11.8 million females. - Les données se rapportent à la population stationnaire sur la base du recensement de 1979 et du recensement préliminaire des logements le plus récent. Sont exclus les réfugiés d'Afghanistan en Iran et au Pakistan et les nomades estimés à 1,5 million. La population totale du pays ainsi ajustée pour 2006 comprend 24,1 millions de personnes (12,3 millions d'hommes et 11,8 millions de femmes).

40 The methodology used for calculating the number of the de facto and de jure population in the 2001 census data differs as follows from the methodology used in previous censuses: the duration that defines a person as being ' temporary present ' or 'temporary absent' is now 'under one year'. The previously applied definition was for '6 months'. - La méthode utilisée pour dénombrer la population de fait et la population de droit dans le contexte du recensement de 2001 diffère de celle qui a été appliquée lors du recensements antérieurs en ce que la durée considérée pour définir la ' présence temporaire 'ou' l'absence temporaire' était dorénavant fixée à 'moins d'un an' alors qu'elle était de '6 mois' auparavant.

41 Excluding usual residents not in country at time of census (Total 4053, Male 2238, Female 1815). - À l'exclusion des résidents habituels qui n'étaient pas dans le pays au moment du recensement (au total 4 053 personnes dont 2 238 hommes et 1 815 femmes).

42 Data have been adjusted for underenumeration, estimated at 4.96 per cent. - Les données ont été ajustées pour compenser les lacunes du dénombrement, estimées à 4,96 p.100.

43 Data refer to projections based on the 2005 population census. - Les données se réfèrent aux projections basées sur le recensement de la population de 2005.

44 Excluding foreign diplomatic personnel and their dependants. - Non compris le personnel diplomatique étranger et les membres de leur famille les accompagnant.

45 Based on the results of the Cambodia Intercensal Population Survey. Data exclude institutional, homeless households and transient poulation. - Les données ne comprennent pas la population des institutions, les ménages sans abri et la population de passage.

46 For statistical purposes, the data for China do not include those for the Hong Kong Special Administrative Region (Hong Kong SAR), Macao Special Administrative Region (Macao SAR) and Taiwan province of China. - Pour la présentation des statistiques, les données pour la Chine ne comprennent pas la Région Administrative Spéciale de Hong Kong (Hong Kong RAS), la Région Administrative Spéciale de Macao (Macao RAS) et Taïwan province de Chine.

47 Data have been adjusted on the basis of the Population Census of 2000. - Les données ont été ajustées à partir des résultats du recensement de la population de 2000.

48 The military personnel are classified as urban population. - Le personnel militaire est classé dans la population urbaine.

49 Data refer to the civilian population of 31 provinces, municipalities and autonomous regions. - Pour la population civile seulement de 31 provinces, municipalités et régions autonomes.

50 Data have been estimated on the basis of the annual National Sample Surveys on Population Changes. - Les données ont été estimées sur la base de l'enquête annuelle "National Sample Survey on Population Changes".

51 Data for 2005 are estimated from the National Sample Survey of 1 per cent population. - Les données pour 2005 ont été estimées à partir de l'enquête nationale qui a porté sur un échantillon de 1 % de la population.

52 Data refer to Hong Kong resident population at the census moment, which covers usual residents and mobile residents. Usual residents refer to two categories of people: (1) Hong Kong permanent residents who had stayed in Hong Kong for at least three months during the six months before or for at least three months during the six months after the census moment, regardless of whether they were in Hong Kong or not at the census moment; and (2) Hong Kong non-permanent residents who were in Hong Kong at the census moment. Mobile Residents, they are Hong Kong permanent residents who had stayed in Hong Kong for at least one month but less than three months during the six months before or for at least one month but less than three months during the six months after the census moment, regardless of whether they were in Hong Kong or not at the census moment. - Les données se rapportent à la population résidente à Hong Kong au moment du recensement. Cette population est composée des résidants habituels et des résidants mobiles. La population résidente est partagée en deux catégories: (1) les résidents permanents qui ont habité à Hong Kong au moins trois mois pendant les six mois précédents ou les six mois suivants le recensement; (2) les habitants non-permanents de Hong Kong qui étaient à Hong Kong au moment du recensement. La population mobile se rapporte aux résidents permanents de Hong Kong qui ont habité à Hong Kong pendant les six mois après le recensement pour une période comprise entre un mois et trois mois, indépendamment du fait qu'ils étaient à Hong Kong au moment du recensement au pays.

53 Based on the results of the By-Census 2006, held during 19 to 31 of August 2006. - Donnes dérivées du recensement partiel de 2006 organisé entre les 19 et 31 août 2006.

54 Data refer to government controlled areas. - Les données se rapportent aux zones contrôlées par le Gouvernement.

55 Including all persons irrespective of citizenship, who at the time of the census resided in the country or intended to reside for a period of at least one year. It does not distinguish between those present or absent at the time of census. - Les chiffres comprennent toute la population, quelle que soit la nationalité, qui à l'époque de recensement avait résidé dans le pays, ou avait l'intention de résider, pendant une période d'au moins un an. Il n'y a pas de distinction entre les personnes présentes ou absentes au moment du recensement.

56 Including data for the Indian-held part of Jammu and Kashmir, the final status of which has not yet been determined. - Y compris les données pour la partie du Jammu et du Cachemire occupée par l'Inde dont le statut définitif n'a pas encore été déterminé.

57 Excluding Mao-Maram, Paomata and Purul sub-divisions of Senapati district of Manipur. The population of Manipur including the estimated population of the

three sub-divisions of Senapati district is 2,291,125 (Males 1,161,173 and females 1,129,952). - Non compris les subdivisions Mao-Maram Paomata et Purul du district de Senapati dans l'État du Manipur. Cet État compte 2 291 125 habitants (1 161 173 hommes et 1 129 952 femmes), y compris la population estimative des trois subdivisions du district de Senapati.

[58] Excluding estimated population for Mao Maram, Paomata and Purul sub-divisions of Senapati district of Manipur. - Hormis la population estimée de Mao Maram, Paomata et les subdivisions Purul du district Senapati de Manipur.

[59] The figure includes an estimated population of 459 557 persons in urban and 1 857 659 persons in rural areas that were not directly enumerated, and a population of 566 403 persons in urban and 1 717 578 persons in rural areas that decline the participation. Also included are 421 399 non permanent residents (the homeless, the crew of ships carrying national flag, boat/floating house people, remote located tribesmen and refugees.) - Y compris la population estimée a 459 557 personnes dans les zones urbaines et de 1 857 659 personnes dans les zones rurales qui n'ont pas été énumérées directement, aussi que 566 403 personnes qui non pas répondu dans les zones urbaines et de 1 717 578 personnes dans les zones rurales. Y compris 421 399 résidants non permanents (les sans abri, l'équipage des bateaux portant le pavillon national, les habitants des embarcations ou des maisons flottantes, les habitants des tribus isolées et les réfugiés.)

[60] Data refer to the "Intercensal Population Survey". Excluding Province Nanggroe Aceh Darussalam, Regency Nias & Nias Selatan, Regency Boven Digul & Teluk Wondama. - Les données concernent l'enquête intercensitaire sur la population. En excluant les provinces de Nanggroe Aceh Darussalam, Regency Nias & Nias Selatan, Regency Boven Digul & Teluk Wondama.

[61] Data refer to the Iranian Year which begins on 21 March and ends on 20 March of the following year. - Les données concernent l'année iranienne, qui commence le 21 mars et se termine le 20 mars de l'année suivante.

[62] Differences between the total country figures and sum of urban and rural areas are due to the inclusion of unsettled population numbering 104 717 (53 065 males and females 51 652). - Les différences entre les chiffres pour l'ensemble du pays et la somme des zones urbaines et rurales s'expliquent par l'inclusion de la population non sédentaire, dont l'effectif est de 104 717 (53 065 de sexe masculin et 51 652 de sexe féminin).

[63] Including data for East Jerusalem and Israeli residents in certain other territories under occupation by Israeli military forces since June 1967. - Y compris les données pour Jérusalem-Est et les résidents israéliens dans certains autres territoires occupés depuis 1967 par les forces armées israéliennes.

[64] Excluding residents who had been registered in the Israeli localities (the Jewish localities) in the Gaza Area and northern Samaria, which were evacuated in August 2005, but did not notify the Ministry of Interior of their new address. These residents are included in total. - Hors résidents enregistrés dans les localités d'Israel (localités juives) de la Bande de Gaza (verify) et du nord de la Samarie, qui ont été évacués en Août 2005, mais qui n'ont pas notifié leur nouvelle adresse au ministère de l'intérieur. Ces résidents sont inclus dans le total.

[65] Excluding diplomatic personnel outside the country and foreign military and civilian personnel and their dependants stationed in the area. - Non compris le personnel diplomatique hors du pays ni les militaires et agents civils étrangers en poste sur le territoire et les membres de leur famille les accompagnant.

[66] Excluding data for Jordanian territory under occupation since June 1967 by Israeli military forces. Excluding foreigners, including registered Palestinian refugees. - Non compris les données pour le territoire jordanien occupé depuis juin 1967 par les forces armées israéliennes. Non compris les étrangers, mais y compris les réfugiés de Palestine enregistrés.

[67] Estimated based on the population census 1995 structure and growth rate at year 2000. - Pour les années 2000 à 2004, on a pris pour base la structure issue du recensement de population de 1995 et le taux de croissance de 2000.

[68] Based on the results of the 2005 Population and Housing Census. - Données fondées sur les résultats du recensement de la population et de l'habitat de 2005.

[69] Based on the results of a household survey. - D'après les résultats d'une enquête des ménages.

[70] Data refer to projections based on the 2000 population census. - Les données se réfèrent aux projections basées sur le recensement de la population de 2000.

[71] Data have been adjusted for underenumeration. Excluding Malaysian citizens and permanent residents who were away or intended to be away from the country for more than six months. Excluding Malaysian military, naval and diplomatic personnel and their families outside the country, and tourists, businessman who intended to be in Malaysia for less than six months. - Les données ont été ajustées pour compenser les lacunes du dénombrement. Non compris les citoyens malaisiens et les résidents permanents qui étaient ou qui ont prévu d'être hors du pays pour six mois ou plus. Non compris le personnel militaire Malaisien, le personnel naval ou diplomatique et leurs familles hors du

pays, et les touristes et les hommes d'affaires qui avaient l'intention de rester en Malaisie moins de six mois.

[72] Data including estimated population from household listing from Village Development Committees and Wards which could not be enumerated at the time of census. - Les données incluent la population estimée par les listes des ménages des comités de développement des villages et des circonscriptions qui n'ont pas pu être énumérée au moment du recensement.

[73] Data for urban include population in refugee camps. - Les données pour la population urbaine comprennent la population dans les camps réfugiés.

[74] Data have been adjusted for underenumeration, estimated at 2.70 per cent. - Les données ont été ajustées pour compenser les lacunes du dénombrement, estimées à 2,70 p. 100.

[75] Excluding data for the Pakistan-held part of Jammu and Kashmir, the final status of which has not yet been determined. - Non compris les données concernant la partie du Jammu et Cachemire occupée par le Pakistan dont le statut définitif n'a pas été déterminé.

[76] Based on the results of the Population Demographic Survey. These estimates do not reflect completely accurately the actual population and vital events of the country. - D'après les résultats de l'Enquête démographique par sondage. Ces estimations ne dénotent pas d'une manière complètement ponctuelle la population actuelle et les statistiques de l'état civil du pays.

[77] Urban population is estimated by applying urban census growth rate of 3.5178 per cent during intercensal period. - La population urbaine est estimée sur la base de taux d'accroissement annuel de 3.5178 pour cent obtenus, pour la période entre deux recensements généraux de la population, par un recensement urbain.

[78] Based on the results of the Pakistan Demographic Survey (PDS 2003). These estimates do not reflect completely accurately the actual population and vital events of the country. - D'après les résultats de Pakistan démographique par sondage 2003. Ces estimations ne dénotent pas d'une manière complètement ponctuelle la population actuelle et les statistiques de l'état civil du pays.

[79] Based on the results of the Pakistan Demographic Survey (PDS 2005). These estimates do not reflect completely accurately the actual population and vital events of the country. - D'après les résultats de Pakistan démographique par sondage 2005. Ces estimations ne dénotent pas d'une manière complètement ponctuelle la population actuelle et les statistiques de l'état civil du pays.

[80] Including diplomats and their families abroad, but excluding foreign diplomats, foreign military personnal, and their families in the country. Excluding foreigners. - Y compris le personnel diplomatique et les membres de leurs familles à l'étranger, mais sans tenir compte du personnel diplomatique et militaire étranger et des membres de leurs familles. Non compris étrangers.

[81] Excluding usual residents not in country at time of census. - À l'exclusion des résidents habituels qui ne sont pas dans le pays au moment du recensement.

[82] Excluding transients afloat and non-locally domiciled military and civilian service personnel and their dependants. - Non compris les personnes de passage à bord de navires, ni les militaires et agents civils domiciliés hors du territoire et les membres de leur famille les accompagnant.

[83] The Population and Housing Census 2001 did not cover the whole area of the country due to the security problems; data refer to the 18 districts for which the census was completed only (in three districts it was not possible to conduct the census at all and in four districts it was partially conducted). - Le recensement de la population et du logement de 2001 n'a pas été réalisé sur la superficie totale du pays à cause de problèmes de sécurité; les données ne concernent que les 18 districts entièrement recensés (3 districts n'ont pas été recensés du tout, et 4 ont été recensés en partie).

[84] Including Palestinian refugees. - Y compris les réfugiés de Palestine.

[85] Also included in Finland. Population statistics are compiled from registers. - Comprise aussi dans Finlande. Les statistiques de la population sont compilées à partir des registres.

[86] Population statistics are compiled from registers. Excluding Faeroe Islands and Greenland shown separately, if available. - Les statistiques de la population sont compilées à partir des registres. Non compris les Iles Féroé et le Gröenland, qui font l'objet de rubriques distinctes, si disponible.

[87] Population statistics are compiled from registers. Including Aland Islands. - Les statistiques de la population sont compilées à partir des registres. Y compris les Îles d'Åland.

[88] Excluding Overseas Departments, namely, French Guiana, Guadeloupe, Martinique and Reunion, shown separately, if available. Excluding diplomatic personnel outside the country and including members of alien armed forces not living in military camps and foreign diplomatic personnel not living in embassies or consulates. - Non compris les départements d'outre mer, c'est-à-dire la Guyane française, la Guadeloupe, la Martinique et la Réunion, qui font l'objet de rubriques distinctes, si disponible. Non compris le personnel diplomatique hors du pays et y compris les militaires étrangers ne vivant pas dans des camps militaires et le personnel diplomatique étranger ne vivant pas dans les ambassades ou les consulats.

[89] Data of the microcensus - a 1% household sample survey - refer to a single reference week in spring (usually last week in April). Excluding homeless persons. Excluding foreign military personnel and foreign diplomatic and consular personnel and their family members in the country. - Les données du microrecensement (enquête sur les ménages, réalisée sur un échantillon de 1 %) concernent une seule semaine de référence au printemps (habituellement la dernière semaine d'avril). Non compris les personnes sans domicile fixe. Non compris le personnel militaire étranger, le personnel diplomatique et consulaire étranger et les membres de leur famille se trouvant dans le pays.

[90] Excluding families of military personnel, visitors and transients. - Non compris les familles des militaires, ni les visiteurs et transients.

[91] Excluding armed forces stationed outside the country, but including alien armed forces stationed in the area. - Non compris les militaires en garnison hors du pays, mais y compris les militaires étrangers en garnison sur le territoire.

[92] Including armed forces stationed outside the country, but excluding alien armed forces stationed in the area. - Y compris les militaires nationaux hors du pays, mais non compris les militaires étrangers en garnison sur le territoire.

[93] Data refer to the Vatican City State. Population statistics are compiled from registers. - Les données se rapportent à l'Etat de la Cité du Vatican. Les statistiques de la population sont compilées à partir des registres.

[94] Including nationals outside the country. - Y compris les nationaux hors du pays.

[95] The regional grouping (urban/rural) was made from 1990 to 2000 according to the administrative division of 1 January 2000 and from 2001 according to the administrative division of 1 January 2004. - Pour les années 1990 à 2000, le découpage régional (zone urbaine/rurale) correspond au découpage administratif en vigueur au 1er janvier 2000; à partir de 2001, il correspond à celui en vigueur au 1er janvier 2004.

[96] Census results based on compilation of continuous accounting and sample surveys. - Les résultat du recensement, d'aprés les résultats des dénombrements et enquêtes par sondage continue.

[97] Including residents temporarily outside the country. Excluding Svalbard and Jan Mayen Island shown separately, if available. - Y compris les résidents se trouvant temporairement hors du pays. Non compris Svalbard et Jan Mayen qui font l'objet de rubriques distinctes, si disponible.

[98] Excluding civilian aliens within country, but including civilian nationals temporarily outside country. - Non compris les civils étrangers dans le pays, mais y compris les civils nationaux temporairement hors du pays.

[99] Excluding Transnistria and the municipality of Bender. - Les données ne tiennent pas compte de l'information sur la Transnistria et la municipalité de Bender.

[100] Data refer to resident population only. - Pour la population résidante seulement.

[101] Figures were updated taking into account the results of the 2002 All-Russian population census. - Les chiffres ont été calculés compte tenu des résultats du recensement de la population de la Fédération de Russie de 2002.

[102] Excluding data for Kosovo and Metohia. - Sans les données pour le Kosovo et Metohie.

[103] Excluding citizens temporarily residing abroad, the sum by urban and rural does not add up to the total. - Les nationaux se trouvant provisoirement à l'étranger ne sont pas pris en compte. La somme des chiffres disponibles pour les zones urbaines et rurales ne correspond donc pas au total.

[104] Excluding Channel Islands (Guernsey and Jersey) and Isle of Man, shown separately, if available. - Non compris les îles Anglo-Normandes (Guernesey et Jersey) et l'île de Man, qui font l'objet de rubriques distinctes, si disponible.

[105] Population estimates for 1994 to 2002 were revised in light of the local studies. - Les estimations de la population pour les années 1994 à 2002 ont été révisées en fonction d'études locales.

[106] Excluding Niue, shown separately, which is part of Cook Islands, but because of remoteness is administered separately. - Non compris Nioué, qui fait l'objet d'une rubrique distincte et qui fait partie des îles Cook, mais qui, en raison de son éloignement, est administrée séparément.

[107] Based on the results of the 1996 population census not necessarily mid year estimated. - À partir des résultats du recensement de la population de 1996, pas nécessairement des estimations en milieu d'année.

[108] Based on the results of the 1996 population census not necessarily mid year estimated. Data refer to national projections. - À partir des résultats du recensement de la population de 1996, pas nécessairement des estimations en milieu d'année. Les données se réfèrent aux projections nationales.

[109] Figures for male and female do not add up to the total, reason for discrepancy not ascertained. - La some des données pour la population masculine et pour la population féminine n'est pas égale au total, les raisons de cette différence ne sont pas expliquées.

Table 7

Table 7 presents population by age, sex and urban/rural residence for the latest available year between 1998 and 2007.

Description of variables: Data in this table are either population census figures or estimates, some of which are based on sample surveys. Data refer to the de facto population unless otherwise noted.

The reference date of the census or estimate appears in the stub of the table. In general, the estimates refer to mid-year (1 July).

Age is defined as age at last birthday, that is, the difference between the date of birth and the reference date of the age distribution expressed in completed solar years. The age classification used in this table is the following: under 1 year, 1-4 years, 5-year groups through 95-99 years, and 100 years or over.

Statistics are presented for one year, the most recent available. However, if more complete disaggregation is available for an earlier year, both are displayed.

The urban/rural classification of population by age and sex is that provided by each country or area; it is presumed to be based on the national census definitions of urban population that have been set forth at the end of the technical notes to table 6.

Estimates of population by age and sex presented in this table have been limited to countries or areas for which estimates have been based on the results of a sample survey or have been constructed by the component method from the results of a population census or sample survey. Estimations derived from distributing estimated total population according to percentages in each age-sex group at the time of a census or sample survey are not included in this table.

Reliability of data: Estimates which are believed to be less reliable are set in *italics* rather than in roman type. No attempt has been made to take account of age-reporting accuracy, the evaluation of which has been described in section 3.1.3 of the Technical Notes. However, the Whipple's Index presented in table 1c of the Demographic Yearbook Special Census Topic Volume 1 (Basic population characteristics) provides an assessment of age heaping for 145 countries for censuses being held between 1985 and 2003. http://unstats.un.org/unsd/demographic/products/dyb/dybcens.htm

Limitations: Statistics on population by age and sex are subject to the same qualifications as have been set forth for population statistics in general and age distributions in particular, as discussed in sections 3 and 3.1.3, respectively, of the Technical Notes.

Comparability of population data classified by age and sex is limited by variations in the definition of total population, discussed in detail in section 3 of the Technical Notes, and by the accuracy of the original enumeration. Both factors are more important in relation to certain age groups than to others. For example, under-enumeration is known to be more prevalent among infants and young children than among older persons. Similarly, the exclusion from the total population of certain groups that tend to be of selected ages (such as the armed forces) can markedly affect the age structure and its comparability with that for other countries or areas. Consideration should be given to the implications of these basic limitations in using the data.

In addition to these general qualifications are the special problems of comparability that arise in relation to age statistics in particular. Age distributions of population are known to suffer from certain deficiencies that have their origin in irregularities in age reporting. Although some of the irregularities tend to be obscured or eliminated when data are tabulated in five-year age groups rather than by single years, precision still continues to be affected, though the degree of distortion is not always readily seen.

Another factor limiting comparability is the age classification employed by the various countries or areas. Age may be based on the year of birth rather than the age at last birthday, in other words, calculated using the day, month and year of birth. Distributions based only on the year of birth are footnoted when known.

The absence of frequencies in the unknown age group does not necessarily indicate completely accurate reporting and tabulation of the age item. The unknowns may have been eliminated by assigning ages to them before tabulation, or by proportionately distributing the unknown category across the age groups after tabulation.

As noted in connection with table 5, intercensal estimates of total population are usually revised to accord with the results of a census of population if inexplicable discontinuities appear to exist. Postcensal age-sex distributions, however, are less likely to be revised in this way. When it is known that a total population estimate for a given year has been revised and the corresponding age distribution has not been, the age distribution is shown as provisional. Distributions of this type should be used with caution when studying trends over a period of years, though their utility for studying age structure for the specified year is probably unimpaired.

The comparability of data by urban/rural residence is affected by the national definitions of urban and rural used in tabulating these data. When known, the definitions of urban used in national population censuses are presented at the end of the technical notes for table 6. As discussed in detail in the technical notes for table 6, these definitions vary considerably from one country or area to another.

Earlier data: Population by age, sex and urban/rural residence has been shown in previous issues of the *Demographic Yearbook*. For more information on specific topics, and years for which data are reported, readers should consult the Historical Index. In addition, population by single years of age, sex and urban/rural residence are shown in the *Demographic Yearbook* Special Census Topics table 1 available online at http://unstats.un.org/unsd/demographic/products/dyb/dybcens.htm.

Tableau 7

Le tableau 7 présente les données les plus récentes (1998-2007) dont on dispose sur la population selon l'âge, le sexe et le lieu de résidence (zone urbaine ou rurale).

Description des variables : les données de ce tableau proviennent de recensements de la population ou correspondent à des estimations fondées, dans certains cas, sur des enquêtes par sondage. Sauf indication contraire, elles se rapportent à la population de fait.

La date du recensement ou de l'estimation figure dans la colonne de gauche du tableau. En général, les estimations se rapportent au milieu de l'année (1er juillet).

L'âge désigne l'âge au dernier anniversaire, c'est-à-dire la différence entre la date de naissance et la date de référence de la répartition par âge exprimée en années solaires révolues. La classification par âge utilisée dans ce tableau est la suivante : moins d'un an, 1 à 4 ans, groupes quinquennaux jusqu'à 95-99 ans et 100 ans ou plus.

Les statistiques portent sur une année, qui correspond à celle pour laquelle on dispose des statistiques les plus récentes. Toutefois, si l'on dispose de répartitions plus complètes pour des années antérieures, les statistiques sont alors présentées pour les deux années.

La classification par zones urbaines et rurales de la population selon l'âge et le sexe est celle qui est communiquée par chaque pays ou zone ; on part du principe qu'elle repose sur les définitions de la population urbaine utilisées pour les recensements de la population nationaux telles qu'elles sont reproduites à la fin des notes techniques du tableau 6.

Les estimations de la population selon l'âge et le sexe qui figurent dans ce tableau ne concernent que les pays ou zones pour lesquels les estimations sont fondées sur les résultats d'une enquête par sondage ou ont été établies par la méthode des composantes à partir des résultats d'un recensement de la population ou d'une enquête par sondage. Les répartitions par âge et par sexe obtenues en appliquant à l'estimation de la population totale les pourcentages enregistrés pour les divers groupes d'âge pour chaque sexe lors d'un recensement ou d'une enquête par sondage n'ont pas été reproduites dans ce tableau.

Fiabilité des données : les estimations considérées comme moins sûres sont indiquées en italique plutôt qu'en caractères romains. On n'a pas tenu compte des inexactitudes dans les déclarations d'âge, dont la méthode d'évaluation est exposée à la section 3.1.3 des Notes techniques. Cependant, l'index de Whipple présenté au tableau 1 c) du volume 1 de l'Annuaire démographique, qui est consacré aux recensements et porte sur les caractéristiques de la population, fournit une évaluation de l'exactitude des déclarations d'âge faites à l'occasion des recensements effectués entre 1985 et 2003 dans 145 pays. http://unstats.un.org/unsd/demographic/products/dyb/dybcens.htm

Insuffisance des données : les statistiques de la population selon l'âge et le sexe appellent les mêmes réserves que celles qui ont été formulées aux sections 3 et 3.1.3 des Notes techniques à propos des statistiques de la population en général et des répartitions par âge en particulier.

La comparabilité des statistiques de la population selon l'âge et le sexe pâtit du manque d'uniformité dans la définition de la population totale (voir la section 3 des Notes techniques) et des lacunes des dénombrements. L'influence de ces deux facteurs varie selon les groupes d'âge. Ainsi, le dénombrement des enfants de moins d'un an et des jeunes enfants comporte souvent plus de lacunes que celui des personnes plus âgées. De même, le fait que certains groupes de personnes appartenant souvent à des groupes d'âge déterminés, par exemple les militaires, ne soient pas pris en compte dans la population totale peut influer sensiblement sur la structure par âge et sur la comparabilité des données avec celles d'autres pays ou zones. Il conviendra de tenir compte de ces facteurs fondamentaux lorsque l'on utilisera les données du tableau.

Outre ces difficultés d'ordre général, la comparabilité pose des problèmes particuliers lorsqu'il s'agit des données par âge. On sait que les répartitions de la population selon l'âge présentent certaines imperfections dues à l'inexactitude des déclarations d'âge. Certaines de ces anomalies ont tendance à s'estomper ou à disparaître lorsque l'on classe les données par groupes d'âge quinquennaux et non par années d'âge, mais une certaine imprécision subsiste, même s'il n'est pas toujours facile de voir à quel point il y a distorsion.

Le degré de comparabilité dépend également de la classification par âge employée dans les divers pays ou zones. L'âge retenu peut être défini par date exacte (jour, mois et année) de naissance ou par celle du dernier anniversaire. Lorsqu'elles étaient connues, les répartitions établies seulement d'après l'année de la naissance ont été signalées en note à la fin du tableau.

Si aucun nombre ne figure dans la rangée réservée aux âges inconnus, cela ne signifie pas nécessairement que les déclarations d'âge et l'exploitation des données par âge aient été tout à fait exactes. C'est souvent une indication que l'on a attribué un âge aux personnes d'âge inconnu avant l'exploitation des données ou qu'elles ont été réparties proportionnellement entre les différents groupes après cette opération.

Comme on l'a indiqué à propos du tableau 5, les estimations intercensitaires de la population totale sont d'ordinaire rectifiées d'après les résultats des recensements de population si l'on constate des discontinuités inexplicables. Les données postcensitaires concernant la répartition de la population par âge et par sexe ont toutefois moins de chance d'être rectifiées de cette manière. Lorsque l'on savait qu'une estimation de la population totale pour une année donnée avait été rectifiée sans qu'il en soit de même pour la répartition par âge correspondante, cette dernière a été indiquée comme ayant un caractère provisoire. Les répartitions de ce type doivent être utilisées avec prudence lorsque l'on étudie les tendances sur un certain nombre d'années, quoique leur utilité pour l'étude de la structure par âge de la population pour l'année visée reste probablement entière.

La comparabilité des données selon le lieu de résidence (zone urbaine ou rurale) peut être limitée par les définitions nationales des termes « urbain » et « rural » utilisées pour la mise en tableaux de ces données. Les définitions du terme « urbain » utilisées pour les recensements nationaux de population ont été présentées à la fin des notes techniques du tableau 6 lorsqu'elles étaient connues. Comme on l'a précisé dans les notes techniques relatives au tableau 6, ces définitions varient considérablement d'un pays ou d'une zone à l'autre.

Données publiées antérieurement : des statistiques concernant la population selon l'âge, le sexe et le lieu de résidence (zone urbaine ou rurale) ont été présentées dans des éditions antérieures de l'*Annuaire démographique*. Pour plus de précisions concernant les années et les sujets pour lesquels des données ont été publiées, se reporter à l'index historique.

7. Population by age, sex and urban/rural residence: latest available year, 1998 - 2007
Population selon l'âge, le sexe et la résidence, urbaine/rurale: dernière année disponible, 1998 - 2007

Continent, country or area, date, code and age (in years) / Continent, pays ou zone, date, code et âge (en annèes)	Total			Urban - Urbaine			Rural - Rurale		
	Both sexes Les deux sexes	Male Masculin	Female Féminin	Both sexes Les deux sexes	Male Masculin	Female Féminin	Both sexes Les deux sexes	Male Masculin	Female Féminin
AFRICA - AFRIQUE									
Algeria - Algérie									
1 VII 2003 (ESDJ)									
Total	31 847 995	16 090 568	15 757 427	...	...	...	...	...	...
0	604 019	308 412	295 607	...	...	...	...	...	...
1 - 4	2 310 513	1 180 730	1 129 783	...	...	...	...	...	...
5 - 9	3 224 819	1 647 090	1 577 729	...	...	...	...	...	...
10 - 14	3 642 440	1 856 114	1 786 326	...	...	...	...	...	...
15 - 19	3 808 498	1 939 408	1 869 089	...	...	...	...	...	...
20 - 24	3 522 547	1 791 140	1 731 407	...	...	...	...	...	...
25 - 29	2 959 388	1 493 925	1 465 463	...	...	...	...	...	...
30 - 34	2 508 416	1 259 600	1 248 816	...	...	...	...	...	...
35 - 39	2 102 178	1 056 627	1 045 551	...	...	...	...	...	...
40 - 44	1 680 817	845 183	835 634	...	...	...	...	...	...
45 - 49	1 378 726	694 140	684 586	...	...	...	...	...	...
50 - 54	1 081 550	545 636	535 914	...	...	...	...	...	...
55 - 59	776 901	382 388	394 513	...	...	...	...	...	...
60 - 64	659 350	320 650	338 700	...	...	...	...	...	...
65 - 69	591 984	286 760	305 224	...	...	...	...	...	...
70 - 74	452 969	219 670	233 299	...	...	...	...	...	...
75 - 79	282 819	137 992	144 827	...	...	...	...	...	...
80 +	260 063	125 104	134 959	...	...	...	...	...	...
Benin - Bénin									
11 II 2002 (CDJC)									
Total	6 769 914	3 284 119	3 485 795	2 630 133	1 280 418	1 349 715	4 139 781	2 003 701	2 136 080
0	235 342	118 243	117 099	82 945	41 797	41 148	152 397	76 446	75 951
1 - 4	939 907	475 297	464 610	309 993	157 189	152 804	629 914	318 108	311 806
5 - 9	1 155 377	589 653	565 724	380 207	188 422	191 785	775 170	401 231	373 939
10 - 14	838 749	438 376	400 373	332 753	162 989	169 764	505 996	275 387	230 609
15 - 19	653 251	321 984	331 267	294 811	144 462	150 349	358 440	177 522	180 918
20 - 24	563 947	243 515	320 432	262 496	123 275	139 221	301 451	120 240	181 211
25 - 29	532 056	228 090	303 966	232 948	107 420	125 528	299 108	120 670	178 438
30 - 34	414 166	192 429	221 737	180 416	88 668	91 748	233 750	103 761	129 989
35 - 39	340 632	157 551	183 081	143 773	69 970	73 803	196 859	87 581	109 278
40 - 44	264 488	125 792	138 696	109 427	54 554	54 873	155 061	71 238	83 823
45 - 49	196 056	94 805	101 251	81 020	40 280	40 740	115 036	54 525	60 511
50 - 54	167 901	81 461	86 440	63 992	31 615	32 377	103 909	49 846	54 063
55 - 59	93 493	46 214	47 279	36 952	18 405	18 547	56 541	27 809	28 732
60 - 64	116 796	53 543	63 253	38 629	17 488	21 141	78 167	36 055	42 112
65 - 69	63 847	28 630	35 217	22 857	10 048	12 809	40 990	18 582	22 408
70 - 74	71 231	32 523	38 708	22 048	9 550	12 498	49 183	22 973	26 210
75 - 79	32 158	14 609	17 549	10 617	4 473	6 144	21 541	10 136	11 405
80 - 84	41 705	18 397	23 308	11 461	4 501	6 960	30 244	13 896	16 348
85 - 89	13 113	6 037	7 076	3 860	1 497	2 363	9 253	4 540	4 713
90 - 94	12 256	5 945	6 311	3 413	1 457	1 956	8 843	4 488	4 355
95 +	23 098	10 753	12 345	5 317	2 201	3 116	17 781	8 552	9 229
Unknown - Inconnu	345	272	73	198	157	41	147	115	32
Botswana[1]									
1 VII 2004 (ESDF)									
Total	1 711 334	828 082	883 252	393 528	191 287	202 241	1 317 806	636 795	681 011
0 - 4	...	...	...	39 462	19 821	19 641	142 574	71 938	70 636
0	40 211	20 179	20 032	...	...	...	...	...	...
1 - 4	182 036	91 759	90 277	...	...	...	...	...	...
5 - 9	209 001	105 382	103 619	36 523	17 780	18 743	172 478	87 602	84 876
10 - 14	206 554	104 108	102 446	35 391	16 470	18 921	171 163	87 638	83 525
15 - 19	200 428	100 765	99 663	42 174	18 910	23 264	158 254	81 855	76 399
20 - 24	184 195	92 070	92 125	58 457	28 634	29 823	125 738	63 436	62 302
25 - 29	160 484	78 938	81 546	54 633	26 777	27 856	105 851	52 161	53 690
30 - 34	124 469	61 673	62 796	41 938	21 392	20 546	82 531	40 281	42 250
35 - 39	88 744	42 494	46 250	27 627	14 270	13 357	61 117	28 224	32 893
40 - 44	68 717	28 867	39 850	19 497	9 029	10 468	49 220	19 838	29 382
45 - 49	59 897	23 659	36 238	14 618	6 738	7 880	45 279	16 921	28 358
50 - 54	45 006	18 356	26 650	9 248	4 692	4 556	35 758	13 664	22 094
55 - 59	33 955	14 131	19 824	5 674	2 896	2 778	28 281	11 235	17 046
60 - 64	29 417	12 772	16 645	3 332	1 711	1 621	26 085	11 061	15 024
65 - 69	24 103	10 638	13 465	1 995	972	1 023	22 108	9 666	12 442

Continent, country or area, date, code and age (in years) / Continent, pays ou zone, date, code et âge (en années)	Total			Urban - Urbaine			Rural - Rurale		
	Both sexes Les deux sexes	Male Masculin	Female Féminin	Both sexes Les deux sexes	Male Masculin	Female Féminin	Both sexes Les deux sexes	Male Masculin	Female Féminin
AFRICA - AFRIQUE									
Botswana[1]									
1 VII 2004 (ESDF)									
70 - 74	16 916	7 281	9 635	1 066	469	597	15 850	6 812	9 038
75 +	37 201	15 010	22 191	1 893	726	1 167	35 308	14 284	21 024
Burkina Faso									
9 XII 2006 (CDJC)									
Total	14 017 262	6 768 739	7 248 523	3 181 967	1 588 895	1 593 072	10 835 295	5 179 844	5 655 451
0	466 516	235 090	231 426	87 021	44 072	42 949	379 495	191 018	188 477
1 - 4	1 970 397	995 520	974 877	333 623	169 737	163 886	1 636 774	825 783	810 991
5 - 9	2 315 710	1 176 473	1 139 237	401 898	200 004	201 894	1 913 812	976 469	937 343
10 - 14	1 746 588	900 103	846 485	369 532	178 639	190 893	1 377 056	721 464	655 592
15 - 19	1 475 285	710 323	764 962	411 383	192 566	218 817	1 063 902	517 757	546 145
20 - 24	1 185 378	530 425	654 953	366 029	178 980	187 049	819 349	351 445	467 904
25 - 29	1 009 285	448 431	560 854	296 420	150 350	146 070	712 865	298 081	414 784
30 - 34	794 820	363 408	431 412	228 658	122 850	105 808	566 162	240 558	325 604
35 - 39	656 824	298 236	358 588	172 705	92 889	79 816	484 119	205 347	278 772
40 - 44	549 287	250 143	299 144	136 961	71 800	65 161	412 326	178 343	233 983
45 - 49	427 739	195 016	232 723	99 671	52 052	47 619	328 068	142 964	185 104
50 - 54	358 810	166 281	192 529	78 866	41 122	37 744	279 944	125 159	154 785
55 - 59	273 563	132 254	141 309	56 234	29 228	27 006	217 329	103 026	114 303
60 - 64	238 962	111 176	127 786	45 740	21 983	23 757	193 222	89 193	104 029
65 - 69	163 609	80 542	83 067	29 765	14 189	15 576	133 844	66 353	67 491
70 - 74	136 282	63 727	72 555	23 129	10 103	13 026	113 153	53 624	59 529
75 - 79	77 113	37 186	39 927	12 366	5 449	6 917	64 747	31 737	33 010
80 - 84	50 317	21 791	28 526	8 171	2 957	5 214	42 146	18 834	23 312
85 - 89	21 694	9 645	12 049	3 512	1 230	2 282	18 182	8 415	9 767
90 - 94	11 529	4 480	7 049	1 898	619	1 279	9 631	3 861	5 770
95 +	13 067	4 727	8 340	1 956	467	1 489	11 111	4 260	6 851
Unknown - Inconnu	74 487	33 762	40 725	16 429	7 609	8 820	58 058	26 153	31 905
Cape Verde - Cap-Vert									
1 VII 2003 (ESDF)									
Total	460 968	223 254	237 715	257 412	125 652	131 759	203 556	97 600	105 956
0 - 4	58 940	30 004	28 936	30 116	15 352	14 765	28 823	14 652	14 171
5 - 9	61 218	30 867	30 351	30 927	15 643	15 284	30 291	15 224	15 067
10 - 14	64 803	32 445	32 358	34 166	16 918	17 248	30 636	15 526	15 110
15 - 19	57 898	28 923	28 975	33 909	16 551	17 358	23 990	12 372	11 618
20 - 24	42 677	21 383	21 294	26 883	13 427	13 456	15 794	7 956	7 838
25 - 29	31 691	15 870	15 821	20 027	9 970	10 057	11 664	5 901	5 763
30 - 34	27 198	13 321	13 877	16 627	8 322	8 306	10 570	4 999	5 571
35 - 39	26 745	12 770	13 975	16 748	8 330	8 419	9 996	4 440	5 556
40 - 44	22 729	10 461	12 268	13 844	6 826	7 018	8 886	3 635	5 251
45 - 49	16 084	6 733	9 351	9 359	4 438	4 921	6 726	2 296	4 430
50 - 54	9 378	3 674	5 704	5 496	2 386	3 110	3 882	1 288	2 594
55 - 59	5 466	2 224	3 242	2 921	1 271	1 651	2 545	953	1 592
60 - 64	7 569	2 919	4 650	3 580	1 404	2 176	3 989	1 515	2 474
65 - 69	9 285	3 660	5 625	4 224	1 629	2 595	5 062	2 032	3 030
70 - 74	7 654	3 244	4 410	3 316	1 270	2 046	4 338	1 974	2 364
75 - 79	5 041	2 183	2 858	2 264	853	1 410	2 778	1 330	1 448
80 +	6 593	2 573	4 020	3 005	1 064	1 941	3 589	1 510	2 079
1 VII 2007 (ESDF)									
Total	491 419	237 842	253 577	...	...	...	...	...	...
0	12 122	6 100	6 022	...	...	...	...	...	...
1 - 4	46 545	23 327	23 218	...	...	...	...	...	...
5 - 9	58 312	29 295	29 017	...	...	...	...	...	...
10 - 14	60 588	30 429	30 159	...	...	...	...	...	...
15 - 19	63 603	31 749	31 854	...	...	...	...	...	...
20 - 24	53 153	26 395	26 758	...	...	...	...	...	...
25 - 29	38 559	19 117	19 442	...	...	...	...	...	...
30 - 34	29 240	14 412	14 828	...	...	...	...	...	...
35 - 39	26 579	12 712	13 867	...	...	...	...	...	...
40 - 44	25 912	12 266	13 646	...	...	...	...	...	...
45 - 49	20 995	9 534	11 461	...	...	...	...	...	...
50 - 54	14 454	6 010	8 444	...	...	...	...	...	...
55 - 59	8 012	3 212	4 800	...	...	...	...	...	...
60 - 64	5 387	2 172	3 215	...	...	...	...	...	...

Continent, country or area, date, code and age (in years) / Continent, pays ou zone, date, code et âge (en années)	Total			Urban - Urbaine			Rural - Rurale		
	Both sexes Les deux sexes	Male Masculin	Female Féminin	Both sexes Les deux sexes	Male Masculin	Female Féminin	Both sexes Les deux sexes	Male Masculin	Female Féminin
AFRICA - AFRIQUE									
Cape Verde - Cap-Vert									
1 VII 2007 (ESDF)									
65 - 69	7 990	3 096	4 894	...	...	...	...	...	...
70 - 74	8 168	3 241	4 927	...	...	...	...	...	...
75 - 79	6 135	2 554	3 581	...	...	...	...	...	...
80 + ...	5 665	2 221	3 444	...	...	...	...	...	...
Congo									
1 VII 2004 (ESDF)									
Total....................	3 231 326	...	...	...	...	...	...	...	...
0 - 4.....................	544 478	...	...	...	...	...	...	...	...
5 - 9.....................	484 376	...	...	...	...	...	...	...	...
10 - 14	414 902	...	...	...	...	...	...	...	...
15 - 19	357 708	...	...	...	...	...	...	...	...
20 - 24	291 466	...	...	...	...	...	...	...	...
25 - 29	231 040	...	...	...	...	...	...	...	...
30 - 34	171 583	...	...	...	...	...	...	...	...
35 - 39	142 178	...	...	...	...	...	...	...	...
40 - 44	130 546	...	...	...	...	...	...	...	...
45 - 49	116 005	...	...	...	...	...	...	...	...
50 - 54	95 970	...	...	...	...	...	...	...	...
55 - 59	80 783	...	...	...	...	...	...	...	...
60 - 64	66 565	...	...	...	...	...	...	...	...
65 - 69	48 793	...	...	...	...	...	...	...	...
70 + ...	54 933	...	...	...	...	...	...	...	...
Egypt - Égypte									
1 VII 2000 (ESDF)									
Total....................	63 976 000	32 695 000	31 281 000	...	...	...	...	...	...
0 - 4.....................	7 394 000	3 783 000	3 611 000	...	...	...	...	...	...
5 - 9.....................	8 225 000	4 245 000	3 980 000	...	...	...	...	...	...
10 - 14	8 481 000	4 392 000	4 089 000	...	...	...	...	...	...
15 - 19	7 445 000	3 882 000	3 563 000	...	...	...	...	...	...
20 - 24	5 474 000	2 848 000	2 626 000	...	...	...	...	...	...
25 - 29	4 714 000	2 266 000	2 448 000	...	...	...	...	...	...
30 - 34	4 293 000	2 149 000	2 144 000	...	...	...	...	...	...
35 - 39	4 164 000	2 064 000	2 100 000	...	...	...	...	...	...
40 - 44	3 422 000	1 740 000	1 682 000	...	...	...	...	...	...
45 - 49	2 909 000	1 516 000	1 393 000	...	...	...	...	...	...
50 - 54	2 180 000	1 071 000	1 109 000	...	...	...	...	...	...
55 - 59	1 593 000	835 000	758 000	...	...	...	...	...	...
60 - 64	1 510 000	761 000	749 000	...	...	...	...	...	...
65 - 69	1 003 000	546 000	457 000	...	...	...	...	...	...
70 - 74	667 000	339 000	328 000	...	...	...	...	...	...
75 + ...	502 000	258 000	244 000	...	...	...	...	...	...
Ethiopia - Éthiopie[2]									
28 V 2007 (CDFC)									
Total....................	73 918 505	37 296 657	36 621 848	11 956 170	5 942 170	6 014 000	61 962 335	31 354 487	30 607 848
0 - 4.....................	10 785 103	5 477 291	5 307 812	1 173 321	597 436	575 885	9 611 782	4 879 855	4 731 927
5 - 9.....................	12 004 737	6 117 281	5 887 456	1 299 097	645 961	653 136	10 705 640	5 471 320	5 234 320
10 - 14	10 458 181	5 437 318	5 020 863	1 389 876	668 524	721 352	9 068 305	4 768 794	4 299 511
15 - 19	8 787 740	4 474 378	4 313 362	1 967 309	944 887	1 022 422	6 820 431	3 529 491	3 290 940
20 - 24	6 425 164	3 110 675	3 314 489	1 521 285	756 529	764 756	4 903 879	2 354 146	2 549 733
25 - 29	5 680 569	2 631 202	3 049 367	1 241 440	601 559	639 881	4 439 129	2 029 643	2 409 486
30 - 34	4 229 468	2 091 932	2 137 536	821 141	435 846	385 295	3 408 327	1 656 086	1 752 241
35 - 39	3 774 499	1 825 390	1 949 109	698 954	358 508	340 446	3 075 545	1 466 882	1 608 663
40 - 44	2 876 111	1 465 605	1 410 506	476 737	261 562	215 175	2 399 374	1 204 043	1 195 331
45 - 49	2 247 330	1 149 510	1 097 820	365 716	190 024	175 692	1 881 614	959 486	922 128
50 - 54	1 892 344	928 329	964 015	290 068	138 817	151 251	1 602 276	789 512	812 764
55 - 59	1 170 688	633 409	537 279	179 133	89 608	89 525	991 555	543 801	447 754
60 - 64	1 236 192	646 290	589 902	179 417	84 909	94 508	1 056 775	561 381	495 394
65 - 69	806 195	446 338	359 857	121 482	59 677	61 805	684 713	386 661	298 052
70 - 74	676 415	359 371	317 044	104 132	47 738	56 394	572 283	311 633	260 650
75 - 79	349 227	203 160	146 067	127 062	60 585	66 477	719 297	430 136	289 161
80 - 84	286 274	158 884	127 390	...	...	...	...	...	...
85 - 89	98 830	61 158	37 672	...	...	...	...	...	...
90 + ...	112 028	67 519	44 509	...	...	...	...	...	...

7. Population by age, sex and urban/rural residence: latest available year, 1998 - 2007
Population selon l'âge, le sexe et la résidence, urbaine/rurale: dernière année disponible, 1998 - 2007 (continued - suite)

Continent, country or area, date, code and age (in years) / Continent, pays ou zone, date, code et âge (en années)	Total			Urban - Urbaine			Rural - Rurale		
	Both sexes Les deux sexes	Male Masculin	Female Féminin	Both sexes Les deux sexes	Male Masculin	Female Féminin	Both sexes Les deux sexes	Male Masculin	Female Féminin
AFRICA - AFRIQUE									
Ghana									
26 III 2000 (CDFC)									
Total...................	18 912 079	9 357 382	9 554 697	8 274 270	4 043 830	4 230 440	10 637 809	5 313 552	5 324 257
0	525 258	262 041	263 217	196 042	98 044	97 998	329 216	163 997	165 219
1 - 4	2 244 163	1 117 729	1 126 434	837 690	415 237	422 453	1 406 473	702 492	703 981
5 - 9	2 775 206	1 390 652	1 384 554	1 053 432	517 610	535 822	1 721 774	873 042	848 732
10 - 14	2 262 216	1 151 131	1 111 085	963 577	461 218	502 359	1 298 639	689 913	608 726
15 - 19	1 883 753	961 162	922 591	918 094	441 479	476 615	965 659	519 683	445 976
20 - 24	1 600 820	763 051	837 769	836 838	407 200	429 638	763 982	355 851	408 131
25 - 29	1 487 299	695 494	791 805	747 897	358 913	388 984	739 402	336 581	402 821
30 - 34	1 206 809	566 439	640 370	582 893	279 843	303 050	623 916	286 596	337 320
35 - 39	1 029 765	490 864	538 901	485 638	231 910	253 728	544 127	258 954	285 173
40 - 44	886 931	443 284	443 647	403 917	201 666	202 251	483 014	241 618	241 396
45 - 49	720 357	377 315	343 042	318 875	167 117	151 758	401 482	210 198	191 284
50 - 54	568 369	279 950	288 419	240 038	120 107	119 931	328 331	159 843	168 488
55 - 59	355 842	182 843	172 999	154 952	80 607	74 345	200 890	102 236	98 654
60 - 64	366 351	177 347	189 004	142 687	70 401	72 286	223 664	106 946	116 718
65 - 69	258 709	129 090	129 619	103 807	51 472	52 335	154 902	77 618	77 284
70 - 74	225 158	106 513	118 645	83 860	38 523	45 337	141 298	67 990	73 308
75 - 79	144 830	74 268	70 562	56 031	27 696	28 335	88 799	46 572	42 227
80 - 84	140 847	66 941	73 906	52 469	24 266	28 203	88 378	42 675	45 703
85 - 89	107 558	58 254	49 304	46 202	25 229	20 973	61 356	33 025	28 331
90 - 94	57 242	28 258	28 984	22 228	10 699	11 529	35 014	17 559	17 455
95 +	64 596	34 756	29 840	27 103	14 593	12 510	37 493	20 163	17 330
Kenya									
1 VII 2005 (ESDF)									
Total...................	35 267 222	17 457 906	17 809 316	6 213 505	3 688 113	2 525 392	29 053 718	13 769 794	15 283 924
0 - 4	6 238 991	3 150 182	3 088 809	982 463	542 222	440 241	5 256 528	2 607 960	2 648 568
5 - 9	4 694 561	2 367 882	2 326 679	634 554	347 165	287 388	4 060 007	2 020 717	2 039 291
10 - 14	3 973 404	2 001 411	1 971 993	471 546	262 014	209 532	3 501 858	1 739 397	1 762 461
15 - 19	4 082 140	2 061 657	2 020 483	631 251	340 802	290 450	3 450 889	1 720 855	1 730 033
20 - 24	3 627 797	1 833 154	1 794 643	910 302	537 287	373 015	2 717 495	1 295 867	1 421 628
25 - 29	2 953 347	1 398 489	1 554 858	812 771	480 022	332 749	2 140 576	918 467	1 222 109
30 - 34	2 387 831	1 119 233	1 268 598	602 678	380 498	222 181	1 785 153	738 735	1 046 417
35 - 39	1 778 184	864 349	913 835	391 067	266 270	124 797	1 387 117	598 079	789 038
40 - 44	1 394 011	685 786	708 225	275 799	191 704	84 096	1 118 212	494 082	624 129
45 - 49	1 038 421	507 834	530 587	177 566	125 206	52 361	860 855	382 628	478 226
50 - 54	829 200	403 131	426 069	122 953	86 594	36 359	706 247	316 537	389 710
55 - 59	681 227	329 709	351 518	76 409	52 171	24 238	604 818	277 538	327 280
60 - 64	546 365	262 036	284 329	50 927	32 721	18 206	495 438	229 315	266 123
65 - 69	420 546	193 429	227 117	30 973	19 350	11 623	389 573	174 079	215 494
70 - 74	300 941	136 132	164 809	21 116	12 614	8 502	279 825	123 518	156 307
75 +	320 257	143 493	176 764	21 129	11 474	9 655	299 128	132 019	167 109
Lesotho									
1 VII 2001 (SSDJ)									
Total...................	2 157 537	1 065 484	1 092 053	288 895	131 861	157 034	1 868 642	933 623	935 019
0	45 867	24 441	21 426	5 590	3 177	2 413	40 277	21 264	19 013
1 - 4	184 467	92 420	92 047	21 097	10 832	10 265	163 370	81 588	81 782
5 - 9	250 417	127 720	122 697	27 655	13 408	14 247	222 762	114 312	108 450
10 - 14	280 429	141 486	138 943	29 492	14 094	15 398	250 937	127 392	123 545
15 - 19	286 404	145 591	140 813	35 686	14 075	21 611	250 719	131 517	119 202
20 - 24	225 779	116 163	109 616	35 176	14 235	20 941	190 603	101 928	88 675
25 - 29	159 700	79 705	79 995	30 051	12 477	17 574	129 648	67 227	62 421
30 - 34	114 507	56 175	58 332	23 915	11 542	12 373	90 592	44 633	45 959
35 - 39	110 264	55 375	54 889	21 547	11 162	10 385	88 717	44 213	44 504
40 - 44	93 645	43 925	49 720	15 044	7 468	7 576	78 602	36 457	42 145
45 - 49	81 488	41 152	40 336	11 468	5 651	5 817	70 019	35 501	34 518
50 - 54	77 212	33 959	43 253	9 388	3 592	5 796	67 824	30 367	37 457
55 - 59	56 352	28 197	28 155	5 927	2 782	3 145	50 425	25 415	25 010
60 - 64	48 107	21 105	27 002	4 770	1 866	2 904	43 337	19 239	24 098
65 - 69	49 001	21 165	27 836	4 284	1 949	2 335	44 717	19 216	25 501
70 - 74	29 628	11 671	17 957	1 801	843	958	27 828	10 829	16 999
75 +	45 242	14 815	30 427	3 208	982	2 226	42 033	13 832	28 201
Unknown - Inconnu.......	19 028	10 419	8 609	2 796	1 726	1 070	16 232	8 693	7 539

Population selon l'âge, le sexe et la résidence, urbaine/rurale: dernière année disponible, 1998 - 2007 (continued - suite)

Continent, country or area, date, code and age (in years) Continent, pays ou zone, date, code et âge (en années)	Total			Urban - Urbaine			Rural - Rurale		
	Both sexes Les deux sexes	Male Masculin	Female Féminin	Both sexes Les deux sexes	Male Masculin	Female Féminin	Both sexes Les deux sexes	Male Masculin	Female Féminin
AFRICA - AFRIQUE									
Malawi									
1 VII 1999 (ESDF)									
Total.....................	10 152 753	4 978 411	5 174 342	1 467 066	719 376	747 690	8 685 689	4 426 650	4 259 039
0.....................	467 027	241 864	225 163	67 485	33 811	33 674	399 542	208 053	191 489
1 - 4.....................	1 634 594	843 949	790 645	236 198	117 978	118 220	1 398 396	725 971	672 425
5 - 9.....................	1 461 434	723 812	737 622	205 389	101 432	103 957	1 215 996	624 158	591 839
10 - 14.....................	1 257 259	629 337	627 922	176 048	87 044	89 003	1 042 283	535 625	506 658
15 - 19.....................	1 101 529	540 963	560 566	152 575	76 254	76 321	903 312	469 225	434 087
20 - 24.....................	994 625	444 395	550 230	133 503	65 463	68 040	790 398	402 825	387 573
25 - 29.....................	823 533	399 681	423 852	118 832	53 234	65 599	703 541	327 572	375 969
30 - 34.....................	626 286	316 923	309 363	98 293	44 601	53 692	581 941	274 452	307 489
35 - 39.....................	500 728	247 753	252 975	74 820	37 408	37 413	442 970	230 186	212 784
40 - 44.....................	372 511	185 328	187 183	58 683	28 775	29 908	347 428	177 066	170 362
45 - 49.....................	333 107	166 203	166 904	44 012	21 581	22 431	260 571	132 800	127 771
50 - 54.....................	255 412	128 321	127 091	38 144	18 704	19 440	225 828	115 093	110 735
55 +.....................	634 704	306 053	328 651	63 084	33 091	29 993	373 485	203 626	169 859
1 VII 2007 (ESDF)[3]									
Total.....................	13 187 632	6 490 146	6 697 486	...	...	...	...	...	...
0.....................	587 233	296 537	290 696	...	...	...	...	...	...
1 - 4.....................	2 062 464	1 035 969	1 026 495	...	...	...	...	...	...
5 - 9.....................	2 114 186	1 054 849	1 059 337	...	...	...	...	...	...
10 - 14.....................	1 497 864	738 039	759 825	...	...	...	...	...	...
15 - 19.....................	1 350 047	669 930	680 117	...	...	...	...	...	...
20 - 24.....................	1 156 120	574 156	581 964	...	...	...	...	...	...
25 - 29.....................	1 021 330	482 757	538 573	...	...	...	...	...	...
30 - 34.....................	901 688	402 593	499 095	...	...	...	...	...	...
35 - 39.....................	708 602	357 116	351 486	...	...	...	...	...	...
40 - 44.....................	533 474	267 755	265 719	...	...	...	...	...	...
45 - 49.....................	418 956	205 315	213 641	...	...	...	...	...	...
50 - 54.....................	311 635	154 150	157 485	...	...	...	...	...	...
55 +.....................	524 033	250 980	273 053	...	...	...	...	...	...
Mali									
1 IV 1998 (CDJC)									
Total.....................	9 709 570	4 804 745	4 904 825	2 614 841	1 309 621	1 305 220	7 094 729	3 495 124	3 599 605
0 - 4.....................	1 664 300	839 795	824 505	394 798	199 839	194 959	1 269 502	639 956	629 546
5 - 9.....................	1 627 268	830 211	797 057	387 621	196 124	191 497	1 239 647	634 087	605 560
10 - 14.....................	1 227 098	637 495	589 603	340 917	170 681	170 236	886 181	466 814	419 367
15 - 19.....................	1 021 750	492 480	529 270	313 002	147 667	165 335	708 748	344 813	363 935
20 - 24.....................	773 917	364 333	409 584	246 230	122 593	123 637	527 687	241 740	285 947
25 - 29.....................	648 030	292 369	355 661	199 937	96 978	102 959	448 093	195 391	252 702
30 - 34.....................	572 134	264 339	307 795	168 907	83 909	84 998	403 227	180 430	222 797
35 - 39.....................	484 352	233 444	250 908	142 538	73 329	69 209	341 814	160 115	181 699
40 - 44.....................	401 782	194 819	206 963	111 861	59 475	52 386	289 921	135 344	154 577
45 - 49.....................	309 015	156 517	152 498	83 404	44 470	38 934	225 611	112 047	113 564
50 - 54.....................	280 669	136 501	144 168	69 208	34 825	34 383	211 461	101 676	109 785
55 - 59.....................	205 322	107 461	97 861	49 697	26 230	23 467	155 625	81 231	74 394
60 - 64.....................	201 703	100 684	101 019	44 471	22 049	22 422	157 232	78 635	78 597
65 - 69.....................	129 879	69 606	60 273	28 324	14 597	13 727	101 555	55 009	46 546
70 - 74.....................	107 360	54 940	52 420	22 374	10 936	11 438	84 986	44 004	40 982
75 +.....................	54 991	29 751	25 240	11 552	5 919	5 633	43 439	23 832	19 607
Mauritania - Mauritanie									
1 VII 2005 (ESDF)									
Total.....................	2 905 727	1 450 418	1 455 309	...	...	...	...	...	...
0 - 4.....................	473 161	242 179	230 982	...	...	...	...	...	...
5 - 9.....................	417 913	214 175	203 738	...	...	...	...	...	...
10 - 14.....................	360 193	185 840	174 353	...	...	...	...	...	...
15 - 19.....................	300 592	153 780	146 812	...	...	...	...	...	...
20 - 24.....................	267 559	130 687	136 872	...	...	...	...	...	...
25 - 29.....................	213 382	100 660	112 722	...	...	...	...	...	...
30 - 34.....................	186 169	87 170	98 999	...	...	...	...	...	...
35 - 39.....................	152 901	72 861	80 040	...	...	...	...	...	...
40 - 44.....................	133 205	63 934	69 271	...	...	...	...	...	...
45 - 49.....................	103 483	51 959	51 524	...	...	...	...	...	...
50 - 54.....................	94 773	46 624	48 149	...	...	...	...	...	...
55 - 59.....................	61 455	30 423	31 032	...	...	...	...	...	...

7. Population by age, sex and urban/rural residence: latest available year, 1998 - 2007
Population selon l'âge, le sexe et la résidence, urbaine/rurale: dernière année disponible, 1998 - 2007 (continued - suite)

Continent, country or area, date, code and age (in years) / Continent, pays ou zone, date, code et âge (en années)	Total			Urban - Urbaine			Rural - Rurale		
	Both sexes Les deux sexes	Male Masculin	Female Féminin	Both sexes Les deux sexes	Male Masculin	Female Féminin	Both sexes Les deux sexes	Male Masculin	Female Féminin
AFRICA - AFRIQUE									
Mauritania - Mauritanie									
1 VII 2005 (ESDF)									
60 - 64	40 130	20 549	19 581	...	...	...	...	...	...
65 - 69	41 849	20 925	20 924	...	...	...	...	...	...
70 - 74	24 539	12 283	12 256	...	...	...	...	...	...
75 +	34 423	16 369	18 054	...	...	...	...	...	...
Mauritius - Maurice									
2 VII 2000 (CDJC)									
Total	1 178 848	583 756	595 092	503 045	247 844	255 201	675 803	335 912	339 891
0	18 915	9 574	9 341	7 127	3 608	3 519	11 788	5 966	5 822
1 - 4	75 388	38 066	37 322	29 620	14 938	14 682	45 768	23 128	22 640
5 - 9	105 189	53 037	52 152	42 660	21 428	21 232	62 529	31 609	30 920
10 - 14	97 740	49 428	48 312	41 020	20 818	20 202	56 720	28 610	28 110
15 - 19	102 088	51 671	50 417	41 369	20 985	20 384	60 719	30 686	30 033
20 - 24	110 892	55 108	55 784	44 167	21 778	22 389	66 725	33 330	33 395
25 - 29	93 797	46 749	47 048	36 979	18 021	18 958	56 818	28 728	28 090
30 - 34	99 515	49 964	49 551	40 103	19 977	20 126	59 412	29 987	29 425
35 - 39	101 946	51 621	50 325	44 743	22 491	22 252	57 203	29 130	28 073
40 - 44	90 406	45 798	44 608	40 283	20 482	19 801	50 123	25 316	24 807
45 - 49	77 931	39 133	38 798	35 122	17 793	17 329	42 809	21 340	21 469
50 - 54	56 939	27 790	29 149	25 928	12 558	13 370	31 011	15 232	15 779
55 - 59	40 491	19 228	21 263	19 033	9 016	10 017	21 458	10 212	11 246
60 - 64	33 097	15 301	17 796	16 474	7 711	8 763	16 623	7 590	9 033
65 - 69	25 768	11 758	14 010	13 159	6 067	7 092	12 609	5 691	6 918
70 - 74	21 694	9 491	12 203	11 050	4 886	6 164	10 644	4 605	6 039
75 - 79	14 910	6 047	8 863	7 697	3 128	4 569	7 213	2 919	4 294
80 - 84	7 132	2 584	4 548	3 713	1 372	2 341	3 419	1 212	2 207
85 - 89	3 498	1 049	2 449	1 916	564	1 352	1 582	485	1 097
90 - 94	1 104	272	832	637	163	474	467	109	358
95 +	289	42	247	173	31	142	116	11	105
Unknown - Inconnu	119	45	74	72	29	43	47	16	31
1 VII 2007 (ESDJ)									
Total	1 260 403	622 926	637 477	...	...	...	...	...	...
0 - 4	92 127	46 939	45 188	...	...	...	...	...	...
5 - 9	97 795	49 883	47 912	...	...	...	...	...	...
10 - 14	104 289	52 387	51 902	...	...	...	...	...	...
15 - 19	105 154	53 496	51 658	...	...	...	...	...	...
20 - 24	93 817	47 412	46 405	...	...	...	...	...	...
25 - 29	113 218	56 477	56 741	...	...	...	...	...	...
30 - 34	97 653	48 470	49 183	...	...	...	...	...	...
35 - 39	93 474	46 420	47 054	...	...	...	...	...	...
40 - 44	102 017	51 210	50 807	...	...	...	...	...	...
45 - 49	91 550	45 673	45 877	...	...	...	...	...	...
50 - 54	79 199	39 446	39 753	...	...	...	...	...	...
55 - 59	64 030	31 005	33 025	...	...	...	...	...	...
60 - 64	41 166	19 085	22 081	...	...	...	...	...	...
65 - 69	29 202	13 118	16 084	...	...	...	...	...	...
70 - 74	23 546	10 102	13 444	...	...	...	...	...	...
75 - 79	15 268	6 048	9 220	...	...	...	...	...	...
80 - 84	10 904	4 025	6 879	...	...	...	...	...	...
85 +	5 994	1 730	4 264	...	...	...	...	...	...
Mayotte									
31 VII 2007 (CDJC)									
Total	186 387	91 405	94 982	...	...	...	...	...	...
0	6 424	3 255	3 169	...	...	...	...	...	...
1 - 4	25 429	12 948	12 481	...	...	...	...	...	...
5 - 9	27 239	13 739	13 500	...	...	...	...	...	...
10 - 14	23 403	11 483	11 920	...	...	...	...	...	...
15 - 19	18 724	9 144	9 580	...	...	...	...	...	...
20 - 24	13 660	5 789	7 871	...	...	...	...	...	...
25 - 29	14 987	6 262	8 725	...	...	...	...	...	...
30 - 34	14 376	6 651	7 725	...	...	...	...	...	...
35 - 39	12 390	6 468	5 922	...	...	...	...	...	...
40 - 44	8 375	4 385	3 990	...	...	...	...	...	...
45 - 49	6 133	3 261	2 872	...	...	...	...	...	...

Continent, country or area, date, code and age (in years) Continent, pays ou zone, date, code et âge (en années)	Total			Urban - Urbaine			Rural - Rurale		
	Both sexes Les deux sexes	Male Masculin	Female Féminin	Both sexes Les deux sexes	Male Masculin	Female Féminin	Both sexes Les deux sexes	Male Masculin	Female Féminin

AFRICA - AFRIQUE

Mayotte
31 VII 2007 (CDJC)

50 - 54	4 763	2 508	2 255	...	...	...	...	...	...
55 - 59	3 566	1 948	1 618	...	...	...	...	...	...
60 - 64	2 522	1 329	1 193	...	...	...	...	...	...
65 - 69	1 621	833	788	...	...	...	...	...	...
70 - 74	1 266	671	595	...	...	...	...	...	...
75 - 79	689	348	341	...	...	...	...	...	...
80 - 84	459	234	225	...	...	...	...	...	...
85 - 89	199	89	110	...	...	...	...	...	...
90 - 94	101	35	66	...	...	...	...	...	...
95 +	61	25	36	...	...	...	...	...	...

Morocco - Maroc
1 VII 2007 (ESDF)

Total	30 841 000	15 246 000	15 595 000	17 404 000	8 572 000	8 832 000	13 437 000	6 674 000	6 763 000
0 - 4	2 876 000	1 469 000	1 407 000	1 480 000	754 000	726 000	1 397 000	715 000	681 000
5 - 9	2 961 000	1 507 000	1 453 000	1 514 000	768 000	746 000	1 447 000	739 000	708 000
10 - 14	3 154 000	1 605 000	1 550 000	1 609 000	813 000	795 000	1 545 000	791 000	754 000
15 - 19	3 238 000	1 634 000	1 605 000	1 689 000	846 000	843 000	1 549 000	788 000	761 000
20 - 24	3 053 000	1 504 000	1 549 000	1 693 000	836 000	857 000	1 361 000	669 000	692 000
25 - 29	2 741 000	1 323 000	1 417 000	1 611 000	781 000	830 000	1 130 000	543 000	588 000
30 - 34	2 328 000	1 114 000	1 214 000	1 410 000	670 000	740 000	918 000	444 000	474 000
35 - 39	2 045 000	974 000	1 072 000	1 283 000	608 000	675 000	763 000	366 000	397 000
40 - 44	1 872 000	892 000	980 000	1 195 000	566 000	628 000	677 000	326 000	351 000
45 - 49	1 734 000	854 000	879 000	1 101 000	545 000	557 000	632 000	310 000	323 000
50 - 54	1 370 000	703 000	667 000	865 000	451 000	414 000	505 000	252 000	253 000
55 - 59	1 009 000	508 000	501 000	609 000	314 000	295 000	400 000	193 000	206 000
60 - 64	700 000	328 000	372 000	400 000	187 000	213 000	299 000	141 000	159 000
65 - 69	638 000	294 000	344 000	352 000	159 000	193 000	286 000	135 000	151 000
70 - 74	466 000	225 000	241 000	259 000	121 000	138 000	207 000	104 000	103 000
75 +	656 000	311 000	344 000	334 000	152 000	182 000	322 000	159 000	162 000

Mozambique
1 VII 2000 (ESDF)

Total	17 690 584	8 284 793	9 405 791	...	...	...	...	...	...
0 - 4	3 139 293	1 514 640	1 624 653	...	...	...	...	...	...
5 - 9	2 664 689	1 282 460	1 382 229	...	...	...	...	...	...
10 - 14	2 208 552	1 059 016	1 149 536	...	...	...	...	...	...
15 - 19	1 966 758	940 308	1 026 450	...	...	...	...	...	...
20 - 24	1 540 328	743 941	796 387	...	...	...	...	...	...
25 - 29	1 312 794	598 600	714 194	...	...	...	...	...	...
30 - 34	1 023 631	438 932	584 699	...	...	...	...	...	...
35 - 39	858 865	372 869	485 996	...	...	...	...	...	...
40 - 44	745 586	341 179	404 407	...	...	...	...	...	...
45 - 49	621 564	286 675	334 889	...	...	...	...	...	...
50 - 54	496 069	226 219	269 850	...	...	...	...	...	...
55 - 59	388 778	173 800	214 978	...	...	...	...	...	...
60 - 64	289 060	126 794	162 266	...	...	...	...	...	...
65 - 69	201 364	86 207	115 157	...	...	...	...	...	...
70 - 74	124 004	50 747	73 257	...	...	...	...	...	...
75 - 79	66 792	26 277	40 515	...	...	...	...	...	...
80 +	42 457	16 129	26 328	...	...	...	...	...	...

Namibia - Namibie
27 VIII 2001 (CDFC)

Total	1 830 330	887 721	942 572	603 612	300 358[4]	303 236[4]	1 226 718	587 363[4]	639 336[4]
0 - 4	241 229	120 044	121 185	67 484	33 494	33 990	173 745	86 550	87 195
0	46 852	23 281	23 571	...	...	...	...	...	...
1 - 4	194 377	96 763	97 614	...	...	...	...	...	...
5 - 9	246 964	121 785	125 179	59 123	28 683	30 440	187 841	93 102	94 739
10 - 14	230 287	113 081	117 206	55 162	25 564	29 598	175 125	87 517	87 608
15 - 19	202 298	99 307	102 991	55 865	25 383	30 482	146 433	73 924	72 509
20 - 24	174 484	86 382	88 102	70 592	34 483	36 109	103 892	51 899	51 993
25 - 29	150 783	74 304	76 479	73 635	37 316	36 319	77 148	36 988	40 160
30 - 34	118 529	57 125	61 404	58 312	29 851	28 461	60 217	27 274	32 943
35 - 39	96 416	45 083	51 333	46 071	23 521	22 550	50 345	21 562	28 783
40 - 44	74 050	34 170	39 880	33 152	16 966	16 186	40 898	17 204	23 694

Continent, country or area, date, code and age (in years) / Continent, pays ou zone, date, code et âge (en années)	Total			Urban - Urbaine			Rural - Rurale		
	Both sexes Les deux sexes	Male Masculin	Female Féminin	Both sexes Les deux sexes	Male Masculin	Female Féminin	Both sexes Les deux sexes	Male Masculin	Female Féminin
AFRICA - AFRIQUE									
Namibia - Namibie									
27 VIII 2001 (CDFC)									
45 - 49	57 749	26 942	30 807	23 576	12 615	10 961	34 173	14 327	19 846
50 - 54	47 779	21 999	25 780	16 798	9 193	7 605	30 981	12 806	18 175
55 - 59	35 209	16 600	18 609	10 890	5 893	4 997	24 319	10 707	13 612
60 - 64	34 378	15 569	18 809	8 512	4 192	4 320	25 866	11 377	14 489
65 - 69	25 262	11 399	13 863	5 458	2 596	2 862	19 804	8 803	11 001
70 - 74	22 052	9 313	12 739	3 707	1 619	2 088	18 345	7 694	10 651
75 - 79	16 007	6 382	9 625	2 531	1 068	1 463	13 476	5 314	8 162
80 - 84	13 818	5 359	8 459	1 753	680	1 073	12 065	4 679	7 386
85 - 89	5 407	2 033	3 374	973	341	632	4 434	1 692	2 742
90 - 94	2 555	927	1 628	376	152	224	2 179	775	1 404
95 +	2 712	897	1 815	262	111	151	2 450	786	1 664
Unknown - Inconnu	32 325	19 020	13 305	9 362	6 637	2 725	22 963	12 383	10 580
Niger[5]									
1 VII 2006 (ESDJ)									
Total	12 929 300	6 470 600	6 458 700	2 295 300	1 151 700	1 143 600	10 634 000	5 318 900	5 315 100
0 - 4	2 454 500	1 257 600	1 196 900	337 600	170 900	166 700	2 116 900	1 086 700	1 030 200
5 - 9	2 190 400	1 128 900	1 061 500	360 200	183 300	176 900	1 830 200	945 600	884 600
10 - 14	1 731 900	878 700	853 200	355 700	179 800	175 900	1 376 200	698 900	677 300
15 - 19	1 250 800	616 500	634 300	273 100	136 500	136 600	977 700	480 000	497 700
20 - 24	986 400	473 700	512 700	187 300	94 000	93 300	799 100	379 700	419 400
25 - 29	849 900	398 400	451 500	156 500	77 000	79 500	693 400	321 400	372 000
30 - 34	735 700	347 900	387 800	138 100	66 600	71 500	597 600	281 300	316 300
35 - 39	654 600	323 700	330 900	122 100	61 300	60 800	532 500	262 400	270 100
40 - 44	543 400	273 700	269 700	98 900	51 500	47 400	444 500	222 200	222 300
45 - 49	405 800	206 600	199 200	72 900	37 800	35 100	332 900	168 800	164 100
50 - 54	321 700	163 000	158 700	57 400	27 500	29 900	264 300	135 500	128 800
55 - 59	267 500	131 000	136 500	47 200	21 900	25 300	220 300	109 100	111 200
60 - 64	198 100	96 500	101 600	33 500	17 900	15 600	164 600	78 600	86 000
65 - 69	118 100	59 400	58 700	19 600	10 700	8 900	98 500	48 700	49 800
70 - 74	78 700	40 500	38 200	13 200	6 300	6 900	65 500	34 200	31 300
75 - 79	54 800	28 400	26 400	9 500	3 300	6 200	45 300	25 100	20 200
80 +	87 000	46 100	40 900	12 500	5 400	7 100	74 500	40 700	33 800
Nigeria - Nigéria[6]									
1 VII 2003 (ESDF)									
Total	126 152 844	63 241 808	62 911 036	...	...	...	...	...	...
0 - 4	22 090 300	11 214 033	10 876 267	...	...	...	...	...	...
5 - 9	18 333 245	9 362 226	8 971 019	...	...	...	...	...	...
10 - 14	15 408 885	7 804 986	7 603 899	...	...	...	...	...	...
15 - 19	12 867 025	6 446 554	6 420 471	...	...	...	...	...	...
20 - 24	10 991 665	5 543 883	5 447 782	...	...	...	...	...	...
25 - 29	9 891 507	4 951 575	4 939 932	...	...	...	...	...	...
30 - 34	8 076 673	3 913 158	4 163 515	...	...	...	...	...	...
35 - 39	6 511 687	3 017 320	3 494 367	...	...	...	...	...	...
40 - 44	5 541 919	2 616 888	2 925 031	...	...	...	...	...	...
45 - 49	4 682 410	2 287 112	2 395 298	...	...	...	...	...	...
50 - 54	3 658 941	1 835 806	1 823 135	...	...	...	...	...	...
55 - 59	2 708 234	1 411 256	1 296 978	...	...	...	...	...	...
60 - 64	1 983 965	1 050 256	933 709	...	...	...	...	...	...
65 - 69	1 357 083	726 454	630 629	...	...	...	...	...	...
70 - 74	950 824	501 708	449 116	...	...	...	...	...	...
75 - 79	612 840	309 402	303 438	...	...	...	...	...	...
80 +	485 641	249 191	236 450	...	...	...	...	...	...
Réunion									
1 I 2007 (ESDJ)									
Total	790 500	382 883	407 617	...	...	...	...	...	...
0 - 4	67 825	34 866	32 959	...	...	...	...	...	...
5 - 9	68 797	35 060	33 737	...	...	...	...	...	...
10 - 14	69 729	35 129	34 600	...	...	...	...	...	...
15 - 19	69 692	35 296	34 396	...	...	...	...	...	...
20 - 24	55 894	27 317	28 577	...	...	...	...	...	...
25 - 29	51 073	23 552	27 521	...	...	...	...	...	...
30 - 34	55 592	26 083	29 509	...	...	...	...	...	...
35 - 39	62 685	29 719	32 966	...	...	...	...	...	...

Continent, country or area, date, code and age (in years) Continent, pays ou zone, date, code et âge (en années)	Total			Urban - Urbaine			Rural - Rurale		
	Both sexes Les deux sexes	Male Masculin	Female Féminin	Both sexes Les deux sexes	Male Masculin	Female Féminin	Both sexes Les deux sexes	Male Masculin	Female Féminin
AFRICA - AFRIQUE									
Réunion									
1 I 2007 (ESDJ)									
40 - 44	66 083	31 945	34 138	...	...	...	...	...	...
45 - 49	52 373	25 548	26 825	...	...	...	...	...	...
50 - 54	46 331	22 306	24 025	...	...	...	...	...	...
55 - 59	35 403	17 546	17 857	...	...	...	...	...	...
60 - 64	26 615	12 522	14 093	...	...	...	...	...	...
65 - 69	21 530	9 920	11 610	...	...	...	...	...	...
70 - 74	16 473	7 195	9 278	...	...	...	...	...	...
75 - 79	11 337	4 597	6 740	...	...	...	...	...	...
80 - 84	7 596	2 815	4 781	...	...	...	...	...	...
85 - 89	3 687	1 060	2 627	...	...	...	...	...	...
90 - 94	1 403	361	1 042	...	...	...	...	...	...
95 + ...	382	46	336	...	...	...	...	...	...
Rwanda									
16 VIII 2002 (CDJC)									
Total.........	8 128 553	3 879 448	4 249 105	1 372 604	727 172	645 432	6 755 949	3 152 276	3 603 673
0.........	325 221	161 653	163 568	46 968	23 496	23 472	278 253	138 157	140 096
1 - 4.........	995 010	493 437	501 573	147 083	73 621	73 462	847 927	419 816	428 111
5 - 9.........	1 141 039	563 351	577 688	157 009	77 648	79 361	984 030	485 703	498 327
10 - 14.........	1 095 225	536 876	558 349	149 787	71 947	77 840	945 438	464 929	480 509
15 - 19.........	1 078 839	526 563	552 276	184 874	89 576	95 298	893 965	436 987	456 978
20 - 24.........	810 681	382 561	428 120	177 151	98 145	79 006	633 530	284 416	349 114
25 - 29.........	555 509	253 180	302 329	130 102	74 049	56 053	425 407	179 131	246 276
30 - 34.........	448 439	208 742	239 697	100 840	59 871	40 969	347 599	148 871	198 728
35 - 39.........	382 636	177 816	204 820	76 430	46 117	30 313	306 206	131 699	174 507
40 - 44.........	363 067	168 934	194 133	63 795	38 834	24 961	299 272	130 100	169 172
45 - 49.........	268 262	122 615	145 647	43 450	26 007	17 443	224 812	96 608	128 204
50 - 54.........	193 382	86 925	106 457	30 845	17 673	13 172	162 537	69 252	93 285
55 - 59.........	123 868	50 480	73 388	18 782	9 561	9 221	105 086	40 919	64 167
60 - 64.........	111 809	45 221	66 588	15 483	7 293	8 190	96 326	37 928	58 398
65 - 69.........	84 928	35 178	49 750	11 333	5 166	6 167	73 595	30 012	43 583
70 - 74.........	71 020	30 970	40 050	8 790	4 025	4 765	62 230	26 945	35 285
75 - 79.........	37 989	16 255	21 734	4 451	1 923	2 528	33 538	14 332	19 206
80 - 84.........	26 788	12 081	14 707	3 295	1 378	1 917	23 493	10 703	12 790
85 +.........	14 841	6 610	8 231	2 136	842	1 294	12 705	5 768	6 937
Saint Helena ex. dep. -									
Sainte-Hélène sans dép.									
8 III 1998 (CDJC)									
Total.........	4 913	2 481	2 432	...	...	...	...	...	...
0.........	60	33	27	...	...	...	...	...	...
1 - 4.........	252	139	113	...	...	...	...	...	...
5 - 9.........	369	197	172	...	...	...	...	...	...
10 - 14.........	368	199	169	...	...	...	...	...	...
15 - 19.........	452	217	235	...	...	...	...	...	...
20 - 24.........	300	154	146	...	...	...	...	...	...
25 - 29.........	370	185	185	...	...	...	...	...	...
30 - 34.........	329	150	179	...	...	...	...	...	...
35 - 39.........	391	181	210	...	...	...	...	...	...
40 - 44.........	336	181	155	...	...	...	...	...	...
45 - 49.........	340	173	167	...	...	...	...	...	...
50 - 54.........	346	200	146	...	...	...	...	...	...
55 - 59.........	230	124	106	...	...	...	...	...	...
60 - 64.........	202	127	75	...	...	...	...	...	...
65 - 69.........	190	86	104	...	...	...	...	...	...
70 - 74.........	143	51	92	...	...	...	...	...	...
75 - 79.........	111	41	70	...	...	...	...	...	...
80 - 84.........	69	25	44	...	...	...	...	...	...
85 - 89.........	26	7	19	...	...	...	...	...	...
90 - 94.........	18	7	11	...	...	...	...	...	...
95 +.........	1	-	1	...	...	...	...	...	...
Unknown - Inconnu	10	4	6	...	...	...	...	...	...

Continent, country or area, date, code and age (in years) / Continent, pays ou zone, date, code et âge (en années)	Total			Urban - Urbaine			Rural - Rurale		
	Both sexes Les deux sexes	Male Masculin	Female Féminin	Both sexes Les deux sexes	Male Masculin	Female Féminin	Both sexes Les deux sexes	Male Masculin	Female Féminin
AFRICA - AFRIQUE									
Saint Helena: Ascension - Sainte-Hélène: Ascension 8 III 1998 (CDJC)									
Total.....................	712	458	254	...	...	...	...	...	...
0.........................	8	4	4	...	...	...	...	...	...
1 - 4.....................	15	9	6	...	...	...	...	...	...
5 - 9.....................	30	11	19	...	...	...	...	...	...
10 - 14...................	37	21	16	...	...	...	...	...	...
15 - 19...................	30	21	9	...	...	...	...	...	...
20 - 24...................	93	55	38	...	...	...	...	...	...
25 - 29...................	115	81	34	...	...	...	...	...	...
30 - 34...................	105	67	38	...	...	...	...	...	...
35 - 39...................	68	42	26	...	...	...	...	...	...
40 - 44...................	67	43	24	...	...	...	...	...	...
45 - 49...................	63	42	21	...	...	...	...	...	...
50 - 54...................	49	37	12	...	...	...	...	...	...
55 - 59...................	25	21	4	...	...	...	...	...	...
60 - 64...................	5	2	3	...	...	...	...	...	...
65 - 69...................	1	1	-	...	...	...	...	...	...
70 +......................	1	1	-	...	...	...	...	...	...
Sao Tome and Principe - Sao Tomé-et-Principe 25 VIII 2001 (CDFC)									
Total.....................	136 554	67 422	69 132	73 907	35 679	38 228	62 647	31 743	30 904
0.........................	4 588	2 299	2 289	2 433	1 221	1 212	2 155	1 078	1 077
1 - 4.....................	16 111	8 149	7 962	8 440	4 325	4 115	7 671	3 824	3 847
5 - 9.....................	18 794	9 587	9 207	9 780	4 972	4 808	9 014	4 615	4 399
10 - 14...................	18 468	9 416	9 052	9 829	4 883	4 946	8 639	4 533	4 106
15 - 19...................	17 311	8 663	8 648	9 762	4 701	5 061	7 549	3 962	3 587
20 - 24...................	13 981	6 870	7 111	7 926	3 783	4 143	6 055	3 087	2 968
25 - 29...................	9 703	4 795	4 908	5 333	2 564	2 769	4 370	2 231	2 139
30 - 34...................	7 684	3 700	3 984	4 235	1 960	2 275	3 449	1 740	1 709
35 - 39...................	6 567	3 050	3 517	3 639	1 632	2 007	2 928	1 418	1 510
40 - 44...................	5 367	2 465	2 902	3 066	1 413	1 653	2 301	1 052	1 249
45 - 49...................	3 984	1 864	2 120	2 261	1 026	1 235	1 723	838	885
50 - 54...................	3 020	1 408	1 612	1 659	758	901	1 361	650	711
55 - 59...................	2 397	1 119	1 278	1 247	559	688	1 150	560	590
60 - 64...................	2 710	1 301	1 409	1 288	568	720	1 422	733	689
65 - 69...................	2 108	1 043	1 065	1 014	482	532	1 094	561	533
70 - 74...................	1 648	780	868	829	366	463	819	414	405
75 - 79...................	1 124	513	611	593	251	342	531	262	269
80 - 84...................	616	262	354	349	140	209	267	122	145
85 +......................	373	138	235	224	75	149	149	63	86
Senegal - Sénégal 31 XII 2002 (ESDJ)									
Total.....................	9 856 145	4 812 096	5 044 049	4 472 867	2 176 338	2 296 529	5 383 278	2 635 758	2 747 520
0 - 4.....................	1 396 011	725 436	670 575	540 412	282 408	258 004	855 599	443 028	412 571
5 - 9.....................	1 425 971	739 950	686 021	527 762	271 844	255 918	898 209	468 106	430 103
10 - 14...................	1 289 319	658 358	630 961	557 386	276 522	280 864	731 933	381 836	350 097
15 - 19...................	1 168 374	558 305	610 069	579 770	273 149	306 621	588 604	285 156	303 448
20 - 24...................	959 723	446 822	512 901	508 140	237 658	270 482	451 583	209 164	242 419
25 - 29...................	772 787	350 167	422 620	394 247	184 840	209 407	378 540	165 327	213 213
30 - 34...................	625 810	279 009	346 801	314 614	145 862	168 752	311 196	133 147	178 049
35 - 39...................	503 200	220 367	282 833	251 349	113 057	138 292	251 851	107 310	144 541
40 - 44...................	419 262	196 261	223 001	206 247	100 334	105 913	213 015	95 927	117 088
45 - 49...................	314 237	155 833	158 404	161 336	80 908	80 428	152 901	74 925	77 976
50 - 54...................	278 642	134 998	143 644	131 682	65 842	65 840	146 960	69 156	77 804
55 - 59...................	171 436	85 926	85 510	80 404	39 673	40 731	91 032	46 253	44 779
60 - 64...................	180 125	85 511	94 614	75 125	35 707	39 418	105 000	49 804	55 196
65 - 69...................	112 922	58 685	54 237	49 083	23 920	25 163	63 839	34 765	29 074
70 - 74...................	112 041	53 339	58 702	45 116	21 034	24 082	66 925	32 305	34 620
75 - 79...................	57 616	31 086	26 530	23 930	12 032	11 898	33 686	19 054	14 632
80 +......................	68 669	32 043	36 626	26 264	11 548	14 716	42 405	20 495	21 910

Continent, country or area, date, code and age (in years) / Continent, pays ou zone, date, code et âge (en années)	Total			Urban - Urbaine			Rural - Rurale		
	Both sexes Les deux sexes	Male Masculin	Female Féminin	Both sexes Les deux sexes	Male Masculin	Female Féminin	Both sexes Les deux sexes	Male Masculin	Female Féminin
AFRICA - AFRIQUE									
Seychelles									
1 VII 2006 (ESDF)									
Total....................	84 600	42 875	41 725	...	...	...	...	...	...
0 - 4.....................	7 023	3 568	3 455	...	...	...	...	...	...
5 - 9.....................	6 102	3 055	3 047	...	...	...	...	...	...
10 - 14...................	6 981	3 696	3 285	...	...	...	...	...	...
15 - 19...................	7 258	3 690	3 568	...	...	...	...	...	...
20 - 24...................	8 008	4 477	3 531	...	...	...	...	...	...
25 - 29...................	7 108	3 854	3 254	...	...	...	...	...	...
30 - 34...................	7 885	4 103	3 782	...	...	...	...	...	...
35 - 39...................	6 564	3 247	3 317	...	...	...	...	...	...
40 - 44...................	6 207	2 985	3 222	...	...	...	...	...	...
45 - 49...................	6 204	3 324	2 880	...	...	...	...	...	...
50 - 54...................	3 479	1 829	1 650	...	...	...	...	...	...
55 - 59·..................	3 057	1 570	1 487	...	...	...	...	...	...
60 - 64...................	2 089	1 004	1 085	...	...	...	...	...	...
65 - 69...................	2 085	839	1 246	...	...	...	...	...	...
70 - 74...................	1 789	710	1 079	...	...	...	...	...	...
75 - 79...................	1 307	508	799	...	...	...	...	...	...
80 +.....................	1 454	416	1 038	...	...	...	...	...	...
Sierra Leone									
1 VII 2003 (ESDF)									
Total....................	5 280 406	2 606 045	2 674 361	...	...	...	...	...	...
0	205 242	102 685	102 557	...	...	...	...	...	...
1 - 4.....................	657 985	331 968	326 016	...	...	...	...	...	...
5 - 9.....................	794 093	399 695	394 398	...	...	...	...	...	...
10 - 14...................	516 752	273 918	242 834	...	...	...	...	...	...
15 - 19...................	513 263	240 312	272 951	...	...	...	...	...	...
20 - 24...................	408 352	182 703	225 649	...	...	...	...	...	...
25 - 29...................	423 009	188 100	234 910	...	...	...	...	...	...
30 - 34...................	329 828	149 713	180 116	...	...	...	...	...	...
35 - 39...................	297 142	146 203	150 940	...	...	...	...	...	...
40 - 44...................	220 272	108 870	111 402	...	...	...	...	...	...
45 - 49...................	193 199	104 586	88 612	...	...	...	...	...	...
50 - 54...................	155 484	80 832	74 652	...	...	...	...	...	...
55 - 59...................	111 025	60 805	50 221	...	...	...	...	...	...
60 - 64...................	116 884	59 762	57 122	...	...	...	...	...	...
65 - 69...................	84 034	44 224	39 811	...	...	...	...	...	...
70 - 74...................	67 884	36 953	30 932	...	...	...	...	...	...
75 - 79...................	50 153	27 772	22 381	...	...	...	...	...	...
80 - 84...................	38 623	19 711	18 912	...	...	...	...	...	...
85 - 89...................	27 246	14 469	12 777	...	...	...	...	...	...
90 +.....................	34 069	17 392	16 677	...	...	...	...	...	...
Unknown - Inconnu.......	35 894	15 402	20 492	...	...	...	...	...	...
Somalia - Somalie									
1 VII 2002 (SSDF)									
Total....................	6 799 079	3 499 523	3 299 556	2 310 817	1 168 410	1 142 407	4 488 262	2 331 113	2 157 149
0 - 4.....................	1 235 105	634 959	600 146	408 646	206 987	201 659	826 459	427 972	398 487
5 - 9.....................	1 049 189	544 431	504 758	352 471	179 293	173 178	696 718	365 138	331 580
10 - 14...................	870 180	455 323	414 857	297 807	151 845	145 962	572 373	303 478	268 895
15 - 19...................	725 723	373 328	352 395	250 718	125 641	125 077	475 005	247 687	227 318
20 - 24...................	581 690	280 786	300 904	202 030	95 671	106 359	379 660	185 115	194 545
25 - 29...................	491 651	231 254	260 397	170 250	78 983	91 267	321 401	152 271	169 130
30 - 34...................	428 269	198 101	230 168	146 024	67 081	78 943	282 245	131 020	151 225
35 - 39...................	366 113	175 050	191 063	123 698	58 860	64 838	242 415	116 190	126 225
40 - 44...................	311 989	164 941	147 048	104 080	54 778	49 302	207 909	110 163	97 746
45 - 49...................	248 939	139 351	109 588	82 971	46 198	36 773	165 968	93 153	72 815
50 - 54...................	174 517	105 972	68 545	58 869	35 355	23 514	115 648	70 617	45 031
55 - 59...................	124 841	79 206	45 635	42 868	26 625	16 243	81 973	52 581	29 392
60 - 64...................	80 530	51 293	29 237	28 988	17 492	11 496	51 542	33 801	17 741
65 - 69...................	51 554	32 843	18 711	19 396	11 603	7 793	32 158	21 240	10 918
70 - 74...................	28 997	17 795	11 202	11 675	6 878	4 797	17 322	10 917	6 405
75 - 79...................	12 860	6 152	6 708	5 828	3 320	2 508	7 032	2 832	4 200
80 +.....................	16 932	8 738	8 194	4 498	1 800	2 698	12 434	6 938	5 496

Continent, country or area, date, code and age (in years) / Continent, pays ou zone, date, code et âge (en années)	Total			Urban - Urbaine			Rural - Rurale		
	Both sexes Les deux sexes	Male Masculin	Female Féminin	Both sexes Les deux sexes	Male Masculin	Female Féminin	Both sexes Les deux sexes	Male Masculin	Female Féminin
AFRICA - AFRIQUE									
South Africa - Afrique du Sud[7]									
1 VII 2007 (ESDF)									
Total.....................	48 287 320	23 231 447	25 055 873	...	...	...	...	...	...
0 - 4....................	5 197 817	2 631 264	2 566 553	...	...	...	...	...	...
5 - 9....................	5 266 681	2 663 826	2 602 855	...	...	...	...	...	...
10 - 14..................	5 272 253	2 661 840	2 610 413	...	...	...	...	...	...
15 - 19..................	5 115 828	2 576 036	2 539 792	...	...	...	...	...	...
20 - 24..................	4 704 277	2 306 426	2 397 851	...	...	...	...	...	...
25 - 29..................	4 334 740	2 102 214	2 232 526	...	...	...	...	...	...
30 - 34..................	3 912 753	1 879 343	2 033 410	...	...	...	...	...	...
35 - 39..................	3 005 229	1 390 530	1 614 699	...	...	...	...	...	...
40 - 44..................	2 407 265	1 091 321	1 315 944	...	...	...	...	...	...
45 - 49..................	2 238 361	1 013 306	1 225 055	...	...	...	...	...	...
50 - 54..................	1 896 863	855 022	1 041 841	...	...	...	...	...	...
55 - 59..................	1 537 496	688 106	849 390	...	...	...	...	...	...
60 - 64..................	1 213 169	533 864	679 305	...	...	...	...	...	...
65 - 69..................	900 567	378 363	522 204	...	...	...	...	...	...
70 - 74..................	613 776	239 518	374 258	...	...	...	...	...	...
75 - 79..................	374 150	132 589	241 561	...	...	...	...	...	...
80 +....................	296 095	87 879	208 216	...	...	...	...	...	...
Tunisia - Tunisie									
1 VII 2007 (ESDF)									
Total.....................	10 225 100	5 105 100	5 120 000	...	...	...	...	...	...
0 - 4....................	823 800	421 300	402 400	...	...	...	...	...	...
5 - 9....................	810 300	418 200	392 100	...	...	...	...	...	...
10 - 14..................	891 500	456 900	434 600	...	...	...	...	...	...
15 - 19..................	1 035 800	530 500	505 200	...	...	...	...	...	...
20 - 24..................	1 049 900	527 300	522 600	...	...	...	...	...	...
25 - 29..................	940 700	461 700	479 000	...	...	...	...	...	...
30 - 34..................	803 400	384 600	418 800	...	...	...	...	...	...
35 - 39..................	704 900	340 000	364 900	...	...	...	...	...	...
40 - 44..................	697 300	337 800	359 600	...	...	...	...	...	...
45 - 49..................	608 000	305 500	302 500	...	...	...	...	...	...
50 - 54..................	510 300	255 300	255 000	...	...	...	...	...	...
55 - 59..................	371 000	182 500	188 500	...	...	...	...	...	...
60 - 64..................	266 900	127 300	139 600	...	...	...	...	...	...
65 - 69..................	237 900	117 400	120 500	...	...	...	...	...	...
70 - 74..................	213 900	105 500	108 400	...	...	...	...	...	...
75 - 79..................	141 400	72 300	69 000	...	...	...	...	...	...
80 +....................	118 100	60 900	57 200	...	...	...	...	...	...
Uganda - Ouganda									
12 IX 2002 (CDFC)									
Total.....................	24 442 084	11 929 803	12 512 281	2 999 387	1 449 684	1 549 703	21 442 697	10 480 119	10 962 578
0.......................	1 007 407	505 006	502 401	104 439	52 481	51 958	902 968	452 525	450 443
1 - 4....................	3 537 016	1 767 120	1 769 896	347 233	172 444	174 789	3 189 783	1 594 676	1 595 107
5 - 9....................	4 001 052	1 998 157	2 002 895	399 119	193 271	205 848	3 601 933	1 804 886	1 797 047
10 - 14..................	3 509 151	1 757 111	1 752 040	391 236	180 572	210 664	3 117 915	1 576 539	1 541 376
15 - 19..................	2 708 143	1 324 222	1 383 921	407 299	180 461	226 838	2 300 844	1 143 761	1 157 083
20 - 24..................	2 175 580	981 994	1 193 586	392 217	180 869	211 348	1 783 363	801 125	982 238
25 - 29..................	1 778 541	831 129	947 412	308 026	152 765	155 261	1 470 515	678 364	792 151
30 - 34..................	1 420 073	708 138	711 935	215 168	116 304	98 864	1 204 905	591 834	613 071
35 - 39..................	1 020 968	492 372	528 596	138 208	72 826	65 382	882 760	419 546	463 214
40 - 44..................	828 317	400 433	427 884	96 870	50 662	46 208	731 447	349 771	381 676
45 - 49..................	542 862	257 694	285 168	58 821	30 676	28 145	484 041	227 018	257 023
50 - 54..................	486 060	223 345	262 715	44 728	22 839	21 889	441 332	200 506	240 826
55 - 59..................	325 875	149 792	176 083	25 198	12 690	12 508	300 677	137 102	163 575
60 - 64..................	363 765	173 325	190 440	24 371	11 139	13 232	339 394	162 186	177 208
65 - 69..................	226 029	115 081	110 948	14 175	6 657	7 518	211 854	108 424	103 430
70 - 74..................	217 160	102 858	114 302	12 538	5 157	7 381	204 622	97 701	106 921
75 - 79..................	105 318	54 213	51 105	6 582	2 824	3 758	98 736	51 389	47 347
80 - 84..................	112 785	52 143	60 642	7 542	2 926	4 616	105 243	49 217	56 026
85 - 89..................	31 184	15 009	16 175	2 146	821	1 325	29 038	14 188	14 850
90 - 94..................	27 871	13 036	14 835	2 126	786	1 340	25 745	12 250	13 495
95 +....................	16 927	7 625	9 302	1 345	514	831	15 582	7 111	8 471

Continent, country or area, date, code and age (in years) / Continent, pays ou zone, date, code et âge (en années)	Total			Urban - Urbaine			Rural - Rurale		
	Both sexes Les deux sexes	Male Masculin	Female Féminin	Both sexes Les deux sexes	Male Masculin	Female Féminin	Both sexes Les deux sexes	Male Masculin	Female Féminin
AFRICA - AFRIQUE									
United Republic of Tanzania - République Unie de Tanzanie									
24 VIII 2002 (CDFC)									
Total	34 443 603	16 829 861	17 613 742	...	...	...	...	...	...
0 - 4	5 664 907	2 830 545	2 834 362	...	...	...	...	...	...
5 - 9	5 130 448	2 573 993	2 556 455	...	...	...	...	...	...
10 - 14	4 443 257	2 233 401	2 209 856	...	...	...	...	...	...
15 - 19	3 595 735	1 761 329	1 834 406	...	...	...	...	...	...
20 - 24	3 148 513	1 402 077	1 746 436	...	...	...	...	...	...
25 - 29	2 801 965	1 309 661	1 492 304	...	...	...	...	...	...
30 - 34	2 229 046	1 087 599	1 141 447	...	...	...	...	...	...
35 - 39	1 669 873	824 338	845 535	...	...	...	...	...	...
40 - 44	1 348 508	669 549	678 959	...	...	...	...	...	...
45 - 49	984 823	478 522	506 301	...	...	...	...	...	...
50 - 54	883 820	428 501	455 319	...	...	...	...	...	...
55 - 59	590 667	290 117	300 550	...	...	...	...	...	...
60 - 64	604 956	287 502	317 454	...	...	...	...	...	...
65 - 69	439 671	213 635	226 036	...	...	...	...	...	...
70 - 74	377 852	180 246	197 606	...	...	...	...	...	...
75 - 79	221 354	113 205	108 149	...	...	...	...	...	...
80 +	308 208	145 641	162 567	...	...	...	...	...	...
Zambia - Zambie									
25 X 2000 (CDFC)									
Total	9 337 425	4 594 290	4 743 135	3 347 069	1 662 739	1 684 330	5 990 356	2 931 551	3 058 805
0	339 228	168 841	170 387	101 775	50 699	51 076	237 453	118 142	119 311
1 - 4	1 317 492	656 948	660 544	420 759	209 814	210 945	896 733	447 134	449 599
5 - 9	1 461 082	729 181	731 901	500 572	247 117	253 455	960 510	482 064	478 446
10 - 14	1 205 646	601 279	604 367	428 831	206 305	222 526	776 815	394 974	381 841
15 - 19	1 069 996	513 320	556 676	415 197	195 518	219 679	654 799	317 802	336 997
20 - 24	908 672	416 083	492 589	376 695	174 331	202 364	531 977	241 752	290 225
25 - 29	741 148	361 901	379 247	308 436	155 070	153 366	432 712	206 831	225 881
30 - 34	557 873	282 439	275 434	225 707	119 524	106 183	332 166	162 915	169 251
35 - 39	429 987	211 356	218 631	169 148	87 763	81 385	260 839	123 593	137 246
40 - 44	325 776	161 179	164 597	125 995	66 050	59 945	199 781	95 129	104 652
45 - 49	245 320	122 486	122 834	91 507	50 128	41 379	153 813	72 358	81 455
50 - 54	203 612	97 850	105 762	65 547	37 513	28 034	138 065	60 337	77 728
55 - 59	144 838	71 905	72 933	39 418	22 860	16 558	105 420	49 045	56 375
60 - 64	131 475	62 678	68 797	29 438	15 308	14 130	102 037	47 370	54 667
65 - 69	100 493	52 499	47 994	20 294	10 642	9 652	80 199	41 857	38 342
70 - 74	68 935	37 066	31 869	12 763	6 634	6 129	56 172	30 432	25 740
75 - 79	40 649	23 301	17 348	7 217	3 793	3 424	33 432	19 508	13 924
80 - 84	24 242	13 311	10 931	4 418	2 206	2 212	19 824	11 105	8 719
85 +	20 961	10 667	10 294	3 352	1 464	1 888	17 609	9 203	8 406
Zimbabwe									
17 VIII 2002 (CDFC)									
Total	11 631 657	5 634 180	5 997 477	4 029 707	1 988 176	2 041 531	7 601 950	3 646 004	3 955 946
0	340 331	170 054	170 277	117 756	59 103	58 653	222 575	110 951	111 624
1 - 4	1 335 738	668 008	667 730	422 397	210 186	212 211	913 341	457 822	455 519
5 - 9	1 533 700	764 453	769 247	424 731	207 986	216 745	1 108 969	556 467	552 502
10 - 14	1 512 244	754 587	757 657	381 331	180 444	200 887	1 130 913	574 143	556 770
15 - 19	1 503 576	736 686	766 890	511 394	217 513	293 881	992 182	519 173	473 009
20 - 24	1 222 907	564 034	658 873	566 584	260 105	306 479	656 323	303 929	352 394
25 - 29	987 777	473 984	513 793	474 294	242 497	231 797	513 483	231 487	281 996
30 - 34	730 127	369 836	360 291	345 675	191 527	154 148	384 452	178 309	206 143
35 - 39	504 489	235 692	268 797	222 381	116 670	105 711	282 108	119 022	163 086
40 - 44	434 429	194 702	239 727	168 100	87 760	80 340	266 329	106 942	159 387
45 - 49	356 605	165 437	191 168	128 388	70 668	57 720	228 217	94 769	133 448
50 - 54	301 258	128 029	173 229	87 458	48 199	39 259	213 800	79 830	133 970
55 - 59	210 915	98 417	112 498	55 467	31 214	24 253	155 448	67 203	88 245
60 - 64	193 867	94 447	99 420	42 546	23 384	19 162	151 321	71 063	80 258
65 - 69	132 152	64 301	67 851	26 735	14 234	12 501	105 417	50 067	55 350
70 - 74	122 775	60 311	62 464	20 371	10 602	9 769	102 404	49 709	52 695
75 +	...	...	...	23 687	10 598	13 089	140 574	61 352	79 222
75 - 79	64 470	29 997	34 473	...	...	...	...	...	...

7. Population by age, sex and urban/rural residence: latest available year, 1998 - 2007
Population selon l'âge, le sexe et la résidence, urbaine/rurale: dernière année disponible, 1998 - 2007 (continued - suite)

Continent, country or area, date, code and age (in years) / Continent, pays ou zone, date, code et âge (en annèes)	Total			Urban - Urbaine			Rural - Rurale		
	Both sexes Les deux sexes	Male Masculin	Female Féminin	Both sexes Les deux sexes	Male Masculin	Female Féminin	Both sexes Les deux sexes	Male Masculin	Female Féminin
AFRICA - AFRIQUE									
Zimbabwe									
17 VIII 2002 (CDFC)									
80 - 84	59 045	26 764	32 281	...	...	...	...	...	...
85 - 89	19 084	7 727	11 357	...	...	...	...	...	...
90 - 94	9 188	3 752	5 436	...	...	...	...	...	...
95 +	12 474	3 710	8 764	...	...	...	...	...	...
Unknown - Inconnu	44 506	19 252	25 254	10 412	5 486	4 926	34 094	13 766	20 328
AMERICA, NORTH - AMÉRIQUE DU NORD									
Anguilla[8]									
9 V 2001 (CDFC)									
Total	11 430	5 628	5 802	...	...	...	...	...	...
0	252	131	121	...	...	...	...	...	...
1 - 4	821	394	427	...	...	...	...	...	...
5 - 9	993	502	491	...	...	...	...	...	...
10 - 14	1 136	563	573	...	...	...	...	...	...
15 - 19	966	477	489	...	...	...	...	...	...
20 - 24	788	375	413	...	...	...	...	...	...
25 - 29	873	440	433	...	...	...	...	...	...
30 - 34	999	494	505	...	...	...	...	...	...
35 - 39	1 040	507	533	...	...	...	...	...	...
40 - 44	881	429	452	...	...	...	...	...	...
45 - 49	714	364	350	...	...	...	...	...	...
50 - 54	468	236	232	...	...	...	...	...	...
55 - 59	323	166	157	...	...	...	...	...	...
60 - 64	304	144	160	...	...	...	...	...	...
65 - 69	288	159	129	...	...	...	...	...	...
70 - 74	211	82	129	...	...	...	...	...	...
75 - 79	155	65	90	...	...	...	...	...	...
80 - 84	102	52	50	...	...	...	...	...	...
85 - 89	79	31	48	...	...	...	...	...	...
90 - 94	30	15	15	...	...	...	...	...	...
95 +	7	2	5	...	...	...	...	...	...
Antigua and Barbuda - Antigua-et-Barbuda									
1 VII 2005 (ESDF)									
Total	82 786	38 878	43 908	...	...	...	...	...	...
0	1 537	765	772	...	...	...	...	...	...
1 - 4	6 269	3 230	3 039	...	...	...	...	...	...
5 - 9	7 954	3 966	3 988	...	...	...	...	...	...
10 - 14	7 635	3 699	3 937	...	...	...	...	...	...
15 - 19	6 812	3 230	3 582	...	...	...	...	...	...
20 - 24	6 527	3 119	3 408	...	...	...	...	...	...
25 - 29	6 889	3 169	3 719	...	...	...	...	...	...
30 - 34	7 518	3 344	4 174	...	...	...	...	...	...
35 - 39	7 199	3 251	3 948	...	...	...	...	...	...
40 - 44	5 977	2 697	3 280	...	...	...	...	...	...
45 - 49	4 658	2 176	2 482	...	...	...	...	...	...
50 - 54	3 518	1 659	1 859	...	...	...	...	...	...
55 - 59	2 573	1 162	1 411	...	...	...	...	...	...
60 - 64	2 028	929	1 099	...	...	...	...	...	...
65 - 69	1 700	778	922	...	...	...	...	...	...
70 - 74	1 442	633	809	...	...	...	...	...	...
75 - 79	1 100	507	593	...	...	...	...	...	...
80 - 84	783	332	451	...	...	...	...	...	...
85 - 89	437	160	278	...	...	...	...	...	...
90 - 94	197	65	132	...	...	...	...	...	...
95 +	32	9	23	...	...	...	...	...	...
Aruba[9]									
1 VII 2007 (ESDJ)									
Total	104 005	49 614	54 391	...	...	...	...	...	...
0	1 241	633	608	...	...	...	...	...	...

Continent, country or area, date, code and age (in years) / Continent, pays ou zone, date, code et âge (en années)	Total			Urban - Urbaine			Rural - Rurale		
	Both sexes Les deux sexes	Male Masculin	Female Féminin	Both sexes Les deux sexes	Male Masculin	Female Féminin	Both sexes Les deux sexes	Male Masculin	Female Féminin
AMERICA, NORTH - AMÉRIQUE DU NORD									
Aruba[9]									
1 VII 2007 (ESDJ)									
1 - 4	5 153	2 632	2 522	...	...	...	...	...	...
5 - 9	7 240	3 653	3 587	...	...	...	...	...	...
10 - 14	7 753	3 942	3 811	...	...	...	...	...	...
15 - 19	7 337	3 698	3 639	...	...	...	...	...	...
20 - 24	5 999	2 983	3 015	...	...	...	...	...	...
25 - 29	6 301	2 982	3 319	...	...	...	...	...	...
30 - 34	7 383	3 473	3 910	...	...	...	...	...	...
35 - 39	8 895	4 180	4 716	...	...	...	...	...	...
40 - 44	9 633	4 549	5 084	...	...	...	...	...	...
45 - 49	9 508	4 501	5 007	...	...	...	...	...	...
50 - 54	7 757	3 580	4 178	...	...	...	...	...	...
55 - 59	6 027	2 828	3 199	...	...	...	...	...	...
60 - 64	4 502	2 083	2 419	...	...	...	...	...	...
65 - 69	3 421	1 548	1 873	...	...	...	...	...	...
70 - 74	2 620	1 088	1 532	...	...	...	...	...	...
75 - 79	1 689	706	983	...	...	...	...	...	...
80 - 84	836	335	501	...	...	...	...	...	...
85 - 89	429	154	275	...	...	...	...	...	...
90 - 94	193	51	142	...	...	...	...	...	...
95 +	91	18	73	...	...	...	...	...	...
Bahamas									
1 VII 2007 (ESDF)									
Total	334 000	162 300	171 700	...	...	...	...	...	...
0 - 4	28 800	14 800	14 000	...	...	...	...	...	...
5 - 9	28 400	14 300	14 100	...	...	...	...	...	...
10 - 14	31 300	15 700	15 600	...	...	...	...	...	...
15 - 19	29 600	14 600	15 000	...	...	...	...	...	...
20 - 24	26 600	13 200	13 400	...	...	...	...	...	...
25 - 29	25 000	12 300	12 700	...	...	...	...	...	...
30 - 34	26 900	13 000	13 900	...	...	...	...	...	...
35 - 39	27 400	13 100	14 300	...	...	...	...	...	...
40 - 44	26 700	12 800	13 900	...	...	...	...	...	...
45 - 49	23 400	11 200	12 200	...	...	...	...	...	...
50 - 54	17 700	8 500	9 200	...	...	...	...	...	...
55 - 59	12 900	6 100	6 800	...	...	...	...	...	...
60 - 64	10 000	4 600	5 400	...	...	...	...	...	...
65 - 69	7 900	3 600	4 300	...	...	...	...	...	...
70 - 74	5 400	2 400	3 000	...	...	...	...	...	...
75 - 79	3 300	1 300	2 000	...	...	...	...	...	...
80 +	2 700	800	1 900	...	...	...	...	...	...
Barbados - Barbade									
1 V 2000 (CDFC)									
Total	250 010	119 926	130 084	...	...	...	...	...	...
0 - 4	17 239	8 763	8 476	...	...	...	...	...	...
5 - 9	18 749	9 479	9 270	...	...	...	...	...	...
10 - 14	18 613	9 425	9 188	...	...	...	...	...	...
15 - 19	18 636	9 434	9 202	...	...	...	...	...	...
20 - 24	17 804	8 913	8 891	...	...	...	...	...	...
25 - 29	19 738	9 758	9 980	...	...	...	...	...	...
30 - 34	19 588	9 574	10 014	...	...	...	...	...	...
35 - 39	21 257	10 155	11 102	...	...	...	...	...	...
40 - 44	20 055	9 544	10 511	...	...	...	...	...	...
45 - 49	16 774	8 007	8 767	...	...	...	...	...	...
50 - 54	13 638	6 563	7 075	...	...	...	...	...	...
55 - 59	9 583	4 376	5 207	...	...	...	...	...	...
60 - 64	8 925	3 969	4 956	...	...	...	...	...	...
65 - 69	8 319	3 648	4 671	...	...	...	...	...	...
70 +	21 092	8 318	12 774	...	...	...	...	...	...
Belize[10]									
1 VII 2006 (ESDF)									
Total	301 298	149 598	151 700	151 994	73 576	78 418	149 394	76 101	73 293
0 - 4	36 761	18 145	18 616	17 720	8 446	9 274	19 808	10 070	9 738

7. Population by age, sex and urban/rural residence: latest available year, 1998 - 2007
Population selon l'âge, le sexe et la résidence, urbaine/rurale: dernière année disponible, 1998 - 2007 (continued - suite)

Continent, country or area, date, code and age (in years) / Continent, pays ou zone, date, code et âge (en années)	Total			Urban - Urbaine			Rural - Rurale		
	Both sexes Les deux sexes	Male Masculin	Female Féminin	Both sexes Les deux sexes	Male Masculin	Female Féminin	Both sexes Les deux sexes	Male Masculin	Female Féminin
AMERICA, NORTH - AMÉRIQUE DU NORD									
Belize[10]									
1 VII 2006 (ESDF)									
5 - 9	40 974	20 850	20 124	19 294	9 792	9 502	21 574	11 011	10 563
10 - 14	40 474	20 611	19 862	19 185	9 790	9 395	21 185	10 775	10 410
15 - 19	33 960	17 192	16 769	16 629	8 785	7 844	17 246	8 369	8 877
20 - 24	24 423	11 939	12 484	12 728	5 973	6 755	11 631	5 939	5 692
25 - 29	20 990	9 733	11 256	11 262	5 018	6 244	9 673	4 693	4 980
30 - 34	20 405	9 522	10 883	11 277	5 183	6 094	9 075	4 318	4 757
35 - 39	18 464	8 747	9 718	9 745	4 294	5 451	8 672	4 433	4 239
40 - 44	15 793	7 735	8 058	8 174	3 931	4 243	7 579	3 787	3 792
45 - 49	12 378	6 295	6 065	6 555	3 305	3 250	5 791	2 976	2 815
50 - 54	9 686	4 983	4 703	5 176	2 385	2 791	4 485	2 586	1 899
55 - 59	6 637	3 363	3 264	3 385	1 636	1 749	3 235	1 720	1 515
60 - 64	5 692	2 913	2 778	2 838	1 376	1 462	2 839	1 531	1 308
65 - 69	4 877	2 547	2 330	2 584	1 201	1 383	2 281	1 341	940
70 - 74	3 867	2 073	1 794	2 203	999	1 204	1 654	1 069	585
75 - 79	2 708	1 374	1 330	1 511	716	795	1 191	656	535
80 - 84	1 578	782	798	794	327	467	784	453	331
85 +	1 629	794	835	934	419	515	691	374	317
1 VII 2007 (ESDF)									
Total	311 500	154 700	156 800	...	...	...	...	...	...
0 - 4	37 300	18 500	18 800	...	...	...	...	...	...
5 - 9	42 200	21 400	20 800	...	...	...	...	...	...
10 - 14	41 800	21 300	20 500	...	...	...	...	...	...
15 - 19	35 300	17 900	17 400	...	...	...	...	...	...
20 - 24	25 000	12 300	12 700	...	...	...	...	...	...
25 - 29	21 600	10 000	11 600	...	...	...	...	...	...
30 - 34	20 900	9 700	11 200	...	...	...	...	...	...
35 - 39	19 200	9 100	10 100	...	...	...	...	...	...
40 - 44	16 600	8 100	8 500	...	...	...	...	...	...
45 - 49	13 000	6 600	6 400	...	...	...	...	...	...
50 - 54	10 200	5 200	5 000	...	...	...	...	...	...
55 - 59	7 100	3 600	3 500	...	...	...	...	...	...
60 - 64	6 000	3 100	2 900	...	...	...	...	...	...
65 - 69	5 100	2 700	2 400	...	...	...	...	...	...
70 - 74	4 000	2 100	1 900	...	...	...	...	...	...
75 - 79	2 900	1 500	1 400	...	...	...	...	...	...
80 - 84	1 600	800	800	...	...	...	...	...	...
85 +	1 700	800	900	...	...	...	...	...	...
Bermuda - Bermudes									
1 VII 2007 (ESDJ)									
Total	64 009	30 577	33 432	...	...	...	...	...	...
0 - 4	3 812	1 955	1 857	...	...	...	...	...	...
5 - 9	3 817	1 939	1 878	...	...	...	...	...	...
10 - 14	3 793	1 902	1 891	...	...	...	...	...	...
15 - 19	3 714	1 824	1 890	...	...	...	...	...	...
20 - 24	3 611	1 776	1 835	...	...	...	...	...	...
25 - 29	4 018	1 880	2 138	...	...	...	...	...	...
30 - 34	4 560	2 169	2 391	...	...	...	...	...	...
35 - 39	5 137	2 515	2 622	...	...	...	...	...	...
40 - 44	5 728	2 869	2 859	...	...	...	...	...	...
45 - 49	5 759	2 769	2 990	...	...	...	...	...	...
50 - 54	4 873	2 304	2 569	...	...	...	...	...	...
55 - 59	4 150	1 974	2 176	...	...	...	...	...	...
60 - 64	3 345	1 561	1 784	...	...	...	...	...	...
65 - 69	2 420	1 079	1 341	...	...	...	...	...	...
70 - 74	2 040	882	1 158	...	...	...	...	...	...
75 - 79	1 547	629	918	...	...	...	...	...	...
80 - 84	998	350	648	...	...	...	...	...	...
85 +	687	200	487	...	...	...	...	...	...

7. Population by age, sex and urban/rural residence: latest available year, 1998 - 2007
Population selon l'âge, le sexe et la résidence, urbaine/rurale: dernière année disponible, 1998 - 2007 (continued - suite)

Continent, country or area, date, code and age (in years) / Continent, pays ou zone, date, code et âge (en années)	Total			Urban - Urbaine			Rural - Rurale		
	Both sexes Les deux sexes	Male Masculin	Female Féminin	Both sexes Les deux sexes	Male Masculin	Female Féminin	Both sexes Les deux sexes	Male Masculin	Female Féminin
AMERICA, NORTH - AMÉRIQUE DU NORD									
British Virgin Islands - Îles Vierges britanniques									
21 V 2001 (CDFC)									
Total	20 647	10 627	10 020						
0 - 4	1 787	913	874	...	...	...	...	...	...
5 - 9	1 865	946	919	...	...	...	...	...	...
10 - 14	1 768	880	888	...	...	...	...	...	...
15 - 19	1 529	778	751	...	...	...	...	...	...
20 - 24	1 465	752	713	...	...	...	...	...	...
25 - 29	1 483	756	727	...	...	...	...	...	...
30 - 34	1 826	913	913	...	...	...	...	...	...
35 - 39	2 085	1 091	994	...	...	...	...	...	...
40 - 44	1 910	991	919	...	...	...	...	...	...
45 - 49	1 501	777	724	...	...	...	...	...	...
50 - 54	1 128	614	514	...	...	...	...	...	...
55 - 59	774	421	353	...	...	...	...	...	...
60 - 64	523	267	256	...	...	...	...	...	...
65 - 69	337	177	160	...	...	...	...	...	...
70 - 74	282	145	137	...	...	...	...	...	...
75 - 79	204	113	91	...	...	...	...	...	...
80 +	180	93	87	...	...	...	...	...	...
Canada									
16 V 2006 (CDJC)[9]									
Total	31 612 895	15 475 970	16 136 925	25 350 585	12 289 025	13 061 560	6 262 315	3 186 950	3 075 365
0 - 4	1 690 540	864 600	825 940	1 365 015	697 760	667 255	325 520	166 840	158 680
5 - 9	1 809 375	926 860	882 515	1 430 755	732 775	697 980	378 620	194 080	184 540
10 - 14	2 079 925	1 065 860	1 014 060	1 623 165	830 685	792 480	456 760	235 180	221 580
15 - 19	2 140 490	1 095 285	1 045 210	1 680 870	855 915	824 960	459 620	239 370	220 250
20 - 24	2 080 385	1 047 950	1 032 440	1 756 075	877 305	878 775	324 310	170 645	153 660
25 - 29	1 985 580	975 945	1 009 635	1 701 100	833 530	867 575	284 480	142 420	142 060
30 - 34	2 020 230	987 715	1 032 510	1 690 870	824 815	866 050	329 360	162 900	166 460
35 - 39	2 208 270	1 083 495	1 124 780	1 810 135	886 375	923 760	398 140	197 125	201 015
40 - 44	2 610 455	1 285 535	1 324 925	2 088 760	1 024 215	1 064 540	521 705	261 320	260 380
45 - 49	2 620 600	1 290 130	1 330 470	2 067 000	1 009 375	1 057 620	553 600	280 755	272 850
50 - 54	2 357 300	1 158 970	1 198 335	1 833 675	891 450	942 230	523 625	267 525	256 100
55 - 59	2 084 620	1 026 390	1 058 230	1 601 975	777 985	823 990	482 650	248 405	234 240
60 - 64	1 589 870	780 135	809 730	1 205 570	579 700	625 870	384 295	200 430	183 860
65 - 69	1 234 575	593 810	640 770	949 745	443 420	506 330	284 835	150 390	134 440
70 - 74	1 053 785	493 465	560 325	834 670	378 835	455 840	219 110	114 630	104 485
75 - 79	879 575	386 485	493 090	718 780	305 230	413 550	160 800	81 255	79 545
80 - 84	646 705	251 420	395 285	544 780	204 705	340 075	101 920	46 710	55 210
85 - 89	342 685	114 585	228 100	292 910	95 160	197 750	49 770	19 425	30 345
90 - 94	139 105	38 455	100 650	120 735	32 340	88 400	18 370	6 115	12 255
95 - 99	34 185	8 080	26 110	29 890	6 790	23 105	4 300	1 290	3 010
100 +	4 635	805	3 825	4 110	685	3 430	525	125	400
1 VII 2007 (ESDJ)									
Total	32 976 026	16 332 277	16 643 749	...	...	...	...	...	...
0 - 4	1 740 197	890 661	849 536	...	...	...	...	...	...
5 - 9	1 812 357	927 173	885 184	...	...	...	...	...	...
10 - 14	2 060 492	1 057 116	1 003 376	...	...	...	...	...	...
15 - 19	2 197 739	1 126 189	1 071 550	...	...	...	...	...	...
20 - 24	2 271 632	1 161 774	1 109 858	...	...	...	...	...	...
25 - 29	2 273 269	1 148 527	1 124 742	...	...	...	...	...	...
30 - 34	2 242 048	1 129 576	1 112 472	...	...	...	...	...	...
35 - 39	2 354 583	1 185 058	1 169 525	...	...	...	...	...	...
40 - 44	2 640 068	1 326 386	1 313 682	...	...	...	...	...	...
45 - 49	2 711 573	1 356 416	1 355 157	...	...	...	...	...	...
50 - 54	2 441 285	1 209 633	1 231 652	...	...	...	...	...	...
55 - 59	2 108 785	1 040 492	1 068 293	...	...	...	...	...	...
60 - 64	1 698 594	834 869	863 725	...	...	...	...	...	...
65 - 69	1 274 574	614 494	660 080	...	...	...	...	...	...
70 - 74	1 047 929	492 229	555 700	...	...	...	...	...	...
75 - 79	894 652	398 597	496 055	...	...	...	...	...	...
80 - 84	650 806	257 633	393 173	...	...	...	...	...	...

Continent, country or area, date, code and age (in years) / Continent, pays ou zone, date, code et âge (en années)	Total			Urban - Urbaine			Rural - Rurale		
	Both sexes Les deux sexes	Male Masculin	Female Féminin	Both sexes Les deux sexes	Male Masculin	Female Féminin	Both sexes Les deux sexes	Male Masculin	Female Féminin
AMERICA, NORTH - AMÉRIQUE DU NORD									
Canada									
1 VII 2007 (ESDJ)									
85 - 89	369 260	125 527	243 733	...	...	...	...	...	...
90 +	186 183	49 927	136 256	...	...	...	...	...	...
Cayman Islands - Îles Caïmanes									
1 VII 2006 (ESDJ)									
Total	51 992	26 340	25 652	...	...	...	...	...	...
0 - 14	8 749	4 625	4 124	...	...	...	...	...	...
15 - 19	2 727	1 494	1 233	...	...	...	...	...	...
20 - 24	2 766	1 507	1 259	...	...	...	...	...	...
25 - 34	10 622	5 396	5 226	...	...	...	...	...	...
35 - 44	11 425	5 687	5 738	...	...	...	...	...	...
45 - 54	8 223	4 063	4 160	...	...	...	...	...	...
55 - 64	4 169	2 208	1 961	...	...	...	...	...	...
65 +	3 311	1 360	1 951	...	...	...	...	...	...
Costa Rica									
1 VII 2007 (ESDJ)									
Total	4 443 100	2 195 652	2 247 448	2 619 591	1 273 998	1 345 593	1 823 509	921 654	901 855
0 - 4	336 499	179 028	157 471	180 246	95 283	84 963	156 253	83 745	72 508
5 - 9	386 717	200 379	186 338	200 441	104 992	95 449	186 276	95 387	90 889
10 - 14	453 341	241 136	212 205	240 169	127 373	112 796	213 172	113 763	99 409
15 - 19	464 534	234 496	230 038	265 720	132 988	132 732	198 814	101 508	97 306
20 - 24	438 286	216 975	221 311	274 275	134 439	139 836	164 011	82 536	81 475
25 - 29	340 846	160 122	180 724	207 614	99 285	108 329	133 232	60 837	72 395
30 - 39	619 168	298 936	320 232	357 715	173 225	184 490	261 453	125 711	135 742
40 - 49	568 373	271 893	296 480	350 248	162 307	187 941	218 125	109 586	108 539
50 - 59	415 724	197 179	218 545	274 792	128 083	146 709	140 932	69 096	71 836
60 - 69	213 102	100 241	112 861	134 864	59 091	75 773	78 238	41 150	37 088
70 +	202 926	93 400	109 526	132 210	56 670	75 540	70 716	36 730	33 986
Unknown - Inconnu	3 584	1 867	1 717	1 297	262	1 035	2 287	1 605	682
Cuba[11]									
1 VII 2007 (ESDJ)									
Total	11 237 916	5 627 694	5 610 222	8 478 510	4 171 388	4 307 122	2 759 406	1 456 305	1 303 100
0 - 4	614 013	316 448	297 565	451 440	232 709	218 731	162 573	83 739	78 834
5 - 9	712 124	366 591	345 533	518 978	267 006	251 972	193 146	99 585	93 561
10 - 14	718 535	368 816	349 719	524 188	268 640	255 548	194 347	100 176	94 170
15 - 19	850 253	437 261	412 992	629 490	321 726	307 764	220 762	115 534	105 228
20 - 24	785 266	404 830	380 436	586 917	299 765	287 152	198 348	105 064	93 284
25 - 29	660 534	341 828	318 705	488 552	251 777	236 775	171 981	90 051	81 930
30 - 34	911 841	465 276	446 565	672 872	341 758	331 114	238 969	123 518	115 451
35 - 39	1 050 886	529 137	521 749	783 369	389 641	393 728	267 516	139 496	128 020
40 - 44	1 092 253	543 196	549 057	845 729	414 013	431 716	246 524	129 182	117 341
45 - 49	765 536	377 013	388 523	593 292	286 276	307 016	172 244	90 737	81 506
50 - 54	643 709	314 126	329 582	499 293	237 419	261 874	144 415	76 707	67 708
55 - 59	605 943	295 838	310 105	474 123	225 398	248 725	131 820	70 440	61 380
60 - 64	525 620	254 448	271 171	409 959	192 461	217 497	115 661	61 987	53 674
65 - 69	431 958	210 931	221 027	334 164	156 634	177 530	97 793	54 296	43 497
70 - 74	317 887	152 452	165 435	243 900	110 667	133 233	73 987	41 785	32 202
75 - 79	237 154	111 529	125 625	182 540	80 049	102 491	54 614	31 480	23 134
80 - 84	161 743	73 266	88 477	124 357	51 779	72 578	37 386	21 487	15 899
85 +	152 658	64 705	87 952	115 342	43 667	71 675	37 315	21 038	16 277
Dominica - Dominique									
31 XII 2006 (ESDF)									
Total	71 180	36 238	34 942	...	...	...	...	...	...
0 - 4	6 317	3 250	3 067	...	...	...	...	...	...
5 - 9	7 554	3 951	3 603	...	...	...	...	...	...
10 - 14	7 105	3 558	3 547	...	...	...	...	...	...
15 - 19	6 818	3 452	3 366	...	...	...	...	...	...
20 - 24	4 578	2 438	2 140	...	...	...	...	...	...
25 - 29	5 121	2 601	2 520	...	...	...	...	...	...
30 - 34	5 663	2 886	2 777	...	...	...	...	...	...
35 - 39	5 296	2 841	2 455	...	...	...	...	...	...
40 - 44	4 476	2 417	2 059	...	...	...	...	...	...

Continent, country or area, date, code and age (in years) / Continent, pays ou zone, date, code et âge (en années)	Total			Urban - Urbaine			Rural - Rurale		
	Both sexes Les deux sexes	Male Masculin	Female Féminin	Both sexes Les deux sexes	Male Masculin	Female Féminin	Both sexes Les deux sexes	Male Masculin	Female Féminin
AMERICA, NORTH - AMÉRIQUE DU NORD									
Dominica - Dominique									
31 XII 2006 (ESDF)									
45 - 49	3 561	1 947	1 614	...	...	...	...	...	...
50 - 54	2 820	1 467	1 353	...	...	...	...	...	...
55 - 59	2 391	1 209	1 182	...	...	...	...	...	...
60 - 64	2 255	1 022	1 233	...	...	...	...	...	...
65 - 69	2 324	1 091	1 233	...	...	...	...	...	...
70 - 74	1 844	871	973	...	...	...	...	...	...
75 - 79	1 332	596	736	...	...	...	...	...	...
80 - 84	901	354	547	...	...	...	...	...	...
85 + ...	825	288	537	...	...	...	...	...	...
Dominican Republic - République dominicaine[3]									
1 VII 2005 (ESDF)									
Total..................	9 226 449	4 615 274	4 611 175	5 816 828	2 881 652	2 935 176	3 409 621	1 733 622	1 675 999
0 - 4.................	1 053 698	537 020	516 678	647 199	333 736	313 462	406 499	203 284	203 216
5 - 9.................	1 012 877	515 417	497 460	610 854	313 263	297 591	402 023	202 154	199 869
10 - 14.............	1 003 497	509 330	494 167	613 179	309 875	303 304	390 318	199 455	190 863
15 - 19.............	939 086	472 387	466 699	594 518	294 994	299 524	344 568	177 393	167 175
20 - 24.............	858 031	426 160	431 871	560 000	274 859	285 141	298 031	151 301	146 730
25 - 29.............	752 009	370 156	381 853	495 914	242 677	253 237	256 095	127 479	128 616
30 - 34.............	671 024	328 762	342 262	439 246	213 800	225 445	231 778	114 962	116 817
35 - 39.............	598 719	294 757	303 962	391 353	190 886	200 466	207 366	103 871	103 496
40 - 44.............	529 396	263 036	266 360	341 232	167 303	173 930	188 164	95 733	92 430
45 - 49.............	447 748	223 705	224 043	287 124	140 961	146 163	160 624	82 744	77 880
50 - 54.............	358 315	179 332	178 983	224 993	110 493	114 500	133 322	68 839	64 483
55 - 59.............	274 722	137 121	137 601	170 336	83 126	87 211	104 386	53 995	50 390
60 - 64.............	213 703	106 527	107 176	129 578	62 264	67 314	84 125	44 263	39 862
65 - 69.............	184 331	91 256	93 075	111 233	52 921	58 312	73 098	38 335	34 763
70 - 74.............	141 054	69 467	71 587	84 217	39 297	44 920	56 837	30 170	26 667
75 - 79.............	94 982	46 287	48 695	57 425	26 094	31 331	37 557	20 193	17 364
80 +.................	93 257	44 554	48 703	58 427	25 104	33 323	34 830	19 450	15 380
El Salvador									
12 V 2007 (CDJC)									
Total..................	5 744 113	2 719 371	3 024 742	3 598 836	1 676 313	1 922 523	2 145 277	1 043 058	1 102 219
0 - 4.................	555 893	283 272	272 621	324 299	165 397	158 902	231 594	117 875	113 719
5 - 9.................	684 727	349 150	335 577	390 873	199 184	191 689	293 854	149 966	143 888
10 - 14.............	706 347	359 523	346 824	404 755	205 222	199 533	301 592	154 301	147 291
15 - 19.............	600 565	298 384	302 181	355 376	174 488	180 888	245 189	123 896	121 293
20 - 24.............	486 542	228 001	258 541	309 107	143 779	165 328	177 435	84 222	93 213
25 - 29.............	457 890	206 963	250 927	306 456	138 320	168 136	151 434	68 643	82 791
30 - 34.............	402 249	178 400	223 849	274 037	121 278	152 759	128 212	57 122	71 090
35 - 39.............	353 147	156 514	196 633	242 566	106 882	135 684	110 581	49 632	60 949
40 - 44.............	303 631	132 218	171 413	209 958	90 559	119 399	93 673	41 659	52 014
45 - 49.............	252 122	109 957	142 165	170 464	73 027	97 437	81 658	36 930	44 728
50 - 54.............	215 734	95 275	120 459	143 882	62 014	81 868	71 852	33 261	38 591
55 - 59.............	183 075	81 718	101 357	119 193	51 574	67 619	63 882	30 144	33 738
60 - 64.............	151 864	68 207	83 657	97 101	41 821	55 280	54 763	26 386	28 377
65 - 69.............	125 157	55 781	69 376	79 690	33 492	46 198	45 467	22 289	23 178
70 - 74.............	97 457	43 449	54 008	62 075	25 726	36 349	35 382	17 723	17 659
75 - 79.............	75 984	33 658	42 326	48 760	20 096	28 664	27 224	13 562	13 662
80 - 84.............	46 870	20 401	26 469	30 578	12 261	18 317	16 292	8 140	8 152
85 + ...	44 859	18 500	26 359	29 666	11 193	18 473	15 193	7 307	7 886
Greenland - Groenland									
1 I 2005 (ESDJ)									
Total..................	56 969	30 319	26 650	47 086	24 884	22 202	9 883	5 435	4 448
0	797	405	392	639	324	315	158	81	77
1 - 4.................	3 540	1 793	1 747	2 866	1 449	1 417	674	344	330
5 - 9.................	4 763	2 419	2 344	3 833	1 969	1 864	930	450	480
10 - 14.............	5 220	2 638	2 582	4 187	2 128	2 059	1 033	510	523
15 - 19.............	4 483	2 256	2 227	3 739	1 872	1 867	744	384	360
20 - 24.............	3 943	2 054	1 889	3 292	1 680	1 612	651	374	277
25 - 29.............	3 428	1 790	1 638	2 832	1 436	1 396	596	354	242
30 - 34.............	3 635	2 001	1 634	3 015	1 660	1 355	620	341	279

Continent, country or area, date, code and age (in years) / Continent, pays ou zone, date, code et âge (en années)	Total			Urban - Urbaine			Rural - Rurale		
	Both sexes Les deux sexes	Male Masculin	Female Féminin	Both sexes Les deux sexes	Male Masculin	Female Féminin	Both sexes Les deux sexes	Male Masculin	Female Féminin
AMERICA, NORTH - AMÉRIQUE DU NORD									
Greenland - Groenland									
1 I 2005 (ESDJ)									
35 - 39	5 627	3 025	2 602	4 699	2 501	2 198	928	524	404
40 - 44	5 627	3 030	2 597	4 736	2 518	2 218	891	512	379
45 - 49	4 442	2 537	1 905	3 721	2 102	1 619	721	435	286
50 - 54	3 431	1 955	1 476	2 863	1 610	1 253	568	345	223
55 - 59	2 637	1 627	1 010	2 228	1 362	866	409	265	144
60 - 64	2 253	1 291	962	1 862	1 064	798	391	227	164
65 - 69	1 317	699	618	1 056	557	499	261	142	119
70 - 74	970	467	503	806	388	418	164	79	85
75 - 79	575	238	337	483	192	291	92	46	46
80 - 84	188	70	118	152	52	100	36	18	18
85 - 89	68	16	52	54	13	41	14	3	11
90 - 94	23	8	15	22	7	15	1	1	-
95 +	1	-	1	-	-	-	1	-	1
1 I 2007 (ESDJ)[12]									
Total	56 648	30 005	26 643	...	...	...	...	...	...
0 - 6	6 002	3 036	2 966	...	...	...	...	...	...
7 - 14	7 757	3 928	3 829	...	...	...	...	...	...
15 - 17	2 844	1 460	1 384	...	...	...	...	...	...
18 - 24	5 865	2 960	2 905	...	...	...	...	...	...
25 - 59	28 440	15 591	12 849	...	...	...	...	...	...
60 - 66	3 077	1 783	1 294	...	...	...	...	...	...
67 +	2 663	1 247	1 416	...	...	...	...	...	...
Grenada - Grenade									
1 VII 2000 (ESDF)									
Total	101 308	50 200	51 108	...	...	...	...	...	...
0 - 4	10 412	5 292	5 120	...	...	...	...	...	...
5 - 9	11 547	5 798	5 749	...	...	...	...	...	...
10 - 14	13 546	6 837	6 709	...	...	...	...	...	...
15 - 19	11 911	6 077	5 834	...	...	...	...	...	...
20 - 24	9 267	4 686	4 581	...	...	...	...	...	...
25 - 29	7 290	3 883	3 407	...	...	...	...	...	...
30 - 34	5 977	2 999	2 978	...	...	...	...	...	...
35 - 39	6 537	3 294	3 243	...	...	...	...	...	...
40 - 44	5 364	2 628	2 736	...	...	...	...	...	...
45 - 49	3 780	1 955	1 825	...	...	...	...	...	...
50 - 54	2 904	1 371	1 533	...	...	...	...	...	...
55 - 59	2 472	1 160	1 312	...	...	...	...	...	...
60 - 64	2 383	1 078	1 305	...	...	...	...	...	...
65 - 69	2 356	1 010	1 346	...	...	...	...	...	...
70 +	5 562	2 132	3 430	...	...	...	...	...	...
Guadeloupe									
1 I 2007 (ESDJ)									
Total	403 000	189 420	213 580	...	...	...	...	...	...
0 - 4	28 517	14 685	13 832	...	...	...	...	...	...
5 - 9	31 036	15 875	15 161	...	...	...	...	...	...
10 - 14	32 237	16 567	15 670	...	...	...	...	...	...
15 - 19	31 874	16 294	15 580	...	...	...	...	...	...
20 - 24	21 829	11 116	10 713	...	...	...	...	...	...
25 - 29	19 335	8 519	10 816	...	...	...	...	...	...
30 - 34	27 098	11 718	15 380	...	...	...	...	...	...
35 - 39	30 749	13 486	17 263	...	...	...	...	...	...
40 - 44	34 082	15 252	18 830	...	...	...	...	...	...
45 - 49	29 615	13 995	15 620	...	...	...	...	...	...
50 - 54	25 418	11 648	13 770	...	...	...	...	...	...
55 - 59	23 118	10 654	12 464	...	...	...	...	...	...
60 - 64	18 392	8 596	9 796	...	...	...	...	...	...
65 - 69	14 438	6 598	7 840	...	...	...	...	...	...
70 - 74	12 587	5 620	6 967	...	...	...	...	...	...
75 - 79	9 298	3 785	5 513	...	...	...	...	...	...
80 - 84	6 897	2 691	4 206	...	...	...	...	...	...
85 - 89	3 956	1 540	2 416	...	...	...	...	...	...

Continent, country or area, date, code and age (in years) / Continent, pays ou zone, date, code et âge (en années)	Total			Urban - Urbaine			Rural - Rurale		
	Both sexes Les deux sexes	Male Masculin	Female Féminin	Both sexes Les deux sexes	Male Masculin	Female Féminin	Both sexes Les deux sexes	Male Masculin	Female Féminin
AMERICA, NORTH - AMÉRIQUE DU NORD									
Guadeloupe									
1 I 2007 (ESDJ)									
90 - 94	1 785	584	1 201	...	...	...	...	...	...
95 + ...	739	197	542	...	...	...	...	...	...
Guatemala[13]									
1 VII 2005 (ESDF)									
Total.....................	12 699 780	6 197 399	6 502 381	6 345 918	3 059 570	3 286 348	6 353 862	3 137 829	3 216 033
0 - 4	2 036 312	1 035 549	1 000 763	866 844	447 724	419 120	1 169 468	587 825	581 643
5 - 9	1 823 642	921 924	901 718	790 225	405 750	384 475	1 033 417	516 174	517 243
10 - 14	1 624 119	815 791	808 328	755 292	378 704	376 587	868 827	437 087	431 741
15 - 19	1 379 574	685 359	694 215	715 501	351 554	363 947	664 073	333 805	330 268
20 - 24	1 180 264	571 385	608 879	636 046	306 874	329 172	544 218	264 511	279 707
25 - 29	952 695	446 309	506 386	523 699	243 461	280 237	428 996	202 848	226 149
30 - 34	753 145	340 378	412 767	416 357	184 973	231 384	336 788	155 405	181 383
35 - 39	600 160	270 907	329 253	326 576	144 824	181 752	273 584	126 083	147 501
40 - 44	492 747	225 243	267 504	270 162	120 913	149 248	222 585	104 330	118 256
45 - 49	409 688	191 635	218 053	221 123	100 439	120 685	188 565	91 196	97 368
50 - 54	367 062	175 311	191 751	201 790	92 775	109 014	165 272	82 536	82 737
55 - 59	310 913	149 593	161 320	171 480	79 044	92 436	139 433	70 549	68 884
60 - 64	233 643	113 686	119 957	128 803	58 925	69 878	104 840	54 761	50 079
65 - 69	192 992	94 128	98 864	111 865	51 579	60 285	81 127	42 549	38 579
70 - 74	156 267	74 463	81 804	93 750	42 080	51 669	62 517	32 383	30 135
75 - 79	107 429	50 340	57 089	66 759	29 241	37 519	40 670	21 099	19 570
80 + ...	79 128	35 398	43 730	49 648	20 709	28 939	29 480	14 689	14 791
Haiti - Haïti									
1 VII 1999 (ESDJ)									
Total.....................	7 803 232	3 834 240	3 968 992	2 731 843	1 234 809	1 497 034	5 071 389	2 599 431	2 471 958
0	242 106	122 835	119 271	68 885	36 499	32 386	173 221	86 336	86 885
1 - 4	913 669	462 018	451 651	252 773	130 783	121 990	660 896	331 235	329 661
5 - 9	1 034 513	521 302	513 211	321 389	154 420	166 969	713 124	366 882	346 242
10 - 14	925 920	466 007	459 913	363 812	161 340	202 472	562 108	304 667	257 441
15 - 19	810 881	407 544	403 337	375 052	156 361	218 691	435 829	251 183	184 646
20 - 24	696 906	347 026	349 880	337 696	153 000	184 696	359 210	194 026	165 184
25 - 29	612 995	301 403	311 592	272 739	124 048	148 691	340 256	177 355	162 901
30 - 34	526 616	255 640	270 976	198 846	88 085	110 761	327 770	167 555	160 215
35 - 39	452 327	216 102	236 225	135 215	57 299	77 916	317 112	158 803	158 309
40 - 44	370 430	173 392	197 038	106 911	42 010	64 901	263 519	131 382	132 137
45 - 49	306 075	141 518	164 557	71 946	29 912	42 034	234 129	111 606	122 523
50 - 54	247 324	114 254	133 070	70 080	31 126	38 954	177 244	83 128	94 116
55 - 59	201 858	93 663	108 195	51 060	22 494	28 566	150 798	71 169	79 629
60 - 64	161 143	74 625	86 518	40 580	18 949	21 631	120 563	55 676	64 887
65 - 69	122 392	56 450	65 942	28 310	12 719	15 591	94 082	43 731	50 351
70 - 74	84 796	38 744	46 052	18 717	7 726	10 991	66 079	31 018	35 061
75 - 79	52 884	23 831	29 053	11 309	5 008	6 301	41 575	18 823	22 752
80 + ...	40 397	17 886	22 511	6 523	3 030	3 493	33 874	14 856	19 018
Honduras									
1 VII 2007 (ESDF)									
Total.....................	7 536 952	3 717 577	3 819 375	3 752 579	1 793 588	1 958 991	3 784 373	1 923 989	1 860 384
0 - 4	1 063 247	541 070	522 177	478 059	243 771	234 288	585 188	297 299	287 889
5 - 9	1 009 399	511 733	497 666	432 422	221 023	211 399	576 977	290 710	286 267
10 - 14	920 850	464 403	456 447	414 394	208 459	205 935	506 456	255 944	250 512
15 - 19	802 793	402 792	400 001	398 138	192 053	206 085	404 655	210 739	193 916
20 - 24	710 751	353 317	357 434	390 899	179 723	211 176	319 852	173 594	146 258
25 - 29	626 413	308 283	318 130	352 025	165 114	186 911	274 388	143 169	131 219
30 - 34	522 679	255 818	266 861	286 860	136 186	150 674	235 819	119 632	116 187
35 - 39	425 045	205 171	219 874	235 598	109 749	125 849	189 447	95 422	94 025
40 - 44	334 632	157 492	177 140	184 004	84 081	99 923	150 628	73 411	77 217
45 - 49	276 277	128 813	147 464	149 861	67 682	82 179	126 416	61 131	65 285
50 - 54	227 421	105 428	121 993	118 577	52 986	65 591	108 844	52 442	56 402
55 - 59	180 676	83 643	97 033	92 810	40 714	52 096	87 866	42 929	44 937
60 - 64	137 652	63 863	73 789	67 361	29 245	38 116	70 291	34 618	35 673
65 - 69	107 540	49 404	58 136	52 443	22 197	30 246	55 097	27 207	27 890
70 - 74	82 118	37 134	44 984	41 131	17 107	24 024	40 987	20 027	20 960

Continent, country or area, date, code and age (in years) / Continent, pays ou zone, date, code et âge (en années)	Total			Urban - Urbaine			Rural - Rurale		
	Both sexes Les deux sexes	Male Masculin	Female Féminin	Both sexes Les deux sexes	Male Masculin	Female Féminin	Both sexes Les deux sexes	Male Masculin	Female Féminin
AMERICA, NORTH - AMÉRIQUE DU NORD									
Honduras									
1 VII 2007 (ESDF)									
75 - 79	54 593	24 368	30 225	28 183	11 568	16 615	26 410	12 800	13 610
80 +	54 866	24 845	30 021	29 814	11 930	17 884	25 052	12 915	12 137
Jamaica - Jamaïque[9]									
1 VII 2007 (ESDJ)									
Total	2 687 241	1 324 277	1 362 964	1 400 045[14]	667 050[14]	732 995[14]	1 287 196[14]	657 227[14]	629 969[14]
0	44 297	22 468	21 829	...	...	...	...	...	...
1 - 4	181 099	92 187	88 912	91 926[14]	46 791[14]	45 135[14]	89 173[14]	45 396[14]	43 777[14]
5 - 9	251 187	127 655	123 532	123 448[14]	62 326[14]	61 122[14]	127 739[14]	65 329[14]	62 410[14]
10 - 14	277 844	143 534	134 310	136 577[14]	70 150[14]	66 427[14]	141 267[14]	73 384[14]	67 883[14]
15 - 19	249 369	127 495	121 874	127 634[14]	63 829[14]	63 805[14]	121 735[14]	63 666[14]	58 069[14]
20 - 24	208 353	101 013	107 340	115 717[14]	54 318[14]	61 399[14]	92 636[14]	46 695[14]	45 941[14]
25 - 29	215 094	102 110	112 984	121 404[14]	55 338[14]	66 065[14]	93 690[14]	46 772[14]	46 919[14]
30 - 34	220 090	104 166	115 924	123 412[14]	56 019[14]	67 393[14]	96 678[14]	48 147[14]	48 531[14]
35 - 39	224 563	106 101	118 462	124 820[14]	56 218[14]	68 601[14]	99 743[14]	49 883[14]	49 861[14]
40 - 44	190 733	94 542	96 191	103 696[14]	48 612[14]	55 084[14]	87 037[14]	45 930[14]	41 107[14]
45 - 49	131 943	65 412	66 531	72 029[14]	33 813[14]	38 216[14]	59 914[14]	31 599[14]	28 315[14]
50 - 54	114 111	59 675	54 436	60 494[14]	29 973[14]	30 521[14]	53 617[14]	29 702[14]	23 915[14]
55 - 59	84 706	44 394	40 312	42 647[14]	21 207[14]	21 441[14]	42 059[14]	23 187[14]	18 871[14]
60 - 64	68 305	33 356	34 949	33 038[14]	15 293[14]	17 745[14]	35 267[14]	18 063[14]	17 204[14]
65 - 69	64 678	31 159	33 519	30 110[14]	13 714[14]	16 396[14]	34 568[14]	17 445[14]	17 123[14]
70 - 74	58 668	27 832	30 836	26 697[14]	11 959[14]	14 738[14]	31 971[14]	15 873[14]	16 098[14]
75 - 79	44 935	19 592	25 343	19 830[14]	7 912[14]	11 918[14]	25 105[14]	11 680[14]	13 425[14]
80 - 84	28 688	11 395	17 293	12 227[14]	4 465[14]	7 762[14]	16 461[14]	6 930[14]	9 532[14]
85 - 89	17 762	6 637	11 125	7 535[14]	2 460[14]	5 075[14]	10 227[14]	4 177[14]	6 050[14]
90 - 94	7 204	2 454	4 750	3 094[14]	908[14]	2 186[14]	4 110[14]	1 546[14]	2 564[14]
95 +	3 612	1 100	2 512	1 515[14]	393[14]	1 122[14]	2 097[14]	707[14]	1 390[14]
Martinique									
1 I 2007 (ESDJ)									
Total	400 000	186 357	213 643	...	...	...	...	...	...
0 - 4	25 063	12 766	12 297	...	...	...	...	...	...
5 - 9	28 130	14 293	13 837	...	...	...	...	...	...
10 - 14	29 511	14 892	14 619	...	...	...	...	...	...
15 - 19	31 317	15 934	15 383	...	...	...	...	...	...
20 - 24	23 432	11 690	11 742	...	...	...	...	...	...
25 - 29	18 951	8 699	10 252	...	...	...	...	...	...
30 - 34	24 510	10 500	14 010	...	...	...	...	...	...
35 - 39	30 761	13 525	17 236	...	...	...	...	...	...
40 - 44	34 010	15 221	18 789	...	...	...	...	...	...
45 - 49	31 270	14 495	16 775	...	...	...	...	...	...
50 - 54	26 225	12 081	14 144	...	...	...	...	...	...
55 - 59	22 722	10 380	12 342	...	...	...	...	...	...
60 - 64	18 820	8 829	9 991	...	...	...	...	...	...
65 - 69	15 943	7 224	8 719	...	...	...	...	...	...
70 - 74	14 295	6 356	7 939	...	...	...	...	...	...
75 - 79	10 675	4 529	6 146	...	...	...	...	...	...
80 - 84	7 488	2 834	4 654	...	...	...	...	...	...
85 - 89	4 193	1 376	2 817	...	...	...	...	...	...
90 - 94	1 951	570	1 381	...	...	...	...	...	...
95 +	733	163	570	...	...	...	...	...	...
Mexico - Mexique									
17 X 2005 (CDJC)									
Total	103 263 388	50 249 955	53 013 433	78 986 852	38 300 417	40 686 435	24 276 536	11 949 538	12 326 998
0	1 866 929	953 071	913 858	1 375 346	701 965	673 381	491 583	251 106	240 477
1 - 4	8 319 314	4 222 842	4 096 472	6 099 968	3 098 431	3 001 537	2 219 346	1 124 411	1 094 935
5 - 9	10 511 738	5 339 127	5 172 611	7 612 581	3 868 547	3 744 034	2 899 157	1 470 580	1 428 577
10 - 14	10 952 123	5 545 910	5 406 213	7 809 172	3 950 685	3 858 487	3 142 951	1 595 225	1 547 726
15 - 19	10 109 021	4 995 906	5 113 115	7 519 867	3 724 606	3 795 261	2 589 154	1 271 300	1 317 854
20 - 24	8 964 629	4 253 440	4 711 189	7 051 808	3 376 247	3 675 561	1 912 821	877 193	1 035 628
25 - 29	8 103 358	3 805 724	4 297 634	6 430 726	3 033 228	3 397 498	1 672 632	772 496	900 136
30 - 34	7 933 951	3 745 974	4 187 977	6 362 249	3 001 742	3 360 507	1 571 702	744 232	827 470
35 - 39	7 112 526	3 371 372	3 741 154	5 690 767	2 688 582	3 002 185	1 421 759	682 790	738 969

Continent, country or area, date, code and age (in years) Continent, pays ou zone, date, code et âge (en années)	Total			Urban - Urbaine			Rural - Rurale		
	Both sexes Les deux sexes	Male Masculin	Female Féminin	Both sexes Les deux sexes	Male Masculin	Female Féminin	Both sexes Les deux sexes	Male Masculin	Female Féminin
AMERICA, NORTH -									
AMÉRIQUE DU NORD									
Mexico - Mexique									
17 X 2005 (CDJC)									
40 - 44	6 017 268	2 871 549	3 145 719	4 827 524	2 293 754	2 533 770	1 189 744	577 795	611 949
45 - 49	5 015 255	2 388 149	2 627 106	3 986 038	1 885 334	2 100 704	1 029 217	502 815	526 402
50 - 54	4 090 650	1 959 720	2 130 930	3 227 317	1 530 942	1 696 375	863 333	428 778	434 555
55 - 59	3 117 071	1 497 981	1 619 090	2 392 022	1 135 166	1 256 856	725 049	362 815	362 234
60 - 64	2 622 476	1 243 788	1 378 688	1 935 880	900 574	1 035 306	686 596	343 214	343 382
65 - 69	1 958 069	922 592	1 035 477	1 428 290	654 658	773 632	529 779	267 934	261 845
70 - 74	1 496 691	703 277	793 414	1 082 372	489 557	592 815	414 319	213 720	200 599
75 - 79	1 048 315	490 840	557 475	747 992	334 692	413 300	300 323	156 148	144 175
80 - 84	657 011	296 351	360 660	468 965	201 082	267 883	188 046	95 269	92 777
85 - 89	345 154	150 617	194 537	244 298	100 594	143 704	100 856	50 023	50 833
90 - 94	132 325	54 391	77 934	93 124	35 731	57 393	39 201	18 660	20 541
95 - 99	61 145	24 439	36 706	40 465	14 930	25 535	20 680	9 509	11 171
100 +	17 649	6 696	10 953	10 007	3 491	6 516	7 642	3 205	4 437
Unknown - Inconnu	2 810 720	1 406 199	1 404 521	2 550 074	1 275 879	1 274 195	260 646	130 320	130 326
1 VII 2007 (ESDJ)[3]									
Total	105 790 725	52 066 743	53 723 982	...	...	...	...	...	...
0 - 4	9 866 329	5 043 765	4 822 564	...	...	...	...	...	...
5 - 9	10 985 475	5 612 554	5 372 921	...	...	...	...	...	...
10 - 14	10 887 338	5 532 006	5 355 332	...	...	...	...	...	...
15 - 19	10 472 794	5 258 911	5 213 883	...	...	...	...	...	...
20 - 24	9 630 652	4 740 119	4 890 533	...	...	...	...	...	...
25 - 29	8 898 375	4 309 904	4 588 471	...	...	...	...	...	...
30 - 34	8 449 816	4 090 733	4 359 083	...	...	...	...	...	...
35 - 39	7 739 332	3 759 849	3 979 483	...	...	...	...	...	...
40 - 44	6 780 934	3 297 930	3 483 004	...	...	...	...	...	...
45 - 49	5 670 043	2 747 983	2 922 060	...	...	...	...	...	...
50 - 54	4 474 538	2 151 832	2 322 706	...	...	...	...	...	...
55 - 59	3 458 963	1 648 719	1 810 244	...	...	...	...	...	...
60 - 64	2 693 850	1 269 379	1 424 471	...	...	...	...	...	...
65 - 69	2 061 449	957 820	1 103 629	...	...	...	...	...	...
70 - 74	1 505 828	687 031	818 797	...	...	...	...	...	...
75 - 79	1 028 863	458 044	570 819	...	...	...	...	...	...
80 - 84	639 577	275 999	363 578	...	...	...	...	...	...
85 - 89	338 414	141 162	197 252	...	...	...	...	...	...
90 - 94	148 119	59 684	88 435	...	...	...	...	...	...
95 - 99	50 611	19 734	30 877	...	...	...	...	...	...
100 +	9 425	3 585	5 840	...	...	...	...	...	...
Montserrat									
12 V 2001 (CDFC)									
Total	4 491	2 418	2 073	...	...	...	...	...	...
0 - 4	311	153	158	...	...	...	...	...	...
5 - 9	277	153	124	...	...	...	...	...	...
10 - 14	281	148	133	...	...	...	...	...	...
15 - 19	273	149	124	...	...	...	...	...	...
20 - 24	206	113	93	...	...	...	...	...	...
25 - 29	319	169	150	...	...	...	...	...	...
30 - 34	346	176	170	...	...	...	...	...	...
35 - 39	382	211	171	...	...	...	...	...	...
40 - 44	325	171	154	...	...	...	...	...	...
45 - 49	335	196	139	...	...	...	...	...	...
50 - 54	282	170	112	...	...	...	...	...	...
55 - 59	239	136	103	...	...	...	...	...	...
60 - 64	203	108	95	...	...	...	...	...	...
65 - 69	148	76	72	...	...	...	...	...	...
70 - 74	169	94	75	...	...	...	...	...	...
75 - 79	139	72	67	...	...	...	...	...	...
80 - 84	107	47	60	...	...	...	...	...	...
85 - 89	67	32	35	...	...	...	...	...	...
90 - 94	38	14	24	...	...	...	...	...	...
95 +	21	9	12	...	...	...	...	...	...
Unknown - Inconnu	23	21	2	...	...	...	...	...	...

Continent, country or area, date, code and age (in years) / Continent, pays ou zone, date, code et âge (en années)	Total			Urban - Urbaine			Rural - Rurale		
	Both sexes Les deux sexes	Male Masculin	Female Féminin	Both sexes Les deux sexes	Male Masculin	Female Féminin	Both sexes Les deux sexes	Male Masculin	Female Féminin
AMERICA, NORTH - AMÉRIQUE DU NORD									
Netherlands Antilles - Antilles néerlandaises									
1 I 2007 (ESDJ)									
Total	193 549	90 140	103 410	...	...	...	...	...	...
0	2 614	1 337	1 277	...	...	...	...	...	...
1 - 4	10 953	5 515	5 438	...	...	...	...	...	...
5 - 9	14 467	7 287	7 180	...	...	...	...	...	...
10 - 14	15 469	7 812	7 657	...	...	...	...	...	...
15 - 19	14 292	7 102	7 190	...	...	...	...	...	...
20 - 24	10 714	5 152	5 562	...	...	...	...	...	...
25 - 29	10 823	4 967	5 856	...	...	...	...	...	...
30 - 34	13 532	6 212	7 320	...	...	...	...	...	...
35 - 39	15 798	7 247	8 551	...	...	...	...	...	...
40 - 44	17 054	7 676	9 378	...	...	...	...	...	...
45 - 49	16 124	7 197	8 927	...	...	...	...	...	...
50 - 54	13 386	6 022	7 364	...	...	...	...	...	...
55 - 59	11 035	5 045	5 990	...	...	...	...	...	...
60 - 64	8 646	3 849	4 797	...	...	...	...	...	...
65 - 69	6 316	2 804	3 512	...	...	...	...	...	...
70 - 74	5 064	2 212	2 852	...	...	...	...	...	...
75 - 79	3 357	1 370	1 987	...	...	...	...	...	...
80 - 84	2 170	799	1 371	...	...	...	...	...	...
85 - 89	1 124	357	767	...	...	...	...	...	...
90 - 94	451	136	315	...	...	...	...	...	...
95 - 99	141	32	109	...	...	...	...	...	...
100 +	20	10	10	...	...	...	...	...	...
Nicaragua									
4 VI 2005 (CDJC)									
Total	5 144 553	2 535 461	2 609 092	2 877 002	1 369 108	1 507 894	2 267 551	1 166 353	1 101 198
0 - 4	604 898	308 912	295 986	300 378	153 228	147 150	304 520	155 684	148 836
5 - 9	641 753	327 983	313 770	311 313	158 300	153 013	330 440	169 683	160 757
10 - 14	681 548	348 625	332 923	352 150	177 521	174 629	329 398	171 104	158 294
15 - 19	586 162	293 677	292 485	327 709	159 022	168 687	258 453	134 655	123 798
20 - 24	539 616	266 097	273 519	317 002	150 922	166 080	222 614	115 175	107 439
25 - 29	412 085	199 201	212 884	240 061	111 455	128 606	172 024	87 746	84 278
30 - 34	338 425	161 457	176 968	201 286	91 594	109 692	137 139	69 863	67 276
35 - 39	293 828	136 016	157 812	181 314	80 264	101 050	112 514	55 752	56 762
40 - 44	248 728	116 604	132 124	158 072	71 301	86 771	90 656	45 303	45 353
45 - 49	202 894	95 992	106 902	126 895	57 662	69 233	75 999	38 330	37 669
50 - 54	159 136	76 190	82 946	98 972	45 019	53 953	60 164	31 171	28 993
55 - 59	119 848	56 927	62 921	71 834	32 009	39 825	48 014	24 918	23 096
60 - 64	92 948	44 597	48 351	54 816	24 250	30 566	38 132	20 347	17 785
65 - 69	72 900	34 473	38 427	43 613	18 820	24 793	29 287	15 653	13 634
70 - 74	55 526	26 500	29 026	33 641	14 640	19 001	21 885	11 860	10 025
75 - 79	40 668	18 988	21 680	25 131	10 552	14 579	15 537	8 436	7 101
80 - 84	25 503	11 457	14 046	15 606	6 274	9 332	9 897	5 183	4 714
85 - 89	15 052	6 490	8 562	9 342	3 528	5 814	5 710	2 962	2 748
90 - 94	6 652	2 771	3 881	4 186	1 513	2 673	2 466	1 258	1 208
95 +	6 383	2 504	3 879	3 681	1 234	2 447	2 702	1 270	1 432
Panama									
1 VII 2000 (ESDF)									
Total	2 855 703	1 440 801	1 414 902	1 604 823	782 928	821 895	1 250 880	657 873	593 007
0	59 949	30 595	29 354	30 248	15 460	14 788	29 701	15 135	14 566
1 - 4	241 433	123 553	117 880	121 253	62 069	59 184	120 180	61 484	58 696
5 - 9	300 852	153 986	146 866	150 849	77 061	73 786	150 003	76 925	73 079
10 - 14	291 489	148 579	142 911	148 812	75 471	73 342	142 678	73 109	69 569
15 - 19	271 684	137 805	133 878	146 537	73 631	72 906	125 147	64 174	60 974
20 - 24	254 772	129 237	125 536	146 169	72 295	73 875	108 605	56 944	51 661
25 - 29	250 152	125 922	124 230	150 336	71 923	78 413	99 816	53 999	45 817
30 - 34	230 835	115 884	114 951	141 488	67 582	73 906	89 347	48 302	41 045
35 - 39	203 446	101 421	102 025	126 268	59 890	66 378	77 178	41 531	35 647
40 - 44	170 180	84 702	85 478	105 158	50 101	55 057	65 022	34 601	30 421
45 - 49	140 684	70 369	70 315	86 739	41 477	45 262	53 945	28 892	25 053
50 - 54	115 342	58 278	57 064	69 710	33 225	36 485	45 632	25 053	20 579

Continent, country or area, date, code and age (in years) / Continent, pays ou zone, date, code et âge (en années)	Total			Urban - Urbaine			Rural - Rurale		
	Both sexes Les deux sexes	Male Masculin	Female Féminin	Both sexes Les deux sexes	Male Masculin	Female Féminin	Both sexes Les deux sexes	Male Masculin	Female Féminin
AMERICA, NORTH - AMÉRIQUE DU NORD									
Panama									
1 VII 2000 (ESDF)									
55 - 59	93 684	47 379	46 305	53 771	25 760	28 011	39 913	21 619	18 294
60 - 64	73 087	36 664	36 423	40 256	18 795	21 461	32 831	17 869	14 962
65 - 69	55 236	27 712	27 524	30 061	13 914	16 147	25 175	13 798	11 377
70 - 74	43 900	21 495	22 405	24 076	10 692	13 384	19 824	10 803	9 021
75 - 79	30 250	14 158	16 092	17 010	7 216	9 794	13 240	6 942	6 298
80 +	28 727	13 063	15 664	16 083	6 367	9 716	12 644	6 696	5 948
1 VII 2006 (ESDF)									
Total	3 283 959	1 656 469	1 627 490	...	...	...	...	...	...
0 - 4	345 075	176 208	168 867	...	...	...	...	...	...
5 - 9	332 782	169 919	162 863	...	...	...	...	...	...
10 - 14	311 909	159 197	152 712	...	...	...	...	...	...
15 - 19	302 064	153 919	148 145	...	...	...	...	...	...
20 - 24	282 585	143 601	138 984	...	...	...	...	...	...
25 - 29	266 603	134 923	131 680	...	...	...	...	...	...
30 - 34	263 104	132 469	130 635	...	...	...	...	...	...
35 - 39	244 441	122 883	121 558	...	...	...	...	...	...
40 - 44	211 442	105 789	105 653	...	...	...	...	...	...
45 - 49	175 069	87 052	88 017	...	...	...	...	...	...
50 - 54	143 081	71 107	71 974	...	...	...	...	...	...
55 - 59	115 497	57 850	57 647	...	...	...	...	...	...
60 - 64	92 979	46 371	46 608	...	...	...	...	...	...
65 - 69	70 241	34 763	35 478	...	...	...	...	...	...
70 - 74	53 174	26 002	27 172	...	...	...	...	...	...
75 - 79	38 088	18 127	19 961	...	...	...	...	...	...
80 +	35 825	16 289	19 536	...	...	...	...	...	...
Puerto Rico - Porto Rico[15]									
1 VII 2007 (ESDJ)									
Total	3 942 375	1 892 503	2 049 872	...	...	...	...	...	...
0	48 044	24 571	23 473	...	...	...	...	...	...
1 - 4	197 144	100 723	96 421	...	...	...	...	...	...
5 - 9	275 933	140 819	135 114	...	...	...	...	...	...
10 - 14	300 165	153 700	146 465	...	...	...	...	...	...
15 - 19	297 823	151 646	146 177	...	...	...	...	...	...
20 - 24	279 892	140 623	139 269	...	...	...	...	...	...
25 - 29	287 001	141 168	145 833	...	...	...	...	...	...
30 - 34	267 172	130 054	137 118	...	...	...	...	...	...
35 - 39	263 370	127 511	135 859	...	...	...	...	...	...
40 - 44	267 222	126 210	141 012	...	...	...	...	...	...
45 - 49	256 927	119 468	137 459	...	...	...	...	...	...
50 - 54	242 853	111 499	131 354	...	...	...	...	...	...
55 - 59	228 560	104 411	124 149	...	...	...	...	...	...
60 - 64	207 370	94 540	112 830	...	...	...	...	...	...
65 - 69	163 339	73 797	89 542	...	...	...	...	...	...
70 - 74	130 561	58 452	72 109	...	...	...	...	...	...
75 - 79	96 756	41 396	55 360	...	...	...	...	...	...
80 - 84	68 759	27 858	40 901	...	...	...	...	...	...
85 - 89	39 878	15 595	24 283	...	...	...	...	...	...
90 - 94	17 539	6 429	11 110	...	...	...	...	...	...
95 - 99	6 067	2 033	4 034	...	...	...	...	...	...
100 +	916	295	621	...	...	...	...	...	...
Saint Kitts and Nevis - Saint-Kitts-et-Nevis									
1 VII 2000 (ESDF)									
Total	40 410	20 400	20 010	...	...	...	...	...	...
0 - 4	4 250	2 130	2 120	...	...	...	...	...	...
5 - 9	4 100	2 140	1 960	...	...	...	...	...	...
10 - 14	4 040	2 120	1 920	...	...	...	...	...	...
15 - 19	3 870	2 000	1 870	...	...	...	...	...	...
20 - 24	3 620	1 880	1 740	...	...	...	...	...	...
25 - 29	3 240	1 640	1 600	...	...	...	...	...	...
30 - 34	3 100	1 550	1 550	...	...	...	...	...	...
35 - 39	2 910	1 430	1 480	...	...	...	...	...	...

Continent, country or area, date, code and age (in years) Continent, pays ou zone, date, code et âge (en années)	Total			Urban - Urbaine			Rural - Rurale		
	Both sexes Les deux sexes	Male Masculin	Female Féminin	Both sexes Les deux sexes	Male Masculin	Female Féminin	Both sexes Les deux sexes	Male Masculin	Female Féminin
AMERICA, NORTH - AMÉRIQUE DU NORD									
Saint Kitts and Nevis - Saint-Kitts-et-Nevis									
1 VII 2000 (ESDF)									
40 - 44	2 520	1 270	1 250	...	...	...	...	...	...
45 - 49	1 880	900	980	...	...	...	...	...	...
50 - 54	1 390	710	680	...	...	...	...	...	...
55 - 59	1 100	560	540	...	...	...	...	...	...
60 - 64	820	400	420	...	...	...	...	...	...
65 - 69	840	410	430	...	...	...	...	...	...
70 - 74	810	380	430	...	...	...	...	...	...
75 - 79	700	330	370	...	...	...	...	...	...
80 - 84	470	240	230	...	...	...	...	...	...
85 +	750	310	440	...	...	...	...	...	...
Saint Lucia - Sainte-Lucie									
22 V 2001 (CDFC)									
Total	157 164	76 741	80 423	42 310	20 208	22 102	111 559	54 897	56 662
0	973	458	515	238	120	118	735	338	397
1 - 4	12 958	6 485	6 473	3 203	1 627	1 576	9 755	4 858	4 897
5 - 9	16 382	8 260	8 122	3 906	1 963	1 943	12 476	6 297	6 179
10 - 14	16 605	8 323	8 282	4 023	2 005	2 018	12 582	6 318	6 264
15 - 19	16 348	8 051	8 297	4 296	2 116	2 180	12 052	5 935	6 117
20 - 24	13 369	6 635	6 734	3 886	1 947	1 939	9 483	4 688	4 795
25 - 29	12 572	6 112	6 460	3 592	1 788	1 804	8 980	4 324	4 656
30 - 34	11 419	5 652	5 767	2 822	1 481	1 341	8 597	4 171	4 426
35 - 39	11 167	5 397	5 770	3 238	1 576	1 662	7 929	3 821	4 108
40 - 44	9 041	4 410	4 631	2 531	1 193	1 338	6 510	3 217	3 293
45 - 49	6 811	3 401	3 410	2 109	995	1 114	4 702	2 406	2 296
50 - 54	5 830	2 926	2 904	1 958	1 000	958	3 872	1 926	1 946
55 - 59	4 479	2 103	2 376	1 353	599	754	3 126	1 504	1 622
60 - 64	3 856	1 788	2 068	1 030	416	614	2 826	1 372	1 454
65 - 69	3 573	1 661	1 912	1 043	440	603	2 530	1 221	1 309
70 - 74	2 776	1 326	1 450	909	399	510	1 867	927	940
75 - 79	2 217	991	1 226	684	283	401	1 533	708	825
80 - 84	1 570	647	923	483	176	307	1 087	471	616
85 - 89	897	352	545	272	81	191	625	271	354
90 - 94	323	128	195	120	39	81	203	89	114
95 +	143	53	90	54	18	36	89	35	54
1 VII 2007 (ESDF)									
Total	168 338	82 426	85 912	...	...	...	...	...	...
0 - 4	14 625	7 389	7 236	...	...	...	...	...	...
5 - 9	14 012	6 932	7 080	...	...	...	...	...	...
10 - 14	16 891	8 509	8 382	...	...	...	...	...	...
15 - 19	17 592	8 790	8 802	...	...	...	...	...	...
20 - 24	16 793	8 225	8 568	...	...	...	...	...	...
25 - 29	14 136	6 953	7 183	...	...	...	...	...	...
30 - 34	12 914	6 229	6 685	...	...	...	...	...	...
35 - 39	11 807	5 700	6 107	...	...	...	...	...	...
40 - 44	11 511	5 557	5 954	...	...	...	...	...	...
45 - 49	9 705	4 720	4 985	...	...	...	...	...	...
50 - 54	7 159	3 609	3 550	...	...	...	...	...	...
55 - 59	5 444	2 683	2 761	...	...	...	...	...	...
60 - 64	4 295	1 977	2 318	...	...	...	...	...	...
65 - 69	3 571	1 643	1 928	...	...	...	...	...	...
70 - 74	3 109	1 439	1 670	...	...	...	...	...	...
75 - 79	2 143	970	1 173	...	...	...	...	...	...
80 +	2 631	1 101	1 530	...	...	...	...	...	...
Saint Vincent and the Grenadines - Saint-Vincent-et-les Grenadines[16]									
14 V 2001 (CDFC)									
Total	106 253	53 626	52 627	...	...	...	...	...	...
0 - 4	9 975	5 128	4 847	...	...	...	...	...	...
5 - 9	11 457	5 739	5 718	...	...	...	...	...	...

7. Population by age, sex and urban/rural residence: latest available year, 1998 - 2007
Population selon l'âge, le sexe et la résidence, urbaine/rurale: dernière année disponible, 1998 - 2007 (continued - suite)

Continent, country or area, date, code and age (in years) — Continent, pays ou zone, date, code et âge (en années)	Total			Urban - Urbaine			Rural - Rurale		
	Both sexes Les deux sexes	Male Masculin	Female Féminin	Both sexes Les deux sexes	Male Masculin	Female Féminin	Both sexes Les deux sexes	Male Masculin	Female Féminin
AMERICA, NORTH - AMÉRIQUE DU NORD									
Saint Vincent and the Grenadines - Saint-Vincent-et-les Grenadines[16]									
14 V 2001 (CDFC)									
10 - 14	11 143	5 650	5 493	...	...	...	...	...	...
15 - 19	11 293	5 676	5 617	...	...	...	...	...	...
20 - 24	9 715	4 975	4 740	...	...	...	...	...	...
25 - 29	8 515	4 350	4 165	...	...	...	...	...	...
30 - 34	7 672	4 018	3 654	...	...	...	...	...	...
35 - 39	8 069	4 194	3 875	...	...	...	...	...	...
40 - 44	6 695	3 447	3 248	...	...	...	...	...	...
45 - 49	4 729	2 415	2 314	...	...	...	...	...	...
50 - 54	3 733	1 938	1 795	...	...	...	...	...	...
55 - 59	2 783	1 393	1 390	...	...	...	...	...	...
60 - 64	2 734	1 310	1 424	...	...	...	...	...	...
65 - 69	2 551	1 226	1 325	...	...	...	...	...	...
70 - 74	1 951	891	1 060	...	...	...	...	...	...
75 - 79	1 514	634	880	...	...	...	...	...	...
80 - 84	943	385	558	...	...	...	...	...	...
85 +	781	257	524	...	...	...	...	...	...
Trinidad and Tobago - Trinité-et-Tobago[17]									
1 VII 2007 (ESDF)									
Total	1 303 188	...	...	...	...	...	...	...	...
0 - 14	330 283	...	...	...	...	...	...	...	...
15 - 19	142 955	...	...	...	...	...	...	...	...
20 - 24	115 601	...	...	...	...	...	...	...	...
25 - 29	99 729	...	...	...	...	...	...	...	...
30 - 34	95 174	...	...	...	...	...	...	...	...
35 - 39	105 890	...	...	...	...	...	...	...	...
40 - 44	93 293	...	...	...	...	...	...	...	...
45 - 49	77 242	...	...	...	...	...	...	...	...
50 - 54	64 452	...	...	...	...	...	...	...	...
55 - 59	48 002	...	...	...	...	...	...	...	...
60 - 64	38 309	...	...	...	...	...	...	...	...
65 +	92 258	...	...	...	...	...	...	...	...
Turks and Caicos Islands - Îles Turques et Caïques									
10 IX 2001 (CDFC)									
Total	19 886[9]	9 897	9 989	...	...	...	...	...	...
0	775[9]	258	517	...	...	...	...	...	...
1 - 4	1 550[9]	795	754	...	...	...	...	...	...
5 - 9	1 731[9]	850	882	...	...	...	...	...	...
10 - 14	1 637[9]	833	804	...	...	...	...	...	...
15 - 19	1 288[9]	636	652	...	...	...	...	...	...
20 - 24	1 376[9]	634	741	...	...	...	...	...	...
25 - 29	2 024[9]	1 001	1 023	...	...	...	...	...	...
30 - 34	2 317[9]	1 177	1 139	...	...	...	...	...	...
35 - 39	2 070[9]	1 073	998	...	...	...	...	...	...
40 - 44	1 590[9]	827	763	...	...	...	...	...	...
45 - 49	1 167[9]	610	557	...	...	...	...	...	...
50 - 54	809[9]	440	370	...	...	...	...	...	...
55 - 59	507[9]	283	224	...	...	...	...	...	...
60 - 64	288[9]	145	143	...	...	...	...	...	...
65 - 69	240[9]	114	125	...	...	...	...	...	...
70 - 74	198[9]	75	123	...	...	...	...	...	...
75 - 79	129[9]	53	76	...	...	...	...	...	...
80 - 84	110[9]	55	55	...	...	...	...	...	...
85 - 89	58[9]	33	25	...	...	...	...	...	...
90 - 94	19[9]	2	17	...	...	...	...	...	...
95 - 99	4[9]	3	2	...	...	...	...	...	...
100 +	-[9]	-	-	...	...	...	...	...	...

7. Population by age, sex and urban/rural residence: latest available year, 1998 - 2007

Population selon l'âge, le sexe et la résidence, urbaine/rurale: dernière année disponible, 1998 - 2007 (continued - suite)

Continent, country or area, date, code and age (in years) / Continent, pays ou zone, date, code et âge (en années)	Total			Urban - Urbaine			Rural - Rurale		
	Both sexes Les deux sexes	Male Masculin	Female Féminin	Both sexes Les deux sexes	Male Masculin	Female Féminin	Both sexes Les deux sexes	Male Masculin	Female Féminin
AMERICA, NORTH - AMÉRIQUE DU NORD									
United States of America - États-Unis d'Amérique[18]									
1 IV 2000 (CDJC)									
Total	281 421 906	138 053 563	143 368 343	222 360 539	108 375 797	113 984 742	59 061 367	29 677 766	29 383 601
0	3 805 648	1 949 017	1 856 631	3 108 179	1 591 301	1 516 878	697 469	357 716	339 753
1 - 4	15 370 150	7 861 716	7 508 434	12 426 799	6 352 829	6 073 970	2 943 351	1 508 887	1 434 464
5 - 9	20 549 505	10 523 277	10 026 228	16 303 052	8 338 164	7 964 888	4 246 453	2 185 113	2 061 340
10 - 14	20 528 072	10 520 197	10 007 875	15 865 132	8 114 898	7 750 234	4 662 940	2 405 299	2 257 641
15 - 19	20 219 890	10 391 004	9 828 886	15 862 692	8 092 790	7 769 902	4 357 198	2 298 214	2 058 984
20 - 24	18 964 001	9 687 814	9 276 187	16 062 564	8 150 162	7 912 402	2 901 437	1 537 652	1 363 785
25 - 29	19 381 336	9 798 760	9 582 576	16 247 338	8 210 254	8 037 084	3 133 998	1 588 506	1 545 492
30 - 34	20 510 388	10 321 769	10 188 619	16 761 355	8 449 017	8 312 338	3 749 033	1 872 752	1 876 281
35 - 39	22 706 664	11 318 696	11 387 968	17 967 717	8 957 072	9 010 645	4 738 947	2 361 624	2 377 323
40 - 44	22 441 863	11 129 102	11 312 761	17 434 999	8 608 239	8 826 760	5 006 864	2 520 863	2 486 001
45 - 49	20 092 404	9 889 506	10 202 898	15 431 618	7 528 331	7 903 287	4 660 786	2 361 175	2 299 611
50 - 54	17 585 548	8 607 724	8 977 824	13 395 145	6 480 878	6 914 267	4 190 403	2 126 846	2 063 557
55 - 59	13 469 237	6 508 729	6 960 508	10 060 185	4 791 948	5 268 237	3 409 052	1 716 781	1 692 271
60 - 64	10 805 447	5 136 627	5 668 820	8 026 903	3 738 462	4 288 441	2 778 544	1 398 165	1 380 379
65 - 69	9 533 545	4 400 362	5 133 183	7 180 256	3 236 555	3 943 701	2 353 289	1 163 807	1 189 482
70 - 74	8 857 441	3 902 912	4 954 529	6 865 515	2 943 669	3 921 846	1 991 926	959 243	1 032 683
75 - 79	7 415 813	3 044 456	4 371 357	5 901 375	2 367 269	3 534 106	1 514 438	677 187	837 251
80 - 84	4 945 367	1 834 897	3 110 470	3 982 799	1 445 556	2 537 243	962 568	389 341	573 227
85 - 89	2 789 818	876 501	1 913 317	2 274 316	695 943	1 578 373	515 502	180 558	334 944
90 - 94	1 112 531	282 325	830 206	920 357	227 019	693 338	192 174	55 306	136 868
95 - 99	286 784	58 115	228 669	239 942	47 265	192 677	46 842	10 850	35 992
100 +	50 454	10 057	40 397	42 301	8 176	34 125	8 153	1 881	6 272
1 VII 2007 (ESDJ)									
Total	301 621 157	148 658 898	152 962 259	...	...	...	...	...	...
0	4 257 020	2 178 808	2 078 212	...	...	...	...	...	...
1 - 4	16 467 105	8 424 049	8 043 056	...	...	...	...	...	...
5 - 9	19 849 628	10 148 578	9 701 050	...	...	...	...	...	...
10 - 14	20 314 309	10 399 927	9 914 382	...	...	...	...	...	...
15 - 19	21 473 690	11 006 869	10 466 821	...	...	...	...	...	...
20 - 24	21 032 396	10 852 937	10 179 459	...	...	...	...	...	...
25 - 29	21 057 706	10 776 189	10 281 517	...	...	...	...	...	...
30 - 34	19 533 220	9 906 361	9 626 859	...	...	...	...	...	...
35 - 39	21 176 460	10 654 911	10 521 549	...	...	...	...	...	...
40 - 44	21 984 829	10 963 823	11 021 006	...	...	...	...	...	...
45 - 49	22 861 373	11 302 842	11 558 531	...	...	...	...	...	...
50 - 54	21 013 387	10 292 071	10 721 316	...	...	...	...	...	...
55 - 59	18 236 259	8 847 222	9 389 037	...	...	...	...	...	...
60 - 64	14 475 817	6 927 866	7 547 951	...	...	...	...	...	...
65 - 69	10 752 441	5 019 063	5 733 378	...	...	...	...	...	...
70 - 74	8 599 708	3 867 910	4 731 798	...	...	...	...	...	...
75 - 79	7 324 882	3 106 968	4 217 914	...	...	...	...	...	...
80 - 84	5 698 629	2 205 705	3 492 924	...	...	...	...	...	...
85 - 89	3 476 545	1 205 125	2 271 420	...	...	...	...	...	...
90 - 94	1 502 489	445 129	1 057 360	...	...	...	...	...	...
95 - 99	452 493	110 237	342 256	...	...	...	...	...	...
100 +	80 771	16 308	64 463	...	...	...	...	...	...
United States Virgin Islands - Îles Vierges américaines[15]									
1 VII 2007 (ESDJ)									
Total	109 821	52 089	57 732	...	...	...	...	...	...
0 - 4	7 557	3 886	3 671	...	...	...	...	...	...
5 - 9	7 656	3 939	3 717	...	...	...	...	...	...
10 - 14	8 545	4 193	4 352	...	...	...	...	...	...
15 - 19	8 355	4 081	4 274	...	...	...	...	...	...
20 - 24	6 967	3 199	3 768	...	...	...	...	...	...
25 - 29	5 378	2 462	2 916	...	...	...	...	...	...
30 - 34	6 116	2 703	3 413	...	...	...	...	...	...
35 - 39	7 390	3 341	4 049	...	...	...	...	...	...
40 - 44	7 995	3 779	4 216	...	...	...	...	...	...
45 - 49	8 132	3 885	4 247	...	...	...	...	...	...

7. Population by age, sex and urban/rural residence: latest available year, 1998 - 2007
Population selon l'âge, le sexe et la résidence, urbaine/rurale: dernière année disponible, 1998 - 2007 (continued - suite)

Continent, country or area, date, code and age (in years) / Continent, pays ou zone, date, code et âge (en années)	Total			Urban - Urbaine			Rural - Rurale		
	Both sexes Les deux sexes	Male Masculin	Female Féminin	Both sexes Les deux sexes	Male Masculin	Female Féminin	Both sexes Les deux sexes	Male Masculin	Female Féminin
AMERICA, NORTH - AMÉRIQUE DU NORD									
United States Virgin Islands - Îles Vierges américaines[15] 1 VII 2007 (ESDJ)									
50 - 54	7 627	3 530	4 097	...	...	...	...	...	...
55 - 59	7 507	3 570	3 937	...	...	...	...	...	...
60 - 64	7 374	3 594	3 780	...	...	...	...	...	...
65 - 69	4 973	2 426	2 547	...	...	...	...	...	...
70 - 74	3 620	1 618	2 002	...	...	...	...	...	...
75 - 79	2 293	1 026	1 267	...	...	...	...	...	...
80 +	2 336	857	1 479	...	...	...	...	...	...
AMERICA, SOUTH - AMÉRIQUE DU SUD									
Argentina - Argentine 1 VII 2007 (ESDF)									
Total	39 356 383	19 273 494	20 082 889	35 719 891	17 383 239	18 336 652	3 636 492	1 890 255	1 746 237
0 - 4	3 354 118	1 706 530	1 647 588	2 950 721	1 506 848	1 443 873	403 397	199 682	203 715
5 - 9	3 374 055	1 715 351	1 658 704	2 965 206	1 512 592	1 452 614	408 849	202 759	206 090
10 - 14	3 450 884	1 753 350	1 697 534	3 066 507	1 561 531	1 504 976	384 377	191 819	192 558
15 - 19	3 404 602	1 728 405	1 676 197	3 072 570	1 554 613	1 517 957	332 032	173 792	158 240
20 - 24	3 262 839	1 651 069	1 611 770	2 983 385	1 504 098	1 479 287	279 454	146 971	132 483
25 - 29	3 277 050	1 648 462	1 628 588	3 018 626	1 514 016	1 504 610	258 424	134 446	123 978
30 - 34	2 951 890	1 477 980	1 473 910	2 716 531	1 355 379	1 361 152	235 359	122 601	112 758
35 - 39	2 499 574	1 247 052	1 252 522	2 296 723	1 138 308	1 158 415	202 851	108 744	94 107
40 - 44	2 295 845	1 137 747	1 158 098	2 104 199	1 032 715	1 071 484	191 646	105 032	86 614
45 - 49	2 160 250	1 050 175	1 110 075	1 978 231	951 166	1 027 065	182 019	99 009	83 010
50 - 54	2 018 437	970 839	1 047 598	1 846 296	876 956	969 340	172 141	93 883	78 258
55 - 59	1 798 950	858 209	940 741	1 645 654	772 848	872 806	153 296	85 361	67 935
60 - 64	1 515 506	710 473	805 033	1 384 606	637 770	746 836	130 900	72 703	58 197
65 - 69	1 255 661	566 698	688 963	1 153 839	511 469	642 370	101 822	55 229	46 593
70 - 74	1 045 588	443 870	601 718	965 498	402 055	563 443	80 090	41 815	38 275
75 - 79	829 500	324 995	504 505	770 054	294 719	475 335	59 446	30 276	29 170
80 +	861 634	282 289	579 345	801 245	256 156	545 089	60 389	26 133	34 256
Bolivia (Plurinational State of) - Bolivie (État plurinational de) 1 VII 2007 (ESDF)									
Total	9 827 522	4 900 162	4 927 360	6 400 366	3 114 403	3 285 963	3 427 156	1 785 759	1 641 397
0 - 4	1 293 134	659 355	633 779	789 556	399 930	389 625	503 579	259 425	244 154
5 - 9	1 215 036	619 415	595 621	749 562	377 597	371 965	465 474	241 818	223 656
10 - 14	1 145 858	583 750	562 108	735 450	366 297	369 153	410 408	217 453	192 955
15 - 19	1 035 164	525 644	509 520	721 012	354 467	366 545	314 152	171 178	142 975
20 - 24	898 751	453 775	444 976	646 365	318 833	327 531	252 387	134 941	117 445
25 - 29	785 260	393 514	391 746	553 318	269 659	283 659	231 942	123 854	108 088
30 - 34	697 867	346 506	351 361	484 117	232 577	251 540	213 750	113 929	99 821
35 - 39	590 361	291 071	299 289	398 780	189 772	209 008	191 581	101 299	90 282
40 - 44	484 217	237 087	247 129	323 460	153 201	170 258	160 757	83 886	76 871
45 - 49	408 397	198 147	210 250	261 700	122 976	138 724	146 697	75 172	71 526
50 - 54	340 239	163 007	177 233	211 960	98 187	113 773	128 279	64 819	63 460
55 - 59	278 398	132 037	146 361	164 695	75 399	89 296	113 703	56 638	57 065
60 - 64	217 288	102 145	115 143	122 773	54 957	67 816	94 515	47 187	47 328
65 - 69	169 908	78 392	91 516	92 835	40 940	51 896	77 073	37 452	39 621
70 - 74	127 389	57 146	70 242	68 862	29 437	39 425	58 526	27 709	30 817
75 - 79	84 659	36 750	47 910	46 451	19 020	27 431	38 208	17 730	20 478
80 +	55 594	22 421	33 173	29 470	11 154	18 316	26 125	11 268	14 857
Brazil - Brésil[19] 1 VIII 2000 (CDJC)									
Total	169 799 170	83 576 015	86 223 155	137 953 959	66 882 993	71 070 966	31 845 211	16 693 022	15 152 189
0	3 213 310	1 635 916	1 577 394	2 518 464	1 282 941	1 235 523	694 846	352 975	341 871
1 - 4	13 162 418	6 691 010	6 471 408	10 242 356	5 207 423	5 034 933	2 920 062	1 483 587	1 436 475
5 - 9	16 542 327	8 402 353	8 139 974	12 821 519	6 500 814	6 320 705	3 720 808	1 901 539	1 819 269
10 - 14	17 348 067	8 777 639	8 570 428	13 530 190	6 803 898	6 726 292	3 817 877	1 973 741	1 844 136

Continent, country or area, date, code and age (in years) / Continent, pays ou zone, date, code et âge (en années)	Total			Urban - Urbaine			Rural - Rurale		
	Both sexes Les deux sexes	Male Masculin	Female Féminin	Both sexes Les deux sexes	Male Masculin	Female Féminin	Both sexes Les deux sexes	Male Masculin	Female Féminin
AMERICA, SOUTH - AMÉRIQUE DU SUD									
Brazil - Brésil[19]									
1 VIII 2000 (CDJC)									
15 - 19	17 939 815	9 019 130	8 920 685	14 403 539	7 132 822	7 270 717	3 536 276	1 886 308	1 649 968
20 - 24	16 141 515	8 048 218	8 093 297	13 352 132	6 549 365	6 802 767	2 789 383	1 498 853	1 290 530
25 - 29	13 849 665	6 814 328	7 035 337	11 570 969	5 606 425	5 964 544	2 278 696	1 207 903	1 070 793
30 - 34	13 028 944	6 363 983	6 664 961	10 918 396	5 248 443	5 669 953	2 110 548	1 115 540	995 008
35 - 39	12 261 529	5 955 875	6 305 654	10 326 271	4 929 130	5 397 141	1 935 258	1 026 745	908 513
40 - 44	10 546 694	5 116 439	5 430 255	8 913 019	4 249 804	4 663 215	1 633 675	866 635	767 040
45 - 49	8 721 541	4 216 418	4 505 123	7 309 621	3 472 375	3 837 246	1 411 920	744 043	667 877
50 - 54	7 062 601	3 415 678	3 646 923	5 833 659	2 764 708	3 068 951	1 228 942	650 970	577 972
55 - 59	5 444 715	2 585 244	2 859 471	4 387 995	2 032 135	2 355 860	1 056 720	553 109	503 611
60 - 64	4 600 929	2 153 209	2 447 720	3 712 213	1 676 323	2 035 890	888 716	476 886	411 830
65 - 69	3 581 106	1 639 325	1 941 781	2 916 899	1 284 812	1 632 087	664 207	354 513	309 694
70 - 74	2 742 302	1 229 329	1 512 973	2 249 617	966 115	1 283 502	492 685	263 214	229 471
75 - 79	1 779 587	780 571	999 016	1 456 665	610 767	845 898	322 922	169 804	153 118
80 - 84	1 036 034	428 501	607 533	841 798	331 002	510 796	194 236	97 499	96 737
85 - 89	534 871	208 088	326 783	436 121	160 379	275 742	98 750	47 709	51 041
90 - 94	180 426	65 117	115 309	147 784	50 531	97 253	32 642	14 586	18 056
95 - 99	56 198	19 221	36 977	45 682	14 899	30 783	10 516	4 322	6 194
100 +	24 576	10 423	14 153	19 050	7 882	11 168	5 526	2 541	2 985
1 VII 2007 (ESDF)									
Total	187 641 714	92 154 636	95 487 078	...	...	...	...	...	...
0	3 177 307	1 614 626	1 562 681	...	...	...	...	...	...
1 - 4	13 404 084	6 803 677	6 600 407	...	...	...	...	...	...
5 - 9	17 263 594	8 756 622	8 506 972	...	...	...	...	...	...
10 - 14	16 563 563	8 390 298	8 173 265	...	...	...	...	...	...
15 - 19	16 862 028	8 510 869	8 351 159	...	...	...	...	...	...
20 - 24	17 787 136	8 933 098	8 854 038	...	...	...	...	...	...
25 - 29	16 621 980	8 294 149	8 327 831	...	...	...	...	...	...
30 - 34	14 558 360	7 234 136	7 324 224	...	...	...	...	...	...
35 - 39	13 624 658	6 698 334	6 926 324	...	...	...	...	...	...
40 - 44	12 996 286	6 254 562	6 741 724	...	...	...	...	...	...
45 - 49	11 299 674	5 360 532	5 939 142	...	...	...	...	...	...
50 - 54	9 040 809	4 252 732	4 788 077	...	...	...	...	...	...
55 - 59	7 054 571	3 299 865	3 754 706	...	...	...	...	...	...
60 - 64	5 390 506	2 485 189	2 905 317	...	...	...	...	...	...
65 - 69	4 310 718	1 962 623	2 348 095	...	...	...	...	...	...
70 - 74	3 186 865	1 414 668	1 772 197	...	...	...	...	...	...
75 - 79	2 216 428	946 562	1 269 866	...	...	...	...	...	...
80 +	2 283 147	942 094	1 341 053	...	...	...	...	...	...
Chile - Chili									
1 VII 2007 (ESDF)									
Total	16 598 074	8 216 068	8 382 006	14 421 386	7 057 476	7 363 910	2 176 688	1 158 592	1 018 096
0 - 4	1 241 807	632 443	609 364	1 088 180	553 946	534 234	153 627	78 497	75 130
5 - 9	1 291 875	657 604	634 271	1 125 983	572 681	553 302	165 892	84 923	80 969
10 - 14	1 424 672	724 842	699 830	1 231 326	625 450	605 876	193 346	99 392	93 954
15 - 19	1 473 222	748 763	724 459	1 270 790	643 199	627 591	202 432	105 564	96 868
20 - 24	1 378 214	698 803	679 411	1 200 637	602 454	598 183	177 577	96 349	81 228
25 - 29	1 230 960	621 408	609 552	1 085 541	541 671	543 870	145 419	79 737	65 682
30 - 34	1 211 746	608 268	603 478	1 068 820	531 630	537 190	142 926	76 638	66 288
35 - 39	1 237 878	618 433	619 445	1 081 883	535 394	546 489	155 995	83 039	72 956
40 - 44	1 249 772	621 630	628 142	1 084 936	532 270	552 666	164 836	89 360	75 476
45 - 49	1 153 894	571 201	582 693	1 002 675	487 435	515 240	151 219	83 766	67 453
50 - 54	943 745	463 699	480 046	821 774	395 629	426 145	121 971	68 070	53 901
55 - 59	754 605	365 837	388 768	654 794	310 621	344 173	99 811	55 216	44 595
60 - 64	614 872	291 812	323 060	528 870	245 088	283 782	86 002	46 724	39 278
65 - 69	475 442	219 052	256 390	403 020	180 219	222 801	72 422	38 833	33 589
70 - 74	364 698	160 202	204 496	305 980	129 358	176 622	58 718	30 844	27 874
75 - 79	271 869	112 029	159 840	229 356	90 254	139 102	42 513	21 775	20 738
80 +	278 803	100 042	178 761	236 821	80 177	156 644	41 982	19 865	22 117
Colombia - Colombie									
22 V 2005 (CDFC)									
Total	41 468 384	20 336 117	21 132 267	31 510 379	15 086 536	16 423 843	9 958 005	5 249 581	4 708 424
0 - 4	4 108 861	2 106 179	2 002 682	2 907 910	1 488 395	1 419 515	1 200 951	617 784	583 167

Continent, country or area, date, code and age (in years) / Continent, pays ou zone, date, code et âge (en années)	Total			Urban - Urbaine			Rural - Rurale		
	Both sexes Les deux sexes	Male Masculin	Female Féminin	Both sexes Les deux sexes	Male Masculin	Female Féminin	Both sexes Les deux sexes	Male Masculin	Female Féminin
AMERICA, SOUTH - AMÉRIQUE DU SUD									
Colombia - Colombie									
22 V 2005 (CDFC)									
5 - 9	4 295 913	2 197 689	2 098 224	3 100 659	1 579 043	1 521 616	1 195 254	618 646	576 608
10 - 14	4 339 046	2 214 464	2 124 582	3 178 643	1 605 865	1 572 778	1 160 403	608 599	551 804
15 - 19	3 933 754	1 975 856	1 957 898	2 965 058	1 455 429	1 509 629	968 696	520 427	448 269
20 - 24	3 641 839	1 783 320	1 858 519	2 842 949	1 359 536	1 483 413	798 890	423 784	375 106
25 - 29	3 280 767	1 590 993	1 689 774	2 571 489	1 219 188	1 352 301	709 278	371 805	337 473
30 - 34	2 917 290	1 401 139	1 516 151	2 278 122	1 068 019	1 210 103	639 168	333 120	306 048
35 - 39	2 919 161	1 392 512	1 526 649	2 299 732	1 067 002	1 232 730	619 429	325 510	293 919
40 - 44	2 732 504	1 304 948	1 427 556	2 184 613	1 013 532	1 171 081	547 891	291 416	256 475
45 - 49	2 291 308	1 088 238	1 203 070	1 823 533	837 758	985 775	467 775	250 480	217 295
50 - 54	1 835 340	876 301	959 039	1 446 551	665 396	781 155	388 789	210 905	177 884
55 - 59	1 450 658	692 733	757 925	1 119 383	512 610	606 773	331 275	180 123	151 152
60 - 64	1 104 733	524 576	580 157	835 144	377 919	457 225	269 589	146 657	122 932
65 - 69	921 054	428 876	492 178	685 621	301 907	383 714	235 433	126 969	108 464
70 - 74	702 518	321 765	380 753	522 246	225 926	296 320	180 272	95 839	84 433
75 - 79	504 438	228 608	275 830	377 004	160 491	216 513	127 434	68 117	59 317
80 - 84	278 875	121 846	157 029	210 501	86 244	124 257	68 374	35 602	32 772
85 - 89	144 936	60 648	84 288	110 851	43 721	67 130	34 085	16 927	17 158
90 - 94	49 438	19 579	29 859	38 439	14 411	24 028	10 999	5 168	5 831
95 - 99	12 786	4 654	8 132	9 698	3 322	6 376	3 088	1 332	1 756
100 +	3 165	1 193	1 972	2 233	822	1 411	932	371	561
1 VII 2007 (ESDF)[20]									
Total	43 926 034	21 682 836	22 243 198	...	...	...	...	...	...
0	856 434	438 146	418 288	...	...	...	...	...	...
1 - 4	3 439 029	1 757 458	1 681 571	...	...	...	...	...	...
5 - 9	4 415 126	2 251 440	2 163 686	...	...	...	...	...	...
10 - 14	4 495 984	2 302 379	2 193 605	...	...	...	...	...	...
15 - 19	4 286 606	2 197 690	2 088 916	...	...	...	...	...	...
20 - 24	3 855 756	1 928 333	1 927 423	...	...	...	...	...	...
25 - 29	3 466 275	1 697 826	1 768 449	...	...	...	...	...	...
30 - 34	3 073 361	1 493 610	1 579 751	...	...	...	...	...	...
35 - 39	2 961 535	1 424 079	1 537 456	...	...	...	...	...	...
40 - 44	2 892 357	1 387 661	1 504 696	...	...	...	...	...	...
45 - 49	2 520 308	1 204 957	1 315 351	...	...	...	...	...	...
50 - 54	2 036 481	973 648	1 062 833	...	...	...	...	...	...
55 - 59	1 613 784	773 678	840 106	...	...	...	...	...	...
60 - 64	1 229 541	587 891	641 650	...	...	...	...	...	...
65 - 69	972 196	455 851	516 345	...	...	...	...	...	...
70 - 74	766 836	350 403	416 433	...	...	...	...	...	...
75 - 79	505 470	228 046	277 424	...	...	...	...	...	...
80 +	538 955	229 740	309 215	...	...	...	...	...	...
Ecuador - Équateur[21]									
1 VII 2007 (ESDF)									
Total	13 605 485	6 820 843	6 784 642	8 785 745	4 358 292	4 427 453	4 819 740	2 462 551	2 357 189
0 - 4	1 438 625	734 197	704 428	864 047	446 747	417 300	574 578	287 450	287 128
5 - 9	1 446 895	737 670	709 225	865 056	443 410	421 646	581 839	294 260	287 579
10 - 14	1 412 506	719 249	693 257	863 567	437 044	426 523	548 939	282 205	266 734
15 - 19	1 353 756	687 501	666 255	880 566	436 634	443 932	473 190	250 867	222 323
20 - 24	1 258 168	635 945	622 223	862 431	427 259	435 172	395 737	208 686	187 051
25 - 29	1 131 520	568 927	562 593	802 479	398 044	404 435	329 041	170 883	158 158
30 - 34	1 009 487	505 194	504 293	718 921	357 196	361 725	290 566	147 998	142 568
35 - 39	901 056	449 252	451 804	622 353	309 101	313 252	278 703	140 151	138 552
40 - 44	789 066	392 340	396 726	528 204	261 158	267 046	260 862	131 182	129 680
45 - 49	676 734	335 363	341 371	432 068	212 209	219 859	244 666	123 154	121 512
50 - 54	581 681	286 890	294 791	365 469	177 693	187 776	216 212	109 197	107 015
55 - 59	452 839	222 432	230 407	280 709	134 383	146 326	172 130	88 049	84 081
60 - 64	345 489	168 422	177 067	211 477	99 673	111 804	134 012	68 749	65 263
65 - 69	279 449	134 370	145 079	170 258	78 765	91 493	109 191	55 605	53 586
70 - 74	218 245	103 081	115 164	131 651	59 351	72 300	86 594	43 730	42 864
75 - 79	158 694	73 544	85 150	95 616	42 002	53 614	63 078	31 542	31 536
80 +	151 275	66 466	84 809	90 873	37 623	53 250	60 402	28 843	31 559

7. Population by age, sex and urban/rural residence: latest available year, 1998 - 2007
Population selon l'âge, le sexe et la résidence, urbaine/rurale: dernière année disponible, 1998 - 2007 (continued - suite)

Continent, country or area, date, code and age (in years) / Continent, pays ou zone, date, code et âge (en années)	Total			Urban - Urbaine			Rural - Rurale		
	Both sexes Les deux sexes	Male Masculin	Female Féminin	Both sexes Les deux sexes	Male Masculin	Female Féminin	Both sexes Les deux sexes	Male Masculin	Female Féminin
AMERICA, SOUTH - AMÉRIQUE DU SUD									
Falkland Islands (Malvinas) - Îles Falkland (Malvinas)[22]									
8 X 2006 (CDFC)									
Total....................	2 955	1 569	1 386	...	...	...	...	...	...
0 - 4...................	156	79	77	...	...	...	...	...	...
5 - 9...................	161	75	86	...	...	...	...	...	...
10 - 14.................	154	71	83	...	...	...	...	...	...
15 - 19.................	155	90	65	...	...	...	...	...	...
20 - 24.................	207	89	118	...	...	...	...	...	...
25 - 29.................	232	126	106	...	...	...	...	...	...
30 - 34.................	266	131	135	...	...	...	...	...	...
35 - 39.................	291	165	126	...	...	...	...	...	...
40 - 44.................	261	156	105	...	...	...	...	...	...
45 - 49.................	249	128	121	...	...	...	...	...	...
50 - 54.................	215	123	92	...	...	...	...	...	...
55 - 59.................	194	113	81	...	...	...	...	...	...
60 - 64.................	148	87	61	...	...	...	...	...	...
65 - 69.................	98	57	41	...	...	...	...	...	...
70 - 74.................	68	36	32	...	...	...	...	...	...
75 - 79.................	48	18	30	...	...	...	...	...	...
80 +....................	52	25	27	...	...	...	...	...	...
French Guiana - Guyane française									
1 I 2007 (ESDJ)									
Total....................	213 500	105 549	107 951	...	...	...	...	...	...
0 - 4...................	27 373	13 887	13 486	...	...	...	...	...	...
5 - 9...................	25 800	12 954	12 846	...	...	...	...	...	...
10 - 14.................	22 869	11 489	11 380	...	...	...	...	...	...
15 - 19.................	19 846	9 907	9 939	...	...	...	...	...	...
20 - 24.................	15 801	7 693	8 108	...	...	...	...	...	...
25 - 29.................	15 019	6 884	8 135	...	...	...	...	...	...
30 - 34.................	16 120	7 599	8 521	...	...	...	...	...	...
35 - 39.................	15 792	7 535	8 257	...	...	...	...	...	...
40 - 44.................	13 983	6 909	7 074	...	...	...	...	...	...
45 - 49.................	11 689	5 932	5 757	...	...	...	...	...	...
50 - 54.................	9 581	4 898	4 683	...	...	...	...	...	...
55 - 59.................	7 027	3 676	3 351	...	...	...	...	...	...
60 - 64.................	4 480	2 390	2 090	...	...	...	...	...	...
65 - 69.................	2 825	1 452	1 373	...	...	...	...	...	...
70 - 74.................	2 109	1 023	1 086	...	...	...	...	...	...
75 - 79.................	1 330	594	736	...	...	...	...	...	...
80 - 84.................	939	391	548	...	...	...	...	...	...
85 - 89.................	595	241	354	...	...	...	...	...	...
90 - 94.................	217	68	149	...	...	...	...	...	...
95 +....................	105	27	78	...	...	...	...	...	...
Guyana									
15 IX 2002 (CDFC)									
Total....................	751 223	376 034	375 189	213 705	103 127	110 578	537 518	272 907	264 611
0 - 4...................	88 996	45 291	43 705	22 436	11 372	11 064	66 560	33 919	32 642
5 - 9...................	96 671	49 119	47 552	25 254	12 909	12 345	71 416	36 210	35 206
10 - 14.................	81 497	41 218	40 279	22 393	11 215	11 178	59 104	30 002	29 101
15 - 19.................	66 922	33 496	33 426	19 559	9 737	9 822	47 363	23 759	23 604
20 - 24.................	64 409	31 908	32 501	19 443	9 301	10 142	44 966	22 608	22 359
25 - 29.................	61 086	30 232	30 854	18 068	8 439	9 629	43 017	21 792	21 225
30 - 34.................	57 942	29 088	28 854	16 403	7 687	8 717	41 538	21 401	20 137
35 - 39.................	52 735	26 441	26 295	14 716	6 779	7 937	38 020	19 662	18 358
40 - 44.................	46 488	23 338	23 150	13 203	6 194	7 009	33 285	17 144	16 141
45 - 49.................	35 810	17 952	17 859	10 609	4 910	5 699	25 202	13 042	12 160
50 - 54.................	28 149	14 207	13 942	8 459	4 008	4 450	19 690	10 198	9 492
55 - 59.................	18 129	8 980	9 149	5 539	2 628	2 911	12 590	6 352	6 238
60 - 64.................	15 005	7 191	7 813	4 540	2 081	2 459	10 465	5 110	5 354
65 - 69.................	11 741	5 575	6 167	3 671	1 649	2 021	8 071	3 925	4 145
70 - 74.................	8 543	3 965	4 578	2 784	1 212	1 571	5 759	2 753	3 006

Continent, country or area, date, code and age (in years) / Continent, pays ou zone, date, code et âge (en annèes)	Total			Urban - Urbaine			Rural - Rurale		
	Both sexes Les deux sexes	Male Masculin	Female Féminin	Both sexes Les deux sexes	Male Masculin	Female Féminin	Both sexes Les deux sexes	Male Masculin	Female Féminin
AMERICA, SOUTH - AMÉRIQUE DU SUD									
Guyana									
15 IX 2002 (CDFC)									
75 +	11 746	5 217	6 529	3 977	1 640	2 337	7 769	3 577	4 192
Unknown - Inconnu	5 354	2 818	2 536	2 699	1 394	1 305	2 655	1 424	1 231
Paraguay									
28 VIII 2002 (CDFC)									
Total	5 163 198	2 603 242	2 559 956	2 928 437	1 422 339	1 506 098	2 234 761	1 180 903	1 053 858
0	115 558	59 043	56 515	62 098	31 869	30 229	53 460	27 174	26 286
1 - 4	491 743	250 996	240 747	256 692	130 582	126 110	235 051	120 414	114 637
5 - 9	663 294	338 199	325 095	341 612	173 363	168 249	321 682	164 836	156 846
10 - 14	644 714	328 120	316 594	331 808	165 636	166 172	312 906	162 484	150 422
15 - 19	576 807	292 731	284 076	327 674	156 108	171 566	249 133	136 623	112 510
20 - 24	472 545	238 527	234 018	294 654	139 622	155 032	177 891	98 905	78 986
25 - 29	359 766	179 299	180 467	221 966	105 928	116 038	137 800	73 371	64 429
30 - 34	333 192	167 025	166 167	204 138	98 568	105 570	129 054	68 457	60 597
35 - 39	307 521	153 333	154 188	186 657	89 705	96 952	120 864	63 628	57 236
40 - 44	284 082	145 797	138 285	170 959	84 148	86 811	113 123	61 649	51 474
45 - 49	227 719	116 069	111 650	135 829	66 659	69 170	91 890	49 410	42 480
50 - 54	182 317	93 396	88 921	106 049	52 006	54 043	76 268	41 390	34 878
55 - 59	135 707	68 353	67 354	78 597	37 878	40 719	57 110	30 475	26 635
60 - 64	114 843	56 778	58 065	64 874	29 968	34 906	49 969	26 810	23 159
65 - 69	80 528	38 292	42 236	45 618	20 151	25 467	34 910	18 141	16 769
70 - 74	70 708	33 286	37 422	40 227	17 320	22 907	30 481	15 966	14 515
75 - 79	47 931	21 703	26 228	27 650	11 307	16 343	20 281	10 396	9 885
80 - 84	29 287	12 433	16 854	16 753	6 289	10 464	12 534	6 144	6 390
85 - 89	16 412	6 750	9 662	9 573	3 548	6 025	6 839	3 202	3 637
90 +	8 524	3 112	5 412	5 009	1 684	3 325	3 515	1 428	2 087
1 VII 2007 (ESDF)									
Total	6 119 641	...	...	3 513 944	...	...	2 605 697	...	...
0 - 4	733 206	...	...	398 085	...	...	335 121	...	...
5 - 9	714 130	...	...	385 722	...	...	328 408	...	...
10 - 14	690 550	...	...	365 757	...	...	324 793	...	...
15 - 19	657 891	...	...	349 734	...	...	308 157	...	...
20 - 24	606 010	...	...	342 353	...	...	263 657	...	...
25 - 29	504 826	...	...	315 032	...	...	189 794	...	...
30 - 34	399 296	...	...	261 625	...	...	137 671	...	...
35 - 39	349 789	...	...	223 785	...	...	126 004	...	...
40 - 44	318 487	...	...	197 120	...	...	121 367	...	...
45 - 49	279 668	...	...	169 359	...	...	110 309	...	...
50 - 54	239 890	...	...	143 561	...	...	96 329	...	...
55 - 59	189 338	...	...	110 985	...	...	78 353	...	...
60 - 64	141 589	...	...	82 208	...	...	59 381	...	...
65 - 69	108 862	...	...	62 020	...	...	46 842	...	...
70 - 74	77 342	...	...	43 874	...	...	33 468	...	...
75 - 79	56 815	...	...	32 583	...	...	24 232	...	...
80 +	51 952	...	...	30 141	...	...	21 811	...	...
Peru - Pérou									
21 X 2007 (CDFC)									
Total	27 412 157	13 622 640	13 789 517	20 810 288	10 226 205	10 584 083	6 601 869	3 396 435	3 205 434
0	500 672	254 537	246 135	358 482	182 489	175 993	142 190	72 048	70 142
1 - 4	2 223 948	1 134 711	1 089 237	1 555 226	794 601	760 625	668 722	340 110	328 612
5 - 9	2 683 928	1 367 011	1 316 917	1 859 901	947 778	912 123	824 027	419 233	404 794
10 - 14	2 948 985	1 503 335	1 445 650	2 087 424	1 057 152	1 030 272	861 561	446 183	415 378
15 - 19	2 730 785	1 373 374	1 357 411	2 089 243	1 036 420	1 052 823	641 542	336 954	304 588
20 - 24	2 531 554	1 255 746	1 275 808	1 998 613	979 819	1 018 794	532 941	275 927	257 014
25 - 29	2 291 865	1 127 632	1 164 233	1 823 271	883 850	939 421	468 594	243 782	224 812
30 - 34	2 074 691	1 015 656	1 059 035	1 662 397	800 459	861 938	412 294	215 197	197 097
35 - 39	1 871 852	906 060	965 792	1 486 744	708 812	777 932	385 108	197 248	187 860
40 - 44	1 642 059	807 852	834 207	1 307 657	632 580	675 077	334 402	175 272	159 130
45 - 49	1 371 385	671 823	699 562	1 086 018	524 146	561 872	285 367	147 677	137 690
50 - 54	1 152 647	561 032	591 615	918 681	441 358	477 323	233 966	119 674	114 292
55 - 59	892 143	438 763	453 380	699 471	340 282	359 189	192 672	98 481	94 191
60 - 64	730 956	360 165	370 791	558 001	272 891	285 110	172 955	87 274	85 681
65 - 69	579 302	284 585	294 717	434 809	211 932	222 877	144 493	72 653	71 840

7. Population by age, sex and urban/rural residence: latest available year, 1998 - 2007
Population selon l'âge, le sexe et la résidence, urbaine/rurale: dernière année disponible, 1998 - 2007 (continued - suite)

Continent, country or area, date, code and age (in years) / Continent, pays ou zone, date, code et âge (en années)	Total			Urban - Urbaine			Rural - Rurale		
	Both sexes Les deux sexes	Male Masculin	Female Féminin	Both sexes Les deux sexes	Male Masculin	Female Féminin	Both sexes Les deux sexes	Male Masculin	Female Féminin
AMERICA, SOUTH - AMÉRIQUE DU SUD									
Peru - Pérou									
21 X 2007 (CDFC)									
70 - 74	452 998	220 472	232 526	337 533	162 379	175 154	115 465	58 093	57 372
75 - 79	343 999	167 439	176 560	256 025	122 120	133 905	87 974	45 319	42 655
80 - 84	203 636	93 831	109 805	153 704	70 169	83 535	49 932	23 662	26 270
85 +	184 752	78 616	106 136	137 088	56 968	80 120	47 664	21 648	26 016
Suriname									
2 VIII 2004 (CDJC)[23]									
Total	492 829	248 046	244 783	328 932[24]	164 444[24]	164 488[24]	163 897[24]	83 602[24]	80 295[24]
0 - 4	51 837	26 252	25 585	31 603[24]	16 152[24]	15 451[24]	20 234[24]	10 100[24]	10 134[24]
5 - 9	49 409	25 200	24 209	30 886[24]	15 639[24]	15 247[24]	18 523[24]	9 561[24]	8 962[24]
10 - 14	45 143	22 889	22 254	28 942[24]	14 536[24]	14 406[24]	16 201[24]	8 353[24]	7 848[24]
15 - 19	46 508	23 465	23 043	31 775[24]	16 181[24]	15 594[24]	14 733[24]	7 284[24]	7 449[24]
20 - 24	43 843	22 437	21 406	30 989[24]	16 056[24]	14 933[24]	12 854[24]	6 381[24]	6 473[24]
25 - 29	37 901	19 006	18 895	25 895[24]	12 853[24]	13 042[24]	12 006[24]	6 153[24]	5 853[24]
30 - 34	38 994	19 828	19 166	26 462[24]	13 226[24]	13 236[24]	12 532[24]	6 602[24]	5 930[24]
35 - 39	37 279	19 179	18 100	25 388[24]	12 845[24]	12 543[24]	11 891[24]	6 334[24]	5 557[24]
40 - 44	33 985	17 657	16 328	23 386[24]	11 870[24]	11 516[24]	10 599[24]	5 787[24]	4 812[24]
45 - 49	25 635	12 643	12 992	17 893[24]	8 565[24]	9 328[24]	7 742[24]	4 078[24]	3 664[24]
50 - 54	20 420	9 933	10 487	14 421[24]	6 955[24]	7 466[24]	5 999[24]	2 978[24]	3 021[24]
55 - 59	14 982	6 955	8 027	10 487[24]	4 806[24]	5 681[24]	4 495[24]	2 149[24]	2 346[24]
60 - 64	13 259	6 200	7 059	9 309[24]	4 428[24]	4 881[24]	3 950[24]	1 772[24]	2 178[24]
65 - 69	10 602	5 148	5 454	7 101[24]	3 521[24]	3 580[24]	3 501[24]	1 627[24]	1 874[24]
70 - 74	8 659	4 103	4 556	5 745[24]	2 708[24]	3 037[24]	2 914[24]	1 395[24]	1 519[24]
75 - 79	5 152	2 419	2 733	3 410[24]	1 576[24]	1 834[24]	1 742[24]	843[24]	899[24]
80 - 84	2 853	1 235	1 618	1 905[24]	779[24]	1 126[24]	948[24]	456[24]	492[24]
85 - 89	1 075	392	677	770[24]	274[24]	496[24]	299[24]	118[24]	181[24]
90 - 94	490	196	294	371[24]	157[24]	214[24]	119[24]	39[24]	80[24]
95 +	129	34	95	94[24]	24[24]	70[24]	35[24]	10[24]	25[24]
Unknown - Inconnu	4 704	2 885	1 819	2 100[24]	1 293[24]	807[24]	2 604[24]	1 592[24]	1 012[24]
1 VII 2007 (ESDJ)[25]									
Total	509 970	257 181	252 789	...	...	...	...	...	...
0	9 769	4 889	4 880	...	...	...	...	...	...
1 - 4	40 951	21 022	19 929	...	...	...	...	...	...
5 - 9	50 987	26 030	24 957	...	...	...	...	...	...
10 - 14	48 453	24 646	23 807	...	...	...	...	...	...
15 - 19	46 014	23 357	22 657	...	...	...	...	...	...
20 - 24	43 838	22 293	21 545	...	...	...	...	...	...
25 - 29	41 642	21 239	20 403	...	...	...	...	...	...
30 - 34	39 555	20 225	19 330	...	...	...	...	...	...
35 - 39	37 120	18 995	18 125	...	...	...	...	...	...
40 - 44	33 306	16 963	16 343	...	...	...	...	...	...
45 - 49	29 097	14 715	14 382	...	...	...	...	...	...
50 - 54	24 032	11 983	12 049	...	...	...	...	...	...
55 - 59	18 996	9 274	9 722	...	...	...	...	...	...
60 - 64	15 053	7 236	7 817	...	...	...	...	...	...
65 - 69	11 475	5 426	6 049	...	...	...	...	...	...
70 - 74	8 529	3 976	4 553	...	...	...	...	...	...
75 - 79	5 922	2 727	3 195	...	...	...	...	...	...
80 +	5 231	2 185	3 046	...	...	...	...	...	...
Uruguay[3]									
1 VII 2007 (ESDF)									
Total	3 323 906	1 605 466	1 718 440	3 114 125	1 487 391	1 626 734	209 781	118 075	91 706
0 - 4	242 203	123 899	118 304	228 281	116 715	111 566	13 922	7 184	6 738
5 - 9	262 811	134 189	128 622	247 056	126 031	121 025	15 755	8 158	7 597
10 - 14	273 563	139 779	133 784	257 219	131 180	126 039	16 344	8 599	7 745
15 - 19	265 255	135 301	129 954	249 970	126 894	123 076	15 285	8 407	6 878
20 - 24	251 509	127 102	124 407	237 262	118 980	118 282	14 247	8 122	6 125
25 - 29	241 626	120 060	121 566	227 428	112 001	115 427	14 198	8 059	6 139
30 - 34	234 045	115 461	118 584	219 620	107 321	112 299	14 425	8 140	6 285
35 - 39	209 938	102 958	106 980	196 037	95 015	101 022	13 901	7 943	5 958
40 - 44	205 917	100 030	105 887	191 965	92 016	99 949	13 952	8 014	5 938
45 - 49	203 712	99 066	104 646	190 025	91 037	98 988	13 687	8 029	5 658

Continent, country or area, date, code and age (in years) / Continent, pays ou zone, date, code et âge (en annèes)	Total			Urban - Urbaine			Rural - Rurale		
	Both sexes Les deux sexes	Male Masculin	Female Féminin	Both sexes Les deux sexes	Male Masculin	Female Féminin	Both sexes Les deux sexes	Male Masculin	Female Féminin
AMERICA, SOUTH - AMÉRIQUE DU SUD									
Uruguay[3]									
1 VII 2007 (ESDF)									
50 - 54	183 183	88 143	95 040	170 289	80 536	89 753	12 894	7 607	5 287
55 - 59	162 352	76 765	85 587	150 078	69 445	80 633	12 274	7 320	4 954
60 - 64	141 169	65 407	75 762	130 320	58 843	71 477	10 849	6 564	4 285
65 - 69	127 300	56 691	70 609	117 899	51 026	66 873	9 401	5 665	3 736
70 - 74	112 247	46 825	65 422	104 743	42 422	62 321	7 504	4 403	3 101
75 - 79	95 987	37 533	58 454	90 572	34 448	56 124	5 415	3 085	2 330
80 - 84	61 871	22 114	39 757	58 731	20 470	38 261	3 140	1 644	1 496
85 - 89	33 094	10 314	22 780	31 405	9 528	21 877	1 689	786	903
90 - 94	12 001	2 940	9 061	11 338	2 678	8 660	663	262	401
95 +	4 123	889	3 234	3 887	805	3 082	236	84	152
Venezuela (Bolivarian Republic of) - Venezuela (République bolivarienne du)[26]									
1 VII 2002 (ESDF)									
Total	25 219 910	12 678 275	12 541 635	22 163 339	11 021 146	11 142 193	3 056 571	1 657 129	1 399 442
0 - 4	...	...	...	2 365 585	1 212 601	1 152 984	431 255	216 828	214 427
0	566 727	289 817	276 910	...	...	...	...	...	...
1 - 4	2 230 113	1 139 612	1 090 501	...	...	...	...	...	...
5 - 9	2 731 128	1 394 224	1 336 904	2 338 027	1 195 058	1 142 969	393 101	199 166	193 935
10 - 14	2 712 386	1 383 578	1 328 808	2 355 253	1 197 602	1 157 651	357 133	185 976	171 157
15 - 19	2 568 391	1 306 597	1 261 794	2 258 881	1 135 863	1 123 018	309 510	170 734	138 776
20 - 24	2 336 801	1 182 579	1 154 222	2 075 006	1 035 987	1 039 019	261 795	146 592	115 203
25 - 29	2 055 341	1 034 449	1 020 892	1 827 634	907 988	919 646	227 707	126 461	101 246
30 - 34	1 871 230	938 046	933 184	1 675 269	828 977	846 292	195 961	109 069	86 892
35 - 39	1 744 170	872 099	872 071	1 567 126	772 287	794 839	177 044	99 812	77 232
40 - 44	1 506 179	751 648	754 531	1 358 018	667 128	690 890	148 161	84 520	63 641
45 - 49	1 266 420	631 252	635 168	1 141 806	559 946	581 860	124 614	71 306	53 308
50 - 54	1 044 891	520 661	524 230	935 412	457 944	477 468	109 479	62 717	46 762
55 - 59	800 903	396 302	404 601	708 958	343 000	365 958	91 945	53 302	38 643
60 - 64	590 879	287 629	303 250	516 207	244 396	271 811	74 672	43 233	31 439
65 - 69	450 395	214 998	235 397	391 277	180 798	210 479	59 118	34 200	24 918
70 - 74	344 553	160 308	184 245	299 965	135 041	164 924	44 588	25 267	19 321
75 - 79	232 921	104 448	128 473	203 220	87 769	115 451	29 701	16 679	13 022
80 +	166 482	70 028	96 454	145 695	58 761	86 934	20 787	11 267	9 520
1 VII 2006 (ESDF)									
Total	27 030 656	13 570 418	13 460 238	...	...	...	...	...	...
0 - 4	2 856 707	1 460 640	1 396 067	...	...	...	...	...	...
5 - 9	2 759 835	1 409 395	1 350 440	...	...	...	...	...	...
10 - 14	2 721 953	1 389 093	1 332 860	...	...	...	...	...	...
15 - 19	2 699 011	1 373 741	1 325 270	...	...	...	...	...	...
20 - 24	2 503 978	1 266 811	1 237 167	...	...	...	...	...	...
25 - 29	2 271 616	1 142 181	1 129 435	...	...	...	...	...	...
30 - 34	1 976 161	989 242	986 919	...	...	...	...	...	...
35 - 39	1 835 406	915 953	919 453	...	...	...	...	...	...
40 - 44	1 697 633	845 497	852 136	...	...	...	...	...	...
45 - 49	1 426 744	708 896	717 848	...	...	...	...	...	...
50 - 54	1 202 803	596 434	606 369	...	...	...	...	...	...
55 - 59	969 382	479 399	489 983	...	...	...	...	...	...
60 - 64	719 188	351 303	367 885	...	...	...	...	...	...
65 - 69	518 392	247 676	270 716	...	...	...	...	...	...
70 - 74	386 812	180 043	206 769	...	...	...	...	...	...
75 - 79	280 119	126 443	153 676	...	...	...	...	...	...
80 +	204 916	87 671	117 245	...	...	...	...	...	...
ASIA - ASIE									
Armenia - Arménie									
1 VII 2007 (ESDJ)									
Total	3 226 520	1 559 978	1 666 542	2 067 650	982 632	1 085 018	1 158 870	577 346	581 524
0	38 454	20 487	17 967	24 341	12 855	11 486	14 113	7 632	6 481

Continent, country or area, date, code and age (in years) Continent, pays ou zone, date, code et âge (en années)	Total			Urban - Urbaine			Rural - Rurale		
	Both sexes Les deux sexes	Male Masculin	Female Féminin	Both sexes Les deux sexes	Male Masculin	Female Féminin	Both sexes Les deux sexes	Male Masculin	Female Féminin
ASIA - ASIE									
Armenia - Arménie 1 VII 2007 (ESDJ)									
1 - 4	143 622	77 072	66 550	90 928	48 327	42 601	52 694	28 745	23 949
5 - 9	195 531	104 301	91 230	116 707	61 632	55 075	78 824	42 669	36 155
10 - 14	246 814	127 825	118 989	143 474	74 250	69 224	103 340	53 575	49 765
15 - 19	317 858	161 512	156 346	189 346	95 939	93 407	128 512	65 573	62 939
20 - 24	312 778	157 563	155 215	197 721	98 220	99 501	115 057	59 343	55 714
25 - 29	268 776	133 852	134 924	179 612	88 256	91 356	89 164	45 596	43 568
30 - 34	220 430	107 373	113 057	147 808	71 467	76 341	72 622	35 906	36 716
35 - 39	198 364	95 033	103 331	126 882	59 599	67 283	71 482	35 434	36 048
40 - 44	231 693	109 376	122 317	142 816	64 408	78 408	88 877	44 968	43 909
45 - 49	269 590	128 109	141 481	176 443	80 437	96 006	93 147	47 672	45 475
50 - 54	207 961	96 816	111 145	146 330	66 085	80 245	61 631	30 731	30 900
55 - 59	149 793	68 195	81 598	110 956	49 929	61 027	38 837	18 266	20 571
60 - 64	76 367	33 157	43 210	56 008	24 201	31 807	20 359	8 956	11 403
65 - 69	126 087	53 305	72 782	84 161	35 782	48 379	41 926	17 523	24 403
70 - 74	99 292	41 332	57 960	60 971	25 178	35 793	38 321	16 154	22 167
75 - 79	79 107	31 388	47 719	46 460	18 053	28 407	32 647	13 335	19 312
80 - 84	34 225	10 809	23 416	20 786	6 462	14 324	13 439	4 347	9 092
85 +	9 778	2 473	7 305	5 900	1 552	4 348	3 878	921	2 957
Azerbaijan - Azerbaïdjan 1 VII 2007 (ESDF)									
Total	8 581 300	4 231 500	4 349 800	4 431 200	2 171 600	2 259 600	4 150 100	2 059 900	2 090 200
0	150 400	81 100	69 300	71 800	38 500	33 300	78 600	42 600	36 000
1 - 4	509 600	274 400	235 200	234 200	126 600	107 600	275 400	147 800	127 600
5 - 9	561 700	299 800	261 900	252 700	136 200	116 500	309 000	163 600	145 400
10 - 14	793 500	411 400	382 100	372 400	194 700	177 700	421 100	216 700	204 400
15 - 19	927 600	475 500	452 100	470 800	242 000	228 800	456 800	233 500	223 300
20 - 24	858 000	437 700	420 300	450 100	230 100	220 000	407 900	207 600	200 300
25 - 29	711 700	353 600	358 100	376 800	187 100	189 700	334 900	166 500	168 400
30 - 34	617 100	294 300	322 800	312 700	144 700	168 000	304 400	149 600	154 800
35 - 39	643 000	303 100	339 900	324 400	147 800	176 600	318 600	155 300	163 300
40 - 44	677 400	318 800	358 600	358 500	164 700	193 800	318 900	154 100	164 800
45 - 49	654 900	314 700	340 200	371 300	178 200	193 100	283 600	136 500	147 100
50 - 54	439 400	210 500	228 900	262 600	125 900	136 700	176 800	84 600	92 200
55 - 59	292 000	138 700	153 300	181 100	86 900	94 200	110 900	51 800	59 100
60 - 64	142 500	65 300	77 200	88 500	40 900	47 600	54 000	24 400	29 600
65 - 69	219 100	95 700	123 400	117 800	52 000	65 800	101 300	43 700	57 600
70 - 74	190 500	81 500	109 000	91 700	38 900	52 800	98 800	42 600	56 200
75 - 79	117 200	49 300	67 900	56 600	23 200	33 400	60 600	26 100	34 500
80 - 84	48 400	17 900	30 500	24 900	9 100	15 800	23 500	8 800	14 700
85 - 89	17 500	5 400	12 100	8 300	2 800	5 500	9 200	2 600	6 600
90 - 94	5 600	1 600	4 000	2 400	800	1 600	3 200	800	2 400
95 - 99	3 100	800	2 300	1 000	300	700	2 100	500	1 600
100 +	1 100	400	700	600	200	400	500	200	300
Bahrain - Bahreïn[9] 1 VII 2007 (ESDF)									
Total	1 039 297	632 074	407 223	...	...	...	...	...	...
0 - 4	74 530	37 799	36 731	...	...	...	...	...	...
5 - 9	73 454	37 590	35 864	...	...	...	...	...	...
10 - 14	71 629	36 632	34 997	...	...	...	...	...	...
15 - 19	69 131	35 260	33 871	...	...	...	...	...	...
20 - 24	97 360	57 615	39 745	...	...	...	...	...	...
25 - 29	136 162	91 555	44 607	...	...	...	...	...	...
30 - 34	128 248	85 383	42 865	...	...	...	...	...	...
35 - 39	111 214	74 399	36 815	...	...	...	...	...	...
40 - 44	90 421	58 281	32 140	...	...	...	...	...	...
45 - 49	72 128	46 859	25 269	...	...	...	...	...	...
50 - 54	48 835	32 887	15 948	...	...	...	...	...	...
55 - 59	27 201	17 878	9 324	...	...	...	...	...	...
60 - 64	12 734	7 188	5 546	...	...	...	...	...	...
65 - 69	9 666	4 901	4 764	...	...	...	...	...	...
70 - 74	6 236	2 997	3 240	...	...	...	...	...	...
75 - 79	4 607	2 218	2 389	...	...	...	...	...	...

Continent, country or area, date, code and age (in years) / Continent, pays ou zone, date, code et âge (en annèes)	Total			Urban - Urbaine			Rural - Rurale		
	Both sexes Les deux sexes	Male Masculin	Female Féminin	Both sexes Les deux sexes	Male Masculin	Female Féminin	Both sexes Les deux sexes	Male Masculin	Female Féminin
ASIA - ASIE									
Bahrain - Bahreïn[9]									
1 VII 2007 (ESDF)									
80 - 84	2 545	1 263	1 281	...	...	...	...	...	...
85 + ...	3 196	1 369	1 827	...	...	...	...	...	...
Bhutan - Bhoutan									
30 V 2005 (CDFC)									
Total.....................	634 982	333 595	301 387	196 111	105 559	90 552	438 871	228 036	210 835
0.....................	12 314	6 096	6 218	4 108	2 050	2 058	8 206	4 046	4 160
1 - 4.....................	50 239	25 393	24 846	15 095	7 659	7 436	35 144	17 734	17 410
5 - 9.....................	70 399	35 547	34 852	19 254	9 589	9 665	51 145	25 958	25 187
10 - 14.....................	77 007	38 728	38 279	22 332	10 904	11 428	54 675	27 824	26 851
15 - 19.....................	75 236	37 504	37 732	27 628	13 659	13 969	47 608	23 845	23 763
20 - 24.....................	70 574	40 254	30 320	28 922	16 884	12 038	41 652	23 370	18 282
25 - 29.....................	57 358	31 386	25 972	21 766	12 170	9 596	35 592	19 216	16 376
30 - 34.....................	42 806	23 208	19 598	15 161	8 527	6 634	27 645	14 681	12 964
35 - 39.....................	38 729	21 124	17 605	13 061	7 613	5 448	25 668	13 511	12 157
40 - 44.....................	29 900	16 022	13 878	8 475	5 068	3 407	21 425	10 954	10 471
45 - 49.....................	27 662	14 895	12 767	6 664	3 984	2 680	20 998	10 911	10 087
50 - 54.....................	22 047	11 779	10 268	4 509	2 769	1 740	17 538	9 010	8 528
55 - 59.....................	16 392	8 764	7 628	2 700	1 532	1 168	13 692	7 232	6 460
60 - 64.....................	14 574	7 564	7 010	2 134	1 084	1 050	12 440	6 480	5 960
65 - 69.....................	11 361	5 999	5 362	1 621	845	776	9 740	5 154	4 586
70 - 74.....................	8 742	4 493	4 249	1 233	579	654	7 509	3 914	3 595
75 - 79.....................	5 245	2 677	2 568	741	337	404	4 504	2 340	2 164
80 - 84.....................	2 884	1 452	1 432	452	200	252	2 432	1 252	1 180
85 - 89.....................	1 082	528	554	193	80	113	889	448	441
90 - 94.....................	297	121	176	40	19	21	257	102	155
95 - 99.....................	104	48	56	18	6	12	86	42	44
100 +.....................	30	13	17	4	1	3	26	12	14
1 VII 2007 (ESDF)[27]									
Total.....................	658 888	345 298	313 590	...	...	...	...	...	...
0.....................	14 169	6 894	7 275	...	...	...	...	...	...
1 - 4.....................	54 011	27 289	26 722	...	...	...	...	...	...
5 - 9.....................	67 205	34 102	33 103	...	...	...	...	...	...
10 - 14.....................	74 948	37 823	37 125	...	...	...	...	...	...
15 - 19.....................	76 381	37 672	38 709	...	...	...	...	...	...
20 - 24.....................	73 004	39 722	33 282	...	...	...	...	...	...
25 - 29.....................	63 148	35 554	27 594	...	...	...	...	...	...
30 - 34.....................	47 480	25 672	21 808	...	...	...	...	...	...
35 - 39.....................	39 956	21 764	18 192	...	...	...	...	...	...
40 - 44.....................	32 929	17 777	15 152	...	...	...	...	...	...
45 - 49.....................	28 039	15 037	13 002	...	...	...	...	...	...
50 - 54.....................	24 140	12 919	11 221	...	...	...	...	...	...
55 - 59.....................	17 764	9 479	8 285	...	...	...	...	...	...
60 - 64.....................	14 525	7 579	6 946	...	...	...	...	...	...
65 - 69.....................	11 870	6 178	5 692	...	...	...	...	...	...
70 - 74.....................	8 913	4 611	4 302	...	...	...	...	...	...
75 - 79.....................	5 712	2 908	2 804	...	...	...	...	...	...
80 +.....................	4 694	2 318	2 376	...	...	...	...	...	...
Brunei Darussalam - Brunéi Darussalam									
21 VIII 2001 (CDFC)									
Total.....................	332 844	168 974	163 870	238 699	120 046	118 653	94 145	48 928	45 217
0 - 14.....................	100 912	52 304	48 608	72 076	37 396	34 680	28 836	14 908	13 928
15 - 19.....................	27 963	14 014	13 949	20 019	10 085	9 934	7 944	3 929	4 015
20 - 24.....................	32 604	15 390	17 214	23 592	10 885	12 707	9 012	4 505	4 507
25 - 29.....................	35 773	17 884	17 889	25 856	12 573	13 283	9 917	5 311	4 606
30 - 34.....................	34 375	16 878	17 497	24 973	11 931	13 042	9 402	4 947	4 455
35 - 39.....................	28 764	14 581	14 183	21 112	10 461	10 651	7 652	4 120	3 532
40 - 44.....................	24 198	12 984	11 214	17 808	9 544	8 264	6 390	3 440	2 950
45 - 49.....................	17 149	9 150	7 999	12 402	6 637	5 765	4 747	2 513	2 234
50 - 54.....................	10 687	5 542	5 145	7 609	4 013	3 596	3 078	1 529	1 549
55 - 59.....................	6 140	3 249	2 891	4 153	2 197	1 956	1 987	1 052	935
60 - 64.....................	4 962	2 432	2 530	3 217	1 544	1 673	1 745	888	857
65 - 69.....................	3 757	1 768	1 989	2 366	1 102	1 264	1 391	666	725

7. Population by age, sex and urban/rural residence: latest available year, 1998 - 2007
Population selon l'âge, le sexe et la résidence, urbaine/rurale: dernière année disponible, 1998 - 2007 (continued - suite)

Continent, country or area, date, code and age (in years) / Continent, pays ou zone, date, code et âge (en annèes)	Total			Urban - Urbaine			Rural - Rurale		
	Both sexes Les deux sexes	Male Masculin	Female Féminin	Both sexes Les deux sexes	Male Masculin	Female Féminin	Both sexes Les deux sexes	Male Masculin	Female Féminin
ASIA - ASIE									
Brunei Darussalam - Brunéi Darussalam									
21 VIII 2001 (CDFC)									
70 - 74	2 441	1 263	1 178	1 530	758	772	911	505	406
75 - 79	1 582	793	789	1 027	492	535	555	301	254
80 - 84	844	423	421	548	264	284	296	159	137
85 - 89	397	188	209	252	98	154	145	90	55
90 - 94	197	86	111	111	47	64	86	39	47
95 - 99	66	33	33	33	14	19	33	19	14
100 +	33	12	21	15	5	10	18	7	11
1 VII 2007 (ESDF)									
Total	390 000	206 900	183 100	...	...	...	...	...	...
0 - 4	34 900	18 600	16 300	...	...	...	...	...	...
5 - 9	35 000	18 900	16 100	...	...	...	...	...	...
10 - 14	35 200	19 100	16 100	...	...	...	...	...	...
15 - 19	33 500	17 800	15 700	...	...	...	...	...	...
20 - 24	40 400	20 200	20 200	...	...	...	...	...	...
25 - 29	43 900	23 000	20 900	...	...	...	...	...	...
30 - 34	39 800	20 800	19 000	...	...	...	...	...	...
35 - 39	33 700	17 800	15 900	...	...	...	...	...	...
40 - 44	27 900	15 900	12 000	...	...	...	...	...	...
45 - 49	21 900	12 100	9 800	...	...	...	...	...	...
50 - 54	15 500	8 200	7 300	...	...	...	...	...	...
55 - 59	10 000	5 200	4 800	...	...	...	...	...	...
60 - 64	5 800	3 000	2 800	...	...	...	...	...	...
65 - 69	5 000	2 500	2 500	...	...	...	...	...	...
70 - 74	3 300	1 700	1 600	...	...	...	...	...	...
75 - 79	2 300	1 200	1 100	...	...	...	...	...	...
80 - 84	1 100	500	600	...	...	...	...	...	...
85 +	800	400	400	...	...	...	...	...	...
Cambodia - Cambodge									
3 III 1998 (CDFC)									
Total	11 437 656	5 511 408	5 926 248	1 795 575	878 186	917 389	9 642 081	4 633 222	5 008 859
0	231 609	118 075	113 534	32 869	16 851	16 018	198 740	101 224	97 516
1 - 4	1 235 183	629 217	605 966	160 680	82 377	78 303	1 074 503	546 840	527 663
5 - 9	1 772 820	903 976	868 844	239 934	122 652	117 282	1 532 886	781 324	751 562
10 - 14	1 658 196	851 139	807 057	246 998	126 217	120 781	1 411 198	724 922	686 276
15 - 19	1 344 258	664 184	680 074	233 677	113 229	120 448	1 110 581	550 955	559 626
20 - 24	745 687	354 100	391 587	128 884	63 561	65 323	616 803	290 539	326 264
25 - 29	888 540	426 968	461 572	157 736	79 241	78 495	730 804	347 727	383 077
30 - 34	782 682	370 090	412 592	137 139	69 093	68 046	645 543	300 997	344 546
35 - 39	695 868	325 331	370 537	123 310	61 255	62 055	572 558	264 076	308 482
40 - 44	497 067	199 722	297 345	92 433	40 499	51 934	404 634	159 223	245 411
45 - 49	415 931	175 052	240 879	72 681	32 868	39 813	343 250	142 184	201 066
50 - 54	312 463	132 413	180 050	50 505	22 227	28 278	261 958	110 186	151 772
55 - 59	256 930	110 189	146 741	37 186	16 284	20 902	219 744	93 905	125 839
60 - 64	204 994	86 602	118 392	28 433	11 627	16 806	176 561	74 975	101 586
65 - 69	166 928	70 660	96 268	21 891	8 614	13 277	145 037	62 046	82 991
70 - 74	112 213	46 769	65 444	14 851	5 535	9 316	97 362	41 234	56 128
75 - 79	67 528	27 838	39 690	9 135	3 337	5 798	58 393	24 501	33 892
80 - 84	30 652	12 159	18 493	4 288	1 515	2 773	26 364	10 644	15 720
85 - 89	13 368	5 029	8 339	1 874	592	1 282	11 494	4 437	7 057
90 - 94	2 867	1 026	1 841	453	157	296	2 414	869	1 545
95 +	1 872	869	1 003	618	455	163	1 254	414	840
1 VII 2004 (SSDF)[28]									
Total	12 824 170	6 197 128	6 627 042	...	...	...	...	...	...
0	314 512	165 946	148 566	...	...	...	...	...	...
1 - 4	1 105 489	567 442	538 047	...	...	...	...	...	...
5 - 9	1 638 623	847 582	791 040	...	...	...	...	...	...
10 - 14	1 892 316	967 807	924 509	...	...	...	...	...	...
15 - 19	1 499 278	761 411	737 867	...	...	...	...	...	...
20 - 24	1 305 670	633 237	672 433	...	...	...	...	...	...
25 - 29	717 482	345 923	371 559	...	...	...	...	...	...
30 - 34	814 752	388 580	426 172	...	...	...	...	...	...
35 - 39	797 807	372 679	425 128	...	...	...	...	...	...

Continent, country or area, date, code and age (in years) / Continent, pays ou zone, date, code et âge (en annèes)	Total			Urban - Urbaine			Rural - Rurale		
	Both sexes Les deux sexes	Male Masculin	Female Féminin	Both sexes Les deux sexes	Male Masculin	Female Féminin	Both sexes Les deux sexes	Male Masculin	Female Féminin
ASIA - ASIE									
Cambodia - Cambodge									
1 VII 2004 (SSDF)[28]									
40 - 44	687 814	305 922	381 893	...	...	...	...	...	...
45 - 49	529 666	213 901	315 765	...	...	...	...	...	...
50 - 54	429 213	174 662	254 552	...	...	...	...	...	...
55 - 59	331 469	140 436	191 033	...	...	...	...	...	...
60 - 64	258 291	109 132	149 159	...	...	...	...	...	...
65 - 69	200 689	84 610	116 079	...	...	...	...	...	...
70 - 74	143 581	54 578	89 003	...	...	...	...	...	...
75 - 79	89 402	35 620	53 782	...	...	...	...	...	...
80 - 84	44 885	19 066	25 820	...	...	...	...	...	...
85 - 89	16 012	5 401	10 612	...	...	...	...	...	...
90 - 94	5 144	2 135	3 009	...	...	...	...	...	...
95 +	2 075	1 058	1 017	...	...	...	...	...	...
China - Chine[29]									
1 XI 2000 (CDJC)									
Total	1242612226	640 275 969	602 336 257	458 770 983	235 264 707	223 506 276	783 841 243	405 011 262	378 829 981
0	13 793 799	7 460 206	6 333 593	4 449 020	2 376 585	2 072 435	9 344 779	5 083 621	4 261 158
1 - 4	55 184 575	30 188 488	24 996 087	17 669 697	9 525 854	8 143 843	37 514 878	20 662 634	16 852 244
5 - 9	90 152 587	48 303 208	41 849 379	26 588 363	14 180 433	12 407 930	63 564 224	34 122 775	29 441 449
10 - 14	125 396 633	65 344 739	60 051 894	35 802 884	18 701 307	17 101 577	89 593 749	46 643 432	42 950 317
15 - 19	103 031 165	52 878 170	50 152 995	42 231 585	21 086 911	21 144 674	60 799 580	31 791 259	29 008 321
20 - 24	94 573 174	47 937 766	46 635 408	41 021 887	20 651 361	20 370 526	53 551 287	27 286 405	26 264 882
25 - 29	117 602 265	60 230 758	57 371 507	48 788 516	24 820 721	23 967 795	68 813 749	35 410 037	33 403 712
30 - 34	127 314 298	65 360 456	61 953 842	49 723 640	25 760 568	23 963 072	77 590 658	39 599 888	37 990 770
35 - 39	109 147 295	56 141 391	53 005 904	44 518 164	23 269 889	21 248 275	64 629 131	32 871 502	31 757 629
40 - 44	81 242 945	42 243 187	38 999 758	33 518 610	17 499 183	16 019 427	47 724 335	24 744 004	22 980 331
45 - 49	85 521 045	43 939 603	41 581 442	31 708 706	16 245 324	15 463 382	53 812 339	27 694 279	26 118 060
50 - 54	63 304 200	32 804 125	30 500 075	22 335 748	11 462 314	10 873 434	40 968 452	21 341 811	19 626 641
55 - 59	46 370 375	24 061 506	22 308 869	16 004 389	8 077 159	7 927 230	30 365 986	15 984 347	14 381 639
60 - 64	41 703 848	21 674 478	20 029 370	14 944 552	7 519 377	7 425 175	26 759 296	14 155 101	12 604 195
65 - 69	34 780 460	17 549 348	17 231 112	12 174 470	6 128 605	6 045 865	22 605 990	11 420 743	11 185 247
70 - 74	25 574 149	12 436 154	13 137 995	8 479 487	4 216 193	4 263 294	17 094 662	8 219 961	8 874 701
75 - 79	15 928 330	7 175 811	8 752 519	5 000 134	2 291 543	2 708 591	10 928 196	4 884 268	6 043 928
80 - 84	7 989 158	3 203 868	4 785 290	2 472 016	1 004 359	1 467 657	5 517 142	2 199 509	3 317 633
85 - 89	3 030 698	1 056 941	1 973 757	994 079	347 550	646 529	2 036 619	709 391	1 327 228
90 - 94	783 594	229 758	553 836	276 586	80 189	196 397	507 008	149 569	357 439
95 - 99	169 756	51 373	118 383	62 255	17 827	44 428	107 501	33 546	73 955
100 +	17 877	4 635	13 242	6 195	1 455	4 740	11 682	3 180	8 502
China, Hong Kong SAR - Chine, Hong Kong RAS									
1 VII 2006 (ESDJ)									
Total	6 857 100	3 270 100	3 587 000	...	...	...	...	...	...
0	42 600	22 900	19 700	...	...	...	...	...	...
1 - 4	170 400	87 500	82 900	...	...	...	...	...	...
5 - 9	314 100	162 300	151 800	...	...	...	...	...	...
10 - 14	412 100	211 300	200 800	...	...	...	...	...	...
15 - 19	436 200	222 300	213 900	...	...	...	...	...	...
20 - 24	472 400	225 600	246 800	...	...	...	...	...	...
25 - 29	502 300	223 800	278 500	...	...	...	...	...	...
30 - 34	548 400	238 800	309 600	...	...	...	...	...	...
35 - 39	579 400	248 000	331 400	...	...	...	...	...	...
40 - 44	669 700	304 400	365 300	...	...	...	...	...	...
45 - 49	659 400	323 700	335 700	...	...	...	...	...	...
50 - 54	531 600	264 000	267 600	...	...	...	...	...	...
55 - 59	422 500	214 700	207 800	...	...	...	...	...	...
60 - 64	243 900	127 600	116 300	...	...	...	...	...	...
65 - 69	241 800	125 200	116 600	...	...	...	...	...	...
70 - 74	228 300	112 400	115 900	...	...	...	...	...	...
75 - 79	178 600	82 300	96 300	...	...	...	...	...	...
80 - 84	112 700	44 800	67 900	...	...	...	...	...	...
85 +	90 700	28 500	62 200	...	...	...	...	...	...

7. Population by age, sex and urban/rural residence: latest available year, 1998 - 2007
Population selon l'âge, le sexe et la résidence, urbaine/rurale: dernière année disponible, 1998 - 2007 (continued - suite)

Continent, country or area, date, code and age (in years) / Continent, pays ou zone, date, code et âge (en années)	Total			Urban - Urbaine			Rural - Rurale		
	Both sexes Les deux sexes	Male Masculin	Female Féminin	Both sexes Les deux sexes	Male Masculin	Female Féminin	Both sexes Les deux sexes	Male Masculin	Female Féminin
ASIA - ASIE									
China, Macao SAR - Chine, Macao RAS[9]									
1 VII 2007 (ESDJ)									
Total	525 800	259 100	266 700	...	...	...	...	...	...
0 - 4	17 500	9 100	8 300	...	...	...	...	...	...
5 - 9	22 000	11 400	10 600	...	...	...	...	...	...
10 - 14	34 500	17 700	16 700	...	...	...	...	...	...
15 - 19	46 100	23 400	22 700	...	...	...	...	...	...
20 - 24	49 800	24 000	25 900	...	...	...	...	...	...
25 - 29	39 600	19 100	20 500	...	...	...	...	...	...
30 - 34	42 500	20 300	22 200	...	...	...	...	...	...
35 - 39	46 200	21 000	25 200	...	...	...	...	...	...
40 - 44	50 100	23 200	26 900	...	...	...	...	...	...
45 - 49	52 300	26 600	25 700	...	...	...	...	...	...
50 - 54	43 300	23 300	20 000	...	...	...	...	...	...
55 - 59	28 200	15 000	13 200	...	...	...	...	...	...
60 - 64	16 600	8 800	7 800	...	...	...	...	...	...
65 - 69	9 900	5 200	4 700	...	...	...	...	...	...
70 - 74	9 300	4 100	5 200	...	...	...	...	...	...
75 +	17 800	6 900	11 000	...	...	...	...	...	...
Cyprus - Chypre[30]									
1 X 2001 (CDJC)									
Total	689 565	338 497	351 068	474 450	231 128	243 322	215 115	107 369	107 746
0	8 024	4 068	3 956	5 443	2 765	2 678	2 581	1 303	1 278
1 - 4	34 558	17 625	16 933	23 296	11 821	11 475	11 262	5 804	5 458
5 - 9	51 718	26 502	25 216	34 111	17 402	16 709	17 607	9 100	8 507
10 - 14	53 178	27 396	25 782	35 772	18 332	17 440	17 406	9 064	8 342
15 - 19	54 603	28 132	26 471	36 725	18 872	17 853	17 878	9 260	8 618
20 - 24	51 803	26 208	25 595	36 231	18 178	18 053	15 572	8 030	7 542
25 - 29	48 272	23 096	25 176	35 248	16 654	18 594	13 024	6 442	6 582
30 - 34	48 233	22 682	25 551	34 899	16 196	18 703	13 334	6 486	6 848
35 - 39	51 561	24 813	26 748	36 645	17 304	19 341	14 916	7 509	7 407
40 - 44	52 289	25 602	26 687	37 070	17 786	19 284	15 219	7 816	7 403
45 - 49	45 580	22 705	22 875	32 005	15 647	16 358	13 575	7 058	6 517
50 - 54	42 587	21 027	21 560	30 186	14 803	15 383	12 401	6 224	6 177
55 - 59	34 554	16 930	17 624	24 216	11 883	12 333	10 338	5 047	5 291
60 - 64	30 747	14 968	15 779	20 763	10 239	10 524	9 984	4 729	5 255
65 - 69	25 445	11 905	13 540	16 669	7 943	8 726	8 776	3 962	4 814
70 - 74	20 965	9 375	11 590	13 157	5 885	7 272	7 808	3 490	4 318
75 - 79	15 974	7 073	8 901	9 899	4 338	5 561	6 075	2 735	3 340
80 - 84	9 802	4 232	5 570	6 010	2 522	3 488	3 792	1 710	2 082
85 - 89	5 861	2 423	3 438	3 523	1 368	2 155	2 338	1 055	1 283
90 - 94	1 975	825	1 150	1 269	532	737	706	293	413
95 - 99	411	148	263	252	89	163	159	59	100
100 +	40	14	26	25	8	17	15	6	9
Unknown - Inconnu	1 385	748	637	1 036	561	475	349	187	162
1 VII 2007 (ESDJ)									
Total	783 971	386 457	397 514	...	...	...	...	...	...
0	8 668	4 513	4 155	...	...	...	...	...	...
1 - 4	32 670	16 800	15·870	...	...	...	...	...	...
5 - 9	43 812	22 376	21 436	...	...	...	...	...	...
10 - 14	52 959	27 068	25 892	...	...	...	...	...	...
15 - 19	56 395	28 720	27 675	...	...	...	...	...	...
20 - 24	64 955	32 084	32 871	...	...	...	...	...	...
25 - 29	66 283	33 188	33 096	...	...	...	...	...	...
30 - 34	58 666	29 221	29 445	...	...	...	...	...	...
35 - 39	54 835	26 796	28 039	...	...	...	...	...	...
40 - 44	56 490	27 619	28 871	...	...	...	...	...	...
45 - 49	56 675	28 263	28 412	...	...	...	...	...	...
50 - 54	50 058	24 717	25 341	...	...	...	...	...	...
55 - 59	46 207	22 604	23 604	...	...	...	...	...	...
60 - 64	37 631	18 157	19 474	...	...	...	...	...	...
65 - 69	31 935	15 467	16 468	...	...	...	...	...	...
70 - 74	24 740	11 478	13 262	...	...	...	...	...	...
75 - 79	18 600	8 145	10 455	...	...	...	...	...	...

Continent, country or area, date, code and age (in years) / Continent, pays ou zone, date, code et âge (en années)	Total			Urban - Urbaine			Rural - Rurale		
	Both sexes Les deux sexes	Male Masculin	Female Féminin	Both sexes Les deux sexes	Male Masculin	Female Féminin	Both sexes Les deux sexes	Male Masculin	Female Féminin
ASIA - ASIE									
Cyprus - Chypre[30]									
1 VII 2007 (ESDJ)									
80 - 84	*12 210*	*5 159*	*7 051*	...	...	...	...	...	...
85 +	*9 577*	*3 769*	*5 808*	...	...	...	...	...	...
Georgia - Géorgie[1]									
1 VII 2000 (ESDF)[1]									
Total	4 945 553	2 364 247	2 581 306	2 860 786	1 348 715	1 512 071	2 084 767	1 015 532	1 069 235
0	42 247	22 938	19 309	26 206	14 152	12 054	16 041	8 786	7 255
1 - 4	197 055	104 267	92 788	119 229	63 120	56 109	77 826	41 147	36 679
5 - 9	361 619	185 741	175 878	208 452	107 038	101 414	153 167	78 703	74 464
10 - 14	409 671	209 366	200 305	229 154	116 874	112 280	180 517	92 492	88 025
15 - 19	388 789	198 066	190 723	222 064	113 224	108 840	166 725	84 842	81 883
20 - 24	376 407	191 927	184 480	213 454	108 613	104 841	162 953	83 314	79 639
25 - 29	350 129	181 759	168 370	213 415	110 488	102 927	136 714	71 271	65 443
30 - 34	363 659	175 712	187 947	214 156	100 573	113 583	149 503	75 139	74 364
35 - 39	403 179	191 543	211 636	241 215	109 394	131 821	161 964	82 149	79 815
40 - 44	353 366	168 218	185 148	216 428	98 958	117 470	136 938	69 260	67 678
45 - 49	305 841	143 921	161 920	193 528	88 504	105 024	112 313	55 417	56 896
50 - 54	216 111	100 444	115 667	137 119	62 640	74 479	78 992	37 804	41 188
55 - 59	225 223	99 437	125 786	130 629	56 530	74 099	94 594	42 907	51 687
60 - 64	280 405	126 438	153 967	155 346	68 463	86 883	125 059	57 975	67 084
65 - 69	242 085	102 877	139 208	123 373	51 091	72 282	118 712	51 786	66 926
70 - 74	218 503	85 840	132 663	111 805	41 553	70 252	106 698	44 287	62 411
75 - 79	113 417	34 835	78 582	56 587	16 900	39 687	56 830	17 935	38 895
80 - 84	59 039	24 600	34 439	29 156	12 606	16 550	29 883	11 994	17 889
85 - 89	27 302	11 583	15 719	13 332	5 601	7 731	13 970	5 982	7 988
90 - 94	8 410	3 605	4 805	4 432	1 819	2 613	3 978	1 786	2 192
95 - 99	2 730	1 020	1 710	1 510	527	983	1 220	493	727
100 +	366	110	256	196	47	149	170	63	107
1 VII 2007 (ESDF)									
Total	4 388 400	2 079 000	2 309 400	...	...	...	...	...	...
0 - 4	233 600	123 300	110 300	...	...	...	...	...	...
5 - 9	239 400	125 800	113 600	...	...	...	...	...	...
10 - 14	294 200	151 700	142 500	...	...	...	...	...	...
15 - 19	368 400	186 900	181 500	...	...	...	...	...	...
20 - 24	358 800	181 000	177 800	...	...	...	...	...	...
25 - 29	329 500	164 100	165 400	...	...	...	...	...	...
30 - 34	310 200	151 700	158 500	...	...	...	...	...	...
35 - 39	299 900	144 000	155 900	...	...	...	...	...	...
40 - 44	313 200	146 700	166 500	...	...	...	...	...	...
45 - 49	331 900	154 300	177 600	...	...	...	...	...	...
50 - 54	280 300	128 800	151 500	...	...	...	...	...	...
55 - 59	241 800	109 600	132 200	...	...	...	...	...	...
60 - 64	144 100	63 800	80 300	...	...	...	...	...	...
65 - 69	222 500	91 800	130 700	...	...	...	...	...	...
70 - 74	176 200	72 100	104 100	...	...	...	...	...	...
75 - 79	135 400	52 000	83 400	...	...	...	...	...	...
80 - 84	72 900	23 700	49 200	...	...	...	...	...	...
85 +	36 100	7 700	28 400	...	...	...	...	...	...
India - Inde[31]									
1 III 2001 (CDFC)									
Total	1028610328	532 156 772	496 453 556	286 119 689	150 554 098	135 565 591	742 490 639	381 602 674	360 887 965
0 - 4	110 447 164	57 119 612	53 327 552	25 338 754	13 262 414	12 076 340	85 108 410	43 857 198	41 251 212
5 - 9	128 316 790	66 734 833	61 581 957	29 860 545	15 640 135	14 220 410	98 456 245	51 094 698	47 361 547
10 - 14	124 846 858	65 632 877	59 213 981	32 464 536	17 030 132	15 434 404	92 382 322	48 602 745	43 779 577
15 - 19	100 215 890	53 939 991	46 275 899	30 154 067	16 191 573	13 962 494	70 061 823	37 748 418	32 313 405
20 - 24	89 764 132	46 321 150	43 442 982	28 365 228	15 193 668	13 171 560	61 398 904	31 127 482	30 271 422
25 - 29	83 422 393	41 557 546	41 864 847	25 737 253	13 180 373	12 556 880	57 685 140	28 377 173	29 307 967
30 - 34	74 274 044	37 361 916	36 912 128	22 445 165	11 673 137	10 772 028	51 828 879	25 688 779	26 140 100
35 - 39	70 574 085	36 038 727	34 535 358	21 615 541	11 157 103	10 458 438	48 958 544	24 881 624	24 076 920
40 - 44	55 738 297	29 878 715	25 859 582	17 173 126	9 458 276	7 714 850	38 565 171	20 420 439	18 144 732
45 - 49	47 408 976	24 867 886	22 541 090	14 453 974	7 844 213	6 609 761	32 955 002	17 023 673	15 931 329
50 - 54	36 587 559	19 851 608	16 735 951	10 809 961	6 038 917	4 771 044	25 777 598	13 812 691	11 964 907
55 - 59	27 653 347	13 583 022	14 070 325	7 682 278	4 010 268	3 672 010	19 971 069	9 572 754	10 398 315
60 - 64	27 516 779	13 586 347	13 930 432	6 864 810	3 439 621	3 425 189	20 651 969	10 146 726	10 505 243

7. Population by age, sex and urban/rural residence: latest available year, 1998 - 2007
Population selon l'âge, le sexe et la résidence, urbaine/rurale: dernière année disponible, 1998 - 2007 (continued - suite)

Continent, country or area, date, code and age (in years) / Continent, pays ou zone, date, code et âge (en années)	Total			Urban - Urbaine			Rural - Rurale		
	Both sexes Les deux sexes	Male Masculin	Female Féminin	Both sexes Les deux sexes	Male Masculin	Female Féminin	Both sexes Les deux sexes	Male Masculin	Female Féminin
ASIA - ASIE									
India - Inde[31]									
1 III 2001 (CDFC)									
65 - 69	19 806 955	9 472 103	10 334 852	4 990 199	2 401 397	2 588 802	14 816 756	7 070 706	7 746 050
70 - 74	14 708 644	7 527 688	7 180 956	3 579 168	1 780 696	1 798 472	11 129 476	5 746 992	5 382 484
75 - 79	6 551 225	3 263 209	3 288 016	1 721 085	851 088	869 997	4 830 140	2 412 121	2 418 019
80 + ...	8 038 718	3 918 980	4 119 738	2 022 345	935 920	1 086 425	6 016 373	2 983 060	3 033 313
Unknown - Inconnu	2 738 472	1 500 562	1 237 910	841 654	465 167	376 487	1 896 818	1 035 395	861 423
Indonesia - Indonésie									
31 X 2005 (SSDF)[32]									
Total	213 375 287	107 274 528	106 100 759	92 005 069	46 055 993	45 949 076	121 370 218	61 218 535	60 151 683
0 - 4	19 095 151	9 732 578	9 362 573	8 117 666	4 129 250	3 988 416	10 977 485	5 603 328	5 374 157
5 - 9	21 563 945	11 089 478	10 474 467	8 573 265	4 417 551	4 155 714	12 990 680	6 671 927	6 318 753
10 - 14	21 306 096	10 956 648	10 349 448	8 472 639	4 343 105	4 129 534	12 833 457	6 613 543	6 219 914
15 - 19	19 796 921	10 103 778	9 693 143	8 585 104	4 254 987	4 330 117	11 211 817	5 848 791	5 363 026
20 - 24	19 445 179	9 533 960	9 911 219	9 594 049	4 647 995	4 946 054	9 851 130	4 885 965	4 965 165
25 - 29	18 680 093	9 078 324	9 601 769	8 955 039	4 392 942	4 562 097	9 725 054	4 685 382	5 039 672
30 - 34	17 420 029	8 543 620	8 876 409	7 945 419	3 905 345	4 040 074	9 474 610	4 638 275	4 836 335
35 - 39	16 454 100	8 186 060	8 268 040	7 267 101	3 642 139	3 624 962	9 186 999	4 543 921	4 643 078
40 - 44	14 489 902	7 273 553	7 216 349	6 311 684	3 162 768	3 148 916	8 178 218	4 110 785	4 067 433
45 - 49	12 382 818	6 303 669	6 079 149	5 294 629	2 706 752	2 587 877	7 088 189	3 596 917	3 491 272
50 - 54	9 941 064	5 175 796	4 765 268	4 154 253	2 167 922	1 986 331	5 786 811	3 007 874	2 778 937
55 - 59	7 262 179	3 755 532	3 506 647	2 830 595	1 440 270	1 390 325	4 431 584	2 315 262	2 116 322
60 - 64	5 611 827	2 748 283	2 863 544	2 193 103	1 079 057	1 114 046	3 418 724	1 669 226	1 749 498
65 - 69	4 112 165	1 957 037	2 155 128	1 565 522	750 321	815 201	2 546 643	1 206 716	1 339 927
70 - 74	2 989 927	1 448 024	1 541 903	1 101 672	519 815	581 857	1 888 255	928 209	960 046
75 - 79	1 573 741	786 789	786 952	604 849	297 376	307 473	968 892	489 413	479 479
80 - 84	797 616	392 368	405 248	283 683	136 765	146 918	513 933	255 603	258 330
85 - 89	287 470	135 751	151 719	97 793	36 302	61 491	189 677	99 449	90 228
90 - 94	104 195	48 039	56 156	40 139	18 078	22 061	64 056	29 961	34 095
95 + ...	60 869	25 241	35 628	16 865	7 253	9 612	44 004	17 988	26 016
1 VII 2007 (ESDJ)									
Total	225 642 000	112 966 900	112 675 100	...	...	...	...	...	...
0 - 4	20 952 200	10 721 200	10 231 000	...	...	...	...	...	...
5 - 9	20 060 200	10 218 300	9 841 900	...	...	...	...	...	...
10 - 14	21 041 500	10 700 200	10 341 300	...	...	...	...	...	...
15 - 19	21 373 600	10 884 100	10 489 500	...	...	...	...	...	...
20 - 24	21 051 500	10 604 200	10 447 300	...	...	...	...	...	...
25 - 29	20 385 300	10 014 000	10 371 300	...	...	...	...	...	...
30 - 34	19 149 200	9 276 300	9 872 900	...	...	...	...	...	...
35 - 39	17 431 600	8 596 800	8 834 800	...	...	...	...	...	...
40 - 44	15 489 100	7 729 900	7 759 200	...	...	...	...	...	...
45 - 49	13 234 700	6 698 900	6 535 800	...	...	...	...	...	...
50 - 54	10 486 600	5 416 600	5 070 000	...	...	...	...	...	...
55 - 59	7 819 800	4 023 500	3 796 300	...	...	...	...	...	...
60 - 64	5 727 900	2 843 200	2 884 700	...	...	...	...	...	...
65 - 69	4 457 700	2 123 600	2 334 100	...	...	...	...	...	...
70 - 74	3 413 300	1 562 400	1 850 900	...	...	...	...	...	...
75 + ...	3 567 800	1 553 700	2 014 100	...	...	...	...	...	...
Iran (Islamic Republic of) - Iran (République islamique d')[33]									
28 X 2006 (CDJC)									
Total	70 495 782	35 866 362	34 629 420	48 259 964	24 576 442	23 683 522	22 131 101	11 236 855	10 894 246
0 - 4	5 463 978	2 801 568	2 662 410	3 565 916	1 829 001	1 736 915	1 887 392	967 079	920 313
5 - 9	5 509 057	2 820 524	2 688 533	3 598 374	1 842 333	1 756 041	1 899 692	972 653	927 039
10 - 14	6 708 594	3 441 245	3 267 349	4 277 679	2 191 218	2 086 461	2 418 523	1 243 833	1 174 690
15 - 19	8 726 761	4 442 901	4 283 860	5 776 097	2 935 673	2 840 424	2 936 385	1 499 970	1 436 415
20 - 24	9 011 422	4 511 851	4 499 571	6 259 429	3 100 943	3 158 486	2 739 796	1 404 789	1 335 007
25 - 29	7 224 952	3 660 167	3 564 785	5 077 373	2 562 557	2 514 816	2 137 610	1 092 578	1 045 032
30 - 34	5 553 531	2 837 969	2 715 562	3 928 775	2 010 887	1 917 888	1 618 164	823 809	794 355
35 - 39	4 921 124	2 511 545	2 409 579	3 593 610	1 844 232	1 749 378	1 322 078	664 694	657 384
40 - 44	4 089 158	2 081 679	2 007 479	3 033 650	1 557 353	1 476 297	1 050 975	522 251	528 724
45 - 49	3 522 761	1 792 481	1 730 280	2 573 962	1 325 730	1 248 232	944 457	464 636	479 821
50 - 54	2 755 420	1 386 063	1 369 357	1 979 657	1 023 518	956 139	771 985	360 739	411 246
55 - 59	1 887 981	923 536	964 445	1 315 505	665 561	649 944	569 871	256 680	313 191

Continent, country or area, date, code and age (in years) / Continent, pays ou zone, date, code et âge (en années)	Total			Urban - Urbaine			Rural - Rurale		
	Both sexes Les deux sexes	Male Masculin	Female Féminin	Both sexes Les deux sexes	Male Masculin	Female Féminin	Both sexes Les deux sexes	Male Masculin	Female Féminin
ASIA - ASIE									
Iran (Islamic Republic of) - Iran (République islamique d')[33]									
28 X 2006 (CDJC)									
60 - 64	1 464 452	726 449	738 003	979 809	497 943	481 866	482 256	227 163	255 093
65 - 69	1 197 550	622 470	575 080	775 173	405 012	370 161	420 834	216 509	204 325
70 - 74	1 119 318	598 231	521 087	692 753	363 249	329 504	425 040	233 970	191 070
75 - 79	694 122	372 570	321 552	426 926	220 338	206 588	266 407	151 703	114 704
80 - 84	445 060	236 980	208 080	279 444	142 408	137 036	165 176	94 298	70 878
85 - 89	127 660	63 992	63 668	82 379	39 265	43 114	45 155	24 656	20 499
90 - 94	39 378	18 792	20 586	24 393	11 007	13 386	14 919	7 742	7 177
95 - 99	16 652	7 754	8 898	9 802	4 284	5 518	6 822	3 453	3 369
100 +	16 851	7 595	9 256	9 258	3 930	5 328	7 564	3 650	3 914
Iraq									
1 VII 2007 (ESDF)									
Total	29 682 081	14 943 516	14 738 565	19 752 833	9 970 074	9 782 759	9 929 248	4 973 442	4 955 806
0 - 4	4 970 829	2 548 402	2 422 427	3 093 542	1 585 669	1 507 873	1 877 287	962 733	914 554
5 - 9	4 222 028	2 166 818	2 055 210	2 665 680	1 367 692	1 297 988	1 556 348	799 126	757 222
10 - 14	3 605 956	1 833 813	1 772 143	2 313 228	1 174 857	1 138 371	1 292 728	658 956	633 772
15 - 19	3 206 547	1 631 272	1 575 275	2 097 711	1 067 009	1 030 702	1 108 836	564 263	544 573
20 - 24	2 745 916	1 394 941	1 350 975	1 836 580	933 972	902 608	909 336	460 969	448 367
25 - 29	2 342 651	1 184 126	1 158 525	1 595 244	808 530	786 714	747 407	375 596	371 811
30 - 34	1 969 141	987 662	981 479	1 367 432	689 466	677 966	601 709	298 196	303 513
35 - 39	1 623 309	806 089	817 220	1 147 326	574 647	572 679	475 983	231 442	244 541
40 - 44	1 280 968	624 348	656 620	925 668	457 710	467 958	355 300	166 638	188 662
45 - 49	1 024 602	494 742	529 860	748 849	368 114	380 735	275 753	126 628	149 125
50 - 54	790 298	378 954	411 344	581 704	284 864	296 840	208 594	94 090	114 504
55 - 59	611 439	292 240	319 199	451 250	220 282	230 968	160 189	71 958	88 231
60 - 64	453 767	218 171	235 596	333 655	163 325	170 330	120 112	54 846	65 266
65 - 69	325 970	154 180	171 790	238 913	114 733	124 180	87 057	39 447	47 610
70 - 74	214 454	98 274	116 180	156 363	72 358	84 005	58 091	25 916	32 175
75 - 79	133 345	58 821	74 524	94 738	41 841	52 897	38 607	16 980	21 627
80 +	160 861	70 663	90 198	104 950	45 005	59 945	55 911	25 658	30 253
Israel - Israël[34]									
1 VII 2007 (ESDJ)									
Total	7 180 115	3 549 216	3 630 899	6 589 632[35]	3 247 280[35]	3 342 352[35]	589 011[35]	301 124[35]	287 887[35]
0	149 263	76 594	72 669	...	...	...	...	...	...
1 - 4	582 047	298 484	283 563	528 923[35]	271 229[35]	257 694[35]	52 908[35]	27 142[35]	25 766[35]
5 - 9	683 760	350 787	332 973	622 120[35]	319 200[35]	302 920[35]	61 451[35]	31 494[35]	29 958[35]
10 - 14	621 221	318 525	302 697	562 694[35]	288 038[35]	274 656[35]	58 361[35]	30 422[35]	27 940[35]
15 - 19	581 395	297 353	284 042	524 730[35]	267 388[35]	257 343[35]	56 601[35]	29 926[35]	26 676[35]
20 - 24	570 534	290 439	280 095	523 841[35]	265 543[35]	258 299[35]	46 424[35]	24 702[35]	21 722[35]
25 - 29	543 992	273 325	270 667	502 444[35]	251 883[35]	250 562[35]	41 394[35]	21 364[35]	20 030[35]
30 - 34	534 144	268 531	265 613	493 751[35]	248 201[35]	245 550[35]	40 365[35]	20 308[35]	20 058[35]
35 - 39	457 552	228 206	229 346	419 462[35]	209 312[35]	210 150[35]	38 027[35]	18 856[35]	19 171[35]
40 - 44	393 912	194 040	199 872	359 575[35]	176 757[35]	182 818[35]	34 266[35]	17 248[35]	17 018[35]
45 - 49	382 415	185 099	197 317	350 758[35]	169 044[35]	181 715[35]	31 606[35]	16 028[35]	15 578[35]
50 - 54	371 776	178 481	193 295	342 674[35]	163 486[35]	179 188[35]	29 035[35]	14 957[35]	14 078[35]
55 - 59	352 322	168 218	184 105	326 546[35]	154 810[35]	171 737[35]	25 723[35]	13 387[35]	12 337[35]
60 - 64	250 685	119 328	131 358	232 484[35]	110 026[35]	122 458[35]	18 186[35]	9 288[35]	8 899[35]
65 - 69	199 228	91 386	107 842	187 185[35]	85 183[35]	102 002[35]	12 041[35]	6 198[35]	5 843[35]
70 - 74	176 620	77 990	98 630	166 471[35]	73 088[35]	93 383[35]	10 147[35]	4 903[35]	5 244[35]
75 - 79	142 152	59 559	82 593	134 290[35]	56 159[35]	78 131[35]	7 856[35]	3 398[35]	4 458[35]
80 - 84	109 545	42 235	67 310	103 378[35]	39 661[35]	63 717[35]	6 161[35]	2 571[35]	3 590[35]
85 - 89	53 555	21 811	31 744	50 304[35]	20 417[35]	29 887[35]	3 249[35]	1 393[35]	1 856[35]
90 - 94	19 202	6 953	12 249	17 785[35]	6 409[35]	11 376[35]	1 416[35]	544[35]	872[35]
95 +	4 800	1 876	2 924	4 383[35]	1 709[35]	2 674[35]	416[35]	168[35]	248[35]
Japan - Japon									
1 X 2005 (CDJC)									
Total	127 767 994	62 348 977	65 419 017	110 264 324	53 886 000	56 378 324	17 503 670	8 462 977	9 040 693
0 - 4	5 578 087	2 854 502	2 723 585	4 852 006	2 482 703	2 369 303	726 081	371 799	354 282
5 - 9	5 928 495	3 036 503	2 891 992	5 109 001	2 616 615	2 492 386	819 494	419 888	399 606
10 - 14	6 014 652	3 080 678	2 933 974	5 127 976	2 626 071	2 501 905	886 676	454 607	432 069
15 - 19	6 568 380	3 373 430	3 194 950	5 651 131	2 902 583	2 748 548	917 249	470 847	446 402

7. Population by age, sex and urban/rural residence: latest available year, 1998 - 2007
Population selon l'âge, le sexe et la résidence, urbaine/rurale: dernière année disponible, 1998 - 2007 (continued - suite)

Continent, country or area, date, code and age (in years) / Continent, pays ou zone, date, code et âge (en années)	Total			Urban - Urbaine			Rural - Rurale		
	Both sexes Les deux sexes	Male Masculin	Female Féminin	Both sexes Les deux sexes	Male Masculin	Female Féminin	Both sexes Les deux sexes	Male Masculin	Female Féminin
ASIA - ASIE									
Japan - Japon									
1 X 2005 (CDJC)									
20 - 24	7 350 598	3 754 822	3 595 776	6 502 213	3 325 698	3 176 515	848 385	429 124	419 261
25 - 29	8 280 049	4 198 551	4 081 498	7 321 003	3 708 770	3 612 233	959 046	489 781	469 265
30 - 34	9 754 857	4 933 265	4 821 592	8 660 059	4 375 975	4 284 084	1 094 798	557 290	537 508
35 - 39	8 735 781	4 402 787	4 332 994	7 742 640	3 907 842	3 834 798	993 141	494 945	498 196
40 - 44	8 080 596	4 065 470	4 015 126	7 062 486	3 557 472	3 505 014	1 018 110	507 998	510 112
45 - 49	7 725 861	3 867 500	3 858 361	6 616 303	3 310 680	3 305 623	1 109 558	556 820	552 738
50 - 54	8 796 499	4 383 240	4 413 259	7 480 089	3 718 540	3 761 549	1 316 410	664 700	651 710
55 - 59	10 255 164	5 077 369	5 177 795	8 818 349	4 353 419	4 464 930	1 436 815	723 950	712 865
60 - 64	8 544 629	4 154 529	4 390 100	7 385 888	3 589 046	3 796 842	1 158 741	565 483	593 258
65 - 69	7 432 610	3 545 006	3 887 604	6 353 609	3 033 231	3 320 378	1 079 001	511 775	567 226
70 - 74	6 637 497	3 039 743	3 597 754	5 584 991	2 560 738	3 024 253	1 052 506	479 005	573 501
75 - 79	5 262 801	2 256 317	3 006 484	4 347 080	1 866 530	2 480 550	915 721	389 787	525 934
80 - 84	3 412 393	1 222 635	2 189 758	2 791 585	1 002 599	1 788 986	620 808	220 036	400 772
85 - 89	1 849 260	555 126	1 294 134	1 508 536	453 182	1 055 354	340 724	101 944	238 780
90 - 94	840 870	210 586	630 284	685 165	172 256	512 909	155 705	38 330	117 375
95 - 99	211 221	41 426	169 795	171 626	33 755	137 871	39 595	7 671	31 924
100 +	25 353	3 760	21 593	20 442	3 037	17 405	4 911	723	4 188
Unknown - Inconnu	482 341	291 732	190 609	472 146	285 258	186 888	10 195	6 474	3 721
1 VII 2007 (ESDF)[36]									
Total	127 772 000	62 301 000	65 471 000	...	...	...	...	...	...
0 - 4	5 455 000	2 794 000	2 661 000	...	...	...	...	...	...
5 - 9	5 892 000	3 021 000	2 871 000	...	...	...	...	...	...
10 - 14	5 995 000	3 071 000	2 924 000	...	...	...	...	...	...
15 - 19	6 323 000	3 241 000	3 082 000	...	...	...	...	...	...
20 - 24	7 290 000	3 738 000	3 552 000	...	...	...	...	...	...
25 - 29	7 847 000	3 992 000	3 855 000	...	...	...	...	...	...
30 - 34	9 436 000	4 783 000	4 653 000	...	...	...	...	...	...
35 - 39	9 374 000	4 735 000	4 640 000	...	...	...	...	...	...
40 - 44	8 141 000	4 099 000	4 042 000	...	...	...	...	...	...
45 - 49	7 705 000	3 863 000	3 842 000	...	...	...	...	...	...
50 - 54	8 135 000	4 058 000	4 077 000	...	...	...	...	...	...
55 - 59	10 596 000	5 243 000	5 353 000	...	...	...	...	...	...
60 - 64	8 314 000	4 051 000	4 264 000	...	...	...	...	...	...
65 - 69	7 792 000	3 725 000	4 067 000	...	...	...	...	...	...
70 - 74	6 893 000	3 175 000	3 718 000	...	...	...	...	...	...
75 - 79	5 520 000	2 386 000	3 134 000	...	...	...	...	...	...
80 - 84	3 821 000	1 440 000	2 381 000	...	...	...	...	...	...
85 +	3 241 000	887 000	2 354 000	...	...	...	...	...	...
Jordan - Jordanie[37]									
1 X 2004 (CDFC)									
Total	5 103 639	2 626 287	2 477 352	3 997 383	2 055 431	1 941 952	1 106 256	570 856	535 400
0	122 757	62 643	60 114	94 974	48 529	46 445	27 783	14 114	13 669
1 - 4	527 574	270 573	257 001	408 893	209 140	199 753	118 681	61 433	57 248
5 - 9	642 871	329 133	313 738	495 583	253 774	241 809	147 288	75 359	71 929
10 - 14	610 129	313 083	297 046	469 321	240 723	228 598	140 808	72 360	68 448
15 - 19	559 838	287 693	272 145	431 275	221 213	210 062	128 563	66 480	62 083
20 - 24	540 193	279 600	260 593	421 400	217 092	204 308	118 793	62 508	56 285
25 - 29	456 261	239 774	216 487	355 950	186 570	169 380	100 311	53 204	47 107
30 - 34	399 169	207 178	191 991	316 235	164 238	151 997	82 934	42 940	39 994
35 - 39	323 426	167 737	155 689	259 736	134 829	124 907	63 690	32 908	30 782
40 - 44	241 400	123 945	117 455	196 923	101 442	95 481	44 477	22 503	21 974
45 - 49	170 456	87 098	83 358	138 372	70 890	67 482	32 084	16 208	15 876
50 - 54	128 240	64 607	63 633	102 179	51 210	50 969	26 061	13 397	12 664
55 - 59	113 721	55 765	57 956	92 893	45 618	47 275	20 828	10 147	10 681
60 - 64	98 787	52 084	46 703	80 269	42 634	37 635	18 518	9 450	9 068
65 - 69	71 823	37 095	34 728	57 484	29 956	27 528	14 339	7 139	7 200
70 - 74	46 820	23 467	23 353	36 958	18 503	18 455	9 862	4 964	4 898
75 - 79	24 268	12 651	11 617	19 160	9 923	9 237	5 108	2 728	2 380
80 +	...	...	...	16 376	7 369	9 007	5 684	2 768	2 916
80 - 84	13 585	6 144	7 441	...	...	...	...	...	...
85 - 89	5 032	2 444	2 588	...	...	...	...	...	...
90 - 94	2 316	1 012	1 304	...	...	...	...	...	...

Continent, country or area, date, code and age (in years) / Continent, pays ou zone, date, code et âge (en années)	Total			Urban - Urbaine			Rural - Rurale		
	Both sexes Les deux sexes	Male Masculin	Female Féminin	Both sexes Les deux sexes	Male Masculin	Female Féminin	Both sexes Les deux sexes	Male Masculin	Female Féminin
ASIA - ASIE									
Jordan - Jordanie[37]									
1 X 2004 (CDFC)									
95 +	1 127	537	590	...	...	...	...	...	...
Unknown - Inconnu	3 846	2 024	1 822	3 402	1 778	1 624	444	246	198
31 XII 2007 (ESDF)									
Total	5 723 000	2 950 000	2 773 000	...	...	...	...	...	...
0 - 4	729 870	374 650	355 220	...	...	...	...	...	...
5 - 9	721 270	369 930	351 340	...	...	...	...	...	...
10 - 14	684 990	352 230	332 760	...	...	...	...	...	...
15 - 19	628 070	323 320	304 750	...	...	...	...	...	...
20 - 24	606 180	314 180	292 000	...	...	...	...	...	...
25 - 29	512 270	269 630	242 640	...	...	...	...	...	...
30 - 34	448 230	233 050	215 180	...	...	...	...	...	...
35 - 39	363 220	188 800	174 420	...	...	...	...	...	...
40 - 44	270 680	139 240	131 440	...	...	...	...	...	...
45 - 49	191 390	97 940	93 450	...	...	...	...	...	...
50 - 54	143 840	72 570	71 270	...	...	...	...	...	...
55 - 59	127 430	62 540	64 890	...	...	...	...	...	...
60 - 64	110 820	58 410	52 410	...	...	...	...	...	...
65 - 69	80 150	41 590	38 560	...	...	...	...	...	...
70 - 74	52 290	26 550	25 740	...	...	...	...	...	...
75 - 79	27 290	14 160	13 130	...	...	...	...	...	...
80 - 84	15 350	6 790	8 560	...	...	...	...	...	...
85 - 89	5 680	2 650	3 030	...	...	...	...	...	...
90 - 94	2 840	1 180	1 660	...	...	...	...	...	...
95 +	1 140	590	550	...	...	...	...	...	...
Kazakhstan									
1 VII 2007 (ESDF)									
Total	15 484 192	7 450 418	8 033 774	8 195 389	3 815 422	4 379 967	7 288 803	3 634 996	3 653 807
0	308 243	158 166	150 077	...	...	...	...	...	...
1 - 4	1 050 343	538 852	511 491	550 468	282 725	267 743	499 875	256 127	243 748
5 - 9	1 084 632	556 007	528 625	498 831	256 322	242 509	585 801	299 685	286 116
10 - 14	1 267 596	646 397	621 199	550 257	280 758	269 499	717 339	365 639	351 700
15 - 19	1 534 489	779 522	754 967	727 177	366 809	360 368	807 312	412 713	394 599
20 - 24	1 506 595	762 842	743 753	775 796	385 516	390 280	730 799	377 326	353 473
25 - 29	1 266 450	636 125	630 325	729 699	350 046	379 653	536 751	286 079	250 672
30 - 34	1 161 480	572 236	589 244	640 035	298 731	341 304	521 445	273 505	247 940
35 - 39	1 079 993	527 509	552 484	604 582	281 577	323 005	475 411	245 932	229 479
40 - 44	1 065 688	511 107	554 581	591 171	272 504	318 667	474 517	238 603	235 914
45 - 49	1 083 082	509 797	573 285	610 336	276 491	333 845	472 746	233 306	239 440
50 - 54	851 737	387 426	464 311	483 165	211 119	272 046	368 572	176 307	192 265
55 - 59	676 073	296 191	379 882	391 097	164 609	226 488	284 976	131 582	153 394
60 - 64	340 897	142 559	198 338	191 410	76 240	115 170	149 487	66 319	83 168
65 - 69	493 271	191 116	302 155	273 100	99 160	173 940	220 171	91 956	128 215
70 - 74	315 134	117 678	197 456	178 404	62 259	116 145	136 730	55 419	81 311
75 - 79	223 576	72 860	150 716	130 807	39 953	90 854	92 769	32 907	59 862
80 - 84	123 843	32 525	91 318	74 009	18 575	55 434	49 834	13 950	35 884
85 - 89	36 944	8 417	28 527	21 796	5 033	16 763	15 148	3 384	11 764
90 - 94	10 808	2 099	8 709	5 816	1 216	4 600	4 992	883	4 109
95 - 99	2 561	681	1 880	1 172	368	804	1 389	313	1 076
100 +	757	306	451	298	152	146	459	154	305
Kuwait - Koweït									
1 VII 2007 (ESDF)									
Total	2 410 829	1 430 584	980 245	...	...	...	...	...	...
0 - 4	235 551	121 319	114 232	...	...	...	...	...	...
5 - 9	212 568	109 379	103 189	...	...	...	...	...	...
10 - 14	182 842	94 980	87 862	...	...	...	...	...	...
15 - 19	165 140	85 781	79 359	...	...	...	...	...	...
20 - 24	216 277	123 117	93 160	...	...	...	...	...	...
25 - 29	306 240	193 199	113 041	...	...	...	...	...	...
30 - 34	291 538	187 331	104 207	...	...	...	...	...	...
35 - 39	256 756	167 846	88 910	...	...	...	...	...	...
40 - 44	192 117	124 581	67 536	...	...	...	...	...	...
45 - 49	139 641	92 449	47 192	...	...	...	...	...	...
50 - 54	89 163	58 551	30 612	...	...	...	...	...	...

Continent, country or area, date, code and age (in years) / Continent, pays ou zone, date, code et âge (en années)	Total			Urban - Urbaine			Rural - Rurale		
	Both sexes Les deux sexes	Male Masculin	Female Féminin	Both sexes Les deux sexes	Male Masculin	Female Féminin	Both sexes Les deux sexes	Male Masculin	Female Féminin
ASIA - ASIE									
Kuwait - Koweït									
1 VII 2007 (ESDF)									
55 - 59	52 917	33 315	19 602	...	...	...	...	...	...
60 - 64	30 356	17 668	12 688	...	...	...	...	...	...
65 - 69	18 593	10 297	8 296	...	...	...	...	...	...
70 - 74	10 917	5 724	5 193	...	...	...	...	...	...
75 - 79	5 784	2 916	2 868	...	...	...	...	...	...
80 +	4 429	2 131	2 298	...	...	...	...	...	...
Kyrgyzstan - Kirghizstan[38]									
1 VII 2007 (ESDJ)									
Total	5 267 040	2 633 650	2 633 390	1 870 994	925 941	945 053	3 396 046	1 707 709	1 688 337
0	178 639	120 791	57 848	98 563	79 729	18 834	80 076	41 062	39 014
1 - 4	419 761	215 028	204 733	133 165	68 196	64 969	286 596	146 832	139 764
5 - 9	485 751	247 748	238 003	140 354	71 713	68 641	345 397	176 035	169 362
10 - 14	560 478	284 366	276 112	157 968	79 781	78 187	402 510	204 585	197 925
15 - 19	584 303	295 724	288 579	173 247	86 417	86 830	411 056	209 307	201 749
20 - 24	527 173	264 698	262 475	168 020	81 034	86 986	359 153	183 664	175 489
25 - 29	435 113	218 263	216 850	183 207	87 130	96 077	251 906	131 133	120 773
30 - 34	382 834	191 379	191 455	152 309	72 837	79 472	230 525	118 542	111 983
35 - 39	348 971	173 798	175 173	141 919	67 610	74 309	207 052	106 188	100 864
40 - 44	320 476	157 051	163 425	126 184	59 977	66 207	194 292	97 074	97 218
45 - 49	303 307	146 616	156 691	118 156	55 104	63 052	185 151	91 512	93 639
50 - 54	218 090	103 639	114 451	85 270	39 034	46 236	132 820	64 605	68 215
55 - 59	153 208	71 893	81 315	61 435	27 788	33 647	91 773	44 105	47 668
60 - 64	70 473	32 186	38 287	29 330	12 697	16 633	41 143	19 489	21 654
65 - 69	94 703	41 053	53 650	36 143	14 733	21 410	58 560	26 320	32 240
70 - 74	74 186	30 421	43 765	26 988	10 157	16 831	47 198	20 264	26 934
75 - 79	59 584	22 773	36 811	20 358	6 825	13 533	39 226	15 948	23 278
80 - 84	32 508	11 545	20 963	12 047	3 469	8 578	20 461	8 076	12 385
85 - 89	11 274	3 111	8 163	4 108	1 129	2 979	7 166	1 982	5 184
90 - 94	3 674	808	2 866	1 341	317	1 024	2 333	491	1 842
95 - 99	2 039	576	1 463	620	201	419	1 419	375	1 044
100 +	495	183	312	262	63	199	233	120	113
Lao People's Democratic Republic - République démocratique populaire lao[39]									
1 VII 2007 (ESDF)									
Total	5 874 000	2 929 000	2 945 000	...	...	...	...	...	...
0 - 4	776 000	391 500	384 300	...	...	...	...	...	...
5 - 9	730 000	368 100	361 600	...	...	...	...	...	...
10 - 14	768 000	391 700	376 500	...	...	...	...	...	...
15 - 19	697 000	351 900	344 700	...	...	...	...	...	...
20 - 24	552 000	273 000	279 000	...	...	...	...	...	...
25 - 29	450 000	221 100	228 700	...	...	...	...	...	...
30 - 34	373 000	182 900	190 400	...	...	...	...	...	...
35 - 39	336 000	166 100	169 500	...	...	...	...	...	...
40 - 44	288 000	143 300	144 600	...	...	...	...	...	...
45 - 49	238 000	118 900	119 000	...	...	...	...	...	...
50 - 54	194 000	95 600	98 800	...	...	...	...	...	...
55 - 59	141 000	68 500	72 700	...	...	...	...	...	...
60 - 64	108 000	51 300	56 200	...	...	...	...	...	...
65 - 69	83 000	39 500	43 600	...	...	...	...	...	...
70 - 74	61 000	28 000	32 300	...	...	...	...	...	...
75 +	80 000	36 800	43 200	...	...	...	...	...	...
Lebanon - Liban[40]									
3 III 2007 (SSDF)									
Total	3 759 134	1 857 659	1 901 475	...	...	...	...	...	...
0 - 4	261 021	136 514	124 507	...	...	...	...	...	...
5 - 9	312 902	160 577	152 325	...	...	...	...	...	...
10 - 14	354 049	183 613	170 436	...	...	...	...	...	...
15 - 19	363 626	195 984	167 642	...	...	...	...	...	...
20 - 24	367 778	191 471	176 307	...	...	...	...	...	...
25 - 29	305 933	148 321	157 612	...	...	...	...	...	...
30 - 34	276 775	132 105	144 670	...	...	...	...	...	...
35 - 39	249 550	111 833	137 717	...	...	...	...	...	...

7. Population by age, sex and urban/rural residence: latest available year, 1998 - 2007
Population selon l'âge, le sexe et la résidence, urbaine/rurale: dernière année disponible, 1998 - 2007 (continued - suite)

Continent, country or area, date, code and age (in years) / Continent, pays ou zone, date, code et âge (en années)	Total			Urban - Urbaine			Rural - Rurale		
	Both sexes Les deux sexes	Male Masculin	Female Féminin	Both sexes Les deux sexes	Male Masculin	Female Féminin	Both sexes Les deux sexes	Male Masculin	Female Féminin
ASIA - ASIE									
Lebanon - Liban[40]									
3 III 2007 (SSDF)									
40 - 44	233 003	102 405	130 598	...	...	...	...	...	...
45 - 49	208 752	95 595	113 157	...	...	...	...	...	...
50 - 54	179 899	84 091	95 808	...	...	...	...	...	...
55 - 59	143 376	66 993	76 383	...	...	...	...	...	...
60 - 64	140 030	65 701	74 329	...	...	...	...	...	...
65 - 69	122 014	59 900	62 114	...	...	...	...	...	...
70 - 74	105 259	53 267	51 992	...	...	...	...	...	...
75 - 79	71 315	38 353	32 962	...	...	...	...	...	...
80 - 84	45 481	21 083	24 398	...	...	...	...	...	...
85 +	18 371	9 853	8 518	...	...	...	...	...	...
Malaysia - Malaisie[41]									
1 VII 2007 (ESDF)									
Total	27 173 580	13 832 952	13 340 628	17 221 551	8 726 982	8 494 569	9 952 029	5 105 970	4 846 059
0 - 4	3 116 235	1 608 747	1 507 488	1 936 603	996 536	940 067	1 179 632	612 211	567 421
5 - 9	2 919 373	1 503 184	1 416 189	1 797 471	922 072	875 399	1 121 902	581 112	540 790
10 - 14	2 713 030	1 399 304	1 313 726	1 641 533	845 101	796 432	1 071 497	554 203	517 294
15 - 19	2 579 814	1 321 107	1 258 707	1 555 291	795 773	759 518	1 024 523	525 334	499 189
20 - 24	2 458 414	1 248 839	1 209 575	1 498 300	757 031	741 269	960 114	491 808	468 306
25 - 29	2 210 567	1 118 197	1 092 370	1 414 573	708 881	705 692	795 994	409 316	386 678
30 - 34	1 975 168	997 724	977 444	1 323 724	661 934	661 790	651 444	335 790	315 654
35 - 39	1 872 283	947 691	924 592	1 243 383	624 201	619 182	628 900	323 490	305 410
40 - 44	1 732 411	879 091	853 320	1 136 425	574 305	562 120	595 986	304 786	291 200
45 - 49	1 516 399	774 095	742 304	999 598	509 089	490 509	516 801	265 006	251 795
50 - 54	1 273 626	652 240	621 386	842 541	431 086	411 455	431 085	221 154	209 931
55 - 59	952 607	488 428	464 179	627 253	321 558	305 695	325 354	166 870	158 484
60 - 64	666 654	340 733	325 921	435 988	223 147	212 841	230 666	117 586	113 080
65 - 69	485 747	238 452	247 295	315 854	155 240	160 614	169 893	83 212	86 681
70 - 74	331 323	152 885	178 438	214 514	98 657	115 857	116 809	54 228	62 581
75 - 79	190 287	86 339	103 948	122 746	55 010	67 736	67 541	31 329	36 212
80 - 84	107 345	45 818	61 527	68 961	28 442	40 519	38 384	17 376	21 008
85 - 89	44 017	18 807	25 210	29 447	12 127	17 320	14 570	6 680	7 890
90 - 94	18 436	7 404	11 032	11 863	4 655	7 208	6 573	2 749	3 824
95 +	9 844	3 867	5 977	5 483	2 137	3 346	4 361	1 730	2 631
Maldives									
21 III 2006 (CDFC)[42]									
Total	298 968	151 459	147 509	103 693	51 992	51 701	195 275	99 467	95 808
0	5 462	2 777	2 685	1 601	832	769	3 861	1 945	1 916
1 - 4	20 709	10 585	10 124	5 743	2 912	2 831	14 966	7 673	7 293
5 - 9	29 867	15 352	14 515	7 538	3 829	3 709	22 329	11 523	10 806
10 - 14	36 999	19 111	17 888	10 082	5 171	4 911	26 917	13 940	12 977
15 - 19	39 904	20 155	19 749	15 656	7 457	8 199	24 248	12 698	11 550
20 - 24	34 809	16 933	17 876	15 535	7 401	8 134	19 274	9 532	9 742
25 - 29	24 581	11 915	12 666	10 176	5 054	5 122	14 405	6 861	7 544
30 - 34	20 635	10 022	10 613	8 137	4 089	4 048	12 498	5 933	6 565
35 - 39	18 174	8 780	9 394	6 616	3 381	3 235	11 558	5 399	6 159
40 - 44	15 871	7 828	8 043	5 529	2 731	2 798	10 342	5 097	5 245
45 - 49	13 569	6 872	6 697	4 394	2 207	2 187	9 175	4 665	4 510
50 - 54	7 936	4 147	3 789	2 601	1 415	1 186	5 335	2 732	2 603
55 - 59	5 859	3 046	2 813	1 863	987	876	3 996	2 059	1 937
60 - 64	5 566	2 852	2 714	1 520	752	768	4 046	2 100	1 946
65 - 69	5 678	3 014	2 664	1 265	619	646	4 413	2 395	2 018
70 - 74	4 186	2 333	1 853	765	363	402	3 421	1 970	1 451
75 - 79	2 377	1 444	933	409	217	192	1 968	1 227	741
80 - 84	1 064	617	447	204	92	112	860	525	335
85 - 89	396	241	155	94	48	46	302	193	109
90 - 94	159	89	70	34	14	20	125	75	50
95 +	84	52	32	19	8	11	65	44	21
Unknown - Inconnu	5 083	3 294	1 789	3 912	2 413	1 499	1 171	881	290
1 VII 2007 (ESDF)									
Total	304 869	154 391	150 478	...	...	...	...	...	...
0	5 749	2 948	2 801	...	...	...	...	...	...
1 - 4	21 312	10 929	10 383	...	...	...	...	...	...
5 - 9	29 248	15 069	14 179	...	...	...	...	...	...

Continent, country or area, date, code and age (in years) Continent, pays ou zone, date, code et âge (en années)	Total			Urban - Urbaine			Rural - Rurale		
	Both sexes Les deux sexes	Male Masculin	Female Féminin	Both sexes Les deux sexes	Male Masculin	Female Féminin	Both sexes Les deux sexes	Male Masculin	Female Féminin
ASIA - ASIE									
Maldives									
1 VII 2007 (ESDF)									
10 - 14	36 506	18 969	17 537	...	...	...	...	...	...
15 - 19	40 808	20 839	19 969	...	...	...	...	...	...
20 - 24	37 242	18 318	18 924	...	...	...	...	...	...
25 - 29	26 860	13 075	13 785	...	...	...	...	...	...
30 - 34	21 620	10 557	11 063	...	...	...	...	...	...
35 - 39	19 017	9 232	9 785	...	...	...	...	...	...
40 - 44	16 620	8 196	8 424	...	...	...	...	...	...
45 - 49	14 585	7 382	7 203	...	...	...	...	...	...
50 - 54	9 051	4 721	4 330	...	...	...	...	...	...
55 - 59	6 144	3 216	2 928	...	...	...	...	...	...
60 - 64	5 571	2 857	2 714	...	...	...	...	...	...
65 - 69	5 722	3 015	2 707	...	...	...	...	...	...
70 - 74	4 487	2 476	2 011	...	...	...	...	...	...
75 - 79	2 469	1 484	985	...	...	...	...	...	...
80 +	1 858	1 108	750	...	...	...	...	...	...
Mongolia - Mongolie									
5 I 2000 (CDFC)									
Total	2 373 493	1 177 981	1 195 512	1 344 516	657 081	687 435	1 028 977	520 900	508 077
0	49 804	25 356	24 448	23 778	12 119	11 659	26 026	13 237	12 789
1 - 4	196 219	99 126	97 093	91 687	46 096	45 591	104 532	53 030	51 502
5 - 9	285 664	144 315	141 349	150 401	75 700	74 701	135 263	68 615	66 648
10 - 14	317 434	159 294	158 140	179 974	89 670	90 304	137 460	69 624	67 836
15 - 19	263 358	133 327	130 031	154 244	75 040	79 204	109 114	58 287	50 827
20 - 24	235 751	118 023	117 728	135 694	66 010	69 684	100 057	52 013	48 044
25 - 29	216 652	107 962	108 690	125 644	61 274	64 370	91 008	46 688	44 320
30 - 34	187 872	92 473	95 399	113 537	54 332	59 205	74 335	38 141	36 194
35 - 39	172 606	84 846	87 760	108 347	52 275	56 072	64 259	32 571	31 688
40 - 44	127 220	62 619	64 601	79 563	38 840	40 723	47 657	23 779	23 878
45 - 49	82 888	40 562	42 326	50 873	25 089	25 784	32 015	15 473	16 542
50 - 54	57 835	27 707	30 128	35 016	17 094	17 922	22 819	10 613	12 206
55 - 59	55 895	27 379	28 516	30 397	15 011	15 386	25 498	12 368	13 130
60 - 64	42 292	20 778	21 514	21 889	10 658	11 231	20 403	10 120	10 283
65 - 69	35 415	15 982	19 433	18 480	8 145	10 335	16 935	7 837	9 098
70 - 74	20 239	8 766	11 473	10 946	4 579	6 367	9 293	4 187	5 106
75 - 79	14 843	5 832	9 011	7 963	3 197	4 766	6 880	2 635	4 245
80 - 84	7 036	2 329	4 707	3 777	1 281	2 496	3 259	1 048	2 211
85 - 89	3 376	991	2 385	1 746	519	1 227	1 630	472	1 158
90 - 94	869	257	612	441	125	316	428	132	296
95 - 99	196	53	143	104	24	80	92	29	63
100 +	29	4	25	15	3	12	14	1	13
1 VII 2007 (ESDF)									
Total	2 614 981	1 274 853	1 340 128	...	...	...	...	...	...
0 - 4	226 100	114 212	111 888	...	...	...	...	...	...
5 - 9	246 409	124 470	121 939	...	...	...	...	...	...
10 - 14	274 100	137 799	136 301	...	...	...	...	...	...
15 - 19	308 843	152 783	156 060	...	...	...	...	...	...
20 - 24	263 022	127 430	135 592	...	...	...	...	...	...
25 - 29	228 988	111 064	117 924	...	...	...	...	...	...
30 - 34	214 602	104 307	110 295	...	...	...	...	...	...
35 - 39	193 351	93 057	100 294	...	...	...	...	...	...
40 - 44	176 035	84 204	91 831	...	...	...	...	...	...
45 - 49	150 411	72 073	78 338	...	...	...	...	...	...
50 - 54	103 682	49 866	53 816	...	...	...	...	...	...
55 - 59	69 211	32 778	36 433	...	...	...	...	...	...
60 - 64	51 871	24 109	27 762	...	...	...	...	...	...
65 - 69	43 755	20 418	23 337	...	...	...	...	...	...
70 +	64 601	26 283	38 318	...	...	...	...	...	...
Myanmar									
1 VII 2004 (ESDF)									
Total	54 299 000	27 000 000	27 299 000	...	...	...	...	...	...
0 - 4	6 407 000	3 235 000	3 172 000	...	...	...	...	...	...
5 - 9	5 933 000	2 974 000	2 959 000	...	...	...	...	...	...
10 - 14	5 382 000	2 715 000	2 667 000	...	...	...	...	...	...

Continent, country or area, date, code and age (in years) Continent, pays ou zone, date, code et âge (en annèes)	Total			Urban - Urbaine			Rural - Rurale		
	Both sexes Les deux sexes	Male Masculin	Female Féminin	Both sexes Les deux sexes	Male Masculin	Female Féminin	Both sexes Les deux sexes	Male Masculin	Female Féminin
ASIA - ASIE									
Myanmar									
1 VII 2004 (ESDF)									
15 - 19	4 824 000	2 512 000	2 312 000	...	...	...	...	...	...
20 - 24	4 748 000	2 429 000	2 319 000	...	...	...	...	...	...
25 - 29	4 490 000	2 265 000	2 225 000	...	...	...	...	...	...
30 - 34	4 135 000	2 059 000	2 076 000	...	...	...	...	...	...
35 - 39	3 760 000	1 845 000	1 915 000	...	...	...	...	...	...
40 - 44	3 287 000	1 604 000	1 683 000	...	...	...	...	...	...
45 - 49	2 759 000	1 340 000	1 419 000	...	...	...	...	...	...
50 - 54	2 293 000	1 107 000	1 186 000	...	...	...	...	...	...
55 - 59	1 818 000	872 000	946 000	...	...	...	...	...	...
60 - 64	1 478 000	698 000	780 000	...	...	...	...	...	...
65 +	2 985 000	1 345 000	1 640 000	...	...	...	...	...	...
Nepal - Népal									
22 VI 2001 (CDJC)									
Total	22 736 934	11 359 378	11 377 556	...	...	...	...	...	...
0	494 813	252 519	242 294	...	...	...	...	...	...
1 - 4	2 260 400	1 143 196	1 117 204	...	...	...	...	...	...
5 - 9	3 211 442	1 633 087	1 578 355	...	...	...	...	...	...
10 - 14	2 981 932	1 533 806	1 448 126	...	...	...	...	...	...
15 - 19	2 389 002	1 185 826	1 203 176	...	...	...	...	...	...
20 - 24	2 016 768	946 742	1 070 026	...	...	...	...	...	...
25 - 29	1 725 478	821 014	904 464	...	...	...	...	...	...
30 - 34	1 489 503	726 040	763 463	...	...	...	...	...	...
35 - 39	1 310 653	651 351	659 302	...	...	...	...	...	...
40 - 44	1 088 044	539 993	548 051	...	...	...	...	...	...
45 - 49	923 373	469 695	453 678	...	...	...	...	...	...
50 - 54	766 054	392 659	373 395	...	...	...	...	...	...
55 - 59	602 093	318 610	283 483	...	...	...	...	...	...
60 - 64	520 908	262 255	258 653	...	...	...	...	...	...
65 - 69	387 223	196 053	191 170	...	...	...	...	...	...
70 - 74	273 789	141 678	132 111	...	...	...	...	...	...
75 - 79	165 764	82 335	83 429	...	...	...	...	...	...
80 - 84	84 255	41 192	43 063	...	...	...	...	...	...
85 - 89	27 947	13 630	14 317	...	...	...	...	...	...
90 - 94	11 421	5 082	6 339	...	...	...	...	...	...
95 +	6 072	2 615	3 457	...	...	...	...	...	...
Occupied Palestinian Territory - Territoire palestinien occupé									
1 VII 2007 (ESDF)									
Total	3 719 189	1 887 628	1 831 561	...	...	...	...	...	...
0	113 198	57 890	55 308	...	...	...	...	...	...
1 - 4	445 471	227 743	217 728	...	...	...	...	...	...
5 - 9	536 853	274 271	262 582	...	...	...	...	...	...
10 - 14	507 389	259 043	248 346	...	...	...	...	...	...
15 - 19	439 680	224 489	215 191	...	...	...	...	...	...
20 - 24	336 418	172 078	164 340	...	...	...	...	...	...
25 - 29	278 625	142 311	136 314	...	...	...	...	...	...
30 - 34	235 845	119 454	116 391	...	...	...	...	...	...
35 - 39	198 447	100 897	97 550	...	...	...	...	...	...
40 - 44	167 434	86 984	80 450	...	...	...	...	...	...
45 - 49	132 844	69 042	63 802	...	...	...	...	...	...
50 - 54	91 483	46 778	44 705	...	...	...	...	...	...
55 - 59	68 263	33 758	34 505	...	...	...	...	...	...
60 - 64	51 166	23 137	28 029	...	...	...	...	...	...
65 - 69	39 523	17 020	22 503	...	...	...	...	...	...
70 - 74	30 691	12 892	17 799	...	...	...	...	...	...
75 - 79	24 668	10 753	13 915	...	...	...	...	...	...
80 +	21 191	9 088	12 103	...	...	...	...	...	...
Oman									
1 VII 2007 (ESDF)									
Total	2 743 499	1 622 119	1 121 380	1 984 191	1 188 568	795 623	759 308	433 551	325 757
0 - 4	259 945	134 151	125 794	176 322	91 094	85 228	83 624	43 058	40 566
5 - 9	254 440	132 245	122 195	168 556	87 920	80 637	85 884	44 325	41 559

Continent, country or area, date, code and age (in years) / Continent, pays ou zone, date, code et âge (en années)	Total			Urban - Urbaine			Rural - Rurale		
	Both sexes Les deux sexes	Male Masculin	Female Féminin	Both sexes Les deux sexes	Male Masculin	Female Féminin	Both sexes Les deux sexes	Male Masculin	Female Féminin
ASIA - ASIE									
Oman									
1 VII 2007 (ESDF)									
10 - 14	275 869	143 042	132 828	183 032	95 012	88 020	92 837	48 030	44 807
15 - 19	293 938	150 988	142 950	200 347	103 823	96 524	93 591	47 165	46 426
20 - 24	309 246	166 750	142 495	227 808	123 300	104 508	81 437	43 450	37 987
25 - 29	334 966	204 681	130 286	255 464	156 020	99 444	79 502	48 661	30 841
30 - 34	287 722	190 882	96 840	225 523	149 061	76 461	62 199	41 820	20 379
35 - 39	218 460	153 147	65 313	170 304	120 034	50 271	48 156	33 113	15 042
40 - 44	178 056	127 274	50 782	138 562	100 451	38 111	39 493	26 822	12 671
45 - 49	120 405	86 718	33 687	92 002	67 654	24 348	28 402	19 064	9 339
50 - 54	81 706	56 463	25 243	60 886	43 339	17 547	20 820	13 124	7 696
55 - 59	46 244	29 510	16 734	32 865	21 494	11 371	13 379	8 016	5 363
60 - 64	35 975	21 247	14 728	23 589	13 987	9 602	12 386	7 260	5 126
65 - 69	18 316	10 563	7 754	11 760	6 740	5 019	6 557	3 822	2 734
70 - 74	15 083	7 968	7 114	9 313	4 853	4 460	5 769	3 115	2 654
75 - 79	5 592	2 870	2 722	3 441	1 721	1 719	2 152	1 149	1 003
80 +	7 537	3 621	3 916	4 417	2 065	2 352	3 120	1 556	1 564
Pakistan[43]									
1 VII 2005 (SSDJ)									
Total	144 367 294	74 247 400	70 119 892	51 408 193	26 556 848	24 851 345	92 959 101	47 690 551	45 268 549
0 - 4	18 971 026	9 656 635	9 314 391	5 932 014	3 015 028	2 916 986	13 039 012	6 641 607	6 397 405
5 - 9	21 573 188	11 218 573	10 354 615	6 835 118	3 555 562	3 279 556	14 738 070	7 663 011	7 075 059
10 - 14	19 513 093	10 186 363	9 326 730	6 701 856	3 410 218	3 291 638	12 811 238	6 776 145	6 035 093
15 - 19	16 874 343	8 902 456	7 971 887	6 387 003	3 337 741	3 049 262	10 487 340	5 564 715	4 922 625
20 - 24	13 468 490	6 802 814	6 665 676	5 322 798	2 762 611	2 560 187	8 145 692	4 040 203	4 105 489
25 - 29	10 187 927	5 015 427	5 172 500	3 872 119	1 977 753	1 894 366	6 315 808	3 037 674	3 278 134
30 - 34	8 053 014	3 858 275	4 194 739	3 052 640	1 504 155	1 548 485	5 000 374	2 354 120	2 646 254
35 - 39	7 932 058	3 940 131	3 991 927	3 105 338	1 564 925	1 540 412	4 826 721	2 375 206	2 451 515
40 - 44	6 527 614	3 298 363	3 229 250	2 544 022	1 307 515	1 236 507	3 983 592	1 990 849	1 992 743
45 - 49	5 942 581	3 065 341	2 877 239	2 265 071	1 192 329	1 072 742	3 677 510	1 873 012	1 804 498
50 - 54	4 355 411	2 287 807	2 067 603	1 619 128	864 977	754 151	2 736 283	1 422 830	1 313 452
55 - 59	3 438 121	1 844 892	1 593 229	1 268 466	684 544	583 922	2 169 655	1 160 347	1 009 307
60 - 64	2 780 283	1 498 457	1 281 826	946 920	509 777	437 143	1 833 362	988 679	844 683
65 - 69	1 966 091	1 087 559	878 532	653 384	366 720	286 664	1 312 707	720 839	591 868
70 - 74	1 358 407	766 308	592 100	460 361	256 659	203 702	898 046	509 649	388 398
75 - 79	653 594	371 304	282 290	214 340	123 783	90 558	439 253	247 522	191 732
80 - 84	456 670	254 863	201 807	133 693	67 439	66 254	322 977	187 423	135 553
85 +	315 383	191 832	123 551	93 922	55 112	38 810	221 461	136 720	84 741
Philippines									
1 VII 2005 (ESDJ)									
Total	84 241 341	42 401 391	41 839 950	...	...	...	...	...	...
0 - 4	9 658 747	4 937 632	4 721 115	...	...	...	...	...	...
5 - 9	9 475 534	4 832 467	4 643 067	...	...	...	...	...	...
10 - 14	9 293 498	4 792 979	4 500 519	...	...	...	...	...	...
15 - 19	8 647 659	4 418 572	4 229 087	...	...	...	...	...	...
20 - 24	7 888 468	3 983 027	3 905 441	...	...	...	...	...	...
25 - 29	7 098 788	3 557 779	3 541 009	...	...	...	...	...	...
30 - 34	6 302 487	3 141 953	3 160 534	...	...	...	...	...	...
35 - 39	5 532 786	2 756 653	2 776 133	...	...	...	...	...	...
40 - 44	4 748 786	2 374 463	2 374 323	...	...	...	...	...	...
45 - 49	4 012 576	2 006 056	2 006 520	...	...	...	...	...	...
50 - 54	3 260 652	1 629 315	1 631 337	...	...	...	...	...	...
55 - 59	2 615 769	1 296 672	1 319 097	...	...	...	...	...	...
60 - 64	1 976 901	963 875	1 013 026	...	...	...	...	...	...
65 - 69	1 471 403	704 079	767 324	...	...	...	...	...	...
70 - 74	1 021 557	475 228	546 329	...	...	...	...	...	...
75 - 79	672 613	298 154	374 459	...	...	...	...	...	...
80 +	563 117	232 487	330 630	...	...	...	...	...	...
Qatar									
1 VII 2007 (ESDF)									
Total	1 226 210	920 415	305 795	...	...	...	...	...	...
0	15 564	7 999	7 565	...	...	...	...	...	...
1 - 4	53 017	27 094	25 923	...	...	...	...	...	...
5 - 9	62 288	31 957	30 331	...	...	...	...	...	...
10 - 14	53 580	27 413	26 167	...	...	...	...	...	...

7. Population by age, sex and urban/rural residence: latest available year, 1998 - 2007
Population selon l'âge, le sexe et la résidence, urbaine/rurale: dernière année disponible, 1998 - 2007 (continued - suite)

Continent, country or area, date, code and age (in years) / Continent, pays ou zone, date, code et âge (en années)	Total			Urban - Urbaine			Rural - Rurale		
	Both sexes Les deux sexes	Male Masculin	Female Féminin	Both sexes Les deux sexes	Male Masculin	Female Féminin	Both sexes Les deux sexes	Male Masculin	Female Féminin
ASIA - ASIE									
Qatar									
1 VII 2007 (ESDF)									
15 - 19	55 144	32 213	22 931	...	...	...	...	...	...
20 - 24	155 749	129 066	26 683	...	...	...	...	...	...
25 - 29	213 050	173 996	39 054	...	...	...	...	...	...
30 - 34	176 747	140 762	35 985	...	...	...	...	...	...
35 - 39	148 497	119 673	28 824	...	...	...	...	...	...
40 - 44	108 543	86 533	22 010	...	...	...	...	...	...
45 - 49	79 255	63 013	16 242	...	...	...	...	...	...
50 - 54	52 336	42 033	10 303	...	...	...	...	...	...
55 - 59	26 606	20 983	5 623	...	...	...	...	...	...
60 - 64	12 694	9 302	3 392	...	...	...	...	...	...
65 - 69	5 974	3 878	2 096	...	...	...	...	...	...
70 - 74	3 701	2 324	1 377	...	...	...	...	...	...
75 - 79	1 620	1 031	589	...	...	...	...	...	...
80 - 84	950	574	376	...	...	...	...	...	...
85 - 89	450	279	171	...	...	...	...	...	...
90 +	445	292	153	...	...	...	...	...	...
Republic of Korea - République de Corée									
1 XI 2005 (CDJC)[44]									
Total	47 041 434	23 465 650	23 575 784	38 337 699	19 145 912	19 191 787	8 703 735	4 319 738	4 383 997
0	413 805	213 786	200 019	343 865	177 539	166 326	69 940	36 247	33 693
1 - 4	1 968 545	1 023 515	945 030	1 624 142	844 076	780 066	344 403	179 439	164 964
5 - 9	3 168 887	1 654 228	1 514 659	2 624 437	1 370 557	1 253 880	544 450	283 671	260 779
10 - 14	3 434 891	1 816 318	1 618 573	2 898 270	1 533 726	1 364 544	536 621	282 592	254 029
15 - 19	3 100 523	1 626 378	1 474 145	2 629 214	1 378 088	1 251 126	471 309	248 290	223 019
20 - 24	3 662 123	1 915 902	1 746 221	3 147 034	1 611 993	1 535 041	515 089	303 909	211 180
25 - 29	3 671 847	1 858 332	1 813 515	3 174 220	1 589 865	1 584 355	497 627	268 467	229 160
30 - 34	4 096 282	2 059 913	2 036 369	3 485 192	1 739 536	1 745 656	611 090	320 377	290 713
35 - 39	4 112 785	2 065 668	2 047 117	3 474 836	1 726 349	1 748 487	637 949	339 319	298 630
40 - 44	4 123 041	2 082 427	2 040 614	3 479 360	1 738 972	1 740 388	643 681	343 455	300 226
45 - 49	3 900 899	1 961 859	1 939 040	3 252 059	1 626 493	1 625 566	648 840	335 366	313 474
50 - 54	2 855 297	1 426 597	1 428 700	2 314 379	1 157 586	1 156 793	540 918	269 011	271 907
55 - 59	2 278 438	1 126 997	1 151 441	1 773 373	882 089	891 284	505 065	244 908	260 157
60 - 64	1 888 853	897 384	991 469	1 370 485	665 921	704 564	518 368	231 463	286 905
65 - 69	1 680 067	755 949	924 118	1 106 537	508 208	598 329	573 530	247 741	325 789
70 - 74	1 252 734	514 241	738 493	773 269	319 475	453 794	479 465	194 766	284 699
75 - 79	766 870	270 632	496 238	466 206	161 741	304 465	300 664	108 891	191 773
80 - 84	432 259	136 705	295 554	261 192	79 567	181 625	171 067	57 138	113 929
85 +	233 288	58 819	174 469	139 629	34 131	105 498	93 659	24 688	68 971
1 VII 2007 (ESDJ)									
Total	48 456 369	24 344 276	24 112 093	...	...	...	...	...	...
0 - 4	2 304 672	1 196 791	1 107 881	...	...	...	...	...	...
5 - 9	2 990 578	1 563 013	1 427 565	...	...	...	...	...	...
10 - 14	3 438 459	1 822 845	1 615 614	...	...	...	...	...	...
15 - 19	3 197 412	1 688 591	1 508 821	...	...	...	...	...	...
20 - 24	3 385 985	1 758 983	1 627 002	...	...	...	...	...	...
25 - 29	3 943 482	2 032 943	1 910 539	...	...	...	...	...	...
30 - 34	4 021 897	2 069 079	1 952 818	...	...	...	...	...	...
35 - 39	4 359 887	2 225 172	2 134 715	...	...	...	...	...	...
40 - 44	4 132 876	2 120 333	2 012 543	...	...	...	...	...	...
45 - 49	4 201 427	2 124 565	2 076 862	...	...	...	...	...	...
50 - 54	3 302 849	1 665 071	1 637 778	...	...	...	...	...	...
55 - 59	2 416 320	1 201 674	1 214 646	...	...	...	...	...	...
60 - 64	1 950 162	936 578	1 013 584	...	...	...	...	...	...
65 - 69	1 784 083	812 552	971 531	...	...	...	...	...	...
70 - 74	1 381 006	581 198	799 808	...	...	...	...	...	...
75 - 79	873 196	316 378	556 818	...	...	...	...	...	...
80 - 84	482 988	153 795	329 193	...	...	...	...	...	...
85 - 89	208 960	58 265	150 695	...	...	...	...	...	...
90 - 94	62 708	13 651	49 057	...	...	...	...	...	...
95 +	17 422	2 799	14 623	...	...	...	...	...	...

7. Population by age, sex and urban/rural residence: latest available year, 1998 - 2007
Population selon l'âge, le sexe et la résidence, urbaine/rurale: dernière année disponible, 1998 - 2007 (continued - suite)

Continent, country or area, date, code and age (in years) / Continent, pays ou zone, date, code et âge (en années)	Total			Urban - Urbaine			Rural - Rurale		
	Both sexes Les deux sexes	Male Masculin	Female Féminin	Both sexes Les deux sexes	Male Masculin	Female Féminin	Both sexes Les deux sexes	Male Masculin	Female Féminin
ASIA - ASIE									
Saudi Arabia - Arabie saoudite									
1 VII 2006 (ESDF)									
Total....................	23 678 849	13 090 839	10 588 009	...	...	...	...	...	...
0 - 4.....................	2 754 108	1 399 669	1 354 439	...	...	...	...	...	...
5 - 9.....................	2 595 789	1 310 112	1 285 677	...	...	...	...	...	...
10 - 14	2 430 136	1 215 671	1 214 465	...	...	...	...	...	...
15 - 19	2 206 139	1 093 786	1 112 353	...	...	...	...	...	...
20 - 24	2 095 772	1 081 896	1 013 876	...	...	...	...	...	...
25 - 29	2 316 893	1 329 970	986 922	...	...	...	...	...	...
30 - 34	2 336 313	1 402 957	933 355	...	...	...	...	...	...
35 - 39	1 992 635	1 237 652	754 983	...	...	...	...	...	...
40 - 44	1 532 030	988 595	543 437	...	...	...	...	...	...
45 - 49	1 119 319	716 867	402 452	...	...	...	...	...	...
50 - 54	779 419	483 487	295 933	...	...	...	...	...	...
55 - 59	513 520	300 719	212 801	...	...	...	...	...	...
60 - 64	348 682	189 197	159 485	...	...	...	...	...	...
65 - 69	244 232	126 042	118 189	...	...	...	...	...	...
70 - 74	170 480	86 502	83 979	...	...	...	...	...	...
75 - 79	112 027	57 538	54 489	...	...	...	...	...	...
80 + ...	131 354	70 180	61 174	...	...	...	...	...	...
Singapore - Singapour									
1 VII 2007 (ESDJ)									
Total....................	3 583 100	1 775 500	1 807 600	...	...	...	...	...	...
0 - 4.....................	193 600	99 100	94 500	...	...	...	...	...	...
5 - 9.....................	229 600	118 400	111 200	...	...	...	...	...	...
10 - 14	255 300	131 400	123 900	...	...	...	...	...	...
15 - 19	257 300	131 600	125 700	...	...	...	...	...	...
20 - 24	218 500	110 600	107 900	...	...	...	...	...	...
25 - 29	254 500	122 000	132 500	...	...	...	...	...	...
30 - 34	294 500	141 500	153 000	...	...	...	...	...	...
35 - 39	302 000	147 400	154 600	...	...	...	...	...	...
40 - 44	321 000	161 200	159 800	...	...	...	...	...	...
45 - 49	315 600	159 600	156 000	...	...	...	...	...	...
50 - 54	279 200	140 800	138 400	...	...	...	...	...	...
55 - 59	220 900	110 300	110 600	...	...	...	...	...	...
60 - 64	135 500	66 700	68 800	...	...	...	...	...	...
65 - 69	113 800	53 800	60 000	...	...	...	...	...	...
70 - 74	78 600	36 200	42 400	...	...	...	...	...	...
75 - 79	56 800	24 400	32 400	...	...	...	...	...	...
80 - 84	31 500	12 300	19 200	...	...	...	...	...	...
85 + ...	25 000	8 300	16 700	...	...	...	...	...	...
Sri Lanka									
17 VII 2001 (CDFC)[45]									
Total....................	16 929 689	8 425 607	8 504 082	2 467 301	1 252 173	1 215 128	14 462 388[46]	7 173 434[46]	7 288 954[46]
0 - 4.....................	1 439 761	733 775	705 986	190 571	97 476	93 095	1 249 190[46]	636 299[46]	612 891[46]
5 - 9.....................	1 483 591	754 518	729 073	187 979	96 025	91 954	1 295 612[46]	658 493[46]	637 119[46]
10 - 14	1 525 674	777 519	748 155	191 194	97 360	93 834	1 334 480[46]	680 159[46]	654 321[46]
15 - 19	1 646 827	834 695	812 132	235 729	120 467	115 262	1 411 098[46]	714 228[46]	696 870[46]
20 - 24	1 591 126	798 288	792 838	274 372	143 696	130 676	1 316 754[46]	654 592[46]	662 162[46]
25 - 29	1 340 562	660 586	679 976	223 920	115 973	107 947	1 116 642[46]	544 613[46]	572 029[46]
30 - 34	1 290 121	636 734	653 387	200 909	104 230	96 679	1 089 212[46]	532 504[46]	556 708[46]
35 - 39	1 258 112	622 957	635 155	187 868	95 408	92 460	1 070 244[46]	527 549[46]	542 695[46]
40 - 44	1 170 941	583 894	587 047	170 722	86 768	83 954	1 000 219[46]	497 126[46]	503 093[46]
45 - 49	1 030 560	509 247	521 313	147 346	74 582	72 764	883 214[46]	434 665[46]	448 549[46]
50 - 54	917 139	452 311	464 828	135 177	68 548	66 629	781 962[46]	383 763[46]	398 199[46]
55 - 59	671 403	324 223	347 180	99 601	49 225	50 376	571 802[46]	274 998[46]	296 804[46]
60 - 64	496 177	241 081	255 096	72 657	35 246	37 411	423 520[46]	205 835[46]	217 685[46]
65 - 69	404 749	188 007	216 742	56 403	26 252	30 151	348 346[46]	161 755[46]	186 591[46]
70 - 74	303 473	142 030	161 443	42 974	19 404	23 570	260 499[46]	122 626[46]	137 873[46]
75 - 79	193 171	89 023	104 148	27 286	11 953	15 333	165 885[46]	77 070[46]	88 815[46]
80 - 84	105 036	48 757	56 279	14 558	6 264	8 294	90 478[46]	42 493[46]	47 985[46]
85 - 89	42 962	19 839	23 123	5 758	2 357	3 401	37 204[46]	17 482[46]	19 722[46]
90 - 94	13 096	5 870	7 226	1 708	708	1 000	11 388[46]	5 162[46]	6 226[46]

Continent, country or area, date, code and age (in years) / Continent, pays ou zone, date, code et âge (en années)	Total			Urban - Urbaine			Rural - Rurale		
	Both sexes Les deux sexes	Male Masculin	Female Féminin	Both sexes Les deux sexes	Male Masculin	Female Féminin	Both sexes Les deux sexes	Male Masculin	Female Féminin
ASIA - ASIE									
Sri Lanka									
17 VII 2001 (CDFC)[45]									
95 - 99	3 904	1 684	2 220	413	163	250	3 491[46]	1 521[46]	1 970[46]
100 +	1 304	569	735	156	68	88	1 148[46]	501[46]	647[46]
1 VII 2007 (ESDF)									
Total	20 010 000	9 888 000	10 122 000						
0 - 4	1 730 000	880 000	850 000	...	...	...	...	...	...
5 - 9	1 781 000	900 000	881 000	...	...	...	...	...	...
10 - 14	1 820 000	929 000	891 000	...	...	...	...	...	...
15 - 19	1 951 000	999 000	952 000	...	...	...	...	...	...
20 - 24	1 841 000	910 000	931 000	...	...	...	...	...	...
25 - 29	1 561 000	751 000	810 000	...	...	...	...	...	...
30 - 34	1 501 000	732 000	769 000	...	...	...	...	...	...
35 - 39	1 481 000	722 000	759 000	...	...	...	...	...	...
40 - 44	1 370 000	672 000	698 000	...	...	...	...	...	...
45 - 49	1 210 000	593 000	617 000	...	...	...	...	...	...
50 - 54	1 091 000	534 000	557 000	...	...	...	...	...	...
55 - 59	801 000	386 000	415 000	...	...	...	...	...	...
60 - 64	591 000	287 000	304 000	...	...	...	...	...	...
65 - 69	490 000	227 000	263 000	...	...	...	...	...	...
70 - 74	360 000	168 000	192 000	...	...	...	...	...	...
75 +	431 000	198 000	233 000	...	...	...	...	...	...
Syrian Arab Republic - République arabe syrienne[47]									
1 VII 2007 (ESDF)									
Total	19 172 000	9 798 000	9 374 000	10 257 000	5 265 000	4 992 000	8 915 000	4 533 000	4 382 000
0 - 4	2 662 000	1 367 000	1 295 000	1 354 000	695 000	659 000	1 308 000	672 000	636 000
5 - 9	2 584 000	1 327 000	1 257 000	1 328 000	684 000	644 000	1 256 000	643 000	613 000
10 - 14	2 319 000	1 196 000	1 123 000	1 205 000	621 000	584 000	1 114 000	575 000	539 000
15 - 19	2 242 000	1 143 000	1 099 000	1 164 000	595 000	569 000	1 078 000	548 000	530 000
20 - 24	1 972 000	997 000	975 000	1 055 000	531 000	524 000	917 000	466 000	451 000
25 - 29	1 543 000	774 000	769 000	835 000	421 000	414 000	708 000	353 000	355 000
30 - 34	1 264 000	639 000	625 000	707 000	358 000	349 000	557 000	281 000	276 000
35 - 39	1 090 000	549 000	541 000	625 000	316 000	309 000	465 000	233 000	232 000
40 - 44	904 000	461 000	443 000	538 000	279 000	259 000	366 000	182 000	184 000
45 - 49	687 000	357 000	330 000	407 000	217 000	190 000	280 000	140 000	140 000
50 - 54	554 000	286 000	268 000	313 000	168 000	145 000	241 000	118 000	123 000
55 - 59	391 000	203 000	188 000	222 000	117 000	105 000	169 000	86 000	83 000
60 - 64	318 000	157 000	161 000	175 000	89 000	86 000	143 000	68 000	75 000
65 +	642 000	342 000	300 000	329 000	174 000	155 000	313 000	168 000	145 000
Tajikistan - Tadjikistan									
1 VII 2007 (ESDF)									
Total	7 139 772	3 581 930	3 557 842	1 877 204	943 033	934 171	5 262 569	2 638 898	2 623 671
0	188 189	96 091	92 099	46 726	23 872	22 854	141 463	72 219	69 244
1 - 4	689 639	354 266	335 374	168 404	86 479	81 925	521 236	267 787	253 449
5 - 9	840 191	429 027	411 164	204 862	104 716	100 146	635 330	324 311	311 019
10 - 14	863 247	438 139	425 108	207 261	105 568	101 693	655 986	332 571	323 415
15 - 19	871 357	442 027	429 330	219 572	113 498	106 074	651 786	328 530	323 256
20 - 24	756 501	381 333	375 168	194 162	100 629	93 533	562 340	280 705	281 635
25 - 29	577 281	289 722	287 560	157 434	84 699	72 735	419 847	205 023	214 825
30 - 34	472 119	231 988	240 131	127 880	61 163	66 717	344 239	170 825	173 414
35 - 39	425 623	208 788	216 836	125 807	60 035	65 772	299 817	148 753	151 064
40 - 44	382 070	187 288	194 782	113 910	55 130	58 780	268 160	132 159	136 002
45 - 49	335 257	165 549	169 708	100 613	49 300	51 313	234 644	116 250	118 395
50 - 54	220 261	108 337	111 924	65 694	31 757	33 938	154 567	76 581	77 986
55 - 59	147 153	72 245	74 908	44 974	21 694	23 280	102 179	50 551	51 628
60 - 64	72 617	38 180	34 437	20 588	10 146	10 442	52 029	28 034	23 995
65 - 69	97 971	49 594	48 377	27 621	13 359	14 262	70 351	36 236	34 115
70 - 74	81 237	38 325	42 912	20 958	9 550	11 408	60 280	28 775	31 505
75 - 79	65 484	31 396	34 088	16 474	7 195	9 279	49 010	24 201	24 809
80 - 84	34 924	15 116	19 808	9 369	3 371	5 998	25 555	11 745	13 810
85 - 89	13 015	3 697	9 318	3 282	673	2 609	9 733	3 024	6 709
90 - 94	3 456	542	2 915	1 002	96	906	2 454	446	2 009
95 - 99	1 475	238	1 237	468	79	390	1 007	159	848
100 +	710	46	665	149	28	121	561	18	544

Continent, country or area, date, code and age (in years) Continent, pays ou zone, date, code et âge (en années)	Total			Urban - Urbaine			Rural - Rurale		
	Both sexes Les deux sexes	Male Masculin	Female Féminin	Both sexes Les deux sexes	Male Masculin	Female Féminin	Both sexes Les deux sexes	Male Masculin	Female Féminin
ASIA - ASIE									
Thailand - Thaïlande[3]									
1 VII 2007 (ESDJ)									
Total	66 041 512	32 467 223	33 574 289	20 117 497	9 733 251	10 384 246	45 924 015	22 733 972	23 190 043
0 - 4	4 705 877	2 394 925	2 310 952	1 502 265	760 630	741 635	3 203 612	1 634 295	1 569 317
5 - 9	4 729 295	2 424 155	2 305 140	1 345 820	685 393	660 427	3 383 475	1 738 762	1 644 713
10 - 14	5 086 526	2 605 315	2 481 211	1 364 860	694 082	670 778	3 721 666	1 911 233	1 810 433
15 - 19	5 256 415	2 688 028	2 568 387	1 414 162	713 833	700 329	3 842 253	1 974 195	1 868 058
20 - 24	5 284 582	2 689 620	2 594 962	1 503 526	745 794	757 732	3 781 056	1 943 826	1 837 230
25 - 29	5 346 391	2 700 109	2 646 282	1 762 528	858 588	903 940	3 583 863	1 841 521	1 742 342
30 - 34	5 465 792	2 694 774	2 771 018	1 875 586	901 232	974 354	3 590 206	1 793 542	1 796 664
35 - 39	5 591 964	2 702 715	2 889 249	1 835 841	873 977	961 864	3 756 123	1 828 738	1 927 385
40 - 44	5 416 443	2 619 933	2 796 510	1 725 618	823 663	901 955	3 690 825	1 796 270	1 894 555
45 - 49	4 925 031	2 383 289	2 541 742	1 545 608	738 891	806 717	3 379 423	1 644 398	1 735 025
50 - 54	4 042 161	1 942 720	2 099 441	1 248 621	593 216	655 405	2 793 540	1 349 504	1 444 036
55 - 59	3 044 220	1 452 795	1 591 425	922 002	435 929	486 073	2 122 218	1 016 866	1 105 352
60 - 64	2 312 904	1 086 173	1 226 731	676 088	314 720	361 368	1 636 816	771 453	865 363
65 - 69	1 862 044	847 454	1 014 590	540 492	243 966	296 526	1 321 552	603 488	718 064
70 - 74	1 413 263	617 154	796 109	409 255	177 534	231 721	1 004 008	439 620	564 388
75 - 79	863 565	356 742	506 823	241 444	97 381	144 063	622 121	259 361	362 760
80 +	695 039	261 322	433 717	203 781	74 422	129 359	491 258	186 900	304 358
Turkey - Turquie									
22 X 2000 (CDFC)									
Total	67 803 927	34 346 735	33 457 192	44 006 274	22 427 603	21 578 671	23 797 653	11 919 132	11 878 521
0	1 244 675	640 760	603 915	782 345	402 411	379 934	462 330	238 349	223 981
1 - 4	5 340 147	2 755 930	2 584 217	3 305 208	1 705 098	1 600 110	2 034 939	1 050 832	984 107
5 - 9	6 756 617	3 485 746	3 270 871	4 239 171	2 186 546	2 052 625	2 517 446	1 299 200	1 218 246
10 - 14	6 878 656	3 570 657	3 307 999	4 390 792	2 300 010	2 090 782	2 487 864	1 270 647	1 217 217
15 - 19	7 209 475	3 691 218	3 518 257	4 740 001	2 485 382	2 254 619	2 469 474	1 205 836	1 263 638
20 - 24	6 690 146	3 426 714	3 263 432	4 616 663	2 412 166	2 204 497	2 073 483	1 014 548	1 058 935
25 - 29	5 895 255	2 976 430	2 918 825	4 043 777	2 043 057	2 000 720	1 851 478	933 373	918 105
30 - 34	5 009 655	2 552 370	2 457 285	3 438 737	1 744 883	1 693 854	1 570 918	807 487	763 431
35 - 39	4 854 387	2 453 579	2 400 808	3 324 212	1 671 781	1 652 431	1 530 175	781 798	748 377
40 - 44	4 068 756	2 083 531	1 985 225	2 781 023	1 424 039	1 356 984	1 287 733	659 492	628 241
45 - 49	3 368 769	1 710 757	1 658 012	2 251 799	1 153 832	1 097 967	1 116 970	556 925	560 045
50 - 54	2 717 349	1 356 391	1 360 958	1 724 916	874 700	850 216	992 433	481 691	510 742
55 - 59	2 058 422	1 016 254	1 042 168	1 225 906	612 521	613 385	832 516	403 733	428 783
60 - 64	1 829 288	864 299	964 989	1 030 176	484 922	545 254	799 112	379 377	419 735
65 - 69	1 645 517	794 881	850 636	883 840	417 194	466 646	761 677	377 687	383 990
70 - 74	1 172 643	517 870	654 773	635 253	270 034	365 219	537 390	247 836	289 554
75 - 79	577 597	254 443	323 154	321 179	135 075	186 104	256 418	119 368	137 050
80 - 84	246 692	98 797	147 895	137 630	52 964	84 666	109 062	45 833	63 229
85 - 89	138 361	55 298	83 063	77 087	28 707	48 380	61 274	26 591	34 683
90 - 94	52 426	18 616	33 810	28 975	9 770	19 205	23 451	8 846	14 605
95 - 99	19 504	7 402	12 102	10 919	4 100	6 819	8 585	3 302	5 283
100 +	6 209	2 256	3 953	3 183	1 118	2 065	3 026	1 138	1 888
Unknown - Inconnu	23 381	12 536	10 845	13 482	7 293	6 189	9 899	5 243	4 656
1 VII 2007 (ESDF)[9]									
Total	73 876 000	37 241 000	36 636 000	...	...	...	...	...	...
0 - 4	6 532 000	3 336 000	3 196 000	...	...	...	...	...	...
5 - 9	6 963 000	3 549 000	3 415 000	...	...	...	...	...	...
10 - 14	6 979 000	3 549 000	3 430 000	...	...	...	...	...	...
15 - 19	6 382 000	3 255 000	3 127 000	...	...	...	...	...	...
20 - 24	6 418 000	3 281 000	3 137 000	...	...	...	...	...	...
25 - 29	6 767 000	3 456 000	3 311 000	...	...	...	...	...	...
30 - 34	6 517 000	3 319 000	3 198 000	...	...	...	...	...	...
35 - 39	5 595 000	2 825 000	2 770 000	...	...	...	...	...	...
40 - 44	4 757 000	2 389 000	2 368 000	...	...	...	...	...	...
45 - 49	4 182 000	2 118 000	2 065 000	...	...	...	...	...	...
50 - 54	3 548 000	1 797 000	1 751 000	...	...	...	...	...	...
55 - 59	2 706 000	1 347 000	1 359 000	...	...	...	...	...	...
60 - 64	2 065 000	1 001 000	1 064 000	...	...	...	...	...	...
65 - 69	1 717 000	809 000	908 000	...	...	...	...	...	...
70 - 74	1 336 000	609 000	726 000	...	...	...	...	...	...
75 +	1 412 000	601 000	811 000	...	...	...	...	...	...

7. Population by age, sex and urban/rural residence: latest available year, 1998 - 2007
Population selon l'âge, le sexe et la résidence, urbaine/rurale: dernière année disponible, 1998 - 2007 (continued - suite)

Continent, country or area, date, code and age (in years) / Continent, pays ou zone, date, code et âge (en annèes)	Total			Urban - Urbaine			Rural - Rurale		
	Both sexes Les deux sexes	Male Masculin	Female Féminin	Both sexes Les deux sexes	Male Masculin	Female Féminin	Both sexes Les deux sexes	Male Masculin	Female Féminin
ASIA - ASIE									
Turkmenistan - Turkménistan[9]									
1 VII 2003 (ESDF)									
Total	5 123 940	2 571 866	2 552 073	...	...	...	...	...	...
0 - 4	571 355	277 748	293 607	...	...	...	...	...	...
5 - 9	613 767	300 841	312 925	...	...	...	...	...	...
10 - 14	645 136	316 247	328 889	...	...	...	...	...	...
15 - 19	579 113	284 926	294 186	...	...	...	...	...	...
20 - 24	479 053	235 762	243 291	...	...	...	...	...	...
25 - 29	423 109	210 578	212 531	...	...	...	...	...	...
30 - 34	380 948	194 438	186 510	...	...	...	...	...	...
35 - 39	341 403	173 922	167 481	...	...	...	...	...	...
40 - 44	316 309	161 800	154 509	...	...	...	...	...	...
45 - 49	233 504	120 701	112 803	...	...	...	...	...	...
50 - 54	161 151	84 220	76 931	...	...	...	...	...	...
55 - 59	85 927	44 454	41 472	...	...	...	...	...	...
60 - 64	92 992	49 068	43 924	...	...	...	...	...	...
65 - 69	76 006	41 263	34 743	...	...	...	...	...	...
70 - 74	61 177	34 393	26 784	...	...	...	...	...	...
75 +	62 987	41 503	21 484	...	...	...	...	...	...
United Arab Emirates - Émirats arabes unis									
1 VII 2007 (ESDF)									
Total	4 488 000	3 084 000	1 404 000	...	...	...	...	...	...
0 - 4	304 902	157 706	147 196	...	...	...	...	...	...
5 - 9	290 912	151 500	139 412	...	...	...	...	...	...
10 - 14	268 177	141 127	127 050	...	...	...	...	...	...
15 - 19	249 456	130 703	118 753	...	...	...	...	...	...
20 - 24	473 105	298 875	174 230	...	...	...	...	...	...
25 - 29	728 573	535 448	193 125	...	...	...	...	...	...
30 - 34	706 268	542 748	163 520	...	...	...	...	...	...
35 - 39	551 459	427 884	123 575	...	...	...	...	...	...
40 - 44	374 763	289 607	85 156	...	...	...	...	...	...
45 - 49	246 986	191 526	55 460	...	...	...	...	...	...
50 - 54	151 602	117 587	34 015	...	...	...	...	...	...
55 - 59	72 965	55 989	16 976	...	...	...	...	...	...
60 - 64	29 496	20 399	9 097	...	...	...	...	...	...
65 - 69	15 433	9 818	5 615	...	...	...	...	...	...
70 - 74	9 990	5 738	4 252	...	...	...	...	...	...
75 - 79	4 556	2 605	1 951	...	...	...	...	...	...
80 +	9 357	4 740	4 617	...	...	...	...	...	...
Uzbekistan - Ouzbékistan									
1 VII 2001 (ESDF)									
Total	24 964 433	12 442 510	12 521 923	9 256 101	4 573 055	4 683 046	15 708 332	7 869 455	7 838 877
0	513 043	263 408	249 635	158 893	81 393	77 500	354 150	182 015	172 135
1 - 4	2 219 863	1 138 212	1 081 651	693 448	355 999	337 449	1 526 415	782 213	744 202
5 - 9	3 237 989	1 653 776	1 584 213	1 015 989	519 360	496 629	2 222 000	1 134 416	1 087 584
10 - 14	3 203 022	1 627 673	1 575 349	1 049 577	533 870	515 707	2 153 445	1 093 803	1 059 642
15 - 19	2 821 926	1 422 296	1 399 630	984 385	497 725	486 660	1 837 541	924 571	912 970
20 - 24	2 296 834	1 157 998	1 138 836	841 326	425 348	415 978	1 455 508	732 650	722 858
25 - 29	2 030 200	1 023 174	1 007 026	788 176	397 184	390 992	1 242 024	625 990	616 034
30 - 34	1 749 557	861 368	888 189	726 099	372 846	353 253	1 023 458	488 522	534 936
35 - 39	1 672 397	816 665	855 732	660 932	323 492	337 440	1 011 465	493 173	518 292
40 - 44	1 479 057	728 780	750 277	612 755	297 460	315 295	866 302	431 320	434 982
45 - 49	1 034 628	506 734	527 894	464 375	223 425	240 950	570 253	283 309	286 944
50 - 54	696 648	337 634	359 014	340 008	161 069	178 939	356 640	176 565	180 075
55 - 59	394 997	197 700	197 297	185 073	88 314	96 759	209 924	109 386	100 538
60 - 64	553 697	265 428	288 269	254 409	115 715	138 694	299 288	149 713	149 575
65 - 69	399 550	185 653	213 897	171 869	75 277	96 592	227 681	110 376	117 305
70 - 74	325 230	143 466	181 764	146 702	57 100	89 602	178 528	86 366	92 162
75 - 79	185 449	67 568	117 881	87 515	27 439	60 076	97 934	40 129	57 805
80 - 84	78 794	23 459	55 335	39 138	10 729	28 409	39 656	12 730	26 926
85 - 89	41 343	10 761	30 582	20 793	4 904	15 889	20 550	5 857	14 693
90 - 94	19 195	6 220	12 975	9 150	2 774	6 376	10 045	3 446	6 599

Continent, country or area, date, code and age (in years) / Continent, pays ou zone, date, code et âge (en années)	Total			Urban - Urbaine			Rural - Rurale		
	Both sexes Les deux sexes	Male Masculin	Female Féminin	Both sexes Les deux sexes	Male Masculin	Female Féminin	Both sexes Les deux sexes	Male Masculin	Female Féminin
ASIA - ASIE									
Uzbekistan - Ouzbékistan									
1 VII 2001 (ESDF)									
95 - 99	10 114	4 171	5 943	4 954	1 461	3 493	5 160	2 710	2 450
100 + ...	900	366	534	535	171	364	365	195	170
1 VII 2003 (ESDF)[9]									
Total......................	25 567 663	12 809 713	12 757 950	...	...	...	...	...	...
0 - 4......................	2 584 779	1 257 871	1 326 908	...	...	...	...	...	...
5 - 9......................	3 057 832	1 492 224	1 565 608	...	...	...	...	...	...
10 - 14....................	3 247 432	1 593 319	1 654 113	...	...	...	...	...	...
15 - 19....................	3 036 011	1 502 977	1 533 033	...	...	...	...	...	...
20 - 24....................	2 440 283	1 210 643	1 229 640	...	...	...	...	...	...
25 - 29....................	2 077 200	1 032 960	1 044 240	...	...	...	...	...	...
30 - 34....................	1 852 315	929 765	922 550	...	...	...	...	...	...
35 - 39....................	1 654 410	848 383	806 026	...	...	...	...	...	...
40 - 44....................	1 586 930	807 669	779 261	...	...	...	...	...	...
45 - 49....................	1 170 247	595 727	574 520	...	...	...	...	...	...
50 - 54....................	821 154	423 337	397 817	...	...	...	...	...	...
55 - 59....................	426 436	218 173	208 263	...	...	...	...	...	...
60 - 64....................	499 732	256 051	243 680	...	...	...	...	...	...
65 - 69....................	416 696	220 394	196 302	...	...	...	...	...	...
70 - 74....................	324 533	182 720	141 812	...	...	...	...	...	...
75 +......................	371 669	237 497	134 172	...	...	...	...	...	...
Viet Nam									
1 IV 1999 (CDFC)									
Total......................	76 323 173	37 469 117	38 854 056	18 076 823	8 825 112	9 251 711	58 246 350	28 644 005	29 602 345
0	1 263 599	647 832	615 767	232 977	120 215	112 762	1 030 622	527 617	503 005
1 - 4......................	5 908 643	3 034 911	2 873 732	1 184 870	611 659	573 211	4 723 773	2 423 252	2 300 521
5 - 9......................	9 033 162	4 634 400	4 398 762	1 746 284	899 731	846 553	7 286 878	3 734 669	3 552 209
10 - 14....................	9 066 562	4 654 315	4 412 247	1 775 015	913 513	861 502	7 291 547	3 740 802	3 550 745
15 - 19....................	8 222 280	4 141 058	4 081 222	1 902 373	944 176	958 197	6 319 907	3 196 882	3 123 025
20 - 24....................	6 925 387	3 430 084	3 495 303	1 787 592	869 997	917 595	5 137 795	2 560 087	2 577 708
25 - 29....................	6 568 174	3 281 300	3 286 874	1 730 659	845 461	885 198	4 837 515	2 435 839	2 401 676
30 - 34....................	6 033 706	3 003 421	3 030 285	1 582 568	776 373	806 195	4 451 138	2 227 048	2 224 090
35 - 39....................	5 586 620	2 726 540	2 860 080	1 547 320	759 866	787 454	4 039 300	1 966 674	2 072 626
40 - 44....................	4 550 060	2 180 363	2 369 697	1 317 660	641 149	676 511	3 232 400	1 539 214	1 693 186
45 - 49....................	3 137 258	1 465 289	1 671 969	872 584	405 712	466 872	2 264 674	1 059 577	1 205 097
50 - 54....................	2 104 316	964 240	1 140 076	571 834	259 517	312 317	1 532 482	704 723	827 759
55 - 59....................	1 787 007	782 143	1 004 864	463 473	209 785	253 688	1 323 534	572 358	751 176
60 - 64....................	1 747 308	759 708	987 600	409 484	179 982	229 502	1 337 824	579 726	758 098
65 - 69....................	1 646 775	725 600	921 175	367 000	164 733	202 267	1 279 775	560 867	718 908
70 - 74....................	1 211 104	500 522	710 582	262 578	111 897	150 681	948 526	388 625	559 901
75 - 79....................	821 749	307 069	514 680	170 797	63 805	106 992	650 952	243 264	407 688
80 - 84....................	418 244	144 203	274 041	89 323	30 036	59 287	328 921	114 167	214 754
85 +......................	291 219	86 119	205 100	62 432	17 505	44 927	228 787	68 614	160 173
Yemen - Yémen									
31 XII 2007 (ESDF)									
Total......................	21 538 995	10 551 463	10 987 532	...	...	...	...	...	...
0 - 4......................	3 214 848	1 571 365	1 643 483	...	...	...	...	...	...
5 - 9......................	3 342 236	1 626 640	1 715 596	...	...	...	...	...	...
10 - 14....................	3 138 981	1 482 165	1 656 816	...	...	...	...	...	...
15 - 19....................	2 709 342	1 324 632	1 384 710	...	...	...	...	...	...
20 - 24....................	2 069 808	1 012 321	1 057 487	...	...	...	...	...	...
25 - 29....................	1 609 588	810 850	798 738	...	...	...	...	...	...
30 - 34....................	1 058 035	524 368	533 667	...	...	...	...	...	...
35 - 39....................	993 236	521 941	471 295	...	...	...	...	...	...
40 - 44....................	796 335	407 965	388 370	...	...	...	...	...	...
45 - 49....................	639 759	329 288	310 471	...	...	...	...	...	...
50 - 54....................	545 804	266 941	278 863	...	...	...	...	...	...
55 - 59....................	314 541	150 219	164 322	...	...	...	...	...	...
60 - 64....................	355 195	168 650	186 545	...	...	...	...	...	...
65 - 69....................	200 326	94 621	105 705	...	...	...	...	...	...
70 - 74....................	239 210	114 259	124 951	...	...	...	...	...	...
75 - 79....................	102 931	47 167	55 764	...	...	...	...	...	...
80 - 84....................	109 209	52 740	56 469	...	...	...	...	...	...

Continent, country or area, date, code and age (in years) / Continent, pays ou zone, date, code et âge (en années)	Total			Urban - Urbaine			Rural - Rurale		
	Both sexes Les deux sexes	Male Masculin	Female Féminin	Both sexes Les deux sexes	Male Masculin	Female Féminin	Both sexes Les deux sexes	Male Masculin	Female Féminin
ASIA - ASIE									
Yemen - Yémen									
31 XII 2007 (ESDF)									
85 +	86 202	39 951	46 251	...	...	...	...	...	...
Unknown - Inconnu	13 409	5 380	8 029	...	...	...	...	...	...
EUROPE									
Åland Islands - Îles d'Åland[48]									
1 VII 2007 (ESDJ)									
Total	27 038	13 407	13 631	10 863	5 151	5 712	16 175	8 256	7 919
0 - 4	1 436	748	688	497	252	245	940	497	443
5 - 9	1 509	795	715	527	278	249	982	517	466
10 - 14	1 686	844	842	600	296	304	1 086	549	538
15 - 19	1 717	903	815	655	334	321	1 063	569	494
20 - 24	1 263	662	602	676	329	347	588	333	255
25 - 29	1 502	781	722	793	404	390	709	377	332
30 - 34	1 666	861	805	727	377	350	939	484	455
35 - 39	1 843	914	930	708	336	373	1 135	578	557
40 - 44	2 019	1 009	1 010	746	361	385	1 274	648	626
45 - 49	1 876	931	945	692	323	369	1 184	608	576
50 - 54	2 013	970	1 043	826	379	447	1 187	591	596
55 - 59	2 030	1 000	1 031	828	374	454	1 202	626	577
60 - 64	1 860	945	916	753	360	393	1 107	585	523
65 - 69	1 314	692	622	487	240	247	827	452	375
70 - 74	1 055	501	555	415	181	235	640	320	320
75 - 79	851	385	466	331	140	191	521	246	275
80 - 84	742	288	455	309	113	196	434	175	259
85 - 89	420	122	298	196	58	138	225	65	160
90 - 94	176	53	124	81	18	63	96	35	61
95 - 99	59	9	51	21	3	18	39	6	33
100 +	4	-	4	1	-	1	3	-	3
Albania - Albanie									
1 VII 2007 (ESDF)									
Total	3 161 337	1 587 496	1 573 841	...	...	...	...	...	...
0 - 4	235 302	123 046	112 256	...	...	...	...	...	...
5 - 9	253 793	132 777	121 016	...	...	...	...	...	...
10 - 14	286 308	147 958	138 350	...	...	...	...	...	...
15 - 19	313 936	161 708	152 228	...	...	...	...	...	...
20 - 24	295 727	147 905	147 822	...	...	...	...	...	...
25 - 29	235 258	113 683	121 575	...	...	...	...	...	...
30 - 34	206 086	98 976	107 110	...	...	...	...	...	...
35 - 39	209 124	101 371	107 753	...	...	...	...	...	...
40 - 44	206 518	102 083	104 435	...	...	...	...	...	...
45 - 49	211 488	107 301	104 187	...	...	...	...	...	...
50 - 54	173 514	88 893	84 621	...	...	...	...	...	...
55 - 59	141 043	72 321	68 722	...	...	...	...	...	...
60 - 64	109 574	56 104	53 470	...	...	...	...	...	...
65 - 69	105 484	52 256	53 228	...	...	...	...	...	...
70 - 74	80 010	40 034	39 976	...	...	...	...	...	...
75 - 79	53 319	24 567	28 752	...	...	...	...	...	...
80 - 84	27 870	10 696	17 174	...	...	...	...	...	...
85 - 89	13 478	4 789	8 689	...	...	...	...	...	...
90 - 94	3 013	907	2 106	...	...	...	...	...	...
95 +	492	121	371	...	...	...	...	...	...
Andorra - Andorre[12]									
31 XII 2007 (ESDF)									
Total	83 137	43 515	39 622	...	...	...	...	...	...
0 - 4	3 770	1 985	1 785	...	...	...	...	...	...
5 - 9	4 418	2 285	2 133	...	...	...	...	...	...
10 - 14	3 967	2 138	1 829	...	...	...	...	...	...
15 - 19	3 924	2 028	1 896	...	...	...	...	...	...
20 - 24	4 790	2 479	2 311	...	...	...	...	...	...
25 - 29	7 029	3 622	3 407	...	...	...	...	...	...
30 - 34	8 181	4 195	3 986	...	...	...	...	...	...

7. Population by age, sex and urban/rural residence: latest available year, 1998 - 2007
Population selon l'âge, le sexe et la résidence, urbaine/rurale: dernière année disponible, 1998 - 2007 (continued - suite)

Continent, country or area, date, code and age (in years) / Continent, pays ou zone, date, code et âge (en années)	Total			Urban - Urbaine			Rural - Rurale		
	Both sexes Les deux sexes	Male Masculin	Female Féminin	Both sexes Les deux sexes	Male Masculin	Female Féminin	Both sexes Les deux sexes	Male Masculin	Female Féminin
EUROPE									
Andorra - Andorre[12]									
31 XII 2007 (ESDF)				...	...	...	...	...	...
35 - 39	8 140	4 200	3 940	...	...	...	...	...	...
40 - 44	7 889	4 196	3 693	...	...	...	...	...	...
45 - 49	6 944	3 715	3 229	...	...	...	...	...	...
50 - 54	5 714	3 126	2 588	...	...	...	...	...	...
55 - 59	4 658	2 566	2 092	...	...	...	...	...	...
60 - 64	3 775	2 069	1 706	...	...	...	...	...	...
65 - 69	2 555	1 302	1 253	...	...	...	...	...	...
70 - 74	2 243	1 183	1 060	...	...	...	...	...	...
75 - 79	1 997	983	1 014	...	...	...	...	...	...
80 - 84	1 480	701	779	...	...	...	...	...	...
85 - 89	909	403	506	...	...	...	...	...	...
90 - 94	399	171	228	...	...	...	...	...	...
95 +	355	168	187	...	...	...	...	...	...
Austria - Autriche									
15 V 2001 (CDJC)									
Total	8 032 926	3 889 189	4 143 737	5 368 693	2 564 828	2 803 865	2 664 233	1 324 361	1 339 872
0	77 060	39 641	37 419	50 942	26 172	24 770	26 118	13 469	12 649
1 - 4	332 964	170 439	162 525	215 492	110 553	104 939	117 472	59 886	57 586
5 - 9	469 735	240 593	229 142	296 471	151 887	144 584	173 264	88 706	84 558
10 - 14	473 723	242 791	230 932	294 674	151 245	143 429	179 049	91 546	87 503
15 - 19	483 957	247 452	236 505	300 985	153 733	147 252	182 972	93 719	89 253
20 - 24	472 777	240 171	232 606	309 267	154 636	154 631	163 510	85 535	77 975
25 - 29	539 031	268 179	270 852	364 619	178 639	185 980	174 412	89 540	84 872
30 - 34	668 281	337 121	331 160	456 030	227 926	228 104	212 251	109 195	103 056
35 - 39	704 872	358 748	346 124	473 632	239 432	234 200	231 240	119 316	111 924
40 - 44	625 783	316 280	309 503	416 601	207 478	209 123	209 182	108 802	100 380
45 - 49	525 207	261 903	263 304	352 245	172 161	180 084	172 962	89 742	83 220
50 - 54	514 535	255 906	258 629	356 937	174 415	182 522	157 598	81 491	76 107
55 - 59	452 265	220 827	231 438	326 907	157 892	169 015	125 358	62 935	62 423
60 - 64	451 057	217 191	233 866	305 628	145 952	159 676	145 429	71 239	74 190
65 - 69	332 596	152 844	179 752	215 372	97 381	117 991	117 224	55 463	61 761
70 - 74	327 321	140 193	187 128	217 723	90 939	126 784	109 598	49 254	60 344
75 - 79	290 140	97 886	192 254	202 551	66 803	135 748	87 589	31 083	56 506
80 - 84	151 242	45 800	105 442	108 554	32 170	76 384	42 688	13 630	29 058
85 - 89	96 166	25 556	70 610	70 458	18 358	52 100	25 708	7 198	18 510
90 - 94	37 255	8 413	28 842	28 193	6 138	22 055	9 062	2 275	6 787
95 +	6 959	1 255	5 704	5 412	918	4 494	1 547	337	1 210
1 VII 2007 (ESDJ)									
Total	8 315 379	4 046 289	4 269 090	...	...	...	...	...	...
0	76 900	39 165	37 735	...	...	...	...	...	...
1 - 4	321 370	164 712	156 658	...	...	...	...	...	...
5 - 9	413 672	212 286	201 386	...	...	...	...	...	...
10 - 14	474 214	242 953	231 261	...	...	...	...	...	...
15 - 19	498 111	255 251	242 860	...	...	...	...	...	...
20 - 24	522 809	263 991	258 818	...	...	...	...	...	...
25 - 29	536 268	270 481	265 787	...	...	...	...	...	...
30 - 34	551 441	274 914	276 527	...	...	...	...	...	...
35 - 39	665 233	334 139	331 094	...	...	...	...	...	...
40 - 44	716 446	362 934	353 512	...	...	...	...	...	...
45 - 49	650 291	328 209	322 082	...	...	...	...	...	...
50 - 54	543 080	268 839	274 241	...	...	...	...	...	...
55 - 59	496 120	243 273	252 847	...	...	...	...	...	...
60 - 64	433 325	208 400	224 925	...	...	...	...	...	...
65 - 69	460 558	217 012	243 546	...	...	...	...	...	...
70 - 74	298 930	133 295	165 635	...	...	...	...	...	...
75 - 79	278 558	114 914	163 644	...	...	...	...	...	...
80 - 84	220 197	70 910	149 287	...	...	...	...	...	...
85 - 89	111 630	30 341	81 289	...	...	...	...	...	...
90 - 94	35 639	8 191	27 448	...	...	...	...	...	...
95 +	10 587	2 079	8 508	...	...	...	...	...	...

7. Population by age, sex and urban/rural residence: latest available year, 1998 - 2007
Population selon l'âge, le sexe et la résidence, urbaine/rurale: dernière année disponible, 1998 - 2007 (continued - suite)

Continent, country or area, date, code and age (in years) / Continent, pays ou zone, date, code et âge (en années)	Total			Urban - Urbaine			Rural - Rurale		
	Both sexes Les deux sexes	Male Masculin	Female Féminin	Both sexes Les deux sexes	Male Masculin	Female Féminin	Both sexes Les deux sexes	Male Masculin	Female Féminin
EUROPE									
Belarus - Bélarus									
1 VII 2007 (ESDF)									
Total	9 702 116	4 528 222	5 173 894	7 091 407	3 302 285	3 789 122	2 610 709	1 225 937	1 384 772
0	99 725	51 368	48 357	74 102	38 248	35 854	25 623	13 120	12 503
1 - 4	357 935	183 783	174 152	265 995	136 672	129 323	91 940	47 111	44 829
5 - 9	454 291	233 702	220 589	331 263	170 540	160 723	123 028	63 162	59 866
10 - 14	520 729	267 229	253 500	364 169	186 989	177 180	156 560	80 240	76 320
15 - 19	731 113	374 674	356 439	558 670	282 406	276 264	172 443	92 268	80 175
20 - 24	838 496	426 771	411 725	660 657	331 467	329 190	177 839	95 304	82 535
25 - 29	747 409	380 494	366 915	611 519	309 567	301 952	135 890	70 927	64 963
30 - 34	687 191	342 625	344 566	536 750	264 548	272 202	150 441	78 077	72 364
35 - 39	671 848	330 055	341 793	504 864	242 465	262 399	166 984	87 590	79 394
40 - 44	722 587	351 262	371 325	540 679	254 044	286 635	181 908	97 218	84 690
45 - 49	820 728	392 554	428 174	619 928	284 698	335 230	200 800	107 856	92 944
50 - 54	702 435	325 539	376 896	537 087	239 589	297 498	165 348	85 950	79 398
55 - 59	593 161	265 947	327 214	452 106	196 698	255 408	141 055	69 249	71 806
60 - 64	343 259	144 447	198 812	242 390	102 077	140 313	100 869	42 370	58 499
65 - 69	447 664	168 896	278 768	287 169	109 440	177 729	160 495	59 456	101 039
70 - 74	381 428	131 229	250 199	208 341	72 165	136 176	173 087	59 064	114 023
75 - 79	319 353	98 634	220 719	158 640	48 723	109 917	160 713	49 911	110 802
80 - 84	183 790	43 615	140 175	93 864	23 295	70 569	89 926	20 320	69 606
85 +	78 974	15 398	63 576	43 214	8 654	34 560	35 760	6 744	29 016
Belgium - Belgique									
1 I 2006 (ESDJ)									
Total	10 511 382	5 143 821	5 367 561	...	...	...	...	...	...
0	118 366	60 747	57 619	...	...	...	...	...	...
1 - 4	462 002	236 121	225 881	...	...	...	...	...	...
5 - 9	592 003	302 269	289 734	...	...	...	...	...	...
10 - 14	623 731	319 008	304 723	...	...	...	...	...	...
15 - 19	632 604	323 106	309 498	...	...	...	...	...	...
20 - 24	637 168	320 284	316 884	...	...	...	...	...	...
25 - 29	667 765	335 194	332 571	...	...	...	...	...	...
30 - 34	703 395	354 866	348 529	...	...	...	...	...	...
35 - 39	766 820	388 525	378 295	...	...	...	...	...	...
40 - 44	818 710	413 953	404 757	...	...	...	...	...	...
45 - 49	782 371	393 789	388 582	...	...	...	...	...	...
50 - 54	714 021	357 987	356 034	...	...	...	...	...	...
55 - 59	675 073	336 999	338 074	...	...	...	...	...	...
60 - 64	508 336	248 736	259 600	...	...	...	...	...	...
65 - 69	487 826	230 477	257 349	...	...	...	...	...	...
70 - 74	462 644	207 712	254 932	...	...	...	...	...	...
75 - 79	392 695	161 235	231 460	...	...	...	...	...	...
80 - 84	286 129	103 843	182 286	...	...	...	...	...	...
85 - 89	115 585	35 057	80 528	...	...	...	...	...	...
90 - 94	51 424	11 898	39 526	...	...	...	...	...	...
95 - 99	11 416	1 865	9 551	...	...	...	...	...	...
100 +	1 298	150	1 148	...	...	...	...	...	...
Bulgaria - Bulgarie									
1 VII 2007 (ESDF)									
Total	7 659 764	3 710 315	3 949 449	5 414 260	2 604 175	2 810 085	2 245 504	1 106 140	1 139 364
0	71 023	36 606	34 417	53 031	27 347	25 684	17 992	9 259	8 733
1 - 4	276 267	142 089	134 178	202 203	103 916	98 287	74 064	38 173	35 891
5 - 9	325 387	167 205	158 182	230 443	118 379	112 064	94 944	48 826	46 118
10 - 14	354 995	182 039	172 956	247 323	126 811	120 512	107 672	55 228	52 444
15 - 19	481 521	247 033	234 488	348 230	177 521	170 709	133 291	69 512	63 779
20 - 24	530 159	271 591	258 568	413 706	209 977	203 729	116 453	61 614	54 839
25 - 29	561 424	287 771	273 653	434 496	219 330	215 166	126 928	68 441	58 487
30 - 34	580 078	295 522	284 556	445 655	224 795	220 860	134 423	70 727	63 696
35 - 39	550 054	278 957	271 097	413 366	205 913	207 453	136 688	73 044	63 644
40 - 44	506 009	253 823	252 186	376 617	184 489	192 128	129 392	69 334	60 058
45 - 49	532 703	263 927	268 776	397 187	191 640	205 547	135 516	72 287	63 229
50 - 54	544 286	264 294	279 992	402 215	190 697	211 518	142 071	73 597	68 474
55 - 59	551 207	260 512	290 695	393 864	183 165	210 699	157 343	77 347	79 996
60 - 64	470 692	215 356	255 336	308 802	141 313	167 489	161 890	74 043	87 847
65 - 69	387 131	169 837	217 294	227 151	98 830	128 321	159 980	71 007	88 973

7. Population by age, sex and urban/rural residence: latest available year, 1998 - 2007
Population selon l'âge, le sexe et la résidence, urbaine/rurale: dernière année disponible, 1998 - 2007 (continued - suite)

Continent, country or area, date, code and age (in years) / Continent, pays ou zone, date, code et âge (en années)	Total			Urban - Urbaine			Rural - Rurale		
	Both sexes Les deux sexes	Male Masculin	Female Féminin	Both sexes Les deux sexes	Male Masculin	Female Féminin	Both sexes Les deux sexes	Male Masculin	Female Féminin
EUROPE									
Bulgaria - Bulgarie									
1 VII 2007 (ESDF)									
70 - 74	376 864	158 528	218 336	209 259	84 948	124 311	167 605	73 580	94 025
75 - 79	290 323	116 685	173 638	162 416	62 772	99 644	127 907	53 913	73 994
80 - 84	184 981	68 991	115 990	102 019	36 730	65 289	82 962	32 261	50 701
85 - 89	67 413	23 802	43 611	37 016	12 635	24 381	30 397	11 167	19 230
90 - 94	14 035	4 693	9 342	7 597	2 435	5 162	6 438	2 258	4 180
95 - 99	2 931	968	1 963	1 531	491	1 040	1 400	477	923
100 +	281	86	195	133	41	92	148	45	103
Croatia - Croatie									
31 III 2001 (CDJC)									
Total	4 437 460	2 135 900	2 301 560	2 471 328	1 171 950	1 299 378	1 966 132	963 950	1 002 182
0	42 942	22 097	20 845	23 438	12 112	11 326	19 504	9 985	9 519
1 - 4	194 580	99 621	94 959	104 707	53 579	51 128	89 873	46 042	43 831
5 - 9	248 528	127 274	121 254	134 027	68 669	65 358	114 501	58 605	55 896
10 - 14	268 584	137 175	131 409	144 935	74 118	70 817	123 649	63 057	60 592
15 - 19	298 606	152 676	145 930	165 511	84 240	81 271	133 095	68 436	64 659
20 - 24	305 631	155 739	149 892	176 487	88 565	87 922	129 144	67 174	61 970
25 - 29	294 497	148 666	145 831	171 776	84 620	87 156	122 721	64 046	58 675
30 - 34	295 431	147 920	147 511	169 076	82 749	86 327	126 355	65 171	61 184
35 - 39	317 273	158 506	158 767	177 369	85 563	91 806	139 904	72 943	66 961
40 - 44	333 403	166 499	166 904	189 206	89 569	99 637	144 197	76 930	67 267
45 - 49	333 576	168 290	165 286	195 040	93 697	101 343	138 536	74 593	63 943
50 - 54	299 773	148 224	151 549	178 220	84 433	93 787	121 553	63 791	57 762
55 - 59	229 775	108 673	121 102	134 170	61 988	72 182	95 605	46 685	48 920
60 - 64	262 016	120 667	141 349	142 207	65 853	76 354	119 809	54 814	64 995
65 - 69	252 947	110 459	142 488	131 008	58 413	72 595	121 939	52 046	69 893
70 - 74	203 885	81 884	122 001	102 578	41 358	61 220	101 307	40 526	60 781
75 - 79	137 201	44 149	93 052	69 924	22 818	47 106	67 277	21 331	45 946
80 - 84	56 954	17 040	39 914	29 302	8 963	20 339	27 652	8 077	19 575
85 - 89	30 833	8 682	22 151	16 108	4 575	11 533	14 725	4 107	10 618
90 - 94	10 265	2 571	7 694	5 386	1 310	4 076	4 879	1 261	3 618
95 - 99	1 371	302	1 069	753	153	600	618	149	469
100 +	84	21	63	54	16	38	30	5	25
Unknown - Inconnu	19 305	8 765	10 540	10 046	4 589	5 457	9 259	4 176	5 083
1 VII 2007 (ESDJ)									
Total	4 435 982	2 137 984	2 297 998	...	...	...	...	...	...
0	40 812	21 036	19 776	...	...	...	...	...	...
1 - 4	164 315	84 454	79 861	...	...	...	...	...	...
5 - 9	229 007	117 287	111 720	...	...	...	...	...	...
10 - 14	255 254	130 493	124 761	...	...	...	...	...	...
15 - 19	267 726	136 855	130 871	...	...	...	...	...	...
20 - 24	298 732	152 470	146 262	...	...	...	...	...	...
25 - 29	314 711	159 956	154 755	...	...	...	...	...	...
30 - 34	301 351	152 152	149 199	...	...	...	...	...	...
35 - 39	295 101	148 042	147 059	...	...	...	...	...	...
40 - 44	317 532	158 407	159 125	...	...	...	...	...	...
45 - 49	330 182	163 761	166 421	...	...	...	...	...	...
50 - 54	337 507	167 468	170 039	...	...	...	...	...	...
55 - 59	297 201	145 087	152 114	...	...	...	...	...	...
60 - 64	223 918	103 765	120 153	...	...	...	...	...	...
65 - 69	236 926	104 800	132 126	...	...	...	...	...	...
70 - 74	219 448	90 287	129 161	...	...	...	...	...	...
75 - 79	165 427	61 627	103 800	...	...	...	...	...	...
80 - 84	94 625	28 315	66 310	...	...	...	...	...	...
85 +	46 207	11 722	34 485	...	...	...	...	...	...
Czech Republic - République tchèque									
31 XII 2007 (ESDJ)									
Total	10 381 130	5 082 934	5 298 196	7 643 756	3 714 094	3 929 662	2 737 374	1 368 840	1 368 534
0	114 410	58 331	56 079	84 205	42 814	41 391	30 205	15 517	14 688
1 - 4	401 835	206 602	195 233	292 342	150 635	141 707	109 493	55 967	53 526
5 - 9	454 698	233 886	220 812	325 750	167 350	158 400	128 948	66 536	62 412
10 - 14	505 980	259 486	246 494	359 089	183 609	175 480	146 891	75 877	71 014
15 - 19	646 427	331 037	315 390	468 796	239 535	229 261	177 631	91 502	86 129

7. Population by age, sex and urban/rural residence: latest available year, 1998 - 2007
Population selon l'âge, le sexe et la résidence, urbaine/rurale: dernière année disponible, 1998 - 2007 (continued - suite)

Continent, country or area, date, code and age (in years) Continent, pays ou zone, date, code et âge (en annèes)	Total			Urban - Urbaine			Rural - Rurale		
	Both sexes Les deux sexes	Male Masculin	Female Féminin	Both sexes Les deux sexes	Male Masculin	Female Féminin	Both sexes Les deux sexes	Male Masculin	Female Féminin
EUROPE									
Czech Republic - République tchèque									
31 XII 2007 (ESDJ)									
20 - 24	699 734	361 040	338 694	516 949	266 843	250 106	182 785	94 197	88 588
25 - 29	808 152	415 373	392 779	602 422	308 994	293 428	205 730	106 379	99 351
30 - 34	933 399	478 255	455 144	689 680	351 450	338 230	243 719	126 805	116 914
35 - 39	743 224	381 515	361 709	546 791	277 823	268 968	196 433	103 692	92 741
40 - 44	712 886	364 627	348 259	529 222	267 507	261 715	183 664	97 120	86 544
45 - 49	641 799	324 914	316 885	472 417	236 091	236 326	169 382	88 823	80 559
50 - 54	751 234	373 028	378 206	553 578	270 459	283 119	197 656	102 569	95 087
55 - 59	770 281	374 358	395 923	567 509	271 499	296 010	202 772	102 859	99 913
60 - 64	684 237	322 001	362 236	512 380	237 154	275 226	171 857	84 847	87 010
65 - 69	473 794	213 332	260 462	354 147	158 139	196 008	119 647	55 193	64 454
70 - 74	362 952	152 247	210 705	268 206	112 076	156 130	94 746	40 171	54 575
75 - 79	327 542	125 281	202 261	241 996	92 444	149 552	85 546	32 837	52 709
80 - 84	223 609	73 516	150 093	165 941	54 629	111 312	57 668	18 887	38 781
85 - 89	96 575	27 446	69 129	71 760	20 327	51 433	24 815	7 119	17 696
90 - 94	21 891	5 277	16 614	16 045	3 780	12 265	5 846	1 497	4 349
95 - 99	5 927	1 262	4 665	4 188	867	3 321	1 739	395	1 344
100 +	544	120	424	343	69	274	201	51	150
Denmark - Danemark[49]									
1 VII 2007 (ESDJ)									
Total	5 457 415	2 702 894	2 754 521	...	...	...	...	...	...
0	64 408	33 110	31 298	...	...	...	...	...	...
1 - 4	260 006	133 064	126 942	...	...	...	...	...	...
5 - 9	333 694	170 638	163 056	...	...	...	...	...	...
10 - 14	352 798	181 026	171 772	...	...	...	...	...	...
15 - 19	327 933	168 414	159 519	...	...	...	...	...	...
20 - 24	297 843	151 640	146 203	...	...	...	...	...	...
25 - 29	321 345	161 115	160 230	...	...	...	...	...	...
30 - 34	371 319	186 131	185 188	...	...	...	...	...	...
35 - 39	388 442	196 788	191 654	...	...	...	...	...	...
40 - 44	427 204	217 326	209 878	...	...	...	...	...	...
45 - 49	377 079	190 700	186 379	...	...	...	...	...	...
50 - 54	362 337	182 176	180 161	...	...	...	...	...	...
55 - 59	358 460	179 255	179 205	...	...	...	...	...	...
60 - 64	370 957	184 861	186 096	...	...	...	...	...	...
65 - 69	260 093	126 427	133 666	...	...	...	...	...	...
70 - 74	201 334	93 914	107 420	...	...	...	...	...	...
75 - 79	157 138	68 627	88 511	...	...	...	...	...	...
80 - 84	118 463	45 887	72 576	...	...	...	...	...	...
85 - 89	71 015	23 077	47 938	...	...	...	...	...	...
90 - 94	28 006	7 276	20 730	...	...	...	...	...	...
95 - 99	6 826	1 342	5 484	...	...	...	...	...	...
100 +	715	100	615	...	...	...	...	...	...
Estonia - Estonie									
1 VII 2007 (ESDF)									
Total	1 341 672	617 828	723 844	931 163	418 873	512 290	410 509	198 955	211 554
0	15 269	7 895	7 374	10 790	5 607	5 183	4 479	2 288	2 191
1 - 4	54 939	28 255	26 684	38 606	19 840	18 766	16 333	8 415	7 918
5 - 9	61 654	31 814	29 840	41 481	21 414	20 067	20 173	10 400	9 773
10 - 14	67 362	34 536	32 826	42 580	21 825	20 755	24 782	12 711	12 071
15 - 19	99 902	51 218	48 684	64 224	32 888	31 336	35 678	18 330	17 348
20 - 24	105 493	53 588	51 905	70 447	35 672	34 775	35 046	17 916	17 130
25 - 29	96 703	49 113	47 590	71 683	35 060	36 623	25 020	14 053	10 967
30 - 34	92 398	46 192	46 206	68 982	33 591	35 391	23 416	12 601	10 815
35 - 39	91 981	45 146	46 835	65 189	31 440	33 749	26 792	13 706	13 086
40 - 44	88 531	42 568	45 963	61 260	28 702	32 558	27 271	13 866	13 405
45 - 49	96 516	45 260	51 256	67 223	30 254	36 969	29 293	15 006	14 287
50 - 54	91 674	41 721	49 953	65 079	28 342	36 737	26 595	13 379	13 216
55 - 59	85 563	37 571	47 992	60 780	25 531	35 249	24 783	12 040	12 743
60 - 64	63 682	26 732	36 950	43 388	17 388	26 000	20 294	9 344	10 950
65 - 69	73 073	28 367	44 706	51 074	19 031	32 043	21 999	9 336	12 663
70 - 74	59 066	21 026	38 040	40 664	14 019	26 645	18 402	7 007	11 395
75 - 79	49 754	15 711	34 043	34 991	10 807	24 184	14 763	4 904	9 859

Continent, country or area, date, code and age (in years) / Continent, pays ou zone, date, code et âge (en annèes)	Total			Urban - Urbaine			Rural - Rurale		
	Both sexes Les deux sexes	Male Masculin	Female Féminin	Both sexes Les deux sexes	Male Masculin	Female Féminin	Both sexes Les deux sexes	Male Masculin	Female Féminin
EUROPE									
Estonia - Estonie									
1 VII 2007 (ESDF)									
80 - 84	30 657	7 544	23 113	21 297	5 170	16 127	9 360	2 374	6 986
85 - 89	11 819	2 469	9 350	7 896	1 658	6 238	3 923	811	3 112
90 - 94	4 107	779	3 328	2 612	457	2 155	1 495	322	1 173
95 - 99	1 160	207	953	675	109	566	485	98	387
100 +	177	30	147	87	14	73	90	16	74
Unknown - Inconnu	192	86	106	155	54	101	37	32	5
Faeroe Islands - Îles Féroé									
1 VII 2007 (ESDJ)									
Total	48 278	25 090	23 188	...	...	...	...	...	...
0	659	305	354	...	...	...	...	...	...
1 - 4	2 838	1 484	1 354	...	...	...	...	...	...
5 - 9	3 509	1 816	1 693	...	...	...	...	...	...
10 - 14	3 717	1 914	1 803	...	...	...	...	...	...
15 - 19	3 978	2 067	1 911	...	...	...	...	...	...
20 - 24	2 846	1 600	1 246	...	...	...	...	...	...
25 - 29	2 574	1 412	1 162	...	...	...	...	...	...
30 - 34	3 018	1 651	1 367	...	...	...	...	...	...
35 - 39	3 270	1 716	1 554	...	...	...	...	...	...
40 - 44	3 580	1 923	1 657	...	...	...	...	...	...
45 - 49	3 179	1 654	1 525	...	...	...	...	...	...
50 - 54	2 985	1 569	1 416	...	...	...	...	...	...
55 - 59	2 981	1 543	1 438	...	...	...	...	...	...
60 - 64	2 515	1 363	1 152	...	...	...	...	...	...
65 - 69	1 937	1 022	915	...	...	...	...	...	...
70 - 74	1 510	776	734	...	...	...	...	...	...
75 - 79	1 350	610	740	...	...	...	...	...	...
80 - 84	987	374	613	...	...	...	...	...	...
85 - 89	579	207	372	...	...	...	...	...	...
90 - 94	213	64	149	...	...	...	...	...	...
95 - 99	47	17	30	...	...	...	...	...	...
100 +	6	3	3	...	...	...	...	...	...
Finland - Finlande[50]									
1 VII 2007 (ESDJ)									
Total	5 288 720	2 590 265	2 698 455	3 431 735	1 656 013	1 775 722	1 856 985	934 252	922 733
0	58 852	30 087	28 765	40 034	20 457	19 578	18 818	9 631	9 187
1 - 4	231 026	117 948	113 078	151 725	77 492	74 234	79 301	40 457	38 845
5 - 9	287 734	147 060	140 675	180 975	92 423	88 552	106 760	54 637	52 123
10 - 14	320 274	163 223	157 052	198 944	101 319	97 626	121 330	61 904	59 426
15 - 19	328 634	167 799	160 835	208 201	104 101	104 100	120 433	63 698	56 735
20 - 24	329 635	168 602	161 033	246 910	122 104	124 806	82 726	46 499	36 227
25 - 29	332 825	170 374	162 451	252 252	127 932	124 321	80 573	42 443	38 130
30 - 34	319 770	164 254	155 516	230 208	118 296	111 912	89 562	45 959	43 604
35 - 39	330 260	168 275	161 986	225 029	114 283	110 746	105 231	53 992	51 240
40 - 44	374 801	190 284	184 518	246 905	123 887	123 018	127 896	66 397	61 500
45 - 49	374 842	188 973	185 869	238 195	118 006	120 189	136 647	70 967	65 681
50 - 54	389 725	194 874	194 851	243 058	117 583	125 476	146 667	77 292	69 375
55 - 59	406 920	202 810	204 110	253 077	121 492	131 585	153 843	81 318	72 525
60 - 64	331 451	162 361	169 091	208 239	98 807	109 432	123 212	63 554	59 659
65 - 69	256 161	120 381	135 781	154 446	70 121	84 325	101 715	50 260	51 456
70 - 74	207 672	92 411	115 261	121 155	51 765	69 390	86 517	40 646	45 871
75 - 79	183 139	73 431	109 708	104 933	40 090	64 843	78 206	33 341	44 865
80 - 84	128 985	43 369	85 616	72 706	23 146	49 560	56 279	20 223	36 056
85 - 89	66 337	17 635	48 702	37 617	9 462	28 155	28 721	8 173	20 548
90 - 94	24 070	5 160	18 910	13 881	2 751	11 130	10 189	2 410	7 780
95 - 99	5 178	900	4 278	3 000	466	2 535	2 178	435	1 743
100 +	434	58	376	249	35	214	186	23	163
France[51]									
1 VII 2006 (ESDJ)									
Total	61 352 572	29 814 775	31 537 797	...	...	...	...	...	...
0 - 4	3 842 363	1 964 230	1 878 133	...	...	...	...	...	...
5 - 9	3 755 290	1 922 521	1 832 769	...	...	...	...	...	...
10 - 14	3 672 769	1 880 577	1 792 192	...	...	...	...	...	...
15 - 19	3 919 043	1 999 228	1 919 815	...	...	...	...	...	...

Continent, country or area, date, code and age (in years) / Continent, pays ou zone, date, code et âge (en années)	Total			Urban - Urbaine			Rural - Rurale		
	Both sexes Les deux sexes	Male Masculin	Female Féminin	Both sexes Les deux sexes	Male Masculin	Female Féminin	Both sexes Les deux sexes	Male Masculin	Female Féminin
EUROPE									
France[51]									
1 VII 2006 (ESDJ)									
20 - 24	3 915 414	1 974 970	1 940 444	...	...	...	...	...	...
25 - 29	3 884 568	1 954 080	1 930 488	...	...	...	...	...	...
30 - 34	4 151 104	2 083 850	2 067 254	...	...	...	...	...	...
35 - 39	4 326 731	2 154 834	2 171 897	...	...	...	...	...	...
40 - 44	4 394 732	2 169 635	2 225 097	...	...	...	...	...	...
45 - 49	4 252 628	2 085 968	2 166 660	...	...	...	...	...	...
50 - 54	4 136 856	2 026 869	2 109 987	...	...	...	...	...	...
55 - 59	4 131 216	2 035 812	2 095 404	...	...	...	...	...	...
60 - 64	2 884 929	1 412 212	1 472 717	...	...	...	...	...	...
65 - 69	2 508 620	1 185 538	1 323 082	...	...	...	...	...	...
70 - 74	2 466 138	1 097 370	1 368 768	...	...	...	...	...	...
75 - 79	2 176 611	893 167	1 283 444	...	...	...	...	...	...
80 - 84	1 675 202	612 738	1 062 464	...	...	...	...	...	...
85 - 89	782 286	250 325	531 961	...	...	...	...	...	...
90 - 94	353 618	87 538	266 080	...	...	...	...	...	...
95 - 99	104 330	19 848	84 482	...	...	...	...	...	...
100 +	18 124	3 465	14 659	...	...	...	...	...	...
Germany - Allemagne									
1 VII 2007 (ESDJ)									
Total	82 266 372	40 287 729	41 978 643	...	...	...	...	...	...
0	679 314	348 957	330 357	...	...	...	...	...	...
1 - 4	2 807 282	1 440 169	1 367 113	...	...	...	...	...	...
5 - 9	3 851 558	1 975 248	1 876 311	...	...	...	...	...	...
10 - 14	4 023 378	2 064 506	1 958 872	...	...	...	...	...	...
15 - 19	4 702 664	2 410 500	2 292 165	...	...	...	...	...	...
20 - 24	4 851 885	2 464 986	2 386 900	...	...	...	...	...	...
25 - 29	4 947 929	2 504 274	2 443 655	...	...	...	...	...	...
30 - 34	4 747 000	2 408 497	2 338 503	...	...	...	...	...	...
35 - 39	6 218 677	3 178 363	3 040 314	...	...	...	...	...	...
40 - 44	7 194 199	3 688 837	3 505 362	...	...	...	...	...	...
45 - 49	6 619 775	3 365 882	3 253 893	...	...	...	...	...	...
50 - 54	5 747 019	2 883 611	2 863 408	...	...	...	...	...	...
55 - 59	5 189 241	2 577 901	2 611 340	...	...	...	...	...	...
60 - 64	4 277 437	2 102 234	2 175 203	...	...	...	...	...	...
65 - 69	5 391 600	2 583 009	2 808 591	...	...	...	...	...	...
70 - 74	4 095 329	1 872 865	2 222 464	...	...	...	...	...	...
75 - 79	3 056 099	1 275 672	1 780 427	...	...	...	...	...	...
80 - 84	2 178 644	710 156	1 468 488	...	...	...	...	...	...
85 - 89	1 136 782	301 044	835 738	...	...	...	...	...	...
90 - 94	381 321	84 737	296 584	...	...	...	...	...	...
95 +	169 242	46 285	122 957	...	...	...	...	...	...
Gibraltar[52]									
12 XI 2001 (CDFC)									
Total	27 495	13 644	13 851	...	...	...	...	...	...
0	143	74	69	...	...	...	...	...	...
1 - 4	1 315	693	622	...	...	...	...	...	...
5 - 9	1 773	932	841	...	...	...	...	...	...
10 - 14	1 831	956	875	...	...	...	...	...	...
15 - 19	1 801	917	884	...	...	...	...	...	...
20 - 24	1 764	912	852	...	...	...	...	...	...
25 - 29	1 770	867	903	...	...	...	...	...	...
30 - 34	1 916	959	957	...	...	...	...	...	...
35 - 39	2 044	1 008	1 036	...	...	...	...	...	...
40 - 44	1 995	987	1 008	...	...	...	...	...	...
45 - 49	1 904	988	916	...	...	...	...	...	...
50 - 54	1 944	1 056	888	...	...	...	...	...	...
55 - 59	1 610	844	766	...	...	...	...	...	...
60 - 64	1 379	691	688	...	...	...	...	...	...
65 - 69	1 247	611	636	...	...	...	...	...	...
70 - 74	1 037	477	560	...	...	...	...	...	...
75 - 79	895	329	566	...	...	...	...	...	...
80 - 84	605	186	419	...	...	...	...	...	...
85 - 89	306	100	206	...	...	...	...	...	...

Continent, country or area, date, code and age (in years) / Continent, pays ou zone, date, code et âge (en années)	Total			Urban - Urbaine			Rural - Rurale		
	Both sexes Les deux sexes	Male Masculin	Female Féminin	Both sexes Les deux sexes	Male Masculin	Female Féminin	Both sexes Les deux sexes	Male Masculin	Female Féminin
EUROPE									
Gibraltar[52]									
12 XI 2001 (CDFC)									
90 - 94	134	25	109	...	...	...	...	...	...
95 +	34	9	25	...	...	...	...	...	...
Unknown - Inconnu	48	23	25	...	...	...	...	...	...
Greece - Grèce[53]									
1 VII 2007 (ESDF)									
Total	11 192 849	5 543 018	5 649 831	...	...	...	...	...	...
0	111 873	57 798	54 075	...	...	...	...	...	...
1 - 4	427 385	220 471	206 914	...	...	...	...	...	...
5 - 9	513 228	264 417	248 811	...	...	...	...	...	...
10 - 14	546 198	280 679	265 519	...	...	...	...	...	...
15 - 19	586 550	304 053	282 497	...	...	...	...	...	...
20 - 24	685 570	356 860	328 710	...	...	...	...	...	...
25 - 29	828 024	431 688	396 336	...	...	...	...	...	...
30 - 34	868 937	448 605	420 332	...	...	...	...	...	...
35 - 39	883 053	451 164	431 889	...	...	...	...	...	...
40 - 44	830 515	417 608	412 907	...	...	...	...	...	...
45 - 49	794 674	394 923	399 751	...	...	...	...	...	...
50 - 54	738 452	365 305	373 147	...	...	...	...	...	...
55 - 59	679 712	332 394	347 318	...	...	...	...	...	...
60 - 64	616 461	295 227	321 234	...	...	...	...	...	...
65 - 69	574 200	261 366	312 834	...	...	...	...	...	...
70 - 74	585 196	260 590	324 606	...	...	...	...	...	...
75 - 79	476 409	208 489	267 920	...	...	...	...	...	...
80 - 84	285 877	120 763	165 114	...	...	...	...	...	...
85 - 89	121 773	51 937	69 836	...	...	...	...	...	...
90 - 94	28 227	13 301	14 926	...	...	...	...	...	...
95 - 99	7 902	4 589	3 313	...	...	...	...	...	...
100 +	2 633	791	1 842	...	...	...	...	...	...
Guernsey - Guernesey									
1 III 2006 (ESDF)									
Total	61 029	30 034	30 995	...	...	...	...	...	...
0 - 9	6 095	3 159	2 936	...	...	...	...	...	...
10 - 19	7 281	3 703	3 578	...	...	...	...	...	...
20 - 29	7 876	3 993	3 883	...	...	...	...	...	...
30 - 39	9 020	4 440	4 580	...	...	...	...	...	...
40 - 49	9 566	4 751	4 815	...	...	...	...	...	...
50 - 59	8 525	4 305	4 220	...	...	...	...	...	...
60 - 69	5 721	2 859	2 862	...	...	...	...	...	...
70 - 79	4 231	1 884	2 347	...	...	...	...	...	...
80 - 89	2 248	827	1 421	...	...	...	...	...	...
90 +	466	113	353	...	...	...	...	...	...
Hungary - Hongrie									
1 VII 2007 (ESDF)									
Total	10 055 780	4 774 320	5 281 460	6 737 792	3 156 954	3 580 839	3 317 988	1 617 367	1 700 621
0	97 567	49 946	47 621	65 575	33 636	31 939	31 993	16 310	15 683
1 - 4	385 283	198 088	187 196	254 117	130 434	123 683	131 167	67 654	63 513
5 - 9	482 944	247 525	235 419	304 279	155 925	148 354	178 665	91 600	87 065
10 - 14	553 434	283 639	269 795	345 153	176 475	168 678	208 282	107 164	101 118
15 - 19	621 743	317 976	303 767	409 703	207 014	202 689	212 041	110 963	101 078
20 - 24	657 889	334 301	323 588	443 918	222 824	221 094	213 971	111 477	102 494
25 - 29	772 395	395 014	377 382	545 092	273 870	271 222	227 304	121 144	106 160
30 - 34	835 545	425 043	410 503	584 701	293 823	290 878	250 845	131 220	119 625
35 - 39	719 982	364 759	355 224	486 126	243 708	242 418	233 857	121 051	112 806
40 - 44	617 118	308 117	309 001	404 048	198 122	205 926	213 070	109 995	103 075
45 - 49	644 028	313 193	330 835	416 340	196 582	219 758	227 688	116 611	111 077
50 - 54	796 412	378 727	417 686	535 520	246 638	288 883	260 892	132 089	128 803
55 - 59	689 053	317 635	371 419	468 193	210 312	257 881	220 861	107 323	113 538
60 - 64	567 881	250 943	316 939	393 360	171 806	221 554	174 522	79 137	95 385
65 - 69	493 349	202 416	290 933	331 119	135 670	195 449	162 230	66 746	95 484
70 - 74	412 325	156 539	255 786	271 833	103 749	168 084	140 492	52 791	87 702
75 - 79	341 075	120 319	220 756	227 050	80 987	146 064	114 025	39 332	74 693
80 - 84	226 814	70 503	156 311	152 750	47 433	105 318	74 064	23 071	50 994

Continent, country or area, date, code and age (in years) / Continent, pays ou zone, date, code et âge (en années)	Total			Urban - Urbaine			Rural - Rurale		
	Both sexes Les deux sexes	Male Masculin	Female Féminin	Both sexes Les deux sexes	Male Masculin	Female Féminin	Both sexes Les deux sexes	Male Masculin	Female Féminin
EUROPE									
Hungary - Hongrie									
1 VII 2007 (ESDF)									
85 - 89	102 539	29 133	73 407	71 072	20 374	50 698	31 468	8 759	22 709
90 +	38 406	10 510	27 897	27 850	7 577	20 273	10 556	2 933	7 624
Iceland - Islande[12]									
1 VII 2007 (ESDJ)									
Total	311 396	158 866	152 530	289 119	146 168	142 951	22 277	12 698	9 579
0	4 455	2 325	2 130	4 224	2 200	2 024	231	125	106
1 - 4	17 229	8 757	8 472	16 340	8 296	8 044	889	461	428
5 - 9	21 224	10 730	10 494	19 939	10 055	9 884	1 285	675	610
10 - 14	22 623	11 582	11 041	21 081	10 815	10 266	1 542	767	775
15 - 19	23 320	11 992	11 328	21 471	10 995	10 476	1 849	997	852
20 - 24	21 983	11 239	10 744	20 461	10 400	10 061	1 522	839	683
25 - 29	23 707	12 350	11 357	22 403	11 587	10 816	1 304	763	541
30 - 34	22 836	12 095	10 741	21 453	11 239	10 214	1 383	856	527
35 - 39	21 449	11 289	10 160	19 858	10 289	9 569	1 591	1 000	591
40 - 44	23 049	11 947	11 102	21 192	10 826	10 366	1 857	1 121	736
45 - 49	22 450	11 788	10 662	20 604	10 686	9 918	1 846	1 102	744
50 - 54	20 336	10 666	9 670	18 700	9 662	9 038	1 636	1 004	632
55 - 59	17 246	8 898	8 348	15 865	8 103	7 762	1 381	795	586
60 - 64	13 561	6 904	6 657	12 495	6 290	6 205	1 066	614	452
65 - 69	9 655	4 757	4 898	8 850	4 312	4 538	805	445	360
70 - 74	8 654	4 093	4 561	7 960	3 709	4 251	694	384	310
75 - 79	7 890	3 622	4 268	7 221	3 238	3 983	669	384	285
80 - 84	5 410	2 273	3 137	5 025	2 073	2 952	385	200	185
85 - 89	2 987	1 146	1 841	2 754	1 026	1 728	233	120	113
90 - 94	1 058	349	709	965	308	657	93	41	52
95 - 99	247	60	187	233	56	177	14	4	10
100 +	27	4	23	25	3	22	2	1	1
Ireland - Irlande									
28 IV 2002 (CDFC)									
Total	3 917 203	1 946 164	1 971 039	2 334 282	1 133 507	1 200 775	1 582 921	812 657	770 264
0	54 499	27 805	26 694	34 126	17 447	16 679	20 373	10 358	10 015
1 - 4	223 131	114 235	108 896	132 464	67 852	64 612	90 667	46 383	44 284
5 - 9	264 090	135 890	128 200	148 750	76 507	72 243	115 340	59 383	55 957
10 - 14	285 708	146 114	139 594	156 518	79 813	76 705	129 190	66 301	62 889
15 - 19	313 188	160 413	152 775	180 794	90 629	90 165	132 394	69 784	62 610
20 - 24	328 334	165 292	163 042	229 323	110 629	118 694	99 011	54 663	44 348
25 - 29	312 693	156 100	156 593	218 159	106 459	111 700	94 534	49 641	44 893
30 - 34	304 676	152 377	152 299	198 557	98 235	100 322	106 119	54 142	51 977
35 - 39	290 906	144 530	146 376	175 440	85 989	89 451	115 466	58 541	56 925
40 - 44	271 984	135 301	136 683	156 586	76 632	79 954	115 398	58 669	56 729
45 - 49	249 604	124 981	124 623	139 387	67 871	71 516	110 217	57 110	53 107
50 - 54	230 843	116 585	114 258	128 125	62 642	65 483	102 718	53 943	48 775
55 - 59	197 294	99 827	97 467	109 812	53 573	56 239	87 482	46 254	41 228
60 - 64	154 252	77 559	76 693	87 940	42 559	45 381	66 312	35 000	31 312
65 - 69	133 474	65 290	68 184	75 006	34 910	40 096	58 468	30 380	28 088
70 - 74	112 129	51 719	60 410	61 997	26 751	35 246	50 132	24 968	25 164
75 - 79	89 815	37 377	52 438	48 176	18 610	29 566	41 639	18 767	22 872
80 - 84	58 857	22 283	36 574	31 005	10 617	20 388	27 852	11 666	16 186
85 - 89	29 629	9 444	20 185	15 533	4 387	11 146	14 096	5 057	9 039
90 - 94	9 871	2 617	7 254	5 329	1 201	4 128	4 542	1 416	3 126
95 - 99	1 972	379	1 593	1 115	168	947	857	211	646
100 +	254	46	208	140	26	114	114	20	94
1 VII 2007 (ESDF)									
Total	4 356 931	2 177 582	2 179 349	...	...	...	...	...	...
0 - 4	316 911	162 664	154 247	...	...	...	...	...	...
5 - 9	297 786	152 243	145 543	...	...	...	...	...	...
10 - 14	277 414	142 287	135 127	...	...	...	...	...	...
15 - 19	285 819	145 483	140 336	...	...	...	...	...	...
20 - 24	342 584	171 565	171 019	...	...	...	...	...	...
25 - 29	405 698	204 631	201 068	...	...	...	...	...	...
30 - 34	360 068	182 868	177 201	...	...	...	...	...	...
35 - 39	334 175	170 157	164 018	...	...	...	...	...	...
40 - 44	306 701	153 982	152 719	...	...	...	...	...	...

Continent, country or area, date, code and age (in years) Continent, pays ou zone, date, code et âge (en annèes)	Total			Urban - Urbaine			Rural - Rurale		
	Both sexes Les deux sexes	Male Masculin	Female Féminin	Both sexes Les deux sexes	Male Masculin	Female Féminin	Both sexes Les deux sexes	Male Masculin	Female Féminin
EUROPE									
Ireland - Irlande									
1 VII 2007 (ESDF)									
45 - 49	281 426	141 212	140 214	...	...	...	...	...	...
50 - 54	253 537	127 504	126 034	...	...	...	...	...	...
55 - 59	228 657	115 450	113 208	...	...	...	...	...	...
60 - 64	192 427	96 967	95 460	...	...	...	...	...	...
65 - 69	145 218	72 000	73 218	...	...	...	...	...	...
70 - 74	119 613	56 872	62 741	...	...	...	...	...	...
75 - 79	92 608	40 922	51 686	...	...	...	...	...	...
80 - 84	65 207	24 948	40 259	...	...	...	...	...	...
85 +	51 087	15 832	35 255	...	...	...	...	...	...
Isle of Man - Île de Man									
30 IV 2007 (ESDJ)									
Total	80 885	39 995	40 889	...	...	...	...	...	...
0	876	459	417	...	...	...	...	...	...
1 - 4	3 309	1 720	1 590	...	...	...	...	...	...
5 - 9	4 454	2 396	2 058	...	...	...	...	...	...
10 - 14	4 912	2 494	2 419	...	...	...	...	...	...
15 - 19	5 060	2 603	2 457	...	...	...	...	...	...
20 - 24	4 499	2 285	2 213	...	...	...	...	...	...
25 - 29	4 546	2 246	2 300	...	...	...	...	...	...
30 - 34	4 993	2 408	2 585	...	...	...	...	...	...
35 - 39	6 061	3 028	3 033	...	...	...	...	...	...
40 - 44	6 343	3 193	3 150	...	...	...	...	...	...
45 - 49	6 042	3 031	3 011	...	...	...	...	...	...
50 - 54	5 324	2 713	2 611	...	...	...	...	...	...
55 - 59	5 607	2 810	2 798	...	...	...	...	...	...
60 - 64	5 004	2 531	2 472	...	...	...	...	...	...
65 - 69	3 869	1 908	1 960	...	...	...	...	...	...
70 - 74	3 215	1 543	1 672	...	...	...	...	...	...
75 - 79	2 686	1 176	1 510	...	...	...	...	...	...
80 - 84	2 095	799	1 296	...	...	...	...	...	...
85 - 89	1 259	442	816	...	...	...	...	...	...
90 +	730	208	522	...	...	...	...	...	...
Italy - Italie									
1 I 2007 (ESDJ)									
Total	59 131 287	28 718 441	30 412 846	...	...	...	...	...	...
0	554 966	285 688	269 278	...	...	...	...	...	...
1 - 4	2 220 845	1 140 917	1 079 928	...	...	...	...	...	...
5 - 9	2 747 128	1 413 120	1 334 008	...	...	...	...	...	...
10 - 14	2 798 961	1 438 889	1 360 072	...	...	...	...	...	...
15 - 19	2 941 233	1 513 012	1 428 221	...	...	...	...	...	...
20 - 24	3 109 753	1 583 603	1 526 150	...	...	...	...	...	...
25 - 29	3 676 293	1 860 591	1 815 702	...	...	...	...	...	...
30 - 34	4 533 258	2 291 216	2 242 042	...	...	...	...	...	...
35 - 39	4 800 563	2 423 049	2 377 514	...	...	...	...	...	...
40 - 44	4 824 533	2 421 687	2 402 846	...	...	...	...	...	...
45 - 49	4 213 028	2 096 037	2 116 991	...	...	...	...	...	...
50 - 54	3 798 683	1 872 198	1 926 485	...	...	...	...	...	...
55 - 59	3 827 042	1 871 043	1 955 999	...	...	...	...	...	...
60 - 64	3 292 249	1 586 769	1 705 480	...	...	...	...	...	...
65 - 69	3 330 888	1 566 182	1 764 706	...	...	...	...	...	...
70 - 74	2 860 272	1 283 854	1 576 418	...	...	...	...	...	...
75 - 79	2 461 918	1 021 855	1 440 063	...	...	...	...	...	...
80 - 84	1 795 994	655 411	1 140 583	...	...	...	...	...	...
85 - 89	842 446	266 112	576 334	...	...	...	...	...	...
90 - 94	390 675	103 718	286 957	...	...	...	...	...	...
95 - 99	99 062	21 465	77 597	...	...	...	...	...	...
100 +	11 497	2 025	9 472	...	...	...	...	...	...
Jersey									
11 III 2001 (CDJC)									
Total	87 186	42 484	44 702	...	...	...	...	...	...
0	856	417	439	...	...	...	...	...	...
1 - 4	3 857	1 986	1 871	...	...	...	...	...	...
5 - 9	5 016	2 616	2 400	...	...	...	...	...	...

7. Population by age, sex and urban/rural residence: latest available year, 1998 - 2007
Population selon l'âge, le sexe et la résidence, urbaine/rurale: dernière année disponible, 1998 - 2007 (continued - suite)

Continent, country or area, date, code and age (in years) / Continent, pays ou zone, date, code et âge (en années)	Total			Urban - Urbaine			Rural - Rurale		
	Both sexes Les deux sexes	Male Masculin	Female Féminin	Both sexes Les deux sexes	Male Masculin	Female Féminin	Both sexes Les deux sexes	Male Masculin	Female Féminin
EUROPE									
Jersey									
11 III 2001 (CDJC)									
10 - 14	5 038	2 569	2 469	...	...	...	...	...	...
15 - 19	4 628	2 356	2 272	...	...	...	...	...	...
20 - 24	5 243	2 488	2 755	...	...	...	...	...	...
25 - 29	6 196	2 988	3 208	...	...	...	...	...	...
30 - 34	7 646	3 761	3 885	...	...	...	...	...	...
35 - 39	7 898	3 921	3 977	...	...	...	...	...	...
40 - 44	7 011	3 467	3 544	...	...	...	...	...	...
45 - 49	6 238	3 073	3 165	...	...	...	...	...	...
50 - 54	6 240	3 132	3 108	...	...	...	...	...	...
55 - 59	4 664	2 319	2 345	...	...	...	...	...	...
60 - 64	4 325	2 148	2 177	...	...	...	...	...	...
65 - 69	3 619	1 790	1 829	...	...	...	...	...	...
70 - 74	3 019	1 373	1 646	...	...	...	...	...	...
75 - 79	2 432	1 051	1 381	...	...	...	...	...	...
80 - 84	1 591	560	1 031	...	...	...	...	...	...
85 - 89	1 101	340	761	...	...	...	...	...	...
90 - 94	444	105	339	...	...	...	...	...	...
95 - 99	109	19	90	...	...	...	...	...	...
100 +	15	5	10	...	...	...	...	...	...
Latvia - Lettonie									
1 VII 2007 (ESDJ)									
Total	2 276 100	1 048 969	1 227 131	1 545 560	693 369	852 191	730 540	355 600	374 940
0	22 992	11 676	11 316	15 908	8 053	7 855	7 084	3 623	3 461
1 - 4	84 389	43 287	41 102	57 691	29 577	28 114	26 698	13 710	12 988
5 - 9	95 441	48 659	46 782	61 470	31 273	30 197	33 971	17 386	16 585
10 - 14	112 564	57 653	54 911	69 030	35 234	33 796	43 534	22 419	21 115
15 - 19	171 502	87 512	83 990	107 260	54 373	52 887	64 242	33 139	31 103
20 - 24	184 491	93 812	90 679	123 287	61 533	61 754	61 204	32 279	28 925
25 - 29	161 604	82 149	79 455	113 369	56 022	57 347	48 235	26 127	22 108
30 - 34	158 896	80 322	78 574	111 513	54 737	56 776	47 383	25 585	21 798
35 - 39	158 859	78 761	80 098	109 065	52 429	56 636	49 794	26 332	23 462
40 - 44	159 160	77 543	81 617	107 431	50 401	57 030	51 729	27 142	24 587
45 - 49	172 624	82 213	90 411	118 172	53 861	64 311	54 452	28 352	26 100
50 - 54	151 531	69 671	81 860	106 521	46 778	59 743	45 010	22 893	22 117
55 - 59	138 769	61 122	77 647	98 339	41 267	57 072	40 430	19 855	20 575
60 - 64	112 903	46 913	65 990	77 495	30 939	46 556	35 408	15 974	19 434
65 - 69	129 327	50 058	79 269	89 190	33 541	55 649	40 137	16 517	23 620
70 - 74	100 045	34 803	65 242	68 017	23 202	44 815	32 028	11 601	20 427
75 - 79	82 597	25 843	56 754	57 428	17 974	39 454	25 169	7 869	17 300
80 - 84	51 266	11 368	39 898	35 996	8 185	27 811	15 270	3 183	12 087
85 - 89	19 091	4 063	15 028	13 029	2 891	10 138	6 062	1 172	4 890
90 - 94	6 224	1 211	5 013	4 113	868	3 245	2 111	343	1 768
95 - 99	1 637	289	1 348	1 107	202	905	530	87	443
100 +	188	41	147	129	29	100	59	12	47
Liechtenstein									
1 VII 2007 (ESDF)									
Total	35 322	17 426	17 896	...	...	...	...	...	...
0	377	187	190	...	...	...	...	...	...
1 - 4	1 480	764	716	...	...	...	...	...	...
5 - 9	2 005	999	1 006	...	...	...	...	...	...
10 - 14	2 122	1 060	1 062	...	...	...	...	...	...
15 - 19	2 174	1 120	1 054	...	...	...	...	...	...
20 - 24	2 139	1 066	1 073	...	...	...	...	...	...
25 - 29	2 247	1 149	1 098	...	...	...	...	...	...
30 - 34	2 449	1 214	1 235	...	...	...	...	...	...
35 - 39	3 006	1 520	1 486	...	...	...	...	...	...
40 - 44	3 064	1 505	1 559	...	...	...	...	...	...
45 - 49	2 916	1 420	1 496	...	...	...	...	...	...
50 - 54	2 615	1 317	1 298	...	...	...	...	...	...
55 - 59	2 385	1 225	1 160	...	...	...	...	...	...
60 - 64	2 049	1 055	994	...	...	...	...	...	...
65 - 69	1 467	715	752	...	...	...	...	...	...
70 - 74	1 017	448	569	...	...	...	...	...	...

7. Population by age, sex and urban/rural residence: latest available year, 1998 - 2007
Population selon l'âge, le sexe et la résidence, urbaine/rurale: dernière année disponible, 1998 - 2007 (continued - suite)

Continent, country or area, date, code and age (in years) / Continent, pays ou zone, date, code et âge (en annèes)	Total			Urban - Urbaine			Rural - Rurale		
	Both sexes Les deux sexes	Male Masculin	Female Féminin	Both sexes Les deux sexes	Male Masculin	Female Féminin	Both sexes Les deux sexes	Male Masculin	Female Féminin
EUROPE									
Liechtenstein									
1 VII 2007 (ESDF)									
75 - 79	726	316	410	...	...	...	...	...	...
80 - 84	602	186	416	...	...	...	...	...	...
85 - 89	345	123	222	...	...	...	...	...	...
90 - 94	113	34	79	...	...	...	...	...	...
95 - 99	22	3	19	...	...	...	...	...	...
100 +	2	-	2	...	...	...	...	...	...
Lithuania - Lituanie									
1 VII 2007 (ESDJ)									
Total	3 375 618	1 571 979	1 803 639	2 255 508	1 028 619	1 226 889	1 120 110	543 360	576 750
0	31 629	16 119	15 510	21 018	10 732	10 286	10 611	5 387	5 224
1 - 4	120 855	61 893	58 962	77 433	39 712	37 721	43 422	22 181	21 241
5 - 9	167 765	86 417	81 348	106 471	54 681	51 790	61 294	31 736	29 558
10 - 14	207 312	106 035	101 277	131 693	67 330	64 363	75 619	38 705	36 914
15 - 19	263 595	134 401	129 194	166 797	84 554	82 243	96 798	49 847	46 951
20 - 24	270 361	137 683	132 678	178 681	89 435	89 246	91 680	48 248	43 432
25 - 29	228 465	116 592	111 873	165 888	81 000	84 888	62 577	35 592	26 985
30 - 34	225 851	112 497	113 354	165 438	80 000	85 438	60 413	32 497	27 916
35 - 39	247 190	121 482	125 708	173 124	83 317	89 807	74 066	38 165	35 901
40 - 44	254 490	124 128	130 362	174 999	82 446	92 553	79 491	41 682	37 809
45 - 49	264 498	125 204	139 294	182 596	82 655	99 941	81 902	42 549	39 353
50 - 54	212 378	97 963	114 415	147 746	65 064	82 682	64 632	32 899	31 733
55 - 59	189 867	83 635	106 232	130 297	54 661	75 636	59 570	28 974	30 596
60 - 64	161 149	67 188	93 961	106 920	42 872	64 048	54 229	24 316	29 913
65 - 69	163 860	64 004	99 856	105 088	39 945	65 143	58 772	24 059	34 713
70 - 74	143 320	51 658	91 662	87 536	31 193	56 343	55 784	20 465	35 319
75 - 79	115 550	37 794	77 756	69 494	22 916	46 578	46 056	14 878	31 178
80 - 84	70 677	18 378	52 299	41 885	10 849	31 036	28 792	7 529	21 263
85 - 89	26 571	6 386	20 185	15 444	3 652	11 792	11 127	2 734	8 393
90 - 94	7 851	1 839	6 012	5 076	1 131	3 945	2 775	708	2 067
95 - 99	2 017	563	1 454	1 574	396	1 178	443	167	276
100 +	367	120	247	310	78	232	57	42	15
Luxembourg									
1 VII 2007 (ESDJ)									
Total	479 993	237 700	242 293	...	...	...	...	...	...
0	5 489	2 786	2 703	...	...	...	...	...	...
1 - 4	22 501	11 698	10 803	...	...	...	...	...	...
5 - 9	29 428	15 069	14 359	...	...	...	...	...	...
10 - 14	30 128	15 399	14 729	...	...	...	...	...	...
15 - 19	28 259	14 466	13 793	...	...	...	...	...	...
20 - 24	28 378	14 498	13 880	...	...	...	...	...	...
25 - 29	32 409	16 237	16 172	...	...	...	...	...	...
30 - 34	35 433	17 664	17 769	...	...	...	...	...	...
35 - 39	39 796	19 962	19 834	...	...	...	...	...	...
40 - 44	41 154	21 029	20 125	...	...	...	...	...	...
45 - 49	37 191	18 966	18 225	...	...	...	...	...	...
50 - 54	32 417	16 388	16 029	...	...	...	...	...	...
55 - 59	27 796	14 279	13 517	...	...	...	...	...	...
60 - 64	22 353	11 252	11 101	...	...	...	...	...	...
65 - 69	19 185	9 070	10 115	...	...	...	...	...	...
70 - 74	16 699	7 598	9 101	...	...	...	...	...	...
75 - 79	15 175	6 473	8 702	...	...	...	...	...	...
80 - 84	9 689	3 263	6 426	...	...	...	...	...	...
85 - 89	4 581	1 257	3 324	...	...	...	...	...	...
90 - 94	1 681	339	1 342	...	...	...	...	...	...
95 +	251	7	244	...	...	...	...	...	...
Malta - Malte									
1 VII 2007 (ESDJ)									
Total	409 092	203 381	205 711	...	...	...	...	...	...
0	3 866	2 026	1 840	...	...	...	...	...	...
1 - 4	15 924	8 117	7 807	...	...	...	...	...	...
5 - 9	21 802	11 098	10 704	...	...	...	...	...	...
10 - 14	25 778	13 317	12 461	...	...	...	...	...	...
15 - 19	28 689	14 627	14 062	...	...	...	...	...	...

Continent, country or area, date, code and age (in years) Continent, pays ou zone, date, code et âge (en années)	Total			Urban - Urbaine			Rural - Rurale		
	Both sexes Les deux sexes	Male Masculin	Female Féminin	Both sexes Les deux sexes	Male Masculin	Female Féminin	Both sexes Les deux sexes	Male Masculin	Female Féminin
EUROPE									
Malta - Malte									
1 VII 2007 (ESDJ)									
20 - 24	29 323	15 198	14 125	...	...	...	...	...	...
25 - 29	30 404	15 738	14 666	...	...	...	...	...	...
30 - 34	29 200	15 072	14 128	...	...	...	...	...	...
35 - 39	25 340	12 995	12 345	...	...	...	...	...	...
40 - 44	26 244	13 403	12 841	...	...	...	...	...	...
45 - 49	30 275	15 222	15 053	...	...	...	...	...	...
50 - 54	29 392	14 815	14 577	...	...	...	...	...	...
55 - 59	30 326	15 141	15 185	...	...	...	...	...	...
60 - 64	26 010	12 659	13 351	...	...	...	...	...	...
65 - 69	16 991	7 938	9 053	...	...	...	...	...	...
70 - 74	15 532	6 820	8 712	...	...	...	...	...	...
75 - 79	11 358	4 555	6 803	...	...	...	...	...	...
80 - 84	7 603	2 922	4 681	...	...	...	...	...	...
85 - 89	3 712	1 342	2 370	...	...	...	...	...	...
90 +	1 323	376	947	...	...	...	...	...	...
Monaco									
21 VI 2000 (CDJC)									
Total	32 020	15 544	16 476	...	...	...	...	...	...
0	145	69	76	...	...	...	...	...	...
1 - 4	1 223	644	579	...	...	...	...	...	...
5 - 9	1 462	747	715	...	...	...	...	...	...
10 - 14	1 407	746	661	...	...	...	...	...	...
15 - 19	1 337	706	631	...	...	...	...	...	...
20 - 24	1 297	661	636	...	...	...	...	...	...
25 - 29	1 638	830	808	...	...	...	...	...	...
30 - 34	2 346	1 184	1 162	...	...	...	...	...	...
35 - 39	2 386	1 205	1 181	...	...	...	...	...	...
40 - 44	2 328	1 151	1 177	...	...	...	...	...	...
45 - 49	2 178	1 107	1 071	...	...	...	...	...	...
50 - 54	2 584	1 264	1 320	...	...	...	...	...	...
55 - 59	2 405	1 163	1 242	...	...	...	...	...	...
60 - 64	2 083	1 018	1 065	...	...	...	...	...	...
65 - 69	1 794	854	940	...	...	...	...	...	...
70 - 74	1 704	803	901	...	...	...	...	...	...
75 - 79	1 598	704	894	...	...	...	...	...	...
80 - 84	937	347	590	...	...	...	...	...	...
85 - 89	669	216	453	...	...	...	...	...	...
90 - 94	374	96	278	...	...	...	...	...	...
95 - 99	96	20	76	...	...	...	...	...	...
100 +	11	2	9	...	...	...	...	...	...
Unknown - Inconnu	18	7	11	...	...	...	...	...	...
Montenegro - Monténégro									
1 VII 2005 (ESDJ)									
Total	623 277	306 839	316 439	389 678	189 222	200 456	233 600	117 617	115 983
0	7 608	3 955	3 653	5 955	3 099	2 857	1 653	857	796
1 - 4	32 446	16 825	15 621	21 794	11 385	10 410	10 652	5 441	5 212
5 - 9	41 691	21 538	20 153	25 956	13 384	12 572	15 736	8 155	7 581
10 - 14	44 850	23 240	21 610	28 168	14 562	13 607	16 682	8 679	8 003
15 - 19	48 434	24 827	23 607	30 696	15 743	14 953	17 738	9 085	8 654
20 - 24	50 240	25 620	24 621	32 191	16 025	16 166	18 050	9 595	8 455
25 - 29	46 344	23 172	23 172	29 900	14 472	15 429	16 444	8 701	7 744
30 - 34	42 712	21 016	21 697	27 289	12 974	14 315	15 423	8 042	7 382
35 - 39	41 245	20 470	20 775	26 243	12 442	13 801	15 002	8 028	6 974
40 - 44	43 851	21 791	22 060	28 410	13 510	14 900	15 442	8 281	7 161
45 - 49	44 446	22 386	22 061	29 026	14 106	14 920	15 421	8 280	7 141
50 - 54	42 291	21 072	21 219	27 752	13 546	14 207	14 539	7 526	7 013
55 - 59	32 875	15 504	17 372	20 870	9 810	11 060	12 006	5 694	6 312
60 - 64	25 855	11 740	14 115	14 653	6 648	8 005	11 202	5 092	6 110
65 - 69	29 533	13 403	16 130	16 268	7 374	8 894	13 265	6 029	7 236
70 - 74	22 462	9 894	12 568	11 857	5 240	6 617	10 605	4 654	5 951
75 - 79	15 359	6 429	8 930	7 556	3 135	4 421	7 803	3 295	4 509
80 - 84	7 506	2 791	4 715	3 551	1 302	2 250	3 955	1 490	2 466
85 - 89	2 172	744	1 428	962	307	655	1 210	437	773

7. Population by age, sex and urban/rural residence: latest available year, 1998 - 2007
Population selon l'âge, le sexe et la résidence, urbaine/rurale: dernière année disponible, 1998 - 2007 (continued - suite)

Continent, country or area, date, code and age (in years) / Continent, pays ou zone, date, code et âge (en années)	Total			Urban - Urbaine			Rural - Rurale		
	Both sexes Les deux sexes	Male Masculin	Female Féminin	Both sexes Les deux sexes	Male Masculin	Female Féminin	Both sexes Les deux sexes	Male Masculin	Female Féminin
EUROPE									
Montenegro - Monténégro									
1 VII 2005 (ESDJ)									
90 - 94	1 004	306	698	433	115	318	571	191	380
95 - 99	284	95	189	116	34	82	168	61	107
100 +	75	25	50	36	14	22	40	11	29
1 VII 2007 (ESDJ)									
Total	626 187	308 352	317 836	...	...	...	...	...	...
0	7 699	4 061	3 639	...	...	...	...	...	...
1 - 4	31 255	16 280	14 975	...	...	...	...	...	...
5 - 9	40 476	20 969	19 507	...	...	...	...	...	...
10 - 14	43 622	22 560	21 062	...	...	...	...	...	...
15 - 19	46 987	24 139	22 848	...	...	...	...	...	...
20 - 24	50 309	25 747	24 562	...	...	...	...	...	...
25 - 29	47 739	24 105	23 634	...	...	...	...	...	...
30 - 34	43 777	21 411	22 366	...	...	...	...	...	...
35 - 39	41 068	20 299	20 769	...	...	...	...	...	...
40 - 44	42 821	21 256	21 565	...	...	...	...	...	...
45 - 49	44 195	22 028	22 167	...	...	...	...	...	...
50 - 54	43 483	21 803	21 681	...	...	...	...	...	...
55 - 59	37 172	17 770	19 402	...	...	...	...	...	...
60 - 64	24 890	11 318	13 572	...	...	...	...	...	...
65 - 69	28 481	12 779	15 702	...	...	...	...	...	...
70 - 74	23 680	10 416	13 265	...	...	...	...	...	...
75 - 79	16 179	6 852	9 328	...	...	...	...	...	...
80 - 84	8 355	3 218	5 137	...	...	...	...	...	...
85 - 89	2 901	1 003	1 898	...	...	...	...	...	...
90 - 94	746	231	516	...	...	...	...	...	...
95 - 99	277	99	178	...	...	...	...	...	...
100 +	81	13	68	...	...	...	...	...	...
Netherlands - Pays-Bas									
1 I 2007 (ESDJ)									
Total	16 357 992	8 088 514	8 269 478	10 806 179	5 313 030	5 493 149	5 551 813	2 775 484	2 776 329
0 - 4	966 881	494 914	471 967	641 934	328 599	313 335	324 947	166 315	158 632
5 - 9	1 005 997	514 058	491 939	639 106	326 491	312 615	366 891	187 567	179 324
10 - 14	985 737	504 748	480 989	619 119	316 894	302 225	366 618	187 854	178 764
15 - 19	998 488	510 433	488 055	649 081	328 719	320 362	349 407	181 714	167 693
20 - 24	966 035	488 388	477 647	700 523	345 657	354 866	265 512	142 731	122 781
25 - 29	989 477	495 146	494 331	731 987	362 567	369 420	257 490	132 579	124 911
30 - 34	1 068 148	534 023	534 125	759 940	381 076	378 864	308 208	152 947	155 261
35 - 39	1 295 476	653 937	641 539	872 784	442 824	429 960	422 692	211 113	211 579
40 - 44	1 309 824	663 663	646 161	859 026	435 639	423 387	450 798	228 024	222 774
45 - 49	1 235 769	622 404	613 365	801 581	402 508	399 073	434 188	219 896	214 292
50 - 54	1 132 228	569 839	562 389	728 092	363 770	364 322	404 136	206 069	198 067
55 - 59	1 111 042	560 626	550 416	705 554	353 972	351 582	405 488	206 654	198 834
60 - 64	924 538	464 275	460 263	574 602	286 478	288 124	349 936	177 797	172 139
65 - 69	707 492	345 852	361 640	442 633	213 774	228 859	264 859	132 078	132 781
70 - 74	584 965	270 832	314 133	368 716	167 795	200 921	216 249	103 037	113 212
75 - 79	475 053	200 533	274 520	308 196	127 988	180 208	166 857	72 545	94 312
80 - 84	339 154	123 040	216 114	225 874	80 731	145 143	113 280	42 309	70 971
85 - 89	180 861	54 177	126 684	122 262	36 018	86 244	58 599	18 159	40 440
90 - 94	65 609	15 047	50 562	44 751	9 860	34 891	20 858	5 187	15 671
95 - 99	13 823	2 378	11 445	9 472	1 550	7 922	4 351	828	3 523
100 +	1 395	201	1 194	946	120	826	449	81	368
Norway - Norvège[54]									
3 XI 2001 (CDJC)									
Total	4 520 947	2 240 281	2 280 666	3 458 699	1 694 153	1 764 546	1 018 422	522 925	495 497
0	57 205	29 340	27 865	44 798	23 002	21 796	11 828	6 048	5 780
1 - 4	240 268	123 153	117 115	186 738	95 742	90 996	51 255	26 232	25 023
5 - 9	307 650	158 230	149 420	235 620	121 061	114 559	69 433	35 833	33 600
10 - 14	300 609	153 989	146 620	227 068	116 054	111 014	71 100	36 697	34 403
15 - 19	267 596	137 494	130 102	199 238	102 194	97 044	66 278	34 188	32 090
20 - 24	273 126	138 679	134 447	211 551	106 040	105 511	59 030	31 337	27 693
25 - 29	316 989	160 678	156 311	255 685	128 167	127 518	57 993	30 759	27 234
30 - 34	351 386	178 688	172 698	280 044	141 397	138 647	67 654	35 193	32 461
35 - 39	338 689	173 595	165 094	265 141	134 740	130 401	70 226	36 890	33 336

Continent, country or area, date, code and age (in years) / Continent, pays ou zone, date, code et âge (en annèes)	Total			Urban - Urbaine			Rural - Rurale		
	Both sexes Les deux sexes	Male Masculin	Female Féminin	Both sexes Les deux sexes	Male Masculin	Female Féminin	Both sexes Les deux sexes	Male Masculin	Female Féminin
EUROPE									
Norway - Norvège[54]									
3 XI 2001 (CDJC)									
40 - 44	319 293	162 807	156 486	246 090	124 014	122 076	70 273	37 050	33 223
45 - 49	309 642	157 276	152 366	236 578	118 274	118 304	70 375	37 421	32 954
50 - 54	301 283	154 010	147 273	227 967	114 779	113 188	70 543	37 669	32 874
55 - 59	269 320	136 414	132 906	203 022	101 540	101 482	63 778	33 413	30 365
60 - 64	190 808	93 953	96 855	140 947	67 923	73 024	47 966	25 008	22 958
65 - 69	163 197	77 766	85 431	119 675	55 351	64 324	41 888	21 553	20 335
70 - 74	161 097	73 389	87 708	118 670	52 350	66 320	40 811	20 243	20 568
75 - 79	151 839	63 682	88 157	111 134	44 980	66 154	38 918	17 898	21 020
80 - 84	113 628	41 784	71 844	83 558	29 286	54 272	28 500	11 877	16 623
85 - 89	60 467	18 752	41 715	44 821	12 816	32 005	14 644	5 617	9 027
90 - 94	22 093	5 668	16 425	16 645	3 797	12 848	4 988	1 744	3 244
95 - 99	4 307	849	3 458	3 333	580	2 753	872	239	633
100 +	455	85	370	376	66	310	69	16	53
1 VII 2007 (ESDJ)[55]									
Total	4 709 153	2 342 739	2 366 414	...	...	...	...	...	...
0	58 678	30 066	28 613	...	...	...	...	...	...
1 - 4	233 116	119 036	114 080	...	...	...	...	...	...
5 - 9	300 578	153 772	146 806	...	...	...	...	...	...
10 - 14	314 283	161 530	152 753	...	...	...	...	...	...
15 - 19	311 920	160 025	151 895	...	...	...	...	...	...
20 - 24	281 536	143 692	137 845	...	...	...	...	...	...
25 - 29	292 598	147 652	144 946	...	...	...	...	...	...
30 - 34	324 828	164 650	160 178	...	...	...	...	...	...
35 - 39	360 546	183 613	176 934	...	...	...	...	...	...
40 - 44	346 893	177 940	168 953	...	...	...	...	...	...
45 - 49	321 932	164 514	157 418	...	...	...	...	...	...
50 - 54	309 711	156 911	152 800	...	...	...	...	...	...
55 - 59	293 378	149 359	144 019	...	...	...	...	...	...
60 - 64	269 707	135 625	134 083	...	...	...	...	...	...
65 - 69	184 667	89 630	95 037	...	...	...	...	...	...
70 - 74	148 878	69 029	79 850	...	...	...	...	...	...
75 - 79	137 530	60 027	77 503	...	...	...	...	...	...
80 - 84	113 900	44 388	69 512	...	...	...	...	...	...
85 - 89	71 911	23 251	48 661	...	...	...	...	...	...
90 - 94	26 346	6 781	19 565	...	...	...	...	...	...
95 - 99	5 613	1 147	4 466	...	...	...	...	...	...
100 +	610	107	503	...	...	...	...	...	...
Unknown - Inconnu	-	-	-	...	...	...	...	...	...
Poland - Pologne[56]									
1 VII 2007 (ESDF)									
Total	38 115 967	18 417 074	19 698 893	23 350 920	11 070 886	12 280 034	14 765 047	7 346 188	7 418 859
0	378 014	194 530	183 484	219 405	112 837	106 568	158 609	81 693	76 916
1 - 4	1 427 110	733 918	693 192	819 211	421 613	397 598	607 899	312 305	295 594
5 - 9	1 888 593	968 662	919 931	1 031 673	529 514	502 159	856 920	439 148	417 772
10 - 14	2 266 445	1 158 694	1 107 751	1 216 235	621 707	594 528	1 050 210	536 987	513 223
15 - 19	2 748 261	1 405 049	1 343 212	1 558 072	793 118	764 954	1 190 189	611 931	578 258
20 - 24	3 242 556	1 648 659	1 593 897	1 972 995	994 723	978 272	1 269 561	653 936	615 625
25 - 29	3 142 934	1 593 318	1 549 616	2 004 762	1 000 128	1 004 634	1 138 172	593 190	544 982
30 - 34	2 883 255	1 459 707	1 423 548	1 833 736	917 194	916 542	1 049 519	542 513	507 006
35 - 39	2 447 142	1 236 704	1 210 438	1 483 319	740 150	743 169	963 823	496 554	467 269
40 - 44	2 407 374	1 209 326	1 198 048	1 438 024	701 213	736 811	969 350	508 113	461 237
45 - 49	2 829 137	1 399 451	1 429 686	1 762 386	835 509	926 877	1 066 751	563 942	502 809
50 - 54	3 018 357	1 464 734	1 553 623	1 990 242	925 212	1 065 030	1 028 115	539 522	488 593
55 - 59	2 648 527	1 252 286	1 396 241	1 775 229	812 361	962 868	873 298	439 925	433 373
60 - 64	1 667 358	758 259	909 099	1 108 377	494 727	613 650	558 981	263 532	295 449
65 - 69	1 478 119	633 892	844 227	944 372	396 484	547 888	533 747	237 408	296 339
70 - 74	1 382 249	554 480	827 769	858 962	339 711	519 251	523 287	214 769	308 518
75 - 79	1 147 670	419 828	727 842	683 762	249 582	434 180	463 908	170 246	293 662
80 - 84	717 823	220 601	497 222	419 128	126 823	292 305	298 695	93 778	204 917
85 +	395 043	104 976	290 067	231 030	58 280	172 750	164 013	46 696	117 317

Continent, country or area, date, code and age (in years) / Continent, pays ou zone, date, code et âge (en années)	Total			Urban - Urbaine			Rural - Rurale		
	Both sexes Les deux sexes	Male Masculin	Female Féminin	Both sexes Les deux sexes	Male Masculin	Female Féminin	Both sexes Les deux sexes	Male Masculin	Female Féminin
EUROPE									
Portugal									
12 III 2001 (CDFC)									
Total	10 356 117	5 000 141	5 355 976	5 680 711	2 713 204	2 967 507	4 675 406	2 286 937	2 388 469
0	110 914	56 866	54 048	63 392	32 505	30 887	47 522	24 361	23 161
1 - 4	428 577	219 103	209 474	238 914	122 152	116 762	189 663	96 951	92 712
5 - 9	537 521	275 199	262 322	291 377	149 224	142 153	246 144	125 975	120 169
10 - 14	579 590	296 385	283 205	306 265	156 159	150 106	273 325	140 226	133 099
15 - 19	688 686	351 422	337 264	364 989	185 544	179 445	323 697	165 878	157 819
20 - 24	790 901	400 087	390 814	446 459	222 820	223 639	344 442	177 267	167 175
25 - 29	814 661	409 243	405 418	477 253	237 314	239 939	337 408	171 929	165 479
30 - 34	761 457	379 363	382 094	436 577	215 220	221 357	324 880	164 143	160 737
35 - 39	770 781	378 783	391 998	431 579	208 353	223 226	339 202	170 430	168 772
40 - 44	728 518	357 528	370 990	410 550	197 035	213 515	317 968	160 493	157 475
45 - 49	686 134	333 382	352 752	392 185	186 726	205 459	293 949	146 656	147 293
50 - 54	642 516	309 484	333 032	373 939	178 079	195 860	268 577	131 405	137 172
55 - 59	571 452	268 899	302 553	320 755	151 997	168 758	250 697	116 902	133 795
60 - 64	550 916	256 179	294 737	289 014	133 942	155 072	261 902	122 237	139 665
65 - 69	538 165	244 230	293 935	271 583	120 482	151 101	266 582	123 748	142 834
70 - 74	453 962	196 615	257 347	225 235	93 945	131 290	228 727	102 670	126 057
75 - 79	348 066	143 439	204 627	169 460	66 449	103 011	178 606	76 990	101 616
80 - 84	201 706	76 014	125 692	96 249	33 700	62 549	105 457	42 314	63 143
85 - 89	108 419	36 167	72 252	53 184	16 295	36 889	55 235	19 872	35 363
90 - 94	36 063	10 241	25 822	18 088	4 583	13 505	17 975	5 658	12 317
95 - 99	6 523	1 417	5 106	3 350	639	2 711	3 173	778	2 395
100 +	589	95	494	314	41	273	275	54	221
1 VII 2007 (ESDJ)									
Total	10 608 335	5 134 372	5 473 963	...	...	...	...	...	...
0	103 684	53 188	50 496	...	...	...	...	...	...
1 - 4	438 412	225 993	212 419	...	...	...	...	...	...
5 - 9	549 683	281 868	267 816	...	...	...	...	...	...
10 - 14	541 467	276 697	264 770	...	...	...	...	...	...
15 - 19	584 467	298 331	286 136	...	...	...	...	...	...
20 - 24	666 301	339 784	326 517	...	...	...	...	...	...
25 - 29	784 567	396 486	388 081	...	...	...	...	...	...
30 - 34	849 867	427 413	422 454	...	...	...	...	...	...
35 - 39	795 174	397 196	397 979	...	...	...	...	...	...
40 - 44	786 641	387 421	399 221	...	...	...	...	...	...
45 - 49	751 877	368 606	383 271	...	...	...	...	...	...
50 - 54	688 805	333 523	355 282	...	...	...	...	...	...
55 - 59	653 340	313 130	340 210	...	...	...	...	...	...
60 - 64	574 830	266 661	308 169	...	...	...	...	...	...
65 - 69	515 058	235 184	279 875	...	...	...	...	...	...
70 - 74	491 118	214 798	276 320	...	...	...	...	...	...
75 - 79	393 397	161 865	231 533	...	...	...	...	...	...
80 - 84	264 456	98 957	165 499	...	...	...	...	...	...
85 +	175 196	57 276	117 920	...	...	...	...	...	...
Republic of Moldova - République de Moldova[57]									
1 VII 2007 (ESDJ)									
Total	3 576 910	1 719 246	1 857 664	1 477 062	694 308	782 754	2 099 848	1 024 938	1 074 910
0	37 469	19 343	18 126	13 844	7 149	6 695	23 625	12 194	11 431
1 - 4	148 343	76 290	72 053	53 834	27 999	25 835	94 509	48 291	46 218
5 - 9	195 202	100 096	95 106	66 562	34 337	32 225	128 640	65 759	62 881
10 - 14	258 109	131 520	126 589	88 407	45 202	43 205	169 702	86 318	83 384
15 - 19	334 989	170 169	164 820	137 600	68 957	68 643	197 389	101 212	96 177
20 - 24	346 837	176 258	170 579	173 019	83 539	89 480	173 818	92 719	81 099
25 - 29	293 890	148 868	145 022	132 937	64 972	67 965	160 953	83 896	77 057
30 - 34	255 725	127 328	128 397	111 460	54 493	56 967	144 265	72 835	71 430
35 - 39	229 956	112 970	116 986	98 636	46 910	51 726	131 320	66 060	65 260
40 - 44	244 364	117 566	126 798	104 869	48 023	56 846	139 495	69 543	69 952
45 - 49	286 438	136 129	150 309	124 049	55 847	68 202	162 389	80 282	82 107
50 - 54	251 349	117 418	133 931	109 942	48 845	61 097	141 407	68 573	72 834
55 - 59	204 517	93 031	111 486	88 406	39 540	48 866	116 111	53 491	62 620
60 - 64	120 914	53 157	67 757	49 033	22 201	26 832	71 881	30 956	40 925
65 - 69	125 812	51 426	74 386	47 031	19 502	27 529	78 781	31 924	46 857

228

Continent, country or area, date, code and age (in years) / Continent, pays ou zone, date, code et âge (en années)	Total			Urban - Urbaine			Rural - Rurale		
	Both sexes Les deux sexes	Male Masculin	Female Féminin	Both sexes Les deux sexes	Male Masculin	Female Féminin	Both sexes Les deux sexes	Male Masculin	Female Féminin
EUROPE									
Republic of Moldova - République de Moldova[57]									
1 VII 2007 (ESDJ)									
70 - 74	101 232	39 396	61 836	33 130	12 528	20 602	68 102	26 868	41 234
75 - 79	78 092	28 590	49 502	24 385	8 485	15 900	53 707	20 105	33 602
80 - 84	42 542	13 322	29 220	13 712	4 022	9 690	28 830	9 300	19 530
85 - 89	16 438	5 019	11 419	4 771	1 349	3 422	11 667	3 670	7 997
90 - 94	3 671	1 081	2 590	1 106	331	775	2 565	750	1 815
95 - 99	893	236	657	283	66	217	610	170	440
100 +	128	33	95	46	11	35	82	22	60
Romania - Roumanie									
1 VII 2007 (ESDJ)									
Total	21 537 563	10 496 720	11 040 843	11 877 659	5 683 983	6 193 676	9 659 904	4 812 737	4 847 167
0	212 871	109 249	103 622	115 564	59 468	56 096	97 307	49 781	47 526
1 - 4	849 666	436 617	413 049	439 777	226 112	213 665	409 889	210 505	199 384
5 - 9	1 090 284	559 856	530 428	508 002	260 810	247 192	582 282	299 046	283 236
10 - 14	1 135 618	581 356	554 262	543 039	277 866	265 173	592 579	303 490	289 089
15 - 19	1 541 828	786 763	755 065	858 375	434 411	423 964	683 453	352 352	331 101
20 - 24	1 640 127	839 745	800 382	978 954	491 194	487 760	661 173	348 551	312 622
25 - 29	1 740 686	890 529	850 157	1 051 807	523 889	527 918	688 879	366 640	322 239
30 - 34	1 715 518	878 737	836 781	981 904	488 907	492 997	733 614	389 830	343 784
35 - 39	1 929 137	975 816	953 321	1 127 775	540 616	587 159	801 362	435 200	366 162
40 - 44	1 200 174	602 225	597 949	722 561	338 110	384 451	477 613	264 115	213 498
45 - 49	1 392 744	687 380	705 364	879 145	407 681	471 464	513 599	279 699	233 900
50 - 54	1 544 281	746 431	797 850	990 079	469 629	520 450	554 202	276 802	277 400
55 - 59	1 360 523	644 226	716 297	792 392	378 596	413 796	568 131	265 630	302 501
60 - 64	984 384	451 848	532 536	495 877	228 210	267 667	488 507	223 638	264 869
65 - 69	1 004 068	436 752	567 316	465 393	202 338	263 055	538 675	234 414	304 261
70 - 74	918 177	383 369	534 808	393 810	161 814	231 996	524 367	221 555	302 812
75 - 79	690 768	275 630	415 138	288 262	111 589	176 673	402 506	164 041	238 465
80 - 84	403 440	149 339	254 101	165 468	58 314	107 154	237 972	91 025	146 947
85 - 89	137 160	45 472	91 688	58 760	18 029	40 731	78 400	27 443	50 957
90 - 94	35 113	11 542	23 571	16 327	5 013	11 314	18 786	6 529	12 257
95 - 99	9 140	3 255	5 885	3 749	1 185	2 564	5 391	2 070	3 321
100 +	1 856	583	1 273	639	202	437	1 217	381	836
Russian Federation - Fédération de Russie									
1 VII 2007 (ESDJ)									
Total	142 008 838	65 717 075	76 291 763	103 773 035	47 517 937	56 255 098	38 235 803	18 199 138	20 036 665
0	1 598 051	821 696	776 355	1 114 062	573 227	540 835	483 989	248 469	235 520
1 - 4	5 850 956	3 004 892	2 846 064	4 150 873	2 133 933	2 016 940	1 700 083	870 959	829 124
5 - 9	6 481 478	3 317 155	3 164 323	4 451 199	2 280 288	2 170 911	2 030 279	1 036 867	993 412
10 - 14	6 893 736	3 522 313	3 371 423	4 632 962	2 369 281	2 263 681	2 260 774	1 153 032	1 107 742
15 - 19	10 206 862	5 206 143	5 000 719	7 027 727	3 566 473	3 461 254	3 179 135	1 639 670	1 539 465
20 - 24	12 764 030	6 458 795	6 305 235	9 611 964	4 804 078	4 807 886	3 152 066	1 654 717	1 497 349
25 - 29	11 475 294	5 744 111	5 731 183	8 864 295	4 398 855	4 465 440	2 610 999	1 345 256	1 265 743
30 - 34	10 492 913	5 191 091	5 301 822	8 030 800	3 942 107	4 088 693	2 462 113	1 248 984	1 213 129
35 - 39	9 702 459	4 779 381	4 923 078	7 301 802	3 571 723	3 730 079	2 400 657	1 207 658	1 192 999
40 - 44	9 804 060	4 726 010	5 078 050	7 151 028	3 392 493	3 758 535	2 653 032	1 333 517	1 319 515
45 - 49	11 954 654	5 631 975	6 322 679	8 739 058	4 015 031	4 724 027	3 215 596	1 616 944	1 598 652
50 - 54	10 947 652	4 969 299	5 978 353	8 112 584	3 580 477	4 532 107	2 835 068	1 388 822	1 446 246
55 - 59	9 349 636	4 076 788	5 272 848	7 084 819	3 015 074	4 069 745	2 264 817	1 061 714	1 203 103
60 - 64	4 898 103	2 017 151	2 880 952	3 783 051	1 538 600	2 244 451	1 115 052	478 551	636 501
65 - 69	6 601 783	2 428 946	4 172 837	4 731 020	1 721 800	3 009 220	1 870 763	707 146	1 163 617
70 - 74	5 198 439	1 781 447	3 416 992	3 627 483	1 216 477	2 411 006	1 570 956	564 970	1 005 986
75 - 79	4 213 458	1 257 377	2 956 081	2 847 348	831 121	2 016 227	1 366 110	426 256	939 854
80 - 84	2 505 423	584 772	1 920 651	1 753 154	418 321	1 334 833	752 269	166 451	585 818
85 - 89	770 747	146 285	624 462	548 202	108 882	439 320	222 545	37 403	185 142
90 - 94	224 397	38 672	185 725	158 408	29 822	128 586	65 989	8 850	57 139
95 - 99	56 125	9 828	46 297	39 467	7 612	31 855	16 658	2 216	14 442
100 +	18 582	2 948	15 634	11 729	2 262	9 467	6 853	686	6 167
San Marino - Saint-Marin									
1 VII 2004 (ESDF)									
Total	29 457	14 442	15 015	...	...	...	...	...	...
0	308	160	149	...	...	...	...	...	...

7. Population by age, sex and urban/rural residence: latest available year, 1998 - 2007

Population selon l'âge, le sexe et la résidence, urbaine/rurale: dernière année disponible, 1998 - 2007 (continued - suite)

Continent, country or area, date, code and age (in years) / Continent, pays ou zone, date, code et âge (en années)	Total			Urban - Urbaine			Rural - Rurale		
	Both sexes Les deux sexes	Male Masculin	Female Féminin	Both sexes Les deux sexes	Male Masculin	Female Féminin	Both sexes Les deux sexes	Male Masculin	Female Féminin
EUROPE									
San Marino - Saint-Marin									
1 VII 2004 (ESDF)									
1 - 4	1 274	678	596	...	...	...	...	...	...
5 - 9	1 508	800	708	...	...	...	...	...	...
10 - 14	1 383	707	676	...	...	...	...	...	...
15 - 19	1 292	672	620	...	...	...	...	...	...
20 - 24	1 519	779	740	...	...	...	...	...	...
25 - 29	2 038	983	1 055	...	...	...	...	...	...
30 - 34	2 559	1 256	1 304	...	...	...	...	...	...
35 - 39	2 863	1 385	1 478	...	...	...	...	...	...
40 - 44	2 617	1 297	1 320	...	...	...	...	...	...
45 - 49	2 067	1 054	1 013	...	...	...	...	...	...
50 - 54	1 876	932	944	...	...	...	...	...	...
55 - 59	1 819	892	927	...	...	...	...	...	...
60 - 64	1 526	751	775	...	...	...	...	...	...
65 - 69	1 383	688	696	...	...	...	...	...	...
70 - 74	1 207	553	655	...	...	...	...	...	...
75 - 79	946	413	533	...	...	...	...	...	...
80 - 84	765	290	475	...	...	...	...	...	...
85 - 89	321	102	219	...	...	...	...	...	...
90 - 94	163	47	116	...	...	...	...	...	...
95 - 99	29	9	20	...	...	...	...	...	...
100 +	2	-	2	...	...	...	...	...	...
Serbia - Serbie[58]									
1 VII 2007 (ESDJ)									
Total	7 381 579	3 588 957	3 792 622	4 270 400	2 037 012	2 233 388	3 111 179	1 551 945	1 559 234
0	69 100	35 635	33 465	45 551	23 519	22 032	23 549	12 116	11 433
1 - 4	302 869	155 955	146 914	190 423	98 006	92 417	112 446	57 949	54 497
5 - 9	365 362	186 902	178 460	202 604	104 069	98 535	162 758	82 833	79 925
10 - 14	405 427	208 289	197 138	225 384	115 939	109 445	180 043	92 350	87 693
15 - 19	446 332	228 507	217 825	254 792	129 851	124 941	191 540	98 656	92 884
20 - 24	500 542	255 127	245 415	302 444	151 281	151 163	198 098	103 846	94 252
25 - 29	513 378	260 965	252 413	323 839	160 226	163 613	189 539	100 739	88 800
30 - 34	508 798	255 674	253 124	314 355	153 377	160 978	194 443	102 297	92 146
35 - 39	477 059	237 651	239 408	285 420	138 355	147 065	191 639	99 296	92 343
40 - 44	483 448	238 686	244 762	285 371	136 080	149 291	198 077	102 606	95 471
45 - 49	522 462	256 981	265 481	309 482	145 314	164 168	212 980	111 667	101 313
50 - 54	594 432	292 754	301 678	353 139	166 205	186 934	241 293	126 549	114 744
55 - 59	552 830	267 105	285 725	333 059	154 913	178 146	219 771	112 192	107 579
60 - 64	368 236	171 670	196 566	211 853	96 648	115 205	156 383	75 022	81 361
65 - 69	389 709	175 718	213 991	209 090	92 445	116 645	180 619	83 273	97 346
70 - 74	379 415	164 805	214 610	191 731	83 244	108 487	187 684	81 561	106 123
75 - 79	285 337	117 392	167 945	130 955	51 700	79 255	154 382	65 692	88 690
80 - 84	151 810	55 934	95 876	71 038	25 708	45 330	80 772	30 226	50 546
85 - 89	52 537	18 795	33 742	23 698	8 092	15 606	28 839	10 703	18 136
90 - 94	8 238	2 904	5 334	4 071	1 329	2 742	4 167	1 575	2 592
95 - 99	3 403	1 221	2 182	1 678	557	1 121	1 725	664	1 061
100 +	855	287	568	423	154	269	432	133	299
Slovakia - Slovaquie									
1 VII 2007 (ESDJ)									
Total	5 397 766	2 621 095	2 776 671	2 985 680	1 433 808	1 551 872	2 412 086	1 187 287	1 224 799
0	53 971	27 673	26 298	28 558	14 665	13 893	25 413	13 008	12 405
1 - 4	211 135	108 362	102 773	109 519	56 288	53 231	101 616	52 074	49 542
5 - 9	271 108	138 951	132 157	133 209	68 105	65 104	137 899	70 846	67 053
10 - 14	324 842	166 290	158 552	163 483	83 499	79 984	161 359	82 791	78 568
15 - 19	395 132	201 798	193 334	214 834	109 709	105 125	180 298	92 089	88 209
20 - 24	439 215	224 049	215 166	248 899	126 781	122 118	190 316	97 268	93 048
25 - 29	466 285	237 832	228 453	270 102	137 347	132 755	196 183	100 485	95 698
30 - 34	453 089	230 710	222 379	256 889	129 519	127 370	196 200	101 191	95 009
35 - 39	370 709	187 676	183 033	205 519	101 267	104 252	165 190	86 409	78 781
40 - 44	377 216	189 101	188 115	213 774	102 624	111 150	163 442	86 477	76 965
45 - 49	386 905	192 986	193 919	226 283	108 052	118 231	160 622	84 934	75 688
50 - 54	404 342	197 446	206 896	241 830	114 248	127 582	162 512	83 198	79 314
55 - 59	350 151	166 395	183 756	205 250	95 558	109 692	144 901	70 837	74 064
60 - 64	248 739	111 207	137 532	139 702	61 692	78 010	109 037	49 515	59 522

Continent, country or area, date, code and age (in years) / Continent, pays ou zone, date, code et âge (en années)	Total			Urban - Urbaine			Rural - Rurale		
	Both sexes Les deux sexes	Male Masculin	Female Féminin	Both sexes Les deux sexes	Male Masculin	Female Féminin	Both sexes Les deux sexes	Male Masculin	Female Féminin
EUROPE									
Slovakia - Slovaquie									
1 VII 2007 (ESDJ)									
65 - 69	202 946	84 977	117 969	106 510	44 604	61 906	96 436	40 373	56 063
70 - 74	165 945	64 402	101 543	84 757	33 431	51 326	81 188	30 971	50 217
75 - 79	137 113	48 493	88 620	68 203	24 691	43 512	68 910	23 802	45 108
80 - 84	88 990	28 047	60 943	43 731	14 194	29 537	45 259	13 853	31 406
85 - 89	36 591	10 867	25 724	17 893	5 516	12 377	18 698	5 351	13 347
90 - 94	9 464	2 657	6 807	4 771	1 359	3 412	4 693	1 298	3 395
95 - 99	3 215	922	2 293	1 638	509	1 129	1 577	413	1 164
100 +	663	254	409	326	150	176	337	104	233
Slovenia - Slovénie									
1 VII 2007 (ESDJ)									
Total	2 019 406	995 125	1 024 281	1 006 767	490 610	516 157	1 012 639	504 515	508 124
0	19 595	10 043	9 552	9 576	4 927	4 649	10 019	5 116	4 903
1 - 4	72 479	37 208	35 271	34 692	17 811	16 881	37 787	19 397	18 390
5 - 9	90 658	46 806	43 852	41 731	21 606	20 125	48 927	25 200	23 727
10 - 14	98 320	50 493	47 827	44 251	22 612	21 639	54 069	27 881	26 188
15 - 19	116 906	60 324	56 582	54 564	28 076	26 488	62 342	32 248	30 094
20 - 24	135 658	70 525	65 133	66 402	34 925	31 477	69 256	35 600	33 656
25 - 29	153 990	80 515	73 475	77 506	40 685	36 821	76 484	39 830	36 654
30 - 34	151 880	79 094	72 786	75 707	39 442	36 265	76 173	39 652	36 521
35 - 39	145 716	75 053	70 663	71 851	36 781	35 070	73 865	38 272	35 593
40 - 44	157 574	80 259	77 315	79 162	39 538	39 624	78 412	40 721	37 691
45 - 49	154 407	78 825	75 582	78 497	39 199	39 298	75 910	39 626	36 284
50 - 54	158 637	81 760	76 877	82 691	41 605	41 086	75 946	40 155	35 791
55 - 59	138 072	69 941	68 131	71 963	35 513	36 450	66 109	34 428	31 681
60 - 64	101 952	49 044	52 908	53 030	24 382	28 648	48 922	24 662	24 260
65 - 69	97 647	44 974	52 673	50 047	22 429	27 618	47 600	22 545	25 055
70 - 74	85 848	36 020	49 828	43 577	18 259	25 318	42 271	17 761	24 510
75 - 79	70 016	25 789	44 227	35 319	12 850	22 469	34 697	12 939	21 758
80 - 84	44 628	12 585	32 043	22 902	6 740	16 162	21 726	5 845	15 881
85 - 89	18 341	4 405	13 936	9 513	2 407	7 106	8 828	1 998	6 830
90 - 94	5 421	1 162	4 259	2 872	654	2 218	2 549	508	2 041
95 - 99	1 512	278	1 234	832	155	677	680	123	557
100 +	149	22	127	82	14	68	67	8	59
Spain - Espagne									
1 VII 2007 (ESDJ)									
Total	44 873 567	22 155 286	22 718 281	...	...	...	...	...	...
0 - 4	2 326 240	1 197 493	1 128 747	...	...	...	...	...	...
5 - 9	2 131 569	1 094 666	1 036 903	...	...	...	...	...	...
10 - 14	2 077 205	1 066 819	1 010 386	...	...	...	...	...	...
15 - 19	2 283 954	1 174 294	1 109 660	...	...	...	...	...	...
20 - 24	2 803 160	1 435 516	1 367 644	...	...	...	...	...	...
25 - 29	3 664 374	1 892 661	1 771 713	...	...	...	...	...	...
30 - 34	3 988 215	2 069 773	1 918 442	...	...	...	...	...	...
35 - 39	3 773 748	1 941 281	1 832 467	...	...	...	...	...	...
40 - 44	3 565 055	1 805 317	1 759 738	...	...	...	...	...	...
45 - 49	3 228 712	1 614 563	1 614 149	...	...	...	...	...	...
50 - 54	2 773 472	1 372 172	1 401 300	...	...	...	...	...	...
55 - 59	2 508 910	1 226 360	1 282 550	...	...	...	...	...	...
60 - 64	2 283 746	1 099 986	1 183 760	...	...	...	...	...	...
65 - 69	1 875 052	882 271	992 781	...	...	...	...	...	...
70 - 74	1 900 208	857 229	1 042 979	...	...	...	...	...	...
75 - 79	1 644 791	698 499	946 292	...	...	...	...	...	...
80 - 84	1 149 412	444 237	705 175	...	...	...	...	...	...
85 - 89	606 034	203 693	402 341	...	...	...	...	...	...
90 - 94	227 515	63 167	164 348	...	...	...	...	...	...
95 - 99	56 535	13 922	42 613	...	...	...	...	...	...
100 +	5 660	1 367	4 293	...	...	...	...	...	...
Sweden - Suède[12]									
1 VII 2007 (ESDJ)									
Total	9 148 092	4 543 722	4 604 370	...	...	...	...	...	...
0	107 018	55 056	51 962	...	...	...	...	...	...
1 - 4	411 927	211 176	200 751	...	...	...	...	...	...
5 - 9	472 130	242 511	229 619	...	...	...	...	...	...

7. Population by age, sex and urban/rural residence: latest available year, 1998 - 2007

Population selon l'âge, le sexe et la résidence, urbaine/rurale: dernière année disponible, 1998 - 2007 (continued - suite)

Continent, country or area, date, code and age (in years) / Continent, pays ou zone, date, code et âge (en années)	Total			Urban - Urbaine			Rural - Rurale		
	Both sexes Les deux sexes	Male Masculin	Female Féminin	Both sexes Les deux sexes	Male Masculin	Female Féminin	Both sexes Les deux sexes	Male Masculin	Female Féminin
EUROPE									
Sweden - Suède[12]									
1 VII 2007 (ESDJ)									
10 - 14	554 587	283 857	270 730	...	...	...	...	...	...
15 - 19	628 375	322 963	305 413	...	...	...	...	...	...
20 - 24	549 552	281 434	268 118	...	...	...	...	...	...
25 - 29	551 093	281 427	269 667	...	...	...	...	...	...
30 - 34	597 623	304 553	293 071	...	...	...	...	...	...
35 - 39	628 970	319 908	309 062	...	...	...	...	...	...
40 - 44	663 975	339 489	324 486	...	...	...	...	...	...
45 - 49	586 537	297 740	288 797	...	...	...	...	...	...
50 - 54	582 049	294 005	288 044	...	...	...	...	...	...
55 - 59	605 560	303 607	301 953	...	...	...	...	...	...
60 - 64	613 776	308 132	305 644	...	...	...	...	...	...
65 - 69	443 520	218 493	225 028	...	...	...	...	...	...
70 - 74	351 314	165 129	186 186	...	...	...	...	...	...
75 - 79	309 483	135 655	173 828	...	...	...	...	...	...
80 - 84	252 241	101 424	150 817	...	...	...	...	...	...
85 - 89	162 105	56 790	105 315	...	...	...	...	...	...
90 - 94	60 978	17 191	43 787	...	...	...	...	...	...
95 - 99	13 853	2 966	10 887	...	...	...	...	...	...
100 +	1 433	222	1 211	...	...	...	...	...	...
Switzerland - Suisse									
1 VII 2007 (ESDJ)									
Total	7 551 117	3 703 187	3 847 930	...	...	...	...	...	...
0	37 108	19 031	18 077	...	...	...	...	...	...
1 - 4	293 458	150 788	142 670	...	...	...	...	...	...
5 - 9	382 894	197 254	185 640	...	...	...	...	...	...
10 - 14	421 095	216 462	204 633	...	...	...	...	...	...
15 - 19	452 369	232 234	220 135	...	...	...	...	...	...
20 - 24	446 387	225 859	220 528	...	...	...	...	...	...
25 - 29	475 605	236 938	238 667	...	...	...	...	...	...
30 - 34	506 254	251 869	254 385	...	...	...	...	...	...
35 - 39	583 007	290 987	292 020	...	...	...	...	...	...
40 - 44	644 765	325 183	319 582	...	...	...	...	...	...
45 - 49	592 121	298 626	293 495	...	...	...	...	...	...
50 - 54	519 250	261 727	257 523	...	...	...	...	...	...
55 - 59	478 293	238 586	239 707	...	...	...	...	...	...
60 - 64	448 029	221 763	226 266	...	...	...	...	...	...
65 - 69	353 188	168 613	184 575	...	...	...	...	...	...
70 - 74	295 401	134 399	161 002	...	...	...	...	...	...
75 - 79	250 562	105 570	144 992	...	...	...	...	...	...
80 - 84	191 061	71 823	119 238	...	...	...	...	...	...
85 - 89	115 412	38 501	76 911	...	...	...	...	...	...
90 - 94	47 989	13 376	34 613	...	...	...	...	...	...
95 +	16 869	3 598	13 271	...	...	...	...	...	...
The Former Yugoslav Republic of Macedonia - L'ex-République yougoslave de Macédoine									
1 VII 2007 (ESDF)									
Total	2 043 559	1 024 489	1 019 070	...	...	...	...	...	...
0	22 393	11 566	10 827	...	...	...	...	...	...
1 - 4	90 971	46 836	44 135	...	...	...	...	...	...
5 - 9	123 879	63 954	59 925	...	...	...	...	...	...
10 - 14	144 613	74 442	70 171	...	...	...	...	...	...
15 - 19	160 730	82 768	77 962	...	...	...	...	...	...
20 - 24	165 092	84 604	80 488	...	...	...	...	...	...
25 - 29	160 339	82 597	77 742	...	...	...	...	...	...
30 - 34	152 865	77 862	75 003	...	...	...	...	...	...
35 - 39	147 569	74 748	72 821	...	...	...	...	...	...
40 - 44	148 730	75 599	73 131	...	...	...	...	...	...
45 - 49	145 053	73 787	71 266	...	...	...	...	...	...
50 - 54	139 009	70 445	68 564	...	...	...	...	...	...
55 - 59	121 041	58 923	62 118	...	...	...	...	...	...
60 - 64	89 766	42 928	46 838	...	...	...	...	...	...

Continent, country or area, date, code and age (in years) / Continent, pays ou zone, date, code et âge (en annèes)	Total			Urban - Urbaine			Rural - Rurale		
	Both sexes Les deux sexes	Male Masculin	Female Féminin	Both sexes Les deux sexes	Male Masculin	Female Féminin	Both sexes Les deux sexes	Male Masculin	Female Féminin
EUROPE									
The Former Yugoslav Republic of Macedonia - L'ex-République yougoslave de Macédoine									
1 VII 2007 (ESDF)									
65 - 69	80 240	37 633	42 607	...	...	...	...	...	...
70 - 74	71 160	32 377	38 783	...	...	...	...	...	...
75 - 79	45 640	19 606	26 034	...	...	...	...	...	...
80 - 84	23 623	9 633	13 990	...	...	...	...	...	...
85 - 89	7 815	3 152	4 663	...	...	...	...	...	...
90 - 94	1 683	645	1 038	...	...	...	...	...	...
95 +	581	200	381	...	...	...	...	...	...
Unknown - Inconnu	767	184	583	...	...	...	...	...	...
Ukraine									
1 I 2007 (ESDJ)									
Total	46 465 691	21 434 680	25 031 011	31 521 751	14 460 756	17 060 995	14 943 940	6 973 924	7 970 016
0	456 726	234 110	222 616	304 397	156 224	148 173	152 329	77 886	74 443
1 - 4	1 632 984	840 107	792 877	1 076 673	554 061	522 612	556 311	286 046	270 265
5 - 9	1 975 375	1 013 270	962 105	1 210 009	621 622	588 387	765 366	391 648	373 718
10 - 14	2 541 354	1 302 181	1 239 173	1 563 531	801 537	761 994	977 823	500 644	477 179
15 - 19	3 393 423	1 737 770	1 655 653	2 322 636	1 179 782	1 142 854	1 070 787	557 988	512 799
20 - 24	3 873 350	1 977 600	1 895 750	2 861 262	1 456 104	1 405 158	1 012 088	521 496	490 592
25 - 29	3 451 651	1 740 002	1 711 649	2 488 916	1 242 176	1 246 740	962 735	497 826	464 909
30 - 34	3 346 629	1 659 422	1 687 207	2 358 324	1 157 539	1 200 785	988 305	501 883	486 422
35 - 39	3 140 431	1 537 592	1 602 839	2 159 219	1 031 745	1 127 474	981 212	505 847	475 365
40 - 44	3 310 823	1 581 508	1 729 315	2 295 465	1 062 029	1 233 436	1 015 358	519 479	495 879
45 - 49	3 672 421	1 716 437	1 955 984	2 588 466	1 170 592	1 417 874	1 083 955	545 845	538 110
50 - 54	3 273 944	1 478 267	1 795 677	2 344 778	1 027 641	1 317 137	929 166	450 626	478 540
55 - 59	2 948 819	1 288 972	1 659 847	2 108 585	903 378	1 205 207	840 234	385 594	454 640
60 - 64	1 844 703	749 847	1 094 856	1 221 605	497 206	724 399	623 098	252 641	370 457
65 - 69	2 885 630	1 105 406	1 780 224	1 859 547	714 072	1 145 475	1 026 083	391 334	634 749
70 - 74	1 754 765	641 782	1 112 983	1 048 787	388 778	660 009	705 978	253 004	452 974
75 - 79	1 622 559	519 690	1 102 869	941 844	309 240	632 604	680 715	210 450	470 265
80 - 84	934 754	227 792	706 962	536 518	135 465	401 053	398 236	92 327	305 909
85 - 89	294 948	63 282	231 666	167 786	38 885	128 901	127 162	24 397	102 765
90 - 94	94 077	16 918	77 159	54 574	11 018	43 556	39 503	5 900	33 603
95 - 99	14 563	2 471	12 092	7 668	1 481	6 187	6 895	990	5 905
100 +	1 762	254	1 508	1 161	181	980	601	73	528
United Kingdom of Great Britain and Northern Ireland - Royaume-Uni de Grande-Bretagne et d'Irlande du Nord[59]									
29 IV 2001 (CDFC)									
Total	58 789 194	28 579 869	30 209 325	47 007 427	22 769 606	24 237 821	11 781 767	5 810 263	5 971 504
0	660 025	337 154	322 871	545 015	278 159	266 856	115 010	58 995	56 015
1 - 4	2 826 228	1 448 534	1 377 694	2 305 860	1 181 014	1 124 846	520 368	267 520	252 848
5 - 9	3 738 042	1 914 727	1 823 315	3 009 441	1 541 475	1 467 966	728 601	373 252	355 349
10 - 14	3 880 557	1 987 606	1 892 951	3 103 939	1 588 218	1 515 721	776 618	399 388	377 230
15 - 19	3 663 782	1 870 508	1 793 274	2 968 710	1 505 467	1 463 243	695 072	365 041	330 031
20 - 24	3 545 984	1 765 257	1 780 727	3 041 392	1 493 532	1 547 860	504 592	271 725	232 867
25 - 29	3 867 015	1 895 469	1 971 546	3 299 342	1 610 026	1 689 316	567 673	285 443	282 230
30 - 34	4 493 532	2 199 767	2 293 765	3 723 844	1 824 665	1 899 179	769 688	375 102	394 586
35 - 39	4 625 777	2 277 678	2 348 099	3 727 542	1 835 623	1 891 919	898 235	442 055	456 180
40 - 44	4 151 613	2 056 545	2 095 068	3 290 231	1 629 251	1 660 980	861 382	427 294	434 088
45 - 49	3 735 986	1 851 391	1 884 595	2 911 582	1 441 854	1 469 728	824 404	409 537	414 867
50 - 54	4 040 576	2 003 158	2 037 418	3 082 777	1 526 738	1 556 039	957 799	476 420	481 379
55 - 59	3 339 004	1 651 396	1 687 608	2 514 831	1 238 414	1 276 417	824 173	412 982	411 191
60 - 64	2 880 074	1 409 684	1 470 390	2 203 267	1 070 975	1 132 292	676 807	338 709	338 098
65 - 69	2 596 939	1 241 382	1 355 557	2 005 735	948 325	1 057 410	591 204	293 057	298 147
70 - 74	2 339 319	1 059 156	1 280 163	1 821 307	812 938	1 008 369	518 012	246 218	271 794
75 - 79	1 967 088	817 738	1 149 350	1 542 567	632 032	910 535	424 521	185 706	238 815
80 - 84	1 313 592	482 707	830 885	1 030 404	373 231	657 173	283 188	109 476	173 712
85 - 89	752 035	226 520	525 515	589 543	174 135	415 408	162 492	52 385	110 107
90 - 94	293 961	68 682	225 279	229 205	52 178	177 027	64 756	16 504	48 252

Continent, country or area, date, code and age (in years) / Continent, pays ou zone, date, code et âge (en années)	Total			Urban - Urbaine			Rural - Rurale		
	Both sexes Les deux sexes	Male Masculin	Female Féminin	Both sexes Les deux sexes	Male Masculin	Female Féminin	Both sexes Les deux sexes	Male Masculin	Female Féminin
EUROPE									
United Kingdom of Great Britain and Northern Ireland - Royaume-Uni de Grande-Bretagne et d'Irlande du Nord[59]									
29 IV 2001 (CDFC)									
95 - 99	68 655	12 920	55 735	53 532	9 866	43 666	15 123	3 054	12 069
100 +	9 410	1 890	7 520	7 361	1 490	5 871	2 049	400	1 649
1 VII 2007 (ESDF)									
Total	60 975 355	29 916 107	31 059 248	...	...	...	...	...	...
0	755 742	387 490	368 252	...	...	...	...	...	...
1 - 4	2 836 856	1 453 443	1 383 413	...	...	...	...	...	...
5 - 9	3 424 180	1 750 416	1 673 764	...	...	...	...	...	...
10 - 14	3 704 261	1 898 270	1 805 991	...	...	...	...	...	...
15 - 19	4 015 768	2 068 706	1 947 062	...	...	...	...	...	...
20 - 24	4 140 505	2 124 464	2 016 041	...	...	...	...	...	...
25 - 29	3 966 264	1 991 986	1 974 278	...	...	...	...	...	...
30 - 34	3 893 213	1 943 984	1 949 229	...	...	...	...	...	...
35 - 39	4 534 061	2 245 779	2 288 282	...	...	...	...	...	...
40 - 44	4 714 031	2 331 980	2 382 051	...	...	...	...	...	...
45 - 49	4 250 229	2 098 919	2 151 310	...	...	...	...	...	...
50 - 54	3 729 877	1 842 351	1 887 526	...	...	...	...	...	...
55 - 59	3 748 112	1 844 944	1 903 168	...	...	...	...	...	...
60 - 64	3 483 180	1 700 736	1 782 444	...	...	...	...	...	...
65 - 69	2 697 243	1 296 389	1 400 854	...	...	...	...	...	...
70 - 74	2 360 446	1 101 784	1 258 662	...	...	...	...	...	...
75 - 79	1 971 880	861 145	1 110 735	...	...	...	...	...	...
80 - 84	1 451 778	570 490	881 288	...	...	...	...	...	...
85 - 89	872 646	294 703	577 943	...	...	...	...	...	...
90 +	425 083	108 128	316 955	...	...	...	...	...	...
OCEANIA - OCÉANIE									
American Samoa - Samoas américaines[15]									
1 IV 2000 (CDJC)									
Total	57 291	29 264	28 027	...	...	...	...	...	...
0 - 4	7 820	4 008	3 812	...	...	...	...	...	...
5 - 9	7 788	4 058	3 730	...	...	...	...	...	...
10 - 14	6 604	3 389	3 215	...	...	...	...	...	...
15 - 19	5 223	2 747	2 476	...	...	...	...	...	...
20 - 24	4 476	2 328	2 148	...	...	...	...	...	...
25 - 29	4 356	2 218	2 138	...	...	...	...	...	...
30 - 34	4 351	2 167	2 184	...	...	...	...	...	...
35 - 39	4 059	1 980	2 079	...	...	...	...	...	...
40 - 44	3 302	1 654	1 648	...	...	...	...	...	...
45 - 49	2 660	1 331	1 329	...	...	...	...	...	...
50 - 54	2 073	1 071	1 002	...	...	...	...	...	...
55 - 59	1 474	817	657	...	...	...	...	...	...
60 - 64	1 204	636	568	...	...	...	...	...	...
65 - 69	790	407	383	...	...	...	...	...	...
70 - 74	555	231	324	...	...	...	...	...	...
75 +	556	222	334	...	...	...	...	...	...
Australia - Australie									
1 VII 2006 (ESDJ)									
Total	20 701 488	10 290 338	10 411 150	17 231 649	8 522 861	8 708 788	3 469 839	1 767 477	1 702 362
0 - 4	1 308 651	672 183	636 468	1 085 661	557 306	528 355	222 990	114 877	108 113
5 - 9	1 340 779	687 357	653 422	1 089 290	557 659	531 631	251 489	129 698	121 791
10 - 14	1 400 713	719 258	681 455	1 132 412	580 720	551 692	268 301	138 538	129 763
15 - 19	1 414 666	726 266	688 400	1 188 711	606 789	581 922	225 955	119 477	106 478
20 - 24	1 469 432	747 927	721 505	1 308 888	663 056	645 832	160 544	84 871	75 673
25 - 29	1 406 466	708 376	698 090	1 242 936	625 379	617 557	163 530	82 997	80 533
30 - 34	1 493 153	743 386	749 767	1 292 900	643 576	649 324	200 253	99 810	100 443
35 - 39	1 527 431	759 543	767 888	1 294 818	643 128	651 690	232 613	116 415	116 198

Continent, country or area, date, code and age (in years) / Continent, pays ou zone, date, code et âge (en années)	Total			Urban - Urbaine			Rural - Rurale		
	Both sexes Les deux sexes	Male Masculin	Female Féminin	Both sexes Les deux sexes	Male Masculin	Female Féminin	Both sexes Les deux sexes	Male Masculin	Female Féminin
OCEANIA - OCÉANIE									
Australia - Australie									
1 VII 2006 (ESDJ)									
40 - 44	1 534 709	762 579	772 130	1 278 134	633 218	644 916	256 575	129 361	127 214
45 - 49	1 495 288	741 136	754 152	1 230 792	605 775	625 017	264 496	135 361	129 135
50 - 54	1 363 680	679 033	684 647	1 114 075	549 246	564 829	249 605	129 787	119 818
55 - 59	1 271 559	636 723	634 836	1 029 336	510 564	518 772	242 223	126 159	116 064
60 - 64	987 847	496 072	491 775	784 895	390 914	393 981	202 952	105 158	97 794
65 - 69	779 169	385 226	393 943	614 069	299 188	314 881	165 100	86 038	79 062
70 - 74	629 138	302 778	326 360	500 701	236 890	263 811	128 437	65 888	62 549
75 - 79	551 488	252 158	299 330	444 809	199 835	244 974	106 679	52 323	54 356
80 - 84	405 328	166 000	239 328	333 439	134 515	198 924	71 889	31 485	40 404
85 +	...	...	...	265 783	85 103	180 680	56 208	19 234	36 974
85 - 89	214 338	75 405	138 933	...	...	...	...	...	...
90 - 94	85 816	24 167	61 649	...	...	...	...	...	...
95 - 99	19 396	4 305	15 091	...	...	...	...	...	...
100 +	2 441	460	1 981	...	...	...	...	...	...
1 VII 2007 (ESDJ)									
Total	21 017 222	10 451 718	10 565 504	...	...	...	...	...	...
0 - 4	1 330 561	683 643	646 918	...	...	...	...	...	...
5 - 9	1 341 929	687 822	654 107	...	...	...	...	...	...
10 - 14	1 401 134	719 203	681 931	...	...	...	...	...	...
15 - 19	1 440 254	739 842	700 412	...	...	...	...	...	...
20 - 24	1 491 506	759 299	732 207	...	...	...	...	...	...
25 - 29	1 445 850	730 017	715 833	...	...	...	...	...	...
30 - 34	1 471 568	734 004	737 564	...	...	...	...	...	...
35 - 39	1 567 896	779 420	788 476	...	...	...	...	...	...
40 - 44	1 522 050	756 909	765 141	...	...	...	...	...	...
45 - 49	1 523 882	755 264	768 618	...	...	...	...	...	...
50 - 54	1 388 533	690 531	698 002	...	...	...	...	...	...
55 - 59	1 269 680	634 147	635 533	...	...	...	...	...	...
60 - 64	1 063 250	533 356	529 894	...	...	...	...	...	...
65 - 69	805 321	399 003	406 318	...	...	...	...	...	...
70 - 74	643 801	309 975	333 826	...	...	...	...	...	...
75 - 79	550 607	253 017	297 590	...	...	...	...	...	...
80 - 84	414 513	172 184	242 329	...	...	...	...	...	...
85 - 89	230 321	82 671	147 650	...	...	...	...	...	...
90 - 94	89 901	25 889	64 012	...	...	...	...	...	...
95 - 99	21 805	4 923	16 882	...	...	...	...	...	...
100 +	2 860	599	2 261	...	...	...	...	...	...
Cook Islands - Îles Cook[60]									
1 XII 2006 (CDFC)									
Total	19 569	9 932	9 637	...	...	...	...	...	...
0 - 14	5 098	2 649	2 449	...	...	...	...	...	...
15 - 44	8 865	4 405	4 460	...	...	...	...	...	...
45 - 59	3 287	1 689	1 598	...	...	...	...	...	...
60 +	2 319	1 189	1 130	...	...	...	...	...	...
Fiji - Fidji									
16 IX 2007 (CDFC)									
Total	837 271	427 176	410 095	424 846	212 454	212 392	412 425	214 722	197 703
0 - 4	82 718	42 835	39 883	39 209	20 264	18 945	43 509	22 571	20 938
5 - 9	78 019	40 441	37 578	35 981	18 528	17 453	42 038	21 913	20 125
10 - 14	82 384	42 369	40 015	38 916	19 790	19 126	43 468	22 579	20 889
15 - 19	79 518	40 818	38 700	42 458	21 051	21 407	37 060	19 767	17 293
20 - 24	80 352	41 325	39 027	45 837	22 896	22 941	34 515	18 429	16 086
25 - 29	73 487	37 390	36 097	40 669	20 260	20 409	32 818	17 130	15 688
30 - 34	63 535	32 825	30 710	33 612	17 017	16 595	29 923	15 808	14 115
35 - 39	56 552	28 778	27 774	29 288	14 674	14 614	27 264	14 104	13 160
40 - 44	56 274	28 598	27 676	28 147	14 058	14 089	28 127	14 540	13 587
45 - 49	50 322	25 835	24 487	25 556	12 780	12 776	24 766	13 055	11 711
50 - 54	40 009	20 215	19 794	20 581	10 118	10 463	19 428	10 097	9 331
55 - 59	31 161	15 735	15 426	15 667	7 715	7 952	15 494	8 020	7 474
60 - 64	24 120	11 956	12 164	11 655	5 647	6 008	12 465	6 309	6 156
65 - 69	16 808	8 098	8 710	7 597	3 509	4 088	9 211	4 589	4 622
70 - 74	10 110	4 716	5 394	4 360	1 887	2 473	5 750	2 829	2 921
75 +	...	...	...	5 313	2 260	3 053	6 589	2 982	3 607

Continent, country or area, date, code and age (in years) / Continent, pays ou zone, date, code et âge (en années)	Total			Urban - Urbaine			Rural - Rurale		
	Both sexes Les deux sexes	Male Masculin	Female Féminin	Both sexes Les deux sexes	Male Masculin	Female Féminin	Both sexes Les deux sexes	Male Masculin	Female Féminin
OCEANIA - OCÉANIE									
Fiji - Fidji									
16 IX 2007 (CDFC)									
75 - 79	6 138	2 811	3 327	...	...	...	...	...	...
80 - 84	3 236	1 376	1 860	...	...	...	...	...	...
85 - 89	1 638	702	936	...	...	...	...	...	...
90 - 94	572	212	360	...	...	...	...	...	...
95 + ...	318	141	177	...	...	...	...	...	...
French Polynesia - Polynésie française									
1 I 1999 (ESDF)									
Total.	227 525	117 738	109 787	...	...	...	...	...	...
0	4 268	2 177	2 091	...	...	...	...	...	...
1 - 4	18 470	9 604	8 866	...	...	...	...	...	...
5 - 9	25 518	13 178	12 340	...	...	...	...	...	...
10 - 14	25 533	13 055	12 478	...	...	...	...	...	...
15 - 19	22 126	11 290	10 836	...	...	...	...	...	...
20 - 24	19 077	9 884	9 193	...	...	...	...	...	...
25 - 29	19 574	10 141	9 433	...	...	...	...	...	...
30 - 34	19 667	10 179	9 488	...	...	...	...	...	...
35 - 39	17 032	8 941	8 091	...	...	...	...	...	...
40 - 44	14 421	7 640	6 781	...	...	...	...	...	...
45 - 49	11 037	5 830	5 207	...	...	...	...	...	...
50 - 54	9 001	4 790	4 211	...	...	...	...	...	...
55 - 59	7 202	3 845	3 357	...	...	...	...	...	...
60 - 64	5 518	2 899	2 619	...	...	...	...	...	...
65 - 69	3 998	2 042	1 956	...	...	...	...	...	...
70 - 74	2 600	1 244	1 356	...	...	...	...	...	...
75 - 79	1 365	585	780	...	...	...	...	...	...
80 + ...	1 118	414	704	...	...	...	...	...	...
Guam[15]									
1 IV 2000 (CDJC)									
Total.	154 805	79 181	75 624	...	...	...	...	...	...
0	3 535	1 862	1 673	...	...	...	...	...	...
1 - 4	13 250	6 945	6 305	...	...	...	...	...	...
5 - 9	16 090	8 270	7 820	...	...	...	...	...	...
10 - 14	14 281	7 232	7 049	...	...	...	...	...	...
15 - 19	12 379	6 273	6 106	...	...	...	...	...	...
20 - 24	11 989	6 140	5 849	...	...	...	...	...	...
25 - 29	12 944	6 584	6 360	...	...	...	...	...	...
30 - 34	12 906	6 727	6 179	...	...	...	...	...	...
35 - 39	12 751	6 692	6 059	...	...	...	...	...	...
40 - 44	10 390	5 344	5 046	...	...	...	...	...	...
45 - 49	9 042	4 608	4 434	...	...	...	...	...	...
50 - 54	7 506	3 813	3 693	...	...	...	...	...	...
55 - 59	4 993	2 548	2 445	...	...	...	...	...	...
60 - 64	4 534	2 190	2 344	...	...	...	...	...	...
65 - 69	3 399	1 628	1 771	...	...	...	...	...	...
70 - 74	2 461	1 287	1 174	...	...	...	...	...	...
75 - 79	1 384	681	703	...	...	...	...	...	...
80 - 84	616	234	382	...	...	...	...	...	...
85 - 89	248	83	165	...	...	...	...	...	...
90 - 94	79	30	49	...	...	...	...	...	...
95 - 99	22	9	13	...	...	...	...	...	...
100 + ...	6	1	5	...	...	...	...	...	...
Kiribati									
7 XII 2005 (CDFC)									
Total.	92 533	45 612	46 921	40 311	19 435	20 876	52 222	26 177	26 045
0 - 4	10 917	5 613	5 304	4 587	2 379	2 208	6 330	3 234	3 096
5 - 9	12 466	6 315	6 151	4 908	2 438	2 470	7 558	3 877	3 681
10 - 14	10 810	5 597	5 213	4 297	2 185	2 112	6 513	3 412	3 101
15 - 19	10 793	5 511	5 282	4 634	2 288	2 346	6 159	3 223	2 936
20 - 24	8 574	4 247	4 327	4 568	2 132	2 436	4 006	2 115	1 891
25 - 29	6 782	3 274	3 508	3 385	1 631	1 754	3 397	1 643	1 754
30 - 34	5 561	2 631	2 930	2 567	1 196	1 371	2 994	1 435	1 559
35 - 39	6 459	3 095	3 364	2 774	1 304	1 470	3 685	1 791	1 894

Continent, country or area, date, code and age (in years) / Continent, pays ou zone, date, code et âge (en années)	Total			Urban - Urbaine			Rural - Rurale		
	Both sexes Les deux sexes	Male Masculin	Female Féminin	Both sexes Les deux sexes	Male Masculin	Female Féminin	Both sexes Les deux sexes	Male Masculin	Female Féminin
OCEANIA - OCÉANIE									
Kiribati									
7 XII 2005 (CDFC)									
40 - 44	5 253	2 575	2 678	2 286	1 093	1 193	2 967	1 482	1 485
45 - 49	4 298	2 046	2 252	1 915	905	1 010	2 383	1 141	1 242
50 - 54	3 150	1 479	1 671	1 396	639	757	1 754	840	914
55 - 59	2 450	1 143	1 307	1 038	458	580	1 412	685	727
60 - 64	1 740	802	938	708	309	399	1 032	493	539
65 - 69	1 288	547	741	516	219	297	772	328	444
70 - 74	1 111	428	683	403	150	253	708	278	430
75 +	881	309	572	329	109	220	552	200	352
Marshall Islands - Îles Marshall									
1 VII 2007 (ESDF)									
Total	52 701	27 022	25 679	...	...	...	...	...	...
0 - 4	7 632	3 916	3 716	...	...	...	...	...	...
5 - 9	7 297	3 768	3 529	...	...	...	...	...	...
10 - 14	6 668	3 422	3 246	...	...	...	...	...	...
15 - 19	6 568	3 378	3 189	...	...	...	...	...	...
20 - 24	6 194	3 215	2 979	...	...	...	...	...	...
25 - 29	3 949	1 999	1 951	...	...	...	...	...	...
30 - 34	2 556	1 282	1 274	...	...	...	...	...	...
35 - 39	2 304	1 174	1 129	...	...	...	...	...	...
40 - 44	2 202	1 130	1 073	...	...	...	...	...	...
45 - 49	2 053	1 018	1 034	...	...	...	...	...	...
50 - 54	1 798	919	878	...	...	...	...	...	...
55 - 59	1 428	784	645	...	...	...	...	...	...
60 - 64	839	438	400	...	...	...	...	...	...
65 - 69	478	242	236	...	...	...	...	...	...
70 - 74	344	159	185	...	...	...	...	...	...
75 +	392	177	216	...	...	...	...	...	...
Micronesia (Federated States of) - Micronésie (États fédérés de)									
1 IV 2000 (CDJC)									
Total	107 008	54 191	52 817	...	...	...	...	...	...
0	2 906	1 528	1 378	...	...	...	...	...	...
1 - 4	11 877	6 051	5 826	...	...	...	...	...	...
5 - 9	14 169	7 310	6 859	...	...	...	...	...	...
10 - 14	14 220	7 481	6 739	...	...	...	...	...	...
15 - 19	13 237	6 754	6 483	...	...	...	...	...	...
20 - 24	9 525	4 886	4 639	...	...	...	...	...	...
25 - 29	7 603	3 695	3 908	...	...	...	...	...	...
30 - 34	6 489	3 124	3 365	...	...	...	...	...	...
35 - 39	6 015	2 994	3 021	...	...	...	...	...	...
40 - 44	5 559	2 801	2 758	...	...	...	...	...	...
45 - 49	4 647	2 393	2 254	...	...	...	...	...	...
50 - 54	3 209	1 654	1 555	...	...	...	...	...	...
55 - 59	1 898	899	999	...	...	...	...	...	...
60 - 64	1 733	830	903	...	...	...	...	...	...
65 - 69	1 487	699	788	...	...	...	...	...	...
70 - 74	993	457	536	...	...	...	...	...	...
75 - 79	727	310	417	...	...	...	...	...	...
80 - 84	328	138	190	...	...	...	...	...	...
85 +	386	187	199	...	...	...	...	...	...
Nauru									
23 IX 2002 (CDFC)									
Total	10 065	5 136	4 929	...	...	...	...	...	...
0 - 4	1 266	648	618	...	...	...	...	...	...
5 - 9	1 359	718	641	...	...	...	...	...	...
10 - 14	1 213	640	573	...	...	...	...	...	...
15 - 19	1 010	502	508	...	...	...	...	...	...
20 - 24	961	500	461	...	...	...	...	...	...
25 - 29	786	397	389	...	...	...	...	...	...
30 - 34	728	375	353	...	...	...	...	...	...
35 - 39	743	375	369	...	...	...	...	...	...

Continent, country or area, date, code and age (in years) / Continent, pays ou zone, date, code et âge (en années)	Total			Urban - Urbaine			Rural - Rurale		
	Both sexes Les deux sexes	Male Masculin	Female Féminin	Both sexes Les deux sexes	Male Masculin	Female Féminin	Both sexes Les deux sexes	Male Masculin	Female Féminin
OCEANIA - OCÉANIE									
Nauru									
23 IX 2002 (CDFC)									
40 - 44	622	292	331	...	...	...	...	...	...
45 - 49	492	236	256	...	...	...	...	...	...
50 - 54	337	162	175	...	...	...	...	...	...
55 - 59	183	95	88	...	...	...	...	...	...
60 - 64	126	79	47	...	...	...	...	...	...
65 - 69	58	31	27	...	...	...	...	...	...
70 - 74	37	18	19	...	...	...	...	...	...
75 - 79	19	6	13	...	...	...	...	...	...
80 - 84	9	2	7	...	...	...	...	...	...
85 - 89	5	1	4	...	...	...	...	...	...
90 +	1	-	1	...	...	...	...	...	...
Unknown - Inconnu	110	59	49	...	...	...	...	...	...
New Caledonia - Nouvelle-Calédonie									
1 I 2007 (ESDF)									
Total	240 390	121 299	119 091	...	...	...	...	...	...
0	4 210	2 177	2 033	...	...	...	...	...	...
1 - 4	16 218	8 355	7 863	...	...	...	...	...	...
5 - 9	22 553	11 543	11 010	...	...	...	...	...	...
10 - 14	22 218	11 493	10 725	...	...	...	...	...	...
15 - 19	21 670	11 018	10 652	...	...	...	...	...	...
20 - 24	18 831	9 538	9 293	...	...	...	...	...	...
25 - 29	17 301	8 557	8 744	...	...	...	...	...	...
30 - 34	19 144	9 457	9 687	...	...	...	...	...	...
35 - 39	18 980	9 378	9 602	...	...	...	...	...	...
40 - 44	17 280	8 779	8 501	...	...	...	...	...	...
45 - 49	14 592	7 269	7 323	...	...	...	...	...	...
50 - 54	12 011	6 144	5 867	...	...	...	...	...	...
55 - 59	10 671	5 641	5 030	...	...	...	...	...	...
60 - 64	8 303	4 392	3 911	...	...	...	...	...	...
65 - 69	6 326	3 127	3 199	...	...	...	...	...	...
70 - 74	4 267	2 042	2 225	...	...	...	...	...	...
75 - 79	2 903	1 259	1 644	...	...	...	...	...	...
80 - 84	1 630	675	955	...	...	...	...	...	...
85 - 89	754	284	470	...	...	...	...	...	...
90 - 94	386	132	254	...	...	...	...	...	...
95 +	142	39	103	...	...	...	...	...	...
New Zealand - Nouvelle-Zélande[9]									
1 VII 2006 (ESDJ)									
Total	4 184 580	2 048 340	2 136 260	3 604 440	1 750 350	1 824 130	580 150	297 980	282 140
0 - 4	286 000	146 210	139 790	246 390	126 030	120 370	39 610	20 180	19 430
0	59 060	30 150	28 910	...	...	...	...	...	...
1 - 4	226 940	116 060	110 880	...	...	...	...	...	...
5 - 9	291 880	149 230	142 650	247 050	126 170	120 890	44 820	23 060	21 760
10 - 14	310 430	159 520	150 920	260 530	133 610	126 920	49 910	25 910	24 000
15 - 19	313 560	159 400	154 160	273 210	137 880	135 340	40 350	21 530	18 820
20 - 24	291 180	145 850	145 330	267 620	132 880	134 740	23 570	12 980	10 590
25 - 29	260 370	126 770	133 600	235 270	114 240	121 030	25 100	12 530	12 570
30 - 34	286 010	136 320	149 700	251 280	119 430	131 850	34 730	16 880	17 850
35 - 39	312 560	149 140	163 430	269 030	128 200	140 830	43 530	20 940	22 600
40 - 44	322 490	155 940	166 540	272 260	131 200	141 060	50 230	24 740	25 490
45 - 49	305 160	149 120	156 040	254 900	123 470	131 430	50 260	25 640	24 610
50 - 54	263 650	129 930	133 720	218 660	106 580	112 070	44 990	23 340	21 650
55 - 59	243 010	120 080	122 930	201 070	98 350	102 720	41 940	21 730	20 210
60 - 64	186 660	91 900	94 760	155 090	75 170	79 920	31 570	16 730	14 840
65 - 69	155 530	75 620	79 910	131 320	62 470	68 860	24 210	13 150	11 050
70 - 74	120 170	57 380	62 790	104 670	48 800	55 870	15 500	8 580	6 910
75 - 79	103 600	47 570	56 030	93 090	41 810	51 280	10 510	5 760	4 750
80 - 84	74 180	30 180	44 000	68 390	27 290	41 100	5 790	2 890	2 890
85 +	...	...	...	54 610	16 770	37 840	3 530	1 410	2 120
85 - 89	39 080	13 160	25 920	...	...	...	...	...	...
90 +	19 060	5 020	14 040	...	...	...	...	...	...

7. Population by age, sex and urban/rural residence: latest available year, 1998 - 2007
Population selon l'âge, le sexe et la résidence, urbaine/rurale: dernière année disponible, 1998 - 2007 (continued - suite)

Continent, country or area, date, code and age (in years) / Continent, pays ou zone, date, code et âge (en années)	Total			Urban - Urbaine			Rural - Rurale		
	Both sexes Les deux sexes	Male Masculin	Female Féminin	Both sexes Les deux sexes	Male Masculin	Female Féminin	Both sexes Les deux sexes	Male Masculin	Female Féminin
OCEANIA - OCÉANIE									
New Zealand - Nouvelle-Zélande[9]									
1 VII 2007 (ESDJ)									
Total....................	4 228 000	2 070 500	2 157 400	...	...	...	...	...	...
0 - 4.....................	292 110	149 670	142 440	...	...	...	...	...	...
5 - 9.....................	289 910	148 230	141 680	...	...	...	...	...	...
10 - 14...................	306 140	157 040	149 100	...	...	...	...	...	...
15 - 19...................	319 510	162 720	156 790	...	...	...	...	...	...
20 - 24...................	293 140	147 270	145 870	...	...	...	...	...	...
25 - 29...................	265 940	130 010	135 930	...	...	...	...	...	...
30 - 34...................	277 860	132 580	145 280	...	...	...	...	...	...
35 - 39...................	314 500	149 900	164 600	...	...	...	...	...	...
40 - 44...................	318 530	153 700	164 830	...	...	...	...	...	...
45 - 49...................	313 020	152 440	160 580	...	...	...	...	...	...
50 - 54...................	270 020	132 880	137 140	...	...	...	...	...	...
55 - 59...................	243 100	120 070	123 030	...	...	...	...	...	...
60 - 64...................	197 540	97 240	100 300	...	...	...	...	...	...
65 - 69...................	163 160	79 400	83 750	...	...	...	...	...	...
70 - 74...................	122 410	58 360	64 050	...	...	...	...	...	...
75 - 79...................	104 390	48 150	56 240	...	...	...	...	...	...
80 - 84...................	75 740	31 420	44 320	...	...	...	...	...	...
85 - 89...................	41 290	14 130	27 170	...	...	...	...	...	...
90 +.....................	19 670	5 320	14 350	...	...	...	...	...	...
Niue - Nioué									
1 VII 2006 (ESDJ)									
Total....................	1 679	815	864	...	...	...	...	...	...
0 - 4.....................	137	58	79	...	...	...	...	...	...
5 - 9.....................	136	65	71	...	...	...	...	...	...
10 - 14...................	145	77	68	...	...	...	...	...	...
15 - 19...................	175	96	79	...	...	...	...	...	...
20 - 24...................	137	56	81	...	...	...	...	...	...
25 - 29...................	103	53	50	...	...	...	...	...	...
30 - 34...................	97	49	48	...	...	...	...	...	...
35 - 39...................	96	50	46	...	...	...	...	...	...
40 - 44...................	101	50	51	...	...	...	...	...	...
45 - 49...................	104	60	44	...	...	...	...	...	...
50 - 54...................	121	60	61	...	...	...	...	...	...
55 - 59...................	67	27	40	...	...	...	...	...	...
60 - 64...................	61	30	31	...	...	...	...	...	...
65 - 69...................	82	32	50	...	...	...	...	...	...
70 - 74...................	62	30	32	...	...	...	...	...	...
75 +.....................	55	22	33	...	...	...	...	...	...
Norfolk Island - Île Norfolk									
8 VIII 2006 (CDFC)									
Total....................	2 523	1 218	1 305	...	...	...	...	...	...
0 - 4.....................	116	60	56	...	...	...	...	...	...
5 - 9.....................	127	67	60	...	...	...	...	...	...
10 - 14...................	116	58	58	...	...	...	...	...	...
15 - 19...................	78	34	44	...	...	...	...	...	...
20 - 24...................	64	22	42	...	...	...	...	...	...
25 - 29...................	96	48	48	...	...	...	...	...	...
30 - 34...................	140	70	70	...	...	...	...	...	...
35 - 39...................	156	78	78	...	...	...	...	...	...
40 - 44...................	170	86	84	...	...	...	...	...	...
45 - 49...................	194	95	99	...	...	...	...	...	...
50 - 54...................	212	95	117	...	...	...	...	...	...
55 - 59...................	255	126	129	...	...	...	...	...	...
60 - 64...................	222	109	113	...	...	...	...	...	...
65 - 69...................	184	81	103	...	...	...	...	...	...
70 +.....................	377	182	195	...	...	...	...	...	...
Unknown - Inconnu.......	16	7	9	...	...	...	...	...	...

7. Population by age, sex and urban/rural residence: latest available year, 1998 - 2007

Population selon l'âge, le sexe et la résidence, urbaine/rurale: dernière année disponible, 1998 - 2007 (continued - suite)

Continent, country or area, date, code and age (in years) / Continent, pays ou zone, date, code et âge (en années)	Total			Urban - Urbaine			Rural - Rurale		
	Both sexes Les deux sexes	Male Masculin	Female Féminin	Both sexes Les deux sexes	Male Masculin	Female Féminin	Both sexes Les deux sexes	Male Masculin	Female Féminin
OCEANIA - OCÉANIE									
Northern Mariana Islands - Îles Mariannes septentrionales[61]									
1 VII 2003 (ESDF)[62]									
Total	63 419	27 488	35 931	56 941	24 932	32 009	6 478	2 556	3 922
0 - 4	4 555	2 498	2 057	4 230	2 285	1 945	325	213	112
5 - 9	5 534	2 836	2 698	5 212	2 656	2 556	322	180	142
10 - 14	4 586	2 362	2 224	4 322	2 216	2 106	264	145	119
15 - 19	3 825	1 848	1 977	3 538	1 684	1 854	287	165	122
20 - 24	7 253	1 671	5 582	6 101	1 492	4 609	1 152	179	973
25 - 29	8 449	2 405	6 044	7 055	2 026	5 029	1 394	379	1 015
30 - 34	8 085	2 900	5 185	7 168	2 597	4 571	917	303	614
35 - 39	6 330	3 033	3 297	5 928	2 834	3 094	402	199	203
40 - 44	5 117	2 615	2 502	4 547	2 320	2 227	569	294	275
45 - 49	4 105	2 270	1 835	3 815	2 102	1 713	290	168	122
50 - 54	2 263	1 240	1 023	1 995	1 107	888	268	133	135
55 - 59	1 505	729	776	1 339	623	716	166	106	60
60 - 64	886	616	270	804	564	240	82	52	30
65 - 69	370	246	124	333	209	124	38	38	-
70 - 74	329	95	234	327	93	234	2	2	-
75 +	227	124	103	227	124	103	-	-	-
1 VII 2005 (ESDF)									
Total	65 927	30 712	35 215	...	...	...	...	...	...
0 - 4	5 335	2 775	2 560	...	...	...	...	...	...
5 - 9	5 244	2 961	2 283	...	...	...	...	...	...
10 - 14	5 621	3 034	2 587	...	...	...	...	...	...
15 - 19	4 971	2 235	2 736	...	...	...	...	...	...
20 - 24	6 260	1 634	4 626	...	...	...	...	...	...
25 - 29	6 238	1 837	4 401	...	...	...	...	...	...
30 - 34	6 576	2 860	3 716	...	...	...	...	...	...
35 - 39	6 562	3 177	3 385	...	...	...	...	...	...
40 - 44	6 000	3 140	2 860	...	...	...	...	...	...
45 - 49	5 148	2 763	2 385	...	...	...	...	...	...
50 - 54	3 207	1 837	1 370	...	...	...	...	...	...
55 - 59	2 124	1 131	993	...	...	...	...	...	...
60 - 64	1 174	583	591	...	...	...	...	...	...
65 - 69	662	413	249	...	...	...	...	...	...
70 - 74	308	142	166	...	...	...	...	...	...
75 +	498	190	308	...	...	...	...	...	...
Palau - Palaos									
1 IV 2005 (CDJC)									
Total	19 907	10 699	9 208	...	...	...	...	...	...
0 - 4	1 363	685	678	...	...	...	...	...	...
5 - 9	1 521	805	716	...	...	...	...	...	...
10 - 14	1 914	964	950	...	...	...	...	...	...
15 - 19	1 462	715	747	...	...	...	...	...	...
20 - 24	1 266	712	554	...	...	...	...	...	...
25 - 29	1 583	942	641	...	...	...	...	...	...
30 - 34	1 856	1 072	784	...	...	...	...	...	...
35 - 39	1 965	1 132	833	...	...	...	...	...	...
40 - 44	1 887	1 096	791	...	...	...	...	...	...
45 - 49	1 534	842	692	...	...	...	...	...	...
50 - 54	1 182	624	558	...	...	...	...	...	...
55 - 59	732	393	339	...	...	...	...	...	...
60 - 64	506	254	252	...	...	...	...	...	...
65 - 69	373	170	203	...	...	...	...	...	...
70 - 74	257	119	138	...	...	...	...	...	...
75 - 79	214	71	143	...	...	...	...	...	...
80 - 84	151	56	95	...	...	...	...	...	...
85 +	141	47	94	...	...	...	...	...	...
Papua New Guinea - Papouasie-Nouvelle-Guinée									
9 VII 2000 (CDFC)									
Total	5 190 786	2 691 744	2 499 042	686 301	372 453	313 848	4 504 485	2 319 291	2 185 194
0	125 718	65 539	60 179	16 930	8 991	7 939	108 788	56 548	52 240

Continent, country or area, date, code and age (in years) / Continent, pays ou zone, date, code et âge (en annèes)	Total			Urban - Urbaine			Rural - Rurale		
	Both sexes Les deux sexes	Male Masculin	Female Féminin	Both sexes Les deux sexes	Male Masculin	Female Féminin	Both sexes Les deux sexes	Male Masculin	Female Féminin
OCEANIA - OCÉANIE									
Papua New Guinea - Papouasie-Nouvelle-Guinée									
9 VII 2000 (CDFC)									
1 - 4	600 962	312 237	288 725	71 219	37 178	34 041	529 743	275 059	254 684
5 - 9	727 370	381 339	346 031	86 078	45 216	40 862	641 292	336 123	305 169
10 - 14	620 874	330 965	289 909	75 022	39 374	35 648	545 852	291 591	254 261
15 - 19	554 481	293 277	261 204	78 912	41 679	37 233	475 569	251 598	223 971
20 - 24	474 801	239 863	234 938	79 915	43 166	36 749	394 886	196 697	198 189
25 - 29	448 414	219 680	228 734	70 866	37 802	33 064	377 548	181 878	195 670
30 - 34	384 260	191 662	192 598	57 156	30 983	26 173	327 104	160 679	166 425
35 - 39	330 337	166 656	163 681	48 585	26 512	22 073	281 752	140 144	141 608
40 - 44	252 368	128 910	123 458	36 195	20 956	15 239	216 173	107 954	108 219
45 - 49	198 757	104 867	93 890	25 337	15 595	9 742	173 420	89 272	84 148
50 - 54	151 013	79 899	71 114	16 428	10 414	6 014	134 585	69 485	65 100
55 - 59	108 708	59 308	49 400	9 692	6 131	3 561	99 016	53 177	45 839
60 - 64	89 503	48 530	40 973	6 723	4 247	2 476	82 780	44 283	38 497
65 - 69	57 221	31 351	25 870	3 641	2 141	1 500	53 580	29 210	24 370
70 - 74	35 134	19 657	15 477	1 930	1 105	825	33 204	18 552	14 652
75 - 79	16 864	9 782	7 082	880	498	382	15 984	9 284	6 700
80 - 84	8 669	5 041	3 628	489	295	194	8 180	4 746	3 434
85 - 89	3 315	1 984	1 331	176	99	77	3 139	1 885	1 254
90 +	2 017	1 197	820	127	71	56	1 890	1 126	764
Pitcairn									
31 XII 2007 (ESDF)									
Total	64	38	26	...	...	...	...	...	...
0	1	-	1	...	...	...	...	...	...
1 - 4	2	1	1	...	...	...	...	...	...
5 - 9	4	3	1	...	...	...	...	...	...
10 - 14	1	1	-	...	...	...	...	...	...
15 - 19	2	-	2	...	...	...	...	...	...
20 - 24	3	2	1	...	...	...	...	...	...
25 - 29	2	1	1	...	...	...	...	...	...
30 - 34	4	4	-	...	...	...	...	...	...
35 - 39	3	1	2	...	...	...	...	...	...
40 - 44	8	7	1	...	...	...	...	...	...
45 - 49	8	5	3	...	...	...	...	...	...
50 - 54	8	5	3	...	...	...	...	...	...
55 - 59	5	3	2	...	...	...	...	...	...
60 - 64	2	-	2	...	...	...	...	...	...
65 - 69	2	1	1	...	...	...	...	...	...
70 - 74	2	-	2	...	...	...	...	...	...
75 - 79	3	2	1	...	...	...	...	...	...
80 +	2	1	1	...	...	...	...	...	...
Unknown - Inconnu	2	1	1	...	...	...	...	...	...
Samoa									
5 XI 2001 (CDFC)									
Total	176 710	92 050	84 660	...	...	...	...	...	...
0 - 4	26 028	13 631	12 397	...	...	...	...	...	...
5 - 9	24 917	13 024	11 893	...	...	...	...	...	...
10 - 14	20 985	10 948	10 037	...	...	...	...	...	...
15 - 19	17 608	9 488	8 120	...	...	...	...	...	...
20 - 24	14 281	7 549	6 732	...	...	...	...	...	...
25 - 29	13 197	6 910	6 287	...	...	...	...	...	...
30 - 34	12 258	6 545	5 713	...	...	...	...	...	...
35 - 39	10 385	5 378	5 007	...	...	...	...	...	...
40 - 44	8 855	4 628	4 227	...	...	...	...	...	...
45 - 49	6 833	3 538	3 295	...	...	...	...	...	...
50 - 54	5 081	2 538	2 543	...	...	...	...	...	...
55 - 59	4 417	2 217	2 200	...	...	...	...	...	...
60 - 64	3 659	1 835	1 824	...	...	...	...	...	...
65 - 69	2 975	1 452	1 523	...	...	...	...	...	...
70 - 74	2 272	1 036	1 236	...	...	...	...	...	...
75 - 79	1 639	731	908	...	...	...	...	...	...
80 - 84	680	312	368	...	...	...	...	...	...
85 - 89	240	80	160	...	...	...	...	...	...

7. Population by age, sex and urban/rural residence: latest available year, 1998 - 2007
Population selon l'âge, le sexe et la résidence, urbaine/rurale: dernière année disponible, 1998 - 2007 (continued - suite)

Continent, country or area, date, code and age (in years) / Continent, pays ou zone, date, code et âge (en années)	Total			Urban - Urbaine			Rural - Rurale		
	Both sexes Les deux sexes	Male Masculin	Female Féminin	Both sexes Les deux sexes	Male Masculin	Female Féminin	Both sexes Les deux sexes	Male Masculin	Female Féminin

OCEANIA - OCÉANIE

Samoa
5 XI 2001 (CDFC)

90 - 94	64	18	46	...	...	...	...	...	...
95 - 99	27	5	22	...	...	...	...	...	...
100 +..................	6	1	5	...	...	...	...	...	...
Unknown - Inconnu	303	186	117	...	...	...	...	...	...

Tokelau - Tokélaou
19 X 2006 (CDFC)

Total....................	1 151	583	568	...	...	...	...	...	...
0 - 4....................	123	63	60	...	...	...	...	...	...
5 - 9....................	143	66	77	...	...	...	...	...	...
10 - 14..................	155	86	69	...	...	...	...	...	...
15 - 19..................	115	69	46	...	...	...	...	...	...
20 - 24..................	66	31	35	...	...	...	...	...	...
25 - 29..................	52	30	22	...	...	...	...	...	...
30 - 34..................	65	29	36	...	...	...	...	...	...
35 - 39..................	72	36	36	...	...	...	...	...	...
40 - 44..................	69	34	35	...	...	...	...	...	...
45 - 49..................	67	31	36	...	...	...	...	...	...
50 - 54..................	48	26	22	...	...	...	...	...	...
55 - 59..................	46	21	25	...	...	...	...	...	...
60 - 64..................	36	22	14	...	...	...	...	...	...
65 - 69..................	33	12	21	...	...	...	...	...	...
70 - 74..................	23	10	13	...	...	...	...	...	...
75 +....................	38	17	21	...	...	...	...	...	...

Tonga
30 XI 2006 (CDFC)

Total....................	101 991	51 772	50 219	23 658	11 860	11 798	78 333	39 912	38 421
0 - 4....................	13 782	7 174	6 608	3 015	1 514	1 501	10 767	5 660	5 107
5 - 9....................	12 804	6 745	6 059	2 721	1 447	1 274	10 083	5 298	4 785
10 - 14..................	12 320	6 412	5 908	2 631	1 357	1 274	9 689	5 055	4 634
15 - 19..................	10 280	5 383	4 897	2 362	1 196	1 166	7 918	4 187	3 731
20 - 24..................	9 191	4 648	4 543	2 503	1 276	1 227	6 688	3 372	3 316
25 - 29..................	7 304	3 639	3 665	1 872	913	959	5 432	2 726	2 706
30 - 34..................	6 337	3 146	3 191	1 551	787	764	4 786	2 359	2 427
35 - 39..................	6 229	3 112	3 117	1 448	711	737	4 781	2 401	2 380
40 - 44..................	5 014	2 578	2 436	1 240	647	593	3 774	1 931	1 843
45 - 49..................	3 982	1 923	2 059	982	458	524	3 000	1 465	1 535
50 - 54..................	3 465	1 634	1 831	844	406	438	2 621	1 228	1 393
55 - 59..................	2 849	1 359	1 490	639	323	316	2 210	1 036	1 174
60 - 64..................	2 470	1 169	1 301	556	260	296	1 914	909	1 005
65 - 69..................	2 174	1 092	1 082	466	211	255	1 708	881	827
70 - 74..................	1 586	777	809	340	152	188	1 246	625	621
75 +....................	2 082	894	1 188	462	183	279	1 620	711	909
Unknown - Inconnu	122	87	35	26	19	7	96	68	28

1 VII 2007 (ESDF)[63]

Total....................	103 289	52 771	50 518	...	...	...	...	...	...
0 - 4....................	12 005	6 182	5 823	...	...	...	...	...	...
5 - 9....................	11 544	5 977	5 567	...	...	...	...	...	...
10 - 14..................	12 134	6 309	5 826	...	...	...	...	...	...
15 - 19..................	11 300	6 047	5 253	...	...	...	...	...	...
20 - 24..................	10 818	5 632	5 186	...	...	...	...	...	...
25 - 29..................	8 296	4 241	4 055	...	...	...	...	...	...
30 - 34..................	5 693	2 859	2 834	...	...	...	...	...	...
35 - 39..................	5 572	2 820	2 752	...	...	...	...	...	...
40 - 44..................	5 113	2 580	2 533	...	...	...	...	...	...
45 - 49..................	4 369	2 113	2 256	...	...	...	...	...	...
50 - 54..................	3 857	1 836	2 021	...	...	...	...	...	...
55 - 59..................	3 205	1 507	1 698	...	...	...	...	...	...
60 - 64..................	2 856	1 367	1 489	...	...	...	...	...	...
65 - 69..................	2 453	1 244	1 209	...	...	...	...	...	...
70 - 74..................	1 877	967	909	...	...	...	...	...	...
75 +....................	2 196	1 090	1 105	...	...	...	...	...	...

Continent, country or area, date, code and age (in years) / Continent, pays ou zone, date, code et âge (en années)	Total			Urban - Urbaine			Rural - Rurale		
	Both sexes Les deux sexes	Male Masculin	Female Féminin	Both sexes Les deux sexes	Male Masculin	Female Féminin	Both sexes Les deux sexes	Male Masculin	Female Féminin
OCEANIA - OCÉANIE									
Tuvalu									
1 XI 2002 (CDFC)									
Total..................	9 561	4 729	4 832	...	...	...	...	...	...
0	182	92	90	...	...	...	...	...	...
1 - 4	996	528	468	...	...	...	...	...	...
5 - 9	1 201	612	589	...	...	...	...	...	...
10 - 14	1 079	591	488	...	...	...	...	...	...
15 - 19	826	474	352	...	...	...	...	...	...
20 - 24	682	326	356	...	...	...	...	...	...
25 - 29	523	245	278	...	...	...	...	...	...
30 - 34	545	278	267	...	...	...	...	...	...
35 - 39	684	331	353	...	...	...	...	...	...
40 - 44	697	310	387	...	...	...	...	...	...
45 - 49	580	261	319	...	...	...	...	...	...
50 - 54	467	199	268	...	...	...	...	...	...
55 - 59	276	129	147	...	...	...	...	...	...
60 - 64	280	131	149	...	...	...	...	...	...
65 - 69	207	84	123	...	...	...	...	...	...
70 - 74	167	75	92	...	...	...	...	...	...
75 - 79	101	40	61	...	...	...	...	...	...
80 - 84	56	20	36	...	...	...	...	...	...
85 - 89	10	1	9	...	...	...	...	...	...
90 + ...	2	2	-	...	...	...	...	...	...
Vanuatu[64]									
1 VII 2004 (ESDF)									
Total....................	*215 541*	*110 141*	*105 399*	...	...	...	...	...	...
0 - 4....................	*33 815*	*17 435*	*16 380*	...	...	...	...	...	...
5 - 9....................	*27 846*	*14 474*	*13 372*	...	...	...	...	...	...
10 - 14	*27 125*	*14 025*	*13 100*	...	...	...	...	...	...
15 - 19	*23 437*	*12 132*	*11 305*	...	...	...	...	...	...
20 - 24	*18 951*	*9 684*	*9 267*	...	...	...	...	...	...
25 - 29	*16 235*	*8 027*	*8 207*	...	...	...	...	...	...
30 - 34	*14 670*	*7 175*	*7 494*	...	...	...	...	...	...
35 - 39	*12 560*	*6 214*	*6 346*	...	...	...	...	...	...
40 - 44	*10 429*	*5 221*	*5 208*	...	...	...	...	...	...
45 - 49	*8 303*	*4 221*	*4 082*	...	...	...	...	...	...
50 - 54	*6 476*	*3 333*	*3 143*	...	...	...	...	...	...
55 - 59	*5 083*	*2 632*	*2 452*	...	...	...	...	...	...
60 - 64	*3 824*	*1 996*	*1 828*	...	...	...	...	...	...
65 - 69	*2 714*	*1 417*	*1 296*	...	...	...	...	...	...
70 - 74	*1 810*	*957*	*854*	...	...	...	...	...	...
75 + ...	*2 265*	*1 198*	*1 066*	...	...	...	...	...	...

FOOTNOTES - NOTES

Italics: estimates which are less reliable. - Italiques: estimations moins sûres.

'Code' indicates the source of data, as follows:
CDFC - Census, de facato, complete tabulation
CDFS - Census, de facto, sample tabulation
CDJC - Census, de jure, complete tabulation
CDJS - Census, de jure, sample tabulation
SSDF - Sample survey, de facto
SSDJ - Sample survey, de jure
ESDF - Estimates, de facto
ESDJ - Estimates, de jure

Le 'Code' indique la source des données, comme suit:
CDFC - Recensement, population de fait, tabulation complète
CDFS - Recensement, population de fait, tabulation par sondage
CDJC - Recensement, population de droit, tabulation complète
CDJS - Recensement, population de droit, tabulation par sondage
SSDF - Enquête par sondage, population de fait
SSDJ - Enquête par sondage, population de droit

ESDF - Estimations, population de fait
ESDJ - Estimations, population de droit

[1] Unrevised data. - Les données n'ont pas été révisées.
[2] Total includes the estimated population of eight rural kebeles (21,410) in Elidar wereda (Affar Region). - Le total comprend l'effectif estimé de la population de huit kebele ruraux (21 410 habitants) du woreda d'Elidar (région Afar).
[3] Data refer to national projections. - Les données se réfèrent aux projections nationales.
[4] The number of males and/or females excludes persons whose sex is not stated (18 urban, 19 rural). - Il n'est pas tenu compte dans le nombre d'hommes et de femmes des personnes dont le sexe n'est pas indiqué (18 en zone urbaine et 19 en zone rurale).
[5] Unrevised data. Data refer to national projections. - Les données n'ont pas été révisées. Les données se réfèrent aux projections nationales.
[6] Data refer to national projections. Data as reported by national statistical authorities. - Les données se réfèrent aux projections nationales. Les données comme elles ont été déclarées par l'institut national de la statistique.
[7] Mid-year estimates have been adjusted for underenumeration, at latest census. - Les estimations au millieu de l'année tiennent compte d'un ajustement

destiné à compenser les lacunes du dénombrement lors du dernier recensement.

[8] Excluding persons who were not contacted at the time of the census. - La population non comprend pas les personnes qui n'ont pas été contactées à l'heure du recensement.

[9] Because of rounding, totals are not in all cases the sum of the parts. - Les chiffres étant arrondis, les totaux ne correspondent pas toujours rigoureusement à la somme des chiffres partiels.

[10] Data as reported by national statistical authorities. Summation of frequencies gives a different total; reason for discrepancy not ascertained. - Les données comme elles ont été déclarées par l'institut national de la statistique. La somme des fréquences un total différent; on ne sait pas comment s'explique la divergence.

[11] As a result of the adjusting method used to calculate midyear population by five-year age groups and by single years of age, there are dicrepancies for ages 0 to 19. - En raison de la méthode d'ajustement servant au calcul de la population médiane par groupes d'âge quinquennaux et par année d'âge, il existe des écarts pour les âges compris entre 0 et 19 ans.

[12] Population statistics are compiled from registers. - Les statistiques de la population sont compilées à partir des registres.

[13] Reason for discrepancy between these figures and corresponding figures shown elsewhere not ascertained. - On ne sait pas comment s'explique la divergence entre ces chiffres et les chiffres correspondants indiqués ailleurs.

[14] Urban and rural distribution derived from census count, held constant and applied to current estimates. - La répartition urbain/rural se réfère aux chiffres du recensement, maintenus constants et appliqués aux estimations actuelles.

[15] Including armed forces stationed in the area. - Y compris les militaires en garnison sur le territoire.

[16] Data have not been adjusted for underenumeration. Excluding the institutional population. - Les données n'ont pas été ajustées pour compenser les lacunes du dénombrement. Non compris la population dans les institutions.

[17] Based on the results of the population census. - D'après le résultats du recensement de la population.

[18] Excluding armed forces overseas and civilian citizens absent from country for an extended period of time. - Non compris les militaires à l'étranger, et les civils hors du pays pendant une période prolongée.

[19] Data include persons in remote areas, military personnel outside the country, merchant seamen at sea, civilian seasonal workers outside the country, and other civilians outside the country, and exclude nomads, foreign military, civilian aliens temporarily in the country, transients on ships and Indian jungle population. - Y compris les personnes vivant dans des régions éloignées, le personel militaire en dehors du pays, les marins marchands, les ouvriers saisonniers en dehors du pays, et autres civils en dehors du pays, et non compris les nomades, les militaires étrangers, les étrangers civils temporairement dans le pays, les transiteurs sur des bateaux et les Indiens de la jungle.

[20] Data have been adjusted on the basis of the Population Census of 2005. - Données ajustées sur la base du recensement de la population de 2005.

[21] Data refer to national projections. Excluding nomadic Indian tribes. - Les données se réfèrent aux projections nationales. Non compris les tribus d'Indiens nomades.

[22] A dispute exists between the governments of Argentina and the United Kingdom of Great Britain and Northern Ireland concerning sovereignty over the Falkland Islands (Malvinas). - La souveraineté sur les îles Falkland (Malvinas) fait l'objet d'un différend entre le Gouvernement argentin et le Gouvernement du Royaume-Uni de Grande-Bretagne et d'Irlande du Nord.

[23] Totals may not add up because cases with age unknown and/or sex unknown have been prorated. - Les totaux peuvent ne pas tomber juste du fait que l'on a calculé au prorata les cas pour lesquels l'âge ou le sexe n'était pas connu.

[24] The districts of Paramaribo and Wanica are considered urban areas, whereas the rest of the districts are considered more or less rural districts (areas). - Les districts de Paramaribo et de Wanica sont considérés comme des zones urbaines, les autres districts étant considérés comme des zones rurales à divers degrés.

[25] The unknown age and sex is proportionately distributed over all age groups and both sexes. - La population d'âge ou de sexe inconnu est répartie proportionnellement dans tous les groupes d'âge et dans chaque sexe.

[26] Excluding Indian jungle population. - Non compris les Indiens de la jungle.

[27] Data refer to projections based on the 2005 population census. - Les données se réfèrent aux projections basées sur le recensement de la population de 2005.

[28] Based on the results of the Cambodia Intercensal Population Survey. Data exclude institutional, homeless households and transient poulation. - Les données ne comprennent pas la population des institutions, les ménages sans abri et la population de passage.

[29] For statistical purposes, the data for China do not include those for the Hong Kong Special Administrative Region (Hong Kong SAR), Macao Special Administrative Region (Macao SAR) and Taiwan province of China. - Pour la présentation des statistiques, les données pour la Chine ne comprennent pas la Région Administrative Spéciale de Hong Kong (Hong Kong RAS), la Région Administrative Spéciale de Macao (Macao RAS) et Taïwan province de Chine.

[30] Data refer to government controlled areas. - Les données se rapportent aux zones contrôlées par le Gouvernement.

[31] Including data for the Indian-held part of Jammu and Kashmir, the final status of which has not yet been determined. Excluding Mao-Maram, Paomata and Purul sub-divisions of Senapati district of Manipur. The population of Manipur including the estimated population of the three sub-divisions of Senapati district is 2,291,125 (Males 1,161,173 and females 1,129,952). - Y compris les données pour la partie du Jammu et du Cachemire occupée par l'Inde dont le statut définitif n'a pas encore été déterminé. Non compris les subdivisions Mao-Maram Paomata et Purul du district de Senapati dans l'État du Manipur. Cet État compte 2 291 125 habitants (1 161 173 hommes et 1 129 952 femmes), y compris la population estimative des trois subdivisions du district de Senapati.

[32] Data refer to the "Intercensal Population Survey". Excluding Province Nanggroe Aceh Darussalam, Regency Nias & Nias Selatan, Regency Boven Digul & Teluk Wondama. - Les données concernent l'enquête intercensitaire sur la population. En excluant les provinces de Nanggroe Aceh Darussalam, Regency Nias & Nias Selatan, Regency Boven Digul & Teluk Wondama.

[33] Differences between the total country figures and sum of urban and rural areas are due to the inclusion of unsettled population numbering 104 717 (53 065 males and females 51 652). - Les différences entre les chiffres pour l'ensemble du pays et la somme des zones urbaines et rurales s'expliquent par l'inclusion de la population non sédentaire, dont l'effectif est de 104 717 (53 065 de sexe masculin et 51 652 de sexe féminin).

[34] Including data for East Jerusalem and Israeli residents in certain other territories under occupation by Israeli military forces since June 1967. - Y compris les données pour Jérusalem-Est et les résidents israéliens dans certains autres territoires occupés depuis 1967 par les forces armées israéliennes.

[35] Excluding residents who had been registered in the Israeli localities (the Jewish localities) in the Gaza Area and northern Samaria, which were evacuated in August 2005, but did not notify the Ministry of Interior of their new address. These residents are included in total. - Hors résidents enregistrés dans les localités d'Israel (localités juives) de la Bande de Gaza (verify) et du nord de la Samarie, qui ont été évacués en Août 2005, mais qui n'ont pas notifié leur nouvelle adresse au ministère de l'intérieur. Ces résidents sont inclus dans le total.

[36] Excluding diplomatic personnel outside the country and foreign military and civilian personnel and their dependants stationed in the area. Because of rounding, totals are not in all cases the sum of the parts. - Non compris le personnel diplomatique hors du pays ni les militaires et agents civils étrangers en poste sur le territoire et les membres de leur famille les accompagnant. Les chiffres étant arrondis, les totaux ne correspondent pas toujours rigoureusement à la somme des chiffres partiels.

[37] Excluding data for Jordanian territory under occupation since June 1967 by Israeli military forces. Excluding foreigners, including registered Palestinian refugees. - Non compris les données pour le territoire jordanien occupé depuis juin 1967 par les forces armées israéliennes. Non compris les étrangers, mais y compris les réfugiés de Palestine enregistrés.

[38] Data refer to constant population as reported by national statistical authorities, meaning that it does not include migrant population. - Les données se rapportent à la population constante déclarée par les autorités statistiques nationales; la population migrante n'est donc pas comprise.

[39] Based on the results of the 2005 Population and Housing Census. Because of rounding, totals are not in all cases the sum of the parts. - Données fondées sur les résultats du recensement de la population et de l'habitat de 2005. Les chiffres étant arrondis, les totaux ne correspondent pas toujours rigoureusement à la somme des chiffres partiels.

[40] Based on the results of a household survey. - D'après les résultats d'une enquête des ménages.

[41] Data refer to projections based on the 2000 population census. - Les données se réfèrent aux projections basées sur le recensement de la population de 2000.

[42] Total Population is taken as de facto and de jure together. - Population totale considérée comme de fait et de droit.

[43] Excluding data for the Pakistan-held part of Jammu and Kashmir, the final status of which has not yet been determined. Based on the results of the Pakistan Demographic Survey (PDS 2005). These estimates do not reflect completely accurately the actual population and vital events of the country. - Non compris les données concernant la partie du Jammu et Cachemire occupée par le Pakistan dont le statut définitif n'a été déterminé. D'après les résultats de Pakistan démographique par sondage 2005. Ces estimations ne dénotent pas d'une manière complètement ponctuelle la population actuelle et les statistiques de l'état civil du pays.

[44] Excluding foreigners. - Non compris étrangers.

[45] The Population and Housing Census 2001 did not cover the whole area of the country due to the security problems; data refer to the 18 districts for which the census was completed only (in three districts it was not possible to conduct the census at all and in four districts it was partially conducted). Unrevised data. - Le recensement de la population et du logement de 2001 n'a pas été réalisé sur la superficie totale du pays à cause de problèmes de sécurité; les données ne concernent que les 18 districts entièrement recensés (3 districts n'ont pas été recensés du tout, et 4 ont été recensés en partie). Les données n'ont pas été révisées.

[46] Data for rural areas include data of estate sectors consist of all plantations which are 20 acres or more in extent and with ten or more resident labourers. - Les données pour les zones rurales comprennent celles pour les domaines, dont l'ensemble des plantations de plus de 10 hectares comptant au moins 10 travailleurs résidents.

[47] Including Palestinian refugees. - Y compris les réfugiés de Palestine.

[48] Population statistics are compiled from registers. Also included in Finland. - Les statistiques de la population sont compilées à partir des registres. Comprise aussi dans Finlande.

[49] Population statistics are compiled from registers. Excluding Faeroe Islands and Greenland shown separately, if available. - Les statistiques de la population sont compilées à partir des registres. Non compris les Îles Féröé et le Gröenland, qui font l'objet de rubriques distinctes, si disponible.

[50] Population statistics are compiled from registers. Including Aland Islands. - Les statistiques de la population sont compilées à partir des registres. Y compris les Îles d'Åland.

[51] Excluding diplomatic personnel outside the country and including members of alien armed forces not living in military camps and foreign diplomatic personnel not living in embassies or consulates. Excluding Overseas Departments, namely, French Guiana, Guadeloupe, Martinique and Reunion, shown separately, if available. - Non compris le personnel diplomatique hors du pays et y compris les militaires étrangers ne vivant pas dans des camps militaires et le personnel diplomatique étranger ne vivant pas dans les ambassades ou les consulats. Non compris les départements d'outre mer, c'est-à-dire la Guyane française, la Guadeloupe, la Martinique et la Réunion, qui font l'objet de rubriques distinctes, si disponible.

[52] Excluding families of military personnel, visitors and transients. - Non compris les familles des militaires, ni les visiteurs et transients.

[53] Excluding armed forces stationed outside the country, but including alien armed forces stationed in the area. - Non compris les militaires en garnison hors du pays, mais y compris les militaires étrangers en garnison sur le territoire.

[54] Excluding Svalbard and Jan Mayen Island shown separately, if available. - Non compris Svalbard et Jan Mayen qui font l'objet de rubriques distinctes, si disponible.

[55] Including residents temporarily outside the country. - Y compris les résidents se trouvant temporairement hors du pays.

[56] Excluding civilian aliens within country, but including civilian nationals temporarily outside country. - Non compris les civils étrangers dans le pays, mais y compris les civils nationaux temporairement hors du pays.

[57] Excluding Transnistria and the municipality of Bender. - Les données ne tiennent pas compte de l'information sur la Transnistria et la municipalité de Bender.

[58] Excluding data for Kosovo and Metohia. - Sans les données pour le Kosovo et Metohie.

[59] Excluding Channel Islands (Guernsey and Jersey) and Isle of Man, shown separately, if available. - Non compris les îles Anglo-Normandes (Guernesey et Jersey) et l'île de Man, qui font l'objet de rubriques distinctes, si disponible.

[60] Excluding Niue, shown separately, which is part of Cook Islands, but because of remoteness is administered separately. - Non compris Nioué, qui fait l'objet d'une rubrique distincte et qui fait partie des îles Cook, mais qui, en raison de son éloignement, est administrée séparément.

[61] Data refer to the island of Saipan only. - Les données se réfèrent uniquement à l'île de Saipan.

[62] Based on the results of a sample survey. - D'après les résultats de l'enquête par sondage.

[63] Based on the results of the 1996 population census not necessarily mid year estimated. Data refer to national projections. - À partir des résultats du recensement de la population de 1996, pas nécessairement des estimations en milieu d'année. Les données se réfèrent aux projections nationales.

[64] Data refer to national projections. Figures for male and female do not add up to the total, reason for discrepancy not ascertained. - Les données se réfèrent aux projections nationales. La some des données pour la population masculine et pour la population féminine n'est pas égale au total, les raisons de cette différence ne sont pas expliquées.

Table 8

Table 8 presents population of capital cities and cities of 100 000 or more inhabitants for the latest available year between 1988 and 2007.

Description of variables: Since the way in which cities are delimited differs from one country or area to another, the table not only presents data for the so-called city proper, but also for the urban agglomeration, if available.

City proper is defined as a locality with legally fixed boundaries and an administratively recognized urban status, usually characterized by some form of local government.

Urban agglomeration has been defined as comprising the city or town proper and also the suburban fringe or densely settled territory lying outside of, but adjacent to, the city boundaries.

For some countries or areas, however, the data relate to entire administrative divisions known, for example, as shi or municipalities (municipios) which are composed of a populated centre and adjoining territory, some of which may contain other, often separate urban localities or may be distinctively rural in character. For this group of countries or areas the type of civil division is given in a footnote.

The surface area of the city or urban agglomeration is presented, when available.

City names are presented in the original language of the country or area in which the cities are located. In cases where the original names are not in the Roman alphabet, they have been romanized. Cities are listed in English alphabetical order.

Capital cities are shown in the table regardless of their population size. The names of the capital cities are printed in capital letters. The designation of any specific city as a capital city is as reported by the country or area.

The table also covers cities whose urban agglomeration's population exceeds 100 000; that is, while the urban agglomeration should have a population of 100 000 or more to be included in the table, the city proper may be of a smaller population size.

The reference date of each population figure appears in the stub of the table. Estimates based on results of sample surveys and city censuses as well as those derived from other sources are noted in the "code" column.

Reliability of data: Specific information is generally not available on the reliability of the estimates of the population of cities or urban agglomerations presented in this table.

In the absence of such quality assessment, data from population censuses, sample surveys and city censuses are considered to be reliable and, therefore, set in Roman type. Other estimates are considered to be reliable if they are based on a complete census (or a sample survey), and have been adjusted by a continuous population register or adjusted on the basis of the calculated balance of births, deaths, and migration.

Limitations: Statistics on the population of capital cities and cities of 100 000 or more inhabitants are subject to the same qualifications as have been set forth for population statistics in general as discussed in section 3 of the Technical Notes.

International comparability of data on city population is limited to a great extent by variations in national concepts and definitions. Although an effort is made to reduce the sources of non-comparability somewhat by presenting the data for both city proper and urban agglomeration, many serious problems of comparability remain.

Data presented in the "city proper" column for some countries represent an urban administrative area legally distinguished from surrounding rural territory, while for other countries these data represent a commune or an equally small administrative unit. In still other countries, the administrative units may be relatively extensive and thereby include considerable territories beyond the urban centre itself.

City data are also especially affected by whether the data refer to *de facto* or *de jure* population, as well as variations among countries in how each of these concepts is applied. With reference to the total population, the difference between the *de facto* and *de jure* population is discussed at length in section 3.1.1 of the Technical Notes.

Data on city populations based on intercensal estimates present additional problems: comparability is impaired by the different methods used in making the estimates and by the loss of precision in applying to selected segments of the population, methods best suited for the whole population. For example, it is far more difficult to apply the component method of estimating population growth to cities than it is to the entire country.

Births and deaths occurring in the cities do not all originate in the population present in or resident of that area. Therefore, the use of natural increase to estimate the probable size of the city population is a potential source of error. Internal migration is another component of population change that cannot be measured with accuracy in many areas. Because of these factors, estimates in this table may be less valuable in general and in particular limited for purposes of international comparison.

City data, even when set in Roman type, are often not as reliable as estimates for the total population of the country or area. Furthermore, because the sources of these data include censuses (national or city), surveys and estimates, the years to which they refer vary widely. In addition, because city boundaries may alter over time, comparisons covering different years should be carried out with caution.

Earlier data: Population of capital cities and cities with a population of 100 000 or more have been shown in previous issues of the *Demographic Yearbook*. For more information on specific topics and years for which data are reported, readers should consult the Historical Index.

Tableau 8

Le tableau 8 présente les données les plus récentes pour la période 1988 – 2007 dont on dispose sur la population des capitales et des villes de 100 000 habitants ou plus.

Description des variables : étant donné que les villes ne sont pas délimitées de la même manière dans tous les pays ou zones, on s'est efforcé de donner, dans ce tableau, des chiffres correspondant non seulement aux villes proprement dites, mais aussi, le cas échéant, aux agglomérations urbaines.

On entend par villes proprement dites les localités qui ont des limites juridiquement définies et sont administrativement considérées comme villes, ce qui se caractérise généralement par l'existence d'une autorité locale.

L'agglomération urbaine comprend, par définition, la ville proprement dite ainsi que la proche banlieue, c'est-à-dire la zone fortement peuplée qui est extérieure, mais contiguë aux limites de la ville.

En outre, dans certains pays ou zones, les données se rapportent à des divisions administratives entières, connues par exemple sous le nom de shi ou de municipios, qui comportent une agglomération et le territoire avoisinant, lequel peut englober d'autres agglomérations urbaines tout à fait distinctes ou être à caractère essentiellement rural. Pour ce groupe de pays ou zones, le type de division administrative est indiqué en note.

On trouvera à la fin du tableau la superficie de la ville ou agglomération urbaine chaque fois que possible.

Les noms des villes sont indiqués dans la langue du pays ou zone où ces villes sont situées. Les noms de villes qui ne sont pas à l'origine libellés en caractères latins ont été romanisés. Les villes sont énumérées dans l'ordre alphabétique anglais.

Les capitales figurent dans le tableau quel que soit le chiffre de leur population et leur nom a été imprimé en lettres majuscules. Ne sont indiquées comme capitales que les villes ainsi désignées par le pays ou zone intéressé.

En ce qui concerne les autres villes, le tableau indique celles dont la population est égale ou supérieure à 100 000 habitants. Ce chiffre limite s'applique à l'agglomération urbaine et non à la ville proprement dite, dont la population peut être moindre.

L'année à laquelle se réfère le chiffre correspondant à chaque population figure dans la colonne de gauche du tableau. La colonne « Code » permet de savoir si les estimations sont fondées sur les résultats d'enquêtes par sondage ou de recensements municipaux ou sont tirées d'autres sources.

Fiabilité des données : on ne possède généralement pas de renseignements précis sur la fiabilité des estimations de la population des villes ou agglomérations urbaines présentées dans ce tableau.

Les données provenant de recensements de la population, d'enquêtes par sondage ou de recensements municipaux sont jugées sûres et figurent par conséquent en caractères romains. D'autres estimations sont considérées comme sûres si elles sont fondées sur un recensement complet (ou une enquête par sondage) et ont été ajustées en fonction des données provenant d'un registre permanent de population ou en fonction de la balance, établie par le calcul des naissances, des décès et des migrations.

Insuffisance des données : les statistiques portant sur la population des capitales et des villes de 100 000 habitants ou plus appellent toutes les réserves qui ont été formulées à la section 3 des Notes techniques à propos des statistiques de la population en général.

La comparabilité internationale des données portant sur la population des villes est compromise dans une large mesure par la diversité des définitions nationales. Bien que l'on se soit efforcé de réduire les facteurs de non-comparabilité en présentant à la fois dans le tableau les données relatives aux villes proprement dites et celles concernant les agglomérations urbaines, de graves problèmes de comparabilité n'en subsistent pas moins.

Pour certains pays, les données figurant dans la colonne intitulée « Ville proprement dite » correspondent à une zone administrative urbaine juridiquement distincte du territoire rural environnant, tandis que pour d'autres pays ces données correspondent à une commune ou petite unité administrative analogue. Pour d'autres encore, les unités administratives en cause peuvent être relativement étendues et englober par conséquent un vaste territoire au-delà du centre urbain lui-même.

L'emploi de données se rapportant tantôt à la population de fait, tantôt à la population de droit, ainsi que les différences de traitement de ces deux notions d'un pays à l'autre influent particulièrement sur les statistiques urbaines. En ce qui concerne la population totale, la différence entre population de fait et population de droit est expliquée en détail à la section 3.1.1 des Notes techniques.

Les statistiques relatives à la population urbaine qui sont fondées sur des estimations intercensitaires posent encore plus de problèmes que les données issues de recensement. Leur comparabilité est compromise par la diversité des méthodes employées pour établir les estimations et par l'imprécision qui résulte de l'application de certaines méthodes à telles ou telles composantes de la population alors qu'elles sont conçues pour être appliquées à l'ensemble de la population. La méthode des composantes, par exemple, est beaucoup plus difficile à appliquer en vue de l'estimation de l'accroissement de la population lorsqu'il s'agit de villes que lorsqu'il s'agit d'un pays tout entier.

Les naissances et décès qui surviennent dans les villes ne correspondent pas tous à la population présente ou résidente. En conséquence, des erreurs peuvent se produire si l'on établit pour les villes des estimations fondées sur l'accroissement naturel de la population. Les migrations intérieures constituent un second élément d'estimation que, dans bien des régions, on ne peut pas toujours mesurer avec exactitude. Pour ces raisons, les estimations présentées dans ce tableau risquent dans l'ensemble d'être peu fiables et leur valeur est particulièrement limitée du point de vue des comparaisons internationales.

Même lorsqu'elles figurent en caractères romains, il arrive souvent que les statistiques urbaines ne soient pas aussi fiables que les estimations concernant la population totale de la zone ou du pays considéré. De surcroît, comme ces statistiques proviennent aussi bien de recensements (nationaux ou municipaux) que d'enquêtes ou d'estimations, les années auxquelles elles se rapportent sont extrêmement variables. Enfin, comme les limites urbaines varient parfois d'une époque à une autre, il y a lieu d'être prudent lorsque l'on compare des données se rapportant à des années différentes.

Données publiées antérieurement : des statistiques concernant la population des capitales et des villes de 100 000 habitants ou plus ont été présentées dans des éditions antérieures de l'*Annuaire démographique*. Pour plus de précisions concernant les années et les sujets pour lesquels des données ont été publiées, se reporter à l'index.

8. Population of capital cities and cities of 100 000 or more inhabitants: latest available year, 1988 - 2007
Population des capitales et des villes de 100 000 habitants ou plus: dernière année disponible, 1988 - 2007

Continent, country or area, date, code and city / Continent, pays ou zone, date, code et ville	City proper - Ville proprement dite				Urban agglomeration - Agglomération urbaine			
	Population			Surface area - Superficie (km²)	Population			Surface area - Superficie (km²)
	Both sexes - Les deux sexes	Male - Masculin	Female - Féminin		Both sexes - Les deux sexes	Male - Masculin	Female - Féminin	

AFRICA - AFRIQUE

Algeria - Algérie								
25 VI 1998 (CDJC)								
ALGIERS (EL DJAZAIR)	1 569 897	...	...	...	...	...	...	...
Annaba	352 523	...	...	...	...	...	...	...
Batna	246 800	...	...	...	...	...	...	...
Béchar	134 523	...	...	...	...	...	...	...
Bejaïa	144 405	...	...	...	...	...	...	...
Beskra	177 060	...	...	...	...	...	...	...
Bordj Bou Arreridj	129 004	...	...	...	...	...	...	...
Bordj el Kiffan	103 690	...	...	...	...	...	...	...
Ech Cheliff (El Asnam)	174 314	...	...	...	...	...	...	...
El Boulaïda (Blida)	229 788	...	...	...	...	...	...	...
El Djelfa	158 679	...	...	...	...	...	...	...
El Eulma	104 758	...	...	...	...	...	...	...
El Wad	105 151	...	...	...	...	...	...	...
Ghardaïa	127 959	...	...	...	...	...	...	...
Ghilizane	104 644	...	...	...	...	...	...	...
Guelma	108 682	...	...	...	...	...	...	...
Jijel	106 306	...	...	...	...	...	...	...
Lemdiyya (Medea)	128 427	...	...	...	...	...	...	...
Mestghanem (Mostaganem)	125 911	...	...	...	...	...	...	...
M'Sila	102 151	...	...	...	...	...	...	...
Qacentina (Constantine)	465 021	...	...	...	...	...	...	...
Saïda	113 533	...	...	...	...	...	...	...
Sidi-bel-Abbès	183 931	...	...	...	...	...	...	...
Skikda	153 531	...	...	...	...	...	...	...
Souq Ahras	114 512	...	...	...	...	...	...	...
Stif (Sétif)	214 842	...	...	...	...	...	...	...
Tbessa	154 335	...	...	...	...	...	...	...
Tihert	148 850	...	...	...	...	...	...	...
Tilimsen (Tlemcen)	156 258	...	...	...	...	...	...	...
Touggourt	114 183	...	...	...	...	...	...	...
Wahran (Oran)	705 335	...	...	...	...	...	...	...
Wargla	139 381	...	...	...	...	...	...	...
Angola								
1 VII 1993 (ESDF)								
Huambo	...	...	...	...	400 000	...	...	...
LUANDA	...	...	...	...	1 822 407	855 676	936 731	...
Benin - Bénin								
1 VII 2000 (ESDF)								
Cotonou	650 660	318 752	331 908	79	...	...	...	...
Parakou	144 627	73 603	71 024	441	...	...	...	...
PORTO-NOVO	232 756	113 737	119 019	50	...	...	...	...
Botswana								
17 VIII 2001 (CDFC)								
Francistown	83 023	40 147	42 876	79	113 315	...	...	...
GABORONE	186 007	91 851	94 156	169	282 150	...	...	...
Burkina Faso								
9 XII 2006 (CDJC)								
Bobo Diuolasso	489 967	244 136	245 831	...	...	...	...	...
OUAGADOUGOU	1 475 839	745 616	730 223	...	...	...	...	...
Burundi								
16 VIII 1990 (CDFC)								
BUJUMBURA	235 440	129 195	106 245	...	...	...	...	...
Cameroon - Cameroun								
1 VII 1998 (ESDF)								
Bafoussam	205 620	...	...	...	...	...	...	...
Bamenda	252 083	...	...	...	...	...	...	...
Bertoua	129 067	...	...	...	...	...	...	...
Douala	1 382 900	...	...	...	...	...	...	...
Edéa	101 200	...	...	...	...	...	...	...
Garoua	293 081	...	...	...	...	...	...	...
Kousséri	233 280	...	...	...	...	...	...	...
Kumba	110 860	...	...	...	...	...	...	...
Loum	115 781	...	...	...	...	...	...	...
Maroua	225 469	...	...	...	...	...	...	...

8. Population of capital cities and cities of 100 000 or more inhabitants: latest available year, 1988 - 2007
Population des capitales et des villes de 100 000 habitants ou plus: dernière année disponible, 1988 - 2007 (continued - suite)

Continent, country or area, date, code and city / Continent, pays ou zone, date, code et ville	City proper - Ville proprement dite				Urban agglomeration - Agglomération urbaine			
	Population			Surface area - Superficie (km²)	Population			Surface area - Superficie (km²)
	Both sexes - Les deux sexes	Male - Masculin	Female - Féminin		Both sexes - Les deux sexes	Male - Masculin	Female - Féminin	
AFRICA - AFRIQUE								
Cameroon - Cameroun								
1 VII 1998 (ESDF)								
Ngaoundéré	156 804	...	...	...	...	...	...	...
Nkongsamba	104 908	...	...	...	...	...	...	...
YAOUNDE	1 293 000	...	...	...	...	...	...	...
Cape Verde - Cap-Vert								
23 VI 1990 (CDFC)								
PRAIA	61 644	...	...					
Central African Republic - République centrafricaine								
8 XII 1988 (CDFC)								
BANGUI	451 690			...	...			...
Chad - Tchad								
8 IV 1993 (CDFC)								
N'DJAMENA	530 965	...	...	...	...	...		...
Comoros - Comores								
15 IX 1991 (CDFC)								
MORONI	30 365	...	...	...	...	...		
Côte d'Ivoire								
1 III 1988 (CDFC)								
Abidjan	1 929 079							
Bouake	329 850	...	...	...		...		...
Daloa	121 842	...	...	...	362 192	...	...	...
Korhogo	109 445	...	...	...	127 923	...	...	...
YAMOUSSOUKRO	106 786	...	...	...	112 888	...	...	...
Djibouti					126 191			
1 VII 1995 (ESDF)								
DJIBOUTI	383 000			...	...	...	...	...
Egypt - Égypte								
11 XI 2006 (CDFC)								
CAIRO	6 758 581	3 433 198	3 325 383	...	...	...	...	...
Eritrea - Érythrée								
1 VII 1990 (ESDF)								
ASMARA	358 100	...	...	...	...	...		...
Ethiopia - Éthiopie								
1 VII 2002 (ESDF)								
ADDIS ABABA	2 646 000	1 273 000	1 373 000					
Awassa	103 725	52 308	51 417	...	...	...	...	...
Bahir Dar	140 084	72 736	67 348	...	...	...	...	...
Debre Zeit	108 632	53 648	54 984	28	...	...	...	...
Dessie	141 616	72 578	69 038	15	...	...	...	...
Dire Dawa	237 012	118 880	118 132	18	...	...	...	...
Gondar	163 097	82 229	80 868	40	...	...	...	...
Harar	105 000	53 000	52 000	...	...	...	...	...
Jimma	131 708	67 138	64 570	...	...	...	...	...
Mekele	141 433	71 990	69 443	24	...	...	...	...
Nazareth	189 362	94 822	94 540	...	...	...	...	...
Gabon								
31 VII 1993 (CDFC)								
LIBREVILLE	362 386	184 192	178 194	...	418 616	212 383	206 233	...
Gambia - Gambie								
15 IV 1993 (CDFC)								
BANJU	42 326	22 268	20 058	12	...	...	...	...
Ghana								
26 III 2000 (CDFC)								
ACCRA	1 658 937	817 404	841 533					
Kumasi	1 170 270	587 012	583 258	...	...	...	...	...
Sekondi	114 157	56 697	57 460	...	...	...	...	...
Takoradi	175 436	86 794	88 642	...	...	...	...	...
Tamale	202 317	100 854	101 463	...	...	...	...	...
Tema	141 479	68 467	73 012	...	...	...	...	...
Guinea - Guinée								
1 XII 1996 (CDFC)								
CONAKRY	1 091 500	...	...	...	...	...		
Kankan	...	...	...	...	261 341	...	...	...
Kindia	...	...	...	...	287 607	...	...	...

8. Population of capital cities and cities of 100 000 or more inhabitants: latest available year, 1988 - 2007
Population des capitales et des villes de 100 000 habitants ou plus: dernière année disponible, 1988 - 2007 (continued - suite)

Continent, country or area, date, code and city / Continent, pays ou zone, date, code et ville	City proper - Ville proprement dite				Urban agglomeration - Agglomération urbaine			
	Population			Surface area - Superficie (km²)	Population			Surface area - Superficie (km²)
	Both sexes - Les deux sexes	Male - Masculin	Female - Féminin		Both sexes - Les deux sexes	Male - Masculin	Female - Féminin	
AFRICA - AFRIQUE								
Guinea - Guinée								
1 XII 1996 (CDFC)								
Labé	...	...	...	...	249 515	...	...	...
Nzérékoré	...	...	...	...	282 772	...	...	...
Guinea-Bissau - Guinée-Bissau								
1 XII 1991 (CDFC)								
BISSAU	197 600	...	...	...	...	...	...	...
Kenya								
1 VII 2006 (ESDF)								
Kisumu	600 789	...	...	475	...	...	...	...
Mombasa	862 092	...	...	230	...	...	...	...
NAIROBI	2 948 109	...	...	696	...	...	...	...
Nakuru	1 571 162	...	...	290	...	...	...	...
Libyan Arab Jamahiriya - Jamahiriya arabe libyenne								
1 VII 1990 (ESDF)								
Al Khums	200 000	...	...	...	...	...	...	...
BENGHAZI[1]	800 000	...	...	...	...	...	...	...
Misurata	360 000	...	...	...	...	...	...	...
Sebha	150 000	...	...	...	...	...	...	...
TRIPOLI[1]	1 500 000	...	...	...	...	...	...	...
Zuwarah	280 000	...	...	...	...	...	...	...
Madagascar								
1 VII 2005 (ESDF)								
ANTANANARIVO[2]	1 015 140	495 393	519 747	72	...	...	...	...
Antsirabe	...	...	...	...	180 180	87 691	92 489	...
Fianarantsoa	...	...	...	...	165 220	80 410	84 810	...
Mahajanga	...	...	...	...	152 785	74 359	78 426	...
Toamasina	...	...	...	...	203 469	99 026	104 443	...
Toliara	...	...	...	...	113 993	55 479	58 514	...
Malawi								
1 VII 2007 (ESDF)								
Blantyre City	778 827[3]	400 493[3]	378 334[3]	220	...	...	...	...
LILONGWE	744 436[3]	384 178[3]	360 258[3]	328	...	...	...	...
Malawi: Mzuzu City	150 065[3]	76 627[3]	73 438[3]	48	...	...	...	...
Malawi: Zomba City	113 106[3]	57 693[3]	55 413[3]	39	...	...	...	...
Mauritania - Mauritanie								
1 XI 2000 (CDFC)								
NOUAKCHOTT	558 195	...	...	...	...	...	...	...
Mauritius - Maurice								
1 VII 2007 (ESDJ)								
Beau Bassin - Rose Hill	109 411	53 276	56 135	20	...	...	...	...
PORT LOUIS	148 877	73 822	75 055	46	...	...	...	...
Vacoas - Phoenix	106 574	52 437	54 137	54	...	...	...	...
Morocco - Maroc								
1 VII 2007 (ESDF)								
Agadir	527 000	...	...	...	...	...	...	...
Béni-Mellal	959 000	...	...	...	...	...	...	...
Casablanca (Dar-el-Beida)[4]	2 995 000	...	...	...	...	...	...	...
El-Jadida	1 132 000	...	...	...	...	...	...	...
Fès	1 026 000	...	...	...	...	...	...	...
Inezgane ait Melloul	462 000	...	...	...	...	...	...	...
Kénitra	1 214 000	...	...	...	...	...	...	...
Khemisset	532 000	...	...	...	...	...	...	...
Khouribga	502 000	...	...	...	...	...	...	...
Laayoune	227 000	...	...	...	...	...	...	...
Larache	479 000	...	...	...	...	...	...	...
Marrakech[4]	1 126 000	...	...	...	...	...	...	...
Meknès	739 000	...	...	...	...	...	...	...
Mohammedia	336 000	...	...	...	...	...	...	...
Nador	740 000	...	...	...	...	...	...	...
Oujda	489 000	...	...	...	...	...	...	...
RABAT	642 000	...	...	...	...	...	...	...
Safi	888 000	...	...	...	...	...	...	...
Salé	879 000	...	...	...	...	...	...	...
Settat	980 000	...	...	...	...	...	...	...
Skhirate-Témara	447 000	...	...	...	...	...	...	...

8. Population of capital cities and cities of 100 000 or more inhabitants: latest available year, 1988 - 2007
Population des capitales et des villes de 100 000 habitants ou plus: dernière année disponible, 1988 - 2007 (continued - suite)

Continent, country or area, date, code and city / Continent, pays ou zone, date, code et ville	City proper - Ville proprement dite				Urban agglomeration - Agglomération urbaine			
	Population			Surface area - Superficie (km²)	Population			Surface area - Superficie (km²)
	Both sexes - Les deux sexes	Male - Masculin	Female - Féminin		Both sexes - Les deux sexes	Male - Masculin	Female - Féminin	
AFRICA - AFRIQUE								
Morocco - Maroc								
1 VII 2007 (ESDF)								
Tanger	811 000	...	...	...	...	...	...	...
Taza	750 000	...	...	...	...	...	...	...
Tétouan	545 000	...	...	...	...	...	...	...
Mozambique								
1 VIII 1997 (CDFC)								
Beira	397 368	...	...	...	...	...	...	...
Chimoio	171 056	...	...	...	...	...	...	...
MAPUTO	966 837	...	...	...	...	...	...	...
Matola	424 662	...	...	...	1 391 499	...	...	...
Mocuba	124 650	...	...	...	...	...	...	...
Nacala	158 248	...	...	...	...	...	...	...
Nampula	303 346	...	...	...	...	...	...	...
Quelimane	150 116	...	...	...	...	...	...	...
Tete	101 984	...	...	...	...	...	...	...
Namibia - Namibie								
27 VIII 2001 (CDFC)								
WINDHOEK	...	...	...	...	233 529	117 306	116 222	...
Niger								
20 V 2001 (CDJC)								
Maradi	148 017	...	...	...	...	...	...	...
NIAMEY	707 951	358 500	349 451	...	...	...	...	...
Zinder	170 575	...	...	...	...	...	...	...
Nigeria - Nigéria								
26 XI 1991 (CDFC)								
Aba	500 183	...	...	...	...	...	...	...
Abeokuta	352 735	...	...	...	...	...	...	...
ABUJA	107 069	...	...	...	378 671	...	...	...
Ado-Ekiti	156 122	...	...	...	...	...	...	...
Akure	239 124	...	...	...	...	...	...	...
Awka	104 682	...	...	...	...	...	...	...
Bauchi	206 537	...	...	...	...	...	...	...
Benin City	762 719	...	...	...	...	...	...	...
Bida	111 245	...	...	...	...	...	...	...
Calabar	310 839	...	...	...	...	...	...	...
Damaturu	141 897	...	...	...	...	...	...	...
Ede	142 363	...	...	...	...	...	...	...
Effon-Alaiye	158 977	...	...	...	...	...	...	...
Enugu	407 756	...	...	...	...	...	...	...
Gboko	101 281	...	...	...	...	...	...	...
Gombe	163 604	...	...	...	...	...	...	...
Gusau	132 393	...	...	...	...	...	...	...
Ibadan	1 835 300	...	...	...	...	...	...	...
Ife	186 856	...	...	...	...	...	...	...
Ijebu-Ode	124 313	...	...	...	...	...	...	...
Ikare	103 843	...	...	...	...	...	...	...
Ikire	111 435	...	...	...	...	...	...	...
Ikorodu	184 674	...	...	...	...	...	...	...
Ikot Ekpene	119 402	...	...	...	...	...	...	...
Ilawe-Ekiti	104 049	...	...	...	...	...	...	...
Ilesha	139 445	...	...	...	...	...	...	...
Ilorin	532 089	...	...	...	...	...	...	...
Ise	108 136	...	...	...	...	...	...	...
Iseyin	170 936	...	...	...	...	...	...	...
Iwo	125 645	...	...	...	...	...	...	...
Jimeta	141 724	...	...	...	...	...	...	...
Jos	510 300	...	...	...	...	...	...	...
Kaduna	993 642	...	...	...	...	...	...	...
Kano	2 166 554	...	...	...	...	...	...	...
Katsina	259 315	...	...	...	...	...	...	...
Lagos	5 195 247	...	...	...	...	...	...	...
Maiduguri	618 278	...	...	...	...	...	...	...
Makurdi	151 515	...	...	...	...	...	...	...
Minna	189 191	...	...	...	...	...	...	...
Mubi	128 900	...	...	...	...	...	...	...

8. Population of capital cities and cities of 100 000 or more inhabitants: latest available year, 1988 - 2007
Population des capitales et des villes de 100 000 habitants ou plus: dernière année disponible, 1988 - 2007 (continued - suite)

Continent, country or area, date, code and city / Continent, pays ou zone, date, code et ville	City proper - Ville proprement dite				Urban agglomeration - Agglomération urbaine			
	Population			Surface area - Superficie (km²)	Population			Surface area - Superficie (km²)
	Both sexes - Les deux sexes	Male - Masculin	Female - Féminin		Both sexes - Les deux sexes	Male - Masculin	Female - Féminin	
AFRICA - AFRIQUE								
Nigeria - Nigéria								
26 XI 1991 (CDFC)								
Nnewi	121 065	...	...	...	...	...	...	...
Ogbomosho	433 030	...	...	...	...	...	...	...
Okene	312 775	...	...	...	...	...	...	...
Okpogho	105 127	...	...	...	...	...	...	...
Ondo	146 051	...	...	...	...	...	...	...
Onitsha	350 280	...	...	...	...	...	...	...
Oshogbo	250 951	...	...	...	...	...	...	...
Owerri	119 711	...	...	...	...	...	...	...
Owo	157 181	...	...	...	...	...	...	...
Oyo	369 894	...	...	...	...	...	...	...
Port Harcourt	703 421	...	...	...	...	...	...	...
Sagamu	127 513	...	...	...	...	...	...	...
Sango Otta	103 332	...	...	...	...	...	...	...
Sapele	109 576	...	...	...	...	...	...	...
Sokoto	329 639	...	...	...	...	...	...	...
Suleja	105 075	...	...	...	...	...	...	...
Ugep	134 773	...	...	...	...	...	...	...
Umuahia	147 167	...	...	...	...	...	...	...
Warri	363 382	...	...	...	...	...	...	...
Zaria	612 257	...	...	...	...	...	...	...
Réunion								
1 I 2006 (CDJC)								
SAINT-DENIS	138 314	64 552	73 762	143[5]	...	...	...	...
Rwanda								
15 VIII 1991 (CDJC)								
KIGALI	233 640	125 550	108 090	...	...	...	...	...
Saint Helena ex. dep. - Sainte-Hélène sans dép.								
8 III 1998 (CDFC)								
JAMESTOWN	884	452	432	4	...	...	...	...
Sao Tome and Principe - Sao Tomé-et-Principe								
25 VIII 2001 (CDJC)								
SAO TOME	...	...	...	...	49 957	24 003	25 954	...
Senegal - Sénégal								
31 XII 2007 (ESDF)								
DAKAR	1 075 582	...	...	500	...	...	...	...
Diourbel	101 215	...	...	...	...	...	...	...
Guediawaye	293 737	...	...	...	...	...	...	...
Kaolack	185 976	...	...	...	...	...	...	...
Mbour	181 825	...	...	...	...	...	...	...
Pikine[6]	874 062	...	...	...	...	...	...	...
Rufisque	162 055	...	...	...	...	...	...	...
Saint Louis	171 263	...	...	...	...	...	...	...
Thiès	181 825	...	...	...	...	...	...	...
Ziguinchor	158 370	...	...	...	...	...	...	...
Seychelles								
29 VIII 1997 (CDFC)								
VICTORIA	...	...	...	...	24 701	...	...	...
Somalia - Somalie								
1 VII 2001 (ESDF)								
MOGADISHU	1 212 000	...	...	...	...	...	...	...
South Africa - Afrique du Sud								
10 X 1996 (CDFC)								
Alexandra	171 284	...	...	...	...	...	...	...
Benoni	366 343	...	...	...	...	...	...	...
Bloemfontein	350 504	...	...	...	...	...	...	...
Boksburg	263 179	...	...	...	...	...	...	...
Botshabelo	177 971	...	...	...	...	...	...	...
CAPE TOWN[7]	987 007	...	...	...	...	...	...	...
Durban	669 242	...	...	...	...	...	...	...
Germiston	164 252	...	...	...	...	...	...	...
Johannesburg	752 349	...	...	...	...	...	...	...
Kathlehong	344 803	...	...	...	...	...	...	...
Kempton Park	344 426	...	...	...	...	...	...	...
Khayelitsa	314 239	...	...	...	...	...	...	...

8. Population of capital cities and cities of 100 000 or more inhabitants: latest available year, 1988 - 2007
Population des capitales et des villes de 100 000 habitants ou plus: dernière année disponible, 1988 - 2007 (continued - suite)

Continent, country or area, date, code and city / Continent, pays ou zone, date, code et ville	City proper - Ville proprement dite				Urban agglomeration - Agglomération urbaine			
	Population			Surface area - Superficie (km²)	Population			Surface area - Superficie (km²)
	Both sexes - Les deux sexes	Male - Masculin	Female - Féminin		Both sexes - Les deux sexes	Male - Masculin	Female - Féminin	
AFRICA - AFRIQUE								
South Africa - Afrique du Sud								
10 X 1996 (CDFC)								
Kimberley	206 070	...	...	...	...	...	...	...
Mangaung	176 525	...	...	...	...	...	...	...
Pietermaritzburg	405 385	...	...	...	...	...	...	...
Port Elizabeth	775 255	...	...	...	...	...	...	...
PRETORIA[7]	692 348	340 363	351 985	...	...	...	...	...
Roodepoort	279 340	...	...	...	...	...	...	...
Soweto	904 165	...	...	...	...	...	...	...
Springs	163 304	...	...	...	...	...	...	...
Tembisa	237 676	...	...	...	...	...	...	...
Umlazi	339 715	...	...	...	...	...	...	...
Vereeniging	379 638	...	...	...	...	...	...	...
Sudan - Soudan								
15 IV 1993 (CDFC)								
Al-Fasher	141 884	...	...	...	...	...	...	...
Al-Gadarif	191 164	...	...	...	...	...	...	...
Al-Gezira	211 362	...	...	...	...	...	...	...
Al-Obeid	229 425	...	...	...	...	...	...	...
Juba	114 980	...	...	...	...	...	...	...
Kassala	234 622	...	...	...	...	...	...	...
KHARTOUM	947 483	...	...	...	2 919 773	...	...	...
Khartoum North	700 887	...	...	...		...	...	...
Kosti	173 599	...	...	...	...	...	...	...
Nyala	227 183	...	...	...	...	...	...	...
Omdurman	1 271 403	...	...	...	...	...	...	...
Port Sudan	308 195	...	...	...	...	...	...	...
Togo								
1 VII 1990 (ESDF)								
LOME	450 000	...	...	...	...	...	...	...
Tunisia - Tunisie								
1 VII 1998 (ESDF)								
Bizerte	105 520	...	...	...	...	...	...	...
Gabes	104 950	...	...	...	...	...	...	...
Kairouan	110 280	...	...	...	...	...	...	...
Sfax	248 800	...	...	...	...	...	...	...
TUNIS	702 330	...	...	...	...	...	...	...
Uganda - Ouganda								
12 IX 2002 (CDFC)								
Gulu	113 144	...	...	...	...	...	...	...
KAMPALA	1 208 544	588 433	620 111	...	...	...	...	...
United Republic of Tanzania - République Unie de Tanzanie								
28 VIII 1988 (CDFC)								
Arusha	134 708	69 875	64 833					
Dar es Salaam	1 360 850	715 925	644 925	...	...	...	...	...
DODOMA	203 833	101 437	102 396	...	...	...	...	...
Mbeya	152 844	74 259	78 585	...	...	...	...	...
Morogoro	117 760	59 144	58 616	...	...	...	...	...
Mwanza	223 013	113 779	109 234	...	...	...	...	...
Shinyanga	100 724	50 117	50 607	...	...	...	...	...
Tanga	187 455	96 259	91 196	...	...	...	...	...
Zanzibar	157 634	77 787	79 847	...	...	...	...	...
Western Sahara - Sahara occidental[8]								
1 VII 1999 (ESDF)								
EL AAIUN	169 000	...	...	...				
Zambia - Zambie								
1 VII 2000 (ESDF)								
Chingola	164 964	82 643	82 321	1 678				
Kabwe	170 387	84 041	86 346	1 572	...	...	...	...
Kitwe	362 423	180 865	181 558	777	...	...	...	...
Luanshya	144 009	72 449	71 560	811	...	...	...	...
LUSAKA	1 057 212	528 891	528 321	360	...	...	...	...
Mufulira	137 272	68 253	69 019	1 637	...	...	...	...
Ndola	371 221	185 043	186 178	1 103	...	...	...	...

Continent, country or area, date, code and city / Continent, pays ou zone, date, code et ville	City proper - Ville proprement dite				Urban agglomeration - Agglomération urbaine			
	Population			Surface area - Superficie (km²)	Population			Surface area - Superficie (km²)
	Both sexes - Les deux sexes	Male - Masculin	Female - Féminin		Both sexes - Les deux sexes	Male - Masculin	Female - Féminin	
AFRICA - AFRIQUE								
Zimbabwe								
17 VIII 2002 (CDFC)								
Bulawayo	676 650	323 550	353 100	479	...	...	...	...
Gweru	140 806	67 689	73 117	...	...	...	...	...
HARARE	1 435 784	720 021	715 763	872	...	...	...	...
Mutare	170 466	85 006	85 460	...	...	...	...	...
AMERICA, NORTH - AMÉRIQUE DU NORD								
Anguilla								
1 VII 2001 (ESDF)								
THE VALLEY	4 904	...	...	...	...	...	...	...
Antigua and Barbuda - Antigua-et-Barbuda								
28 V 1991 (CDFC)								
ST. JOHN	22 342	...	...	...	...	...	...	...
Aruba								
6 X 1991 (CDJC)								
ORANJESTAD	20 045	9 441	10 604	...	...	...	...	...
Bahamas								
1 V 2000 (CDFC)								
NASSAU	...	...	...	...	210 832	101 558	109 274	80
Belize								
1 VII 2000 (ESDF)								
BELMOPAN	*8 305*	*4 050*	*4 255*	...	...	...	...	...
Bermuda - Bermudes								
20 V 2000 (CDJC)								
HAMILTON	969[9]	508[9]	461[9]	0[10]	...	...	...	...
British Virgin Islands - Îles Vierges britanniques								
1 VII 1992 (ESDF)								
ROAD TOWN	3 500	...	...	...	...	...	...	...
Canada								
1 VII 2007 (ESDJ)								
Abbotsford	...	...	...	...	164 638	82 807	81 831	626
Calgary	...	...	...	...	1 139 126	577 035	562 091	5 083
Edmonton	...	...	...	...	1 081 275	543 902	537 373	9 419
Greater Sudbury / Grand Sudbury	...	...	...	...	162 653	79 949	82 704	3 536
Halifax	...	...	...	...	385 457	187 823	197 634	5 496
Hamilton	...	...	...	...	720 426	354 129	366 297	1 372
Kingston	...	...	...	...	154 985	76 621	78 364	1 907
Kitchener	...	...	...	...	468 002	232 636	235 366	827
London	...	...	...	...	469 714	229 935	239 779	2 333
Montréal	...	...	...	...	3 695 790	1 809 363	1 886 427	4 047
Oshawa	...	...	...	...	347 999	172 536	175 463	903
Ottawa - Gatineau[11]	...	...	...	...	1 168 788	574 109	594 679	5 318
Québec	...	...	...	...	728 924	355 758	373 166	3 154
Regina	...	...	...	...	201 514	98 585	102 929	3 408
Saguenay	...	...	...	...	151 803	75 428	76 375	1 754
Saint John	...	...	...	...	126 382	61 090	65 292	3 360
Saskatoon	...	...	...	...	241 439	118 510	122 929	5 192
Sherbrooke	...	...	...	...	166 503	81 442	85 061	1 108
St. Catharines	...	...	...	...	395 839	193 794	202 045	1 406
St. John's	...	...	...	...	183 493	88 646	94 847	805
Thunder Bay	...	...	...	...	124 109	61 314	62 795	2 548
Toronto	...	...	...	...	5 509 874	2 707 521	2 802 353	5 903
Trois-Rivières	...	...	...	...	143 846	69 552	74 294	880
Vancouver	...	...	...	...	2 285 893	1 131 142	1 154 751	2 879
Victoria	...	...	...	...	337 411	163 211	174 200	695
Windsor	...	...	...	...	331 149	164 476	166 673	1 023
Winnipeg	...	...	...	...	712 671	350 908	361 763	4 151
Cayman Islands - Îles Caïmanes								
1 IV 2007 (SSDJ)								
GEORGE TOWN	28 836	...	...	...	...	...	...	...

8. Population of capital cities and cities of 100 000 or more inhabitants: latest available year, 1988 - 2007
Population des capitales et des villes de 100 000 habitants ou plus: dernière année disponible, 1988 - 2007 (continued - suite)

Continent, country or area, date, code and city / Continent, pays ou zone, date, code et ville	City proper - Ville proprement dite				Urban agglomeration - Agglomération urbaine			
	Population			Surface area - Superficie (km²)	Population			Surface area - Superficie (km²)
	Both sexes - Les deux sexes	Male - Masculin	Female - Féminin		Both sexes - Les deux sexes	Male - Masculin	Female - Féminin	
AMERICA, NORTH - AMÉRIQUE DU NORD								
Costa Rica								
1 VII 2007 (ESDJ)								
Alajuela	252 358	128 575	123 783	388	...	...	...	...
Cartago	148 065	74 654	73 411	288	...	...	...	...
Heredia	117 492	57 969	59 523	283	...	...	...	...
Limón	104 763	53 323	51 440	1 766	...	...	...	...
Puntarenas	117 269	60 662	56 607	1 842	...	...	...	...
SAN JOSE	348 558	172 006	176 552	45	...	...	...	...
Cuba								
1 VII 2007 (ESDJ)								
Bayamo	146 531	...	...	27	...	...	...	...
Camagüey	307 414	...	...	82	...	...	...	...
Ciego de Avila	110 119	...	...	21	...	...	...	...
Cienfuegos	142 678	...	...	46	...	...	...	...
Guantánamo	208 298	...	...	34	...	...	...	...
Holguín	275 994	...	...	58	...	...	...	...
LA HABANA	2 162 452	...	...	721	...	...	...	...
Las Tunas	151 472	...	...	31	...	...	...	...
Matanzas	130 781	...	...	44	...	...	...	...
Pinar del Río	137 916	...	...	32	...	...	...	...
Santa Clara	208 230	...	...	44	...	...	...	...
Santiago de Cuba	426 493	...	...	70	...	...	...	...
Dominica - Dominique								
12 V 1991 (CDFC)								
ROSEAU	16 243	...	...	...	...	...	...	...
Dominican Republic - République dominicaine								
18 X 2002 (CDJC)								
La Romana	202 488	98 113	104 375	263	191 303	92 460	98 843	26
San Pedro de Macoris	217 141	105 070	112 071	146	193 713	93 246	100 467	38
Santiago de los Caballeros	622 101	302 619	319 482	529	507 418	244 935	262 483	91
SANTO DOMINGO	913 540	430 698	482 842	91	913 540	430 698	482 842	91
Santo Domingo East - Santo Domingo Este	787 129	377 240	409 889	169	480 749	227 837	252 912	75
Santo Domingo North - Santo Domingo Norte	321 178	158 466	162 712	387	266 987	131 342	135 645	61
Santo Domingo West - Santo Domingo Oeste	280 912	135 836	145 076	56	226 310	109 128	117 182	33
El Salvador								
1 VII 2005 (ESDF)								
Ahuachapan	121 123[12]	...	...	245	...	...	...	...
Apopa	205 488[12]	...	...	52	...	...	...	...
Ciudad Delgado	170 014[12]	...	...	33	...	...	...	...
Cuscatancingo	111 011[12]	...	...	5	...	...	...	...
Ilopango	152 465[12]	...	...	35	...	...	...	...
Mejicanos	207 153[12]	...	...	22	...	...	...	...
Nueva San Salvador	186 635[12]	...	...	112	...	...	...	...
San Martin	134 152[12]	...	...	56	...	...	...	...
San Miguel	274 231[12]	...	...	594	...	...	...	...
SAN SALVADOR	507 665[12]	...	...	886	...	...	...	...
Santa Ana	270 339[12]	...	...	400	...	...	...	...
Sonsonate	108 118[12]	...	...	233	...	...	...	...
Soyapango	294 604[12]	...	...	30	...	...	...	...
Greenland - Groenland								
1 VII 2000 (ESDJ)								
NUUK (GODTHAB)	13 552	7 265	6 287	...	...	...	...	...
Guadeloupe								
8 III 1999 (CDJC)								
BASSE-TERRE	12 377	5 687	6 690	...	44 747	21 252	23 495	...
Pointe-à-Pitre	...	...	...	...	171 773	...	...	...
Guatemala								
1 VII 2001 (ESDF)								
CUIDAD DE GUATEMALA	1 022 001	491 891	530 110	228	...	...	...	...
Escuintla	114 626	57 893	56 733	332	...	...	...	...
Mixco	452 134	221 928	230 206	99	...	...	...	...
Quetzaltenango	152 223	76 272	75 951	120	...	...	...	...
Villa Nueva	390 329	192 238	198 091	114	...	...	...	...

8. Population of capital cities and cities of 100 000 or more inhabitants: latest available year, 1988 - 2007
Population des capitales et des villes de 100 000 habitants ou plus: dernière année disponible, 1988 - 2007 (continued - suite)

Continent, country or area, date, code and city / Continent, pays ou zone, date, code et ville	City proper - Ville proprement dite				Urban agglomeration - Agglomération urbaine			
	Population			Surface area - Superficie (km²)	Population			Surface area - Superficie (km²)
	Both sexes - Les deux sexes	Male - Masculin	Female - Féminin		Both sexes - Les deux sexes	Male - Masculin	Female - Féminin	
AMERICA, NORTH - AMÉRIQUE DU NORD								
Haiti - Haïti								
1 VII 1999 (ESDJ)								
Cap-Haitien..............................	113 555	50 064	63 491	10	...	...	...	...
Carrefour.................................	336 222	146 838	189 384	23	...	...	...	...
Delmas....................................	284 079	124 774	159 305	26	...	...	...	...
PORT-AU-PRINCE	990 558	436 170	554 388	21	...	...	...	...
Honduras								
1 VII 2003 (ESDF)								
La Ceiba	137 815	67 691	70 124	...	...	...	...	...
San Pedro Sula	518 736	251 514	267 222	...	...	...	...	...
TEGUCIGALPA.........................	858 437	411 687	446 749	...	...	...	...	...
Jamaica - Jamaïque								
10 IX 2001 (CDJC)								
KINGSTON...............................	579 137	272 587	306 550	22	...	...	...	...
Portmore.................................	156 467	72 292	84 175	...	...	...	...	...
Spanish Town	131 510	63 791	67 719	...	...	...	...	...
Martinique								
1 I 2006 (CDJC)								
FORT-DE-FRANCE.....................	90 347	40 128	50 219	...	133 281	59 945	73 336	...
Mexico - Mexique[13]								
1 VII 2006 (ESDJ)								
Acapulco (de Juárez)[14]	...	...	...	...	638 084	...	...	...
Aguascalientes[14]	...	...	...	...	718 643	...	...	...
Campeche.............................	216 473	...	...	...	...	...	...	...
Cancun[14]....................................	...	...	...	...	545 138	...	...	...
Celaya	320 881	...	...	...	...	...	...	...
Chihuahua[14]	...	...	...	...	766 513	...	...	...
Ciudad Del Carmen.....................	160 500	...	...	...	...	...	...	...
Ciudad Victoria	282 527	...	...	...	...	...	...	...
Coatzacoalcos[14]	...	...	...	...	423 095	...	...	...
Colimas[14]...................................	...	...	...	...	227 198	...	...	...
Cuernavaca[14].............................	...	...	...	...	725 033	...	...	...
Culiacán Rosales	620 768	...	...	...	...	...	...	...
Durango (Victoria de Durango)...............	479 450	...	...	...	...	...	...	...
Guadalajara[14]	...	...	...	...	3 833 866	...	...	...
Hermosillo.............................	661 057	...	...	...	...	...	...	...
Irapuato	346 706	...	...	...	...	...	...	...
Juárez[14]....................................	...	...	...	...	1 333 234	...	...	...
La Paz[14]....................................	...	...	...	...	192 157	...	...	...
León (de los Aldama)[14]	...	...	...	...	1 284 692	...	...	...
Manzanillo	114 630	...	...	...	...	...	...	...
Matamoros[14]...............................	...	...	...	...	430 923	...	...	...
Mérida[14]....................................	...	...	...	...	889 435	...	...	...
Mexicali[14]..................................	...	...	...	...	668 736	...	...	...
MEXICO, CIUDAD DE[14]	...	...	...	...	18 204 965	...	...	...
Monclova[14].................................	...	...	...	...	267 575	...	...	...
Monterrey[14]...............................	...	...	...	...	3 473 088	...	...	...
Morelia[14]..................................	...	...	...	...	654 303	...	...	...
Nuevo Laredo[14]............................	...	...	...	...	355 666	...	...	...
Oaxaca de Juárez[14].......................	...	...	...	...	500 338	...	...	...
Orizaba[14]..................................	...	...	...	...	481 444	...	...	...
Pachuca (de Soto)[14]	...	...	...	...	321 799	...	...	...
Puebla de Zaragoza[14]	...	...	...	...	1 887 827	...	...	...
Querétaro[14]................................	...	...	...	...	695 149	...	...	...
Reynosa[14].................................	...	...	...	...	532 192	...	...	...
Salamanca	145 860	...	...	...	...	...	...	...
Saltillo[14]..................................	...	...	...	...	701 570	...	...	...
San Luis Potosí[14].........................	...	...	...	...	934 645	...	...	...
Tampico[14]..................................	...	...	...	...	644 494	...	...	...
Tepic[14]	...	...	...	...	303 613	...	...	...
Tijuana[14]..................................	...	...	...	...	1 311 774	...	...	...
Tlaxcala[14].................................	...	...	...	...	503 693	...	...	...
Toluca (de Lerdo)[14]	...	...	...	...	1 069 710	...	...	...
Torreón[14]..................................	...	...	...	...	883 021	...	...	...
Tuxtla Gutiérrez[14].........................	...	...	...	...	501 681	...	...	...

8. Population of capital cities and cities of 100 000 or more inhabitants: latest available year, 1988 - 2007
Population des capitales et des villes de 100 000 habitants ou plus: dernière année disponible, 1988 - 2007 (continued - suite)

Continent, country or area, date, code and city / Continent, pays ou zone, date, code et ville	City proper - Ville proprement dite				Urban agglomeration - Agglomération urbaine			
	Population			Surface area - Superficie (km²)	Population			Surface area - Superficie (km²)
	Both sexes - Les deux sexes	Male - Masculin	Female - Féminin		Both sexes - Les deux sexes	Male - Masculin	Female - Féminin	
AMERICA, NORTH - AMÉRIQUE DU NORD								
Mexico - Mexique[13]								
1 VII 2006 (ESDJ)								
Veracruz[14]	...	...	...	...	637 345	...	...	...
Villahermosa[14]	...	...	...	...	378 618	...	...	...
Zacatecas[14]	...	...	...	...	235 325	...	...	...
Netherlands Antilles - Antilles néerlandaises								
27 I 1992 (CDJC)								
WILLEMSTAD	2 345	...	...	...	...	...	...	...
Nicaragua								
4 VI 2005 (CDJC)								
Leon	...	...	...	...	139 433	64 973	74 460	...
MANAGUA	...	...	...	...	908 892	430 389	478 503	...
Panama								
1 VII 2000 (ESDF)								
PANAMA DE PANAMA[15]	484 261	230 747	253 514	107	...	...	...	...
San Miguelito	331 692	161 901	169 791	50	...	...	...	...
Puerto Rico - Porto Rico								
1 VII 2007 (ESDJ)								
Arecibo	102 495[16]	49 923[16]	52 572[16]	327	...	...	...	...
Bayamón	220 629[16]	105 446[16]	115 183[16]	115	...	...	...	...
Caguas	142 984[16]	67 000[16]	75 984[16]	152	...	...	...	...
Carolina	187 607[16]	86 860[16]	100 747[16]	118	...	...	...	...
Guaynabo	102 838[16]	48 886[16]	53 952[16]	70	...	...	...	...
Ponce	180 376[16]	87 283[16]	93 093[16]	301	...	...	...	...
SAN JUAN	424 951[16]	195 961[16]	228 990[16]	124	...	...	...	...
Saint Lucia - Sainte-Lucie								
22 V 2001 (CDFC)								
CASTRIES	11 092	5 238	5 854	...	...	...	...	...
Saint Pierre and Miquelon - Saint Pierre-et-Miquelon								
8 III 1999 (CDFC)								
SAINT-PIERRE...............................	5 618	...	...	...	...	...	...	...
Saint Vincent and the Grenadines - Saint-Vincent-et-les Grenadines								
12 V 1991 (CDFC)								
KINGSTOWN..................................	15 466	...	...	...	...	...	...	...
Trinidad and Tobago - Trinité-et-Tobago								
1 VII 1996 (ESDF)								
PORT-OF-SPAIN	43 396	20 739	22 657	12	...	...	...	...
Turks and Caicos Islands - Îles Turques et Caïques								
1 VII 2006 (ESDJ)								
GRAND TURK.................................	5 718	2 846	2 872	17	...	...	...	...
United States of America - États-Unis d'Amérique								
1 VII 2007 (ESDJ)								
Abilene (TX)[17]	116 219	...	...	274	...	...	...	...
Akron (OH)[17]	207 934	...	...	161	...	...	...	...
Albuquerque (NM)[17]	518 271	...	...	487	...	...	...	...
Alexandria (VA)[17]	140 024	...	...	39	...	...	...	...
Allentown (PA)[17]	107 117	...	...	45	...	...	...	...
Amarillo (TX)[17]	186 106	...	...	254	...	...	...	...
Anaheim (CA)[17]	333 249	...	...	127	...	...	...	...
Anchorage (AK)[17]	279 671	...	...	4 396	...	...	...	...
Ann Arbor (MI)[17]	115 092	...	...	71	...	...	...	...
Arlington (TX)[17]	371 038	...	...	67	...	...	...	...
Arlington (VA)[17]	204 568	...	...	246	...	...	...	...
Arvada (CO)[17]	106 328	...	...	90	...	...	...	...
Athens (GA)[17]	112 760	...	...	301	...	...	...	...
Atlanta (GA)[17]	519 145	...	...	343	...	...	...	...
Augusta (GA)[17]	192 142	...	...	783	...	...	...	...
Aurora (CO)[17]	311 794	...	...	388	...	...	...	...
Aurora (IL)[17]	170 855	...	...	115	...	...	...	...
Austin (TX)[17]	743 074	...	...	688	...	...	...	...
Bakersfield (CA)[17]	315 837	...	...	335	...	...	...	...
Baltimore (MD)[17]	637 455	...	...	210	...	...	...	...
Baton Rouge (LA)[17]	227 071	...	...	200	...	...	...	...

8. Population of capital cities and cities of 100 000 or more inhabitants: latest available year, 1988 - 2007
Population des capitales et des villes de 100 000 habitants ou plus: dernière année disponible, 1988 - 2007 (continued - suite)

Continent, country or area, date, code and city Continent, pays ou zone, date, code et ville	City proper - Ville proprement dite				Urban agglomeration - Agglomération urbaine			
	Population			Surface area - Superficie (km²)	Population			Surface area - Superficie (km²)
	Both sexes - Les deux sexes	Male - Masculin	Female - Féminin		Both sexes - Les deux sexes	Male - Masculin	Female - Féminin	
AMERICA, NORTH - AMÉRIQUE DU NORD								
United States of America - États-Unis d'Amérique								
1 VII 2007 (ESDJ)								
Beaumont (TX)[17]	109 579	...	...	214	...	...	...	...
Bellevue (WA)[17]	121 347	...	...	82	...	...	...	...
Berkeley (CA)[17]	101 377	...	...	27	...	...	...	...
Billings (MT)[17]	101 876	...	...	108	...	...	...	...
Birmingham (AL)[17]	229 800	...	...	386	...	...	...	...
Boise City (ID)[17]	202 832	...	...	187	...	...	...	...
Boston (MA)[17]	599 351	...	...	125	...	...	...	...
Bridgeport (CT)[17]	136 695	...	...	41	...	...	...	...
Brownsville (TX)[17]	172 806	...	...	343	...	...	...	...
Buffalo (NY)[17]	272 632	...	...	105	...	...	...	...
Burbank (CA)[17]	103 286	...	...	45	...	...	...	...
Cambridge (MA)[17]	101 388	...	...	17	...	...	...	...
Cape Coral (FL)[17]	156 981	...	...	272	...	...	...	...
Carrollton (TX)[17]	123 799	...	...	94	...	...	...	...
Cary (NC)[17]	121 796	...	...	134	...	...	...	...
Cedar Rapids (IA)[17]	126 396	...	...	182	...	...	...	...
Chandler (AZ)[17]	246 399	...	...	166	...	...	...	...
Charleston (SC)[17]	110 015	...	...	262	...	...	...	...
Charlotte (NC)[17]	671 588	...	...	728	...	...	...	...
Chattanooga (TN)[17]	169 884	...	...	351	...	...	...	...
Chesapeake (VA)[17]	219 154	...	...	883	...	...	...	...
Chicago (IL)[17]	2 836 658	...	...	589	...	...	...	...
Chula Vista (CA)[17]	217 478	...	...	130	...	...	...	...
Cincinnati (OH)[17]	332 458	...	...	202	...	...	...	...
Clarksville (TN)[17]	119 284	...	...	249	...	...	...	...
Clearwater (FL)[17]	106 642	...	...	66	...	...	...	...
Cleveland (OH)[17]	438 042	...	...	201	...	...	...	...
Colorado Springs (CO)[17]	376 427	...	...	502	...	...	...	...
Columbia (SC)[17]	124 818	...	...	335	...	...	...	...
Columbus (GA)[17]	187 046	...	...	561	...	...	...	...
Columbus (OH)[17]	747 755	...	...	560	...	...	...	...
Concord (CA)[17]	120 844	...	...	79	...	...	...	...
Coral Springs (FL)[17]	126 875	...	...	62	...	...	...	...
Corona (CA)[17]	150 308	...	...	100	...	...	...	...
Corpus Christi (TX)[17]	285 507	...	...	412	...	...	...	...
Costa Mesa (CA)[17]	108 978	...	...	41	...	...	...	...
Dallas (TX)[17]	1 240 499	...	...	881	...	...	...	...
Daly City (CA)[17]	100 882	...	...	20	...	...	...	...
Dayton (OH)[17]	155 461	...	...	144	...	...	...	...
Denton (TX)[17]	115 506	...	...	204	...	...	...	...
Denver (CO)[17]	588 349	...	...	397	...	...	...	...
Des Moines (IA)[17]	196 998	...	...	209	...	...	...	...
Detroit (MI)[17]	916 952	...	...	359	...	...	...	...
Downey (CA)[17]	108 109	...	...	32	...	...	...	...
Durham (NC)[17]	217 847	...	...	270	...	...	...	...
El Monte (CA)[17]	122 272	...	...	25	...	...	...	...
El Paso (TX)[17]	606 913	...	...	657	...	...	...	...
Elgin (IL)[17]	104 288	...	...	94	...	...	...	...
Elizabeth (NJ)[17]	124 862	...	...	32	...	...	...	...
Elk Grove (CA)[17]	131 212	...	...	109	...	...	...	...
Erie (PA)[17]	103 650	...	...	49	...	...	...	...
Escondido (CA)[17]	136 246	...	...	95	...	...	...	...
Eugene (OR)[17]	149 004	...	...	108	...	...	...	...
Evansville (IN)[17]	116 253	...	...	108	...	...	...	...
Fairfield (CA)[17]	103 992	...	...	97	...	...	...	...
Fayetteville (NC)[17]	171 853	...	...	236	...	...	...	...
Flint (MI)[17]	114 662	...	...	87	...	...	...	...
Fontana (CA)[17]	183 502	...	...	107	...	...	...	...
Fort Collins (CO)[17]	133 899	...	...	132	...	...	...	...
Fort Lauderdale (FL)[17]	183 606	...	...	90	...	...	...	...
Fort Wayne (IN)[17]	251 247	...	...	283	...	...	...	...
Fort Worth (TX)[17]	681 818	...	...	845	...	...	...	...

8. Population of capital cities and cities of 100 000 or more inhabitants: latest available year, 1988 - 2007
Population des capitales et des villes de 100 000 habitants ou plus: dernière année disponible, 1988 - 2007 (continued - suite)

Continent, country or area, date, code and city / Continent, pays ou zone, date, code et ville	City proper - Ville proprement dite				Urban agglomeration - Agglomération urbaine			
	Population			Surface area - Superficie (km²)	Population			Surface area - Superficie (km²)
	Both sexes - Les deux sexes	Male - Masculin	Female - Féminin		Both sexes - Les deux sexes	Male - Masculin	Female - Féminin	

AMERICA, NORTH - AMÉRIQUE DU NORD

United States of America - États-Unis d'Amérique
1 VII 2007 (ESDJ)

Fremont (CA)[17]	201 334	...	...	199	...	...	...	...
Fresno (CA)[17]	470 508	...	...	286	...	...	...	...
Fullerton (CA)[17]	132 066	...	...	58	...	...	...	...
Gainesville (FL)[17]	114 375	...	...	138	...	...	...	...
Garden Grove (CA)[17]	165 610	...	...	47	...	...	...	...
Garland (TX)[17]	218 792	...	...	148	...	...	...	...
Gilbert (AZ)[17]	207 550	...	...	171	...	...	...	...
Glendale (AZ)[17]	253 152	...	...	153	...	...	...	...
Glendale (CA)[17]	196 979	...	...	79	...	...	...	...
Grand Prairie (TX)[17]	158 422	...	...	186	...	...	...	...
Grand Rapids (MI)[17]	193 627	...	...	115	...	...	...	...
Green Bay (WI)[17]	100 781	...	...	118	...	...	...	...
Greensboro (NC)[17]	247 183	...	...	304	...	...	...	...
Hampton (VA)[17]	146 439	...	...	133	...	...	...	...
Hartford (CT)[17]	124 563	...	...	45	...	...	...	...
Hayward (CA)[17]	140 943	...	...	115	...	...	...	...
Henderson (NV)[17]	249 386	...	...	273	...	...	...	...
Hialeah (FL)[17]	212 217	...	...	55	...	...	...	...
High Point City (NC)[17]	100 432	...	...	139	...	...	...	...
Hollywood (FL)[17]	142 473	...	...	71	...	...	...	...
Honolulu (HI)[17]	375 571	...	...	222	...	...	...	...
Houston (TX)[17]	2 208 180	...	...	1 551	...	...	...	...
Huntington Beach (CA)[17]	192 885	...	...	68	...	...	...	...
Huntsville (AL)[17]	171 327	...	...	488	...	...	...	...
Independence (MO)[17]	110 704	...	...	201	...	...	...	...
Indianapolis (IN)[17]	795 458	...	...	937	...	...	...	...
Inglewood (CA)[17]	113 376	...	...	24	...	...	...	...
Irvine (CA)[17]	201 160	...	...	172	...	...	...	...
Irving (TX)[17]	199 505	...	...	173	...	...	...	...
Jackson (MS)[17]	175 710	...	...	272	...	...	...	...
Jacksonville (FL)[17]	805 605	...	...	1 935	...	...	...	...
Jersey City (NJ)[17]	242 389	...	...	38	...	...	...	...
Joliet (IL)[17]	144 316	...	...	135	...	...	...	...
Kansas City (KS)	142 320[17]	...	...	323	...	...	...	...
Kansas City (MO)	450 375[17]	...	...	814	...	...	...	...
Killeen (TX)[17]	112 434	...	...	116	...	...	...	...
Knoxville (TN)[17]	183 546	...	...	253	...	...	...	...
Lafayette (LA)[17]	113 544	...	...	127	...	...	...	...
Lakewood (CO)[17]	140 305	...	...	108	...	...	...	...
Lancaster (CA)[17]	143 616	...	...	244	...	...	...	...
Lansing (MI)[17]	114 947	...	...	93	...	...	...	...
Laredo (TX)[17]	217 506	...	...	220	...	...	...	...
Las Vegas (NV)[17]	558 880	...	...	347	...	...	...	...
Lexington-Fayette (KY)[17]	279 044	...	...	735	...	...	...	...
Lincoln (NE)[17]	248 744	...	...	219	...	...	...	...
Little Rock (AR)[17]	187 452	...	...	303	...	...	...	...
Long Beach (CA)[17]	466 520	...	...	131	...	...	...	...
Los Angeles (CA)[17]	3 834 340	...	...	1 214	...	...	...	...
Louisville (KY)[17]	557 789	...	...	842	...	...	...	...
Lowell (MA)[17]	103 512	...	...	35	...	...	...	...
Lubbock (TX)[17]	217 326	...	...	308	...	...	...	...
Madison (WI)[17]	228 775	...	...	197	...	...	...	...
Manchester (NH)[17]	108 874	...	...	86	...	...	...	...
McAllen (TX)[17]	127 245	...	...	123	...	...	...	...
McKinney City (TX)[17]	115 620	...	...	162	...	...	...	...
Memphis (TN)[17]	674 028	...	...	815	...	...	...	...
Mesa (AZ)[17]	452 933	...	...	341	...	...	...	...
Mesquite (TX)[17]	131 738	...	...	119	...	...	...	...
Miami (FL)[17]	409 719	...	...	93	...	...	...	...
Midland City (TX)[17]	103 880	...	...	181	...	...	...	...
Milwaukee (WI)[17]	602 191	...	...	249	...	...	...	...
Minneapolis (MN)[17]	377 392	...	...	142	...	...	...	...

8. Population of capital cities and cities of 100 000 or more inhabitants: latest available year, 1988 - 2007
Population des capitales et des villes de 100 000 habitants ou plus: dernière année disponible, 1988 - 2007 (continued - suite)

Continent, country or area, date, code and city Continent, pays ou zone, date, code et ville	City proper - Ville proprement dite				Urban agglomeration - Agglomération urbaine			
	Population			Surface area - Superficie (km²)	Population			Surface area - Superficie (km²)
	Both sexes - Les deux sexes	Male - Masculin	Female - Féminin		Both sexes - Les deux sexes	Male - Masculin	Female - Féminin	

AMERICA, NORTH - AMÉRIQUE DU NORD

United States of America - États-Unis d'Amérique
1 VII 2007 (ESDJ)

Miramar (FL)[17]	108 240	...	...	77	...	...	...	...
Mobile (AL)[17]	191 411	...	...	304	...	...	...	...
Modesto (CA)[17]	203 955	...	...	93	...	...	...	...
Montgomery (AL)[17]	204 086	...	...	403	...	...	...	...
Moreno Valley (CA)[17]	188 936	...	...	133	...	...	...	...
Naperville (IL)[17]	142 479	...	...	100	...	...	...	...
Nashville-Davidson (TN)[17]	590 807	...	...	1 224	...	...	...	...
New Haven (CT)[17]	123 932	...	...	49	...	...	...	...
New Orleans (LA)[17]	239 124	...	...	439	...	...	...	...
New York (NY)[17]	8 274 527	...	...	786	...	...	...	...
Newark (NJ)[17]	280 135	...	...	63	...	...	...	...
Newport News (VA)[17]	179 153	...	...	177	...	...	...	...
Norfolk (VA)[17]	235 747	...	...	140	...	...	...	...
Norman (OK)[17]	106 707	...	...	466	...	...	...	...
North Las Vegas (NV)[17]	212 114	...	...	211	...	...	...	...
Norwalk (CA)[17]	103 720	...	...	25	...	...	...	...
Oakland (CA)[17]	401 489	...	...	145	...	...	...	...
Oceanside (CA)[17]	168 602	...	...	105	...	...	...	...
Oklahoma City (OK)[17]	547 274	...	...	1 570	...	...	...	...
Olathe (KS)[17]	118 034	...	...	152	...	...	...	...
Omaha (NE)[17]	424 482	...	...	304	...	...	...	...
Ontario (CA)[17]	170 936	...	...	129	...	...	...	...
Orange (CA)[17]	134 299	...	...	64	...	...	...	...
Orlando (FL)[17]	227 907	...	...	262	...	...	...	...
Overland Park (KS)[17]	169 403	...	...	167	...	...	...	...
Oxnard (CA)[17]	184 725	...	...	70	...	...	...	...
Palm Bay City (FL)[17]	100 116	...	...	170	...	...	...	...
Palmdale (CA)[17]	140 882	...	...	275	...	...	...	...
Pasadena (CA)[17]	143 400	...	...	60	...	...	...	...
Pasadena (TX)[17]	146 518	...	...	114	...	...	...	...
Paterson (NJ)[17]	146 545	...	...	22	...	...	...	...
Pembroke Pines (FL)[17]	146 828	...	...	85	...	...	...	...
Peoria (AZ)[17]	146 743	...	...	457	...	...	...	...
Peoria (IL)[17]	113 546	...	...	122	...	...	...	...
Philadelphia (PA)[17]	1 449 634	...	...	347	...	...	...	...
Phoenix (AZ)[17]	1 552 259	...	...	1 329	...	...	...	...
Pittsburgh (PA)[17]	311 218	...	...	144	...	...	...	...
Plano (TX)[17]	260 796	...	...	186	...	...	...	...
Pomona (CA)[17]	152 631	...	...	59	...	...	...	...
Pompano Beach (FL)[17]	102 745	...	...	62	...	...	...	...
Port St. Lucie (FL)[17]	151 391	...	...	292	...	...	...	...
Portland (OR)[17]	550 396	...	...	346	...	...	...	...
Portsmouth (VA)[17]	101 967	...	...	87	...	...	...	...
Providence (RI)[17]	172 459	...	...	48	...	...	...	...
Provo (UT)[17]	117 592	...	...	106	...	...	...	...
Pueblo (CO)[17]	103 805	...	...	123	...	...	...	...
Raleigh (NC)[17]	375 806	...	...	353	...	...	...	...
Rancho Cucamonga (CA)[17]	170 266	...	...	100	...	...	...	...
Reno (NV)[17]	214 853	...	...	260	...	...	...	...
Richmond (CA)	101 454[17]	...	...	78	...	...	...	...
Richmond (VA)	200 123[17]	...	...	155	...	...	...	...
Riverside (CA)[17]	294 437	...	...	207	...	...	...	...
Rochester (NY)[17]	206 759	...	...	93	...	...	...	...
Rockford (IL)[17]	156 596	...	...	154	...	...	...	...
Roseville (CA)[17]	108 759	...	...	94	...	...	...	...
Sacramento (CA)[17]	460 242	...	...	251	...	...	...	...
Salem (OR)[17]	151 913	...	...	121	...	...	...	...
Salinas (CA)[17]	143 517	...	...	50	...	...	...	...
Salt Lake City (UT)[17]	180 651	...	...	283	...	...	...	...
San Antonio (TX)[17]	1 328 984	...	...	1 318	...	...	...	...
San Bernardino (CA)[17]	199 285	...	...	153	...	...	...	...
San Buenaventura (CA)[17]	103 219	...	...	55	...	...	...	...

8. Population of capital cities and cities of 100 000 or more inhabitants: latest available year, 1988 - 2007
Population des capitales et des villes de 100 000 habitants ou plus: dernière année disponible, 1988 - 2007 (continued - suite)

Continent, country or area, date, code and city / Continent, pays ou zone, date, code et ville	City proper - Ville proprement dite				Urban agglomeration - Agglomération urbaine			
	Population			Surface area - Superficie (km²)	Population			Surface area - Superficie (km²)
	Both sexes - Les deux sexes	Male - Masculin	Female - Féminin		Both sexes - Les deux sexes	Male - Masculin	Female - Féminin	
AMERICA, NORTH - AMÉRIQUE DU NORD								
United States of America - États-Unis d'Amérique								
1 VII 2007 (ESDJ)								
San Diego (CA)[17]	1 266 731	...	...	844	...	...	...	...
San Francisco (CA)[17]	764 976	...	...	121	...	...	...	...
San Jose (CA)[17]	939 899	...	...	456	...	...	...	...
Santa Ana (CA)[17]	339 555	...	...	70	...	...	...	...
Santa Clara (CA)[17]	109 756	...	...	48	...	...	...	...
Santa Clarita (CA)[17]	169 951	...	...	139	...	...	...	...
Santa Rosa (CA)[17]	154 241	...	...	106	...	...	...	...
Savannah (GA)[17]	130 331	...	...	231	...	...	...	...
Scottsdale (AZ)[17]	235 677	...	...	477	...	...	...	...
Seattle (WA)[17]	594 210	...	...	217	...	...	...	...
Shreveport (LA)[17]	199 569	...	...	273	...	...	...	...
Simi Valley (CA)[17]	120 464	...	...	108	...	...	...	...
Sioux Falls (SD)[17]	151 505	...	...	166	...	...	...	...
South Bend (IN)[17]	104 069	...	...	105	...	...	...	...
Spokane (WA)[17]	200 975	...	...	152	...	...	...	...
Springfield (IL)[17]	117 090	...	...	150	...	...	...	...
Springfield (MA)[17]	149 938	...	...	83	...	...	...	...
Springfield (MO)[17]	154 777	...	...	207	...	...	...	...
St. Louis (MO)[17]	350 759	...	...	160	...	...	...	...
St. Paul (MN)[17]	277 251	...	...	135	...	...	...	...
St. Petersburg (FL)[17]	246 407	...	...	160	...	...	...	...
Stamford (CT)[17]	118 475	...	...	98	...	...	...	...
Sterling Heights (MI)[17]	127 349	...	...	95	...	...	...	...
Stockton (CA)[17]	287 245	...	...	148	...	...	...	...
Sunnyvale (CA)[17]	131 140	...	...	57	...	...	...	...
Syracuse (NY)[17]	139 079	...	...	65	...	...	...	...
Tacoma (WA)[17]	196 520	...	...	129	...	...	...	...
Tallahassee (FL)[17]	168 979	...	...	259	...	...	...	...
Tampa (FL)[17]	336 823	...	...	294	...	...	...	...
Tempe (AZ)[17]	174 091	...	...	103	...	...	...	...
Thornton (CO)[17]	110 880	...	...	84	...	...	...	...
Thousand Oaks (CA)[17]	123 349	...	...	142	...	...	...	...
Toledo (OH)[17]	295 029	...	...	209	...	...	...	...
Topeka (KS)[17]	122 642	...	...	154	...	...	...	...
Torrance (CA)[17]	141 420	...	...	53	...	...	...	...
Tucson (AZ)[17]	525 529	...	...	586	...	...	...	...
Tulsa (OK)[17]	384 037	...	...	509	...	...	...	...
Vallejo (CA)[17]	115 552	...	...	79	...	...	...	...
Vancouver (WA)[17]	161 436	...	...	116	...	...	...	...
Victorville City (CA)[17]	107 221	...	...	190	...	...	...	...
Virginia Beach (VA)[17]	434 743	...	...	645	...	...	...	...
Visalia (CA)[17]	118 603	...	...	92	...	...	...	...
Waco (TX)[17]	122 222	...	...	227	...	...	...	...
Warren (MI)[17]	134 223	...	...	89	...	...	...	...
WASHINGTON (DC)[17]	588 292	...	...	158	...	...	...	...
Waterbury (CT)[17]	107 174	...	...	74	...	...	...	...
West Covina (CA)[17]	106 388	...	...	42	...	...	...	...
West Jordan (UT)[17]	102 445	...	...	84	...	...	...	...
West Valley City (UT)[17]	122 374	...	...	92	...	...	...	...
Westminster (CO)[17]	106 195	...	...	82	...	...	...	...
Wichita (KS)[17]	361 420	...	...	406	...	...	...	...
Wichita Falls (TX)[17]	101 590	...	...	184	...	...	...	...
Winston-Salem (NC)[17]	215 348	...	...	340	...	...	...	...
Worcester (MA)[17]	173 966	...	...	97	...	...	...	...
Yonkers (NY)[17]	199 244	...	...	47	...	...	...	...
United States Virgin Islands - Îles Vierges américaines[16]								
1 IV 2000 (CDJC)								
CHARLOTTE AMALIE	11 004	...	...	...	18 914	...	...	...

8. Population of capital cities and cities of 100 000 or more inhabitants: latest available year, 1988 - 2007
Population des capitales et des villes de 100 000 habitants ou plus: dernière année disponible, 1988 - 2007 (continued - suite)

Continent, country or area, date, code and city / Continent, pays ou zone, date, code et ville	City proper - Ville proprement dite				Urban agglomeration - Agglomération urbaine			
	Population			Surface area - Superficie (km²)	Population			Surface area - Superficie (km²)
	Both sexes - Les deux sexes	Male - Masculin	Female - Féminin		Both sexes - Les deux sexes	Male - Masculin	Female - Féminin	
AMERICA, SOUTH - AMÉRIQUE DU SUD								
Argentina - Argentine								
15 V 1991 (CDFC)								
Avellaneda	344 024	...	...	...	...	...	...	...
Bahía Blanca	260 096	...	...	...	...	...	...	...
BUENOS AIRES	2 965 403	...	...	...	11 298 030	...	...	...
Catamarca	109 882	...	...	...	132 626	...	...	...
Comodoro Rivadavia	124 104	...	...	...	...	...	...	...
Concordia	116 485	...	...	...	...	...	...	...
Córdoba	1 157 507	...	...	...	1 208 554	...	...	...
Corrientes	258 103	...	...	...	...	...	...	...
Formosa	147 636	...	...	...	...	...	...	...
General San Martín	406 809	...	...	...	...	...	...	...
La Matanza	1 120 088	...	...	...	...	...	...	...
La Plata	521 936	...	...	...	642 979	...	...	...
Lanus	468 561	...	...	...	...	...	...	...
Lomas de Zamora	574 330	...	...	...	...	...	...	...
Mar del Plata	512 880	...	...	...	...	...	...	...
Mendoza	121 620	...	...	...	773 113	...	...	...
Morón	643 553	...	...	...	...	...	...	...
Neuquén	167 296	...	...	...	183 579	...	...	...
Paraná	207 041	...	...	...	211 936	...	...	...
Posadas	201 273	...	...	...	210 755	...	...	...
Quilmes	511 234	...	...	...	...	...	...	...
Resistencia	229 212	...	...	...	292 287	...	...	...
Río Cuarto	134 355	...	...	...	138 853	...	...	...
Rosario	907 718	...	...	...	1 118 905	...	...	...
Salta	367 550	...	...	...	370 904	...	...	...
San Fernando	141 063	...	...	...	...	...	...	...
San Isidro	299 023	...	...	...	...	...	...	...
San Juan	119 423	...	...	...	352 691	...	...	...
San Miguel de Tucumán	470 809	...	...	...	622 324	...	...	...
San Nicolás	119 302	...	...	...	...	...	...	...
San Salvador de Jujuy	178 748	...	...	...	180 102	...	...	...
Santa Fé	353 063	...	...	...	406 388	...	...	...
Santiago del Estero	189 947	...	...	...	263 471	...	...	...
Vicente López	289 505	...	...	...	...	...	...	...
Bolivia (Plurinational State of) - Bolivie (État plurinational de)								
1 VII 2007 (ESDF)								
Cochabamba	595 226	284 000	311 226	...	...	...	...	...
El Alto	858 932	419 653	439 279	...	...	...	...	...
LA PAZ[18]	835 186	397 546	437 640	...	...	...	...	...
Oruro	216 702	104 281	112 420	...	...	...	...	...
Potosí	150 647	72 477	78 170	...	...	...	...	...
Santa Cruz	1 451 597	706 110	745 486	...	...	...	...	...
SUCRE[18]	256 225	123 697	132 528	...	...	...	...	...
Tarija	176 787	85 385	91 402	...	...	...	...	...
Brazil - Brésil								
1 VII 2005 (ESDF)								
Abaeteluba	133 316[12]	...	...	1 090	...	...	...	...
Açailândia[12]	106 357	...	...	...	...	...	...	...
Aguas Lindas de Goiás[12]	168 919	...	...	...	...	...	...	...
Alagoinhas	139 818[12]	...	...	761	...	...	...	...
Almirante Tamandaré[12]	113 589	...	...	...	...	...	...	...
Alvorada[12]	214 953	...	...	...	...	...	...	...
Americana[12]	203 845	...	...	...	...	...	...	...
Ananindeua	498 095[12]	...	...	485	...	...	...	...
Anápolis[12]	318 808	...	...	...	...	...	...	...
Angra dos Reis[12]	144 137	...	...	...	...	...	...	...
Aparecida de Goiania[12]	453 104	...	...	...	...	...	...	...
Apucarana	117 260[12]	...	...	556	...	...	...	...
Aracaju	505 286[12]	...	...	151	...	...	...	...
Araçatuba	181 598[12]	...	...	2 668	...	...	...	...
Araguaina[12]	130 105	...	...	...	...	...	...	...
Araguario[12]	109 876	...	...	...	...	...	...	...

8. Population of capital cities and cities of 100 000 or more inhabitants: latest available year, 1988 - 2007
Population des capitales et des villes de 100 000 habitants ou plus: dernière année disponible, 1988 - 2007 (continued - suite)

Continent, country or area, date, code and city / Continent, pays ou zone, date, code et ville	City proper - Ville proprement dite				Urban agglomeration - Agglomération urbaine			
	Population			Surface area - Superficie (km²)	Population			Surface area - Superficie (km²)
	Both sexes - Les deux sexes	Male - Masculin	Female - Féminin		Both sexes - Les deux sexes	Male - Masculin	Female - Féminin	
AMERICA, SOUTH - AMÉRIQUE DU SUD								
Brazil - Brésil								
1 VII 2005 (ESDF)								
Arapiraca[12]	202 390	...	...	...	...	...	...	...
Arapongas[12]	100 855	...	...	...	...	...	...	...
Araraquara[12]	199 657	...	...	...	...	...	...	...
Araras[12]	116 566	...	...	...	...	...	...	...
Araruama[12]	110 378	...	...	...	...	...	...	...
Araucária[12]	118 313	...	...	...	...	...	...	...
Atibaia[12]	129 751	...	...	...	...	...	...	...
Bagé	122 461[12]	...	...	7 185	...	...	...	...
Barbacena[12]	124 601	...	...	...	...	...	...	...
Barra Mansa	176 151[12]	...	...	830	...	...	...	...
Barreiras[12]	138 037	...	...	...	...	...	...	...
Barretos[12]	110 195	...	...	...	...	...	...	...
Barueri[12]	265 549	...	...	...	...	...	...	...
Bauru	356 680[12]	...	...	702	...	...	...	...
Belém	1 428 368[12]	...	...	736	...	...	...	...
Belford Roxo[12]	489 002	...	...	...	...	...	...	...
Belo Horizonte	2 399 920[12]	...	...	335	...	...	...	...
Bento Gonçalves[12]	104 423	...	...	...	...	...	...	...
Betim	407 003[12]	...	...	376	...	...	...	...
Birigui[12]	108 472	...	...	...	...	...	...	...
Blumenou	298 603[12]	...	...	509	...	...	...	...
Boa Vista[12]	249 655	...	...	...	...	...	...	...
Botucatu[12]	121 274	...	...	...	...	...	...	...
Bragança[12]	103 751	...	...	...	...	...	...	...
Bragança Paulista	143 621[12]	...	...	770	...	...	...	...
BRASILIA	2 383 784[12]	...	...	5 794	...	...	...	...
Cabo de Santo Agostinho[12]	172 150	...	...	...	...	...	...	...
Cabo Frio[12]	165 591	...	...	...	...	...	...	...
Cachoeirinha[12]	121 880	...	...	...	...	...	...	...
Cachoeiro de Itapemirim	198 150[12]	...	...	892	...	...	...	...
Camacari	197 144[12]	...	...	718	...	...	...	...
Camaragibe[12]	150 354	...	...	...	...	...	...	...
Cametá[12]	106 816	...	...	...	...	...	...	...
Campina Grande	379 871[12]	...	...	970	...	...	...	...
Campinas	1 059 420[12]	...	...	781	...	...	...	...
Campo Grande	765 247[12]	...	...	8 091	...	...	...	...
Campo Largo[12]	107 756	...	...	...	...	...	...	...
Campos dos Goytacazes	429 667[12]	...	...	4 536	...	...	...	...
Canoas[12]	333 322	...	...	...	...	...	...	...
Carapicuíba[12]	389 634	...	...	...	...	...	...	...
Cariacica	361 058[12]	...	...	279	...	...	...	...
Caruaru	283 152[12]	...	...	936	...	...	...	...
Cascavel	284 083[12]	...	...	2 074	...	...	...	...
Castanhal	158 462[12]	...	...	1 003	...	...	...	...
Catanduva[12]	116 984	...	...	...	...	...	...	...
Caucaia	313 584[12]	...	...	1 293	...	...	...	...
Caxias	144 387[12]	...	...	6 724	...	...	...	...
Caxias do Sul	412 053[12]	...	...	1 601	...	...	...	...
Chapecó[12]	173 262	...	...	...	...	...	...	...
Codo	115 098[12]	...	...	4 923	...	...	...	...
Colatina	111 789[12]	...	...	2 094	...	...	...	...
Colombo[12]	231 787	...	...	...	...	...	...	...
Conselheiro Lafaiete[12]	113 019	...	...	...	...	...	...	...
Contagem	603 376[12]	...	...	167	...	...	...	...
Coronel Fabriciano[12]	104 851	...	...	...	...	...	...	...
Corumbá[12]	101 089	...	...	...	...	...	...	...
Cotia[12]	179 685	...	...	...	...	...	...	...
Crato[12]	115 087	...	...	...	...	...	...	...
Criciúma[12]	188 233	...	...	...	...	...	...	...
Cubatao[12]	121 002	...	...	...	...	...	...	...
Cuiabá	542 861[12]	...	...	3 922	...	...	...	...

Continent, country or area, date, code and city / Continent, pays ou zone, date, code et ville	City proper - Ville proprement dite				Urban agglomeration - Agglomération urbaine			
	Population			Surface area - Superficie (km²)	Population			Surface area - Superficie (km²)
	Both sexes - Les deux sexes	Male - Masculin	Female - Féminin		Both sexes - Les deux sexes	Male - Masculin	Female - Féminin	

AMERICA, SOUTH - AMÉRIQUE DU SUD

Brazil - Brésil
1 VII 2005 (ESDF)

Curitiba	1 788 559[12]	...	...	427	...	...	...	...
Diadema[12]	395 333	...	...	...	...	...	...	...
Divinópolis	207 983[12]	...	...	716	...	...	...	...
Dourados	186 357[12]	...	...	4 082	...	...	...	...
Duque de Caxias	855 010[12]	...	...	463	...	...	...	...
Embu[12]	245 855	...	...	...	...	...	...	...
Erechim[12]	100 251	...	...	...	...	...	...	...
Feira de Santana	535 820[12]	...	...	1 344	...	...	...	...
Ferraz de Vasconcelos[12]	176 532	...	...	...	...	...	...	...
Florianópolis	406 564[12]	...	...	440	...	...	...	...
Fortaleza	2 416 920[12]	...	...	336	...	...	...	...
Foz do Iguaçu	309 113[12]	...	...	596	...	...	...	...
Franca[12]	328 121	...	...	...	...	...	...	...
Francisco Morato[12]	170 585	...	...	...	...	...	...	...
Franco da Rocha[12]	124 816	...	...	...	...	...	...	...
Garanhuns	128 398[12]	...	...	456	...	...	...	...
Goiânia	1 220 412[12]	...	...	788	...	...	...	...
Governador Valadares	259 405[12]	...	...	2 447	...	...	...	...
Gravataí[12]	270 763	...	...	...	...	...	...	...
Guaíba[12]	105 808	...	...	...	...	...	...	...
Guarapari[12]	108 120	...	...	...	...	...	...	...
Guarapuava	169 007[12]	...	...	5 365	...	...	...	...
Guaratinguetá[12]	113 012	...	...	...	...	...	...	...
Guarujá[12]	305 171	...	...	...	...	...	...	...
Guarulhos[12]	1 283 253	...	...	...	...	...	...	...
Hortolandia[12]	201 795	...	...	...	...	...	...	...
Ibirité[12]	173 617	...	...	...	...	...	...	...
Ilhéus	220 932[12]	...	...	1 712	...	...	...	...
Imperatriz	232 560[12]	...	...	6 014	...	...	...	...
Indaiatuba[12]	181 124	...	...	...	...	...	...	...
Ipatinga	236 463[12]	...	...	231	...	...	...	...
Itabiraí[12]	107 721	...	...	...	...	...	...	...
Itaboraí	220 981[12]	...	...	569	...	...	...	...
Itabuna[12]	205 070	...	...	...	...	...	...	...
Itajaí[12]	168 088	...	...	...	...	...	...	...
Itapecerica da Serra[12]	162 239	...	...	...	...	...	...	...
Itapetininga	143 097[12]	...	...	2 035	...	...	...	...
Itapevi[12]	202 683	...	...	...	...	...	...	...
Itapipoca[12]	107 012	...	...	...	...	...	...	...
Itaquaquecetuba[12]	352 755	...	...	...	...	...	...	...
Itu	156 100[12]	...	...	640	...	...	...	...
Jaboatao dos Guarapes[12]	651 355	...	...	...	...	...	...	...
Jacareí[12]	211 559	...	...	...	...	...	...	...
Jandira[12]	113 323	...	...	...	...	...	...	...
Jaraguá do Sul[12]	131 786	...	...	...	...	...	...	...
Jaú[12]	125 399	...	...	...	...	...	...	...
Jequié	148 992[12]	...	...	3 113	...	...	...	...
Ji-Paraná[12]	113 453	...	...	...	...	...	...	...
Joao Pessoa[12]	672 081	...	...	...	...	...	...	...
Joinville	496 051[12]	...	...	1 080	...	...	...	...
Juazeiro	208 299[12]	...	...	5 615	...	...	...	...
Juàzeiro do Norte[12]	240 638	...	...	...	...	...	...	...
Juiz de Fora	509 125[12]	...	...	1 424	...	...	...	...
Jundiaí	348 621[12]	...	...	432	...	...	...	...
Lages	168 384[12]	...	...	5 287	...	...	...	...
Lauro de Freitas[12]	146 150	...	...	...	...	...	...	...
Limeira[12]	279 554	...	...	...	...	...	...	...
Linhares	123 000[12]	...	...	4 388	...	...	...	...
Londrina	495 696[12]	...	...	2 129	...	...	...	...
Luziânia	187 262[12]	...	...	4 653	...	...	...	...
Macae[12]	160 725	...	...	...	...	...	...	...

Continent, country or area, date, code and city / Continent, pays ou zone, date, code et ville	City proper - Ville proprement dite				Urban agglomeration - Agglomération urbaine			
	Population			Surface area - Superficie (km²)	Population			Surface area - Superficie (km²)
	Both sexes - Les deux sexes	Male - Masculin	Female - Féminin		Both sexes - Les deux sexes	Male - Masculin	Female - Féminin	
AMERICA, SOUTH - AMÉRIQUE DU SUD								
Brazil - Brésil								
1 VII 2005 (ESDF)								
Macapá[12]	368 367	...	...	...	...	...	...	...
Maceió	922 458[12]	...	...	517	...	...	...	...
Magé	237 000[12]	...	...	744	...	...	...	...
Manaus	1 688 524[12]	...	...	11 349	...	...	...	...
Maraba	200 801[12]	...	...	14 320	...	...	...	...
Maracanau[12]	196 422	...	...		...	...	...	...
Maranguape[12]	100 279	...	...	...	...	...	...	...
Marília	224 093[12]	...	...	1 194	...	...	...	...
Maringá	324 397[12]	...	...	490	...	...	...	...
Mauá[12]	413 943	...	...	...	...	...	...	...
Mesquita[12]	185 552	...	...		...	...	...	...
Moji das Cruzes	372 419[12]	...	...	749	...	...	...	...
Moji-Guaçu	141 559[12]	...	...	960	...	...	...	...
Montes Claros	348 991[12]	...	...	4 135	...	...	...	...
Mossoró	229 787[12]	...	...	2 108	...	...	...	...
Natal[12]	789 896	...	...		...	...	...	...
Nilópolis[12]	150 475	...	...		...	...	...	...
Niterói	476 669[12]	...	...	131	...	...	...	...
Nossa Senhora do Socorro[12]	179 060	...	...		...	...	...	...
Nova Friburgo	178 102[12]	...	...	930	...	...	...	...
Nova Iguaçu	844 583[12]	...	...	795	...	...	...	...
Nôvo Hamburgo[12]	258 754	...	...	...	...	...	...	...
Olinda[12]	387 494	...	...	...	...	...	...	...
Osasco[12]	714 950	...	...	...	...	...	...	...
Ourinhos[12]	106 350	...	...	...	...	...	...	...
Palhoça[12]	128 102	...	...	...	...	...	...	...
Palmas[12]	220 889	...	...		...	...	...	...
Paranaguá	147 934[12]	...	...	1 015	...	...	...	...
Parintins[12]	112 636	...	...		...	...	...	...
Parnaíba	143 675[12]	...	...	1 053	...	...	...	...
Parnamirim[12]	170 055	...	...	...	...	...	...	...
Passo Fundo	188 302[12]	...	...	1 596	...	...	...	...
Passos[12]	106 516	...	...		...	...	...	...
Patos de Minas	139 354[12]	...	...	3 336	...	...	...	...
Paulista[12]	299 744	...	...	...	...	...	...	...
Paulo Afonso[12]	103 776	...	...	...	...	...	...	...
Pelotas	346 452[12]	...	...	1 924	...	...	...	...
Petrolina	260 004[12]	...	...	6 116	...	...	...	...
Petrópolis	310 216[12]	...	...	771	...	...	...	...
Pindamonhangaba	143 737[12]	...	...	719	...	...	...	...
Pinhais[12]	123 288	...	...	...	...	...	...	...
Piracicaba	366 442[12]	...	...	1 426	...	...	...	...
Poà[12]	110 213	...	...	...	...	...	...	...
Poços de Caldas	154 477[12]	...	...	533	...	...	...	...
Ponta Grossa	304 973[12]	...	...	2 212	...	...	...	...
Porto Alegre[12]	1 440 939	...	...	...	...	...	...	...
Porto Seguro[12]	140 692	...	...		...	...	...	...
Porto Velho[12]	380 974	...	...	...	...	...	...	...
Pouso Alegre[12]	125 209	...	...	...	...	...	...	...
Praia Grande[12]	245 386	...	...		...	...	...	...
Presidente Prudente	206 704[12]	...	...	554	...	...	...	...
Queimados[12]	139 118	...	...	...	...	...	...	...
Recife[12]	1 515 052	...	...	...	...	...	...	...
Resende[12]	119 729	...	...		...	...	...	...
Ribeirao das Neves[12]	322 969	...	...	...	...	...	...	...
Ribeiro Pires[12]	118 864	...	...		...	...	...	...
Ribeirao Prêto[12]	559 650	...	...		...	...	...	...
Rio Branco[12]	314 127	...	...		...	...	...	...
Rio Claro	190 373[12]	...	...	503	...	...	...	...
Rio de Janeiro	6 136 652[12]	...	...	1 256	...	...	...	...
Rio Grande	196 982[12]	...	...	2 825	...	...	...	...

8. Population of capital cities and cities of 100 000 or more inhabitants: latest available year, 1988 - 2007
Population des capitales et des villes de 100 000 habitants ou plus: dernière année disponible, 1988 - 2007 (continued - suite)

Continent, country or area, date, code and city / Continent, pays ou zone, date, code et ville	City proper - Ville proprement dite				Urban agglomeration - Agglomération urbaine			
	Population			Surface area - Superficie (km²)	Population			Surface area - Superficie (km²)
	Both sexes - Les deux sexes	Male - Masculin	Female - Féminin		Both sexes - Les deux sexes	Male - Masculin	Female - Féminin	
AMERICA, SOUTH - AMÉRIQUE DU SUD								
Brazil - Brésil								
1 VII 2005 (ESDF)								
Rio Verde	136 229[12]	...	...	9 136	...	...	...	...
Rondonópolis	169 814[12]	...	...	4 594	...	...	...	...
Sabára[12]	134 282	...	...	...	...	...	...	...
Salto[12]	108 552	...	...	...	...	...	...	...
Salvador	2 714 018[12]	...	...	313	...	...	...	...
Santa Bárbara D'Oeste[12]	188 417	...	...	...	...	...	...	...
Santa Cruz do Sul[12]	119 803	...	...	...	...	...	...	...
Santa Luzia (Minas Gerais)[12]	219 699	...	...	...	...	...	...	...
Santa Maria	270 073[12]	...	...	3 279	...	...	...	...
Santa Rita[12]	131 684	...	...	...	...	...	...	...
Santarém[12]	276 074	...	...	...	...	...	...	...
Santo André[12]	673 234	...	...	...	...	...	...	...
Santos	418 375[12]	...	...	725	...	...	...	...
Sao Bernardo do Campo	803 906[12]	...	...	319	...	...	...	...
Sao Caetano do Sul[12]	133 241	...	...	...	...	...	...	...
Sao Carlo	218 702[12]	...	...	1 120	...	...	...	...
Sao Gonçalo[12]	973 372	...	...	...	...	...	...	...
Sao Joao de Meriti[12]	466 996	...	...	...	...	...	...	...
Sao José[12]	201 103	...	...	...	...	...	...	...
Sao José de Ribamar[12]	134 593	...	...	...	...	...	...	...
Sao José do Rio Prêto	415 508[12]	...	...	586	...	...	...	...
Sao José dos Campos	610 965[12]	...	...	1 186	...	...	...	...
Sao José dos Pinhais	261 125[12]	...	...	923	...	...	...	...
Sao Leopoldo[12]	212 498	...	...	...	...	...	...	...
Sao Luís	998 385[12]	...	...	822	...	...	...	...
Sao Paulo	11 016 703[12]	...	...	1 493	...	...	...	...
Sao Vicente[12]	329 370	...	...	...	...	...	...	...
Sapucaia do Sul[12]	135 956	...	...	...	...	...	...	...
Serra	394 370[12]	...	...	549	...	...	...	...
Sertaozinho[12]	106 407	...	...	...	...	...	...	...
Sete Lagoas[12]	215 069	...	...	...	...	...	...	...
Simoes Filho[12]	109 930	...	...	...	...	...	...	...
Sobral	175 814[12]	...	...	1 646	...	...	...	...
Sorocaba[12]	578 068	...	...	...	...	...	...	...
Sumaré	237 900[12]	...	...	208	...	...	...	...
Susano[12]	280 318	...	...	...	...	...	...	...
Taboao da Serra[12]	225 405	...	...	...	...	...	...	...
Tatuí[12]	107 115	...	...	...	...	...	...	...
Taubaté[12]	271 660	...	...	...	...	...	...	...
Teixeira de Freitas[12]	123 557	...	...	...	...	...	...	...
Teófilo Otoni[12]	127 530	...	...	...	...	...	...	...
Teresina	801 971[12]	...	...	1 356	...	...	...	...
Teresópolis	150 921[12]	...	...	768	...	...	...	...
Timon	146 139[12]	...	...	1 702	...	...	...	...
Toledo[12]	107 033	...	...	...	...	...	...	...
Uberaba	285 094[12]	...	...	4 524	...	...	...	...
Uberlândia	600 368[12]	...	...	4 040	...	...	...	...
Uruguaiana	136 364[12]	...	...	6 763	...	...	...	...
Valparaíso de Goiás[12]	123 921	...	...	...	...	...	...	...
Varginha[12]	124 502	...	...	...	...	...	...	...
Varzea Grande	254 736[12]	...	...	900	...	...	...	...
Varzea Paulista[12]	110 449	...	...	...	...	...	...	...
Viamao[12]	261 971	...	...	...	...	...	...	...
Vila Velha[12]	405 374	...	...	...	...	...	...	...
Vitória[12]	317 085	...	...	...	...	...	...	...
Vitória da Conquista	290 042[12]	...	...	3 743	...	...	...	...
Vitória de Santo Antao	125 563[12]	...	...	344	...	...	...	...
Volta Redonda[12]	258 145	...	...	...	...	...	...	...
Chile - Chili								
1 VII 2007 (ESDF)								
Antofagasta	347 941	180 783	167 158	44	...	...	...	...
Arica	171 651	82 387	89 264	42	...	...	...	...

268

Continent, country or area, date, code and city / Continent, pays ou zone, date, code et ville	City proper - Ville proprement dite				Urban agglomeration - Agglomération urbaine			
	Population			Surface area - Superficie (km²)	Population			Surface area - Superficie (km²)
	Both sexes - Les deux sexes	Male - Masculin	Female - Féminin		Both sexes - Les deux sexes	Male - Masculin	Female - Féminin	
AMERICA, SOUTH - AMÉRIQUE DU SUD								
Chile - Chili								
1 VII 2007 (ESDF)								
Calama	145 369	74 205	71 164	18	...	...	...	...
Chiguallante	107 411	50 546	56 865	...	...	...	...	...
Chillán	157 560	74 831	82 729	33	...	...	...	...
Concepción	220 607	106 620	113 987	56	...	...	...	...
Copiapó	147 870	74 203	73 667	48	...	...	...	...
Coquimbo	177 930	87 333	90 597	42	...	...	...	...
Iquique	179 302	87 030	92 272	22	...	...	...	...
La Serena	179 163	86 790	92 373	66	...	...	...	...
Los Angeles	134 359	65 096	69 263	27	...	...	...	...
Osorno	143 028	69 804	73 224	32	...	...	...	...
Puente Alto	646 724	317 042	329 682	64	...	...	...	...
Puerto Montt	188 125	94 118	94 007	40	...	...	...	...
Punta Arenas	120 463	60 449	60 014	39	...	...	...	...
Quilpué	147 758	71 695	76 063	38	...	...	...	...
Rancagua	229 065	113 411	115 654	50	...	...	...	...
San Bernardo	281 244	138 412	142 832	52	...	...	...	...
SANTIAGO	4 960 815[19]	2 403 691[19]	2 557 124[19]	727	...	...	...	...
Talca	209 323	100 904	108 419	46	...	...	...	...
Talcahuano	150 900	72 690	78 210	51	...	...	...	...
Temuco	256 732	123 544	133 188	46	...	...	...	...
Valdivia	137 560	67 120	70 440	42	...	...	...	...
Valparaíso	274 233	135 824	138 409	47	...	...	...	...
Villa Alemana	117 225	57 057	60 168	...	...	...	...	...
Viña del Mar	291 803	139 828	151 975	87	...	...	...	...
Colombia - Colombie[20]								
1 VII 2007 (ESDF)								
Apartadó	...	...	...	...	139 913	...	...	607
Armenia	...	...	...	...	284 120	...	...	115
Barrancabermeja	...	...	...	...	190 864	...	...	1 274
Barranquilla	...	...	...	...	1 163 007	...	...	166
Bello	...	...	...	...	388 460	...	...	151
Bucaramanga	...	...	...	...	520 080	...	...	154
Buenaventura	...	...	...	...	342 260	...	...	6 785
Cali	...	...	...	...	2 169 801	...	...	552
Cartagena	...	...	...	...	912 674	...	...	570
Cartago	...	...	...	...	126 134	...	...	260
Chía	...	...	...	...	103 568	...	...	76
Ciénaga	...	...	...	...	102 400	...	...	1 366
Cúcuta	...	...	...	...	600 049	...	...	1 098
Dosquebradas	...	...	...	...	183 250	...	...	80
Duitama	...	...	...	...	108 776	...	...	229
Envigado	...	...	...	...	183 251	...	...	51
Facatativá	...	...	...	...	112 486	...	...	160
Florencia	...	...	...	...	148 978	...	...	2 292
Floridablanca	...	...	...	...	257 631	...	...	101
Fusagasugá	...	...	...	...	113 888	...	...	206
Girardot	...	...	...	...	101 192	...	...	...
Girón	...	...	...	...	144 089	...	...	681
Gudalajara de Buga	...	...	...	...	116 510	...	...	873
Ibagué	...	...	...	...	509 796	...	...	1 439
Ipiales	...	...	...	...	114 609	...	...	1 707
Itagüi	...	...	...	...	242 403	...	...	17
Lorica	...	...	...	...	111 782	...	...	890
Magangué	...	...	...	...	121 651	...	...	1 102
Maicao	...	...	...	...	131 285	...	...	2 229
Malambo	...	...	...	...	105 324	...	...	108
Manizales	...	...	...	...	383 483	...	...	477
Medellín	...	...	...	...	2 264 776	...	...	387
Montería	...	...	...	...	390 996	...	...	3 043
Neiva	...	...	...	...	322 098	...	...	1 468
Palmira	...	...	...	...	288 382	...	...	1 044
Pasto	...	...	...	...	394 074	...	...	1 181
Pereira	...	...	...	...	448 971	...	...	702
Piedecuesta	...	...	...	...	123 371	...	...	481

8. Population of capital cities and cities of 100 000 or more inhabitants: latest available year, 1988 - 2007
Population des capitales et des villes de 100 000 habitants ou plus: dernière année disponible, 1988 - 2007 (continued - suite)

Continent, country or area, date, code and city / Continent, pays ou zone, date, code et ville	City proper - Ville proprement dite				Urban agglomeration - Agglomération urbaine			
	Population			Surface area - Superficie (km²)	Population			Surface area - Superficie (km²)
	Both sexes - Les deux sexes	Male - Masculin	Female - Féminin		Both sexes - Les deux sexes	Male - Masculin	Female - Féminin	
AMERICA, SOUTH - AMÉRIQUE DU SUD								
Colombia - Colombie[20]								
1 VII 2007 (ESDF)								
Pitalito	...	...	...	...	107 091	...	...	653
Popayán	...	...	...	...	261 694	...	...	464
Quibdo	...	...	...	...	113 542	...	...	3 075
Riohacha	...	...	...	...	184 847	...	...	3 276
Rionegro	...	...	...	...	104 453	...	...	198
San Andres de Tumaco	...	...	...	...	167 545	...	...	3 778
SANTA FE DE BOGOTA	...	...	...	...	7 050 228	...	...	1 605
Santa Marta	...	...	...	...	428 374	...	...	2 369
Sincelejo	...	...	...	...	245 180	...	...	292
Soacha	...	...	...	...	423 435	...	...	187
Sogamoso	...	...	...	...	116 718	...	...	214
Soledad	...	...	...	...	490 825	...	...	67
Tuluá	...	...	...	...	192 082	...	...	818
Tunja	...	...	...	...	161 209	...	...	118
Turbo	...	...	...	...	128 868	...	...	3 090
Uribia	...	...	...	...	128 473	...	...	7 904
Valledupar	...	...	...	...	373 872	...	...	4 225
Villavicencio	...	...	...	...	400 475	...	...	1 328
Yopal	...	...	...	...	113 250	...	...	2 532
Zipaquirá	...	...	...	...	105 830	...	...	194
Ecuador - Équateur								
1 VII 2007 (ESDF)								
Ambato	200 641	...	...	27	...	...	...	...
Babahoyo	106 196	...	...	...	...	...	...	...
Cuenca	359 730	...	...	47	...	...	...	...
Durán	192 909	...	...	...	...	...	...	...
Esmeraldas	115 468	...	...	8	...	...	...	...
Guayaquil	2 194 442	...	...	193	...	...	...	...
Ibarra	140 095	...	...	39	...	...	...	...
Loja	143 382	...	...	21	...	...	...	...
Machala	236 589	...	...	23	...	...	...	...
Manta	202 698	...	...	38	...	...	...	...
Milagro	125 385	...	...	17	...	...	...	...
Portoviejo	229 089	...	...	38	...	...	...	...
Quevedo	137 665	...	...	20	...	...	...	...
QUITO	1 559 295	...	...	170	...	...	...	...
Riobamba	167 260	...	...	24	...	...	...	...
Santo Domingo de los Colorados	222 663	...	...	43	...	...	...	...
Falkland Islands (Malvinas) - Îles Falkland (Malvinas)								
8 X 2006 (CDFC)								
STANLEY	2 115	...	...	...	...	...	...	...
French Guiana - Guyane française[5]								
1 I 2006 (CDJC)								
CAYENNE	58 004	27 412	30 591	24	75 740	36 484	39 256	70
Guyana								
1 VII 2001 (ESDF)								
GEORGETOWN	...	...	...	...	280 000	...	...	...
Paraguay								
28 VIII 2002 (CDFC)								
ASUNCION	513 399	...	...	117	1 620 483[21]	...	...	...
Capiatá	154 469	...	...	...	...	...	...	...
Ciudad del Este	223 350	...	...	57	333 535	...	...	...
Fernando de la Mora	114 332	...	...	...	...	...	...	...
Lambaré	119 984	...	...	...	...	...	...	...
Luque	170 433	...	...	...	...	...	...	...
San Lorenzo	202 745	...	...	91	...	...	...	...
Peru - Pérou								
21 X 2007 (CDFC)								
Arequipa	784 651	...	...	...	...	...	...	...
Ayacucho	151 019	...	...	...	...	...	...	...
Cajamarca	162 326	...	...	...	...	...	...	...
Callao	876 877	...	...	...	...	...	...	...
Chiclayo	524 442	...	...	...	...	...	...	...

8. Population of capital cities and cities of 100 000 or more inhabitants: latest available year, 1988 - 2007
Population des capitales et des villes de 100 000 habitants ou plus: dernière année disponible, 1988 - 2007 (continued - suite)

Continent, country or area, date, code and city Continent, pays ou zone, date, code et ville	City proper - Ville proprement dite				Urban agglomeration - Agglomération urbaine			
	Population			Surface area - Superficie (km²)	Population			Surface area - Superficie (km²)
	Both sexes - Les deux sexes	Male - Masculin	Female - Féminin		Both sexes - Les deux sexes	Male - Masculin	Female - Féminin	
AMERICA, SOUTH - AMÉRIQUE DU SUD								
Peru - Pérou								
21 X 2007 (CDFC)								
Chimbote	334 568	...	...	...	...	...	...	...
Chincha Alta	153 598	...	...	...	...	...	...	...
Cuzco	348 935	...	...	...	...	...	...	...
Huancayo	323 054	...	...	...	...	...	...	...
Huánuco	149 210	...	...	...	...	...	...	...
Ica	219 856	...	...	...	...	...	...	...
Iquitos	370 962	...	...	...	...	...	...	...
Juliaca	216 716	...	...	...	...	...	...	...
LIMA	8 445 211	...	...	...	...	...	...	...
Piura	377 496	...	...	...	...	...	...	...
Pucallpa	204 772	...	...	...	...	...	...	...
Puno	120 229	...	...	...	...	...	...	...
Sullana	181 954	...	...	...	...	...	...	...
Tacna	242 451	...	...	...	...	...	...	...
Tarapoto	117 184	...	...	...	...	...	...	...
Trujillo	682 834	...	...	...	...	...	...	...
Suriname								
2 VIII 2004 (CDJC)								
PARAMARIBO	...	...	...	...	242 946	120 292	122 405	182
Uruguay								
1 VII 2006 (ESDF)								
MONTEVIDEO	1 345 010	627 495	717 515	530	...	...	...	...
Venezuela (Bolivarian Republic of) - Venezuela (République bolivarienne du)								
1 VII 1998 (ESDF)								
Acarigua-Araure	227 684	...	...	1 065	...	...	...	...
Barcelona	301 595	...	...	463	...	...	...	...
Barcelona-Puerto La Cruz	484 149	...	...	707	...	...	...	...
Barinas	221 558	...	...	848	...	...	...	...
Barquisimeto	810 809	...	...	2 645	...	...	...	...
Cabimas	213 290	...	...	175	...	...	...	...
CARACAS	1 975 294	...	...	433	...	...	...	...
Carúpano	116 107	...	...	203	...	...	...	...
Catia la Mar	117 013	...	...	76	...	...	...	...
Ciudad Bolívar	278 525	...	...	5 851	...	...	...	...
Ciudad Guayana	641 998	...	...	1 612	...	...	...	...
Coro	167 048	...	...	438	...	...	...	...
Cumaná	265 621	...	...	405	...	...	...	...
Guarenas	169 202	...	...	180	...	...	...	...
Los Teques	176 292	...	...	98	...	...	...	...
Maracaibo	1 706 547	...	...	604	...	...	...	...
Maracay	458 761	...	...	169	...	...	...	...
Maturín	262 167	...	...	...	...	...	...	...
Mérida	272 437	...	...	482	...	...	...	...
Puerto Cabello	176 347	...	...	309	...	...	...	...
Punto Fijo	118 126	...	...	31	...	...	...	...
San Cristóbal	272 374	...	...	248	...	...	...	...
San Fernando de Apure	121 949	...	...	...	...	...	...	...
Turmero	203 434	...	...	208	...	...	...	...
Valencia	1 263 888	...	...	1 212	...	...	...	...
Valera	121 090	...	...	55	...	...	...	...
ASIA - ASIE								
Afghanistan								
1 VII 1988 (ESDF)								
Herat	*177 300*	...	...	...	...	...	...	...
KABUL	*1 424 400*	...	...	...	...	...	...	...
Kandahar (Quandahar)	*225 500*	...	...	...	...	...	...	...
Mazar-i-Sharif	*130 600*	...	...	...	...	...	...	...

Continent, country or area, date, code and city / Continent, pays ou zone, date, code et ville	City proper - Ville proprement dite				Urban agglomeration - Agglomération urbaine			
	Population			Surface area - Superficie (km²)	Population			Surface area - Superficie (km²)
	Both sexes - Les deux sexes	Male - Masculin	Female - Féminin		Both sexes - Les deux sexes	Male - Masculin	Female - Féminin	
ASIA - ASIE								
Armenia - Arménie								
Armenia - Arménie								
1 VII 2007 (ESDJ)								
Gyumri (Leninakan)	147 350	70 384	76 966	50	...	...	...	...
Vanadzoz (Kirovakan)	105 100	50 052	55 048	25	...	...	...	...
YEREVAN	1 106 383	516 769	589 614	227	...	...	...	...
Azerbaijan - Azerbaïdjan								
1 VII 2007 (ESDF)								
BAKU	1 905 156	936 113	969 043	2 130	...	...	...	...
Ganja	308 723	149 028	159 695	110	...	...	...	...
Sumgayit	298 216	146 869	151 347	80	...	...	...	...
Bahrain - Bahreïn								
1 VII 2006 (ESDF)								
MANAMA	*176 909*	*113 503*	*63 406*	30	...	...	...	...
Bangladesh								
22 I 2001 (CDFC)								
Barisal	...	...	...	...	192 810	103 785	89 025	20
Bogra	...	...	...	...	154 807	82 368	72 439	11
Brahmanbaria	...	...	...	...	129 278	66 890	62 388	18
Chittagong	...	...	...	...	2 023 489	1 127 516	895 973	168
Comilla	...	...	...	...	166 519	88 927	77 592	11
DHAKA	...	...	...	...	5 333 571	3 025 395	2 308 176	154
Dinajpur	...	...	...	...	157 914	82 068	75 846	19
Gazipur	...	...	...	...	122 801	65 522	57 279	49
Jamalpur	...	...	...	...	120 955	62 059	58 896	53
Jessore	...	...	...	...	176 655	94 203	82 452	15
Kadamrasul	...	...	...	...	128 561	66 799	61 762	6
Khulna	...	...	...	...	770 498	412 661	357 837	60
Mymensingh	...	...	...	...	227 204	119 172	108 032	22
Naogaon	...	...	...	...	124 046	65 406	58 640	37
Narayanganj	...	...	...	...	241 393	131 168	110 225	13
Narsingdi	...	...	...	...	124 204	67 575	56 629	9
Nawabganj	...	...	...	...	152 223	75 375	76 848	34
Pabna	...	...	...	...	116 305	60 666	55 639	27
Rajshahi	...	...	...	...	388 811	208 525	180 286	97
Rangpur	...	...	...	...	241 310	124 296	117 014	51
Saidpur	...	...	...	...	112 609	58 289	54 320	34
Sirajganj	...	...	...	...	128 144	66 673	61 471	28
Tangail	...	...	...	...	128 785	66 856	61 929	29
Tongi	...	...	...	...	283 099	156 335	126 764	30
Bhutan - Bhoutan								
30 V 2005 (CDFC)								
THIMPHU	79 185	42 465	36 720	...	...	...	...	...
Brunei Darussalam - Brunéi Darussalam								
21 VIII 2001 (CDFC)								
BANDAR SERI BEGAWAN	27 285	13 639	13 646	100	...	...	...	...
Cambodia - Cambodge								
1 VII 2002 (ESDF)								
Bat Dambang	*171 382*	*82 785*	*88 597*	114	...	...	...	...
PHNOM PENH	*703 963*	*339 763*	*364 200*	21	*1 234 444*	...	...	...
Seam Reab	*140 966*	*69 052*	*71 914*	292	...	...	...	...
China - Chine								
1 XI 2000 (CDJC)								
Acheng	638 894	327 774	311 120	...	...	...	...	...
Akeshu	561 822	295 811	266 011	...	...	...	...	...
Aletai	178 510	91 207	87 303	...	...	...	...	...
Anda	473 091	243 349	229 742	...	...	...	...	...
Anguo	378 830	189 944	188 886	...	...	...	...	...
Ankang	843 426	443 270	400 156	...	...	...	...	...
Anlu	611 990	314 089	297 901	...	...	...	...	...
Anning	295 173	161 481	133 692	...	...	...	...	...
Anqing	582 751	293 884	288 867	...	...	...	...	...
Anqiu	1 096 782	554 403	542 379	...	...	...	...	...
Anshan	1 556 285	787 838	768 447	...	...	...	...	...
Anshun	767 307	395 894	371 413	...	...	...	...	...
Anyang	768 992	390 120	378 872	...	...	...	...	...

Continent, country or area, date, code and city Continent, pays ou zone, date, code et ville	City proper - Ville proprement dite				Urban agglomeration - Agglomération urbaine			
	Population			Surface area - Superficie (km²)	Population			Surface area - Superficie (km²)
	Both sexes - Les deux sexes	Male - Masculin	Female - Féminin		Both sexes - Les deux sexes	Male - Masculin	Female - Féminin	
ASIA - ASIE								
China - Chine								
1 XI 2000 (CDJC)								
Atushi	200 345	101 867	98 478					
Baicheng	484 979	244 453	240 526	...	...	...	...	...
Baise	340 483	177 310	163 173	...	...	...	...	...
Baishan	335 400	172 109	163 291	...	...	...	...	...
Baiyin	460 982	243 672	217 310	...	...	...	...	...
Baoding	902 496	455 625	446 871	...	...	...	...	...
Baoji	600 377	308 493	291 884	...	...	...	...	...
Baoshan	846 865	430 076	416 789	...	...	...	...	...
Baotou	1 671 181	862 495	808 686	...	...	...	...	...
Bazhong	1 185 862	616 323	569 539	...	...	...	...	...
Bazhou	557 901	285 321	272 580	...	...	...	...	...
Bei'an	442 474	226 743	215 731	...	...	...	...	...
Beihai	558 635	290 544	268 091	...	...	...	...	...
BEIJING (PEKING)	11 509 595	6 020 903	5 488 692	...	...	...	...	...
Beiliu	1 049 035	557 967	491 068	...	...	...	...	...
Beining	527 217	270 153	257 064	...	...	...	...	...
Beipiao	573 836	291 584	282 252	...	...	...	...	...
Bengbu	809 399	413 444	395 955	...	...	...	...	...
Benxi	980 069	495 102	484 967	...	...	...	...	...
Bijie	1 128 230	589 537	538 693	...	...	...	...	...
Binzhou	600 883	299 952	300 931	...	...	...	...	...
Bole	224 869	116 506	108 363	...	...	...	...	...
Botou	550 888	280 209	270 679	...	...	...	...	...
Bozhou	1 351 939	697 126	654 813	...	...	...	...	...
Cangzhou	443 561	223 648	219 913	...	...	...	...	...
Cenxi	731 623	384 212	347 411	...	...	...	...	...
Changchun	3 225 557	1 647 216	1 578 341	...	...	...	...	...
Changde	1 346 739	686 467	660 272	...	...	...	...	...
Changge	646 306	332 022	314 284	...	...	...	...	...
Changji	387 169	202 275	184 894	...	...	...	...	...
Changle	689 815	358 963	330 852	...	...	...	...	...
Changning	795 223	428 332	366 891	...	...	...	...	...
Changsha	2 122 873	1 099 304	1 023 569	...	...	...	...	...
Changshu	1 239 637	598 034	641 603	...	...	...	...	...
Changyi	683 182	340 763	342 419	...	...	...	...	...
Changzhi	648 981	332 246	316 735	...	...	...	...	...
Changzhou	1 081 845	552 850	528 995	...	...	...	...	...
Chaohu	778 864	396 961	381 903	...	...	...	...	...
Chaoyang (Guangdong)	2 470 812	1 256 428	1 214 384	...	...	...	...	...
Chaoyang (Liaoning)	475 038	238 128	236 910	...	...	...	...	...
Chaozhou	363 582	181 260	182 322	...	...	...	...	...
Chengde	437 251	221 221	216 030	...	...	...	...	...
Chengdu	4 333 541	2 258 996	2 074 545	...	...	...	...	...
Chenghai	860 003	428 157	431 846	...	...	...	...	...
Chenzhou	655 014	340 799	314 215	...	...	...	...	...
Chibi	510 926	267 233	243 693	...	...	...	...	...
Chifeng	1 153 723	589 450	564 273	...	...	...	...	...
Chishui	251 780	130 227	121 553	...	...	...	...	...
Chizhou	555 489	280 395	275 094	...	...	...	...	...
Chongqing	9 691 901	5 013 398	4 678 503	...	...	...	...	...
Chongzhou	650 698	330 345	320 353	...	...	...	...	...
Chuxiong	503 682	261 315	242 367	...	...	...	...	...
Chuzhou	493 735	251 117	242 618	...	...	...	...	...
Cixi	1 214 537	615 279	599 258	...	...	...	...	...
Conghua	517 552	264 150	253 402	...	...	...	...	...
Da'an	430 512	219 682	210 830	...	...	...	...	...
Dafeng	756 766	383 391	373 375	...	...	...	...	...
Dali	521 169	262 564	258 605	...	...	...	...	...
Dalian	3 245 191	1 641 485	1 603 706	...	...	...	...	...
Dandong	780 414	389 277	391 137	...	...	...	...	...
Dangyang	495 946	253 125	242 821	...	...	...	...	...
Danjiangkou	501 126	262 922	238 204	...	...	...	...	...
Danyang	877 232	442 296	434 936	...	...	...	...	...
Danzhou	835 465	442 636	392 829	...	...	...	...	...

Continent, country or area, date, code and city / Continent, pays ou zone, date, code et ville	City proper - Ville proprement dite				Urban agglomeration - Agglomération urbaine			
	Population			Surface area - Superficie (km²)	Population			Surface area - Superficie (km²)
	Both sexes - Les deux sexes	Male - Masculin	Female - Féminin		Both sexes - Les deux sexes	Male - Masculin	Female - Féminin	
ASIA - ASIE								
China - Chine								
1 XI 2000 (CDJC)								
Daqing	1 380 051	704 765	675 286	...	...	...	...	...
Dashiqiao	714 670	370 713	343 957	...	...	...	...	...
Datong	1 526 744	785 754	740 990	...	...	...	...	...
Daye	873 859	460 417	413 442	...	...	...	...	...
Dazhou	384 525	192 819	191 706	...	...	...	...	...
Dehui	878 349	448 146	430 203	...	...	...	...	...
Dengfeng	609 085	321 081	288 004	...	...	...	...	...
Dengta	502 149	259 895	242 254	...	...	...	...	...
Dengzhou	1 290 656	677 791	612 865	...	...	...	...	...
Dexing	297 784	155 178	142 606	...	...	...	...	...
Deyang	628 876	324 823	304 053	...	...	...	...	...
Dezhou	552 445	277 994	274 451	...	...	...	...	...
Dingzhou	1 107 903	559 214	548 689	...	...	...	...	...
Dongfang	358 318	188 840	169 478	...	...	...	...	...
Donggang	640 340	324 344	315 996	...	...	...	...	...
Dongguan	6 445 777	3 035 742	3 410 035	...	...	...	...	...
Dongsheng	252 566	129 512	123 054	...	...	...	...	...
Dongtai	1 164 653	583 122	581 531	...	...	...	...	...
Dongxing	108 131	58 939	49 192	...	...	...	...	...
Dongyang	753 094	375 565	377 529	...	...	...	...	...
Dongying	788 844	407 241	381 603	...	...	...	...	...
Dujiangyan	621 980	314 845	307 135	...	...	...	...	...
Dunhua	480 834	247 966	232 868	...	...	...	...	...
Dunhuang	187 578	96 679	90 899	...	...	...	...	...
Duyun	463 426	241 421	222 005	...	...	...	...	...
Emeishan	423 070	217 201	205 869	...	...	...	...	...
Enping	464 898	240 765	224 133	...	...	...	...	...
Enshi	755 725	397 284	358 441	...	...	...	...	...
Ezhou	1 023 285	533 940	489 345	...	...	...	...	...
Fangchenggang	422 514	233 979	188 535	...	...	...	...	...
Feicheng	948 602	476 032	472 570	...	...	...	...	...
Fengcheng (Jiangxi)	1 216 412	644 029	572 383	...	...	...	...	...
Fengcheng (Liaoning)	560 384	288 402	271 982	...	...	...	...	...
Fenghua	471 558	239 252	232 306	...	...	...	...	...
Fengnan	550 872	285 442	265 430	...	...	...	...	...
Fengzhen	264 204	137 562	126 642	...	...	...	...	...
Fenyang	387 046	199 129	187 917	...	...	...	...	...
Foshan	768 656	398 973	369 683	...	...	...	...	...
Fu'an	554 057	296 379	257 678	...	...	...	...	...
Fuding	521 070	276 419	244 651	...	...	...	...	...
Fujin	420 579	215 650	204 929	...	...	...	...	...
Fukang	152 965	80 372	72 593	...	...	...	...	...
Fuqing	1 174 540	597 890	576 650	...	...	...	...	...
Fuquan	292 720	155 972	136 748	...	...	...	...	...
Fushun	1 434 447	722 549	711 898	...	...	...	...	...
Fuxin	627 855	311 912	315 943	...	...	...	...	...
Fuyang (Anhui)	628 633	324 172	304 461	...	...	...	...	...
Fuyang (Zhejiang)	1 719 057	878 560	840 497	...	...	...	...	...
Fuzhou (Fujian)	2 124 435	1 086 638	1 037 797	...	...	...	...	...
Fuzhou (Jiangxi)	1 007 391	533 936	473 455	...	...	...	...	...
Gaizhou	883 811	455 641	428 170	...	...	...	...	...
Ganzhou	494 600	254 272	240 328	...	...	...	...	...
Gaoan	788 329	416 678	371 651	...	...	...	...	...
Gaobeidian	538 582	268 027	270 555	...	...	...	...	...
Gaocheng	758 269	380 317	377 952	...	...	...	...	...
Gaomi	842 403	420 956	421 447	...	...	...	...	...
Gaoming	301 041	159 746	141 295	...	...	...	...	...
Gaoping	471 671	236 439	235 232	...	...	...	...	...
Gaoyao	625 125	314 474	310 651	...	...	...	...	...
Gaoyou	797 752	392 863	404 889	...	...	...	...	...
Gaozhou	1 219 132	639 497	579 635	...	...	...	...	...
Geermu	135 897	73 572	62 325	...	...	...	...	...
Gejiu	453 311	243 377	209 934	...	...	...	...	...
Genhe	157 337	80 485	76 852	...	...	...	...	...

Continent, country or area, date, code and city Continent, pays ou zone, date, code et ville	City proper - Ville proprement dite				Urban agglomeration - Agglomération urbaine			
	Population			Surface area - Superficie (km²)	Population			Surface area - Superficie (km²)
	Both sexes - Les deux sexes	Male - Masculin	Female - Féminin		Both sexes - Les deux sexes	Male - Masculin	Female - Féminin	
ASIA - ASIE								
China - Chine								
1 XI 2000 (CDJC)								
Gongyi	777 202	395 784	381 418					
Gongzhuling	1 041 735	532 134	509 601	...	...	...	...	...
Guangan	1 093 103	561 454	531 649	...	...	...	...	...
Guanghan	577 298	289 596	287 702	...	...	...	...	...
Guangshui	885 936	458 607	427 329	...	...	...	...	...
Guangyuan	905 057	467 422	437 635	...	...	...	...	...
Guangzhou	8 524 826	4 445 052	4 079 774	...	...	...	...	...
Guigang	1 413 128	731 298	681 830	...	...	...	...	...
Guilin	804 571	414 004	390 567	...	...	...	...	...
Guiping	1 359 035	716 617	642 418	...	...	...	...	...
Guixi	535 517	282 662	252 855	...	...	...	...	...
Guiyang	2 985 105	1 568 544	1 416 561	...	...	...	...	...
Gujiao	205 702	110 105	95 597	...	...	...	...	...
Haerbin	3 481 504	1 759 609	1 721 895	...	...	...	...	...
Haicheng	1 181 130	606 805	574 325	...	...	...	...	...
Haikou	830 192	431 774	398 418	...	...	...	...	...
Hailaer	262 184	132 849	129 335	...	...	...	...	...
Hailin	435 677	222 525	213 152	...	...	...	...	...
Hailun	720 008	368 751	351 257	...	...	...	...	...
Haimen	942 952	431 066	511 886	...	...	...	...	...
Haining	666 080	331 349	334 731	...	...	...	...	...
Haiyang	654 594	329 202	325 392	...	...	...	...	...
Hami	388 714	201 005	187 709	...	...	...	...	...
Hancheng	387 041	201 881	185 160	...	...	...	...	...
Hanchuan	1 057 396	552 093	505 303	...	...	...	...	...
Handan	1 329 734	693 882	635 852	...	...	...	...	...
Hangzhou	2 451 319	1 301 103	1 150 216	...	...	...	...	...
Hanzhong	503 871	258 142	245 729	...	...	...	...	...
Hebi	495 336	260 212	235 124	...	...	...	...	...
Hechi	318 348	167 526	150 822	...	...	...	...	...
Hechuan	1 420 520	732 503	688 017	...	...	...	...	...
Hefei	1 659 075	879 749	779 326	...	...	...	...	...
Hegang	694 640	354 262	340 378	...	...	...	...	...
Heihe	192 764	97 488	95 276	...	...	...	...	...
Hejian	757 581	383 621	373 960	...	...	...	...	...
Hejin	368 572	195 677	172 895	...	...	...	...	...
Helong	215 266	110 051	105 215	...	...	...	...	...
Hengshui	422 761	212 417	210 344	...	...	...	...	...
Hengyang	879 051	450 222	428 829	...	...	...	...	...
Heshan (Guangdong)	405 779	202 461	203 318	...	...	...	...	...
Heshan (Guangxi)	131 249	69 205	62 044	...	...	...	...	...
Hetian	186 127	94 034	92 093	...	...	...	...	...
Heyuan	227 773	115 330	112 443	...	...	...	...	...
Heze	1 280 031	656 790	623 241	...	...	...	...	...
Hezhou	850 023	446 208	403 815	...	...	...	...	...
Honghu	877 775	459 997	417 778	...	...	...	...	...
Hongjiang	485 061	250 434	234 627	...	...	...	...	...
Houma	225 123	113 997	111 126	...	...	...	...	...
Huadian	444 415	228 624	215 791	...	...	...	...	...
Huaian	1 200 679	619 541	581 138	...	...	...	...	...
Huaibei	741 195	382 444	358 751	...	...	...	...	...
Huaihua	346 522	178 221	168 301	...	...	...	...	...
Huainan	1 357 228	701 205	656 023	...	...	...	...	...
Huaiyin	555 052	282 186	272 866	...	...	...	...	...
Huanggang	373 568	194 607	178 961	...	...	...	...	...
Huanghua	483 273	251 128	232 145	...	...	...	...	...
Huangshan	406 200	208 004	198 196	...	...	...	...	...
Huangshi (Hubei)	653 722	334 712	319 010	...	...	...	...	...
Huayin	242 488	125 006	117 482	...	...	...	...	...
Huaying	352 257	183 962	168 295	...	...	...	...	...
Huazhou	1 007 796	529 550	478 246	...	...	...	...	...
Huhehaote	1 406 955	724 328	682 627	...	...	...	...	...
Huixian	776 326	394 763	381 563	...	...	...	...	...
Huiyang	862 822	429 006	433 816	...	...	...	...	...

Continent, country or area, date, code and city / Continent, pays ou zone, date, code et ville	City proper - Ville proprement dite				Urban agglomeration - Agglomération urbaine			
	Population			Surface area - Superficie (km²)	Population			Surface area - Superficie (km²)
	Both sexes - Les deux sexes	Male - Masculin	Female - Féminin		Both sexes - Les deux sexes	Male - Masculin	Female - Féminin	

ASIA - ASIE

China - Chine
1 XI 2000 (CDJC)

Huizhou	591 686	292 216	299 470	...	...	...	...	...
Hulin	311 509	160 842	150 667	...	...	...	...	...
Huludao	900 936	456 211	444 725	...	...	...	...	...
Hunchun	211 091	108 873	102 218	...	...	...	...	...
Huozhou	274 955	142 316	132 639	...	...	...	...	...
Huzhou	1 145 414	573 421	571 993	...	...	...	...	...
Jiamusi	859 944	433 369	426 575	...	...	...	...	...
Ji'an (Jiangxi)	473 113	244 476	228 637	...	...	...	...	...
Jian (Jilin)	239 849	124 475	115 374	...	...	...	...	...
Jiande	473 062	242 606	230 456	...	...	...	...	...
Jiangdu	1 053 023	512 151	540 872	...	...	...	...	...
Jiangjin	1 322 890	686 106	636 784	...	...	...	...	...
Jiangmen	536 317	271 693	264 624	...	...	...	...	...
Jiangshan	473 222	241 301	231 921	...	...	...	...	...
Jiangyan	861 321	419 333	441 988	...	...	...	...	...
Jiangyin	1 315 472	665 719	649 753	...	...	...	...	...
Jiangyou	849 761	436 112	413 649	...	...	...	...	...
Jianou	478 651	249 624	229 027	...	...	...	...	...
Jianyang (Fujian)	317 848	167 066	150 782	...	...	...	...	...
Jianyang (Sichuan)	1 412 523	728 353	684 170	...	...	...	...	...
Jiaohe	474 109	243 510	230 599	...	...	...	...	...
Jiaonan	827 771	419 331	408 440	...	...	...	...	...
Jiaozhou	783 478	388 207	395 271	...	...	...	...	...
Jiaozuo	747 299	384 395	362 904	...	...	...	...	...
Jiaxing	881 923	445 646	436 277	...	...	...	...	...
Jiayuguan	159 541	85 959	73 582	...	...	...	...	...
Jieshou	640 878	327 384	313 494	...	...	...	...	...
Jiexiu	372 993	190 675	182 318	...	...	...	...	...
Jieyang	633 570	324 831	308 739	...	...	...	...	...
Jilin	1 953 134	984 762	968 372	...	...	...	...	...
Jimo	1 111 202	553 261	557 941	...	...	...	...	...
Jinan	2 999 934	1 539 067	1 460 867	...	...	...	...	...
Jinchang	204 902	106 725	98 177	...	...	...	...	...
Jincheng	304 221	157 663	146 558	...	...	...	...	...
Jingdezhen	444 720	228 747	215 973	...	...	...	...	...
Jinggangshan	145 769	74 722	71 047	...	...	...	...	...
Jinghong	443 672	229 846	213 826	...	...	...	...	...
Jingjiang	639 665	316 885	322 780	...	...	...	...	...
Jingmen	583 373	300 284	283 089	...	...	...	...	...
Jingzhou	1 177 150	598 951	578 199	...	...	...	...	...
Jinhua	424 859	216 773	208 086	...	...	...	...	...
Jining (Inner Mongolia)	272 448	136 913	135 535	...	...	...	...	...
Jining (Shandong)	1 050 522	530 322	520 200	...	...	...	...	...
Jinjiang	1 479 259	772 066	707 193	...	...	...	...	...
Jinshi	243 242	126 619	116 623	...	...	...	...	...
Jintan	533 350	256 798	276 552	...	...	...	...	...
Jinzhong	534 357	274 957	259 400	...	...	...	...	...
Jinzhou (Hebei)	520 942	265 012	255 930	...	...	...	...	...
Jinzhou (Liaoning)	861 991	430 777	431 214	...	...	...	...	...
Jishou	294 297	151 422	142 875	...	...	...	...	...
Jiujiang	551 329	280 126	271 203	...	...	...	...	...
Jiuquan	346 258	177 943	168 315	...	...	...	...	...
Jiutai	799 729	411 067	388 662	...	...	...	...	...
Jixi	910 782	467 547	443 235	...	...	...	...	...
Jiyuan	626 478	323 554	302 924	...	...	...	...	...
Jizhou	373 825	187 005	186 820	...	...	...	...	...
Jurong	594 316	302 713	291 603	...	...	...	...	...
Kaifeng	796 171	398 133	398 038	...	...	...	...	...
Kaili	433 236	230 692	202 544	...	...	...	...	...
Kaiping	668 692	326 560	342 132	...	...	...	...	...
Kaiyuan (Liaoning)	529 736	271 422	258 314	...	...	...	...	...
Kaiyuan (Yunnan)	292 039	152 771	139 268	...	...	...	...	...
Kashi (Xinjiang)	340 640	172 136	168 504	...	...	...	...	...
Kelamayi	270 232	143 500	126 732	...	...	...	...	...

Continent, country or area, date, code and city Continent, pays ou zone, date, code et ville	City proper - Ville proprement dite				Urban agglomeration - Agglomération urbaine			
	Population			Surface area - Superficie (km²)	Population			Surface area - Superficie (km²)
	Both sexes - Les deux sexes	Male - Masculin	Female - Féminin		Both sexes - Les deux sexes	Male - Masculin	Female - Féminin	
ASIA - ASIE								
China - Chine								
1 XI 2000 (CDJC)								
Kuerle	381 943	199 344	182 599					
Kuitun	285 299	148 740	136 559	...	...	...	...	...
Kunming	3 035 406	1 615 096	1 420 310	...	...	...	...	...
Kunshan	750 074	377 433	372 641	...	...	...	...	...
Laiwu	1 233 525	626 549	606 976	...	...	...	...	...
Laixi	728 796	366 400	362 396	...	...	...	...	...
Laiyang	897 681	453 293	444 388	...	...	...	...	...
Laizhou	889 361	450 192	439 169	...	...	...	...	...
Langfang	715 388	363 094	352 294	...	...	...	...	...
Langzhong	787 809	400 390	387 419	...	...	...	...	...
Lanxi	607 196	314 090	293 106	...	...	...	...	...
Lanzhou	2 087 759	1 092 661	995 098	...	...	...	...	...
Laohekou	509 468	257 204	252 264	...	...	...	...	...
Lasa	223 001	117 004	105 997	...	...	...	...	...
Lechang	423 444	223 788	199 656	...	...	...	...	...
Leiyang	1 180 235	631 431	548 804	...	...	...	...	...
Leizhou	1 268 298	674 213	594 085	...	...	...	...	...
Leling	615 833	313 642	302 191	...	...	...	...	...
Lengshuijiang	339 701	175 071	164 630	...	...	...	...	...
Leping	729 639	381 937	347 702	...	...	...	...	...
Leqing	1 162 765	605 494	557 271	...	...	...	...	...
Leshan	1 120 158	567 028	553 130	...	...	...	...	...
Lianjiang	1 205 764	642 214	563 550	...	...	...	...	...
Lianyuan	996 893	521 941	474 952	...	...	...	...	...
Lianyungang	687 242	354 350	332 892	...	...	...	...	...
Lianzhou	409 360	212 292	197 068	...	...	...	...	...
Liaocheng	950 319	474 976	475 343	...	...	...	...	...
Liaoyang	728 492	365 833	362 659	...	...	...	...	...
Liaoyuan	462 233	234 701	227 532	...	...	...	...	...
Lichuan	786 984	417 988	368 996	...	...	...	...	...
Liling	934 396	484 127	450 269	...	...	...	...	...
Linan	514 238	261 852	252 386	...	...	...	...	...
Linfen	724 403	367 377	357 026	...	...	...	...	...
Lingbao	722 890	377 872	345 018	...	...	...	...	...
Linghai	647 310	332 906	314 404	...	...	...	...	...
Lingwu	249 890	128 364	121 526	...	...	...	...	...
Lingyuan	620 121	324 554	295 567	...	...	...	...	...
Linhai	948 618	479 625	468 993	...	...	...	...	...
Linhe	510 965	260 835	250 130	...	...	...	...	...
Linjiang	184 901	94 904	89 997	...	...	...	...	...
Linqing	694 247	348 411	345 836	...	...	...	...	...
Linxia	202 498	104 017	98 481	...	...	...	...	...
Linxiang	448 452	235 723	212 729	...	...	...	...	...
Linyi	1 938 510	988 940	949 570	...	...	...	...	...
Linzhou	982 254	501 659	480 595	...	...	...	...	...
Lishi	235 678	121 253	114 425	...	...	...	...	...
Lishui	348 241	178 908	169 333	...	...	...	...	...
Liupanshui	995 055	523 692	471 363	...	...	...	...	...
Liuyang	1 307 572	680 610	626 962	...	...	...	...	...
Liuzhou	1 220 392	634 909	585 483	...	...	...	...	...
Liyang	740 871	375 694	365 177	...	...	...	...	...
Longhai	816 318	415 936	400 382	...	...	...	...	...
Longjing	261 551	132 150	129 401	...	...	...	...	...
Longkou	671 335	337 507	333 828	...	...	...	...	...
Longquan	250 398	131 534	118 864	...	...	...	...	...
Longyan	543 731	298 481	245 250	...	...	...	...	...
Loudi	398 577	205 172	193 405	...	...	...	...	...
Lu'an	1 559 037	807 902	751 135	...	...	...	...	...
Lucheng	213 944	111 293	102 651	...	...	...	...	...
Lufeng	1 164 767	600 959	563 808	...	...	...	...	...
Luoding	866 190	449 131	417 059	...	...	...	...	...
Luohe	304 105	150 273	153 832	...	...	...	...	...
Luoyang	1 491 680	759 425	732 255	...	...	...	...	...
Luquan	397 449	202 340	195 109	...	...	...	...	...

8. Population of capital cities and cities of 100 000 or more inhabitants: latest available year, 1988 - 2007
Population des capitales et des villes de 100 000 habitants ou plus: dernière année disponible, 1988 - 2007 (continued - suite)

Continent, country or area, date, code and city / Continent, pays ou zone, date, code et ville	City proper - Ville proprement dite				Urban agglomeration - Agglomération urbaine			
	Population			Surface area - Superficie (km²)	Population			Surface area - Superficie (km²)
	Both sexes - Les deux sexes	Male - Masculin	Female - Féminin		Both sexes - Les deux sexes	Male - Masculin	Female - Féminin	

ASIA - ASIE

China - Chine
1 XI 2000 (CDJC)

Luxi (Yunnan)............	337 406	172 038	165 368	...	...	...	...	...
Luzhou................	1 252 884	636 652	616 232	...	...	...	...	...
Ma'anshan............	567 576	292 994	274 582	...	...	...	...	...
Macheng..............	1 129 047	595 391	533 656	...	...	...	...	...
Manzhouli.............	181 112	92 853	88 259	...	...	...	...	...
Maoming..............	644 301	335 713	308 588	...	...	...	...	...
Meihekou.............	617 674	317 226	300 448	...	...	...	...	...
Meishan..............	799 309	402 889	396 420	...	...	...	...	...
Meizhou..............	354 302	178 658	175 644	...	...	...	...	...
Mianyang.............	1 162 962	604 414	558 548	...	...	...	...	...
Mianzhu..............	515 830	263 098	252 732	...	...	...	...	...
Miluo................	658 867	342 113	316 754	...	...	...	...	...
Mingguang............	569 585	290 126	279 459	...	...	...	...	...
Miquan...............	180 952	95 368	85 584	...	...	...	...	...
Mishan...............	438 277	224 565	213 712	...	...	...	...	...
Mudanjiang...........	1 014 206	512 000	502 206	...	...	...	...	...
Muling...............	310 096	158 623	151 473	...	...	...	...	...
Nanan................	1 385 276	700 218	685 058	...	...	...	...	...
Nanchang.............	1 844 253	952 504	891 749	...	...	...	...	...
Nanchong.............	1 771 920	922 452	849 468	...	...	...	...	...
Nanchuan.............	631 853	326 307	305 546	...	...	...	...	...
Nangong.............	467 356	234 978	232 378	...	...	...	...	...
Nanhai...............	2 133 741	1 111 731	1 022 010	...	...	...	...	...
Nanjing..............	3 624 234	1 935 931	1 688 303	...	...	...	...	...
Nankang.............	694 987	338 836	356 151	...	...	...	...	...
Nanning.............	1 766 701	924 916	841 785	...	...	...	...	...
Nanping.............	488 818	257 352	231 466	...	...	...	...	...
Nantong.............	771 386	386 206	385 180	...	...	...	...	...
Nanxiong............	372 844	185 330	187 514	...	...	...	...	...
Nanyang.............	1 584 715	814 822	769 893	...	...	...	...	...
Nehe................	672 295	343 873	328 422	...	...	...	...	...
Neijiang.............	1 391 931	709 053	682 878	...	...	...	...	...
Ningan..............	437 328	223 201	214 127	...	...	...	...	...
Ningbo..............	1 567 499	804 850	762 649	...	...	...	...	...
Ningde..............	400 293	213 131	187 162	...	...	...	...	...
Ningguo.............	381 842	199 915	181 927	...	...	...	...	...
Panjin..............	602 541	309 377	293 164	...	...	...	...	...
Panshi..............	530 470	273 219	257 251	...	...	...	...	...
Panzhihua...........	690 739	363 585	327 154	...	...	...	...	...
Penglai.............	500 408	252 726	247 682	...	...	...	...	...
Pengzhou............	770 749	389 697	381 052	...	...	...	...	...
Pingdingshan........	900 903	470 362	430 541	...	...	...	...	...
Pingdu..............	1 321 975	670 685	651 290	...	...	...	...	...
Pinghu..............	507 899	249 848	258 051	...	...	...	...	...
Pingliang...........	454 996	236 426	218 570	...	...	...	...	...
Pingxiang (Guangxi)...	107 046	57 445	49 601	...	...	...	...	...
Pingxiang (Jiangxi)...	783 445	402 198	381 247	...	...	...	...	...
Pizhou..............	1 539 922	791 332	748 590	...	...	...	...	...
Pulandian...........	757 844	385 636	372 208	...	...	...	...	...
Puning..............	1 856 402	954 242	902 160	...	...	...	...	...
Putian..............	443 926	216 578	227 348	...	...	...	...	...
Puyang..............	448 290	229 387	218 903	...	...	...	...	...
Qianan..............	632 704	323 330	309 374	...	...	...	...	...
Qianjiang...........	992 438	506 290	486 148	...	...	...	...	...
Qidong..............	1 057 073	495 819	561 254	...	...	...	...	...
Qingdao.............	2 720 972	1 359 527	1 361 445	...	...	...	...	...
Qingtongxia.........	248 640	129 121	119 519	...	...	...	...	...
Qingyuan............	506 680	258 819	247 861	...	...	...	...	...
Qingzhen............	471 305	248 079	223 226	...	...	...	...	...
Qingzhou............	894 468	450 090	444 378	...	...	...	...	...
Qinhuangdao.........	817 487	411 355	406 132	...	...	...	...	...
Qinyang.............	446 404	224 725	221 679	...	...	...	...	...
Qinzhou.............	1 035 504	578 428	457 076	...	...	...	...	...
Qionghai............	449 845	236 560	213 285	...	...	...	...	...

Continent, country or area, date, code and city Continent, pays ou zone, date, code et ville	City proper - Ville proprement dite				Urban agglomeration - Agglomération urbaine			
	Population			Surface area - Superficie (km²)	Population			Surface area - Superficie (km²)
	Both sexes - Les deux sexes	Male - Masculin	Female - Féminin		Both sexes - Les deux sexes	Male - Masculin	Female - Féminin	

ASIA - ASIE

China - Chine
1 XI 2000 (CDJC)

Qionglai	631 577	321 382	310 195					
Qiongshan	678 149	355 557	322 592	...	...	...	...	...
Qiqihaer	1 540 089	776 191	763 898	...	...	...	...	...
Qitaihe	486 704	254 500	232 204	...	...	...	...	...
Qixia	651 357	331 148	320 209	...	...	...	...	...
Quanzhou	1 192 286	616 826	575 460	...	...	...	...	...
Qufu	625 313	317 685	307 628	...	...	...	...	...
Qujing	648 956	333 756	315 200	...	...	...	...	...
Quzhou	286 271	148 054	138 217	...	...	...	...	...
Renhuai	520 759	270 091	250 668	...	...	...	...	...
Renqiu	768 900	390 649	378 251	...	...	...	...	...
Rizhao	1 148 190	576 050	572 140	...	...	...	...	...
Rongcheng	732 147	368 156	363 991	...	...	...	...	...
Rugao	1 362 533	659 720	702 813	...	...	...	...	...
Ruian	1 207 788	627 593	580 195	...	...	...	...	...
Ruichang	398 844	209 755	189 089	...	...	...	...	...
Ruijin	535 499	280 328	255 171	...	...	...	...	...
Ruili	155 210	80 532	74 678	...	...	...	...	...
Rushan	580 326	291 047	289 279	...	...	...	...	...
Ruzhou	923 245	474 090	449 155	...	...	...	...	...
Sanhe	456 882	229 788	227 094	...	...	...	...	...
Sanmenxia	288 746	149 846	138 900	...	...	...	...	...
Sanming	337 105	178 031	159 074	...	...	...	...	...
Sanshui	440 119	230 835	209 284	...	...	...	...	...
Sanya	482 296	254 293	228 003	...	...	...	...	...
Shahe	474 260	243 171	231 089	...	...	...	...	...
Shanghai	14 348 535	7 414 274	6 934 261	...	...	...	...	...
Shangqiu	1 428 983	729 319	699 664	...	...	...	...	...
Shangrao	327 703	164 698	163 005	...	...	...	...	...
Shangyu	722 523	354 917	367 606	...	...	...	...	...
Shangzhi	582 764	298 966	283 798	...	...	...	...	...
Shangzhou	530 883	279 160	251 723	...	...	...	...	...
Shantou	1 270 112	636 189	633 923	...	...	...	...	...
Shanwei	409 677	211 746	197 931	...	...	...	...	...
Shaoguan	535 979	282 515	253 464	...	...	...	...	...
Shaowu	288 401	151 117	137 284	...	...	...	...	...
Shaoxing	633 118	310 860	322 258	...	...	...	...	...
Shaoyang	607 868	309 563	298 305	...	...	...	...	...
Shengzhou	671 221	345 614	325 607	...	...	...	...	...
Shenyang	5 303 053	2 700 380	2 602 673	...	...	...	...	...
Shenzhen	7 008 831	3 454 392	3 554 439	...	...	...	...	...
Shenzhou	568 558	289 086	279 472	...	...	...	...	...
Shifang	432 579	218 447	214 132	...	...	...	...	...
Shihezi	590 115	305 253	284 862	...	...	...	...	...
Shijiazhuang	1 969 975	1 005 476	964 499	...	...	...	...	...
Shishi	498 786	264 700	234 086	...	...	...	...	...
Shishou	602 649	310 486	292 163	...	...	...	...	...
Shiyan	589 824	309 552	280 272	...	...	...	...	...
Shizuishan	314 296	163 261	151 035	...	...	...	...	...
Shouguang	1 081 991	548 020	533 971	...	...	...	...	...
Shuangcheng	749 182	382 673	366 509	...	...	...	...	...
Shuangliao	404 499	206 071	198 428	...	...	...	...	...
Shuangyashan	487 294	248 542	238 752	...	...	...	...	...
Shulan	660 065	340 293	319 772	...	...	...	...	...
Shunde	1 694 152	893 580	800 572	...	...	...	...	...
Shuozhou	563 896	290 621	273 275	...	...	...	...	...
Sihui	409 804	209 936	199 868	...	...	...	...	...
Simao	230 834	120 071	110 763	...	...	...	...	...
Siping	492 841	247 416	245 425	...	...	...	...	...
Songyuan	538 469	273 101	265 368	...	...	...	...	...
Songzi	859 941	437 980	421 961	...	...	...	...	...
Suihua	800 207	405 382	394 825	...	...	...	...	...
Suining	1 355 388	696 590	658 798	...	...	...	...	...
Suizhou	1 598 752	818 936	779 816	...	...	...	...	...

Continent, country or area, date, code and city / Continent, pays ou zone, date, code et ville	City proper - Ville proprement dite				Urban agglomeration - Agglomération urbaine			
	Population			Surface area - Superficie (km²)	Population			Surface area - Superficie (km²)
	Both sexes - Les deux sexes	Male - Masculin	Female - Féminin		Both sexes - Les deux sexes	Male - Masculin	Female - Féminin	

ASIA - ASIE

China - Chine
1 XI 2000 (CDJC)

Suqian	244 651	124 719	119 932	...	...	...	...	...
Suzhou (Anhui)	1 601 181	819 067	782 114	...	...	...	...	...
Suzhou (Jiangsu)	1 344 709	686 919	657 790	...	...	...	...	...
Tacheng	149 210	76 056	73 154	...	...	...	...	...
Tai'an	1 538 211	775 346	762 865	...	...	...	...	...
Taicang	515 063	250 788	264 275	...	...	...	...	...
Taishan	948 716	478 773	469 943	...	...	...	...	...
Taixing	1 235 454	618 158	617 296	...	...	...	...	...
Taiyuan	2 558 382	1 321 216	1 237 166	...	...	...	...	...
Taizhou (Jiangsu)	607 660	303 078	304 582	...	...	...	...	...
Taizhou (Zhejiang)	1 491 963	766 497	725 466	...	...	...	...	...
Tangshan	1 711 311	863 091	848 220	...	...	...	...	...
Taonan	441 096	224 878	216 218	...	...	...	...	...
Tengzhou	1 548 817	811 999	736 818	...	...	...	...	...
Tianchang	590 745	297 550	293 195	...	...	...	...	...
Tianjin	7 499 181	3 825 069	3 674 112	...	...	...	...	...
Tianmen	1 613 739	849 283	764 456	...	...	...	...	...
Tianshui	1 146 986	594 508	552 478	...	...	...	...	...
Tiefa	239 636	121 471	118 165	...	...	...	...	...
Tieli	354 601	181 024	173 577	...	...	...	...	...
Tieling	433 799	217 795	216 004	...	...	...	...	...
Tongcheng	660 772	321 098	339 674	...	...	...	...	...
Tongchuan	404 257	211 294	192 963	...	...	...	...	...
Tonghua	460 148	231 960	228 188	...	...	...	...	...
Tongjiang	164 595	85 426	79 169	...	...	...	...	...
Tongliao	793 913	400 930	392 983	...	...	...	...	...
Tongling	362 477	188 130	174 347	...	...	...	...	...
Tongren	308 583	163 632	144 951	...	...	...	...	...
Tongshi	100 836	53 146	47 690	...	...	...	...	...
Tongxiang	713 399	360 567	352 832	...	...	...	...	...
Tongzhou	1 371 498	652 777	718 721	...	...	...	...	...
Tulufan	251 652	129 183	122 469	...	...	...	...	...
Tumen	132 368	67 067	65 301	...	...	...	...	...
Urumqi	1 753 298	911 328	841 970	...	...	...	...	...
Wafangdian	956 063	489 377	466 686	...	...	...	...	...
Wanning	513 604	272 751	240 853	...	...	...	...	...
Wanyuan	536 685	278 918	257 767	...	...	...	...	...
Weifang	1 380 300	696 720	683 580	...	...	...	...	...
Weihai	609 219	307 867	301 352	...	...	...	...	...
Weihui	464 371	233 151	231 220	...	...	...	...	...
Weinan	888 866	451 028	437 838	...	...	...	...	...
Wenchang	509 271	260 432	248 839	...	...	...	...	...
Wendeng	675 061	335 330	339 731	...	...	...	...	...
Wenling	1 162 783	604 031	558 752	...	...	...	...	...
Wenzhou	1 915 548	1 028 001	887 547	...	...	...	...	...
Wuan	720 196	373 108	347 088	...	...	...	...	...
Wuchang	888 782	454 587	434 195	...	...	...	...	...
Wuchuan	822 482	429 336	393 146	...	...	...	...	...
Wudalianchi	338 689	176 002	162 687	...	...	...	...	...
Wugang (Henan)	313 089	164 347	148 742	...	...	...	...	...
Wugang (Hunan)	694 847	363 904	330 943	...	...	...	...	...
Wuhai	427 553	223 947	203 606	...	...	...	...	...
Wuhan	8 312 700	4 306 729	4 005 971	...	...	...	...	...
Wuhu	697 197	359 560	337 637	...	...	...	...	...
Wujiang	857 104	426 423	430 681	...	...	...	...	...
Wujin	1 420 204	719 200	701 004	...	...	...	...	...
Wulanhaote	269 162	135 406	133 756	...	...	...	...	...
Wusu	190 359	100 288	90 071	...	...	...	...	...
Wuwei	946 506	488 872	457 634	...	...	...	...	...
Wuxi	1 425 766	732 231	693 535	...	...	...	...	...
Wuxian	1 128 429	557 717	570 712	...	...	...	...	...
Wuxue	719 426	381 959	337 467	...	...	...	...	...
Wuyishan	212 156	112 006	100 150	...	...	...	...	...
Wuzhong	355 442	181 909	173 533	...	...	...	...	...

Continent, country or area, date, code and city / Continent, pays ou zone, date, code et ville	City proper - Ville proprement dite				Urban agglomeration - Agglomération urbaine			
	Population			Surface area - Superficie (km²)	Population			Surface area - Superficie (km²)
	Both sexes - Les deux sexes	Male - Masculin	Female - Féminin		Both sexes - Les deux sexes	Male - Masculin	Female - Féminin	
ASIA - ASIE								
China - Chine								
1 XI 2000 (CDJC)								
Wuzhou	381 043	193 424	187 619	...	...	...	...	...
Xiamen	2 053 070	1 061 697	991 373	...	...	...	...	...
Xi'an	4 481 508	2 320 642	2 160 866	...	...	...	...	...
Xiangcheng	1 052 468	546 760	505 708	...	...	...	...	...
Xiangfan	871 388	443 899	427 489	...	...	...	...	...
Xiangtan	707 783	363 619	344 164	...	...	...	...	...
Xiangxiang	807 718	413 489	394 229	...	...	...	...	...
Xianning	567 598	295 836	271 762	...	...	...	...	...
Xiantao	1 474 078	774 487	699 591	...	...	...	...	...
Xianyang	953 860	493 153	460 707	...	...	...	...	...
Xiaogan	883 123	454 917	428 206	...	...	...	...	...
Xiaoshan	1 233 348	613 229	620 119	...	...	...	...	...
Xiaoyi	414 154	215 941	198 213	...	...	...	...	...
Xichang	615 212	318 658	296 554	...	...	...	...	...
Xifeng	317 669	163 228	154 441	...	...	...	...	...
Xilinhaote	173 796	89 527	84 269	...	...	...	...	...
Xingcheng	524 527	269 567	254 960	...	...	...	...	...
Xinghua	1 441 659	745 856	695 803	...	...	...	...	...
Xingning	871 507	436 749	434 758	...	...	...	...	...
Xingping	551 523	284 879	266 644	...	...	...	...	...
Xingtai	536 282	272 661	263 621	...	...	...	...	...
Xingyang	619 840	316 049	303 791	...	...	...	...	...
Xingyi	719 605	375 079	344 526	...	...	...	...	...
Xinhui	932 425	467 557	464 868	...	...	...	...	...
Xining	854 466	440 359	414 107	...	...	...	...	...
Xinji	623 219	314 536	308 683	...	...	...	...	...
Xinle	439 644	220 811	218 833	...	...	...	...	...
Xinmi	779 014	406 291	372 723	...	...	...	...	...
Xinmin	653 719	333 683	320 036	...	...	...	...	...
Xintai	1 344 395	687 569	656 826	...	...	...	...	...
Xinxiang	775 941	394 224	381 717	...	...	...	...	...
Xinyang	1 255 750	644 031	611 719	...	...	...	...	...
Xinyi (Guangdong)	907 978	464 088	443 890	...	...	...	...	...
Xinyi (Jiangsu)	962 656	491 509	471 147	...	...	...	...	...
Xinyu	778 391	408 940	369 451	...	...	...	...	...
Xinzheng	609 173	315 462	293 711	...	...	...	...	...
Xinzhou	496 608	251 708	244 900	...	...	...	...	...
Xishan	1 181 073	599 540	581 533	...	...	...	...	...
Xuancheng	822 707	428 470	394 237	...	...	...	...	...
Xuanwei	1 292 825	691 846	600 979	...	...	...	...	...
Xuchang	373 387	188 476	184 911	...	...	...	...	...
Xuzhou	1 679 626	866 686	812 940	...	...	...	...	...
Ya'an	334 475	171 237	163 238	...	...	...	...	...
Yakeshi	405 806	207 451	198 355	...	...	...	...	...
Yan'an	403 868	209 240	194 628	...	...	...	...	...
Yancheng	683 663	347 576	336 087	...	...	...	...	...
Yangchun	840 581	440 930	399 651	...	...	...	...	...
Yangjiang	538 069	276 769	261 300	...	...	...	...	...
Yangquan	655 317	346 209	309 108	...	...	...	...	...
Yangzhong	301 672	150 538	151 134	...	...	...	...	...
Yangzhou	711 993	362 425	349 568	...	...	...	...	...
Yanji	432 339	223 342	208 997	...	...	...	...	...
Yanshi	816 026	414 890	401 136	...	...	...	...	...
Yantai	1 724 404	871 452	852 952	...	...	...	...	...
Yanzhou	598 387	303 581	294 806	...	...	...	...	...
Yibin	809 099	419 397	389 702	...	...	...	...	...
Yichang	712 738	371 510	341 228	...	...	...	...	...
Yicheng	522 835	266 340	256 495	...	...	...	...	...
Yichun (Heilongjiang)	814 016	413 071	400 945	...	...	...	...	...
Yichun (Jiangxi)	920 357	480 945	439 412	...	...	...	...	...
Yidu	385 779	196 716	189 063	...	...	...	...	...
Yima	136 543	73 411	63 132	...	...	...	...	...
Yinchuan	807 487	415 203	392 284	...	...	...	...	...
Yingcheng	650 485	340 907	309 578	...	...	...	...	...

Continent, country or area, date, code and city / Continent, pays ou zone, date, code et ville	City proper - Ville proprement dite				Urban agglomeration - Agglomération urbaine			
	Population			Surface area - Superficie (km²)	Population			Surface area - Superficie (km²)
	Both sexes - Les deux sexes	Male - Masculin	Female - Féminin		Both sexes - Les deux sexes	Male - Masculin	Female - Féminin	
ASIA - ASIE								
China - Chine								
1 XI 2000 (CDJC)								
Yingde	810 446	421 964	388 482	...	...	...	...	...
Yingko	698 059	353 751	344 308	...	...	...	...	...
Yingtan	178 406	92 050	86 356	...	...	...	...	...
Yining	357 519	179 862	177 657	...	...	...	...	...
Yiwu	912 670	461 103	451 567	...	...	...	...	...
Yixing	1 164 275	592 095	572 180	...	...	...	...	...
Yiyang	1 228 881	629 842	599 039	...	...	...	...	...
Yizheng	610 356	311 144	299 212	...	...	...	...	...
Yizhou	549 434	288 084	261 350	...	...	...	...	...
Yongan	334 852	180 109	154 743	...	...	...	...	...
Yongcheng	1 264 607	654 047	610 560	...	...	...	...	...
Yongchuan	984 730	507 848	476 882	...	...	...	...	...
Yongji	421 244	214 446	206 798	...	...	...	...	...
Yongkang	557 067	290 946	266 121	...	...	...	...	...
Yongzhou	976 539	508 021	468 518	...	...	...	...	...
Yuanjiang	700 236	363 730	336 506	...	...	...	...	...
Yuanping	471 853	244 751	227 102	...	...	...	...	...
Yucheng	494 301	248 103	246 198	...	...	...	...	...
Yueyang	912 993	471 170	441 823	...	...	...	...	...
Yuhang	817 715	419 877	397 838	...	...	...	...	...
Yulin (Guangxi)	918 229	491 729	426 500	...	...	...	...	...
Yulin (Shaanxi)	451 337	232 951	218 386	...	...	...	...	...
Yumen	188 931	99 832	89 099	...	...	...	...	...
Yuncheng	604 381	304 489	299 892	...	...	...	...	...
Yunfu	261 636	136 789	124 847	...	...	...	...	...
Yushu	1 155 670	592 213	563 457	...	...	...	...	...
Yuxi	409 044	206 139	202 905	...	...	...	...	...
Yuyao	852 719	429 835	422 884	...	...	...	...	...
Yuzhou	1 122 669	587 728	534 941	...	...	...	...	...
Zaoyang	1 054 374	538 588	515 786	...	...	...	...	...
Zaozhuang	1 996 798	1 025 190	971 608	...	...	...	...	...
Zengcheng	899 644	466 540	433 104	...	...	...	...	...
Zhalantun	409 051	211 922	197 129	...	...	...	...	...
Zhangjiagang	957 223	466 771	490 452	...	...	...	...	...
Zhangjiajie	453 723	234 454	219 269	...	...	...	...	...
Zhangjiakou	903 348	455 048	448 300	...	...	...	...	...
Zhangping	264 757	140 779	123 978	...	...	...	...	...
Zhangqiu	977 324	485 925	491 399	...	...	...	...	...
Zhangshu	527 823	273 691	254 132	...	...	...	...	...
Zhangye	486 688	248 469	238 219	...	...	...	...	...
Zhangzhou	567 884	291 597	276 287	...	...	...	...	...
Zhanjiang	1 350 665	707 187	643 478	...	...	...	...	...
Zhaodong	832 657	424 694	407 963	...	...	...	...	...
Zhaoqing	507 834	254 086	253 748	...	...	...	...	...
Zhaotong	727 959	377 931	350 028	...	...	...	...	...
Zhaoyuan	593 705	297 504	296 201	...	...	...	...	...
Zhengzhou	2 589 387	1 347 037	1 242 350	...	...	...	...	...
Zhenjiang	695 663	364 429	331 234	...	...	...	...	...
Zhijiang	508 835	257 013	251 822	...	...	...	...	...
Zhongshan	2 363 322	1 175 587	1 187 735	...	...	...	...	...
Zhongxiang	1 021 998	516 758	505 240	...	...	...	...	...
Zhoukou	323 738	162 443	161 295	...	...	...	...	...
Zhoushan	715 685	362 426	353 259	...	...	...	...	...
Zhuanghe	835 062	422 677	412 385	...	...	...	...	...
Zhucheng	1 053 695	531 390	522 305	...	...	...	...	...
Zhuhai	833 908	414 067	419 841	...	...	...	...	...
Zhuji	1 070 675	535 820	534 855	...	...	...	...	...
Zhumadian	338 036	170 485	167 551	...	...	...	...	...
Zhuozhou	546 754	275 834	270 920	...	...	...	...	...
Zhuzhou	879 996	454 057	425 939	...	...	...	...	...
Zibo	2 817 479	1 429 838	1 387 641	...	...	...	...	...
Zigong	1 051 384	532 479	518 905	...	...	...	...	...
Zixing	351 581	181 632	169 949	...	...	...	...	...
Ziyang	1 016 034	527 326	488 708	...	...	...	...	...

8. Population of capital cities and cities of 100 000 or more inhabitants: latest available year, 1988 - 2007
Population des capitales et des villes de 100 000 habitants ou plus: dernière année disponible, 1988 - 2007 (continued - suite)

Continent, country or area, date, code and city / Continent, pays ou zone, date, code et ville	City proper - Ville proprement dite				Urban agglomeration - Agglomération urbaine			
	Population			Surface area - Superficie (km²)	Population			Surface area - Superficie (km²)
	Both sexes - Les deux sexes	Male - Masculin	Female - Féminin		Both sexes - Les deux sexes	Male - Masculin	Female - Féminin	
ASIA - ASIE								
China - Chine								
1 XI 2000 (CDJC)								
Zoucheng	1 101 003	571 761	529 242	...	...	...	...	...
Zunhua	683 662	348 121	335 541	...	...	...	...	...
Zunyi	691 694	358 839	332 855	...	...	...	...	...
China, Hong Kong SAR - Chine, Hong Kong RAS								
1 VII 2007 (ESDJ)								
HONG KONG SAR	6 925 900	...	...	1 104	...	...	...	...
China, Macao SAR - Chine, Macao RAS								
1 VII 2007 (ESDJ)								
MACAO	525 800	259 100	266 700	29	...	...	...	...
Cyprus - Chypre								
1 I 2006 (ESDJ)								
LEFKOSIA[22]	...	...	...	...	224 500	...	...	...
Lemesos[23]	...	...	...	...	176 900	...	...	...
Democratic People's Republic of Korea - République populaire démocratique de Corée								
31 XII 1993 (CDFC)								
Chongjin	582 480	...	...	...	...	...	...	...
Haeju	229 172	...	...	...	...	...	...	...
Hamhung	709 730	...	...	...	...	...	...	...
Hyesan	178 020	...	...	...	...	...	...	...
Kaesong	334 433	...	...	...	...	...	...	...
Kanggye	223 410	...	...	...	...	...	...	...
Nampho	731 448	...	...	...	...	...	...	...
Phyongsong	272 934	...	...	...	...	...	...	...
PYONGYANG	2 741 260	...	...	...	...	...	...	...
Sariwon	254 146	...	...	...	...	...	...	...
Sinuiji	326 011	...	...	...	...	...	...	...
Wonsan	300 148	...	...	...	...	...	...	...
Georgia - Géorgie								
1 VII 2007 (ESDF)								
Batumi	122 200	...	...	...	...	...	...	...
Kutaisi	189 100	...	...	...	...	...	...	...
Rustavi	117 600	...	...	...	...	...	...	...
TBILISI	1 108 600	...	...	...	...	...	...	...
India - Inde[24]								
1 III 2001 (CDFC)								
Abohar	124 339	66 445	57 894	23	...	...	...	...
Achalpur	107 316	55 687	51 629	17	...	...	...	...
Adilabad	109 529	55 641	53 888	16	129 403	65 501	63 902	21
Adityapur	119 233	63 837	55 396	50	...	...	...	...
Adoni	157 305	79 639	77 666	30	162 458	82 345	80 113	...
Agartala	189 998	94 742	95 256	16	...	...	...	...
Agra	1 275 134	690 599	584 535	121	1 331 339	720 707	610 632	141
Ahmedabad	3 520 085	1 867 249	1 652 836	191	4 525 013	2 401 422	2 123 591	438
Ahmednagar	307 615	159 564	148 051	18	347 549	184 765	162 784	30
Aizawl	228 280	115 986	112 294	110	...	...	...	...
Ajmer	485 575	254 164	231 411	218	490 520	256 695	233 825	223
Akola	400 520	206 649	193 871	23	...	...	...	...
Alandur	146 287	74 836	71 451	20	...	...	...	...
Alappuzha	177 029	85 725	91 304	70	282 675	137 244	145 431	84
Aligarh	669 087	356 725	312 362	40	...	...	...	...
Alipurduar	...	...	...	...	114 035	58 503	55 532	26
Allahabad	975 393	539 772	435 621	63	1 042 229	576 122	466 107	86
Alwar	260 593	139 585	121 008	...	266 203	143 699	122 504	58
Ambala	139 279	74 016	65 263	17	168 316	92 977	75 339	38
Ambala Sadar	106 568	55 750	50 818	...	...	...	...	...
Ambarnath	203 804	107 325	96 479	36	...	...	...	...
Ambattur	310 967	160 282	150 685	40	...	...	...	...
Amravati	549 510	284 247	265 263	122	...	...	...	...
Amritsar	966 862	518 388	448 474	136	1 003 917	538 744	465 173	...
Amroha	165 129	86 943	78 186	6	...	...	...	...
Anand	130 685	68 074	62 611	21	218 486	115 295	103 191	60
Anantapur	218 808	110 979	107 829	...	243 143	123 713	119 430	...
Anklesvar	...	...	...	...	112 643	60 249	52 394	...

8. Population of capital cities and cities of 100 000 or more inhabitants: latest available year, 1988 - 2007
Population des capitales et des villes de 100 000 habitants ou plus: dernière année disponible, 1988 - 2007 (continued - suite)

Continent, country or area, date, code and city / Continent, pays ou zone, date, code et ville	City proper - Ville proprement dite				Urban agglomeration - Agglomération urbaine			
	Population			Surface area - Superficie (km²)	Population			Surface area - Superficie (km²)
	Both sexes - Les deux sexes	Male - Masculin	Female - Féminin		Both sexes - Les deux sexes	Male - Masculin	Female - Féminin	
ASIA - ASIE								
India - Inde[24]								
1 III 2001 (CDFC)								
Arcot	...	...	...	...	126 671	62 787	63 884	19
Arrah	203 380	109 867	93 513	31	...	...	...	...
Asansol	475 439	250 886	224 553	128	1 067 369	564 837	502 532	352
Ashoknagar Kalyangarh	111 607	56 490	55 117	...	...	...	...	...
Aurangabad	873 311	459 295	414 016	139	892 483	469 237	423 246	148
Avadi	229 403	117 991	111 412	65	...	...	...	...
Bahadurgarh	119 846	65 859	53 987	21	131 925	72 873	59 052	30
Baharampur	160 143	81 737	78 406	17	170 322	86 969	83 353	19
Bahraich	168 323	89 581	78 742	13	...	...	...	...
Baidyabati	108 229	56 394	51 835	8	...	...	...	...
Baleshwar	106 082	55 691	50 391	...	156 430	82 106	74 324	42
Ballia	101 465	54 496	46 969	16	...	...	...	...
Bally	260 906	149 603	111 303	12	...	...	...	...
Balurghat	135 737	68 871	66 866	10	143 321	72 764	70 557	12
Banda	134 839	72 632	62 207	16	139 436	75 174	64 262	28
Bangalore	4 301 326	2 242 835	2 058 491	...	5 701 446	2 988 561	2 712 885	540
Bangaon	102 163	52 537	49 626	25	...	...	...	...
Bankura	128 781	66 429	62 352	19	...	...	...	...
Bansberia	104 412	55 389	49 023	9	...	...	...	...
Baranagar	250 768	132 559	118 209	7	...	...	...	...
Barasat	231 521	118 374	113 147	31	...	...	...	...
Barddhaman	285 602	148 562	137 040	23	...	...	...	...
Bareilly	718 395	378 848	339 547	106	748 353	397 304	351 049	125
Baripada	...	...	...	...	100 651	53 606	47 045	38
Barrackpur	144 391	76 299	68 092	11	...	...	...	...
Barshi	104 785	53 848	50 937	36	...	...	...	...
Basirhat	113 159	57 965	55 194	22	...	...	...	...
Basti	107 601	57 053	50 548	19	...	...	...	...
Batala	125 677	66 508	59 169	9	147 872	78 393	69 479	...
Bathinda	217 256	116 946	100 310	110	...	...	...	...
Beawar	123 759	64 417	59 342	18	125 981	65 586	60 395	24
Begusarai	...	...	...	...	107 623	57 541	50 082	12
Belgaum	399 653	204 598	195 055	100	506 480	261 639	244 841	173
Bellary	316 766	162 699	154 067	66	...	...	...	...
Bettiah	116 670	61 753	54 917	8	...	...	...	...
Bhadravati	160 662	81 351	79 311	...	...	...	...	...
Bhadreswar	106 071	58 040	48 031	6	...	...	...	...
Bhagalpur	340 767	182 806	157 961	30	350 133	187 723	162 410	31
Bhalswa Jahangir Pur	152 339	83 802	68 537	7	...	...	...	...
Bharatpur	204 587	110 057	94 530	41	205 235	110 397	94 838	51
Bharuch	148 140	76 506	71 634	18	176 364	91 281	85 083	20
Bhatpara	442 385	243 157	199 228	30	...	...	...	...
Bhavani	...	...	...	...	104 646	52 998	51 648	10
Bhavnagar	511 085	266 838	244 247	90	517 708	270 278	247 430	91
Bheemavaram	137 409	69 473	67 936	26	142 064	71 929	70 135	26
Bhilai Nagar	556 366	291 070	265 296	141	...	...	...	...
Bhilwara	280 128	148 794	131 334	118	...	...	...	...
Bhind	153 752	82 945	70 807	17	...	...	...	...
Bhiwandi	598 741	367 565	231 176	26	621 427	382 184	239 243	28
Bhiwani	169 531	91 697	77 834	28	...	...	...	...
Bhopal	1 437 354	757 408	679 946	285	1 458 416	768 391	690 025	298
Bhubaneswar	648 032	360 739	287 293	135	658 220	366 134	292 086	148
Bhuj	...	...	...	...	136 429	71 056	65 373	25
Bhusawal	172 372	89 208	83 164	13	187 564	97 243	90 321	25
Bid	138 196	71 827	66 369	8	...	...	...	...
Bidar	172 877	89 934	82 943	...	174 257	90 662	83 595	47
Bidhan Nagar	164 221	83 220	81 001	34	...	...	...	...
Bihar	232 071	122 019	110 052	24	...	...	...	...
Bijapur	228 175	117 375	110 800	...	253 891	130 416	123 475	75
Bikaner	529 690	283 067	246 623	166	...	...	...	...
Bilaspur	275 694	143 518	132 176	36	335 293	174 351	160 942	46
Birnagar	...	...	...	...	115 127	59 232	55 895	40
Bokaro Steel City	393 805	213 231	180 574	163	497 780	268 969	228 811	188
Bommanahalli	201 652	108 108	93 544	36	...	...	...	...

Continent, country or area, date, code and city / Continent, pays ou zone, date, code et ville	City proper - Ville proprement dite				Urban agglomeration - Agglomération urbaine			
	Population			Surface area - Superficie (km²)	Population			Surface area - Superficie (km²)
	Both sexes - Les deux sexes	Male - Masculin	Female - Féminin		Both sexes - Les deux sexes	Male - Masculin	Female - Féminin	

ASIA - ASIE

India - Inde[24]
  1 III 2001 (CDFC)

Botad	100 194	52 752	47 442	10				
Brahmapur	307 792	160 354	147 438	80	...	...	...	...
Budaun	148 029	78 141	69 888	4	...	...	...	
Bulandshahr	176 425	93 531	82 894	12	...	...	...	
Burhanpur	193 725	99 751	93 974	13				
Byatarayanapura	181 744	95 508	86 236	45	...			
Chakdaha	...	...	...	...	101 320	51 485	49 835	
Champdani	103 246	57 842	45 404	6	...			
Chandan Nagar	162 187	84 181	78 006	22	...			
Chandausi	103 749	55 127	48 622	9	...			
Chandigarh	808 515	450 122	358 393	79	...			
Chandrapur	289 450	151 202	138 248	56	...			
Chapra	179 190	95 494	83 696	17	...			
Chennai (Madras)	4 343 645	2 219 539	2 124 106	174	6 560 242	3 355 524	3 204 718	702
Cherthala	...	...	...	...	141 558	68 756	72 802	92
Chhatarpur	...	...	...	...	109 078	58 421	50 657	17
Chhindwara	122 247	63 584	58 663	11	153 552	79 889	73 663	22
Chikmagalur	101 251	51 694	49 557	33				
Chirala	...	...	...	...	166 294	82 954	83 340	48
Chirkunda	...	...	...	...	106 227	56 536	49 691	26
Chitradurga	122 702	62 845	59 857	24	125 170	64 112	61 058	26
Chittoor	152 654	76 879	75 775	33				
Churu	...	...	...	...	101 874	53 079	48 795	30
Coimbatore	930 882	477 937	452 945	106	1 461 139	748 376	712 763	379
Coonoor	...	...	...	...	101 490	51 208	50 282	44
Cuddalore	158 634	80 012	78 622	28	...			
Cuddapah	126 505	63 669	62 836	42	262 506	133 224	129 282	78
Cuttack	534 654	285 838	248 816	149	587 182	314 101	273 081	195
Dallo Pura	132 621	71 362	61 259	2				
Damoh	112 185	58 962	53 223	16	127 967	67 321	60 646	36
Darbhanga	267 348	142 377	124 971	19	...			
Darjiling	107 197	55 963	51 234	11	108 830	56 769	52 061	13
Dasarahalli	264 940	143 909	121 031	23	...			
Davangere	364 523	187 987	176 536		...	...	...	
Dehradun	426 674	224 546	202 128	52	530 263	283 064	247 199	103
Dehri	119 057	63 540	55 517	21	...			
Delhi	9 879 172	5 412 497	4 466 675	554	12 877 470[25]	7 069 371[25]	5 808 099[25]	889[25]
Delhi Cantonment	124 917	75 827	49 090	43	...			
Deoghar	...	...	...	...	112 525	61 442	51 083	22
Deoli	119 468	66 594	52 874	10	...			
Deoria	104 227	54 681	49 546	16	...			
Dewas	231 672	121 075	110 597	100	...			
Dhanbad	199 258	108 512	90 746	23	1 065 327	579 150	486 177	223
Dharmavaram	103 357	52 785	50 572	40	...			
Dhule	341 755	177 772	163 983	46	...			
Dibrugarh	121 893	65 118	56 775	25	137 661	73 307	64 354	26
Dinapur Nizamat	131 176	69 419	61 757	12	...			
Dindigul	196 955	99 124	97 831	14	...			
Dohad	...	...	...	...	112 026	57 642	54 384	26
Dumdum	101 296	52 890	48 406	9	...			
Durg	232 517	119 315	113 202	66	...	...	...	
Durgapur	493 405	263 721	229 684	154	...			
Durg-Bhilai Nagar	...	...	...	...	927 864	482 304	445 560	341
Eluru	190 062	92 790	97 272	15	215 804	105 476	110 328	
English Bazar	161 456	82 845	78 611	...	224 415	115 356	109 059	19
Erode	150 541	76 462	74 079	8	389 906	198 842	191 064	132
Etah	107 110	56 763	50 347	13	...			
Etawah	210 453	111 749	98 704	9	...	...	...	
Faizabad	144 705	75 935	68 770	33	208 162	114 330	93 832	63
Faridabad	1 055 938	581 069	474 869	199	...			
Farrukhabad-cum-Fategarh	228 333	120 829	107 504	17	242 997	129 643	113 354	21
Fatehpur	152 078	80 011	72 067	57	...			
Firozabad	279 102	148 263	130 839	9	432 866	230 802	202 064	12
Gadag-Betgeri	154 982	78 713	76 269	35	...	...	...	

8. Population of capital cities and cities of 100 000 or more inhabitants: latest available year, 1988 - 2007
Population des capitales et des villes de 100 000 habitants ou plus: dernière année disponible, 1988 - 2007 (continued - suite)

Continent, country or area, date, code and city / Continent, pays ou zone, date, code et ville	City proper - Ville proprement dite				Urban agglomeration - Agglomération urbaine			
	Population			Surface area - Superficie (km²)	Population			Surface area - Superficie (km²)
	Both sexes - Les deux sexes	Male - Masculin	Female - Féminin		Both sexes - Les deux sexes	Male - Masculin	Female - Féminin	

ASIA - ASIE

India - Inde[24]
1 III 2001 (CDFC)

City	Both sexes	Male	Female	Surface	Both sexes	Male	Female	Surface
Gajuwaka	259 180	133 469	125 711	128	...	...	...	...
Gandhidham	151 693	79 379	72 314	30	...	...	...	...
Gandhinagar	195 985	103 876	92 109	57	...	...	...	...
Ganganagar	210 713	115 321	95 392	21	222 858	121 865	100 993	...
Gangapur City	...	...	...	...	105 396	56 009	49 387	12
Gangawati	...	...	...	29	101 392	51 211	50 181	16
Gaya	385 432	204 483	180 949	4	394 945	210 410	184 535	32
Ghatlodiya	106 684	56 219	50 465	145	...	...	...	...
Ghaziabad	968 256	521 026	447 230	...	...	...	...	...
Ghazipur	...	...	...	...	103 298	54 371	48 927	20
Giridih	...	...	...	20	105 634	55 490	50 144	11
Godhra	121 879	63 176	58 703	15	131 172	67 969	63 203	23
Gonda	120 301	66 207	54 094	18	...	...	...	...
Gondiya	120 902	61 418	59 484	141	...	...	...	...
Gorakhpur	622 701	329 807	292 894	13	...	...	...	...
Gudivada	113 054	55 867	57 187	...	...	...	...	...
Gudiyatham	...	...	...	...	100 115	49 794	50 321	14
Gulbarga	422 569	219 409	203 160	46	430 265	223 594	206 671	43
Guna	137 175	72 538	64 637	41	...	...	...	...
Guntakul	117 103	59 211	57 892	46	...	...	...	...
Guntur	514 461	257 775	256 686	15	...	...	...	...
Gurgaon	172 955	92 934	80 021	...	228 820	123 377	105 443	24
Guruvayur	...	...	...	217	138 681	64 554	74 127	57
Guwahati	809 895	440 288	369 607	167	818 809	446 311	372 498	217
Gwalior	827 026	442 343	384 683	18	865 548	465 057	400 491	180
Habra	127 602	65 141	62 461	20	239 209	121 631	117 578	37
Hajipur	119 412	63 838	55 574	69	...	...	...	...
Haldia	170 673	89 893	80 780	11	...	...	...	...
Haldwani-cum-Kathgodam	129 015	68 755	60 260	8	158 896	84 541	74 355	...
Halisahar	124 510	67 151	57 359	13	...	...	...	...
Hanumangarh	129 556	69 532	60 024	52	...	...	...	...
Haora (Howrah)	1 007 532	547 068	460 464	14	...	...	...	...
Hapur	211 983	113 175	98 808	6	...	...	...	...
Hardoi	112 486	59 876	52 610	15	...	...	...	...
Hardwar	175 340	94 736	80 604	27	220 767	119 234	101 533	42
Hassan	116 574	59 743	56 831	8	133 262	68 242	65 020	30
Hathras	123 244	65 778	57 466	26	126 355	67 436	58 919	8
Hazaribag	127 269	67 900	59 369	38	135 473	72 288	63 185	27
Hindupur	125 074	64 132	60 942	45	...	...	...	...
Hisar	256 689	140 083	116 606	35	263 186	143 795	119 391	49
Hoshiarpur	149 668	79 454	70 214	28	...	...	...	...
Hospet	164 240	83 767	80 473	213	...	...	...	...
Hubli-Dharwad	786 195	403 085	383 110	17	...	...	...	...
Hugli-Chinsurah	170 206	86 788	83 418	173	...	...	...	...
Hyderabad	3 637 483	1 883 064	1 754 419	30	5 742 036	2 973 472	2 768 564	822
Ichalakaranji	257 610	136 063	121 547	33	285 860	150 977	134 883	38
Imphal	221 492	109 815	111 677	130	250 234	123 859	126 375	37
Indore	1 474 968	774 540	700 428	...	1 516 918	796 673	720 245	165
Itarsi	...	...	...	119	107 831	56 347	51 484	24
Jabalpur	932 484	488 479	444 005	...	1 098 000	580 038	517 962	205
Jagadhri	101 290	55 844	45 446	...	...	...	...	...
Jagdalpur	...	...	...	485	103 123	52 909	50 214	26
Jaipur	2 322 575	1 237 765	1 084 810	102	...	...	...	...
Jalandhar	706 043	379 439	326 604	62	714 077	383 624	330 453	...
Jalgaon	368 618	193 496	175 122	82	...	...	...	...
Jalna	235 795	121 922	113 873	13	...	...	...	...
Jalpaiguri	100 348	50 629	49 719	40	...	...	...	...
Jammu	369 959	198 956	171 003	26	612 163	334 452	277 711	202
Jamnagar	443 518	232 845	210 673	60	556 956	292 168	264 788	...
Jamshedpur	573 096	301 433	271 663	73	1 104 713	581 829	522 884	160
Jamuria	129 484	68 695	60 789	25	...	...	...	...
Jaunpur	160 055	84 203	75 852	36	...	...	...	...
Jetpur Navagadh	104 312	54 768	49 544	58	...	...	...	...
Jhansi	383 644	202 745	180 899	...	460 278	244 169	216 109	84

Continent, country or area, date, code and city Continent, pays ou zone, date, code et ville	City proper - Ville proprement dite				Urban agglomeration - Agglomération urbaine			
	Population			Surface area - Superficie (km²)	Population			Surface area - Superficie (km²)
	Both sexes - Les deux sexes	Male - Masculin	Female - Féminin		Both sexes - Les deux sexes	Male - Masculin	Female - Féminin	
ASIA - ASIE								
India - Inde[24]								
1 III 2001 (CDFC)								
Jhunjhunun	100 485	52 781	47 704	37	...	...	...	...
Jind	135 855	73 407	62 448	15	...	...	...	...
Jodhpur	851 051	454 075	396 976	79	860 818	459 198	401 620	90
Jorhat	...	...	...	...	137 814	73 213	64 601	69
Junagadh	168 515	86 980	81 535	13	252 108	130 461	121 647	...
Kaithal	117 285	63 098	54 187	44	...	...	...	...
Kakinada	296 329	146 476	149 853	39	376 861	187 064	189 797	58
Kalol	100 008	53 110	46 898	17	112 013	59 539	52 474	30
Kalyan	1 193 512	633 508	560 004	105	...	...	...	...
Kamarhati	314 507	168 555	145 952	11	...	...	...	...
Kamptee	...	...	...	...	136 491	71 270	65 221	37
Kancheepuram	153 140	77 069	76 071	12	188 733	95 068	93 665	40
Kanchrapara	126 191	65 264	60 927	9	...	...	...	...
Kanhangad	65 503	31 627	33 876	40	129 367	62 002	67 365	84
Kannur	...	...	...	...	498 207	237 108	261 099	154
Kanpur	2 551 337	1 374 121	1 177 216	267	2 715 555	1 465 142	1 250 413	301
Kapra	159 002	82 579	76 423	65	...	...	...	...
Karaikkudi	...	...	...	...	125 717	62 479	63 238	43
Karawal Nagar	148 624	80 495	68 129	5	...	...	...	...
Karimnagar	205 653	105 336	100 317	24	218 302	111 875	106 427	...
Karnal	207 640	110 595	97 045	22	221 236	117 875	103 361	24
Karur	...	...	...	...	153 365	77 207	76 158	33
Katihar	175 199	93 617	81 582	25	190 873	102 161	88 712	...
Khammam	159 544	80 574	78 970	...	198 620	100 930	97 690	26
Khandwa	172 242	88 950	83 292	36	...	...	...	...
Khanna	103 099	55 276	47 823	25	...	...	...	...
Kharagpur	188 761	97 721	91 040	91	272 865	140 730	132 135	125
Khardaha	116 470	61 214	55 256	7	...	...	...	...
Khargone	...	...	...	...	103 448	53 921	49 527	33
Kirari Suleman Nagar	154 633	85 362	69 271	5	...	...	...	...
Kishangarh	116 222	61 075	55 147	25	...	...	...	...
Koch Bihar	...	...	...	...	103 008	52 275	50 733	17
Kochi	595 575	294 756	300 819	95	1 355 972	670 340	685 632	453
Kolar	113 907	58 060	55 847	18	...	...	...	...
Kolhapur	493 167	255 778	237 389	67	505 541	262 258	243 283	67
Kolkata (Calcutta)	4 572 876	2 500 040	2 072 836	185	13 205 697[26]	7 064 138[26]	6 141 559[26]	1 034[26]
Kollam	361 560	177 677	183 883	41	380 091	186 924	193 167	68
Korba	315 690	164 768	150 922	35	...	...	...	...
Kota	694 316	368 451	325 865	221	703 150	373 094	330 056	226
Kothagudem	...	...	...	...	105 266	52 318	52 948	25
Kottayam	...	...	...	...	172 878	84 960	87 918	64
Kozhikode	436 556	211 888	224 668	84	880 247	429 163	451 084	235
Krishnanagar	139 110	70 576	68 534	16	148 709	75 495	73 214	18
Krishnarajapura	186 210	97 412	88 798	25	...	...	...	...
Kukatpalle	292 289	153 331	138 958	72	...	...	...	...
Kulti	289 903	152 821	137 082	100	...	...	...	...
Kumbakonam	139 954	69 785	70 169	13	160 767	80 188	80 579	15
Kurnool	269 122	136 619	132 503	15	342 973	174 190	168 783	46
Lakhimpur	121 486	65 236	56 250	7	...	...	...	...
Lal Bahadur Nagar	268 689	138 667	130 022	85	...	...	...	...
Lalitpur	111 892	58 993	52 899	...	...	...	...	...
Latur	299 985	156 547	143 438	21	...	...	...	...
Loni	120 945	65 278	55 667	7	...	...	...	...
Lucknow	2 185 927	1 156 151	1 029 776	310	2 245 509	1 189 466	1 056 043	338
Ludhiana	1 398 467	793 142	605 325	159	...	...	...	...
Machilipatnam	179 353	89 100	90 253	27	...	...	...	...
Madanapalle	...	...	...	...	107 449	54 497	52 952	13
Madhyamgram	155 451	79 728	75 723	21	...	...	...	...
Madurai	928 869	469 396	459 473	52	1 203 095	608 531	594 564	141
Mahadevapura	135 794	72 882	62 912	53	...	...	...	...
Mahbubnagar	130 986	67 007	63 979	14	139 662	71 516	68 146	14
Mahesana	...	...	...	...	141 453	74 866	66 587	...
Maheshtala	385 266	202 304	182 962	44	...	...	...	...
Mainpuri	...	...	...	...	104 851	55 462	49 389	17

8. Population of capital cities and cities of 100 000 or more inhabitants: latest available year, 1988 - 2007
Population des capitales et des villes de 100 000 habitants ou plus: dernière année disponible, 1988 - 2007 (continued - suite)

Continent, country or area, date, code and city / Continent, pays ou zone, date, code et ville	City proper - Ville proprement dite				Urban agglomeration - Agglomération urbaine			
	Population			Surface area - Superficie (km²)	Population			Surface area - Superficie (km²)
	Both sexes - Les deux sexes	Male - Masculin	Female - Féminin		Both sexes - Les deux sexes	Male - Masculin	Female - Féminin	
ASIA - ASIE								
India - Inde[24]								
1 III 2001 (CDFC)								
Malappuram	...	...	...	...	170 409	83 709	86 700	111
Malegaon	409 403	208 864	200 539	13	...	...	...	...
Malerkotla	107 009	56 767	50 242	21	...	...	...	...
Malkajgiri	193 863	98 972	94 891	18	...	...	...	...
Mancherial	...	...	...	...	118 195	60 371	57 824	62
Mandsaur	116 505	60 269	56 236	...	117 555	60 859	56 696	...
Mandya	131 179	66 551	64 628	17	...	...	...	...
Mangalore	399 565	200 630	198 935	118	539 387	269 562	269 825	201
Mango	166 125	87 375	78 750	19	...	...	...	...
Mathura	302 770	162 021	140 749	9	323 315	174 335	148 980	22
Maunath Bhanjan	212 657	109 958	102 699	9	...	...	...	...
Medinipur	149 769	76 503	73 266	15	...	...	...	...
Meerut	1 068 772	568 081	500 691	142	1 161 716	621 481	540 235	178
Mira-Bhayandar	520 388	286 391	233 997	79	...	...	...	...
Mirzapur-cum-Vindhyachal	205 053	109 647	95 406	39	...	...	...	...
Modinagar	113 218	60 468	52 750	16	139 929	74 788	65 141	23
Moga	125 573	66 888	58 685	16	135 279	72 043	63 236	...
Moradabad	641 583	340 314	301 269	89	...	...	...	...
Morena	150 959	82 305	68 654	12	...	...	...	...
Mormugoa	...	...	...	...	104 758	55 954	48 804	40
Morvi	145 719	75 745	69 974	25	178 055	92 639	85 416	...
Motihari	100 683	54 261	46 422	14	108 428	59 148	49 280	16
Mughalsarai	...	...	...	...	116 308	61 579	54 729	29
Mumbai (Bombay)	11 978 450	6 619 966	5 358 484	603	16 434 386	9 021 789	7 412 597	1 133
Munger	188 050	101 264	86 786	18	...	...	...	...
Murwara (Katni)	187 029	97 843	89 186	107	...	...	...	...
Muzaffarnagar	316 729	167 397	149 332	...	331 668	175 283	156 385	12
Muzaffarpur	305 525	164 000	141 525	26	...	...	...	...
Mysore	755 379	383 480	371 899	89	799 228	406 363	392 865	132
Nabadwip	115 016	58 287	56 729	12	125 341	63 574	61 767	13
Nadiad	192 913	100 322	92 591	28	196 793	102 336	94 457	30
Nagaon	107 667	56 815	50 852	...	123 265	64 895	58 370	16
Nagercoil	208 179	102 907	105 272	24	...	...	...	...
Nagpur	2 052 066	1 059 765	992 301	218	2 129 500	1 102 009	1 027 491	229
Naihati	215 303	113 777	101 526	12	...	...	...	...
Nala Sopara	184 538	98 870	85 668	...	...	...	...	...
Nalgonda	110 286	56 299	53 987	12	111 380	56 848	54 532	51
Nanded	430 733	224 843	205 890	21	...	...	...	...
Nandyal	152 676	77 273	75 403	15	157 120	79 500	77 620	...
Nangloi Jat	150 948	82 687	68 261	7	...	...	...	...
Nashik	1 077 236	575 737	501 499	259	1 152 326	616 088	536 238	322
Navghar-Manikpur	116 723	61 757	54 966	...	...	...	...	...
Navi Mumbai (New Bombay)	704 002	395 705	308 297	133	...	...	...	...
Navsari	134 017	69 794	64 223	...	232 411	122 282	110 129	...
Neemuch	107 663	56 588	51 075	13	112 852	59 320	53 532	13
Nellore	378 428	190 522	187 906	48	404 775	203 823	200 952	...
NEW DELHI[27]	302 363	165 723	136 640	43	...	...	...	...
Neyveli	127 552	65 348	62 204	97	138 035	70 746	67 289	116
Nizamabad	288 722	146 198	142 524	37	...	...	...	...
Noida	305 058	168 958	136 100	90	...	...	...	...
North Barrackpur	123 668	63 796	59 872	9	...	...	...	...
North Dumdum	220 042	113 034	107 008	26	...	...	...	...
Ongole	150 471	76 511	73 960	27	153 829	78 242	75 587	27
Orai	139 318	74 703	64 615	20	...	...	...	...
Ozhukarai	217 707	110 042	107 665	35	...	...	...	...
Palakkad	130 767	64 379	66 388	30	197 369	96 928	100 441	59
Palanpur	110 419	58 055	52 364	20	122 300	64 365	57 935	40
Pali	187 641	99 267	88 374	84	...	...	...	...
Pallavaram	144 623	73 385	71 238	18	...	...	...	...
Palwal	100 722	53 648	47 074	8	...	...	...	...
Panchkula Urban Estate	140 925	75 897	65 028	26	...	...	...	...
Panihati	348 438	180 307	168 131	19	...	...	...	...
Panipat	261 740	143 644	118 096	21	354 148	194 850	159 298	...
Panvel	104 058	54 963	49 095	12	...	...	...	...

8. Population of capital cities and cities of 100 000 or more inhabitants: latest available year, 1988 - 2007
Population des capitales et des villes de 100 000 habitants ou plus: dernière année disponible, 1988 - 2007 (continued - suite)

Continent, country or area, date, code and city / Continent, pays ou zone, date, code et ville	City proper - Ville proprement dite				Urban agglomeration - Agglomération urbaine			
	Population			Surface area - Superficie (km²)	Population			Surface area - Superficie (km²)
	Both sexes - Les deux sexes	Male - Masculin	Female - Féminin		Both sexes - Les deux sexes	Male - Masculin	Female - Féminin	
ASIA - ASIE								
India - Inde[24]								
1 III 2001 (CDFC)								
Parbhani	259 329	133 959	125 370	58	...	...	...	...
Patan	112 219	59 097	53 122	14	113 749	59 955	53 794	...
Pathankot	157 925	86 520	71 405	22	168 485	92 003	76 482	...
Patiala	303 151	162 573	140 578	65	323 884	173 682	150 202	...
Patna	1 366 444	746 344	620 100	99	1 697 976	922 971	775 005	135
Phagwara	...	...	...	...	102 253	55 335	46 918	...
Phusro	...	...	...	...	174 402	93 700	80 702	84
Pilibhit	124 245	65 853	58 392	10	...	...	...	...
Pimpri Chinchwad	1 012 472	547 050	465 422	171	...	...	...	...
Pollachi	...	...	...	...	128 458	64 657	63 801	29
Pondicherry	220 865	109 389	111 476	20	505 959	253 375	252 584	72
Porbandar	133 051	68 201	64 850	12	197 382	101 824	95 558	...
Proddatur	150 309	75 372	74 937	7	...	...	...	...
Pudukkottai	109 217	54 614	54 603	13	...	...	...	...
Pune	2 538 473	1 321 338	1 217 135	430	3 760 636	1 980 621	1 780 015	669
Puri	157 837	82 269	75 568	17	...	...	...	...
Purnia	171 687	92 826	78 861	45	197 211	106 313	90 898	60
Puruliya	113 806	59 092	54 714	14	...	...	...	...
Quthbullapur	231 108	120 690	110 418	47	...	...	...	...
Rae Bareli	169 333	88 911	80 422	50	...	...	...	...
Raichur	207 421	105 763	101 658	...	...	...	...	...
Raiganj	165 212	87 458	77 754	11	175 047	92 703	82 344	15
Raigarh	111 154	57 650	53 504	18	115 908	60 101	55 807	21
Raipur	605 747	314 584	291 163	56	700 113	364 436	335 677	116
Rajahmundry	315 251	158 454	156 797	52	413 616	207 869	205 747	64
Rajapalayam	122 307	61 221	61 086	10	...	...	...	...
Rajarhat Gopalpur	271 811	140 218	131 593	35	...	...	...	...
Rajendranagar	143 240	74 889	68 351	52	...	...	...	...
Rajkot	967 476	506 993	460 483	105	1 003 015	525 898	477 117	163
Rajnandgaon	143 770	72 949	70 821	78	...	...	...	...
Rajpur Sonarpur	336 707	174 140	162 567	55	...	...	...	...
Ramagundam	236 600	120 687	115 913	28	237 686	121 250	116 436	...
Ramgarh	...	...	...	...	110 496	61 591	48 905	50
Rampur	281 494	146 652	134 842	20	...	...	...	...
Ranaghat	...	...	...	...	145 285	73 933	71 352	25
Ranchi	847 093	450 727	396 366	177	863 495	459 462	404 033	182
Raniganj	111 116	59 270	51 846	23	...	...	...	...
Ratlam	222 202	114 370	107 832	39	234 419	120 874	113 545	41
Raurkela	224 987	121 240	103 747	133	484 874	258 731	226 143	157
Raurkela Industrialship	206 693	109 394	97 299	122	...	...	...	...
Rewa	183 274	98 793	84 481	55	...	...	...	...
Rewari	100 684	53 935	46 749	12	...	...	...	...
Rishra	113 305	62 585	50 720	6	...	...	...	...
Robertson Pet	141 424	70 619	70 805	...	157 084	78 578	78 506	...
Rohtak	286 807	154 148	132 659	28	294 577	158 287	136 290	...
Roorkee	...	...	...	...	115 278	64 240	51 038	17
S.A.S. Nagar (Mohali)	123 484	65 642	57 842	24	...	...	...	...
Sagar	232 133	122 385	109 748	36	308 922	162 919	146 003	52
Saharanpur	455 754	241 508	214 246	26	...	...	...	...
Saharasa	125 167	67 718	57 449	21	...	...	...	...
Salem	696 760	353 933	342 827	91	751 438	382 211	369 227	108
Sambalpur	153 643	79 683	73 960	50	226 469	117 745	108 724	90
Sambhal	182 478	97 011	85 467	16	...	...	...	...
Sangli-Miraj-Kupwad	436 781	224 300	212 481	118	447 774	229 958	217 816	121
Santipur	138 235	70 089	68 146	25	...	...	...	...
Sasaram	131 172	69 682	61 490	11	...	...	...	...
Satara	108 048	55 938	52 110	...	...	...	...	...
Satna	225 464	120 277	105 187	...	229 307	122 401	106 906	...
Sawai Madhopur	...	...	...	...	101 997	53 903	48 094	60
Secunderabad	206 102	104 335	101 767	40	...	...	...	...
Serampore	197 857	105 415	92 442	15	...	...	...	...
Serilingampalle	153 364	79 225	74 139	98	...	...	...	...
Shahjahanpur	296 662	160 178	136 484	13	321 885	174 276	147 609	23
Shillong	132 867	66 106	66 761	10	267 662	134 497	133 165	25

8. Population of capital cities and cities of 100 000 or more inhabitants: latest available year, 1988 - 2007
Population des capitales et des villes de 100 000 habitants ou plus: dernière année disponible, 1988 - 2007 (continued - suite)

Continent, country or area, date, code and city / Continent, pays ou zone, date, code et ville	City proper - Ville proprement dite				Urban agglomeration - Agglomération urbaine			
	Population			Surface area - Superficie (km²)	Population			Surface area - Superficie (km²)
	Both sexes - Les deux sexes	Male - Masculin	Female - Féminin		Both sexes - Les deux sexes	Male - Masculin	Female - Féminin	
ASIA - ASIE								
India - Inde[24]								
1 III 2001 (CDFC)								
Shimla	142 555	81 186	61 369	29	144 975	82 840	62 135	30
Shimoga	274 352	140 224	134 128	...	...	...	...	...
Shivapuri	146 892	78 433	68 459	81	...	...	...	...
Sikar	185 323	96 379	88 944	23	185 925	96 697	89 228	...
Silchar	142 199	72 679	69 520	16	184 105	94 306	89 799	...
Siliguri	472 374	250 645	221 729	42	...	...	...	...
Singrauli	185 190	100 149	85 041	...	...	...	...	...
Sirsa	160 735	85 993	74 742	19	...	...	...	...
Sitapur	151 908	79 767	72 141	26	...	...	...	...
Sivakasi	...	...	...	...	121 358	60 841	60 517	27
Siwan	109 919	58 262	51 657	13	...	...	...	...
Solapur	872 478	444 734	427 744	179	...	...	...	...
Sonipat	214 974	117 020	97 954	28	225 074	122 480	102 594	...
South Dum Dum	392 444	200 298	192 146	14	...	...	...	...
Srikakulam	109 905	54 926	54 979	12	117 320	58 753	58 567	14
Srinagar	898 440	484 627	413 813	184	988 210	537 512	450 698	243
Sultan Pur Majra	164 426	88 729	75 697	3	...	...	...	...
Sultanpur	100 065	53 189	46 876	12	...	...	...	...
Surat	2 433 835	1 372 415	1 061 420	112	2 811 614	1 597 156	1 214 458	237
Surendranagar Dudhrej	156 161	81 377	74 784	39	...	...	...	...
Tadepalligudem	102 622	50 925	51 697	21	...	...	...	...
Tambaram	137 933	70 419	67 514	21	...	...	...	...
Tenali	153 756	77 404	76 352	15	...	...	...	...
Tezpur	...	...	...	...	105 377	59 869	45 508	23
Thane	1 262 551	675 147	587 404	128	...	...	...	...
Thanesar	119 687	65 525	54 162	33	122 319	66 978	55 341	36
Thanjavur	215 314	106 625	108 689	15	...	...	...	...
Thiruvananthapuram	744 983	366 235	378 748	142	889 635	437 407	452 228	178
Thoothukkudi (Tuticorin)	216 054	107 758	108 296	13	243 415	121 428	121 987	140
Thrissur	317 526	154 248	163 278	...	330 122	160 443	169 679	88
Tinsukia	...	...	...	...	108 123	59 561	48 562	26
Tiruchchirappalli	752 066	376 125	375 941	147	866 354	434 321	432 033	196
Tirunelveli	411 831	203 232	208 599	109	433 352	214 133	219 219	135
Tirupati	228 202	118 187	110 015	16	303 521	155 468	148 053	20
Tiruppur	344 543	179 930	164 613	27	550 826	286 862	263 964	147
Tiruvannamalai	130 567	66 125	64 442	14	...	...	...	...
Tiruvottiyur	212 281	108 720	103 561	21	...	...	...	...
Titagarh	124 213	70 705	53 508	3	...	...	...	...
Tonk	135 689	70 255	65 434	61	...	...	...	...
Tumkur	248 929	129 273	119 656	...	...	...	...	...
Udaipur	389 438	205 335	184 103	64	...	...	...	...
Udupi	113 112	55 893	57 219	64	127 124	62 596	64 528	73
Ujjain	430 427	223 998	206 429	...	431 162	224 475	206 687	92
Ulhasnagar	473 731	251 888	221 843	13	...	...	...	...
Uluberia	202 135	105 843	96 292	34	...	...	...	...
Unnao	144 662	76 254	68 408	21	...	...	...	...
Uppal Kalan	117 217	60 857	56 360	20	...	...	...	...
Uttarpara Kotrung	150 363	78 808	71 555	16	...	...	...	...
Vadakara	...	...	...	...	124 083	59 803	64 280	51
Vadodara	1 306 227	684 013	622 214	108	1 491 045	782 251	708 794	214
Valsad	...	...	...	...	145 592	75 216	70 376	...
Vaniyambadi	...	...	...	...	103 950	51 886	52 064	16
Varanasi	1 091 918	582 096	509 822	92	1 203 961	643 043	560 918	111
Vasai	...	...	...	...	174 396	91 030	83 366	...
Vejalpur	113 445	58 878	54 567	7	...	...	...	...
Vellore	177 230	87 977	89 253	12	386 746	193 176	193 570	62
Veraval	141 357	72 148	69 209	38	158 032	80 889	77 143	41
Vidisha	125 453	66 572	58 881	6	...	...	...	...
Vijayawada	851 282	431 243	420 039	60	1 039 518	527 307	512 211	101
Virar	118 928	63 704	55 224	20	...	...	...	...
Visakhapatnam	982 904	501 406	481 498	112	1 345 938	687 985	657 953	326
Vizianagarm	174 651	86 375	88 276	21	195 801	97 032	98 769	30
Wadhwan	...	...	...	...	219 585	114 175	105 410	59
Warangal	530 636	268 954	261 682	68	579 216	293 709	285 507	97

8. Population of capital cities and cities of 100 000 or more inhabitants: latest available year, 1988 - 2007
Population des capitales et des villes de 100 000 habitants ou plus: dernière année disponible, 1988 - 2007 (continued - suite)

Continent, country or area, date, code and city / Continent, pays ou zone, date, code et ville	City proper - Ville proprement dite				Urban agglomeration - Agglomération urbaine			
	Population			Surface area - Superficie (km²)	Population			Surface area - Superficie (km²)
	Both sexes - Les deux sexes	Male - Masculin	Female - Féminin		Both sexes - Les deux sexes	Male - Masculin	Female - Féminin	
ASIA - ASIE								
India - Inde[24]								
1 III 2001 (CDFC)								
Wardha	111 118	57 499	53 619	8	...	...	...	...
Yamunanagar	189 696	101 782	87 914	16	306 740	166 137	140 603	42
Yavatmal	120 676	61 780	58 896	10	139 835	71 908	67 927	13
Indonesia - Indonésie								
31 X 2005 (SSDF)								
Ambon	204 218[28]	102 464[28]	101 754[28]	359				
Balikpapan	440 552[28]	223 192[28]	217 360[28]	503	...	...	...	...
Bandar Lampung	790 057[28]	397 214[28]	392 843[28]	193	...	...	...	...
Bandjarmasin	576 413[28]	289 619[28]	286 794[28]	72				
Bandung	2 288 570[28]	1 150 954[28]	1 137 616[28]	1 670	...	...	...	...
Batam	587 227[28]	277 877[28]	309 350[28]	969	...	...	...	...
Bengkulu	252 768[28]	122 801[28]	129 967[28]	145				
Binjai	222 299[28]	112 218[28]	110 081[28]	9				
Bitung	131 999[28]	69 469[28]	62 530[28]	304				
Blitar	126 776[28]	62 310[28]	64 466[28]	33				
Bogor	891 467[28]	440 346[28]	451 121[28]	119				
Cirebon (Tjirebon)	312 771[28]	156 411[28]	156 360[28]	37	...	...	...	...
Denpasar	574 610[28]	288 621[28]	285 989[28]	124	...	...	...	...
Gorontalo	137 461[28]	65 153[28]	72 308[28]	65	...	...	...	...
JAKARTA	8 820 603[28]	4 380 888[28]	4 439 715[28]	740	...	...	...	...
Jambi	409 202[28]	212 043[28]	197 159[28]	205	...	...	...	...
Jayapura	164 220[28]	86 625[28]	77 595[28]	740	...	...	...	...
Kediri	248 640[28]	122 227[28]	126 413[28]	63	...	...	...	...
Madiun	171 390[28]	81 758[28]	89 632[28]	34	...	...	...	...
Magelang	124 374[28]	60 761[28]	63 613[28]	18	...	...	...	...
Makasar (Ujung Pandang)	1 168 258[28]	562 358[28]	605 900[28]	199	...	...	...	...
Malang	773 174[28]	386 100[28]	387 074[28]	145	...	...	...	...
Manado	370 139[28]	184 415[28]	185 724[28]	157	...	...	...	...
Mataram	342 896[28]	173 511[28]	169 385[28]	61	...	...	...	...
Medan	2 029 797[28]	984 046[28]	1 045 751[28]	265	...	...	...	...
Mojokerto	111 860[28]	54 738[28]	57 122[28]	16	...	...	...	...
Padang	686 908[28]	336 655[28]	350 253[28]	694	...	...	...	...
Pakalongan	263 921[28]	128 347[28]	135 574[28]	45	...	...	...	...
Pakanbaru	703 956[28]	351 598[28]	352 358[28]	632	...	...	...	...
Palangkaraya	148 139[28]	74 497[28]	73 642[28]	2 400	...	...	...	...
Palembang	1 323 169[28]	651 161[28]	672 008[28]	369	...	...	...	...
Pangkal Pinang	139 385[28]	70 995[28]	68 390[28]	89	...	...	...	...
Pare Pare	101 453[28]	50 153[28]	51 300[28]	99	...	...	...	...
Pasuruan	166 519[28]	84 375[28]	82 144[28]	35	...	...	...	...
Pematang Siantar	229 525[28]	114 684[28]	114 841[28]	80	...	...	...	...
Pontianak	501 843[28]	252 304[28]	249 539[28]	108	...	...	...	...
Probolinggo	168 734[28]	83 946[28]	84 788[28]	57	...	...	...	...
Salatiga	152 913[28]	74 184[28]	78 729[28]	57	...	...	...	...
Samarinda	505 664[28]	262 407[28]	243 257[28]	781	...	...	...	...
Semarang	1 352 869[28]	674 649[28]	678 220[28]	374	...	...	...	...
Sukabumi	280 373[28]	145 910[28]	134 463[28]	48	...	...	...	...
Surabaya	2 611 506[28]	1 270 795[28]	1 340 711[28]	351	...	...	...	...
Surakarta	506 397[28]	251 977[28]	254 420[28]	44	...	...	...	...
Tangerang	1 451 595[28]	740 589[28]	711 006[28]	187	...	...	...	...
Tanjung Balai	133 897[28]	65 893[28]	68 004[28]	68	...	...	...	...
Tebing Tinggi	134 548[28]	65 801[28]	68 747[28]	32	...	...	...	...
Tegal	238 676[28]	119 457[28]	119 219[28]	35	...	...	...	...
Yogyakarta	433 539[28]	216 222[28]	217 317[28]	33	...	...	...	...
Iran (Islamic Republic of) - Iran (République islamique d')								
28 X 2006 (CDJC)								
Abadan	219 772	...	...	...	...	...	...	...
Ahwaz	985 614	...	...	...	...	...	...	...
Amol	199 698	...	...	...	...	...	...	...
Andimeshk	120 177	...	...	...	...	...	...	...
Arak	446 760	...	...	...	...	...	...	...

8. Population of capital cities and cities of 100 000 or more inhabitants: latest available year, 1988 - 2007
Population des capitales et des villes de 100 000 habitants ou plus: dernière année disponible, 1988 - 2007 (continued - suite)

Continent, country or area, date, code and city / Continent, pays ou zone, date, code et ville	City proper - Ville proprement dite				Urban agglomeration - Agglomération urbaine			
	Population			Surface area - Superficie (km²)	Population			Surface area - Superficie (km²)
	Both sexes - Les deux sexes	Male - Masculin	Female - Féminin		Both sexes - Les deux sexes	Male - Masculin	Female - Féminin	
ASIA - ASIE								
Iran (Islamic Republic of) - Iran (République islamique d')								
28 X 2006 (CDJC)								
Ardabil	418 262	...	...	...	...	...	...	...
Babol	201 335	...	...	...	...	...	...	...
Bandar Anzali	110 643	...	...	...	...	...	...	...
Bandar-e-Abbas	379 301	...	...	...	...	...	...	...
Bandar-e-Mahshahr	111 448	...	...	...	...	...	...	...
Behbahan	101 178	...	...	...	...	...	...	...
Birjand	166 138	...	...	...	...	...	...	...
Bojnurd	176 726	...	...	...	...	...	...	...
Borujerd	229 541	...	...	...	...	...	...	...
Bukand	150 703	...	...	...	...	...	...	...
Bushehr	169 966	...	...	...	...	...	...	...
Dezful	235 819	...	...	...	...	...	...	...
Dorud	101 219	...	...	...	...	...	...	...
Esfahan	1 602 110	...	...	...	...	...	...	...
Golestan (Soltanabad)	231 905	...	...	...	...	...	...	...
Gonbad-e-Kavus	129 167	...	...	...	...	...	...	...
Gorgan	274 438	...	...	...	...	...	...	...
Hamadan	479 640	...	...	...	...	...	...	...
Ilam	160 355	...	...	...	...	...	...	...
Iranshahr	100 642	...	...	...	...	...	...	...
Islam Shahr (Qasemabad)	357 389	...	...	...	...	...	...	...
Izeh	104 364	...	...	...	...	...	...	...
Jahrom	105 285	...	...	...	...	...	...	...
Karaj	1 386 030	...	...	...	...	...	...	...
Kashan	253 509	...	...	...	...	...	...	...
Kerman	515 114	...	...	...	...	...	...	...
Kermanshah	794 863	...	...	...	...	...	...	...
Khomeini shahr	223 071	...	...	...	...	...	...	...
Khoramabad	333 945	...	...	...	...	...	...	...
Khoramshahr	125 859	...	...	...	...	...	...	...
Khoy	181 465	...	...	...	...	...	...	...
Mahabad	135 780	...	...	...	...	...	...	...
Malard	228 713	...	...	...	...	...	...	...
Malayer	156 289	...	...	...	...	...	...	...
Marand	114 841	...	...	...	...	...	...	...
Maraqeh	149 929	...	...	...	...	...	...	...
Marvadsht	124 350	...	...	...	...	...	...	...
Mashhad	2 427 316	...	...	...	...	...	...	...
Masjed Soleyman	108 682	...	...	...	...	...	...	...
Miandoab	114 153	...	...	...	...	...	...	...
Najafabad	208 647	...	...	...	...	...	...	...
Nasim Shahr	135 846	...	...	...	...	...	...	...
Neyshabur	208 860	...	...	...	...	...	...	...
Orumiyeh	583 255	...	...	...	...	...	...	...
Pakdasht	126 937	...	...	...	...	...	...	...
Qaem shahr	174 768	...	...	...	...	...	...	...
Qarchak	174 006	...	...	...	...	...	...	...
Qazvin	355 338	...	...	...	...	...	...	...
Qods	230 147	...	...	...	...	...	...	...
Qom	964 706	...	...	...	...	...	...	...
Quchan	101 313	...	...	...	...	...	...	...
Rafsanjan	139 219	...	...	...	...	...	...	...
Rasht	557 366	...	...	...	...	...	...	...
Sabzewar	214 582	...	...	...	...	...	...	...
Sanandaj	316 862	...	...	...	...	...	...	...
Saqez	133 331	...	...	...	...	...	...	...
Sari	261 293	...	...	...	...	...	...	...
Saveh	180 548	...	...	...	...	...	...	...
Semnan	126 780	...	...	...	...	...	...	...
Shahinshahr	127 412	...	...	...	...	...	...	...
Shahr-e-Kord	131 612	...	...	...	...	...	...	...
Shahreza	109 601	...	...	...	...	...	...	...
Shahriar	189 421	...	...	...	...	...	...	...

Continent, country or area, date, code and city / Continent, pays ou zone, date, code et ville	City proper - Ville proprement dite				Urban agglomeration - Agglomération urbaine			
	Population			Surface area - Superficie (km²)	Population			Surface area - Superficie (km²)
	Both sexes - Les deux sexes	Male - Masculin	Female - Féminin		Both sexes - Les deux sexes	Male - Masculin	Female - Féminin	
ASIA - ASIE								
Iran (Islamic Republic of) - Iran (République islamique d')								
28 X 2006 (CDJC)								
Shahrud	132 379	...	...	...	...	...	...	...
Shiraz	1 227 331	...	...	...	...	...	...	...
Sirjan	170 916	...	...	...	...	...	...	...
Tabriz	1 398 060	...	...	...	...	...	...	...
TEHRAN	7 088 287	...	...	...	...	...	...	...
Torbat-e-heydariyeh	121 300	...	...	...	...	...	...	...
Varamin	208 996	...	...	...	...	...	...	...
Yazd	432 194	...	...	...	...	...	...	...
Zabol	136 956	...	...	...	...	...	...	...
Zahedan	567 449	...	...	...	...	...	...	...
Zanjan	349 713	...	...	...	...	...	...	...
Israel - Israël								
1 VII 2007 (ESDJ)								
Ashdod	205 594[29]	101 046[29]	104 549[29]	47	...	...	...	...
Ashqelon	108 327[29]	52 820[29]	55 508[29]	48	...	...	...	...
Bat Yam	129 265[29]	61 060[29]	68 205[29]	8	...	...	...	...
Be'er Sheva	185 781[29]	90 311[29]	95 471[29]	53	...	...	...	...
Bene Beraq	149 450[29]	75 147[29]	74 304[29]	7	...	...	...	...
Haifa	265 611[29]	127 538[29]	138 074[29]	64	...	...	...	...
Holon	167 928[29]	80 771[29]	87 157[29]	19	...	...	...	...
JERUSALEM[30]	740 475	368 950	371 525	125	...	...	...	...
Netanya	175 150[29]	84 610[29]	90 540[29]	29	...	...	...	...
Petah Tiqwa	186 532[29]	90 430[29]	96 103[29]	36	...	...	...	...
Ramat Gan	129 774[29]	60 997[29]	68 777[29]	13	...	...	...	...
Rehovot	105 371[29]	51 466[29]	53 905[29]	23	...	...	...	...
Rishon Leziyyon	223 153[29]	108 842[29]	114 311[29]	59	...	...	...	...
Tel Aviv-Yafo	387 234[29]	186 918[29]	200 316[29]	52	...	...	...	...
Japan - Japon								
1 X 2005 (CDJC)								
Abiko	131 205[31]	64 853[31]	66 352[31]	43	...	...	...	...
Ageo	220 232[31]	110 102[31]	110 130[31]	46	...	...	...	...
Aizuwakamatsu	122 248[31]	58 067[31]	64 181[31]	343	...	...	...	...
Akashi	291 027[31]	141 749[31]	149 278[31]	49	...	...	...	...
Akishima	110 143[31]	55 446[31]	54 697[31]	17	...	...	...	...
Akita	333 109[31]	158 107[31]	175 002[31]	906	...	...	...	...
Amagasaki	462 647[31]	226 084[31]	236 563[31]	50	...	...	...	...
Anjo	170 250[31]	87 022[31]	83 228[31]	86	...	...	...	...
Aomori	311 508[31]	145 965[31]	165 543[31]	825	...	...	...	...
Asahikawa	355 004[31]	165 387[31]	189 617[31]	748	...	...	...	...
Asaka	124 393[31]	65 460[31]	58 933[31]	18	...	...	...	...
Ashikaga	159 756[31]	78 120[31]	81 636[31]	178	...	...	...	...
Atsugi	222 403[31]	116 150[31]	106 253[31]	94	...	...	...	...
Beppu	126 959[31]	57 392[31]	69 567[31]	125	...	...	...	...
Chiba	924 319[31]	462 961[31]	461 358[31]	272	...	...	...	...
Chigasaki	228 420[31]	113 272[31]	115 148[31]	36	...	...	...	...
Chikusei	112 581[31]	55 795[31]	56 786[31]	205	...	...	...	...
Chofu	216 119[31]	109 098[31]	107 021[31]	22	...	...	...	...
Daito	126 504[31]	62 840[31]	63 664[31]	18	...	...	...	...
Ebetsu	125 601[31]	60 807[31]	64 794[31]	188	...	...	...	...
Ebina	123 764[31]	63 089[31]	60 675[31]	26	...	...	...	...
Fuchu	245 623[31]	127 575[31]	118 048[31]	29	...	...	...	...
Fuji	236 474[31]	117 069[31]	119 405[31]	214	...	...	...	...
Fujieda	129 248[31]	62 921[31]	66 327[31]	141	...	...	...	...
Fujimi	104 748[31]	52 491[31]	52 257[31]	20	...	...	...	...
Fujimino	101 960[31]	51 349[31]	50 611[31]	15	...	...	...	...
Fujinomiya	121 779[31]	60 113[31]	61 666[31]	315	...	...	...	...
Fujisawa	396 014[31]	198 365[31]	197 649[31]	70	...	...	...	...
Fukaya	103 529[31]	51 692[31]	51 837[31]	69	...	...	...	...
Fukui	252 220[31]	122 750[31]	129 470[31]	341	...	...	...	...
Fukuoka	1 401 279[31]	673 097[31]	728 182[31]	341	...	...	...	...

293

Continent, country or area, date, code and city / Continent, pays ou zone, date, code et ville	City proper - Ville proprement dite				Urban agglomeration - Agglomération urbaine			
	Population			Surface area - Superficie (km²)	Population			Surface area - Superficie (km²)
	Both sexes - Les deux sexes	Male - Masculin	Female - Féminin		Both sexes - Les deux sexes	Male - Masculin	Female - Féminin	

ASIA - ASIE

Japan - Japon
1 X 2005 (CDJC)

Fukushima	290 869[31]	140 013[31]	150 856[31]	746	...	...	...	...
Fukuyama	418 509[31]	201 999[31]	216 510[31]	461	...	...	...	...
Funabashi	569 835[31]	288 667[31]	281 168[31]	86	...	...	...	...
Gifu	399 931[31]	189 633[31]	210 298[31]	195	...	...	...	...
Habikino	118 695[31]	56 447[31]	62 248[31]	26	...	...	...	...
Hachinohe	244 700[31]	117 446[31]	127 254[31]	305	...	...	...	...
Hachioji	560 012[31]	286 154[31]	273 858[31]	186	...	...	...	...
Hadano	168 317[31]	86 664[31]	81 653[31]	104	...	...	...	...
Hakodate	294 264[31]	134 868[31]	159 396[31]	678	...	...	...	...
Hakusan	109 450[31]	53 129[31]	56 321[31]	755	...	...	...	...
Hamamatsu	804 032[31]	399 704[31]	404 328[31]	1 511	...	...	...	...
Handa	115 845[31]	57 626[31]	58 219[31]	47	...	...	...	...
Higashihiroshima	184 430[31]	93 960[31]	90 470[31]	635	...	...	...	...
Higashikurume	115 330[31]	57 123[31]	58 207[31]	13	...	...	...	...
Higashimurayama	144 929[31]	71 635[31]	73 294[31]	17	...	...	...	...
Higashiosaka	513 821[31]	251 708[31]	262 113[31]	62	...	...	...	...
Hikone	109 779[31]	54 136[31]	55 643[31]	98	...	...	...	...
Himeji	482 304[31]	232 553[31]	249 751[31]	276	...	...	...	...
Hino	176 538[31]	90 636[31]	85 902[31]	28	...	...	...	...
Hirakata	404 044[31]	195 236[31]	208 808[31]	65	...	...	...	...
Hiratsuka	258 958[31]	132 156[31]	126 802[31]	68	...	...	...	...
Hirosaki	173 221[31]	79 299[31]	93 922[31]	274	...	...	...	...
Hiroshima	1 154 391[31]	559 345[31]	595 046[31]	905	...	...	...	...
Hitachi	199 218[31]	99 212[31]	100 006[31]	226	...	...	...	...
Hitachinaka	153 639[31]	77 331[31]	76 308[31]	99	...	...	...	...
Hofu	116 818[31]	56 332[31]	60 486[31]	189	...	...	...	...
Ibaraki	267 961[31]	131 135[31]	136 826[31]	77	...	...	...	...
Ichihara	280 255[31]	143 404[31]	136 851[31]	368	...	...	...	...
Ichikawa	466 608[31]	239 659[31]	226 949[31]	57	...	...	...	...
Ichinomiya	371 687[31]	181 614[31]	190 073[31]	114	...	...	...	...
Ichinoseki	125 818[31]	60 793[31]	65 025[31]	1 133	...	...	...	...
Iga	100 623[31]	48 675[31]	51 948[31]	558	...	...	...	...
Iida	108 624[31]	51 706[31]	56 918[31]	659	...	...	...	...
Ikeda	101 616[31]	49 682[31]	51 934[31]	22	...	...	...	...
Ikoma	113 686[31]	53 937[31]	59 749[31]	53	...	...	...	...
Imabari	173 983[31]	80 745[31]	93 238[31]	420	...	...	...	...
Inazawa	136 965[31]	67 754[31]	69 211[31]	79	...	...	...	...
Iruma	148 576[31]	73 574[31]	75 002[31]	45	...	...	...	...
Isahaya	144 034[31]	68 154[31]	75 880[31]	312	...	...	...	...
Isehara	100 579[31]	51 630[31]	48 949[31]	56	...	...	...	...
Isesaki	202 447[31]	101 019[31]	101 428[31]	139	...	...	...	...
Ishinomaki	167 324[31]	80 553[31]	86 771[31]	556	...	...	...	...
Itami	192 250[31]	94 232[31]	98 018[31]	25	...	...	...	...
Iwaki	354 492[31]	172 169[31]	182 323[31]	1 231	...	...	...	...
Iwakuni	103 507[31]	49 240[31]	54 267[31]	222	...	...	...	...
Iwata	170 899[31]	86 262[31]	84 637[31]	164	...	...	...	...
Izumi (Osaka)	177 856[31]	86 339[31]	91 517[31]	85	...	...	...	...
Izumo	146 307[31]	69 901[31]	76 406[31]	543	...	...	...	...
Joetsu	208 082[31]	100 884[31]	107 198[31]	973	...	...	...	...
Kadoma	131 706[31]	65 229[31]	66 477[31]	12	...	...	...	...
Kagoshima	604 367[31]	281 389[31]	322 978[31]	547	...	...	...	...
Kakamigahara	144 174[31]	70 696[31]	73 478[31]	88	...	...	...	...
Kakegawa	117 857[31]	58 862[31]	58 995[31]	266	...	...	...	...
Kakogawa	267 100[31]	130 694[31]	136 406[31]	139	...	...	...	...
Kamagaya	102 812[31]	50 969[31]	51 843[31]	21	...	...	...	...
Kamakura	171 158[31]	81 443[31]	89 715[31]	40	...	...	...	...
Kanazawa	454 607[31]	220 679[31]	233 928[31]	468	...	...	...	...
Karatsu	128 564[31]	59 962[31]	68 602[31]	425	...	...	...	...
Kariya	142 134[31]	74 800[31]	67 334[31]	50	...	...	...	...
Kashihara	124 728[31]	59 792[31]	64 936[31]	40	...	...	...	...

8. Population of capital cities and cities of 100 000 or more inhabitants: latest available year, 1988 - 2007
Population des capitales et des villes de 100 000 habitants ou plus: dernière année disponible, 1988 - 2007 (continued - suite)

Continent, country or area, date, code and city / Continent, pays ou zone, date, code et ville	City proper - Ville proprement dite				Urban agglomeration - Agglomération urbaine			
	Population			Surface area - Superficie (km²)	Population			Surface area - Superficie (km²)
	Both sexes - Les deux sexes	Male - Masculin	Female - Féminin		Both sexes - Les deux sexes	Male - Masculin	Female - Féminin	

ASIA - ASIE

Japan - Japon
1 X 2005 (CDJC)

Kashiwa	380 963[31]	190 138[31]	190 825[31]	115	...	...	...	...
Kasuga	108 402[31]	52 815[31]	55 587[31]	14	...	...	...	...
Kasugai	295 802[31]	147 732[31]	148 070[31]	93	...	...	...	...
Kawachinagano	117 239[31]	55 618[31]	61 621[31]	110	...	...	...	...
Kawagoe	333 795[31]	168 943[31]	164 852[31]	109	...	...	...	...
Kawaguchi	480 079[31]	246 310[31]	233 769[31]	56	...	...	...	...
Kawanishi	157 668[31]	74 928[31]	82 740[31]	53	...	...	...	...
Kawasaki	1 327 011[31]	687 080[31]	639 931[31]	143	...	...	...	...
Kiryu	128 037[31]	61 796[31]	66 241[31]	275	...	...	...	...
Kisarazu	122 234[31]	60 947[31]	61 287[31]	139	...	...	...	...
Kishiwada	201 000[31]	96 866[31]	104 134[31]	72	...	...	...	...
Kitakyushu[32]	993 525[31]	466 779[31]	526 746[31]	488	...	...	...	...
Kitami	110 715[31]	53 484[31]	57 231[31]	421	...	...	...	...
Kobe	1 525 393[31]	724 427[31]	800 966[31]	552	...	...	...	...
Kochi	333 484[31]	155 025[31]	178 459[31]	264	...	...	...	...
Kodaira	183 796[31]	91 756[31]	92 040[31]	20	...	...	...	...
Kofu	194 244[31]	95 535[31]	98 709[31]	172	...	...	...	...
Koga	145 265[31]	72 399[31]	72 866[31]	124	...	...	...	...
Koganei	114 112[31]	57 696[31]	56 416[31]	11	...	...	...	...
Kokubunji	117 604[31]	58 889[31]	58 715[31]	11	...	...	...	...
Komaki	147 182[31]	74 526[31]	72 656[31]	63	...	...	...	...
Komatsu	109 084[31]	52 782[31]	56 302[31]	371	...	...	...	...
Konosu	119 594[31]	59 595[31]	59 999[31]	67	...	...	...	...
Koriyama	338 834[31]	167 071[31]	171 763[31]	757	...	...	...	...
Koshigaya	315 792[31]	158 721[31]	157 071[31]	60	...	...	...	...
Kumagaya	191 107[31]	95 743[31]	95 364[31]	137	...	...	...	...
Kumamoto	669 603[31]	316 048[31]	353 555[31]	267	...	...	...	...
Kurashiki	469 377[31]	227 334[31]	242 043[31]	354	...	...	...	...
Kure	251 003[31]	120 435[31]	130 568[31]	353	...	...	...	...
Kurume	306 434[31]	145 210[31]	161 224[31]	230	...	...	...	...
Kusatsu	121 159[31]	63 071[31]	58 088[31]	48	...	...	...	...
Kushiro	181 516[31]	86 007[31]	95 509[31]	222	...	...	...	...
Kuwana	138 963[31]	68 145[31]	70 818[31]	137	...	...	...	...
Kyoto	1 474 811[31]	703 210[31]	771 601[31]	828	...	...	...	...
Machida	405 534[31]	200 197[31]	205 337[31]	72	...	...	...	...
Maebashi	318 584[31]	155 480[31]	163 104[31]	241	...	...	...	...
Marugame	110 085[31]	53 090[31]	56 995[31]	112	...	...	...	...
Matsubara	127 276[31]	61 776[31]	65 500[31]	17	...	...	...	...
Matsudo	472 579[31]	237 562[31]	235 017[31]	61	...	...	...	...
Matsue	196 603[31]	94 638[31]	101 965[31]	530	...	...	...	...
Matsumoto	227 627[31]	112 083[31]	115 544[31]	919	...	...	...	...
Matsusaka	168 973[31]	81 320[31]	87 653[31]	624	...	...	...	...
Matsuyama	514 937[31]	242 463[31]	272 474[31]	429	...	...	...	...
Mihara	104 196[31]	49 729[31]	54 467[31]	471	...	...	...	...
Minoh	127 135[31]	61 286[31]	65 849[31]	48	...	...	...	...
Misato	128 278[31]	65 307[31]	62 971[31]	30	...	...	...	...
Mishima	112 241[31]	55 054[31]	57 187[31]	62	...	...	...	...
Mitaka	177 016[31]	88 579[31]	88 437[31]	17	...	...	...	...
Mito	262 603[31]	127 435[31]	135 168[31]	217	...	...	...	...
Miyakonojo	133 062[31]	62 426[31]	70 636[31]	306	...	...	...	...
Miyazaki	310 123[31]	145 263[31]	164 860[31]	287	...	...	...	...
Moriguchi	147 465[31]	71 972[31]	75 493[31]	13	...	...	...	...
Morioka	287 192[31]	137 262[31]	149 930[31]	489	...	...	...	...
Musashino	137 525[31]	66 628[31]	70 897[31]	11	...	...	...	...
Nagano	378 512[31]	183 065[31]	195 447[31]	731	...	...	...	...
Nagaoka	236 344[31]	115 726[31]	120 618[31]	526	...	...	...	...
Nagareyama	152 641[31]	75 643[31]	76 998[31]	35	...	...	...	...
Nagasaki	442 699[31]	203 292[31]	239 407[31]	339	...	...	...	...
Nagoya	2 215 062[31]	1 099 582[31]	1 115 480[31]	326	...	...	...	...

8. Population of capital cities and cities of 100 000 or more inhabitants: latest available year, 1988 - 2007
Population des capitales et des villes de 100 000 habitants ou plus: dernière année disponible, 1988 - 2007 (continued - suite)

Continent, country or area, date, code and city / Continent, pays ou zone, date, code et ville	City proper - Ville proprement dite				Urban agglomeration - Agglomération urbaine			
	Population			Surface area - Superficie (km²)	Population			Surface area - Superficie (km²)
	Both sexes - Les deux sexes	Male - Masculin	Female - Féminin		Both sexes - Les deux sexes	Male - Masculin	Female - Féminin	

ASIA - ASIE

Japan - Japon
  1 X 2005 (CDJC)

Naha	312 393[31]	150 463[31]	161 930[31]	39	...	...	...	...
Nara	370 102[31]	174 469[31]	195 633[31]	277	...	...	...	...
Narashino	158 785[31]	80 308[31]	78 477[31]	21	...	...	...	...
Narita	100 717[31]	50 592[31]	50 125[31]	131	...	...	...	...
Nasushiobara	115 032[31]	57 184[31]	57 848[31]	593	...	...	...	...
Neyagawa	241 816[31]	118 593[31]	123 223[31]	25	...	...	...	...
Niigata	785 134[31]	378 725[31]	406 409[31]	650	...	...	...	...
Niihama	123 952[31]	59 190[31]	64 762[31]	234	...	...	...	...
Niiza	153 305[31]	77 310[31]	75 995[31]	23	...	...	...	...
Nishinomiya	465 337[31]	221 205[31]	244 132[31]	99	...	...	...	...
Nishio	104 321[31]	52 584[31]	51 737[31]	76	...	...	...	...
Nishitokyo	189 735[31]	94 046[31]	95 689[31]	16	...	...	...	...
Nobeoka	121 635[31]	56 816[31]	64 819[31]	284	...	...	...	...
Noda	151 240[31]	75 797[31]	75 443[31]	104	...	...	...	...
Numazu	208 005[31]	102 259[31]	105 746[31]	187	...	...	...	...
Obihiro	170 580[31]	81 906[31]	88 674[31]	619	...	...	...	...
Odawara	198 741[31]	97 501[31]	101 240[31]	114	...	...	...	...
Ogaki	151 030[31]	73 398[31]	77 632[31]	80	...	...	...	...
Oita	462 317[31]	221 539[31]	240 778[31]	501	...	...	...	...
Okayama	674 746[31]	324 623[31]	350 123[31]	659	...	...	...	...
Okazaki	354 704[31]	179 294[31]	175 410[31]	227	...	...	...	...
Okinawa	126 400[31]	60 896[31]	65 504[31]	49	...	...	...	...
Ome	142 354[31]	71 731[31]	70 623[31]	103	...	...	...	...
Omuta	131 090[31]	59 452[31]	71 638[31]	82	...	...	...	...
Onomichi	114 486[31]	54 018[31]	60 468[31]	212	...	...	...	...
Osaka	2 628 811[31]	1 280 325[31]	1 348 486[31]	222	...	...	...	...
Ota	213 299[31]	107 556[31]	105 743[31]	176	...	...	...	...
Otaru	142 161[31]	64 436[31]	77 725[31]	243	...	...	...	...
Otsu	301 672[31]	146 353[31]	155 319[31]	302	...	...	...	...
Oyama	160 150[31]	80 723[31]	79 427[31]	172	...	...	...	...
Saga	206 967[31]	98 013[31]	108 954[31]	355	...	...	...	...
Sagamihara	628 698[31]	318 986[31]	309 712[31]	90	...	...	...	...
Saijo	113 371[31]	54 144[31]	59 227[31]	509	...	...	...	...
Saitama	1 176 314[31]	590 972[31]	585 342[31]	217	...	...	...	...
Sakai	830 966[31]	400 294[31]	430 672[31]	150	...	...	...	...
Saku	100 462[31]	49 041[31]	51 421[31]	424	...	...	...	...
Sakura	171 246[31]	84 050[31]	87 196[31]	104	...	...	...	...
Sanda	113 572[31]	54 881[31]	58 691[31]	210	...	...	...	...
Sanjo	104 749[31]	50 660[31]	54 089[31]	432	...	...	...	...
Sano	123 926[31]	60 917[31]	63 009[31]	356	...	...	...	...
Sapporo	1 880 863[31]	889 054[31]	991 809[31]	1 121	...	...	...	...
Sasebo	248 041[31]	116 726[31]	131 315[31]	308	...	...	...	...
Satsumasendai	102 370[31]	48 195[31]	54 175[31]	684	...	...	...	...
Sayama	158 074[31]	80 072[31]	78 002[31]	49	...	...	...	...
Sendai	1 025 098[31]	500 597[31]	524 501[31]	784	...	...	...	...
Seto	131 925[31]	65 471[31]	66 454[31]	112	...	...	...	...
Shibata	104 634[31]	50 431[31]	54 203[31]	533	...	...	...	...
Shimonoseki	290 693[31]	134 741[31]	155 952[31]	716	...	...	...	...
Shizuoka	700 886[31]	340 999[31]	359 887[31]	1 374	...	...	...	...
Shunan	152 387[31]	73 058[31]	79 329[31]	656	...	...	...	...
Soka	236 316[31]	120 673[31]	115 643[31]	27	...	...	...	...
Suita	353 885[31]	173 154[31]	180 731[31]	36	...	...	...	...
Suzuka	193 114[31]	96 577[31]	96 537[31]	195	...	...	...	...
Tachikawa	172 566[31]	85 889[31]	86 677[31]	24	...	...	...	...
Tajimi	103 821[31]	50 283[31]	53 538[31]	78	...	...	...	...
Takamatsu	337 902[31]	163 509[31]	174 393[31]	274	...	...	...	...
Takaoka	167 685[31]	80 216[31]	87 469[31]	151	...	...	...	...
Takarazuka	219 862[31]	103 495[31]	116 367[31]	102	...	...	...	...
Takasaki	245 100[31]	120 607[31]	124 493[31]	111	...	...	...	...
Takatsuki	351 826[31]	170 102[31]	181 724[31]	105	...	...	...	...

Continent, country or area, date, code and city / Continent, pays ou zone, date, code et ville	City proper - Ville proprement dite				Urban agglomeration - Agglomération urbaine			
	Population			Surface area - Superficie (km²)	Population			Surface area - Superficie (km²)
	Both sexes - Les deux sexes	Male - Masculin	Female - Féminin		Both sexes - Les deux sexes	Male - Masculin	Female - Féminin	
ASIA - ASIE								
Japan - Japon								
1 X 2005 (CDJC)								
Tama	145 877[31]	73 140[31]	72 737[31]	21	...	...	...	...
Toda	116 696[31]	61 254[31]	55 442[31]	18	...	...	...	...
Tokai	104 339[31]	54 737[31]	49 602[31]	43	...	...	...	...
Tokorozawa	336 100[31]	169 176[31]	166 924[31]	72	...	...	...	...
Tokushima	267 833[31]	127 241[31]	140 592[31]	191	...	...	...	...
TOKYO[33]	8 489 653[31]	4 210 749[31]	4 278 904[31]	621	12 576 601[31]	6 264 895[31]	6 311 706[31]	2 187
Tomakomai	172 758[31]	83 935[31]	88 823[31]	561	...	...	...	...
Tondabayashi	123 837[31]	58 946[31]	64 891[31]	40	...	...	...	...
Toride	111 327[31]	54 899[31]	56 428[31]	70	...	...	...	...
Tottori	201 740[31]	98 333[31]	103 407[31]	766	...	...	...	...
Toyama	421 239[31]	204 407[31]	216 832[31]	1 242	...	...	...	...
Toyohashi	372 479[31]	186 116[31]	186 363[31]	261	...	...	...	...
Toyokawa	120 967[31]	60 337[31]	60 630[31]	65	...	...	...	...
Toyonaka	386 623[31]	186 440[31]	200 183[31]	36	...	...	...	...
Toyota	412 141[31]	218 286[31]	193 855[31]	918	...	...	...	...
Tsu	165 182[31]	80 544[31]	84 638[31]	102	...	...	...	...
Tsuchiura	135 058[31]	67 254[31]	67 804[31]	82	...	...	...	...
Tsukuba	200 528[31]	103 110[31]	97 418[31]	284	...	...	...	...
Tsuruoka	142 384[31]	67 676[31]	74 708[31]	1 311	...	...	...	...
Tsuyama	110 569[31]	52 418[31]	58 151[31]	506	...	...	...	...
Ube	178 955[31]	85 444[31]	93 511[31]	288	...	...	...	...
Ueda	123 680[31]	60 383[31]	63 297[31]	177	...	...	...	...
Uji	189 591[31]	92 286[31]	97 305[31]	68	...	...	...	...
Urasoe	106 049[31]	52 128[31]	53 921[31]	19	...	...	...	...
Urayasu	155 290[31]	79 275[31]	76 015[31]	17	...	...	...	...
Uruma	113 535[31]	56 598[31]	56 937[31]	86	...	...	...	...
Utsunomiya	457 673[31]	229 006[31]	228 667[31]	312	...	...	...	...
Wakayama	375 591[31]	176 825[31]	198 766[31]	209	...	...	...	...
Yachiyo	180 729[31]	89 601[31]	91 128[31]	51	...	...	...	...
Yaizu	120 109[31]	58 484[31]	61 625[31]	46	...	...	...	...
Yamagata	256 012[31]	122 903[31]	133 109[31]	381	...	...	...	...
Yamaguchi	191 677[31]	91 263[31]	100 414[31]	730	...	...	...	...
Yamato	221 220[31]	111 802[31]	109 418[31]	27	...	...	...	...
Yao	273 487[31]	132 627[31]	140 860[31]	42	...	...	...	...
Yatsushiro	136 886[31]	63 823[31]	73 063[31]	680	...	...	...	...
Yokkaichi	303 845[31]	149 692[31]	154 153[31]	205	...	...	...	...
Yokohama	3 579 628[31]	1 803 579[31]	1 776 049[31]	437	...	...	...	...
Yokosuka	426 178[31]	214 029[31]	212 149[31]	101	...	...	...	...
Yokote	103 652[31]	48 811[31]	54 841[31]	694	...	...	...	...
Yonago	149 584[31]	71 053[31]	78 531[31]	132	...	...	...	...
Zama	128 174[31]	65 860[31]	62 314[31]	18	...	...	...	...
Jordan - Jordanie								
31 XII 2007 (ESDF)								
AMMAN	1 204 110	619 290	584 820	...	...	...	...	...
Irbid	275 054	141 172	133 882	...	...	...	...	...
Russiefa	253 964	132 081	121 883	...	...	...	...	...
Zarqa	440 736	227 717	213 019	...	...	...	...	...
Kazakhstan								
1 I 2007 (ESDF)								
Aktau	167 460	81 111	86 349	29	...	...	...	...
Aktobe	262 830	121 555	141 275	234	...	...	...	...
Almaty	1 287 246	585 212	702 034	32	...	...	...	...
ASTANA	574 448	282 259	292 189	71	...	...	...	...
Atirau	155 173	73 044	82 129	347	...	...	...	...
Ekibastuz	120 387	56 198	64 189	31	...	...	...	...
Karaganda	453 271	205 812	247 459	50	...	...	...	...
Koktshetau	129 244	58 671	70 573	43	...	...	...	...
Kustanai	208 262	93 905	114 357	21	...	...	...	...
Kyzylorda	164 103	77 841	86 262	236	...	...	...	...
Pavlodar	300 226	136 399	163 827	56	...	...	...	...

8. Population of capital cities and cities of 100 000 or more inhabitants: latest available year, 1988 - 2007
Population des capitales et des villes de 100 000 habitants ou plus: dernière année disponible, 1988 - 2007 (continued - suite)

Continent, country or area, date, code and city / Continent, pays ou zone, date, code et ville	City proper - Ville proprement dite				Urban agglomeration - Agglomération urbaine			
	Population			Surface area - Superficie (km²)	Population			Surface area - Superficie (km²)
	Both sexes - Les deux sexes	Male - Masculin	Female - Féminin		Both sexes - Les deux sexes	Male - Masculin	Female - Féminin	
ASIA - ASIE								
Kazakhstan								
1 I 2007 (ESDF)								
Petropavlovsk (Severo- Kazakhstanskaya oblast)	192 449	86 468	105 981	22	...	...	...	...
Rudni	109 759	50 564	59 195	19	...	...	...	...
Semipalatinsk	279 910	125 830	154 080	9	...	...	...	...
Shimkent	535 125	254 225	280 900	36	...	...	...	...
Taldykorgan	110 686	49 456	61 230	39	...	...	...	...
Taraz	338 454	154 901	183 553	13	...	...	...	...
Temirtau	162 567	74 482	88 085	30	...	...	...	...
Uralsk	205 277	92 630	112 647	71	...	...	...	...
Ust-Kamenogorsk	287 693	129 006	158 687	54	...	...	...	...
Kuwait - Koweït								
20 IV 2005* (CDFC)								
KUWAIT CITY	32 403	26 706	5 697	...	...	...	...	...
Kyrgyzstan - Kirghizstan								
1 VII 2007 (ESDJ)								
BISHKEK	798 300	380 900	417 400	...	810 200	386 800	423 400	127
Osh	223 200	106 600	116 600	...	249 800	119 800	130 000	182
Lao People's Democratic Republic - République démocratique populaire lao								
1 III 1995 (CDFC)								
VIENTIANE	...	...	...	...	528 100	...	...	...
Lebanon - Liban[34]								
3 III 2007 (SSDF)								
BEIRUT	361 366	166 282	195 084	...	...	...	...	...
Malaysia - Malaisie[35]								
1 VII 2007 (ESDF)								
Alor Setar	145 926	...	...	...	...	...	...	...
Ampang/Ulu Kelang	117 251	...	...	...	...	...	...	...
Bintulu	123 355	...	...	...	...	...	...	...
George Town	192 798	...	...	...	...	...	...	...
Ipoh	471 575	...	...	...	...	...	...	...
Johor Bahru	508 085	...	...	...	...	...	...	...
Kajang dan Sungai Chua	108 817	...	...	...	...	...	...	...
Klang	348 991	...	...	...	...	...	...	...
Kota Bharu	236 868	...	...	...	...	...	...	...
Kota Kinabalu	278 568	...	...	...	...	...	...	...
KUALA LUMPUR	1 551 306	...	...	...	...	...	...	...
Kuala Terengganu	191 852	...	...	...	...	...	...	...
Kuantan	325 066	...	...	...	...	...	...	...
Kuching	197 335	...	...	...	...	...	...	...
Miri	161 891	...	...	...	...	...	...	...
Petaling Jaya	231 050	...	...	...	...	...	...	...
Sandakan	204 656	...	...	...	...	...	...	...
Seleyang Baru	180 420	...	...	...	...	...	...	...
Seremban	273 941	...	...	...	...	...	...	...
Shah Alam	177 030	...	...	...	...	...	...	...
Sibu	185 286	...	...	...	...	...	...	...
Subang Jaya	182 674	...	...	...	...	...	...	...
Sungai Petani	198 822	...	...	...	...	...	...	...
Taiping	195 214	...	...	...	...	...	...	...
Tawau	126 802	...	...	...	...	...	...	...
Maldives								
21 III 2006 (CDFC)								
MALE'	103 693	51 992	51 701	2	...	...	...	...
Mongolia - Mongolie								
1 VII 2007 (ESDF)								
ULAANBAATAR	1 012 733	488 848	523 886	201	...	...	...	...
Nepal - Népal								
22 VI 2001 (CDJC)								
Biratnagar	166 674	87 664	79 010	58	...	...	...	...
Birgunj	112 484	60 956	51 528	21	...	...	...	...
KATHMANDU	671 846	360 103	311 743	49	...	...	...	...
Lalitpur	162 991	84 502	78 489	15	...	...	...	...
Pokhara	156 312	79 563	76 749	55	...	...	...	...

Continent, country or area, date, code and city Continent, pays ou zone, date, code et ville	City proper - Ville proprement dite				Urban agglomeration - Agglomération urbaine			
	Population			Surface area - Superficie (km²)	Population			Surface area - Superficie (km²)
	Both sexes - Les deux sexes	Male - Masculin	Female - Féminin		Both sexes - Les deux sexes	Male - Masculin	Female - Féminin	
ASIA - ASIE								
Occupied Palestinian Territory - Territoire palestinien occupé								
1 VII 2007 (ESDF)								
Gaza	443 095	...	...	38				
Hebron	160 702	...	...	49	...	...	...	...
Jabalya	120 881	...	...	...	...	...	...	...
Khan Yunis	140 697	...	...	...	...	...	...	...
Nablus	124 780	...	...	26	...	...	...	...
Oman								
7 XII 2003 (CDFC)								
As Seeb	223 449	128 068	95 381					
As Suwayq	101 122	54 997	46 125		...	...	...	...
Bawshar	150 420	91 687	58 733		...	...	...	...
MUSCAT	24 893	13 695	11 198		...	...	...	...
Mutrah	153 526	96 878	56 648		...	...	...	...
Salalah	156 530	92 489	64 041		...	...	...	...
Sohar	104 312	57 695	46 617		...	...	...	...
Pakistan[36]								
2 III 1998 (CDFC)								
Abbotabad	106 101	61 698	44 403		...	...	...	...
Bahawalnagar	111 313	57 779	53 534		...	...	...	...
Bahawalpur	408 395	222 228	186 167		...	...	...	...
Burewala	152 097	78 726	73 371		...	...	...	...
Chiniot	172 522	90 474	82 048		...	...	...	...
Chishtian	102 287	52 427	49 860		...	...	...	...
Dadu	102 550	53 508	49 042		...	...	...	...
Daska	102 883	52 359	50 524		...	...	...	...
Dera Ghazi Khan	190 542	98 738	91 804		...	...	...	...
Faisalabad (Lyallpur)	2 008 861	1 053 085	955 776		...	...	...	...
Gojra	117 872	60 598	57 274		...	...	...	...
Gujranwala	1 132 509	588 512	543 997		...	...	...	...
Gujrat	251 792	128 524	123 268		...	...	...	...
Hafizabad	133 678	69 231	64 447		...	...	...	...
Hyderabad	1 166 894	612 283	554 611		...	...	...	...
ISLAMABAD	529 180	290 717	238 463		...	...	...	...
Jacobabad	138 780	71 854	66 926		...	...	...	...
Jaranwala	106 785	55 619	51 166		...	...	...	...
Jhang	293 366	153 123	140 243		...	...	...	...
Jhelum	147 392	79 169	68 223		...	...	...	...
Kamoke	152 288	78 848	73 440		...	...	...	...
Karachi	9 339 023	5 029 900	4 309 123		...	...	...	...
Kasur	245 321	129 553	115 768		...	...	...	...
Khairpur	105 637	55 358	50 279		...	...	...	...
Khanewal	133 986	69 145	64 841		...	...	...	...
Khanpur	120 382	62 371	58 011		...	...	...	...
Kohat	126 627	71 505	55 122		...	...	...	...
Lahore	5 143 495	2 707 220	2 436 275		...	...	...	...
Larkana	270 283	140 622	129 661		...	...	...	...
Mangora	173 868	91 742	82 126		...	...	...	...
Mardan	245 926	129 247	116 679		...	...	...	...
Mirpur Khas	189 671	97 940	91 731		...	...	...	...
Multan	1 197 384	637 911	559 473		...	...	...	...
Muridke	111 951	58 210	53 741		...	...	...	...
Muzaffargarh	123 404	66 556	56 848		...	...	...	...
Nawabshah	189 244	98 116	91 128		...	...	...	...
Okara	201 815	104 245	97 570		...	...	...	...
Pakpattan	109 033	56 676	52 357		...	...	...	...
Peshawar	982 816	521 901	460 915		...	...	...	...
Quetta	565 137	307 759	257 378		...	...	...	...
Rahimyar Khan	233 537	121 446	112 091		...	...	...	...
Rawalpindi	1 409 768	750 530	659 238		...	...	...	...
Sadiqabad	144 391	75 217	69 174		...	...	...	...
Sahiwal	208 778	108 992	99 786		...	...	...	...
Sargodha	458 440	239 837	218 603		...	...	...	...
Shakkarpur	134 883	69 713	65 170		...	...	...	...
Sheikhu Pura	280 263	146 739	133 524		...	...	...	...

8. Population of capital cities and cities of 100 000 or more inhabitants: latest available year, 1988 - 2007
Population des capitales et des villes de 100 000 habitants ou plus: dernière année disponible, 1988 - 2007 (continued - suite)

Continent, country or area, date, code and city / Continent, pays ou zone, date, code et ville	City proper - Ville proprement dite				Urban agglomeration - Agglomération urbaine			
	Population			Surface area - Superficie (km²)	Population			Surface area - Superficie (km²)
	Both sexes - Les deux sexes	Male - Masculin	Female - Féminin		Both sexes - Les deux sexes	Male - Masculin	Female - Féminin	
ASIA - ASIE								
Pakistan[36]								
2 III 1998 (CDFC)								
Sialkote	421 502	227 398	194 104	...	...	...	...	...
Sukkur	335 551	175 679	159 872	...	...	...	...	...
Tandoadam................................	104 907	54 670	50 237	...	...	...	...	...
Wah Cantonment	198 891	104 230	94 661	...	...	...	...	...
Philippines								
1 V 2000 (CDJC)								
Angeles	267 788	132 972	134 816	60	...	...	...	...
Bacolod	429 076	209 729	219 347	156	...	...	...	...
Bago	141 721	72 777	68 944	402	...	...	...	...
Baguio	252 386	124 208	128 178	58	...	...	...	...
Basilan	332 828	166 413	166 415	...	...	...	...	...
Batangas	247 588	123 740	123 848	283	...	...	...	...
Butuan	267 279	135 735	131 544	816	...	...	...	...
Cabanatuan	222 859	111 461	111 398	283	...	...	...	...
Cadiz..	141 954	72 701	69 253	467	...	...	...	...
Cagayan de Oro	461 877	228 524	233 353	413	...	...	...	...
Calbayog	147 187	75 157	72 030	...	...	...	...	...
Cebu	718 821	351 640	367 181	281	...	...	...	...
Cotabato	163 849	79 853	83 996	144	...	...	...	...
Dagupan	130 328	64 468	65 860	37	...	...	...	...
Davao	1 147 116	573 242	573 874	1 211	...	...	...	...
Digos..	125 171	63 107	62 064	...	...	...	...	...
Dumaguete	102 265	49 378	52 887	34	...	...	...	...
General Santos	411 822	207 496	264 326	402	...	...	...	...
Gingoog....................................	102 379	52 302	50 077	...	...	...	...	...
Iligan	285 061	141 641	143 420	673	...	...	...	...
Iloilo	366 391	177 620	188 771	56	...	...	...	...
Kabankalan...............................	149 769	76 479	73 290	697	...	...	...	...
Kalookan (caloocan)	1 177 604	587 890	589 714	56	...	...	...	...
Kidapawan	101 205	51 278	49 927	...	...	...	...	...
Koronadal	133 786	67 493	66 293	...	...	...	...	...
Lapu-Lapu.................................	217 019	106 099	110 920	...	...	...	...	...
Las Piñas..................................	472 780	229 776	243 004	33	...	...	...	...
Legasp	157 010	78 141	78 869	154	...	...	...	...
Lipa	218 447	109 938	108 509	209	...	...	...	...
Lucena City...............................	196 075	97 380	98 695	80	...	...	...	...
Makati	471 379	226 422	244 957	18	...	...	...	...
Malabalay	123 672	63 381	60 291	969	...	...	...	...
Malabon	338 855	168 587	170 268	...	...	...	...	...
Malolos.....................................	175 291	86 600	88 691	67	...	...	...	...
Mandaluyong.............................	278 474	135 287	143 187	9	...	...	...	...
Mandaue	259 728	128 501	131 227	12	...	...	...	...
MANILA	1 581 082	770 491	810 591	614	...	...	...	...
Marawi	131 090	63 110	67 980	23	...	...	...	...
Marikina	391 170	191 585	199 585	22	...	...	...	...
Muntinlupa	379 310	187 381	191 929	40	...	...	...	...
Naga	137 810	68 040	69 770	85	...	...	...	...
Navotas	230 403	115 697	114 706	...	...	...	...	...
Olongapo...................................	194 260	95 585	98 675	185	...	...	...	...
Ormoc.......................................	154 297	78 612	75 685	...	...	...	...	...
Ozamis......................................	110 420	54 986	55 434	...	...	...	...	...
Pagadian...................................	142 585	71 009	71 576	332	...	...	...	...
Paranaque	449 811	217 828	231 983	47	...	...	...	...
Pasay	354 908	175 041	179 867	14	...	...	...	...
Pasig..	505 058	246 047	259 011	49	...	...	...	...
Puerto Princesa	161 912	83 045	78 867	2 381	...	...	...	...
Quezon City	2 173 831	1 064 780	1 109 051	172	...	...	...	...
Roxas.......................................	126 352	62 542	63 810	95	...	...	...	...
Sagay City.................................	129 765	65 935	63 830	330	...	...	...	...
San Carlos (Negros Occidental)......	118 259	60 073	58 186	452	...	...	...	...
San Carlos (Pangasinan)	154 264	77 652	76 612	...	...	...	...	...
San Fernando City......................	221 857	111 798	110 059	68	...	...	...	...
San Juan...................................	117 680	54 604	63 076	6	...	...	...	...
San Pablo	207 927	102 685	105 242	...	...	...	...	...

Continent, country or area, date, code and city / Continent, pays ou zone, date, code et ville	City proper - Ville proprement dite				Urban agglomeration - Agglomération urbaine			
	Population			Surface area - Superficie (km²)	Population			Surface area - Superficie (km²)
	Both sexes - Les deux sexes	Male - Masculin	Female - Féminin		Both sexes - Les deux sexes	Male - Masculin	Female - Féminin	
ASIA - ASIE								
Philippines								
1 V 2000 (CDJC)								
Silay	107 722	54 419	53 303	215	...	...	...	...
Surigao	118 534	59 253	59 281	225	...	...	...	...
Tacloban	178 639	88 490	90 149	...	...	...	...	...
Taguig	467 375	233 712	233 663	...	...	...	...	...
Tagum	179 531	90 004	89 527	...	...	...	...	...
Tarlac	262 481	132 532	129 949	...	...	...	...	...
Toledo	141 174	71 719	69 455	...	...	...	...	...
Tuguegarao	120 645	60 270	60 375	145	...	...	...	...
Valenzuela	485 433	244 373	241 060	47	...	...	...	...
Zamboanga	601 794	302 089	299 705	464	...	...	...	...
Qatar								
1 VII 2007 (ESDF)								
Al-Khoor	...	...	...	...	144 459	133 620	10 839	1 552
Al-Rayyan	...	...	...	...	291 727	185 697	106 030	5 818
DOHA	...	...	...	...	635 201	477 437	157 764	234
Republic of Korea - République de Corée								
1 VII 2006 (ESDF)								
Busan (Pusan)	3 554 003	1 767 568	1 786 435	765	...	...	...	...
Daegu (Taegu)	2 484 022	1 247 963	1 236 059	884	...	...	...	...
Daejeon (Taejon)	1 476 736	743 507	733 229	540	...	...	...	...
Gwangju (Kwangchu)	1 443 226	720 228	722 998	501	...	...	...	...
Incheon	2 596 317	1 313 256	1 283 061	1 002	...	...	...	...
SEOUL	10 020 123	4 994 996	5 025 127	605	...	...	...	...
Ulsan	1 074 516	556 396	518 120	1 057	...	...	...	...
Saudi Arabia - Arabie saoudite								
15 IX 2004 (CDFC)								
Abha	201 912	113 102	88 810		...	...	...	...
Ad-Dammam	744 321	450 494	293 827	...	...	...	...	...
Al-Hawiyah	132 078	69 481	62 597	...	...	...	...	...
Al-Hufuf	287 841	155 924	131 917	...	...	...	...	...
Al-Jubayl	222 544	135 659	86 885	...	...	...	...	...
Al-Kharj	200 958	109 112	91 846	...	...	...	...	...
Al-Khubar	165 799	101 818	63 981	...	...	...	...	...
Al-Madinah	918 889	493 929	424 960	...	...	...	...	...
Al-Mubarraz	285 067	150 449	134 618	...	...	...	...	...
Al-Qurrayyat	100 436	52 869	47 567	...	...	...	...	...
Ar'ar	145 237	77 744	67 493	...	...	...	...	...
Ath-Thuqbah	191 826	117 165	74 661	...	...	...	...	...
At-Ta'if	521 273	274 531	246 742	...	...	...	...	...
Buraydah	378 422	211 317	167 105	...	...	...	...	...
Hafar al-Batin	231 978	122 781	109 197	...	...	...	...	...
Ha'il	267 005	142 015	124 990	...	...	...	...	...
Jiddah	2 801 481	1 619 932	1 181 549	...	...	...	...	...
Jizan	100 694	57 988	42 706	...	...	...	...	...
Khamis Mushayt	372 695	208 397	164 298	...	...	...	...	...
Makkah	1 294 168	704 672	589 496	...	...	...	...	...
Najran (Aba as-Suud)	246 880	133 405	113 475	...	...	...	...	...
RIYADH	4 087 152	2 354 246	1 732 906	...	...	...	...	...
Sekaka	122 686	66 672	56 014	...	...	...	...	...
Tabuk	441 351	241 913	199 438	...	...	...	...	...
Unayzah	128 930	71 841	57 089	...	...	...	...	...
Yanbu al-Bahr	188 430	105 966	82 464	...	...	...	...	...
Singapore - Singapour								
1 VII 2007 (ESDF)								
SINGAPORE	4 588 600	...	...		...	...		
Sri Lanka								
1 VII 1990 (ESDF)								
COLOMBO	615 000	...	...	...	...	...	...	...
Dehiwala-Mount Lavinia	196 000	...	...	...	...	...	...	...
Jaffna	129 000	...	...	...	...	...	...	...
Kandy	104 000	...	...	...	...	...	...	...
Moratuwa	170 000	...	...	...	...	...	...	...

8. Population of capital cities and cities of 100 000 or more inhabitants: latest available year, 1988 - 2007
Population des capitales et des villes de 100 000 habitants ou plus: dernière année disponible, 1988 - 2007 (continued - suite)

Continent, country or area, date, code and city / Continent, pays ou zone, date, code et ville	City proper - Ville proprement dite				Urban agglomeration - Agglomération urbaine			
	Population			Surface area - Superficie (km²)	Population			Surface area - Superficie (km²)
	Both sexes - Les deux sexes	Male - Masculin	Female - Féminin		Both sexes - Les deux sexes	Male - Masculin	Female - Féminin	
ASIA - ASIE								
Syrian Arab Republic - République arabe syrienne								
1 VII 2007 (ESDF)								
Aleppo	4 337 000	2 231 000	2 106 000	...	...	...	...	...
Al-Hasakeh	1 361 000	692 000	669 000	...	...	...	...	...
Al-Rakka	843 000	429 000	414 000	...	...	...	...	...
DAMASCUS	1 658 000	846 000	812 000	...	...	...	...	...
Deir El-Zor	1 077 000	544 000	533 000	...	...	...	...	...
Hama	1 474 000	756 000	718 000	...	...	...	...	...
Homs	1 629 000	835 000	794 000	...	...	...	...	...
Lattakia	935 000	473 000	462 000	...	...	...	...	...
Tajikistan - Tadjikistan								
1 VII 2007 (ESDF)								
DUSHANBE	670 168	348 864	321 304	...	...	...	...	...
Khujand	155 316	...	...	...	...	...	...	...
Thailand - Thaïlande								
1 VII 2007 (ESDJ)					...	6 842 000[3]	3 206 000[3]	3 636 000[3]	1 569
BANGKOK	...	...	...	...	225 568[3]	110 815[3]	114 753[3]	10 323
Buri Ram	...	...	...	...	132 285[3]	63 362[3]	68 923[3]	5 351
Chachoengsao	...	...	...	...	161 998[3]	78 645[3]	83 353[3]	12 778
Chaiyaphum	...	...	...	...	145 962[3]	70 197[3]	75 765[3]	6 338
Chanthaburi	...	...	...	...	378 682[3]	179 471[3]	199 211[3]	20 107
Chiang Mai	...	...	...	...	216 119[3]	105 355[3]	110 764[3]	11 678
Chiang Rai	...	...	...	...	640 205[3]	310 927[3]	329 278[3]	4 363
Chon Buri	...	...	...	...	100 464[3]	48 882[3]	51 582[3]	6 009
Chumphon	...	...	...	...	213 483[3]	105 518[3]	107 965[3]	6 947
Kalasin	...	...	...	...	145 737[3]	69 198[3]	76 539[3]	19 483
Kanchanaburi	...	...	...	...	396 112[3]	192 712[3]	203 400[3]	10 886
Khon Kaen	...	...	...	...	414 207[3]	293 479[3]	120 728[3]	12 534
Lampang	...	...	...	...	114 798[3]	55 269[3]	59 529[3]	4 506
Lamphun	...	...	...	...	102 252[3]	50 681[3]	51 571[3]	11 425
Loei	...	...	...	...	141 465[3]	72 098[3]	69 367[3]	6 200
Lop Buri	...	...	...	...	105 967[3]	51 045[3]	54 922[3]	5 292
Maha Sarakham	...	...	...	...	209 584[3]	101 115[3]	108 469[3]	2 168
Nakhon Pathom	...	...	...	...	544 647[3]	264 759[3]	279 888[3]	20 494
Nakhon Ratchasima	...	...	...	...	231 251[3]	109 854[3]	121 397[3]	9 598
Nakhon Sawan	...	...	...	...	275 176[3]	132 684[3]	142 492[3]	9 943
Nakhon Si Thammarat	...	...	...	...	166 920[3]	82 285[3]	84 635[3]	4 475
Narathiwat	...	...	...	...	110 223[3]	54 525[3]	55 698[3]	3 859
Nong Bua Lam Phu	...	...	...	...	174 476[3]	86 781[3]	87 695[3]	7 332
Nong Khai	...	...	...	...	573 988[3]	276 350[3]	297 638[3]	1 004
Nonthaburi	...	...	...	...	331 940[3]	161 211[3]	170 729[3]	1 526
Pathum Thani	...	...	...	...	122 367[3]	60 797[3]	61 570[3]	1 940
Pattani	...	...	...	...	118 521[3]	58 029[3]	60 492[3]	6 335
Phayao	...	...	...	...	142 675[3]	68 707[3]	73 968[3]	12 668
Phetchabun	...	...	...	...	154 512[3]	74 081[3]	80 431[3]	6 225
Phetchaburi	...	...	...	...	112 684[3]	53 481[3]	59 203[3]	4 531
Phichit	...	...	...	...	142 655[3]	67 453[3]	75 202[3]	10 816
Phitsanulok	...	...	...	...	256 675[3]	123 714[3]	132 961[3]	2 557
Phra Nakhon Si Ayutthaya	...	...	...	...	106 396[3]	51 180[3]	55 216[3]	6 539
Phrae	...	...	...	...	120 880[3]	58 371[3]	62 509[3]	543
Phuket	...	...	...	...	151 051[3]	72 731[3]	78 320[3]	6 368
Prachuap Khiri Khan	...	...	...	...	260 167[3]	125 151[3]	135 016[3]	5 197
Ratchaburi	...	...	...	...	230 000[3]	114 232[3]	115 768[3]	3 552
Rayong	...	...	...	...	157 176[3]	76 629[3]	80 547[3]	8 299
Roi Et	...	...	...	...	142 877[3]	70 398[3]	72 479[3]	9 606
Sakon Nakhon	...	...	...	...	704 329[3]	335 239[3]	369 090[3]	622
Samut Prakan	...	...	...	...	230 121[3]	112 012[3]	118 109[3]	417
Samut Songkhram	...	...	...	...	215 544[3]	106 661[3]	108 883[3]	3 577
Saraburi	...	...	...	...	132 251[3]	64 555[3]	67 696[3]	8 840
Si Sa Ket	...	...	...	...	528 941[3]	253 699[3]	275 242[3]	7 394
Songkhla	...	...	...	...	113 240[3]	53 579[3]	59 661[3]	6 596
Sukhothai	...	...	...	...	140 744[3]	66 768[3]	73 976[3]	5 358
Suphan Buri	...	...	...	...				

8. Population of capital cities and cities of 100 000 or more inhabitants: latest available year, 1988 - 2007
Population des capitales et des villes de 100 000 habitants ou plus: dernière année disponible, 1988 - 2007 (continued - suite)

Continent, country or area, date, code and city Continent, pays ou zone, date, code et ville	City proper - Ville proprement dite				Urban agglomeration - Agglomération urbaine			
	Population			Surface area - Superficie (km²)	Population			Surface area - Superficie (km²)
	Both sexes - Les deux sexes	Male - Masculin	Female - Féminin		Both sexes - Les deux sexes	Male - Masculin	Female - Féminin	
ASIA - ASIE								
Thailand - Thaïlande								
1 VII 2007 (ESDJ)								
Surat Thani	...	...	...	...	336 834[3]	164 573[3]	172 261[3]	12 892
Tak	...	...	...	...	109 054[3]	53 478[3]	55 576[3]	16 407
Trang	...	...	...	...	126 507[3]	61 110[3]	65 397[3]	4 918
Ubon Ratchathani	...	...	...	...	268 865[3]	132 125[3]	136 740[3]	15 745
Udon Thani	...	...	...	...	403 118[3]	199 058[3]	204 060[3]	11 730
Uttaradit	...	...	...	...	108 830[3]	51 715[3]	57 115[3]	7 839
Yala	...	...	...	...	107 063[3]	51 943[3]	55 120[3]	4 521
Timor-Leste								
1 VII 2001 (ESDF)								
DILI	56 000	...	...	...	...	...	...	...
Turkey - Turquie								
1 VII 2007 (ESDF)								
Adana[37]	...	...	...	...	1 251 863	...	...	...
Adiyaman	241 260	...	...	...	...	...	...	...
Afyon	1 488 350	...	...	...	...	...	...	...
Aksaray	157 232	...	...	...	...	...	...	...
Alanya (Antalya)	115 927	...	...	...	...	...	...	...
ANKARA[38]	...	...	...	...	3 953 344	...	...	...
Antalya	763 205	...	...	...	...	...	...	...
Aydin	164 525	...	...	...	...	...	...	...
Balikesir	241 682	...	...	...	...	...	...	...
Bandirma	109 000	...	...	...	...	...	...	...
Batman	321 222	...	...	...	...	...	...	...
Bursa[39]	...	...	...	...	1 597 162	...	...	...
Ceyhan	122 699	...	...	...	...	...	...	...
Corlu	199 714	...	...	...	...	...	...	...
Corum	190 430	...	...	...	...	...	...	...
Denizli	320 460	...	...	...	...	...	...	...
Derince[40]	111 659	...	...	...	...	...	...	...
Diyarbakir	662 954	...	...	...	...	...	...	...
Edirne	125 753	...	...	...	...	...	...	...
Elazig	297 703	...	...	...	...	...	...	...
Erzincan	112 069	...	...	...	...	...	...	...
Erzurum	443 423	...	...	...	...	...	...	...
Eskisehir	512 972	...	...	...	...	...	...	...
Gaziantep[41]	...	...	...	...	1 024 411	...	...	...
Gebze	325 021	...	...	...	...	...	...	...
Hatay	153 581	...	...	...	...	...	...	...
Içel	604 236	...	...	...	...	...	...	...
Inegol	125 507	...	...	...	...	...	...	...
Iskenderun	154 706	...	...	...	...	...	...	...
Isparta	168 872	...	...	...	...	...	...	...
Istanbul[42]	...	...	...	...	10 822 846	...	...	...
Izmir[43]	...	...	...	...	2 583 670	...	...	...
Kahramanmaras	393 583	...	...	...	...	...	...	...
Karaman	124 603	...	...	...	...	...	...	...
Kayseri[44]	...	...	...	...	710 735	...	...	...
Kirikkale	207 613	...	...	...	...	...	...	...
Kiziltepe	157 834	...	...	...	...	...	...	...
Kocaeli	186 951	...	...	...	...	...	...	...
Konya	...	...	...	...	994 883	...	...	...
Kütahya	186 516	...	...	...	...	...	...	...
Malatya	454 249	...	...	...	...	...	...	...
Manavgat (Antalya)	100 588	...	...	...	...	...	...	...
Manisa	250 943	...	...	...	...	...	...	...
Nazilli	119 972	...	...	...	...	...	...	...
Ordu	112 746	...	...	...	...	...	...	...
Osmaniye	209 907	...	...	...	...	...	...	...
Patnos (Agri)	108 507	...	...	...	...	...	...	...
Sakarya	276 713	...	...	...	...	...	...	...
Samsun	393 334	...	...	...	...	...	...	...
Sanliurfa	438 134	...	...	...	...	...	...	...
Siirt	118 567	...	...	...	...	...	...	...

Continent, country or area, date, code and city Continent, pays ou zone, date, code et ville	City proper - Ville proprement dite				Urban agglomeration - Agglomération urbaine			
	Population			Surface area - Superficie (km²)	Population			Surface area - Superficie (km²)
	Both sexes - Les deux sexes	Male - Masculin	Female - Féminin		Both sexes - Les deux sexes	Male - Masculin	Female - Féminin	
ASIA - ASIE								
Turkey - Turquie								
1 VII 2007 (ESDF)								
Sivas	258 746	...	...	...	...	...	...	...
Siverek	184 121	...	...	...	...	...	...	...
Tarsus	227 595	...	...	...	...	...	...	...
Tekirdag	119 518	...	...	...	...	...	...	...
Tokat	132 929	...	...	...	...	...	...	...
Trabzon	242 445	...	...	...	...	...	...	...
Turgutlu (Manisa)	105 565	...	...	...	...	...	...	...
Turhal	113 457	...	...	...	...	...	...	...
Usak	156 672	...	...	...	...	...	...	...
Van	381 653	...	...	...	...	...	...	...
Viransehir	182 095	...	...	...	...	...	...	...
Turkmenistan - Turkménistan								
1 VII 1990 (ESDF)								
ASHKHABAD	407 000	...	...	...	...	...	...	...
Tashauz	114 000	...	...	...	...	...	...	...
Türkmenabat (Chardzhou)	164 000	...	...	...	...	...	...	...
United Arab Emirates - Émirats arabes unis								
1 VII 2002 (ESDF)								
ABU DHABI	527 000	359 000	168 000	...	...	...	...	...
Ajman	205 000	122 000	83 000	...	...	...	...	...
Al-Ayn	328 000	215 000	113 000	...	...	...	...	...
Al-Sharjah	488 000	317 000	171 000	...	...	...	...	...
Dubai	1 089 000	759 000	330 000	...	...	...	...	...
Uzbekistan - Ouzbékistan								
1 VII 2001 (ESDF)								
Almalyk	113 114	56 317	56 797	...	...	...	...	...
Andizhan	338 366	165 159	173 207	...	...	...	...	...
Angren	128 757	64 060	64 697	...	...	...	...	...
Banjzak	131 512	68 441	63 071	...	...	...	...	...
Bukhara	237 361	118 613	118 748	...	...	...	...	...
Chirchik	141 742	70 203	71 539	...	...	...	...	...
Fergana	183 037	87 142	95 895	...	...	...	...	...
Karshi	204 690	104 159	100 531	...	...	...	...	...
Kokand	197 450	95 872	101 578	...	...	...	...	...
Margilan	149 646	73 899	75 747	...	...	...	...	...
Namangan	391 297	197 962	193 335	...	...	...	...	...
Navoi	138 082	70 577	67 505	...	...	...	...	...
Nukus	212 012	103 918	108 094	...	...	...	...	...
Samarkand	361 339	178 608	182 731	...	...	...	...	...
TASHKENT	2 137 218	1 043 213	1 094 005	...	...	...	...	...
Termez	116 467	60 031	56 436	...	...	...	...	...
Urgentch	138 609	67 667	70 942	...	...	...	...	...
Viet Nam								
1 VII 1992 (ESDF)								
Buonmathuot	282 095	...	...	...	...	...	...	...
Campha	209 086	...	...	...	...	...	...	...
Cantho	215 587	...	...	...	...	...	...	...
Da Nang	382 674	...	...	...	...	...	...	...
Dalat	106 409	...	...	...	...	...	...	...
Haiphong	783 133	...	...	22	...	...	...	...
HANOI	1 073 760	...	...	46	...	...	...	...
Ho Chi Minh[45]	3 015 743	...	...	140	...	...	...	...
Hon Gai	127 484	...	...	...	...	...	...	...
Hué	219 149	...	...	...	...	...	...	...
Longxuyen	132 681	...	...	...	...	...	...	...
Mytho	108 404	...	...	...	...	...	...	...
Namdinh	171 699	...	...	...	...	...	...	...
Nhatrang	221 331	...	...	...	...	...	...	...
Qui Nhon	163 385	...	...	...	...	...	...	...
Rach Gia	141 132	...	...	...	...	...	...	...
Thai Nguyen	127 643	...	...	...	...	...	...	...
Vinh	112 455	...	...	...	...	...	...	...
Vungtau	145 145	...	...	...	...	...	...	...

8. Population of capital cities and cities of 100 000 or more inhabitants: latest available year, 1988 - 2007
Population des capitales et des villes de 100 000 habitants ou plus: dernière année disponible, 1988 - 2007 (continued - suite)

Continent, country or area, date, code and city / Continent, pays ou zone, date, code et ville	City proper - Ville proprement dite				Urban agglomeration - Agglomération urbaine			
	Population			Surface area - Superficie (km²)	Population			Surface area - Superficie (km²)
	Both sexes - Les deux sexes	Male - Masculin	Female - Féminin		Both sexes - Les deux sexes	Male - Masculin	Female - Féminin	
ASIA - ASIE								
Yemen - Yémen								
16 XII 1994 (CDFC)								
Adan	398 294	...	...	...	...	...	...	...
Al-Hudaydah (Hodeidah)	298 452	...	...	...	...	...	...	...
Al-Mukalla	122 359	...	...	...	...	...	...	...
Ibb	103 312	...	...	...	...	...	...	...
SANA'A	954 448	...	...	...	...	...	...	...
Ta'izz	317 571	...	...	...	...	...	...	...
EUROPE								
Åland Islands - Îles d'Åland[46]								
1 VII 2007 (ESDJ)								
MARIEHAMN	10 863[47]	5 151[47]	5 712[47]	12	...	...	...	...
Albania - Albanie[48]								
1 VII 2003 (ESDF)								
TIRANA	392 863	194 006	198 857	31	...	...	...	...
Andorra - Andorre[47]								
31 XII 2007 (ESDF)								
ANDORRA LA VELLA	...	...	...	...	24 574	12 426	12 148	...
Austria - Autriche								
1 I 2007 (ESDJ)								
Graz	247 698[49]	118 671[49]	129 027[49]	128	...	...	...	...
Innsbruck	117 693[49]	55 814[49]	61 879[49]	105	...	...	...	...
Linz	188 894[49]	89 606[49]	99 288[49]	96	...	...	...	...
Salzburg	149 018[49]	69 899[49]	79 119[49]	66	...	...	...	...
WIEN	1 664 146[49]	794 835[49]	869 311[49]	415	...	...	...	...
Belarus - Bélarus								
1 VII 2006 (ESDF)								
Baranovichi	167 911	77 765	90 146	50	...	...	...	...
Bobruisk	218 756	102 058	116 698	90	...	...	...	...
Borisov	149 788	70 652	79 136	46	...	...	...	...
Brest	302 348	139 140	163 208	75	...	...	...	...
Gomel	...	...	...	...	492 032	224 323	267 709	118
Grodno	320 166	147 515	172 651	93	...	...	...	...
MINSK	1 789 098	826 797	962 301	306	...	...	...	...
Mogilev	368 481	169 991	198 490	108	...	...	...	...
Mozir	111 693	53 330	58 363	38	...	...	...	...
Novopolotsk	...	...	...	...	106 764	50 784	55 980	54
Orsha	...	...	...	...	139 994	66 633	73 361	51
Pinsk	129 779	60 705	69 074	44	...	...	...	...
Soligorsk	100 805	47 716	53 089	11	...	...	...	...
Vitebsk	...	...	...	...	352 247	157 421	194 826	96
Belgium - Belgique								
1 I 2006 (ESDJ)								
Antwerpen (Anvers)	461 496[50]	226 280[50]	235 216[50]	205	...	...	...	...
Brugge	117 224[50]	56 769[50]	60 455[50]	138	...	...	...	...
BRUXELLES (BRUSSEL)	144 784[50]	72 270[50]	72 514[50]	161	1 018 804	489 684	529 120	...
Charleroi	201 300[50]	97 421[50]	103 879[50]	102	...	...	...	...
Gent (Gand)	233 120[50]	114 061[50]	119 059[50]	156	...	...	...	...
Liège (Luik)	187 086[50]	91 363[50]	95 723[50]	69	...	...	...	...
Namur	107 178[50]	51 489[50]	55 689[50]	176	...	...	...	...
Bosnia and Herzegovina - Bosnie-Herzégovine								
31 III 1991 (CDJC)								
Banja Luka	195 692	97 110	98 582	1 239	...	...	...	...
Doboj	102 549	51 144	51 405	697	...	...	...	...
Mostar	126 628	62 291	64 337	1 227	...	...	...	...
Prijedor	112 543	56 092	56 451	834	...	...	...	...
SARAJEVO	527 049	257 284	269 765	2 095	...	...	...	...
Tuzla	131 318	64 514	66 804	303	...	...	...	...
Zenica	145 517	72 985	72 532	505	...	...	...	...

Continent, country or area, date, code and city / Continent, pays ou zone, date, code et ville	City proper - Ville proprement dite				Urban agglomeration - Agglomération urbaine			
	Population			Surface area - Superficie (km²)	Population			Surface area - Superficie (km²)
	Both sexes - Les deux sexes	Male - Masculin	Female - Féminin		Both sexes - Les deux sexes	Male - Masculin	Female - Féminin	
EUROPE								
Bulgaria - Bulgarie[51]								
1 VII 2007 (ESDF)								
Bourgas	188 201	90 374	97 827	...	...	...	...	...
Plévène	112 976	54 421	58 555	...	...	...	...	...
Plovdiv	344 456	163 946	180 510	...	...	...	...	...
Roussé	157 144	75 521	81 623	...	...	...	...	...
SOFIA	1 155 403	547 477	607 926	...	...	...	...	...
Stara Zagora	140 950	68 198	72 752	...	...	...	...	...
Varna	312 724	151 591	161 133	...	...	...	...	...
Croatia - Croatie								
31 III 2001 (CDJC)								
Osijek	90 411[52]	41 592[52]	48 819[52]	...	114 616[53]	53 497[53]	61 119[53]	...
Rijeka	143 800[52]	68 382[52]	75 418[52]	...	144 043[53]	68 511[53]	75 532[53]	...
Split	175 140[52]	83 720[52]	91 420[52]	...	188 694[53]	90 484[53]	98 210[53]	...
ZAGREB	691 724[52]	321 507[52]	370 217[52]	....	779 145[53]	363 992[53]	415 153[53]	...
Czech Republic - République tchèque								
1 I 2007 (ESDJ)								
Brno	366 680	174 592	192 088	230	...	...	...	...
Olomouc	100 168	47 269	52 899	103	...	...	...	...
Ostrava	309 098	149 167	159 931	214	...	...	...	...
Plzen	163 392	78 688	84 704	138	...	...	...	...
PRAHA	1 188 126	570 881	617 245	496	...	...	...	...
Denmark - Danemark[54]								
1 VII 2007 (ESDJ)								
Ålborg	194 049	96 802	97 247	560	...	...	...	...
Århus	295 599	144 867	150 732	469	...	...	...	...
KOBENHAVN	505 141	249 300	255 841	88	...	...	...	...
Odense	186 085	91 082	95 003	304	...	...	...	...
Estonia - Estonie								
1 VII 2007 (ESDF)								
TALLINN	397 235	179 375	217 860	158	...	...	...	...
Tartu	102 190	45 675	56 515	39	...	...	...	...
Faeroe Islands - Îles Féroé								
1 VII 1992 (ESDJ)								
THORSHAVN	14 671	...	...	63	16 218	...	...	79
Finland - Finlande[55]								
1 VII 2007 (ESDJ)								
Espoo	236 533	116 092	120 442	312	...	...	...	...
HELSINKI	566 526	264 536	301 991	186	...	...	...	...
Oulu	130 882	63 897	66 985	369	...	...	...	...
Tampere	207 117	99 571	107 547	523	...	...	...	...
Turku	175 320	82 280	93 041	246	...	...	...	...
Vantaa	191 117	93 418	97 699	241	...	...	...	...
France[56]								
8 III 1999 (CDJC)								
Aix-en-Provence	134 280[57]	62 220[57]	72 060[57]	186	...	...	...	...
Amiens	135 406[57]	63 513[57]	71 893[57]	49	...	...	...	...
Angers	151 406[57]	69 235[57]	82 171[57]	43	...	...	...	...
Besançon	117 693[57]	54 692[57]	63 001[57]	65	...	...	...	...
Bordeaux	215 277[57]	99 637[57]	115 640[57]	49	...	...	...	...
Boulogne-Billancourt	106 384[57]	49 840[57]	56 544[57]	6	...	...	...	...
Brest	149 495[57]	71 431[57]	78 064[57]	50	...	...	...	...
Caen	114 079[57]	52 605[57]	61 474[57]	26	...	...	...	...
Clermont-Ferrand	136 968[57]	63 702[57]	73 266[57]	43	...	...	...	...
Dijon	150 144[57]	69 331[57]	80 813[57]	40	...	...	...	...
Grenoble	153 531[57]	73 311[57]	80 220[57]	18	...	...	...	...
Le Havre	190 806[57]	90 882[57]	99 924[57]	47	...	...	...	...
Le Mans	145 994[57]	68 982[57]	77 012[57]	53	...	...	...	...
Lille[58]	184 445[57]	86 196[57]	98 249[57]	30	...	...	...	...
Limoges	134 055[57]	62 106[57]	71 949[57]	77	...	...	...	...
Lyon[59]	444 852[57]	206 422[57]	238 430[57]	48	...	...	...	...
Marseille	796 525[57]	376 082[57]	420 443[57]	241	...	...	...	...
Metz	123 720[57]	59 670[57]	64 050[57]	42	...	...	...	...
Montpellier	225 748[57]	103 437[57]	122 311[57]	57	...	...	...	...

Continent, country or area, date, code and city / Continent, pays ou zone, date, code et ville	City proper - Ville proprement dite				Urban agglomeration - Agglomération urbaine			
	Population			Surface area - Superficie (km²)	Population			Surface area - Superficie (km²)
	Both sexes - Les deux sexes	Male - Masculin	Female - Féminin		Both sexes - Les deux sexes	Male - Masculin	Female - Féminin	
EUROPE								
France[56]								
8 III 1999 (CDJC)								
Mulhouse	110 129[57]	53 963[57]	56 166[57]	22	...	...	...	...
Nancy	103 533[57]	47 345[57]	56 188[57]	15	...	...	...	...
Nantes	270 474[57]	126 599[57]	143 875[57]	65	...	...	...	...
Nice	343 166[57]	157 148[57]	186 018[57]	72	...	...	...	...
Nîmes	133 391[57]	62 451[57]	70 940[57]	162	...	...	...	...
Orléans	113 077[57]	53 728[57]	59 349[57]	27	...	...	...	...
PARIS	2 125 017[57]	995 844[57]	1 129 173[57]	105	...	...	...	...
Perpignan	105 027[57]	47 870[57]	57 157[57]	68	...	...	...	...
Reims	187 183[57]	88 707[57]	98 476[57]	47	...	...	...	...
Rennes	206 221[57]	95 224[57]	110 997[57]	50	...	...	...	...
Rouen	106 356[57]	49 432[57]	56 924[57]	21	...	...	...	...
Saint-Étienne	180 393[57]	84 135[57]	96 258[57]	80	...	...	...	...
Strasbourg[58]	263 682[57]	124 926[57]	138 756[57]	78	...	...	...	...
Toulon	160 549[57]	74 964[57]	85 585[57]	43	...	...	...	...
Toulouse	390 174[57]	185 107[57]	205 067[57]	118	...	...	...	...
Tours	132 637[57]	60 117[57]	72 520[57]	34	...	...	...	...
Villeurbanne	124 451[57]	59 519[57]	64 932[57]	15	...	...	...	...
Germany - Allemagne								
1 VII 1999 (ESDJ)								
Aachen	243 825	121 671	122 154	161	...	...	...	...
Augsburg	254 867	121 846	133 021	147	...	...	...	...
Bergisch Gladbach	106 150	50 723	55 427	83	...	...	...	...
BERLIN	3 386 667	1 644 575	1 742 092	891	...	...	...	...
Bielefeld	321 125	152 701	168 424	258	...	...	...	...
Bochum	392 830	190 433	202 397	145	...	...	...	...
Bonn	301 048	143 416	157 632	141	...	...	...	...
Bottrop	121 097	58 490	62 607	101	...	...	...	...
Braunschweig	246 322	119 350	126 972	192	...	...	...	...
Bremen	540 330	259 439	280 891	327	...	...	...	...
Bremerhaven	122 735	59 991	62 744	78	...	...	...	...
Chemnitz	263 222	125 123	138 099	176	...	...	...	...
Cottbus	110 894	53 712	57 182	150	...	...	...	...
Darmstadt	137 776	67 680	70 096	122	...	...	...	...
Dortmund	590 213	286 880	303 333	280	...	...	...	...
Dresden	476 668	229 565	247 103	237	...	...	...	...
Duisburg	519 793	252 735	267 058	233	...	...	...	...
Düsseldorf	568 855	268 630	300 225	217	...	...	...	...
Erfurt	201 267	96 937	104 330	269	...	...	...	...
Erlangen	100 750	48 939	51 811	77	...	...	...	...
Essen	599 515	286 350	313 165	210	...	...	...	...
Frankfurt am Main	643 821	314 431	329 390	248	...	...	...	...
Freiburg im Breisgau	202 455	96 025	106 430	153	...	...	...	...
Fürth	109 771	52 773	56 998	63	...	...	...	...
Gelsenkirchen	281 979	135 781	146 198	105	...	...	...	...
Gera	114 718	55 211	59 507	152	...	...	...	...
Göttingen	124 775	60 334	64 441	117	...	...	...	...
Hagen	205 201	98 338	106 863	160	...	...	...	...
Halle	254 360	121 314	133 046	135	...	...	...	...
Hamburg	1 704 735	824 686	880 049	755	...	...	...	...
Hamm	181 804	89 307	92 497	226	...	...	...	...
Hannover	514 718	245 017	269 701	204	...	...	...	...
Heidelberg	139 672	65 694	73 978	109	...	...	...	...
Heilbronn	119 526	58 400	61 126	100	...	...	...	...
Herne	175 661	85 577	90 084	51	...	...	...	...
Hildesheim	104 013	48 910	55 103	93	...	...	...	...
Ingolstadt	114 826	56 417	58 409	133	...	...	...	...
Kaiserslautern	100 025	49 247	50 778	140	...	...	...	...
Karlsruhe	277 204	134 775	142 429	173	...	...	...	...
Kassel	196 211	93 058	103 153	107	...	...	...	...
Kiel	233 795	113 274	120 521	117	...	...	...	...
Koblenz	108 003	51 340	56 663	105	...	...	...	...
Köln	962 507	466 543	495 964	405	...	...	...	...
Krefeld	241 769	117 087	124 682	138	...	...	...	...

8. Population of capital cities and cities of 100 000 or more inhabitants: latest available year, 1988 - 2007
Population des capitales et des villes de 100 000 habitants ou plus: dernière année disponible, 1988 - 2007 (continued - suite)

Continent, country or area, date, code and city / Continent, pays ou zone, date, code et ville	City proper - Ville proprement dite				Urban agglomeration - Agglomération urbaine			
	Population			Surface area - Superficie (km²)	Population			Surface area - Superficie (km²)
	Both sexes - Les deux sexes	Male - Masculin	Female - Féminin		Both sexes - Les deux sexes	Male - Masculin	Female - Féminin	
EUROPE								
Germany - Allemagne								
1 VII 1999 (ESDJ)								
Leipzig	489 532	235 789	253 743	176	...	...	...	...
Leverkusen	160 841	78 116	82 725	79	...	...	...	...
Lübeck	213 326	101 024	112 302	214	...	...	...	...
Ludwigshafen am Rhein	163 771	81 257	82 514	78	...	...	...	...
Magdeburg	235 073	112 839	122 234	193	...	...	...	...
Mainz	183 134	89 093	94 041	98	...	...	...	...
Mannheim	307 730	151 145	156 585	145	...	...	...	...
Moers	106 837	51 824	55 013	68	...	...	...	...
Mönchengladbach	263 697	126 721	136 976	170	...	...	...	...
Mülheim an der Ruhr	173 895	82 677	91 218	91	...	...	...	...
München	1 194 560	571 363	623 197	311	...	...	...	...
Münster (Westf.)	264 670	123 825	140 845	303	...	...	...	...
Neuss	149 702	72 522	77 180	99	...	...	...	...
Nürnberg	486 628	233 415	253 213	186	...	...	...	...
Oberhausen	222 349	107 562	114 787	77	...	...	...	...
Offenbach am Main	116 627	57 539	59 088	45	...	...	...	...
Oldenburg	154 125	73 572	80 553	103	...	...	...	...
Osnabrück	164 539	77 981	86 558	120	...	...	...	...
Paderborn	137 647	67 010	70 637	179	...	...	...	...
Pforzheim	117 227	55 738	61 489	98	...	...	...	...
Potsdam	128 983	62 651	66 332	109	...	...	...	...
Recklinghausen	125 022	60 456	64 566	66	...	...	...	...
Regensburg	125 236	59 600	65 636	81	...	...	...	...
Remscheid	120 125	57 923	62 202	75	...	...	...	...
Reutlingen	110 343	53 564	56 779	87	...	...	...	...
Rostock	203 279	99 627	103 652	181	...	...	...	...
Saarbrücken	183 836	87 875	95 961	167	...	...	...	...
Salzgitter	112 934	54 808	58 126	224	...	...	...	...
Schwerin	102 878	49 428	53 450	130	...	...	...	...
Siegen	109 225	53 585	55 640	115	...	...	...	...
Solingen	165 583	79 712	85 871	89	...	...	...	...
Stuttgart	582 443	284 977	297 466	207	...	...	...	...
Ulm	116 103	56 511	59 592	119	...	...	...	...
Wiesbaden	268 716	129 032	139 684	204	...	...	...	...
Witten	103 384	49 545	53 839	72	...	...	...	...
Wolfsburg	121 954	59 761	62 193	204	...	...	...	...
Wuppertal	368 993	176 350	192 643	168	...	...	...	...
Würzburg	127 350	58 801	68 549	88	...	...	...	...
Zwickau	104 146	49 513	54 633	73	...	...	...	...
Gibraltar								
14 X 1991 (CDFC)								
GIBRALTAR	28 074	...	...	...				
Greece - Grèce								
18 III 2001 (CDJC)								
ATHINAI	789 166[60]	374 900[60]	414 266[60]	39	...	...	...	...
Calithèa	115 150[60]	54 137[60]	61 013[60]	5	...	...	...	...
Iraclion	135 761[60]	66 956[60]	68 805[60]	52	...	...	...	...
Larissa	131 095[60]	64 000[60]	67 095[60]	88	...	...	...	...
Patrai	168 530[60]	82 981[60]	85 549[60]	57	...	...	...	...
Pésterion	146 743[60]	72 391[60]	74 352[60]	10	...	...	...	...
Pireas[60]	181 933	87 362	94 571	...	...	...	...	...
Thessaloniki[60]	385 406	180 122	205 284	...	...	...	...	...
Guernsey - Guernesey								
29 IV 2001 (CDJC)								
ST. PETER PORT	16 488	...	...					
Holy See - Saint-Siège[61]								
1 VII 2000* (CDFC)								
VATICAN CITY	798[47]	529[47]	269[47]	0[62]	...	...	...	...
Hungary - Hongrie								
1 VII 2007 (ESDF)								
BUDAPEST	1 699 213	774 927	924 286	525	...	...	...	...
Debrecen	204 604	94 646	109 958	462	...	...	...	...
Györ	128 537	60 354	68 183	175	...	...	...	...

8. Population of capital cities and cities of 100 000 or more inhabitants: latest available year, 1988 - 2007
Population des capitales et des villes de 100 000 habitants ou plus: dernière année disponible, 1988 - 2007 (continued - suite)

Continent, country or area, date, code and city Continent, pays ou zone, date, code et ville	City proper - Ville proprement dite				Urban agglomeration - Agglomération urbaine			
	Population			Surface area - Superficie (km²)	Population			Surface area - Superficie (km²)
	Both sexes - Les deux sexes	Male - Masculin	Female - Féminin		Both sexes - Les deux sexes	Male - Masculin	Female - Féminin	
EUROPE								
Hungary - Hongrie								
1 VII 2007 (ESDF)								
Kecskemét	110 082	51 015	59 067	321				
Miskolc	171 867	79 408	92 459	237	...	...	...	...
Nyiregyhaza	116 586	53 872	62 715	275	...	...	...	...
Pécs	156 657	71 943	84 714	163	...	...	...	...
Szeged	165 961	76 087	89 875	281	...	...	...	...
Székesfehérvar	101 678	47 670	54 008	171	...	...	...	...
Iceland - Islande								
1 VII 2007 (ESDJ)								
REYKJAVIK	117 598[63]	58 637[63]	58 961[63]	100	194 460[63]	97 201[63]	97 259[63]	...
Ireland - Irlande								
28 IV 2002 (CDFC)								
Cork	123 062	59 263	63 799	40	186 239	90 348	95 891	...
DUBLIN	495 781	237 813	257 968	118	1 004 614	485 209	519 405	...
Isle of Man - Île de Man								
23 IV 2006 (CDJC)								
DOUGLAS	26 218	13 000	13 218	...	...	...	...	...
Italy - Italie								
1 VII 2007 (ESDJ)								
Ancona	101 671	48 365	53 306	124	...	...	...	...
Bari	325 984	157 100	168 884	116	...	...	...	...
Bergamo	115 921	54 198	61 724	40	...	...	...	...
Bologna	373 385	174 629	198 756	141	...	...	...	...
Brescia	190 552	90 275	100 277	91	...	...	...	...
Cagliari	159 852	74 526	85 326	86	...	...	...	...
Catania	302 854	142 822	160 033	181	...	...	...	...
Ferrara	132 843	62 092	70 751	404	...	...	...	...
Firenze	366 434	171 390	195 044	102	...	...	...	...
Foggia	153 590	74 117	79 473	508	...	...	...	...
Forli	113 041	54 510	58 531	228	...	...	...	...
Genova	618 001	290 333	327 669	244	...	...	...	...
Giugliano in Campania	109 419	53 897	55 522	94	...	...	...	...
Latina	113 503	54 627	58 876	278	...	...	...	...
Livorno	160 518	76 705	83 813	104	...	...	...	...
Messina	245 741	117 243	128 498	211	...	...	...	...
Milano	1 306 086	617 637	688 449	182	...	...	...	...
Modena	180 275	86 701	93 574	183	...	...	...	...
Monza	121 703	58 470	63 233	33	...	...	...	...
Napoli	979 691	466 667	513 024	117	...	...	...	...
Novara	102 706	49 252	53 455	103	...	...	...	...
Padova	210 643	99 177	111 466	93	...	...	...	...
Palermo	668 686	318 461	350 226	159	...	...	...	...
Parma	176 429	83 750	92 680	261	...	...	...	...
Perugia	161 667	77 089	84 578	450	...	...	...	...
Pescara	122 430	57 692	64 738	33	...	...	...	...
Prato	184 742	90 440	94 302	98	...	...	...	...
Ravenna	150 070	73 076	76 994	653	...	...	...	...
Reggio di Calabria	184 274	88 616	95 658	236	...	...	...	...
Reggio nell'Emilia	158 599	77 382	81 217	232	...	...	...	...
Rimini	136 603	65 928	70 675	134	...	...	...	...
ROMA	2 626 640	1 234 647	1 391 993	1 308	...	...	...	...
Salerno	133 805	62 521	71 285	59	...	...	...	...
Sassari	128 252	61 771	66 482	546	...	...	...	...
Siracusa	123 148	59 991	63 158	204	...	...	...	...
Taranto	196 976	93 795	103 181	210	...	...	...	...
Terni	109 693	51 967	57 726	212	...	...	...	...
Torino	900 589	429 749	470 840	130	...	...	...	...
Trento	111 381	53 370	58 011	158	...	...	...	...
Trieste	205 711	96 058	109 653	84	...	...	...	...
Venezia	269 357	127 676	141 681	416	...	...	...	...
Verona	260 049	123 730	136 320	207	...	...	...	...
Vicenza	114 250	54 444	59 806	81	...	...	...	...
Jersey								
11 III 2001 (CDJC)								
ST. HELIER	28 310	13 669	14 641	9	...	...	...	...

8. Population of capital cities and cities of 100 000 or more inhabitants: latest available year, 1988 - 2007
Population des capitales et des villes de 100 000 habitants ou plus: dernière année disponible, 1988 - 2007 (continued - suite)

Continent, country or area, date, code and city Continent, pays ou zone, date, code et ville	City proper - Ville proprement dite				Urban agglomeration - Agglomération urbaine			
	Population			Surface area - Superficie (km²)	Population			Surface area - Superficie (km²)
	Both sexes - Les deux sexes	Male - Masculin	Female - Féminin		Both sexes - Les deux sexes	Male - Masculin	Female - Féminin	
EUROPE								
Latvia - Lettonie								
1 VII 2007 (ESDJ)								
Daugavpils	107 025	47 548	59 477	72	...	...	...	...
RIGA	719 928	319 946	399 982	303	...	...	...	...
Liechtenstein								
1 VII 2007 (ESDF)								
VADUZ	5 091	2 463	2 628	17	...	...	...	...
Lithuania - Lituanie[64]								
1 VII 2007 (ESDJ)								
Kaunas	356 849	159 998	196 851	157	...	...	...	...
Klaipeda	185 296	85 083	100 213	98	...	...	...	...
Panevezhis	114 117	51 931	62 186	50	...	...	...	...
Shauliai	127 728	58 132	69 596	81	...	...	...	...
VILNIUS	543 494	246 472	297 022	394	...	...	...	...
Luxembourg								
1 VII 2007 (ESDJ)								
LUXEMBOURG-VILLE	84 644	...	...	51	...	...	...	...
Malta - Malte								
1 VII 2007 (ESDJ)								
VALLETTA	6 318[65]	3 089[65]	3 229[65]	1	...	...	...	...
Monaco								
1 VII 2000 (ESDJ)								
MONACO	*32 020*	*15 544*	*16 476*	...	...	...	...	...
Netherlands - Pays-Bas								
1 I 2007 (ESDJ)								
Almere[66]	180 924	89 697	91 227	130	...	...	...	...
Amersfoort	139 054[66]	68 011[66]	71 043[66]	63[66]	167 664	82 103	85 561	122
AMSTERDAM	742 884[66]	365 705[66]	377 179[66]	166[66]	1 022 487	501 962	520 525	367
Apeldoorn[66]	155 564	76 397	79 167	340	...	...	...	...
Arnhem	142 569[66]	70 548[66]	72 021[66]	98[66]	144 096	71 294	72 802	126
Breda[66]	170 349	82 722	87 627	127	...	...	...	...
Dordrecht	118 541[66]	58 085[66]	60 456[66]	79[66]	235 811	115 530	120 281	139
Ede[66]	107 500	52 635	54 865	318	...	...	...	...
Eindhoven	209 699[66]	106 060[66]	103 639[66]	88[66]	322 633	162 121	160 512	199
Emmen[66]	108 832	53 807	55 025	337	...	...	...	...
Enschede[66]	154 476	78 530	75 946	141	...	...	...	...
Geleen-Sittard	...	...	...	...	139 293	68 558	70 735	121
Groningen	181 613[66]	89 805[66]	91 808[66]	78[66]	200 422	98 635	101 787	124
Haarlem	146 960[66]	71 262[66]	75 698[66]	29[66]	189 563	91 216	98 347	76
Haarlemmermeer[66]	138 255	68 860	69 395	179	...	...	...	...
Heerlen-Kerkrade	...	...	...	...	207 762	102 155	105 607	109
Leiden	117 485[66]	57 273[66]	60 212[66]	22[66]	249 480	121 814	127 666	77
Maastricht[66]	119 038	57 245	61 793	57	...	...	...	...
Nijmegen[66]	160 907	76 965	83 942	54	...	...	...	...
Rotterdam	584 058[66]	285 800[66]	298 258[66]	206[66]	985 950	482 471	503 479	329
s-Gravenhage	...	...	...	...	619 414	301 614	317 800	180
s-Hertogenbosch	135 648[66]	66 669[66]	68 979[66]	84[66]	160 887	79 112	81 775	118
The Hague[66]	473 941	232 529	241 412	82	...	...	...	...
Tilburg	201 259[66]	99 623[66]	101 636[66]	117[66]	223 343	110 606	112 737	159
Utrecht	288 401[66]	139 298[66]	149 103[66]	95[66]	423 153	205 706	217 447	167
Zaanstad[66]	141 402	69 713	71 689	74	...	...	...	...
Zoetermeer[66]	118 024	57 832	60 192	35	...	...	...	...
Zwolle[66]	114 635	55 680	58 955	112	...	...	...	...
Norway - Norvège[67]								
1 VII 2007 (ESDJ)								
Bergen	246 183	122 077	124 107	445	...	...	...	...
OSLO	554 551	272 318	282 233	426	...	...	...	...
Stavanger	118 451	59 097	59 354	68	...	...	...	...
Trondheim	163 461	81 160	82 301	322	...	...	...	...
Poland - Pologne[68]								
1 VII 2007 (ESDF)								
Bialystok	294 817	138 111	156 706	102	...	...	...	...
Bielsko-Biala	176 182	83 114	93 068	125	...	...	...	...
Bydgoszcz	362 397	169 854	192 543	175	...	...	...	...
Bytom	185 793	89 897	95 896	69	...	...	...	...

Continent, country or area, date, code and city / Continent, pays ou zone, date, code et ville	City proper - Ville proprement dite				Urban agglomeration - Agglomération urbaine			
	Population			Surface area - Superficie (km²)	Population			Surface area - Superficie (km²)
	Both sexes - Les deux sexes	Male - Masculin	Female - Féminin		Both sexes - Les deux sexes	Male - Masculin	Female - Féminin	
EUROPE								
Poland - Pologne[68]								
1 VII 2007 (ESDF)								
Chorzów	113 739	54 222	59 517	33				
Czestochowa	244 137	114 884	129 253	160	...	...	...	...
Dabrowa Górnicza	129 281	62 331	66 950	189	...	...	...	...
Elblag	126 876	60 671	66 205	80	...	...	...	...
Gdansk	456 103	216 041	240 062	262	...	...	...	...
Gdynia	251 183	119 709	131 474	135	...	...	...	...
Gliwice	197 874	95 400	102 474	134	...	...	...	...
Gorzów Wielkopolski	125 438	59 762	65 676	86	...	...	...	...
Kalisz	108 311	50 547	57 764	69	...	...	...	...
Katowice	313 461	148 273	165 188	165	...	...	...	...
Kielce	206 796	97 989	108 807	110	...	...	...	...
Koszalin	107 448	51 177	56 271	83	...	...	...	...
Kraków	756 336	353 691	402 645	327	...	...	...	...
Legnica	105 025	49 830	55 195	56	...	...	...	...
Lódz	756 666	344 347	412 319	293	...	...	...	...
Lublin	352 786	162 704	190 082	147	...	...	...	...
Olsztyn	175 098	81 242	93 856	88	...	...	...	...
Opole	127 246	59 644	67 602	97	...	...	...	...
Plock	127 017	60 771	66 246	88	...	...	...	...
Poznan	564 035	262 793	301 242	262	...	...	...	...
Radom	225 292	107 549	117 743	112	...	...	...	...
Ruda Slaska	144 914	70 545	74 369	78	...	...	...	...
Rybnik	141 262	69 236	72 026	148	...	...	...	...
Rzeszów	166 684	78 826	87 858	77	...	...	...	...
Sosnowiec	223 284	106 189	117 095	91	...	...	...	...
Szczecin	408 583	194 206	214 377	301	...	...	...	...
Tarnów	116 527	55 274	61 253	72	...	...	...	...
Torun	206 765	95 827	110 938	116	...	...	...	...
Tychy	130 355	63 200	67 155	82	...	...	...	...
Walbrzych	124 357	58 604	65 753	85	...	...	...	...
WARSZAWA	1 704 717	784 184	920 533	517	...	...	...	...
Wloclawek	118 957	56 000	62 957	84	...	...	...	...
Wroclaw	633 950	296 432	337 518	293	...	...	...	...
Zabrze	189 656	91 706	97 950	80	...	...	...	...
Zielona Góra	118 045	55 315	62 730	58	...	...		...
Portugal								
1 VII 2007 (ESDJ)								
Amadora	173 962	83 117	90 846	24				
LISBOA	504 726	229 585	275 141	85	...	...	...	...
Porto	224 795	101 743	123 053	41	...	...	...	...
Republic of Moldova - République de Moldova								
1 VII 2007 (ESDJ)								
Balti (Beltsy)	142 703	65 376	77 327	41	147 607	67 711	79 896	78
CHIŞINĂU (KISHINEV)	660 726	307 719	353 007	123	782 693	367 534	415 159	572
Romania - Roumanie								
1 VII 2007 (ESDJ)								
Arad	167 238	78 116	89 122	267	...	...	...	...
Bacau	178 203	85 427	92 776	43	...	...	...	...
Baia Mare	139 870	66 994	72 876	233	...	...	...	...
Botosani	115 739	55 472	60 267	41	...	...	...	...
Braila	215 316	102 865	112 451	33	...	...	...	...
Brasov	277 945	132 365	145 580	267	...	...	...	...
BUCURESTI	1 931 838	899 960	1 031 878	238	...	...	...	...
Buzau	134 619	64 456	70 163	81	...	...	...	...
Cluj-Napoca	310 243	145 894	164 349	180	...	...	...	...
Constanta	304 279	143 620	160 659	127	...	...	...	...
Craiova	299 429	143 123	156 306	81	...	...	...	...
Drobeta Turnu-Severin	107 882	52 219	55 663	55	...	...	...	...
Galati	293 523	142 358	151 165	246	...	...	...	...
Iasi	315 214	149 187	166 027	94	...	...	...	...
Oradea	205 077	96 776	108 301	111	...	...	...	...
Piatra Neamt	108 085	51 421	56 664	77	...	...	...	...
Pitesti	168 958	80 804	88 154	41	...	...	...	...
Ploiesti	230 240	108 482	121 758	58	...	...	...	...

Continent, country or area, date, code and city / Continent, pays ou zone, date, code et ville	City proper - Ville proprement dite				Urban agglomeration - Agglomération urbaine			
	Population			Surface area - Superficie (km²)	Population			Surface area - Superficie (km²)
	Both sexes - Les deux sexes	Male - Masculin	Female - Féminin		Both sexes - Les deux sexes	Male - Masculin	Female - Féminin	
EUROPE								
Romania - Roumanie								
1 VII 2007 (ESDJ)								
Rimnicu Vilcea	111 342	53 416	57 926	90	...	...	...	...
Satu-Mare	113 688	53 750	59 938	150	...	...	...	...
Sibiu	154 458	72 264	82 194	122	...	...	...	...
Suceava	106 397	51 103	55 294	52	...	...	...	...
Timisoara	307 347	144 002	163 345	49	...	...	...	...
Tirgu-Mures	145 943	69 266	76 677	130	...	...	...	...
Russian Federation - Fédération de Russie								
1 VII 2007 (ESDJ)								
Abakan	163 146	74 831	88 315	...	112 508	...	...	...
Achinsk	111 230	50 037	61 193	...	...	...	...	...
Almetievsk	141 917	65 953	75 964	...	...	...	...	...
Angarsk	243 339	111 310	132 029	...	...	...	...	...
Arkhangelsk	348 661	155 248	193 413	...	354 633	...	...	...
Armavir	189 554	84 723	104 831	...	208 258	...	...	...
Artem (Primorskiy Krai)	102 381	47 855	54 526	...	111 821	...	...	...
Arzamas	106 184	47 975	58 209	...	...	...	...	...
Asbest	...	...	...	...	103 581	...	...	...
Astrakhan	501 638	229 139	272 499	...	...	...	...	...
Balakovo	198 914	89 990	108 924	...	200 155	...	...	...
Balashikha	186 792	87 293	99 499	...	...	...	...	...
Barnaul	598 671	266 279	332 392	...	648 700	...	...	...
Bataisk	102 146	48 137	54 009	...	...	...	...	...
Belgorod	350 598	158 930	191 668	...	...	...	...	...
Belovo	...	...	...	...	136 906	...	...	...
Berezniki	166 477	74 093	92 384	...	...	...	...	...
Biisk	222 249	98 970	123 279	...	223 707	...	...	...
Blagoveshchensk (Amurskaya oblast)	208 197	95 275	112 922	...	213 424	...	...	...
Bratsk	252 584	114 139	138 445	...	...	...	...	...
Bryansk	415 063	184 356	230 707	...	433 486	...	...	...
Chaykovsky	...	...	...	...	108 630	...	...	...
Cheboksary	441 425	197 667	243 758	...	453 032	...	...	...
Chelyabinsk	1 091 992	489 751	602 241	...	...	...	...	...
Cherepovets	307 915	140 308	167 607	...	...	...	...	...
Cherkessk	116 290	52 004	64 286	...	...	...	...	...
Chita	305 957	142 479	163 478	...	306 296	...	...	...
Derbent	108 351	51 919	56 432	...	...	...	...	...
Dimitrovgrad	127 286	59 078	68 208	...	...	...	...	...
Dzerzhinsk (Nizhegorodskaya oblast)	248 713	110 448	138 265	...	257 352	...	...	...
Ekaterinburg	1 319 028	593 598	725 430	...	1 350 354	...	...	...
Elektrostal	145 861	65 274	80 587	...	...	...	...	...
Elets	112 458	50 782	61 676	...	...	...	...	...
Elista	102 702	46 399	56 303	...	106 664	...	...	...
Engels	202 615	92 691	109 924	...	239 017	...	...	...
Groznyi	224 070	102 864	121 206	...	...	...	...	...
Hasaviurt	126 560	60 657	65 903	...	...	...	...	...
Irkutsk	575 843	258 740	317 103	...	...	...	...	...
Ivanovo	407 716	178 356	229 360	...	...	...	...	...
Izhevsk	614 479	276 117	338 362	...	...	...	...	...
Kaliningrad (Kaliningradskaya oblast)	422 013	196 941	225 072	...	...	...	...	...
Kaluga	327 228	145 116	182 112	...	341 340	...	...	...
Kamensk-Uralsky	181 272	80 737	100 535	...	182 798	...	...	...
Kamyshin	119 265	56 643	62 622	...	...	...	...	...
Kazan	1 118 116	495 897	622 219	...	...	...	...	...
Kemerovo	519 924	232 444	287 480	...	...	...	...	...
Khabarovsk	577 377	267 027	310 350	...	...	...	...	...
Khimki	182 276	82 376	99 900	...	...	...	...	...
Kirov	465 411	204 956	260 455	...	487 166	...	...	...
Kiselevsk	103 595	47 046	56 549	...	108 173	...	...	...
Kislovodsk	128 880	58 299	70 581	...	134 607	...	...	...
Kolomna	147 958	68 064	79 894	...	...	...	...	...
Komsomolsk-na-Amure	272 007	126 343	145 664	...	...	...	...	...
Kopeysk	137 307	66 648	70 659	...	139 455	...	...	...
Korolev (Moskovskaya oblast)	174 090	78 043	96 047	...	...	...	...	...
Kostroma	272 540	121 626	150 914	...	...	...	...	...

Continent, country or area, date, code and city / Continent, pays ou zone, date, code et ville	City proper - Ville proprement dite				Urban agglomeration - Agglomération urbaine			
	Population			Surface area - Superficie (km²)	Population			Surface area - Superficie (km²)
	Both sexes - Les deux sexes	Male - Masculin	Female - Féminin		Both sexes - Les deux sexes	Male - Masculin	Female - Féminin	

EUROPE

Russian Federation - Fédération de Russie
1 VII 2007 (ESDJ)

Kovrov	150 661	69 539	81 122	...	...	...	...	...
Krasnodar	709 345	322 226	387 119	...	...	...	...	...
Krasnoyarsk	931 800	419 740	512 060	...	779 767	...	...	...
Kurgan	325 272	145 016	180 256	...	932 512	...	...	...
Kursk	407 027	181 214	225 813	...	...	...	...	...
Kyzyl	108 192	49 706	58 486	...	...	...	...	...
Leninsk-Kuznetsky	105 898	48 751	57 147	...	108 249	...	...	...
Lipetsk	502 558	228 419	274 139	...	...	...	...	...
Lyubertsy	158 911	70 242	88 669	...	...	...	...	...
Magadan	99 909	46 719	53 190	...	107 355	...	...	...
Magnitogorsk	409 767	187 001	222 766	...	...	...	...	...
Maikop	155 079	69 510	85 569	...	173 742	...	...	...
Makhachkala	465 566	222 910	242 656	...	551 955	...	...	...
Mezhdurechensk	103 654	48 320	55 334	...	...	...	...	...
Miass	153 114	69 023	84 091	...	167 208	...	...	...
MOSKVA	10 456 490	4 969 687	5 486 803	...	...	...	...	...
Murmansk	316 126	145 614	170 512	...	...	...	...	...
Murom	120 100	53 186	66 914	...	...	...	...	...
Mytishchi	163 061	72 773	90 288	...	...	...	...	...
Naberezhnye Tchelny	506 244	233 690	272 554	...	...	...	...	...
Nakhodka	169 251	81 900	87 351	...	170 250	...	...	...
Naltchik	269 999	121 382	148 617	...	295 779	...	...	...
Nazran	133 253	63 441	69 812	...	...	...	...	...
Neftekamsk	117 903	54 531	63 372	...	129 178	...	...	...
Nefteyugansk	115 186	56 529	58 657	...	...	...	...	...
Nevinnomyssk	129 157	60 469	68 688	...	...	...	...	...
Nizhnekamsk	226 498	105 777	120 721	...	...	...	...	...
Nizhnevartovsk	242 744	118 685	124 059	...	...	...	...	...
Nizhny Novgorod	1 276 524	562 293	714 231	...	1 284 556	...	...	...
Nizhny Tagil	376 622	172 450	204 172	...	...	...	...	...
Noginsk	115 862	52 065	63 797	...	...	...	...	...
Norilsk	207 853	103 518	104 335	...	208 971	...	...	...
Novocheboksarsk	126 176	58 969	67 207	...	126 464	...	...	...
Novocherkassk	177 508	84 400	93 108	...	...	...	...	...
Novokuybishevsk	111 249	49 793	61 456	...	113 299	...	...	...
Novokuznetsk	561 547	252 852	308 695	...	...	...	...	...
Novomoskovsk (Tulskaya oblast)	124 901	55 748	69 153	...	...	...	...	...
Novorossiysk	228 544	109 214	119 330	...	281 110	...	...	...
Novoshakhtinsk	114 573	51 965	62 608	...	...	...	...	...
Novosibirsk	1 391 216	630 908	760 308	...	...	...	...	...
Novotroitsk	102 694	48 759	53 935	...	110 233	...	...	...
Novy Urengoy	117 672	58 830	58 842	...	...	...	...	...
Noyabrsk	110 121	54 471	55 650	...	...	...	...	...
Obninsk	105 430	48 379	57 051	...	...	...	...	...
Odintsovo	129 541	61 097	68 444	...	...	...	...	...
Oktyabrsky	107 934	49 699	58 235	...	...	...	...	...
Omsk	1 132 937	514 446	618 491	...	...	...	...	...
Orekhovo-Zuevo	121 813	53 040	68 773	...	...	...	...	...
Orel	321 872	142 938	178 934	...	...	...	...	...
Orenburg	528 014	241 051	286 963	...	542 955	...	...	...
Orsk	245 804	108 541	137 263	...	...	...	...	...
Penza	508 510	228 506	280 004	...	...	...	...	...
Perm	988 695	442 891	545 804	...	988 707	...	...	...
Pervouralsk	133 801	60 095	73 706	...	158 832	...	...	...
Petropavlovsk-Kamchatsky	195 016	97 002	98 014	...	...	...	...	...
Petrozavodsk	267 524	117 677	149 847	...	...	...	...	...
Podolsk	179 683	80 000	99 683	...	...	...	...	...
Prokopyevsk	213 960	96 661	117 299	...	215 168	...	...	...
Pskov	194 516	86 748	107 768	...	...	...	...	...
Pyatigorsk	139 706	62 646	77 060	...	206 270	...	...	...
Rostov-na-Donu	1 050 172	477 693	572 479	...	...	...	...	...
Rubtsovsk	156 727	74 030	82 697	...	...	...	...	...
Ryazan	511 512	230 969	280 543	...	...	...	...	...
Rybinsk	211 962	94 518	117 444	...	...	...	...	...

8. Population of capital cities and cities of 100 000 or more inhabitants: latest available year, 1988 - 2007
Population des capitales et des villes de 100 000 habitants ou plus: dernière année disponible, 1988 - 2007 (continued - suite)

Continent, country or area, date, code and city / Continent, pays ou zone, date, code et ville	City proper - Ville proprement dite				Urban agglomeration - Agglomération urbaine			
	Population			Surface area - Superficie (km²)	Population			Surface area - Superficie (km²)
	Both sexes - Les deux sexes	Male - Masculin	Female - Féminin		Both sexes - Les deux sexes	Male - Masculin	Female - Féminin	

EUROPE

Russian Federation - Fédération de Russie
1 VII 2007 (ESDJ)

Salavat	156 098	74 603	81 495	...	...	...	...	...
Samara (Samarskaya oblast)	1 137 208	509 592	627 616	...	1 137 254	...	...	...
Saransk	295 366	130 984	164 382	...	322 413	...	...	...
Saratov	838 769	373 908	464 861	...	...	...	...	...
Sergiev Posad	110 206	49 687	60 519	...	...	...	...	...
Serov	98 487	43 797	54 690	...	100 369	...	...	...
Serpukhov	124 016	56 021	67 995	...	...	...	...	...
Severodvinsk	192 308	88 274	104 034	...	...	...	...	...
Seversk	107 121	49 955	57 166	...	...	...	...	...
Shakhty	245 127	110 882	134 245	...	...	...	...	...
Shchelkovo	112 903	52 561	60 342	...	...	...	...	...
Smolensk	317 126	140 100	177 026	...	...	...	...	...
Sochi	332 670	151 028	181 642	...	...	...	...	...
St. Petersburg	4 569 616	2 046 237	2 523 379	...	...	...	...	...
Stary Oskol	219 682	100 657	119 025	...	...	...	...	...
Stavropol	361 721	165 314	196 407	...	361 920	...	...	...
Sterlitamak	267 260	121 519	145 741	...	...	...	...	...
Surgut	292 021	142 199	149 822	...	...	...	...	...
Syktivkar	230 075	104 353	125 722	...	245 371	...	...	...
Syzran	179 405	81 172	98 233	...	180 223	...	...	...
Taganrog	262 541	117 282	145 259	...	...	...	...	...
Tambov	280 797	124 928	155 869	...	...	...	...	...
Tobolsk	99 904	45 476	54 428	...	104 121	...	...	...
Tolyatti	705 380	329 334	376 046	...	718 208	...	...	...
Tomsk	494 754	228 230	266 524	...	514 318	...	...	...
Tula	501 997	220 675	281 322	...	...	...	...	...
Tver	406 388	178 286	228 102	...	...	...	...	...
Tyumen	554 942	255 284	299 658	...	583 459	...	...	...
Ufa	1 022 017	464 871	557 146	...	1 029 221	...	...	...
Uhta	103 464	48 930	54 534	...	127 168	...	...	...
Ulan-Ude	341 913	156 610	185 303	...	372 858	...	...	...
Ulyanovsk	609 339	277 094	332 245	...	630 390	...	...	...
Ussuriisk	153 661	73 790	79 871	...	180 943	...	...	...
Velikie Luky	100 717	44 478	56 239	...	...	...	...	...
Velikiy Novgorod	216 436	93 862	122 574	...	...	...	...	...
Vladikavkaz (Osetinskaya ASSR)	313 266	146 094	167 172	...	330 581	...	...	...
Vladimir	339 675	152 448	187 227	...	...	...	...	...
Vladivostok	579 811	270 451	309 360	...	606 361	...	...	...
Volgodonsk	169 882	77 348	92 534	...	...	...	...	...
Volgograd	985 126	447 331	537 795	...	1 019 750	...	...	...
Vologda	286 199	126 919	159 280	...	293 764	...	...	...
Volzhsky	306 842	140 152	166 690	...	317 730	...	...	...
Vorkuta	...	...	...	...	118 496	...	...	...
Voronezh	840 309	374 372	465 937	...	...	...	...	...
Yakutsk	250 700	114 519	136 181	...	271 374	...	...	...
Yaroslave	604 589	267 696	336 893	...	...	...	...	...
Yoshkar-Ola	249 212	111 838	137 374	...	273 037	...	...	...
Yuzhno-Sakhalinsk	173 492	80 585	92 907	...	181 035	...	...	...
Zheleznodorozhny	120 768	54 322	66 446	...	...	...	...	...
Zheleznogorsk	...	...	...	...	102 696	...	...	...
Zhukovsky	102 548	46 660	55 888	...	...	...	...	...
Zlatoust	189 059	85 881	103 178	...	191 465	...	...	...

San Marino - Saint-Marin
1 VII 2004 (ESDF)

SAN MARINO	4 464	2 168	2 296	...	...	...	...	...

Serbia - Serbie
1 VII 2007 (ESDJ)

BEOGRAD (BELGRADE)	1 313 994	612 949	701 045	389	1 611 333[69]	761 457[69]	849 876[69]	3 215[69]
Čačak	73 739	35 387	38 352	38	116 254[69]	56 429[69]	59 825[69]	642[69]
Kragujevac	146 681	70 901	75 780	83	174 626[69]	84 799[69]	89 827[69]	847[69]
Kraljevo	64 307	31 028	33 279	22	119 994[69]	58 797[69]	61 197[69]	1 529[69]
Kruševac	57 016	27 115	29 901	11	128 758[69]	62 570[69]	66 188[69]	854[69]
Leskovac	68 537	33 426	35 111	24	151 964[69]	75 638[69]	76 326[69]	1 025[69]

8. Population of capital cities and cities of 100 000 or more inhabitants: latest available year, 1988 - 2007
Population des capitales et des villes de 100 000 habitants ou plus: dernière année disponible, 1988 - 2007 (continued - suite)

Continent, country or area, date, code and city / Continent, pays ou zone, date, code et ville	City proper - Ville proprement dite				Urban agglomeration - Agglomération urbaine			
	Population			Surface area - Superficie (km²)	Population			Surface area - Superficie (km²)
	Both sexes - Les deux sexes	Male - Masculin	Female - Féminin		Both sexes - Les deux sexes	Male - Masculin	Female - Féminin	
EUROPE								
Serbia - Serbie								
1 VII 2007 (ESDJ)								
Niš	177 571	85 387	92 184	43	239 645[69]	116 800[69]	122 845[69]	597[69]
Novi Sad	252 881	118 186	134 695	103	319 259[69]	151 071[69]	168 188[69]	699[69]
Pancevo	91 907	44 151	47 756	162	125 769[69]	61 141[69]	64 628[69]	756[69]
Šabac	54 468	25 716	28 752	31	120 000[69]	58 577[69]	61 423[69]	795[69]
Smederevo	63 526	30 887	32 639	40	109 007[69]	53 706[69]	55 301[69]	481[69]
Subotica	107 157	50 897	56 260	164	145 752[69]	69 967[69]	75 785[69]	1 007[69]
Zrenjanin	77 778	37 167	40 611	50	127 416[69]	61 833[69]	65 583[69]	1 327[69]
Slovakia - Slovaquie								
1 VII 2007 (ESDJ)								
BRATISLAVA	426 808	199 890	226 918	368				
Kosice	234 663	111 878	122 785	243	...	...	...	...
Slovenia - Slovénie								
1 VII 2007 (ESDJ)								
LJUBLJANA	250 953	116 626	134 327	164	252 639	117 452	135 187	171
Maribor	88 679	41 577	47 102	38	106 245	50 216	56 029	99
Spain - Espagne								
1 I 2006 (ESDJ)								
Albacete	161 508	79 498	82 010	12 431				
Alcalá de Henares	201 380	101 351	100 029	...	...	...	...	...
Alcobendas	104 118	50 765	53 353	...	...	...	...	...
Alcorcón	164 633	81 380	83 253	...	...	...	...	...
Algeciras	112 937	57 853	55 084	...	...	...	...	...
Alicante	322 431	156 772	165 659	2 008	...	...	...	...
Almería	185 309	91 235	94 074	2 962	...	...	...	...
Badajoz	143 748	69 853	73 895	15 302	...	...	...	...
Badalona	221 520	112 117	109 403	...	...	...	...	...
Barcelona	1 605 602	761 870	843 732	991	...	...	...	...
Bilbao	354 145	167 652	186 493	413	...	...	...	...
Burgos	173 676	83 580	90 096	1 084	...	...	...	...
Cádiz	130 561	62 374	68 187	112	...	...	...	...
Cartagena	208 609	106 497	102 112	...	...	...	...	...
Castellón de la Plana	172 110	85 208	86 902	1 075	...	...	...	...
Córdoba	322 867	155 543	167 324	12 533	...	...	...	...
Coruña (A)	243 320	113 431	129 889	...	...	...	...	...
Donostia - San Sebastián	183 308	86 116	97 192	615	...	...	...	...
Dos Hermanas	114 672	56 871	57 801	...	...	...	...	...
Elche	219 032	109 595	109 437	...	...	...	...	...
Fuenlabrada	193 715	98 089	95 626	...	...	...	...	...
Getafe	156 320	77 584	78 736	...	...	...	...	...
Gijón	274 472	130 229	144 243	...	...	...	...	...
Granada	237 929	110 698	127 231	882	...	...	...	...
Hospitalet de Llobregat	248 150	121 707	126 443	...	...	...	...	...
Huelva	145 763	70 688	75 075	1 513	...	...	...	...
Jaén	116 769	56 459	60 310	4 243	...	...	...	...
Jérez de la Frontera	199 544	97 424	102 120	...	...	...	...	...
La Coruña	243 320	113 431	129 889	376	...	...	...	...
Las Palmas de Gran Canaria	377 056	184 295	192 761	1 005	...	...	...	...
Leganés	182 471	90 850	91 621	...	...	...	...	...
León	136 985	63 255	73 730	392	...	...	...	...
Lleida	125 677	62 347	63 330	2 120	...	...	...	...
Logroño	147 036	71 617	75 419	796	...	...	...	...
MADRID	3 128 600	1 469 284	1 659 316	6 058	...	...	...	...
Málaga	560 631	270 672	289 959	3 930	...	...	...	...
Marbella	125 519	61 899	63 620	...	...	...	...	...
Mataró	118 748	59 683	59 065	...	...	...	...	...
Móstoles	206 301	102 998	103 303	...	...	...	...	...
Murcia	416 996	207 800	209 196	8 865	...	...	...	...
Ourense	108 137	50 362	57 775	845	...	...	...	...
Oviedo	214 883	100 072	114 811	1 866	...	...	...	...
Palma de Mallorca	375 048	183 443	191 605	2 008	...	...	...	...
Palmas de Gran Canaria	377 056	184 295	192 761	...	...	...	...	...
Pamplona	195 769	93 775	101 994	238	...	...	...	...
Reus	101 767	50 697	51 070	...	...	...	...	...

8. Population of capital cities and cities of 100 000 or more inhabitants: latest available year, 1988 - 2007
Population des capitales et des villes de 100 000 habitants ou plus: dernière année disponible, 1988 - 2007 (continued - suite)

Continent, country or area, date, code and city / Continent, pays ou zone, date, code et ville	City proper - Ville proprement dite				Urban agglomeration - Agglomération urbaine			
	Population			Surface area - Superficie (km²)	Population			Surface area - Superficie (km²)
	Both sexes - Les deux sexes	Male - Masculin	Female - Féminin		Both sexes - Les deux sexes	Male - Masculin	Female - Féminin	
EUROPE								
Spain - Espagne								
1 I 2006 (ESDJ)								
Sabadell	200 545	98 312	102 233	...	...	...	...	...
Salamanca	159 754	74 349	85 405	386	...	...	...	...
San Cristóbal de La Laguna	142 161	69 995	72 166	...	...	...	...	...
Santa Coloma de Gramanet	119 056	60 583	58 473	...	...	...	...	...
Santa Cruz de Tenerife	223 148	107 638	115 510	1 506	...	...	...	...
Santander	182 926	85 243	97 683	348	...	...	...	...
Sevilla	704 414	335 792	368 622	1 413	...	...	...	...
Tarragona	131 158	64 783	66 375	624	...	...	...	...
Terrassa	199 817	99 579	100 238	...	...	...	...	...
Torrejón de Ardoz	112 114	55 605	56 509	...	...	...	...	...
Valencia	805 304	388 401	416 903	1 346	...	...	...	...
Valladolid	319 943	152 976	166 967	1 975	...	...	...	...
Vigo	293 255	139 869	153 386	...	...	...	...	...
Vitoria-Gasteiz	227 568	112 028	115 540	2 768	...	...	...	...
Zaragoza	649 181	314 460	334 721	10 631	...	...	...	...
Sweden - Suède								
1 VII 2007 (ESDJ)								
Göteborg	491 630	242 916	248 714	449	...	...	...	...
Helsingborg	124 188	60 672	63 516	346	...	...	...	...
Jönköping	122 952	60 462	62 490	1 485	...	...	...	...
Linköping	139 474	70 239	69 235	1 431	...	...	...	...
Malmö	278 523	135 997	142 526	154	...	...	...	...
Norrköping	126 072	62 323	63 749	1 491	...	...	...	...
Orebro	129 703	63 123	66 581	1 371	...	...	...	...
STOCKHOLM	789 024	384 243	404 781	187	...	...	...	...
Umeå	111 503	55 549	55 955	2 316	...	...	...	...
Uppsala	186 364	91 149	95 215	2 465	...	...	...	...
Västerås	133 324	66 056	67 269	956	...	...	...	...
Switzerland - Suisse								
1 I 2007 (ESDJ)								
Baden-Brugg	25 558	12 720	12 838	19	109 631	54 420	55 211	124
Bâle	163 438	77 597	85 841	24	486 431	234 914	251 517	481
BERNE	122 256	57 388	64 868	52	344 167	164 906	179 261	481
Genève	178 574	84 216	94 358	16	495 262	237 855	257 407	457
Lausanne	117 664	55 513	62 151	41	311 494	150 036	161 458	312
Lugano	49 449	22 984	26 465	26	127 962	60 627	67 335	222
Luzern	57 691	26 863	30 828	16	199 683	97 235	102 448	198
Olten-Zofingen	26 971	13 055	13 916	23	105 038	51 778	53 260	183
St. Gallen	70 319	33 744	36 575	39	145 403	70 614	74 789	175
Winterthur	94 094	45 632	48 462	68	129 331	63 186	66 145	151
Zug	24 507	12 193	12 314	22	102 487	51 548	50 939	180
Zürich	348 680	169 162	179 518	88	1 106 451	543 825	562 626	937
The Former Yugoslav Republic of Macedonia - L'ex-République yougoslave de Macédoine								
1 VII 2007 (ESDF)								
Kumanovo	106 407	53 671	52 736	...	...	...	...	...
SKOPLJE	524 470	257 361	267 109	...	...	...	...	...
Ukraine								
1 I 2007 (ESDJ)								
Alchevsk	115 438	52 841	62 597	30	...	...	...	...
Belaya Tserkov (Bila Crkva)	203 892	94 415	109 477	42	...	...	...	...
Berdyansk	118 540	52 910	65 630	41	121 712	54 419	67 293	205
Cherkassy	288 455	132 272	156 183	60	289 222	132 674	156 548	76
Chernigov	293 047	135 723	157 324	49	...	...	...	...
Chernovtsy	241 235	110 678	130 557	71	...	...	...	...
Dneprodzerzhinsk	246 184	110 720	135 464	84	253 040	113 831	139 209	138
Dnepropetrovsk	1 029 340	468 183	561 157	250	1 031 638	469 306	562 332	405
Donetsk (Donestskaya oblast)	979 521	434 486	545 035	305	995 904	441 937	553 967	557
Evpatoriya	104 131	46 439	57 692	21	119 565	53 459	66 106	54
Gorlovka	270 188	121 404	148 784	162	291 267	130 969	160 298	399
Ivano-Frankovsk	218 356	103 356	115 000	34	234 012	110 693	123 319	90
Kertch	151 382	68 262	83 120	43	...	...	...	...
Kharkov	1 441 613	658 961	782 652	239	...	...	...	...
Kherson	308 757	139 161	169 596	58	346 136	156 504	189 632	304

8. Population of capital cities and cities of 100 000 or more inhabitants: latest available year, 1988 - 2007
Population des capitales et des villes de 100 000 habitants ou plus: dernière année disponible, 1988 - 2007 (continued - suite)

Continent, country or area, date, code and city / Continent, pays ou zone, date, code et ville	City proper - Ville proprement dite				Urban agglomeration - Agglomération urbaine			
	Population			Surface area - Superficie (km²)	Population			Surface area - Superficie (km²)
	Both sexes - Les deux sexes	Male - Masculin	Female - Féminin		Both sexes - Les deux sexes	Male - Masculin	Female - Féminin	
EUROPE								
Ukraine								
1 I 2007 (ESDJ)								
Khmelnitsky (Hmilnyk)	255 512	118 708	136 804	50	...	...	...	...
KIEV	2 676 789	1 239 333	1 437 456	834	...	...	...	...
Kirovograd	240 035	108 698	131 337	59	248 059	112 345	135 714	74
Kramatorsk	171 330	76 348	94 982	53	205 470	92 164	113 306	349
Krementchug	229 136	104 843	124 293	44	...	...	...	...
Kryvy Rig	685 762	310 778	374 984	243	689 141	312 478	376 663	470
Lugansk	442 577	196 507	246 070	120	481 712	214 827	266 885	269
Lutsk	203 447	91 901	111 546	43	...	...	...	...
Lvov	728 799	342 257	386 542	94	754 713	354 550	400 163	168
Lysychansk	109 043	49 346	59 697	45	125 749	56 999	68 750	87
Makeyevka	368 064	166 652	201 412	161	408 299	185 379	222 920	460
Mariupol	474 190	216 498	257 692	134	496 208	226 867	269 341	200
Melitopol	158 460	71 883	86 577	47	...	...	...	...
Mykolaiv (Nikolaevskaya oblast)	502 909	227 845	275 064	112	...	...	...	...
Nikopol	131 261	58 891	72 370	46	...	...	...	...
Odessa	982 920	455 858	527 062	130	...	...	...	...
Pavlograd	112 622	52 147	60 475	48	...	...	...	...
Poltava	299 208	137 492	161 716	77	...	...	...	...
Rivne	244 807	112 338	132 469	40	...	...	...	...
Sevastopol	338 118	153 921	184 197	55	377 269	172 036	205 233	866
Severodonetsk	114 837	51 571	63 266	22	124 873	56 302	68 571	65
Simferopol	334 228	147 189	187 039	49	356 800	157 524	199 276	90
Slavyansk	118 800	51 926	66 874	59	138 492	60 963	77 529	74
Sumy	277 654	125 999	151 655	62	280 488	127 345	153 143	127
Ternopol	216 772	101 198	115 574	34	...	...	...	...
Uzhgorod	114 897	53 375	61 522	23	...	...	...	...
Vinnutsya	363 249	166 616	196 633	56	...	...	...	...
Zaporozhye	786 159	355 550	430 609	169	788 769	356 722	432 047	328
Zhitomir	273 004	126 250	146 754	55	...	...	...	...
United Kingdom of Great Britain and Northern Ireland - Royaume-Uni de Grande-Bretagne et d'Irlande du Nord[70]								
29 IV 2001 (CDFC)								
Aberdeen	...	...	...	...	212 125	103 818	108 307	...
Aberdeenshire	...	...	...	...	226 871	112 470	114 401	...
Aldershot	...	...	...	...	243 344	121 127	122 217	...
Angus	...	...	...	...	108 400	52 458	55 942	...
Basildon/North Benfleet	...	...	...	...	101 492	48 649	52 843	...
Bedford/Kempston	...	...	...	...	101 928	50 341	51 587	...
Belfast[71]	...	...	...	...	276 459	129 321	147 138	...
Birkenhead	...	...	...	...	319 675	152 133	167 542	...
Blackburn/Darwen	...	...	...	...	136 655	66 834	69 821	...
Blackpool	...	...	...	...	261 088	124 698	136 390	...
Bournemouth	...	...	...	...	383 713	182 875	200 838	...
Brighton/Worthing/Littlehampton	...	...	...	...	461 181	220 275	240 906	...
Bristol	...	...	...	...	551 066	269 689	281 377	...
Burnley/Nelson	...	...	...	...	149 796	72 657	77 139	...
Cambridge	...	...	...	...	131 465	65 343	66 122	...
Cardiff[72]	...	...	...	...	327 706	156 272	171 434	...
Cheltenham/Charlton Kings	...	...	...	...	110 320	53 526	56 794	...
Chesterfield/Staveley	...	...	...	...	100 879	49 204	51 675	...
Colchester	...	...	...	...	104 390	51 652	52 738	...
Coventry/Bedworth	...	...	...	...	336 452	166 666	169 786	...
Crawley	...	...	...	...	180 177	88 404	91 773	...
Dearne Valley	...	...	...	...	207 726	100 992	106 734	...
Derby	...	...	...	...	236 738	115 644	121 094	...
Doncaster	...	...	...	...	127 851	62 127	65 724	...
Dumfries & Galloway	...	...	...	...	147 765	71 303	76 462	...
Dundee	...	...	...	...	145 663	69 140	76 523	...
East Ayrshire	...	...	...	...	120 235	57 842	62 393	...
East Dunbartonshire	...	...	...	...	108 243	52 014	56 229	...
Eastbourne	...	...	...	...	106 562	49 369	57 193	...
Edinburgh[73]	...	...	...	...	448 624	214 711	233 913	...
Exeter	...	...	...	...	106 772	52 045	54 727	...

8. Population of capital cities and cities of 100 000 or more inhabitants: latest available year, 1988 - 2007
Population des capitales et des villes de 100 000 habitants ou plus: dernière année disponible, 1988 - 2007 (continued - suite)

Continent, country or area, date, code and city / Continent, pays ou zone, date, code et ville	City proper - Ville proprement dite				Urban agglomeration - Agglomération urbaine			
	Population			Surface area - Superficie (km²)	Population			Surface area - Superficie (km²)
	Both sexes - Les deux sexes	Male - Masculin	Female - Féminin		Both sexes - Les deux sexes	Male - Masculin	Female - Féminin	
EUROPE								
United Kingdom of Great Britain and Northern Ireland - Royaume-Uni de Grande-Bretagne et d'Irlande du Nord[70]								
29 IV 2001 (CDFC)								
Falkirk	...	...	...	...	145 191	70 016	75 175	...
Fife	...	...	...	...	349 429	167 628	181 801	...
Glasgow	...	...	...	...	577 869	272 309	305 560	...
Gloucester	...	...	...	...	136 203	66 669	69 534	...
Grimsby/Cleethorpes	...	...	...	...	138 842	67 360	71 482	...
Hastings/Bexhill	...	...	...	...	126 386	59 247	67 139	...
High Wycombe	...	...	...	...	118 229	57 857	60 372	...
Highland	...	...	...	...	208 914	102 297	106 617	...
Ipswich	...	...	...	...	141 658	69 468	72 190	...
Kingston-upon-Hull	...	...	...	...	301 416	146 926	154 490	...
Leicester	...	...	...	...	441 213	214 060	227 153	...
Lincoln	...	...	...	...	104 221	50 794	53 427	...
Liverpool	...	...	...	...	816 216	389 119	427 097	...
LONDON[74]	...	...	...	...	8 278 251	4 007 297	4 270 954	...
Luton/Dunstable	...	...	...	...	236 318	117 707	118 611	...
Manchester	...	...	...	...	2 244 931	1 090 898	1 154 033	...
Mansfield	...	...	...	...	158 114	76 884	81 230	...
Milton Keynes	...	...	...	...	184 506	91 441	93 065	...
Newport	...	...	...	...	139 298	66 884	72 414	...
North Ayrshire	...	...	...	...	135 817	64 238	71 579	...
North Lanarkshire	...	...	...	...	321 067	153 966	167 101	...
Northampton	...	...	...	...	197 199	96 670	100 529	...
Norwich	...	...	...	...	194 839	94 523	100 316	...
Nottingham	...	...	...	...	666 358	327 851	338 507	...
Nuneaton	...	...	...	...	132 236	64 837	67 399	...
Oxford	...	...	...	...	143 016	70 462	72 554	...
Perth & Kinross	...	...	...	...	134 949	65 172	69 777	...
Peterborough	...	...	...	...	136 292	66 139	70 153	...
Plymouth	...	...	...	...	243 795	119 076	124 719	...
Portsmouth	...	...	...	...	442 252	216 341	225 911	...
Preston	...	...	...	...	264 601	129 665	134 936	...
Reading/Wokingham	...	...	...	...	369 804	185 475	184 329	...
Renfrewshire	...	...	...	...	172 867	82 525	90 342	...
Scottish Borders	...	...	...	...	106 764	51 361	55 403	...
Sheffield	...	...	...	...	640 720	312 619	328 101	...
Slough	...	...	...	...	141 848	70 286	71 562	...
South Ayrshire	...	...	...	...	112 097	53 406	58 691	...
South Lanarkshire	...	...	...	...	302 216	144 206	158 010	...
Southampton	...	...	...	...	304 400	151 534	152 866	...
Southend	...	...	...	...	269 415	129 650	139 765	...
Southport/Formby	...	...	...	...	115 882	54 337	61 545	...
St. Albans/Hatfield	...	...	...	...	114 710	56 585	58 125	...
Sunderland	...	...	...	...	182 974	88 892	94 082	...
Swansea	...	...	...	...	270 506	130 648	139 858	...
Swindon	...	...	...	...	155 432	77 551	77 881	...
Teesside	...	...	...	...	365 323	176 475	188 848	...
Telford	...	...	...	...	138 241	67 770	70 471	...
Thanet	...	...	...	...	119 144	56 266	62 878	...
The Medway Towns	...	...	...	...	231 659	114 069	117 590	...
The Potteries	...	...	...	...	362 403	176 467	185 936	...
Torbay	...	...	...	...	110 366	52 551	57 815	...
Tyneside	...	...	...	...	879 996	425 119	454 877	...
Warrington	...	...	...	...	158 195	77 334	80 861	...
West Lothian	...	...	...	...	158 714	76 701	82 013	...
West Midlands	...	...	...	...	2 284 093	1 109 397	1 174 696	...
West Yorkshire	...	...	...	...	1 499 465	724 818	774 647	...
Wigan	...	...	...	...	166 840	81 254	85 586	...
York	...	...	...	...	137 505	66 142	71 363	...

8. Population of capital cities and cities of 100 000 or more inhabitants: latest available year, 1988 - 2007
Population des capitales et des villes de 100 000 habitants ou plus: dernière année disponible, 1988 - 2007 (continued - suite)

Continent, country or area, date, code and city / Continent, pays ou zone, date, code et ville	City proper - Ville proprement dite				Urban agglomeration - Agglomération urbaine			
	Population			Surface area - Superficie (km²)	Population			Surface area - Superficie (km²)
	Both sexes - Les deux sexes	Male - Masculin	Female - Féminin		Both sexes - Les deux sexes	Male - Masculin	Female - Féminin	
OCEANIA - OCÉANIE								
American Samoa - Samoas américaines[16]								
1 IV 2000 (CDJC)								
PAGO PAGO	4 278	2 086	2 192	...	...	...	...	...
Australia - Australie								
1 VII 2007* (ESDJ)								
Adelaide[75]	1 158 259[76]	...	...	1 830	...	...	...	...
Albury-Wodonga[77]	101 842[76]	...	...	4 410	...	...	...	...
Brisbane[75]	1 857 594[76]	...	...	5 900	...	...	...	...
Cairns[77]	135 856[76]	...	...	490	...	...	...	...
CANBERRA[75]	339 573[76]	...	...	810	...	...	...	...
Darwin[75]	117 395[76]	...	...	3 120	...	...	...	...
Geelong[77]	169 544[76]	...	...	390	...	...	...	...
Gold Coast[77]	583 657[76]	...	...	1 320	...	...	...	...
Greater Wollongong[77]	280 159[76]	...	...	1 090	...	...	...	...
Hobart[75]	207 484[76]	...	...	1 360	...	...	...	...
Launceston[77]	104 071[76]	...	...	800	...	...	...	...
Melbourne[75]	3 806 092[76]	...	...	7 690	...	...	...	...
Newcastle[77]	523 662[76]	...	...	4 050	...	...	...	...
Perth[75]	1 554 769[76]	...	...	5 390	...	...	...	...
Sunshine Coast[77]	230 429[76]	...	...	460	...	...	...	...
Sydney[75]	4 336 374[76]	...	...	12 140	...	...	...	...
Toowoomba[77]	123 406[76]	...	...	550	...	...	...	...
Townsville[77]	157 174[76]	...	...	460	...	...	...	...
Cook Islands - Îles Cook[78]								
1 XII 2001 (CDFC)								
RAROTONGA	12 188	...	...	...	...	...	...	...
Fiji - Fidji								
25 VIII 1996 (CDFC)								
SUVA	77 366	38 518	38 848	...	167 975	83 910	84 065	...
French Polynesia - Polynésie française								
7 XI 2002 (CDFC)								
PAPEETE	26 181	...	...	...	124 864	...	...	...
Guam								
1 IV 2000 (CDJC)								
AGANA	1 100[16]	672[16]	428[16]	3	...	...	...	...
Kiribati								
7 XI 2000* (CDFC)								
TARAWA	...	...	...	...	36 717	...	...	...
Marshall Islands - Îles Marshall								
1 VI 1999 (CDFC)								
MAJURO	23 676	12 075	11 601	...	...	...	...	...
Micronesia (Federated States of) - Micronésie (États fédérés de)								
1 IV 2000 (CDJC)								
PALIKIR	6 227	...	...	...	...	...	...	...
Nauru								
17 IV 1992 (CDFC)								
YAREN	672	...	...	...	...	...	...	...
New Caledonia - Nouvelle-Calédonie								
16 IV 1996 (CDFC)								
NOUMEA	76 293	38 443	37 850	46	118 823	60 327	58 496	1 643
New Zealand - Nouvelle-Zélande[79]								
1 VII 2006 (ESDJ)								
Auckland	428 300	209 600	218 700	664	1 272 800	621 800	650 900	1 084
Christchurch	361 800	175 500	186 300	1 540	374 500	181 700	192 800	608
Dunedin	122 300	58 800	63 500	3 342	114 400	54 800	59 600	255
Hamilton	134 400	64 700	69 700	98	191 700	92 800	99 000	1 099
Lower Hutt	101 300	49 600	51 700	377	...	...	...	...
Manukau	347 100	169 400	177 700	683	...	...	...	...
Napier-Hastings	...	...	...	...	121 900	58 800	63 200	389
North Shore	216 900	106 200	110 700	129	...	...	...	...
Tauranga	106 700	51 100	55 600	168	112 100	53 800	58 300	178
Waitakere	195 300	95 400	100 000	367	...	...	...	...
WELLINGTON	187 700	91 200	96 500	290	375 600	183 400	192 200	447

Continent, country or area, date, code and city / Continent, pays ou zone, date, code et ville	City proper - Ville proprement dite				Urban agglomeration - Agglomération urbaine			
	Population			Surface area - Superficie (km²)	Population			Surface area - Superficie (km²)
	Both sexes - Les deux sexes	Male - Masculin	Female - Féminin		Both sexes - Les deux sexes	Male - Masculin	Female - Féminin	
OCEANIA - OCÉANIE								
Niue - Nioué								
7 IX 2001 (CDFC)								
ALOFI....................	615	...	...	...	...	...	...	...
Norfolk Island - Île Norfolk								
1 VII 1997 (ESDF)								
KINGSTON....................	*800*	...	...	...	...	...	...	...
Northern Mariana Islands - Îles Mariannes septentrionales								
1 IV 2000 (CDFC)								
GARAPAN....................	3 588	...	...	...	...	...	...	...
Palau - Palaos								
15 IV 2000 (CDFC)								
KOROR	10 600	...	...	...	...	...	...	...
Papua New Guinea - Papouasie-Nouvelle-Guinée								
9 VII 2000 (CDFC)								
PORT MORESBY	254 158	138 974	115 184	...	...	...	...	...
Pitcairn								
31 XII 1993 (ESDF)								
ADAMSTOWN....................	53	25	28	0[80]	...	...	...	...
Samoa								
5 XI 2001 (CDFC)								
APIA	38 836	...	...	...	...	...	...	...
Solomon Islands - Îles Salomon								
21 XI 1999 (CDFC)								
HONIARA	49 107	...	...	...	...	...	...	...
Tonga								
1 VII 2000 (ESDF)								
NUKU'ALOFA	*21 538*	*10 625*	*10 913*	...	*30 336*	*15 115*	*15 221*	...
Tuvalu								
1 XI 2002 (CDFC)								
FUNAFUTI	4 492	2 281	2 211	...	...	...	...	...
Vanuatu								
16 XI 1999 (CDJC)								
PORT VILA....................	29 356	...	...	...	...	...	...	...
Wallis and Futuna Islands - Îles Wallis et Futuna								
3 X 1996 (CDFC)								
META-UTU	1 137	...	...	...	...	...	...	...

FOOTNOTES - NOTES

The capital city of each country is shown in capital letters. Figures in italics are estimates of questionnable reliability. For definition of city proper and urban agglomeration, method of evaluation and limitations of data see Technical Notes for this table. - Le nom de la capitale de chaque pays est imprimé en majuscules. Les chiffres en italique sont des estimations dont la fiabilité n'est pas assurée. Pour la définition de la ville proprement dite et de l'agglomération urbaine, et pour les méthodes d'évaluation et les insuffisances de données, voir les notes techniques pour ce tableau.

Italics: estimates which are less reliable. - Italiques: estimations moins sûres.

* Provisional. - Données provisoires.

'Code' indicates the source of data, as follows:
CDFC - Census, de facto, complete tabulation
CDFS - Census, de facto, sample tabulation
CDJC - Census, de jure, complete tabulation
CDJS - Census, de jure, sample tabulation
SSDF - Sample survey, de facto
SSDJ - Sample survey, de jure
ESDF - Estimates, de facto
ESDJ - Estimates, de jure

Le 'Code' indique la source des données, comme suit:
CDFC - Recensement, population de fait, tabulation complète

CDFS - Recensement, population de fait, tabulation par sondage
CDJC - Recensement, population de droit, tabulation complète
CDJS - Recensement, population de droit, tabulation par sondage
SSDF - Enquête par sondage, population de fait
SSDJ - Enquête par sondage, population de droit
ESDF - Données estimatées, population de fait
ESDJ - Données estimatées, population de droit

[1] Dual capitals. - Le pays a deux capitales.
[2] Data refer to the urban commune of Antananarivo. - Pour la commune urbaine de Antananarivo.
[3] Data refer to national projections. - Les données se réfèrent aux projections nationales.
[4] Data include those for two or more cities. - Les données présentées concernent deux villes ou plus.
[5] Data refer to communes, which may contain an urban centre as well as rural areas. - Commune(s) pouvant comprendre un centre urbain et une zone rurale.
[6] Included in urban agglomeration of Dakar. - Comprise dans l'agglomération urbaine de Dakar.
[7] Pretoria is the administrative capital, Cape Town the legislative capital. - Pretoria est la capitale administrative, Le Cap la capitale législative.
[8] Comprising the Northern Region (former Saguia el Hamra) and Southern Region (former Rio de Oro). - Comprend la région septentrionale (ancien Saguia-el-Hamra) et la région méridionale (ancien Rio de Oro).
[9] Excluding the institutional population. - Non compris la population dans les institutions.
[10] Surface area is 0.28 Km2. - Superficie: 0,28 Km2.

[11] Ottawa is the capital city, but the data are reported for the Ottawa-Gatineau urban agglomeration. - Ottawa est la capitale, mais les données se rapportent à l'agglomération urbaine d'Ottawa-Gatineau.

[12] Data refer to municipalities, which may contain an urban centre as well as rural areas. - Pour municipios qui peuvent comprendre un centre urbain et aussi une zone rurale.

[13] The definition of locality is based on the 2000 Population census. Data refer to national projections. - La localité est définie survant le recensement general de la population de 2000. Les données se réfèrent aux projections nationales.

[14] Urban agglomeration (Metropolitan area) refers to 2 or more municipalities where there is only one urban concentration. - L'agglomération urbaine (zone métropolitaine) se rapporte à 2 municipalités ou plus où il y a seulement une concentration urbaine.

[15] Including municipalities of Bella Vista, Betania, Calidonia, Curundu, El Chorillo, Juan Diaz, Parque Lefevre, Pedregal, Pueblo Nuevo, Rio Abajo, San Felipe, San Francisco and Santa Ana. - Y compris les corregimientos de Bella Vista, Betania, Calidonia, Curundu, El Chorillo, Juan Diaz, Parque Lefevre, Pedregal, Pueblo Nuevo, Rio Abajo, San Felipe, San Francisco et Santa Ana.

[16] Including armed forces stationed in the area. - Y compris les militaires en garnison sur le territoire.

[17] Excluding armed forces overseas and civilian citizens absent from country for an extended period of time. City refers to a type of incorporated place in 49 states and the District of Columbia, that has an elected government and provides a range of government functions and services. Also included are Honolulu, Hawaii Census Designated Place (CDP), for which the Census Bureau reports data under agreement with the State of Hawaii (instead of the combined city and county of Honolulu), and Arlington, VA CDP (which is coextensive with Arlington County - an entirely urban county that provides the same levels of services and functions as a municipality. - Non compris les militaires à l'étranger, et les civils hors du pays pendant une période prolongée. Par ville, on entend un lieu doté de la personnalité morale dans 49 États et dans le district de Columbia, qui a un gouvernement élu et fournit tout un ensemble de fonctions et de services publics. Sont également inclus Honolulu, lieu chargé du recensement pour Hawaii, pour lequel le Census Bureau établit les données en accord avec l'État de Hawaii (au lieu de la ville et du comté d'Honolulu), et Arlington, lieu chargé du recensement pour la Virginie, qui est de même étendue que le comté d'Arlington, lequel est un comté entièrement urbain qui offre les mêmes niveaux de services et de fonctions qu'une municipalité.

[18] La Paz is the actual capital and the seat of the Government but Sucre is the legal capital and the seat of the judiciary. - La Paz est la capitale effective et le siège du gouvernement, mais Sucre est la capitale constitutionnelle et la siège du pouvoir judiciaire.

[19] 'Metropolitan area' Grand Santiago. - 'Zone métropolitaine' Grand Santiago.

[20] Urban agglomeration refers to the urban part of the municipality with a proper city center. - L'agglomération urbaine se rapporte à la partie urbaine de la municipalité avec un centre de la ville.

[21] Data for urban agglomeration refer to 'metropolitan area', comprising Asuncion proper and localities of Trinidad, Zeballos Cué, Campo Grande and Lamboré. - Les données pour l'agglomération urbaine se rapportent à la 'zone métropolitaine' comprenant la ville d'Asuncion proprement dite et les localités de Trinidad, Zeballos Cué, Campo Grande et Lamboré.

[22] Lefkosia urban agglomeration is composed of Lefkosia municipality, Agios Dometios, Egkomi, Strovolos, Aglangia, Lakatameia, Anthoupoli, Latsia and Geri. - L'agglomération urbaine de Lefkosia se comprend de la municipalité de Lefkosia et Agios Dometios, Egkomi, Strovolos, Aglangia, Lakatameia, Anthoupoli, Latsia et Geri.

[23] Lemesos urban agglomeration is composed of Lemesos municipality, Mesa Geitonia, Agios Athanasios, Germasogeia, Pano Polemidia, Ypsonas, Kato Polemidia, and parts of Mouttagiaka, Agios Tychon, Parekklisia, Monagrouli, Moni, Pyrgos and Tserkezoi. - L'agglomération urbaine de Lemesos se comprend de la municipalité de Lemesos et Mesa Geitonia, Agios Athanasios, Germasogeia, Pano Polemidia, Ypsonas, Kato Polemidia, et certaines parties des Mouttagiaka, Agios Tychon, Parekklisia, Monagrouli, Moni, Pyrgos et Tserkezoi.

[24] Including data for the Indian-held part of Jammu and Kashmir, the final status of which has not yet been determined. - Y compris les données pour la partie du Jammu et du Cachemire occupée par l'Inde dont le statut définitif n'a pas encore été déterminé.

[25] Data for urban agglomeration include New Delhi. - Les données pour l'agglomération urbaine y compris New Delhi.

[26] Data for urban agglomeration include Bally, Baranagar, Barrackpur, Bhatpara, Calcutta Municipal Corporation, Chandan Nagar, Garden Reach, Houghly-Chinsura, Howrah, Jadarpur, Kamarhati, Naihati, Panihati, Serampore, South Dum Dum, South Suburban, and Titagarh. - Les données pour l'agglomération urbaine y compris Bally, Baranagar, Barrackpur, Bhatpara, Calcutta Municipal Corporation, Chandan Nagar, Garden Reach, Houghly

Chinsura, Howrah, Jadarpur, Kamarhati, Naihati, Panihati, Serampopre, South Dum Dum, South Suburban et Titagarh.

[27] Included in urban agglomeration of Delhi. Data refer to the New Delhi Municipal Council. - Comprise dans l'agglomération urbaine de Delhi. Les données se rapportent au New Delhi Municipal Council.

[28] Data refer to the "Intercensal Population Survey". Excluding Province Nanggroe Aceh Darussalam, Regency Nias & Nias Selatan, Regency Boven Digul & Teluk Wondama. - Les données concernent l'enquête intercensitaire sur la population. En excluant les provinces de Nanggroe Aceh Darussalam, Regency Nias & Nias Selatan, Regency Boven Digul & Teluk Wondama.

[29] Designation and data provided by Israel. The position of the United Nations on the question of Jerusalem is contained in General Assembly resolution 181 (II) and subsequent resolutions of the General Assembly and the Security Council concerning this question. - Appelation de données fournies par Israel. La position des Nations Unies concernant la question de Jérusalem est décrite dans la resolution 181 (II) de l'Assemblée générale et résolutions ultérieures de l'Assemblée générale et du Conseil de sécurité sur cette question.

[30] Designation and data provided by Israel. The position of the United Nations on the question of Jerusalem is contained in General Assembly resolution 181 (II) and subsequent resolutions of the General Assembly and the Security Council concerning this question. Including East Jerusalem. - Appelation de données fournies par Israel. La position des Nations Unies concernant la question de Jérusalem est décrite dans la resolution 181 (II) de l'Assemblée générale et résolutions ultérieures de l'Assemblée générale et du Conseil de sécurité sur cette question. Y compris Jérusalem-Est.

[31] Except for Tokyo, all data refer to shi, a minor division which may include some scattered or rural population as well as an urban centre. Excluding diplomatic personnel outside the country and foreign military and civilian personnel and their dependants stationed in the area. - Sauf pour Tokyo, toutes les données se rapportent à des shi, petites divisions administratives qui peuvent comprendre des peuplements dispersés ou ruraux en plus d'un centre urbain. Non compris le personnel diplomatique hors du pays ni les militaires et agents civils étrangers en poste sur le territoire et les membres de leur famille les accompagnant.

[32] Including Kokura, Moji, Tobata, Wakamatsu and Yahata (Yawata). - Y compris Kokura, Moji, Tobata, Wakamatsu et Yahata (Yawata).

[33] Data for city proper refer to 23 wards (ku) of the old city. The urban agglomeration figures refer to Tokyo-to (Tokyo Prefecture), comprising the 23 wards plus 14 urban counties (shi), 18 towns (machi) and 8 villages. The 'Tokyo Metropolitan Area' comprises the 23 wards of Tokyo-to plus 21 cities, 20 towns and 2 villages. The 'Keihin Metropolitan Area' (Tokyo-Yokohama Metropolitan Area) plus 9 cities (one of which is Yokohama City) and two towns, with a total population of 20 485 542 on 1 October 1965. - Les données concernant la ville proprement dite se rapportent aux 23 circonscriptions de Tokyo-to (préfecture de Tokyo), comprenant les 23 circonscriptions plus 14 cantons urbains (Shi), 18 villes (machi) et 8 villages (mura). La 'zone métropolitaine de Tokyo' comprend les 23 circonscriptions de Tokyo-to plus 21 municipalités, 20 villes et 2 villages. La 'zone métropolitaine de Keihin' (zone métropolitaine de Tokyo-Yokohama) comprend la zone métropolitaine de Tokyo, plus 9 municipalités, dont l'une est Yokohama et 2 villes, elle comptait 20 485 542 habitants au 1er octobre 1965.

[34] Based on the results of a household survey. - D'après les résultats d'une enquête des ménages.

[35] Data refer to projections by Local Authority Area. - Les données se réfèrent aux projections de la collectivité locale.

[36] Excluding data for the Pakistan-held part of Jammu and Kashmir, the final status of which has not yet been determined, and for Junagardh, Manavadar, Gilgit and Baltistan. - Non compris les données pour la partie de Jammu-Cachemire occupée par le Pakistan dont le status definitif n'a pas encore été déterminé, et le Junagardh, le Manavadar, le Gilgit et le Baltistan.

[37] Covering Seyhan and Yuregir districts in Adana. - Y compris la population des districts de Seyhan et de Yuregir.

[38] Covering Altindag, Cankaya, Etimesgut, Golbasi, Kecioren, Mamak, Sincan, and Yenimahalle districts in Ankara. - Y compris la population des districts de Altindag, de Cankaya, de Etimesgut, de Golbasi, de Kecioren, de Mamak, de Sincan, et de Yenimahalle.

[39] Covering Nilufer, Osmangazi and Yildirim districts in Bursa. - Y compris la population des districts de Nilufer, de Osmangazi et de Yildirim.

[40] District centre. - Le centre du district.

[41] Covering Sahinbey and Sehitkamil districts in Gaziantep. - Y compris la population des districts de Sahinbey et de Sehitkamil.

[42] Covering Adalar, Avcilar, Bagcilar, Bahcelievler, Bakirkoy, Bayrampasa, Besiktas, Beykoz, Beyoglu, Eminonu, Esenler, Eyup, Fatih, Gaziosmanpasa, Gungoren, Kadikoy, Kagithane, Kartal, Kucukcekmece, Maltepe, Pendik, Sariyer, Sisli, Sultanbeyli, Tuzla, Umraniye, Uskudar, Zentinburnu districts in Istanbul. - Y compris la population des districts de Adalar, de Avcilar, de Bagcilar, de

321

Bahcelievler, de Bakirkoy, de Bayrampasa, de Besiktas, de Beykoz, de Beyoglu, de Eminonu, de Esenler, de Eyup, de Fatih, de Gaziosmanpasa, de Gungoren, de Kadikoy, de Kagithane, de Kartal, de Kucukcekmece, de Maltepe, de Pendik, de Sariyer, de Sisli, de Sultanbeyli, de Tuzla, de Umraniye, de Uskudar, et de Zentinburnu.

[43] Covering Bolcova, Bornova, Buca, Cigli, Gaziemir, Guzelbahce, Karsiyaka, Konak and Narlidere districts in Izmir. - Y compris la population des districts de Bolcova, de Bornova, de Buca, de Cigli, de Gaziemir, de Guzelbahce, de Karsiyaka, de Konak et de Narlidere.

[44] Covering Kocasinan and Melikgazi districts in Kayseri. - Y compris la population des districts de Kocasinan et de Melikgazi.

[45] Including Cholon. - Y compris Cholon.

[46] Also included in Finland. - Comprise aussi dans Finlande.

[47] Population statistics are compiled from registers. - Les statistiques de la population sont compilées à partir des registres.

[48] City is defined as a residential center that has a zoning and urbanisation plan approved by law. - Une ville est définie comme centre résidentiel soumis à un règlement de zonage et à un plan d'urbanisation approuvés par voie législative.

[49] City proper refers to commune or municipality. - La ville proprement dite se rapporte à la commune ou à la municipalité

[50] Data for cities proper refer to communes which may contain an urban centre and a rural area. - Les données concernant les villes proprement dites se rapportent à des communes qui peuvent comprendre un centre urbain et une zone rurale.

[51] City is a settlement with a status of city according to the administrative-territorial division of the country at the end of the respective year. Urban agglomeration refers to the urban part of the municipality with a proper city center. - La ville est une agglomération avec un statut de ville selon la division administratif-territoriale du pays à la fin de l'année respective. L'agglomération urbaine se rapporte à la partie urbaine de la municipalité avec un centre de la ville.

[52] Data for city proper refer to settlements. - Les données pour la ville proprement dite concernent les établissements.

[53] Data for urban agglomeration refer to the city. - Les données pour l'agglomération urbaine concernent la ville.

[54] Excluding Faeroe Islands and Greenland shown separately, if available. - Non compris les Iles Féroé et le Gröenland, qui font l'objet de rubriques distinctes, si disponible.

[55] Including Aland Islands. - Y compris les Îles d'Åland.

[56] Excluding Overseas Departments, namely, French Guiana, Guadeloupe, Martinique and Reunion, shown separately, if available. Data for cities proper refer to communes which are centres for urban agglomeration. - Non compris les départements d'outre mer, c'est-à-dire la Guyane française, la Guadeloupe, la Martinique et la Réunion, qui font l'objet de rubriques distinctes, si disponible. Les données concernant les villes proprement dites se rapportent à des communes qui sont des centres d'agglomérations urbaines.

[57] De jure population, but excluding diplomatic personnel outside the country and including foreign diplomatic personnel not living in embassies or consulates. - Population de droit, mais non compris le personnel diplomatique hors du pays et y compris le personnel diplomatique étranger qui ne vit pas dans les ambassades ou les consulats.

[58] Data refer to French territory of this international agglomeration. - Les données se rapportent aux habitants de cette agglomération internationale qui vivent en territoire francais.

[59] Including Villeurbanne. - Y compris Villeurbanne.

[60] Including armed forces stationed outside the country, but excluding alien armed forces stationed in the area. - Y compris les militaires nationaux hors du pays, mais non compris les militaires étrangers en garnison sur le territoire.

[61] Data refer to the Vatican City State. - Les données se rapportent à l'Etat de la Cité du Vatican.

[62] Surface area is 0.44 Km2. - Superficie: 0,44 Km2.

[63] The boundaries of a city are related to the boundaries of a commune. The urban agglomeration of the capital area is much bigger and includes the following communes: Bessastaðahreppur, Garðabær, Hafnarfjörður, Kjósarhreppur, Kópavogur, Mosfellsbær ,Reykjavík, Seltjarnarnes. - Les limites d'une ville correspondent aux limites d'une commune. L'agglomération urbaine de la capitale est beaucoup plus étendue et comprend les communes suivantes : Bessastaðahreppur, Garðabær, Hafnarfjörður, Kjósarhreppur, Kópavogur, Mosfellsbær ,Reykjavík, Seltjarnarnes.

[64] City refers to densely built-up residential areas with a resident population of more than 3000 persons. - Une ville est définie comme une zone résidentielle agglomérée avec une population permanente de plus de 3000 personnes.

[65] Including civilian nationals temporarily outside the country. - Y compris les civils nationaux temporairement hors du pays.

[66] Data for cities proper refer to administrative units (municipalities). - Les données concernant les villes proprement dites se rapportent à des unités administratives (municipalités).

[67] Excluding Svalbard and Jan Mayen Island shown separately, if available. - Non compris Svalbard et Jan Mayen qui font l'objet de rubriques distinctes, si disponible.

[68] City is defined as an administratively separated area entitled to civil (municipal) rights. - Une ville est définie comme une zone administrativement distincte dotée de droits municipaux.

[69] Data for urban agglomeration refer to communes which are administrative divisions. - Les données pour l'agglomération urbaine se rapportent aux communes qui sont des divisions administrative.

[70] Data refer to urban areas with 100,000+ residents. Excluding Channel Islands (Guernsey and Jersey) and Isle of Man, shown separately, if available. - Les données se rapportent aux zones urbaines avec plus de 100 000 résidents. Non compris les îles Anglo-Normandes (Guernesey et Jersey) et l'île de Man, qui font l'objet de rubriques distinctes, si disponible.

[71] Capital of Northern Ireland. - Capitale de l'Irlande du Nord.

[72] Capital of Wales for certain purposes. - Considérée à certains égards comme la capitale du pays de Galles.

[73] Capital of Scotland. - Capitale de l'Ecosse.

[74] 'Greater London' conurbation as reconstituted in 1965 and comprising 32 new Greater London Boroughs. - Ensemble urbain du 'Grand Londres', tel qu'il a été reconstitué en 1965, comprenant 32 nouveaux Greater London Boroughs.

[75] Statistical division, which is a relatively stable area that includes a large buffer around each city to reduce the need to change boundaries as the city grows. - Division statistique, définie comme zone relativement stable comprenant une zone-tampon assez étendue autour de chaque ville, ce qui permet de ne pas avoir à en modifier aussi souvent les limites à mesure que la ville s'étend.

[76] For all regions it is not possible to distinguish between 'city proper' and 'urban agglomeration' areas, therefore data has been include under 'city proper'. - - Il n'est pas possible de distinguer pour toutes les régions entre 'ville proprement dite' et 'agglomération urbaine', et les données sont donc présentées sous 'ville proprement dite'.

[77] Statistical district, which includes a much smaller buffer and basically just represent the urban area of that city. - District statistique, comprenant une zone-tampon beaucoup plus restreinte, et représentant pour l'essentiel la seule zone urbaine de la ville considérée.

[78] Excluding Niue, shown separately, which is part of Cook Islands, but because of remoteness is administered separately. - Non compris Nioué, qui fait l'objet d'une rubrique distincte et qui fait partie des îles Cook, mais qui, en raison de son éloignement, est administrée séparément.

[79] Excluding inland water and oceanic areas. - Exclut les eaux intérieures et les zones océaniques.

[80] Surface area is 0.24 Km2. - Superficie: 0,24 Km2.

Table 9

Table 9 presents live births and crude live birth rates by urban/rural residence for as many years as possible between 2003 and 2007.

Description of variables: Live birth is defined as the complete expulsion or extraction from its mother of a product of conception, irrespective of the duration of pregnancy, which after such separation, breathes or shows any other evidence of life such as beating of the heart, pulsation of the umbilical cord, or definite movements of voluntary muscles, whether or not the umbilical cord has been cut or the placenta is attached; each product of such a birth is considered live-born[1].

Statistics on the number of live births are obtained from civil registers unless otherwise noted. For those countries or areas where civil registration statistics on live births are considered reliable the birth rates shown have been calculated on the basis of registered live births.

For certain countries, there is a discrepancy between the total number of live births shown in this table and those shown in subsequent tables for the same year. Usually this discrepancy arises because the total number of live births occurring in a given year is revised although the remaining tabulations are not.

Rate computation: Crude live birth rates are the annual number of live births per 1 000 mid-year population.

Rates by urban/rural residence are the annual number of live births, in the appropriate urban or rural category, per 1 000 corresponding mid-year population. Rates are calculated only for data considered complete, that is, coded with a "C" and for estimates, coded "|". These rates are calculated by the Statistics Division of the United Nations based on the appropriate reference population (for example: total population, nationals only etc.) if known and available. If the reference population is not known or unavailable the total population is used to calculate the rates. Therefore, if the population that is used to calculate the rates is different from the correct reference population, the rates presented might under- or overstate the true situation in a country or area.

Rates presented in this table are limited to those countries or areas having a minimum number of 30 live births in a given year.

In addition, some rates were obtained from sample surveys, using different methods[2]; to distinguish them from civil registration data, estimated rates are identified by a footnote.

Reliability of data: Each country or area has been asked to indicate the estimated completeness of the live births recorded in its civil register. These national assessments are indicated by the quality codes "C" and "U" that appear in the first column of this table.

"C" indicates that the data are estimated to be virtually complete, that is, representing at least 90 per cent of the live births occurring each year, while "U" indicates that data are estimated to be incomplete, that is, representing less than 90 per cent of the live births occurring each year. A third code "..." indicates that no information was provided regarding completeness.

Data from civil registers that are reported as incomplete or of unknown completeness (coded "U" or "...") are considered unreliable. They appear in italics in this table and rates are not calculated for these data.

These quality codes apply only to data from civil registers. If data from other sources are presented, the symbol "|" is shown instead of the quality code. For more information about the quality of vital statistics data in general, and the information available on the basis of the completeness estimates in particular, see section 4.2 of the Technical Notes.

Limitations: Statistics on live births are subject to the same qualifications as have been set forth for vital statistics in general and birth statistics in particular as discussed in section 4 of the Technical Notes.

The reliability of data, an indication of which is described above, is an important factor in considering the limitations. In addition, some live births are tabulated by date of registration and not by date of occurrence; these have been indicated by a plus sign "+". Whenever the lag between the date of occurrence and date of registration is prolonged and, therefore, a large proportion of the live birth registrations are delayed, birth statistics for any given year may be seriously affected.

Another factor that limits international comparability is the practice of some countries or areas not to include in live birth statistics infants who were born alive but died before the registration of the birth or within the first 24 hours of life, thus underestimating the total number of life births. Statistics of this type are footnoted.

In addition, it should be noted that rates are affected also by the quality and limitations of the population estimates that are used in their computation. The problems of under-enumeration or over-enumeration and, to some extent, the differences in definition of total population have been discussed in section 3 of the Technical Notes dealing with population data in general, and specific information pertaining to individual countries or areas is given in the footnotes to table 3.

The rates estimated from the results of sample surveys are subject to possibilities of considerable error as a result of omissions in reporting of births, or as a result of erroneous reporting of births that occurred outside the reference period. However, rates estimated from sample surveys have the advantage of the availability of a built-in and strictly corresponding population base.

It should be emphasized that crude birth rates - like crude death, marriage and divorce rates - may be seriously affected by the age-sex structure of the populations to which they relate. Nevertheless, they do provide a simple measure of the level of and changes in natality.

The urban/rural classification of birth may refer to the residence of mother or the place of delivery, as the national practices vary and is provided by each country or area. In addition, the comparability of data by urban/rural residence is affected by the national definition of urban and rural used in tabulating these data. It is assumed, in the absence of specific information to the contrary, that the definitions of urban and rural used in connection with the national population census were also used in the compilation of the vital statistics for each country or area. However, it cannot be ruled out that, for a given country or area, different definitions of urban and rural are used for the vital statistics data and the population census data respectively. When known, the definitions of urban used in national population census are presented at the end of the technical notes to table 6. As discussed in detail in the technical notes to table 6, these definitions vary considerably from one area or country to another. Urban/rural differentials in vital rates may also be affected by whether the vital events have been tabulated in terms of place of occurrence or place of usual residence. This problem is discussed in more detail in section 4.1.4.1 of the Technical notes.

Earlier data: Live births have been shown in each issue of the *Demographic Yearbook*. Data included in this table update the series covering a period of years as follows:

Issue	Years Covered
Special Edition on Natality, CD, 1999	
- Numbers	1980 - 1999
- Rates	1985 - 1999
Historical Supplement, CD, 1997	1948 – 1997
44th issue, 1992	1983 – 1992
38th issue, 1986	1967 – 1986
33rd issue, 1981	1962 – 1981
Historical Supplement, 1979	1948 - 1977

For further information on years covered prior to 1948, readers should consult the Historical Index.

NOTES

[1] *Principles and Recommendations for a Vital Statistics System Revision 2,* Sales No. E. 01.XVII.10, United Nations, New York, 2001.
[2] *Manual X: Indirect Techniques for Demographic Estimation,* United Nations publication, Sales No. E.83.XIII.2, United Nations, New York, 1983.

Tableau 9

Le tableau 9 présente des données sur les naissances vivantes et les taux bruts de natalité selon le lieu de résidence (zone urbaine ou rurale) pour le plus grand nombre d'années possible entre 2003 et 2007.

Description des variables : La naissance vivante est l'expulsion ou l'extraction complète du corps de la mère, indépendamment de la durée de gestation, d'un produit de la conception qui, après cette séparation, respire ou manifeste tout autre signe de vie, tel que battement de cœur, pulsation du cordon ombilical ou contraction effective d'un muscle soumis à l'action de la volonté, que le cordon ombilical ait été coupé ou non et que le placenta soit ou non demeuré attaché ; tout produit d'une telle naissance est considéré comme « enfant né vivant »[1].

Sauf indication contraire, les statistiques relatives au nombre de naissances vivantes sont établies sur la base des registres de l'état civil. Pour les pays ou zones où les statistiques obtenues auprès des services de l'état civil sont jugées sûres, les taux de natalité indiqués ont été calculés par la Division de statistique de l'ONU d'après les naissances vivantes enregistrées.

Pour quelques pays il y a une discordance entre le nombre total des décès présenté dans ce tableau et ceux présentés après pour la même année. Habituellement ces différences apparaissent lorsque le nombre total des décès pour une certaine année a été révisé alors que les autres tabulations ne l'ont pas été.

Calcul des taux : Les taux bruts de natalité représentent le nombre annuel de naissances vivantes pour 1 000 habitants au milieu de l'année.

Les taux selon le lieu de résidence (zone urbaine ou rurale) représentent le nombre annuel de naissances vivantes, classées selon la catégorie urbaine ou rurale appropriée pour 1 000 habitants au milieu de l'année. Les taux ont été calculés seulement pour les données considérées complètes, c'est-à-dire celles associées au code "C". Ces taux sont calculés par la division de statistique des Nations Unies sur la base de la population de référence adéquate (par exemple : population totale, nationaux seulement, etc.) si connue et disponible. Si la population de référence n'est pas connue ou n'est pas disponible, la population totale est utilisée pour calculer les taux. Par conséquent, si la population utilisée pour calculer les taux est différente de la population de référence adéquate, les taux présentés sont susceptibles de sous ou sur estimer la situation réelle d'un pays ou d'un territoire.

Les taux présentés dans ce tableau se rapportent seulement aux pays ou zones où l'on a enregistré un nombre minimal de 30 naissances vivantes au cours d'une année donnée.

Dans certains cas, les données ont été calculées à partir d'enquêtes par sondage, en utilisant différentes techniques indirectes d'estimation démographique[2]. Pour les distinguer des données qui proviennent des registres de l'état civil, les taux estimatifs ont été signalés par une note.

Fiabilité des données : Il a été demandé à chaque pays ou zone d'indiquer le degré estimatif de complétude des données sur les naissances vivantes figurant dans ses registres d'état civil. Ces évaluations nationales sont signalées par les codes de qualité "C" et "U" qui apparaissent dans la deuxième colonne du tableau.

La lettre "C" indique que les données sont jugées à peu près complètes, c'est-à-dire qu'elles représentent au moins 90 p. 100 des naissances vivantes survenues chaque année ; la lettre "U" signifie que les données sont jugées incomplètes, c'est-à-dire qu'elles représentent moins de 90 p. 100 des naissances vivantes survenues chaque année. Un troisième code, "...", indique qu'aucun renseignement n'a été communiqué quant à la complétude des données.

Les données provenant des registres de l'état civil qui sont déclarées incomplètes ou dont le degré de complétude n'est pas connu (code "U" ou "...") sont jugées douteuses. Elles apparaissent en italique dans le tableau. Les taux pour ces données ne sont pas calculés.

Les codes de qualité ne s'appliquent qu'aux données provenant des registres de l'état civil. Si l'on présente des données autres que celles de l'état civil, le signe "|" est utilisé à la place du code de qualité. Pour plus de précisions sur la qualité des données reposant sur les statistiques de l'état civil en général et les estimations de complétude en particulier, voir la section 4.2 des Notes techniques.

Insuffisance des données : Les statistiques concernant les naissances vivantes appellent toutes les réserves qui ont été formulées à propos des statistiques de l'état civil en général et des statistiques des naissances en particulier (voir la section 4 des Notes techniques).

La fiabilité des données, au sujet de laquelle des indications ont été fournies plus haut, est un facteur important. Il faut également tenir compte du fait que, dans certains cas, les données relatives aux naissances vivantes sont exploitées selon la date de l'enregistrement et non selon la date de l'événement ; ces cas ont été signalés par le signe '+'. Chaque fois que le décalage entre l'événement et son enregistrement est grand et qu'une forte proportion des naissances vivantes fait l'objet d'un enregistrement tardif, les statistiques des naissances vivantes pour une année donnée peuvent être considérablement faussées.

Un autre facteur qui nuit à la comparabilité internationale est la pratique de certains pays ou zones qui consiste à ne pas inclure dans les statistiques des naissances vivantes les enfants nés vivants mais décédés avant l'enregistrement de leur naissance ou dans les 24 heures qui ont suivi la naissance, pratique qui conduit à sous-estimer le nombre total de naissances vivantes. Lorsque ce facteur a joué, cela a été signalé en note à la fin du tableau.

La qualité et les limitations des estimations concernant la population ont également une incidence sur le calcul des taux. Les problèmes liés au sur-dénombrement ou au sous-dénombrement et, dans une certaine mesure, aux différences dans la définition de la population totale ont été abordés à la section 3 des Notes techniques relative aux données sur la population en général et des précisions sur certains pays ou zones sont données dans les notes se rapportant au tableau 3.

Les taux estimatifs fondés sur les résultats d'enquêtes par sondage comportent des possibilités d'erreurs considérables dues soit à des omissions dans les déclarations, soit au fait que l'on a déclaré à tort des naissances survenues en réalité hors de la période considérée. Toutefois, les taux estimatifs fondés sur les résultats d'enquêtes par sondage présentent un gros avantage : le chiffre de population utilisé comme base est, par définition, rigoureusement correspondant.

Il faut souligner que les taux bruts de natalité, de même que les taux bruts de mortalité, de nuptialité et de divortialité, peuvent varier très sensiblement selon la structure par âge et par sexe de la population à laquelle ils se rapportent. Ils offrent néanmoins un moyen simple de mesurer le niveau et l'évolution de la natalité.

La classification des naissances selon le lieu de résidence (zone urbaine ou rurale) peut se rapporter au lieu de résidence de la mère ou au lieu d'occurrence et correspond à celle indiquée par chaque pays ou zone. En outre, la comparabilité des données selon le lieu de résidence (zone urbaine ou rurale) peut être limitée par les définitions nationales des termes « urbain » et « rural » utilisées pour la mise en tableaux de ces données. En l'absence d'indications contraires, on a supposé que les mêmes définitions avaient servi pour le recensement national de la population et pour l'établissement des statistiques de l'état civil pour chaque pays ou zone. Toutefois, il n'est pas exclu que, pour une zone ou un pays donné, des définitions différentes aient été retenues. Les définitions du terme « urbain » utilisées pour les recensements nationaux de population ont été présentées à la fin des notes techniques du tableau 6 lorsqu'elles étaient connues. Comme on l'a précisé dans les notes techniques relatives au tableau 6, ces définitions varient considérablement d'un pays ou d'une zone à l'autre. La différence entre ces taux pour les zones urbaines et rurales pourra aussi être faussée selon que les faits d'état civil auront été classés d'après le lieu de l'événement ou le lieu de résidence habituel. Ce problème est examiné plus en détail à la section 4.1.4.1 des Notes techniques.

Données publiées antérieurement : Les différentes éditions de l'*Annuaire démographique* contiennent des données sur les naissances vivantes. Les données qui figurent dans le tableau 9 actualisent les données qui portaient sur les périodes suivantes :

Éditions	Années considérées
Édition spéciale sur les statistiques de la natalité (CD-ROM), 1999	
- Nombre	1980 – 1999

- Taux	1985 – 1999
Supplément historique (CD-ROM), 1997	1948 – 1997
44ᵉ édition, 1992	1983 – 1992
38ᵉ édition,1986	1967 – 1986
33ᵉ édition, 1981	1962 – 1981
Supplément rétrospectif, 1979	1948 – 1977

Pour plus de détails concernant les années antérieures à 1948, se reporter à l'index historique.

NOTES

[1] *Principes et recommandations pour un système de statistique de l'état civil, deuxième révision*, numéro de vente : F.01.XVII.10, publication des Nations Unies, New York, 2003.
[2] *Manuel X, techniques indirectes d'estimation démographique*, numéro de vente : F.83.XIII.2, publication des Nations Unies, New York, 1984.

9. Live births and crude live birth rates, by urban/rural residence: 2003 - 2007
Naissances vivantes et taux bruts de natalité selon la résidence, urbaine/rurale: 2003 - 2007

Continent, country or area, and urban/rural residence — Continent, pays ou zone et résidence, urbaine/rurale	Code[a]	Number - Nombre					Rate - Taux				
		2003	2004	2005	2006	2007	2003	2004	2005	2006	2007
AFRICA - AFRIQUE											
Algeria - Algérie[1]											
Total	C	649 000	669 000	703 000	739 000	783 000	20.4	20.7	21.4	22.1	23.0
Burkina Faso[2]											
Total	I	...	...	...	612 840	...	...	...	...	46.7	...
Urban - Urbaine	I	...	...	...	107 657	...	...	...	...	50.4	...
Rural - Rurale	I	...	...	...	505 183	...	...	...	...	46.0	...
Cape Verde - Cap-Vert											
Total	C	13 334	...	...	...	...	28.9	...	...	...	...
Congo[3]											
Total	+U	*44 132*	*44 473*	...	...	...	...	...	...	...	...
Egypt - Égypte											
Total	C	1 777 418	1 779 500	1 800 972	1 853 746	1 949 569	26.2	25.7	25.5	25.7	26.5
Urban - Urbaine	C	769 791	712 431	723 044	740 228	763 798	26.4	24.0	24.0	24.1	24.1
Rural - Rurale	C	1 007 627	1 067 069	1 077 928	1 113 518	1 185 771	25.9	26.9	26.6	27.0	28.3
Kenya											
Total	U	*495 433*	...	...	...	...	...	...	...	...	...
Malawi[4]											
Total	U	*578 978*	*590 774*	*602 590*	*614 410*	*626 181*	...	...	...	...	...
Mauritius - Maurice											
Total	+C	19 343	19 230	18 820	17 604	17 034	15.8	15.6	15.1	14.1	13.5
Urban - Urbaine	+C	7 580	7 268	7 115	6 691	6 467	14.6	13.9	13.6	12.7	12.2
Rural - Rurale	+C	11 763	11 962	11 705	10 913	10 567	16.7	16.8	16.3	15.0	14.4
Mayotte											
Total	C	7 197	7 452	...	...	...	...	...	...	...	...
Réunion[5]											
Total	C	14 427	14 545	14 610	14 495	14 808	19.1	19.0	18.8	18.4	18.6
Saint Helena ex. dep. - Sainte-Hélène sans dép.											
Total	C	37	34	34	35	42	...	...	...	...	10.6
Seychelles											
Total	+C	1 498	1 435	1 536	1 467	1 499	18.1	17.4	18.5	17.3	17.6
South Africa - Afrique du Sud											
Total	U	*926 592*	*971 142*	*998 257*	*999 874*	*911 494*	...	...	...	...	...
Tunisia - Tunisie											
Total	C	168 022	166 551	170 999	173 390	177 503	17.1	16.8	17.1	17.1	17.4
Zambia - Zambie[4]											
Total	U	...	...	...	*509 766*		...	...	...	...	...
AMERICA, NORTH - AMÉRIQUE DU NORD											
Anguilla											
Total	+C	139	164	167	183	148	11.4	13.1	12.2	12.8	9.9
Aruba											
Total	C	1 244	1 193	1 263	1 227	1 239	13.1	12.2	12.5	11.9	11.9
Bahamas											
Total	U	*5 054*	*5 154*	*5 548*	*5 296*	*5 854*	...	...	...	...	...
Barbados - Barbade											
Total	+C	*3 748	*3 473	*3 508	*3 414	*3 537	*13.8	*12.7	*12.8	*12.5	*12.9
Belize											
Total	U	*7 440*	*8 083*	*8 396*	...	...	...	...	...	...	...
Bermuda - Bermudes[6]											
Total	C	834	831	835	798		13.2	13.1	13.1	12.5	...
British Virgin Islands - Îles Vierges britanniques											
Total	C	269	318	...	...	...	12.6	14.7	...	...	...
Canada[7]											
Total	C	335 202	337 422	342 176	*350 181	...	10.6	10.5	10.6	*10.7	...
Cayman Islands - Îles Caïmanes[8]											
Total	C	623	611	699	710	744	14.3	13.8	14.5	13.7	13.8
Costa Rica											
Total	C	72 938	72 247	71 548	71 291	73 144	17.8	17.3	16.8	16.4	16.5
Urban - Urbaine	C	33 674	31 203	30 602	29 515	28 883	14.0	12.7	12.2	11.5	11.0
Rural - Rurale	C	39 264	41 044	40 946	41 776	44 261	23.4	24.0	23.4	23.4	24.3

Continent, country or area, and urban/rural residence / Continent, pays ou zone et résidence, urbaine/rurale	Code[a]	Number - Nombre					Rate - Taux				
		2003	2004	2005	2006	2007	2003	2004	2005	2006	2007
AMERICA, NORTH - AMÉRIQUE DU NORD											
Cuba											
Total	C	136 795	127 192	120 716	111 323	112 472	12.2	11.3	10.7	9.9	10.0
Urban - Urbaine	C	100 429	92 129	88 922	83 389	84 828	11.8	10.8	10.5	9.8	10.0
Rural - Rurale	C	36 366	35 063	31 794	27 934	27 644	13.4	12.8	11.6	10.2	10.0
Dominica - Dominique											
Total	+C	1 056	1 066	1 009	1 058	...	15.0	15.1	14.3	14.9	...
Dominican Republic - République dominicaine											
Total	U	*151 466*	*139 215*	*131 101*	*121 038*	*106 405*	...	...	...	...	...
Urban - Urbaine[9]	U	*114 331*	*103 182*	*97 573*	*89 728*	*77 590*	...	...	...	...	...
Rural - Rurale[9]	U	*30 394*	*30 350*	*27 800*	*24 476*	*21 091*	...	...	...	...	...
El Salvador											
Total	C	124 476	119 710	112 769	107 111	106 471	18.8	17.7	16.4	15.3	15.0
Urban - Urbaine	C	73 311	71 430	69 236	70 810	68 439	18.6	17.8	16.9	16.9	16.0
Rural - Rurale	C	51 165	48 280	43 533	36 301	38 032	18.9	17.6	15.7	13.0	13.5
Greenland - Groenland											
Total	C	895	893	887	842	853	15.8	15.7	15.6	14.8	15.1
Urban - Urbaine	C	717	...	...	...	...	15.3	...	...	...	...
Rural - Rurale	C	178	...	...	...	...	17.8	...	...	...	...
Guadeloupe[5]											
Total	C	7 047	7 273	7 551	7 193	6 862	16.1	16.4	16.9	15.7	17.0
Guatemala											
Total	C	375 092	383 704	374 066	368 399	...	31.0	31.0	29.5	28.3	...
Urban - Urbaine	C	...	...	160 158	158 159	...	...	...	...	...	...
Rural - Rurale	C	...	...	213 908	210 240	...	...	...	...	...	...
Honduras											
Total	+U	*218 173*	*220 040*	*221 759*	*222 512*		...	...			
Urban - Urbaine	+U	*95 182*	*96 862*	*98 408*	*99 818*		...	...	...	...	...
Rural - Rurale	+U	*122 991*	*123 178*	*123 351*	*122 694*		...	...	...	...	...
Jamaica - Jamaïque[10]											
Total	C	47 110	47 127	47 255	46 277	45 590	17.9	17.9	17.8	17.4	17.0
Martinique[5]											
Total	C	5 430	5 255	5 032	5 370	5 317	13.9	13.3	12.7	13.4	13.3
Urban - Urbaine	C	4 867	4 743	4 551	4 858	4 822	...	...	...	...	...
Rural - Rurale	C	563	512	481	512	495	...	...	...	...	...
Mexico - Mexique[11]											
Total	+U	*2 165 318*	*2 154 927*	*2 141 083*	...	...	...	...	...	...	...
Urban - Urbaine[9]	+U	*1 564 908*	*1 575 037*	*1 589 256*	...	...	...	...	...	...	...
Rural - Rurale[9]	+U	*550 595*	*531 186*	*504 990*	...	...	...	...	...	...	...
Montserrat											
Total	+C	40	47	63	49	43	8.9	10.0	13.2	10.5	8.9
Netherlands Antilles - Antilles néerlandaises[12]											
Total	C	2 488	2 388	2 553	2 578	*2 558	14.1	13.4	13.9	13.6	*13.2
Nicaragua											
Total	+U	*120 784*	*121 402*	*121 380*	*123 886*	*128 171*	...	...	...	...	...
Urban - Urbaine	+U	*63 105*	*62 412*	*62 960*	*62 438*	*64 803*	...	...	...	...	...
Rural - Rurale	+U	*57 679*	*58 990*	*58 420*	*61 448*	*63 368*	...	...	...	...	...
Panama											
Total	C	61 753	62 743	63 645	65 764	67 364	19.8	19.8	19.7	20.0	20.2
Urban - Urbaine	C	38 568	38 797	38 902	40 113	41 146	...	...	19.0	19.2	...
Rural - Rurale	C	23 185	23 946	24 743	25 651	26 218	...	...	21.0	21.6	...
Puerto Rico - Porto Rico											
Total	C	50 803	51 239	50 687	48 744	...	13.1	13.2	13.0	12.4	...
Urban - Urbaine[9]	C	26 642	26 866	27 809	...	...	...	...	...	...	...
Rural - Rurale[9]	C	24 151	24 355	22 867	...	...	...	...	...	...	...
Saint Lucia - Sainte-Lucie											
Total	C	2 486	2 322	*2 298	...	...	15.5	14.3	*14.0	...	...
Saint Vincent and the Grenadines - Saint-Vincent-et-les Grenadines											
Total	+C	1 923	1 804	1 779	...	...	18.3	17.3	17.1	...	...
Trinidad and Tobago - Trinité-et-Tobago											
Total	C	17 989	17 235	...	...	...	14.0	13.4	...	...	...

Continent, country or area, and urban/rural residence / Continent, pays ou zone et résidence, urbaine/rurale	Code[a]	Number - Nombre					Rate - Taux				
		2003	2004	2005	2006	2007	2003	2004	2005	2006	2007
AMERICA, NORTH - AMÉRIQUE DU NORD											
Turks and Caicos Islands - Îles Turques et Caïques											
Total	C	213	300	318	409	512	8.5	10.9	10.4	12.3	14.7
United States of America - États-Unis d'Amérique											
Total	C	4 089 950	4 112 052	4 138 349	4 265 555	4 317 119	14.1	14.0	14.0	14.3	14.3
United States Virgin Islands - Îles Vierges américaines											
Total	C	1 610	1 672	1 686	1 763	1 771	14.8	15.3	15.4	16.1	16.1
AMERICA, SOUTH - AMÉRIQUE DU SUD											
Argentina - Argentine											
Total	C	697 952	736 261	712 220	...	700 792	18.4	19.3	18.5	...	17.8
Total	+C	...	...	...	696 451	...	...	...	...	17.9	...
Bolivia (Plurinational State of) - Bolivie (État plurinational de)											
Total	U	204 683	177 306	160 052	135 069	*96 856	...	...	...	...	...
Brazil - Brésil[13]											
Total	U	2 822 462	2 813 704	2 874 542	2 798 964	2 750 667	...	...	...	...	...
Chile - Chili											
Total	C	234 486	230 352	230 831	231 383	...	14.7	14.3	14.2	14.1	...
Urban - Urbaine	C	209 572	204 612	205 297	208 709	...	15.2	14.7	14.5	14.6	...
Rural - Rurale	C	24 914	25 740	25 534	22 674	...	11.8	12.1	11.9	10.5	...
Colombia - Colombie											
Total	U	710 702	723 099	719 968	714 450	*685 609	...	...	...	...	...
Urban - Urbaine[9]	U	546 406	554 045	554 388	555 009	*538 128	...	...	...	...	...
Rural - Rurale[9]	U	149 345	154 369	152 392	147 921	*136 463	...	...	...	...	...
Ecuador - Équateur[14]											
Total	U	262 004	254 362	252 725	278 591	195 051[15]	...	...	...	...	...
Urban - Urbaine[15]	U	137 189	132 618	131 539	...	159 061	...	...	...	...	...
Rural - Rurale[15]	U	41 360	36 275	36 785	...	35 990	...	...	...	...	...
Falkland Islands (Malvinas) - Îles Falkland (Malvinas)											
Total	+C	34	44	18	27	...	...	...	...	...	...
French Guiana - Guyane française[5]											
Total	C	5 553	5 312	5 998	6 276	6 386	30.7	28.4	30.0	31.9	29.9
Urban - Urbaine	C	4 292	4 234	4 688	4 990	5 003	...	...	...	...	...
Rural - Rurale	C	1 261	1 078	1 310	1 286	1 383	...	...	...	...	...
Paraguay											
Total	U	45 669	49 857	51 444	...	...	...	...	...	...	...
Peru - Pérou[16]											
Total	+U	383 919	344 804	*310 611	*307 779	*508 384	...	...	...	...	...
Suriname[17]											
Total	C	9 634	9 062	8 657	9 311	9 769	20.0	18.6	17.4	18.5	19.2
Urban - Urbaine[18]	C	6 053	5 632	5 427	5 726	6 103	...	...	...	...	...
Rural - Rurale[18]	C	3 581	3 430	3 230	3 585	3 666	...	...	...	...	...
Uruguay											
Total	C	50 631	50 052	47 150	47 231	47 372	15.3	15.2	14.3	14.2	14.3
Venezuela (Bolivarian Republic of) - Venezuela (République bolivarienne du)[13]											
Total	C	555 614	637 799	665 997	646 225	615 371	21.6	24.4	25.1	23.9	22.4

9. Live births and crude live birth rates, by urban/rural residence: 2003 - 2007
Naissances vivantes et taux bruts de natalité selon la résidence, urbaine/rurale: 2003 - 2007 (continued - suite)

Continent, country or area, and urban/rural residence — Continent, pays ou zone et résidence, urbaine/rurale	Code[a]	Number - Nombre					Rate - Taux				
		2003	2004	2005	2006	2007	2003	2004	2005	2006	2007
ASIA - ASIE											
Armenia - Arménie											
Total	C	35 793[19]	37 520[19]	37 499[19]	37 639[20]	40 105	11.1	11.7	11.7	11.7	12.4
Urban - Urbaine	C	22 629[19]	23 628[19]	23 762[19]	23 793[20]	25 519	11.0	11.5	11.5	11.5	12.3
Rural - Rurale	C	13 164[19]	13 892[19]	13 737[19]	13 846[20]	14 586	11.5	12.1	11.9	12.0	12.6
Azerbaijan - Azerbaïdjan[19]											
Total	+C	113 467	131 609	141 901	148 946	151 963	13.8	15.8	16.9	17.6	17.7
Urban - Urbaine	+C	51 057	59 026	64 362	70 541	73 102	12.0	13.8	14.9	16.1	16.5
Rural - Rurale	+C	62 410	72 583	77 539	78 405	78 861	15.6	18.0	19.1	19.1	19.0
Bahrain - Bahreïn											
Total	C	14 560	14 968	15 198	15 053	16 062	19.0	18.2	17.1	15.7	15.5
Bangladesh[21]											
Total	I	...	...	...	...	...	20.9	20.8	20.7	20.6	20.9
Urban - Urbaine	I	...	...	...	...	...	17.9	17.8	17.8	17.5	17.4
Rural - Rurale	I	...	...	...	...	...	21.7	21.6	21.7	21.7	22.1
Bhutan - Bhoutan[22]											
Total	I	...	...	12 538	...	...	...	...	19.7	...	...
Urban - Urbaine	I	...	...	3 845	...	...	...	...	...	...	...
Rural - Rurale	I	...	...	8 693	...	...	...	...	...	...	...
Brunei Darussalam - Brunéi Darussalam											
Total	+C	7 047	7 163	6 933	6 526	6 314	20.2	19.9	18.7	17.0	16.2
Cambodia - Cambodge											
Total	U	375 799	384 267				...	...	...	...	...
China - Chine[23]											
Total	I	15 990 000[24]	15 930 000[24]	16 170 000[25]	15 840 000[24]	15 940 000[24]	12.4	12.3	12.4	12.1	12.0
China, Hong Kong SAR - Chine, Hong Kong RAS											
Total	C	46 965	49 796	57 098	65 626	*70 875	7.0	7.3	8.4	9.6	*10.2
China, Macao SAR - Chine, Macao RAS											
Total	C	3 212	3 308	3 671	4 058	4 537	7.2	7.3	7.8	8.1	8.6
Cyprus - Chypre[26]											
Total	C	8 088	8 309	8 243	8 731	8 575	11.2	11.3	10.9	11.3	10.9
Urban - Urbaine[9]	C	4 854	5 366	5 672	5 184	...	...	...	...	...	...
Rural - Rurale[9]	C	2 692	2 863	2 512	2 875	...	...	...	...	...	...
Georgia - Géorgie[19]											
Total	C	46 194	49 572	46 512	47 795	49 287	10.7	11.5	10.7	10.9	11.2
Urban - Urbaine	C	34 589	31 037	31 174	33 547	34 301	15.3	13.8	13.6	14.5	14.9
Rural - Rurale	C	11 605	18 535	15 338	14 248	14 986	5.6	9.0	7.4	6.8	7.2
India - Inde[27]											
Total	I	...	...	...	...	...	24.8	24.1	23.8	23.5	23.1
Urban - Urbaine	I	...	...	...	...	...	19.8	19.0	19.1	18.8	18.6
Rural - Rurale	I	...	...	...	...	...	26.4	25.9	25.6	25.2	24.7
Iran (Islamic Republic of) - Iran (République islamique d')[28]											
Total	C	1 171 573	1 154 368	1 233 873	1 253 506	1 286 716	17.4	16.9	17.8	17.8	18.0
Urban - Urbaine	C	768 845	759 162	815 445	844 813	872 658	17.1	16.5	17.3	17.1	17.6
Rural - Rurale	C	402 728	395 206	418 428	408 693	414 058	17.9	17.7	18.8	...	18.9
Iraq											
Total	U	*691 269	*840 257	*896 340	*902 934	...	...	...	...	...	...
Israel - Israël[29]											
Total	C	144 936	145 207	143 913	148 170	151 679	21.7	21.3	20.8	21.0	21.1
Urban - Urbaine[9]	C	131 658	131 794	130 294	133 924	138 143	21.5	21.2	20.5	20.7	21.0
Rural - Rurale[9]	C	13 272	13 404	13 517	14 084	13 478	23.4	23.0	23.7	24.5	22.9
Japan - Japon[30]											
Total	C	1 123 610	1 110 721	1 062 530	1 092 674	1 089 818	8.9	8.8	8.4	8.7	8.6
Urban - Urbaine[31]	C	917 627	916 299	917 831	984 329	987 851	...	...	...	...	...
Rural - Rurale[31]	C	205 813	194 246	144 529	108 169	101 807	...	...	...	...	...
Jordan - Jordanie[32]											
Total	C	148 294	150 248	152 276	162 972	185 011	27.1	28.1	27.8	29.1	32.3
Kazakhstan[19]											
Total	C	247 946	273 028	278 977	301 756	321 963	16.6	18.2	18.4	19.7	20.8
Urban - Urbaine	C	138 680	155 997	163 952	175 582	174 343	16.3	18.2	18.9	20.0	21.3
Rural - Rurale	C	109 266	117 031	115 025	126 174	147 620	17.0	18.2	17.7	19.3	20.3
Kuwait - Koweït											
Total	C	43 982	47 274	50 941	52 759	53 587	21.0	21.8	22.7	22.7	22.2

Continent, country or area, and urban/rural residence / Continent, pays ou zone et résidence, urbaine/rurale	Code[a]	Number - Nombre					Rate - Taux				
		2003	2004	2005	2006	2007	2003	2004	2005	2006	2007
ASIA - ASIE											
Kyrgyzstan - Kirghizstan											
Total	C	105 490	109 939[33]	109 839	120 737	123 251	20.9	21.6	21.4	23.3	23.5
Urban - Urbaine	C	31 866	37 381[33]	35 600	39 414	41 402	17.8	20.6	19.4	21.4	22.4
Rural - Rurale	C	73 624	72 558[33]	74 239	81 323	81 849	22.6	22.1	22.4	24.3	24.2
Lebanon - Liban											
Total	C	71 702	73 900	73 973	72 790	80 896	...	19.7	...	...	21.5
Malaysia - Malaisie											
Total	C	480 083	477 768	469 204	465 112	*456 443	19.2	18.7	18.0	17.5	*16.8
Urban - Urbaine	C	304 013	300 655	295 513	295 561	...	19.4	18.7	17.9	17.6	...
Rural - Rurale	C	176 070	177 113	173 691	169 551	...	18.8	18.6	18.0	17.3	...
Maldives											
Total	C	5 157	5 220	5 543	5 829	6 569	18.1	18.0	18.9	19.5	21.5
Urban - Urbaine	C	1 966	2 145	2 457	2 707	3 083	25.1	27.0	...	...	...
Rural - Rurale	C	3 191	3 075	3 086	3 122	3 486	15.4	14.6	...	...	...
Mongolia - Mongolie											
Total	C	45 723	45 501	45 326	49 092	56 636	18.4	18.1	17.8	19.0	21.7
Urban - Urbaine	C	24 315	25 812	26 462	29 717	36 256	16.9	17.4	17.4	19.0	22.8
Rural - Rurale	C	21 408	19 689	18 864	19 375	20 380	20.4	19.0	18.4	19.0	19.9
Myanmar											
Total	U	*685 443*	*791 600*	*836 124*	...	...	...	...	...	...	...
Urban - Urbaine	U	*228 981*	*228 680*	*233 307*	...	...	...	...	...	...	...
Rural - Rurale	U	*456 462*	*562 920*	*602 817*	...	...	...	...	...	...	...
Occupied Palestinian Territory - Territoire palestinien occupé											
Total	C	106 355	111 245	109 439	108 874	108 674	32.1	32.6	31.2	30.1	29.2
Oman											
Total	U	*40 062*[34]	*40 584*[34]	*42 065*[34]	*44 116*[34]	*48 041*[35]	...	...	...	...	...
Pakistan[36]											
Total	I	3 683 290[37]	...	3 772 494[38]	...	...	24.9	...	24.5	...	...
Urban - Urbaine	I	1 194 081[37]	...	1 226 151[38]	...	...	24.3	...	23.4	...	...
Rural - Rurale	I	2 489 209[37]	...	2 546 343[38]	...	...	25.1	...	25.1	...	...
Philippines											
Total	C	1 669 442	1 710 994	1 688 918	...	...	20.6	20.7	20.0	...	...
Qatar											
Total	C	12 856	13 190	13 401	14 120	15 681	17.9	17.4	15.1	13.6	12.8
Republic of Korea - République de Corée[39]											
Total[40]	C	493 471	476 052	438 062	451 514	*496 710	10.2	9.8	9.0	9.2	*10.3
Urban - Urbaine	C	400 980	388 402	357 588	371 084	...	10.4	10.0	9.2	9.4	...
Rural - Rurale	C	86 525	84 303	77 406	77 020	...	8.8	8.7	8.0	8.2	...
Saudi Arabia - Arabie saoudite											
Total	...	*567 433*	*574 211*	*582 582*	*589 223*	...	...	...	...	...	...
Singapore - Singapour											
Total	C	37 485	37 174	37 492	38 317	39 490	9.1	8.9	8.8	8.7	8.6
Sri Lanka											
Total	+C	370 642	360 220	370 424	371 264	380 069	19.3	18.5	18.8	18.7	19.0
Urban - Urbaine	+C	243 388	...	...	...	...	...	...	...	...	...
Rural - Rurale	+C	127 255	...	...	...	...	...	...	...	...	...
Syrian Arab Republic - République arabe syrienne[41]											
Total	U	*609 774*	*598 221*	*634 170*	*656 599*	*727 439*	...	...	...	...	...
Tajikistan - Tadjikistan[42]											
Total	U	*177 938*	*179 563*	*180 790*	*186 463*	*200 010*	...	...	...	...	...
Urban - Urbaine	U	*45 182*	*44 304*	*42 563*	*44 298*	*51 384*	...	...	...	...	...
Rural - Rurale	U	*132 756*	*135 259*	*138 227*	*142 165*	*148 626*	...	...	...	...	...
Thailand - Thaïlande											
Total	+U	*742 183*	*813 069*	*809 485*	*793 623*	*797 588*	...	...	...	...	...
Turkey - Turquie[43]											
Total	I	1 291 000	1 286 000	1 281 000	1 277 000	1 275 000	18.4	18.1	17.8	17.5	17.3
United Arab Emirates - Émirats arabes unis											
Total	...		*61 165*	*63 113*	*64 623*	*62 969*	...	...	...	...	...

9. Live births and crude live birth rates, by urban/rural residence: 2003 - 2007
Naissances vivantes et taux bruts de natalité selon la résidence, urbaine/rurale: 2003 - 2007 (continued - suite)

Continent, country or area, and urban/rural residence / Continent, pays ou zone et résidence, urbaine/rurale	Code[a]	Number - Nombre					Rate - Taux				
		2003	2004	2005	2006	2007	2003	2004	2005	2006	2007
ASIA - ASIE											
Viet Nam											
Total	C	1 292 086	1 249 191	1 252 882	1 243 463	1 326 464	16.0	15.2	15.1	14.8	15.6
Urban - Urbaine	C	336 600	307 427	320 544	320 456	358 119	16.1	14.1	14.4	14.1	15.3
Rural - Rurale	C	955 486	941 764	932 338	923 007	968 345	15.9	15.6	15.3	15.0	15.7
Yemen - Yémen											
Total	U	130 112	153 945	167 830	298 437	256 288	...	...	...	...	...
EUROPE											
Åland Islands - Îles d'Åland[44]											
Total	C	262	281	268	295	286	10.0	10.6	10.1	11.0	10.6
Urban - Urbaine	C	102	122	94	113	109	9.6	11.4	8.7	10.5	10.0
Rural - Rurale	C	160	159	174	182	177	10.2	10.1	10.9	11.3	10.9
Albania - Albanie											
Total	C	47 012	43 022	39 612	34 229	33 163	15.1	13.8	12.6	10.9	10.5
Urban - Urbaine	C	19 447	18 859	...	...	...	14.1	13.4	...	...	...
Rural - Rurale	C	27 565	24 163	...	...	...	15.9	14.0	...	...	...
Andorra - Andorre											
Total	C	721	814	828	843	826	10.3	10.9	10.5	10.5	10.0
Austria - Autriche											
Total	C	76 944	78 968	78 190	77 914	76 250	9.5	9.7	9.5	9.4	9.2
Belarus - Bélarus[19]											
Total	C	88 512	88 943	90 508	96 721	103 626	9.0	9.1	9.3	9.9	10.7
Urban - Urbaine	C	64 814	65 038	66 259	71 186	77 137	9.2	9.2	9.4	10.1	10.9
Rural - Rurale	C	23 698	23 905	24 249	25 535	26 489	8.4	8.6	8.9	9.6	10.1
Belgium - Belgique[45]											
Total	C	112 149	115 618	118 002	121 382	120 663	10.8	11.1	11.3	11.5	11.4
Urban - Urbaine	C	110 451	113 921	116 288	119 696	119 040	10.8	11.1	11.3	11.5	11.4
Rural - Rurale	C	1 698	1 697	1 714	1 686	1 623	11.4	11.3	11.4	11.1	10.6
Bosnia and Herzegovina - Bosnie-Herzégovine											
Total	C	35 234	35 151	34 627	34 033	33 835	9.2	9.1	9.0	8.9	...
Bulgaria - Bulgarie											
Total	C	67 359	69 886	71 075	73 978	75 349	8.6	9.0	9.2	9.6	9.8
Urban - Urbaine	C	48 597	50 390	52 280	55 043	56 257	8.9	9.3	9.6	10.1	10.4
Rural - Rurale	C	18 762	19 496	18 795	18 935	19 092	7.9	8.3	8.1	8.3	8.5
Croatia - Croatie											
Total	C	39 668	40 307	42 492	41 446	41 910	8.9	9.1	9.6	9.3	9.4
Urban - Urbaine	C	21 837	22 420	23 421	23 085	23 302	...	...	...	...	...
Rural - Rurale	C	17 831	17 887	19 071	18 361	18 608	...	...	...	...	...
Czech Republic - République tchèque											
Total	C	93 685	97 664	102 211	105 831	114 632	9.2	9.6	10.0	10.3	11.1
Urban - Urbaine	C	69 120	72 231	75 719	78 561	84 759	9.2	9.6	10.0	10.4	11.1
Rural - Rurale	C	24 565	25 433	26 492	27 270	29 873	9.2	9.5	9.9	10.1	11.0
Denmark - Danemark[46]											
Total	C	64 599	64 609	64 282	64 984	64 082	12.0	12.0	11.9	12.0	11.7
Estonia - Estonie											
Total	C	13 036	13 992	14 350	14 877	15 775	9.6	10.4	10.7	11.1	11.8
Urban - Urbaine	C	9 049	9 892	10 233	10 554	11 134	9.7	10.6	11.0	11.3	12.0
Rural - Rurale	C	3 987	4 100	4 117	4 323	4 641	9.6	9.9	10.0	10.5	11.3
Faeroe Islands - Îles Féroé											
Total	C	705	713	712	661	674	14.7	14.8	14.8	13.7	14.0
Finland - Finlande[47]											
Total	C	56 630	57 758	57 745	58 840	58 729	10.9	11.0	11.0	11.2	11.1
Urban - Urbaine	C	37 303	37 816	38 181	39 003	40 318	11.5	11.7	11.7	11.8	11.7
Rural - Rurale	C	19 327	19 942	19 564	19 837	18 411	9.8	10.1	10.0	10.2	9.9
France[48]											
Total	C	761 464	767 816	774 355	796 896	785 985	12.6	12.7	12.7	13.0	12.7
Urban - Urbaine[49]	C	574 477	578 024	581 681	596 949	587 384	...	...	...	...	...
Rural - Rurale[49]	C	185 572	188 475	191 223	198 494	197 161	...	...	...	...	...
Germany - Allemagne											
Total	C	706 721	705 622	685 795	672 724	684 862	8.6	8.6	8.3	8.2	8.3
Gibraltar[50]											
Total	+C	372	421	418	373	400	13.0	14.7	14.5	12.8	13.7

9. Live births and crude live birth rates, by urban/rural residence: 2003 - 2007
Naissances vivantes et taux bruts de natalité selon la résidence, urbaine/rurale: 2003 - 2007 (continued - suite)

Continent, country or area, and urban/rural residence / Continent, pays ou zone et résidence, urbaine/rurale	Co-de[a]	Number - Nombre					Rate - Taux				
		2003	2004	2005	2006	2007	2003	2004	2005	2006	2007
EUROPE											
Greece - Grèce											
Total.....................	C	104 420	105 655	107 545	112 042	111 926	9.5	9.6	9.7	10.0	10.0
Urban - Urbaine	C	...	...	73 816	76 996	76 513	...	...	...	...	...
Rural - Rurale	C	...	...	33 729	35 046	35 413	...	...	...	...	...
Guernsey - Guernesey											
Total.....................	C	650	586	638	598	645	...	9.7	...	9.8	10.4
Hungary - Hongrie											
Total.....................	C	94 647	95 137	97 496	99 871	97 613	9.3	9.4	9.7	9.9	9.7
Urban - Urbaine[51]........	C	59 280	60 331	63 785	66 223	65 417	9.0	9.2	9.6	9.8	9.7
Rural - Rurale[51]..........	C	34 465	33 983	32 860	32 789	31 525	9.7	9.6	9.6	9.9	9.5
Iceland - Islande											
Total.....................	C	4 143	4 234	4 280	4 415	4 560	14.3	14.5	14.5	14.5	14.6
Urban - Urbaine	C	3 906	...	4 054	4 204	4 315	14.6	...	14.7	14.9	14.9
Rural - Rurale	C	237	...	226	211	245	11.1	...	10.8	9.4	11.0
Ireland - Irlande											
Total[52].................	C	61 529	61 972	61 372	...	...	15.5	15.3	14.9	...	...
Total.....................	+C	...	...	...	*64 237	*70 620	...	...	...	*15.2	*16.3
Isle of Man - Île de Man											
Total.....................	+C	860	862	901	905	919	11.1	11.1	11.4	11.3	11.4
Italy - Italie											
Total.....................	C	544 063	562 599	554 022	560 010	563 933	9.4	9.7	9.5	9.5	9.5
Jersey[11]											
Total.....................	+C	1 009	973	970	962	1 031	11.5	11.1	11.0	10.8	11.4
Latvia - Lettonie											
Total.....................	C	21 006	20 334	21 497	22 264	23 273	9.0	8.8	9.3	9.7	10.2
Urban - Urbaine	C	13 891	13 820	14 591	15 342	16 123	8.8	8.8	9.3	9.9	10.4
Rural - Rurale	C	7 115	6 514	6 906	6 922	7 150	9.5	8.8	9.4	9.4	9.8
Liechtenstein											
Total.....................	C	347	372	381	361	*351	10.2	10.8	11.0	10.3	*9.9
Lithuania - Lituanie											
Total.....................	C	30 598	30 419	30 541	31 265	32 346	8.9	8.9	8.9	9.2	9.6
Urban - Urbaine	C	19 140	19 464	19 914	20 691	21 656	8.3	8.5	8.8	9.1	9.6
Rural - Rurale	C	11 458	10 955	10 627	10 574	10 690	10.0	9.6	9.3	9.4	9.5
Luxembourg											
Total.....................	C	5 303	5 452	5 371	5 514	5 477	11.7	11.9	11.5	11.7	11.4
Malta - Malte											
Total.....................	C	4 050	3 887	3 858	3 885	3 871	10.2	9.7	9.6	9.6	9.5
Monaco											
Total.....................	C	842	825	894	880[53]	...	...	...	...	...	...
Montenegro - Monténégro											
Total.....................	C	8 342	7 848	7 352	7 531	7 834	13.4	12.6	11.8	12.1	12.5
Urban - Urbaine	C	6 328	6 144	5 786	6 598	6 200	16.4	15.9	14.8	16.8	15.7
Rural - Rurale	C	2 014	1 704	1 555	933	1 634	8.6	7.3	6.7	4.0	7.1
Netherlands - Pays-Bas[54]											
Total.....................	C	200 297	194 007	187 910	185 057	181 336	12.3	11.9	11.5	11.3	11.1
Urban - Urbaine	C	132 805	130 945	128 609	126 775	125 067	12.6	12.3	11.9	11.7	11.6
Rural - Rurale	C	67 492	63 062	59 301	58 282	56 269	11.9	11.3	10.7	10.5	10.1
Norway - Norvège[55]											
Total.....................	C	56 458	56 951	56 756	58 545	58 459	12.4	12.4	12.3	12.6	12.4
Poland - Pologne											
Total.....................	C	351 072	356 131	364 383	374 244	387 873	9.2	9.3	9.5	9.8	10.2
Urban - Urbaine	C	199 583	204 898	211 200	218 000	225 638	8.5	8.7	9.0	9.3	9.7
Rural - Rurale	C	151 489	151 233	153 183	156 244	162 235	10.3	10.3	10.4	10.6	11.0
Portugal[11]											
Total.....................	C	112 515	109 298	109 399	105 449	102 492	10.8	10.4	10.4	10.0	9.7
Republic of Moldova - République de Moldova[56]											
Total.....................	C	36 471	38 272	37 695	37 587	37 973	10.1	10.6	10.5	10.5	10.6
Urban - Urbaine	C	12 788	14 060	13 583	13 579	13 679	8.6	9.5	9.2	9.2	9.3
Rural - Rurale	C	23 683	24 212	24 112	24 008	24 294	11.1	11.4	11.4	11.4	11.6
Romania - Roumanie											
Total.....................	C	212 459	216 261	221 020	219 483	214 728	9.8	10.0	10.2	10.2	10.0
Urban - Urbaine	C	100 915	111 348	117 780	119 477	116 367	8.7	9.4	9.9	10.0	9.8
Rural - Rurale	C	111 544	104 913	103 240	100 006	98 361	11.0	10.7	10.6	10.3	10.2

Continent, country or area, and urban/rural residence / Continent, pays ou zone et résidence, urbaine/rurale	Code[a]	Number - Nombre					Rate - Taux				
		2003	2004	2005	2006	2007	2003	2004	2005	2006	2007
EUROPE											
Russian Federation - Fédération de Russie[19]											
Total	C	1 477 301	1 502 477	1 457 376	1 479 637	1 610 122	10.2	10.4	10.2	10.4	11.3
Urban - Urbaine	C	1 050 565	1 074 247	1 036 870	1 044 540	1 120 741	9.9	10.2	9.9	10.0	11.3
Rural - Rurale	C	426 736	428 230	420 506	435 097	489 381	11.1	11.1	10.9	11.3	12.8
San Marino - Saint-Marin											
Total	+C	300	306	284	302	292	10.3	10.4	9.2	9.6	9.2
Serbia - Serbie[57]											
Total	+C	79 025	78 186	72 180	70 997	68 102	10.6	10.5	9.7	9.6	9.2
Urban - Urbaine	+C	47 968	47 998	46 754	46 401	44 776	11.3	11.3	11.0	10.9	10.5
Rural - Rurale	+C	31 057	30 188	25 426	24 596	23 326	9.6	9.4	8.0	7.8	7.5
Slovakia - Slovaquie											
Total	C	51 713	53 747	54 430	53 904	54 424	9.6	10.0	10.1	10.0	10.1
Urban - Urbaine	C	26 798	28 399	28 816	28 411	28 970	8.9	9.5	9.6	9.5	9.7
Rural - Rurale	C	24 915	25 348	25 614	25 493	25 454	10.5	10.6	10.7	10.6	10.6
Slovenia - Slovénie											
Total	C	17 321	17 961	18 157	18 932	19 823	8.7	9.0	9.1	9.4	9.8
Urban - Urbaine	C	8 425	8 745	8 869	9 190	9 629	8.7	9.0	9.2	9.5	9.6
Rural - Rurale	C	8 896	9 216	9 288	9 742	10 194	9.1	9.4	9.4	9.8	10.1
Spain - Espagne											
Total	C	441 881	454 591	466 371	481 102	493 702	10.5	10.6	10.7	10.9	11.0
Sweden - Suède											
Total	C	99 157	100 928	101 346	105 913	107 421	11.1	11.2	11.2	11.7	11.7
Switzerland - Suisse											
Total	C	71 848	73 082	72 903	73 371	74 494	9.8	9.9	9.8	9.8	9.9
Urban - Urbaine	C	52 789	53 844	54 021	54 465	55 235	9.8	9.9	9.9	9.9	10.0
Rural - Rurale	C	19 059	19 238	18 882	18 906	19 259	9.7	9.7	9.5	9.5	9.6
The Former Yugoslav Republic of Macedonia - L'ex-République yougoslave de Macédoine											
Total	C	27 011	23 361	22 482	22 585	22 688	13.3	11.5	11.0	11.1	11.1
Urban - Urbaine	C	...	...	12 519	12 653	12 761	...	...	...	...	...
Rural - Rurale	C	...	...	9 963	9 932	9 927	...	...	...	...	...
Ukraine											
Total	C	408 589[19]	427 259[19]	426 086[19]	460 368[58]	472 657[58]	8.5	9.0	9.1	9.8	10.1
Urban - Urbaine	C	266 415[19]	284 361[19]	284 257[19]	306 635[58]	314 065[58]	8.3	...	...	...	9.9
Rural - Rurale	C	142 174[19]	142 898[19]	141 829[19]	153 733[58]	158 592[58]	9.1	...	...	...	10.7
United Kingdom of Great Britain and Northern Ireland - Royaume-Uni de Grande-Bretagne et d'Irlande du Nord[59]											
Total	C	695 549[60]	715 996	722 549	748 563	772 245	11.7	12.0	12.0	12.4	12.7
OCEANIA - OCÉANIE											
American Samoa - Samoas américaines											
Total	C	1 608	1 713	1 720	1 442	...	25.7	26.7	26.3	21.6	...
Australia - Australie[61]											
Total	+C	250 518	253 652	259 177	265 423	284 466	12.6	12.6	12.7	12.8	13.5
Urban - Urbaine	+C	206 563	209 419	214 793	220 349	236 494	12.8	12.8	12.9	13.0	13.7
Rural - Rurale	+C	43 955	44 233	44 384	45 074	47 972	11.8	11.9	11.8	11.8	12.5
Cook Islands - Îles Cook[62]											
Total	+C	298	295	280	*278	*287	16.2	14.5	13.9	*13.4	*13.6
Fiji - Fidji											
Total	+C	17 701	17 189	17 826	18 394	19 298	21.7	20.9	21.6	22.2	23.1
Urban - Urbaine	+C	8 332	8 508	...	...	...	...	...	...	...	...
Rural - Rurale	+C	9 369	8 681	...	...	...	...	...	...	...	...
French Polynesia - Polynésie française											
Total	C	4 501	4 431	4 467	4 592	4 434	18.2	17.7	17.7	17.9	17.1
Guam[63]											
Total	C	3 298	3 427	*3 203	*3 414	*3 501	19.8	20.6	*19.0	*20.0	*20.2

9. Live births and crude live birth rates, by urban/rural residence: 2003 - 2007
Naissances vivantes et taux bruts de natalité selon la résidence, urbaine/rurale: 2003 - 2007 (continued - suite)

Continent, country or area, and urban/rural residence — Continent, pays ou zone et résidence, urbaine/rurale	Code[a]	Number - Nombre					Rate - Taux				
		2003	2004	2005	2006	2007	2003	2004	2005	2006	2007
OCEANIA - OCÉANIE											
Marshall Islands - Îles Marshall[64]											
Total	+U	*1 565*	*1 512*	*1 589*	*1 576*	...	...	...	...	...	...
Micronesia (Federated States of) - Micronésie (États fédérés de)											
Total	U	*2 483*	...	...	...	...	...	...	...	...	...
New Caledonia - Nouvelle-Calédonie											
Total	C	4 102	4 006	4 035	4 224	4 093	18.2	17.4	17.2	17.7	16.9
Urban - Urbaine	C	...	...	...	...	2 678	...	...	...	...	...
Rural - Rurale	C	...	...	...	...	1 415	...	...	...	...	...
New Zealand - Nouvelle-Zélande											
Total	+C	56 134	58 073	57 745	59 193	64 044	13.9	14.2	14.0	14.1	15.1
Urban - Urbaine[9]	+C	49 166	50 933	50 300	51 540	55 822	14.2	14.5	14.1	14.3	15.3
Rural - Rurale[9]	+C	6 878	7 060	7 391	7 518	8 065	12.2	12.4	12.9	13.0	13.8
Niue - Nioué[65]											
Total	C	33	18	23	35	28	19.2	...	...	20.8	...
Northern Mariana Islands - Îles Mariannes septentrionales											
Total	U	*1 355*	*1 350*	*1 335*	*1 422*	*1 385*	...	...	...	...	...
Palau - Palaos											
Total	C	312	259	279	259	...	15.4	12.6	14.0	12.0	...
Papua New Guinea - Papouasie-Nouvelle-Guinée											
Total	U	*192 817*	...	...	...	...	...	...	...	...	...
Pitcairn											
Total	C	...	...	...	...	1	...	...	...	...	...
Samoa											
Total	C	*2 070	*1 679	...	...	...	*11.5	*9.2	...	...	...
Tonga											
Total	+C	2 781	*2 628	...	2 945	...	27.4	*25.8	...	28.6	...
Tuvalu											
Total	U	*185*	*190*	*231*	*184*	...	...	...	...	...	...
Wallis and Futuna Islands - Îles Wallis et Futuna											
Total	C	290	241	223	220	...	19.4	...	...	...	...

FOOTNOTES - NOTES

Italics: data from civil registers which are incomplete or of unknown completeness. - Italiques: données incomplètes ou dont le degré d'exactitude n'est pas connu, provenant des registres de l'état civil.

* Provisional. - Données provisoires.

[a] 'Code' indicates the source of data, as follows:
C - Civil registration, estimated over 90% complete
U - Civil registration, estimated less than 90% complete
| - Other source, estimated reliable
+ - Data tabulated by date of registration rather than occurence.
... - Information not available

Le 'Code' indique la source des données, comme suit:
C - Registres de l'état civil considérés complets à 90 p. 100 au moins.
U - Registres de l'état civil qui ne sont pas considérés complets à 90 p. 100 au moins.
| - Autre source, considérée pas douteuses.
+ - Données exploitées selon la date de l'enregistrement et non la date de l'événement.
... - Information pas disponible.

[1] Excluding live-born infants who died before their birth was registered. Data refer to Algerian population only. - Non compris les enfants nés vivants décédés avant l'enregistrement de leur naissance. Les données ne concernent que la population algérienne.
[2] Data refer to the twelve months preceding the census in December. Data refer to mothers aged 15-49. - Les données se rapportent aux douze mois précédant le recensement de décembre. Les données se réfèrent aux mères âgées de 15 à 49 ans.
[3] Data from civil registration centers of Brazzaville, Pointe-Noire, Dolisie, Nkayi, Mossendijo and Ouesso communes. - Données issues des centres d'enregistrement des faits d'état-civil des communes de Brazzaville, Pointe-Noire, Dolisie, Nkayi, Mossendijo et Ouesso.
[4] Data refer to national projections. - Les données se réfèrent aux projections nationales.
[5] Excluding live-born infants who died before their birth was registered. - Non compris les enfants nés vivants décédés avant l'enregistrement de leur naissance.
[6] Excluding non-residents and foreign service personnel and their dependants. - À l'exclusion des non-résidents et du personnel diplomatique et de leurs charges de famille.
[7] Including Canadian residents temporarily in the United States, but excluding United States residents temporarily in Canada. - Y compris les résidents canadiens se trouvant temporairement aux Etats-Unis, mais ne comprenant pas les résidents des Etats-Unis se trouvant temporairement au Canada.
[8] Resident births outside the islands are excluded. - Non compris les naissances de résidents hors des îles.

[9] The total number includes 'Unknown residence', but the categories urban and rural do not. - Le nombre total inclue 'Résidence inconnue ', mais les catégories Urbain et Rural ne l'incluent pas.

[10] Data have been adjusted for underenumeration. - Les données ont été ajustées pour compenser les lacunes du dénombrement.

[11] Data refer to resident mothers. - Données concernant les mères résidentes.

[12] Data refer to resident population only. - Pour la population résidante seulement.

[13] Excluding Indian jungle population. - Non compris les Indiens de la jungle.

[14] Excluding nomadic Indian tribes. - Non compris les tribus d'Indiens nomades.

[15] Excluding events registered late. - Non compris les enregistrements tardifs.

[16] Data refer to registered events only. - Les données ne concernent que les événements enregistrés.

[17] Including births to non-resident mothers. - Y compris les naissances chez des mères non résidentes.

[18] The districts of Paramaribo and Wanica are considered urban areas, whereas the rest of the districts are considered more or less rural districts (areas). - Les districts de Paramaribo et de Wanica sont considérés comme des zones urbaines, les autres districts étant considérés comme des zones rurales à divers degrés.

[19] Excluding infants born alive of less than 28 weeks' gestation, of less than 1 000 grams in weight and 35 centimeters in length, who die within seven days of birth. - Non compris les enfants nés vivants après moins de 28 semaines de gestations, pesant moins de 1 000 grammes, mesurant moins de 35 centimètres et décédés dans les sept jours qui ont suivi leur naissance.

[20] Since 16 October 2005 the definition of WHO on livebirths has been put into force in accordance with the 10th revision of the International Classification of Diseases. - Depuis le 16 octobre 2005, la définition de l'OMS concernant les naissances vivantes est en vigueur conformément à la dixième révision de la Classification internationale des maladies.

[21] Rates were obtained by the Sample Vital Registration System of Bangladesh. - Taux obtenus au moyen du Sample Vital Registration System du Bangladesh.

[22] Data refer to the twelve months preceding the census in May. - Les données se rapportent aux douze mois précédant le recensement de mai.

[23] For statistical purposes, the data for China do not include those for the Hong Kong Special Administrative Region (Hong Kong SAR), Macao Special Administrative Region (Macao SAR) and Taiwan province of China. - Pour la présentation des statistiques, les données pour la Chine ne comprennent pas la Région Administrative Spéciale de Hong Kong (Hong Kong RAS), la Région Administrative Spéciale de Macao (Macao RAS) et Taïwan province de Chine.

[24] Data have been estimated on the basis of the annual National Sample Surveys on Population Changes. - Les données ont été estimées sur la base de l'enquête annuelle "National Sample Survey on Population Changes".

[25] Data for 2005 are estimated from the National Sample Survey of 1 per cent population. - Les données pour 2005 ont été estimées à partir de l'enquête nationale qui a porté sur un échantillon de 1 % de la population.

[26] Data refer to government controlled areas. - Les données se rapportent aux zones contrôlées par le Gouvernement.

[27] Including data for the Indian-held part of Jammu and Kashmir, the final status of which has not yet been determined. Rates were obtained by the Sample Registration System of India, actually a large demographic survey. - Y compris les données pour la partie du Jammu et du Cachemire occupée par l'Inde dont le statut définitif n'a pas encore été déterminé. Les taux ont été obtenus par le Système de l'enregistrement par échantillon de l'Inde qui est une large enquête démographique.

[28] Data refer to the Iranian Year which begins on 21 March and ends on 20 March of the following year. - Les données concernent l'année iranienne, qui commence le 21 mars et se termine le 20 mars de l'année suivante.

[29] Including data for East Jerusalem and Israeli residents in certain other territories under occupation by Israeli military forces since June 1967. - Y compris les données pour Jérusalem-Est et les résidents israéliens dans certains autres territoires occupés depuis 1967 par les forces armées israéliennes.

[30] Data refer to Japanese nationals in Japan only. - Les données se raportent aux nationaux japonais au Japon seulement.

[31] The total number includes 'Unknown residence', but the categories urban and rural do not. Urban and rural distribution refers to the residence of the child. - Le nombre total inclue 'Résidence inconnue ', mais les catégories Urbain et Rural ne l'incluent pas. La répartition urbain/rural se réfère au domicile de l'enfant.

[32] Excluding data for Jordanian territory under occupation since June 1967 by Israeli military forces. Excluding foreigners, including registered Palestinian refugees. - Non compris les données pour le territoire jordanien occupé depuis juin 1967 par les forces armées israéliennes. Non compris les étrangers, mais y compris les réfugiés de Palestine enregistrés.

[33] Since 2004, WHO criteria have been adopted in the country. - Depuis 2004, le pays a adopté les critères de l'OMS.

[34] Data refer to the recorded events in Ministry of Health hospitals and health centres only. - Les données se rapportent aux faits d'état civil enregistrés dans les hôpitaux et les dispensaires du Ministère de la santé seulement.

[35] Data from Births and Deaths Notification System (Ministry of Health institutions and all other health care providers). - Les données proviennent du système de notification des naissances et des décès (établissements du Ministère de la santé et tous autres prestataires de soins de santé).

[36] Excluding data for the Pakistan-held part of Jammu and Kashmir, the final status of which has not yet been determined. - Non compris les données concernant la partie du Jammu et Cachemire occupée par le Pakistan dont le statut définitif n'a pas été déterminé.

[37] Based on the results of the Pakistan Demographic Survey (PDS 2003) . - Données extraites de l'enquête démographique effectuée par le Pakistan en 2003.

[38] Based on the results of the Pakistan Demographic Survey (PDS 2005). - Données extraites de l'enquête démographique effectuée par le Pakistan en 2005.

[39] Excluding alien armed forces, civilian aliens employed by armed forces, and foreign diplomatic personnel and their dependants. - Non compris les militaires étrangers, les civils étrangers employés par les forces armées ni le personnel diplomatique étranger et les membres de leur famille les accompagnant.

[40] Including nationals outside the country. - Y compris les nationaux hors du pays.

[41] Excluding nomad population and Palestinian refugees. Excluding live-born infants who died before their birth was registered. - Non compris la population nomade et les réfugiés de Palestine. Non compris les enfants nés vivants décédés avant l'enregistrement de leur naissance.

[42] Excluding infants born alive of less than 28 weeks' gestation, of less than 1 000 grams in weight and 35 centimeters in length, who die within seven days of birth. Data have been adjusted for under-registration. - Non compris les enfants nés vivants après moins de 28 semaines de gestations, pesant moins de 1 000 grammes, mesurant moins de 35 centimètres et décédés dans les sept jours qui ont suivi leur naissance. Y compris un ajustement pour sous-enregistrement.

[43] Data are estimates based on Address Based Population Registration System and other survey. - Les données sont des estimations basées sur le registre national de la population basé sur l'adresse et d'autres enquêtes.

[44] Also included in Finland. - Comprise aussi dans Finlande.

[45] Including armed forces stationed outside the country, but excluding alien armed forces stationed in the area. - Y compris les militaires nationaux hors du pays, mais non compris les militaires étrangers en garnison sur le territoire.

[46] Excluding Faeroe Islands and Greenland shown separately, if available. - Non compris les Iles Féroé et le Gröenland, qui font l'objet de rubriques distinctes, si disponible.

[47] Including nationals temporarily outside the country. Including Aland Islands. - Y compris les nationaux se trouvant temporairement hors du pays. Y compris les Îles d'Åland.

[48] Including armed forces stationed outside the country. Excluding Overseas Departments, namely, French Guiana, Guadeloupe, Martinique and Reunion, shown separately, if available. - Y compris les militaires nationaux hors du pays. Non compris les départements d'outre mer, c'est-à-dire la Guyane française, la Guadeloupe, la Martinique et la Réunion, qui font l'objet de rubriques distinctes, si disponible.

[49] Data for urban and rural, excluding nationals outside the country. - Les données pour la résidence urbaine et rurale , non compris les nationaux hors du pays.

[50] Excluding armed forces. - Non compris les militaires en garnison.

[51] Total includes the data of foreigners, persons of unknown residence and homeless, but the categories urban and rural do not. - Total incluant les étrangers, les personnes de résidence inconnue et les sans-abri, ce qui n'est pas le cas pour les catégories urbaines et rurales.

[52] Data refer to events registered within one year of occurrence. - Evénements enregistrés dans l'année qui suit l'événement.

[53] Including residents outside the country. - Y compris les résidents hors du pays.

[54] Including residents outside the country if listed in a Netherlands population register. - Y compris les résidents hors du pays, s'ils sont inscrits sur un registre de population néerlandais.

[55] Excluding Svalbard and Jan Mayen Island shown separately, if available. - Non compris Svalbard et Jan Mayen qui font l'objet de rubriques distinctes, si disponible.

[56] Excluding Transnistria and the municipality of Bender. Excluding infants born alive of less than 28 weeks' gestation, of less than 1 000 grams in weight and 35 centimeters in length, who die within seven days of birth. - Les données ne tiennent pas compte de l'information sur la Transnistria et la municipalité de Bender. Non compris les enfants nés vivants après moins de 28 semaines de gestations, pesant moins de 1 000 grammes, mesurant moins de 35 centimètres et décédés dans les sept jours qui ont suivi leur naissance.

[57] Excluding data for Kosovo and Metohia. - Sans les données pour le Kosovo et Metohie.

[58] Data refer to births with weight 500g and more (if weight is unknown - with length 25 centimeters and more, or with gestation during 22 weeks or more). - Données concernant les nouveau-nés de 500 grammes ou plus (si le poids est inconnu – de 25 centimètres de long ou plus, ou après une grossesse de 22 semaines ou plus).

[59] Data tabulated by date of occurrence for England and Wales, and by date of registration for Northern Ireland and Scotland. Excluding Channel Islands (Guernsey and Jersey) and Isle of Man, shown separately, if available. - Données exploitées selon la date de l'événement pour l'Angleterre et le pays de Galles, et selon la date de l'enregistrement pour l'Irlande du Nord et l'Ecosse. Non compris les îles Anglo-Normandes (Guernesey et Jersey) et l'île de Man, qui font l'objet de rubriques distinctes, si disponible.

[60] Excluding births to non-resident mothers of Northern Ireland. - Les données ne tiennent pas compte des enfants nés de mères non résidentes en Irlande du Nord.

[61] Excluding data where usual residence was undefined, offshore or migratory and unknown. - En excluant les données lorsque le lieu du domicile n'est pas précisé, est à l'étranger, est mouvant ou inconnu.

[62] Excluding Niue, shown separately, which is part of Cook Islands, but because of remoteness is administered separately. - Non compris Nioué, qui fait l'objet d'une rubrique distincte et qui fait partie des îles Cook, mais qui, en raison de son éloignement, est administrée séparément.

[63] Including United States military personnel, their dependants and contract employees. - Y compris les militaires des Etats-Unis, les membres de leur famille les accompagnant et les agents contractuels des Etats-Unis.

[64] Excluding United States military personnel, their dependants and contract employees. - Non compris les militaires des Etats-Unis, les membres de leur famille les accompagnant et les agents contractuels des Etats-Unis.

[65] Includes children born in New Zealand to women resident in Niue who chose to travel to New Zealand to give birth. - Y compris les enfants nés en Nouvelle-Zélande de femmes résidant à Nioué qui ont choisi de se rendre en Nouvelle-Zélande pour accoucher.

Table 10

Table 10 presents live births by age of mother and sex of the child and live-birth rates by age of mother for the latest available year between 1998 and 2007.

Description of variables: Age is defined as age at last birthday, that is, the difference between the date of birth and the date of the occurrence of the event, expressed in completed solar years. The age classification used in this table is the following: under 15 years, 5-year age groups through 45-49 years, and 50 years and over. Deviating age groups are shown if so provided by a country or area.

Rate computation: Live-birth rates specific to age of mother are the annual number of births to women in each age group per 1 000 female population in the same age group. These rates are calculated by the Statistics Division of the United Nations.

Since relatively few births occur to women below 15 or above 50 years of age, birth rates for women under 20 years of age and for those 45 years of age or over are computed on the female population aged 15-19 and 45-49, respectively. Similarly, the rate for women of "All ages" is based on all live births irrespective of age of mother, and is computed on the female population aged 15-49 years. This rate for "All ages" is known as the general fertility rate.

Births to mothers of unknown age are distributed proportionally across the age groups, by the Statistics Division of the United Nations, in accordance with the distribution of births by age of mother prior to the calculation of the rates.

The population used in computing the rates is the estimated or enumerated distribution of females by age. First priority was given to an estimate and second priority to census returns of the year to which the births referred.

Rates presented in this table are limited to those for countries or areas having at least a total of 100 live births in a given year.

Reliability of data: Data from civil registers of live births which are reported as incomplete (less than 90 per cent completeness) or of unknown completeness are considered unreliable and are set in *italics* rather than in roman type. Rates are not computed if the data on live births from civil registers are reported as incomplete (less than 90 per cent completeness) or of unknown completeness. Table 9 and the technical notes for that table provide more detailed information on the completeness of live-birth registration. For more information about the quality of vital statistics data in general, see section 4.2 of the Technical Notes.

Limitations: Statistics on live births by age of mother are subject to the same qualifications as have been set forth for vital statistics in general and birth statistics in particular as discussed in section 4 of the Technical Notes. These include differences in the completeness of registration, the method used to determine age of mother and the quality of the reported information relating to age of mother.

The reliability of the data described above, is an important factor in considering the limitations. In addition, some live births are tabulated by date of registration and not by date of occurrence; these are indicated in the table by a plus sign "+". Whenever the lag between the date of occurrence and date of registration is prolonged and, therefore, a large proportion of the live-birth registrations are delayed, birth statistics for any given year may be seriously affected. For example, the age of the mother will almost always refer to the date of registration rather than to the date of birth of the child. Hence, in those countries or areas where registration of births is delayed, possibly for years, statistics on births by age of mother should be used with caution.

Another factor which limits international comparability is the practice of some countries or areas of not including in live-birth statistics infants who were born alive but died before the registration of the birth or within the first 24 hours of life, thus underestimating the total number of live births. Statistics of this type are footnoted.

Because these statistics are classified according to age, they are subject to the limitations with respect to accuracy of age reporting similar to those already discussed in connection with section 3.1.3 of the Technical Notes. The factors influencing the accuracy of reporting may be somewhat dissimilar in vital statistics (because of the differences in the method of taking a census and registering a birth) but, in general, the same errors can be observed. The absence of frequencies in the unknown age group does not necessarily indicate completely accurate reporting and tabulation of the age item. It is often an indication that the unknowns have been eliminated by assigning ages to them before tabulation, or by proportionate distribution after tabulation.

On the other hand, large frequencies in the unknown age category may indicate that a large proportion of the births are born outside of wedlock, the records for which tend to be incomplete so far as characteristics of the parents are concerned.

Another limitation of age reporting may result from calculating age of mother at birth of child (or at time of registration) from year of birth rather than from day, month and year of birth. Information on this factor is given in footnotes when known.

In few countries, data by age refer to deliveries rather than to live births causing under-enumeration in the event of a multiple birth. This practice leads to lack of strict comparability, both among countries or areas relying on this practice and between data shown in this table and table 9.

Rates shown in this table are subject to the same limitations that affect the corresponding statistics on live births. In cases of rates based on births tabulated by date of registration and not by date of occurrence; the effect of including delayed registration on the distribution of births by age of mother may be noted in the age-specific fertility rates for women at older ages. In some cases, high age-specific rates for women aged 45 years and over may reflect age of mother at registration of birth and not fertility at these older ages.

Earlier data: Live births and live-birth rates by age of mother have been shown for the latest available year in each issue of the Yearbook. Data included in this table update the series covering period of years as follows:

Issue	Years Covered
Special Edition on Natality, CD, 1999	1990 – 1998
Historical Supplement, CD, 1997	1948 – 1997
44th issue, 1992	1983 – 1992
38th issue, 1986	1977 – 1988
33rd issue, 1981	1972 – 1980
Historical Supplement, 1979	1948 – 1977

For further information on years covered prior to 1948, readers should consult the Historical Index.

Tableau 10

Le tableau 10 présente les données les plus récentes pour la période 1998 -2007 dont on dispose sur les naissances vivantes selon l'âge de la mère et le sexe de l'enfant et les taux des naissances vivantes selon l'âge de la mère.

Description des variables : l'âge désigne l'âge au dernier anniversaire, c'est-à-dire la différence entre la date de naissance et la date de l'événement exprimée en années solaires révolues. La classification par âge utilisée dans ce tableau comprend les catégories suivantes : moins de 15 ans, groupes quinquennaux jusqu'à 45-49 ans, 50 ans et plus, et âge inconnu. Des groupes d'âge différents sont parfois utilisés lorsque les pays ou territoires ont fourni les données dans une autre classification.

Les taux de natalité selon l'âge de la mère représentent le nombre annuel de naissances vivantes intervenues dans un groupe d'âge donné pour 1 000 femmes du groupe d'âge. Ces taux ont été calculés par la Division de statistique de l'ONU.

Étant donné que le nombre de naissances parmi les femmes de moins de 15 ans ou de plus de 50 ans est relativement peu élevé, les taux de natalité parmi les femmes âgées de moins de 20 ans et celles de 45 ans et plus ont été calculés sur la base des populations féminines âgées de 15 à 19 ans et de 45 à 49 ans, respectivement. De même, le taux pour les femmes de « tous âges » est fondé sur la totalité des naissances vivantes, indépendamment de l'âge de la mère et ce chiffre est rapporté à l'effectif de la population féminine âgée de 15 à 49 ans. Ce taux « tous âges » est le taux global de fécondité.

Les naissances pour lesquelles l'âge de la mère était inconnu ont été réparties par la Division de statistique de l'ONU, avant le calcul des taux, suivant les proportions observées pour celles où l'âge de la mère était connu.

Les chiffres de population utilisés pour le calcul des taux proviennent de dénombrements ou de répartitions estimatives de la population féminine selon l'âge. On a utilisé de préférence les estimations de la population; à défaut, on s'est contenté des données censitaires se rapportant à l'année des naissances.

Les taux présentés dans ce tableau ne concernent que les pays ou zones où l'on a enregistré un total d'au moins 100 naissances vivantes dans une année donnée.

Fiabilité des données : les données sur les naissances vivantes provenant des registres de l'état civil qui sont déclarées incomplètes (degré de complétude inférieur à 90 p. 100) ou dont le degré de complétude n'est pas connu sont jugées douteuses et apparaissent en italique et non en caractères romains. On a choisi de ne pas faire figurer les taux calculés à partir de données sur les naissances vivantes issues de registres de l'état civil qui sont déclarées incomplètes (degré de complétude inférieur à 90 p. 100) ou dont le degré de complétude n'est pas connu. Le tableau 9 et les notes techniques qui s'y rapportent présentent des renseignements plus détaillés sur le degré de complétude de l'enregistrement des naissances vivantes. Pour plus de précisions sur la qualité des statistiques de l'état civil en général, voir la section 4.2 des Notes techniques.

Insuffisance des données : les statistiques relatives aux naissances vivantes selon l'âge de la mère appellent toutes les réserves qui ont été formulées à propos des statistiques de l'état civil en général et des statistiques de naissances en particulier (voir la section 4 des Notes techniques). Ceci inclut les différences de complétude d'enregistrement des faits d'état civil, de méthode pour déterminer l'âge de la mère et de qualité d'information concernant l'âge de la mère.

La fiabilité des données, au sujet de laquelle des indications ont été données plus haut, est un facteur important. Il faut également tenir compte du fait que, dans certains cas, les données relatives aux naissances vivantes sont exploitées selon la date de l'enregistrement et non la date de l'événement ; ces cas ont été signalés dans le tableau par le signe '+'. Chaque fois que le décalage entre l'événement et son enregistrement est grand et qu'une forte proportion des naissances vivantes fait l'objet d'un enregistrement tardif, les statistiques des naissances vivantes pour une année donnée peuvent être considérablement faussées. Par exemple, l'âge de la mère représente presque toujours son âge à la date de l'enregistrement et non à la date de la naissance de l'enfant. Ainsi, dans les pays ou zones où l'enregistrement des naissances est tardif, le retard atteignant parfois plusieurs années, il faut utiliser avec prudence les statistiques concernant les naissances selon l'âge de la mère.

Un autre facteur qui nuit à la comparabilité internationale est la pratique de certains pays ou zones qui consiste à ne pas inclure dans les statistiques des naissances vivantes les enfants nés vivants mais décédés avant l'enregistrement de leur naissance ou dans les 24 heures qui ont suivi la naissance, pratique qui conduit à sous-estimer le nombre total de naissances vivantes. Quand pareil facteur a joué, cela a été signalé en note à la fin du tableau.

Étant donné que les statistiques du tableau 10 sont classées selon l'âge, elles appellent les mêmes réserves concernant l'exactitude des déclarations d'âge que celles formulées à la section 3.1.3 des Notes techniques. Dans le cas des statistiques de l'état civil, les facteurs qui interviennent à cet égard sont parfois différents, étant donné que le recensement de la population et l'enregistrement des naissances se font par des méthodes différentes, mais, d'une manière générale, les erreurs observées seront les mêmes. Si aucun nombre ne figure dans la rangée réservée aux âges inconnus, cela ne signifie pas nécessairement que les déclarations d'âge et l'exploitation des données par âge ont été tout à fait exactes. C'est souvent une indication que l'on a attribué un âge aux personnes d'âge inconnu avant l'exploitation des données ou qu'elles ont été réparties proportionnellement entre les différents groupes après cette opération.

À l'inverse, lorsque le nombre des personnes d'âge inconnu est important, cela peut signifier que la proportion de naissances parmi les mères célibataires est élevée, étant donné qu'en pareil cas l'acte de naissance ne contient pas tous les renseignements concernant les parents.

Les déclarations par âge peuvent comporter des distorsions, du fait que l'âge de la mère au moment de la naissance d'un enfant (ou de la déclaration de naissance) est donné par année de naissance et non par date exacte (jour, mois et année).

Dans quelques pays, la classification par âges se réfère aux accouchements, et non aux naissances vivantes, ce qui conduit à un sous-dénombrement en cas de naissances gémellaires. Cette pratique nuit à la comparabilité des données, à la fois entre pays ou zones qui recourent à cette méthode et entre les données présentées dans le tableau 10 et celles du tableau 9.

Les taux présentés dans ce tableau sont sujets aux mêmes limitations qui affectent les statistiques correspondantes de naissances vivantes. Dans le cas des taux basés sur des naissances par date d'enregistrement et non par date d'occurrence, l'effet peut être visible sur les taux de fécondité par âge des femmes aux âges plus élevés. Dans certains cas, les taux de fécondité des femmes de plus de 45 ans peuvent refléter l'âge de la mère à l'enregistrement plus que la fécondité à ces âges.

Données publiées antérieurement : les différentes éditions de l'*Annuaire démographique* regroupent les dernières statistiques dont on disposait à l'époque sur les naissances vivantes selon l'âge de la mère et les taux des naissances vivantes selon l'âge de la mère. Les données qui figurent dans ce tableau actualisent les données qui portaient sur les périodes suivantes :

Éditions	Années considérées
Édition spéciale sur les statistiques de la natalité (CD-ROM), 1999	1990 – 1998
Supplément historique (CD-ROM), 1997	1948 – 1997
44e édition, 1992	1983 – 1992
38e édition, 1986	1977 – 1988
33e édition, 1981	1972 – 1980
Supplément rétrospectif, 1979	1948 – 1977

Pour plus de détails concernant les années antérieures à 1948, se reporter à l'index historique.

10. Live-births by age of mother and sex of child and live-birth rates by age of mother: latest available year, 1998 - 2007
Naissances vivantes selon l'âge de la mère et le sexe de l'enfant et taux de natalité selon l'âge de la mère : dernière année disponible, 1998 - 2007

Continent, country or area, year, code and age of mother (in years) / Continent, pays ou zone, année, code et âge de la mère (en années)	Number - Nombre			Rate Taux
	Total	Male Masculin	Female Féminin	
AFRICA - AFRIQUE				
Egypt - Égypte				
2006 (C)				
Total	1 853 746	951 085	902 661	...
0 - 14	-	-	-	...
15 - 19	77 837	36 171	41 666	...
20 - 24	433 135	223 554	209 581	...
25 - 29	483 538	248 979	234 559	...
30 - 34	250 837	127 874	122 963	...
35 - 39	121 711	62 184	59 527	...
40 - 44	34 751	17 797	16 954	...
45 +	6 972	3 472	3 500	...
Unknown - Inconnu	444 965	231 054	213 911	..
Kenya				
2000 (U)				
Total	470 712	...	...	...
0 - 14	1 033	...	...	...
15 - 19	72 510	...	...	...
20 - 24	151 037	...	...	...
25 - 29	117 804	...	...	...
30 - 34	76 286	...	...	...
35 - 39	33 301	...	...	...
40 - 44	9 096	...	...	...
45 - 49	1 571	...	...	...
50 +	218	...	...	..
Unknown - Inconnu	7 856	...	...	..
Libyan Arab Jamahiriya - Jamahiriya arabe libyenne				
2002 (C)				
Total	111 053	57 722	53 331	...
0 - 19	1 196	592	604	...
20 - 24	15 018	7 845	7 173	...
25 - 29	32 713	16 877	15 836	...
30 - 34	33 325	17 384	15 941	...
35 - 39	18 702	9 777	8 925	...
40 - 44	6 422	3 296	3 126	...
45 +	676	364	312	...
Unknown - Inconnu	3 001	1 587	1 414	..
Mauritius - Maurice				
2007 (C)				
Total	16 894	8 618	8 276	48.6
0 - 14	43	26	17	..
15 - 19	1 749	895	854	34.5
20 - 24	4 289	2 223	2 066	94.3
25 - 29	5 658	2 886	2 772	101.7
30 - 34	3 086	1 544	1 542	64.0
35 - 39	1 323	658	665	28.7
40 - 44	396	197	199	7.9
45 - 49	20	11	9	♦0.4
50 +	-	-	-	..
Unknown - Inconnu	330	178	152	..
Morocco - Maroc				
2001 (C)				
Total	541 298	277 242	264 056	66.7
0 - 14	1 016	525	491	..
15 - 19	45 049	23 151	21 898	28.3
20 - 24	131 163	67 353	63 810	88.3
25 - 29	136 599	69 989	66 610	102.3
30 - 34	117 851	60 300	57 551	104.4
35 - 39	75 484	38 586	36 898	73.6
40 - 44	27 453	13 958	13 495	32.1
45 - 49	3 974	1 998	1 976	5.9
50 +	1 105	556	549	..
Unknown - Inconnu	1 604	826	778	..

Continent, country or area, year, code and age of mother (in years) / Continent, pays ou zone, année, code et âge de la mère (en années)	Number - Nombre			Rate Taux
	Total	Male Masculin	Female Féminin	
AFRICA - AFRIQUE				
Namibia - Namibie[1]				
2001 (I)				
Total	45 157	22 643	22 514	100.1
12 - 14	74	37	37	..
15 - 19	5 278	2 638	2 640	51.2
20 - 24	11 964	5 997	5 967	135.8
25 - 29	11 056	5 563	5 493	144.6
30 - 34	8 429	4 259	4 170	137.3
35 - 39	5 292	2 636	2 656	103.1
40 - 44	2 383	1 187	1 196	59.8
45 +	681	326	355	22.1
Réunion				
2007 (C)				
Total	14 808	7 711	7 097	69.2
0 - 14	23	11	12	..
15 - 19	1 517	769	748	44.1
20 - 24	3 348	1 752	1 596	117.2
25 - 29	3 968	2 075	1 893	144.2
30 - 34	3 429	1 779	1 650	116.2
35 - 39	1 931	1 009	922	58.6
40 - 44	572	307	265	16.8
45 +	20	9	11	♦0.7
Saint Helena ex. dep. - Sainte-Hélène sans dép.				
2000 (C)				
Total	56	32	24	...
15 - 19	7	3	4	...
20 - 24	16	10	6	...
25 - 29	12	5	7	...
30 - 34	13	9	4	...
35 - 39	7	4	3	...
40 - 44	1	1	-	...
Seychelles				
2006 (+C)				
Total	1 467	757	710	62.3
0 - 14	4	-	4	...
15 - 19	196	107	89	54.9
20 - 24	364	193	171	103.1
25 - 29	422	199	223	129.7
30 - 34	301	166	135	79.6
35 - 39	149	77	72	44.9
40 - 44	30	15	15	♦9.3
45 +	1	-	1	♦0.3
2007 (+C)				
Total	1 499	...	...	...
0 - 14	8	...	...	...
15 - 19	208	...	...	..
20 - 24	362	...	...	...
25 - 29	400	...	...	...
30 - 34	296	...	...	...
35 - 39	167	...	...	...
40 - 44	53	...	...	...
45 +	5	...	...	...
South Africa - Afrique du Sud[2]				
2007 (U)				
Total	858 866	432 282	426 584	...
0 - 14	804	381	423	..
15 - 19	93 451	47 102	46 349	...
20 - 24	246 545	124 213	122 332	...
25 - 29	222 601	112 241	110 360	...
30 - 34	165 240	83 254	81 986	...
35 - 39	95 875	47 952	47 923	...
40 - 44	29 099	14 544	14 555	...
45 - 49	4 196	2 093	2 103	...

10. Live-births by age of mother and sex of child and live-birth rates by age of mother: latest available year, 1998 - 2007
Naissances vivantes selon l'âge de la mère et le sexe de l'enfant et taux de natalité selon l'âge de la mère : dernière année disponible, 1998 - 2007 (continued - suite)

Continent, country or area, year, code and age of mother (in years) / Continent, pays ou zone, année, code et âge de la mère (en années)	Number - Nombre			Rate Taux
	Total	Male Masculin	Female Féminin	
AFRICA - AFRIQUE				
South Africa - Afrique du Sud[2]				
2007 (U)				
50 + ...	659	310	349	..
Unknown - Inconnu	396	192	204	..
Tunisia - Tunisie				
2007 (C)				
Total....................	177 503	...	...	60.1
0 - 14....................	-	...	...	..
15 - 19	2 555	...	...	6.0
20 - 24	23 334	...	...	52.6
25 - 29	47 786	...	...	117.4
30 - 34	44 906	...	...	126.2
35 - 39	24 726	...	...	79.8
40 - 44	6 964	...	...	22.8
45 + ...	510	...	...	2.0
Unknown - Inconnu	26 721	...	...	..
AMERICA, NORTH - AMÉRIQUE DU NORD				
Anguilla				
2006 (+C)				
Total....................	183	...	...	...
0 - 14....................	2	...	...	...
15 - 19	26	...	...	...
20 - 24	56	...	...	...
25 - 29	42	...	...	...
30 - 34	26	...	...	...
35 - 39	27	...	...	...
40 + ...	4	...	...	...
Unknown - Inconnu	-	...	...	...
Aruba				
2007 (C)				
Total....................	1 239	642	597	43.2
0 - 14....................	3	2	1	..
15 - 19	149	78	71	41.0
20 - 24	305	157	148	101.2
25 - 29	314	149	165	94.7
30 - 34	280	159	121	71.7
35 - 39	149	79	70	31.6
40 - 44	36	17	19	7.1
45 + ...	2	1	1	◆0.4
50 + ...	-	-	-	..
Unknown - Inconnu	1	-	1	..
Bahamas[3]				
2007 (U)				
Total....................	5 182	2 659	2 523	...
0 - 14....................	6	1	5	..
15 - 19	604	318	286	...
20 - 24	1 204	607	597	...
25 - 29	1 283	652	631	...
30 - 34	1 153	593	560	...
35 - 39	709	379	330	...
40 - 44	193	93	100	...
45 + ...	10	7	3	...
Unknown - Inconnu	20	9	11	..
Belize				
1998 (U)				
Total....................	5 986	3 047	2 939	...
0 - 14....................	24	14	10	..
15 - 19	1 081	530	551	...
20 - 24	1 783	916	867	...
25 - 29	1 454	749	705	...
30 - 34	893	472	421	...

Continent, country or area, year, code and age of mother (in years) / Continent, pays ou zone, année, code et âge de la mère (en années)	Number - Nombre			Rate Taux
	Total	Male Masculin	Female Féminin	
AMERICA, NORTH - AMÉRIQUE DU NORD				
Belize				
1998 (U)				
35 - 39....................	465	234	231	...
40 - 44....................	108	53	55	...
45 + ...	18	8	10	...
Unknown - Inconnu	160	71	89	..
2002 (U)				
Total[4]....................	7 356	...	...	...
0 - 14....................	22	...	...	...
15 - 19	1 237	...	...	...
20 - 24	2 233	...	...	...
25 - 29	1 712	...	...	...
30 - 34	1 106	...	...	...
35 - 39	566	...	...	...
40 - 44	165	...	...	...
45 + ...	17	...	...	...
Unknown - Inconnu	298	...	...	...
Bermuda - Bermudes				
1998 (C)				
Total....................	825	416	409	...
0 - 14....................	-	-	-	...
15 - 19	66	34	32	...
20 - 24	142	63	79	...
25 - 29	187	102	85	...
30 - 34	265	139	126	...
35 - 39	141	68	73	...
40 + ...	24	10	14	...
2003 (C)				
Total....................	834	...	...	48.9
15 - 19	79	...	...	42.4
20 - 24	116	...	...	68.8
25 - 29	203	...	...	91.9
30 - 34	250	...	...	93.5
35 - 39	148	...	...	52.2
40 + ...	38	...	...	6.6
Canada[5]				
2005 (C)				
Total....................	342 176	175 376	166 800	41.8
0 - 14....................	118	60	58	..
15 - 19	13 895	7 184	6 711	13.3
20 - 24	55 318	28 372	26 946	50.5
25 - 29	105 566	54 041	51 525	97.4
30 - 34	107 524	54 966	52 558	97.6
35 - 39	49 526	25 413	24 113	42.1
40 - 44	9 728	5 076	4 652	7.1
45 - 49	396	209	187	0.3
50 + ...	22	11	11	..
Unknown - Inconnu	83	44	39	..
Costa Rica				
2007 (C)				
Total....................	73 144	37 471	35 673	58.6
0 - 14....................	500	277	223	..
15 - 19	13 981	7 128	6 853	61.0
20 - 24	22 928	11 833	11 095	103.9
25 - 29	17 915	9 139	8 776	99.4
30 - 34	10 928	5 567	5 361	...
35 - 39	5 176	2 644	2 532	...
40 - 44	1 405	713	692	...
45 - 49	99	51	48	...
Unknown - Inconnu	212	119	93	..
Cuba				
2007 (C)				
Total....................	112 472	57 984	54 488	37.3
0 - 14....................	316	162	154	..
15 - 19	17 599	9 020	8 579	42.6
20 - 24	33 910	17 539	16 371	89.2

10. Live-births by age of mother and sex of child and live-birth rates by age of mother: latest available year, 1998 - 2007
Naissances vivantes selon l'âge de la mère et le sexe de l'enfant et taux de natalité selon l'âge de la mère : dernière année disponible, 1998 - 2007 (continued - suite)

Continent, country or area, year, code and age of mother (in years) / Continent, pays ou zone, année, code et âge de la mère (en années)	Number - Nombre			Rate Taux
	Total	Male Masculin	Female Féminin	
AMERICA, NORTH - AMÉRIQUE DU NORD				
Cuba				
2007 (C)				
25 - 29	25 082	13 014	12 068	78.7
30 - 34	21 868	11 173	10 695	49.0
35 - 39	11 535	5 977	5 558	22.1
40 - 44	2 065	1 047	1 018	3.8
45 - 49	57	35	22	0.1
50 +	18	7	11	..
Unknown - Inconnu	22	10	12	..
Dominica - Dominique				
2006 (+C)				
Total	1 056	505	551	62.4
0 - 14	3	-	3	
15 - 19	154	80	74	45.8
20 - 24	250	115	135	116.8
25 - 29	197	91	106	78.2
30 - 34	207	99	108	74.5
35 - 39	179	86	93	72.9
40 - 44	59	29	30	28.7
45 - 49	5	3	2	♦3.1
Dominican Republic - République dominicaine				
2007 (U)				
Total	106 405	54 128	52 277	...
0 - 14	623	308	315	...
15 - 19	15 158	7 758	7 400	...
20 - 24	32 662	16 625	16 037	...
25 - 29	29 510	15 088	14 422	...
30 - 34	17 232	8 705	8 527	...
35 - 39	7 219	3 606	3 613	...
40 - 44	1 589	770	819	...
45 - 49	158	80	78	...
50 +	130	61	69	...
Unknown - Inconnu	2 124	1 127	997	...
El Salvador				
2007 (C)				
Total	106 471	55 742	50 729	68.9
12 - 14	1 067	549	518	
15 - 19	22 272	11 661	10 611	73.9
20 - 24	30 060	15 770	14 290	116.5
25 - 29	25 793	13 601	12 192	103.0
30 - 34	16 619	8 706	7 913	74.4
35 - 39	7 903	4 079	3 824	40.3
40 - 44	2 312	1 147	1 165	13.5
45 - 49	173	90	83	1.2
50 +	22	11	11	..
Unknown - Inconnu	250	128	122	..
Greenland - Groenland				
2007 (C)				
Total	853	447	406	...
0 - 14	-	-	-	
15 - 19	100	55	45	...
20 - 24	264	144	120	...
25 - 29	215	106	109	...
30 - 34	149	76	73	...
35 - 39	99	52	47	...
40 - 44	26	14	12	...
45 - 49	-	-	-	...
50 +	-	-	-	...
Grenada - Grenade				
2000 (+C)				
Total	1 883	...	...	76.5
0 - 14	9	...	...	
15 - 19	310	...	...	53.1
20 - 24	490	...	...	107.0
25 - 29	452	...	...	132.7

Continent, country or area, year, code and age of mother (in years) / Continent, pays ou zone, année, code et âge de la mère (en années)	Number - Nombre			Rate Taux
	Total	Male Masculin	Female Féminin	
AMERICA, NORTH - AMÉRIQUE DU NORD				
Grenada - Grenade				
2000 (+C)				
30 - 34	339	...	...	113.8
35 - 39	208	...	...	64.1
40 - 44	73	...	...	26.7
45 +	2	...	...	♦1.1
Guadeloupe				
2003 (C)				
Total	7 047	3 543	3 504	60.4
0 - 14	7	2	5	..
15 - 19	431	215	216	25.5
20 - 24	1 148	588	560	81.3
25 - 29	1 815	912	903	132.3
30 - 34	2 001	1 005	996	108.6
35 - 39	1 280	637	643	64.6
40 - 44	352	177	175	19.3
45 +	13	7	6	♦0.8
Guatemala				
2006 (C)				
Total	368 399	187 190	181 209	...
0 - 14	2 209	1 101	1 108	...
15 - 19	65 284	33 335	31 949	...
20 - 24	107 634	54 736	52 898	...
25 - 29	86 944	44 413	42 531	...
30 - 34	56 080	28 468	27 612	...
35 - 39	32 668	16 478	16 190	...
40 - 44	12 790	6 341	6 449	...
45 - 49	2 280	1 141	1 139	...
50 +	1 009	487	522	..
Unknown - Inconnu	1 501	690	811	..
Jamaica - Jamaïque[6]				
2006 (C)				
Total	42 387	21 671	20 716	...
0 - 14	211	111	100	...
15 - 19	7 809	4 029	3 780	...
20 - 24	11 699	5 972	5 727	...
25 - 29	9 283	4 722	4 561	...
30 - 34	7 339	3 781	3 558	...
35 - 39	4 455	2 280	2 175	...
40 - 44	1 496	232	764	...
45 +	79	35	44	...
Unknown - Inconnu	16	9	7	..
Martinique				
2007 (C)				
Total	5 317	2 676	2 641	51.0
0 - 14	2	1	1	..
15 - 19	305	165	140	19.8
20 - 24	911	447	464	77.6
25 - 29	1 202	617	585	117.2
30 - 34	1 376	678	698	98.2
35 - 39	1 105	560	545	64.1
40 - 44	393	194	199	20.9
45 +	23	14	9	♦1.4
Mexico - Mexique[7]				
2005 (+U)				
Total	2 141 083	1 090 593[8]	1 050 217[8]	...
0 - 14	5 977	3 064[8]	2 912[8]	...
15 - 19	349 273	178 502[8]	170 725[8]	...
20 - 24	637 184	325 036[8]	312 078[8]	...
25 - 29	553 779	281 644[8]	272 071[8]	...
30 - 34	376 779	191 928[8]	184 801[8]	...
35 - 39	163 801	82 890[8]	80 884[8]	...
40 - 44	39 789	20 108[8]	19 673[8]	...
45 - 49	3 977	1 948[8]	2 028[8]	...

10. Live-births by age of mother and sex of child and live-birth rates by age of mother: latest available year, 1998 - 2007
Naissances vivantes selon l'âge de la mère et le sexe de l'enfant et taux de natalité selon l'âge de la mère : dernière année disponible, 1998 - 2007 (continued - suite)

Continent, country or area, year, code and age of mother (in years) / Continent, pays ou zone, année, code et âge de la mère (en années)	Total	Male Masculin	Female Féminin	Rate Taux
AMERICA, NORTH - AMÉRIQUE DU NORD				
Mexico - Mexique[7]				
2005 (+U)				
50 +	868	435[8]	433[8]	..
Unknown - Inconnu	9 656	5 038[8]	4 612[8]	..
Montserrat				
1999 (+C)				
Total	45	19	26	...
0 - 14	-	-	-	...
15 - 19	7	5	2	...
20 - 24	10	4	6	...
25 - 29	11	4	7	...
30 - 34	12	4	8	...
35 - 39	5	2	3	...
40 - 44	-	-	-	...
45 - 49	-	-	-	...
50 +	-	-	-	..
Unknown - Inconnu	-	-	-	
Netherlands Antilles - Antilles néerlandaises[9]				
2007* (C)				
Total	2 558	1 289	1 269	48.5
0 - 14	4	1	3	..
15 - 19	220	108	112	31.7
20 - 24	515	237	278	96.0
25 - 29	599	321	278	106.1
30 - 34	591	301	290	83.7
35 - 39	423	218	205	51.3
40 - 44	108	50	58	11.9
45 - 49	5	3	2	♦0.6
50 +	1	-	1	..
Unknown - Inconnu	92	50	42	..
Nicaragua				
2007 (+U)				
Total	128 171	66 220	61 951	...
0 - 14	1 503	793	710	...
15 - 19	32 239	16 508	15 731	...
20 - 24	40 172	20 751	19 421	...
25 - 29	28 544	14 833	13 711	...
30 - 34	15 830	8 155	7 675	...
35 - 39	7 642	4 034	3 608	...
40 - 44	1 988	1 019	969	...
45 - 49	224	114	110	...
50 +	29	13	16	...
Panama				
2007 (C)				
Total	67 364	34 465	32 899	...
0 - 14	550	272	278	..
15 - 19	12 337	6 263	6 074	...
20 - 24	19 645	10 048	9 597	...
25 - 29	16 057	8 213	7 844	...
30 - 34	11 258	5 817	5 441	...
35 - 39	5 760	2 963	2 797	...
40 - 44	1 340	678	662	...
45 - 49	125	67	58	...
50 +	17	9	8	..
Unknown - Inconnu	275	135	140	..
Puerto Rico - Porto Rico				
2006 (C)				
Total	48 744	25 151	23 593	49.4
0 - 14	170	89	81	..
15 - 19	8 728	4 533	4 195	59.8
20 - 24	15 416	7 927	7 489	106.7
25 - 29	12 702	6 550	6 152	87.7
30 - 34	7 728	3 992	3 736	56.1
35 - 39	3 239	1 681	1 558	23.8
AMERICA, NORTH - AMÉRIQUE DU NORD				
Puerto Rico - Porto Rico				
2006 (C)				
40 - 44	716	361	355	5.1
45 - 49	27	11	16	♦0.2
50 +	2	-	2	..
Unknown - Inconnu	16	7	9	..
Saint Kitts and Nevis - Saint-Kitts-et-Nevis				
2001 (+C)				
Total	803	...	...	...
10 - 14	3	...	...	...
15 - 19	164	...	...	...
20 - 24	241	...	...	...
25 - 29	166	...	...	...
30 - 34	148	...	...	...
35 - 39	67	...	...	...
40 - 44	14	...	...	...
Saint Lucia - Sainte-Lucie				
2002 (C)[4]				
Total	2 529	1 299	1 230	58.2
0 - 14	8	5	3	..
15 - 19	447	223	224	51.4
20 - 24	686	356	330	96.1
25 - 29	569	284	285	83.9
30 - 34	469	238	231	76.4
35 - 39	277	156	121	45.9
40 - 44	71	36	35	14.1
45 - 49	2	1	1	♦0.6
2005* (C)				
Total	2 298	...	...	49.4
0 - 14	7	...	...	..
15 - 19	390	...	...	43.9
20 - 24	639	...	...	79.5
25 - 29	549	...	...	79.0
30 - 34	396	...	...	61.2
35 - 39	245	...	...	40.2
40 - 44	62	...	...	10.9
45 - 49	10	...	...	♦2.3
Saint Vincent and the Grenadines - Saint-Vincent-et-les Grenadines				
2003 (+C)				
Total	1 923	975	948	...
0 - 14	10	4	6	..
15 - 19	388	193	195	...
20 - 24	547	286	261	...
25 - 29	430	208	222	...
30 - 34	304	163	141	...
35 - 39	182	82	100	...
40 - 44	55	34	21	...
45 - 49	4	2	2	...
50 +	-	-	-	..
Unknown - Inconnu	3	3	-	..
Trinidad and Tobago - Trinité-et-Tobago				
2004 (C)				
Total	17 235	8 748	8 487	...
0 - 14	32	13	19	...
15 - 19	2 278	1 139	1 139	...
20 - 24	5 206	2 697	2 509	...
25 - 29	4 419	2 252	2 167	...
30 - 34	3 144	1 564	1 580	...
35 - 39	1 642	818	824	...
40 - 44	473	242	231	...
45 - 49	22	11	11	...

Continent, country or area, year, code and age of mother (in years) / Continent, pays ou zone, année, code et âge de la mère (en années)	Number - Nombre			Rate Taux
	Total	Male Masculin	Female Féminin	

AMERICA, NORTH - AMÉRIQUE DU NORD

Trinidad and Tobago - Trinité-et-Tobago
2004 (C)

50 +	1	1	-	..
Unknown - Inconnu	18	11	7	..

Turks and Caicos Islands - Îles Turques et Caïques
2005 (C)

Total	318	158	160	...
0 - 14	1	-	1	..
15 - 19	28	13	15	...
20 - 24	65	29	36	...
25 - 29	83	40	43	...
30 - 34	76	47	29	...
35 - 39	52	23	29	...
40 - 44	11	5	6	...
45 +	2	1	1	...

United States of America - États-Unis d'Amérique
2004 (C)

Total	4 112 052	...	...	56.1
0 - 14	6 781	...	...	..
15 - 19	415 262	...	...	41.2
20 - 24	1 034 454	...	...	101.8
25 - 29	1 104 485	...	...	115.2
30 - 34	965 663	...	...	95.4
35 - 39	475 606	...	...	45.3
40 - 44	103 679	...	...	9.0
45 - 49	5 748	...	...	0.5
50 +	374	...	...	..

United States Virgin Islands - Îles Vierges américaines
2007 (C)

Total	1 771	...	...	65.9
0 - 14	2	...	...	..
15 - 19	226	...	...	53.1
20 - 24	550	...	...	146.6
25 - 29	424	...	...	146.1
30 - 34	319	...	...	93.9
35 - 39	196	...	...	48.6
40 +	46	...	...	5.5
Unknown - Inconnu	8	...	...	..

AMERICA, SOUTH - AMÉRIQUE DU SUD

Argentina - Argentine
2007 (C)

Total	700 792	...	...	70.7
0 - 14	2 841	...	...	..
15 - 19	106 720	...	...	64.3
20 - 24	174 679	...	...	109.4
25 - 29	175 632	...	...	108.9
30 - 34	139 393	...	...	95.5
35 - 39	73 532	...	...	59.3
40 - 44	19 879	...	...	17.3
45 - 49	1 428	...	...	1.3
50 +	69	...	...	..
Unknown - Inconnu	6 619	...	...	..

Brazil - Brésil[4]
2007 (U)

Total	2 755 176	1 417 887	1 337 289	...
0 - 14	22 276	11 371	10 905	..
15 - 19	531 898	273 683	258 215	..
20 - 24	799 660	411 991	387 669	..

AMERICA, SOUTH - AMÉRIQUE DU SUD

Brazil - Brésil[4]
2007 (U)

25 - 29	683 734	352 112	331 622	...
30 - 34	431 445	222 022	209 423	...
35 - 39	210 688	108 147	102 541	...
40 - 44	56 376	28 708	27 668	...
45 - 49	4 142	2 057	2 085	...
50 +	470	242	228	...
Unknown - Inconnu	14 487	7 554	6 933	..

Chile - Chili
2006 (C)

Total	231 383	118 203	113 180	52.4
0 - 14	954	498	456	
15 - 19	36 819	18 749	18 070	51.0
20 - 24	54 312	27 714	26 598	81.6
25 - 29	52 387	26 917	25 470	88.0
30 - 34	49 335	25 125	24 210	80.8
35 - 39	28 767	14 685	14 082	46.4
40 - 44	8 372	4 304	4 068	13.3
45 - 49	430	210	220	0.8
50 +	7	1	6	..

Colombia - Colombie
2007* (U)

Total	685 859	352 271	333 588	...
0 - 14	6 381	3 281	3 100	...
15 - 19	153 068	78 711	74 357	...
20 - 24	200 891	103 232	97 659	...
25 - 29	156 925	80 547	76 378	...
30 - 34	96 035	49 327	46 708	...
35 - 39	53 581	27 444	26 137	...
40 - 44	15 194	7 749	7 445	...
45 - 49	1 244	642	602	...
50 +	175	96	79	...
Unknown - Inconnu	2 365	1 242	1 123	...

Ecuador - Équateur[10]
2007 (U)

Total	195 051	99 958	95 093	...
0 - 14	990	538	452	...
15 - 19	35 838	18 479	17 359	...
20 - 24	57 944	29 812	28 132	...
25 - 29	45 800	23 529	22 271	...
30 - 34	28 650	14 481	14 169	...
35 - 39	15 407	7 842	7 565	...
40 - 44	4 918	2 498	2 420	...
45 - 49	681	329	352	...
50 +	-	-	-	...
Unknown - Inconnu	4 823	2 450	2 373	...

French Guiana - Guyane française[11]
2007 (C)

Total	6 386	3 269	3 117	114.5
0 - 14	23	12	11	..
15 - 19	828	428	400	83.3
20 - 24	1 477	726	751	182.2
25 - 29	1 590	821	769	195.5
30 - 34	1 312	707	605	154.0
35 - 39	844	414	430	102.2
40 - 44	289	152	137	40.9
45 - 49	22	8	14	◆3.8
50 +	1	1	-	..

Peru - Pérou[3]
2006* (+U)

Total	307 779	157 216	150 563	...
0 - 14	932	491	441	..
15 - 19	42 981	22 134	20 847	...

10. Live-births by age of mother and sex of child and live-birth rates by age of mother: latest available year, 1998 - 2007
Naissances vivantes selon l'âge de la mère et le sexe de l'enfant et taux de natalité selon l'âge de la mère : dernière année disponible, 1998 - 2007 (continued - suite)

Continent, country or area, year, code and age of mother (in years) — Continent, pays ou zone, année, code et âge de la mère (en années)	Number - Nombre			Rate Taux
	Total	Male Masculin	Female Féminin	

AMERICA, SOUTH - AMÉRIQUE DU SUD

Peru - Pérou[3]
2006* (+U)

20 - 24	79 862	40 718	39 144	...
25 - 29	75 205	38 516	36 689	...
30 - 34	59 529	30 327	29 202	...
35 - 39	36 372	18 489	17 883	...
40 - 44	11 796	5 964	5 832	...
45 - 49	1 008	526	482	...
50 +	93	50	43	...
Unknown - Inconnu	1	1	-	..

Suriname
2007 (C)

Total	9 769	...	...	73.6
0 - 14	65	...	...	..
15 - 19	1 485	...	...	65.5
20 - 24	2 818	...	...	130.8
25 - 29	2 487	...	...	121.9
30 - 34	1 716	...	...	88.8
35 - 39	943	...	...	52.0
40 - 44	243	...	...	14.9
45 +	12	...	...	◆0.8
Unknown - Inconnu	-	...	...	..

Uruguay
2000 (C)

Total	52 770[12]	27 119	25 641	65.7
0 - 14	206[12]	91	116	..
15 - 19	8 268[12]	4 293	3 974	63.3
20 - 24	13 173[12]	6 729	6 442	106.3
25 - 29	12 404[12]	6 460	5 943	107.0
30 - 34	11 342[12]	5 792	5 547	100.0
35 - 39	5 373[12]	2 765	2 606	48.1
40 - 44	1 340[12]	669	670	12.9
45 +	71	34	37	0.7
Unknown - Inconnu	593[12]	286	306	..

2007 (C)

Total	47 372	...	...	58.3
0 - 14	213	...	...	..
15 - 19	7 562	...	...	58.8
20 - 24	11 341	...	...	92.2
25 - 29	11 082	...	...	92.2
30 - 34	10 141	...	...	86.5
35 - 39	5 111	...	...	48.3
40 - 44	1 307	...	...	12.5
45 +	91	...	...	0.9
Unknown - Inconnu	524	...	...	..

Venezuela (Bolivarian Republic of) - Venezuela (République bolivarienne du)[13]
2002 (C)

Total	492 678	254 969	237 709	74.3
0 - 14	5 148	2 660	2 488	..
15 - 19	100 062	51 874	48 188	80.6
20 - 24	146 417	75 965	70 452	129.0
25 - 29	110 318	56 888	53 430	109.9
30 - 34	73 522	38 081	35 441	80.1
35 - 39	36 756	18 951	17 805	42.9
40 - 44	10 443	5 408	5 035	14.1
45 - 49	1 376	685	691	2.2
50 +	412	186	226	..
Unknown - Inconnu	8 224	4 271	3 953	..

ASIA - ASIE

Armenia - Arménie
2007 (C)

Total	40 105	21 460	18 645	43.3
15 - 19	3 980	2 059	1 921	25.5
20 - 24	19 050	9 978	9 072	122.7
25 - 29	11 487	6 285	5 202	85.1
30 - 34	4 118	2 305	1 813	36.4
35 - 39	1 178	665	513	11.4
40 - 44	263	153	110	2.2
45 - 49	29	15	14	◆0.2

Azerbaijan - Azerbaïdjan[14]
2007 (+C)

Total	151 963	82 005	69 958	58.6
0 - 14	1	1	-	..
15 - 19	17 801	9 237	8 564	39.4
20 - 24	64 813	34 286	30 527	154.2
25 - 29	42 110	23 029	19 081	117.6
30 - 34	17 777	10 075	7 702	55.1
35 - 39	7 276	4 139	3 137	21.4
40 - 44	1 936	1 092	844	5.4
45 - 49	225	129	96	0.7
50 +	24	17	7	..

Bahrain - Bahreïn
2002 (C)

Total	13 576	6 953	6 623	80.5
15 - 19	349	185	164	13.7
20 - 24	2 645	1 359	1 286	96.7
25 - 29	4 147	2 098	2 049	151.2
30 - 34	3 413	1 779	1 634	120.0
35 - 39	2 299	1 175	1 124	87.3
40 - 44	655	322	333	32.0
45 - 49	51	27	24	3.9
50 +	9	5	4	..
Unknown - Inconnu	8	3	5	..

2007 (C)

Total	16 062	...	...	62.9
0 - 14	3	...	...	..
15 - 19	431	...	...	12.7
20 - 24	3 556	...	...	89.5
25 - 29	5 168	...	...	115.9
30 - 34	3 897	...	...	90.9
35 - 39	2 166	...	...	58.9
40 - 44	740	...	...	23.0
45 - 49	91	...	...	3.6
50 +	5	...	...	..
Unknown - Inconnu	5	...	...	..

Bhutan - Bhoutan[15]
2005 (I)

Total	12 538	6 306	6 232	79.4
15 - 19	1 376	711	665	36.5
20 - 24	4 211	2 156	2 055	138.9
25 - 29	3 677	1 814	1 863	141.6
30 - 34	1 753	880	873	89.4
35 - 39	960	463	497	54.5
40 - 44	434	207	227	31.3
45 - 49	127	75	52	9.9

Brunei Darussalam - Brunéi Darussalam
2002 (+C)

Total	7 464	3 818	3 646	...
0 - 14	7	4	3	..
15 - 19	387	187	200	...
20 - 24	1 585	819	766	...
25 - 29	2 125	1 072	1 053	...
30 - 34	1 967	994	973	...
35 - 39	1 052	560	492	

Continent, country or area, year, code and age of mother (in years) / Continent, pays ou zone, année, code et âge de la mère (en années)	Number - Nombre			Rate Taux
	Total	Male Masculin	Female Féminin	

ASIA - ASIE

Brunei Darussalam - Brunéi Darussalam
2002 (+C)

40 - 44	317	169	148	...
45 - 49	21	12	9	...
50 +	-	-	-	...
Unknown - Inconnu	3	1	2	...

Cambodia - Cambodge
2004 (U)

Total[4]	320 594	...	...	...
15 - 19	23 238	...	...	...
20 - 24	106 787	...	...	...
25 - 29	66 573	...	...	...
30 - 34	57 861	...	...	...
35 - 39	43 391	...	...	...
40 - 44	19 386	...	...	...
45 - 49	3 358	...	...	...

China, Hong Kong SAR - Chine, Hong Kong RAS
2006 (C)

Total	65 626	34 595	31 031	31.5
0 - 14	9	2	7	..
15 - 19	885	455	430	4.1
20 - 24	9 071	4 713	4 358	36.8
25 - 29	18 814	9 902	8 912	67.6
30 - 34	23 035	12 219	10 816	74.4
35 - 39	11 750	6 206	5 544	35.5
40 - 44	1 958	1 043	915	5.4
45 - 49	100	52	48	0.3
50 +	2	1	1	..
Unknown - Inconnu	2	2	-	..

China, Macao SAR - Chine, Macao RAS
2007 (C)

Total	4 537	2 342	2 195	26.8
0 - 14	-	-	-	..
15 - 19	75	41	34	3.3
20 - 24	833	430	403	32.2
25 - 29	1 312	638	674	64.0
30 - 34	1 391	721	670	62.7
35 - 39	771	424	347	30.6
40 - 44	148	83	65	5.5
45 - 49	7	5	2	♦0.3

Cyprus - Chypre[16]
2007 (C)

Total	8 575	4 466	4 109	41.1
12 - 14	-	-	-	..
15 - 19	145	77	68	5.2
20 - 24	1 314	678	636	40.0
25 - 29	3 109	1 640	1 469	94.0
30 - 34	2 653	1 374	1 279	90.1
35 - 39	1 134	588	546	40.5
40 - 44	187	96	91	6.5
45 - 49	22	6	16	♦0.8
50 +	7	4	3	..
Unknown - Inconnu	4	3	1	..

Georgia - Géorgie[14]
2006 (C)

Total	47 795	25 236	22 559	40.3
0 - 14	25	13	12	..
15 - 19	6 608	3 478	3 130	36.6
20 - 24	17 666	9 301	8 365	100.8
25 - 29	12 409	6 487	5 922	76.0
30 - 34	6 831	3 673	3 158	43.3
35 - 39	2 929	1 597	1 332	18.9

ASIA - ASIE

Georgia - Géorgie[14]
2006 (C)

40 - 44	791	423	368	4.6
45 - 49	87	49	38	0.5
50 +	34	15	19	..
Unknown - Inconnu	415	200	215	..

Iraq[17]
2000 (U)

Total	471 886	...	...	...
15 - 19	21 367	...	...	...
20 - 24	115 973	...	...	...
25 - 29	149 287	...	...	...
30 - 34	110 981	...	...	...
35 - 39	52 196	...	...	...
40 - 44	16 717	...	...	...
45 +	5 365	...	...	...

Israel - Israël[18]
2007 (C)

Total	151 679	77 830	73 849	87.8
0 - 14	2	2	-	..
15 - 19	3 927	2 087	1 840	13.9
20 - 24	29 166	14 988	14 178	104.3
25 - 29	46 465	23 916	22 549	172.0
30 - 34	44 429	22 662	21 767	167.6
35 - 39	22 009	11 269	10 740	96.1
40 - 44	4 875	2 526	2 349	24.4
45 - 49	437	206	231	2.2
50 +	79	38	41	..
Unknown - Inconnu	290	136	154	..

Japan - Japon[19]
2007 (C)

Total	1 089 818	559 847	529 971	39.4
0 - 14	39	21	18	..
15 - 19	15 211	7 941	7 270	4.9
20 - 24	126 180	64 524	61 656	35.5
25 - 29	324 041	167 088	156 953	84.1
30 - 34	412 611	211 630	200 981	88.7
35 - 39	186 568	95 849	90 719	40.2
40 - 44	24 553	12 490	12 063	6.1
45 - 49	590	294	296	0.2
50 +	19	9	10	..
Unknown - Inconnu	6	1	5	..

Kazakhstan[14]
2007 (C)

Total	321 963	165 543	156 420	73.2
0 - 14	17	7	10	..
15 - 19	22 095	11 325	10 770	29.3
20 - 24	108 852	56 023	52 829	146.5
25 - 29	92 963	47 753	45 210	147.6
30 - 34	59 935	30 808	29 127	101.8
35 - 39	30 333	15 608	14 725	55.0
40 - 44	7 119	3 673	3 446	12.8
45 - 49	331	183	148	0.6
50 +	14	7	7	..
Unknown - Inconnu	304	156	148	..

Kuwait - Koweït
2007 (C)

Total	53 587	27 458	26 129	90.3
15 - 19	1 210	635	575	15.7
20 - 24	11 644	6 019	5 625	128.5
25 - 29	17 011	8 764	8 247	154.7
30 - 34	13 149	6 756	6 393	129.7
35 - 39	7 012	3 530	3 482	81.1
40 - 44	1 899	946	953	28.9

10. Live-births by age of mother and sex of child and live-birth rates by age of mother: latest available year, 1998 - 2007
Naissances vivantes selon l'âge de la mère et le sexe de l'enfant et taux de natalité selon l'âge de la mère : dernière année disponible, 1998 - 2007 (continued - suite)

Continent, country or area, year, code and age of mother (in years) / Continent, pays ou zone, année, code et âge de la mère (en années)	Total	Male Masculin	Female Féminin	Rate Taux
ASIA - ASIE				
Kuwait - Koweït				
2007 (C)				
45 +	202	103	99	4.4
Unknown - Inconnu	1 460	705	755	..
Kyrgyzstan - Kirghizstan				
2007 (C)				
Total	123 251	63 359	59 892	84.7
0 - 14	3	1	2	..
15 - 19	8 500	4 366	4 134	29.5
20 - 24	46 105	23 853	22 252	175.9
25 - 29	34 166	17 498	16 668	157.8
30 - 34	20 454	10 464	9 990	107.0
35 - 39	10 521	5 392	5 129	60.1
40 - 44	2 912	1 489	1 423	17.8
45 - 49	389	204	185	2.5
50 +	24	8	16	..
Unknown - Inconnu	177	84	93	..
Malaysia - Malaisie				
2007* (C)				
Total	456 443	235 359	221 084	64.7
0 - 14	617	329	288	..
15 - 19	14 535	7 662	6 873	11.6
20 - 24	79 113	40 839	38 274	65.6
25 - 29	151 150	77 666	73 484	138.8
30 - 34	122 935	63 365	59 570	126.2
35 - 39	66 320	34 233	32 087	71.9
40 - 44	18 610	9 583	9 027	21.9
45 - 49	1 700	909	791	2.3
50 +	90	47	43	..
Unknown - Inconnu	1 373	726	647	..
Maldives				
2007 (C)				
Total	6 569	3 393	3 176	73.7
10 - 14	2	-	2	..
15 - 19	275	137	138	13.8
20 - 24	2 440	1 278	1 162	129.0
25 - 29	1 998	1 023	975	145.0
30 - 34	1 168	602	566	105.6
35 - 39	527	272	255	53.9
40 - 44	141	72	69	16.7
45 - 49	15	6	9	♦2.1
50 +	1	1	-	..
Unknown - Inconnu	2	2	-	..
Mongolia - Mongolie				
2007 (C)				
Total	56 636	28 750	27 886	71.7
0 - 14	75	44	31	..
15 - 19	2 842	1 458	1 384	18.2
20 - 24	18 269	9 252	9 017	134.7
25 - 29	17 533	8 927	8 606	148.7
30 - 34	11 067	5 619	5 448	100.3
35 - 39	5 277	2 662	2 615	52.6
40 - 44	1 354	681	673	14.7
45 - 49	195	93	102	2.5
50 +	24	14	10	..
Oman[20]				
2007 (U)				
Total	48 041	24 456	23 585	...
0 - 14	18	11	7	..
15 - 19	1 033	546	487	...
20 - 24	10 029	5 131	4 898	...
25 - 29	16 887	8 588	8 299	...
30 - 34	11 763	5 945	5 818	...
35 - 39	5 676	2 884	2 792	...
40 - 44	2 098	1 071	1 027	...
ASIA - ASIE				
Oman[20]				
2007 (U)				
45 - 49	457	238	219	...
50 +	80	42	38	..
Pakistan[21]				
2005 (|)				
Total	3 772 494	1 993 492	1 779 002	110.6
15 - 19	161 490	90 049	71 441	20.3
20 - 24	1 050 830	556 310	494 520	157.6
25 - 29	1 166 365	611 186	555 179	225.5
30 - 34	754 513	395 425	359 088	179.9
35 - 39	425 352	222 186	203 166	106.6
40 - 44	161 914	86 273	75 641	50.1
45 +	52 030	32 063	19 967	18.1
Philippines				
2005 (C)				
Total	1 688 918	878 084	810 834	76.8
0 - 14	811	401	410	..
15 - 19	143 142	74 351	68 791	33.9
20 - 24	471 118	245 037	226 081	120.9
25 - 29	471 888	246 133	225 755	133.5
30 - 34	325 129	169 167	155 962	103.1
35 - 39	197 594	102 383	95 211	71.3
40 - 44	67 145	34 469	32 676	28.3
45 - 49	8 277	4 158	4 119	4.1
50 +	556	297	259	..
Unknown - Inconnu	3 258	1 688	1 570	..
Qatar				
2007 (C)				
Total	15 681	8 056	7 625	81.8
0 - 14	-	-	-	..
15 - 19	366	184	182	16.0
20 - 24	2 932	1 520	1 412	109.9
25 - 29	5 038	2 613	2 425	129.0
30 - 34	4 138	2 124	2 014	115.0
35 - 39	2 416	1 243	1 173	83.8
40 - 44	712	332	380	32.4
45 - 49	65	32	33	4.0
50 +	11	7	4	..
Unknown - Inconnu	3	1	2	..
Republic of Korea - République de Corée[22]				
2006 (C)				
Total	451 514	233 845	217 669	...
0 - 14	33	17	16	..
15 - 19	3 236	1 808	1 428	...
20 - 24	30 801	15 904	14 897	...
25 - 29	173 711	89 737	83 974	...
30 - 34	189 454	98 060	91 394	...
35 - 39	47 628	24 930	22 698	...
40 - 44	5 398	2 770	2 628	...
45 - 49	357	152	205	...
50 +	35	22	13	..
Unknown - Inconnu	861	445	416	...
Saudi Arabia - Arabie saoudite				
2005 (...)				
Total	582 582	298 396	284 186	...
15 - 19	25 652	13 139	12 513	...
20 - 24	153 901	78 827	75 074	...
25 - 29	194 252	99 495	94 757	...
30 - 34	135 325	69 313	66 012	...
35 - 39	57 941	29 677	28 264	...
40 - 44	14 373	7 362	7 011	...
45 - 49	1 137	583	555	...

10. Live-births by age of mother and sex of child and live-birth rates by age of mother: latest available year, 1998 - 2007
Naissances vivantes selon l'âge de la mère et le sexe de l'enfant et taux de natalité selon l'âge de la mère : dernière année disponible, 1998 - 2007 (continued - suite)

Continent, country or area, year, code and age of mother (in years) / Continent, pays ou zone, année, code et âge de la mère (en années)	Total	Male Masculin	Female Féminin	Rate Taux
ASIA - ASIE				
Singapore - Singapour 2007 (C)				
Total	39 490	20 438[23]	19 051[23]	39.9
0 - 14	15	5	10	..
15 - 19	805	431	374	6.4
20 - 24	3 548	1 840	1 708	32.9
25 - 29	11 229	5 879	5 350	84.7
30 - 34	15 655	8 071[23]	7 583[23]	102.3
35 - 39	7 081	3 626	3 455	45.8
40 - 44	1 124	563	561	7.0
45 - 49	31	22	9	0.2
50 +	1	-	1	..
Unknown - Inconnu	1	1	-	..
Sri Lanka 2001 (+C)				
Total	358 581	183 409	175 172	76.6
0 - 14	118	68	50	..
15 - 19	27 515	14 105	13 410	33.9
20 - 24	92 239	47 239	45 000	116.3
25 - 29	105 303	54 028	51 275	154.9
30 - 34	83 231	42 415	40 816	127.4
35 - 39	39 712	20 259	19 453	62.5
40 - 44	9 597	4 875	4 722	16.3
45 - 49	816	399	417	1.6
50 +	50	21	29	..
Tajikistan - Tadjikistan[14] 1999 (U)				
Total	114 015	60 552	53 463	...
15 - 19	10 026	5 239	4 787	...
20 - 24	38 400	20 275	18 125	...
25 - 29	30 752	16 431	14 321	...
30 - 34	20 245	10 744	9 501	...
35 - 39	10 957	5 873	5 084	...
40 - 44	2 819	1 532	1 287	...
45 - 49	234	128	106	...
50 +	37	25	12	..
Unknown - Inconnu	545	305	240	..
Thailand - Thaïlande 2007 (+U)				
Total	797 588	410 921	386 667	..
0 - 14	2 616	1 363	1 253	..
15 - 19	116 086	59 678	56 408	..
20 - 24	196 390	101 219	95 171	...
25 - 29	215 888	111 698	104 190	...
30 - 34	163 888	84 114	79 774	...
35 - 39	80 129	41 272	38 857	...
40 - 44	19 043	9 727	9 316	...
45 - 49	1 320	683	637	...
50 +	63	31	32	..
Unknown - Inconnu	2 159	1 130	1 029	..
United Arab Emirates - Émirats arabes unis 2003 (...)				
Total	61 165	31 241	29 924	...
15 - 19	2 647	1 415	1 232	...
20 - 24	12 551	6 386	6 165	...
25 - 29	18 710	9 605	9 105	...
30 - 34	14 699	7 484	7 215	...
35 - 39	7 670	3 876	3 794	...
40 - 44	2 796	1 409	1 387	...
45 - 49	620	316	304	...
50 +	101	51	50	..
Unknown - Inconnu	1 371	699	672	..
ASIA - ASIE				
Uzbekistan - Ouzbékistan[14] 2000 (C)				
Total	527 580	...	...	82.7
15 - 19	28 179	...	...	21.1
20 - 24	228 743	...	...	205.4
25 - 29	160 082	...	...	161.4
30 - 34	78 316	...	...	89.7
35 - 39	26 866	...	...	31.5
40 - 44	4 979	...	...	7.0
45 - 49	348	...	...	0.7
50 +	67	...	...	..
EUROPE				
Åland Islands - Îles d'Åland[24] 2007 (C)				
Total	286	144	142	49.1
0 - 14	-	-	-	..
15 - 19	5	3	2	♦6.1
20 - 24	31	11	20	51.5
25 - 29	79	39	40	109.5
30 - 34	117	65	52	145.4
35 - 39	40	18	22	43.0
40 - 44	14	8	6	♦13.9
45 - 49	-	-	-	..
50 +	-	-	-	..
Albania - Albanie 2004 (C)				
Total	43 022	22 859	20 163	51.8
15 - 19	2 249	1 213	1 036	14.5
20 - 24	13 516	7 006	6 510	99.3
25 - 29	14 476	7 669	6 807	127.6
30 - 34	8 491	4 597	3 894	78.8
35 - 39	3 239	1 800	1 439	30.0
40 - 44	736	419	317	6.7
45 - 49	64	38	26	0.7
50 +	12	7	5	..
Unknown - Inconnu	239	110	129	..
2007 (C)				
Total	33 163	...	...	39.2
0 - 19	1 705	...	...	11.3
20 - 24	10 330	...	...	70.4
25 - 29	11 053	...	...	91.6
30 - 34	6 504	...	...	61.2
35 - 39	2 683	...	...	25.1
40 - 44	554	...	...	5.3
45 - 49	76	...	...	0.7
50 +	22	...	...	..
Unknown - Inconnu	236	...	...	..
Andorra - Andorre 2007 (C)				
Total	826	435	391	36.8
12 - 14	-	-	-	..
15 - 19	13	8	5	♦6.9
20 - 24	87	46	41	37.6
25 - 29	223	127	96	65.5
30 - 34	308	156	152	77.3
35 - 39	163	83	80	41.4
40 - 44	31	14	17	8.4
45 - 49	1	1	-	♦0.3
50 +	-	-	-	..
Unknown - Inconnu	-	-	-	..

10. Live-births by age of mother and sex of child and live-birth rates by age of mother: latest available year, 1998 - 2007
Naissances vivantes selon l'âge de la mère et le sexe de l'enfant et taux de natalité selon l'âge de la mère : dernière année disponible, 1998 - 2007 (continued - suite)

Continent, country or area, year, code and age of mother (in years) / Continent, pays ou zone, année, code et âge de la mère (en années)	Number - Nombre			Rate Taux
	Total	Male Masculin	Female Féminin	

Continent, country or area, year, code and age of mother (in years) / Continent, pays ou zone, année, code et âge de la mère (en années)	Total	Male Masculin	Female Féminin	Rate Taux
EUROPE				
Austria - Autriche				
2007 (C)				
Total.....................	76 250	38 940	37 310	37.2
12 - 14	6	2	4	..
15 - 19	2 717	1 415	1 302	11.2
20 - 24	13 209	6 787	6 422	51.0
25 - 29	23 409	11 950	11 459	88.1
30 - 34	22 606	11 506	11 100	81.7
35 - 39	11 806	6 026	5 780	35.7
40 - 44	2 384	1 197	1 187	6.7
45 - 49	107	55	52	0.3
50 + ...	6	2	4	..
Belarus - Bélarus[14]				
2006 (C)				
Total.....................	96 721	49 849	46 872	36.6
0 - 14.................	10	5	5	..
15 - 19	8 238	4 234	4 004	21.9
20 - 24	36 120	18 613	17 507	88.9
25 - 29	29 846	15 372	14 474	83.0
30 - 34	15 950	8 229	7 721	46.3
35 - 39	5 488	2 846	2 642	16.1
40 - 44	935	488	447	2.4
45 - 49	47	23	24	0.1
50 + ...	-	-	-	..
Unknown - Inconnu	87	39	48	..
Bosnia and Herzegovina - Bosnie-Herzégovine				
2006 (C)				
Total.....................	34 033	...	...	...
0 - 14.................	7	...	...	...
15 - 19	2 065	...	...	...
20 - 24	9 964	...	...	...
25 - 29	11 370	...	...	...
30 - 34	6 969	...	...	...
35 - 39	2 555	...	...	...
40 - 44	507	...	...	...
45 - 49	29	...	...	...
50 + ...	1	...	...	..
Unknown - Inconnu	566	...	...	..
Bulgaria - Bulgarie				
2007 (C)				
Total.....................	75 349	38 822	36 527	40.9
12 - 14	407	205	202	..
15 - 19	9 673	5 057	4 616	41.3
20 - 24	20 147	10 324	9 823	77.9
25 - 29	23 427	12 122	11 305	85.6
30 - 34	15 970	8 185	7 785	56.1
35 - 39	4 977	2 542	2 435	18.4
40 - 44	699	367	332	2.8
45 - 49	31	13	18	0.1
50 + ...	4	-	4	..
Unknown - Inconnu	14	7	7	..
Croatia - Croatie				
2007 (C)				
Total.....................	41 910	21 460	20 450	39.8
12 - 14	5	4	1	.
15 - 19	1 772	893	879	13.6
20 - 24	8 887	4 562	4 325	60.8
25 - 29	14 731	7 609	7 122	95.3
30 - 34	11 152	5 613	5 539	74.8
35 - 39	4 417	2 294	2 123	30.1
40 - 44	866	445	421	5.4
45 - 49	38	21	17	0.2
50 + ...	3	-	3	..
Unknown - Inconnu	39	19	20	..
EUROPE				
Czech Republic - République tchèque				
2007 (C)				
Total.....................	114 632	58 475	56 157	45.3
12 - 14.................	18	10	8	..
15 - 19	3 516	1 758	1 758	11.1
20 - 24	16 241	8 290	7 951	48.0
25 - 29	42 169	21 519	20 650	107.4
30 - 34	40 187	20 470	19 717	88.3
35 - 39	10 831	5 588	5 243	29.9
40 - 44	1 605	811	794	4.6
45 - 49	59	26	33	0.2
50 + ...	6	3	3	..
Unknown - Inconnu	-	-	-	..
Denmark - Danemark[25]				
2007 (C)				
Total.....................	64 082	32 815	31 267	51.7
12 - 14	3	2	1	..
15 - 19	904	449	455	5.7
20 - 24	6 185	3 170	3 015	42.3
25 - 29	20 262	10 335	9 927	126.5
30 - 34	24 138	12 437	11 701	130.3
35 - 39	10 606	5 404	5 202	55.3
40 - 44	1 918	981	937	9.1
45 - 49	65	37	28	0.3
50 + ...	1	-	1	..
Unknown - Inconnu	-	-	-	..
Estonia - Estonie				
2007 (C)				
Total.....................	15 775	8 100	7 675	46.6
12 - 14	5	2	3	..
15 - 19	1 167	584	583	24.0
20 - 24	3 720	1 920	1 800	71.7
25 - 29	4 930	2 532	2 398	103.6
30 - 34	3 739	1 898	1 841	80.9
35 - 39	1 847	971	876	39.4
40 - 44	354	188	166	7.7
45 - 49	13	5	8	♦0.3
50 + ...	-	-	...	..
Unknown - Inconnu	-	-	-	..
Faeroe Islands - Îles Féroé				
2005 (C)				
Total.....................	713	...	...	...
0 - 14	-	...	...	...
15 - 19	24	...	...	...
20 - 24	119	...	...	...
25 - 29	229	...	...	...
30 - 34	196	...	...	...
35 - 39	124	...	...	...
40 - 44	19	...	...	...
45 - 49	2	...	...	...
50 + ...	-	...	...	...
Finland - Finlande[26]				
2007 (C)				
Total.....................	58 729	30 136	28 593	50.1
12 - 14	2	1	1	..
15 - 19	1 464	773	691	9.1
20 - 24	9 467	4 812	4 655	58.8
25 - 29	18 673	9 469	9 204	114.9
30 - 34	18 206	9 517	8 689	117.1
35 - 39	8 721	4 434	4 287	53.8
40 - 44	2 095	1 080	1 015	11.4
45 - 49	98	48	50	0.5
50 + ...	3	2	1	..
Unknown - Inconnu	-	-	-	..

10. Live-births by age of mother and sex of child and live-birth rates by age of mother: latest available year, 1998 - 2007
Naissances vivantes selon l'âge de la mère et le sexe de l'enfant et taux de natalité selon l'âge de la mère : dernière année disponible, 1998 - 2007 (continued - suite)

Continent, country or area, year, code and age of mother (in years) — Continent, pays ou zone, année, code et âge de la mère (en années)	Number - Nombre			Rate Taux
	Total	Male Masculin	Female Féminin	
EUROPE				
France[27]				
2007 (C)				
Total.....................	785 985	402 297	383 688	54.5
12 - 14	93	46	47	..
15 - 19	19 630	9 955	9 675	10.3
20 - 24	117 285	60 127	57 158	60.6
25 - 29	261 454	133 901	127 553	133.9
30 - 34	242 449	124 083	118 366	119.2
35 - 39	119 070	60 848	58 222	54.8
40 - 44	24 834	12 747	12 087	11.2
45 - 49	1 113	560	553	0.5
50 + ...	57	30	27	..
Unknown - Inconnu	-	-	-	..
Germany - Allemagne				
2007 (C)				
Total.....................	684 862	351 839	333 023	35.6
0 - 14...................	148	74	74	..
15 - 19	22 712	11 725	10 987	9.9
20 - 24	104 696	53 744	50 952	43.9
25 - 29	203 168	104 499	98 669	83.2
30 - 34	204 865	105 288	99 577	87.6
35 - 39	123 185	63 162	60 023	40.5
40 - 44	24 955	12 768	12 187	7.1
45 - 49	936	476	460	0.3
50 + ...	38	24	14	..
Unknown - Inconnu	159	79	80	..
Gibraltar				
2002 (C)				
Total.....................	375	...	...	...
15 - 19	25	...	...	...
20 - 24	59	...	...	...
25 - 29	120	...	...	...
30 - 34	115	...	...	...
35 - 39	46	...	...	...
40 - 44	10	...	...	...
Greece - Grèce				
2007 (C)				
Total.....................	111 926	57 959	53 967	41.9
12 - 14	76	38	38	..
15 - 19	3 129	1 571	1 558	11.1
20 - 24	14 592	7 644	6 948	44.4
25 - 29	33 216	17 192	16 024	83.8
30 - 34	38 254	19 797	18 457	91.0
35 - 39	18 731	9 664	9 067	43.4
40 - 44	3 515	1 844	1 671	8.5
45 - 49	361	184	177	0.9
50 + ...	52	25	27	..
Unknown - Inconnu	-	-	-	..
Guernsey - Guernesey				
2000 (C)				
Total.....................	644	336	308	...
15 - 19	42	15	27	...
20 - 24	84	49	35	...
25 - 29	192	101	91	...
30 - 34	200	102	98	...
35 - 39	106	60	46	...
40 - 44	20	9	11	...
Hungary - Hongrie				
2007 (C)				
Total.....................	97 613	50 033	47 580	40.5
12 - 14	102	43	59	..
15 - 19	5 889	2 943	2 946	19.4
20 - 24	14 671	7 476	7 195	45.3
25 - 29	32 263	16 703	15 560	85.5
30 - 34	32 339	16 580	15 759	78.8
35 - 39	10 542	5 380	5 162	29.7

Continent, country or area, year, code and age of mother (in years) — Continent, pays ou zone, année, code et âge de la mère (en années)	Number - Nombre			Rate Taux
	Total	Male Masculin	Female Féminin	
EUROPE				
Hungary - Hongrie				
2007 (C)				
40 - 44	1 746	881	865	5.7
45 - 49	60	26	34	0.2
50 + ...	1	1	-	..
Unknown - Inconnu	-	-	-	..
Iceland - Islande				
2007 (C)				
Total.....................	4 560	2 359	2 201	59.9
0 - 14...................	-	-	-	..
15 - 19	160	85	75	14.1
20 - 24	838	434	404	78.0
25 - 29	1 521	804	717	133.9
30 - 34	1 307	690	617	121.7
35 - 39	610	286	324	60.0
40 - 44	113	50	63	10.2
45 - 49	10	9	1	♦0.9
50 + ...	1	1	-	..
Unknown - Inconnu	-	-	-	..
Ireland - Irlande				
2006* (+C)				
Total.....................	64 237	33 085	31 152	57.9
0 - 14...................	10	7	3	..
15 - 19	2 352	1 239	1 113	16.4
20 - 24	8 345	4 345	4 000	48.8
25 - 29	14 891	7 616	7 275	79.4
30 - 34	22 002	11 426	10 576	131.9
35 - 39	13 856	7 029	6 827	89.3
40 - 44	2 648	1 348	1 300	17.8
45 - 49	94	52	42	0.7
50 + ...	4	1	3	..
Unknown - Inconnu	35	22	13	..
2007* (+C)				
Total.....................	70 620	...	...	61.6
0 - 15...................	65	...	...	..
0 - 19...................	2 464	...	...	..
20 - 24	8 863	...	...	51.8
25 - 29	16 336	...	...	81.3
30 - 34	24 151	...	...	136.3
35 - 39	15 728	...	...	95.9
40 - 44	2 937	...	...	19.2
45 + ...	121	...	...	0.9
Unknown - Inconnu	20	...	...	..
Italy - Italie[7]				
2005 (C)				
Total.....................	544 030	280 606	263 424	..
0 - 14...................	3	2	1	..
15 - 19	9 416	4 863	4 553	...
20 - 24	50 715	26 262	24 453	...
25 - 29	135 713	69 895	65 818	...
30 - 34	198 611	102 392	96 219	...
35 - 39	117 659	60 755	56 904	...
40 - 44	23 874	12 310	11 564	...
45 - 49	880	467	413	...
50 + ...	113	59	54	...
Unknown - Inconnu	7 046	3 601	3 445	...
Jersey				
2007 (+C)				
Total.....................	1 031	515	516	...
0 - 14...................	-	-	-	...
15 - 19	29	14	15	...
20 - 24	114	56	58	...
25 - 29	228	114	114	...
30 - 34	325	170	155	...
35 - 39	273	134	139	...
40 - 44	61	27	34	...

Continent, country or area, year, code and age of mother (in years) / Continent, pays ou zone, année, code et âge de la mère (en années)	Number - Nombre			Rate Taux
	Total	Male Masculin	Female Féminin	

EUROPE

	Total	Male Masculin	Female Féminin	Rate Taux
Jersey				
2007 (+C)				
45 - 49	1	-	1	...
50 +	-	-	-	..
Latvia - Lettonie				
2007 (C)				
Total	23 273	11 838	11 435	39.8
0 - 14	2	1	1	..
15 - 19	1 501	752	749	17.9
20 - 24	6 152	3 199	2 953	67.9
25 - 29	7 182	3 681	3 501	90.4
30 - 34	5 142	2 566	2 576	65.5
35 - 39	2 645	1 298	1 347	33.0
40 - 44	607	319	288	7.4
45 - 49	30	17	13	0.3
50 +	3	1	2	..
Unknown - Inconnu	9	4	5	..
Liechtenstein				
2007* (C)				
Total	351	184	167	39.0
12 - 14	-	-	-	..
15 - 19	2	-	2	◆1.9
20 - 24	35	20	15	32.6
25 - 29	94	53	41	85.6
30 - 34	117	56	61	94.7
35 - 39	88	47	41	59.2
40 - 44	15	8	7	◆9.6
45 - 49	-	-	-	-
Unknown - Inconnu	-	-	-	..
Lithuania - Lituanie				
2007 (C)				
Total	32 346	16 544	15 802	36.7
12 - 14	11	7	4	..
15 - 19	2 411	1 226	1 185	18.7
20 - 24	8 418	4 237	4 181	63.4
25 - 29	10 814	5 545	5 269	96.7
30 - 34	7 038	3 685	3 353	62.1
35 - 39	3 047	1 547	1 500	24.2
40 - 44	582	281	301	4.5
45 - 49	25	16	9	◆0.2
50 +	-	-	...	..
Unknown - Inconnu	-	-	-	..
Luxembourg				
2007 (C)				
Total	5 477	2 754	2 723	45.7
12 - 14	-	-	-	..
15 - 19	141	66	75	10.2
20 - 24	640	332	308	46.1
25 - 29	1 583	796	787	97.9
30 - 34	1 853	929	924	104.3
35 - 39	1 065	531	534	53.7
40 - 44	185	94	91	9.2
45 - 49	7	4	3	◆0.4
50 +	-	-	...	..
Unknown - Inconnu	3	2	1	..
Malta - Malte				
2007 (C)				
Total	3 871	2 036	1 835	39.8
13 - 14	4	2	2	..
15 - 19	235	133	102	16.7
20 - 24	649	348	301	46.0
25 - 29	1 299	693	606	88.6
30 - 34	1 189	598	591	84.2
35 - 39	412	223	189	33.4
40 - 44	78	37	41	6.1
Unknown - Inconnu	2	1	1	..

EUROPE

	Total	Male Masculin	Female Féminin	Rate Taux
Montenegro - Monténégro				
2007 (C)				
Total	7 834	4 136	3 698	49.6
0 - 14	1	-	1	..
15 - 19	393	214	179	17.4
20 - 24	1 953	1 033	920	80.4
25 - 29	2 641	1 365	1 276	112.9
30 - 34	1 803	947	856	81.5
35 - 39	804	452	352	39.1
40 - 44	148	76	72	6.9
45 - 49	7	2	5	◆0.3
50 +	2	2	-	..
Unknown - Inconnu	82	45	37	..
Netherlands - Pays-Bas[28]				
2007 (C)				
Total	181 336	92 560	88 776	46.6
15 - 19	2 543	1 298	1 245	5.2
20 - 24	18 715	9 584	9 131	39.2
25 - 29	52 427	26 720	25 707	106.1
30 - 34	67 042	34 266	32 776	125.5
35 - 39	35 378	17 990	17 388	55.1
40 - 44	5 060	2 621	2 439	7.8
45 - 49	158	75	83	0.3
50 +	13	6	7	..
Norway - Norvège[29]				
2007 (C)				
Total	58 459	30 004	28 455	53.2
12 - 14	4	3	1	..
15 - 19	1 381	707	674	9.1
20 - 24	8 332	4 265	4 067	60.5
25 - 29	17 720	9 099	8 621	122.3
30 - 34	19 727	10 090	9 637	123.2
35 - 39	9 576	4 974	4 602	54.1
40 - 44	1 638	821	817	9.7
45 - 49	62	34	28	0.4
50 +	-	-	-	..
Unknown - Inconnu	19	11	8	..
Poland - Pologne				
2006 (C)				
Total	374 244	192 518	181 726	38.1
0 - 14	44	26	18	..
15 - 19	19 186	9 853	9 333	13.9
20 - 24	93 569	48 100	45 469	57.7
25 - 29	139 853	72 056	67 797	91.1
30 - 34	86 825	44 609	42 216	62.8
35 - 39	28 487	14 667	13 820	24.0
40 - 44	5 975	3 059	2 916	4.9
45 - 49	304	148	156	0.2
50 +	1	-	1	..
Portugal[7]				
2007 (C)				
Total	102 492	52 683	49 809	39.4
13 - 14	70	32	38	..
15 - 19	4 774	2 413	2 361	16.7
20 - 24	14 397	7 426	6 971	44.1
25 - 29	29 539	15 149	14 390	76.1
30 - 34	34 959	18 035	16 924	82.8
35 - 39	15 670	8 059	7 611	39.4
40 - 44	2 959	1 513	1 446	7.4
45 - 49	118	54	64	0.3
50 +	4	-	4	..
Unknown - Inconnu	2	2	-	..

10. Live-births by age of mother and sex of child and live-birth rates by age of mother: latest available year, 1998 - 2007
Naissances vivantes selon l'âge de la mère et le sexe de l'enfant et taux de natalité selon l'âge de la mère : dernière année disponible, 1998 - 2007 (continued - suite)

Continent, country or area, year, code and age of mother (in years) / Continent, pays ou zone, année, code et âge de la mère (en années)	Number - Nombre			Rate Taux
	Total	Male Masculin	Female Féminin	

EUROPE

	Total	Male Masculin	Female Féminin	Rate Taux
Republic of Moldova - République de Moldova[30]				
2006 (C)				
Total	37 587	19 310	18 277	37.1
0 - 14	8	5	3	..
15 - 19	4 873	2 513	2 360	28.7
20 - 24	14 762	7 584	7 178	86.7
25 - 29	10 537	5 415	5 122	71.7
30 - 34	5 237	2 695	2 542	40.0
35 - 39	1 815	918	897	16.0
40 - 44	350	178	172	2.7
45 - 49	4	1	3	-
50 +	-	-	-	..
Unknown - Inconnu	1	1	-	..
Romania - Roumanie				
2007 (C)				
Total	214 728	110 459	104 269	39.0
12 - 14	562	299	263	..
15 - 19	26 607	13 663	12 944	35.2
20 - 24	53 250	27 417	25 833	66.5
25 - 29	68 851	35 559	33 292	81.0
30 - 34	45 512	23 334	22 178	54.4
35 - 39	17 473	8 931	8 542	18.3
40 - 44	2 345	1 197	1 148	3.9
45 - 49	120	56	64	0.2
50 +	8	3	5	..
Russian Federation - Fédération de Russie[14]				
2007 (C)				
Total	1 610 122	828 772	781 350	41.6
12 - 14	377	204	173	..
15 - 19	151 460	77 824	73 636	30.3
20 - 24	549 262	282 154	267 108	87.2
25 - 29	487 804	251 645	236 159	85.2
30 - 34	287 605	148 159	139 446	54.3
35 - 39	110 780	57 031	53 749	22.5
40 - 44	20 099	10 355	9 744	4.0
45 - 49	1 049	554	495	0.2
50 +	47	21	26	..
Unknown - Inconnu	1 639	825	814	..
San Marino - Saint-Marin				
2003 (+C)				
Total	300	161	139	40.1
0 - 14	1	-	1	..
15 - 19	4	1	3	♦6.4
20 - 24	17	10	7	♦22.2
25 - 29	72	40	32	66.4
30 - 34	121	66	55	91.5
35 - 39	73	36	37	50.0
40 - 44	11	8	3	♦9.0
45 +	1	-	1	♦1.0
2004 (+C)				
Total	306	...	...	40.7
15 - 19	1	...	...	♦1.6
20 - 24	15	...	...	♦20.3
25 - 29	69	...	...	65.4
30 - 34	134	...	...	102.8
35 - 39	75	...	...	50.7
40 - 44	11	...	...	♦8.3
45 - 49	1	...	...	♦1.0
Serbia - Serbie[31]				
2006 (+C)				
Total	70 997	36 599	34 398	41.0
0 - 14	55	29	26	..
15 - 19	5 045	2 592	2 453	22.8

EUROPE

	Total	Male Masculin	Female Féminin	Rate Taux
Serbia - Serbie[31]				
2006 (+C)				
20 - 24	19 478	10 054	9 424	78.8
25 - 29	23 525	12 019	11 506	93.2
30 - 34	15 845	8 229	7 616	63.7
35 - 39	5 631	2 936	2 695	23.6
40 - 44	985	513	472	4.0
45 - 49	65	32	33	0.2
50 +	16	12	4	..
Unknown - Inconnu	352	183	169	..
Slovakia - Slovaquie				
2007 (C)				
Total	54 424	27 903	26 521	38.2
0 - 14	38	24	14	..
15 - 19	3 979	2 017	1 962	20.6
20 - 24	11 628	5 873	5 755	54.0
25 - 29	19 047	9 852	9 195	83.4
30 - 34	14 525	7 484	7 041	65.3
35 - 39	4 398	2 242	2 156	24.0
40 - 44	772	389	383	4.1
45 - 49	36	22	14	0.2
50 +	1	-	1	..
Slovenia - Slovénie				
2007 (C)				
Total	19 823	10 152	9 671	40.3
12 - 14	1	1	-	..
15 - 19	290	156	134	5.1
20 - 24	2 553	1 304	1 249	39.2
25 - 29	7 521	3 879	3 642	102.4
30 - 34	6 772	3 418	3 354	93.0
35 - 39	2 253	1 182	1 071	31.9
40 - 44	415	205	210	5.4
45 - 49	18	7	11	♦0.2
50 +	-	-	-	..
Unknown - Inconnu	-	-	-	..
Spain - Espagne				
2007 (C)				
Total	493 702	254 590	239 112	43.4
0 - 14	156	80	76	..
15 - 19	14 606	7 555	7 051	13.2
20 - 24	48 487	25 036	23 451	35.5
25 - 29	115 339	59 412	55 927	65.1
30 - 34	189 442	97 673	91 769	98.7
35 - 39	105 858	54 707	51 151	57.8
40 - 44	18 531	9 484	9 047	10.5
45 - 49	1 199	598	601	0.7
50 +	84	45	39	..
Sweden - Suède				
2007 (C)				
Total	107 421	55 259	52 162	52.2
12 - 14	6	2	4	..
15 - 19	1 803	913	890	5.9
20 - 24	13 287	6 858	6 429	49.6
25 - 29	30 321	15 517	14 804	112.4
30 - 34	38 611	19 958	18 653	131.7
35 - 39	19 232	9 851	9 381	62.2
40 - 44	3 978	2 073	1 905	12.3
45 - 49	170	81	89	0.6
50 +	13	6	7	..
Unknown - Inconnu	-	-	-	..
Switzerland - Suisse				
2007 (C)				
Total	74 494	38 184	36 310	40.5
12 - 14	3	1	2	..
15 - 19	950	481	469	4.3
20 - 24	8 020	4 103	3 917	36.4

10. Live-births by age of mother and sex of child and live-birth rates by age of mother: latest available year, 1998 - 2007
Naissances vivantes selon l'âge de la mère et le sexe de l'enfant et taux de natalité selon l'âge de la mère : dernière année disponible, 1998 - 2007 (continued - suite)

Continent, country or area, year, code and age of mother (in years) / Continent, pays ou zone, année, code et âge de la mère (en années)	Number - Nombre Total	Male Masculin	Female Féminin	Rate Taux
EUROPE				
Switzerland - Suisse				
2007 (C)				
25 - 29	20 151	10 289	9 862	84.4
30 - 34	26 701	13 731	12 970	105.0
35 - 39	15 521	8 017	7 504	53.2
40 - 44	2 993	1 494	1 499	9.4
45 - 49	145	61	84	0.5
50 +	10	7	...	..
The Former Yugoslav Republic of Macedonia - L'ex-République yougoslave de Macédoine				
2007 (C)				
Total	22 688	11 772	10 916	42.9
13 - 14	24	8	16	..
15 - 19	1 598	801	797	20.5
20 - 24	6 447	3 333	3 114	80.1
25 - 29	8 262	4 296	3 966	106.3
30 - 34	4 650	2 415	2 235	62.0
35 - 39	1 476	787	689	20.3
40 - 44	209	124	85	2.9
Unknown - Inconnu	6	2	4	..
Ukraine[32]				
2007 (C)				
Total	472 657	...	...	38.6
12 - 14	143	...	...	..
15 - 19	48 425	...	...	29.3
20 - 24	174 577	...	...	92.3
25 - 29	139 976	...	...	82.0
30 - 34	76 252	...	...	45.3
35 - 39	27 174	...	...	17.0
40 - 44	4 871	...	...	2.8
45 - 49	213	...	...	0.1
50 +	17	...	...	..
Unknown - Inconnu	1 009	...	...	..
United Kingdom of Great Britain and Northern Ireland - Royaume-Uni de Grande-Bretagne et d'Irlande du Nord[33]				
2002 (C)[34]				
Total	668 777	343 155	325 622	...
0 - 14	299	148	151	..
12 - 14	297	...	...	..
15 - 19	48 865	25 329	23 536	...
20 - 24	123 845	63 370	60 475	...
25 - 29	171 852	88 469	83 383	...
30 - 34	203 261	103 879	99 382	...
35 - 39	101 379	52 003	49 376	...
40 - 44	18 273	9 457	8 816	...
45 - 49	890	435	455	...
50 +	78	47	31	..
Unknown - Inconnu	35	18	17	..
2004 (C)				
Total	715 996	...	...	49.8
10 - 14	226	...	...	..
15 - 19	50 525	...	...	26.7
20 - 24	134 615	...	...	71.5
25 - 29	179 050	...	...	97.6
30 - 34	213 619	...	...	97.5
35 - 39	114 852	...	...	48.5
40 - 44	22 107	...	...	9.8
45 - 49	923	...	...	0.5
Unknown - Inconnu	26	...	...	..
OCEANIA - OCÉANIE				
American Samoa - Samoas américaines				
2006 (C)				
Total	1 442	...	...	...
0 - 14	1	...	...	...
15 - 19	110	...	...	...
20 - 24	342	...	...	...
25 - 29	410	...	...	...
30 - 34	303	...	...	...
35 - 39	218	...	...	...
40 - 44	55	...	...	...
45 - 49	3	...	...	...
Australia - Australie				
2007 (+C)				
Total	285 213	146 456	138 757	54.8
0 - 14	103	57	46	..
15 - 19	11 101	5 752	5 349	15.9
20 - 24	40 907	20 919	19 988	55.9
25 - 29	75 998	39 063	36 935	106.3
30 - 34	93 072	47 862	45 210	126.3
35 - 39	53 561	27 434	26 127	68.0
40 - 44	9 642	4 942	4 700	12.6
45 - 49	470	255	215	0.6
50 +	36	18	18	..
Unknown - Inconnu	323	154	169	..
Fiji - Fidji				
2004 (+C)				
Total	17 189	8 944	8 245	...
0 - 14	7	1	6	...
15 - 19	1 194	622	572	...
20 - 24	5 684	2 961	2 723	...
25 - 29	5 126	2 665	2 461	...
30 - 34	3 033	1 526	1 507	...
35 - 39	1 592	868	724	...
40 - 44	464	254	210	...
45 - 49	43	23	20	...
50 +	-	-	-	...
Unknown - Inconnu	46	24	22	...
Guam[35]				
2004 (C)				
Total	3 427	1 783	1 644	...
10 - 14	2	1	1	...
15 - 19	352	168	184	...
20 - 24	887	486	401	...
25 - 29	939	483	456	...
30 - 34	738	393	345	...
35 - 39	395	196	199	...
40 - 44	102	50	52	...
45 - 49	10	5	5	...
50 +	-	-	-	...
Unknown - Inconnu	2	1	1	...
Marshall Islands - Îles Marshall[36]				
2006 (+U)				
Total	1 576	...	...	...
0 - 14	2	...	...	...
15 - 19	268	...	...	...
20 - 24	551	...	...	...
25 - 29	431	...	...	...
30 - 34	211	...	...	...
35 - 39	91	...	...	...
40 - 44	19	...	...	...
45 - 49	3	...	...	...
Unknown - Inconnu	-	...	...	...

10. Live-births by age of mother and sex of child and live-birth rates by age of mother: latest available year, 1998 - 2007
Naissances vivantes selon l'âge de la mère et le sexe de l'enfant et taux de natalité selon l'âge de la mère : dernière année disponible, 1998 - 2007 (continued - suite)

Continent, country or area, year, code and age of mother (in years) / Continent, pays ou zone, année, code et âge de la mère (en années)	Number - Nombre			Rate Taux
	Total	Male Masculin	Female Féminin	
OCEANIA - OCÉANIE				
Micronesia (Federated States of) - Micronésie (États fédérés de)				
2003 (U)				
Total[37]	2 485	...	...	...
10 - 14	10	...	...	...
15 - 19	329	...	...	...
20 - 24	675	...	...	...
25 - 29	649	...	...	...
30 - 34	401	...	...	...
35 - 39	275	...	...	...
40 - 44	108	...	...	...
45 +	11	...	...	...
Unknown - Inconnu	27	...	...	...
New Caledonia - Nouvelle-Calédonie				
2007 (C)				
Total	4 093	...	...	64.2
0 - 19	213	...	...	20.0
20 - 24	902	...	...	97.1
25 - 29	1 150	...	...	131.5
30 - 34	1 072	...	...	110.7
35 - 39	611	...	...	63.6
40 - 44	138	...	...	16.2
45 - 49	7	...	...	♦1.0
50 +	-	...	...	..
New Zealand - Nouvelle-Zélande				
2007 (+C)				
Total	64 044	33 013	31 031	59.6
0 - 14	52	29	23	..
15 - 19	4 903	2 571	2 332	31.3
20 - 24	11 093	5 722	5 371	76.0
25 - 29	15 516	8 057	7 459	114.1
30 - 34	18 499	9 496	9 003	127.3
35 - 39	11 600	5 940	5 660	70.5
40 - 44	2 268	1 148	1 120	13.8
45 - 49	109	48	61	0.7
50 +	4	2	2	..
Northern Mariana Islands - Îles Mariannes septentrionales				
2002 (U)				
Total	1 289	...	...	...
0 - 19	110	...	...	...
20 - 24	298	...	...	...
25 - 29	347	...	...	...
30 - 34	317	...	...	...
35 - 39	182	...	...	...
40 +	35	...	...	...
Unknown - Inconnu	-	...	...	..
Palau - Palaos				
2003 (C)				
Total	312	163	149	...
15 - 19	21	13	8	...
20 - 24	71	34	37	...
25 - 29	81	40	41	...
30 - 34	63	35	28	...
OCEANIA - OCÉANIE				
Palau - Palaos				
2003 (C)				
35 - 39	56	29	27	...
40 - 44	16	11	5	...
45 - 49	4	1	3	...
2005 (C)				
Total	279	...	...	55.3
0 - 14	-	...	...	..
15 - 19	23	...	...	♦30.8
20 - 24	65	...	...	117.3
25 - 29	56	...	...	87.4
30 - 34	73	...	...	93.1
35 - 39	40	...	...	48.0
40 - 44	20	...	...	♦25.3
45 - 49	2	...	...	♦2.9
Tonga				
2003 (+C)				
Total	2 781	...	...	114.1
0 - 14	-	...	...	..
15 - 19	94	...	...	17.5
20 - 24	619	...	...	129.9
25 - 29	787	...	...	230.6
30 - 34	643	...	...	222.6
35 - 39	405	...	...	155.0
40 - 44	110	...	...	48.2
45 - 49	10	...	...	♦4.8
50 +	-	...	...	..
Unknown - Inconnu	113	...	...	..
Tuvalu				
2003 (U)				
Total[4]	239	...	...	...
15 - 19	17	...	...	...
20 - 24	76	...	...	...
25 - 29	53	...	...	...
30 - 34	35	...	...	...
35 - 39	37	...	...	...
40 - 44	20	...	...	...
45 - 49	-	...	...	...
Wallis and Futuna Islands - Îles Wallis et Futuna				
2006 (C)				
Total	220	...	...	...
15 - 19	7	...	...	...
20 - 24	45	...	...	...
25 - 29	74	...	...	...
30 - 34	58	...	...	...
35 - 39	20	...	...	...
40 - 44	10	...	...	...

FOOTNOTES - NOTES

♦ Rates based on 30 or fewer births. - Taux basés sur 30 naissances ou moins.

* Provisional. - Données provisoires.

'Code' indicates the source of data, as follows:
C - Civil registration, estimated over 90% complete
U - Civil registration, estimated less than 90% complete
| - Other source, estimated reliable
+ - Data tabulated by date of registration rather than occurrence.
... Information not available

Le 'Code' indique la source des données, comme suit:
C - Registres de l'état civil considérés complets à 90 p. 100 au moins.
U - Registres de l'état civil qui ne sont pas considérés complets à 90 p. 100 au moins.
| - Autre source, considérée fiable.
+ - Données exploitées selon la date de l'enregistrement et non la date de l'événement.
... Information non disponible.

[1] Data refer to the twelve months preceding the census in August. - Les données se rapportent aux douze mois précédant le recensement d'août.

[2] Excluding late registration (after 28/29 February of the following year). - En excluant les enregistrements tardifs (après les 28/29 février de l'année suivante).

[3] Data refer to registered events only. - Les données ne concernent que les événements enregistrés.

[4] Data as reported by national statistical authorities; they may differ from data presented in other tables. - Les données comme elles ont été déclarées par l'institut national de la statistique; elles peuvent être différentes de celles présentées dans d'autres tableaux.

[5] Including Canadian residents temporarily in the United States, but excluding United States residents temporarily in Canada. - Y compris les résidents canadiens se trouvant temporairement aux Etats-Unis, mais ne comprenant pas les résidents des Etats-Unis se trouvant temporairement au Canada.

[6] Data have not been adjusted for underenumeration. - Les données n'ont pas été ajustées pour compenser les lacunes du dénombrement.

[7] Data refer to resident mothers. - Données concernant les mères résidentes.

[8] Total includes unknown sex. - Le total comprend les personnes dont le sexe n'est pas connu.

[9] Data refer to resident population only. - Pour la population résidante seulement.

[10] Excluding nomadic Indian tribes. Excluding events registered late. - Non compris les tribus d'Indiens nomades. Non compris les enregistrements tardifs.

[11] Excluding live-born infants who died before their birth was registered. - Non compris les enfants nés vivants décédés avant l'enregistrement de leur naissance.

[12] Including unknown sex. - Y compris le sexe inconnu.

[13] Excluding Indian jungle population. - Non compris les Indiens de la jungle.

[14] Excluding infants born alive of less than 28 weeks' gestation, of less than 1 000 grams in weight and 35 centimeters in length, who die within seven days of birth. - Non compris les enfants nés vivants après moins de 28 semaines de gestations, pesant moins de 1 000 grammes, mesurant moins de 35 centimètres et décédés dans les sept jours qui ont suivi leur naissance.

[15] Data refer to the twelve months preceding the census in May. - Les données se rapportent aux douze mois précédant le recensement de mai.

[16] Data refer to government controlled areas. - Les données se rapportent aux zones contrôlées par le Gouvernement.

[17] As published by the United Nations Economic and Social Commission for Western Asia. - Publié par la Commission économique et sociale des Nations Unies pour l'Asie occidentale.

[18] Including data for East Jerusalem and Israeli residents in certain other territories under occupation by Israeli military forces since June 1967. - Y compris les données pour Jérusalem-Est et les résidents israéliens dans certains autres territoires occupés depuis 1967 par les forces armées israéliennes.

[19] Data refer to Japanese nationals in Japan only. - Les données se raportent aux nationaux japonais au Japon seulement.

[20] Data from Births and Deaths Notification System (Ministry of Health institutions and all other health care providers). - Les données proviennent du système de notification des naissances et des décès (établissements du Ministère de la santé et tous autres prestataires de soins de santé).

[21] Based on the results of the Pakistan Demographic Survey (PDS 2005). Excluding data for the Pakistan-held part of Jammu and Kashmir, the final status of which has not yet been determined. - Données extraites de l'enquête démographique effectuée par le Pakistan en 2005. Non compris les données concernant la partie du Jammu et Cachemire occupée par le Pakistan dont le statut définitif n'a pas été déterminé.

[22] Excluding alien armed forces, civilian aliens employed by armed forces, and foreign diplomatic personnel and their dependants. Including nationals outside the country. - Non compris les militaires étrangers, les civils étrangers employés par les forces armées ni le personnel diplomatique étranger et les membres de leur famille les accompagnant. Y compris les nationaux hors du pays.

[23] Figures for male and female do not add up to the total, since they do not include the category "Unknown". - La somme des chiffres indiqués pour les sexes masculin et féminin n'est pas égale au total parce qu'elle n'inclut pas la catégorie " inconnue ".

[24] Also included in Finland. - Comprise aussi dans Finlande.

[25] Excluding Faeroe Islands and Greenland shown separately, if available. - Non compris les Iles Féroé et le Gröenland, qui font l'objet de rubriques distinctes, si disponible.

[26] Including nationals temporarily outside the country. Including Aland Islands. - Y compris les nationaux se trouvant temporairement hors du pays. Y compris les Îles d'Åland.

[27] Including armed forces stationed outside the country. Excluding Overseas Departments, namely, French Guiana, Guadeloupe, Martinique and Reunion, shown separately, if available. - Y compris les militaires nationaux hors du pays. Non compris les départements d'outre mer, c'est-à-dire la Guyane française, la Guadeloupe, la Martinique et la Réunion, qui font l'objet de rubriques distinctes, si disponible.

[28] Including residents outside the country if listed in a Netherlands population register. - Y compris les résidents hors du pays, s'ils sont inscrits sur un registre de population néerlandais.

[29] Age classification based on year of birth of mother rather than the exact age of mother at birth of child. Excluding Svalbard and Jan Mayen Island shown separately, if available. - Le classement selon l'âge est basé sur l'année de naissance de la mère et non sur l'age exacte de la mère au moment de naissance de l'enfant. Non compris Svalbard et Jan Mayen qui font l'objet de rubriques distinctes, si disponible.

[30] Excluding infants born alive of less than 28 weeks' gestation, of less than 1 000 grams in weight and 35 centimeters in length, who die within seven days of birth. Excluding Transnistria and the municipality of Bender. - Non compris les enfants nés vivants après moins de 28 semaines de gestations, pesant moins de 1 000 grammes, mesurant moins de 35 centimètres et décédés dans les sept jours qui ont suivi leur naissance. Les données ne tiennent pas compte de l'information sur la Transnistria et la municipalité de Bender.

[31] Excluding data for Kosovo and Metohia. - Sans les données pour le Kosovo et Metohie.

[32] Data refer to births with weight 500g and more (if weight is unknown - with length 25 centimeters and more, or with gestation during 22 weeks or more). - Données concernant les nouveau-nés de 500 grammes ou plus (si le poids est inconnu – de 25 centimètres de long ou plus, ou après une grossesse de 22 semaines ou plus).

[33] Excluding Channel Islands (Guernsey and Jersey) and Isle of Man, shown separately, if available. Data tabulated by date of occurrence for England and Wales, and by date of registration for Northern Ireland and Scotland. - Non compris les îles Anglo-Normandes (Guernesey et Jersey) et l'île de Man, qui font l'objet de rubriques distinctes, si disponible. Données exploitées selon la date de l'événement pour l'Angleterre et le pays de Galles, et selon la date de l'enregistrement pour l'Irlande du Nord et l'Ecosse.

[34] Excluding births to non-resident mothers of Northern Ireland. - Les données ne tiennent pas compte des enfants nés de mères non résidentes en Irlande du Nord.

[35] Including United States military personnel, their dependants and contract employees. - Y compris les militaires des Etats-Unis, les membres de leur famille les accompagnant et les agents contractuels des Etats-Unis.

[36] Excluding United States military personnel, their dependants and contract employees. - Non compris les militaires des Etats-Unis, les membres de leur famille les accompagnant et les agents contractuels des Etats-Unis.

[37] The total births by year may not match due to late births report coming from the Outer Islands of Yap. - Le total des naissances annuelles peut ne pas correspondre, les îles extérieures de Yap ayant communiqué leurs données tardivement.

Table 11

Table 11 presents live births by age of father and live-birth rates by age of father for the latest available year between 1998 and 2007.

Description of variables: Age is defined as age at last birthday, that is, the difference between the date of birth and the date of the occurrence of the event, expressed in completed solar years. The age classification used in this table is the following: under 20 years, 5-year age groups through 60-64 years, 65 years and over, and age unknown. Deviating age groups are shown if so provided by a country or area.

Rate computation: Live-birth rates specific to age of father are the annual number of births to a man in each age group per 1 000 male population in the same age group. These rates are calculated by the Statistics Division of the United Nations.

Since relatively few births occur to men below 15 or above 59 years of age, birth rates for men under 20 years of age and for those 55 years of age or over are computed on the male population aged 15-19 and 55-59, respectively. Similarly, the rate for men of "All ages" is based on all live births irrespective of age of father, and is computed on the male population aged 15-59 years.

Births to fathers of unknown age are distributed proportionately across the age groups, by the Statistics Division of the United Nations, in accordance with the distribution of births by age of father prior to the calculation of the rates.

The population used in computing the rates is the estimated or enumerated distribution of males by age. First priority is given to an estimate and second priority to census returns of the year to which the births refer.

Rates presented in this table are limited to those for countries or areas having at least a total of 100 live births in a given year.

Reliability of data: Data from civil registers of live births which are reported as incomplete (less than 90 per cent completeness) or of unknown completeness are considered unreliable and are set in *italics* rather than in roman type. Rates are not computed if the data on live births from civil registers are reported as incomplete (less than 90 per cent completeness) or of unknown completeness. Table 9 and the technical notes for that table provide more detailed information on the completeness of live-birth registration. For more information about the quality of vital statistics data in general, see section 4.2 of the Technical Notes.

Limitations: Statistics on live births by age of father are subject to the same qualifications as have been set forth for vital statistics in general and birth statistics in particular as discussed in section 4 of the Technical Notes. These include differences in the completeness of registration, the method used to determine age of father and the quality of the reported information relating to age of father.

The reliability of the data described above, is an important factor in considering the limitations. In addition, some live births are tabulated by date of registration and not by date of occurrence; these are indicated in the table by a plus sign "+". Whenever the lag between the date of occurrence and date of registration is prolonged and, therefore, a large proportion of the live-birth registrations are delayed, birth statistics for any given year may be seriously affected. For example, the age of the father will almost always refer to the date of registration rather than to the date of birth of the child. Hence, in those countries or areas where registration of births is delayed, possibly for years, statistics on births by age of father should be used with caution.

Another factor which limits international comparability is the practice of some countries or areas of not including in live-birth statistics infants who were born alive but died before the registration of the birth or within the first 24 hours of life, thus underestimating the total number of live births. Statistics of this type are footnoted.

Because these statistics are classified according to age, they are subject to the limitations with respect to accuracy of age reporting similar to those already discussed in connection with section 3.1.3 of the Technical Notes. The factors influencing the accuracy of reporting may be somewhat dissimilar in vital statistics (because of the differences in the method of taking a census and registering a birth) but, in general, the same errors can be observed. The absence of frequencies in the unknown age group does not necessarily indicate completely accurate reporting and tabulation of the age item. It is often an indication that the unknowns have been eliminated by assigning ages to them before tabulation, or by proportionate distribution after tabulation.

On the other hand, large frequencies in the unknown age category may indicate that a large proportion of the births are born outside of wedlock, the records for which tend to be incomplete so far as characteristics of the parents are concerned.

Another limitation of age reporting may result from calculating age of father at birth of child (or at time of registration) from year of birth rather than from day, month and year of birth. Information on this factor is given in footnotes when known.

In few countries, data by age refer to deliveries rather than to live births causing under-enumeration in the event of a multiple birth. This practice leads to lack of strict comparability, both among countries or areas relying on this practice and between data shown in this table and table 9.

Rates shown in this table are subject to the same limitations that affect the corresponding statistics on live births. In cases of rates based on births tabulated by date of registration and not by date of occurrence; the effect of including delayed registration on the distribution of births by age of father may be noted in the age-specific fertility rates for men at older ages. In some cases, high age-specific rates for men aged 55 years and over may reflect age of father at registration of birth and not fertility at these older ages.

Earlier data: Live births and live-birth rates by age of father have been shown in previous issues of the Yearbook as follows.

Issue	Years Covered
Special Edition on Natality, CD, 1999	1990 – 1998
38th issue, 1986	1977 – 1985
33rd issue, 1981	1972 – 1980
27th issue, 1975	1966 – 1974
21st issue, 1969	1963 – 1968
17th issue, 1965	1955 – 1964
11th issue, 1959	1949 – 1958
6th issue, 1954	1936 – 1953
2nd issue, 1949/50	1942 – 1949

Tableau 11

Le tableau 11 présente les données les plus récentes pour la période 1998 -2007 dont on dispose sur les naissances vivantes selon l'âge du père et les taux des naissances vivantes selon l'âge du père.

Description des variables : l'âge désigne l'âge au dernier anniversaire, c'est-à-dire la différence entre la date de naissance et la date de l'événement exprimée en années solaires révolues. La classification par âge utilisée dans ce tableau comprend les catégories suivantes : moins de 20 ans, groupes quinquennaux jusqu'à 60-64 ans, 65 ans et plus, et âge inconnu. Des groupes d'âge différents sont parfois utilisés lorsque les pays ou territoires ont fourni les données dans une autre classification.

Les taux de natalité selon l'âge du père représentent le nombre annuel de naissances vivantes intervenues dans un groupe d'âge donné pour 1 000 hommes du groupe d'âge. Ces taux ont été calculés par la Division de statistique de l'ONU.

Étant donné que le nombre de naissances parmi les hommes de moins de 15 ans ou de plus de 59 ans est relativement peu élevé, les taux de natalité parmi les hommes âgées de moins de 20 ans et celles de 55 ans et plus ont été calculés sur la base des populations masculines âgées de 15 à 19 ans et de 55 à 59 ans, respectivement. De même, le taux pour les hommes de « tous âges » est fondé sur la totalité des naissances vivantes, indépendamment de l'âge du père et ce chiffre est rapporté à l'effectif de la population masculine âgée de 15 à 59 ans.

Les naissances pour lesquelles l'âge du père était inconnu ont été réparties par la Division de statistique de l'ONU, avant le calcul des taux, suivant les proportions observées pour celles où l'âge du père était connu.

Les chiffres de population utilisés pour le calcul des taux proviennent de dénombrements ou de répartitions estimatives de la population masculine selon l'âge. On a utilisé de préférence les estimations de la population; à défaut, on s'est contenté des données censitaires se rapportant à l'année des naissances.

Les taux présentés dans ce tableau ne concernent que les pays ou zones où l'on a enregistré un total d'au moins 100 naissances vivantes dans une année donnée.

Fiabilité des données : les données sur les naissances vivantes provenant des registres de l'état civil qui sont déclarées incomplètes (degré de complétude inférieur à 90 p. 100) ou dont le degré de complétude n'est pas connu sont jugées douteuses et apparaissent en italique et non en caractères romains. On a choisi de ne pas faire figurer dans le tableau 11 des taux calculés à partir de données sur les naissances vivantes issues de registres de l'état civil qui sont déclarées incomplètes (degré de complétude inférieur à 90 p. 100) ou dont le degré de complétude n'est pas connu. Le tableau 9 et les notes techniques qui s'y rapportent présentent des renseignements plus détaillés sur le degré de complétude de l'enregistrement des naissances vivantes. Pour plus de précisions sur la qualité des statistiques de l'état civil en général, voir la section 4.2 des Notes techniques.

Insuffisance des données : les statistiques relatives aux naissances vivantes selon l'âge du père appellent toutes les réserves qui ont été formulées à propos des statistiques de l'état civil en général et des statistiques de naissances en particulier (voir la section 4 des Notes techniques). Ceci inclut les différences de complétude d'enregistrement des faits d'état civil, de méthode pour déterminer l'âge du père et de qualité d'information concernant l'âge du père.

La fiabilité des données, au sujet de laquelle des indications ont été données plus haut, est un facteur important. Il faut également tenir compte du fait que, dans certains cas, les données relatives aux naissances vivantes sont exploitées selon la date de l'enregistrement et non la date de l'événement ; ces cas ont été signalés dans le tableau par le signe '+'. Chaque fois que le décalage entre l'événement et son enregistrement est grand et qu'une forte proportion des naissances vivantes fait l'objet d'un enregistrement tardif, les statistiques des naissances vivantes pour une année donnée peuvent être considérablement faussées. Par exemple, l'âge du père représente presque toujours son âge à la date de l'enregistrement et non à la date de la naissance de l'enfant. Ainsi, dans les pays ou zones où l'enregistrement des naissances est tardif, le retard atteignant parfois plusieurs années, il faut utiliser avec prudence les statistiques concernant les naissances selon l'âge du père.

361

Un autre facteur qui nuit à la comparabilité internationale est la pratique de certains pays ou zones qui consiste à ne pas inclure dans les statistiques des naissances vivantes les enfants nés vivants mais décédés avant l'enregistrement de leur naissance ou dans les 24 heures qui ont suivi la naissance, pratique qui conduit à sous-estimer le nombre total de naissances vivantes. Quand pareil facteur a joué, cela a été signalé en note à la fin du tableau.

Étant donné que les statistiques du tableau 10 sont classées selon l'âge, elles appellent les mêmes réserves concernant l'exactitude des déclarations d'âge que celles formulées à la section 3.1.3 des Notes techniques. Dans le cas des statistiques de l'état civil, les facteurs qui interviennent à cet égard sont parfois différents, étant donné que le recensement de la population et l'enregistrement des naissances se font par des méthodes différentes, mais, d'une manière générale, les erreurs observées seront les mêmes. Si aucun nombre ne figure dans la rangée réservée aux âges inconnus, cela ne signifie pas nécessairement que les déclarations d'âge et l'exploitation des données par âge ont été tout à fait exactes. C'est souvent une indication que l'on a attribué un âge aux personnes d'âge inconnu avant l'exploitation des données ou qu'elles ont été réparties proportionnellement entre les différents groupes après cette opération.

À l'inverse, lorsque le nombre des personnes d'âge inconnu est important, cela peut signifier que la proportion de naissances parmi les mères célibataires est élevée, étant donné qu'en pareil cas l'acte de naissance ne contient pas tous les renseignements concernant les parents.

Les déclarations par âge peuvent comporter des distorsions, du fait que l'âge du père au moment de la naissance d'un enfant (ou de la déclaration de naissance) est donné par année de naissance et non par date exacte (jour, mois et année).

Dans quelques pays, la classification par âges se réfère aux accouchements, et non aux naissances vivantes, ce qui conduit à un sous-dénombrement en cas de naissances gémellaires. Cette pratique nuit à la comparabilité des données, à la fois entre pays ou zones qui recourent à cette méthode et entre les données présentées dans le tableau 11 et celles du tableau 9.

Les taux présentés dans ce tableau, sont sujets aux mêmes limitations qui affectent les statistiques correspondantes de naissances vivantes. Dans le cas des taux basés sur des naissances par date d'enregistrement et non par date d'occurrence, l'effet peut être visible sur les taux de fécondité par âge des hommes aux âges plus élevés. Dans certains cas, les taux de fécondité des hommes de plus de 55 ans peuvent refléter l'âge du père à l'enregistrement plus que la fécondité à ces âges.

Données publiées antérieurement : Les données sur les naissances vivantes selon l'âge du père et les taux des naissances vivantes selon l'âge du père ont été publié antérieurement dans l'*Annuaire démographique* comme suit :

Éditions	Années considérées
Édition spéciale sur les statistiques de la natalité (CD-ROM), 1999	1990 – 1998
38e édition, 1986	1977 – 1985
33e édition, 1981	1972 – 1980
27e édition, 1975	1966 – 1974
21e édition, 1969	1963 – 1968
17e édition, 1965	1955 – 1964
11e édition, 1959	1949 – 1958
6e édition, 1954	1936 – 1953
2e édition, 1949/50	1942 – 1949

11. Live-births and live-birth rates by age of father: latest available year, 1998 - 2007
Naissances vivantes et taux de natalité selon l'âge du père : dernière année disponible, 1998 - 2007

Continent, country or area, year, code and age of father (in years) / Continent, pays ou zone, année, code et âge du père (en années)	Number - Nombre	Rate Taux
AFRICA - AFRIQUE		
Egypt - Égypte		
2007 (C)		
Total.	1 949 569	...
0 - 19.	3 926	...
20 - 24	142 740	...
25 - 29	358 052	...
30 - 34	401 283	...
35 - 39	273 238	...
40 - 44	138 236	...
45 - 49	56 181	...
50 - 54	21 178	...
55 - 59	9 281	...
60 +	7 179	...
Unknown - Inconnu	537 275	..
Mauritius - Maurice		
2007 (C)		
Total.	16 894	40.3
0 - 19.	232	4.6
20 - 24	1 666	37.1
25 - 29	4 480	83.8
30 - 34	4 683	102.1
35 - 39	2 827	64.4
40 - 44	1 466	30.3
45 - 49	472	10.9
50 - 54	105	2.8
55 - 59	41	1.4
60 - 64	8	..
65 +	4	..
Unknown - Inconnu	910	..
Réunion[1]		
2007 (C)		
Total.	14 808	61.9
0 - 19.	352	10.0
20 - 24	2 409	88.2
25 - 29	3 283	139.4
30 - 34	3 693	141.6
35 - 39	2 860	96.2
40 - 44	1 488	46.6
45 - 49	491	19.2
50 - 54	151	6.8
55 - 59	53	3.0
60 - 64	28	..
AMERICA, NORTH - AMÉRIQUE DU NORD		
Bahamas[2]		
2007 (U)		
Total.	5 182	...
0 - 19.	108	...
20 - 24	696	...
25 - 29	999	...
30 - 34	1 069	...
35 - 39	879	...
40 - 44	446	...
45 - 49	175	...
50 - 54	60	...
55 - 59	24	...
60 - 64	11	...
65 +	10	...
Unknown - Inconnu	705	..
Canada[3]		
2005 (C)		
Total.	342 176	32.6
0 - 19.	3 993	3.9
20 - 24	27 281	25.3
25 - 29	76 137	72.8

Continent, country or area, year, code and age of father (in years) / Continent, pays ou zone, année, code et âge du père (en années)	Number - Nombre	Rate Taux
AMERICA, NORTH - AMÉRIQUE DU NORD		
Canada[3]		
2005 (C)		
30 - 34	106 752	101.0
35 - 39	69 582	62.1
40 - 44	28 113	21.6
45 - 49	7 745	6.3
50 - 54	1 781	1.7
55 - 59	577	0.6
60 - 64	146	..
65 +	46	..
Unknown - Inconnu	20 023	..
Costa Rica		
2007 (C)		
Total.	73 144	53.0
0 - 19.	2 044	12.8
20 - 24	11 233	75.8
25 - 29	13 171	120.4
30 - 34	10 715	...
35 - 39	6 850	...
40 - 44	3 527	...
45 - 49	1 464	...
50 - 54	607	...
55 - 59	223	...
60 - 64	81	..
65 +	43	..
Unknown - Inconnu	23 186	..
Cuba		
2007 (C)		
Total.	112 472	30.3
0 - 19.	2 900	7.6
20 - 24	18 237	51.5
25 - 29	22 256	74.4
30 - 34	24 519	60.3
35 - 39	17 691	38.2
40 - 44	8 792	18.5
45 - 49	2 585	7.8
50 - 54	864	3.1
55 - 59	308	1.2
60 - 64	123	..
65 +	86	..
Unknown - Inconnu	14 111	..
Dominican Republic - République dominicaine		
2007 (U)		
Total.	106 405	...
0 - 19.	1 815	...
20 - 24	16 523	...
25 - 29	25 647	...
30 - 34	21 857	...
35 - 39	13 485	...
40 - 44	7 167	...
45 - 49	3 269	...
50 - 54	1 597	...
55 - 59	739	...
60 - 64	282	...
65 +	181	...
Unknown - Inconnu	13 843	...
El Salvador		
2007 (C)		
Total.	106 471	71.6
12 - 14.	1 067	...
15 - 19.	22 272	74.8
20 - 24	30 060	132.2
25 - 29	25 793	124.9
30 - 34	16 619	93.4
35 - 39	7 903	50.6
40 - 44	2 312	17.5
45 - 49	173	1.6

Continent, country or area, year, code and age of father (in years) Continent, pays ou zone, année, code et âge du père (en années)	Number - Nombre	Rate Taux	Continent, country or area, year, code and age of father (in years) Continent, pays ou zone, année, code et âge du père (en années)	Number - Nombre	Rate Taux
AMERICA, NORTH - AMÉRIQUE DU NORD			**AMERICA, NORTH - AMÉRIQUE DU NORD**		
El Salvador			Martinique[1]		
2007 (C)			2007 (C)		
50 +	22	♦0.1	30 - 34	1 173	111.7
Unknown - Inconnu	250	..	35 - 39	1 293	95.6
Greenland - Groenland			40 - 44	702	46.1
2006 (C)			45 - 49	235	16.2
Total	842	42.0	50 - 54	42	3.5
0 - 19	25	13.3	55 - 59	16	♦1.5
20 - 24	112	67.8	60 +	3	..
25 - 29	152	101.2	Mexico - Mexique[5]		
30 - 34	144	96.1	2005 (+U)		
35 - 39	140	67.1	Total	2 141 083	...
40 - 44	69	28.0	0 - 19	119 886	...
45 - 49	26	12.2	20 - 24	465 158	...
50 - 54	7	♦4.3	25 - 29	531 717	...
55 - 59	1	♦0.8	30 - 34	432 785	...
60 +	1	..	35 - 39	233 644	...
Unknown - Inconnu	165	..	40 - 44	104 465	...
Guadeloupe[1]			45 - 49	42 335	...
2003 (C)			50 +	29 404	...
Total	7 047	55.0	Unknown - Inconnu	181 689	..
0 - 19	112	6.4	Panama		
20 - 24	809	55.5	2007 (C)		
25 - 29	1 303	103.0	Total	67 364	...
30 - 34	1 950	125.6	0 - 19	2 804	...
35 - 39	1 698	102.0	20 - 24	13 326	...
40 - 44	877	53.1	25 - 29	15 367	...
45 - 49	211	15.9	30 - 34	13 275	...
50 - 54	59	5.1	35 - 39	8 852	...
55 - 59	20	♦2.1	40 - 44	4 426	...
60 +	8	..	45 - 49	2 028	...
Guatemala			50 - 54	854	...
2006 (C)			55 - 59	369	...
Total	368 399	...	60 +	302	..
0 - 19	17 875	...	Unknown - Inconnu	5 761	..
20 - 24	77 239	...	Puerto Rico - Porto Rico		
25 - 29	84 377	...	2006 (C)		
30 - 34	59 956	...	Total	48 744	42.4
35 - 39	38 741	...	0 - 19	3 498	24.1
40 - 44	23 591	...	20 - 24	12 504	88.9
45 - 49	11 709	...	25 - 29	13 355	99.1
50 - 54	4 785	...	30 - 34	9 325	73.7
55 - 59	2 150	...	35 - 39	5 008	41.2
60 - 64	941	..	40 - 44	2 085	17.3
65 +	862	..	45 - 49	777	6.8
Unknown - Inconnu	46 173	..	50 - 54	317	3.0
Jamaica - Jamaïque[4]			55 - 59	131	1.3
2006 (C)			60 - 64	51	..
Total	42 399	...	65 +	23	..
0 - 19	496	...	Unknown - Inconnu	1 670	..
20 - 24	3 756	...	Trinidad and Tobago - Trinité-et-Tobago		
25 - 29	5 341	...	2004 (C)		
30 - 34	5 069	...	Total	17 235	...
35 - 39	3 635	...	0 - 19	402	...
40 - 44	2 166	...	20 - 24	3 259	...
45 - 49	986	...	25 - 29	4 442	...
50 - 54	373	...	30 - 34	3 927	...
55 - 59	131	...	35 - 39	2 616	...
60 - 64	53	...	40 - 44	1 521	...
65 +	37	...	45 - 49	587	...
Unknown - Inconnu	20 356	..	50 - 54	207	...
Martinique[1]			55 - 59	84	...
2007 (C)			60 +	43	..
Total	5 317	47.3	Unknown - Inconnu	147	..
0 - 19	98	6.2	United States of America - États-Unis d'Amérique		
20 - 24	710	60.7	2006 (C)		
25 - 29	1 043	119.9	Total	4 265 555	...
			0 - 19	129 959	...

Continent, country or area, year, code and age of father (in years) Continent, pays ou zone, année, code et âge du père (en années)	Number - Nombre	Rate Taux
AMERICA, NORTH - AMÉRIQUE DU NORD		
United States of America - États-Unis d'Amérique		
2006 (C)		
20 - 24	625 254	...
25 - 29	958 146	...
30 - 34	947 453	...
35 - 39	623 458	...
40 + ...	364 393	...
Unknown - Inconnu	616 892	..
AMERICA, SOUTH - AMÉRIQUE DU SUD		
Chile - Chili		
2006 (C)		
Total..	231 383	44.1
0 - 19...	16 088	21.6
20 - 24	46 911	68.5
25 - 29	51 549	85.1
30 - 34	53 116	86.4
35 - 39	35 339	57.1
40 - 44	18 071	28.9
45 - 49	6 810	12.3
50 + ...	3 499	4.4
Unknown - Inconnu	-	..
Colombia - Colombie		
2007* (U)		
Total..	685 859	...
0 - 19...	43 157	...
20 - 24	161 249	...
25 - 29	173 790	...
30 - 34	124 209	...
35 - 39	82 320	...
40 - 44	44 157	...
45 - 49	18 815	...
50 - 54	7 995	...
55 - 59	2 744	...
60 - 64	1 208	..
65 + ...	830	..
Unknown - Inconnu	25 385	..
French Guiana - Guyane française[1]		
2007 (C)		
Total..	6 386	104.6
0 - 19...	323	32.6
20 - 24	1 263	164.2
25 - 29	1 401	203.5
30 - 34	1 334	175.5
35 - 39	1 043	138.4
40 - 44	622	90.0
45 - 49	230	38.8
50 - 54	94	19.2
55 - 59	59	16.1
60 - 64	17	..
65 + ...	-	..
Uruguay		
2004 (C)		
Total..	50 052	52.8
0 - 19...	805	10.3
20 - 24	4 203	57.8
25 - 29	7 179	100.3
30 - 34	7 629	118.5
35 - 39	5 142	87.4
40 - 44	2 622	43.3
45 - 49	978	17.9
50 - 54	420	8.5
55 - 59	117	2.8
60 - 64	43	..

Continent, country or area, year, code and age of father (in years) Continent, pays ou zone, année, code et âge du père (en années)	Number - Nombre	Rate Taux
AMERICA, SOUTH - AMÉRIQUE DU SUD		
Uruguay		
2004 (C)		
65 + ...	32	..
Unknown - Inconnu	20 882	..
Venezuela (Bolivarian Republic of) - Venezuela (République bolivarienne du)[6]		
1998 (C)		
Total..	501 808	73.1
0 - 19...	26 613	26.3
20 - 24	94 692	105.5
25 - 29	106 336	134.3
30 - 34	84 801	113.6
35 - 39	53 635	81.9
40 - 44	28 593	52.8
45 - 49	13 263	29.0
50 + ...	9 631	15.7
Unknown - Inconnu	84 244	..
ASIA - ASIE		
Armenia - Arménie[7]		
2000 (C)		
Total..	29 287	25.2
0 - 19...	3 774	20.0
20 - 24	13 933	84.7
25 - 29	6 776	46.5
30 - 34	2 894	21.3
35 - 39	1 503	10.1
40 - 44	380	2.6
45 - 49	16	♦0.1
55 - 59	11	♦0.2
Azerbaijan - Azerbaïdjan[8]		
2004 (+C)		
Total..	104 940	39.9
0 - 19...	265	0.6
20 - 24	14 809	38.2
25 - 29	38 134	120.9
30 - 34	29 898	101.9
35 - 39	15 057	47.7
40 - 44	5 179	15.6
45 - 49	1 091	4.2
50 - 54	268	1.6
55 + ...	239	2.5
Bahrain - Bahreïn		
2007 (C)		
Total..	16 062	32.1
0 - 14...	-	..
15 - 19	19	♦0.5
20 - 24	930	16.1
25 - 29	3 652	39.9
30 - 34	4 486	52.6
35 - 39	3 447	46.4
40 - 44	2 200	37.8
45 - 49	911	19.5
50 - 54	255	7.8
55 - 59	89	5.0
60 - 64	35	..
65 + ...	30	..
Unknown - Inconnu	8	..
Brunei Darussalam - Brunéi Darussalam		
2002 (+C)		
Total..	7 464	...
0 - 19...	15	...
20 - 24	651	...
25 - 29	1 714	...
30 - 34	1 980	...

Continent, country or area, year, code and age of father (in years) Continent, pays ou zone, année, code et âge du père (en années)	Number - Nombre	Rate Taux	Continent, country or area, year, code and age of father (in years) Continent, pays ou zone, année, code et âge du père (en années)	Number - Nombre	Rate Taux
ASIA - ASIE			**ASIA - ASIE**		
Brunei Darussalam - Brunéi Darussalam			**Japan - Japon**[11]		
2002 (+C)			2007 (C)		
35 - 39	1 402	...	Total	1 067 648	28.3
40 - 44	785	...	0 - 19	4 899	1.5
45 - 49	257	...	20 - 24	81 894	21.9
50 - 54	55	...	25 - 29	255 152	63.9
55 +	33	...	30 - 34	387 735	81.1
Unknown - Inconnu	572	..	35 - 39	237 231	50.1
China, Hong Kong SAR - Chine, Hong Kong RAS			40 - 44	75 279	18.4
2005 (C)			45 - 49	18 360	4.8
Total	57 098	25.3	50 - 54	4 767	1.2
0 - 19	172	0.8	55 - 59	1 814	0.3
20 - 24	2 731	12.3	60 - 64	415	..
25 - 29	9 656	44.8	65 +	100	..
30 - 34	17 371	73.5	Unknown - Inconnu	2	..
35 - 39	13 872	55.3	**Kazakhstan**[12]		
40 - 44	7 458	24.0	2006 (C)		
45 - 49	2 853	9.1	Total	301 756	61.4
50 - 54	1 049	4.2	0 - 19	2 897	4.2
55 - 59	395	2.0	20 - 24	46 772	73.1
60 - 64	132	..	25 - 29	82 596	152.2
65 +	106	...	30 - 34	66 344	134.3
Unknown - Inconnu	1 303	..	35 - 39	41 180	90.8
China, Macao SAR - Chine, Macao RAS			40 - 44	17 594	38.6
2007 (C)			45 - 49	4 336	10.0
Total	4 537	23.2	50 - 54	873	2.7
0 - 19	24	♦1.0	55 - 59	296	1.2
20 - 24	415	17.5	60 - 64	74	..
25 - 29	831	44.1	65 +	74	..
30 - 34	1 262	63.0	Unknown - Inconnu	38 720	..
35 - 39	1 021	49.2	**Kyrgyzstan - Kirghizstan**		
40 - 44	539	23.5	2007 (C)		
45 - 49	246	9.4	Total	123 251	75.9
50 - 54	89	3.9	0 - 19	660	2.6
55 - 59	35	2.4	20 - 24	17 075	73.7
60 - 64	5	..	25 - 29	36 043	188.7
65 +	13	..	30 - 34	27 273	162.9
Unknown - Inconnu	57	..	35 - 39	16 637	109.4
Cyprus - Chypre[9]			40 - 44	7 226	52.6
2006 (C)			45 - 49	2 072	16.2
Total	8 731	35.1	50 - 54	509	5.6
0 - 19	19	♦0.7	55 - 59	195	3.1
20 - 24	565	17.9	60 - 64	57	..
25 - 29	2 290	71.4	65 +	90	..
30 - 34	2 738	97.4	Unknown - Inconnu	15 414	..
35 - 39	1 862	72.1	**Philippines**		
40 - 44	769	28.3	2005 (C)		
45 - 49	269	9.8	Total	1 688 918	67.1
50 +	113	2.5	0 - 19	30 260	7.3
Unknown - Inconnu	106	..	20 - 24	289 106	77.4
Israel - Israël[10]			25 - 29	447 676	134.1
2007 (C)			30 - 34	367 207	124.6
Total	151 679	72.8	35 - 39	245 765	95.0
0 - 19	336	1.2	40 - 44	128 007	57.5
20 - 24	12 051	43.8	45 - 49	51 542	27.4
25 - 29	34 926	134.8	50 - 54	15 967	10.4
30 - 34	47 915	188.2	55 - 59	5 658	4.7
35 - 39	31 019	143.4	60 - 64	1 950	..
40 - 44	12 423	67.5	65 +	1 553	..
45 - 49	3 765	21.5	Unknown - Inconnu	104 227	..
50 - 54	910	5.4	**Qatar**		
55 - 59	277	1.7	2007 (C)		
60 - 64	104	..	Total	15 681	19.4
65 +	69	..	0 - 19	22	♦0.7
Unknown - Inconnu	7 884	..	20 - 24	817	6.3
			25 - 29	3 123	18.0
			30 - 34	4 377	31.1
			35 - 39	3 647	30.5

Continent, country or area, year, code and age of father (in years) / Continent, pays ou zone, année, code et âge du père (en années)	Number - Nombre	Rate Taux
ASIA - ASIE		
Qatar		
2007 (C)		
40 - 44	2 159	25.0
45 - 49	988	15.7
50 +	538	8.5
Unknown - Inconnu	10	..
Republic of Korea - République de Corée[13]		
2006 (C)		
Total	451 514	...
0 - 19	600	...
20 - 24	8 578	...
25 - 29	84 649	...
30 - 34	217 157	...
35 - 39	109 425	...
40 - 44	22 101	...
45 - 49	4 152	...
50 - 54	666	...
55 - 59	128	...
60 - 64	19	..
65 +	3	..
Unknown - Inconnu	4 036	..
Singapore - Singapour		
2007 (C)		
Total	39 490	32.2
0 - 19	182	1.4
20 - 24	1 256	11.5
25 - 29	5 961	49.6
30 - 34	14 278	102.4
35 - 39	11 035	76.0
40 - 44	4 403	27.7
45 - 49	1 329	8.5
50 - 54	343	2.5
55 - 59	90	0.8
60 - 64	22	..
65 +	5	..
Unknown - Inconnu	586	..
Tajikistan - Tadjikistan[12]		
1999 (C)		
Total	114 015	...
0 - 19	1 264	...
20 - 24	22 170	...
25 - 29	32 740	...
30 - 34	25 021	...
35 - 39	15 777	...
40 - 44	6 181	...
45 - 49	1 957	...
50 - 54	588	...
55 - 59	333	...
60 - 64	255	...
65 +	203	..
Unknown - Inconnu	7 526	..
EUROPE		
Åland Islands - Îles d'Åland[14]		
2006 (C)		
Total	120	15.0
0 - 19	-	-
20 - 24	4	♦6.0
25 - 29	13	♦17.1
30 - 34	38	43.4
35 - 39	36	38.7
40 - 44	23	♦23.0
45 - 49	2	♦2.2
50 - 54	3	♦3.1
55 - 59	1	♦1.0

Continent, country or area, year, code and age of father (in years) / Continent, pays ou zone, année, code et âge du père (en années)	Number - Nombre	Rate Taux
EUROPE		
Åland Islands - Îles d'Åland[14]		
2006 (C)		
60 - 64	-	..
65 +	-	..
Unknown - Inconnu	-	..
Albania - Albanie		
2004 (C)		
Total	43 022	45.5
0 - 19	293	1.9
20 - 24	2 812	22.3
25 - 29	11 631	113.3
30 - 34	14 648	148.4
35 - 39	8 622	85.5
40 - 44	3 353	30.6
45 - 49	835	8.5
50 - 54	180	2.3
55 - 59	68	1.1
60 - 64	36	..
Unknown - Inconnu	544	..
Austria - Autriche[7]		
2007 (C)		
Total	47 122	18.1
0 - 19	140	0.5
20 - 24	2 903	11.0
25 - 29	9 826	36.3
30 - 34	14 652	53.3
35 - 39	11 948	35.8
40 - 44	5 411	14.9
45 - 49	1 619	4.9
50 - 54	442	1.6
55 - 59	126	0.5
60 - 64	44	..
65 +	11	..
Belarus - Bélarus[8]		
2007 (C)		
Total	81 701	25.6
0 - 19	999	2.7
20 - 24	19 881	46.6
25 - 29	29 582	77.7
30 - 34	19 060	55.6
35 - 39	8 532	25.9
40 - 44	2 720	7.7
45 - 49	703	1.8
50 - 54	165	0.5
55 +	59	0.2
Bulgaria - Bulgarie		
2007 (C)		
Total	75 349	31.1
0 - 19	1 005	5.0
20 - 24	7 739	35.1
25 - 29	18 599	79.7
30 - 34	19 682	82.1
35 - 39	9 663	42.7
40 - 44	3 032	14.7
45 - 49	961	4.5
50 - 54	312	1.5
55 - 59	83	0.4
60 - 64	28	..
65 +	9	..
Unknown - Inconnu	14 236	..
Croatia - Croatie		
2007 (C)		
Total	41 910	30.3
0 - 19	255	1.9
20 - 24	3 909	26.4
25 - 29	11 626	74.8
30 - 34	13 155	89.0

11. Live-births and live-birth rates by age of father: latest available year, 1998 - 2007
Naissances vivantes et taux de natalité selon l'âge du père : dernière année disponible, 1998 - 2007 (continued - suite)

Continent, country or area, year, code and age of father (in years) — Continent, pays ou zone, année, code et âge du père (en années)	Number - Nombre	Rate Taux
EUROPE		
Croatia - Croatie		
2007 (C)		
35 - 39	7 637	53.1
40 - 44	2 976	19.3
45 - 49	881	5.5
50 - 54	216	1.3
55 - 59	61	0.4
60 - 64	11	..
65 + ...	5	..
Unknown - Inconnu	1 178	..
Czech Republic - République tchèque		
2007 (C)		
Total	114 632	33.7
0 - 19	553	1.8
20 - 24	5 909	18.1
25 - 29	27 197	72.5
30 - 34	41 821	96.8
35 - 39	18 042	52.3
40 - 44	6 750	20.5
45 - 49	2 132	7.3
50 - 54	784	2.3
55 - 59	276	0.8
60 - 64	72	..
65 + ...	21	..
Unknown - Inconnu	11 075	..
Denmark - Danemark[15]		
2007 (C)		
Total	64 082	39.2
0 - 19	30	0.3
20 - 24	760	8.5
25 - 29	6 745	71.2
30 - 34	15 001	137.1
35 - 39	9 949	86.0
40 - 44	3 871	30.3
45 - 49	947	8.4
50 - 54	252	2.4
55 - 59	76	0.7
60 - 64	40	..
65 + ...	8	..
Unknown - Inconnu	26 403	..
Estonia - Estonie		
2007 (C)		
Total	15 775	38.3
0 - 19	234	5.0
20 - 24	1 973	40.0
25 - 29	4 180	92.5
30 - 34	4 107	96.6
35 - 39	2 516	60.5
40 - 44	1 001	25.5
45 - 49	373	9.0
50 - 54	95	2.5
55 - 59	33	1.0
60 - 64	7	..
65 + ...	2	..
Unknown - Inconnu	1 254	..
Finland - Finlande[16]		
2007 (C)		
Total	58 729	36.3
0 - 19	53	0.5
20 - 24	1 980	19.7
25 - 29	7 988	78.8
30 - 34	12 382	126.6
35 - 39	7 868	78.5
40 - 44	3 418	30.2
45 - 49	897	8.0
50 - 54	269	2.3
55 - 59	72	0.6
60 - 64	26	..

Continent, country or area, year, code and age of father (in years) — Continent, pays ou zone, année, code et âge du père (en années)	Number - Nombre	Rate Taux
EUROPE		
Finland - Finlande[16]		
2007 (C)		
65 + ...	6	..
Unknown - Inconnu	23 770	..
France[17]		
2007 (C)		
Total	785 985	42.5
0 - 19	3 726	1.9
20 - 24	53 996	27.4
25 - 29	180 394	91.2
30 - 34	257 634	125.5
35 - 39	178 486	82.6
40 - 44	74 062	34.1
45 - 49	24 801	11.9
50 - 54	8 300	4.1
55 - 59	3 335	1.6
60 - 64	1 122	..
65 + ...	129	..
Unknown - Inconnu	-	..
Germany - Allemagne		
2007 (C)		
Total	684 862	26.9
0 - 19	3 217	1.5
20 - 24	40 602	18.0
25 - 29	126 408	55.1
30 - 34	184 082	83.5
35 - 39	167 942	57.7
40 - 44	76 017	22.5
45 - 49	20 424	6.6
50 - 54	5 485	2.1
55 - 59	1 843	0.8
60 - 64	635	..
65 + ...	292	..
Unknown - Inconnu	57 915	..
Greece - Grèce		
2007 (C)		
Total	111 926	32.0
0 - 19	217	0.8
20 - 24	3 059	9.1
25 - 29	17 382	42.7
30 - 34	37 082	87.7
35 - 39	30 100	70.8
40 - 44	12 860	32.7
45 - 49	3 641	9.8
50 - 54	905	2.6
55 - 59	206	0.7
60 - 64	41	..
65 + ...	5	..
Unknown - Inconnu	6 428	..
Hungary - Hongrie		
2007 (C)		
Total	97 613	30.9
0 - 19	944	3.3
20 - 24	5 820	19.6
25 - 29	21 193	60.4
30 - 34	33 737	89.4
35 - 39	16 576	51.2
40 - 44	5 542	20.3
45 - 49	1 810	6.5
50 - 54	725	2.2
55 - 59	210	0.7
60 - 64	72	..
65 + ...	20	..
Unknown - Inconnu	10 964	..
Iceland - Islande		
2007 (C)		
Total	4 560	44.6
0 - 19	43	3.6

Continent, country or area, year, code and age of father (in years) Continent, pays ou zone, année, code et âge du père (en années)	Number - Nombre	Rate Taux	Continent, country or area, year, code and age of father (in years) Continent, pays ou zone, année, code et âge du père (en années)	Number - Nombre	Rate Taux
EUROPE			**EUROPE**		
Iceland - Islande			Lithuania - Lituanie		
2007 (C)			2007 (C)		
20 - 24	458	41.3	65 +	4	..
25 - 29	1 292	105.9	Unknown - Inconnu	2 507	..
30 - 34	1 400	117.2	Luxembourg		
35 - 39	816	73.2	2007 (C)		
40 - 44	352	29.8	Total	5 477	35.7
45 - 49	94	8.1	0 - 19	36	2.6
50 - 54	26	♦2.5	20 - 24	323	23.0
55 - 59	19	♦2.2	25 - 29	1 048	66.5
60 - 64	2	..	30 - 34	1 684	98.3
65 +	1	..	35 - 39	1 390	71.8
Unknown - Inconnu	57		40 - 44	571	28.0
Ireland - Irlande			45 - 49	182	9.9
2006* (+C)			50 - 54	57	3.6
Total	64 237	46.8	55 - 59	16	♦1.2
0 - 19	714	5.1	60 - 64	1	..
20 - 24	4 382	26.9	65 +	4	..
25 - 29	10 351	57.1	Unknown - Inconnu	165	
30 - 34	19 695	121.1	Malta - Malte		
35 - 39	16 702	111.2	2007 (C)		
40 - 44	6 268	45.2	Total	3 871	29.3
45 - 49	1 585	12.4	0 - 19	57	4.3
50 - 54	374	3.2	20 - 24	228	16.5
55 - 59	119	1.1	25 - 29	947	66.3
60 - 64	27	..	30 - 34	1 248	91.2
65 +	6	..	35 - 39	665	56.4
Unknown - Inconnu	4 014		40 - 44	256	21.0
Italy - Italie			45 - 49	85	6.2
2006 (C)			50 - 54	17	♦1.3
Total	560 010	31.2	55 - 59	8	♦0.6
0 - 19	1 744	1.2	60 - 64	3	..
20 - 24	16 889	11.2	Unknown - Inconnu	357	..
25 - 29	72 846	40.7	Montenegro - Monténégro		
30 - 34	175 527	80.4	2007 (C)		
35 - 39	164 481	71.8	Total	7 834	39.5
40 - 44	73 108	32.3	0 - 19	23	♦1.0
45 - 49	18 642	9.5	20 - 24	566	24.2
50 +	5 896	1.7	25 - 29	1 848	84.4
Unknown - Inconnu	30 877	..	30 - 34	2 078	106.8
Latvia - Lettonie			35 - 39	1 461	79.2
2007 (C)			40 - 44	750	38.8
Total	23 273	32.6	45 - 49	280	14.0
0 - 19	296	3.6	50 - 54	80	4.0
20 - 24	3 608	41.5	55 - 59	24	♦1.5
25 - 29	6 237	81.9	60 - 64	3	..
30 - 34	5 699	76.5	65 +	7	..
35 - 39	3 483	47.7	Unknown - Inconnu	714	..
40 - 44	1 434	19.9	Norway - Norvège[18]		
45 - 49	563	7.4	2007 (C)		
50 - 54	146	2.3	Total	58 459	40.4
55 - 59	74	1.3	0 - 19	311	2.0
60 - 64	20	..	20 - 24	3 844	27.8
65 +	14	..	25 - 29	12 358	86.9
Unknown - Inconnu	1 699	..	30 - 34	18 970	119.7
Lithuania - Lituanie			35 - 39	13 545	76.6
2007 (C)			40 - 44	5 067	29.6
Total	32 346	30.7	45 - 49	1 498	9.5
0 - 19	439	3.5	50 - 54	481	3.2
20 - 24	4 815	37.9	55 - 59	160	1.1
25 - 29	9 786	91.0	60 - 64	43	..
30 - 34	8 179	78.8	65 +	11	..
35 - 39	4 283	38.2	Unknown - Inconnu	2 171	..
40 - 44	1 604	14.0	Poland - Pologne		
45 - 49	529	4.6	2007 (C)		
50 - 54	142	1.6	Total	387 873	30.6
55 - 59	46	0.6	0 - 19	2 701	2.0
60 - 64	12	..	20 - 24	48 192	30.6

Continent, country or area, year, code and age of father (in years) Continent, pays ou zone, année, code et âge du père (en années)	Number - Nombre	Rate Taux	Continent, country or area, year, code and age of father (in years) Continent, pays ou zone, année, code et âge du père (en années)	Number - Nombre	Rate Taux
EUROPE			EUROPE		
Poland - Pologne			Serbia - Serbie[20]		
2007 (C)	125 344	82.5	2007 (+C)	68 102	29.7
25 - 29	116 772	83.8	Total	497	2.5
30 - 34	49 844	42.2	0 - 19	6 499	29.1
35 - 39	18 788	16.3	20 - 24	18 676	81.6
40 - 44	6 099	4.6	25 - 29	19 298	86.1
45 - 49	2 321	0.9	30 - 34	9 817	47.1
50 +	17 812	..	35 - 39	3 417	16.3
Unknown - Inconnu			40 - 44	1 039	4.6
Portugal[5]			45 - 49	462	0.9
2007 (C)	102 492	31.4	50 +	8 397	..
Total	1 374	4.7	Unknown - Inconnu		
0 - 19	8 855	26.5	Slovakia - Slovaquie[7]		
20 - 24	23 251	59.6	2007 (C)	38 758	21.2
25 - 29	35 469	84.3	Total	257	1.3
30 - 34	20 792	53.2	0 - 19	3 181	14.2
35 - 39	7 746	20.3	20 - 24	11 798	49.6
40 - 44	2 332	6.4	25 - 29	14 354	62.2
45 - 49	699	2.1	30 - 34	6 219	33.1
50 - 54	251	0.8	35 - 39	2 214	11.7
55 - 59	68	..	40 - 44	528	2.7
60 - 64	26	..	45 - 49	140	0.7
65 +	1 629	..	50 - 54	42	0.3
Unknown - Inconnu			55 - 59	12	..
Republic of Moldova - République de Moldova[19]			60 - 64	13	..
2007 (C)	37 973	31.7	65 +		
Total	519	3.3	Slovenia - Slovénie		
0 - 19	8 641	53.5	2007 (C)	19 823	29.3
20 - 24	11 975	87.8	Total	71	1.2
25 - 29	8 094	69.4	0 - 19	1 026	14.9
30 - 34	3 684	35.6	20 - 24	5 187	66.1
35 - 39	1 280	11.9	25 - 29	7 212	93.5
40 - 44	437	3.5	30 - 34	3 884	53.1
45 - 49	115	1.1	35 - 39	1 403	17.9
50 - 54	31	0.4	40 - 44	382	5.0
55 - 59	7	..	45 - 49	109	1.4
60 - 64	12	..	50 - 54	45	0.7
65 +	3 178	..	55 - 59	8	..
Unknown - Inconnu			60 - 64	1	..
Romania - Roumanie			65 +	495	..
2007 (C)	214 728	30.4	Unknown - Inconnu		
Total	4 040	5.5	Spain - Espagne		
0 - 19	24 154	31.1	2007 (C)	492 527	33.9
20 - 24	63 157	76.6	Total	3 957	3.4
25 - 29	62 301	76.6	0 - 19	24 595	17.4
30 - 34	31 946	35.4	20 - 24	79 398	42.7
35 - 39	8 568	15.4	25 - 29	174 332	85.7
40 - 44	3 207	5.0	30 - 34	136 444	71.5
45 - 49	1 019	1.5	35 - 39	47 861	27.0
50 - 54	297	0.5	40 - 44	12 767	8.0
55 - 59	87	..	45 - 49	3 346	2.5
60 - 64	23	..	50 - 54	1 025	0.9
65 +	15 929	..	55 - 59	288	..
Unknown - Inconnu			60 - 64	119	..
San Marino - Saint-Marin			65 +	8 395	..
2004 (+C)	306	33.1	Unknown - Inconnu		
Total	7	♦4.8	Sweden - Suède		
0 - 24	46	46.8	2007 (C)	107 421	39.1
25 - 29	116	92.4	Total	514	1.6
30 - 34	85	61.4	0 - 19	6 161	22.2
35 - 39	37	28.5	20 - 24	21 826	78.5
40 - 44	14	♦13.3	25 - 29	36 846	122.5
45 - 49	1	♦0.5	30 - 34	25 345	80.2
50 +			35 - 39	10 859	32.4
			40 - 44	3 146	10.7
			45 - 49	985	3.4
			50 - 54	305	1.0
			55 - 59		

Continent, country or area, year, code and age of father (in years) Continent, pays ou zone, année, code et âge du père (en années)	Number - Nombre	Rate Taux
EUROPE		
Sweden - Suède		
2007 (C)		
60 - 64	112	..
65 +	28	..
Unknown - Inconnu	1 294	
Switzerland - Suisse[7]		
2006 (C)		
Total	62 103	26.5
0 - 19	56	0.2
20 - 24	2 585	11.6
25 - 29	10 921	47.0
30 - 34	20 715	82.0
35 - 39	17 529	59.3
40 - 44	7 325	22.6
45 - 49	2 066	7.1
50 - 54	594	2.3
55 - 59	193	0.8
60 - 64	85	..
65 +	34	..
The Former Yugoslav Republic of Macedonia - L'ex-République yougoslave de Macédoine		
2007 (C)		
Total	22 688	33.3
0 - 19	149	1.9
20 - 24	2 547	32.5
25 - 29	7 448	97.2
30 - 34	6 665	92.3
35 - 39	2 952	42.6
40 - 44	972	13.9
45 - 49	246	3.6
50 - 54	37	0.6
55 - 59	15	♦0.3
60 - 64	3	..
65 +	3	..
Unknown - Inconnu	1 651	..
Ukraine[21]		
2007 (C)		
Total	472 657	32.1
0 - 19	6 594	4.4
20 - 24	99 136	58.3
25 - 29	137 388	91.8
30 - 34	94 891	66.5
35 - 39	45 618	34.5
40 - 44	15 916	11.7
45 - 49	5 172	3.5
50 - 54	1 382	1.1
55 +	611	0.6
Unknown - Inconnu	65 949	..
United Kingdom of Great Britain and Northern Ireland - Royaume-Uni de Grande-Bretagne et d'Irlande du Nord[22]		
2003 (C)		
Total	695 549	38.6
0 - 19	13 848	7.5
20 - 24	70 484	40.7
25 - 29	132 039	77.8
30 - 34	206 797	101.9
35 - 39	143 461	66.2
40 - 44	55 851	27.6
45 - 49	15 730	8.8
50 - 54	4 661	2.7
55 - 59	1 616	0.9
60 - 64	465	..
65 +	280	..
Unknown - Inconnu	50 317	..

Continent, country or area, year, code and age of father (in years) Continent, pays ou zone, année, code et âge du père (en années)	Number - Nombre	Rate Taux
OCEANIA - OCÉANIE		
Australia - Australie		
2007 (+C)		
Total	285 213	43.3
0 - 19	3 910	5.5
20 - 24	23 537	32.0
25 - 29	56 589	80.0
30 - 34	89 233	125.4
35 - 39	66 157	87.6
40 - 44	25 556	34.8
45 - 49	8 109	11.1
50 - 54	2 242	3.3
55 - 59	775	1.3
60 - 64	240	..
65 +	83	..
Unknown - Inconnu[23]	8 782	..
Fiji - Fidji		
2004 (+C)		
Total	17 189	...
0 - 19	45	...
20 - 24	1 677	...
25 - 29	4 265	...
30 - 34	3 706	...
35 - 39	2 382	...
40 - 44	1 242	...
45 - 49	403	...
50 - 54	106	...
55 - 59	44	...
60 +	19	...
Unknown - Inconnu	3 300	..
Guam[24]		
2004 (C)		
Total	3 425	...
0 - 19	113	...
20 - 24	511	...
25 - 29	654	...
30 - 34	651	...
35 - 39	412	...
40 - 44	222	...
45 +	107	...
Unknown - Inconnu	757	..
New Caledonia - Nouvelle-Calédonie		
2007 (C)		
Total	4 093	54.0
0 - 19	27	2.9
20 - 24	354	44.7
25 - 29	741	104.2
30 - 34	993	126.3
35 - 39	761	97.6
40 - 44	348	47.7
45 - 49	121	20.0
50 - 54	35	6.9
55 - 59	17	♦3.6
60 +	5	..
Unknown - Inconnu	691	..
New Zealand - Nouvelle-Zélande		
2007 (+C)		
Total	64 044	50.0
0 - 19	2 273	14.9
20 - 24	7 025	50.9
25 - 29	11 944	98.1
30 - 34	16 913	136.2
35 - 39	13 600	96.9
40 - 44	5 745	39.9
45 - 49	1 782	12.5
50 - 54	487	3.9
55 - 59	147	1.3
60 - 64	34	..

Continent, country or area, year, code and age of father (in years) / Continent, pays ou zone, année, code et âge du père (en années)	Number - Nombre	Rate Taux
OCEANIA - OCÉANIE		
New Zealand - Nouvelle-Zélande		
2007 (+C)		
65 + ...	20	..
Unknown - Inconnu	4 074	..
Palau - Palaos		
2003 (C)		
Total	312	...
0 - 19	6	...
20 - 24	50	...
25 - 29	56	...
30 - 34	76	...
35 - 39	59	...
40 - 44	29	...

Continent, country or area, year, code and age of father (in years) / Continent, pays ou zone, année, code et âge du père (en années)	Number - Nombre	Rate Taux
OCEANIA - OCÉANIE		
Palau - Palaos		
2003 (C)		
45 - 49	17	...
50 - 54	9	...
Unknown - Inconnu	10	..

FOOTNOTES - NOTES

♦ Rates based on 30 or fewer births. - Taux basés sur 30 naissances ou moins.

* Provisional. - Données provisoires.

'Code' indicates the source of data, as follows:
C - Civil registration, estimated over 90% complete
U - Civil registration, estimated less than 90% complete
| - Other source, estimated reliable
+ - Data tabulated by date of registration rather than occurrence.
... Information not available

Le 'Code' indique la source des données, comme suit:
C - Registres de l'état civil considérés complets à 90 p. 100 au moins.
U - Registres de l'état civil qui ne sont pas considérés complets à 90 p. 100 au moins.
| - Autre source, considérée fiable.
+ - Données exploitées selon la date de l'enregistrement et non la date de l'événement.
... Information non disponible.

[1] Excluding live-born infants who died before their birth was registered. - Non compris les enfants nés vivants décédés avant l'enregistrement de leur naissance.
[2] Data refer to registered events only. - Les données ne concernent que les événements enregistrés.
[3] Including Canadian residents temporarily in the United States, but excluding United States residents temporarily in Canada. - Y compris les résidents canadiens se trouvant temporairement aux Etats-Unis, mais ne comprenant pas les résidents des Etats-Unis se trouvant temporairement au Canada.
[4] Data have not been adjusted for underenumeration. - Les données n'ont pas été ajustées pour compenser les lacunes du dénombrement.
[5] Data refer to resident mothers. - Données concernant les mères résidentes.
[6] Excluding Indian jungle population. - Non compris les Indiens de la jungle.
[7] Data refer to live births in wedlock only. - Les données ne concernent que les naissances vivantes de parents mariés.
[8] Excluding infants born alive of less than 28 weeks' gestation, of less than 1 000 grams in weight and 35 centimeters in length, who die within seven days of birth. Data refer to live births in wedlock only. - Non compris les enfants nés vivants après moins de 28 semaines de gestations, pesant moins de 1 000 grammes, mesurant moins de 35 centimètres et décédés dans les sept jours qui ont suivi leur naissance. Les données ne concernent que les naissances vivantes de parents mariés.
[9] Data refer to government controlled areas. - Les données se rapportent aux zones contrôlées par le Gouvernement.
[10] Including data for East Jerusalem and Israeli residents in certain other territories under occupation by Israeli military forces since June 1967. - Y compris les données pour Jérusalem-Est et les résidents israéliens dans certains autres territoires occupés depuis 1967 par les forces armées israéliennes.
[11] Data refer to Japanese nationals in Japan only. Data refer to live births in wedlock only. - Les données se raportent aux nationaux japonais au Japon

seulement. Les données ne concernent que les naissances vivantes de parents mariés.
[12] Excluding infants born alive of less than 28 weeks' gestation, of less than 1 000 grams in weight and 35 centimeters in length, who die within seven days of birth. - Non compris les enfants nés vivants après moins de 28 semaines de gestations, pesant moins de 1 000 grammes, mesurant moins de 35 centimètres et décédés dans les sept jours qui ont suivi leur naissance.
[13] Excluding alien armed forces, civilian aliens employed by armed forces, and foreign diplomatic personnel and their dependants. - Non compris les militaires étrangers, les civils étrangers employés par les forces armées ni le personnel diplomatique étranger et les membres de leur famille les accompagnant.
[14] Data refer to live births in wedlock only. Also included in Finland. - Les données ne concernent que les naissances vivantes de parents mariés. Comprise aussi dans Finlande.
[15] Excluding Faeroe Islands and Greenland shown separately, if available. - Non compris les Iles Féroé et le Gröenland, qui font l'objet de rubriques distinctes, si disponible.
[16] Including nationals temporarily outside the country. Including Aland Islands. - Y compris les nationaux se trouvant temporairement hors du pays. Y compris les Îles d'Åland.
[17] Excluding Overseas Departments, namely, French Guiana, Guadeloupe, Martinique and Reunion, shown separately, if available. Including armed forces stationed outside the country. - Non compris les départements d'outre mer, c'est-à-dire la Guyane française, la Guadeloupe, la Martinique et la Réunion, qui font l'objet de rubriques distinctes, si disponible. Y compris les militaires nationaux hors du pays.
[18] Excluding Svalbard and Jan Mayen Island shown separately, if available. Age classification based on year of birth of father rather than the exact age of father at birth of child. - Non compris Svalbard et Jan Mayen qui font l'objet de rubriques distinctes, si disponible. Le classement selon l'âge est basé sur l'année de naissance de la père et non sur l'age exacte de la père au moment de naissance de l'enfant.
[19] Excluding infants born alive of less than 28 weeks' gestation, of less than 1 000 grams in weight and 35 centimeters in length, who die within seven days of birth. Excluding Transnistria and the municipality of Bender. - Non compris les enfants nés vivants après moins de 28 semaines de gestations, pesant moins de 1 000 grammes, mesurant moins de 35 centimètres et décédés dans les sept jours qui ont suivi leur naissance. Les données ne tiennent pas compte de l'information sur la Transnistria et la municipalité de Bender.
[20] Excluding data for Kosovo and Metohia. - Sans les données pour le Kosovo et Metohie.
[21] Data refer to births with weight 500g and more (if weight is unknown - with length 25 centimeters and more, or with gestation during 22 weeks or more). - Données concernant les nouveau-nés de 500 grammes ou plus (si le poids est inconnu – de 25 centimètres de long ou plus, ou après une grossesse de 22 semaines ou plus).
[22] Data tabulated by date of occurrence for England and Wales, and by date of registration for Northern Ireland and Scotland. Excluding Channel Islands (Guernsey and Jersey) and Isle of Man, shown separately, if available. Excluding births to non-resident mothers of Northern Ireland. - Données exploitées selon la date de l'événement pour l'Angleterre et le pays de Galles, et selon la date de l'enregistrement pour l'Irlande du Nord et l'Ecosse. Non compris les îles Anglo-Normandes (Guernesey et Jersey) et l'île de Man, qui font l'objet de

rubriques distinctes, si disponible. Les données ne tiennent pas compte des enfants nés de mères non résidentes en Irlande du Nord.

[23] Data includes; births born in wedlock where age of father is unknown and ; births born out of wedlock and where the father has not acknowledged the birth and age of father is therefore unknown. - Les données se rapportent aux enfants légitimes pour lesquels l'âge du père n'est pas connu et aux naissances hors mariage non reconnues par le père et pour lesquelles l'âge n'est par conséquent pas connu.

[24] Including United States military personnel, their dependants and contract employees. - Y compris les militaires des Etats-Unis, les membres de leur famille les accompagnant et les agents contractuels des Etats-Unis.

Table 12

Table 12 presents late foetal deaths and late foetal-death ratios by urban/rural residence for as many years as possible between 2003 and 2007.

Description of variables: Late foetal deaths are foetal deaths[1] of 28 or more completed weeks of gestation. Foetal deaths of unknown gestational age are included with those 28 or more weeks.

Statistics on the number of late foetal deaths are obtained from civil registers unless otherwise noted.

The urban/rural classification of late foetal deaths is as provided by each country or area; it is presumed to be based on the national census definitions of urban population that have been set forth at the end of the technical notes for table 6.

Ratio computation: Late foetal-death ratios are the annual number of late foetal deaths per 1 000 live births (as shown in table 9) in the same year. The live-birth base was adopted because it is assumed to be more comparable from one country or area to another than the sum of live births and foetal deaths.

Ratios by urban/rural residence are the annual number of late foetal deaths, in the appropriate urban or rural category, per 1 000 corresponding live births (as shown in table 9). These ratios are calculated by the Statistics Division of the United Nations.

Ratios presented in this table are limited to those for countries or areas and urban/rural areas having at least a total of 30 late foetal deaths in a given year.

Reliability of data: Each country or area is asked to indicate the estimated completeness of the late foetal deaths recorded in its civil register. These national assessments are indicated by the quality codes "C", "U" and "..." that appear in the first column of this table.

"C" indicates that the data are estimated to be virtually complete, that is, representing at least 90 per cent of the late foetal deaths occurring each year, while "U" indicates that data are estimated to be incomplete, that is, representing less than 90 per cent of the late foetal deaths occurring each year. The code "..." indicates that no information was provided regarding completeness.

Data from civil registers which are reported as incomplete or of unknown completeness (coded "U" or "...") are considered unreliable. They appear in italics in this table. Ratios are not computed for data so coded.

For more information about the quality of vital statistics data in general, see section 4.2 of the Technical Notes.

Limitations: Statistics on late foetal deaths are subject to the same qualifications as have been set forth for vital statistics in general and foetal-death statistics in particular as discussed in section 4 of the Technical Notes.

The reliability of the data is a very important factor. Of all vital statistics, the registration of foetal deaths is probably the most incomplete.

Variation in the definition of foetal deaths, and in particular late foetal deaths, also limits international comparability. The criterion of 28 or more completed weeks of gestation to distinguish late foetal deaths is not universally used; some countries or areas use different durations of gestation or other criteria such as size of the foetus. In addition, the difficulty of accurately determining gestational age further reduces comparability. However, to promote comparability, late foetal deaths shown in this table are restricted to those of at least 28 or more completed weeks of gestation. Wherever this is not possible a footnote is provided.

Another factor introducing variation in the definition of late foetal deaths is the practice by some countries or areas of including in late foetal-death statistics infants who were born alive but died before the registration of the birth or within the first 24 hours of life, thus overestimating the total number of late foetal deaths. This has also the effect of inflating the late foetal-death ratios unduly by decreasing the birth denominator and increasing the foetal-death numerator. Statistics of this type are footnoted.

In addition, late foetal-death ratios are subject to the limitations of the data on live births with which they have been calculated. These have been set forth in the technical notes for table 9.

Regarding the computation of the ratios, it must be pointed out that when late foetal deaths and live births are both under registered, the resulting ratios may be of reasonable magnitude. For the countries or areas where live-birth registration is poorest, the late foetal-death ratios may be the largest, effectively masking the completeness of the base data. For this reason, possible variations in birth-registration completeness as well as the reported completeness of late foetal deaths must always be borne in mind in evaluating late foetal-death ratios.

In addition to the indirect effect of live-birth under-registration, late foetal-death ratios may be seriously affected by date-of-registration tabulation of live births. When the annual number of live births registered and reported fluctuates over a wide range due to changes in legislation or to special needs for proof of birth on the part of large segments of the population, then the late foetal-death ratios will also fluctuate, but inversely. Because of these effects, data for countries or areas known to tabulate live births by date of registration should be used with caution.

Finally, it may be noted that the counting of live-born infants as late foetal deaths, because they died before the registration of the birth or within the first 24 hours of life, has the effect of inflating the late foetal-death ratios unduly by decreasing the birth denominator and increasing the foetal-death numerator. This factor should not be overlooked in using data from this table.

The comparability of data by urban/rural residence is affected by the national definitions of urban and rural used in tabulating these data. It is assumed, in the absence of specific information to the contrary, that the definitions of urban and rural used in connection with the national population census were also used in the compilation of the vital statistics for each country or area. However, it cannot be excluded that, for a given country or area, different definitions of urban and rural are used for the vital statistics data and the population census data respectively. When known, the definitions of urban used in national population censuses are presented at the end of the technical notes for table 6. As discussed in detail in the technical notes for table 6, these definitions vary considerably from one country or area to another.

Urban/rural differentials in late foetal death ratios may also be affected by whether the late foetal deaths and live births have been tabulated in terms of place of occurrence or place of usual residence. This problem is discussed in more detail in section 4.1.4.1 of the Technical Notes.

Earlier data: Late foetal deaths and late foetal-death ratios have been shown in each issue of the Demographic Yearbook beginning with the 1951 issue. A special topic CD on natality published in 2001 presents the data for all available years from 1990 to 1998. For more information on specific topics, and years for which data are reported, readers should consult the Historical Index.

NOTES

[1] For definition, see section 4.1.1.3 of the Technical Notes.

Tableau 12

Le tableau 12 présente des données sur les morts fœtales tardives et les rapports de mortinatalité selon le lieu de résidence (zone urbaine ou rurale) pour le plus grand nombre d'années possible entre 2003 et 2007.

Description des variables : Par mort fœtale tardive, on entend le décès d'un fœtus[1] survenu après 28 semaines complètes de gestation au moins. Les morts fœtales pour lesquelles la durée de la période de gestation n'est pas connue sont comprises dans cette catégorie.

Sauf indication contraire, les statistiques du nombre de morts fœtales tardives sont établies sur la base des registres de l'état civil.

La classification des morts fœtales tardives selon le lieu de résidence (zone urbaine ou rurale) est celle qui a été communiquée par chaque pays ou zone ; on part du principe qu'elle repose sur les définitions de la population urbaine utilisées pour les recensements nationaux, telles qu'elles sont reproduites à la fin des notes techniques du tableau 6.

Calcul des rapports : les rapports de mortinatalité représentent le nombre annuel de morts fœtales tardives pour 1 000 naissances vivantes (telles qu'elles sont présentées au tableau 9) survenues pendant la même année. On a pris pour base de calcul les naissances vivantes parce que l'on pense qu'elle sont plus facilement comparables d'un pays ou d'une zone à l'autre que la somme des naissances vivantes et des morts fœtales.

Les rapports selon le lieu de résidence (zone urbaine ou rurale) représentent le nombre annuel de morts fœtales tardives, classées selon la catégorie urbaine ou rurale appropriée pour 1 000 naissances vivantes (telles qu'elles sont présentées au tableau 9) survenues parmi la population correspondante. Ces rapports ont été calculés par la Division de statistique de l'ONU.

Les rapports présentés dans le tableau 12 ne concernent que les pays ou zones où l'on a enregistré un total d'au moins 1 000 morts fœtales tardives pendant une année donnée.

Fiabilité des données : il a été demandé à chaque pays ou zone d'indiquer le degré estimatif de complétude des données sur les morts fœtales tardives figurant dans ses registres d'état civil. Ces évaluations nationales sont signalées par les codes de qualité "C", "U" et "..." qui apparaissent dans la deuxième colonne du tableau.

La lettre "C" indique que les données sont jugées à peu près complètes, c'est-à-dire qu'elles représentent au moins 90 p. 100 des morts fœtales tardives survenues chaque année ; la lettre "U" signifie que les données sont jugées incomplètes, c'est-à-dire qu'elles représentent moins de 90 p.100 des morts fœtales tardives survenues chaque année. Le code "..." indique qu'aucun renseignement n'a été communiqué quant à la complétude des données.

Les données provenant des registres de l'état civil qui sont déclarées incomplètes ou dont le degré de complétude n'est pas connu (code "U" ou "...") sont jugées douteuses. Elles apparaissent en italique dans le tableau ; les rapports, dans ces cas, n'ont pas été calculés.

Pour plus de précisions sur la qualité des données reposant sur les statistiques de l'état civil en général, voir la section 4.2 des Notes techniques.

Insuffisance des données : les statistiques des morts fœtales tardives appellent toutes les réserves qui ont été formulées à propos des statistiques de l'état civil en général et des statistiques concernant les morts fœtales en particulier (voir la section 4 des Notes techniques).

La fiabilité des données est un facteur très important. Les statistiques concernant les morts fœtales sont probablement les moins complètes de toutes les statistiques de l'état civil.

L'hétérogénéité des définitions de la mort fœtale et, en particulier, de la mort fœtale tardive nuit aussi à la comparabilité internationale des données. Le critère des 28 semaines complètes de gestation au moins n'est pas universellement utilisé ; certains pays ou zones retiennent des critères différents pour la durée de la période de gestation ou d'autres critères tels que la taille du fœtus. De surcroît, la comparabilité est rendue malaisée par le fait qu'il est difficile d'établir avec précision l'âge gestationnel. Pour faciliter les comparaisons, les morts fœtales tardives considérées ici sont exclusivement celles qui sont survenues au terme de 28 semaines de gestation au moins. Les exceptions sont signalées en note.

Un autre facteur d'hétérogénéité dans la définition de la mort fœtale tardive est la pratique de certains pays ou zones qui consiste à inclure dans les statistiques des morts fœtales tardives les enfants nés vivants mais décédés avant l'enregistrement de leur naissance ou dans les 24 heures qui ont suivi la naissance, pratique qui conduit à surestimer le nombre total des morts fœtales tardives. Cela donne aussi des rapports de mortinatalité exagérés parce que le dénominateur (nombre de naissances) se trouve alors diminué et le numérateur (morts fœtales) augmenté. Quand pareil facteur a joué, cela a été signalé en note.

Les rapports de mortinatalité appellent en outre toutes les réserves qui ont été formulées à propos des statistiques des naissances vivantes qui ont servi à leur calcul (voir à ce sujet les notes techniques relatives au tableau 9).

En ce qui concerne le calcul des rapports, il convient de noter que, si l'enregistrement des morts fœtales tardives et celui des naissances vivantes sont loin d'être exhaustifs, les rapports de mortinatalité peuvent être raisonnables. C'est parfois pour les pays ou zones où l'enregistrement des naissances vivantes laisse le plus à désirer que les rapports de mortinatalité sont les plus élevés, ce qui masque le caractère incomplet des données de base. Aussi, pour porter un jugement sur la qualité des rapports de mortinatalité, il ne faut jamais oublier que la complétude de l'enregistrement des naissances comme celle de l'enregistrement des morts fœtales tardives peuvent varier sensiblement.

Hormis les effets indirects des lacunes de l'enregistrement des naissances vivantes, il arrive que les rapports de mortinatalité soient considérablement faussés lorsque l'exploitation des données relatives aux naissances se fait d'après la date de l'enregistrement. Si le nombre des naissances vivantes enregistrées vient à varier notablement d'une année à l'autre par suite de modifications de la législation ou parce que de très nombreuses personnes ont besoin de se procurer une attestation de naissance, les rapports de mortinatalité varient également, mais en sens inverse. Il convient donc d'utiliser avec prudence le données des pays ou zones où les statistiques sont établies d'après la date de l'enregistrement.

Enfin, on notera que l'inclusion parmi les morts fœtales tardives des décès d'enfants nés vivants qui sont décédés avant l'enregistrement de leur naissance ou dans les 24 heures qui ont suivi la naissance conduit à des rapports de mortinatalité exagérés parce que le dénominateur (nombre de naissances) se trouve alors diminué et le numérateur (morts fœtales) augmenté. Il importe de ne pas négliger ce facteur lorsque l'on utilise les données du tableau 12.

La comparabilité des données selon le lieu de résidence (zone urbaine ou rurale) peut être limitée par les définitions nationales des termes « urbain » et « rural » utilisées pour la mise en tableaux de ces données. En l'absence d'indications contraires, on a supposé que les mêmes définitions avaient servi pour le recensement national de la population et pour l'établissement des statistiques de l'état civil pour chaque pays ou zone. Toutefois, il n'est pas exclu que, pour une zone ou un pays donné, des définitions différentes aient été retenues. Les définitions du terme « urbain » utilisées pour les recensements nationaux de population ont été présentées à la fin des notes techniques du tableau 6 lorsqu'elles étaient connues. Comme on l'a précisé dans les notes techniques relatives au tableau 6, ces définitions varient considérablement d'un pays ou d'une zone à l'autre.

La différence entre les rapports de mortinatalité pour les zones urbaines et rurales pourra aussi être faussée selon que les morts fœtales tardives et les naissances vivantes auront été classées d'après le lieu de l'événement ou le lieu de résidence habituel. Ce problème est examiné plus en détail à la section 4.1.4.1 des Notes techniques.

Données publiées antérieurement : les éditions de l'*Annuaire démographique* parues à partir de 1951 contiennent des statistiques concernant les morts fœtales tardives et les rapports de mortinatalité. Un CD-ROM sur la natalité paru en 2001 présente les données pour toutes les années disponibles de 1990 à 1998. Pour plus de précisions concernant les années et les sujets pour lesquels des données ont été publiées, se reporter à l'index.

NOTE

[1] Pour la définition, voir la section 4.1.1.3 des Notes techniques.

12. Late foetal deaths and late foetal death ratios, by urban/rural residence: 2003 - 2007
Morts foetales tardives et rapports de mortinatalité, selon la résidence, urbaine/rurale: 2003 - 2007

Continent, country or area, and urban/rural residence / Continent, pays ou zone et résidence, urbaine/rurale	Co-de	Number - Nombre					Ratio - Rapport				
		2003	2004	2005	2006	2007	2003	2004	2005	2006	2007
AFRICA - AFRIQUE											
Egypt - Égypte											
Total	+U	4 605	4 201	4 218	4 557	4 468	...	...	...	...	...
Urban - Urbaine	+U	3 567	3 436	3 549	3 869	3 895	...	...	...	...	...
Rural - Rurale	+U	1 038	765	669	688	573	...	...	...	...	...
Mauritius - Maurice											
Total	+C	220	191	185	147	172	11.4	9.9	9.8	8.4	10.1
Urban - Urbaine	+C	79	70	65	49	...	10.4	9.6	9.1	7.3	...
Rural - Rurale	+C	141	121	120	98	...	12.0	10.1	10.3	9.0	...
Réunion											
Total	C	161	159	166	178	194	11.2	10.9	11.4	12.3	13.1
Seychelles											
Total	+C	...	6	13	7		...	...	...	...	...
South Africa - Afrique du Sud[1]											
Total	...	14 625	15 742	13 719	14 194		...	...	...	...	...
Tunisia - Tunisie											
Total	U	1 550	1 525	1 640	1 576	1 580	...	...	...	...	...
AMERICA, NORTH - AMÉRIQUE DU NORD											
Bahamas											
Total	C	90	96	106	94	119	17.8	18.6	19.1	17.7	20.3
Bermuda - Bermudes											
Total	C	-	-	-	-	...	...	...	...	...	...
Canada[2]											
Total	C	1 027	972	1 012	...	...	3.1	2.9	3.0	...	...
Costa Rica											
Total	C	274	228	227	436	345	3.8	3.2	3.2	6.1	4.7
Urban - Urbaine	C	130	108	107	183	143	3.9	3.5	3.5	6.2	5.0
Rural - Rurale	C	144	120	120	253	202	3.7	2.9	2.9	6.1	4.6
Cuba[3]											
Total	C	1 868	1 675	1 639	1 439	1 017	13.7	13.2	13.6	12.9	9.0
El Salvador											
Total	C	535	572	460	378	369	4.3	4.8	4.1	3.5	3.5
Urban - Urbaine	C	461	510	410	348	349	6.3	7.1	5.9	4.9	5.1
Rural - Rurale	C	74	62	50	30	20	1.4	1.3	1.1	0.8	...
Greenland - Groenland											
Total	C	...	...	3	8	3	...	...	...	...	...
Guadeloupe											
Total	C	151	140	157	...	...	21.4	19.2	20.8	...	...
Guatemala											
Total	C	2 865	3 016	3 136	2 980	...	7.6	7.9	8.4	8.1	...
Martinique											
Total	C	118	98	88	102	98	21.7	18.6	17.5	19.0	18.4
Urban - Urbaine	C	98	91	82	94	87	20.1	19.2	18.0	19.3	18.0
Rural - Rurale	C	20	7	6	8	11	...	...	...	...	...
Mexico - Mexique[4]											
Total	+U	14 508	14 090	13 633	12 812	12 325	...	...	...	...	...
Urban - Urbaine[5]	+U	10 734	10 390	10 101	9 584	2 890	...	...	...	...	...
Rural - Rurale[5]	+U	3 556	3 422	3 385	3 098	753	...	...	...	...	...
Panama											
Total	U	371	378	319	394	415	...	...	...	...	...
Puerto Rico - Porto Rico											
Total	C	206	198	189	205	...	4.1	3.9	3.7	4.2	...
Urban - Urbaine[5]	C	113	124	109	...	...	4.2	4.6	3.9	...	...
Rural - Rurale[5]	C	87	64	74	...	...	3.6	2.6	3.2	...	...
Saint Lucia - Sainte-Lucie											
Total	C	36	39	*31	...	...	14.5	16.8	*13.5	...	...
Trinidad and Tobago - Trinité-et-Tobago											
Total	C	238	244	...	...	...	13.2	14.2	...	...	...
Turks and Caicos Islands - Îles Turques et Caïques											
Total	C	5[6]	1	-	2	-	...	...	...	...	...

12. Late foetal deaths and late foetal death ratios, by urban/rural residence: 2003 - 2007
Morts foetales tardives et rapports de mortinatalité, selon la résidence, urbaine/rurale: 2003 - 2007 (continued - suite)

Continent, country or area, and urban/rural residence / Continent, pays ou zone et résidence, urbaine/rurale	Co-de	Number - Nombre					Ratio - Rapport				
		2003	2004	2005	2006	2007	2003	2004	2005	2006	2007
AMERICA, NORTH - AMÉRIQUE DU NORD											
United States of America - États-Unis d'Amérique											
Total...................	C	12 485	12 761	12 567	...	...	3.1	3.1	3.0	...	...
AMERICA, SOUTH - AMÉRIQUE DU SUD											
Argentina - Argentine											
Total...................	C	4 663	3 812	5 048	4 983	4 833	6.7	5.2	7.1	7.2	6.9
Brazil - Brésil[7]											
Total...................	U	30 201	28 852	26 257	25 564	23 648	...	...	...	...	...
Chile - Chili[8]											
Total...................	C	1 404	1 510	1 841	2 124	...	6.0	6.6	8.0	9.2	...
Urban - Urbaine	C	1 220	1 365	1 740	1 980	...	5.8	6.7	8.5	9.5	...
Rural - Rurale	C	184	145	101	144	...	7.4	5.6	4.0	6.4	...
Colombia - Colombie[9]											
Total...................	...	8 542	8 897	11 428	11 958	11 951	...	...	...	...	...
Urban - Urbaine[5]	...	6 119	6 400	8 405	9 067	9 154	...	...	...	...	...
Rural - Rurale[5]	...	1 886	1 798	2 312	2 246	2 129	...	...	...	...	...
Ecuador - Équateur[10]											
Total...................	...	1 598[8]	1 506[8]	1 361	1 499	1 424	...	...	...	...	...
French Guiana - Guyane française											
Total...................	C	69	60	63	66	83	12.4	11.3	10.5	10.5	13.0
Urban - Urbaine	C	58	55	49	53	69	13.5	13.0	10.5	10.6	13.8
Rural - Rurale	C	11	5	14	13	14	...	...	...	...	...
Suriname[11]											
Total...................	...	229	222	200	221		...	...	...	...	...
Uruguay											
Total...................	C	...	*458	...	...	...	...	*9.2	...	...	...
ASIA - ASIE											
Armenia - Arménie											
Total...................	C	289	290	358	662[12]	563	8.1	7.7	9.5	17.6	14.0
Urban - Urbaine	C	227	224	284	456[12]	342	10.0	9.5	12.0	19.2	13.4
Rural - Rurale	C	62	66	74	206[12]	221	4.7	4.8	5.4	14.9	15.2
Azerbaijan - Azerbaïdjan											
Total...................	+C	431	479	550	603	536	3.8	3.6	3.9	4.0	3.5
Bahrain - Bahreïn											
Total...................	...	34	50	58	59	54	...	...	...	...	...
China, Hong Kong SAR - Chine, Hong Kong RAS											
Total...................	...	189	164	218	...	...	...	...	...	...	...
China, Macao SAR - Chine, Macao RAS											
Total...................	C	8	4	5	9	8	...	...	...	...	...
Georgia - Géorgie											
Total...................	C	811	870	739	712	632	17.6	17.6	15.9	14.9	12.8
Urban - Urbaine	C	791	679	547	539	459	22.9	21.9	17.5	16.1	13.4
Rural - Rurale	C	20	191	192	173	173	...	10.3	12.5	12.1	11.5
Israel - Israël[13]											
Total...................	C	560	420[14]	494	566	565	3.9	2.9	3.4	3.8	3.7
Urban - Urbaine[5]	C	503	378[14]	437	500	507	3.8	2.9	3.4	3.7	3.7
Rural - Rurale[5]	C	53	34[14]	54	62	50	4.0	2.5	4.0	4.4	3.7
Japan - Japon[15]											
Total...................	C	2 692	2 487	2 401	2 367	2 254	2.4	2.2	2.3	2.2	2.1
Urban - Urbaine[5]	C	2 161	2 057	2 083	2 137	2 009	2.4	2.2	2.3	2.2	2.0
Rural - Rurale[5]	C	529	430	318	227	244	2.6	2.2	2.2	2.1	2.4
Kazakhstan											
Total...................	C	1 768	1 729	1 882	1 987	2 112	7.1	6.3	6.7	6.6	6.6
Urban - Urbaine	C	1 169	1 196	1 324	1 416	1 443	8.4	7.7	8.1	8.1	8.3
Rural - Rurale[8]	C	599	533	558	571	669	5.5	4.6	4.9	4.5	4.5

12. Late foetal deaths and late foetal death ratios, by urban/rural residence: 2003 - 2007
Morts foetales tardives et rapports de mortinatalité, selon la résidence, urbaine/rurale: 2003 - 2007 (continued - suite)

Continent, country or area, and urban/rural residence / Continent, pays ou zone et résidence, urbaine/rurale	Co-de	Number - Nombre					Ratio - Rapport				
		2003	2004	2005	2006	2007	2003	2004	2005	2006	2007
ASIA - ASIE											
Kuwait - Koweït											
Total	C	307	355	375	347	374	7.0	7.5	7.4	6.6	7.0
Kyrgyzstan - Kirghizstan											
Total	C	879	1 437[16]	1 586	1 621	1 730	8.3	13.1	14.4	13.4	14.0
Urban - Urbaine	C	470	962[16]	1 022	1 066	1 172	14.7	25.7	28.7	27.0	28.3
Rural - Rurale	C	409	475[16]	564	555	558	5.6	6.5	7.6	6.8	6.8
Malaysia - Malaisie											
Total	C	2 030	2 003	2 075	2 136	*2 057	4.2	4.2	4.4	4.6	*4.5
Urban - Urbaine	C	1 196	1 134	1 195	1 288	...	3.9	3.8	4.0	4.4	...
Rural - Rurale	C	834	869	880	848	...	4.7	4.9	5.1	5.0	...
Maldives[8]											
Total	...	71	47	41	59	58	...	...	...	...	...
Urban - Urbaine	...	28	20	12	27	18	...	...	...	...	...
Rural - Rurale	...	43	27	29	32	40	...	...	...	...	...
Myanmar											
Urban - Urbaine	U	1 819	1 794	1 778	...	...	...	...	...	...	...
Oman[17]											
Total	U	381	346	387	367		...	...	...	...	...
Philippines											
Total	...	4 386	4 565	5 385	...	...	...	...	...	...	...
Qatar											
Total	C	81	64	97	79	95	6.3	4.9	7.2	5.6	6.1
Singapore - Singapour											
Total	+C	95	115	102	99	90	2.5	3.1	2.7	2.6	2.3
Sri Lanka[18]											
Total	+U	948	987	998	...	...	...	...	...	...	...
Tajikistan - Tadjikistan											
Total	U	1 043	1 144	1 267	1 326	1 497	...	...	...	...	...
Urban - Urbaine	U	899	936	1 074	1 134	1 292	...	...	...	...	...
Rural - Rurale	U	144	208	193	192	205	...	...	...	...	...
United Arab Emirates - Émirats arabes unis											
Total	...	188	170	190	...	...	...	...	...	...	...
EUROPE											
Åland Islands - Îles d'Åland[19]											
Total	C	1	-	1	...	...	...	...	...	...	...
Andorra - Andorre											
Total	C	3	5	-	1	...	...	...	...	...	...
Austria - Autriche											
Total	C	229	206	220	222	205	3.0	2.6	2.8	2.8	2.7
Belarus - Bélarus											
Total	C	...	...	326	352	324	...	...	3.6	3.6	3.1
Urban - Urbaine	C	...	...	237	250	223	...	...	3.6	3.5	2.9
Rural - Rurale	C	...	...	89	102	101	...	...	3.7	4.0	3.8
Belgium - Belgique											
Total	C	493	437	442	...	...	4.4	3.8	3.7	...	...
Bosnia and Herzegovina - Bosnie-Herzégovine											
Total	C	150	168	147	160	...	4.3	4.8	4.2	4.7	...
Bulgaria - Bulgarie											
Total	C	549	547	565	517	566	8.2	7.8	7.9	7.0	7.5
Urban - Urbaine	C	348	339	363	349	378	7.2	6.7	6.9	6.3	6.7
Rural - Rurale	C	201	208	202	168	188	10.7	10.7	10.7	8.9	9.8
Croatia - Croatie[20]											
Total	C	180	179	186	182	160	4.5	4.4	4.4	4.4	3.8
Urban - Urbaine	C	94	107	105	99	89	4.3	4.8	4.5	4.3	3.8
Rural - Rurale	C	86	72	81	83	71	4.8	4.0	4.2	4.5	3.8
Czech Republic - République tchèque[8]											
Total	C	272	265	287	299	315	2.9	2.7	2.8	2.8	2.7
Urban - Urbaine	C	209	162	195	213	230	3.0	2.2	2.6	2.7	2.7
Rural - Rurale	C	63	103	92	86	85	2.6	4.0	3.5	3.2	2.8

12. Late foetal deaths and late foetal death ratios, by urban/rural residence: 2003 - 2007
Morts foetales tardives et rapports de mortinatalité, selon la résidence, urbaine/rurale: 2003 - 2007 (continued - suite)

Continent, country or area, and urban/rural residence / Continent, pays ou zone et résidence, urbaine/rurale	Co-de	Number - Nombre					Ratio - Rapport				
		2003	2004	2005	2006	2007	2003	2004	2005	2006	2007
EUROPE											
Denmark - Danemark[21]											
Total	C	239	316	246	...	...	3.7	4.9	3.8	...	...
Estonia - Estonie[8]											
Total	C	63	63	88	56	65	4.8	4.5	6.1	3.8	4.1
Urban - Urbaine	C	45	49	60	38	40	5.0	5.0	5.9	3.6	3.6
Rural - Rurale	C	18	14	28	18	25					
Finland - Finlande[22]											
Total	C	133	117	113	139	148	2.3	2.0	2.0	2.4	2.5
Urban - Urbaine	C	84	73	77	88	99	2.3	1.9	2.0	2.3	2.5
Rural - Rurale	C	49	44	36	51	49	2.5	2.2	1.8	2.6	2.7
France[23]											
Total	C	6 862	7 054	6 964	7 531	7 246	9.0	9.2	9.0	9.5	9.2
Urban - Urbaine[24]	C	5 309	5 469	5 370	5 824	5 604	9.2	9.5	9.2	9.8	9.5
Rural - Rurale[24]	C	1 477	1 510	1 518	1 643	1 575	8.0	8.0	7.9	8.3	8.0
Germany - Allemagne											
Total	C	2 699	2 728	2 487	2 420	2 371	3.8	3.9	3.6	3.6	3.5
Greece - Grèce											
Total	C	416	408	346	316	364	4.0	3.9	3.2	2.8	3.3
Urban - Urbaine	C	...	...	244	226	252	...	...	3.3	2.9	3.3
Rural - Rurale	C	...	...	102	90	112	...	...	3.0	2.6	3.2
Hungary - Hongrie[25]											
Total	C	530	476	506	489	485	5.6	5.0	5.2	4.9	5.0
Urban - Urbaine[26]	C	291	267	298	271	290	4.9	4.4	4.7	4.1	4.4
Rural - Rurale[26]	C	237	208	201	211	193	6.9	6.1	6.1	6.4	6.1
Iceland - Islande											
Total	C	4	15	8	13	7	...	...	...	...	...
Urban - Urbaine	C	4	...	7	12	7	...	...	...	...	...
Rural - Rurale	C	-	...	1	1	7	...	...	...	...	...
Ireland - Irlande[27]											
Total	C	258	236	...	...	...	4.2	3.8	...	...	...
Italy - Italie[8]											
Total	C	*1 660	*1 658	*1 776	*1 628	*1 570	*3.1	*2.9	*3.2	*2.9	*2.8
Latvia - Lettonie											
Total	C	130	136	132[28]	154[28]	121[28]	6.2	6.7	6.1	6.9	5.2
Urban - Urbaine	C	76	90	79[28]	103[28]	83[28]	5.5	6.5	5.4	6.7	5.1
Rural - Rurale	C	54	46	53[28]	51[28]	38[28]	7.6	7.1	7.7	7.4	5.3
Lithuania - Lituanie[20]											
Total	C	168	150	152	137	161	5.5	4.9	5.0	4.4	5.0
Urban - Urbaine	C	106	81	86	79	93	5.5	4.2	4.3	3.8	4.3
Rural - Rurale	C	62	69	66	58	68	5.4	6.3	6.2	5.5	6.4
Luxembourg											
Total	C	17	16	21	14	20	...	...	...	...	...
Malta - Malte[20]											
Total	C	18	15	8	10	12	...	...	...	...	...
Montenegro - Monténégro											
Total	C	42	38	27	20	22	5.0	4.8	...	...	...
Urban - Urbaine	C	25	28	24	...	...	...	...	...	...	...
Rural - Rurale	C	17	10	3	...	...	...	...	...	...	...
Netherlands - Pays-Bas[29]											
Total	C	928	795	760	642	608	4.6	4.1	4.0	3.5	3.4
Urban - Urbaine	C	631	527	517	456	435	4.8	4.0	4.0	3.6	3.5
Rural - Rurale	C	297	268	243	186	173	4.4	4.2	4.1	3.2	3.1
Norway - Norvège[30]											
Total	C	213	210	182	201	241	3.8	3.7	3.2	3.4	4.1
Poland - Pologne											
Total	C	1 322	1 342	1 283	1 338	1 346	3.8	3.8	3.5	3.6	3.5
Urban - Urbaine	C	687	715	687	710	753	3.4	3.5	3.3	3.3	3.3
Rural - Rurale	C	635	627	596	628	593	4.2	4.1	3.9	4.0	3.7
Portugal[31]											
Total	C	349	294	306	324	289	3.1	2.7	2.8	3.1	2.8
Romania - Roumanie											
Total	C	1 290	1 314	1 262	1 143	1 009	6.1	6.1	5.7	5.2	4.7
Urban - Urbaine	C	569	633	589	538	498	5.6	5.7	5.0	4.5	4.3
Rural - Rurale	C	721	681	673	605	511	6.5	6.5	6.5	6.0	5.2

12. Late foetal deaths and late foetal death ratios, by urban/rural residence: 2003 - 2007
Morts foetales tardives et rapports de mortinatalité, selon la résidence, urbaine/rurale: 2003 - 2007 (continued - suite)

Continent, country or area, and urban/rural residence — Continent, pays ou zone et résidence, urbaine/rurale	Co-de	Number - Nombre					Ratio - Rapport				
		2003	2004	2005	2006	2007	2003	2004	2005	2006	2007
EUROPE											
Russian Federation - Fédération de Russie											
Total	C	9 043	8 745	8 328	7 934	8 612	6.1	5.8	5.7	5.4	5.3
Urban - Urbaine	C	6 624	6 416	6 035	5 678	6 061	6.3	6.0	5.8	5.4	5.4
Rural - Rurale	C	2 419	2 329	2 293	2 256	2 551	5.7	5.4	5.5	5.2	5.2
San Marino - Saint-Marin											
Total	+C	2	-	-	-	-	...	...	...	...	...
Serbia - Serbie[32]											
Total	+C	411	419	361	365	343	5.2	5.4	5.0	5.1	5.0
Slovakia - Slovaquie[8]											
Total	C	217	211	195	218	207	4.2	3.9	3.6	4.0	3.8
Urban - Urbaine	C	114	92	93	98	89	4.3	3.2	3.2	3.4	3.1
Rural - Rurale	C	103	119	102	120	118	4.1	4.7	4.0	4.7	4.6
Slovenia - Slovénie											
Total	C	58	62	76	57	101	3.3	3.5	4.2	3.0	5.1
Urban - Urbaine	C	...	32	...	...	41	...	3.7	...	...	4.3
Rural - Rurale	C	...	30	...	...	60	...	3.3	...	...	5.9
Spain - Espagne											
Total	C	1 494	1 438	1 169	1 528	1 511	3.4	3.2	2.5	3.2	3.1
Sweden - Suède											
Total	C	347	318	301	319	326	3.5	3.2	3.0	3.0	3.0
Switzerland - Suisse											
Total	C	306	276	307	342	205	4.3	3.8	4.2	4.7	2.8
Urban - Urbaine	C	232	206	210	249	154	4.4	3.8	3.9	4.6	2.8
Rural - Rurale	C	74	70	97	93	51	3.9	3.6	5.1	4.9	2.6
The Former Yugoslav Republic of Macedonia - L'ex-République yougoslave de Macédoine											
Total	C	232	258	215	201	215	8.6	11.0	9.6	8.9	9.5
Urban - Urbaine	C	...	...	102	112	106	...	...	8.1	8.9	8.3
Rural - Rurale	C	...	...	113	89	109	...	...	11.3	9.0	11.0
Ukraine											
Total	C	1 969	1 986	2 242	2 314	3 070	4.8	4.6	5.3	5.0	6.5
Urban - Urbaine	C	1 361	1 398	1 489	1 532	2 088	5.1	4.9	5.2	5.0	6.6
Rural - Rurale	C	608	588	753	782	982	4.3	4.1	5.3	5.1	6.2
United Kingdom of Great Britain and Northern Ireland - Royaume-Uni de Grande-Bretagne et d'Irlande du Nord[33]											
Total	C	3 989	3 962	...	...	...	5.7	5.5	...	...	...
OCEANIA - OCÉANIE											
Australia - Australie[9]											
Total	+C	759	732	757	...	...	3.0	2.9	2.9	...	...
Urban - Urbaine	+C	504	439	513	...	...	2.4	2.1	2.4	...	...
Rural - Rurale	+C	255	293	244	...	...	5.8	6.6	5.5	...	...
French Polynesia - Polynésie française											
Total	C	35	...	...	...	...	7.8	...	...	...	...
Guam											
Total	C	43	42	...	...	...	13.0	12.3	...	...	...
New Caledonia - Nouvelle-Calédonie											
Total	+C	25	...	...	...	...	...	...	...	...	...
New Zealand - Nouvelle-Zélande[4]											
Total	+C	169	228	174	162	226	3.0	3.9	3.0	2.7	3.5
Urban - Urbaine	+C	150	210	156	139	205	3.1	4.1	3.1	2.7	3.7
Rural - Rurale	+C	19	18	18	23	20	...	...	...	...	...
Palau - Palaos											
Total	C	2	18	5	6	...	...	...	...	...	...

Continent, country or area, and urban/rural residence / Continent, pays ou zone et résidence, urbaine/rurale	Co-de	Number - Nombre					Ratio - Rapport				
		2003	2004	2005	2006	2007	2003	2004	2005	2006	2007
OCEANIA - OCÉANIE											
Papua New Guinea - Papouasie-Nouvelle-Guinée											
Total.....................	U	*991*	...	...	...	...	...	...	...	...	...

FOOTNOTES - NOTES

Italics: data from civil registers which are incomplete or of unknown completeness. - Italiques: données incomplètes ou dont le degré d'exactitude n'est pas connu, provenant des registres de l'état civil.

* Provisional. - Données provisoires.

[1] Data refer to foetal deaths of 26 weeks and over. - Les données se réfèrent aux morts fœtales à plus de 26 semaines.

[2] Including Canadian residents temporarily in the United States, but excluding United States residents temporarily in Canada. - Y compris les résidents canadiens se trouvant temporairement aux Etats-Unis, mais ne comprenant pas les résidents des Etats-Unis se trouvant temporairement au Canada.

[3] Late foetal death is indicated by the fact that the foetus is at least 500 grams or more in weight. - Les décès foetaux tardifs sont caractérisés par le fait que le foetus pèse au moins 500 grammes

[4] Data refer to resident population only. - Pour la population résidante seulement.

[5] The total number includes 'Unknown residence', but the categories urban and rural do not. - Le nombre total inclue 'Résidence inconnue ', mais les catégories Urbain et Rural ne l'incluent pas.

[6] Two of the 5 still births are to non Turks and Caicos nationals. - Deux des cinq mortinaissances concernent des personnes qui n'étaient pas ressortissantes des Îles Turques et Caïques.

[7] Excluding Indian jungle population. - Non compris les Indiens de la jungle.

[8] Data refer to total foetal deaths. - Y compris toutes les morts foetales.

[9] Data include unknown gestational weeks. - Les données comprennnent les cas où le nombre de semaines de gestation n'est pas connu.

[10] Excluding nomadic Indian tribes. - Non compris les tribus d'Indiens nomades.

[11] Data from the 4 hospitals in Paramaribo and that of the hospital of the Nickerie district. - Données provenant de 4 hôpitaux à Paramaribo et d'un hôpital du district de Nickerie.

[12] Since 16 October 2005 the definition of WHO on livebirths has been put into force in accordance with the 10th revision of the International Classification of Diseases. - Depuis le 16 octobre 2005, la définition de l'OMS concernant les naissances vivantes est en vigueur conformément à la dixième révision de la Classification internationale des maladies.

[13] Including data for East Jerusalem and Israeli residents in certain other territories under occupation by Israeli military forces since June 1967. - Y compris les données pour Jérusalem-Est et les résidents israéliens dans certains autres territoires occupés depuis 1967 par les forces armées israéliennes.

[14] Including 8 foetal deaths of unknown gestational age and weight over 1000 grams. - Y compris huit décès intra-utérins pour lesquels l'âge gestationnel est inconnu et le poids est supérieur à 1 000 grammes.

[15] Data refer to Japanese nationals in Japan only. Data exclude unknown duration of pregnancy. - Les données se raportent aux nationaux japonais au Japon seulement. Exception faite des grossesses dont la durée n'est pas connue.

[16] Since 2004, WHO criteria have been adopted in the country. - Depuis 2004, le pays a adopté les critères de l'OMS.

[17] Data refer to the recorded events in Ministry of Health hospitals and health centres only. - Les données se rapportent aux faits d'état civil enregistrés dans les hôpitaux et les dispensaires du Ministère de la santé seulement.

[18] Data refer to certain towns only. - Les données se réfèrent à certaines villes seulement.

[19] Also included in Finland. - Comprise aussi dans Finlande.

[20] Late foetal death is defined as an infant born without any signs of life, weighing at least 500 grams, after of pregnancy of at least 22 weeks. - On dit qu'il y a mort intra-utérine tardive lorsqu'un enfant pesant au minimum 500 grammes naît sans donner aucun signe de vie au terme d'une grossesse qui a duré au moins 22 semaines.

[21] Excluding Faeroe Islands and Greenland shown separately, if available. - Non compris les Iles Féroé et le Gröenland, qui font l'objet de rubriques distinctes, si disponible.

[22] Including nationals temporarily outside the country. Including Aland Islands. - Y compris les nationaux se trouvant temporairement hors du pays. Y compris les Îles d'Aland.

[23] Foetal deaths after at least 180 days (6 calendar months or 26 weeks) of gestation. Excluding Overseas Departments, namely, French Guiana, Guadeloupe, Martinique and Reunion, shown separately, if available. - Morts foetales survenues après 180 jours (6 mois civils ou 26 semaines) au moins de gestation. Non compris les départements d'outre mer, c'est-à-dire la Guyane française, la Guadeloupe, la Martinique et la Réunion, qui font l'objet de rubriques distinctes, si disponible.

[24] Data for urban and rural, excluding nationals outside the country. - Les données pour la résidence urbaine et rurale , non compris les nationaux hors du pays.

[25] Late foetal death is indicated by the fact that the foetus is at least 24 (it has been 28 weeks until 1996) completed weeks of gestational and does not show any sign of life after the separation from its mother; the foetus has to be 30 cm or more in length or 500 grams or more in weight if its gestational age cannot be determined. - Pour qu'il y ait mort foetale tardive, il faut que le décès d'un foetus survienne après 24 semaines complètes de gestation au moins (28 semaines jusqu'en 1996), que le foetus n'ait pas donné signe de vie après avoir été séparé de la mère, qu'il mesure 30 centimètres au moins ou pèse 500 grammes si la durée de la période de gestation n'est pas connue.

[26] Total includes the data of foreigners, persons of unknown residence and homeless, but the categories urban and rural do not. - Total incluant les étrangers, les personnes de résidence inconnue et les sans-abri, ce qui n'est pas le cas pour les catégories urbaines et rurales.

[27] Data refer to events registered within one year of occurrence. - Evénements enregistrés dans l'année qui suit l'événement.

[28] Data refer to the death of a fetus at least 22 completed weeks of gestation. - Les données concernent le décès d'un fœtus après 22 semaines de gestation au moins.

[29] Including residents outside the country if listed in a Netherlands population register. - Y compris les résidents hors du pays, s'ils sont inscrits sur un registre de population néerlandais.

[30] Excluding Svalbard and Jan Mayen Island shown separately, if available. - Non compris Svalbard et Jan Mayen qui font l'objet de rubriques distinctes, si disponible.

[31] Data refer to resident mothers. - Données concernant les mères résidentes.

[32] Excluding data for Kosovo and Metohia. - Sans les données pour le Kosovo et Metohie.

[33] Excluding Channel Islands (Guernsey and Jersey) and Isle of Man, shown separately, if available. - Non compris les îles Anglo-Normandes (Guernesey et Jersey) et l'Île de Man, qui font l'objet de rubriques distinctes, si disponible.

Table 13

Table 13 presents legally induced abortions for as many years as possible between 1998 and 2007.

Description of variables: There are two major categories of abortion: spontaneous and induced. Induced abortions are those initiated by deliberate action undertaken with the intention of terminating pregnancy; all other abortions are considered spontaneous.

The induction of abortion is subject to governmental regulation in most, if not all, countries or areas. This regulation varies from complete prohibition in some countries or areas to abortion on request, with services provided by governmental health authorities, in others. More generally, governments have attempted to define the conditions under which a pregnancy may lawfully be terminated and have established procedures for authorizing abortion in individual cases.

Information on abortion policies is collected by the United Nations Population Division and published in the World Population Policies[1]. An overview is also published a wall chart[2].

Reliability of data: Unlike data on live births and foetal deaths, which are generally collected through systems of vital registration, data on abortion are collected from a variety of sources. Because of this, the quality specification, showing the completeness of civil registers, which is presented for other tables, does not appear here.

Limitations: With regard to the collection of information on abortions, a variety of sources are used, but hospital records are the most common source of information. This implies that most cases that have no contact with hospitals are missed. Data from other sources are probably also incomplete. The data in the present table are limited to legally induced abortions, which, by their nature, might be assumed to be more complete than data on all induced abortions.

Earlier data: Legally induced abortions have been shown previously in all issues of the *Demographic Yearbook* since the 1971 issue.

NOTES

[1] World Population Policies 2007 (United Nations Publication, Sales No. E.08.XIII.8), New York 2008. See also: http://www.un.org/esa/population/publications/wpp2007/Publication_index.htm.
[2] World Abortion Policies 2007 (United Nations Publication, Sales No. E.07.XIII.6), New York, 2007. See also: http://www.un.org/esa/population/publications/2007_Abortion_Policies_Chart/2007AbortionPolicies_wallchart.htm.

Tableau 13

Ce tableau présente des données relatives aux avortements provoqués légalement, pour le plus grand nombre d'années possible entre 1998 et 2007.

Description des variables : l'avortement peut être spontané ou provoqué. L'avortement provoqué est celui qui résulte de manœuvres délibérées, entreprises afin d'interrompre la grossesse ; tous les autres avortements sont considérés comme spontanés.

L'interruption délibérée de la grossesse fait l'objet d'une réglementation officielle dans la plupart des pays ou zones, sinon dans tous. Cette réglementation va de l'interdiction totale à l'autorisation de l'avortement sur demande, pratiqué par des services de santé publique. Le plus souvent, les gouvernements se sont efforcés de définir les circonstances dans lesquelles la grossesse peut être interrompue licitement et de fixer une procédure d'autorisation.

La Division de la population des Nations Unies collecte des informations sur les politiques en matière d'avortement et les publient dans "World Population Policies"[1]. Une vue d'ensemble est également publiée sous forme de poster[2].

Fiabilité des données : à la différence des données sur les naissances vivantes et les morts fœtales, qui proviennent généralement des registres d'état civil, les données sur l'avortement sont tirées de sources diverses. Aussi ne trouve-t-on pas ici une évaluation de la qualité des données semblable à celle qui indique, pour les autres tableaux, le degré d'exhaustivité des données de l'état civil.

Insuffisance des données : en ce qui concerne les renseignements sur l'avortement, un grand nombre de sources sont utilisées, les relevés hospitaliers restant cependant la source la plus commune. Il s'ensuit que la plupart des cas qui ne passent pas par les hôpitaux sont ignorés. Il faut aussi tenir compte du fait que les données provenant d'autres sources sont probablement incomplètes. Les données du tableau 13 se limitent aux avortements provoqués pour raisons légales dont on peut supposer, en raison de leur nature même, que les statistiques sont plus complètes que les données concernant l'ensemble des avortements provoqués.

Données publiées antérieurement : des statistiques concernant les avortements provoqués pour raisons légales sont publiées dans *l'Annuaire démographique* depuis 1971.

NOTES

[1] World Population Policies 2007 (publication des Nations Unies, Numéro de vente E.08.XIII.8), New York 2008. http://www.un.org/esa/population/publications/wpp2007/Publication_index.htm.
[2] World Abortion Policies 2007 (publication des Nations Unies, Numéro de vente E.07.XIII.6), New York, 2007. http://www.un.org/esa/population/publications/2007_Abortion_Policies_Chart/2007AbortionPolicies_wallchart.htm.

13. Legally induced abortions: 1998 - 2007
Avortements provoqués légalement: 1998 - 2007

Continent and country or area Continent et pays ou zone	Number - Nombre									
	1998	1999	2000	2001	2002	2003	2004	2005	2006	2007
AFRICA - AFRIQUE										
Réunion	4 657	4 525	4 379	4 339	4 385	4 129	4 155	4 421	4 523	...
Seychelles	411	536	495	461	460	440	435	413	443	...
South Africa - Afrique du Sud[1]	28 978	...	...	...	...	...	...	...	...	...
AMERICA, NORTH - AMÉRIQUE DU NORD										
Anguilla	...	...	...	...	27	24	26	21	...	...
Canada	110 331	105 666	105 427	106 418	105 154[2]	103 768[2]	100 039[2]	96 815[2]	...	...
Cuba	75 109	80 037	76 293	69 563	70 823	65 628	67 277	62 530	67 903	66 008
Dominican Republic - République dominicaine	31 068	...	...	20 187	28 091	24 899	26 438	29 167	...	...
Greenland - Groenland	915	842	944	809	821	869	...	899	867	...
Martinique	...	2 529	2 627	2 502	2 614	2 394	2 426	2 304	2 392	...
Mexico - Mexique[3]	595	614	541	571	591	676	752	735	799	834
Panama[4]	...	...	11	...	...	...	...	...	...	...
Puerto Rico - Porto Rico	...	...	...	1 229	...	7 781	9 215	6 713	5 538[5]	...
Turks and Caicos Islands - Îles Turques et Caïques[6]	...	...	...	...	39	32	43	32	...	...
AMERICA, SOUTH - AMÉRIQUE DU SUD										
French Guiana - Guyane française	...	1 310	1 409	1 386	1 699	1 783	1 639	1 612	1 661	...
ASIA - ASIE										
Armenia - Arménie	18 286	14 403	11 769	10 419	9 372	10 290	10 487	10 925	11 132	11 501
Azerbaijan - Azerbaïdjan	29 914	20 878	17 501	18 332	16 606	16 903	19 798	19 577	20 864	22 323
Bahrain - Bahreïn	1 680	1 658	1 655	1 747	1 749	...	...	...	...	...
China, Hong Kong SAR - Chine, Hong Kong RAS	22 086	20 891	21 375	20 235	18 651	17 420	15 880	14 190	...	...
Georgia - Géorgie	21 018	18 306	14 951	15 008	13 908	13 834	17 210	19 681	21 204	20 644
Israel - Israël[7]	18 500	18 372	18 689	19 131	19 126	19 671	19 712	19 090	19 452	19 470
Japan - Japon[8]	333 220	337 288	341 146	341 588	329 326	319 831	301 673	289 127	276 352	256 672
Kazakhstan	148 799	137 808	...	...	...	...	...	...	...	...
Kyrgyzstan - Kirghizstan[9]	28 090	25 790	22 044	23 390	18 995	19 225	19 984	20 035	19 762	21 884
Mongolia - Mongolie	9 135	9 200	11 837	12 056	9 977	10 472	8 919	9 064	12 594	15 817
Qatar	71	124	177	127	121	131	172	169	...	...
Singapore - Singapour	13 838	13 753	13 734	13 140	12 749	12 272	12 070	11 482	12 032	11 933
Tajikistan - Tadjikistan	24 514	21 234	22 066	19 087	20 007	18 822	20 495	19 418	17 489	18 986
EUROPE										
Åland Islands - Îles d'Åland[10]	64	76	59	59	61	70	59	68	53	...
Albania - Albanie	18 944	19 930	21 004	17 125	17 500	12 087	10 517	9 403	9 552	9 030
Belarus - Bélarus	145 339	135 824	121 895	101 402	89 895	80 174	71 700	64 655	58 516	46 285
Belgium - Belgique	11 999	12 734	13 762	14 775	14 791	15 595	16 024	16 696	17 640	18 033
Bulgaria - Bulgarie	79 842	72 382	61 378	51 165	50 824	48 035	47 223	41 795	37 272	37 594
Croatia - Croatie	8 907	8 064	7 534	6 574	6 191	5 923	5 232	4 563	4 733	4 573
Czech Republic - République tchèque	42 959	39 382	34 623	32 528	31 142	29 298	27 574	26 453	25 352	25 414
Denmark - Danemark[11]	16 592	16 271	15 681	15 315	14 991	15 622	14 674	15 103	15 053	...
Estonia - Estonie[2]	15 798	14 503	12 743	11 653	10 834	10 619	10 074	9 610	9 378	8 883
Faeroe Islands - Îles Féroé	59	47	49	42	49	37	44	29	41	46
Finland - Finlande[12]	10 751	10 837	10 932	10 738	10 974	10 767	11 162	10 969	10 645	10 533
France[13]	195 368	196 295	...	201 434	205 898	202 591	209 907	205 392	...	...
Germany - Allemagne	131 795	130 471	134 609	134 964	130 387	128 030	129 650	124 023	119 710	116 871
Greece - Grèce	11 838	11 824	18 015	22 223	16 173	15 782	16 135	...	...	...
Guernsey - Guernesey	104	92	89	...	...	...	...	...	...	...
Hungary - Hongrie	68 971	65 981	59 249	56 404	56 075	53 789	52 539	48 689	46 324	43 870
Iceland - Islande	...	935	987	984	926	951	889	867	904	...
Italy - Italie	138 354	138 708	134 740	132 073	131 039	124 118	137 140	129 272	...	...

Continent and country or area / Continent et pays ou zone	Number - Nombre									
	1998	1999	2000	2001	2002	2003	2004	2005	2006	2007
EUROPE										
Latvia - Lettonie	19 964	18 031	17 240	15 647	14 685	14 508	13 723	12 785	11 825	11 814
Lithuania - Lituanie	21 022	18 846	16 259	13 677	12 495	11 513	10 644	9 972	9 536	9 596
Montenegro - Monténégro	...	...	...	...	...	...	...	1 952	...	...
Netherlands - Pays-Bas	24 141	...	...	...	...	...	...	...	...	...
Norway - Norvège[14]	14 028	14 279	14 655	13 887	13 557	13 888	14 071	13 989	14 417	15 118
Poland - Pologne[15]	312	151	138	123	159	174	199	225	339	...
Republic of Moldova - République de Moldova	31 293	27 908	20 395	16 028	15 739	17 551	17 965	16 642	15 742	15 843
Romania - Roumanie	271 496	259 888	257 865	254 855	247 608	224 803	191 038	163 359	150 246	137 226
Russian Federation - Fédération de Russie	...	...	...	2 014 710	1 944 481	1 864 647	1 797 567	1 732 289	1 582 398	1 479 010
Serbia - Serbie[16]	...	43 771	42 322	34 255	30 794	29 856	29 650	26 645	25 665	24 273
Slovakia - Slovaquie	21 109	19 949	...	18 026	17 382	16 222	15 307	14 427	14 243	13 424
Slovenia - Slovénie	9 116	8 707	8 429	7 799	7 327	6 873	6 403	5 851	5 632	5 176
Spain - Espagne	53 847	58 399	63 756	69 857	77 125	79 788	84 985	91 664	...	...
Sweden - Suède	31 008	30 712	30 980	31 772	33 365	34 473	34 454	34 978	36 045	...
Switzerland - Suisse	...	...	...	...	...	...	10 959	10 818	10 594	10 645
Ukraine	525 329	495 760	434 223	369 750	345 967	315 835	289 065	263 590	229 618	210 454
United Kingdom of Great Britain and Northern Ireland - Royaume-Uni de Grande-Bretagne et d'Irlande du Nord[17]	199 887	195 394	197 366	197 913	...	...	...	...	...	...
OCEANIA - OCÉANIE										
New Caledonia - Nouvelle-Calédonie	1 466	...	...	...	...	...	...	...	...	...
New Zealand - Nouvelle-Zélande	15 029	15 501	16 103	16 410	17 380	18 511	18 211	17 531	17 934	18 382

FOOTNOTES - NOTES

* Provisional. - Données provisoires.

[1] Data refer to 1997 - 1998. - Les données se rapportent à 1997 et à 1998.
[2] Data refer to resident population only. - Pour la population résidante seulement.
[3] Data refer to resident population only. Data refer to abortions prescribed by a physician. - Pour la population résidante seulement. Les données se réfèrent aux avortements prescrits par un médecin.
[4] Data refer to abortions granted for medical reasons by the Comision Multidisciplinaria Nacional de Aborto Terapéutico. - Les données se réfèrent aux avortements autorisés pour des raisons médicales par la Comision Multidisciplinaria Nacional de Aborto Terapéutico.
[5] Data refer to the fiscal year 2006-2007. - Les données se réfèrent à l'année budgétaire 2006-2007.
[6] Data refer to abortions performed in hospitals at Grand Turk and Providenciales. - Pour des avortements exécutés dans les hôpitaux dans Grand Turk et Providenciales.
[7] Including data for East Jerusalem and Israeli residents in certain other territories under occupation by Israeli military forces since June 1967. Data refer to applications to commissions for termination of pregnancy and not to authorizations. - Y compris les données pour Jérusalem-Est et les résidents israéliens dans certains autres territoires occupés depuis 1967 par les forces armées israéliennes. Les données relatives aux avortements provoqués légalement se rapportent aux demandes d'autorisation et non aux autorisations elles-mêmes.
[8] Data refer to Japanese nationals in Japan only. - Les données se raportent aux nationaux japonais au Japon seulement.
[9] Based on administrative reporting of the Ministry of Health. - Les données reposent sur les rapports administratifs du Ministère de la santé.
[10] Also included in Finland. - Comprise aussi dans Finlande.
[11] Excluding Faeroe Islands and Greenland shown separately, if available. - Non compris les Iles Féroé et le Grönland, qui font l'objet de rubriques distinctes, si disponible.
[12] Including Aland Islands. - Y compris les Îles d'Åland.
[13] Excluding Overseas Departments, namely, French Guiana, Guadeloupe, Martinique and Reunion, shown separately, if available. Data refer to women between 15 and 49 years of age. - Non compris les départements d'outre mer, c'est-à-dire la Guyane française, la Guadeloupe, la Martinique et la Réunion, qui font l'objet de rubriques distinctes, si disponible. Le total se rapporte uniquement aux femmes dont l'âge est compris entre 15 et 49 ans.
[14] Excluding Svalbard and Jan Mayen Island shown separately, if available. - Non compris Svalbard et Jan Mayen qui font l'objet de rubriques distinctes, si disponible.
[15] Based on hospital and polyclinic records. - D'après les registres des hôpitaux et des polycliniques.
[16] Excluding data for Kosovo and Metohia. Data refer to institutions included in the Health Institutions Network Plan in the Republic of Serbia. - Sans les données pour le Kosovo et Metohie. Les données se rapportent aux institutions membres du "Health Institutions Network Plan" de la République de Serbie.
[17] Data refer to resident population only. Excluding Channel Islands (Guernsey and Jersey) and Isle of Man, shown separately, if available. - Pour la population résidante seulement. Non compris les îles Anglo-Normandes (Guernesey et Jersey) et l'île de Man, qui font l'objet de rubriques distinctes, si disponible.

Table 14

Table 14 presents legally induced abortions by age and number of previous live births of women for the latest available year between 1998 and 2007.

Description of variables: Age is defined as age at last birthday, that is, the difference between the date of birth and the date of the occurrence of the event, expressed in complete solar years. The age classification used in this table is the following: under 15 years, 5-year age groups through 45-49 years and 50 years and over.

Except where otherwise indicated, eight categories are used in classifying the number of previous live births: 0 through 5, 6 or more live births, and, if required, number of live births unknown.

Information on abortion policies is collected by the United Nations Population Division and published in the World Population Policies[1]. An overview is also published a wall chart[2].

Reliability of data: Unlike data on live births and foetal deaths, which are generally collected through systems of vital registration, data on abortion are collected from a variety of sources. Because of this, the quality specification, showing the completeness of civil registers, which is presented for other tables, does not appear here.

Limitations: With regard to the collection of information on abortions, a variety of sources are used, but hospital records are the most common source of information. This implies that most cases that have no contact with hospitals are missed. Data from other sources are probably also incomplete. The data in the present table are limited to legally induced abortions, which, by their nature, might be assumed to be more complete than data on all induced abortions.

In addition, deficiencies in the reporting of age and number of previous live births of the woman, differences in the method used for obtaining the age of the woman, and the proportion of abortions for which age or previous live births of the woman are unknown must all be taken into account in using these data.

Earlier data: Legally induced abortions by age and previous live births of women have been shown previously in most issues of the *Demographic Yearbook* since the 1971 issue. For more information on specific topics and years for which data are reported, readers should consult the Index.

NOTES

[1] World Population Policies 2007 (United Nations Publication, Sales No. E.08.XIII.8), New York 2008. See also: http://www.un.org/esa/population/publications/wpp2007/Publication_index.htm.
[2] World Abortion Policies 2007 (United Nations Publication, Sales No. E.07.XIII.6), New York, 2007. See also: http://www.un.org/esa/population/publications/2007_Abortion_Policies_Chart/2007AbortionPolicies_wallchart.htm.

Tableau 14

Le tableau 14 présente les données les plus récentes dont on dispose sur les avortements provoqués pour des raisons légales, selon l'âge de la mère et le nombre de naissances vivantes précédentes.

Description des variables : Les notes techniques du tableau 13 contiennent une classification des avortements provoqués légalement. L'âge considéré est l'âge au dernier anniversaire, c'est-à-dire la différence entre la date de naissance et la date de l'avortement, exprimée en années solaires révolues. La classification par âge utilisée dans le tableau 14 est la suivante : moins de 15 ans, groupes quinquennaux jusqu'à 45-49 ans, 50 ans et plus, et âge inconnu.

Sauf indication contraire, les naissances vivantes antérieures sont classées dans les huit catégories suivantes: 0 à 5 naissances vivantes, 6 naissances vivantes ou plus et, le cas échéant, nombre de naissances vivantes inconnu.

La Division de la population des Nations Unies collecte des informations sur les politiques en matière d'avortement et les publient dans "World Population Policies"[1]. Une vue d'ensemble est également publiée sous forme de poster[2].

Fiabilité des données : à la différence des données sur les naissances vivantes et les morts fœtales, qui proviennent généralement des registres d'état civil, les données sur l'avortement sont tirées de sources diverses. Aussi ne trouve-t-on pas ici une évaluation de la qualité des données semblable à celle qui indique, pour les autres tableaux, le degré d'exhaustivité des données de l'état civil.

Insuffisance des données : en ce qui concerne les renseignements sur l'avortement, un grand nombre de sources sont utilisées, les relevés hospitaliers restant cependant la source la plus commune. Il s'ensuit que la plupart des cas qui ne passent pas par les hôpitaux sont ignorés. Il faut aussi tenir compte du fait que les données provenant d'autres sources sont probablement incomplètes. Les données du tableau 14 se limitent aux avortements provoqués pour raisons légales dont on peut supposer, en raison de leur nature même, que les statistiques sont plus complètes que les données concernant l'ensemble des avortements provoqués.

En outre, on doit tenir compte, lorsque l'on utilise ces données, des erreurs de déclaration de l'âge de la mère et du nombre des naissances vivantes précédentes, de l'hétérogénéité des méthodes de calcul de l'âge de la mère et de la proportion d'avortements pour lesquels l'âge de la mère ou le nombre des naissances vivantes ne sont pas connus.

Données publiées antérieurement : Depuis 1971, la plupart des éditions de l'*Annuaire démographique* contiennent des statistiques concernant les avortements provoqués pour raisons légales, selon l'âge de la mère et le nombre de naissances vivantes antérieures. Pour plus de précisions concernant les années et les sujets pour lesquels des données ont été publiées, se reporter à l'index.

NOTES

[1] World Population Policies 2007 (publication des Nations Unies, Numéro de vente E.08.XIII.8), New York 2008. http://www.un.org/esa/population/publications/wpp2007/Publication_index.htm.
[2] World Abortion Policies 2007 (publication des Nations Unies, Numéro de vente E.07.XIII.6), New York, 2007. http://www.un.org/esa/population/publications/2007_Abortion_Policies_Chart/2007AbortionPolicies_wallchart.htm.

14. Legally induced abortions by age and number of previous live births of women: latest available year, 1998 - 2007
Avortments provoqués légalement selon l'âge de la femme et selon le nombre des naissances vivantes précédentes: dernière année disponible, 1998 - 2007

Continent, country or area, year and age / Continent, pays ou zone, année et âge	Number of previous live births / Nombre des naissances vivantes précédentes								
	Total	0	1	2	3	4	5	6+	Unknown - Inconnu
AMERICA, NORTH - AMÉRIQUE DU NORD									
Canada[1]									
2005									
Total	96 815	...	...	...	...	...	...	...	...
0 - 14	284	...	...	...	...	...	...	...	...
15 - 19	16 065	...	...	...	...	...	...	...	...
20 - 24	30 359	...	...	...	...	...	...	...	...
25 - 29	21 419	...	...	...	...	...	...	...	...
30 - 34	14 450	...	...	...	...	...	...	...	...
35 - 39	9 973	...	...	...	...	...	...	...	...
40 - 44	4 263	...	...	...	...	...	...	...	...
45 +	-	...	...	...	...	...	...	...	...
Unknown - Inconnu	2	...	...	...	...	...	...	...	...
Cuba									
2007									
Total	66 008	...	...	...	...	...	...	...	...
0 - 19	20 648	...	...	...	...	...	...	...	...
20 - 34	36 292	...	...	...	...	...	...	...	...
35 +	9 068	...	...	...	...	...	...	...	...
Mexico - Mexique[2]									
2007									
Total	834	157	250	171	72	31	11	4	138
0 - 14	3	1	1	-	-	-	-	-	1
15 - 19	94	40	23	-	-	-	-	-	31
20 - 24	202	39	82	33	12	-	-	-	36
25 - 29	197	38	66	45	13	6	-	-	29
30 - 34	154	21	39	41	21	9	5	-	18
35 - 39	107	6	24	34	21	9	3	2	8
40 - 44	30	5	7	5	2	4	3	1	3
45 - 49	2	-	-	1	-	1	-	-	-
50 +	-	-	-	-	-	-	-	-	-
Unknown - Inconnu	45	7	8	12	3	2	-	1	12
Panama[3]									
2000									
Total	11	7	3	-	-	-	-	1	-
15 - 19	2	2	-	-	-	-	-	-	-
20 - 24	4	3	1	-	-	-	-	-	-
25 - 29	2	1	1	-	-	-	-	-	-
30 - 34	2	-	1	-	-	-	-	1	-
35 +	1	1	-	-	-	-	-	-	-
Puerto Rico - Porto Rico[4]									
2006									
Total	5 538	1 991	1 639	1 013	588	229	46	32	-
0 - 14	21	...	...	...	...	...	...	...	...
15 - 19	968	...	...	...	...	...	...	...	...
20 - 24	1 868	...	...	...	...	...	...	...	...
25 - 29	1 413	...	...	...	...	...	...	...	...
30 - 34	767	...	...	...	...	...	...	...	...
35 - 39	351	...	...	...	...	...	...	...	...
40 - 44	129	...	...	...	...	...	...	...	...
45 +	21	...	...	...	...	...	...	...	...
Turks and Caicos Islands - Îles Turques et Caïques[5]									
2005									
Total	32	...	...	...	...	...	...	...	...
15 - 19	4	...	...	...	...	...	...	...	...
20 - 24	7	...	...	...	...	...	...	...	...
25 - 29	9	...	...	...	...	...	...	...	...
30 - 34	6	...	...	...	...	...	...	...	...
35 - 39	4	...	...	...	...	...	...	...	...
40 - 44	1	...	...	...	...	...	...	...	...
45 +	1	...	...	...	...	...	...	...	...

14. Legally induced abortions by age and number of previous live births of women: latest available year, 1998 - 2007
Avortments provoqués légalement selon l'âge de la femme et selon le nombre des naissances vivantes précédentes: dernière année disponible, 1998 - 2007 (continued - suite)

Continent, country or area, year and age Continent, pays ou zone, année et âge	Total	Number of previous live births Nombre des naissances vivantes précédentes							Unknown - Inconnu
		0	1	2	3	4	5	6+	
ASIA - ASIE									
Armenia - Arménie									
2007									
Total....................................	11 501	...	...	...	...	...	...	...	...
15 - 19	548	...	...	...	...	...	...	...	...
20 - 34	8 585	...	...	...	...	...	...	...	...
35 + ...	2 368	...	...	...	...	...	...	...	...
Azerbaijan - Azerbaïdjan									
2007									
Total....................................	22 323								
0 - 14..................................	-	...	...	...	...	...	...	...	...
15 - 19	1 100	...	...	...	...	...	...	...	...
20 - 24	4 944	...	...	...	...	...	...	...	...
25 - 29	6 977	...	...	...	...	...	...	...	...
30 - 34	5 438	...	...	...	...	...	...	...	...
35 + ...	3 864	...	...	...	...	...	...	...	...
China, Hong Kong SAR - Chine, Hong Kong RAS									
2005									
Total....................................	14 190	7 995	2 764	2 774	547	^110			
0 - 14..................................	28	28	-	-	-	^_	...	...	-
15 - 19	1 260	1 215	41	4	-	^_	...	...	-
20 - 24	3 258	2 924	259	58	15	^2	...	...	-
25 - 29	2 883	2 007	554	281	35	^6	...	...	-
30 - 34	2 740	1 136	786	701	103	^14	...	...	-
35 - 39	2 518	516	735	1 012	208	^47	...	...	-
40 - 44	1 353	159	354	644	162	^34	...	...	-
45 + ...	150	10	35	74	24	^7	...	...	-
Unknown - Inconnu	-	-	-	-	-	^_	...	...	-
Georgia - Géorgie									
2007									
Total....................................	20 644								
0 - 14..................................	8	...	...	...	...	...	...	...	...
15 - 19	1 037	...	...	...	...	...	...	...	...
20 - 24	4 708	...	...	...	...	...	...	...	...
25 - 29	6 419	...	...	...	...	...	...	...	...
30 - 34	4 653	...	...	...	...	...	...	...	...
35 - 39	2 869	...	...	...	...	...	...	...	...
40 - 44	834	...	...	...	...	...	...	...	...
45 - 49	110	...	...	...	...	...	...	...	...
50 + ...	6	...	...	...	...	...	...	...	...
Israel - Israël[6]									
2007									
Total....................................	19 470	8 637	2 946	3 809	2 404	949	397	328	-
0 - 14..................................	76	75	1	-	-	-	-	-	-
15 - 19	2 735	2 650	74	9	1	-	-	-	-
20 - 24	4 082	3 237	508	277	53	6	1	1	-
25 - 29	3 827	1 712	874	781	317	93	31	-	-
30 - 34	4 003	692	888	1 325	673	258	100	19	-
35 - 39	3 093	217	441	1 001	838	329	139	67	-
40 - 44	1 488	47	141	376	473	237	114	128	-
45 - 49	157	4	18	38	48	26	12	100	-
50 + ...	9	3	1	2	1	-	-	11	-
Japan - Japon[7]									2
2007									
Total....................................	256 672								
0 - 14..................................	345	...	...	...	...	...	...	...	...
15 - 19	23 640	...	...	...	...	...	...	...	...
20 - 24	62 523	...	...	...	...	...	...	...	...
25 - 29	54 653	...	...	...	...	...	...	...	...
30 - 34	52 718	...	...	...	...	...	...	...	...
35 - 39	44 161	...	...	...	...	...	...	...	...
40 - 44	17 145	...	...	...	...	...	...	...	...
45 - 49	1 447	...	...	...	...	...	...	...	...
50 + ...	24	...	...	...	...	...	...	...	...
Unknown - Inconnu	16	...	...	...	...	...	...	...	...
Kazakhstan									
1999									
Total....................................	137 808	...	...	...	...	...	...	...	...
0 - 14..................................	177	...	...	...	...	...	...	...	...

14. Legally induced abortions by age and number of previous live births of women: latest available year, 1998 - 2007
Avortments provoqués légalement selon l'âge de la femme et selon le nombre des naissances vivantes précédentes: dernière année disponible, 1998 - 2007 (continued - suite)

Continent, country or area, year and age / Continent, pays ou zone, année et âge	Total	Number of previous live births / Nombre des naissances vivantes précédentes							Unknown - Inconnu
		0	1	2	3	4	5	6+	
ASIA - ASIE									
Kazakhstan									
1999									
15 - 18	8 971	...	...	...	...	...	...	...	...
19 - 35	105 204	...	...	...	...	...	...	...	...
36 +	23 456	...	...	...	...	...	...	...	...
Unknown - Inconnu	-	...	...						
Kyrgyzstan - Kirghizstan[8]									
2007									
Total	21 884	...	...	...	...	...	...	...	...
0 - 14	1	...	...	...	...	...	...	...	...
15 - 19	1 910	...	...	...	...	...	...	...	...
20 - 24	5 471	...	...	...	...	...	...	...	...
25 - 29	5 868	...	...	...	...	...	...	...	...
30 - 34	4 481	...	...	...	...	...	...	...	...
35 - 39	2 838	...	...	...	...	...	...	...	...
40 - 44	1 172	...	...	...	...	...	...	...	...
45 +	143	...	...	...	...	...	...	...	...
Singapore - Singapour									
2007									
Total	11 933	5 922	2 115	2 415	1 043	331	73	34	-
0 - 14	24	24	-	-	-	-	-	-	-
15 - 19	1 339	1 234	85	20					
20 - 24	2 980	2 323	405	192	40	18	1	1	
25 - 29	2 906	1 503	678	502	174	35	10	4	
30 - 34	2 275	571	537	743	317	85	14	8	
35 - 39	1 667	200	311	650	332	123	36	15	
40 - 44	681	63	93	277	166	64	12	6	
45 +	61	4	6	31	14	6	-	-	
Tajikistan - Tadjikistan									
2007									
Total	18 986	...	...	...	...	...	...	...	...
0 - 14	1	...	...	...	...	...	...	...	...
15 - 19	1 277	...	...	...	...	...	...	...	...
20 - 34	12 724	...	...	...	...	...	...	...	...
35 +	4 984	...	...	...	...	...	...	...	...
EUROPE									
Åland Islands - Îles d'Åland[9]									
2006									
Total	53	...	...	...	...	...	...	...	...
0 - 14	-	...	...	...	...	...	...	...	...
15 - 19	11	...	...	...	...	...	...	...	...
20 - 24	14	...	...	...	...	...	...	...	...
25 - 29	11	...	...	...	...	...	...	...	...
30 - 34	7	...	...	...	...	...	...	...	...
35 - 39	6	...	...	...	...	...	...	...	...
40 - 44	3	...	...	...	...	...	...	...	...
45 - 49	1	...	...	...	...	...	...	...	...
50 +	-	...	...	...	...	...	...	...	...
Unknown - Inconnu	-	...	...	...	...	...	...	...	...
Belarus - Bélarus									
2007									
Total	46 285	...	...	...	...	...	...	...	...
0 - 14	33	...	...	...	...	...	...	...	...
15 - 19	4 336	...	...	...	...	...	...	...	...
20 - 24	11 699	...	...	...	...	...	...	...	...
25 - 29	11 788	...	...	...	...	...	...	...	...
30 - 34	9 210	...	...	...	...	...	...	...	...
35 - 39	6 320	...	...	...	...	...	...	...	...
40 - 44	2 631	...	...	...	...	...	...	...	...
45 - 49	268	...	...	...	...	...	...	...	...
50 +	-	...	...	...	...	...	...	...	...
Belgium - Belgique									
2003									
Total	15 595	...	...	...	...	...	...	...	...
0 - 14	65	...	...	...	...	...	...	...	...

14. Legally induced abortions by age and number of previous live births of women: latest available year, 1998 - 2007
Avortements provoqués légalement selon l'âge de la femme et selon le nombre des naissances vivantes précédentes: dernière année disponible, 1998 - 2007 (continued - suite)

Continent, country or area, year and age / Continent, pays ou zone, année et âge	Total	Number of previous live births / Nombre des naissances vivantes précédentes							
		0	1	2	3	4	5	6+	Unknown - Inconnu
EUROPE									
Belgium - Belgique									
2003									
15 - 19	2 097	...	...	...	...	...	...	...	...
20 - 24	4 032	...	...	...	...	...	...	...	...
25 - 29	3 411	...	...	...	...	...	...	...	...
30 - 34	3 001	...	...	...	...	...	...	...	...
35 - 39	2 107	...	...	...	...	...	...	...	...
40 - 44	810	...	...	...	...	...	...	...	...
45 - 49	67	...	...	...	...	...	...	...	...
50 +	1	...	...	...	...	...	...	...	...
Unknown - Inconnu	4	...	...	...	...	...	...	...	...
Bulgaria - Bulgarie									
2007									
Total	37 594	...	...	...	...	...	...	...	...
0 - 14	176	...	...	...	...	...	...	...	...
15 - 19	3 536	...	...	...	...	...	...	...	...
20 - 24	9 026	...	...	...	...	...	...	...	...
25 - 29	9 897	...	...	...	...	...	...	...	...
30 - 34	8 414	...	...	...	...	...	...	...	...
35 - 39	4 888	...	...	...	...	...	...	...	...
40 - 44	1 543	...	...	...	...	...	...	...	...
45 - 49	109	...	...	...	...	...	...	...	...
50 +	5	...	...	...	...	...	...	...	...
Unknown - Inconnu	-	...	...	...	...	...	...	...	...
Croatia - Croatie									
2007									
Total	4 573	1 378	894	1 468	516	166	58	53	40
0 - 14	11	11	-	-	-	-	-	-	-
15 - 19	412	372	30	5	-	-	-	-	5
20 - 24	826	498	178	108	26	5	1	1	9
25 - 29	897	247	229	293	83	24	7	4	10
30 - 34	949	138	213	378	139	40	13	19	9
35 - 39	926	60	167	427	164	66	13	19	9
40 - 44	449	20	64	222	90	28	17	19	6
45 - 49	56	5	9	24	12	2	2	8	-
50 +	-	-	-	-	-	-	-	-	-
Unknown - Inconnu	47	27	4	11	2	1	1	-	1
Czech Republic - République tchèque									
2007									
Total	25 414	7 129	6 631	8 413	2 400	570	155	116	-
0 - 14	35	35	-	-	-	-	-	-	-
15 - 19	2 355	2 030	289	34	2	-	-	-	-
20 - 24	4 691	2 680	1 390	484	113	20	3	1	-
25 - 29	5 445	1 555	1 860	1 531	365	87	32	15	-
30 - 34	6 501	626	1 860	2 990	749	193	38	45	-
35 - 39	4 345	157	882	2 277	767	167	57	38	-
40 - 44	1 865	43	316	1 008	362	96	23	17	-
45 - 49	173	2	33	87	42	7	2	-	-
50 +	4	1	1	2	-	-	-	-	-
Unknown - Inconnu	-	-	-	-	-	-	-	-	-
Denmark - Danemark[10]									
2006									
Total	15 053	...	...	...	...	...	...	...	...
15 - 19	2 518	...	...	...	...	...	...	...	...
20 - 24	3 138	...	...	...	...	...	...	...	...
25 - 29	2 861	...	...	...	...	...	...	...	...
30 - 34	2 973	...	...	...	...	...	...	...	...
35 - 39	2 373	...	...	...	...	...	...	...	...
40 - 44	1 107	...	...	...	...	...	...	...	...
45 - 49	83	...	...	...	...	...	...	...	...
50 +	-	...	...	...	...	...	...	...	...
Estonia - Estonie[1]									
2007									
Total	8 883	2 541	2 982	2 420	666	184	53	24	13
0 - 14	18	18	-	-	-	-	-	-	-
15 - 19	1 275	1 079	184	8	1	-	-	-	3
20 - 24	2 145	980	922	218	19	5	-	-	3
25 - 29	1 900	326	799	607	125	33	5	3	1
30 - 34	1 624	95	576	699	193	34	19	4	4

14. Legally induced abortions by age and number of previous live births of women: latest available year, 1998 - 2007
Avortments provoqués légalement selon l'âge de la femme et selon le nombre des naissances vivantes précédentes: dernière année disponible, 1998 - 2007 (continued - suite)

Continent, country or area, year and age / Continent, pays ou zone, année et âge	Total	Number of previous live births / Nombre des naissances vivantes précédentes							Unknown - Inconnu
		0	1	2	3	4	5	6+	
EUROPE									
Estonia - Estonie[1]									
2007									
35 - 39	1 333	34	354	622	224	64	21	12	2
40 - 44	526	9	133	234	94	43	8	4	1
45 - 49	61	-	13	32	10	5	-	1	-
50 +	1	-	1	-	-	-	-	-	-
Unknown - Inconnu	-	-	-						
Faeroe Islands - Îles Féroé									
2005									
Total	29	...	...	...	...	...	...	...	...
0 - 14	-	...	...	...	...	...	...	...	...
15 - 19	6	...	...	...	...	...	...	...	...
20 - 24	2	...	...	...	...	...	...	...	...
25 - 29	5	...	...	...	...	...	...	...	...
30 - 34	8	...	...	...	...	...	...	...	...
35 - 39	5	...	...	...	...	...	...	...	...
40 - 44	3	...	...	...	...	...	...	...	...
45 - 49	-	...	...	...	...	...	...	...	...
50 +	-	...	...	...	...	...	...	...	...
Finland - Finlande[11]									
2007*									
Total	10 533	5 531	2 024	1 858	771	248	61	39	1
0 - 14	50	50	-	-	-	-	-	-	-
15 - 19	2 108	2 002	93	13	-	-	-	-	1
20 - 24	2 904	1 972	645	255	26	4	1	-	1
25 - 29	2 067	906	551	419	137	47	5	2	-
30 - 34	1 586	340	355	540	245	67	27	12	-
35 - 39	1 228	189	260	422	243	89	13	12	-
40 - 44	545	66	112	194	112	35	15	11	-
45 - 49	44	5	8	15	8	6	-	2	-
50 +	-	-	-	-	-	-	-	-	-
Unknown - Inconnu	1	1	-	-	-	-	-	-	-
France[12]									
2004									
Total	209 907	...	...	...	...	...	...	...	...
0 - 14	-	...	...	...	...	...	...	...	...
15 - 19	28 925	...	...	...	...	...	...	...	...
20 - 24	52 929	...	...	...	...	...	...	...	...
25 - 29	44 001	...	...	...	...	...	...	...	...
30 - 34	40 512	...	...	...	...	...	...	...	...
35 - 39	29 706	...	...	...	...	...	...	...	...
40 - 44	12 521	...	...	...	...	...	...	...	...
45 - 49	1 313	...	...	...	...	...	...	...	...
50 +	-	...	...	...	...	...	...	...	...
Germany - Allemagne									
2007									
Total	116 871	47 943	30 342	26 519	8 730	2 298	665	374	-
0 - 14	494	494	-	-	-	-	-	-	-
15 - 19	14 495	13 195	1 191	97	11	1	-	-	-
20 - 24	27 727	17 250	7 386	2 563	443	67	13	5	-
25 - 29	26 413	9 319	8 546	6 309	1 691	408	101	39	-
30 - 34	20 801	4 201	6 089	7 091	2 480	656	181	103	-
35 - 39	18 132	2 490	4 962	6 922	2 635	746	246	131	-
40 - 44	8 133	928	2 025	3 248	1 351	385	116	80	-
45 - 49	665	64	141	284	118	34	8	16	-
50 +	11	2	2	5	1	1	-	-	-
Greece - Grèce									
2003									
Total	15 782	...	...	...	...	...	...	...	...
0 - 14	8	...	...	...	...	...	...	...	...
15 - 19	569	...	...	...	...	...	...	...	...
20 - 29	5 934	...	...	...	...	...	...	...	...
30 - 39	7 557	...	...	...	...	...	...	...	...
40 - 49	1 345	...	...	...	...	...	...	...	...
50 +	48	...	...	...	...	...	...	...	...
Unknown - Inconnu	321	...	...	...	...	...	...	...	...

14. Legally induced abortions by age and number of previous live births of women: latest available year, 1998 - 2007
Avortments provoqués légalement selon l'âge de la femme et selon le nombre des naissances vivantes précédentes: dernière année disponible, 1998 - 2007 (continued - suite)

Continent, country or area, year and age / Continent, pays ou zone, année et âge	Total	Number of previous live births / Nombre des naissances vivantes précédentes							
		0	1	2	3	4	5	6+	Unknown - Inconnu
EUROPE									
Guernsey - Guernesey									
2000									
Total	89	46	21	11	9	1	1	-	-
0 - 14	1	1	-	-	-	-	-	-	-
15 - 19	12	11	1	-	-	-	-	-	-
20 - 24	30	17	13	-	-	-	-	-	-
25 - 29	18	11	3	3	1	-	-	-	-
30 - 34	15	4	3	4	2	1	1	-	-
35 - 39	10	1	1	4	4	-	-	-	-
40 - 44	3	1	-	-	2	-	-	-	-
45 +	-	-	-	-	-	-	-	-	-
Hungary - Hongrie									
2007									
Total	43 870	12 020	10 444	11 407	6 100	2 298	899	702	-
0 - 14	184	184	-	-	-	-	-	-	-
15 - 19	5 109	3 929	923	221	31	4	1	-	-
20 - 24	8 607	3 915	2 373	1 415	680	174	44	6	-
25 - 29	9 929	2 440	2 666	2 438	1 472	593	203	117	-
30 - 34	10 228	1 139	2 555	3 387	1 821	730	327	269	-
35 - 39	7 205	342	1 475	2 814	1 514	581	241	238	-
40 - 44	2 430	64	427	1 053	538	201	77	70	-
45 - 49	172	6	24	76	43	15	6	2	-
50 +	6	1	1	3	1	-	-	-	-
Unknown - Inconnu	-	-	-	-	-	-	-	-	-
Iceland - Islande									
2005									
Total	867	348	239	164	87	29	-	-	-
0 - 14	2	...	...	...	...	...	...	...	...
15 - 19	163	...	...	...	...	...	...	...	...
20 - 24	253	...	...	...	...	...	...	...	...
25 - 29	193	...	...	...	...	...	...	...	...
30 - 34	127	...	...	...	...	...	...	...	...
35 - 39	82	...	...	...	...	...	...	...	...
40 - 44	45	...	...	...	...	...	...	...	...
45 +	2	...	...	...	...	...	...	...	...
Italy - Italie									
2003									
Total	124 118	52 804	28 193	30 616	9 001	2 007	464	216	817
0 - 14	255	242	3	1	-	-	-	-	9
15 - 19	9 725	8 722	744	114	13	2	1	-	129
20 - 24	24 074	17 042	4 694	1 757	251	47	4	3	276
25 - 29	28 656	13 633	7 686	5 655	1 212	217	44	11	198
30 - 34	27 794	7 948	7 527	9 078	2 470	502	107	52	110
35 - 39	22 877	3 840	5 299	9 387	3 273	734	180	95	69
40 - 44	9 580	1 147	2 016	4 191	1 604	449	113	46	14
45 - 49	760	76	133	333	149	47	12	9	1
50 +	36	9	9	12	4	1	1	-	-
Unknown - Inconnu	361	145	82	88	25	8	2	-	11
Latvia - Lettonie									
2007									
Total	11 814	...	...	...	...	...	...	...	...
0 - 14	14	...	...	...	...	...	...	...	...
15 - 19	1 387	...	...	...	...	...	...	...	...
20 - 24	2 845	...	...	...	...	...	...	...	...
25 - 29	2 615	...	...	...	...	...	...	...	...
30 - 34	2 272	...	...	...	...	...	...	...	...
35 - 39	1 819	...	...	...	...	...	...	...	...
40 - 44	758	...	...	...	...	...	...	...	...
45 - 49	101	...	...	...	...	...	...	...	...
50 +	3	...	...	...	...	...	...	...	...
Lithuania - Lituanie									
2007									
Total	9 596	...	...	...	...	...	...	...	...
0 - 14	7	...	...	...	...	...	...	...	...
15 - 19	863	...	...	...	...	...	...	...	...
20 - 24	2 078	...	...	...	...	...	...	...	...
25 - 29	2 093	...	...	...	...	...	...	...	...
30 - 34	2 005	...	...	...	...	...	...	...	...
35 - 39	1 699	...	...	...	...	...	...	...	...

14. Legally induced abortions by age and number of previous live births of women: latest available year, 1998 - 2007
Avortments provoqués légalement selon l'âge de la femme et selon le nombre des naissances vivantes précédentes: dernière année disponible, 1998 - 2007 (continued - suite)

Continent, country or area, year and age / Continent, pays ou zone, année et âge	Total	Number of previous live births / Nombre des naissances vivantes précédentes							Unknown - Inconnu
		0	1	2	3	4	5	6+	
EUROPE									
Lithuania - Lituanie									
2007									
40 - 44	752	...	...	...	...	...	...	...	...
45 - 49	99	...	...	...	...	...	...	...	...
50 +	-	...	...	...	...	...	...	...	...
Montenegro - Monténégro									
2005									
Total	1 952	307	283	677	473	139	45	26	2
0 - 14	3	-	2	1	-	-	-	-	-
15 - 16	5	5	-	-	-	-	-	-	1
17 - 19	46	31	7	4	2	1	-	3	-
20 - 29	685	179	155	219	98	21	10	18	1
30 - 39	982	80	108	365	286	91	33	5	-
40 - 49	223	11	11	86	82	26	2	-	-
50 +	4	1	-	1	2	-	-	-	-
Unknown - Inconnu	4	-	-	1	3	-	-	-	-
Norway - Norvège[13]									
2006									
Total	14 132	...	...	...	...	...	...	...	...
0 - 14	37	...	...	...	...	...	...	...	...
15 - 19	2 307	...	...	...	...	...	...	...	...
20 - 24	3 740	...	...	...	...	...	...	...	...
25 - 29	2 904	...	...	...	...	...	...	...	...
30 - 34	2 495	...	...	...	...	...	...	...	...
35 - 39	1 877	...	...	...	...	...	...	...	...
40 - 44	694	...	...	...	...	...	...	...	...
45 - 49	55	...	...	...	...	...	...	...	...
50 +	-	...	...	...	...	...	...	...	...
Unknown - Inconnu	23	...	...	...	...	...	...	...	...
Poland - Pologne[14]									
2006									
Total	339	...	...	...	...	...	...	...	...
15 - 19	24	...	...	...	...	...	...	...	...
20 - 24	81	...	...	...	...	...	...	...	...
25 - 29	112	...	...	...	...	...	...	...	...
30 - 34	72	...	...	...	...	...	...	...	...
35 +	50	...	...	...	...	...	...	...	...
Republic of Moldova - République de Moldova									
2007									
Total	15 843	...	...	...	...	...	...	...	...
0 - 14	19	...	...	...	...	...	...	...	...
15 - 19	1 409	...	...	...	...	...	...	...	...
20 - 34	11 954	...	...	...	...	...	...	...	...
35 +	2 461	...	...	...	...	...	...	...	...
Romania - Roumanie									
2006									
Total	150 246	...	...	...	...	...	...	...	...
0 - 14	616	...	...	...	...	...	...	...	...
15 - 19	16 656	...	...	...	...	...	...	...	...
20 - 24	30 732	...	...	...	...	...	...	...	...
25 - 29	37 085	...	...	...	...	...	...	...	...
30 - 34	32 951	...	...	...	...	...	...	...	...
35 - 39	25 260	...	...	...	...	...	...	...	...
40 - 44	6 319	...	...	...	...	...	...	...	...
45 - 49	595	...	...	...	...	...	...	...	...
50 +	32	...	...	...	...	...	...	...	...
Russian Federation - Fédération de Russie									
2006									
Total	1 582 398	...	...	...	...	...	...	...	...
0 - 14	1 062	...	...	...	...	...	...	...	...
15 - 19	161 156	...	...	...	...	...	...	...	...
20 - 34	1 123 654	...	...	...	...	...	...	...	...
35 +	296 526	...	...	...	...	...	...	...	...
Serbia - Serbie[15]									
2007									
Total	24 273	5 974	4 604	9 879	2 758	757	173	128	-
0 - 14	16	14	-	2	-	-	-	-	-
15 - 19	967	738	151	63	12	3	-	-	-

14. Legally induced abortions by age and number of previous live births of women: latest available year, 1998 - 2007
Avortments provoqués légalement selon l'âge de la femme et selon le nombre des naissances vivantes précédentes: dernière année disponible, 1998 - 2007 (continued - suite)

Continent, country or area, year and age / Continent, pays ou zone, année et âge	Total	Number of previous live births / Nombre des naissances vivantes précédentes							Unknown - Inconnu
		0	1	2	3	4	5	6+	
EUROPE									
Serbia - Serbie[15]									
2007									
20 - 24	3 496	1 708	858	694	176	52	6	2	-
25 - 29	5 567	1 450	1 295	2 050	515	197	45	15	-
30 - 34	6 318	1 081	1 195	2 950	780	222	45	45	-
35 - 39	5 155	655	708	2 692	827	185	47	41	-
40 - 44	2 444	290	367	1 256	401	82	26	22	-
45 - 49	290	32	30	160	45	16	4	3	-
50 +	20	6	-	12	2	-	-	-	-
Unknown - Inconnu	-	-	-	-	-	-	-	-	-
Slovakia - Slovaquie									
2007									
Total	13 424	3 717	3 442	4 176	1 319	410	189	171	-
0 - 14	16	16	-	-	-	-	-	-	-
15 - 19	1 134	963	141	20	6	4	-	-	-
20 - 24	2 594	1 343	730	387	95	27	9	3	-
25 - 29	3 055	861	1 002	826	233	63	37	33	-
30 - 34	3 418	349	1 007	1 377	439	133	63	50	-
35 - 39	2 168	140	419	1 040	347	111	56	55	-
40 - 44	962	44	133	485	177	71	22	30	-
45 - 49	76	1	10	40	22	1	2	-	-
50 +	1	-	-	1	-	-	-	-	-
Slovenia - Slovénie									
2007									
Total	5 176	1 744	1 197	1 675	436	88	21	12	3
0 - 14	6	6	-	-	-	-	-	-	-
15 - 19	412	394	14	3	-	-	-	-	1
20 - 24	910	663	189	47	9	-	1	-	1
25 - 29	1 111	421	335	294	47	11	2	-	1
30 - 34	1 203	178	349	508	141	16	9	2	-
35 - 39	1 012	61	205	552	149	35	3	7	-
40 - 44	467	19	96	243	77	23	6	3	-
45 - 49	54	2	9	27	13	3	-	-	-
50 +	1	-	-	1	-	-	-	-	-
Unknown - Inconnu	-	-	-	-	-	-	-	-	-
Spain - Espagne									
2004									
Total	84 985	42 757	19 962	15 023	4 772	1 400	^741	...	330
0 - 14	369	365	1	-	-	-	^-	...	3
15 - 19	11 677	10 415	1 057	145	16	4	^-	...	40
20 - 24	22 461	15 193	5 127	1 680	353	33	^13	...	62
25 - 29	20 309	9 931	5 541	3 457	981	239	^77	...	83
30 - 34	15 212	4 630	4 381	4 186	1 329	424	^195	...	67
35 - 39	10 572	1 777	2 846	3 757	1 373	476	^288	...	55
40 - 44	4 072	414	949	1 665	661	211	^153	...	19
45 - 49	313	32	60	133	59	13	^15	...	1
50 +	-	-	-	-	-	-	^-	...	-
Sweden - Suède[16]									
2006									
Total	36 045	19 390	5 498	6 918	2 708	788	236	114	393
0 - 14	236	230	1	-	-	-	-	-	5
15 - 19	7 296	6 945	225	19	6	-	-	-	101
20 - 24	8 638	6 735	1 294	430	63	9	-	-	107
25 - 29	6 740	3 402	1 530	1 314	339	57	15	4	79
30 - 34	5 851	1 343	1 246	2 131	789	216	55	22	49
35 - 39	4 904	529	839	2 081	977	304	92	53	29
40 - 44	2 188	191	338	864	490	192	64	27	22
45 - 49	170	8	21	72	40	10	10	8	1
50 +	2	-	-	1	1	-	-	-	-
Unknown - Inconnu	20	7	4	6	3	-	-	-	1
Switzerland - Suisse									
2007*									
Total	9 469	...	...	...	...	...	...	...	...
0 - 14	9	...	...	...	...	...	...	...	...
15 - 19	1 072	...	...	...	...	...	...	...	...
20 - 24	2 088	...	...	...	...	...	...	...	...
25 - 29	2 110	...	...	...	...	...	...	...	...
30 - 34	1 868	...	...	...	...	...	...	...	...
35 - 39	1 506	...	...	...	...	...	...	...	...

14. Legally induced abortions by age and number of previous live births of women: latest available year, 1998 - 2007
Avortments provoqués légalement selon l'âge de la femme et selon le nombre des naissances vivantes précédentes: dernière année disponible, 1998 - 2007 (continued - suite)

Continent, country or area, year and age / Continent, pays ou zone, année et âge	Number of previous live births / Nombre des naissances vivantes précédentes								
	Total	0	1	2	3	4	5	6+	Unknown - Inconnu
EUROPE									
Switzerland - Suisse									
2007*									
40 - 44	699	...	...	...	...	...	...	...	...
45 - 49	76	...	...	...	...	...	...	...	...
50 +	-	...	...	...	...	...	...	...	...
Unknown - Inconnu	41	...	...	...	...	...	...	...	...
Ukraine									
2007									
Total	210 454	...	...	...	...	...	...	...	...
0 - 14	84	...	...	...	...	...	...	...	...
15 - 19	19 693	...	...	...	...	...	...	...	...
20 - 34	155 379	...	...	...	...	...	...	...	...
35 +	35 298	...	...	...	...	...	...	...	...
United Kingdom of Great Britain and Northern Ireland - Royaume-Uni de Grande-Bretagne et d'Irlande du Nord[17]									
2000									
Total	197 366	105 328	37 645	33 532	13 982	4 683	1 414	753	29
0 - 14	1 170	1 165	4	1	-	-	-	-	-
15 - 19	40 225	35 254	4 393	528	40	4	-	-	6
20 - 24	53 590	35 263	11 732	5 183	1 150	222	25	9	6
25 - 29	42 680	20 273	9 640	8 295	3 212	953	231	71	5
30 - 34	31 928	8 925	7 004	9 504	4 339	1 491	455	205	5
35 - 39	20 684	3 562	3 711	7 438	3 771	1 433	485	279	5
40 - 44	6 526	794	1 081	2 375	1 359	542	203	171	1
45 - 49	490	62	66	189	108	36	14	15	-
50 +	25	4	4	9	2	2	1	3	-
Unknown - Inconnu	48	26	10	10	1	-	-	-	1
2001									
Total	197 913	...	...	...	...	...	...	...	...
0 - 14	1 157	...	...	...	...	...	...	...	...
15 - 19	40 387	...	...	...	...	...	...	...	...
20 - 24	54 878	...	...	...	...	...	...	...	...
25 - 29	41 126	...	...	...	...	...	...	...	...
30 - 34	31 921	...	...	...	...	...	...	...	...
35 - 39	21 096	...	...	...	...	...	...	...	...
40 - 44	6 833	...	...	...	...	...	...	...	...
45 - 49	513	...	...	...	...	...	...	...	...
50 +	-	...	...	...	...	...	...	...	...
Unknown - Inconnu	2	...	...	...	...	...	...	...	...
OCEANIA - OCÉANIE									
New Zealand - Nouvelle-Zélande									
2007									
Total	18 382	9 197	3 582	3 170	1 414	612	241	166	-
0 - 14	104	103	1	-	-	-	-	-	-
15 - 19	4 173	3 606	503	59	5	-	-	-	-
20 - 24	5 445	3 252	1 272	702	169	45	3	2	-
25 - 29	3 574	1 361	788	780	386	183	48	28	-
30 - 34	2 547	557	547	721	391	182	90	59	-
35 - 39	1 814	242	329	682	302	136	72	51	-
40 - 44	667	69	125	207	152	64	25	25	-
45 - 49	58	7	17	19	9	2	3	1	-
50 +	-	-	-	-	-	-	-	-	-

FOOTNOTES - NOTES

* Provisional. - Données provisoires.

^ Indicates an open-ended group, for example 4+. - indique un groupe d'âge ouvert, par exemple 4 ou plus.

[1] Data refer to resident population only. - Pour la population résidante seulement.

[2] Data refer to resident population only. Data refer to abortions prescribed by a physician. - Pour la population résidante seulement. Les données se réfèrent aux avortements prescrits par un médecin.

[3] Data refer to abortions granted for medical reasons by the Comision Multidisciplinaria Nacional de Aborto Terapéutico. - Les données se réfèrent aux avortements autorisés pour des raisons médicales par la Comision Multidisciplinaria Nacional de Aborto Terapéutico.

[4] Data refer to the fiscal year 2006-2007. - Les données se réfèrent à l'année budgétaire 2006-2007.

[5] Data refer to abortions performed in hospitals at Grand Turk and Providenciales. - Pour des avortements exécutés dans les hôpitaux dans Grand Turk et Providenciales.

[6] Including data for East Jerusalem and Israeli residents in certain other territories under occupation by Israeli military forces since June 1967. Data refer to applications to commissions for termination of pregnancy and not to authorizations. - Y compris les données pour Jérusalem-Est et les résidents israéliens dans certains autres territoires occupés depuis 1967 par les forces armées israéliennes. Les données relatives aux avortements provoqués légalement se rapportent aux demandes d'autorisation et non aux autorisations elles-mêmes.

[7] Data refer to Japanese nationals in Japan only. - Les données se raportent aux nationaux japonais au Japon seulement.

[8] Based on administrative reporting of the Ministry of Health. - Les données reposent sur les rapports administratifs du Ministère de la santé.

[9] Also included in Finland. - Comprise aussi dans Finlande.

[10] Excluding Faeroe Islands and Greenland shown separately, if available. - Non compris les Îles Féroé et le Gröenland, qui font l'objet de rubriques distinctes, si disponible.

[11] Including Aland Islands. - Y compris les Îles d'Aland.

[12] Excluding Overseas Departments, namely, French Guiana, Guadeloupe, Martinique and Reunion, shown separately, if available. - Non compris les départements d'outre mer, c'est-à-dire la Guyane française, la Guadeloupe, la Martinique et la Réunion, qui font l'objet de rubriques distinctes, si disponible.

[13] Excluding Svalbard and Jan Mayen Island shown separately, if available. - Non compris Svalbard et Jan Mayen qui font l'objet de rubriques distinctes, si disponible.

[14] Based on hospital and polyclinic records. - D'après les registres des hôpitaux et des polycliniques.

[15] Excluding data for Kosovo and Metohia. Data refer to institutions included in the Health Institutions Network Plan in the Republic of Serbia. - Sans les données pour le Kosovo et Metohie. Les données se rapportent aux institutions membres du "Health Institutions Network Plan" de la République de Serbie.

[16] Data refer to previous deliveries of mother rather than previous live births of mother. - Avortements selon les accouchements précédents de la mère plutôt que selon les naissances vivantes de la mère.

[17] Data refer to resident population only. Excluding Channel Islands (Guernsey and Jersey) and Isle of Man, shown separately, if available. - Pour la population résidante seulement. Non compris les îles Anglo-Normandes (Guernesey et Jersey) et l'île de Man, qui font l'objet de rubriques distinctes, si disponible.

Table 15

Table 15 presents infant deaths and infant mortality rates by urban/rural residence for as many years as possible between 2003 and 2007.

Description of variables: Infant deaths are deaths of live-born infants under one year of age.

Statistics on the number of infant deaths are obtained from civil registers unless otherwise noted. Infant mortality rates are, in most instances, calculated from data on registered infant deaths and registered live births for a country or area where civil registration is considered reliable (that is, with an estimated completeness of 90 per cent or more).

The urban/rural classification of infant deaths is that provided by each reporting country or area; it is presumed to be based on the national census definitions of urban population that have been set forth at the end of the technical notes of table 6.

Rate computation: Infant mortality rates are the annual number of deaths of infants under one year of age per 1 000 live births (as shown in table 9) in the same year.

Rates by urban/rural residence are the annual number of infant deaths, in the appropriate urban or rural category, per 1 000 corresponding live births (as shown in table 9). These rates have been calculated by the Statistics Division of the United Nations.

Rates presented in this table have been limited to those for countries or areas having at least a total of 100 infant deaths in a given year and for which the quality code is represented by a "C" or a symbol "|".

Reliability of data: Each country or area has been asked to indicate the estimated completeness of the infant deaths recorded in its civil register. These national assessments are indicated by the quality codes "C", "U" and "|" that appear in the first column of this table.

"C" indicates that the data are estimated to be virtually complete, that is, representing at least 90 per cent of the infant deaths occurring each year, while "U" indicates that data are estimated to be incomplete that is, representing less than 90 per cent of the infant deaths occurring each year. The code "|" indicates that the source of data is not civil registration, but is still considered reliable. The code "…" indicates that no information was provided regarding completeness.

Data from civil registers that are reported as incomplete or of unknown completeness (coded "U" or "…") are considered unreliable. They appear in italics in this table; rates are not computed for data so coded.

Limitations: Statistics on infant deaths are subject to the same qualifications as have been set forth for vital statistics in general and death statistics in particular as discussed in section 4 of the Technical Notes.

The reliability of the data, an indication of which is described above, is an important factor in considering the limitations. In addition, some infant deaths are tabulated by date of registration and not by date of occurrence; these have been indicated by a plus sign "+". Whenever the lag between the date of occurrence and date of registration is prolonged and, therefore, a large proportion of the infant-death registrations are delayed, infant-death statistics for any given year may be seriously affected.

Another factor that limits international comparability is the practice of some countries or areas not to include in infant-death statistics infants who were born alive but died before the registration of the birth or within the first 24 hours of life, thus underestimating the total number of infant deaths. Statistics of this type are footnoted.

The method of reckoning age at death for infants may also introduce non-comparability. If year alone, rather than completed minutes, hours, days and months elapsed since birth, is used to calculate age at time of death, many of the infants who died during the eleventh month of life and some of those who died at younger ages will be classified as having completed one year of age and thus be excluded. The effect would be to underestimate the number of infant deaths. Information on this factor is given in footnotes when known. Reckoning of infant age is further discussed in the technical notes for table 16.

In addition, infant mortality rates are subject to the limitations of the data on live births with which they have been calculated. These have been set forth in the technical notes for table 9.

Because the two components of the infant mortality rate, infant deaths in the numerator and live births in the denominator, are both obtained from systems of civil registration, the limitations which affect live-birth statistics are very similar to those which have been mentioned above in connection with the infant-death statistics. It is important to consider the reliability of the data (the completeness of registration) and the method of tabulation (by date of occurrence or by date of registration) of live-birth statistics as well as infant-death statistics, both of which are used to calculate infant mortality rates. The quality code and use of italics to indicate unreliable data presented in this table refer only to infant deaths. Similarly, the indication of the basis of tabulation (the use of the symbol "+" to indicate data tabulated by date of registration) presented in this table also refers only to infant deaths. Table 9 provides the corresponding information for live births.

If the registration of infant deaths is more complete than the registration of live births, then infant mortality rates would be biased upwards. If, however, the registration of live births is more complete than registration of infant deaths, infant mortality rates would be biased downwards. If both infant deaths and live births are tabulated by registration, it should be noted that deaths tend to be more promptly reported than births.

Infant mortality rates may be seriously affected by the practice of some countries or areas of not considering infants that were born alive but died before the registration of the birth or within the first 24 hours of life as live-birth and subsequently infant death. Although this practice results in both the number of infant deaths in the numerator and the number of live births in the denominator being underestimated, its impact is greater on the numerator of the infant mortality rate. As a result this practice causes infant mortality rates to be biased downwards.

Infant mortality rates will also be underestimated if the method of reckoning age at death results in an underestimation of the number of infant deaths. This point has been discussed above.

Because of all these factors care should be taken in comparing and rank ordering infant mortality rates.

With respect to the method of calculating infant mortality rates used in this table, it should be noted that no adjustment was made to take account of the fact that a proportion of the infant deaths that occur during a given year are deaths of infants that were born during the preceding year and hence are not taken from the universe of births used to compute the rates. However, unless the number of live births or infant deaths is changing rapidly, the error involved is insignificant.

The comparability of data by urban/rural residence is affected by the national definitions of urban and rural used in tabulating these data. It is assumed, in the absence of specific information to the contrary, that the definitions of urban and rural used in connection with the national population census were also used in the compilation of the vital statistics for each country or area. However, it cannot be denied that, for some countries or areas, different definitions of urban and rural may be used for the vital statistics data and the population census data respectively. When known, the definitions of urban used in national population censuses are presented at the end of the technical notes for table 6. As discussed in detail in the technical notes for table 6, these definitions vary considerably from one country or area to another.

Urban/rural differentials in infant mortality rates may also be affected by whether the infant deaths and live births have been tabulated in terms of place of occurrence or place of usual residence. This problem is discussed in more detail in section 4.1.4.1 of the Technical Notes.

Earlier data: Infant deaths and infant mortality rates have been shown in previous issues of the *Demographic Yearbook*. For more information on specific topics and years for which data are reported, readers should consult the Historical Index.

Tableau 15

Le tableau 15 présente des données sur les décès d'enfants de moins d'un an et les taux de mortalité infantile selon le lieu de résidence (zone urbaine ou rurale) pour le plus grand nombre d'années possible entre 2003 et 2007.

Description des variables : les chiffres se rapportent aux décès d'enfants de moins d'un an.

Sauf indication contraire, les statistiques concernant le nombre de décès d'enfants de moins d'un an sont établies à partir des registres de l'état civil. Dans la plupart des cas, les taux de mortalité infantile sont calculés à partir des données relatives aux décès enregistrés d'enfants de moins d'un an et aux naissances vivantes enregistrées dans un pays ou une zone lorsque les registres de l'état civil sont jugés fiables (exhaustivité estimée à 90 p. 100 ou plus).

La classification des décès d'enfants de moins d'un an selon le lieu de résidence (zone urbaine ou rurale) est celle qui a été communiquée par chaque pays ou zone ; on part du principe qu'elle repose sur les définitions de la population urbaine utilisées pour les recensements nationaux, telles qu'elles sont reproduites à la fin des notes techniques du tableau 6.

Calcul des taux : Les taux de mortalité infantile représentent le nombre annuel de décès d'enfants de moins d'un an pour 1 000 naissances vivantes (fréquences du tableau 9) survenues pendant la même année.

Les taux selon le lieu de résidence (zone urbaine ou rurale) représentent le nombre annuel de décès d'enfants de moins d'un an, classés selon la catégorie urbaine ou rurale appropriée pour 1 000 naissances vivantes survenues parmi la population correspondante (fréquences du tableau 9). Ces taux ont été calculés par la Division de statistique de l'ONU.

Les taux présentés dans ce tableau se rapportent seulement aux pays ou zones où l'on a enregistré au moins un total de 100 décès d'enfants de moins d'un an au cours d'une année donnée et pour lesquels le code de qualité est soit "C", soit "I".

Fiabilité des données : il a été demandé à chaque pays ou zone d'indiquer le degré estimatif de complétude des données sur les décès d'enfants de moins d'un an figurant dans ses registres d'état civil. Ces évaluations nationales sont signalées par les codes de qualité "C", "U" et "I" qui apparaissent dans la deuxième colonne du tableau.

La lettre "C" indique que les données sont jugées à peu près complètes, c'est-à-dire qu'elles représentent au moins 90 p. 100 des décès d'enfants de moins d'un an survenus chaque année ; la lettre "U" signifie que les données sont jugées incomplètes, c'est-à-dire qu'elles représentent moins de 90 p.100 des décès d'enfants de moins d'un an survenus chaque année. Le symbole 'I' indique que la source des données n'est pas un registre de l'état civil, mais est quand même considérée fiable. Le code "..." dénote qu'aucun renseignement n'a été communiqué quant à la complétude des données.

Les données provenant des registres de l'état civil qui sont déclarées incomplètes ou dont le degré de complétude n'est pas connu (code "U" ou "...") sont jugées douteuses. Elles apparaissent en italique dans le tableau ; les taux, dans ces cas là, n'ont pas été calculés.

Insuffisance des données : les statistiques des décès d'enfants de moins d'un an appellent toutes les réserves qui ont été formulées à propos des statistiques de l'état civil en général et des statistiques concernant les décès en particulier (voir la section 4 des notes techniques).

La fiabilité des données, au sujet de laquelle des indications ont été fournies plus haut, est un facteur important. Il faut également tenir compte du fait que, dans certains cas, les données relatives aux décès d'enfants de moins d'un an sont exploitées selon la date de l'enregistrement et non la date de l'événement ; ces cas ont été signalés par le signe "+". Chaque fois que le décalage entre l'événement et son enregistrement est grand et qu'une forte proportion des décès d'enfants de moins d'un an fait l'objet d'un enregistrement tardif, les statistiques des décès d'enfants de moins d'un an pour une année donnée peuvent être considérablement faussées.

Un autre facteur qui nuit à la comparabilité internationale est la pratique de certains pays ou zones qui consiste à ne pas inclure dans les statistiques des décès d'enfants de moins d'un an les enfants nés vivants mais décédés avant l'enregistrement de leur naissance ou dans les 24 heures qui ont suivi la naissance, pratique qui conduit à sous-estimer le nombre total de décès d'enfants de moins d'un an. Quand pareil facteur a joué, cela a été signalé en note.

Les méthodes appliquées pour calculer l'âge au moment du décès peuvent également nuire à la comparabilité des données. Si l'on utilise à cet effet l'année seulement, et non pas les minutes, heures, jours et mois qui se sont écoulés depuis la naissance, de nombreux enfants décédés au cours du onzième mois qui a suivi leur naissance et certains enfants décédés encore plus jeunes seront classés comme décédés à un an révolu et donc exclus des données. Cette pratique conduit à sous-estimer le nombre de décès d'enfants de moins d'un an. Les renseignements dont on dispose sur ce facteur apparaissent en note à la fin du tableau. La question du calcul de l'âge au moment du décès est examinée plus en détail dans les notes techniques se rapportant au tableau 16.

Les taux de mortalité infantile appellent en outre toutes les réserves qui ont été formulées à propos des statistiques des naissances vivantes qui ont servi à leur calcul (voir à ce sujet les notes techniques relatives au tableau 9).

Les deux composantes du taux de mortalité infantile - décès d'enfants de moins d'un an au numérateur et naissances vivantes au dénominateur - étant obtenues à partir des registres de l'état civil, les statistiques des naissances vivantes appellent des réserves presque identiques à celles qui ont été formulées plus haut à propos des statistiques des décès d'enfants de moins d'un an. Il importe de prendre en considération la fiabilité des données (complétude de l'enregistrement) et le mode d'exploitation (selon la date de l'événement ou selon la date de l'enregistrement) dans le cas des statistiques des naissances vivantes tout comme dans le cas de celles des décès d'enfants de moins d'un an, puisque les unes et les autres servent au calcul des taux de mortalité infantile. Dans le tableau 15, le code de qualité et l'emploi de caractères italiques pour signaler les données moins sûres ne concernent que les décès d'enfants de moins d'un an. L'indication du mode d'exploitation des données (emploi du signe "+" pour signaler les données exploitées selon la date de l'enregistrement) ne porte là aussi que sur les décès d'enfants de moins d'un an. Le tableau 9 contient les renseignements correspondants pour les naissances vivantes.

Si l'enregistrement des décès d'enfants de moins d'un an est plus complet que l'enregistrement des naissances vivantes, les taux de mortalité infantile seront entachés d'une erreur par excès. En revanche, si l'enregistrement des naissances vivantes est plus complet que l'enregistrement des décès d'enfants de moins d'un an, les taux de mortalité infantile seront entachés d'une erreur par défaut. Si les décès d'enfants de moins d'un an et les naissances vivantes sont exploitées selon la date de l'enregistrement, il convient de ne pas perdre de vue que les décès sont, en règle générale, déclarés plus rapidement que les naissances.

Les taux de mortalité infantile peuvent être gravement faussés par la pratique de certains pays ou zones qui consiste à ne pas classer dans les naissances vivantes et ensuite dans les décès d'enfants de moins d'un an les enfants nés vivants mais décédés soit avant l'enregistrement de leur naissance, soit dans les 24 heures qui ont suivi la naissance. Cette pratique conduit à sous-estimer aussi bien le nombre des décès d'enfants de moins d'un an, qui constitue le numérateur, que le nombre des naissances vivantes, qui constitue le dénominateur, mais c'est pour le numérateur du taux de mortalité infantile que la distorsion est la plus marquée. Ce système a pour effet d'introduire une erreur par défaut dans les taux de mortalité infantile.

Les taux de mortalité infantile seront également sous-estimés si la méthode utilisée pour calculer l'âge au moment du décès conduit à sous-estimer le nombre de décès d'enfants de moins d'un an. Cette question a été examinée plus haut.

Tous ces facteurs sont importants et il faut donc en tenir compte lorsque l'on compare et classe les taux de mortalité infantile.

En ce qui concerne la méthode de calcul des taux de mortalité infantile utilisée dans le tableau, il convient de noter qu'il n'a pas été tenu compte du fait qu'une partie des décès survenus pendant une année donnée sont des décès d'enfants nés l'année précédente et ne correspondent donc pas à l'ensemble des naissances utilisé pour le calcul des taux. Toutefois, l'erreur n'est pas grave, à moins que le nombre des naissances vivantes ou des décès d'enfants de moins d'un an ne varie rapidement.

La comparabilité des données selon le lieu de résidence (zone urbaine ou rurale) peut être limitée par les définitions nationales des termes « urbain » et « rural » utilisées pour la mise en tableaux de ces données. En l'absence d'indications contraires, on a supposé que les mêmes définitions avaient servi pour le recensement national de la population et pour l'établissement des statistiques de l'état civil pour chaque pays ou zone. Toutefois, il n'est pas exclu que, pour une zone ou un pays donné, des définitions différentes aient été retenues. Les définitions du terme « urbain » utilisées pour les recensements nationaux de population ont été présentées à la fin des notes techniques du tableau 6 lorsqu'elles étaient connues. Comme on l'a précisé dans les notes techniques relatives au tableau 6, ces définitions varient considérablement d'un pays ou d'une zone à l'autre.

La différence entre les taux de mortalité infantile pour les zones urbaines et rurales pourra aussi être faussée selon que les décès d'enfants de moins d'un an et les naissances vivantes auront été classés d'après le lieu de l'événement ou le lieu de résidence habituel. Ce problème est examiné plus en détail à la section 4.1.4.1 des Notes techniques.

Données publiées antérieurement : des statistiques concernant les décès d'enfants de moins d'un an et les taux de mortalité infantile ont déjà été présentées dans des éditions antérieures de l'*Annuaire démographique*. Pour plus de précisions concernant les années et les sujets pour lesquels des données ont été publiées, se reporter à l'index historique.

15. Infant deaths and infant mortality rates, by urban/rural residence: 2003 - 2007
Décès d'enfants de moins d'un an et taux de mortalité infantile, selon la résidence, urbaine/rurale: 2003 - 2007

Continent, country or area, and urban/rural residence — Continent, pays ou zone et résidence, urbaine/rurale	Code[a]	Number - Nombre					Rate - Taux				
		2003	2004	2005	2006	2007	2003	2004	2005	2006	2007
AFRICA - AFRIQUE											
Burkina Faso[1]											
Total	|	...	...	...	16 259	...	...	...	...	26.5	...
Urban - Urbaine	|	...	...	...	1 704	...	...	...	...	15.8	...
Rural - Rurale	|	...	...	...	14 555	...	...	...	...	28.8	...
Egypt - Égypte											
Total	C	38 859	40 177	36 146	35 952	34 612	21.9	22.6	20.1	19.4	17.8
Urban - Urbaine	C	17 021	16 954	16 676	17 792	17 030	22.1	23.8	23.1	24.0	22.3
Rural - Rurale	C	21 838	23 223	19 470	18 160	17 582	21.7	21.8	18.1	16.3	14.8
Kenya											
Total	U	35 515	35 321	35 252	35 786		...	...	...	...	...
Mauritius - Maurice											
Total	+C	250	277	248	249	261	12.9	14.4	13.2	14.1	15.3
Urban - Urbaine	+C	93	90	92	79	106	...	...	...	...	16.4
Rural - Rurale	+C	157	187	156	170	155	13.3	15.6	13.3	15.6	14.7
Réunion[2]											
Total	C	107	104	117	96	91	7.4	7.2	8.0	...	...
Saint Helena ex. dep. - Sainte-Hélène sans dép.											
Total	C	1	-	1	-	-	...	...	...	...	...
Seychelles											
Total	+C	24	17	16	14	16	...	...	...	...	...
South Africa - Afrique du Sud											
Total	...	38 306	41 132	46 122	47 703		...	...	...	...	...
AMERICA, NORTH - AMÉRIQUE DU NORD											
Anguilla											
Total	+C	2	-	3	*1	-	...	...	...	...	...
Aruba											
Total	+U	3	3	6	8	4	...	...	...	...	...
Bahamas											
Total	C	54	57	100	79	69	...	...	18.0	...	...
Barbados - Barbade											
Total	+C	*37	*64	*29	*38	*46	...	...	...	...	...
Belize											
Total	U	...	112	137	...		...	...	...	...	...
Bermuda - Bermudes											
Total	C	2	-	2	6		...	...	...	...	...
Canada[3]											
Total	C	1 765	1 775	1 863	...	...	5.3	5.3	5.4	...	...
Cayman Islands - Îles Caïmanes											
Total	C	6	3	4	8	5	...	...	...	...	...
Costa Rica											
Total	C	737	668	700	692	735	10.1	9.2	9.8	9.7	10.0
Urban - Urbaine	C	388	292	280	301	326	11.5	9.4	9.1	10.2	11.3
Rural - Rurale	C	349	376	420	391	409	8.9	9.2	10.3	9.4	9.2
Cuba											
Total	C	859	736	746	589	592	6.3	5.8	6.2	5.3	5.3
Urban - Urbaine	C	671	...	584	475	401	6.7	...	6.6	5.7	4.7
Rural - Rurale	C	188	...	162	114	191	5.2	...	5.1	4.1	6.9
Dominica - Dominique											
Total	+C	20	14	22	13		...	...	...	...	...
Dominican Republic - République dominicaine											
Total	U	451	359	369	158	60	...	...	...	...	...
Urban - Urbaine[4]	U	336	190	276	127	43	...	...	...	...	...
Rural - Rurale[4]	U	75	66	56	24	13	...	...	...	...	...
El Salvador											
Total	C	1 322	1 255	1 097	1 013	981	10.6	10.5	9.7	9.5	9.2
Urban - Urbaine	C	847	781	718	822	713	11.6	10.9	10.4	11.6	10.4
Rural - Rurale	C	475	474	379	191	268	9.3	9.8	8.7	5.3	7.0

15. Infant deaths and infant mortality rates, by urban/rural residence: 2003 - 2007
Décès d'enfants de moins d'un an et taux de mortalité infantile, selon la résidence, urbaine/rurale: 2003 - 2007 (continued - suite)

Continent, country or area, and urban/rural residence / Continent, pays ou zone et résidence, urbaine/rurale	Co-de[a]	Number - Nombre					Rate - Taux				
		2003	2004	2005	2006	2007	2003	2004	2005	2006	2007
AMERICA, NORTH - AMÉRIQUE DU NORD											
Greenland - Groenland											
Total	C	8	10	7	13	7	...	...	...	...	...
Urban - Urbaine	C	8	...	...	...	...	...	...	...	...	...
Rural - Rurale	C	-	...	...	...	...	...	...	...	...	...
Guadeloupe[2]											
Total	C	56	50	...	...	...	...	...	...	...	...
Guatemala											
Total	C	11 022	10 038	9 947	9 042	...	29.4	26.2	26.6	24.5	...
Urban - Urbaine	C	...	...	5 062	4 993	...	...	...	31.6	31.6	...
Rural - Rurale	C	...	...	4 885	4 049	...	...	...	22.8	19.3	...
Honduras											
Total	+U	6 902	6 740	6 566	6 400	...	...	...	...	...	...
Urban - Urbaine	+U	2 162	2 135	2 104	2 077	...	...	...	...	...	...
Rural - Rurale	+U	4 740	4 605	4 462	4 323	...	...	...	...	...	...
Jamaica - Jamaïque[5]											
Total	U	1 004	1 004	1 007	...	...	...	...	...	...	...
Martinique											
Total	C	34	27	47	44	47	...	...	...	...	...
Urban - Urbaine	C	31	26	35	41	43	...	...	...	...	...
Rural - Rurale	C	3	1	12	3	4	...	...	...	...	...
Mexico - Mexique[6]											
Total	+U	33 331	32 758	32 590	30 890	30 412	...	...	...	...	...
Urban - Urbaine[4]	+U	25 073	24 433	24 372	23 057	22 656	...	...	...	...	...
Rural - Rurale[4]	+U	7 714	7 671	7 639	7 263	7 284	...	...	...	...	...
Netherlands Antilles - Antilles néerlandaises											
Total	C	19	20	26	40	33	...	...	...	...	...
Nicaragua											
Total	+U	2 008	1 827	1 970	1 925	1 955	...	...	...	...	...
Urban - Urbaine	+U	1 091	1 073	934	973	1 072	...	...	...	...	...
Rural - Rurale	+U	917	754	1 036	952	883	...	...	...	...	...
Panama											
Total	U	940	932	980	971	992	...	...	...	...	...
Urban - Urbaine	U	500	546	533	490	500	...	...	...	...	...
Rural - Rurale	U	440	386	447	481	492	...	...	...	...	...
Puerto Rico - Porto Rico											
Total	C	498	416	472	442	...	9.8	8.1	9.3	9.1	...
Urban - Urbaine	C	297[4]	246[4]	285	...	...	11.1	9.2	10.2	...	...
Rural - Rurale	C	199[4]	169[4]	187	...	...	8.2	6.9	8.2	...	...
Saint Lucia - Sainte-Lucie											
Total	C	37	45	*46	...	...	...	...	...	...	...
Saint Vincent and the Grenadines - Saint-Vincent-et-les Grenadines											
Total	+C	35	33	29	...	...	...	...	...	...	...
Trinidad and Tobago - Trinité-et-Tobago											
Total	C	431	284	266	...	...	24.0	16.5	...	...	...
Turks and Caicos Islands - Îles Turques et Caïques											
Total	C	2	-	1	4	2	...	...	...	...	...
United States of America - États-Unis d'Amérique											
Total	C	28 025	27 936	28 440	28 527	...	6.9	6.8	6.9	6.7	...
United States Virgin Islands - Îles Vierges américaines											
Total	C	8	8	9	8	12	...	...	...	...	...
AMERICA, SOUTH - AMÉRIQUE DU SUD											
Argentina - Argentine											
Total	C	11 494	10 576	9 507	8 986	9 300	16.5	14.4	13.3	12.9	13.3

15. Infant deaths and infant mortality rates, by urban/rural residence: 2003 - 2007
Décès d'enfants de moins d'un an et taux de mortalité infantile, selon la résidence, urbaine/rurale: 2003 - 2007 (continued - suite)

Continent, country or area, and urban/rural residence — Continent, pays ou zone et résidence, urbaine/rurale	Code[a]	Number - Nombre					Rate - Taux				
		2003	2004	2005	2006	2007	2003	2004	2005	2006	2007
AMERICA, SOUTH - AMÉRIQUE DU SUD											
Brazil - Brésil[7]											
Total....................	U	48 039	41 851	39 259	37 677	35 159[8]					
Chile - Chili							...	...	...	...	...
Total....................	C	1 935	2 034	1 911	1 839	...					
Urban - Urbaine	C	1 691	1 773	1 637	1 587	...	8.3	8.8	8.3	7.9	...
Rural - Rurale	C	244	261	274	252	...	8.1	8.7	8.0	7.6	...
Colombia - Colombie							9.8	10.1	10.7	11.1	...
Total....................	U	12 210	11 772	11 456	11 049	*9 997					
Urban - Urbaine[4]	U	8 807	8 445	8 160	7 812	*7 221	...	...	...	...	...
Rural - Rurale[4]	U	2 722	2 664	2 643	2 703	*2 351	...	...	...	...	...
Ecuador - Équateur[9]							...	...	...	...	...
Total....................	U	3 985	3 942	3 717	3 715	3 529					
Urban - Urbaine	U	3 085	3 121	2 936	2 923	2 883	...	...	...	...	...
Rural - Rurale	U	900	821	781	792	646	...	...	...	...	...
French Guiana - Guyane française[2]											
Total....................	C	61	55	64	79	77					
Urban - Urbaine	C	43	42	47	58	60	...	...	...	...	...
Rural - Rurale	C	18	13	17	21	17	...	...	...	...	...
Paraguay											
Total....................	U	674	647	539	549	...	...	...	...	...	...
Peru - Pérou[10]											
Total....................	I	14 015	13 135	12 343	11 584	...	36.5	38.1	39.7	37.6	...
Suriname[11]											
Total....................	C	109	120	136	129	134	11.3	13.2	15.7	13.9	13.7
Urban - Urbaine[12]........	C	69[4]	67[4]	87[4]	88	97	...	...	...	...	...
Rural - Rurale[12]..........	C	36[4]	49[4]	48[4]	41	37	...	...	...	...	...
Uruguay											
Total....................	C	*757	659	*601	*497	573	*15.0	13.2	*12.7	*10.5	12.1
ASIA - ASIE											
Armenia - Arménie[13]											
Total....................	C	422	430	460	523	433	11.8	11.5	12.3	13.9	10.8
Urban - Urbaine	C	311	311	351	389	315	13.7	13.2	14.8	16.3	12.3
Rural - Rurale	C	111	119	109	134	118	8.4	8.6	7.9	9.7	8.1
Azerbaijan - Azerbaïdjan[13]											
Total....................	+C	1 649	1 892	1 580	1 882	1 756	14.5	14.4	11.1	12.6	11.6
Urban - Urbaine	+C	719	889	780	1 082	1 036	14.1	15.1	12.1	15.3	14.2
Rural - Rurale	+C	930	1 003	800	800	720	14.9	13.8	10.3	10.2	9.1
Bahrain - Bahreïn											
Total....................	C	107	141	134	115	133	7.3	9.4	8.8	7.6	8.3
Bangladesh[14]											
Total....................	I	...	...	...	...	...	53.0	52.0	49.0	45.0	43.0
Urban - Urbaine	I	...	...	...	...	...	40.0	41.0	44.0	38.0	42.0
Rural - Rurale	I	...	...	...	...	...	57.0	55.0	51.0	47.0	43.0
Bhutan - Bhoutan[15]											
Total....................	I	...	...	503	...	...	...	...	40.1	...	...
Urban - Urbaine	I	...	...	126	...	...	...	...	32.8	...	...
Rural - Rurale	I	...	...	377	...	...	...	...	43.4	...	...
Brunei Darussalam - Brunéi Darussalam											
Total....................	+C	67	63	*51	...	...	...	...	...	...	...
Cambodia - Cambodge											
Total....................	...	80	76	...	...	...	...	...	...	...	...
China, Hong Kong SAR - Chine, Hong Kong RAS											
Total....................	C	109	132	131	*118	*125	2.3	2.7	2.3	*1.8	*1.8
China, Macao SAR - Chine, Macao RAS											
Total....................	C	2	10	12	11	9	...	...	...	...	...
Cyprus - Chypre[16]											
Total....................	C	33	29	38	27	32	...	...	...	...	...

15. Infant deaths and infant mortality rates, by urban/rural residence: 2003 - 2007
Décès d'enfants de moins d'un an et taux de mortalité infantile, selon la résidence, urbaine/rurale: 2003 - 2007 (continued - suite)

Continent, country or area, and urban/rural residence / Continent, pays ou zone et résidence, urbaine/rurale	Code[a]	Number - Nombre					Rate - Taux				
		2003	2004	2005	2006	2007	2003	2004	2005	2006	2007
ASIA - ASIE											
Georgia - Géorgie[13]											
Total	C	1 144	1 178	916	753	656	24.8	23.8	19.7	15.8	13.3
Urban - Urbaine	C	1 057	803	838	651	555	30.6	25.9	26.9	19.4	16.2
Rural - Rurale	C	87	375	78	102	101	...	20.2	...	7.2	6.7
India - Inde[17]											
Total	I	...	...	...	...	...	60.0	58.0	58.0	57.0	55.0
Urban - Urbaine	I	...	...	...	...	...	38.0	40.0	40.0	39.0	37.0
Rural - Rurale	I	...	...	...	...	...	66.0	64.0	64.0	62.0	61.0
Iraq											
Total	U	...	*10 972	*12 460	*48 078	...	...	...	...	...	...
Israel - Israël[18]											
Total[19]	C	717	670	629	598	591	4.9	4.6	4.4	4.0	3.9
Urban - Urbaine	C	641	597	558	536	530	4.9	4.5	4.3	4.0	3.8
Rural - Rurale	C	74	73	70	62	61	...	...	...	...	...
Japan - Japon[20]											
Total	C	3 364	3 122	2 958	2 864	2 828	3.0	2.8	2.8	2.6	2.6
Urban - Urbaine[4]	C	2 728	2 591	2 544	2 581	2 564	3.0	2.8	2.8	2.6	2.6
Rural - Rurale[4]	C	631	529	407	280	259	3.1	2.7	2.8	2.6	2.5
Kazakhstan[13]											
Total	C	3 806	3 901	4 213	4 154	4 646	15.4	14.3	15.1	13.8	14.4
Urban - Urbaine	C	2 340	2 418	2 711	2 730	2 765	16.9	15.5	16.5	15.5	15.9
Rural - Rurale	C	1 466	1 483	1 502	1 424	1 881	13.4	12.7	13.1	11.3	12.7
Kuwait - Koweït											
Total	C	412	422	420	456	449	9.4	8.9	8.2	8.6	8.4
Kyrgyzstan - Kirghizstan											
Total	C	2 186	2 812[21]	3 258	3 526	3 771	20.7	25.6	29.7	29.2	30.6
Urban - Urbaine	C	880	1 427[21]	1 617	1 802	1 963	27.6	38.2	45.4	45.7	47.4
Rural - Rurale	C	1 306	1 385[21]	1 641	1 724	1 808	17.7	19.1	22.1	21.2	22.1
Malaysia - Malaisie											
Total	C	3 148	3 105	3 112	2 877	*2 878	6.6	6.5	6.6	6.2	*6.3
Urban - Urbaine	C	1 781	1 873	1 822	1 701	...	5.9	6.2	6.2	5.8	...
Rural - Rurale	C	1 367	1 232	1 290	1 176	...	7.8	7.0	7.4	6.9	...
Maldives											
Total	C	72	76	67	92	66	...	...	...	...	...
Urban - Urbaine	C	16	21	29	36	28	...	...	...	...	...
Rural - Rurale	C	56	55	38	56	38	...	...	...	...	...
Mongolia - Mongolie											
Total	C	1 051	1 016	938	937	994	23.0	22.3	20.7	19.1	17.6
Urban - Urbaine	C	520	531	520	583	707	21.4	20.6	19.7	19.6	19.5
Rural - Rurale	C	531	485	418	354	287	24.8	24.6	22.2	18.3	14.1
Myanmar											
Total	U	31 873	36 812	38 872	...	...	...	...	...	...	...
Urban - Urbaine	U	10 378	10 340	10 531	...	...	...	...	...	...	...
Rural - Rurale	U	21 495	26 472	28 341	...	...	...	...	...	...	...
Occupied Palestinian Territory - Territoire palestinien occupé											
Total	U	1 150	1 103	1 057	906	794	...	...	...	...	...
Oman[22]											
Total	U	335	336	315	381		...	...	...	...	...
Pakistan[23]											
Total	I	280 729[24]	...	289 169[25]	...	...	76.2	...	76.7	...	...
Urban - Urbaine	I	80 199[24]	...	82 299[25]	...	...	67.2	...	67.1	...	...
Rural - Rurale	I	200 530[24]	...	206 870[25]	...	...	80.6	...	81.2	...	...
Philippines											
Total	C	22 844	22 557	21 674	...	...	13.7	13.2	12.8	...	...
Qatar											
Total	C	137	113	110	114	117	10.7	8.6	8.2	8.1	7.5
Republic of Korea - République de Corée[26]											
Total[27]	C	2 470	2 209	1 822	1 709	*1 703	5.0	4.6	4.2	3.8	*3.4
Urban - Urbaine	C	1 984	1 759	1 438	1 359	...	4.9	4.5	4.0	3.7	...
Rural - Rurale	C	483	447	382	348	...	5.6	5.3	4.9	4.5	...
Saudi Arabia - Arabie saoudite											
Total	...	11 297	11 165	11 078	10 954	...	...	...	...	...	...

15. Infant deaths and infant mortality rates, by urban/rural residence: 2003 - 2007
Décès d'enfants de moins d'un an et taux de mortalité infantile, selon la résidence, urbaine/rurale: 2003 - 2007 (continued - suite)

Continent, country or area, and urban/rural residence — Continent, pays ou zone et résidence, urbaine/rurale	Code[a]	Number - Nombre					Rate - Taux				
		2003	2004	2005	2006	2007	2003	2004	2005	2006	2007
ASIA - ASIE											
Singapore - Singapour											
Total	+C	100	82	95	117	94	2.7	...	...	3.1	...
Tajikistan - Tadjikistan[13]											
Total	U	1 944	2 071	2 129	2 160	2 168	...	...	...	...	...
Urban - Urbaine	U	824	953	983	994	993	...	...	...	...	...
Rural - Rurale	U	1 120	1 118	1 146	1 166	1 175	...	...	...	...	...
Thailand - Thaïlande											
Total	+U	5 349	6 061	6 183	5 855	5 781	...	...	...	...	...
Turkey - Turquie[28]											
Total	I	29 822	26 877	24 211	22 348	21 293	23.1	20.9	18.9	17.5	16.7
United Arab Emirates - Émirats arabes unis											
Total	...		488	550	500	455		...	...	...	...
Viet Nam											
Total	C	27 134	22 610	22 301	19 895	21 223	21.0	18.1	17.8	16.0	16.0
Urban - Urbaine	C	4 376	3 412	3 109	3 205	3 581	13.0	11.1	9.7	10.0	10.0
Rural - Rurale	C	22 758	19 198	19 192	16 690	17 642	23.8	20.4	20.6	18.1	18.2
EUROPE											
Åland Islands - Îles d'Åland[29]											
Total	C	2	1	-	-	-	...	...	...	...	...
Urban - Urbaine	C	-	1	-	-	-	...	...	...	...	...
Rural - Rurale	C	2	-	-	-	-	...	...	...	...	...
Albania - Albanie											
Total	C	395	336	303	253	205	8.4	7.8	7.6	7.4	6.2
Andorra - Andorre											
Total	C	-	2	5	3	1	...	...	...	...	...
Austria - Autriche											
Total	C	343	353	327	281	280	4.5	4.5	4.2	3.6	3.7
Belarus - Bélarus[13]											
Total	C	685	614	640	587	534	7.7	6.9	7.1	6.1	5.2
Urban - Urbaine	C	440	386	398	407	339	6.8	5.9	6.0	5.7	4.4
Rural - Rurale	C	245	228	242	180	195	10.3	9.5	10.0	7.0	7.4
Belgium - Belgique[30]											
Total	C	462	437	441	489	487	4.1	3.8	3.7	4.0	4.0
Urban - Urbaine	C	454	431	432	482	485	4.1	3.8	3.7	4.0	4.0
Rural - Rurale	C	8	6	9	7	2	...	...	...	4.0	4.1
Bosnia and Herzegovina - Bosnie-Herzégovine											
Total	C	268	253	233	255	231	7.6	7.2	6.7	7.5	6.8
Bulgaria - Bulgarie											
Total	C	831	814	739	720	690	12.3	11.6	10.4	9.7	9.2
Urban - Urbaine	C	522	516	464	472	447	10.7	10.2	8.9	8.6	7.9
Rural - Rurale	C	309	298	275	248	243	16.5	15.3	14.6	13.1	12.7
Croatia - Croatie											
Total	C	251	245	242	215	234	6.3	6.1	5.7	5.2	5.6
Urban - Urbaine	C	135	132	151	113	136	6.2	5.9	6.4	4.9	5.8
Rural - Rurale	C	116	113	91	102	98	6.5	6.3	...	5.6	...
Czech Republic - République tchèque											
Total	C	365	366	347	352	360	3.9	3.7	3.4	3.3	3.1
Urban - Urbaine	C	266	268	261	268	259	3.8	3.7	3.4	3.4	3.1
Rural - Rurale	C	99	98	86	84	101	...	...	...	...	3.4
Denmark - Danemark[31]											
Total	C	286	283	280	250	256	4.4	4.4	4.4	3.8	4.0
Estonia - Estonie											
Total	C	91	90	78	66	79	...	...	...	...	...
Urban - Urbaine	C	59	58	53	47	56	...	...	...	...	...
Rural - Rurale	C	32	32	25	19	23	...	...	...	...	...
Finland - Finlande[32]											
Total	C	176	191	174	167	161	3.1	3.3	3.0	2.8	2.7
Urban - Urbaine	C	107	121	103	109	104	2.9	3.2	2.7	2.8	2.6
Rural - Rurale	C	69	70	71	58	57	...	...	...	...	...

15. Infant deaths and infant mortality rates, by urban/rural residence: 2003 - 2007
Décès d'enfants de moins d'un an et taux de mortalité infantile, selon la résidence, urbaine/rurale: 2003 - 2007 (continued - suite)

Continent, country or area, and urban/rural residence / Continent, pays ou zone et résidence, urbaine/rurale	Code[a]	Number - Nombre					Rate - Taux				
		2003	2004	2005	2006	2007	2003	2004	2005	2006	2007
EUROPE											
France[33]											
Total..................	C	3 053	2 988	2 775	2 906	...	4.0	3.9	3.6	3.6	...
Urban - Urbaine[34]........	C	2 403	2 321	2 139	2 271	...	4.2	4.0	3.7	3.8	...
Rural - Rurale[34]..........	C	625	633	610	618	...	3.4	3.4	3.2	3.1	...
Germany - Allemagne											
Total..................	C	2 990	2 918	2 696	2 579	2 656	4.2	4.1	3.9	3.8	3.9
Gibraltar											
Total..................	C	2	...	1	1		...	...	...	...	...
Greece - Grèce											
Total..................	C	420	429	409	415	397	4.0	4.1	3.8	3.7	3.5
Urban - Urbaine	C	...	319	302	299	293	...	...	4.1	3.9	3.8
Rural - Rurale	C	...	110	107	116	104	...	...	3.2	3.3	2.9
Hungary - Hongrie											
Total..................	C	690	628	607	571	577	7.3	6.6	6.2	5.7	5.9
Urban - Urbaine[35]........	C	375	384	369	349	352	6.3	6.4	5.8	5.3	5.4
Rural - Rurale[35]..........	C	308	236	228	215	221	8.9	6.9	6.9	6.6	7.0
Iceland - Islande											
Total..................	C	10	12	10	6	9	...	...	...	...	...
Urban - Urbaine	C	10	...	10	6	9	...	...	...	...	...
Rural - Rurale	C	-	...	-	-	-	...	...	...	...	...
Ireland - Irlande											
Total[36].................	C	326	287	...	...	...	5.3	4.6	...	...	...
Total..................	+C	...	...	*244	*237	...	...	...	*4.0	*3.7	...
Isle of Man - Île de Man											
Total..................	+C	6	2	1	...	...	...	...	...	...	...
Italy - Italie											
Total..................	C	2 134	2 168	2 108	*2 112	*2 085	3.9	3.9	3.8	*3.8	*3.7
Latvia - Lettonie											
Total..................	C	198	191	168	170	203	9.4	9.4	7.8	7.6	8.7
Urban - Urbaine	C	129	117	102	99	123	9.3	8.5	7.0	...	7.6
Rural - Rurale	C	69	74	66	71	80	...	...	...	...	...
Liechtenstein											
Total..................	C	1	1	1	2	*-	...	...	...	...	...
Lithuania - Lituanie[13]											
Total..................	C	206	240	209	213	190	6.7	7.9	6.8	6.8	5.9
Urban - Urbaine	C	108	133	135	167	155	5.6	6.8	6.8	8.1	7.2
Rural - Rurale	C	98	107	74	46	35	...	9.8	...	...	...
Luxembourg											
Total..................	C	26	21	14	14	10	...	...	...	...	...
Malta - Malte											
Total..................	C	23	23	23	14	25	...	...	...	...	...
Montenegro - Monténégro											
Total..................	C	92	61	70	83	58	...	...	...	...	...
Urban - Urbaine	C	86	52	65	...	...	...	...	...	...	...
Rural - Rurale	C	6	9	5	...	...	...	...	...	...	...
Netherlands - Pays-Bas[37]											
Total..................	C	962	852	928	820	736	4.8	4.4	4.9	4.4	4.1
Urban - Urbaine	C	627	554	650	538	530	4.7	4.2	5.1	4.2	4.2
Rural - Rurale	C	335	298	278	282	206	5.0	4.7	4.7	4.8	3.7
Norway - Norvège[38]											
Total..................	C	190	185	175	185	180	3.4	3.2	3.1	3.2	3.1
Poland - Pologne											
Total..................	C	2 470	2 423	2 340	2 238	2 322	7.0	6.8	6.4	6.0	6.0
Urban - Urbaine	C	1 446	1 462	1 339	1 343	1 371	7.2	7.1	6.3	6.2	6.1
Rural - Rurale	C	1 024	961	1 001	895	951	6.8	6.4	6.5	5.7	5.9
Portugal[6]											
Total..................	C	466	418	382	349	353	4.1	3.8	3.5	3.3	3.4
Republic of Moldova - République de Moldova[39]											
Total..................	C	522	464	468	442	428	14.3	12.1	12.4	11.8	11.3
Urban - Urbaine	C	178	167	177	177	141	13.9	11.9	13.0	13.0	10.3
Rural - Rurale	C	344	297	291	265	287	14.5	12.3	12.1	11.0	11.8
Romania - Roumanie											
Total..................	C	3 546	3 641	3 310	3 052	2 574	16.7	16.8	15.0	13.9	12.0
Urban - Urbaine	C	1 381	1 555	1 458	1 341	1 186	13.7	14.0	12.4	11.2	10.2
Rural - Rurale	C	2 165	2 086	1 852	1 711	1 388	19.4	19.9	17.9	17.1	14.1

15. Infant deaths and infant mortality rates, by urban/rural residence: 2003 - 2007
Décès d'enfants de moins d'un an et taux de mortalité infantile, selon la résidence, urbaine/rurale: 2003 - 2007 (continued - suite)

Continent, country or area, and urban/rural residence — Continent, pays ou zone et résidence, urbaine/rurale	Code[a]	Number - Nombre					Rate - Taux				
		2003	2004	2005	2006	2007	2003	2004	2005	2006	2007
EUROPE											
Russian Federation - Fédération de Russie[13]											
Total	C	18 142	17 339	16 073	15 079	14 858	12.3	11.5	11.0	10.2	9.2
Urban - Urbaine	C	12 235	11 596	10 716	9 839	9 497	11.6	10.8	10.3	9.4	8.5
Rural - Rurale	C	5 907	5 743	5 357	5 240	5 361	13.8	13.4	12.7	12.0	11.0
San Marino - Saint-Marin											
Total	+C	2	1	-	-	-	...	...	...	...	...
Serbia - Serbie[40]											
Total	+C	711	633	579	525	484	9.0	8.1	8.0	7.4	7.1
Urban - Urbaine	+C	451	435	378	352	339	9.4	9.1	8.1	7.6	7.6
Rural - Rurale	+C	260	198	201	173	145	8.4	6.6	7.9	7.0	6.2
Slovakia - Slovaquie											
Total	C	406	365	392	355	334	7.9	6.8	7.2	6.6	6.1
Urban - Urbaine	C	176	171	188	153	156	6.6	6.0	6.5	5.4	5.4
Rural - Rurale	C	230	194	204	202	178	9.2	7.7	8.0	7.9	7.0
Slovenia - Slovénie											
Total	C	69	66	75	64	55	...	...	...	...	...
Urban - Urbaine	C	37	34	26	37	19	...	...	...	...	...
Rural - Rurale	C	32	32	49	27	36	...	...	...	...	...
Spain - Espagne											
Total	C	1 733	1 813	1 765	1 812	1 704	3.9	4.0	3.8	3.8	3.5
Sweden - Suède											
Total	C	308	314	246	297	268	3.1	3.1	2.4	2.8	2.5
Switzerland - Suisse											
Total	C	311	309	308	325	293	4.3	4.2	4.2	4.4	3.9
Urban - Urbaine	C	225	220	223	255	221	4.3	4.1	4.1	4.7	4.0
Rural - Rurale	C	86	89	85	70	72	...	...	...	...	...
The Former Yugoslav Republic of Macedonia - L'ex-République yougoslave de Macédoine											
Total	C	305	308	287	260	234	11.3	13.2	12.8	11.5	10.3
Urban - Urbaine	C	...	...	151	144	125	...	...	12.1	11.4	9.8
Rural - Rurale	C	...	...	136	116	109	...	...	13.7	11.7	11.0
Ukraine											
Total	C	3 882[13]	4 024[13]	4 259[13]	4 433[41]	5 188[41]	9.5	9.4	10.0	9.6	11.0
Urban - Urbaine	C	2 531[13]	2 584[13]	2 675[13]	2 828[41]	3 330[41]	9.5	9.1	9.4	9.2	11.0
Rural - Rurale	C	1 351[13]	1 440[13]	1 584[13]	1 605[41]	1 858[41]	9.5	10.1	11.2	10.4	11.7
United Kingdom of Great Britain and Northern Ireland - Royaume-Uni de Grande-Bretagne et d'Irlande du Nord[42]											
Total	C	*3 686	3 606	*3 670	*3 740	...	*5.3	5.0	*5.1	*5.0	...
OCEANIA - OCÉANIE											
American Samoa - Samoas américaines											
Total	C	20	26	12	17	...	...	...	...	...	...
Australia - Australie[43]											
Total	+C	1 195	1 178	1 296	1 247	1 171	4.8	4.6	5.0	4.7	4.1
Urban - Urbaine	+C	922	927	1 041	980	936	4.5	4.4	4.8	4.4	4.0
Rural - Rurale	+C	273	251	255	267	235	6.2	5.7	5.7	5.9	4.9
Cook Islands - Îles Cook[44]											
Total	+C	5	5	6	*3	*3	...	...	...	...	...
Fiji - Fidji											
Total	+C	304	338	...	...	...	17.2	19.7	...	...	...
French Polynesia - Polynésie française											
Total	C	31	20	28	31	30	...	...	...	...	...
Guam[45]											
Total	C	37	42	...	...	...	...	...	...	...	...
New Caledonia - Nouvelle-Calédonie											
Total	C	24	25	...	25	...	...	...	...	...	...

Continent, country or area, and urban/rural residence / Continent, pays ou zone et résidence, urbaine/rurale	Code[a] / Code[a]	Number - Nombre					Rate - Taux				
		2003	2004	2005	2006	2007	2003	2004	2005	2006	2007
OCEANIA - OCÉANIE											
New Zealand - Nouvelle-Zélande[6]											
Total	+C	277	324	295	300	317	4.9	5.6	5.1	5.1	4.9
Urban - Urbaine[4]	+C	231	274	246	251	263	4.7	5.4	4.9	4.9	4.7
Rural - Rurale[4]	+C	27	33	26	33	34	...	...	...	...	...
Northern Mariana Islands - Îles Mariannes septentrionales											
Total	U	7	12	6	9	6	...	...	...	...	...
Palau - Palaos											
Total	C	2	7	6	2	...	...	...	...	...	...
Papua New Guinea - Papouasie-Nouvelle-Guinée											
Total	U	2 082	...	...	...	...	...	...	...	...	...
Pitcairn											
Total	C	...	...	...	-	-	...	...	...	...	...
Tonga											
Total	+C	34	*35	...	...	...	...	...	...	...	...
Tuvalu											
Total	U	4	5	6	...	...	...	...	...	...	...

FOOTNOTES - NOTES

Italics: data from civil registers which are incomplete or of unknown completeness. - Italiques: données incomplètes ou dont le degré d'exactitude n'est pas connu, provenant des registres de l'état civil.

* Provisional. - Données provisoires.

a 'Code' indicates the source of data, as follows:

C - Civil registration, estimated over 90% complete
U - Civil registration, estimated less than 90% complete
| - Other source, estimated reliable
+ - Data tabulated by date of registration rather than occurence.
... - Information not available

Le 'Code' indique la source des données, comme suit:
C - Registres de l'état civil considérés complets à 90 p. 100 au moins.
U - Registres de l'état civil qui ne sont pas considérés complets à 90 p. 100 au moins.
| - Autre source, considérée pas douteuses.
+ - Données exploitées selon la date de l'enregistrement et non la date de l'événement.
... - Information pas disponible.

1 Data refer to the twelve months preceding the census in December. - Les données se rapportent aux douze mois précédant le recensement de décembre.
2 Excluding live-born infants who died before their birth was registered. - Non compris les enfants nés vivants décédés avant l'enregistrement de leur naissance.
3 Including Canadian residents temporarily in the United States, but excluding United States residents temporarily in Canada. - Y compris les résidents canadiens se trouvant temporairement aux Etats-Unis, mais ne comprenant pas les résidents des Etats-Unis se trouvant temporairement au Canada.
4 The total number includes 'Unknown residence', but the categories urban and rural do not. - Le nombre total inclue 'Résidence inconnue ', mais les catégories Urbain et Rural ne l'incluent pas.
5 Data have been adjusted for underenumeration. - Les données ont été ajustées pour compenser les lacunes du dénombrement.
6 Data refer to resident population only. - Pour la population résidante seulement.
7 Excluding Indian jungle population. - Non compris les Indiens de la jungle.
8 Data as reported by national statistical authorities; they may differ from data presented in other tables. - Les données comme elles ont été déclarées par l'institut national de la statistique; elles peuvent être différentes de celles présentées dans d'autres tableaux.
9 Excluding nomadic Indian tribes. - Non compris les tribus d'Indiens nomades.
10 Data refer to national projections. - Les données se réfèrent aux projections nationales.
11 Including non-residents. - Y compris les résidents.
12 The districts of Paramaribo and Wanica are considered urban areas, whereas the rest of the districts are considered more or less rural districts (areas). - Les districts de Paramaribo et de Wanica sont considérés comme des zones urbaines, les autres districts étant considérés comme des zones rurales à divers degrés.
13 Excluding infants born alive of less than 28 weeks' gestation, of less than 1 000 grams in weight and 35 centimeters in length, who die within seven days of birth. - Non compris les enfants nés vivants après moins de 28 semaines de gestation, pesant moins de 1 000 grammes, mesurant moins de 35 centimètres et décédés dans les sept jours qui ont suivi leur naissance.
14 Rates were obtained by the Sample Vital Registration System of Bangladesh. - Taux obtenus au moyen du Sample Vital Registration System du Bangladesh.
15 Data refer to the twelve months preceding the census in May. - Les données se rapportent aux douze mois précédant le recensement de mai.
16 Data refer to government controlled areas. - Les données se rapportent aux zones contrôlées par le Gouvernement.
17 Rates were obtained by the Sample Registration System of India, actually a large demographic survey. Including data for the Indian-held part of Jammu and Kashmir, the final status of which has not yet been determined. - Les taux ont été obtenus par le Système de l'enregistrement par échantillon de l'Inde qui est une large enquête démographique. Y compris les données pour la partie du Jammu et du Cachemire occupée par l'Inde dont le statut définitif n'a pas encore été déterminé.
18 Including data for East Jerusalem and Israeli residents in certain other territories under occupation by Israeli military forces since June 1967. - Y compris les données pour Jérusalem-Est et les résidents israéliens dans certains autres territoires occupés depuis 1967 par les forces armées israéliennes.
19 Including deaths abroad of Israeli residents who were out of the country for less than a year. - Y compris les décès à l'étranger de résidents israéliens qui ont quitté le pays depuis moins d'un an.
20 Data refer to Japanese nationals in Japan only. - Les données se raportent aux nationaux japonais au Japon seulement.
21 Since 2004, WHO criteria have been adopted in the country. - Depuis 2004, le pays a adopté les critères de l'OMS.
22 Data refer to the recorded events in Ministry of Health hospitals and health centres only. - Les données se rapportent aux faits d'état civil enregistrés dans les hôpitaux et les dispensaires du Ministère de la santé seulement.
23 Excluding data for the Pakistan-held part of Jammu and Kashmir, the final status of which has not yet been determined. - Non compris les données

concernant la partie du Jammu et Cachemire occupée par le Pakistan dont le statut définitif n'a pas été déterminé.

[24] Based on the results of the Pakistan Demographic Survey (PDS 2003) . - Données extraites de l'enquête démographique effectuée par le Pakistan en 2003.

[25] Based on the results of the Pakistan Demographic Survey (PDS 2005). - Données extraites de l'enquête démographique effectuée par le Pakistan en 2005.

[26] Excluding alien armed forces, civilian aliens employed by armed forces, and foreign diplomatic personnel and their dependants. - Non compris les militaires étrangers, les civils étrangers employés par les forces armées ni le personnel diplomatique étranger et les membres de leur famille les accompagnant.

[27] Including nationals outside the country. - Y compris les nationaux hors du pays.

[28] Data are estimates based on Address Based Population Registration System and other survey. - Les données sont des estimations basées sur le registre national de la population basé sur l'adresse et d'autres enquêtes.

[29] Also included in Finland. - Comprise aussi dans Finlande.

[30] Including armed forces stationed outside the country, but excluding alien armed forces stationed in the area. - Y compris les militaires nationaux hors du pays, mais non compris les militaires étrangers en garnison sur le territoire.

[31] Excluding Faeroe Islands and Greenland shown separately, if available. - Non compris les Iles Féroé et le Gröenland, qui font l'objet de rubriques distinctes, si disponible.

[32] Including nationals temporarily outside the country. Including Aland Islands. - Y compris les nationaux se trouvant temporairement hors du pays. Y compris les Îles d'Åland.

[33] Including armed forces stationed outside the country. Excluding Overseas Departments, namely, French Guiana, Guadeloupe, Martinique and Reunion, shown separately, if available. - Y compris les militaires nationaux hors du pays. Non compris les départements d'outre mer, c'est-à-dire la Guyane française, la Guadeloupe, la Martinique et la Réunion, qui font l'objet de rubriques distinctes, si disponible.

[34] Data for urban and rural, excluding nationals outside the country. - Les données pour la résidence urbaine et rurale , non compris les nationaux hors du pays.

[35] Total includes the data of foreigners, persons of unknown residence and homeless, but the categories urban and rural do not. - Total incluant les étrangers, les personnes de résidence inconnue et les sans-abri, ce qui n'est pas le cas pour les catégories urbaines et rurales.

[36] Data refer to events registered within one year of occurrence. - Evénements enregistrés dans l'année qui suit l'événement.

[37] Including residents outside the country if listed in a Netherlands population register. - Y compris les résidents hors du pays, s'ils sont inscrits sur un registre de population néerlandais.

[38] Including residents temporarily outside the country. Excluding Svalbard and Jan Mayen Island shown separately, if available. - Y compris les résidents se trouvant temporairement hors du pays. Non compris Svalbard et Jan Mayen qui font l'objet de rubriques distinctes, si disponible.

[39] Excluding infants born alive of less than 28 weeks' gestation, of less than 1 000 grams in weight and 35 centimeters in length, who die within seven days of birth. Excluding Transnistria and the municipality of Bender. - Non compris les enfants nés vivants après moins de 28 semaines de gestations, pesant moins de 1 000 grammes, mesurant moins de 35 centimètres et décédés dans les sept jours qui ont suivi leur naissance. Les données ne tiennent pas compte de l'information sur la Transnistria et la municipalité de Bender.

[40] Excluding data for Kosovo and Metohia. - Sans les données pour le Kosovo et Metohie.

[41] Excluding infants born living with birth weight of less than 500grams (or if birth weight is unknown - with length of less than 25 centimeters, or with gestation period of less than 22 weeks). - Non compris les données concernant les nouveau-nés pesant moins de 500 grammes (si le pods est inconnu – mesurant moins de 25 centimètres ou après moins de 22 semaines de gestations).

[42] Excluding Channel Islands (Guernsey and Jersey) and Isle of Man, shown separately, if available. - Non compris les îles Anglo-Normandes (Guernesey et Jersey) et l'île de Man, qui font l'objet de rubriques distinctes, si disponible.

[43] Excluding data where usual residence was undefined, offshore or migratory and unknown. - En excluant les données lorsque le lieu du domicile n'est pas précisé, est à l'étranger, est mouvant ou inconnu.

[44] Excluding Niue, shown separately, which is part of Cook Islands, but because of remoteness is administered separately. - Non compris Nioué, qui fait l'objet d'une rubrique distincte et qui fait partie des îles Cook, mais qui, en raison de son éloignement, est administrée séparément.

[45] Including United States military personnel, their dependants and contract employees. - Y compris les militaires des Etats-Unis, les membres de leur famille les accompagnant et les agents contractuels des Etats-Unis.

Table 16

Table 16 presents infant deaths and infant mortality rates by age and sex for latest available year between 1998 and 2007.

Description of variables: Age is defined as hours, days and months of life completed, based on the difference between the hour, day, month and year of birth and the hour, day, month and year of death. The age classification used in this table has been expanded from previous years and is now as follows: Main categories are "under 1 day", "1-6 days", "7-27 days" and "28 days – 11 months". Additional subcategories are shown within "7-27 days" and "28 days to 11 months" wherever available.

Rate computation: Infant mortality rates are the annual number of deaths of infants under one year of age per 1 000 live births (as shown in table 9) in the same year.

Infant mortality rates by age and sex are the annual number of infant deaths that occurred in a specific age-sex group per 1 000 live births in the corresponding sex group (as shown in table 9). These rates have been calculated by the Statistics Division of the United Nations. The denominator for all these rates, regardless of age of infant at death, is the number of live births by sex.

Infant deaths of unknown age are included only in the rate for under one year of age. Deaths under the category of sex "unknown" are included in the rate for the total and, hence, these rates, shown in the first column of the table, should agree with the infant mortality rates shown in table 15. Discrepancies are explained in footnotes.

Rates presented in this table have been limited to those for countries or areas having at least a total of 1 000 deaths in a given year. Moreover, rates specific for individual sub-categories based on 30 or fewer infant deaths are identified by the symbol "♦".

Reliability of data: Data from civil registers of infant deaths which are reported as incomplete (less than 90 percent completeness) or of unknown completeness are considered unreliable and are set in italics rather than in roman type. Rates on these data are not computed. Tables 9 and 15 and the technical notes for these tables provide more detailed information on the completeness of infant death registration. For more information about the quality of vital statistics data in general, and the information available on the basis of the completeness of estimates in particular, see section 4.2 of the Technical Notes.

Limitations: Statistics on infant deaths by age and sex are subject to the same qualifications as have been set forth for vital statistics in general and death statistics in particular as discussed in section 4 of the Technical Notes.

The reliability of the data, an indication of which is described above, is an important factor in considering the limitations. In addition, some infant deaths are tabulated by date of registration and not by date of occurrence; these have been indicated by a plus sign "+". Whenever the lag between the date of occurrence and date of registration is prolonged and, therefore, a large proportion of the infant-death registrations are delayed, infant-death statistics for any given year may be seriously affected.

Another factor that limits international comparability is the practice of some countries or areas of not including in infant-death statistics infants who were born alive but died before the registration of the birth or within the first 24 hours of life, thus underestimating the total number of infant deaths. Statistics of this type are footnoted. In this table in particular, this practice may contribute to the lack of comparability among deaths under one year, under 28 days, under one week and under one day.

Variation in the method of reckoning age at the time of death may also introduce non-comparability. Although it is to some degree a limiting factor throughout the age span, it is an especially important consideration with respect to deaths at ages under one day and under one week (early neonatal deaths) and under 28 days (neonatal deaths). As noted above, the recommended method of reckoning infant age at death is to calculate duration of life in minutes, hours and days, as appropriate. This gives age in completed units of time. In some countries or areas, however, infant age is calculated to the nearest day only, that is, age at death for an infant is the difference between the day, month and year of birth and the day, month and year of death. The result of this procedure is to classify as deaths at age one day, many deaths of infants that occurred before the infants had completed 24 hours of life. The under-one-day class is thus understated while the frequency in the 1-6-day age group is inflated.

A special limitation on comparability of neonatal (under 28 days) deaths is the variation in the classification of infant age used. It is evident from the footnotes that some countries or areas continue to report infant age in calendar, rather than lunar month (4-week or 28-day) periods. This failure to tabulate infant deaths under 4 weeks of age in terms of completed days introduces another source of variation between countries or areas. Deaths classified as occurring under one month usually connote deaths within any one calendar month; these frequencies are not strictly comparable with those referring to deaths within 4 weeks or 27 completed days.

In addition, infant mortality rates by age and sex are subject to the limitations of the data on live births with which they have been calculated. These have been set forth in the technical notes for table 9. These limitations have also been discussed in the technical notes for table 15.

In addition, it should be noted that infant mortality rates by age are affected by the problems related to the practice of excluding infants who were born alive but died before the registration of the birth or within the first 24 hours of life from both infant-death and live-birth statistics and the problems related to the reckoning of infant age at death. These factors, which have been described above, may affect certain age groups more than others. In so far as the numbers of infant deaths for the various age groups are underestimated or overestimated, the corresponding rates for the various age groups will also be underestimated or overestimated. The youngest age groups are more likely to be underestimated than other age groups; the youngest age group (under one day) is likely to be the most seriously affected.

Earlier data: Infant deaths and infant mortality rates by age and sex have been shown in previous issues of the *Demographic Yearbook*. For information on specific years covered, readers should consult the Historical Index.

Tableau 16

Le tableau 16 présente les données les plus récentes dont on dispose sur les décès d'enfants de moins d'un an et les taux de mortalité infantile selon l'âge et le sexe.

Description des variables : l'âge est exprimé en heures, jours et mois révolus et est calculé en retranchant la date de la naissance (heure, jour, mois et année) de celle du décès (heure, jour, mois et année). Les tranches d'âge utilisées dans ce tableau ont été étendues par rapport aux années précédentes et se présentent désormais comme suit : les catégories principales sont « moins d'un jour », « 1-6 jours », « 7-27 jours » et « 28 jours à 11 mois ». Des sous-catégories additionnelles pour « 7-27 jours » et « 28 jours à 11 mois » sont présentées lorsque disponibles.

Calcul des taux : les taux de mortalité infantile selon l'âge et le sexe représentent le nombre annuel de décès d'enfants de moins d'un an selon l'âge et le sexe pour 1 000 naissances vivantes d'enfants du même sexe (fréquences du tableau 9) survenues au cours de l'année considérée.

Les taux de mortalité infantile selon l'âge et le sexe représentent le nombre annuel de décès d'enfants de moins d'un an intervenu dans un groupe d'âge donné parmi la population de sexe masculin ou féminin (fréquences du tableau 9) pour 1 000 naissances vivantes survenues parmi la population du même sexe. Ces taux ont été calculés par la Division de statistique de l'ONU. Le dénominateur de tous ces taux, quel que soit l'âge de l'enfant au moment du décès, est le nombre de naissances vivantes selon le sexe.

Il n'est tenu compte des décès d'enfants d'âge « inconnu » que pour le calcul du taux relatif à l'ensemble des décès de moins d'un an. Étant donné que les décès d'enfants de sexe inconnu sont compris dans le numérateur des taux concernant le total qui figurent dans la deuxième colonne du tableau 16, les chiffres obtenus devraient concorder avec les taux de mortalité infantile du tableau 15. Les divergences sont expliquées en note.

Les taux présentés dans le tableau 16 ne concernent que les pays ou zones où l'on a enregistré un total d'au moins 1 000 décès au cours d'une année donnée. Les taux relatifs à des sous-catégories qui sont fondées sur un nombre égal ou inférieur à 30 décès d'enfants âgés de moins d'un an sont signalés par le signe "♦".

Fiabilité des données : les données relatives aux décès d'enfants de moins d'un an provenant de registres de l'état civil qui sont déclarées incomplètes (degré de complétude inférieur à 90 p.100) ou dont le degré de complétude n'est pas connu sont jugées douteuses et apparaissent en italique et non en caractères romains. Les taux à partir de ces données n'ont pas été calculés. Les tableaux 9 et 15 et les notes techniques se rapportant à ces tableaux comportent des renseignements plus détaillés sur le degré de complétude de l'enregistrement des décès d'enfants de moins d'un an. Pour plus de précisions sur la qualité des données reposant sur les statistiques de l'état civil en général et les estimations de complétude en particulier, voir la section 4.2 des Notes techniques.

Insuffisance des données : les statistiques des décès d'enfants de moins d'un an selon l'âge et le sexe appellent toutes les réserves qui ont été formulées à propos des statistiques de l'état civil en général et des statistiques concernant les décès en particulier (voir la section 4 des Notes techniques).

La fiabilité des données, au sujet de laquelle des indications ont été fournies plus haut, est un facteur important. Il faut également tenir compte du fait que, dans certains cas, les données relatives aux décès d'enfants de moins d'un an sont exploitées selon la date de l'enregistrement et non la date de l'événement ; ces cas ont été signalés par le signe "+". Chaque fois que le décalage entre l'événement et son enregistrement est grand et qu'une forte proportion des décès d'enfants de moins d'un an fait l'objet d'un enregistrement tardif, les statistiques des décès d'enfants de moins d'un an pour une année donnée peuvent être considérablement faussées.

Un autre facteur qui nuit à la comparabilité internationale est la pratique de certains pays ou zones qui consiste à ne pas inclure dans les statistiques des décès d'enfants de moins d'un an les enfants nés vivants mais décédés soit avant l'enregistrement de leur naissance, soit dans les 24 heures qui ont suivi la naissance, pratique qui conduit à sous-estimer le nombre total de décès d'enfants de moins d'un an. Quand pareil facteur a joué, cela a été signalé en note. Dans le tableau 16 en particulier, ce système peut limiter la comparabilité des données concernant les décès d'enfants de moins d'un an, de moins de 28 jours, de moins d'une semaine et de moins d'un jour.

Le manque d'uniformité des méthodes suivies pour calculer l'âge au moment du décès nuit également à la comparabilité des données. Ce facteur influe dans une certaine mesure sur les données relatives à la mortalité à tous les âges, mais il a des répercussions particulièrement marquées sur les statistiques des décès de moins d'un jour et de moins d'une semaine (mortalité néo-natale précoce) et de moins de 28 jours (mortalité néo-natale). Comme on l'a dit, l'âge d'un enfant de moins d'un an à son décès est calculé, selon la méthode recommandée, en évaluant la durée de vie en minutes, heures et jours, selon le cas. L'âge est ainsi exprimé en unités de temps révolues. Toutefois, dans certains pays ou zones, l'âge de ces enfants est ramené au jour le plus proche en retranchant la date de la naissance (jour, mois et année) de celle du décès (jour, mois et année). Il s'ensuit que de nombreux décès survenus dans les vingt-quatre heures qui suivent la naissance sont classés comme décès d'un jour. Dans ces conditions, les données concernant les décès de moins d'un jour sont entachées d'une erreur par défaut et celles qui se rapportent aux décès de 1 à 6 jours d'une erreur par excès.

La comparabilité des données relatives à la mortalité néo-natale (moins de 28 jours) est influencée par un facteur spécial : l'hétérogénéité de la classification par âge utilisée pour les enfants de moins d'un an. Les notes figurant à la fin des tableaux montrent que, dans un certain nombre de pays ou zones, on continue d'utiliser le mois civil au lieu du mois lunaire (4 semaines ou 28 jours).

Lorsque les données relatives aux décès de moins de 4 semaines ne sont pas exploitées sur la base de l'âge en jours révolus, il existe une nouvelle cause de non-comparabilité internationale. Les décès de moins d'un mois sont généralement ceux qui se produisent au cours d'un mois civil ; les taux calculés sur la base de ces données ne sont pas strictement comparables à ceux qui sont établis à partir des données concernant les décès survenus dans les 4 semaines ou 27 jours révolus qui suivent la naissance.

Les taux de mortalité infantile selon l'âge et le sexe appellent en outre toutes les réserves qui ont été formulées à propos des statistiques des naissances vivantes qui ont servi à leur calcul (voir à ce sujet les notes techniques relatives au tableau 9). Ces insuffisances ont également été examinées dans les notes techniques relatives au tableau 15.

Il convient de signaler aussi que les taux de mortalité infantile selon l'âge peuvent être gravement faussés par la pratique qui consiste à ne pas classer dans les naissances vivantes et ensuite dans les décès d'enfants de moins d'un an les enfants nés vivants mais décédés soit avant l'enregistrement de leur naissance, soit dans les 24 heures qui ont suivi la naissance, et par les problèmes que pose le calcul de l'âge de l'enfant au moment du décès. Ces facteurs, qui ont été décrits plus haut, peuvent fausser les statistiques concernant certains groupes d'âge plus que d'autres. Si le nombre des décès d'enfants de moins d'un an pour chaque groupe d'âge est sous-estimé ou surestimé, les taux correspondants pour chacun de ces groupes d'âge seront eux aussi sous-estimés ou surestimés. Les risques de sous-estimation sont plus grands pour les groupes les plus jeunes ; c'est pour le groupe d'âge le plus jeune de tous (moins d'un jour) que les données risquent de comporter les plus grosses erreurs.

Données publiées antérieurement : des statistiques des décès d'enfants de moins d'un an et des taux de mortalité infantile selon l'âge et le sexe ont déjà été présentées dans des éditions antérieures de l'*Annuaire démographique*. Pour plus de précisions concernant les années pour lesquelles ces données ont été publiées, se reporter à l'index.

16. Infant deaths and infant mortality rates by age and sex: latest available year, 1998 - 2007
Décès d'enfants de moins d'un an et taux de mortalité infantile selon l'âge et le sexe: dernière année disponible, 1998 - 2007

Continent, country or area, year and age (in days) Continent, pays ou zone, année et âge (en jours)	Number - Nombre			Rate - Taux		
	Both sexes Les deux sexes	Male Masculin	Female Féminin	Both sexes Les deux sexes	Male Masculin	Female Féminin
AFRICA - AFRIQUE						
Egypt - Égypte						
2007 (C)						
Total....................	34 612	18 872	15 740	17.8	18.9	16.5
Less than 1 day - Moins de 1 jour[1]	-	-	-	-	-	-
1 - 6 days - 1 - 6 jours....................	7 407	4 438	2 969	3.8	4.4	3.1
7 - 27 days - 7 - 27 jours....................	8 247	4 680	3 567	4.2	4.7	3.8
7 - 13 days - 7 - 13 jours....................	4 468	2 570	1 898	2.3	2.6	2.0
14 - 20 days - 14 - 20 jours....................	2 408	1 336	1 072	1.2	1.3	1.1
21 - 27 days - 21 - 27 jours....................	1 371	774	597	0.7	0.8	0.6
28 days - 11 months - 28 jours - 11 mois....................	18 958	9 754	9 204	9.7	9.8	9.7
28 days - 1 month - 28 jours - 1 mois....................	4 380	2 296	2 084	2.2	2.3	2.2
2 months - 2 mois....................	2 939	1 484	1 455	1.5	1.5	1.5
3 months - 3 mois....................	2 350	1 206	1 144	1.2	1.2	1.2
4 months - 4 mois....................	2 212	1 133	1 079	1.1	1.1	1.1
5 months - 5 mois....................	1 609	852	757	0.8	0.9	0.8
6 months - 6 mois....................	1 535	778	757	0.8	0.8	0.8
7 months - 7 mois....................	1 043	531	512	0.5	0.5	0.5
8 months - 8 mois....................	857	429	428	0.4	0.4	0.4
9 months - 9 mois....................	871	465	406	0.4	0.5	0.4
10 months - 10 mois....................	631	322	309	0.3	0.3	0.3
11 months - 11 mois....................	531	258	273	0.3	0.3	0.3
Mauritius - Maurice						
2007 (+C)						
Total....................	261	138	123	...	...	...
Less than 1 day - Moins de 1 jour....................	46	26	20	...	...	...
1 - 6 days - 1 - 6 jours....................	94	47	47	...	...	...
7 - 27 days - 7 - 27 jours....................	47	28	19	...	...	...
7 - 13 days - 7 - 13 jours....................	22	13	9	...	...	...
14 - 20 days - 14 - 20 jours....................	18	11	7	...	...	...
21 - 27 days - 21 - 27 jours....................	7	4	3	...	...	...
28 days - 11 months - 28 jours - 11 mois....................	74	37	37	...	...	...
28 days - 1 month - 28 jours - 1 mois....................	24	12	12	...	...	...
2 months - 2 mois....................	11	6	5	...	...	...
3 months - 3 mois....................	10	6	4	...	...	...
4 months - 4 mois....................	7	4	3	...	...	...
5 months - 5 mois....................	3	3	-	...	...	...
6 months - 6 mois....................	7	3	4	...	...	...
7 months - 7 mois....................	2	1	1	...	...	...
8 months - 8 mois....................	2	-	2	...	...	...
9 months - 9 mois....................	1	-	1	...	...	...
10 months - 10 mois....................	3	1	2	...	...	...
11 months - 11 mois....................	4	1	3	...	...	...
Unknown - Inconnu....................	-	-	-	...	...	...
Morocco - Maroc						
2001 (U)						
Total....................	7 379	4 022	3 357	...	...	...
Less than 28 days - Moins de 28 jours....................	1 638	912	726	...	...	...
28 days - 11 months - 28 jours - 11 mois....................	5 729	3 103	2 626	...	...	...
28 days - 1 month - 28 jours - 1 mois....................	1 331	733	598	...	...	...
2 months - 2 mois....................	941	556	385	...	...	...
3 months - 3 mois....................	753	421	332	...	...	...
4 months - 4 mois....................	610	320	290	...	...	...
5 months - 5 mois....................	512	274	238	...	...	...
6 months - 6 mois....................	405	212	193	...	...	...
7 months - 7 mois....................	339	174	165	...	...	...
8 months - 8 mois....................	321	156	165	...	...	...
9 months - 9 mois....................	234	118	116	...	...	...
10 months - 10 mois....................	186	94	92	...	...	...
11 months - 11 mois....................	97	45	52	...	...	...
Unknown - Inconnu....................	12	7	5	...	...	...
Réunion[2]						
2007 (C)						
Total....................	91	48	43	...	...	...
Less than 1 day - Moins de 1 jour....................	24	14	10	...	...	...
1 - 6 days - 1 - 6 jours....................	20	9	11	...	...	...
7 - 27 days - 7 - 27 jours....................	18	7	11	...	...	...
7 - 13 days - 7 - 13 jours....................	7	3	4	...	...	...
14 - 20 days - 14 - 20 jours....................	9	2	7	...	...	...

16. Infant deaths and infant mortality rates by age and sex: latest available year, 1998 - 2007
Décès d'enfants de moins d'un an et taux de mortalité infantile selon l'âge et le sexe: dernière année disponible, 1998 - 2007 (continued - suite)

Continent, country or area, year and age (in days) / Continent, pays ou zone, année et âge (en jours)	Number - Nombre			Rate - Taux		
	Both sexes Les deux sexes	Male Masculin	Female Féminin	Both sexes Les deux sexes	Male Masculin	Female Féminin

AFRICA - AFRIQUE

Réunion[2]
2007 (C)
21 - 27 days - 21 - 27 jours...............................	7	2	5	...	...	...
28 days - 11 months - 28 jours - 11 mois........................	30	18	12	...	...	...

Saint Helena ex. dep. - Sainte-Hélène sans dép.
2005 (C)
Total..	1	1	-	...	...	...
Less than 1 day - Moins de 1 jour	-	-	-	...	...	...
1 - 6 days - 1 - 6 jours.................................	1	1	-	...	...	...
7 - 27 days - 7 - 27 jours...............................	-	-	-	...	...	...
28 days - 11 months - 28 jours - 11 mois.................	-	-	-	...	...	...
Unknown - Inconnu	-	-	-	...	...	...

Seychelles
2006 (+C)
Total..	14	5	9	...	...	...
Less than 1 day - Moins de 1 jour	5	1	4	...	...	...
1 - 6 days - 1 - 6 jours.................................	2	1	1	...	...	...
7 - 27 days - 7 - 27 jours...............................	2	-	2	...	...	...
7 - 13 days - 7 - 13 jours.............................	1	-	1	...	...	...
14 - 20 days - 14 - 20 jours...........................	-	-	-	...	...	...
21 - 27 days - 21 - 27 jours...........................	1	-	1	...	...	...
28 days - 11 months - 28 jours - 11 mois.................	5	3	2	...	...	...
28 days - 1 month - 28 jours - 1 mois....................	1	1	-	...	...	...
2 months - 2 mois.....................................	-	-	-	...	...	...
3 months - 3 mois.....................................	-	-	-	...	...	...
4 months - 4 mois.....................................	1	-	1	...	...	...
5 months - 5 mois.....................................	2	2	-	...	...	...
6 months - 6 mois.....................................	1	-	1	...	...	...
7 months - 7 mois.....................................	-	-	-	...	...	...
8 months - 8 mois.....................................	-	-	-	...	...	...
9 months - 9 mois.....................................	-	-	-	...	...	...
10 months - 10 mois...................................	-	-	-	...	...	...
11 months - 11 mois...................................	-	-	-	...	...	...
Unknown - Inconnu	-	-	-	...	...	...

South Africa - Afrique du Sud
2006 (...)
Total..	47 703	25 178[3]	21 810[3]	...	...	...
Less than 1 day - Moins de 1 jour	2 422	1 387[3]	969[3]	...	...	...
1 - 6 days - 1 - 6 jours.................................	7 217	4 146[3]	2 892[3]	...	...	...
7 - 27 days - 7 - 27 jours...............................	3 640	1 991[3]	1 568[3]	...	...	...
7 - 13 days - 7 - 13 jours.............................	1 613	912[3]	667[3]	...	...	...
14 - 20 days - 14 - 20 jours...........................	1 074	589[3]	460[3]	...	...	...
21 - 27 days - 21 - 27 jours...........................	953	490[3]	441[3]	...	...	...
28 days - 11 months - 28 jours - 11 mois.................	34 424	17 654	16 381	...	...	...
28 days - 1 month - 28 jours - 1 mois....................	4 770	2 509[3]	2 175[3]	...	...	...
2 months - 2 mois.....................................	5 786	2 784[3]	2 934[3]	...	...	...
3 months - 3 mois.....................................	5 472	2 783[3]	2 621[3]	...	...	...
4 months - 4 mois.....................................	3 711	1 958[3]	1 714[3]	...	...	...
5 months - 5 mois.....................................	3 041	1 548[3]	1 465[3]	...	...	...
6 months - 6 mois.....................................	2 704	1 393[3]	1 281[3]	...	...	...
7 months - 7 mois.....................................	2 258	1 181[3]	1 059[3]	...	...	...
8 months - 8 mois.....................................	1 948	1 020[3]	910[3]	...	...	...
9 months - 9 mois.....................................	1 811	954[3]	841[3]	...	...	...
10 months - 10 mois...................................	1 544	803[3]	730[3]	...	...	...
11 months - 11 mois...................................	1 379	721[3]	651[3]	...	...	...

Tunisia - Tunisie
1998 (U)
Total..	3 098	1 775	1 323	...	...	...
Less than 1 day - Moins de 1 jour	464	281	183	...	...	...
1 - 6 days - 1 - 6 jours.................................	847	485	362	...	...	...
7 - 27 days - 7 - 27 jours...............................	559	332	227	...	...	...
7 - 13 days - 7 - 13 jours.............................	282	160	122	...	...	...
14 - 20 days - 14 - 20 jours...........................	173	114	59	...	...	...
21 - 27 days - 21 - 27 jours...........................	104	58	46	...	...	...
28 days - 11 months - 28 jours - 11 mois.................	1 227	677	550	...	...	...
28 days - 1 month - 28 jours - 1 mois....................	292	165	127	...	...	...
2 months - 2 mois.....................................	220	124	96	...	...	...

Continent, country or area, year and age (in days) / Continent, pays ou zone, année et âge (en jours)	Number - Nombre			Rate - Taux		
	Both sexes Les deux sexes	Male Masculin	Female Féminin	Both sexes Les deux sexes	Male Masculin	Female Féminin
AFRICA - AFRIQUE						
Tunisia - Tunisie						
1998 (U)						
3 months - 3 mois	168	92	76	...	...	...
4 months - 4 mois	132	72	60	...	...	...
5 months - 5 mois	89	54	35	...	...	...
6 months - 6 mois	75	40	35	...	...	...
7 months - 7 mois	51	33	18	...	...	...
8 months - 8 mois	64	35	29	...	...	...
9 months - 9 mois	58	28	30	...	...	...
10 months - 10 mois	40	16	24	...	...	...
11 months - 11 mois	38	18	20	...	...	...
Unknown - Inconnu	1	-	1			
AMERICA, NORTH - AMÉRIQUE DU NORD						
Aruba						
2007 (+U)						
Total	4	2	2	...	...	...
Less than 1 day - Moins de 1 jour	-	-	-	...	...	...
1 - 6 days - 1 - 6 jours	2	1	1	...	...	...
7 - 27 days - 7 - 27 jours	1	1	-	...	...	...
7 - 13 days - 7 - 13 jours	1	1	-	...	...	...
14 - 27 days - 14 - 27 jours	-	-	-	...	...	...
28 days - 11 months - 28 jours - 11 mois	1	-	1	...	...	...
28 days - 1 month - 28 jours - 1 mois	-	-	-	...	...	...
2 - 9 months - 2 - 9 mois	-	-	-	...	...	...
10 months - 10 mois	1	-	1	...	...	...
11 months - 11 mois	-	-	-	...	...	...
Bahamas						
2006 (C)						
Total	79	42	37	...	...	...
Less than 1 day - Moins de 1 jour	-	-	-	...	...	...
1 - 6 days - 1 - 6 jours	29	18	11	...	...	...
7 - 27 days - 7 - 27 jours	24	15	9	...	...	...
7 - 13 days - 7 - 13 jours	13	10	3	...	...	...
14 - 20 days - 14 - 20 jours	9	4	5	...	...	...
21 - 27 days - 21 - 27 jours	3	2	1	...	...	...
28 days - 11 months - 28 jours - 11 mois	26	9	17	...	...	...
28 days - 1 month - 28 jours - 1 mois	8	3	5	...	...	...
2 months - 2 mois	3	1	2	...	...	...
3 months - 3 mois	4	2	2	...	...	...
4 months - 4 mois	6	1	5	...	...	...
5 months - 5 mois	1	1	-	...	...	...
6 months - 6 mois	-	-	-	...	...	...
7 months - 7 mois	2	-	2	...	...	...
8 months - 8 mois	1	1	-	...	...	...
9 months - 9 mois	-	-	-	...	...	...
10 months - 10 mois	1	-	1	...	...	...
11 months - 11 mois	-	-	-	...	...	...
Canada[4]						
2005 (C)						
Total	1 863	1 030	833	5.4	5.9	5.0
Less than 1 day - Moins de 1 jour	916	500	416	2.7	2.9	2.5
1 - 6 days - 1 - 6 jours	242	135	107	0.7	0.8	0.6
7 - 27 days - 7 - 27 jours	252	132	120	0.7	0.8	0.7
7 - 13 days - 7 - 13 jours	129	73	56	0.4	0.4	0.3
14 - 20 days - 14 - 20 jours	74	36	38	0.2	0.2	0.2
21 - 27 days - 21 - 27 jours	49	23	26	0.1	♦0.1	♦0.2
28 days - 11 months - 28 jours - 11 mois	453	263	190	1.3	1.5	1.1
28 days - 1 month - 28 jours - 1 mois	129	76	53	0.4	0.4	0.3
2 months - 2 mois	75	41	34	0.2	0.2	0.2
3 months - 3 mois	47	31	16	0.1	0.2	♦0.1
4 months - 4 mois	52	31	21	0.2	0.2	♦0.1
5 months - 5 mois	30	17	13	0.1	♦0.1	♦0.1
6 months - 6 mois	29	14	15	♦0.1	♦0.1	♦0.1
7 months - 7 mois	19	12	7	♦0.1	♦0.1	-
8 months - 8 mois	20	13	7	♦0.1	♦0.1	-

Continent, country or area, year and age (in days) Continent, pays ou zone, année et âge (en jours)	Number - Nombre			Rate - Taux		
	Both sexes Les deux sexes	Male Masculin	Female Féminin	Both sexes Les deux sexes	Male Masculin	Female Féminin
AMERICA, NORTH - AMÉRIQUE DU NORD						
Canada[4]						
2005 (C)						
9 months - 9 mois............	21	10	11	♦0.1	♦0.1	♦0.1
10 months - 10 mois............	14	7	7	-	-	-
11 months - 11 mois............	17	11	6	-	♦0.1	-
Unknown - Inconnu	-	-	-			
Cayman Islands - Îles Caïmanes						
2007 (C)						
Total............	5	4	1	...	...	...
Less than 1 day - Moins de 1 jour............	3	2	1	...	...	...
1 - 6 days - 1 - 6 jours............	2	2	-	...	...	...
7 - 27 days - 7 - 27 jours............	-	-	-	...	...	...
28 days - 11 months - 28 jours - 11 mois............	-	-	-	...	...	...
Costa Rica						
2007 (C)						
Total............	735	417	318	...	...	...
Less than 1 day - Moins de 1 jour............	212	118	94	...	...	...
1 - 6 days - 1 - 6 jours............	193	113	80	...	...	...
7 - 27 days - 7 - 27 jours............	124	70	54	...	...	...
7 - 13 days - 7 - 13 jours............	65	37	28	...	...	...
14 - 20 days - 14 - 20 jours............	32	21	11	...	...	...
21 - 27 days - 21 - 27 jours............	27	12	15	...	...	...
28 days - 11 months - 28 jours - 11 mois............	206	116	90	...	...	...
28 days - 1 month - 28 jours - 1 mois............	61	34	27	...	...	...
2 months - 2 mois............	31	19	12	...	...	...
3 months - 3 mois............	18	11	7	...	...	...
4 months - 4 mois............	20	13	7	...	...	...
5 months - 5 mois............	16	10	6	...	...	...
6 months - 6 mois............	15	7	8	...	...	...
7 months - 7 mois............	10	7	3	...	...	...
8 months - 8 mois............	10	4	6	...	...	...
9 months - 9 mois............	8	3	5	...	...	...
10 months - 10 mois............	6	4	2	...	...	...
11 months - 11 mois............	11	4	7	...	...	...
Unknown - Inconnu............	-	-	-	...	...	...
Cuba						
2007 (C)						
Total............	592	332	260	...	...	...
Less than 1 day - Moins de 1 jour............	65	36	29	...	...	...
1 - 6 days - 1 - 6 jours............	155	96	59	...	...	...
7 - 27 days - 7 - 27 jours............	121	68	53	...	...	...
7 - 13 days - 7 - 13 jours............	59	38	21	...	...	...
14 - 20 days - 14 - 20 jours............	41	23	18	...	...	...
21 - 27 days - 21 - 27 jours............	21	7	14	...	...	...
28 days - 11 months - 28 jours - 11 mois............	251	132	119	...	...	...
28 days - 1 month - 28 jours - 1 mois............	78	45	33	...	...	...
2 months - 2 mois............	43	19	24	...	...	...
3 months - 3 mois............	32	13	19	...	...	...
4 months - 4 mois............	28	15	13	...	...	...
5 months - 5 mois............	14	8	6	...	...	...
6 months - 6 mois............	14	7	7	...	...	...
7 months - 7 mois............	7	6	1	...	...	...
8 months - 8 mois............	4	2	2	...	...	...
9 months - 9 mois............	14	9	5	...	...	...
10 months - 10 mois............	9	4	5	...	...	...
11 months - 11 mois............	8	4	4	...	...	...
Unknown - Inconnu............	-	-	-	...	...	...
El Salvador						
2007 (C)						
Total............	981	579	402	...	...	...
Less than 1 day - Moins de 1 jour............	133	76	57	...	...	...
1 - 6 days - 1 - 6 jours............	166	94	72	...	...	...
7 - 27 days - 7 - 27 jours............	163	99	64	...	...	...
7 - 13 days - 7 - 13 jours............	79	50	29	...	...	...
14 - 20 days - 14 - 20 jours............	52	33	19	...	...	...
21 - 27 days - 21 - 27 jours............	32	16	16	...	...	...
28 days - 11 months - 28 jours - 11 mois............	519	310	209	...	...	...
28 days - 1 month - 28 jours - 1 mois............	119	82	37	...	...	...

16. Infant deaths and infant mortality rates by age and sex: latest available year, 1998 - 2007

Décès d'enfants de moins d'un an et taux de mortalité infantile selon l'âge et le sexe: dernière année disponible, 1998 - 2007 (continued - suite)

Continent, country or area, year and age (in days) / Continent, pays ou zone, année et âge (en jours)	Number - Nombre			Rate - Taux		
	Both sexes Les deux sexes	Male Masculin	Female Féminin	Both sexes Les deux sexes	Male Masculin	Female Féminin
AMERICA, NORTH - AMÉRIQUE DU NORD						
El Salvador						
2007 (C)						
2 months - 2 mois	69	44	25	...	...	...
3 months - 3 mois	64	33	31	...	...	...
4 months - 4 mois	49	29	20	...	...	...
5 months - 5 mois	41	20	21	...	...	...
6 months - 6 mois	37	21	16	...	...	...
7 months - 7 mois	34	22	12	...	...	...
8 months - 8 mois	34	19	15	...	...	...
9 months - 9 mois	25	12	13	...	...	...
10 months - 10 mois	29	17	12	...	...	...
11 months - 11 mois	18	11	7	...	...	...
Greenland - Groenland						
2006 (C)						
Total	13	7	6	...	...	...
Less than 1 day - Moins de 1 jour	8	5	3	...	...	...
1 - 6 days - 1 - 6 jours	-	-	-	...	...	...
7 - 27 days - 7 - 27 jours	-	-	-	...	...	...
28 days - 11 months - 28 jours - 11 mois	5	2	3	...	...	...
28 days - 1 month - 28 jours - 1 mois	5	2	3	...	...	...
2 - 11 months - 2 - 11 mois	-	-	-	...	...	...
Guadeloupe[2]						
2003 (C)						
Total	56	34	22	...	...	...
Less than 1 day - Moins de 1 jour	13	5	8	...	...	...
1 - 6 days - 1 - 6 jours	8	4	4	...	...	...
7 - 27 days - 7 - 27 jours	19	12	7	...	...	...
7 - 13 days - 7 - 13 jours	5	3	2	...	...	...
14 - 20 days - 14 - 20 jours	10	5	5	...	...	...
21 - 27 days - 21 - 27 jours	4	4	-	...	...	...
28 days - 11 months - 28 jours - 11 mois	16	13	3	...	...	...
28 days - 1 month - 28 jours - 1 mois	7	6	1	...	...	...
2 months - 2 mois	4	2	2	...	...	...
3 months - 3 mois	3	3	-	...	...	...
4 months - 4 mois	1	1	-	...	...	...
5 months - 5 mois	-	-	-	...	...	...
6 months - 6 mois	1	1	-	...	...	...
7 months - 7 mois	-	-	-	...	...	...
8 months - 8 mois	-	-	-	...	...	...
9 months - 9 mois	-	-	-	...	...	...
10 months - 10 mois	-	-	-	...	...	...
11 months - 11 mois	-	-	-	...	...	...
Unknown - Inconnu	-	-	-	...	...	...
Guatemala						
2006 (C)						
Total	9 042	5 012	4 030	24.5	26.8	22.2
Less than 1 day - Moins de 1 jour	842	478	364	2.3	2.6	2.0
1 - 6 days - 1 - 6 jours	2 040	1 162	878	5.5	6.2	4.8
7 - 27 days - 7 - 27 jours	1 209	681	528	3.3	3.6	2.9
7 - 13 days - 7 - 13 jours	550	318	232	1.5	1.7	1.3
14 - 20 days - 14 - 20 jours	359	185	174	1.0	1.0	1.0
21 - 27 days - 21 - 27 jours	300	178	122	0.8	1.0	0.7
28 days - 11 months - 28 jours - 11 mois	4 951	2 691	2 260	13.4	14.4	12.5
28 days - 1 month - 28 jours - 1 mois	1 017	564	453	2.8	3.0	2.5
2 months - 2 mois	773	402	371	2.1	2.1	2.0
3 months - 3 mois	527	274	253	1.4	1.5	1.4
4 months - 4 mois	438	248	190	1.2	1.3	1.0
5 months - 5 mois	323	162	161	0.9	0.9	0.9
6 months - 6 mois	367	211	156	1.0	1.1	0.9
7 months - 7 mois	332	171	161	0.9	0.9	0.9
8 months - 8 mois	297	166	131	0.8	0.9	0.7
9 months - 9 mois	296	170	126	0.8	0.9	0.7
10 months - 10 mois	282	152	130	0.8	0.8	0.7
11 months - 11 mois	299	171	128	0.8	0.9	0.7
Martinique						
2003 (C)						
Total	33	14	19	...	...	...
Less than 1 day - Moins de 1 jour	9	4	5	...	...	...

16. Infant deaths and infant mortality rates by age and sex: latest available year, 1998 - 2007
Décès d'enfants de moins d'un an et taux de mortalité infantile selon l'âge et le sexe: dernière année disponible, 1998 - 2007 (continued - suite)

Continent, country or area, year and age (in days) / Continent, pays ou zone, année et âge (en jours)	Number - Nombre			Rate - Taux		
	Both sexes Les deux sexes	Male Masculin	Female Féminin	Both sexes Les deux sexes	Male Masculin	Female Féminin
AMERICA, NORTH - AMÉRIQUE DU NORD						
Martinique						
2003 (C)						
1 - 6 days - 1 - 6 jours	11	5	6	...	...	...
7 - 27 days - 7 - 27 jours	4	1	3	...	...	...
7 - 13 days - 7 - 13 jours	4	1	3	...	...	...
14 - 20 days - 14 - 20 jours	-	-	-	...	...	...
21 - 27 days - 21 - 27 jours	-	-	-	...	...	...
28 days - 11 months - 28 jours - 11 mois	9	4	5	...	...	...
28 days - 1 month - 28 jours - 1 mois	3	1	2	...	...	...
2 months - 2 mois	1	1	-	...	...	...
3 months - 3 mois	1	-	1	...	...	...
4 months - 4 mois	-	-	-	...	...	...
5 months - 5 mois	-	-	-	...	...	...
6 months - 6 mois	1	-	1	...	...	...
7 months - 7 mois	2	1	1	...	...	...
8 months - 8 mois	-	-	-	...	...	...
9 months - 9 mois	-	-	-	...	...	...
10 months - 10 mois	1	1	-	...	...	...
11 months - 11 mois	-	-	-	...	...	...
Unknown - Inconnu	-	-	-	...	...	...
Mexico - Mexique[5]						
2007 (+U)						
Total	30 412	17 183	13 136	...	...	...
Less than 1 day - Moins de 1 jour	6 277	3 456	2 754	...	...	...
1 - 6 days - 1 - 6 jours	7 442	4 379	3 052	...	...	...
7 - 27 days - 7 - 27 jours	5 169	2 928	2 235	...	...	...
7 - 13 days - 7 - 13 jours	2 756	1 570	1 184	...	...	...
14 - 20 days - 14 - 20 jours	1 439	820	616	...	...	...
21 - 27 days - 21 - 27 jours	974	538	435	...	...	...
28 days - 11 months - 28 jours - 11 mois	11 523	6 419	5 095	...	...	...
28 days - 1 month - 28 jours - 1 mois	3 102	1 761	1 335	...	...	...
2 months - 2 mois	2 087	1 183	903	...	...	...
3 months - 3 mois	1 423	776	647	...	...	...
4 months - 4 mois	1 072	613	458	...	...	...
5 months - 5 mois	787	436	351	...	...	...
6 months - 6 mois	716	383	332	...	...	...
7 months - 7 mois	608	331	277	...	...	...
8 months - 8 mois	505	262	243	...	...	...
9 months - 9 mois	435	256	179	...	...	...
10 months - 10 mois	381	205	176	...	...	...
11 months - 11 mois	407	213	194	...	...	...
Unknown - Inconnu	1	1	-	...	...	...
Netherlands Antilles - Antilles néerlandaises						
2004 (C)						
Total	20	13	7	...	...	...
Less than 1 day - Moins de 1 jour	4	3	1	...	...	...
1 - 6 days - 1 - 6 jours	5	2	3	...	...	...
7 - 27 days - 7 - 27 jours	3	2	1	...	...	...
7 - 13 days - 7 - 13 jours	-	-	-	...	...	...
14 - 20 days - 14 - 20 jours	2	1	1	...	...	...
21 - 27 days - 21 - 27 jours	1	1	-	...	...	...
28 days - 11 months - 28 jours - 11 mois	8	6	2	...	...	...
28 days - 1 month - 28 jours - 1 mois	4	3	1	...	...	...
2 months - 2 mois	3	3	-	...	...	...
3 months - 3 mois	-	-	-	...	...	...
4 months - 4 mois	1	-	1	...	...	...
5 - 11 months - 5 - 11 mois	-	-	-	...	...	...
Nicaragua						
2007 (+U)						
Total	1 955	1 083	872	...	...	...
Less than 1 day - Moins de 1 jour	338	191	147	...	...	...
1 - 6 days - 1 - 6 jours	721	413	308	...	...	...
7 - 27 days - 7 - 27 jours	283	161	122	...	...	...
7 - 13 days - 7 - 13 jours	168	98	70	...	...	...
14 - 20 days - 14 - 20 jours	53	30	23	...	...	...
21 - 27 days - 21 - 27 jours	62	33	29	...	...	...
28 days - 11 months - 28 jours - 11 mois	604	313	291	...	...	...
28 days - 1 month - 28 jours - 1 mois	153	77	76	...	...	...

Continent, country or area, year and age (in days) / Continent, pays ou zone, année et âge (en jours)	Number - Nombre			Rate - Taux		
	Both sexes Les deux sexes	Male Masculin	Female Féminin	Both sexes Les deux sexes	Male Masculin	Female Féminin
AMERICA, NORTH - AMÉRIQUE DU NORD						
Nicaragua						
2007 (+U)						
2 months - 2 mois	85	40	45	...	...	...
3 months - 3 mois	75	49	26	...	...	...
4 months - 4 mois	66	41	25	...	...	...
5 months - 5 mois	43	23	20	...	...	...
6 months - 6 mois	54	20	34	...	...	...
7 months - 7 mois	31	13	18	...	...	...
8 months - 8 mois	28	15	13	...	...	...
9 months - 9 mois	25	15	10	...	...	...
10 months - 10 mois	24	9	15	...	...	...
11 months - 11 mois	20	11	9	...	...	...
Unknown - Inconnu	9	5	4	...	...	...
Panama						
2007 (U)						
Total	992	567	425	...	...	...
Less than 1 day - Moins de 1 jour	153	95	58	...	...	...
1 - 6 days - 1 - 6 jours	218	122	96	...	...	...
7 - 27 days - 7 - 27 jours	151	79	72	...	...	...
7 - 13 days - 7 - 13 jours	88	48	40	...	...	...
14 - 20 days - 14 - 20 jours	39	19	20	...	...	...
21 - 27 days - 21 - 27 jours	24	12	12	...	...	...
28 days - 11 months - 28 jours - 11 mois	470	271	199	...	...	...
28 days - 1 month - 28 jours - 1 mois	117	74	43	...	...	...
2 months - 2 mois	66	37	29	...	...	...
3 months - 3 mois	49	27	22	...	...	...
4 months - 4 mois	38	23	15	...	...	...
5 months - 5 mois	34	20	14	...	...	...
6 months - 6 mois	27	16	11	...	...	...
7 months - 7 mois	29	14	15	...	...	...
8 months - 8 mois	32	21	11	...	...	...
9 months - 9 mois	21	7	14	...	...	...
10 months - 10 mois	24	13	11	...	...	...
11 months - 11 mois	33	19	14	...	...	...
Puerto Rico - Porto Rico						
2006 (C)						
Total	442	260	182	...	...	...
Less than 1 day - Moins de 1 jour	108	65	43	...	...	...
1 - 6 days - 1 - 6 jours	150	88	62	...	...	...
7 - 27 days - 7 - 27 jours	76	44	32	...	...	...
7 - 13 days - 7 - 13 jours	38	20	18	...	...	...
14 - 20 days - 14 - 20 jours	23	15	8	...	...	...
21 - 27 days - 21 - 27 jours	15	9	6	...	...	...
28 days - 11 months - 28 jours - 11 mois	108	63	45	...	...	...
28 days - 1 month - 28 jours - 1 mois	30	16	14	...	...	...
2 months - 2 mois	20	12	8	...	...	...
3 months - 3 mois	13	10	3	...	...	...
4 months - 4 mois	7	4	3	...	...	...
5 months - 5 mois	12	8	4	...	...	...
6 months - 6 mois	3	2	1	...	...	...
7 months - 7 mois	8	5	3	...	...	...
8 months - 8 mois	9	3	6	...	...	...
9 months - 9 mois	3	2	1	...	...	...
10 months - 10 mois	1	-	1	...	...	...
11 months - 11 mois	2	1	1	...	...	...
Unknown - Inconnu	-	-	-	...	...	...
Saint Lucia - Sainte-Lucie						
2002 (C)						
Total	36	17	19	...	...	...
Less than 1 day - Moins de 1 jour	11	5	6	...	...	...
1 - 6 days - 1 - 6 jours	16	6	10	...	...	...
7 - 27 days - 7 - 27 jours	2	1	1	...	...	...
7 - 20 days - 7 - 20 jours	-	-	-	...	...	...
21 - 27 days - 21 - 27 jours	2	1	1	...	...	...
28 days - 11 months - 28 jours - 11 mois	7	5	2	...	...	...
28 days - 1 month - 28 jours - 1 mois	-	-	-	...	...	...
2 months - 2 mois	1	1	-	...	...	...
3 months - 3 mois	1	1		...	...	

16. Infant deaths and infant mortality rates by age and sex: latest available year, 1998 - 2007
Décès d'enfants de moins d'un an et taux de mortalité infantile selon l'âge et le sexe: dernière année disponible, 1998 - 2007 (continued - suite)

Continent, country or area, year and age (in days) / Continent, pays ou zone, année et âge (en jours)	Number - Nombre			Rate - Taux		
	Both sexes Les deux sexes	Male Masculin	Female Féminin	Both sexes Les deux sexes	Male Masculin	Female Féminin
AMERICA, NORTH - AMÉRIQUE DU NORD						
Saint Lucia - Sainte-Lucie						
2002 (C)						
4 months - 4 mois	1	1	-	...	...	...
5 months - 5 mois	1	1	-	...	...	...
6 months - 6 mois	-	-	-	...	...	...
7 months - 7 mois	-	-	-	...	...	...
8 months - 8 mois	2	1	1	...	...	...
9 months - 9 mois	-	-	-	...	...	...
10 months - 10 mois	1	-	1	...	...	...
11 months - 11 mois	-	-	-	...	...	...
Unknown - Inconnu	-	-	-	...	...	...
Saint Vincent and the Grenadines - Saint-Vincent-et-les Grenadines						
2005 (+C)						
Total	29	17	12	...	...	...
Less than 1 day - Moins de 1 jour	6	3	3	...	...	...
1 - 6 days - 1 - 6 jours	11	6	5	...	...	...
7 - 27 days - 7 - 27 jours	3	2	1	...	...	...
28 days - 11 months - 28 jours - 11 mois	9	6	3	...	...	...
28 days - 1 month - 28 jours - 1 mois	-	-	-	...	...	...
2 - 11 months - 2 - 11 mois	9	6	3	...	...	...
Trinidad and Tobago - Trinité-et-Tobago						
2002 (C)						
Total	412	247	165	...	...	...
Less than 1 day - Moins de 1 jour	91	51	40	...	...	...
1 - 6 days - 1 - 6 jours	148	92	56	...	...	...
7 - 27 days - 7 - 27 jours	105	71	34	...	...	...
7 - 13 days - 7 - 13 jours	66	44	22	...	...	...
14 - 20 days - 14 - 20 jours	21	16	5	...	...	...
21 - 27 days - 21 - 27 jours	18	11	7	...	...	...
28 days - 11 months - 28 jours - 11 mois	68	33	35	...	...	...
28 days - 1 month - 28 jours - 1 mois	25	12	13	...	...	...
2 - 3 months - 2 - 3 mois	4	2	2	...	...	...
4 - 6 months - 4 - 6 mois	18	9	9	...	...	...
7 - 9 months - 7 - 9 mois	11	4	7	...	...	...
10 - 11 months - 10 - 11 mois	10	6	4	...	...	...
Unknown - Inconnu	-	-	-	...	...	...
United States of America - États-Unis d'Amérique						
2003 (C)						
Total	28 025	15 902	12 123	6.9	7.6	6.1
Less than 1 day - Moins de 1 jour	11 469	6 387	5 082	2.8	3.1	2.5
1 - 6 days - 1 - 6 jours	3 664	2 123	1 541	0.9	1.0	0.8
7 - 27 days - 7 - 27 jours	3 760	2 126	1 634	0.9	1.0	0.8
7 - 13 days - 7 - 13 jours	1 650	923	727	0.4	0.4	0.4
14 - 20 days - 14 - 20 jours	1 203	688	515	0.3	0.3	0.3
21 - 27 days - 21 - 27 jours	907	515	392	0.2	0.2	0.2
28 days - 11 months - 28 jours - 11 mois	9 132	5 266	3 866	2.2	2.5	1.9
28 days - 1 month - 28 jours - 1 mois	2 544	1 437	1 107	0.6	0.7	0.6
2 months - 2 mois	1 747	1 030	717	0.4	0.5	0.4
3 months - 3 mois	1 301	776	525	0.3	0.4	0.3
4 months - 4 mois	901	534	367	0.2	0.3	0.2
5 months - 5 mois	682	389	293	0.2	0.2	0.1
6 months - 6 mois	502	300	202	0.1	0.1	0.1
7 months - 7 mois	366	201	165	0.1	0.1	0.1
8 months - 8 mois	347	192	155	0.1	0.1	0.1
9 months - 9 mois	299	164	135	0.1	0.1	0.1
10 months - 10 mois	232	129	103	0.1	0.1	0.1
11 months - 11 mois	211	114	97	0.1	0.1	-
AMERICA, SOUTH - AMÉRIQUE DU SUD						
Argentina - Argentine						
2006 (C)						
Total	8 986	5 063[3]	3 911[3]	12.9	14.1	11.7
Less than 7 days - Moins de 7 jours	4 312	2 465[3]	1 838[3]	6.2	6.8	5.5
7 - 27 days - 7 - 27 jours	1 591	898[3]	691[3]	2.3	2.5	2.1
28 days - 11 months - 28 jours - 11 mois	3 083	1 700[3]	1 382[3]	4.4	4.7	4.1

16. Infant deaths and infant mortality rates by age and sex: latest available year, 1998 - 2007
Décès d'enfants de moins d'un an et taux de mortalité infantile selon l'âge et le sexe: dernière année disponible, 1998 - 2007 (continued - suite)

Continent, country or area, year and age (in days) / Continent, pays ou zone, année et âge (en jours)	Number - Nombre			Rate - Taux		
	Both sexes Les deux sexes	Male Masculin	Female Féminin	Both sexes Les deux sexes	Male Masculin	Female Féminin
AMERICA, SOUTH - AMÉRIQUE DU SUD						
Brazil - Brésil[6]						
2007 (U)						
Total....	34 986	19 849	15 137	...	...	...
Less than 1 day - Moins de 1 jour	8 232	4 672	3 560	...	...	...
1 - 6 days - 1 - 6 jours	9 235	5 464	3 771	...	...	...
7 - 27 days - 7 - 27 jours	5 924	3 288	2 636	...	...	...
7 - 13 days - 7 - 13 jours	3 095	1 707	1 388	...	...	...
14 - 20 days - 14 - 20 jours	1 645	905	740	...	...	...
21 - 27 days - 21 - 27 jours	1 184	676	508	...	...	...
28 days - 11 months - 28 jours - 11 mois	11 595	6 425	5 170	...	...	...
28 days - 1 month - 28 jours - 1 mois	3 287	1 881	1 406	...	...	...
2 months - 2 mois	1 857	1 018	839	...	...	...
3 months - 3 mois	1 433	773	660	...	...	...
4 months - 4 mois	1 027	556	471	...	...	...
5 months - 5 mois	844	475	369	...	...	...
6 months - 6 mois	736	425	311	...	...	...
7 months - 7 mois	624	327	297	...	...	...
8 months - 8 mois	536	287	249	...	...	...
9 months - 9 mois	454	253	201	...	...	...
10 months - 10 mois	416	223	193	...	...	...
11 months - 11 mois	381	207	174	...	...	...
Chile - Chili						
2006 (C)						
Total....	1 839	1 019	820	7.9	8.6	7.2
Less than 1 day - Moins de 1 jour	658	364	294	2.8	3.1	2.6
1 - 6 days - 1 - 6 jours	337	184	153	1.5	1.6	1.4
7 - 27 days - 7 - 27 jours	254	144	110	1.1	1.2	1.0
7 - 13 days - 7 - 13 jours	140	81	59	0.6	0.7	0.5
14 - 20 days - 14 - 20 jours	68	38	30	0.3	0.3	0.3
21 - 27 days - 21 - 27 jours	46	25	21	0.2	♦0.2	♦0.2
28 days - 11 months - 28 jours - 11 mois	1 133	623	510	4.9	5.3	4.5
28 days - 1 month - 28 jours - 1 mois	295	167	128	1.3	1.4	1.1
2 months - 2 mois	178	99	79	0.8	0.8	0.7
3 months - 3 mois	135	70	65	0.6	0.6	0.6
4 months - 4 mois	86	45	41	0.4	0.4	0.4
5 months - 5 mois	60	38	22	0.3	0.3	♦0.2
6 months - 6 mois	55	29	26	0.2	♦0.2	♦0.2
7 months - 7 mois	52	23	29	0.2	♦0.2	♦0.3
8 months - 8 mois	45	27	18	0.2	♦0.2	♦0.2
9 months - 9 mois	30	16	14	0.1	♦0.1	♦0.1
10 months - 10 mois	32	16	16	0.1	♦0.1	♦0.1
11 months - 11 mois	165	93	72	0.7	0.8	0.6
Unknown - Inconnu	-	-	-	-	-	-
Colombia - Colombie						
2007* (U)						
Total....	10 005	5 686[3]	4 313[3]	...	...	...
Less than 1 day - Moins de 1 jour	2 043	1 167[3]	873[3]	...	...	...
1 - 6 days - 1 - 6 jours	2 168	1 294[3]	873[3]	...	...	...
7 - 27 days - 7 - 27 jours	1 763	980	783	...	...	...
7 - 13 days - 7 - 13 jours	905	520	385	...	...	...
14 - 20 days - 14 - 20 jours	502	269	233	...	...	...
21 - 27 days - 21 - 27 jours	356	191	165	...	...	...
28 days - 11 months - 28 jours - 11 mois	3 759	2 088	1 671	...	...	...
28 days - 1 month - 28 jours - 1 mois	901	497	404	...	...	...
2 months - 2 mois	583	340	243	...	...	...
3 months - 3 mois	455	264	191	...	...	...
4 months - 4 mois	368	189	179	...	...	...
5 months - 5 mois	301	163	138	...	...	...
6 months - 6 mois	245	134	111	...	...	...
7 months - 7 mois	214	119	95	...	...	...
8 months - 8 mois	217	129	88	...	...	...
9 months - 9 mois	160	86	74	...	...	...
10 months - 10 mois	156	77	79	...	...	...
11 months - 11 mois	159	90	69	...	...	...
Unknown - Inconnu	272	157	113	...	...	...

16. Infant deaths and infant mortality rates by age and sex: latest available year, 1998 - 2007
Décès d'enfants de moins d'un an et taux de mortalité infantile selon l'âge et le sexe: dernière année disponible, 1998 - 2007 (continued - suite)

Continent, country or area, year and age (in days) / Continent, pays ou zone, année et âge (en jours)	Number - Nombre			Rate - Taux		
	Both sexes Les deux sexes	Male Masculin	Female Féminin	Both sexes Les deux sexes	Male Masculin	Female Féminin
AMERICA, SOUTH - AMÉRIQUE DU SUD						
Ecuador - Équateur[7]						
2007 (U)						
Total						
Less than 1 day - Moins de 1 jour	3 529	2 027	1 502	...	...	...
1 - 6 days - 1 - 6 jours	655	381	274			
7 - 27 days - 7 - 27 jours	817	481	336	...	...	...
7 - 13 days - 7 - 13 jours	598	361	237			
14 - 20 days - 14 - 20 jours	315	195	120			
21 - 27 days - 21 - 27 jours	159	94	65			
28 days - 11 months - 28 jours - 11 mois	124	72	52	...	...	...
28 days - 1 month - 28 jours - 1 mois	1 459	804	655			
2 months - 2 mois	235	130	105	...	...	...
3 months - 3 mois	247	145	102	...	...	...
4 months - 4 mois	179	106	73			
5 months - 5 mois	157	93	64	...	...	...
6 months - 6 mois	118	61	57			
7 months - 7 mois	101	44	57	...	...	...
8 months - 8 mois	102	46	56			
9 months - 9 mois	103	60	43	...	...	...
10 months - 10 mois	74	41	33			
11 months - 11 mois	74	39	35	...	...	...
French Guiana - Guyane française[8]	69	39	30			...
2003 (C)						
Total						
Less than 1 day - Moins de 1 jour	58	32	26	...	...	...
1 - 6 days - 1 - 6 jours	10	3	7	...	...	...
7 - 27 days - 7 - 27 jours	15	10	5			
7 - 13 days - 7 - 13 jours	16	12	4			
14 - 20 days - 14 - 20 jours	7	5	2	...	...	...
21 - 27 days - 21 - 27 jours	4	3	1			
28 days - 11 months - 28 jours - 11 mois	5	4	1	...	...	...
28 days - 1 month - 28 jours - 1 mois	17	7	10			
2 months - 2 mois	5	3	2	...	...	...
3 months - 3 mois	2	-	2	...	...	...
4 months - 4 mois	-	-	-			
5 months - 5 mois	1	-	1	...	...	...
6 months - 6 mois	2	1	1			
7 months - 7 mois	3	1	2	...	...	...
8 months - 8 mois	2	1	1			
9 months - 9 mois	2	1	1	...	...	...
10 months - 10 mois	-	-	-			
11 months - 11 mois	-	-	-			...
Paraguay						
2006 (U)						
Total						
Less than 28 days - Moins de 28 jours	549	...	...	...	...	...
28 days - 11 months - 28 jours - 11 mois[9]	270	...	...	...		...
Peru - Pérou[10]	279	...	...	...		...
2003 (+U)						
Total						
Less than 1 day - Moins de 1 jour	7 122	3 886[3]	3 233[3]			
1 - 6 days - 1 - 6 jours	1 256	701[3]	553[3]	...	...	...
7 - 27 days - 7 - 27 jours	1 503	836	667			
7 - 13 days - 7 - 13 jours	1 160	647	513	...		
14 - 20 days - 14 - 20 jours	501	295	206			
21 - 27 days - 21 - 27 jours	373	200	173			
28 days - 11 months - 28 jours - 11 mois	286	152	134			
28 days - 1 month - 28 jours - 1 mois	3 203	1 702[3]	1 500[3]			
2 months - 2 mois	990	548	442	...		
3 months - 3 mois	578	305	273			
4 months - 4 mois	345	185	160	...		
5 months - 5 mois	265	128	137			
6 months - 6 mois	195	100	95	...		
7 months - 7 mois	172	84[3]	87[3]	...		
8 months - 8 mois	142	78	64			
9 months - 9 mois	149	85	64	...		
10 months - 10 mois	132	71	61			
11 months - 11 mois	104	55	49	...		
	131	63	68			...

16. Infant deaths and infant mortality rates by age and sex: latest available year, 1998 - 2007
Décès d'enfants de moins d'un an et taux de mortalité infantile selon l'âge et le sexe: dernière année disponible, 1998 - 2007 (continued - suite)

Continent, country or area, year and age (in days)	Number - Nombre			Rate - Taux		
Continent, pays ou zone, année et âge (en jours)	Both sexes Les deux sexes	Male Masculin	Female Féminin	Both sexes Les deux sexes	Male Masculin	Female Féminin
AMERICA, SOUTH - AMÉRIQUE DU SUD						
Uruguay						
2000 (C)						
Total............	742	434[3]	304[3]	...	...	...
Less than 1 day - Moins de 1 jour	152	87[3]	61[3]	...	...	...
1 - 6 days - 1 - 6 jours.............	124	74	50	...	...	...
7 - 27 days - 7 - 27 jours.............	142	90	52	...	...	...
7 - 13 days - 7 - 13 jours.............	71	46	25	...	...	...
14 - 20 days - 14 - 20 jours.............	42	27	15	...	...	...
21 - 27 days - 21 - 27 jours.............	29	17	12	...	...	...
28 days - 11 months - 28 jours - 11 mois.............	324	183	141	...	...	...
28 days - 1 month - 28 jours - 1 mois	96	62	34	...	...	...
2 months - 2 mois	46	23	23	...	...	...
3 months - 3 mois.............	44	25	19	...	...	...
4 months - 4 mois	33	19	14	...	...	...
5 months - 5 mois	26	15	11	...	...	...
6 months - 6 mois.............	18	10	8	...	...	...
7 months - 7 mois.............	12	7	5	...	...	...
8 months - 8 mois.............	14	7	7	...	...	...
9 months - 9 mois.............	17	7	10	...	...	...
10 months - 10 mois.............	9	6	3	...	...	...
11 months - 11 mois.............	9	2	7	...	...	...
Venezuela (Bolivarian Republic of) - Venezuela (République bolivarienne du)[11]						
2001 (C)						
Total............	8 158	4 710	3 448	15.4	17.1	13.5
Less than 28 days - Moins de 28 jours	5 657	3 288	2 369	10.7	12.0	9.3
28 days - 11 months - 28 jours - 11 mois.............	2 501	1 422	1 079	4.7	5.2	4.2
28 days - 1 month - 28 jours - 1 mois	461	250	211	0.9	0.9	0.8
2 months - 2 mois.............	367	222	145	0.7	0.8	0.6
3 months - 3 mois.............	291	165	126	0.5	0.6	0.5
4 months - 4 mois.............	265	154	111	0.5	0.6	0.4
5 months - 5 mois.............	229	126	103	0.4	0.5	0.4
6 months - 6 mois.............	197	112	85	0.4	0.4	0.3
7 months - 7 mois.............	194	106	88	0.4	0.4	0.3
8 months - 8 mois.............	176	97	79	0.3	0.4	0.3
9 months - 9 mois.............	178	101	77	0.3	0.4	0.3
10 - 11 months - 10 - 11 mois.............	143	89	54	0.3	0.3	0.2
ASIA - ASIE						
Armenia - Arménie[12]						
2007 (C)						
Total............	433	268	165	...	...	...
Less than 1 day - Moins de 1 jour	100	58	42	...	...	...
1 - 6 days - 1 - 6 jours.............	182	116	66	...	...	...
7 - 27 days - 7 - 27 jours.............	52	37	15	...	...	...
7 - 13 days - 7 - 13 jours.............	31	22	9	...	...	...
14 - 20 days - 14 - 20 jours.............	8	6	2	...	...	...
21 - 27 days - 21 - 27 jours.............	13	9	4	...	...	...
28 days - 11 months - 28 jours - 11 mois.............	99	57	42	...	...	...
28 days - 1 month - 28 jours - 1 mois	17	11	6	...	...	...
2 months - 2 mois.............	15	10	5	...	...	...
3 months - 3 mois.............	12	10	2	...	...	...
4 months - 4 mois	8	3	5	...	...	...
5 months - 5 mois	8	5	3	...	...	...
6 months - 6 mois.............	9	4	5	...	...	...
7 months - 7 mois.............	12	6	6	...	...	...
8 months - 8 mois.............	6	3	3	...	...	...
9 months - 9 mois.............	4	2	2	...	...	...
10 months - 10 mois.............	3	2	1	...	...	...
11 months - 11 mois.............	5	1	4	...	...	...
Azerbaijan - Azerbaïdjan[12]						
2007 (+C)						
Total............	1 756	966	790	11.6	11.8	11.3
Less than 1 day - Moins de 1 jour	240	132	108	1.6	1.6	1.5
1 - 6 days - 1 - 6 jours.............	446	277	169	2.9	3.4	2.4

Continent, country or area, year and age (in days) / Continent, pays ou zone, année et âge (en jours)	Number - Nombre			Rate - Taux		
	Both sexes Les deux sexes	Male Masculin	Female Féminin	Both sexes Les deux sexes	Male Masculin	Female Féminin
ASIA - ASIE						
Azerbaijan - Azerbaïdjan[12]						
2007 (+C)						
7 - 27 days - 7 - 27 jours	73	43	30	0.5	0.5	0.4
7 - 13 days - 7 - 13 jours	37	23	14	0.2	♦0.3	♦0.2
14 - 20 days - 14 - 20 jours	18	6	12	♦0.1	♦0.1	♦0.2
21 - 27 days - 21 - 27 jours	18	14	4	♦0.1	♦0.2	♦0.1
28 days - 11 months - 28 jours - 11 mois	997	514	483	6.6	6.3	6.9
28 days - 1 month - 28 jours - 1 mois	102	47	55	0.7	0.6	0.8
2 months - 2 mois	91	49	42	0.6	0.6	0.6
3 months - 3 mois	102	55	47	0.7	0.7	0.7
4 months - 4 mois	126	70	56	0.8	0.9	0.8
5 months - 5 mois	116	65	51	0.8	0.8	0.7
6 months - 6 mois	100	35	65	0.7	0.4	0.9
7 months - 7 mois	65	31	34	0.4	0.4	0.5
8 months - 8 mois	92	57	35	0.6	0.7	0.5
9 months - 9 mois	69	39	30	0.5	0.5	0.4
10 months - 10 mois	51	25	26	0.3	♦0.3	♦0.4
11 months - 11 mois	83	41	42	0.5	0.5	0.6
Unknown - Inconnu	-	-	-	-	-	-
Bahrain - Bahreïn						
2006 (C)						
Total	115	60	55			
Less than 7 days - Moins de 7 jours	34	14	20	...	...	...
7 - 27 days - 7 - 27 jours	22	14	8	...	...	...
28 days - 11 months - 28 jours - 11 mois	59	32	27	...	...	...
China, Hong Kong SAR - Chine, Hong Kong RAS						
2005 (C)						
Total	131	78	53			
Less than 1 day - Moins de 1 jour	21	13	8	...	...	...
1 - 6 days - 1 - 6 jours	39	24	15	...	...	...
7 - 27 days - 7 - 27 jours	27	10	17	...	...	...
7 - 13 days - 7 - 13 jours	14	5	9	...	...	...
14 - 20 days - 14 - 20 jours	12	5	7	...	...	...
21 - 27 days - 21 - 27 jours	1	-	1	...	...	...
28 days - 11 months - 28 jours - 11 mois	44	31	13	...	...	...
28 days - 1 month - 28 jours - 1 mois	8	4	4	...	...	...
2 months - 2 mois	8	6	2	...	...	...
3 months - 3 mois	8	6	2	...	...	...
4 months - 4 mois	3	3	-	...	...	...
5 months - 5 mois	3	2	1	...	...	...
6 months - 6 mois	7	4	3	...	...	...
7 months - 7 mois	2	2	-	...	...	...
8 months - 8 mois	-	-	-	...	...	...
9 months - 9 mois	-	-	-	...	...	...
10 months - 10 mois	4	3	1	...	...	...
11 months - 11 mois	1	1	-	...	...	...
Unknown - Inconnu						
China, Macao SAR - Chine, Macao RAS						
2007 (C)						
Total	9	6	3			
Less than 1 day - Moins de 1 jour	3	2	1	...	...	...
1 - 6 days - 1 - 6 jours	-	-	-	...	...	...
7 - 27 days - 7 - 27 jours	2	1	1	...	...	...
7 - 13 days - 7 - 13 jours	2	1	1	...	...	...
14 - 20 days - 14 - 20 jours	-	-	-	...	...	...
21 - 27 days - 21 - 27 jours	4	3	1	...	...	...
28 days - 11 months - 28 jours - 11 mois	-	-	-	...	...	...
28 days - 1 month - 28 jours - 1 mois	-	-	-	...	...	...
2 months - 2 mois	-	-	-	...	...	...
3 months - 3 mois	1	1	-	...	...	...
4 months - 4 mois	-	-	-	...	...	...
5 months - 5 mois	2	1	1	...	...	...
6 months - 6 mois	-	-	-	...	...	...
7 months - 7 mois	1	1	-	...	...	...
8 months - 8 mois	-	-	-	...	...	...
9 months - 9 mois	-	-	-	...	...	...
10 months - 10 mois				...	...	...
11 months - 11 mois				...	...	...

16. Infant deaths and infant mortality rates by age and sex: latest available year, 1998 - 2007
Décès d'enfants de moins d'un an et taux de mortalité infantile selon l'âge et le sexe: dernière année disponible, 1998 - 2007 (continued - suite)

Continent, country or area, year and age (in days) / Continent, pays ou zone, année et âge (en jours)	Number - Nombre			Rate - Taux		
	Both sexes Les deux sexes	Male Masculin	Female Féminin	Both sexes Les deux sexes	Male Masculin	Female Féminin
ASIA - ASIE						
Cyprus - Chypre[13]						
2006 (C)						
Total	27	16	11	...	...	...
Less than 1 day - Moins de 1 jour	9	5	4	...	...	...
1 - 6 days - 1 - 6 jours	6	4	2	...	...	...
7 - 27 days - 7 - 27 jours	4	3	1	...	...	...
28 days - 11 months - 28 jours - 11 mois	7	4	3	...	...	...
28 days - 1 month - 28 jours - 1 mois	1	-	1	...	...	...
2 months - 2 mois	3	3	-	...	...	...
3 months - 3 mois	1	1	-	...	...	...
4 months - 4 mois	-	-	-	...	...	...
5 months - 5 mois	-	-	-	...	...	...
6 months - 6 mois	-	-	-	...	...	...
7 months - 7 mois	-	-	-	...	...	...
8 months - 8 mois	1	-	1	...	...	...
9 months - 9 mois	1	-	1	...	...	...
10 months - 10 mois	-	-	-	...	...	...
11 months - 11 mois	-	-	-	...	...	...
Unknown - Inconnu	1	-	1	...	...	...
Georgia - Géorgie[12]						
2007 (C)						
Total	656	372	284	...	...	...
Less than 1 day - Moins de 1 jour	108	69	39	...	...	...
1 - 6 days - 1 - 6 jours	313	175	138	...	...	...
7 - 27 days - 7 - 27 jours	116	65	51	...	...	...
7 - 13 days - 7 - 13 jours	79	45	34	...	...	...
14 - 20 days - 14 - 20 jours	21	11	10	...	...	...
21 - 27 days - 21 - 27 jours	16	9	7	...	...	...
28 days - 11 months - 28 jours - 11 mois	119	63	56	...	...	...
28 days - 1 month - 28 jours - 1 mois	34	17	17	...	...	...
2 months - 2 mois	17	9	8	...	...	...
3 months - 3 mois	19	11	8	...	...	...
4 months - 4 mois	6	2	4	...	...	...
5 months - 5 mois	14	9	5	...	...	...
6 months - 6 mois	3	2	1	...	...	...
7 months - 7 mois	7	4	3	...	...	...
8 months - 8 mois	7	3	4	...	...	...
9 months - 9 mois	4	2	2	...	...	...
10 months - 10 mois	3	2	1	...	...	...
11 months - 11 mois	5	2	3	...	...	...
Unknown - Inconnu	-	-	-	...	...	...
Israel - Israël[14]						
2007 (C)						
Total	591	318[3]	272[3]	...	...	...
Less than 1 day - Moins de 1 jour	114	63	51	...	...	...
1 - 6 days - 1 - 6 jours	140	79	61	...	...	...
7 - 27 days - 7 - 27 jours	109	56	53	...	...	...
7 - 13 days - 7 - 13 jours	64	30	34	...	...	...
14 - 20 days - 14 - 20 jours	26	14	12	...	...	...
21 - 27 days - 21 - 27 jours	19	12	7	...	...	...
28 days - 11 months - 28 jours - 11 mois	228	120	107	...	...	...
28 days - 1 month - 28 jours - 1 mois	70	38	32	...	...	...
2 months - 2 mois	31	12	19	...	...	...
3 months - 3 mois	30	16	14	...	...	...
4 months - 4 mois	21	16	5	...	...	...
5 months - 5 mois	14	8[3]	5[3]	...	...	...
6 months - 6 mois	13	7	6	...	...	...
7 months - 7 mois	12	8	4	...	...	...
8 months - 8 mois	9	3	6	...	...	...
9 months - 9 mois	11	5	6	...	...	...
10 months - 10 mois	9	3	6	...	...	...
11 months - 11 mois	8	4	4	...	...	...
Japan - Japon[15]						
2007 (C)						
Total	2 828	1 534	1 294	2.6	2.7	2.4
Less than 1 day - Moins de 1 jour	673	353	320	0.6	0.6	0.6
1 - 6 days - 1 - 6 jours	379	203	176	0.3	0.4	0.3

16. Infant deaths and infant mortality rates by age and sex: latest available year, 1998 - 2007
Décès d'enfants de moins d'un an et taux de mortalité infantile selon l'âge et le sexe: dernière année disponible, 1998 - 2007 (continued - suite)

Continent, country or area, year and age (in days) / Continent, pays ou zone, année et âge (en jours)	Number - Nombre			Rate - Taux		
	Both sexes Les deux sexes	Male Masculin	Female Féminin	Both sexes Les deux sexes	Male Masculin	Female Féminin
ASIA - ASIE						
Japan - Japon[15]						
2007 (C)						
7 - 27 days - 7 - 27 jours	382	208	174	0.4	0.4	0.3
7 - 13 days - 7 - 13 jours	170	96	74	0.2	0.2	0.1
14 - 20 days - 14 - 20 jours	112	63	49	0.1	0.1	0.1
21 - 27 days - 21 - 27 jours	100	49	51	0.1	0.1	0.1
28 days - 11 months - 28 jours - 11 mois	1 394	770	624	1.3	1.4	1.2
28 days - 1 month - 28 jours - 1 mois	287	174	113	0.3	0.3	0.2
2 months - 2 mois	193	104	89	0.2	0.2	0.2
3 months - 3 mois	170	88	82	0.2	0.2	0.2
4 months - 4 mois	146	93	53	0.1	0.2	0.1
5 months - 5 mois	131	72	59	0.1	0.1	0.1
6 months - 6 mois	106	58	48	0.1	0.1	0.1
7 months - 7 mois	106	54	52	0.1	0.1	0.1
8 months - 8 mois	83	46	37	0.1	0.1	0.1
9 months - 9 mois	54	23	31	-	-	0.1
10 months - 10 mois	62	28	34	0.1	♦0.1	0.1
11 months - 11 mois	56	30	26	0.1	0.1	-
Unknown - Inconnu	-	-	-	-	-	-
Kazakhstan[12]						
2007 (C)						
Total	4 646	2 744	1 902	14.4	16.6	12.2
Less than 1 day - Moins de 1 jour	492	298	194	1.5	1.8	1.2
1 - 6 days - 1 - 6 jours	1 669	1 015	654	5.2	6.1	4.2
7 - 27 days - 7 - 27 jours	674	400	274	2.1	2.4	1.8
7 - 13 days - 7 - 13 jours	412	248	164	1.3	1.5	1.0
14 - 20 days - 14 - 20 jours	152	93	59	0.5	0.6	0.4
21 - 27 days - 21 - 27 jours	110	59	51	0.3	0.4	0.3
28 days - 11 months - 28 jours - 11 mois	1 809	1 029	780	5.6	6.2	5.0
28 days - 1 month - 28 jours - 1 mois	452	266	186	1.4	1.6	1.2
2 months - 2 mois	249	144	105	0.8	0.9	0.7
3 months - 3 mois	220	117	103	0.7	0.7	0.7
4 months - 4 mois	173	106	67	0.5	0.6	0.4
5 months - 5 mois	152	80	72	0.5	0.5	0.5
6 months - 6 mois	143	90	53	0.4	0.5	0.3
7 months - 7 mois	122	61	61	0.4	0.4	0.4
8 months - 8 mois	108	62	46	0.3	0.4	0.3
9 months - 9 mois	70	39	31	0.2	0.2	0.2
10 months - 10 mois	72	38	34	0.2	0.2	0.2
11 months - 11 mois	48	26	22	0.1	♦0.2	♦0.1
Unknown - Inconnu	2	2	-	-	-	-
Kuwait - Koweït						
2007 (C)						
Total	449	242	207	...	...	...
Less than 1 day - Moins de 1 jour	113	64	49	...	...	...
1 - 6 days - 1 - 6 jours	79	43	36	...	...	...
7 - 27 days - 7 - 27 jours	103	61	42	...	...	...
7 - 13 days - 7 - 13 jours	48	24	24	...	...	...
14 - 20 days - 14 - 20 jours	34	24	10	...	...	...
21 - 27 days - 21 - 27 jours	21	13	8	...	...	...
28 days - 11 months - 28 jours - 11 mois	154	74	80	...	...	...
28 days - 1 month - 28 jours - 1 mois	53	27	26	...	...	...
2 months - 2 mois	26	13	13	...	...	...
3 months - 3 mois	21	14	7	...	...	...
4 months - 4 mois	14	4	10	...	...	...
5 months - 5 mois	9	4	5	...	...	...
6 months - 6 mois	8	4	4	...	...	...
7 months - 7 mois	5	2	3	...	...	...
8 months - 8 mois	5	2	3	...	...	...
9 months - 9 mois	3	2	1	...	...	...
10 months - 10 mois	3	1	2	...	...	...
11 months - 11 mois	7	1	6	...	...	...
Kyrgyzstan - Kirghizstan						
2007 (C)						
Total	3 771	2 142	1 629	30.6	33.8	27.2
Less than 1 day - Moins de 1 jour	1 095	602	493	8.9	9.5	8.2
1 - 6 days - 1 - 6 jours	1 230	697	533	10.0	11.0	8.9

16. Infant deaths and infant mortality rates by age and sex: latest available year, 1998 - 2007
Décès d'enfants de moins d'un an et taux de mortalité infantile selon l'âge et le sexe: dernière année disponible, 1998 - 2007 (continued - suite)

Continent, country or area, year and age (in days) / Continent, pays ou zone, année et âge (en jours)	Number - Nombre			Rate - Taux		
	Both sexes Les deux sexes	Male Masculin	Female Féminin	Both sexes Les deux sexes	Male Masculin	Female Féminin
ASIA - ASIE						
Kyrgyzstan - Kirghizstan						
2007 (C)				2.2	2.3	2.1
7 - 27 days - 7 - 27 jours	271	145	126	1.3	1.3	1.3
7 - 13 days - 7 - 13 jours	159	83	76	0.5	0.5	♦0.5
14 - 20 days - 14 - 20 jours	59	32	27	0.4	0.5	♦0.4
21 - 27 days - 21 - 27 jours	53	30	23	9.5	11.0	8.0
28 days - 11 months - 28 jours - 11 mois	1 175	698	477	1.8	2.0	1.7
28 days - 1 month - 28 jours - 1 mois	226	126	100	1.3	1.6	1.0
2 months - 2 mois	162	101	61	1.0	1.1	0.9
3 months - 3 mois	127	71	56	1.1	1.3	0.8
4 months - 4 mois	130	84	46	0.9	1.0	0.7
5 months - 5 mois	105	64	41	0.9	1.0	0.8
6 months - 6 mois	112	65	47	0.6	0.7	0.6
7 months - 7 mois	79	46	33	0.6	0.7	♦0.4
8 months - 8 mois	70	46	24	0.5	0.6	0.5
9 months - 9 mois	67	36	31	0.4	♦0.4	♦0.4
10 months - 10 mois	54	28	26	0.3	0.5	♦0.2
11 months - 11 mois	43	31	12	-	-	-
Unknown - Inconnu	-	-	-			
Malaysia - Malaisie						
2004 (C)				6.5	7.2	5.7
Total	3 105	1 784	1 321	0.9	1.1	0.8
Less than 1 day - Moins de 1 jour	443	262	181	1.7	2.0	1.4
1 - 6 days - 1 - 6 jours	834	500	334	1.0	1.1	1.0
7 - 27 days - 7 - 27 jours	492	268	224	2.8	3.1	2.5
28 days - 11 months - 28 jours - 11 mois	1 336	754	582	1.2	1.4	1.0
28 days - 2 months - 28 jours - 2 mois	568	335	233	0.8	0.9	0.8
3 - 5 months - 3 - 5 mois	393	216	177	0.5	0.5	0.4
6 - 8 months - 6 - 8 mois	220	122	98	0.3	0.3	0.3
9 - 11 months - 9 - 11 mois	155	81	74			
Maldives						
2007 (C)				...	...	...
Total	66	47	19			
Less than 7 days - Moins de 7 jours	41	26	15			
7 - 27 days - 7 - 27 jours	6	5	1			
28 days - 11 months - 28 jours - 11 mois	19	16	3			
Occupied Palestinian Territory - Territoire palestinien occupé						
2007 (U)				...	...	...
Total	794	420	374	...	...	...
Less than 1 day - Moins de 1 jour	42	24	18	...	...	...
1 - 6 days - 1 - 6 jours	183	113	70	...	...	...
7 - 27 days - 7 - 27 jours	156	79	77	...	...	...
7 - 13 days - 7 - 13 jours	79	44	35	...	...	...
14 - 20 days - 14 - 20 jours	47	19	28	...	...	...
21 - 27 days - 21 - 27 jours	30	16	14	...	...	...
28 days - 11 months - 28 jours - 11 mois	413	204	209	...	...	...
28 days - 1 month - 28 jours - 1 mois	111	64	47	...	...	...
2 months - 2 mois	56	25	31	...	...	...
3 months - 3 mois	50	28	22	...	...	...
4 months - 4 mois	32	14	18	...	...	...
5 months - 5 mois	40	20	20	...	...	...
6 months - 6 mois	28	17	11	...	...	...
7 months - 7 mois	19	8	11	...	...	...
8 months - 8 mois	19	10	9	...	...	...
9 months - 9 mois	22	8	14	...	...	...
10 months - 10 mois	21	5	16	...	...	...
11 months - 11 mois	15	5	10	...	...	...
Oman[16]						
2006 (U)				...	...	...
Total	381	212	170	...	...	...
Less than 7 days - Moins de 7 jours	206	126	81	...	...	...
7 - 27 days - 7 - 27 jours[17]	56	31	25	...	...	...
28 days - 11 months - 28 jours - 11 mois[18]	119	55	64	...	...	...
Pakistan[19]						
2005 (I)				76.7	84.8	67.6
Total	289 169	168 960	120 209	8.0	9.4	6.4
Less than 1 day - Moins de 1 jour	30 052	18 699	11 353	30.1	34.2	25.5
1 - 6 days - 1 - 6 jours	113 531	68 118	45 413			

16. Infant deaths and infant mortality rates by age and sex: latest available year, 1998 - 2007
Décès d'enfants de moins d'un an et taux de mortalité infantile selon l'âge et le sexe: dernière année disponible, 1998 - 2007 (continued - suite)

Continent, country or area, year and age (in days) Continent, pays ou zone, année et âge (en jours)	Number - Nombre			Rate - Taux		
	Both sexes Les deux sexes	Male Masculin	Female Féminin	Both sexes Les deux sexes	Male Masculin	Female Féminin
ASIA - ASIE						
Pakistan[19]						
2005 (I)						
7 - 27 days - 7 - 27 jours	38 734	23 374	15 359	10.3	11.7	8.6
7 - 13 days - 7 - 13 jours	22 706	11 353	11 353	6.0	5.7	6.4
14 - 20 days - 14 - 20 jours	13 357	11 353	2 003	3.5	5.7	1.1
21 - 27 days - 21 - 27 jours	2 671	668	2 003	0.7	0.3	1.1
28 days - 11 months - 28 jours - 11 mois	106 852	58 768	48 084	28.3	29.5	27.0
28 days - 1 month - 28 jours - 1 mois	26 713	12 689	14 025	7.1	6.4	7.9
2 months - 2 mois	14 692	6 678	8 014	3.9	3.3	4.5
3 months - 3 mois	19 367	10 685	8 682	5.1	5.4	4.9
4 months - 4 mois	8 014	5 343	2 671	2.1	2.7	1.5
5 months - 5 mois	6 678	3 339	3 339	1.8	1.7	1.9
6 months - 6 mois	8 682	5 343	3 339	2.3	2.7	1.9
7 months - 7 mois	4 007	2 003	2 003	1.1	1.0	1.1
8 months - 8 mois	5 343	2 003	3 339	1.4	1.0	1.9
9 months - 9 mois	6 010	4 675	1 336	1.6	2.3	0.8
10 months - 10 mois	4 007	3 339	668	1.1	1.7	0.4
11 months - 11 mois	3 339	2 671	668	0.9	1.3	0.4
Philippines						
2005 (C)						
Total	21 674	12 752	8 922	12.8	14.5	11.0
Less than 1 day - Moins de 1 jour	4 117	2 411	1 706	2.4	2.7	2.1
1 - 6 days - 1 - 6 jours	5 709	3 461	2 248	3.4	3.9	2.8
7 - 27 days - 7 - 27 jours	2 656	1 600	1 056	1.6	1.8	1.3
7 - 13 days - 7 - 13 jours	1 434	885	549	0.8	1.0	0.7
14 - 20 days - 14 - 20 jours	726	418	308	0.4	0.5	0.4
21 - 27 days - 21 - 27 jours	496	297	199	0.3	0.3	0.2
28 days - 11 months - 28 jours - 11 mois	9 192	5 280	3 912	5.4	6.0	4.8
28 days - 1 month - 28 jours - 1 mois	2 000	1 229	771	1.2	1.4	1.0
2 months - 2 mois	1 286	753	533	0.8	0.9	0.7
3 months - 3 mois	889	522	367	0.5	0.6	0.5
4 months - 4 mois	817	438	379	0.5	0.5	0.5
5 months - 5 mois	725	411	314	0.4	0.5	0.4
6 months - 6 mois	754	401	353	0.4	0.5	0.4
7 months - 7 mois	663	369	294	0.4	0.4	0.4
8 months - 8 mois	614	325	289	0.4	0.4	0.4
9 months - 9 mois	534	321	213	0.3	0.4	0.3
10 months - 10 mois	431	233	198	0.3	0.3	0.2
11 months - 11 mois	479	278	201	0.3	0.3	0.2
Qatar						
2007 (C)						
Total				...	...	...
Less than 1 day - Moins de 1 jour	117	57	60	...	...	...
1 - 6 days - 1 - 6 jours	-	-	-	...	...	...
7 - 27 days - 7 - 27 jours	58	32	26	...	...	...
7 - 13 days - 7 - 13 jours	20	13	7	...	...	...
14 - 20 days - 14 - 20 jours	8	5	3	...	...	...
21 - 27 days - 21 - 27 jours	8	5	3	...	...	...
28 days - 11 months - 28 jours - 11 mois	4	3	1	...	...	...
28 days - 1 month - 28 jours - 1 mois	39	12	27	...	...	...
2 months - 2 mois	9	4	5	...	...	...
3 months - 3 mois	6	2	4	...	...	...
4 months - 4 mois	6	2	4	...	...	...
5 months - 5 mois	2	-	2	...	...	...
6 months - 6 mois	3	-	3	...	...	...
7 months - 7 mois	8	3	5	...	...	...
8 months - 8 mois	-	-	-	...	...	...
9 months - 9 mois	1	-	1	...	...	...
10 months - 10 mois	1	-	1	...	...	...
11 months - 11 mois	2	1	1	...	...	...
Unknown - Inconnu	1	-	1	...	...	...
	-	-	-	...	...	...
Republic of Korea - République de Corée[20]						
2006 (C)						
Total	1 709	959	750	3.8	4.1	3.4
Less than 7 days - Moins de 7 jours	622	371	251	1.4	1.6	1.2
7 - 27 days - 7 - 27 jours	357	185	172	0.8	0.8	0.8

16. Infant deaths and infant mortality rates by age and sex: latest available year, 1998 - 2007
Décès d'enfants de moins d'un an et taux de mortalité infantile selon l'âge et le sexe: dernière année disponible, 1998 - 2007 (continued - suite)

Continent, country or area, year and age (in days) / Continent, pays ou zone, année et âge (en jours)	Number - Nombre			Rate - Taux		
	Both sexes Les deux sexes	Male Masculin	Female Féminin	Both sexes Les deux sexes	Male Masculin	Female Féminin
ASIA - ASIE						
Republic of Korea - République de Corée[20]						
2006 (C)	730	403	327	1.6	1.7	1.5
28 days - 11 months - 28 jours - 11 mois	200	104	96	0.4	0.4	0.4
28 days - 1 month - 28 jours - 1 mois	530	299	231	1.2	1.3	1.1
2 - 11 months - 2 - 11 mois						
Singapore - Singapour						
2007 (+C)						
Total	94	60[3]	33[3]	...	...	...
Less than 1 day - Moins de 1 jour	8	5[3]	2[3]	...	...	...
1 - 6 days - 1 - 6 jours	23	15	8	...	...	...
7 - 27 days - 7 - 27 jours	21	11	10	...	...	...
7 - 13 days - 7 - 13 jours	13	8	5	...	...	...
14 - 20 days - 14 - 20 jours	6	1	5	...	...	...
21 - 27 days - 21 - 27 jours	2	2	-	...	...	...
28 days - 11 months - 28 jours - 11 mois	42	29	13	...	...	...
28 days - 1 month - 28 jours - 1 mois	13	11	2	...	...	...
2 months - 2 mois	6	3	3	...	...	...
3 months - 3 mois	6	3	3	...	...	...
4 months - 4 mois	4	3	1	...	...	...
5 months - 5 mois	3	2	1	...	...	...
6 months - 6 mois	1	1	-	...	...	...
7 months - 7 mois	1	1	-	...	...	...
8 months - 8 mois	4	3	1	...	...	...
9 months - 9 mois	1	1	-	...	...	...
10 months - 10 mois	-	-	-	...	...	...
11 months - 11 mois	3	1	2	...	...	...
Unknown - Inconnu	-	-		...	...	...
Tajikistan - Tadjikistan[12]						
2006 (U)						
Total	2 160	1 315	845	...	...	...
Less than 1 day - Moins de 1 jour	322	189	133	...	...	...
1 - 6 days - 1 - 6 jours	597	370	227	...	...	...
7 - 27 days - 7 - 27 jours	191	118	73	...	...	...
7 - 13 days - 7 - 13 jours	114	73	41	...	...	...
14 - 20 days - 14 - 20 jours	39	22	17	...	...	...
21 - 27 days - 21 - 27 jours	38	23	15	...	...	...
28 days - 11 months - 28 jours - 11 mois	1 050	638	412	...	...	...
28 days - 1 month - 28 jours - 1 mois	165	102	63	...	...	...
2 months - 2 mois	116	67	49	...	...	...
3 months - 3 mois	123	82	41	...	...	...
4 months - 4 mois	113	65	48	...	...	...
5 months - 5 mois	97	64	33	...	...	...
6 months - 6 mois	95	55	40	...	...	...
7 months - 7 mois	77	50	27	...	...	...
8 months - 8 mois	79	48	31	...	...	...
9 months - 9 mois	63	39	24	...	...	...
10 months - 10 mois	69	39	30	...	...	...
11 months - 11 mois	53	27	26	...	...	...
Thailand - Thaïlande						
2007 (+U)						
Total	5 781	3 269	2 512	...	...	...
Less than 1 day - Moins de 1 jour	622	338	284	...	...	...
1 - 6 days - 1 - 6 jours	1 783	1 045	738	...	...	...
7 - 27 days - 7 - 27 jours	1 028	591	437	...	...	...
7 - 13 days - 7 - 13 jours	562	326	236	...	...	...
14 - 20 days - 14 - 20 jours	276	162	114	...	...	...
21 - 27 days - 21 - 27 jours	190	103	87	...	...	...
28 days - 11 months - 28 jours - 11 mois	2 348	1 295	1 053	...	...	...
28 days - 1 month - 28 jours - 1 mois	658	364	294	...	...	...
2 months - 2 mois	374	207	167	...	...	...
3 months - 3 mois	287	159	128	...	...	...
4 months - 4 mois	225	106	119	...	...	...
5 months - 5 mois	166	85	81	...	...	...
6 months - 6 mois	162	89	73	...	...	...
7 months - 7 mois	125	72	53	...	...	...
8 months - 8 mois	99	62	37	...	...	...
9 months - 9 mois	106	57	49	...	...	...

16. Infant deaths and infant mortality rates by age and sex: latest available year, 1998 - 2007
Décès d'enfants de moins d'un an et taux de mortalité infantile selon l'âge et le sexe: dernière année disponible, 1998 - 2007 (continued - suite)

Continent, country or area, year and age (in days) / Continent, pays ou zone, année et âge (en jours)	Number - Nombre			Rate - Taux		
	Both sexes Les deux sexes	Male Masculin	Female Féminin	Both sexes Les deux sexes	Male Masculin	Female Féminin
ASIA - ASIE						
Thailand - Thaïlande						
2007 (+U)						
10 months - 10 mois	70	43	27	...	...	...
11 months - 11 mois	76	51	25	...	...	...
Turkey - Turquie[21]						
1999 (U)						
Total	15 870	8 931	6 939	...	...	...
Less than 1 day - Moins de 1 jour	-	-	-	...	...	...
1 - 6 days - 1 - 6 jours	8 483	4 876	3 607	...	...	...
7 - 27 days - 7 - 27 jours	1 978	1 093	885	...	...	...
7 - 13 days - 7 - 13 jours	1 119	636	483	...	...	...
14 - 20 days - 14 - 20 jours	582	308	274	...	...	...
21 - 27 days - 21 - 27 jours	277	149	128	...	...	...
28 days - 11 months - 28 jours - 11 mois	5 409	2 962	2 447	...	...	...
28 days - 1 month - 28 jours - 1 mois	993	545	448	...	...	...
2 months - 2 mois	799	438	361	...	...	...
3 months - 3 mois	759	416	343	...	...	...
4 months - 4 mois	540	287	253	...	...	...
5 months - 5 mois	607	345	262	...	...	...
6 months - 6 mois	592	347	245	...	...	...
7 months - 7 mois	325	165	160	...	...	...
8 months - 8 mois	277	152	125	...	...	...
9 months - 9 mois	193	91	102	...	...	...
10 months - 10 mois	194	108	86	...	...	...
11 months - 11 mois	130	68	62	...	...	...
Uzbekistan - Ouzbékistan[12]						
2000 (C)						
Total	10 091	5 805	4 286	19.1	21.4	16.7
Less than 1 day - Moins de 1 jour	607	355	252	1.2	1.3	1.0
1 - 6 days - 1 - 6 jours	2 179	1 352	827	4.1	5.0	3.2
7 - 27 days - 7 - 27 jours	1 279	731	548	2.4	2.7	2.1
7 - 13 days - 7 - 13 jours	719	421	298	1.4	1.6	1.2
14 - 20 days - 14 - 20 jours	343	192	151	0.7	0.7	0.6
21 - 27 days - 21 - 27 jours	217	118	99	0.4	0.4	0.4
28 days - 11 months - 28 jours - 11 mois	6 026	3 367	2 659	11.4	12.4	10.4
28 days - 1 month - 28 jours - 1 mois	976	582	394	1.8	2.1	1.5
2 months - 2 mois	680	363	317	1.3	1.3	1.2
3 months - 3 mois	693	411	282	1.3	1.5	1.1
4 months - 4 mois	691	377	314	1.3	1.4	1.2
5 months - 5 mois	612	324	288	1.2	1.2	1.1
6 months - 6 mois	538	293	245	1.0	1.1	1.0
7 months - 7 mois	486	269	217	0.9	1.0	0.8
8 months - 8 mois	445	259	186	0.8	1.0	0.7
9 months - 9 mois	388	204	184	0.7	0.8	0.7
10 months - 10 mois	274	150	124	0.5	0.6	0.5
11 months - 11 mois	243	135	108	0.5	0.5	0.4
EUROPE						
Albania - Albanie						
2006 (C)						
Total	253	...	...	...	...	...
Less than 1 day - Moins de 1 jour	10	...	...	...	...	...
1 - 6 days - 1 - 6 jours	40	...	...	...	...	...
7 - 27 days - 7 - 27 jours	21	...	...	...	...	...
28 days - 11 months - 28 jours - 11 mois	182	...	...	...	...	...
28 days - 1 month - 28 jours - 1 mois	35	...	...	...	...	...
2 - 11 months - 2 - 11 mois	147	...	...	...	...	...
Andorra - Andorre						
2007 (C)						
Total	1	-	1	...	...	...
Less than 1 day - Moins de 1 jour	-	-	-	...	...	...
1 - 6 days - 1 - 6 jours	-	-	-	...	...	...
7 - 27 days - 7 - 27 jours	1	-	1	...	...	...
7 - 13 days - 7 - 13 jours	-	-	-	...	...	...
14 - 20 days - 14 - 20 jours	1	-	1	...	...	...

16. Infant deaths and infant mortality rates by age and sex: latest available year, 1998 - 2007
Décès d'enfants de moins d'un an et taux de mortalité infantile selon l'âge et le sexe: dernière année disponible, 1998 - 2007 (continued - suite)

Continent, country or area, year and age (in days) Continent, pays ou zone, année et âge (en jours)	Number - Nombre			Rate - Taux		
	Both sexes Les deux sexes	Male Masculin	Female Féminin	Both sexes Les deux sexes	Male Masculin	Female Féminin
EUROPE						
Andorra - Andorre						
2007 (C)						
21 - 27 days - 21 - 27 jours...............................	-	-	-	...	...	...
28 days - 11 months - 28 jours - 11 mois..............	-	-	-	...	...	...
Austria - Autriche						
2007 (C)						
Total.................................	280	158	122	...	...	...
Less than 1 day - Moins dè 1 jour........................	111	68	43	...	...	...
1 - 6 days - 1 - 6 jours..................................	46	23	23	...	...	...
7 - 27 days - 7 - 27 jours...............................	35	22	13	...	...	...
7 - 13 days - 7 - 13 jours............................	16	11	5	...	...	...
14 - 20 days - 14 - 20 jours..........................	12	7	5	...	...	...
21 - 27 days - 21 - 27 jours..........................	7	4	3	...	...	...
28 days - 11 months - 28 jours - 11 mois...............	88	45	43	...	...	...
28 days - 1 month - 28 jours - 1 mois.................	22	14	8	...	...	...
2 months - 2 mois...................................	15	8	7	...	...	...
3 months - 3 mois...................................	9	5	4	...	...	...
4 months - 4 mois...................................	7	2	5	...	...	...
5 months - 5 mois...................................	7	3	4	...	...	...
6 months - 6 mois...................................	4	3	1	...	...	...
7 months - 7 mois...................................	3	-	3	...	...	...
8 months - 8 mois...................................	4	2	2	...	...	...
9 months - 9 mois...................................	4	1	3	...	...	...
10 months - 10 mois..................................	8	5	3	...	...	...
11 months - 11 mois..................................	5	2	3	...	...	...
Belarus - Bélarus[12]						
2007 (C)						
Total.................................	534	309	225	...	...	...
Less than 1 day - Moins de 1 jour.......................	75	39	36	...	...	...
1 - 6 days - 1 - 6 jours..................................	108	64	44	...	...	...
7 - 27 days - 7 - 27 jours...............................	75	48	27	...	...	...
7 - 13 days - 7 - 13 jours............................	21	16	5	...	...	...
14 - 20 days - 14 - 20 jours..........................	37	20	17	...	...	...
21 - 27 days - 21 - 27 jours..........................	17	12	5	...	...	...
28 days - 11 months - 28 jours - 11 mois...............	276	158	118	...	...	...
28 days - 1 month - 28 jours - 1 mois.................	77	43	34	...	...	...
2 months - 2 mois...................................	44	28	16	...	...	...
3 months - 3 mois...................................	32	21	11	...	...	...
4 months - 4 mois...................................	27	15	12	...	...	...
5 months - 5 mois...................................	19	11	8	...	...	...
6 months - 6 mois...................................	28	16	12	...	...	...
7 months - 7 mois...................................	23	9	14	...	...	...
8 months - 8 mois...................................	10	5	5	...	...	...
9 months - 9 mois...................................	9	7	2	...	...	...
10 months - 10 mois..................................	5	2	3	...	...	...
11 months - 11 mois..................................	2	1	1	...	...	...
Belgium - Belgique						
2000 (C)						
Total.................................	554	305	249	...	...	...
Less than 1 day - Moins de 1 jour.......................	91	46	45	...	...	...
1 - 6 days - 1 - 6 jours..................................	153	85	68	...	...	...
7 - 27 days - 7 - 27 jours...............................	90	56	34	...	...	...
28 days - 11 months - 28 jours - 11 mois...............	220	118	102	...	...	...
Bosnia and Herzegovina - Bosnie-Herzégovine						
2006 (C)						
Total.................................	255	158	97	...	...	...
Less than 1 day - Moins de 1 jour.......................	60	38	22	...	...	...
1 - 6 days - 1 - 6 jours..................................	104	66	38	...	...	...
7 - 27 days - 7 - 27 jours...............................	40	21	19	...	...	...
28 days - 11 months - 28 jours - 11 mois...............	51	33	18	...	...	...
28 days - 1 month - 28 jours - 1 mois.................	-	-	-	...	...	...
2 - 11 months - 2 - 11 mois..........................	51	33	18	...	...	...
Bulgaria - Bulgarie						
2007 (C)						
Total.................................	690	388	302	...	...	...
Less than 1 day - Moins de 1 jour.......................	111	63	48	...	...	...
1 - 6 days - 1 - 6 jours..................................	156	99	57	...	...	...

Continent, country or area, year and age (in days) / Continent, pays ou zone, année et âge (en jours)	Number - Nombre			Rate - Taux		
	Both sexes Les deux sexes	Male Masculin	Female Féminin	Both sexes Les deux sexes	Male Masculin	Female Féminin
EUROPE						
Bulgaria - Bulgarie						
2007 (C)						
7 - 27 days - 7 - 27 jours	103	54	49			
7 - 13 days - 7 - 13 jours	40	25	15	...	...	...
14 - 20 days - 14 - 20 jours	37	14	23	...	...	...
21 - 27 days - 21 - 27 jours	26	15	11	...	...	...
28 days - 11 months - 28 jours - 11 mois	320	172	148	...	...	...
28 days - 1 month - 28 jours - 1 mois	105	60	45	...	...	...
2 months - 2 mois	43	21	22	...	...	...
3 months - 3 mois	31	18	13	...	...	...
4 months - 4 mois	35	24	11	...	...	...
5 months - 5 mois	20	7	13	...	...	...
6 months - 6 mois	18	10	8	...	...	...
7 months - 7 mois	15	8	7	...	...	...
8 months - 8 mois	13	6	7	...	...	...
9 months - 9 mois	12	5	7	...	...	...
10 months - 10 mois	16	7	9	...	...	...
11 months - 11 mois	12	6	6	...	...	...
Croatia - Croatie						
2007 (C)						
Total	234	114	120			
Less than 1 day - Moins de 1 jour	73	35	38	...	...	...
1 - 6 days - 1 - 6 jours	63	35	28	...	...	...
7 - 27 days - 7 - 27 jours	31	13	18	...	...	...
7 - 13 days - 7 - 13 jours	19	7	12	...	...	...
14 - 20 days - 14 - 20 jours	4	2	2	...	...	...
21 - 27 days - 21 - 27 jours	8	4	4	...	...	...
28 days - 11 months - 28 jours - 11 mois	67	31	36	...	...	...
28 days - 1 month - 28 jours - 1 mois	23	10	13	...	...	...
2 months - 2 mois	10	5	5	...	...	...
3 months - 3 mois	5	4	1	...	...	...
4 months - 4 mois	10	4	6	...	...	...
5 months - 5 mois	2	2	-	...	...	...
6 months - 6 mois	4	1	3	...	...	...
7 months - 7 mois	5	3	2	...	...	...
8 months - 8 mois	2	-	2	...	...	...
9 months - 9 mois	1	-	1	...	...	...
10 months - 10 mois	3	2	1	...	...	...
11 months - 11 mois	2	-	2	...	...	...
Unknown - Inconnu	-	-	-	...	...	...
Czech Republic - République tchèque						
2007 (C)						
Total	360	218	142			
Less than 1 day - Moins de 1 jour	55	33	22	...	...	...
1 - 6 days - 1 - 6 jours	88	55	33	...	...	...
7 - 27 days - 7 - 27 jours	92	59	33	...	...	...
7 - 13 days - 7 - 13 jours	50	33	17	...	...	...
14 - 20 days - 14 - 20 jours	30	17	13	...	...	...
21 - 27 days - 21 - 27 jours	12	9	3	...	...	...
28 days - 11 months - 28 jours - 11 mois	125	71	54	...	...	...
28 days - 1 month - 28 jours - 1 mois	40	23	17	...	...	...
2 months - 2 mois	21	12	9	...	...	...
3 months - 3 mois	12	7	5	...	...	...
4 months - 4 mois	11	6	5	...	...	...
5 months - 5 mois	11	7	4	...	...	...
6 months - 6 mois	4	3	1	...	...	...
7 months - 7 mois	8	3	5	...	...	...
8 months - 8 mois	8	4	4	...	...	...
9 months - 9 mois	2	1	1	...	...	...
10 months - 10 mois	7	5	2	...	...	...
11 months - 11 mois	1	-	1	...	...	...
Unknown - Inconnu	-	-	-	...	...	...
Denmark - Danemark[22]						
2006 (C)						
Total	250	141	109			
Less than 1 day - Moins de 1 jour	112	65	47	...	...	...
1 - 6 days - 1 - 6 jours	59	26	33	...	...	...

Continent, country or area, year and age (in days) / Continent, pays ou zone, année et âge (en jours)	Number - Nombre			Rate - Taux		
	Both sexes Les deux sexes	Male Masculin	Female Féminin	Both sexes Les deux sexes	Male Masculin	Female Féminin
EUROPE						
Denmark - Danemark[22]						
2006 (C)						
7 - 27 days - 7 - 27 jours	34	23	11	...	...	...
28 days - 11 months - 28 jours - 11 mois........	45	27	18	...	...	...
Estonia - Estonie						
2007 (C)						
Total........	79	42	37	...	...	...
Less than 1 day - Moins de 1 jour	10	6	4	...	...	...
1 - 6 days - 1 - 6 jours	19	8	11	...	...	...
7 - 27 days - 7 - 27 jours	16	8	8	...	...	...
7 - 13 days - 7 - 13 jours	12	6	6	...	...	...
14 - 20 days - 14 - 20 jours	3	2	1	...	...	...
21 - 27 days - 21 - 27 jours	1	-	1	...	...	...
28 days - 11 months - 28 jours - 11 mois........	34	20	14	...	...	...
28 days - 1 month - 28 jours - 1 mois......	15	7	8	...	...	...
2 months - 2 mois..........	4	1	3	...	...	...
3 months - 3 mois..........	3	3	-	...	...	...
4 months - 4 mois..........	1	1	-	...	...	...
5 months - 5 mois..........	1	1	-	...	...	...
6 months - 6 mois..........	3	1	2	...	...	...
7 months - 7 mois..........	2	2	-	...	...	...
8 months - 8 mois..........	1	1	-	...	...	...
9 months - 9 mois..........	2	2	-	...	...	...
10 months - 10 mois..........	2	1	1	...	...	...
11 months - 11 mois..........	-	-	-	...	...	...
Unknown - Inconnu				...	...	...
Finland - Finlande[23]						
2007 (C)						
Total........	161	93	68	...	...	...
Less than 1 day - Moins de 1 jour	51	32	19	...	...	...
1 - 6 days - 1 - 6 jours.........	44	25	19	...	...	...
7 - 27 days - 7 - 27 jours	16	8	8	...	...	...
7 - 13 days - 7 - 13 jours	12	6	6	...	...	...
14 - 20 days - 14 - 20 jours	2	1	1	...	...	...
21 - 27 days - 21 - 27 jours	2	1	1	...	...	...
28 days - 11 months - 28 jours - 11 mois........	50	28	22	...	...	...
28 days - 1 month - 28 jours - 1 mois......	14	11	3	...	...	...
2 months - 2 mois...........	9	4	5	...	...	...
3 months - 3 mois..........	9	5	4	...	...	...
4 months - 4 mois..........	4	1	3	...	...	...
5 months - 5 mois..........	3	3	-	...	...	...
6 months - 6 mois..........	3	3	-	...	...	...
7 months - 7 mois..........	2	-	2	...	...	...
8 months - 8 mois..........	2	-	2	...	...	...
9 months - 9 mois..........	2	-	2	...	...	...
10 months - 10 mois..........	-	-	-	...	...	...
11 months - 11 mois..........	2	1	1	...	...	...
Unknown - Inconnu	-	-	-	...	...	...
France[24]						
2006 (C)						
Total.......	2 906	1 670	1 236	3.6	4.1	3.2
Less than 1 day - Moins de 1 jour	621	344	277	0.8	0.8	0.7
1 - 6 days - 1 - 6 jours	633	385	248	0.8	0.9	0.6
7 - 27 days - 7 - 27 jours	609	362	247	0.8	0.9	0.6
7 - 13 days - 7 - 13 jours	311	186	125	0.4	0.5	0.3
14 - 20 days - 14 - 20 jours	184	110	74	0.2	0.3	0.2
21 - 27 days - 21 - 27 jours	114	66	48	0.1	0.2	0.1
28 days - 11 months - 28 jours - 11 mois........	1 043	579	464	1.3	1.4	1.2
28 days - 1 month - 28 jours - 1 mois......	286	154	132	0.4	0.4	0.3
2 months - 2 mois...........	157	99	58	0.2	0.2	0.2
3 months - 3 mois..........	131	70	61	0.2	0.2	0.1
4 months - 4 mois..........	92	51	41	0.1	0.1	0.1
5 months - 5 mois..........	93	50	43	0.1	0.1	0.1
6 months - 6 mois..........	76	37	39	0.1	0.1	0.1
7 months - 7 mois..........	41	24	17	0.1	♦0.1	-
8 months - 8 mois..........	50	31	19	0.1	♦0.1	0.1
9 months - 9 mois..........	42	25	17	0.1	♦0.1	-
10 months - 10 mois..........	39	22	17	-	♦0.1	-

16. Infant deaths and infant mortality rates by age and sex: latest available year, 1998 - 2007
Décès d'enfants de moins d'un an et taux de mortalité infantile selon l'âge et le sexe: dernière année disponible, 1998 - 2007 (continued - suite)

Continent, country or area, year and age (in days) / Continent, pays ou zone, année et âge (en jours)	Number - Nombre			Rate - Taux		
	Both sexes Les deux sexes	Male Masculin	Female Féminin	Both sexes Les deux sexes	Male Masculin	Female Féminin
EUROPE						
France[24]						
2006 (C)						
11 months - 11 mois	36	16	20	-	-	♦0.1
Unknown - Inconnu	-	-	-	-	-	-
Germany - Allemagne						
2007 (C)						
Total						
Less than 1 day - Moins de 1 jour	2 656	1 518	1 138	3.9	4.3	3.4
1 - 6 days - 1 - 6 jours	825	453	372	1.2	1.3	1.1
7 - 27 days - 7 - 27 jours	599	371	228	0.9	1.1	0.7
7 - 13 days - 7 - 13 jours	398	213	185	0.6	0.6	0.6
14 - 20 days - 14 - 20 jours	203	111	92	0.3	0.3	0.3
21 - 27 days - 21 - 27 jours	110	60	50	0.2	0.2	0.2
28 days - 11 months - 28 jours - 11 mois	85	42	43	0.1	0.1	0.1
28 days - 1 month - 28 jours - 1 mois	834	481	353	1.2	1.4	1.1
2 months - 2 mois	203	111	92	0.3	0.3	0.3
3 months - 3 mois	139	75	64	0.2	0.2	0.2
4 months - 4 mois	106	61	45	0.2	0.2	0.1
5 months - 5 mois	76	40	36	0.1	0.1	0.1
6 months - 6 mois	63	43	20	0.1	0.1	0.1
7 months - 7 mois	55	36	19	0.1	0.1	♦0.1
8 months - 8 mois	50	31	19	0.1	0.1	♦0.1
9 months - 9 mois	44	30	14	0.1	0.1	-
10 months - 10 mois	41	23	18	0.1	♦0.1	♦0.1
11 months - 11 mois	31	13	18	-	-	♦0.1
	26	18	8	-	♦0.1	-
Gibraltar						
2006 (C)						
Total	1	1	-	...	...	...
Less than 7 days - Moins de 7 jours	-	-	-	...	...	...
7 - 27 days - 7 - 27 jours	-	-	-	...	...	...
28 days - 11 months - 28 jours - 11 mois	1	1	-	...	...	...
28 days - 2 months - 28 jours - 2 mois	-	-	-	...	...	...
3 months - 3 mois	1	1	-	...	...	...
4 - 11 months - 4 - 11 mois	-	-	-	...	...	...
Greece - Grèce						
2007 (C)						
Total	394	219	175	...	...	...
Less than 1 day - Moins de 1 jour	55	32	23	...	...	...
1 - 6 days - 1 - 6 jours	107	55	52	...	...	...
7 - 27 days - 7 - 27 jours	88	46	42	...	...	...
7 - 13 days - 7 - 13 jours	47	23	24	...	...	...
14 - 20 days - 14 - 20 jours	23	14	9	...	...	...
21 - 27 days - 21 - 27 jours	18	9	9	...	...	...
28 days - 11 months - 28 jours - 11 mois	144	86	58	...	...	...
28 days - 1 month - 28 jours - 1 mois	47	26	21	...	...	...
2 months - 2 mois	24	16	8	...	...	...
3 months - 3 mois	17	11	6	...	...	...
4 months - 4 mois	11	7	4	...	...	...
5 months - 5 mois	10	7	3	...	...	...
6 months - 6 mois	8	4	4	...	...	...
7 months - 7 mois	9	4	5	...	...	...
8 months - 8 mois	6	4	2	...	...	...
9 months - 9 mois	5	2	3	...	...	...
10 months - 10 mois	5	4	1	...	...	...
11 months - 11 mois	2	1	1	...	...	...
Unknown - Inconnu	-	-	-	...	...	...
Hungary - Hongrie						
2007 (C)						
Total	577	310	267	...	...	...
Less than 1 day - Moins de 1 jour	132	59	73	...	...	...
1 - 6 days - 1 - 6 jours	145	84	61	...	...	...
7 - 27 days - 7 - 27 jours	107	60	47	...	...	...
7 - 13 days - 7 - 13 jours	58	31	27	...	...	...
14 - 20 days - 14 - 20 jours	31	18	13	...	...	...
21 - 27 days - 21 - 27 jours	18	11	7	...	...	...
28 days - 11 months - 28 jours - 11 mois	193	107	86	...	...	...
28 days - 1 month - 28 jours - 1 mois	56	33	23	...	...	...
2 months - 2 mois	29	17	12	...	...	...

16. Infant deaths and infant mortality rates by age and sex: latest available year, 1998 - 2007
Décès d'enfants de moins d'un an et taux de mortalité infantile selon l'âge et le sexe: dernière année disponible, 1998 - 2007 (continued - suite)

Continent, country or area, year and age (in days) Continent, pays ou zone, année et âge (en jours)	Number - Nombre			Rate - Taux		
	Both sexes Les deux sexes	Male Masculin	Female Féminin	Both sexes Les deux sexes	Male Masculin	Female Féminin
EUROPE						
Hungary - Hongrie						
2007 (C)						
3 months - 3 mois	18	9	9	...	...	...
4 months - 4 mois	25	13	12	...	...	...
5 months - 5 mois	15	10	5	...	...	...
6 months - 6 mois	13	8	5	...	...	...
7 months - 7 mois	6	3	3	...	...	...
8 months - 8 mois	11	7	4	...	...	...
9 months - 9 mois	8	4	4	...	...	...
10 months - 10 mois	7	2	5	...	...	...
11 months - 11 mois	5	1	4	...	...	...
Unknown - Inconnu	-	-	-	...	...	...
Iceland - Islande						
2007 (C)						
Total	9	7	2	...	...	...
Less than 1 day - Moins de 1 jour	2	2	-	...	...	...
1 - 6 days - 1 - 6 jours	3	2	1	...	...	...
7 - 27 days - 7 - 27 jours	1	1	-	...	...	...
7 - 13 days - 7 - 13 jours	1	1	-	...	...	...
14 - 20 days - 14 - 20 jours	-	-	-	...	...	...
21 - 27 days - 21 - 27 jours	-	-	-	...	...	...
28 days - 11 months - 28 jours - 11 mois	3	2	1	...	...	...
28 days - 1 month - 28 jours - 1 mois	1	1	-	...	...	...
2 months - 2 mois	-	-	-	...	...	...
3 months - 3 mois	-	-	-	...	...	...
4 months - 4 mois	1	-	1	...	...	...
5 months - 5 mois	-	-	-	...	...	...
6 months - 6 mois	-	-	-	...	...	...
7 months - 7 mois	-	-	-	...	...	...
8 months - 8 mois	-	-	-	...	...	...
9 months - 9 mois	-	-	-	...	...	...
10 months - 10 mois	1	1	-	...	...	...
11 months - 11 mois	-	-	-	...	...	...
Unknown - Inconnu	-	-	-	...	...	...
Ireland - Irlande						
2006* (+C)						
Total	238	136	102	...	...	...
Less than 1 day - Moins de 1 jour	86	48	38	...	...	...
1 - 6 days - 1 - 6 jours	43	23	20	...	...	...
7 - 27 days - 7 - 27 jours	39	20	19	...	...	...
7 - 13 days - 7 - 13 jours	20	11	9	...	...	...
14 - 20 days - 14 - 20 jours	12	5	7	...	...	...
21 - 27 days - 21 - 27 jours	7	4	3	...	...	...
28 days - 11 months - 28 jours - 11 mois	69	45	24	...	...	...
28 days - 1 month - 28 jours - 1 mois	24	17	7	...	...	...
2 months - 2 mois	11	8	3	...	...	...
3 months - 3 mois	5	3	2	...	...	...
4 months - 4 mois	7	3	4	...	...	...
5 months - 5 mois	4	3	1	...	...	...
6 months - 6 mois	8	5	3	...	...	...
7 months - 7 mois	2	1	1	...	...	...
8 months - 8 mois	3	2	1	...	...	...
9 months - 9 mois	2	2	-	...	...	...
10 months - 10 mois	3	1	2	...	...	...
11 months - 11 mois	-	-	-	...	...	...
Unknown - Inconnu	-	-	-	...	...	...
Isle of Man - Île de Man						
2004 (+C)						
Total	2	1	1	...	...	...
Less than 7 days - Moins de 7 jours	-	-	-	...	...	...
7 - 27 days - 7 - 27 jours	1	-	1	...	...	...
7 - 13 days - 7 - 13 jours	1	-	1	...	...	...
14 - 27 days - 14 - 27 jours	-	-	-	...	...	...
28 days - 11 months - 28 jours - 11 mois	1	1	-	...	...	...
28 days - 4 months - 28 jours - 4 mois	-	-	-	...	...	...
5 months - 5 mois	1	1	-	...	...	...
6 - 11 months - 6 - 11 mois	-	-	-	...	...	...

Continent, country or area, year and age (in days) / Continent, pays ou zone, année et âge (en jours)	Number - Nombre			Rate - Taux		
	Both sexes Les deux sexes	Male Masculin	Female Féminin	Both sexes Les deux sexes	Male Masculin	Female Féminin
EUROPE						
Italy - Italie						
2005 (C)						
Total	2 108	1 169	939	3.8	4.1	3.5
Less than 1 day - Moins de 1 jour	558	304	254	1.0	1.1	0.9
1 - 6 days - 1 - 6 jours	515	301	214	0.9	1.1	0.8
7 - 27 days - 7 - 27 jours	436	235	201	0.8	0.8	0.7
7 - 13 days - 7 - 13 jours	223	130	93	0.4	0.5	0.3
14 - 20 days - 14 - 20 jours	139	68	71	0.4	0.2	0.3
21 - 27 days - 21 - 27 jours	74	37	37	0.1	0.1	0.1
28 days - 11 months - 28 jours - 11 mois	599	329	270	1.1	1.2	1.0
28 days - 1 month - 28 jours - 1 mois	183	103	80	0.3	0.4	0.3
2 months - 2 mois	85	53	32	0.2	0.2	0.1
3 months - 3 mois	60	32	28	0.1	0.1	♦0.1
4 months - 4 mois	46	24	22	0.1	♦0.1	♦0.1
5 months - 5 mois	56	30	26	0.1	0.1	♦0.1
6 months - 6 mois	35	23	12	0.1	♦0.1	-
7 months - 7 mois	32	12	20	0.1	-	♦0.1
8 months - 8 mois	31	16	15	0.1	♦0.1	♦0.1
9 months - 9 mois	24	11	13	-	-	♦0.1
10 months - 10 mois	23	9	14	-	-	-
11 months - 11 mois	24	16	8	-	♦0.1	-
Latvia - Lettonie						
2007 (C)						
Total	203	98	105	...	...	...
Less than 1 day - Moins de 1 jour	33	14	19			
1 - 6 days - 1 - 6 jours	63	33	30	...	...	...
7 - 27 days - 7 - 27 jours	37	22	15			
7 - 13 days - 7 - 13 jours	23	13	10	...	...	...
14 - 20 days - 14 - 20 jours	11	6	5			
21 - 27 days - 21 - 27 jours	3	3	-	...	...	...
28 days - 11 months - 28 jours - 11 mois	70	29	41			
28 days - 1 month - 28 jours - 1 mois	2	1	1	...	...	...
2 months - 2 mois	14	3	11			
3 months - 3 mois	10	5	5	...	...	...
4 months - 4 mois	8	2	6			
5 months - 5 mois	6	3	3	...	...	...
6 months - 6 mois	5	2	3			
7 months - 7 mois	6	3	3	...	...	...
8 months - 8 mois	5	3	2			
9 months - 9 mois	7	2	5	...	...	...
10 months - 10 mois	3	2	1			
11 months - 11 mois	4	3	1	...	...	...
Unknown - Inconnu	-	-	-			
Lithuania - Lituanie[12]				...	...	...
2007 (C)						
Total	190	96	94			
Less than 1 day - Moins de 1 jour	35	17	18	...	...	...
1 - 6 days - 1 - 6 jours	44	20	24			
7 - 27 days - 7 - 27 jours	28	16	12	...	...	...
7 - 13 days - 7 - 13 jours	12	8	4			
14 - 20 days - 14 - 20 jours	12	6	6	...	...	...
21 - 27 days - 21 - 27 jours	4	2	2			
28 days - 11 months - 28 jours - 11 mois	83	43	40	...	...	...
28 days - 1 month - 28 jours - 1 mois	22	11	11			
2 months - 2 mois	13	8	5	...	...	...
3 months - 3 mois	15	11	4			
4 months - 4 mois	12	3	9	...	...	...
5 months - 5 mois	3	1	2			
6 months - 6 mois	4	3	1	...	...	...
7 months - 7 mois	3	2	1			
8 months - 8 mois	1	-	1	...	...	...
9 months - 9 mois	3	2	1			
10 months - 10 mois	4	2	2	...	...	...
11 months - 11 mois	3	-	3			
Unknown - Inconnu	-	-	-	...	...	...

Continent, country or area, year and age (in days) / Continent, pays ou zone, année et âge (en jours)	Number - Nombre			Rate - Taux		
	Both sexes Les deux sexes	Male Masculin	Female Féminin	Both sexes Les deux sexes	Male Masculin	Female Féminin
EUROPE						
Luxembourg						
2007 (C)						
Total	10	8	2	...	...	...
Less than 1 day - Moins de 1 jour	-	-	-	...	...	...
1 - 6 days - 1 - 6 jours	4	3	1	...	...	...
7 - 27 days - 7 - 27 jours	3	3	-	...	...	...
7 - 13 days - 7 - 13 jours	2	2	-	...	...	...
14 - 20 days - 14 - 20 jours	1	1	-	...	...	...
21 - 27 days - 21 - 27 jours	-	-	-	...	...	...
28 days - 11 months - 28 jours - 11 mois	3	2	1	...	...	...
28 days - 1 month - 28 jours - 1 mois	-	-	-	...	...	...
2 months - 2 mois	-	-	-	...	...	...
3 months - 3 mois	-	-	-	...	...	...
4 months - 4 mois	1	1	-	...	...	...
5 months - 5 mois	-	-	-	...	...	...
6 months - 6 mois	-	-	-	...	...	...
7 months - 7 mois	1	1	-	...	...	...
8 months - 8 mois	-	-	-	...	...	...
9 months - 9 mois	-	-	-	...	...	...
10 months - 10 mois	-	-	-	...	...	...
11 months - 11 mois	1	-	1	...	...	...
Unknown - Inconnu	-	-	-			
Malta - Malte						
2007 (C)						
Total	25	9	16	...	...	...
Less than 1 day - Moins de 1 jour	-	-	-	...	...	...
1 - 6 days - 1 - 6 jours	18	6	12	...	...	...
7 - 27 days - 7 - 27 jours	3	1	2	...	...	...
7 - 13 days - 7 - 13 jours	2	1	1	...	...	...
14 - 20 days - 14 - 20 jours	1	-	1	...	...	...
21 - 27 days - 21 - 27 jours	-	-	-	...	...	...
28 days - 11 months - 28 jours - 11 mois	4	2	2	...	...	...
28 days - 1 month - 28 jours - 1 mois	-	-	-	...	...	...
2 months - 2 mois	2	1	1	...	...	...
3 months - 3 mois	-	-	-	...	...	...
4 months - 4 mois	1	1	-	...	...	...
5 months - 5 mois	-	-	-	...	...	...
6 months - 6 mois	-	-	-	...	...	...
7 months - 7 mois	-	-	-	...	...	...
8 months - 8 mois	-	-	-	...	...	...
9 months - 9 mois	-	-	-	...	...	...
10 months - 10 mois	-	-	-	...	...	...
11 months - 11 mois	1	-	1	...	...	...
Montenegro - Monténégro						
2007 (C)						
Total	58	36	22	...	...	...
Less than 1 day - Moins de 1 jour	13	9	4	...	...	...
1 - 6 days - 1 - 6 jours	18	14	4	...	...	...
7 - 27 days - 7 - 27 jours	8	2	6	...	...	...
7 - 13 days - 7 - 13 jours	6	2	4	...	...	...
14 - 20 days - 14 - 20 jours	1	-	1	...	...	...
21 - 27 days - 21 - 27 jours	1	-	1	...	...	...
28 days - 11 months - 28 jours - 11 mois	19	11	8	...	...	...
28 days - 1 month - 28 jours - 1 mois	10	5	5	...	...	...
2 months - 2 mois	2	2	-	...	...	...
3 months - 3 mois	2	1	1	...	...	...
4 months - 4 mois	1	1	-	...	...	...
5 months - 5 mois	1	-	1	...	...	...
6 months - 6 mois	2	1	1	...	...	...
7 months - 7 mois	-	-	-	...	...	...
8 months - 8 mois	-	-	-	...	...	...
9 months - 9 mois	-	-	-	...	...	...
10 months - 10 mois	-	-	-	...	...	...
11 months - 11 mois	1	1	-	...	...	...
Unknown - Inconnu	-	-	-	...	...	...

Continent, country or area, year and age (in days) Continent, pays ou zone, année et âge (en jours)	Number - Nombre			Rate - Taux		
	Both sexes Les deux sexes	Male Masculin	Female Féminin	Both sexes Les deux sexes	Male Masculin	Female Féminin
EUROPE						
Netherlands - Pays-Bas[25]						
2006 (C)						
Total...........	820	468	352			
Less than 1 day - Moins de 1 jour	250	141	109	...	...	...
1 - 6 days - 1 - 6 jours...............	219	131	88	...	...	...
7 - 27 days - 7 - 27 jours................	150	87	63	...	...	...
7 - 13 days - 7 - 13 jours	79	44	35	...	...	...
14 - 20 days - 14 - 20 jours................	42	26	16	...	...	...
21 - 27 days - 21 - 27 jours...............	29	17	12	...	...	...
28 days - 11 months - 28 jours - 11 mois......................	200	108	92	...	...	...
28 days - 1 month - 28 jours - 1 mois...........	58	28	30	...	...	...
2 months - 2 mois...............	26	13	13	...	...	...
3 months - 3 mois...............	16	8	8	...	...	...
4 months - 4 mois...............	20	10	10	...	...	...
5 months - 5 mois...............	23	12	11	...	...	...
6 months - 6 mois...............	10	8	2	...	...	...
7 months - 7 mois...............	14	8	6	...	...	...
8 months - 8 mois...............	12	7	5	...	...	...
9 months - 9 mois...............	6	4	2	...	...	...
10 months - 10 mois...............	9	7	2	...	...	...
11 months - 11 mois...............	6	3	3	...	...	...
Norway - Norvège[26]						
2007 (C)						
Total...........	180	97	83			
Less than 1 day - Moins de 1 jour	47	22	25	...	...	...
1 - 6 days - 1 - 6 jours...............	51	32	19	...	...	...
7 - 27 days - 7 - 27 jours...............	19	7	12	...	...	...
7 - 13 days - 7 - 13 jours	8	2	6	...	...	...
14 - 20 days - 14 - 20 jours...............	7	2	5	...	...	...
21 - 27 days - 21 - 27 jours...............	4	3	1	...	...	...
28 days - 11 months - 28 jours - 11 mois............	63	36	27	...	...	...
28 days - 1 month - 28 jours - 1 mois............	22	11	11	...	...	...
2 months - 2 mois...............	6	4	2	...	...	...
3 months - 3 mois...............	10	7	3	...	...	...
4 months - 4 mois...............	4	2	2	...	...	...
5 months - 5 mois...............	6	6	-	...	...	...
6 months - 6 mois...............	3	2	1	...	...	...
7 months - 7 mois...............	3	1	2	...	...	...
8 months - 8 mois...............	5	2	3	...	...	...
9 months - 9 mois...............	1	-	1	...	...	...
10 months - 10 mois...............	2	1	1	...	...	...
11 months - 11 mois...............	1	-	1	...	...	...
Unknown - Inconnu	-	-	-	...	...	...
Poland - Pologne						
2007 (C)						
Total...........	2 322	1 305	1 017			
Less than 1 day - Moins de 1 jour	625	339	286	6.0	6.5	5.4
1 - 6 days - 1 - 6 jours...............	625	350	275	1.6	1.7	1.5
7 - 27 days - 7 - 27 jours...............	424	256	168	1.6	1.8	1.5
7 - 13 days - 7 - 13 jours	205	126	79	1.1	1.3	0.9
14 - 20 days - 14 - 20 jours...............	138	84	54	0.5	0.6	0.4
21 - 27 days - 21 - 27 jours...............	81	46	35	0.4	0.4	0.3
28 days - 11 months - 28 jours - 11 mois............	648	360	288	0.2	0.2	0.2
28 days - 1 month - 28 jours - 1 mois............	223	120	103	1.7	1.8	1.5
2 months - 2 mois...............	110	65	45	0.6	0.6	0.5
3 months - 3 mois...............	87	55	32	0.3	0.3	0.2
4 months - 4 mois...............	62	29	33	0.2	0.3	0.2
5 months - 5 mois...............	36	19	17	0.2	♦0.1	0.2
6 months - 6 mois...............	30	16	14	0.1	♦0.1	♦0.1
7 months - 7 mois...............	26	13	13	0.1	♦0.1	♦0.1
8 months - 8 mois...............	21	13	8	♦0.1	♦0.1	♦0.1
9 months - 9 mois...............	13	10	3	♦0.1	♦0.1	-
10 months - 10 mois...............	15	12	3	-	♦0.1	-
11 months - 11 mois...............	25	8	17	♦0.1	-	♦0.1
Portugal[5]						
2007 (C)						
Total...........	353	186	167	...	...	...
Less than 1 day - Moins de 1 jour	77	36	41	...	...	...

16. Infant deaths and infant mortality rates by age and sex: latest available year, 1998 - 2007
Décès d'enfants de moins d'un an et taux de mortalité infantile selon l'âge et le sexe: dernière année disponible, 1998 - 2007 (continued - suite)

Continent, country or area, year and age (in days) / Continent, pays ou zone, année et âge (en jours)	Number - Nombre			Rate - Taux		
	Both sexes Les deux sexes	Male Masculin	Female Féminin	Both sexes Les deux sexes	Male Masculin	Female Féminin
EUROPE						
Portugal[5]						
2007 (C)						
1 - 6 days - 1 - 6 jours	86	49	37	...	...	...
7 - 27 days - 7 - 27 jours	50	27	23	...	...	...
7 - 13 days - 7 - 13 jours	28	18	10	...	...	...
14 - 20 days - 14 - 20 jours	11	4	7	...	...	...
21 - 27 days - 21 - 27 jours	11	5	6	...	...	...
28 days - 11 months - 28 jours - 11 mois	140	74	66	...	...	...
28 days - 1 month - 28 jours - 1 mois	40	16	24	...	...	...
2 months - 2 mois	28	15	13	...	...	...
3 months - 3 mois	6	4	2	...	...	...
4 months - 4 mois	14	10	4	...	...	...
5 months - 5 mois	11	4	7	...	...	...
6 months - 6 mois	13	10	3	...	...	...
7 months - 7 mois	9	4	5	...	...	...
8 months - 8 mois	5	3	2	...	...	...
9 months - 9 mois	6	3	3	...	...	...
10 months - 10 mois	3	2	1	...	...	...
11 months - 11 mois	5	3	2	...	...	...
Unknown - Inconnu	-	-	-	...	...	...
Republic of Moldova - République de Moldova[27]						
2007 (C)						
Total	428	221	207	...	...	...
Less than 1 day - Moins de 1 jour	55	26	29	...	...	...
1 - 6 days - 1 - 6 jours	138	70	68	...	...	...
7 - 27 days - 7 - 27 jours	66	43	23	...	...	...
7 - 13 days - 7 - 13 jours	38	26	12	...	...	...
14 - 20 days - 14 - 20 jours	13	8	5	...	...	...
21 - 27 days - 21 - 27 jours	15	9	6	...	...	...
28 days - 11 months - 28 jours - 11 mois	163	79	84	...	...	...
28 days - 1 month - 28 jours - 1 mois	25	14	11	...	...	...
2 months - 2 mois	29	14	15	...	...	...
3 months - 3 mois	26	14	12	...	...	...
4 months - 4 mois	16	6	10	...	...	...
5 months - 5 mois	15	6	9	...	...	...
6 months - 6 mois	18	9	9	...	...	...
7 months - 7 mois	6	4	2	...	...	...
8 months - 8 mois	13	5	8	...	...	...
9 months - 9 mois	5	2	3	...	...	...
10 months - 10 mois	6	3	3	...	...	...
11 months - 11 mois	4	2	2	...	...	...
Unknown - Inconnu	6	3	3	...	...	...
Romania - Roumanie						
2007 (C)						
Total	2 574	1 476	1 098	12.0	13.4	10.5
Less than 1 day - Moins de 1 jour	255	152	103	1.2	1.4	1.0
1 - 6 days - 1 - 6 jours	768	452	316	3.6	4.1	3.0
7 - 27 days - 7 - 27 jours	453	248	205	2.1	2.2	2.0
7 - 13 days - 7 - 13 jours	241	133	108	1.1	1.2	1.0
14 - 20 days - 14 - 20 jours	128	68	60	0.6	0.6	0.6
21 - 27 days - 21 - 27 jours	84	47	37	0.4	0.4	0.4
28 days - 11 months - 28 jours - 11 mois	1 098	624	474	5.1	5.6	4.5
28 days - 1 month - 28 jours - 1 mois	321	187	134	1.5	1.7	1.3
2 months - 2 mois	201	117	84	0.9	1.1	0.8
3 months - 3 mois	114	68	46	0.5	0.6	0.4
4 months - 4 mois	122	71	51	0.6	0.6	0.5
5 months - 5 mois	76	35	41	0.4	0.3	0.4
6 months - 6 mois	62	35	27	0.3	0.3	♦0.3
7 months - 7 mois	55	30	25	0.3	0.3	♦0.2
8 months - 8 mois	36	19	17	0.2	♦0.2	♦0.2
9 months - 9 mois	50	29	21	0.2	♦0.3	♦0.2
10 months - 10 mois	32	15	17	0.1	♦0.1	♦0.2
11 months - 11 mois	29	18	11	♦0.1	♦0.2	♦0.1
Russian Federation - Fédération de Russie[12]						
2007 (C)						
Total	14 858	8 598	6 260	9.2	10.4	8.0
Less than 1 day - Moins de 1 jour	1 860	1 017	843	1.2	1.2	1.1
1 - 6 days - 1 - 6 jours	4 200	2 550	1 650	2.6	3.1	2.1

Continent, country or area, year and age (in days) / Continent, pays ou zone, année et âge (en jours)	Number - Nombre			Rate - Taux		
	Both sexes Les deux sexes	Male Masculin	Female Féminin	Both sexes Les deux sexes	Male Masculin	Female Féminin
EUROPE						
Russian Federation - Fédération de Russie[12]						
2007 (C)						
7 - 27 days - 7 - 27 jours	2 653	1 562	1 091	1.6	1.9	1.4
7 - 13 days - 7 - 13 jours	1 325	770	555	0.8	0.9	0.7
14 - 20 days - 14 - 20 jours	778	471	307	0.5	0.6	0.4
21 - 27 days - 21 - 27 jours	550	321	229	0.3	0.4	0.3
28 days - 11 months - 28 jours - 11 mois	6 131	3 461	2 670	3.8	4.2	3.4
28 days - 1 month - 28 jours - 1 mois	1 796	1 045	751	1.1	1.3	1.0
2 months - 2 mois	1 072	607	465	0.7	0.7	0.6
3 months - 3 mois	777	449	328	0.5	0.5	0.4
4 months - 4 mois	635	330	305	0.4	0.4	0.4
5 months - 5 mois	419	228	191	0.3	0.3	0.2
6 months - 6 mois	373	200	173	0.2	0.2	0.2
7 months - 7 mois	276	147	129	0.2	0.2	0.2
8 months - 8 mois	243	148	95	0.2	0.2	0.1
9 months - 9 mois	200	114	86	0.1	0.1	0.1
10 months - 10 mois	189	105	84	0.1	0.1	0.1
11 months - 11 mois	151	88	63	0.1	0.1	0.1
Unknown - Inconnu	14	8	6	-	-	-
San Marino - Saint-Marin						
2003 (+C)						
Total	2	1	1	...	...	...
Less than 1 day - Moins de 1 jour	1	-	1	...	...	...
1 - 6 days - 1 - 6 jours	-	-	-	...	...	...
7 - 27 days - 7 - 27 jours	1	1	-	...	...	...
28 days - 11 months - 28 jours - 11 mois	-	-	-	...	...	...
Serbia - Serbie[28]						
2007 (+C)						
Total	484	288	196	...	...	...
Less than 1 day - Moins de 1 jour	145	97	48	...	...	...
1 - 6 days - 1 - 6 jours	125	78	47	...	...	...
7 - 27 days - 7 - 27 jours	72	33	39	...	...	...
7 - 13 days - 7 - 13 jours	42	15	27	...	...	...
14 - 20 days - 14 - 20 jours	17	9	8	...	...	...
21 - 27 days - 21 - 27 jours	13	9	4	...	...	...
28 days - 11 months - 28 jours - 11 mois	142	80	62	...	...	...
28 days - 1 month - 28 jours - 1 mois	49	26	23	...	...	...
2 months - 2 mois	25	16	9	...	...	...
3 months - 3 mois	20	11	9	...	...	...
4 months - 4 mois	8	3	5	...	...	...
5 months - 5 mois	8	5	3	...	...	...
6 months - 6 mois	12	8	4	...	...	...
7 months - 7 mois	3	1	2	...	...	...
8 months - 8 mois	6	4	2	...	...	...
9 months - 9 mois	3	3	-	...	...	...
10 months - 10 mois	4	3	1	...	...	...
11 months - 11 mois	4	-	4	...	...	...
Unknown - Inconnu	-	-	-	...	...	...
Slovakia - Slovaquie						
2007 (C)						
Total	334	189	145	...	...	...
Less than 1 day - Moins de 1 jour	52	31	21	...	...	...
1 - 6 days - 1 - 6 jours	74	45	29	...	...	...
7 - 27 days - 7 - 27 jours	57	25	32	...	...	...
7 - 13 days - 7 - 13 jours	24	11	13	...	...	...
14 - 20 days - 14 - 20 jours	15	8	7	...	...	...
21 - 27 days - 21 - 27 jours	18	6	12	...	...	...
28 days - 11 months - 28 jours - 11 mois	151	88	63	...	...	...
28 days - 1 month - 28 jours - 1 mois	45	22	23	...	...	...
2 months - 2 mois	35	18	17	...	...	...
3 months - 3 mois	17	10	7	...	...	...
4 months - 4 mois	10	7	3	...	...	...
5 months - 5 mois	11	9	2	...	...	...
6 months - 6 mois	7	5	2	...	...	...
7 months - 7 mois	8	5	3	...	...	...
8 months - 8 mois	7	4	3	...	...	...
9 months - 9 mois	3	3	-	...	...	...

Continent, country or area, year and age (in days) / Continent, pays ou zone, année et âge (en jours)	Number - Nombre			Rate - Taux		
	Both sexes Les deux sexes	Male Masculin	Female Féminin	Both sexes Les deux sexes	Male Masculin	Female Féminin
EUROPE						
Slovakia - Slovaquie						
2007 (C)						
10 months - 10 mois	4	3	1	...	...	...
11 months - 11 mois	4	2	2	...	...	...
Slovenia - Slovénie						
2007 (C)						
Total	55	27	28	...	...	...
Less than 1 day - Moins de 1 jour	16	6	10	...	...	...
1 - 6 days - 1 - 6 jours	13	9	4	...	...	...
7 - 27 days - 7 - 27 jours	10	4	6	...	...	...
7 - 13 days - 7 - 13 jours	5	3	2	...	...	...
14 - 20 days - 14 - 20 jours	2	-	2	...	...	...
21 - 27 days - 21 - 27 jours	3	1	2	...	...	...
28 days - 11 months - 28 jours - 11 mois	16	8	8	...	...	...
28 days - 1 month - 28 jours - 1 mois	5	3	2	...	...	...
2 months - 2 mois	-	-	-	...	...	...
3 months - 3 mois	2	2	-	...	...	...
4 months - 4 mois	1	-	1	...	...	...
5 months - 5 mois	2	1	1	...	...	...
6 months - 6 mois	-	-	-	...	...	...
7 months - 7 mois	6	2	4	...	...	...
8 months - 8 mois	-	-	-	...	...	...
9 months - 9 mois	-	-	-	...	...	...
10 months - 10 mois	-	-	-	...	...	...
11 months - 11 mois	-	-	-	...	...	...
Unknown - Inconnu	-	-	-	...	...	...
Spain - Espagne						
2007 (C)						
Total	1 704	933	771	3.5	3.7	3.2
Less than 1 day - Moins de 1 jour	314	169	145	0.6	0.7	0.6
1 - 6 days - 1 - 6 jours	383	212	171	0.8	0.8	0.7
7 - 27 days - 7 - 27 jours	423	223	200	0.9	0.9	0.8
7 - 13 days - 7 - 13 jours	224	115	109	0.5	0.5	0.5
14 - 20 days - 14 - 20 jours	123	63	60	0.2	0.2	0.3
21 - 27 days - 21 - 27 jours	76	45	31	0.2	0.2	0.1
28 days - 11 months - 28 jours - 11 mois	584	329	255	1.2	1.3	1.1
28 days - 1 month - 28 jours - 1 mois	176	95	81	0.4	0.4	0.3
2 months - 2 mois	98	60	38	0.2	0.2	0.2
3 months - 3 mois	58	31	27	0.1	0.1	♦0.1
4 months - 4 mois	65	41	24	0.1	0.2	♦0.1
5 months - 5 mois	44	22	22	0.1	♦0.1	♦0.1
6 months - 6 mois	40	23	17	0.1	♦0.1	♦0.1
7 months - 7 mois	27	15	12	♦0.1	♦0.1	♦0.1
8 months - 8 mois	18	10	8	-	-	-
9 months - 9 mois	30	16	14	0.1	♦0.1	♦0.1
10 months - 10 mois	17	12	5	-	-	-
11 months - 11 mois	11	4	7	-	-	-
Sweden - Suède						
2007 (C)						
Total	268	148	120	...	...	...
Less than 1 day - Moins de 1 jour	66	40	26	...	...	...
1 - 6 days - 1 - 6 jours	73	36	37	...	...	...
7 - 27 days - 7 - 27 jours	45	27	18	...	...	...
7 - 13 days - 7 - 13 jours	25	14	11	...	...	...
14 - 20 days - 14 - 20 jours	13	10	3	...	...	...
21 - 27 days - 21 - 27 jours	7	3	4	...	...	...
28 days - 11 months - 28 jours - 11 mois	84	45	39	...	...	...
28 days - 1 month - 28 jours - 1 mois	24	13	11	...	...	...
2 months - 2 mois	8	4	4	...	...	...
3 months - 3 mois	14	9	5	...	...	...
4 months - 4 mois	7	5	2	...	...	...
5 months - 5 mois	11	6	5	...	...	...
6 months - 6 mois	3	-	3	...	...	...
7 months - 7 mois	6	5	1	...	...	...
8 months - 8 mois	3	1	2	...	...	...
9 months - 9 mois	5	1	4	...	...	...
10 months - 10 mois	1	1	-	...	...	...

Décès d'enfants de moins d'un an et taux de mortalité infantile selon l'âge et le sexe: dernière année disponible, 1998 - 2007 (continued - suite)

Continent, country or area, year and age (in days) / Continent, pays ou zone, année et âge (en jours)	Number - Nombre			Rate - Taux		
	Both sexes Les deux sexes	Male Masculin	Female Féminin	Both sexes Les deux sexes	Male Masculin	Female Féminin
EUROPE						
Sweden - Suède						
2007 (C)						
11 months - 11 mois	2	-	2	...	...	...
Unknown - Inconnu	-	-	-	...	...	...
Switzerland - Suisse						
2007 (C)						
Total	293	152	141	...	...	...
Less than 1 day - Moins de 1 jour	139	68	71	...	...	...
1 - 6 days - 1 - 6 jours	59	35	24	...	...	...
7 - 27 days - 7 - 27 jours	31	14	17	...	...	...
7 - 13 days - 7 - 13 jours	16	8	8	...	...	...
14 - 20 days - 14 - 20 jours	9	4	5	...	...	...
21 - 27 days - 21 - 27 jours	6	2	4	...	...	...
28 days - 11 months - 28 jours - 11 mois	64	35	29	...	...	...
28 days - 1 month - 28 jours - 1 mois	12	9	3	...	...	...
2 months - 2 mois	13	6	7	...	...	...
3 months - 3 mois	7	2	5	...	...	...
4 months - 4 mois	5	4	1	...	...	...
5 months - 5 mois	6	3	3	...	...	...
6 months - 6 mois	5	2	3	...	...	...
7 months - 7 mois	3	2	1	...	...	...
8 months - 8 mois	6	5	1	...	...	...
9 months - 9 mois	4	1	3	...	...	...
10 months - 10 mois	1	-	1	...	...	...
11 months - 11 mois	2	1	1	...	...	...
The Former Yugoslav Republic of Macedonia - L'ex-République yougoslave de Macédoine						
2007 (C)						
Total	234	...	...	...	...	...
Less than 1 day - Moins de 1 jour	59	...	...	...	...	...
1 - 6 days - 1 - 6 jours	77	...	...	...	...	...
7 - 27 days - 7 - 27 jours	43	...	...	...	...	...
7 - 13 days - 7 - 13 jours	26	...	...	...	...	...
14 - 20 days - 14 - 20 jours	9	...	...	...	...	...
21 - 27 days - 21 - 27 jours	8	...	...	...	...	...
28 days - 11 months - 28 jours - 11 mois	55	...	...	...	...	...
28 days - 1 month - 28 jours - 1 mois	22	...	...	...	...	...
2 months - 2 mois	8	...	...	...	...	...
3 months - 3 mois	6	...	...	...	...	...
4 months - 4 mois	6	...	...	...	...	...
5 months - 5 mois	2	...	...	...	...	...
6 months - 6 mois	1	...	...	...	...	...
7 months - 7 mois	4	...	...	...	...	...
8 months - 8 mois	3	...	...	...	...	...
9 months - 9 mois	1	...	...	...	...	...
10 months - 10 mois	2	...	...	...	...	...
11 months - 11 mois	-	...	...	...	...	...
Ukraine[29]						
2007 (C)						
Total	5 188	3 039	2 149	11.0	12.5	9.4
Less than 1 day - Moins de 1 jour	720	407	313	1.5	1.7	1.4
1 - 6 days - 1 - 6 jours	1 490	909	581	3.2	3.7	2.5
7 - 27 days - 7 - 27 jours	924	552	372	2.0	2.3	1.6
7 - 13 days - 7 - 13 jours	501	301	200	1.1	1.2	0.9
14 - 20 days - 14 - 20 jours	255	150	105	0.5	0.6	0.5
21 - 27 days - 21 - 27 jours	168	101	67	0.4	0.4	0.3
28 days - 11 months - 28 jours - 11 mois	2 054	1 171	883	4.3	4.8	3.8
28 days - 1 month - 28 jours - 1 mois	613	351	262	1.3	1.4	1.1
2 months - 2 mois	343	189	154	0.7	0.8	0.7
3 months - 3 mois	255	150	105	0.5	0.6	0.5
4 months - 4 mois	200	110	90	0.4	0.5	0.4
5 months - 5 mois	145	88	57	0.3	0.4	0.2
6 months - 6 mois	132	74	58	0.3	0.3	0.3
7 months - 7 mois	105	62	43	0.2	0.3	0.2
8 months - 8 mois	79	49	30	0.2	0.2	0.1
9 months - 9 mois	73	37	36	0.2	0.2	0.2
10 months - 10 mois	65	37	28	0.1	0.2	◆0.1

Continent, country or area, year and age (in days) / Continent, pays ou zone, année et âge (en jours)	Number - Nombre			Rate - Taux		
	Both sexes Les deux sexes	Male Masculin	Female Féminin	Both sexes Les deux sexes	Male Masculin	Female Féminin
EUROPE						
Ukraine[29]						
2007 (C)						
11 months - 11 mois	44	24	20	0.1	♦0.1	♦0.1
Unknown - Inconnu	-	-	-	-	-	-
United Kingdom of Great Britain and Northern Ireland - Royaume-Uni de Grande-Bretagne et d'Irlande du Nord[30]						
2003* (C)						
Total	3 686	2 029	1 657	5.3	5.7	4.9
Less than 1 day - Moins de 1 jour	1 073	593	480	1.5	1.7	1.4
1 - 6 days - 1 - 6 jours	873	483	390	1.3	1.4	1.2
7 - 27 days - 7 - 27 jours	583	300	283	0.8	0.8	0.8
28 days - 11 months - 28 jours - 11 mois	1 157	653	504	1.7	1.8	1.5
OCEANIA - OCÉANIE						
Australia - Australie						
2007 (+C)						
Total	1 203	655	548	4.2	4.5	4.0
Less than 1 day - Moins de 1 jour	471	246	225	1.7	1.7	1.6
1 - 6 days - 1 - 6 jours	217	124	93	0.8	0.8	0.7
7 - 27 days - 7 - 27 jours	168	91	77	0.6	0.6	0.6
7 - 13 days - 7 - 13 jours	80	43	37	0.3	0.3	0.3
14 - 20 days - 14 - 20 jours	47	28	19	0.2	♦0.2	♦0.1
21 - 27 days - 21 - 27 jours	41	20	21	0.1	♦0.1	♦0.2
28 days - 11 months - 28 jours - 11 mois	347	194	153	1.2	1.3	1.1
28 days - 1 month - 28 jours - 1 mois	85	51	34	0.3	0.3	0.2
2 months - 2 mois	55	32	23	0.2	0.2	♦0.2
3 months - 3 mois	44	23	21	0.2	♦0.2	♦0.2
4 months - 4 mois	39	17	22	0.1	♦0.1	♦0.2
5 months - 5 mois	39	25	14	0.1	♦0.2	♦0.1
6 months - 6 mois	21	13	8	♦0.1	♦0.1	♦0.1
7 months - 7 mois	15	8	7	♦0.1	♦0.1	♦0.1
8 months - 8 mois	16	8	8	♦0.1	♦0.1	♦0.1
9 months - 9 mois	9	5	4	-	-	♦0.1
10 months - 10 mois	11	4	7	-	-	-
11 months - 11 mois	13	8	5	-	♦0.1	-
Unknown - Inconnu	-	-	-			
French Polynesia - Polynésie française						
2007 (C)						
Total	30	...	...	...	...	...
Less than 7 days - Moins de 7 jours	11	...	...	...	...	...
7 - 27 days - 7 - 27 jours	2	...	...	...	...	...
28 days - 11 months - 28 jours - 11 mois	17	...	...	...	...	...
New Caledonia - Nouvelle-Calédonie						
2007 (C)						
Total	25	15	10	...	...	...
Less than 1 day - Moins de 1 jour	-	-	-	...	...	...
1 - 6 days - 1 - 6 jours	11	9	2	...	...	...
7 - 27 days - 7 - 27 jours	6	2	4	...	...	...
7 - 13 days - 7 - 13 jours	6	2	4	...	...	...
14 - 20 days - 14 - 20 jours	-	-	-	...	...	...
21 - 27 days - 21 - 27 jours	-	-	-	...	...	...
28 days - 11 months - 28 jours - 11 mois	8	4	4	...	...	...
28 days - 1 month - 28 jours - 1 mois	-	-	-	...	...	...
2 months - 2 mois	-	-	-	...	...	...
3 months - 3 mois	-	2	-	...	...	...
4 months - 4 mois	-	-	-	...	...	...
5 months - 5 mois	-	-	-	...	...	...
6 months - 6 mois	2	2	-	...	...	...
7 months - 7 mois	-	-	-	...	...	...
8 months - 8 mois	-	-	-	...	...	...
9 months - 9 mois	-	-	-	...	...	...
10 months - 10 mois	-	-	-	...	...	...
11 months - 11 mois	4	-	4	...	...	...

16. Infant deaths and infant mortality rates by age and sex: latest available year, 1998 - 2007
Décès d'enfants de moins d'un an et taux de mortalité infantile selon l'âge et le sexe: dernière année disponible, 1998 - 2007 (continued - suite)

Continent, country or area, year and age (in days) / Continent, pays ou zone, année et âge (en jours)	Number - Nombre			Rate - Taux		
	Both sexes Les deux sexes	Male Masculin	Female Féminin	Both sexes Les deux sexes	Male Masculin	Female Féminin
OCEANIA - OCÉANIE						
New Zealand - Nouvelle-Zélande[5]						
2007 (+C)						
Total	317	174	143			
Less than 1 day - Moins de 1 jour	96	50	46	...	...	...
1 - 6 days - 1 - 6 jours	44	23	21	...	...	...
7 - 27 days - 7 - 27 jours	31	16	15	...	...	...
7 - 13 days - 7 - 13 jours	15	7	8	...	...	...
14 - 20 days - 14 - 20 jours	6	5	1	...	...	...
21 - 27 days - 21 - 27 jours	10	4	6	...	...	...
28 days - 11 months - 28 jours - 11 mois	146	85	61	...	...	...
28 days - 1 month - 28 jours - 1 mois	35	20	15	...	...	...
2 months - 2 mois	24	13	11	...	...	...
3 months - 3 mois	18	11	7	...	...	...
4 months - 4 mois	22	12	10	...	...	...
5 months - 5 mois	10	4	6	...	...	...
6 months - 6 mois	10	8	2	...	...	...
7 months - 7 mois	5	4	1	...	...	...
8 months - 8 mois	5	4	1	...	...	...
9 months - 9 mois	3	2	1	...	...	...
10 months - 10 mois	9	3	6	...	...	...
11 months - 11 mois	5	4	1	...	...	...

FOOTNOTES - NOTES

Italics: data from civil registers which are incomplete or of unknown completeness. - Italiques: données incomplètes ou dont le degré d'exactitude n'est pas connu, provenant des registres de l'état civil.

♦ Rates based on 30 or fewer infant deaths. — Taux basés sur 30 décès d'enfants ou moins.

* Provisional. - Données provisoires.

'Code' indicates the source of data, as follows:
C - Civil registration, estimated over 90% complete
U - Civil registration, estimated less than 90% complete
| - Other source, estimated reliable
+ - Data tabulated by date of registration rather than occurence.
... - Information not available

Le 'Code' indique la source des données, comme suit:
C - Registres de l'état civil considérés complets à 90 p. 100 au moins.
U - Registres de l'état civil qui ne sont pas considérés complets à 90 p. 100 au moins.
| - Autre source, considérée pas douteuses.
+ - Données exploitées selon la date de l'enregistrement et non la date de l'événement.
... - Information pas disponible.

[1] Data as reported by national statistical authorities. - Les données comme elles ont été déclarées par l'institut national de la statistique.
[2] Excluding live-born infants who died before their birth was registered. - Non compris les enfants nés vivants décédés avant l'enregistrement de leur naissance.
[3] Data for male and female categories exclude infant deaths of unknown sex. - Il n'est pas tenu compte dans les données classées par sexe des décès d'enfant de moins d'un an de sexe inconnu.
[4] Including Canadian residents temporarily in the United States, but excluding United States residents temporarily in Canada. - Y compris les résidents canadiens se trouvant temporairement aux Etats-Unis, mais ne comprenant pas les résidents des Etats-Unis se trouvant temporairement au Canada.
[5] Data refer to resident population only. - Pour la population résidante seulement.
[6] Excluding Indian jungle population. Data as reported by national statistical authorities; they may differ from data presented in other tables. - Non compris les Indiens de la jungle. Les données comme elles ont été déclarées par l'institut

national de la statistique; elles peuvent être différentes de celles présentées dans d'autres tableaux.
[7] Excluding nomadic Indian tribes. - Non compris les tribus d'Indiens nomades.
[8] Excluding live-born infants who died before their birth was registered. Unrevised data. - Non compris les enfants nés vivants décédés avant l'enregistrement de leur naissance. Les données n'ont pas été révisées.
[9] Data refer to infant 30 days - 12 months old. - Les données se réfèrent aux nouveaux-nés âgées de 30 jours à 12 mois.
[10] Data refer to registered events only. Excluding Indian jungle population. - Les données ne concernent que les événements enregistrés. Non compris les Indiens de la jungle.
[11] Excluding Indian jungle population. - Non compris les Indiens de la jungle.
[12] Excluding infants born alive of less than 28 weeks' gestation, of less than 1 000 grams in weight and 35 centimeters in length, who die within seven days of birth. - Non compris les enfants nés vivants après moins de 28 semaines de gestation, pesant moins de 1 000 grammes, mesurant moins de 35 centimètres et décédés dans les sept jours qui ont suivi leur naissance.
[13] Data refer to government controlled areas. - Les données se rapportent aux zones contrôlées par le Gouvernement.
[14] Including deaths abroad of Israeli residents who were out of the country for less than a year. Including data for East Jerusalem and Israeli residents in certain other territories under occupation by Israeli military forces since June 1967. - Y compris les décès à l'étranger de résidents israéliens qui ont quitté le pays depuis moins d'un an. Y compris les données pour Jérusalem-Est et les résidents israéliens dans certains autres territoires occupés depuis 1967 par les forces armées israéliennes.
[15] Data refer to Japanese nationals in Japan only. - Les données se raportent aux nationaux japonais au Japon seulement.
[16] Data refer to the recorded events in Ministry of Health hospitals and health centres only. - Les données se rapportent aux faits d'état civil enregistrés dans les hôpitaux et les dispensaires du Ministère de la santé seulement.
[17] Data refer to infant 7 - 28 days old. - Les données se réfèrent aux nouveaux-nés âgés de 7 à 28 jours.
[18] Data refer to infant 29 days - 11months old. - Les données se réfèrent aux nouveaux-nés âgés de 29 jours à 11 mois.
[19] Based on the results of the Pakistan Demographic Survey (PDS 2005). Excluding data for the Pakistan-held part of Jammu and Kashmir, the final status of which has not yet been determined. - Données extraites de l'enquête démographique effectuée par le Pakistan en 2005. Non compris les données concernant la partie du Jammu et Cachemire occupée par le Pakistan dont le statut définitif n'a pas été déterminé.
[20] Excluding alien armed forces, civilian aliens employed by armed forces, and foreign diplomatic personnel and their dependants. Including nationals outside the country. - Non compris les militaires étrangers, les civils étrangers employés

par les forces armées ni le personnel diplomatique étranger et les membres de leur famille les accompagnant. Y compris les nationaux hors du pays.

[21] Based on the results of the Population Demographic Survey. Deaths in province and district centers. - D'après les résultats de la Population Demographic Survey. Les décès aux centres des provinces et des zones seulement.

[22] Excluding Faeroe Islands and Greenland shown separately, if available. - Non compris les Iles Féroé et le Gröenland, qui font l'objet de rubriques distinctes, si disponible.

[23] Including nationals temporarily outside the country. Including Aland Islands. - Y compris les nationaux se trouvant temporairement hors du pays. Y compris les Îles d'Åland.

[24] Including armed forces stationed outside the country. Excluding Overseas Departments, namely, French Guiana, Guadeloupe, Martinique and Reunion, shown separately, if available. - Y compris les militaires nationaux hors du pays. Non compris les départements d'outre mer, c'est-à-dire la Guyane française, la Guadeloupe, la Martinique et la Réunion, qui font l'objet de rubriques distinctes, si disponible.

[25] Including residents outside the country if listed in a Netherlands population register. - Y compris les résidents hors du pays, s'ils sont inscrits sur un registre de population néerlandais.

[26] Including residents temporarily outside the country. Excluding Svalbard and Jan Mayen Island shown separately, if available. - Y compris les résidents se trouvant temporairement hors du pays. Non compris Svalbard et Jan Mayen qui font l'objet de rubriques distinctes, si disponible.

[27] Excluding Transnistria and the municipality of Bender. Excluding infants born alive of less than 28 weeks' gestation, of less than 1 000 grams in weight and 35 centimeters in length, who die within seven days of birth. - Les données ne tiennent pas compte de l'information sur la Transnistria et la municipalité de Bender. Non compris les enfants nés vivants après moins de 28 semaines de gestations, pesant moins de 1 000 grammes, mesurant moins de 35 centimètres et décédés dans les sept jours qui ont suivi leur naissance.

[28] Excluding data for Kosovo and Metohia. - Sans les données pour le Kosovo et Metohie.

[29] Excluding infants born living with birth weight of less than 500grams (or if birth weight is unknown - with length of less than 25 centimeters, or with gestation period of less than 22 weeks). - Non compris les données concernant les nouveau-nés pesant moins de 500 grammes (si le pods est inconnu – mesurant moins de 25 centimètres ou après moins de 22 semaines de gestations).

[30] Excluding Channel Islands (Guernsey and Jersey) and Isle of Man, shown separately, if available. - Non compris les îles Anglo-Normandes (Guernesey et Jersey) et l'île de Man, qui font l'objet de rubriques distinctes, si disponible.

Table 17

Table 17 presents maternal deaths and maternal mortality rates for as many years available between 1997 and 2006.

Description of variables: Maternal deaths are defined for the purposes of the Demographic Yearbook as those caused by deliveries and complications of pregnancy, childbirth and the puerperium, within 42 days of termination of pregnancy. They are usually defined as deaths coded "38-41" for ICD-9 Basic Tabulation List or as deaths coded "A34", "O00-O95", "O98-O99" for ICD-10, respectively. However, data for ICD-10 shown in this table include deaths due to "O96" and "O97" which refer to deaths from any obstetric cause occurring more than 42 days but less than one year after delivery and death from sequelae of direct obstetric causes occurring one year or more after delivery.

For further information on the definition of maternal mortality from the tenth revisions of the *International Statistical Classification of Diseases and Related Health Problems*[1], see also section 4.3 of the Technical Notes.

Statistics on maternal death presented in this table are provided by the World Health Organisation. They are limited to countries or areas that meet the criterion that cause-of-death statistics are either classified by or convertible to the ninth or tenth revisions mentioned above. Data that are classified by the tenth revision are set in bold in the table.

Rate computation: Maternal mortality rates are the annual number of maternal deaths per 100 000 live births (table 9) in the same year. These rates have been calculated by the Statistics Division of the United Nations. Rates based on 30 or fewer maternal deaths are identified by the symbol "♦".

Reliability of data: Countries and areas that have incomplete (less than 90 per cent completeness) or of unknown completeness of cause of deaths data coverage are considered to provide unreliable data, which are set in *italics* rather than in roman type. Rates on these data are not computed. Information on completeness is normally provided by the World Health Organisation. When this is not the case, information on completeness is set to coincide with that of table 18. Similarly, the reliability of data for the completeness of cause of death is provided by the World Health Organisation[2] and it may differ from the reliability of data for the total number of reported deaths. Therefore, there are cases when the quality code in table 18 does not correspond with the typeface used in this table.

Territorial composition as set in Section 2.2 of "Technical Notes on the Statistical Tables", including or excluding certain population of a country refers only to the denominator.

Limitations: Statistics on maternal deaths are subject to the same qualifications that have been set forth for vital statistics in general and death statistics in particular as discussed in section 4 of the Technical Notes. The reliability of the data, an indication of which is described above, is an important factor in considering the limitations. In addition, maternal-death statistics are subject to all the qualifications relating to cause-of-death statistics. These have been set forth in section 4 of the Technical Notes.

Maternal mortality rates are subject to the limitations of the data on live births with which they have been calculated. These have been set forth in the technical notes for table 9. Specific information pertaining to individual countries or areas is given in the footnotes to table 9.

The calculation of the maternal mortality rates based on the total number of live births approximates the risk of dying from complications of pregnancy, childbirth or puerperium. Ideally this rate should be based on the number of women exposed to the risk of pregnancy, in other words, the number of women conceiving. Since it is impossible to know how many women have conceived, the total number of live births is used in calculating this rate.

Earlier data: Maternal deaths and maternal mortality rates have been shown in previous issues of the *Demographic Yearbook*. For information on specific years covered, the reader should consult the Index.

It should however be noted that in issues prior to 1975, maternal mortality rates were calculated using the female population rather than live births. Therefore, maternal mortality rates published since 1975 are not comparable to the earlier maternal death rates.

NOTES

[1] *International Statistical Classification of Diseases and Related Health Problems*, Tenth Revision, Volume 2, World Health Organization, Geneva, 1992.

[2] For more information on specific method used for countries, see "Mathers CD, Bernard C, Iburg KM, Inoue M, Ma Fat D, Shibuya K et al. *Global burden of disease in 2002: data sources, methods and results*. Geneva, World Health Organization, 2003 (GPE Discussion Paper No. 54).

Tableau 17

Ce tableau présente des statistiques et des taux de mortalité liée à la maternité pour les années disponibles entre 1997 et 2006.

Description des variables : aux fins de *l'Annuaire démographique*, les décès liés à la maternité sont ceux entraînés par l'accouchement ou les complications de la grossesse, de l'accouchement et des suites de couches dans un délai de 42 jours après la terminaison de la grossesse. Ils sont généralement associés aux codes 38 à 41 dans le cas de la liste de base pour la mise en tableaux de la CIM-9 et aux codes A34, O00 à O95 et O98 et O99 dans le cas de la CIM-10. Les statistiques associées à des codes correspondant à la CIM-10 englobent des décès de type O96 et O97, qui désignent les décès liés à des causes obstétriques se produisant après 42 jours mais moins d'un an après l'accouchement et les décès entraînés par les séquelles de complications obstétriques directes qui se produisent un an ou plus après l'accouchement.

Pour plus de précisions concernant les définitions de la mortalité liée à la maternité dans la dixième révision de la *Classification statistique internationale des maladies et des problèmes de santé connexes*[1], se reporter également à la section 4.3 des Notes techniques.

Les statistiques de mortalité liée à la maternité présentées dans le tableau 17 émanent de l'Organisation mondiale de la santé. Elles ne se rapportent qu'aux pays ou zones qui répondent aux critères selon lesquels les statistiques relatives à la cause des décès sont conformes à la liste de la neuvième ou de la dixième révision de la CIM ou peuvent être aisément comparées aux catégories de cette liste. Les données conformes à la dixième révision sont indiquées en gras dans le tableau.

Calcul des taux : les taux de mortalité liée à la maternité représentent le nombre annuel de décès dus à la maternité pour 100 000 naissances vivantes (fréquences du tableau 9) de la même année. Ces taux ont été calculés par la Division de statistique de l'ONU. Les taux fondés sur 30 décès liés à la maternité ou moins sont signalés par le signe "♦".

Fiabilité des données : les statistiques relatives aux pays et aux zones pour lesquels la couverture des données concernant les causes de décès est incomplète (mois de 90 pour cent) ou dont le degré de complétude n'est pas connue sont jugés douteuses et apparaissent en *italique* et non en caractères romains. Les taux correspondant ne sont pas calculés. L'information sur la complétude est normalement fournie par l'Organisation Mondiale de la Santé. Si ce n'est pas le cas, l'information sur la complétude est reprise de tableau 18. De même, la fiabilité des données relatives aux causes de décès est fournie par l'Organisation Mondiale de la Santé[2] et peut différer de la fiabilité des données relatives au nombre de décès enregistrés. En conséquence, il peut apparaitre de différences entre les codes de fiabilité du tableau 18 et du présent tableau.

La composition territoriale est définie dans la Section 2.2 des "Notes Techniques sur les tableaux statistiques". L'inclusion ou l'exclusion de certaines populations d'un pays ne concerne que le dénominateur.

Insuffisance des données : les statistiques de la mortalité liée à la maternité appellent toutes les réserves qui ont été formulées à propos des statistiques de l'état civil en général et des statistiques relatives à la mortalité en particulier (voir la section 4 des Notes techniques). La fiabilité des données, au sujet de laquelle des indications ont été fournies plus haut, est un facteur important. En outre, les statistiques de la mortalité liée à la maternité appellent les mêmes réserves que celles exposées à la section 4 des Notes techniques en ce qui concerne les statistiques des causes de décès.

Les taux de mortalité liée à la maternité appellent également toutes les réserves formulées à propos des statistiques des naissances vivantes qui ont servi à leur calcul (voir à ce sujet les notes techniques relatives au tableau 9). Des précisions sur certains pays ou zones sont données dans les notes se rapportant au tableau 9.

En prenant le nombre total des naissances vivantes comme base pour le calcul des taux de mortalité liée à la maternité, on obtient une mesure approximative de la probabilité de décès dus aux complications de la grossesse, de l'accouchement et des suites de couches. Idéalement, ces taux devraient être calculés sur la base du nombre de femmes exposées aux risques liés à la grossesse, c'est-à-dire sur la base du nombre de femmes qui conçoivent. Étant donné qu'il est impossible de connaître le nombre de femmes ayant conçu, c'est le nombre total de naissances vivantes que l'on utilise pour calculer ces taux.

Données publiées antérieurement : des statistiques concernant les décès liés à la maternité (nombre de décès et taux) ont déjà été présentées dans des éditions antérieures de *l'Annuaire démographique*. Pour plus de précisions concernant les années pour lesquelles ces données ont été publiées, se reporter à l'index.

Il faut souligner que, avant 1975, les taux de mortalité liée à la maternité étaient calculés sur la base de la population féminine et non sur celle du nombre de naissances vivantes. Ils ne sont donc pas comparables à ceux qui figurent dans les éditions de *l'Annuaire démographique* parues après 1975.

NOTES

[1] *Classification statistique internationale des maladies et des problèmes de santé connexes*, dixième révision, volume 2. Genève, Organisation mondiale de la santé, 1992.

[2] Pour plus d'information sur les méthodes spécifiques utilisées pour les pays, voir "Mathers CD, Bernard C, Iburg KM, Inoue M, Ma Fat D, Shibuya K et al. *Global burden of disease in 2002: data sources, methods and results*. Geneva, World Health Organization, 2003 (GPE Discussion Paper No. 54).

17. Maternal deaths and maternal mortality rates: 1997 - 2006
Mortalité liée à la maternité, nombre de décès et taux: 1997 - 2006

Continent and country or area / Continent et pays ou zone	Code[a]	1997	1998	1999	2000	2001	2002	2003	2004	2005	2006
AFRICA - AFRIQUE											
Egypt - Égypte											
Number - Nombre	U	...	...	...	492	...	...	...	...	...	...
Mauritius - Maurice											
Number - Nombre	+C	10	4	7	3	4	1	4	3	4	...
Rate - Taux	+C	♦50.0	♦20.6	♦34.5	♦14.8	♦20.3	♦5.0	♦20.7	♦15.6	♦21.3	...
Réunion											
Number - Nombre	...	...	...	...	...	-	3	3	4	4	...
Seychelles											
Number - Nombre	+C	...	...	...	...	-	1	1	-	1	...
Rate - Taux	+C	...	...	...	...	-	♦67.5	♦66.8	-	♦65.1	...
South Africa - Afrique du Sud											
Number - Nombre	U	623	631	693	737	854	794	898	1 158	1 249	...
AMERICA, NORTH - AMÉRIQUE DU NORD											
Anguilla											
Number - Nombre	+...	...	...	...	-	-	...	-	-	...	...
Antigua and Barbuda - Antigua-et-Barbuda											
Number - Nombre	+U	...	...	...	-	-	...	-	-	...	
Aruba											
Number - Nombre	C	...	...	-	...	...	...	...	...	...	
Bahamas											
Number - Nombre	U	-	1	1	2	...	...	...	...	...	
Barbados - Barbade											
Number - Nombre	C	...	...	...	1	-	...	...	...	...	
Rate - Taux	C	...	...	...	♦26.6	-	...	...	...	...	
Belize											
Number - Nombre	C	3	9	3	5	3	...	...	...	...	
Rate - Taux	C	♦40.8	♦131.5	♦42.2	♦68.4	♦41.6	...	...	...	...	
Bermuda - Bermudes											
Number - Nombre	...	-	-	-	-	...	...	...	...	...	
British Virgin Islands - Îles Vierges britanniques											
Number - Nombre	...	-	-	-	-	-	-	-	...	...	
Canada											
Number - Nombre	C	19	13	8	11	26	15	23	20	...	...
Rate - Taux	C	♦5.5	♦3.8	♦2.4	♦3.4	♦7.8	♦4.6	♦6.9	♦5.9	...	...
Cayman Islands - Îles Caïmanes											
Number - Nombre	...	-	-	-	1	...	...	...	-	...	...
Costa Rica											
Number - Nombre	+U	29	14	15	28	24	27	24	22	24	...
Cuba											
Number - Nombre	C	59	59	66	58	57	65	62	56	66	...
Rate - Taux	C	38.6	39.1	43.8	40.4	41.1	46.0	45.3	44.0	54.7	...
Dominica - Dominique											
Number - Nombre	+C	-	1	-	-	1	1	-	-	...	...
Rate - Taux	+C	-	♦80.9	-	-	♦82.2	♦92.5	-	-	...	...
Dominican Republic - République dominicaine											
Number - Nombre	U	74	64	69	51	64	...	58	85	...	...
El Salvador											
Number - Nombre	+U	42	42	23	31	28	32	27	22	23	...
Grenada - Grenade											
Number - Nombre	U	...	...	...	...	-	1	...	...	...	
Guadeloupe											
Number - Nombre	...	...	...	...	3	2	6	4	3	1	...
Guatemala											
Number - Nombre	U	342	324	316	346	278	280	293	296	...	...
Haiti - Haïti											
Number - Nombre	...	101	...	156	...	180	135	124	...	...	
Martinique											
Number - Nombre	...	...	...	...	2	1	2	2	1	-	
Mexico - Mexique											
Number - Nombre	+C	1 266	1 430	1 411	1 325	1 268	1 324	1 332	1 266	1 269	...
Rate - Taux	+C	57.5	63.8	62.9	57.6	56.9	59.9	61.5	58.7	59.3	...

Continent and country or area / Continent et pays ou zone	Co-de[a]	1997	1998	1999	2000	2001	2002	2003	2004	2005	2006
AMERICA, NORTH - AMÉRIQUE DU NORD											
Montserrat											
Number - Nombre	+C	-	-	-	1	-	-	-	...	...	...
Rate - Taux	+C	-	-	-	♦2083.3	-	-	-	...	...	...
Nicaragua											
Number - Nombre	+U	127	113	138	97	124	114	88	108	93	...
Panama											
Number - Nombre	+U	28	30	31	30	37	38	34	23	...	...
Puerto Rico - Porto Rico											
Number - Nombre	+...	13	8	10	14	6	5	8	...	5	...
Saint Kitts and Nevis - Saint-Kitts-et-Nevis											
Number - Nombre	+C	-	-	-	-	2	-	2	-	-	...
Rate - Taux	+C	-	-	-	-	♦249.1	...	...	...	...	...
Saint Lucia - Sainte-Lucie											
Number - Nombre	C	-	-	1	3	1	1	...	...	...	...
Rate - Taux	C	-	-	♦33.4	♦103.3	♦35.9	♦38.5	...	...	...	...
Saint Pierre and Miquelon - Saint Pierre-et-Miquelon											
Number - Nombre	C	...	...	...	...	...	...	...	...	-	...
Saint Vincent and the Grenadines - Saint-Vincent-et-les Grenadines											
Number - Nombre	+C	1	-	1	1	-	-	-	...	...	...
Rate - Taux	+C	♦43.3	-	♦46.1	♦46.5	-	-	-	...	...	...
Trinidad and Tobago - Trinité-et-Tobago											
Number - Nombre	C	13	8	7	10	7	5	...	...	...	...
Rate - Taux	C	♦70.5	♦44.7	♦38.2	♦55.1	♦38.7	♦29.4	...	...	...	...
Turks and Caicos Islands - Îles Turques et Caïques											
Number - Nombre	...	-	-	-	-	1	-	1	1	-	...
United States of America - États-Unis d'Amérique											
Number - Nombre	C	327	281	406	404	416	379	545	697	760	...
Rate - Taux	C	8.4	7.1	10.3	10.0	10.3	9.4	13.3	17.0	18.4	...
United States Virgin Islands - Îles Vierges américaines											
Number - Nombre	...	1	-	-	1	2	-	-	...	-	...
AMERICA, SOUTH - AMÉRIQUE DU SUD											
Argentina - Argentine											
Number - Nombre	+C	265	260	287	245	309	356	321	313	290	...
Rate - Taux	+C	38.3	38.1	41.8	34.9	45.2	51.2	46.0	42.5	40.7	...
Brazil - Brésil											
Number - Nombre	U	1 791	1 937	1 823	1 648	1 587	1 648	1 597	1 672	...	...
Chile - Chili											
Number - Nombre	C	61	55	60	49	45	42	33	42	48	...
Rate - Taux	C	23.5	21.4	23.9	19.7	18.3	17.6	14.1	18.2	20.8	...
Colombia - Colombie											
Number - Nombre	U	420	721	676	776	689	577	...	546	504	...
Ecuador - Équateur[1]											
Number - Nombre	U	162	153	209	232	187	149	139	129	143	...
French Guiana - Guyane française											
Number - Nombre	...	...	...	...	...	2	2	1	1	1	...
Guyana											
Number - Nombre	U	...	24	17	...	17	20	21	19	24	...
Paraguay											
Number - Nombre	+U	89	96	103	140	132	163	150	154	...	...
Peru - Pérou											
Number - Nombre	+U	246	279	261	263	...	...	...	...	...	...
Suriname											
Number - Nombre	U	5	7	4	9	...	...	...	...	...	...

17. Maternal deaths and maternal mortality rates: 1997 - 2006
Mortalité liée à la maternité, nombre de décès et taux: 1997 - 2006 (continued - suite)

Continent and country or area / Continent et pays ou zone	Code[a]	1997	1998	1999	2000	2001	2002	2003	2004	2005	2006
AMERICA, SOUTH - AMÉRIQUE DU SUD											
Uruguay											
Number - Nombre	C	17	11	6	9	19	...	...	9	...	...
Rate - Taux	C	♦29.3	♦20.1	♦11.1	♦17.1	♦36.6	...	...	♦18.0	...	...
Venezuela (Bolivarian Republic of) - Venezuela (République bolivarienne du)[2]											
Number - Nombre	C	308	256	313	327	356	335	321	318	351	...
Rate - Taux	C	59.6	51.0	59.3	60.1	67.2	68.0	57.8	49.9	52.7	...
ASIA - ASIE											
Armenia - Arménie											
Number - Nombre	C	17	10	12	18	7	3	8	...	...	...
Rate - Taux	C	♦38.7	♦25.4	♦32.9	♦52.5	♦21.8	♦9.3	♦22.4	...	...	...
Azerbaijan - Azerbaïdjan											
Number - Nombre	U	41	51	51	44	27	22	21	34	...	...
Bahrain - Bahreïn											
Number - Nombre	C	2	2	3	2	3	...	...	...	...	...
Rate - Taux	C	♦14.9	♦14.9	♦21.0	♦14.3	♦22.3	...	...	...	...	...
Brunei Darussalam - Brunéi Darussalam											
Number - Nombre	+C	2	3	-	2	...	...	...	...	...	...
Rate - Taux	+C	♦26.8	♦40.5	-	♦26.7	...	...	...	...	...	...
China, Hong Kong SAR - Chine, Hong Kong RAS											
Number - Nombre	...	1	1	1	3	1	1	2	2	2	1
Cyprus - Chypre											
Number - Nombre	C	...	...	-	-	...	...	...	...	...	1
Rate - Taux	C	...	...	-	...	...	...	...	-	...	♦11.5
Georgia - Géorgie											
Number - Nombre	U	13	15	9	4	4	...	...	...	...	...
Israel - Israël											
Number - Nombre	C	12	11	9	5	9	6	3	6	...	...
Rate - Taux	C	♦9.6	♦8.5	♦6.8	♦3.7	♦6.6	♦4.3	♦2.1	♦4.1	...	...
Japan - Japon											
Number - Nombre	C	81	89	79	84	79	90	74	56	66	63
Rate - Taux	C	6.8	7.4	6.7	7.1	6.7	7.8	6.6	5.0	6.2	5.8
Kazakhstan											
Number - Nombre	U	137	122	98	94	87	80	67	63	81	100
Kuwait - Koweït											
Number - Nombre	U	7	3	3	2	1	3	...	...	...	...
Kyrgyzstan - Kirghizstan											
Number - Nombre	U	64	35	44	44	43	54	52	56	66	67
Maldives											
Number - Nombre	+C	...	...	...	4	3	7	-	2	1	...
Rate - Taux	+C	...	...	...	♦74.1	♦61.2	♦139.9	-	♦38.3	♦18.0	...
Philippines											
Number - Nombre	U	1 513	1 579	...	...	...	...	...	...	...	...
Republic of Korea - République de Corée											
Number - Nombre	U	66	63	77	62	70	71	58	59	53	54
Singapore - Singapour											
Number - Nombre	+U	1	5	2	8	4	4	2	1	4	3
Tajikistan - Tadjikistan											
Number - Nombre	U	38	57	45	36	40	57	36	37	28	...
Thailand - Thaïlande											
Number - Nombre	+U	87	63	93	102	...	114	...	...	...	...
Turkmenistan - Turkménistan											
Number - Nombre	U	21	16	...	...	...	...	...	...	...	...
Uzbekistan - Ouzbékistan											
Number - Nombre	U	62	48	80	182	...	143	151	156	145	...

Continent and country or area / Continent et pays ou zone	Code[a]	1997	1998	1999	2000	2001	2002	2003	2004	2005	2006
EUROPE											
Albania - Albanie											
Number - Nombre	C	5	8	2	8	2	5	1	1	...	...
Rate - Taux	C	♦8.1	♦13.3	♦3.5	♦16.0	♦3.7	♦11.0	♦2.1	♦2.3	...	...
Austria - Autriche											
Number - Nombre	C	2	4	1	2	5	2	2	3	3	2
Rate - Taux	C	♦2.4	♦4.9	♦1.3	♦2.6	♦6.6	♦2.6	♦2.6	♦3.8	♦3.8	♦2.6
Belarus - Bélarus											
Number - Nombre	C	23	26	19	20	13	17	18	...	...	...
Rate - Taux	C	♦25.7	♦28.1	♦20.4	♦21.3	♦14.2	♦19.2	♦20.3	...	...	...
Belgium - Belgique											
Number - Nombre	C	10	...	...	...	...	...	...	...	...	...
Rate - Taux	C	♦8.6	...	...	...	...	...	...	...	...	...
Bulgaria - Bulgarie											
Number - Nombre	C	12	10	16	13	13	11	4	7	...	...
Rate - Taux	C	♦18.7	♦15.3	♦22.1	♦17.6	♦19.1	♦16.5	♦5.9	♦10.0	...	...
Croatia - Croatie											
Number - Nombre	C	6	3	5	3	1	4	3	3	3	4
Rate - Taux	C	♦10.8	♦6.4	♦11.1	♦6.9	♦2.4	♦10.0	♦7.6	♦7.4	♦7.1	♦9.7
Czech Republic - République tchèque											
Number - Nombre	C	2	5	6	5	3	3	4	5	3	...
Rate - Taux	C	♦2.2	♦5.5	♦6.7	♦5.5	♦3.3	♦3.1	♦4.3	♦5.1	♦2.9	...
Denmark - Danemark											
Number - Nombre	C	5	2	4	-	2	...	...	...	...	...
Rate - Taux	C	♦7.4	♦3.0	♦6.0	-	♦3.1	...	...	...	...	...
Estonia - Estonie											
Number - Nombre	C	2	2	2	5	1	1	4	4	2	...
Rate - Taux	C	♦15.9	♦16.4	♦16.1	♦38.3	♦7.9	♦7.7	♦30.7	♦28.6	♦13.9	...
Finland - Finlande											
Number - Nombre	C	3	3	2	3	3	3	2	7	3	4
Rate - Taux	C	♦5.1	♦5.3	♦3.5	♦5.3	♦5.3	♦5.4	♦3.5	♦12.1	♦5.2	♦6.8
France											
Number - Nombre	C	70	75	55	50	56	67	56	53	41	...
Rate - Taux	C	9.6	10.2	7.4	6.5	7.3	8.8	7.4	6.9	5.3	...
Germany - Allemagne											
Number - Nombre	C	49	44	37	43	27	21	30	37	28	41
Rate - Taux	C	6.0	5.6	4.8	5.6	♦3.7	♦2.9	♦4.2	5.2	♦4.1	6.1
Greece - Grèce											
Number - Nombre	C	-	7	6	-	4	1	2	3	-	3
Rate - Taux	C	-	♦6.9	♦6.0	-	♦3.9	♦1.0	♦1.9	♦2.8	-	♦2.7
Hungary - Hongrie											
Number - Nombre	C	21	6	4	10	5	8	7	4	5	...
Rate - Taux	C	♦20.9	♦6.2	♦4.2	♦10.2	♦5.2	♦8.3	♦7.4	♦4.2	♦5.1	...
Iceland - Islande											
Number - Nombre	C	-	-	-	-	1	-	-	-	-	-
Rate - Taux	C	-	-	-	-	♦24.4	-	-	-	-	-
Ireland - Irlande											
Number - Nombre	C	3	2	1	1	3	5	-	-	2	-
Rate - Taux	C	♦5.7	♦3.7	♦1.9	♦1.8	♦5.2	♦8.3	-	-	♦3.3	-
Italy - Italie											
Number - Nombre	C	23	18	14	16	11	17	28	...	...	...
Rate - Taux	C	♦4.3	♦3.4	♦2.6	♦2.9	♦2.1	♦3.2	♦5.1	...	...	...
Latvia - Lettonie											
Number - Nombre	+C	8	9	8	5	5	1	3	2	1	2
Rate - Taux	+C	♦42.5	♦48.9	♦41.2	♦24.7	♦25.4	♦5.0	♦14.3	♦9.8	♦4.7	♦9.0
Lithuania - Lituanie											
Number - Nombre	+C	6	5	5	3	4	6	1	5	4	-
Rate - Taux	+C	♦15.9	♦13.5	♦13.7	♦8.8	♦12.7	♦20.0	♦3.3	♦16.4	♦13.1	-
Luxembourg											
Number - Nombre	+C	-	1	-	1	-	-	-	1	1	...
Rate - Taux	+C	-	♦18.6	-	♦17.5	-	-	-	♦18.3	♦18.6	...
Malta - Malte											
Number - Nombre	+C	-	1	1	-	2	-	-	-	-	...
Rate - Taux	+C	-	♦21.4	♦22.7	-	♦50.5	-	-	-	-	...
Netherlands - Pays-Bas											
Number - Nombre	+C	15	23	19	18	14	20	8	10	16	15
Rate - Taux	+C	♦7.8	♦11.5	♦9.5	♦8.7	♦6.9	♦9.9	♦4.0	♦5.2	♦8.5	♦8.1

17. Maternal deaths and maternal mortality rates: 1997 - 2006
Mortalité liée à la maternité, nombre de décès et taux: 1997 - 2006 (continued - suite)

Continent and country or area / Continent et pays ou zone	Co-de[a]	1997	1998	1999	2000	2001	2002	2003	2004	2005	2006
EUROPE											
Norway - Norvège											
Number - Nombre	+C	1	4	5	2	3	2	7	-	2	...
Rate - Taux	+C	♦1.7	♦6.9	♦8.4	♦3.4	♦5.3	♦3.6	♦12.4	-	♦3.5	...
Poland - Pologne											
Number - Nombre	C	...	...	20	30	13	19	14	17	11	11
Rate - Taux	C	...	...	♦5.2	♦7.9	♦3.5	♦5.4	♦4.0	♦4.8	♦3.0	♦2.9
Portugal											
Number - Nombre	+C	6	9	6	3	6	8	8	...	...	...
Rate - Taux	+C	♦5.3	♦7.9	♦5.2	♦2.5	♦5.3	♦7.0	♦7.1	...	...	...
Republic of Moldova - République de Moldova											
Number - Nombre	+U	23	15	11	10	16	11	8	9	8	6
Romania - Roumanie											
Number - Nombre	+C	98	96	98	75	75	47	65	52	37	34
Rate - Taux	+C	41.4	40.5	41.8	32.0	34.0	22.3	30.6	24.0	16.7	15.5
Russian Federation - Fédération de Russie[3]											
Number - Nombre	+C	633	565	537	503	479	469	463	352	370	352
Rate - Taux	+C	50.2	44.0	44.2	39.7	36.5	33.6	31.3	23.4	25.4	23.8
San Marino - Saint-Marin											
Number - Nombre	+U	-	-	-	-	...	-	...	...	-	...
Serbia - Serbie											
Number - Nombre	+C	...	...	...	...	...	...	...	2	10	9
Rate - Taux	+C	...	...	...	...	...	...	...	♦2.6	♦13.9	♦12.7
Slovakia - Slovaquie											
Number - Nombre	C	1	5	5	1	7	4	2	3	2	...
Rate - Taux	C	♦1.7	♦8.7	♦8.9	♦1.8	♦13.7	♦7.9	♦3.9	♦5.6	♦3.7	...
Slovenia - Slovénie											
Number - Nombre	C	2	-	2	2	3	-	-	2	1	3
Rate - Taux	C	♦11.0	-	♦11.4	♦11.0	♦17.2	-	-	♦11.1	♦5.5	♦15.8
Spain - Espagne											
Number - Nombre	C	8	10	14	14	17	14	20	21	18	...
Rate - Taux	C	♦2.2	♦2.7	♦3.7	♦3.5	♦4.2	♦3.3	♦4.5	♦4.6	♦3.9	...
Sweden - Suède											
Number - Nombre	C	3	7	1	4	3	4	2	2	6	...
Rate - Taux	C	♦3.3	♦7.9	♦1.1	♦4.4	♦3.3	♦4.2	♦2.0	♦2.0	♦5.9	...
Switzerland - Suisse											
Number - Nombre	C	3	3	6	5	1	3	4	4	4	...
Rate - Taux	C	♦3.7	♦3.8	♦7.7	♦6.4	♦1.4	♦4.1	♦5.6	♦5.5	♦5.5	...
The Former Yugoslav Republic of Macedonia - L'ex-République yougoslave de Macédoine											
Number - Nombre	C	1	1	2	4	4	3	1	...	...	...
Rate - Taux	C	♦3.4	♦3.4	♦7.3	♦13.6	♦14.8	♦10.8	♦3.7	...	...	...
Ukraine											
Number - Nombre	C	111	114	98	95	90	85	71	56	75	...
Rate - Taux	C	25.1	27.2	25.2	24.7	23.9	21.8	17.4	13.1	17.6	...
United Kingdom of Great Britain and Northern Ireland - Royaume-Uni de Grande-Bretagne et d'Irlande du Nord											
Number - Nombre	+C	39	49	37	46	50	40	53	55	51	50
Rate - Taux	+C	5.4	6.8	5.3	6.8	7.5	6.0	7.6	7.7	7.1	6.7
OCEANIA - OCÉANIE											
Australia - Australie											
Number - Nombre	C	12	5	13	13	12	13	8	...	...	...
Rate - Taux	C	♦4.8	♦2.0	♦5.2	♦5.2	♦4.9	♦5.2	♦3.2	...	...	...
Kiribati											
Number - Nombre	U	3	-	1	-	1	...	...	...	...	...
New Zealand - Nouvelle-Zélande											
Number - Nombre	+C	3	3	4	5	3	8	4	4	...	...
Rate - Taux	+C	♦5.2	♦5.4	♦7.0	♦8.8	♦5.4	♦14.8	♦7.1	♦6.9	...	...

FOOTNOTES - NOTES

Data in bold refer to maternal deaths based on ICD-10 Classification, otherwise data refer to maternal deaths based on ICD-9 Classification. - Les données en typographie gras se rapportent aux décès maternelles basées sur la classification CIM-10, autrement les données se rapportent aux décès maternelles basées sur la classification CIM-9.

Italics: data from civil registers which are incomplete or of unknown completeness. - Italiques: données incomplètes ou dont le degré d'exactitude n'est pas connu, provenant des registres de l'état civil.

* Provisional. - Données provisoires.

♦ Rates based on 30 or fewer deaths. - Taux basés sur 30 décès ou moins.

a 'Code' indicates the source of data, as follows:
  C - Civil registration, estimated over 90% complete
  U - Civil registration, estimated less than 90% complete
  | - Other source, estimated reliable
  + - Data tabulated by date of registration rather than occurence.
  ... - Information not available

Le 'Code' indique la source des données, comme suit:
  C - Registres de l'état civil considérés complèts à 90 p. 100 au moins.
  U - Registres de l'état civil qui ne sont pas considérés complèts à 90 p. 100 au moins.
  | - Autre source, considérée pas douteuses.
  + - Données exploitées selon la date de l'enregistrement et non la date de l'événement.
  ... - Information pas disponible.

1 Excluding nomadic Indian tribes. - Non compris les tribus d'Indiens nomades.
2 Excluding Indian jungle population. - Non compris les Indiens de la jungle.
3 For 2003 and before, data on cause of death do not include the Chechnya region. Therefore, rates must be used with caution as they are based on the total population, which is assumed to include all regions. - Pour 2003 et avant, les données sur les causes de décès ne comprennent par la région de Chechnya. Par conséquent, les taux doivent être utilisés avec précaution car ils sont basés sur la population totale, qui est supposée inclure toutes les régions.

Table 18

Table 18 presents deaths and crude death rates by urban/rural residence for as many years as possible between 2003 and 2007.

Description of variables: Death is defined as the permanent disappearance of all evidence of life at any time after live birth has taken place (post-natal cessation of vital functions without capability of resuscitation).

Statistics on the number of deaths are obtained from civil registers unless otherwise noted. For those countries or areas where civil registration statistics on deaths are considered reliable (estimated completeness of 90 per cent or more), the death rates shown have been calculated on the basis of registered deaths.

The urban/rural classification of deaths is that provided by each country or area; it is presumed to be based on the national census definitions of urban population that have been set forth at the end of the technical notes for table 6.

For certain countries, there is a discrepancy between the total number of deaths shown in this table and those shown in subsequent tables for the same year. Usually this discrepancy arises because the total number of deaths occurring in a given year is revised although the remaining tabulations are not.

Rate computation: Crude death rates are the annual number of deaths per 1 000 mid-year population.

Rates by urban/rural residence are the annual number of deaths, in the appropriate urban or rural category, per 1 000 corresponding mid-year population. These rates are calculated by the Statistics Division of the United Nations based on the appropriate reference population (for example: total population, nationals only etc.) if known and available. If the reference population is not known or unavailable the total population is used to calculate the rates. Therefore, if the population that is used to calculate the rates is different from the correct reference population, the rates presented might under- or overstate the true situation in a country or area.

Rates presented in this table are limited to those countries or areas with a minimum number of 30 deaths in a given year.

Reliability of data: Each country or area has been asked to indicate the estimated completeness of the deaths recorded in its civil register. These national assessments are indicated by the quality codes "C", "U" and "|" that appear in the first column of this table. "C" indicates that the data are estimated to be virtually complete, that is, representing at least 90 per cent of the deaths occurring each year, while "U" indicates that data are estimated to be incomplete that is, representing less than 90 per cent of the deaths occurring each year. The code "|" indicates that the source of data is different than civil registration, but still considered reliable and explained by footnote. The code "..." indicates that no information was provided regarding completeness or no assessment has been done in the country.

Data from civil registers that are reported as incomplete or of unknown completeness (code "U" or "...") are considered unreliable. They appear in italics in this table; rates based on these data are not computed.

Limitations: Statistics on deaths are subject to the same qualifications as have been set forth for vital statistics in general and death statistics in particular as discussed in section 4 of the Introduction.

The reliability of the data, an indication of which is described above, is an important factor in considering the limitations. In addition, some deaths are tabulated by date of registration and not by date of occurrence; these have been indicated with a plus sign "+". Whenever the lag between the date of occurrence and date of registration is prolonged and, therefore, a large proportion of the death registrations are delayed, death statistics for any given year may be seriously affected. However, delays in the registration of deaths are less common and shorter than in the registration of live births.

International comparability in mortality statistics may also be affected by the exclusion of deaths of infants who were born alive but died before the registration of the birth or within the first 24 hours of life. Statistics of this type are footnoted.

In addition, it should be noted that rates are affected also by the quality and limitations of the population estimates that are used in their computation. The problems of under-enumeration or over-enumeration and, to some extent, the differences in definition of total population have been discussed in section 3 of the Introduction dealing with population data in general, and specific information pertaining to individual countries or areas is given in the footnotes to table 3.

Estimated rates based directly on the results of sample surveys are subject to considerable error as a result of omissions in reporting deaths or as a result of erroneous reporting of those that occurred outside the period of reference. However, such rates do have the advantage of having a "built-in" and corresponding base.

It should be emphasized that crude death rates -- like other crude rates, such as of birth, marriage and divorce -- may be seriously affected by the age-sex structure of the populations to which they relate. Nevertheless, they do provide a simple measure of the level and changes in mortality.

The comparability of data by urban/rural residence is affected by the national definitions of urban and rural used in tabulating these data. It is assumed, in the absence of specific information to the contrary, that the definitions of urban and rural used in connection with the national population census were also used in the compilation of the vital statistics for each country or area. However, it cannot be excluded that, for a given country or area, different definitions of urban and rural are used for the vital statistics data and the population census data respectively. When known, the definitions of urban used in national population censuses are presented at the end of the technical notes for table 6. As discussed in detail in the technical notes for table 6, these definitions vary considerably from one country or area to another.

In addition to problems of comparability, vital rates classified by urban/rural residence are also subject to certain types of bias. If, when calculating vital rates, different definitions of urban are used in connection with the vital events and the population data and if this results in a net difference between the numerator and denominator of the rate in the population at risk, then the vital rates would be biased. Urban/rural differentials in vital rates may also be affected by whether the vital events have been tabulated in terms of place of occurrence or place of usual residence. This problem is discussed in more detail in section 4.1.4.1 of the Introduction.

Earlier data: Deaths and crude death rates have been shown in each issue of the Demographic Yearbook. Data included in this table update the series covering a period of years as follows:

Issue	Years Covered
Historical Supplement CD, 1997	1948 – 1997
44th issue, 1992	1983 – 1992
37th issue, 1985	1976 – 1985
32nd issue, 1980	1971 – 1980
Historical Supplement, 1979	1948 – 1977

Tableau 18

Le tableau 18 présente le nombre des décès et les taux bruts de mortalité selon le lieu de résidence (zone urbaine ou rurale) pour le plus grand nombre d'années possible entre 2003 et 2007.

Description des variables : Le décès est défini comme la disparition permanente de tout signe de vie à un moment quelconque postérieur à la naissance vivante (cessation des fonctions vitales après la naissance sans possibilité de réanimation).

Sauf indication contraire, les statistiques relatives au nombre de décès sont établies sur la base des registres d'état civil. Pour les pays ou zones où les données concernant l'enregistrement des décès par les services de l'état civil sont jugées sûres (complétude estimée à 90 p. 100 ou plus), les taux de mortalité ont été calculés d'après les décès enregistrés.

La répartition des décès entre zones urbaines et zones rurales est celle qui a été communiquée par chaque pays ou zone ; on part du principe qu'elle repose sur les définitions de la population urbaine utilisées pour les recensements nationaux, qui sont reproduites à la fin des notes techniques du tableau 6.

Pour quelques pays il y a une discordance entre le nombre total des décès présenté dans ce tableau et ceux présentés après pour la même année. Habituellement ces différences apparaissent lorsque le nombre total des décès pour une certaine année a été révisé alors que les autres tabulations ne l'ont pas été.

Calcul des taux : Les taux bruts de mortalité représentent le nombre annuel de décès pour 1 000 habitants en milieu d'année.

Les taux selon le lieu de résidence (zone urbaine ou rurale) représentent le nombre annuel de décès, classés selon la catégorie urbaine ou rurale appropriée, pour 1 000 habitants en milieu d'année. Ces taux sont calculés par la division de statistique des Nations Unies sur la base de la population de référence adéquate (par exemple : population totale, nationaux seulement, etc.) si connue et disponible. Si la population de référence n'est pas connue ou n'est pas disponible, la population totale est utilisée pour calculer les taux. Par conséquent, si la population utilisée pour calculer les taux est différente de la population de référence adéquate, les taux présentés sont susceptibles de sous ou sur estimer la situation réelle d'un pays ou d'un territoire.

Les taux présentés dans ce tableau se rapportent seulement aux pays ou zones où l'on a enregistré un nombre minimal de 30 décès au cours d'une année donnée.

Fiabilité des données : Il a été demandé à chaque pays ou zone d'indiquer le degré estimatif de complétude des données sur les décès d'enfants de moins d'un an figurant dans ses registres d'état civil. Ces évaluations nationales sont signalées par les codes de qualité "C", "U" et "|" qui apparaissent dans la deuxième colonne du tableau.

La lettre "C" indique que les données sont jugées à peu près complètes, c'est-à-dire qu'elles représentent au moins 90 p. 100 des décès d'enfants de moins d'un an survenus chaque année ; la lettre "U" signifie que les données sont jugées incomplètes, c'est-à-dire qu'elles représentent moins de 90 p.100 des décès d'enfants de moins d'un an survenus chaque année. Le symbole "|" indique que la source des données est fiable mais n'est pas un registre de l'état civil ; le symbole, dans ce cas, est accompagné par une note explicative. Le code "..." dénote qu'aucun renseignement n'a été communiqué quant à la complétude des données.

Les données provenant des registres de l'état civil qui sont déclarées incomplètes ou dont le degré de complétude n'est pas connu (code "U" ou "...") sont jugées douteuses. Elles apparaissent en italique dans le présent tableau et les taux correspondants n'ont pas été calculés.

Insuffisance des données : Les statistiques relatives à la mortalité appellent les mêmes réserves que celles qui ont été formulées à propos des statistiques de l'état civil en général et des statistiques relatives aux décès en particulier (voir la section 4 de l'Introduction).

La fiabilité des données, au sujet de laquelle des indications ont été fournies plus haut, est un facteur important. Il faut également tenir compte du fait que, dans certains cas, les décès sont classés par date d'enregistrement et non par date d'occurrence ; ces cas ont été signalés par le signe "+". Chaque fois que le décalage entre le décès et son enregistrement est grand et qu'une forte proportion des décès fait l'objet d'un enregistrement tardif, les statistiques relatives aux décès survenus pendant l'année peuvent être considérablement faussées.

En règle générale, toutefois, les décès sont enregistrés beaucoup plus rapidement que les naissances vivantes, et les retards prolongés sont rares.

Un autre facteur qui nuit à la comparabilité internationale est la pratique qui consiste à ne pas inclure dans les statistiques de la mortalité les enfants nés vivants mais décédés avant l'enregistrement de leur naissance ou dans les 24 heures qui ont suivi la naissance. Quand pareil facteur a joué, cela a été signalé en note à la fin du tableau.

Il convient de noter par ailleurs que l'exactitude des taux dépend également de la qualité et des limitations des estimations de la population qui sont utilisées pour leur calcul. Le problème des erreurs par excès ou par défaut commises lors du dénombrement et, dans une certaine mesure, le problème de l'hétérogénéité des définitions de la population totale ont été examinés à la section 3 de l'Introduction, relative à la population en général ; des indications concernant certains pays ou zones sont données en note à la fin du tableau 3.

Les taux estimatifs fondés directement sur les résultats d'enquêtes par sondage comportent des possibilités d'erreurs considérables dues soit à des omissions dans les déclarations des décès, soit au fait que l'on a déclaré à tort des décès survenus en réalité hors de la période considérée. Toutefois, ces taux présentent un avantage : le chiffre de population utilisé comme base est connu par définition et rigoureusement correspondant.

Il faut souligner que les taux bruts de mortalité, de même que les taux bruts de natalité, de nuptialité et de divortialité, peuvent varier très sensiblement selon la composition par âge et par sexe de la population à laquelle ils se rapportent. Ils offrent néanmoins un moyen simple de mesurer le niveau et l'évolution de la mortalité.

La comparabilité des données selon le lieu de résidence (zone urbaine ou rurale) peut être limitée par les définitions nationales des termes « urbain » et « rural » utilisées pour le classement de ces données. En l'absence d'indications contraires, on a supposé que les mêmes définitions avaient servi pour le recensement national de la population et pour l'établissement des statistiques de l'état civil pour chaque pays ou zone. Toutefois, il n'est pas exclu que, pour une zone ou un pays donné, des définitions différentes aient été retenues. Les définitions du terme « urbain » utilisées pour les recensements nationaux de population ont été présentées à la fin du tableau 6 lorsqu'elles étaient connues. Comme on l'a précisé dans les notes techniques relatives au tableau 6, ces définitions varient considérablement d'un pays ou d'une zone à l'autre.

Outre les problèmes de comparabilité, les taux démographiques classés selon le lieu de résidence « urbaine » ou « rurale » sont également sujets à des distorsions particulières. Si l'on utilise des définitions différentes du terme « urbain » pour classer les faits d'état civil et les données relatives à la population lors du calcul des taux et qu'il en résulte une différence nette entre le numérateur et le dénominateur pour le taux de la population exposée au risque, les taux démographiques s'en trouveront faussés. La différence entre ces taux pour les zones urbaines et rurales pourra aussi être faussée selon que les faits d'état civil auront été classés d'après le lieu où ils se sont produits ou d'après le lieu de résidence habituel. Ce problème est examiné plus en détail à la section 4.1.4.1 de l' Introduction.

Données publiées antérieurement : les différentes éditions de l'*Annuaire démographique* contiennent des statistiques des décès et des taux bruts de mortalité. Les données qui figurent dans le tableau 18 actualisent les données qui portaient sur les périodes suivantes :

Éditions	**Années considérées**
Supplément historique (CD-ROM), 1997	1948 – 1997
44e édition, 1992	1983 – 1992
37e édition, 1985	1976 – 1985
32e édition, 1980	1971 – 1980
Supplément rétrospectif, 1979	1948 – 1977

18. Deaths and crude death rates, by urban/rural residence: 2003 - 2007
Décès et taux bruts de mortalité, selon la résidence, urbaine/rurale: 2003 - 2007

Continent, country or area, and urban/rural residence / Continent, pays ou zone et résidence, urbaine/rurale	Code[a]	Number - Nombre					Rate - Taux				
		2003	2004	2005	2006	2007	2003	2004	2005	2006	2007
AFRICA - AFRIQUE											
Algeria - Algérie[1]											
Total	U	145 000	141 000	147 000	144 000	149 000		...	...	...	...
Burkina Faso[2]											
Total	I	...	...	...	116 199		...	...	...		...
Urban - Urbaine	I	...	...	...	16 411		...	...	...	8.9	...
Rural - Rurale	I	...	...	...	99 788		...	...	...	7.7	...
Egypt - Égypte										9.1	...
Total	C	440 149	440 790	450 646	451 863	450 596	6.5	6.4	6.4	6.3	6.1
Urban - Urbaine	C	211 719	195 491	198 588	214 008	212 305	7.3	6.6	6.6	7.0	6.7
Rural - Rurale	C	228 430	245 299	252 058	237 855	238 291	5.9	6.2	6.2	5.8	5.7
Kenya											
Total	U	174 950	178 051	168 919	174 856		...	...	...	...	...
Malawi[3]											
Total	U	213 705	210 936	209 019	207 641	206 527	...	...	...	...	...
Mauritius - Maurice											
Total	+C	8 520	8 475	8 646	9 162	8 498	7.0	6.9	7.0	7.3	6.7
Urban - Urbaine	+C	3 942	3 914	3 988	4 142	4 036	7.6	7.5	7.6	7.9	7.6
Rural - Rurale	+C	4 578	4 561	4 658	5 020	4 462	6.5	6.4	6.5	6.9	6.1
Mayotte											
Total	C	...	513	...	...	...	...	...	...	...	...
Namibia - Namibie[3]											
Total	U	29 425	29 262	29 073	28 879	28 673	...	...	...	...	...
Réunion[4]											
Total	C	*4 022	3 958	4 357	4 323	4 045	*5.3	5.2	5.6	5.5	5.1
Saint Helena ex. dep. - Sainte-Hélène sans dép.											
Total	C	44	33	39	52	59	...	...	...	...	14.9
Seychelles											
Total	+C	668	611	673	664	630	8.1	7.4	8.1	7.8	7.4
South Africa - Afrique du Sud											
Total	U	554 199	572 620	593 341	607 184		...	...	...	...	...
Tunisia - Tunisie											
Total	U	59 781	59 269	58 673	57 000	56 741	...	...	...	...	...
Zambia - Zambie[3]											
Total	U	...	...	...	152 549		...	...	...	...	...
AMERICA, NORTH - AMÉRIQUE DU NORD											
Anguilla											
Total	+C	65	52	60	58	70	5.3	4.2	4.4	4.1	4.7
Aruba											
Total	C	501	502	482	537	521	5.3	5.1	4.8	5.2	5.0
Bahamas											
Total	C	1 649	1 655	1 824	1 730	1 798	5.2	5.2	5.6	5.3	5.4
Barbados - Barbade											
Total	+C	*2 274	*2 424	*2 162	*2 317	*2 213	*8.4	*8.9	*7.9	*8.5	*8.1
Belize											
Total	U	1 277	1 298	1 369	...	...	...	...	...	...	...
Bermuda - Bermudes[5]											
Total	C	434	406	437	461	...	6.9	6.4	6.9	7.2	...
British Virgin Islands - Îles Vierges britanniques											
Total	C	104	120	...	...	...	4.9	5.5	...	...	...
Canada[6]											
Total	C	226 169	226 584	230 132	*233 415	...	7.1	7.1	7.1	*7.1	...
Cayman Islands - Îles Caïmanes[7]											
Total	C	153	165	170	181	159	3.5	3.7	3.5	3.5	2.9
Costa Rica											
Total	C	15 800	15 949	16 139	16 766	17 070	3.9	3.8	3.8	3.9	3.8
Urban - Urbaine	C	8 701	8 501	8 429	8 786	8 779	3.6	3.4	3.3	3.4	3.4
Rural - Rurale	C	7 099	7 448	7 710	7 980	8 291	4.2	4.3	4.4	4.5	4.5

Continent, country or area, and urban/rural residence / Continent, pays ou zone et résidence, urbaine/rurale	Code[a]	Number - Nombre					Rate - Taux				
		2003	2004	2005	2006	2007	2003	2004	2005	2006	2007
AMERICA, NORTH - AMÉRIQUE DU NORD											
Cuba											
Total	C	78 434	81 110	84 824	80 831	81 927	7.0	7.2	7.5	7.2	7.3
Urban - Urbaine	C	64 200[8]	66 410[8]	69 969	67 002	66 913	7.6	7.8	8.2	7.9	7.9
Rural - Rurale	C	14 224[8]	14 677[8]	14 855	13 829	15 014	5.2	5.4	5.4	5.0	5.4
Dominica - Dominique											
Total	+C	557	557	489	536	...	7.9	7.9	6.9	7.5	...
Dominican Republic - République dominicaine											
Total	U	28 950	33 370	33 035	30 759	31 204	...	...	...	...	...
Urban - Urbaine[8]	U	20 131	23 407	24 166	21 207	22 563	...	...	...	...	...
Rural - Rurale[8]	U	6 636	7 750	7 434	6 835	6 655	...	...	...	...	...
El Salvador											
Total	C	29 377	30 058	30 933	31 453	31 349	4.4	4.4	4.5	4.5	4.4
Urban - Urbaine	C	20 856	20 576	21 612	24 682	23 358	5.3	5.1	5.3	5.9	5.5
Rural - Rurale	C	8 521	9 482	9 321	6 771	7 991	3.1	3.5	3.4	2.4	2.8
Greenland - Groenland											
Total	C	412	475	466	440	451	7.3	8.3	8.2	7.7	8.0
Urban - Urbaine	C	340	...	...	...	...	7.3	...	...	...	...
Rural - Rurale	C	72	...	...	...	...	7.2	...	...	...	...
Guadeloupe[4]											
Total	C	2 636	2 676	2 904	2 902	2 769	6.0	6.0	6.5	6.3	6.9
Guatemala											
Total	C	66 695	66 991	71 039	69 756	...	5.5	5.4	5.6	5.4	...
Urban - Urbaine	C	...	...	38 444	38 897	...	...	...	...	...	...
Rural - Rurale	C	...	...	32 595	30 859	...	...	...	...	...	...
Haiti - Haïti[9]											
Total	U	8 011	...	...	...	...	...	...	...	...	...
Honduras											
Total	+U	34 754	35 075	35 356	35 682	...	...	...	...	...	...
Urban - Urbaine	+U	13 459	13 867	14 251	14 654	...	...	...	...	...	...
Rural - Rurale	+U	21 295	21 208	21 105	21 028	...	...	...	...	...	...
Jamaica - Jamaïque[10]											
Total	U	16 699	16 905	17 552	16 317	17 048	...	...	...	...	...
Martinique[4]											
Total	C	2 727	2 647	2 610	2 663	2 830	7.0	6.7	6.6	6.7	7.1
Urban - Urbaine	C	2 380	2 289	2 259	2 291	2 482	...	...	...	...	...
Rural - Rurale	C	347	358	351	372	348	...	...	...	...	...
Mexico - Mexique[11]											
Total	+C	470 692	472 273	493 957	493 296	513 122	4.6	4.6	4.8	4.7	4.9
Urban - Urbaine[8]	+C	354 633	353 951	370 267	370 811	384 724	4.6	4.5	4.7	4.6	4.7
Rural - Rurale[8]	+C	109 167	110 999	116 657	116 393	121 743	4.4	4.5	4.8	4.8	5.1
Montserrat											
Total	+C	55	56	59	47	44	12.3	12.0	12.3	10.1	9.1
Netherlands Antilles - Antilles néerlandaises[11]											
Total	C	1 374	1 413	1 304	1 327	1 339	7.8	7.9	7.1	7.0	6.9
Nicaragua											
Total	+U	15 379	15 821	16 770	16 595	17 288	...	...	...	...	...
Urban - Urbaine	+U	10 180	10 957	10 931	11 129	11 456	...	...	...	...	...
Rural - Rurale	+U	5 199	4 864	5 839	5 466	5 832	...	...	...	...	...
Panama											
Total	U	13 248	13 475	14 180	14 358	14 775	...	...	...	...	...
Urban - Urbaine	U	8 638	8 945	9 358	9 396	9 768	...	...	...	...	...
Rural - Rurale	U	4 610	4 530	4 822	4 962	5 007	...	...	...	...	...
Puerto Rico - Porto Rico											
Total	C	28 356	29 066	29 702	28 589	...	7.3	7.5	7.6	7.3	...
Urban - Urbaine[8]	C	15 038	15 627	16 000	...	...	...	...	...	...	...
Rural - Rurale[8]	C	13 283	13 423	13 617	...	...	...	...	...	...	...
Saint Lucia - Sainte-Lucie											
Total	C	1 046	1 114	*1 107	...	...	6.5	6.9	*6.7	...	...
Saint Vincent and the Grenadines - Saint-Vincent-et-les Grenadines											
Total	+C	790	812	813	...	...	7.5	7.8	7.8	...	...

Continent, country or area, and urban/rural residence / Continent, pays ou zone et résidence, urbaine/rurale	Code[a]	Number - Nombre					Rate - Taux				
		2003	2004	2005	2006	2007	2003	2004	2005	2006	2007
AMERICA, NORTH - AMÉRIQUE DU NORD											
Trinidad and Tobago - Trinité-et-Tobago											
Total	C	10 206	9 872	9 885	...	...	8.0	7.6	7.6	...	...
Turks and Caicos Islands - Îles Turques et Caïques											
Total	C	61	46	53	73	114	2.4	1.7	1.7	2.2	3.3
United States of America - États-Unis d'Amérique											
Total	C	2 448 288	2 397 615	2 448 017	2 426 264		8.4	8.2	8.3	8.1	...
United States Virgin Islands - Îles Vierges américaines											
Total	C	615	628	674	629	727	5.6	5.7	6.1	5.7	6.6
AMERICA, SOUTH - AMÉRIQUE DU SUD											
Argentina - Argentine											
Total	C	302 064	294 051	293 529	292 313	315 852	8.0	7.7	7.6	7.5	8.0
Bolivia (Plurinational State of) - Bolivie (État plurinational de)[12]											
Total	U	27 589	27 942	27 129	*25 954	*21 846	...	...	...	...	...
Brazil - Brésil[13]											
Total	U	977 717	998 725	979 854	1 023 545	1 032 450	...	...	...	...	...
Chile - Chili											
Total	C	83 672	86 138	86 102	85 639	...	5.3	5.4	5.3	5.2	...
Urban - Urbaine	C	72 647	74 920	73 900	73 406	...	5.3	5.4	5.2	5.1	...
Rural - Rurale	C	11 025	11 218	12 202	12 233	...	5.2	5.3	5.7	5.7	...
Colombia - Colombie											
Total	U	192 121	188 933	189 022	192 814	*184 530	...	...	...	...	...
Urban - Urbaine[8]	U	144 707	144 135	146 173	148 690	*143 402	...	...	...	...	...
Rural - Rurale[8]	U	37 785	36 720	36 123	37 445	*35 149	...	...	...	...	...
Ecuador - Équateur[14]											
Total	U	53 521	54 729	56 825	57 940	58 016	...	...	...	...	...
Urban - Urbaine	U	40 585	41 783	43 406	43 038	44 644	...	...	...	...	...
Rural - Rurale	U	12 936	12 946	13 419	14 902	13 372	...	...	...	...	...
Falkland Islands (Malvinas) - Îles Falkland (Malvinas)											
Total	+C	20	15	19	20		...	...	...	...	...
French Guiana - Guyane française[4]											
Total	C	721	719	705	711	690	4.0	3.8	3.5	3.6	3.2
Urban - Urbaine	C	590	580	563	552	567	...	...	...	...	...
Rural - Rurale	C	131	139	142	159	123	...	...	...	...	...
Guyana											
Total	+C	4 986	5 141	5 259	5 031	5 066	6.6	6.8	6.9	6.6	6.6
Paraguay											
Total	U	19 593	20 283	17 360	19 298		...	...	...	...	...
Peru - Pérou[12]											
Total	+U	84 265	87 189	88 704	82 620		...	...	...	...	...
Suriname[15]											
Total	C	3 154	3 319	3 392	3 247	3 374	6.5	6.8	6.8	6.4	6.6
Urban - Urbaine[16]	C	2 166	2 298	2 308	2 205	2 334	...	...	...	...	...
Rural - Rurale[16]	C	988	1 021	1 084	1 042	1 040	...	...	...	...	...
Uruguay											
Total	C	32 587	32 222	32 319	31 056	33 706	9.9	9.8	9.8	9.4	10.1
Venezuela (Bolivarian Republic of) - Venezuela (République bolivarienne du)[13]											
Total	C	118 562	110 946	110 301	115 348	118 594	4.6	4.2	4.2	4.3	4.3

Continent, country or area, and urban/rural residence / Continent, pays ou zone et résidence, urbaine/rurale	Code[a]	Number - Nombre					Rate - Taux				
		2003	2004	2005	2006	2007	2003	2004	2005	2006	2007
ASIA - ASIE											
Armenia - Arménie[17]							8.1	8.0	8.2	8.4	8.3
Total	C	26 014	25 679	26 379	27 202	26 830	8.2	8.0	8.3	8.6	8.3
Urban - Urbaine	C	16 870	16 531	17 128	17 689	17 213	8.0	7.9	8.0	8.2	8.3
Rural - Rurale	C	9 144	9 148	9 251	9 513	9 617					
Azerbaijan - Azerbaïdjan[17]							6.0	6.0	6.2	6.2	6.3
Total	+C	49 001	49 568	51 962	52 248	53 655	5.9	6.0	6.3	6.3	6.4
Urban - Urbaine	+C	24 999	25 867	27 347	27 581	28 162	6.0	5.9	6.1	6.0	6.1
Rural - Rurale	+C	24 002	23 701	24 615	24 667	25 493					
Bahrain - Bahreïn							2.8	2.7	2.5	2.4	2.2
Total	C	2 114	2 215	2 222	2 317	2 270					
Bangladesh[18]							5.9	5.8	5.8	5.6	6.2
Total	I	...	...	...	...	...	4.7	4.4	4.9	4.4	5.1
Urban - Urbaine	I	...	...	...	...	...	6.2	6.1	6.1	6.0	6.6
Rural - Rurale	I	...	...	...	...	...					
Bhutan - Bhoutan[19]							...	...	7.1	...	...
Total	I	...	...	4 498	...	...	...	...	...	...	...
Urban - Urbaine	I	...	...	1 048	...	...	...	...	...	...	...
Rural - Rurale	I	...	...	3 450	...	...					
Brunei Darussalam - Brunéi Darussalam							2.9	2.8	2.9	2.9	3.0
Total	+C	1 010	1 010	1 072	1 095	1 174					
Cambodia - Cambodge							...	...	...	...	...
Total	U	*124 981*	*124 391*	...	...	...					
China - Chine[20]							6.4	6.4	6.5	6.8	6.9
Total	I	8 250 000[21]	8 320 000[21]	8 490 000[22]	8 920 000[21]	9 130 000[21]					
China, Hong Kong SAR - Chine, Hong Kong RAS							5.5	5.4	5.7	*5.5	*5.7
Total	C	36 971	36 918	38 830	*37 457	*39 476					
China, Macao SAR - Chine, Macao RAS							3.3	3.4	3.4	3.1	2.9
Total	C	1 474	1 533	1 615	1 566	1 545					
Cyprus - Chypre[23]							7.2	7.1	7.2	6.7	6.9
Total	C	5 200	5 225	5 425	5 127	5 391					
Georgia - Géorgie[17]							10.6	11.3	9.3	9.6	9.4
Total	C	46 055	48 793	40 721	42 255	41 178	12.8	13.1	11.6	11.8	11.4
Urban - Urbaine	C	28 887	29 540	26 577	27 267	26 387	8.3	9.3	6.8	7.2	7.1
Rural - Rurale	C	17 168	19 253	14 144	14 988	14 791					
India - Inde[24]							8.0	7.5	7.6	7.5	7.4
Total	I	...	...	...	...	...	6.0	5.8	6.0	6.0	6.0
Urban - Urbaine	I	...	...	...	...	...	8.7	8.2	8.1	8.1	8.0
Rural - Rurale	I	...	...	...	...	...					
Iran (Islamic Republic of) - Iran (République islamique d')[25]							5.5	5.2	5.2	5.8	5.8
Total	C	368 518	355 213	361 326	408 566	412 735	5.9	5.2	5.1	...	5.3
Urban - Urbaine	C	265 239	240 872	238 235	257 436	260 855	4.6	5.1	5.5	...	6.9
Rural - Rurale	C	103 279	114 341	123 091	151 130	151 880					
Iraq							...	...	...	...	...
Total	U	*95 935	*101 820	*115 775	*211 757	...					
Israel - Israël[26]							5.8	5.6	5.6	5.5	5.5
Total	C	38 499[27]	37 938[28]	39 047	38 776	39 836	5.9	5.7	5.8	5.6	5.7
Urban - Urbaine	C	36 086[8]	35 526[8]	36 656	36 473[8]	37 440[8]	4.2	4.1	4.2	4.0	4.1
Rural - Rurale	C	2 407[8]	2 411[8]	2 374	2 300[8]	2 390[8]					
Japan - Japon[29]							8.0	8.1	8.6	8.6	8.8
Total	C	1 014 951	1 028 602	1 083 796	1 084 450	1 108 334	...	...	...	...	...
Urban - Urbaine[8]	C	750 810	773 413	877 007	936 383	964 905	...	...	...	...	...
Rural - Rurale[8]	C	261 979	253 197	204 723	146 174	141 514					
Jordan - Jordanie[30]							...	...	...	...	...
Total	U	16 937	17 011	17 883	20 397	20 924					
Kazakhstan[17]							10.4	10.1	10.4	10.3	10.2
Total	C	155 277	152 250	157 121	157 210	158 297	11.7	11.4	11.6	11.5	11.3
Urban - Urbaine	C	99 595	98 025	100 651	100 526	92 385	8.7	8.4	8.7	8.7	9.0
Rural - Rurale	C	55 682	54 225	56 470	56 684	65 912					
Kuwait - Koweït							2.1	2.2	2.1	2.3	2.2
Total	C	4 424	4 793	4 784	5 247	5 293					

18. Deaths and crude death rates, by urban/rural residence: 2003 - 2007
Décès et taux bruts de mortalité, selon la résidence, urbaine/rurale: 2003 - 2007 (continued - suite)

Continent, country or area, and urban/rural residence — Continent, pays ou zone et résidence, urbaine/rurale	Code[a]	Number - Nombre					Rate - Taux				
		2003	2004	2005	2006	2007	2003	2004	2005	2006	2007
ASIA - ASIE											
Kyrgyzstan - Kirghizstan											
Total	C	35 941	35 061	36 992	38 566	38 180	7.1	6.9	7.2	7.4	7.3
Urban - Urbaine	C	13 943	14 108	14 526	14 930	14 744	7.8	7.8	7.9	8.1	8.0
Rural - Rurale	C	21 998	20 953	22 466	23 636	23 436	6.8	6.4	6.8	7.0	6.9
Lebanon - Liban											
Total	C	17 187	17 774	18 012	18 787	21 092	...	4.7	...	...	5.6
Malaysia - Malaisie											
Total	C	111 644	112 700	113 714	115 084	*116 672	4.5	4.4	4.4	4.3	*4.3
Urban - Urbaine	C	64 306	66 257	66 775	67 759	...	4.1	4.1	4.1	4.0	...
Rural - Rurale	C	47 338	46 443	46 939	47 325	...	5.1	4.9	4.9	4.8	...
Maldives											
Total	C	1 030	1 015	1 027	1 084	1 119	3.6	3.5	3.5	3.6	3.7
Urban - Urbaine	C	297	294	327	354	372	3.8	3.7	...	...	...
Rural - Rurale	C	733	721	700	730	747	3.5	3.4	...	...	...
Mongolia - Mongolie											
Total	C	16 006	16 404	16 480	16 682	16 259	6.4	6.5	6.5	6.5	6.2
Urban - Urbaine	C	9 480	10 183	10 148	10 811	10 498	6.6	6.9	6.7	6.9	6.6
Rural - Rurale	C	6 526	6 221	6 332	5 871	5 761	6.2	6.0	6.2	5.8	5.6
Myanmar											
Total	U	197 716	230 683	242 549	...	...	...	...	...	...	...
Urban - Urbaine	U	64 428	66 325	67 344	...	...	...	...	...	...	...
Rural - Rurale	U	133 288	164 358	175 205	...	...	...	...	...	...	...
Occupied Palestinian Territory - Territoire palestinien occupé											
Total	U	10 207	10 029	9 645	9 938	9 887		...	...	...	...
Oman											
Total	U	2 701[31]	2 743[31]	2 849[31]	3 027[31]	6 449[32]	...	...	...	...	...
Pakistan[33]											
Total	I	970 428[34]	...	1 019 467[35]	...	...	6.5	...	6.6	...	...
Urban - Urbaine	I	309 451[34]	...	321 394[35]	...	...	6.3	...	6.1	...	...
Rural - Rurale	I	660 977[34]	...	698 073[35]	...	...	6.7	...	6.9	...	...
Philippines											
Total	C	396 331	403 191	426 054			4.9	4.9	5.1	...	...
Qatar											
Total	C	1 311	1 341	1 545	1 750	1 776	1.8	1.8	1.7	1.7	1.4
Republic of Korea - République de Corée[36]											
Total[37]	C	245 817	245 771	245 511	243 934	*244 874	5.1	5.1	5.0	5.0	*5.1
Urban - Urbaine	C	156 802	158 419	159 797	159 877	...	4.1	4.1	4.1	4.1	...
Rural - Rurale	C	87 661	85 774	84 089	82 391	...	8.9	8.8	8.7	8.7	...
Saudi Arabia - Arabie saoudite											
Total	...		89 976	91 243	92 487	93 752	...	...	...	...	...
Singapore - Singapour											
Total	+C	16 036	15 860	16 215	16 393	17 140	3.9	3.8	3.8	3.7	3.7
Sri Lanka											
Total	+C	114 310	112 568	129 822	115 424	116 883	5.9	5.8	6.6	5.8	5.8
Syrian Arab Republic - République arabe syrienne[38]											
Total	U	62 880	68 551	73 928	72 534	76 064	...	...	...	...	...
Tajikistan - Tadjikistan[17]											
Total	U	26 785	26 770	28 913	29 366	30 332	...	...	...	...	...
Urban - Urbaine	U	8 425	8 647	8 917	9 308	9 464	...	...	...	...	...
Rural - Rurale	U	18 360	18 123	19 996	20 058	20 868	...	...	...	...	...
Thailand - Thaïlande											
Total	+U	384 131	393 592	395 374	391 126	393 255	...	...	...	...	...
Turkey - Turquie[39]											
Total	I	430 000	433 000	436 000	440 000	447 000	6.1	6.1	6.1	6.0	6.1
United Arab Emirates - Émirats arabes unis											
Total	...	6 002	6 123	6 361	6 563		...	...	...	...	...
Viet Nam											
Total	C	372 721	351 801	336 405	334 432	382 624	4.6	4.3	4.0	4.0	4.5
Urban - Urbaine	C	90 649	82 477	78 815	82 499	93 222	4.3	3.8	3.5	3.6	4.5
Rural - Rurale	C	282 072	269 324	257 590	251 933	289 402	4.7	4.5	4.2	4.1	4.7

Continent, country or area, and urban/rural residence / Continent, pays ou zone et résidence, urbaine/rurale	Code[a]	Number - Nombre					Rate - Taux				
		2003	2004	2005	2006	2007	2003	2004	2005	2006	2007
ASIA - ASIE											
Yemen - Yémen											
Total	U	20 346	22 255	20 451	21 456	24 449	...	...	...	...	...
EUROPE											
Åland Islands - Îles d'Åland[40]											
Total	C	268	262	259	257	249	10.2	9.9	9.7	9.6	9.2
Urban - Urbaine	C	102	109	110	91	108	9.6	10.2	10.2	8.4	9.9
Rural - Rurale	C	166	153	149	166	141	10.6	9.7	9.4	10.3	8.7
Albania - Albanie											
Total	C	17 967	17 749	17 427	16 935	14 528	5.8	5.7	5.5	5.4	4.6
Urban - Urbaine	C	8 923	9 248	7 040	...	...	6.5	6.6	4.8	...	...
Rural - Rurale	C	9 044	8 501	10 387	...	...	5.2	4.9	6.2	...	...
Andorra - Andorre											
Total	C	221	281	276	260	230	3.2	3.8	3.5	3.2	2.8
Austria - Autriche											
Total	C	77 209	74 292	75 189	74 295	74 625	9.5	9.1	9.1	9.0	9.0
Belarus - Bélarus[17]											
Total	C	143 200	140 064	141 857	138 426	132 993	14.5	14.3	14.5	14.2	13.7
Urban - Urbaine	C	75 420	74 486	76 452	75 437	74 017	10.7	10.6	10.8	10.7	10.4
Rural - Rurale	C	67 780	65 578	65 405	62 989	58 976	23.9	23.6	24.1	23.6	22.6
Belgium - Belgique[41]											
Total	C	107 039	101 946	103 278	101 587	100 658	10.3	9.8	9.9	9.6	9.5
Urban - Urbaine	C	105 406	100 446	101 708	100 118	99 118	10.3	9.8	9.9	9.6	9.5
Rural - Rurale	C	1 633	1 500	1 570	1 469	1 540	10.9	10.0	10.4	9.7	10.0
Bosnia and Herzegovina - Bosnie-Herzégovine											
Total	C	31 757	32 616	34 402	33 221	35 044	8.3	8.5	9.0	8.6	...
Bulgaria - Bulgarie											
Total	C	111 927	110 110	113 374	113 438	113 004	14.3	14.2	14.6	14.7	14.8
Urban - Urbaine	C	64 495	64 638	65 309	66 352	66 486	11.8	11.9	12.0	12.2	12.3
Rural - Rurale	C	47 432	45 472	48 065	47 086	46 518	20.1	19.4	20.8	20.7	20.7
Croatia - Croatie											
Total	C	52 575	49 756	51 790	50 378	52 367	11.8	11.2	11.7	11.3	11.8
Urban - Urbaine	C	25 976	24 418	25 899	25 144	26 241	...	...	...	...	...
Rural - Rurale	C	26 599	25 338	25 891	25 234	26 126	...	...	...	...	...
Czech Republic - République tchèque											
Total	C	111 288	107 177	107 938	104 441	104 636	10.9	10.5	10.5	10.2	10.1
Urban - Urbaine	C	80 561	77 674	78 141	75 900	76 441	10.7	10.3	10.3	10.0	10.0
Rural - Rurale	C	30 727	29 503	29 797	28 541	28 195	11.5	11.0	11.1	10.5	10.3
Denmark - Danemark[42]											
Total	C	57 574	55 806	54 962	55 477	55 604	10.7	10.3	10.1	10.2	10.2
Estonia - Estonie											
Total	C	18 152	17 685	17 316	17 316	17 409	13.4	13.1	12.9	12.9	13.0
Urban - Urbaine[8]	C	12 106	11 937	11 587	11 500	11 611	12.9	12.8	12.4	12.3	12.5
Rural - Rurale[8]	C	6 037	5 745	5 728	5 816	5 797	14.5	13.9	13.9	14.1	14.1
Faeroe Islands - Îles Féroé											
Total	C	404	379	419	416	383	8.4	7.9	8.7	8.6	7.9
Finland - Finlande[43]											
Total	C	48 996	47 600	47 928	48 065	49 077	9.4	9.1	9.1	9.1	9.3
Urban - Urbaine	C	27 156	26 715	27 009	27 199	28 296	8.4	8.2	8.2	8.2	8.2
Rural - Rurale	C	21 840	20 885	20 919	20 866	20 781	11.0	10.5	10.7	10.7	11.2
France[44]											
Total	C	552 339	509 429	527 533	516 416	*516 000	9.2	8.4	8.6	8.4	*8.4
Urban - Urbaine[45]	C	393 958	360 779	373 576	366 641	...	...	...	...	...	...
Rural - Rurale[45]	C	156 493	146 823	152 218	148 125	...	...	...	...	...	...
Germany - Allemagne											
Total	C	853 946	818 271	830 227	821 627	827 155	10.3	9.9	10.1	10.0	10.1
Gibraltar[46]											
Total	C	234	242	249	230	...	8.2	8.4	8.6	7.9	...
Greece - Grèce											
Total	C	105 529	104 942	105 091	105 476	109 895	9.6	9.5	9.5	9.5	9.8
Urban - Urbaine	C	58 197	58 300	58 022	57 700	60 765	...	...	...	...	...
Rural - Rurale	C	47 332	46 642	47 069	47 776	49 130	...	...	...	...	...

18. Deaths and crude death rates, by urban/rural residence: 2003 - 2007
Décès et taux bruts de mortalité, selon la résidence, urbaine/rurale: 2003 - 2007 (continued - suite)

Continent, country or area, and urban/rural residence / Continent, pays ou zone et résidence, urbaine/rurale	Code[a]	Number - Nombre					Rate - Taux				
		2003	2004	2005	2006	2007	2003	2004	2005	2006	2007
EUROPE											
Guernsey - Guernesey											
Total	C	564	537	525	498	513	...	8.9	...	8.2	8.3
Hungary - Hongrie											
Total	C	135 823	132 492	135 732	131 603	132 938	13.4	13.1	13.5	13.1	13.2
Urban - Urbaine[47]	C	84 106	82 363	85 546	84 656	85 832	12.8	12.5	12.8	12.5	12.7
Rural - Rurale[47]	C	51 086	49 473	49 479	46 233	46 475	14.3	14.0	14.5	13.9	14.0
Iceland - Islande											
Total	C	1 827	1 824	1 838	1 903	1 942	6.3	6.2	6.2	6.3	6.2
Urban - Urbaine	C	1 676	1 672	1 693	1 750	1 806	6.3	6.2	6.2	6.2	6.2
Rural - Rurale	C	151	152	145	153	136	7.1	7.0	7.0	6.8	6.1
Ireland - Irlande											
Total[48]	C	29 074	28 665	28 260	...	...	7.3	7.1	6.8	...	...
Total	+C	...	...	...	*27 479	*28 050	...	...	...	*6.5	*6.5
Isle of Man - Île de Man											
Total	+C	852	798	775	768	789	11.0	10.3	9.8	9.6	9.8
Italy - Italie											
Total	C	588 897	545 050	568 328	*560 875	*573 026	10.2	9.4	9.7	*9.5	*9.7
Jersey											
Total	+C	768	745	761	758	708	8.8	8.5	8.6	8.5	7.9
Latvia - Lettonie											
Total	C	32 437	32 024	32 777	33 098	33 042	13.9	13.8	14.2	14.5	14.5
Urban - Urbaine	C	21 038	20 814	21 186	21 535	21 555	13.3	13.3	13.6	13.9	13.9
Rural - Rurale	C	11 399	11 210	11 591	11 563	11 487	15.2	15.1	15.7	15.8	15.7
Liechtenstein											
Total	C	217	198	215	220	*227	6.4	5.7	6.2	6.3	*6.4
Lithuania - Lituanie											
Total	C	40 990	41 340	43 799	44 813	45 624	11.9	12.0	12.8	13.2	13.5
Urban - Urbaine	C	23 082	23 550	25 067	26 194	26 796	10.0	10.3	11.0	11.6	11.9
Rural - Rurale	C	17 908	17 790	18 732	18 619	18 828	15.6	15.5	16.4	16.5	16.8
Luxembourg											
Total	C	4 053	3 578	3 621	3 766	3 866	9.0	7.8	7.8	8.0	8.1
Malta - Malte											
Total	C	3 164	2 999	3 130	3 216	3 111	7.9	7.5	7.8	7.9	7.6
Monaco											
Total	C	617	525	601	535[49]	...	...	...	...	...	...
Montenegro - Monténégro											
Total	C	5 704	5 707	5 839	5 968	5 979	9.2	9.2	9.4	9.6	9.5
Urban - Urbaine	C	3 798	3 585	3 571	...	...	9.9	9.3	9.2	...	...
Rural - Rurale	C	1 906	2 122	2 268	...	...	8.1	9.0	9.7	...	...
Netherlands - Pays-Bas[50]											
Total	C	141 936	136 553	136 402	135 372	133 022	8.7	8.4	8.4	8.3	8.1
Urban - Urbaine	C	94 744	91 388	91 282	90 611	89 272	9.0	8.6	8.5	8.4	8.2
Rural - Rurale	C	47 192	45 165	45 120	44 761	43 750	8.3	8.1	8.1	8.1	7.9
Norway - Norvège[51]											
Total	C	42 478	41 200	41 232	41 253	41 954	9.3	9.0	8.9	8.9	8.9
Poland - Pologne											
Total	C	365 230	363 522	368 285	369 686	377 226	9.6	9.5	9.7	9.7	9.9
Urban - Urbaine	C	216 349	216 515	219 403	222 219	226 495	9.2	9.2	9.4	9.5	9.7
Rural - Rurale	C	148 881	147 007	148 882	147 467	150 731	10.2	10.0	10.1	10.0	10.2
Portugal[11]											
Total	C	108 795	102 010	107 462	101 990	103 512	10.4	9.7	10.2	9.6	9.8
Republic of Moldova - République de Moldova[52]											
Total	C	43 079	41 668	44 689	43 137	43 050	11.9	11.6	12.4	12.0	12.0
Urban - Urbaine	C	13 650	13 319	14 199	13 764	13 855	9.2	9.0	9.6	9.3	9.4
Rural - Rurale	C	29 429	28 349	30 490	29 373	29 195	13.8	13.3	14.4	14.0	13.9
Romania - Roumanie											
Total	C	266 575	258 890	262 101	258 094	251 965	12.3	11.9	12.1	12.0	11.7
Urban - Urbaine	C	112 283	114 316	116 809	116 384	114 562	9.7	9.6	9.8	9.8	9.6
Rural - Rurale	C	154 292	144 574	145 292	141 710	137 403	15.2	14.8	14.9	14.7	14.2
Russian Federation - Fédération de Russie[17]											
Total	C	2 365 826	2 295 402	2 303 935	2 166 703	2 080 445	16.4	16.0	16.1	15.2	14.6
Urban - Urbaine	C	1 657 569	1 606 894	1 595 762	1 501 245	1 445 411	15.6	15.3	15.3	14.4	13.9
Rural - Rurale	C	708 257	688 508	708 173	665 458	635 034	18.4	17.9	18.3	17.3	16.6
San Marino - Saint-Marin											
Total	+C	216	185	219	225	225	7.5	6.3	7.1	7.2	7.1

18. Deaths and crude death rates, by urban/rural residence: 2003 - 2007
Décès et taux bruts de mortalité, selon la résidence, urbaine/rurale: 2003 - 2007 (continued - suite)

Continent, country or area, and urban/rural residence / Continent, pays ou zone et résidence, urbaine/rurale	Co-de[a]	Number - Nombre					Rate - Taux				
		2003	2004	2005	2006	2007	2003	2004	2005	2006	2007
EUROPE											
Serbia - Serbie[53]											
Total.	+C	103 946	104 320	106 771	102 884	102 805	13.9	14.0	14.3	13.9	13.9
Urban - Urbaine	+C	51 817	52 701	54 937	53 073	53 469	12.2	12.4	12.9	12.4	12.5
Rural - Rurale	+C	52 129	51 619	51 834	49 811	49 336	16.1	16.1	16.3	15.8	15.9
Slovakia - Slovaquie											
Total.	C	52 230	51 852	53 475	53 301	53 856	9.7	9.6	9.9	9.9	10.0
Urban - Urbaine	C	25 272	25 041	26 111	26 157	26 347	8.4	8.4	8.7	8.7	8.8
Rural - Rurale	C	26 958	26 811	27 364	27 144	27 509	11.3	11.2	11.4	11.3	11.4
Slovenia - Slovénie											
Total.	C	19 451	18 523	18 825	18 180	18 584	9.7	9.3	9.4	9.1	9.2
Urban - Urbaine	C	8 983	8 725	8 791	8 571	8 336	9.2	9.0	9.1	8.9	8.3
Rural - Rurale	C	10 468	9 798	10 034	9 609	10 248	10.7	10.0	10.2	9.7	10.1
Spain - Espagne											
Total.	C	384 828	371 934	387 355	371 267	385 122	9.2	8.7	8.9	8.4	8.6
Sweden - Suède											
Total.	C	92 961	90 532	91 710	91 177	91 729	10.4	10.1	10.2	10.0	10.0
Switzerland - Suisse											
Total.	C	63 070	60 180	61 124	60 283	61 089	8.6	8.1	8.2	8.1	8.1
Urban - Urbaine	C	46 125	43 993	44 575	44 255	44 559	8.6	8.1	8.2	8.1	8.0
Rural - Rurale	C	16 945	16 187	16 549	16 028	16 530	8.6	8.2	8.3	8.0	8.2
The Former Yugoslav Republic of Macedonia - L'ex-République yougoslave de Macédoine											
Total.	C	18 006	17 944	18 406	18 630	19 594	8.9	8.8	9.0	9.1	9.6
Urban - Urbaine	C	10 597	...	10 645	10 931	11 517	...	...	...	...	...
Rural - Rurale	C	7 409	...	7 761	7 699	8 077	...	...	...	...	...
Ukraine											
Total.	C	765 408[17]	761 261[17]	781 961[17]	758 092[54]	762 877[54]	16.0	16.1	16.6	16.2	16.4
Urban - Urbaine	C	459 965[17]	460 492[17]	471 561[17]	461 774[54]	466 253[54]	14.4	...	...	...	14.7
Rural - Rurale	C	305 443[17]	300 769[17]	310 400[17]	296 318[54]	296 624[54]	19.5	...	...	...	19.9
United Kingdom of Great Britain and Northern Ireland - Royaume-Uni de Grande-Bretagne et d'Irlande du Nord[55]											
Total.	C	*611 188	*584 600	*582 900	*572 200	...	*10.3	*9.8	*9.7	*9.4	...
OCEANIA - OCÉANIE											
American Samoa - Samoas américaines											
Total.	C	257	289	279	267	...	4.1	4.5	4.3	4.0	...
Australia - Australie[56]											
Total.	+C	131 848	132 051	130 274	133 273	137 372	6.6	6.6	6.4	6.4	6.5
Urban - Urbaine	+C	103 848	104 106	102 650	104 889	108 460	6.4	6.3	6.2	6.2	6.3
Rural - Rurale	+C	28 000	27 945	27 624	28 384	28 912	7.5	7.5	7.3	7.5	7.5
Cook Islands - Îles Cook[57]											
Total.	+C	87	99	91	*85	*82	4.7	4.9	4.5	*4.1	*3.9
Fiji - Fidji											
Total.	+C	5 068	5 628	...	...	...	6.2	6.9	...	...	...
Urban - Urbaine	+C	3 211	...	...	...	...	...	...	...	...	...
Rural - Rurale	+C	1 857	...	...	...	...	...	...	...	...	...
French Polynesia - Polynésie française											
Total.	C	1 122	1 131	1 239	1 152	1 215	4.5	4.5	4.9	4.5	4.7
Guam[58]											
Total.	C	700	691	*697	*682	*786	4.2	4.2	*4.1	*4.0	*4.5
Marshall Islands - Îles Marshall											
Total.	+U	306	263	302	318		...	...	...	...	...
Micronesia (Federated States of) - Micronésie (États fédérés de)											
Total.	U	427	...	...	...	...	...	...	...	...	...

18. Deaths and crude death rates, by urban/rural residence: 2003 - 2007
Décès et taux bruts de mortalité, selon la résidence, urbaine/rurale: 2003 - 2007 (continued - suite)

Continent, country or area, and urban/rural residence / Continent, pays ou zone et résidence, urbaine/rurale	Code[a]	Number - Nombre					Rate - Taux				
		2003	2004	2005	2006	2007	2003	2004	2005	2006	2007
OCEANIA - OCÉANIE											
New Caledonia - Nouvelle-Calédonie											
Total	C	1 121	1 100	1 139	1 115	1 207	5.0	4.8	4.9	4.7	5.0
Urban - Urbaine	C	...	...	...	...	664	...	...	...	...	...
Rural - Rurale	C	...	...	...	...	543	...	...	...	...	...
New Zealand - Nouvelle-Zélande[11]											
Total	+C	28 010	28 419	27 034	28 245	28 522	7.0	7.0	6.5	6.7	6.7
Urban - Urbaine[8]	+C	25 279	25 684	24 275	25 398	25 588	7.3	7.3	6.8	7.0	7.0
Rural - Rurale[8]	+C	2 654	2 653	2 628	2 711	2 801	4.7	4.7	4.6	4.7	4.8
Niue - Nioué[59]											
Total	C	16	18	15	19	9					
Northern Mariana Islands - Îles Mariannes septentrionales											
Total	U	*144*	*165*	*189*	*174*	*140*	...	...	...	...	...
Palau - Palaos											
Total	C	136	142	134	144	...	6.7	6.9	6.7	6.6	...
Papua New Guinea - Papouasie-Nouvelle-Guinée											
Total	U	*7 054*	...	...	...	...	...	...	...	...	...
Pitcairn											
Total	C	...	...	...	...	1					
Samoa											
Total	U	*551	*547	...	...	...	...	...	...	...	...
Tonga											
Total	+C	617	559	543	...	...	6.1	5.5	5.3	...	...
Total[60]	I	...	...	...	709	...	...	...	...	6.9	...
Tuvalu											
Total	U	*83*	*89*	*64*	*31*	...	...	...	...	...	...
Wallis and Futuna Islands - Îles Wallis et Futuna											
Total	C	88	72	65	77	...	5.9	...	...	...	...

FOOTNOTES - NOTES

Italics: data from civil registers which are incomplete or of unknown completeness. -
Italiques: données incomplètes ou dont le degré d'exactitude n'est pas connu, provenant des registres de l'état civil.

* Provisional. -
Données provisoires.

[a] 'Code' indicates the source of data, as follows:
C - Civil registration, estimated over 90% complete
U - Civil registration, estimated less than 90% complete
I - Other source, estimated reliable
+ - Data tabulated by date of registration rather than occurence.
... - Information not available

Le 'Code' indique la source des données, comme suit:
C - Registres de l'état civil considérés complets à 90 p. 100 au moins.
U - Registres de l'état civil qui ne sont pas considérés complets à 90 p. 100 au moins.
I - Autre source, considérée pas douteuses.
+ - Données exploitées selon la date de l'enregistrement et non la date de l'événement.
... - Information pas disponible.

[1] Excluding live-born infants who died before their birth was registered. Data refer to Algerian population only. - Non compris les enfants nés vivants décédés avant l'enregistrement de leur naissance. Les données ne concernent que la population algérienne.

[2] Data refer to the twelve months preceding the census in December. - Les données se rapportent aux douze mois précédant le recensement de décembre.

[3] Data refer to national projections. - Les données se réfèrent aux projections nationales.

[4] Excluding live-born infants who died before their birth was registered. - Non compris les enfants nés vivants décédés avant l'enregistrement de leur naissance.

[5] Excluding non-residents and foreign service personnel and their dependants. - À l'exclusion des non-résidents et du personnel diplomatique et de leurs charges de famille.

[6] Including Canadian residents temporarily in the United States, but excluding United States residents temporarily in Canada. - Y compris les résidents canadiens se trouvant temporairement aux Etats-Unis, mais ne comprenant pas les résidents des Etats-Unis se trouvant temporairement au Canada.

[7] Resident deaths outside the islands are excluded if they are not buried in the islands. - Les décès de résidents hors des îles ne sont pas compris s'ils ne sont pas inhumés dans les îles.

[8] The total number includes 'Unknown residence', but the categories urban and rural do not. - Le nombre total inclue 'Résidence inconnue ', mais les catégories Urbain et Rural ne l'incluent pas.

[9] Source: World Health Organization. - Source : Organisation mondiale de la santé.

[10] Data have been adjusted for undercoverage of infant deaths and sudden and violent deaths. - Ajusté pour la sous-estimation de la mortalité infantile, du nombre de morts soudaines et de morts violentes.

[11] Data refer to resident population only. - Pour la population résidante seulement.

[12] Data refer to registered events only. - Les données ne concernent que les événements enregistrés.

[13] Excluding Indian jungle population. - Non compris les Indiens de la jungle.

[14] Excluding nomadic Indian tribes. - Non compris les tribus d'Indiens nomades.

[15] Including non-residents. - Y compris les résidents.

[16] The districts of Paramaribo and Wanica are considered urban areas, whereas the rest of the districts are considered more or less rural districts (areas). - Les districts de Paramaribo et de Wanica sont considérés comme des zones urbaines, les autres districts étant considérés comme des zones rurales à divers degrés.

[17] Excluding infants born alive of less than 28 weeks' gestation, of less than 1 000 grams in weight and 35 centimeters in length, who die within seven days of birth. - Non compris les enfants nés vivants après moins de 28 semaines de gestations, pesant moins de 1 000 grammes, mesurant moins de 35 centimètres et décédés dans les sept jours qui ont suivi leur naissance.

[18] Rates were obtained by the Sample Vital Registration System of Bangladesh. - Taux obtenus au moyen du Sample Vital Registration System du Bangladesh.

[19] Data refer to the twelve months preceding the census in May. - Les données se rapportent aux douze mois précédant le recensement de mai.

[20] For statistical purposes, the data for China do not include those for the Hong Kong Special Administrative Region (Hong Kong SAR), Macao Special Administrative Region (Macao SAR) and Taiwan province of China. - Pour la présentation des statistiques, les données pour la Chine ne comprennent pas la Région Administrative Spéciale de Hong Kong (Hong Kong RAS), la Région Administrative Spéciale de Macao (Macao RAS) et Taïwan province de Chine.

[21] Data have been estimated on the basis of annual National Sample Surveys on Population Changes. - Les données ont été estimées sur la base de l'enquête annuelle "National Sample Survey on Population Changes".

[22] Data for 2005 are estimated from the National Sample Survey of 1 per cent population. - Les données pour 2005 ont été estimées à partir de l'enquête nationale qui a porté sur un échantillon de 1 % de la population.

[23] Data refer to government controlled areas. - Les données se rapportent aux zones contrôlées par le Gouvernement.

[24] Including data for the Indian-held part of Jammu and Kashmir, the final status of which has not yet been determined. Rates were obtained by the Sample Registration System of India, actually a large demographic survey. - Y compris les données pour la partie du Jammu et du Cachemire occupée par l'Inde dont le statut définitif n'a pas encore été déterminé. Les taux ont été obtenus par le Système de l'enregistrement par échantillon de l'Inde qui est une large enquête démographique.

[25] Data refer to the Iranian Year which begins on 21 March and ends on 20 March of the following year. - Les données concernent l'année iranienne, qui commence le 21 mars et se termine le 20 mars de l'année suivante.

[26] Including data for East Jerusalem and Israeli residents in certain other territories under occupation by Israeli military forces since June 1967. - Y compris les données pour Jérusalem-Est et les résidents israéliens dans certains autres territoires occupés depuis 1967 par les forces armées israéliennes.

[27] Including 182 deaths abroad of Israeli residents who were out of the country for less than a year. - Y compris les décès à l'étranger de 182 résidents israéliens qui ont quitté le pays depuis moins d'un an.

[28] Including 183 deaths abroad of Israeli residents who were out of the country for less than a year. - Y compris les décès à l'étranger de 183 résidents israéliens qui ont quitté le pays depuis moins d'un an.

[29] Data refer to Japanese nationals in Japan only. - Les données se raportent aux nationaux japonais au Japon seulement.

[30] Excluding data for Jordanian territory under occupation since June 1967 by Israeli military forces. Excluding foreigners, including registered Palestinian refugees. - Non compris les données pour le territoire jordanien occupé depuis juin 1967 par les forces armées israéliennes. Non compris les étrangers, mais y compris les réfugiés de Palestine enregistrés.

[31] Data refer to the recorded events in Ministry of Health hospitals and health centres only. - Les données se rapportent aux faits d'état civil enregistrés dans les hôpitaux et les dispensaires du Ministère de la santé seulement.

[32] Data from Births and Deaths Notification System (Ministry of Health institutions and all other health care providers). - Les données proviennent du système de notification des naissances et des décès (établissements du Ministère de la santé et tous autres prestataires de soins de santé).

[33] Excluding data for the Pakistan-held part of Jammu and Kashmir, the final status of which has not yet been determined. - Non compris les données concernant la partie du Jammu et Cachemire occupée par le Pakistan dont le statut définitif n'a pas été déterminé.

[34] Based on the results of the Pakistan Demographic Survey (PDS 2003) . - Données extraites de l'enquête démographique effectuée par le Pakistan en 2003.

[35] Based on the results of the Pakistan Demographic Survey (PDS 2005). - Données extraites de l'enquête démographique effectuée par le Pakistan en 2005.

[36] Excluding alien armed forces, civilian aliens employed by armed forces, and foreign diplomatic personnel and their dependants. - Non compris les militaires étrangers, les civils étrangers employés par les forces armées ni le personnel diplomatique étranger et les membres de leur famille les accompagnant.

[37] Including nationals outside the country. - Y compris les nationaux hors du pays.

[38] Excluding nomad population and Palestinian refugees. Excluding live-born infants who died before their birth was registered. - Non compris la population nomade et les réfugiés de Palestine. Non compris les enfants nés vivants décédés avant l'enregistrement de leur naissance.

[39] Data are estimates based on Address Based Population Registration System and other survey. - Les données sont des estimations basées sur le registre national de la population basé sur l'adresse et d'autres enquêtes.

[40] Also included in Finland. - Comprise aussi dans Finlande.

[41] Including armed forces stationed outside the country, but excluding alien armed forces stationed in the area. - Y compris les militaires nationaux hors du pays, mais non compris les militaires étrangers en garnison sur le territoire.

[42] Excluding Faeroe Islands and Greenland shown separately, if available. - Non compris les Iles Féroé et le Gröenland, qui font l'objet de rubriques distinctes, si disponible.

[43] Including nationals temporarily outside the country. Including Aland Islands. - Y compris les nationaux se trouvant temporairement hors du pays. Y compris les Îles d'Åland.

[44] Including armed forces stationed outside the country. Excluding Overseas Departments, namely, French Guiana, Guadeloupe, Martinique and Reunion, shown separately, if available. - Y compris les militaires nationaux hors du pays. Non compris les départements d'outre mer, c'est-à-dire la Guyane française, la Guadeloupe, la Martinique et la Réunion, qui font l'objet de rubriques distinctes, si disponible.

[45] Data for urban and rural, excluding nationals outside the country. - Les données pour la résidence urbaine et rurale , non compris les nationaux hors du pays.

[46] Excluding armed forces. - Non compris les militaires en garnison.

[47] Total includes the data of foreigners, persons of unknown residence and homeless, but the categories urban and rural do not. - Total incluant les étrangers, les personnes de résidence inconnue et les sans-abri, ce qui n'est pas le cas pour les catégories urbaines et rurales.

[48] Data refer to events registered within one year of occurrence. - Evénements enregistrés dans l'année qui suit l'événement.

[49] Including residents outside the country. - Y compris les résidents hors du pays.

[50] Including residents outside the country if listed in a Netherlands population register. - Y compris les résidents hors du pays, s'ils sont inscrits sur un registre de population néerlandais.

[51] Including residents temporarily outside the country. Excluding Svalbard and Jan Mayen Island shown separately, if available. - Y compris les résidents se trouvant temporairement hors du pays. Non compris Svalbard et Jan Mayen qui font l'objet de rubriques distinctes, si disponible.

[52] Excluding infants born alive of less than 28 weeks' gestation, of less than 1 000 grams in weight and 35 centimeters in length, who die within seven days of birth. Excluding Transnistria and the municipality of Bender. - Non compris les enfants nés vivants après moins de 28 semaines de gestations, pesant moins de 1 000 grammes, mesurant moins de 35 centimètres et décédés dans les sept jours qui ont suivi leur naissance. Les données ne tiennent pas compte de l'information sur la Transnistria et la municipalité de Bender.

[53] Excluding data for Kosovo and Metohia. - Sans les données pour le Kosovo et Metohie.

[54] Excluding infants born living with birth weight of less than 500grams (or if birth weight is unknown - with length of less than 25 centimeters, or with gestation period of less than 22 weeks). - Non compris les données concernant les nouveau-nés pesant moins de 500 grammes (si le pods est inconnu – mesurant moins de 25 centimètres ou après moins de 22 semaines de gestations).

[55] Excluding Channel Islands (Guernsey and Jersey) and Isle of Man, shown separately, if available. - Non compris les îles Anglo-Normandes (Guernesey et Jersey) et l'île de Man, qui font l'objet de rubriques distinctes, si disponible.

[56] Excluding data where usual residence was undefined, offshore or migratory and unknown. - En excluant les données lorsque le lieu du domicile n'est pas précisé, est à l'étranger, est mouvant ou inconnu.

[57] Excluding Niue, shown separately, which is part of Cook Islands, but because of remoteness is administered separately. - Non compris Nioué, qui fait l'objet d'une rubrique distincte et qui fait partie des îles Cook, mais qui, en raison de son éloignement, est administrée séparément.

[58] Including United States military personnel, their dependants and contract employees. - Y compris les militaires des Etats-Unis, les membres de leur famille les accompagnant et les agents contractuels des Etats-Unis.

[59] Includes deaths occurred in New Zealand but buried in Niue and deaths occurred in Niue but buried elsewhere. - Y compris les personnes décédées en Nouvelle-Zélande qui sont enterrées à Nioué et les personnes décédées à Nioué qui sont enterrées ailleurs.

[60] Estimate based on results of the population census. - Estimation fondeé sur les résultats du recensement de la population.

Table 19

Table 19 presents deaths and death rates by age and sex for latest available year between 1998 and 2007.

Description of variables: Age is defined as age at last birthday, that is, the difference between the date of birth and the date of the occurrence of the event, expressed in completed solar years. The age classification used in this table is the following: under 1 year, 1-4 years, 5-year age groups through 95-99 years, and 100 years or over.

Rate computation: Death rates specific for age and sex are the annual number of deaths in each age-sex group per 1 000 population in the same age-sex group.

Death rates by age and sex are the annual number of deaths that occurred in a specific age-sex group per 1 000 population in the corresponding age-sex group. These rates are calculated by the Statistics Division of the United Nations.

Deaths at unknown age and the population of unknown age are excluded from age-specific rate calculations but are part of the death rate for all ages combined.

Death rates for infants under one year of age in this table differ from the infant mortality rates shown elsewhere, because the latter are computed per 1 000 live births rather than per 1 000 population.

The population used in computing the rates is estimated or enumerated distributions by age and sex. First priority was given to an estimate and second priority to census returns of the year to which the deaths referred.

Rates presented in this table have been limited to those for countries or areas having at least a total of 1 000 deaths in a given year. Moreover, rates specific for individual sub-categories that are based on 30 or fewer deaths are identified by the symbol "♦".

Reliability of data: Data from civil registers of deaths that are reported as incomplete (less than 90 per cent completeness) or of unknown completeness are considered unreliable and are set in italics rather than in roman type. Table 18 and the technical notes for that table provide more detailed information on the completeness of death registration. For more information about the quality of vital statistics data in general and the information available on the basis of the completeness estimates in particular, see section 4.2 of the Introduction.

Rates are not computed if data from civil registers of deaths are reported as incomplete (less than 90 per cent completeness) or of unknown completeness, and therefore deemed unreliable.

Limitations: Statistics on deaths by age and sex are subject to the same qualifications as are set forth for vital statistics in general and death statistics in particular as discussed in section 4 of the Introduction.

The reliability of the data is an important factor in considering the limitations. In addition, some deaths are tabulated by date of registration and not by date of occurrence; these have been indicated by a plus sign "+". Whenever the lag between the date of occurrence and date of registration is prolonged and, therefore, a large proportion of the death registrations are delayed, death statistics for any given year may be seriously affected. However, delays in the registration of deaths are less common and shorter than in the registration of live births.

International comparability in mortality statistics may also be affected by the exclusion of deaths of infants who were born alive but died before the registration of the birth or within the first 24 hours of life. Statistics of this type are footnoted.

Because these statistics are classified according to age, they are subject to the limitations with respect to accuracy of age reporting similar to those already discussed in connection with section 3.1.3 of the Introduction. The factors influencing the accuracy of reporting may be somewhat dissimilar in vital statistics (because of the differences in the method of taking a census and registering a death) but, in general, the same errors can be observed.

The absence of frequencies in the unknown age group does not necessarily indicate completely accurate reporting and tabulation of the age item. It is often an indication that the unknowns have been eliminated by assigning ages to them before tabulation, or by proportionate distribution after tabulation.

International comparability of statistics on deaths by age is also affected by the use of different methods to determine age at death. If age is obtained from an item that simply requests age at death in completed years or is derived from information on year of birth and death rather than from information on complete date (day, month and year) of birth and death, the number of deaths classified in the under-one-year age group will tend to be reduced and the number of deaths in the next age group will tend to be somewhat increased. A similar bias may affect other age groups but its impact is usually negligible. Information on this factor is given in the footnotes when known.

The comparability of data by urban/rural residence is affected by the national definitions of urban and rural used in tabulating these data. It is assumed, in the absence of specific information to the contrary, that the definitions of urban and rural used in connection with the national population census were also used in the compilation of the vital statistics for each country or area. However, it cannot be excluded that, for a given country or area, different definitions of urban and rural are used for the vital statistics data and the population census data respectively. When known, the definitions of urban used in national population censuses are presented at the end of the technical notes for table 6. As discussed in detail in the technical notes for table 6, these definitions vary considerably from one country or area to another.

Limitations of rates: Rates shown in this table are subject to the same limitations that affect the corresponding frequencies and are set forth in the technical notes for table 18. These include differences in the completeness of registration, the treatment of infants who were born alive but died before the registration of their birth or within the first 24 hours of life, the method used to determine age at death and the quality of the reported information relating to age at death. In addition, some rates are based on deaths tabulated by date of registration and not by date of occurrence; these have been indicated with a plus sign "+".

The problem of obtaining precise correspondence between deaths (numerator) and population (denominator) as regards the inclusion or exclusion of armed forces, refugees, displaced persons and other special groups is particularly difficult where age-specific death rates are concerned. This is the case for Japan and Malta. For Japan, deaths refer to Japanese nationals only while the population include foreigners except foreign military and civilian personnel and their dependants stationed in the area. Similarly for Malta, deaths are for Maltese nationals only while the population include foreigners who hold work and resident permit and reside in the country. One should also note that male rates in the age range 20 to 40 years may be especially affected by this non-correspondence, and care should be exercised in using these rates for comparative purposes.

Even when deaths and population do correspond conceptually, comparability of the rates may be affected by abnormal conditions such as absence from the country or area of large numbers of young men in the military forces or working abroad as temporary workers. Death rates may appear high in the younger ages, simply because a large section of the able-bodied members of the age group, whose death rates under normal conditions might be less than the average for persons of their age, is not included.

Also, in a number of cases the rates shown here for all ages combined differ from crude death rates shown elsewhere, because in this table they are computed on the population for which an appropriate age-sex distribution was available, while the crude death rates shown elsewhere may utilize a different total population. The population by age and sex might refer to a census date within the year rather than to the mid-point, or it might be more or less inclusive as regards ethnic groups, armed forces and so forth. In a few instances, the difference is attributable to the fact that the rates in this table were computed on the mean population whereas the corresponding rates in other tables were computed on an estimate for 1 July.

In addition to problems of comparability, vital rates classified by urban/rural residence are also subject to certain special types of bias. If, when calculating vital rates, different definitions of urban are used in connection with the vital events and the population data and if this results in a net difference between the numerator and denominator of the rate in the population at risk, then the vital rates would be biased. Urban/rural differentials in vital rates may also be affected by whether the vital events have been tabulated in terms of place of occurrence or place of usual residence. This problem is discussed in more detail in section 4.1.4.1 of the Introduction.

Earlier data: Deaths by age and sex and death rates specific for age and sex have been shown for the latest available year in each issue of the Yearbook since the 1955 issue. Data included in this table update the series covering a period of years as follows:

Issue	Years Covered
Historical Supplement, CD, 1997	1948 – 1997
48th issue, 1996	1987 – 1995
44th issue, 1992	1983 – 1992
37th issue, 1985	1976 – 1984
32nd issue, 1980	1971 – 1979
Historical Supplement, 1979	1948 – 1977

Data have been presented by urban/rural residence in each regular issue of the Yearbook since the 1967 issue.

Tableau 19

Le tableau 19 présente les données les plus récentes (1998 - 2007) dont on dispose sur les décès selon l'âge et le sexe et les taux de mortalité.

Description des variables : L'âge considéré est l'âge au dernier anniversaire, c'est-à-dire la différence entre la date de naissance et la date du décès, exprimée en années solaires révolues. La classification par âge est la suivante : moins d'un an, 1 à 4 ans, groupes quinquennaux jusqu'à 95-99 ans et 100 ans et plus.

Calcul des taux : les taux de mortalité selon l'âge et le sexe représentent le nombre annuel de décès survenus pour chaque sexe et chaque groupe d'âge pour 1 000 personnes du même groupe.

Les taux de mortalité selon l'âge et le sexe représentent le nombre annuel de décès survenus dans un groupe d'âge et de sexe pour 1 000 personnes du même groupe. Ces taux ont été calculés par la Division de statistique de l'ONU.

On n'a pas tenu compte des décès à un âge inconnu ni de la population d'âge inconnu, sauf dans les taux de mortalité pour tous les âges combinés.

Il convient de noter que, dans ce tableau, les taux de mortalité des groupes de moins d'un an sont différents des taux de mortalité infantile qui figurent dans d'autres tableaux, ces derniers ayant été établis pour 1 000 naissances vivantes et non pour 1 000 habitants.

Les chiffres de population utilisés pour le calcul des taux proviennent de dénombrements ou de répartitions estimatives de la population selon l'âge et le sexe. On a utilisé de préférence les estimations de la population; à défaut, on s'est contenté des données censitaires se rapportant à l'année des décès.

Les taux présentés dans ce tableau ne se rapportent qu'aux pays ou zones où l'on a enregistré un total d'au moins 1 000 décès pendant l'année. Les taux relatifs à des sous-catégories, qui sont fondés sur 30 décès ou moins, sont signalés par le signe "♦".

Fiabilité des données : Les données sur les décès issues des registres d'état civil qui sont déclarées incomplètes (degré d'exhaustivité inférieur à 90 p.100) ou dont le degré d'exhaustivité n'est pas connu sont jugées douteuses et apparaissent en italique et non en caractères romains. Le tableau 18 et les notes techniques s'y rapportant présentent des renseignements plus détaillés sur le degré d'exhaustivité de l'enregistrement des décès. Pour plus de précisions sur la qualité des statistiques de l'état civil en général et le degré de complétude en particulier, voir la section 4.2 de l'Introduction.

On a choisi de ne pas faire figurer dans le tableau 19 des taux calculés à partir de données sur les décès issues de registres d'état civil qui sont déclarées incomplètes (degré d'exhaustivité inférieur à 90 p. 100) ou dont le degré d'exhaustivité n'est pas connu.

Insuffisance des données : Les statistiques des décès selon l'âge et le sexe appellent les mêmes réserves que les statistiques de l'état civil en général et les statistiques relatives à la mortalité en particulier (voir la section 4 de l'Introduction).

La fiabilité des données est un facteur important. Il faut également tenir compte du fait que, dans certains cas, les données relatives aux décès sont classées par date d'enregistrement et non par date d'occurrence ; ces cas ont été signalés par le signe "+". Chaque fois que le décalage entre le décès et son enregistrement est grand et qu'une forte proportion des décès fait l'objet d'un enregistrement tardif, les statistiques des décès de l'année peuvent être considérablement faussées.

En règle générale, toutefois, les décès sont enregistrés beaucoup plus rapidement que les naissances vivantes, et les retards prolongés sont rares.

Un autre facteur qui nuit à la comparabilité internationale est la pratique de certains pays ou zones qui consiste à ne pas inclure dans les statistiques des décès les enfants nés vivants mais décédés avant l'enregistrement de leur naissance ou dans les 24 heures qui ont suivi la naissance, pratique qui conduit à sous-évaluer le nombre de décès à moins d'un an. Quand pareil facteur a joué, cela a été signalé en note à la fin du tableau.

Étant donné que les statistiques relatives à la mortalité sont classées selon l'âge, elles appellent les mêmes réserves concernant l'exactitude des déclarations d'âge que celles qui ont été formulées à la section 3.1.3 des Introduction. Dans le cas des données d'état civil, les facteurs qui interviennent à cet égard sont parfois un peu différents, du fait que le recensement et l'enregistrement des décès se font par des méthodes différentes, mais, d'une manière générale, les erreurs observées sont les mêmes.

Si aucun nombre ne figure dans la rangée réservée aux âges inconnus, cela ne signifie pas nécessairement que les déclarations d'âge et le classement par âge sont tout à fait exacts. C'est souvent une indication que l'on a attribué un âge aux personnes d'âge inconnu avant l'exploitation des données ou qu'elles ont été réparties proportionnellement entre les différents groupes après cette opération.

Le manque d'uniformité des méthodes suivies pour obtenir l'âge au moment du décès nuit également à la comparabilité internationale des données. Si l'âge est connu, soit d'après la réponse à une simple question sur l'âge du décès en années révolues, soit d'après l'année de la naissance et l'année du décès, et non d'après des renseignements concernant la date exacte (jour, mois et année) de la naissance et du décès, le nombre de décès classés dans la catégorie « moins d'un an » sera entaché d'une erreur par défaut et le chiffre figurant dans la catégorie suivante d'une erreur par excès.

Les données pour les autres groupes d'âge pourront être entachées d'une distorsion analogue, mais les répercussions seront généralement négligeables. Les imperfections, lorsqu'elles étaient connues, ont été signalées en note à la fin du tableau.

La comparabilité des données selon le lieu de résidence (zone urbaine ou rurale) peut être limitée par les définitions nationales des termes « urbain » et « rural » utilisées pour le classement de ces données. En l'absence d'indications contraires, on a supposé que les mêmes définitions avaient servi pour le recensement national de la population et pour l'établissement des statistiques de l'état civil pour chaque pays ou zone. Toutefois, il n'est pas exclu que, pour une zone ou un pays donné, des définitions différentes aient été retenues. Les définitions du terme « urbain » utilisées pour les recensements nationaux de population ont été présentées à la fin du tableau 6 lorsqu'elles étaient connues. Comme on l'a précisé dans les notes techniques relatives au tableau 6, ces définitions varient considérablement d'un pays ou d'une zone à l'autre.

Insuffisance des taux : les taux présentés dans le tableau 19 appellent les mêmes réserves que celles formulées à propos des fréquences correspondantes (voir à ce sujet les notes techniques se rapportant au tableau 18). Leurs imperfections tiennent notamment aux différences d'exhaustivité de l'enregistrement, au classement des enfants nés vivants mais décédés avant l'enregistrement de leur naissance ou dans les 24 heures qui ont suivi la naissance, à la méthode utilisée pour obtenir l'âge au moment du décès, et à la qualité des déclarations concernant l'âge au moment du décès. En outre, dans certains cas, les données relatives aux décès sont classées par date d'enregistrement et non par date de l'événement ; ces cas ont été signalés par le signe "+".

S'agissant des taux de mortalité par âge, il est particulièrement difficile d'établir une correspondance exacte entre les décès (numérateur) et la population (dénominateur) du fait de l'inclusion ou de l'exclusion des militaires, des réfugiés, des personnes déplacées et d'autres groupes spéciaux. C'est le cas pour le Japon et Malte. Pour le Japon, les décès se rapportent aux seuls citoyens japonais alors que la population inclut les étrangers à l'exception des militaires étrangers et des personnels civils ainsi que leurs familles stationnés dans le pays. De même, pour Malte, les décès se rapportent aux nationaux alors que la population inclut les étrangers titulaires d'un permis de séjour et de travail qui résident dans le pays. Les taux de mortalité pour le sexe masculin dans les groupes d'âge de 20 à 40 ans peuvent être tout particulièrement influencés par ce manque de correspondance, et il importe d'être prudent quand on les utilise dans des comparaisons. Il convient d'ajouter que, même lorsque population et décès correspondent, la comparabilité des taux peut être compromise par des conditions anormales telles que l'absence du pays ou de la zone d'un grand nombre de jeunes gens qui sont sous les drapeaux ou qui travaillent à l'étranger comme travailleurs temporaires. Il arrive ainsi que les taux de mortalité paraissent élevés parmi les groupes les plus jeunes simplement parce que l'on en a exclu un grand nombre d'individus en bonne santé pour lesquels le taux de mortalité pourrait être, dans des conditions normales, inférieur à la moyenne observée pour les personnes du même âge.

De même, les taux indiqués pour tous les âges combinés diffèrent dans plusieurs cas des taux bruts de mortalité qui figurent dans d'autres tableaux, parce qu'ils se rapportent à une population pour laquelle on disposait d'une répartition par âge et par sexe appropriée, tandis que les taux bruts de mortalité indiqués ailleurs peuvent avoir été calculés sur la base d'un chiffre de population totale différent. Ainsi, il est possible que les chiffres de population par âge et par sexe proviennent d'un recensement effectué dans le courant de l'année et non au milieu de l'année, et qu'ils se différencient des autres chiffres de population en excluant ou en incluant certains groupes ethniques, les militaires, etc. Quelquefois, la différence tient à ce que les taux du tableau 20 ont été calculés sur la base de la population moyenne, alors que les taux correspondants des autres tableaux reposent sur une estimation au 1er juillet. Les écarts de cet ordre sont insignifiants, mais il n'en a pas été tenu compte dans le tableau.

Outre les problèmes de comparabilité, les taux démographiques classés selon le lieu de résidence (zone urbaine ou rurale) sont également sujets à des distorsions particulières. Si l'on utilise des définitions différentes du terme « urbain » pour classer les faits d'état civil et les données relatives à la population lors du calcul des taux et qu'il en résulte une différence nette entre le numérateur et le dénominateur pour le taux de la population exposée au risque, les taux démographiques s'en trouveront faussés. La différence entre ces taux pour les zones urbaines et rurales pourra aussi être faussée selon que les faits d'état civil auront été classés d'après le lieu où ils se sont produits ou d'après le lieu de résidence habituel.

Ce problème est examiné plus en détail à la section 4.1.4.1 de l'introduction.

Données publiées antérieurement : Les éditions de l'*Annuaire démographique* parues depuis 1955 présentent les statistiques les plus récentes dont on disposait à l'époque sur les décès selon l'âge et le sexe et sur les taux de mortalité selon l'âge et le sexe. Les données qui figurent dans le tableau 19 actualisent les données qui portaient sur les périodes suivantes :

Éditions	Années considérées
Supplément historique (CD-ROM), 1997	1948 – 1997
48e édition, 1996	1987 – 1995
44e édition, 1992	1983 – 1992
37e édition, 1985	1976 – 1984
32e édition, 1980	1971 – 1979
Supplément rétrospectif, 1979	1948 – 1977

Des données selon le lieu de résidence (zone urbaine ou rurale) ont été présentées dans toutes les éditions de l'*Annuaire* depuis celle de 1967, exception faite des éditions spéciales.

19. Deaths and death rates by age and sex: latest available year, 1998 - 2007
Décès et taux de mortalité selon l'âge et le sexe: dernière année disponible, 1998 - 2007

Continent, country or area, date, code and age (in years) / Continent, pays ou zone, date, code et âge (en années)	Number - Nombre Both sexes Les deux sexes	Number - Nombre Male Masculin	Number - Nombre Female Féminin	Rate - Taux Both sexes Les deux sexes	Rate - Taux Male Masculin	Rate - Taux Female Féminin
AFRICA - AFRIQUE						
Algeria - Algérie[1]						
1998 (+U)						
Total	131 708	73 352	58 356			
0	21 169	12 009	9 160	...	...	...
1 - 4	4 475	2 378	2 097	...	...	...
5 - 9	2 759	1 592	1 167	...	...	...
10 - 14	2 272	1 373	899	...	...	...
15 - 19	3 017	1 947	1 070	...	...	...
20 - 24	3 425	2 335	1 090	...	...	...
25 - 29	3 508	2 355	1 153	...	...	...
30 - 34	3 216	1 958	1 258	...	...	...
35 - 39	3 195	1 770	1 425	...	...	...
40 - 44	3 468	1 959	1 509	...	...	...
45 - 49	3 771	2 135	1 636	...	...	...
50 - 54	3 777	2 184	1 593	...	...	...
55 - 59	5 113	2 908	2 205	...	...	...
60 - 64	7 616	4 227	3 389	...	...	...
65 - 69	8 962	4 937	4 025	...	...	...
70 - 74	10 320	5 732	4 588	...	...	...
75 - 79	11 346	6 241	5 105	...	...	...
80 +	30 299	15 312	14 987	...	...	...
Botswana[2]						
2001 (I)						
Total	20 823	10 800	10 023			
0	1 576	815	761	12.4	13.3	11.6
1 - 4	1 187	637	550	36.8	37.5	36.1
5 - 9	484	251	233	7.8	8.3	7.2
10 - 14	249	114	135	2.3	2.4	2.2
15 - 19	386	179	207	1.2	1.1	1.3
20 - 24	1 090	388	702	1.9	1.8	2.0
25 - 29	2 091	848	1 243	6.4	4.8	7.8
30 - 34	2 376	1 235	1 141	14.2	11.8	16.4
35 - 39	2 039	1 132	907	20.9	22.5	19.4
40 - 44	1 595	910	685	21.4	25.4	17.9
45 - 49	1 334	814	520	20.9	25.8	16.7
50 - 54	858	529	329	21.0	27.5	15.3
55 - 59	669	416	253	19.0	24.5	14.0
60 - 64	638	386	252	20.1	26.5	14.3
65 - 69	673	374	299	22.3	28.9	16.5
70 - 74	601	322	279	26.4	33.7	20.8
75 +	2 203	1 055	1 148	28.4	36.2	22.8
75 - 79	569	315	254	60.1	73.2	51.6
80 +	1 634	740	894	...	...	...
Unknown - Inconnu	774	395	379	..		..
Egypt - Égypte						
2007 (C)						
Total	450 596	249 100	201 496			
0	34 612	18 872	15 740	...	...	...
1 - 4	9 551	5 192	4 359	...	...	...
5 - 9	4 502	2 704	1 798	...	...	...
10 - 14	3 927	2 395	1 532	...	...	...
15 - 19	5 838	3 866	1 972	...	...	...
20 - 24	6 991	4 561	2 430	...	...	...
25 - 29	6 656	4 250	2 406	...	...	...
30 - 34	6 483	3 958	2 525	...	...	...
35 - 39	8 053	4 887	3 166	...	...	...
40 - 44	12 343	7 938	4 405	...	...	...
45 - 49	19 434	13 036	6 398	...	...	...
50 - 54	29 321	18 900	10 421	...	...	...
55 - 59	36 839	23 143	13 696	...	...	...
60 - 64	39 591	23 299	16 292	...	...	...
65 - 69	41 830	23 673	18 157	...	...	...
70 - 74	48 735	25 500	23 235	...	...	...
75 - 79	46 016	22 945	23 071	...	...	...
80 - 84	37 289	16 950	20 339	...	...	...
85 +	34 552	13 316	21 236	...	...	...
Unknown - Inconnu	18 033	9 715	8 318	...	..	...

Continent, country or area, date, code and age (in years) / Continent, pays ou zone, date, code et âge (en années)	Number - Nombre			Rate - Taux		
	Both sexes Les deux sexes	Male Masculin	Female Féminin	Both sexes Les deux sexes	Male Masculin	Female Féminin

AFRICA - AFRIQUE

Kenya
2002 (U)

Total	206 089	107 108	98 981	...	...	...
0	32 459	16 735	15 724	...	...	...
1 - 4	22 623	12 166	10 457	...	...	...
5 - 14	11 035	5 889	5 146	...	...	...
15 - 24	15 157	6 083	9 074	...	...	...
25 - 34	29 921	13 485	16 436	...	...	...
35 - 44	27 720	14 714	13 006	...	...	...
45 - 54	19 896	11 770	8 126	...	...	...
55 - 74	26 196	15 183	11 013	...	...	...
75 +	21 082	11 083	9 999	...	...	...

Libyan Arab Jamahiriya - Jamahiriya arabe libyenne
2002 (U)

Total	19 362	11 278	8 084	...	...	...
0	2 194	1 190	1 004	...	...	...
1 - 4	891	546	345	...	...	...
5 - 9	267	142	125	...	...	...
10 - 19	670	432	238	...	...	...
20 - 29	1 100	824	276	...	...	...
30 - 39	1 287	820	467	...	...	...
40 - 49	1 118	621	497	...	...	...
50 - 59	1 492	860	632	...	...	...
60 - 69	2 936	1 754	1 182	...	...	...
70 - 79	3 812	2 254	1 558	...	...	...
80 +	3 595	1 835	1 760	...	...	...

Malawi[3]
1998 (|)

Total	208 040	113 856	94 184	20.9	23.4	18.6
0	44 928	24 977	19 951	122.0	136.9	107.4
1 - 4	59 930	32 821	27 109	46.4	51.2	41.6
5 - 9	16 717	9 200	7 517	11.6	12.9	10.4
10 - 14	9 638	4 849	4 789	7.8	7.9	7.8
15 - 19	7 130	3 427	3 703	6.6	6.5	6.6
20 - 24	11 710	6 947	4 763	12.0	16.0	8.8
25 - 29	9 290	4 853	4 437	11.7	12.3	11.1
30 - 34	8 797	4 481	4 316	14.6	14.8	14.5
35 - 39	7 036	3 678	3 358	14.5	15.4	13.7
40 - 44	6 338	3 713	2 625	17.6	20.6	14.5
45 - 49	5 639	3 705	1 934	16.9	22.3	11.6
50 - 54	3 677	2 160	1 517	15.4	18.0	12.8
55 - 59	3 872	1 739	2 133	22.1	19.3	25.0
60 - 64	2 921	1 620	1 301	19.1	22.4	16.1
65 - 69	2 695	1 257	1 438	19.3	19.1	19.5
70 - 74	2 228	1 358	870	22.7	30.0	16.5
75 - 79	1 599	942	657	24.4	29.3	19.7
80 - 84	1 516	842	674	33.2	41.1	26.8
85 +	2 379	1 287	1 092	51.7	60.6	44.1

Mauritius - Maurice
2007 (+C)

Total	8 498	4 749	3 749	6.7	7.6	5.9
0	261	138	123	15.4	15.8	14.9
1 - 4	31	18	13	0.4	♦0.5	♦0.4
5 - 9	18	11	7	♦0.2	♦0.2	♦0.1
10 - 14	25	16	9	♦0.2	♦0.3	♦0.2
15 - 19	47	31	16	0.4	0.6	♦0.3
20 - 24	84	60	24	0.9	1.3	♦0.5
25 - 29	128	94	34	1.1	1.7	0.6
30 - 34	152	111	41	1.6	2.3	0.8
35 - 39	207	140	67	2.2	3.0	1.4
40 - 44	350	246	104	3.4	4.8	2.0
45 - 49	483	347	136	5.3	7.6	3.0
50 - 54	565	398	167	7.1	10.1	4.2
55 - 59	757	471	286	11.8	15.2	8.7
60 - 64	749	452	297	18.2	23.7	13.5
65 - 69	760	446	314	26.0	34.0	19.5
70 - 74	941	520	421	40.0	51.5	31.3

Continent, country or area, date, code and age (in years) / Continent, pays ou zone, date, code et âge (en années)	Number - Nombre			Rate - Taux		
	Both sexes Les deux sexes	Male Masculin	Female Féminin	Both sexes Les deux sexes	Male Masculin	Female Féminin
AFRICA - AFRIQUE						
Mauritius - Maurice						
2007 (+C)						
75 - 79	935	466	469	61.2	77.1	50.9
80 - 84	972	428	544	89.1	106.3	79.1
85 +	1 033	356	677	172.3	205.8	158.8
Morocco - Maroc						
2001 (U)						
Total	95 612	62 023	33 589			
0	7 379	4 022	3 357	...	...	...
1 - 4	3 066	1 590	1 476	...	...	...
5 - 9	1 300	787	513	...	...	...
10 - 14	1 346	805	541	...	...	...
15 - 19	1 954	1 174	780	...	...	...
20 - 24	2 721	1 734	987	...	...	...
25 - 29	2 685	1 679	1 006	...	...	...
30 - 34	2 784	1 685	1 099	...	...	...
35 - 39	2 884	1 716	1 168	...	...	...
40 - 44	3 683	2 272	1 411	...	...	...
45 - 49	3 798	2 476	1 322	...	...	...
50 - 54	4 385	2 925	1 460	...	...	...
55 - 59	4 949	3 229	1 720	...	...	...
60 - 64	8 122	5 290	2 832	...	...	...
65 - 69	9 255	6 243	3 012	...	...	...
70 - 74	11 272	7 590	3 682	...	...	...
75 - 79	9 110	6 417	2 693	...	...	...
80 +	14 063	9 896	4 167	...	...	...
Unknown - Inconnu	856	493	363	..	..	...
Namibia - Namibie[4]						
2001 (I)						
Total	25 061	12 338[5]	12 137[5]	13.7	13.9	12.9
0 - 4	4 631	2 180[5]	2 343[5]	19.2	18.2	19.3
5 - 9	-938	461[5]	447[5]	3.8	3.8	3.6
10 - 14	508	246[5]	256[5]	2.2	2.2	2.2
15 - 19	658	317[5]	330[5]	3.3	3.2	3.2
20 - 24	1 240	492[5]	740[5]	7.1	5.7	8.4
25 - 29	1 791	799[5]	989[5]	11.9	10.8	12.9
30 - 34	2 032	1 029[5]	988[5]	17.1	18.0	16.1
35 - 39	1 845	1 003[5]	837[5]	19.1	22.2	16.3
40 - 44	1 370	753[5]	615[5]	18.5	22.0	15.4
45 - 49	1 099	609[5]	485[5]	19.0	22.6	15.7
50 - 54	866	547[5]	317[5]	18.1	24.9	12.3
55 - 59	699	419[5]	279[5]	19.9	25.2	15.0
60 - 64	761	431[5]	315[5]	22.1	27.7	16.7
65 - 69	576	310[5]	260[5]	22.8	27.2	18.8
70 - 74	729	405[5]	322[5]	33.1	43.5	25.3
75 - 79	571	266[5]	291[5]	35.7	41.7	30.2
80 - 84	539	228[5]	299[5]	39.0	42.5	35.3
85 - 89	361	162[5]	189[5]	66.8	79.7	56.0
90 - 94	246	102[5]	138[5]	96.3	110.0	84.8
95 +	373	131[5]	242[5]	137.5	146.0	133.3
Unknown - Inconnu	3 228	1 448[5]	1 455[5]	..		..
Réunion[6]						
2007 (C)						
Total	4 045	2 247	1 798	5.1	5.9	4.4
0 - 4	114	58	56	1.7	1.7	1.7
0	99	49	50	...	...	...
1 - 4	15	9	6	...	...	...
5 - 9	6	6	-	♦0.1	♦0.2	-
10 - 14	10	7	3	♦0.1	♦0.2	♦0.1
15 - 19	32	25	7	0.5	♦0.7	♦0.2
20 - 24	44	35	9	0.8	1.3	♦0.3
25 - 29	39	27	12	0.8	♦1.1	♦0.4
30 - 34	55	37	18	1.0	1.4	♦0.6
35 - 39	97	68	29	1.5	2.3	♦0.9
40 - 44	158	106	52	2.4	3.3	1.5
45 - 49	211	150	61	4.0	5.9	2.3

Continent, country or area, date, code and age (in years) Continent, pays ou zone, date, code et âge (en annèes)	Number - Nombre			Rate - Taux		
	Both sexes Les deux sexes	Male Masculin	Female Féminin	Both sexes Les deux sexes	Male Masculin	Female Féminin
AFRICA - AFRIQUE						
Réunion[6]						
2007 (C)						
50 - 54	236	183	53	5.1	8.2	2.2
55 - 59	266	188	78	7.5	10.7	4.4
60 - 64	287	176	111	10.8	14.1	7.9
65 - 69	375	246	129	17.4	24.8	11.1
70 - 74	427	250	177	25.9	34.7	19.1
75 - 79	448	231	217	39.5	50.3	32.2
80 - 84	496	222	274	65.3	78.9	57.3
85 - 89	393	149	244	106.6	140.6	92.9
90 - 94	233	66	167	166.1	182.8	160.3
95 +	118	17	101	308.9	♦369.6	300.6
95 - 99	96	15	81	...	...	...
100 +	22	2	20	...	...	...
Saint Helena ex. dep. - Sainte-Hélène sans dép.						
2007 (C)						
Total	59	31	28	...	...	...
0	-	-	-	...	...	...
1 - 4	-	-	-	...	...	...
5 - 9	-	-	-	...	...	...
10 - 14	-	-	-	...	...	...
15 - 19	-	-	-	...	...	...
20 - 24	2	-	2	...	...	...
25 - 29	1	-	1	...	...	...
30 - 34	2	2	-	...	...	...
35 - 39	-	-	-	...	...	...
40 - 44	1	1	-	...	...	...
45 - 49	3	1	2	...	...	...
50 - 54	4	3	1	...	...	...
55 - 59	5	3	2	...	...	...
60 - 64	9	5	4	...	...	...
65 - 69	7	6	1	...	...	...
70 - 74	4	1	3	...	...	...
75 - 79	9	1	8	...	...	...
80 - 84	4	4	-	...	...	...
85 - 89	5	4	1	...	...	...
90 - 94	2	-	2	...	...	...
95 - 99	1	-	1	...	...	...
100 +						
Seychelles						
2007 (+C)						
Total	630	345	285	...	...	...
0	16	12	4	...	...	...
1 - 4	3	1	2	...	...	...
5 - 9	3	1	2	...	...	...
10 - 14	2	2	-	...	...	...
15 - 19	2	2	-	...	...	...
20 - 24	12	9	3	...	...	...
25 - 29	14	12	2	...	...	...
30 - 34	14	7	7	...	...	...
35 - 39	17	14	3	...	...	...
40 - 44	31	18	13	...	...	...
45 - 49	32	18	14	...	...	...
50 - 54	32	27	5	...	...	...
55 - 59	31	21	10	...	...	...
60 - 64	39	25	14	...	...	...
65 - 69	51	28	23	...	...	...
70 - 74	83	47	36	...	...	...
75 - 79	74	42	32	...	...	...
80 - 84	67	34	33	...	...	...
85 +	107	25	82	...	...	...
South Africa - Afrique du Sud						
2006 (U)						
Total	607 184	306 676[5]	298 804[5]	...	...	...
0	47 703	25 178[5]	21 810[5]	...	...	...
1 - 4	15 893	8 299[5]	7 478[5]	...	...	...
5 - 9	5 544	2 999[5]	2 528[5]	...	...	...

19. Deaths and death rates by age and sex: latest available year, 1998 - 2007
Décès et taux de mortalité selon l'âge et le sexe: dernière année disponible, 1998 - 2007 (continued - suite)

Continent, country or area, date, code and age (in years) / Continent, pays ou zone, date, code et âge (en années)	Number - Nombre			Rate - Taux		
	Both sexes Les deux sexes	Male Masculin	Female Féminin	Both sexes Les deux sexes	Male Masculin	Female Féminin
AFRICA - AFRIQUE						
South Africa - Afrique du Sud						
2006 (U)						
10 - 14	4 273	2 362[5]	1 897[5]			
15 - 19	9 394	4 806[5]	4 552[5]	...	...	...
20 - 24	25 477	10 760[5]	14 626[5]	...	...	...
25 - 29	44 762	18 827[5]	25 853[5]			
30 - 34	59 344	28 576[5]	30 679[5]	...	...	...
35 - 39	55 083	29 177[5]	25 831[5]			
40 - 44	49 527	27 808[5]	21 647[5]			
45 - 49	42 713	24 882[5]	17 787[5]	...	...	...
50 - 54	38 073	22 568[5]	15 466[5]			
55 - 59	34 556	20 458[5]	14 059[5]			
60 - 64	30 167	16 911[5]	13 231[5]	...	...	...
65 - 69	33 358	17 614[5]	15 721[5]			
70 - 74	29 009	13 485[5]	15 498[5]	...	...	...
75 - 79	29 571	12 627[5]	16 920[5]	...	...	...
80 - 84	21 178	8 896[5]	12 262[5]			
85 - 89	18 057	6 098[5]	11 948[5]	...	...	...
90 - 94	7 818	2 315[5]	5 500[5]	...	...	...
95 - 99	2 963	735[5]	2 225[5]	...	...	...
100 +	1 428	481[5]	945[5]	...	...	...
Unknown - Inconnu	1 293	814[5]	341[5]	..		..
Tunisia - Tunisie						
1998 (U)						
Total	42 571	25 319	17 252			
0	3 098	1 775	1 323	...	...	...
1 - 4	2 096	1 196	900	...	...	...
5 - 9	412	252	160	...	...	...
10 - 14	382	236	146	...	...	...
15 - 19	578	408	170	...	...	...
20 - 24	653	459	194	...	...	...
25 - 29	612	425	187	...	...	...
30 - 34	801	528	273	...	...	...
35 - 39	812	519	293			
40 - 44	998	631	367	...	...	...
45 - 49	1 161	737	424			
50 - 54	1 267	805	462			
55 - 59	1 833	1 152	681			
60 - 64	2 920	1 843	1 077			
65 - 69	4 337	2 673	1 664	...	...	...
70 - 74	4 918	2 943	1 975			
75 - 79	5 201	2 930	2 271	...	...	...
80 +	10 199	5 681	4 518	...	...	...
Unknown - Inconnu	293	126	167	..		..
Zimbabwe[2]						
2002 (I)						
Total	200 294	103 741	96 553	17.2	18.4	16.1
0	23 672	12 887	10 785	69.6	75.8	63.3
1 - 4	16 231	8 688	7 543	12.2	13.0	11.3
5 - 9	5 166	2 793	2 373	3.4	3.7	3.1
10 - 14	3 599	1 946	1 653	2.4	2.6	2.2
15 - 19	4 165	1 802	2 363	2.8	2.4	3.1
20 - 24	9 623	3 440	6 183	7.9	6.1	9.4
25 - 29	17 414	6 930	10 484	17.6	14.6	20.4
30 - 34	21 358	10 286	11 072	29.3	27.8	30.7
35 - 39	19 611	10 176	9 435	38.9	43.2	35.1
40 - 44	15 322	8 608	6 714	35.3	44.2	28.0
45 - 49	11 993	6 907	5 086	33.6	41.8	26.6
50 - 54	8 845	5 029	3 816	29.4	39.3	22.0
55 - 59	6 229	3 857	2 372	29.5	39.2	21.1
60 - 64	5 910	3 649	2 261	30.5	38.6	22.7
65 - 69	4 504	2 682	1 822	34.1	41.7	26.9
70 - 74	4 638	2 810	1 828	37.8	46.6	29.3
75 +	11 781	6 066	5 715	71.7	84.3	61.9
Unknown - Inconnu	10 233	5 185	5 048	..	..	..

Continent, country or area, date, code and age (in years) / Continent, pays ou zone, date, code et âge (en années)	Number - Nombre			Rate - Taux		
	Both sexes Les deux sexes	Male Masculin	Female Féminin	Both sexes Les deux sexes	Male Masculin	Female Féminin
AMERICA, NORTH - AMÉRIQUE DU NORD						
Anguilla						
2007 (+C)						
Total	70	43	27	...	...	...
0 - 4	1	-	1	...	...	...
5 - 14	-	-	-	...	...	...
15 - 29	5	4	1	...	...	...
30 - 44	9	6	3	...	...	...
45 - 59	10	7	3	...	...	...
60 - 64	1	1	-	...	...	...
65 - 69	1	1	-	...	...	...
70 - 74	8	3	5	...	...	...
75 - 79	10	8	2	...	...	...
80 - 84	5	4	1	...	...	...
85 +	20	9	11	...	...	...
Antigua and Barbuda - Antigua-et-Barbuda[7]						
2002 (+C)						
Total	444	234	210	...	...	...
0	21	14	7	...	...	...
1 - 4	3	2	1	...	...	...
5 - 9	1	-	1	...	...	...
10 - 14	2	1	1	...	...	...
15 - 19	2	2	-	...	...	...
20 - 24	9	6	3	...	...	...
25 - 29	3	3	-	...	...	...
30 - 34	11	8	3	...	...	...
35 - 39	10	8	2	...	...	...
40 - 44	13	5	8	...	...	...
45 - 49	13	6	7	...	...	...
50 - 54	16	7	9	...	...	...
55 - 59	18	9	9	...	...	...
60 - 64	24	15	9	...	...	...
65 - 69	28	17	11	...	...	...
70 - 74	52	27	25	...	...	...
75 - 79	48	30	18	...	...	...
80 - 84	64	32	32	...	...	...
85 - 89	54	25	29	...	...	...
90 - 94	30	10	20	...	...	...
95 +	22	7	15	...	...	...
Aruba						
2007 (C)						
Total	521	279	242	...	...	...
0	4	2	2	...	...	...
1 - 4	-	-	-	...	...	...
5 - 9	-	-	-	...	...	...
10 - 14	-	-	-	...	...	...
15 - 19	7	6	1	...	...	...
20 - 24	3	2	1	...	...	...
25 - 29	6	3	3	...	...	...
30 - 34	5	3	2	...	...	...
35 - 39	9	4	5	...	...	...
40 - 44	16	11	5	...	...	...
45 - 49	22	13	9	...	...	...
50 - 54	23	14	9	...	...	...
55 - 59	47	28	19	...	...	...
60 - 64	45	28	17	...	...	...
65 - 69	55	31	24	...	...	...
70 - 74	60	37	23	...	...	...
75 - 79	60	39	21	...	...	...
80 - 84	62	30	32	...	...	...
85 - 89	32	8	24	...	...	...
90 - 94	44	13	31	...	...	...
95 - 99	18	7	11	...	...	...
100 +	3	-	3	...	...	...
Bahamas						
2007 (C)						
Total	1 798	1 001	797	5.4	6.2	4.6
0	69	33	36	11.7	10.8	12.6

Continent, country or area, date, code and age (in years) / Continent, pays ou zone, date, code et âge (en années)	Number - Nombre			Rate - Taux		
	Both sexes Les deux sexes	Male Masculin	Female Féminin	Both sexes Les deux sexes	Male Masculin	Female Féminin
AMERICA, NORTH - AMÉRIQUE DU NORD						
Bahamas						
2007 (C)						
1 - 4	6	3	3			
5 - 9	11	7	4	◆0.3	◆0.3	◆0.3
10 - 14	9	6	3	◆0.4	◆0.5	◆0.3
15 - 19	27	23	4	◆0.3	◆0.4	◆0.2
20 - 24	39	26	13	◆0.9	◆1.6	◆0.3
25 - 29	54	40	14	1.5	◆2.0	◆1.0
30 - 34	60	40	20	2.2	3.3	◆1.1
35 - 39	109	66	43	2.2	3.1	◆1.4
40 - 44	105	66	39	4.0	5.0	3.0
45 - 49	130	76	54	3.9	5.2	2.8
50 - 54	138	97	41	5.6	6.8	4.4
55 - 59	116	68	48	7.8	11.4	4.5
60 - 64	125	79	46	9.0	11.1	7.1
65 - 69	159	87	72	12.5	17.2	8.5
70 - 74	150	86	64	20.1	24.2	16.7
75 - 79	144	70	74	27.8	35.8	21.3
80 +	345	126	219	43.6	53.8	37.0
80 - 84	122	46	76	127.8	157.5	115.3
85 - 89	114	44	70	...	...	...
90 - 94	72	26	46	...	...	...
95 - 99	32	9	23	...	...	...
100 +	5	1	4	...	...	...
Unknown - Inconnu	2	2	-	...	...	..
Barbados - Barbade[7]						
2001 (+C)						
Total	1 712	784	928			
0	32	15	17	...	...	...
1 - 4	5	2	3	...	...	...
5 - 9	2	1	1	...	...	...
10 - 14	1	1	-	...	...	...
15 - 19	9	7	2	...	...	...
20 - 24	16	12	4	...	...	...
25 - 29	26	18	8	...	...	...
30 - 34	32	16	16	...	...	...
35 - 39	31	16	15	...	...	...
40 - 44	51	29	22	...	...	...
45 - 49	45	31	14	...	...	...
50 - 54	53	33	20	...	...	...
55 - 59	66	34	32	...	...	...
60 - 64	84	39	45	...	...	...
65 - 69	107	55	52	...	...	...
70 - 74	175	82	93	...	...	...
75 - 79	192	89	103	...	...	...
80 - 84	285	137	148	...	...	...
85 - 89	260	106	154	...	...	...
90 - 94	145	46	99	...	...	...
95 +	92	14	78	...	...	...
Unknown - Inconnu	3	1	2	..	..	...
Belize						
2000 (U)						
Total	1 534	895	639			
0	155	87	68	...	...	...
1 - 4	35	15	20	...	...	...
5 - 9	14	4	10	...	...	...
10 - 14	20	11	9	...	...	...
15 - 19	31	22	9	...	...	...
20 - 24	40	32	8	...	...	...
25 - 29	41	31	10	...	...	...
30 - 34	54	35	19	...	...	...
35 - 39	55	30	25	...	...	...
40 - 44	30	21	9	...	...	...
45 - 49	50	41	9	...	...	...
50 - 54	77	41	36	...	...	...
55 - 59	72	43	29	...	...	...
60 - 64	109	60	49	...	...	...

Continent, country or area, date, code and age (in years) / Continent, pays ou zone, date, code et âge (en années)	Number - Nombre			Rate - Taux		
	Both sexes Les deux sexes	Male Masculin	Female Féminin	Both sexes Les deux sexes	Male Masculin	Female Féminin

AMERICA, NORTH - AMÉRIQUE DU NORD

Belize

2000 (U)

65 - 69	134	69	65	...	...	...
70 - 74	151	102	49	...	...	...
75 - 79	160	93	67	...	...	...
80 +	305	157	148	...	...	...
Unknown - Inconnu	1	1	...	..	..	..

2001 (U)

Total	1 261	...	...	...	...	...
0	120	...	...	...	...	...
1 - 4	32	...	...	...	...	...
5 - 9	15	...	...	...	...	...
10 - 14	12	...	...	...	...	...
15 - 19	35	...	...	...	...	...
20 - 24	41	...	...	...	...	...
25 - 29	54	...	...	...	...	...
30 - 34	51	...	...	...	...	...
35 - 39	56	...	...	...	...	...
40 - 44	53	...	...	...	...	...
45 - 49	62	...	...	...	...	...
50 - 54	53	...	...	...	...	...
55 - 59	57	...	...	...	...	...
60 - 64	68	...	...	...	...	...
65 - 69	98	...	...	...	...	...
70 - 74	122	...	...	...	...	...
75 - 79	87	...	...	...	...	...
80 +	239	...	...	...	...	...
Unknown - Inconnu	6	...	...	..	..	..

Bermuda - Bermudes

1998 (C)

Total	505	265	240	...	...	...
0 - 14	-	-	-	...	...	...
15 - 19	1	1	-	...	...	...
20 - 24	-	-	-	...	...	...
25 - 29	2	2	-	...	...	...
30 - 34	5	3	2	...	...	...
35 - 39	10	6	4	...	...	...
40 - 44	14	5	9	...	...	...
45 - 49	16	10	6	...	...	...
50 - 54	30	17	13	...	...	...
55 - 59	26	16	10	...	...	...
60 - 64	39	26	13	...	...	...
65 - 69	43	26	17	...	...	...
70 - 74	63	35	28	...	...	...
75 - 79	70	31	39	...	...	...
80 - 84	74	41	33	...	...	...
85 - 89	48	16	32	...	...	...
90 - 94	35	14	21	...	...	...
95 - 99	6	2	4	...	...	...
100 +	4	-	4	..	..	..
Unknown - Inconnu	19	14	5			

2003 (C)

Total	434	...	...	...	...	...
0 - 14	2	...	...	...	...	...
15 - 24	2	...	...	...	...	...
25 - 44	31	...	...	...	...	...
45 - 64	81	...	...	...	...	...
65 - 84	197	...	...	...	...	...
85 +	121	...	...	...	...	...

British Virgin Islands - Îles Vierges britanniques[7]

1998 (C)

Total	85	50	35	...	...	...
0	3	2	1	...	...	...
1 - 4	-	-	-	...	...	...
5 - 9	1	1	-	...	...	...
10 - 14	-	-	-	...	...	...
15 - 19	2	2	-	...	...	...

19. Deaths and death rates by age and sex: latest available year, 1998 - 2007
Décès et taux de mortalité selon l'âge et le sexe: dernière année disponible, 1998 - 2007 (continued - suite)

Continent, country or area, date, code and age (in years) / Continent, pays ou zone, date, code et âge (en années)	Number - Nombre			Rate - Taux		
	Both sexes Les deux sexes	Male Masculin	Female Féminin	Both sexes Les deux sexes	Male Masculin	Female Féminin
AMERICA, NORTH - AMÉRIQUE DU NORD						
British Virgin Islands - Îles Vierges britanniques[7]						
1998 (C)						
20 - 24	2	2	-	...	...	...
25 - 29	2	2	-	...	...	...
30 - 34	1	1	-	...	...	...
35 - 39	5	1	4	...	...	...
40 - 44	2	1	1	...	...	...
45 - 49	5	3	2	...	...	...
50 - 54	6	6	-	...	...	...
55 - 59	3	1	2	...	...	...
60 - 64	1	1	-	...	...	...
65 - 69	3	2	1	...	...	...
70 - 74	11	7	4	...	...	...
75 - 79	15	8	7	...	...	...
80 - 84	9	5	4	...	...	...
85 - 89	8	3	5	...	...	...
90 - 94	3	1	2	...	...	...
95 +	3	1	2	...	...	...
Canada[8]						
2005 (C)						
Total	230 132	116 006	114 126	7.1	7.3	7.0
0	1 863	1 030	833	5.5	6.0	5.1
1 - 4	282	170	112	0.2	0.2	0.2
5 - 9	198	120	78	0.1	0.1	0.1
10 - 14	311	186	125	0.1	0.2	0.1
15 - 19	986	672	314	0.5	0.6	0.3
20 - 24	1 342	973	369	0.6	0.8	0.3
25 - 29	1 265	920	345	0.6	0.8	0.3
30 - 34	1 541	1 043	498	0.7	0.9	0.5
35 - 39	2 177	1 412	765	0.9	1.2	0.7
40 - 44	3 874	2 418	1 456	1.4	1.8	1.1
45 - 49	5 828	3 521	2 307	2.2	2.7	1.8
50 - 54	7 937	4 812	3 125	3.4	4.2	2.7
55 - 59	10 878	6 665	4 213	5.4	6.7	4.1
60 - 64	13 269	8 045	5 224	8.8	10.8	6.8
65 - 69	16 400	9 945	6 455	13.7	17.3	10.4
70 - 74	23 429	13 760	9 669	22.5	28.2	17.5
75 - 79	31 682	17 391	14 291	36.7	46.0	29.4
80 - 84	38 443	18 707	19 736	61.5	77.4	51.5
85 - 89	34 288	14 090	20 198	106.3	131.6	93.8
90 +	34 136	10 124	24 012	201.4	227.1	192.2
Unknown - Inconnu	3	2	1	..	..	..
Cayman Islands - Îles Caïmanes[9]						
2006 (C)						
Total	181	111	70			
0	8	4	4	...	...	...
1 - 4	-	-	-	...	...	...
5 - 9	-	-	-	...	...	...
10 - 14	-	-	-	...	...	...
15 - 19	4	3	1	...	...	...
20 - 24	3	3	-	...	...	...
25 - 29	6	5	1	...	...	...
30 - 34	2	2	-	...	...	...
35 - 39	5	4	1	...	...	...
40 - 44	4	3	1	...	...	...
45 - 49	8	4	4	...	...	...
50 - 54	7	5	2	...	...	...
55 - 59	9	7	2	...	...	...
60 - 64	14	10	4	...	...	...
65 - 69	11	7	4	...	...	...
70 - 74	20	12	8	...	...	...
75 - 79	19	11	8	...	...	...
80 - 84	24	14	10	...	...	...
85 - 89	18	7	11	...	...	...
90 - 94	8	4	4	...	...	...
95 - 99	4	1	3	...	...	...

Continent, country or area, date, code and age (in years) Continent, pays ou zone, date, code et âge (en années)	Number - Nombre			Rate - Taux		
	Both sexes Les deux sexes	Male Masculin	Female Féminin	Both sexes Les deux sexes	Male Masculin	Female Féminin
AMERICA, NORTH - AMÉRIQUE DU NORD						
Cayman Islands - Îles Caïmanes[9]						
2006 (C)						
100 +..........	-	-	-	...	...	...
Unknown - Inconnu...................	7	5	2	..	..	...
Costa Rica						
2006 (C)						
Total..................	16 766	9 697	7 069	3.9	4.5	3.2
0 - 4..................	791	452	339	2.3	2.6	2.1
0..................	692	398	294	...	...	...
1 - 4..................	99	54	45	...	...	...
5 - 9..................	91	52	39	0.2	0.3	0.2
10 - 14..................	107	70	37	0.2	0.3	0.2
15 - 19..................	241	172	69	0.5	0.7	0.3
20 - 24..................	347	256	91	0.8	1.2	0.4
25 - 29..................	380	289	91	1.1	1.8	0.5
30 - 39..................	760	534	226	1.3	1.9	0.7
30 - 34..................	342	242	100	...	...	...
35 - 39..................	418	292	126	...	...	...
40 - 49..................	1 273	832	441	2.2	2.9	1.5
40 - 44..................	556	378	178	...	...	...
45 - 49..................	717	454	263	...	...	...
50 - 59..................	1 755	1 067	688	4.5	5.9	3.4
50 - 54..................	855	523	332	...	...	...
55 - 59..................	900	544	356	...	...	...
60 - 69..................	2 398	1 426	972	11.7	15.1	8.7
60 - 64..................	1 052	622	430	...	...	...
65 - 69..................	1 346	804	542	...	...	...
70 +..................	8 598	4 526	4 072	44.6	51.4	38.9
70 - 74..................	1 505	897	608	...	...	...
75 - 79..................	1 959	1 123	836	...	...	...
80 - 84..................	1 842	1 000	842	...	...	...
85 +..................	3 292	1 506	1 786	...	...	...
Unknown - Inconnu..................	25	21	4	..	..	..
Cuba						
2007 (C)						
Total..................	81 927	44 033	37 894	7.3	7.8	6.8
0..................	592	332	260	5.3	5.8	4.8
1 - 4..................	160	84	76	0.3	0.3	0.3
5 - 9..................	132	85	47	0.2	0.2	0.1
10 - 14..................	178	119	59	0.2	0.3	0.2
15 - 19..................	365	251	114	0.4	0.6	0.3
20 - 24..................	453	302	151	0.6	0.7	0.4
25 - 29..................	435	291	144	0.7	0.9	0.5
30 - 34..................	837	543	294	0.9	1.2	0.7
35 - 39..................	1 225	803	422	1.2	1.5	0.8
40 - 44..................	2 034	1 248	786	1.9	2.3	1.4
45 - 49..................	2 394	1 442	952	3.1	3.8	2.5
50 - 54..................	3 257	1 974	1 283	5.1	6.3	3.9
55 - 59..................	4 693	2 762	1 931	7.7	9.3	6.2
60 - 64..................	6 196	3 619	2 577	11.8	14.2	9.5
65 - 69..................	7 733	4 495	3 238	17.9	21.3	14.6
70 - 74..................	8 829	4 828	4 001	27.8	31.7	24.2
75 - 79..................	10 487	5 751	4 736	44.2	51.6	37.7
80 - 84..................	11 325	5 770	5 555	70.0	78.8	62.8
85 +..................	20 594	9 327	11 267	134.9	144.1	128.1
85 - 89..................	10 136	4 870	5 266	...	...	...
90 - 94..................	6 863	3 031	3 832	...	...	...
95 - 99..................	2 945	1 173	1 772	...	...	...
100 +..................	650	253	397	...	...	...
Unknown - Inconnu..................	8	7	1	..	..	..
Dominica - Dominique						
2006 (+C)						
Total..................	536	285	251	...	...	...
0..................	13	11	2	...	...	...
1 - 4..................	1	1	-	...	...	...
5 - 9..................	1	1	-	...	...	...
10 - 14..................	2	2	-	...	...	...

Continent, country or area, date, code and age (in years) / Continent, pays ou zone, date, code et âge (en années)	Number - Nombre			Rate - Taux		
	Both sexes Les deux sexes	Male Masculin	Female Féminin	Both sexes Les deux sexes	Male Masculin	Female Féminin
AMERICA, NORTH - AMÉRIQUE DU NORD						
Dominica - Dominique						
2006 (+C)						
15 - 19	8	7	1			
20 - 24	9	6	3	...	...	...
25 - 29	5	3	2	...	...	...
30 - 34	9	5	4	...	...	...
35 - 39	8	6	2	...	...	...
40 - 44	8	5	3	...	...	...
45 - 49	23	7	16	...	...	...
50 - 54	17	9	8	...	...	...
55 - 59	19	11	8	...	...	...
60 - 64	19	13	6	...	...	...
65 - 69	34	16	18	...	...	...
70 - 74	57	26	31	...	...	...
75 - 79	76	39	37	...	...	...
80 - 84	68	38	30	...	...	...
85 +	152	73	79	...	...	...
Unknown - Inconnu	7	6	1	...	...	...
Dominican Republic - République dominicaine						
2007 (U)						
Total	31 204	17 848	13 356			
0	60	28	32	...	...	...
1 - 4	413	217	196	...	...	...
5 - 9	105	54	51	...	...	...
10 - 14	135	81	54	...	...	...
15 - 19	295	194	101	...	...	...
20 - 24	455	302	153			
25 - 29	507	323	184	...	...	...
30 - 34	605	414	191			
35 - 39	633	391	242			
40 - 44	735	460	275			
45 - 49	747	434	313			
50 - 54	1 008	585	423	...	...	...
55 - 59	1 138	655	483			
60 - 64	1 331	799	532	...	...	...
65 - 69	1 636	909	727			
70 - 74	2 018	1 107	911			
75 - 79	2 400	1 376	1 024			
80 - 84	1 960	1 066	894			
85 - 89	1 563	853	710			
90 - 94	792	407	385			
95 - 99	401	206	195			
100 +	188	86	102			
Unknown - Inconnu	12 079	6 901	5 178	...	...	...
El Salvador						
2007 (C)						
Total	31 349	18 317	13 032			
0	981	579	402	5.5	6.7	4.3
1 - 4	286	160	126	9.6	11.2	8.0
5 - 9	179	102	77	0.6	0.7	0.6
10 - 14	287	174	113	0.3	0.3	0.2
15 - 19	922	696	226	0.4	0.5	0.3
20 - 24	1 170	966	204	1.5	2.3	0.7
25 - 29	1 469	1 225	244	2.4	4.2	0.8
30 - 34	1 286	1 036	250	3.2	5.9	1.0
35 - 39	1 173	864	309	3.2	5.8	1.1
40 - 44	1 164	794	370	3.3	5.5	1.6
45 - 49	1 352	891	461	3.8	6.0	2.2
50 - 54	1 461	912	549	5.4	8.1	3.2
55 - 59	1 748	1 062	686	6.8	9.6	4.6
60 - 64	1 758	1 015	743	9.5	13.0	6.8
65 - 69	2 351	1 284	1 067	11.6	14.9	8.9
70 - 74	2 555	1 342	1 213	18.8	23.0	15.4
75 - 79	3 086	1 543	1 543	26.2	30.9	22.5
80 - 84	3 088	1 484	1 604	40.6	45.8	36.5
85 +	5 033	2 188	2 845	65.9	72.7	60.6
				112.2	118.3	107.9

19. Deaths and death rates by age and sex: latest available year, 1998 - 2007
Décès et taux de mortalité selon l'âge et le sexe: dernière année disponible, 1998 - 2007 (continued - suite)

Continent, country or area, date, code and age (in years) Continent, pays ou zone, date, code et âge (en années)	Number - Nombre			Rate - Taux		
	Both sexes Les deux sexes	Male Masculin	Female Féminin	Both sexes Les deux sexes	Male Masculin	Female Féminin
AMERICA, NORTH - AMÉRIQUE DU NORD						
Greenland - Groenland						
2003 (C)						
Total..........	412	235	177	...	...	...
0...........	8	6	2	...	...	...
1 - 4........	4	2	2	...	...	...
5 - 9........	1	-	1	...	...	...
10 - 14......	2	2	-	...	...	...
15 - 19......	12	7	5	...	...	...
20 - 24......	17	13	4	...	...	...
25 - 29......	5	3	2	...	...	...
30 - 34......	10	5	5	...	...	...
35 - 39......	16	12	4	...	...	...
40 - 44......	15	11	4	...	...	...
45 - 49......	21	13	8	...	...	...
50 - 54......	23	13	10	...	...	...
55 - 59......	36	25	11	...	...	...
60 - 64......	32	18	14	...	...	...
65 - 69......	61	40	21	...	...	...
70 - 74......	64	29	35	...	...	...
75 - 79......	38	19	19	...	...	...
80 - 84......	32	13	19	...	...	...
85 +........	15	4	11	...	...	...
Grenada - Grenade						
2000 (+C)						
Total..........	716	365	351	...	...	...
0...........	27	10	17	...	...	...
1 - 4........	1	1	-	...	...	...
5 - 9........	1	1	-	...	...	...
10 - 14......	4	4	-	...	...	...
15 - 19......	8	2	6	...	...	...
20 - 24......	11	9	2	...	...	...
25 - 29......	17	13	4	...	...	...
30 - 34......	21	11	10	...	...	...
35 - 39......	17	7	10	...	...	...
40 - 44......	14	9	5	...	...	...
45 - 49......	21	13	8	...	...	...
50 - 54......	27	15	12	...	...	...
55 - 59......	24	17	7	...	...	...
60 - 64......	50	30	20	...	...	...
65 - 69......	61	35	26	...	...	...
70 - 74......	81	52	29	...	...	...
75 - 79......	96	50	46	...	...	...
80 - 84......	69	27	42	...	...	...
85 - 89......	84	34	50	...	...	...:
90 - 94......	52	16	36	...	...	...
95 - 99......	24	8	16	...	...	...
100 +........	6	1	5	...	...	...
Guadeloupe[6]						
2003 (C)						
Total..........	2 636	1 405	1 231	6.0	6.7	5.4
0...........	56	34	22	8.1	9.7	♦6.5
1 - 4........	9	5	4	♦0.3	♦0.3	♦0.3
5 - 9........	5	4	1	♦0.1	♦0.2	♦0.1
10 - 14......	5	3	2	♦0.1	♦0.2	♦0.1
15 - 19......	21	18	3	♦0.6	♦1.0	♦0.2
20 - 24......	23	19	4	♦0.8	♦1.3	♦0.3
25 - 29......	23	17	6	♦0.9	♦1.3	♦0.4
30 - 34......	39	31	8	1.1	2.0	♦0.4
35 - 39......	60	40	20	1.6	2.4	♦1.0
40 - 44......	76	47	29	2.2	2.8	♦1.6
45 - 49......	102	71	31	3.5	5.3	2.0
50 - 54......	112	87	25	4.5	7.5	♦1.9
55 - 59......	128	85	43	6.3	8.7	4.1
60 - 64......	177	96	81	10.9	12.7	9.3
65 - 69......	213	126	87	14.9	19.1	11.2
70 - 74......	257	141	116	22.7	28.5	18.2
75 - 79......	316	180	136	34.1	45.4	25.6

19. Deaths and death rates by age and sex: latest available year, 1998 - 2007
Décès et taux de mortalité selon l'âge et le sexe: dernière année disponible, 1998 - 2007 (continued - suite)

Continent, country or area, date, code and age (in years) / Continent, pays ou zone, date, code et âge (en annèes)	Number - Nombre			Rate - Taux		
	Both sexes Les deux sexes	Male Masculin	Female Féminin	Both sexes Les deux sexes	Male Masculin	Female Féminin
AMERICA, NORTH - AMÉRIQUE DU NORD						
Guadeloupe[6]						
2003 (C)						
80 - 84	356	185	171	53.8	68.2	43.8
85 - 89	329	124	205	96.8	98.9	95.6
90 +	329	92	237	148.6	142.2	151.2
90 - 94	205	65	140	...	...	...
95 - 99	96	19	77	...	...	...
100 +	28	8	20	...	...	...
Guatemala						
2006 (C)						
Total	69 756	40 650	29 106			
0	9 042	5 012	4 030	...	...	...
1 - 4	3 567	1 900	1 667	...	...	...
5 - 9	1 016	556	460	...	...	...
10 - 14	922	519	403	...	...	...
15 - 19	2 271	1 597	674	...	...	...
20 - 24	3 053	2 342	711	...	...	...
25 - 29	3 227	2 448	779	...	...	...
30 - 34	2 777	2 054	723	...	...	...
35 - 39	2 721	1 905	816	...	...	...
40 - 44	2 765	1 835	930	...	...	...
45 - 49	2 829	1 803	1 026	...	...	...
50 - 54	3 048	1 846	1 202	...	...	...
55 - 59	3 342	1 857	1 485	...	...	...
60 - 64	3 420	1 870	1 550	...	...	...
65 - 69	3 955	2 124	1 831	...	...	...
70 +	21 532	10 787	10 745	...	...	...
Unknown - Inconnu	269	195	74	...	...	...
Haiti - Haïti[7]						
2003 (U)						
Total	8 011	4 135	3 876			
0	724	388	336	...	...	...
1 - 4	501	270	231	...	...	...
5 - 9	161	85	76	...	...	...
10 - 14	135	66	69	...	...	...
15 - 19	216	114	102	...	...	...
20 - 24	324	158	166	...	...	...
25 - 29	371	179	192	...	...	...
30 - 34	442	229	213	...	...	...
35 - 39	392	215	177	...	...	...
40 - 44	434	234	200	...	...	...
45 - 49	363	190	173	...	...	...
50 - 54	346	177	169	...	...	...
55 - 59	316	176	140	...	...	...
60 - 64	397	205	192	...	...	...
65 - 69	378	196	182	...	...	...
70 - 74	460	245	215	...	...	...
75 - 79	416	223	193	...	...	...
80 - 84	417	208	209	...	...	...
85 - 89	266	110	156	...	...	...
90 - 94	162	57	105	...	...	...
95 +	132	48	84	...	...	...
Unknown - Inconnu	658	362	296	...	...	...
Jamaica - Jamaïque[10]						
2005 (U)						
Total	17 552	9 473	8 079			
0	1 007	517	490	...	...	...
1 - 4	197	98	99	...	...	...
5 - 9	75	45	30	...	...	...
10 - 14	73	32	41	...	...	...
15 - 19	248	195	53	...	...	...
20 - 24	505	404	101	...	...	...
25 - 29	550	398	152	...	...	...
30 - 34	555	386	169	...	...	...
35 - 39	568	350	218	...	...	...
40 - 44	597	370	227	...	...	...
45 - 49	597	329	268	...	...	...

19. Deaths and death rates by age and sex: latest available year, 1998 - 2007
Décès et taux de mortalité selon l'âge et le sexe: dernière année disponible, 1998 - 2007 (continued - suite)

Continent, country or area, date, code and age (in years) / Continent, pays ou zone, date, code et âge (en années)	Number - Nombre			Rate - Taux		
	Both sexes Les deux sexes	Male Masculin	Female Féminin	Both sexes Les deux sexes	Male Masculin	Female Féminin
AMERICA, NORTH - AMÉRIQUE DU NORD						
Jamaica - Jamaïque[10]						
2005 (U)	636	382	254	...	...	...
50 - 54	670	397	273	...	...	...
55 - 59	981	566	415	...	...	...
60 - 64	1 159	658	501	...	...	...
65 - 69	1 701	974	727	...	...	...
70 - 74	7 433	3 372	4 061	...	...	...
75 +						
Martinique[6]						
2007 (C)	2 830	1 439	1 391	7.1	7.7	6.5
Total	51	31	20	2.0	2.4	♦1.6
0 - 4	47	28	19	...	...	...
0	4	3	1	...	...	...
1 - 4	4	3	1	♦0.1	♦0.2	♦0.1
5 - 9	7	5	2	♦0.2	♦0.3	♦0.1
10 - 14	16	12	4	♦0.5	♦0.8	♦0.3
15 - 19	26	22	4	♦1.1	♦1.9	♦0.3
20 - 24	19	13	6	♦1.0	♦1.5	♦0.6
25 - 29	35	22	13	1.4	♦2.1	♦0.9
30 - 34	36	22	14	1.2	♦1.6	♦0.8
35 - 39	53	31	22	1.6	2.0	♦1.2
40 - 44	64	46	18	2.0	3.2	♦1.1
45 - 49	107	68	39	4.1	5.6	2.8
50 - 54	97	57	40	4.3	5.5	3.2
55 - 59	146	91	55	7.8	10.3	5.5
60 - 64	226	135	91	14.2	18.7	10.4
65 - 69	305	173	132	21.3	27.2	16.6
70 - 74	382	200	182	35.8	44.2	29.6
75 - 79	443	217	226	59.2	76.6	48.6
80 - 84	388	168	220	92.5	122.1	78.1
85 - 89	269	91	178	137.9	159.6	128.9
90 - 94	156	32	124	212.8	196.3	217.5
95 +						
Mexico - Mexique[11]						
2007 (+C)	513 122	284 012[5]	228 936[5]	4.9	5.5	4.3
Total	30 412	17 183[5]	13 136[5]	15.7	17.3	13.8
0	6 046	3 301[5]	2 744[5]	0.8	0.8	0.7
1 - 4	2 965	1 630[5]	1 334[5]	0.3	0.3	0.2
5 - 9	3 564	2 118[5]	1 446[5]	0.3	0.4	0.3
10 - 14	7 930	5 494[5]	2 435[5]	0.8	1.0	0.5
15 - 19	9 963	7 344[5]	2 616[5]	1.0	1.5	0.5
20 - 24	11 095	8 200[5]	2 894[5]	1.2	1.9	0.6
25 - 29	12 950	9 438[5]	3 512[5]	1.5	2.3	0.8
30 - 34	14 848	10 479[5]	4 368[5]	1.9	2.8	1.1
35 - 39	17 546	11 626[5]	5 919[5]	2.6	3.5	1.7
40 - 44	21 895	13 973[5]	7 919[5]	3.9	5.1	2.7
45 - 49	26 662	16 180[5]	10 478[5]	6.0	7.5	4.5
50 - 54	31 497	18 241[5]	13 254[5]	9.1	11.1	7.3
55 - 59	36 888	20 548[5]	16 338[5]	13.7	16.2	11.5
60 - 64	42 479	23 225[5]	19 249[5]	20.6	24.2	17.4
65 - 69	49 124	26 245[5]	22 876[5]	32.6	38.2	27.9
70 - 74	52 418	26 855[5]	25 561[5]	50.9	58.6	44.8
75 - 79	51 134	25 377[5]	25 753[5]	79.9	91.9	70.8
80 - 84	41 080	18 821[5]	22 256[5]	121.4	133.3	112.8
85 - 89	24 440	10 153[5]	14 283[5]	165.0	170.1	161.5
90 - 94	12 391	4 789[5]	7 599[5]	244.8	242.7	246.1
95 - 99	3 882	1 342[5]	2 540[5]	411.9	374.3	434.9
100 +	1 913	1 450[5]	426[5]	..		..
Unknown - Inconnu						
Montserrat						
1999 (+C)	59	39	20	...	...	...
Total	-	-	-	...	...	...
0	-	-	-	...	...	...
1 - 4	-	-	-	...	...	...
5 - 9	-	-	-	...	...	...
10 - 14						

19. Deaths and death rates by age and sex: latest available year, 1998 - 2007
Décès et taux de mortalité selon l'âge et le sexe: dernière année disponible, 1998 - 2007 (continued - suite)

Continent, country or area, date, code and age (in years) / Continent, pays ou zone, date, code et âge (en annèes)	Number - Nombre			Rate - Taux		
	Both sexes Les deux sexes	Male Masculin	Female Féminin	Both sexes Les deux sexes	Male Masculin	Female Féminin
AMERICA, NORTH - AMÉRIQUE DU NORD						
Montserrat						
1999 (+C)						
15 - 19	1	-	1	...	...	...
20 - 24	-	-	-	...	...	...
25 - 29	-	-	-	...	...	...
30 - 34	-	-	-	...	...	...
35 - 39	-	-	-	...	...	...
40 - 44	-	-	-	...	...	...
45 - 49	1	1	-	...	...	...
50 - 54	1	1	-	...	...	...
55 - 59	2	2	-	...	...	...
60 - 64	3	2	1	...	...	...
65 - 69	3	2	1	...	...	...
70 - 74	7	6	1	...	...	...
75 - 79	5	4	1	...	...	...
80 - 84	15	8	7	...	...	...
85 - 89	11	5	6	...	...	...
90 +	9	7	2	...	...	...
Unknown - Inconnu	1	1	-	..	..	..
Netherlands Antilles - Antilles néerlandaises[11]						
2006 (C)						
Total	1 327	706	621	7.0	8.0	6.1
0 - 4	41	22	19	3.0	♦3.2	♦2.8
0	40	21	19	...	...	...
1 - 4	1	1	-	...	...	...
5 - 9	3	2	1	♦0.2	♦0.3	♦0.1
10 - 14	1	1	-	♦0.1	♦0.1	-
15 - 19	7	4	3	♦0.5	♦0.6	♦0.4
20 - 24	11	10	1	♦1.1	♦2.0	♦0.2
25 - 29	9	6	3	♦0.8	♦1.2	♦0.5
30 - 34	14	10	4	♦1.0	♦1.6	♦0.6
35 - 39	25	16	9	♦1.6	♦2.3	♦1.1
40 - 44	33	18	15	2.0	♦2.4	♦1.6
45 - 49	61	38	23	3.9	5.5	♦2.7
50 - 54	59	35	24	4.6	6.1	♦3.3
55 - 59	89	51	38	8.3	10.4	6.6
60 - 64	113	72	41	13.9	19.7	9.1
65 - 69	107	69	38	17.4	25.5	11.0
70 - 74	146	86	60	30.2	40.5	22.1
75 - 79	172	87	85	52.8	65.4	44.1
80 - 84	172	88	84	81.3	114.1	62.5
85 +	264	91	173	157.7	178.3	148.6
85 - 89	141	58	83	...	...	...
90 - 94	85	25	60	...	...	...
95 - 99	33	8	25	...	...	...
100 +	5	-	5	...	...	...
Nicaragua						
2007 (+U)						
Total	17 288	9 772	7 516	...	...	...
0	1 955	1 083	872	...	...	...
1 - 4	295	151	144	...	...	...
5 - 9	150	84	66	...	...	...
10 - 14	205	115	90	...	...	...
15 - 19	404	281	123	...	...	...
20 - 24	548	401	147	...	...	...
25 - 29	552	403	149	...	...	...
30 - 34	545	393	152	...	...	...
35 - 39	557	378	179	...	...	...
40 - 44	598	410	188	...	...	...
45 - 49	759	469	290	...	...	...
50 - 54	931	560	371	...	...	...
55 - 59	979	567	412	...	...	...
60 - 64	999	544	455	...	...	...
65 - 69	1 145	663	482	...	...	...
70 - 74	1 379	728	651	...	...	...
75 - 79	1 462	770	692	...	...	...
80 +	3 825	1 772	2 053	...	...	...

19. Deaths and death rates by age and sex: latest available year, 1998 - 2007
Décès et taux de mortalité selon l'âge et le sexe: dernière année disponible, 1998 - 2007 (continued - suite)

Continent, country or area, date, code and age (in years) / Continent, pays ou zone, date, code et âge (en années)	Number - Nombre			Rate - Taux		
	Both sexes Les deux sexes	Male Masculin	Female Féminin	Both sexes Les deux sexes	Male Masculin	Female Féminin
AMERICA, NORTH - AMÉRIQUE DU NORD						
Panama						
2007 (U)						
Total	14 775	8 664	6 111	...	...	...
0	992	567	425	...	...	...
1 - 4	380	209	171	...	...	...
5 - 9	109	64	45	...	...	...
10 - 14	118	72	46	...	...	...
15 - 19	240	163	77	...	...	...
20 - 24	361	275	86	...	...	...
25 - 29	369	260	109	...	...	...
30 - 34	377	264	113	...	...	...
35 - 39	425	294	131	...	...	...
40 - 44	454	298	156	...	...	...
45 - 49	496	316	180	...	...	...
50 - 54	607	372	235	...	...	...
55 - 59	720	447	273	...	...	...
60 - 64	852	547	305	...	...	...
65 - 69	1 005	615	390	...	...	...
70 - 74	1 195	713	482	...	...	...
75 - 79	1 465	831	634	...	...	...
80 - 84	1 617	913	704	...	...	...
85 +	2 918	1 387	1 531	...	...	...
Unknown - Inconnu	75	57	18	..		..
Puerto Rico - Porto Rico						
2006 (C)						
Total	28 589	15 913	12 676	7.3	8.4	6.2
0	442	260	182	8.9	10.2	7.5
1 - 4	45	20	25	0.2	♦0.2	♦0.3
5 - 9	22	12	10	♦0.1	♦0.1	♦0.1
10 - 14	37	22	15	0.1	♦0.1	♦0.1
15 - 19	203	167	36	0.7	1.1	0.2
20 - 24	428	366	62	1.5	2.5	0.4
25 - 29	427	351	76	1.5	2.5	0.5
30 - 34	391	312	79	1.5	2.4	0.6
35 - 39	508	363	145	1.9	2.9	1.1
40 - 44	692	467	225	2.6	3.7	1.6
45 - 49	931	653	278	3.6	5.5	2.0
50 - 54	1 142	768	374	4.8	7.1	2.9
55 - 59	1 642	1 090	552	7.1	10.3	4.4
60 - 64	2 125	1 298	827	10.9	14.6	7.8
65 - 69	2 376	1 436	940	15.0	19.9	10.9
70 - 74	2 889	1 602	1 287	22.9	28.6	18.4
75 - 79	3 293	1 780	1 513	35.3	44.6	28.3
80 +	10 927	4 890	6 037	86.6	98.0	79.2
80 - 84	3 933	1 920	2 013	...	...	...
85 - 89	3 381	1 536	1 845	...	...	...
90 - 94	2 373	965	1 408	...	...	...
95 - 99	965	372	593	...	...	...
100 +	275	97	178	...	...	...
Unknown - Inconnu	69	56	13	..		..
Saint Kitts and Nevis - Saint-Kitts-et-Nevis						
2001 (+C)						
Total	352	181	171	...		...
0	10	3	7	...		...
1 - 4	6	1	5	...		...
5 - 9	3	3	-	...		...
10 - 14	2	1	1	...		...
15 - 19	2	1	1	...		...
20 - 24	2	1	1	...		...
25 - 29	6	4	2	...		...
30 - 34	5	3	2	...		...
35 - 39	8	6	2	...		...
40 - 44	9	6	3	...		...
45 - 49	22	16	6	...		...
50 - 54	9	4	5	...		...
55 - 59	12	8	4	...		...
60 - 64	13	9	4	...		...

19. Deaths and death rates by age and sex: latest available year, 1998 - 2007
Décès et taux de mortalité selon l'âge et le sexe: dernière année disponible, 1998 - 2007 (continued - suite)

Continent, country or area, date, code and age (in years) / Continent, pays ou zone, date, code et âge (en années)	Number - Nombre			Rate - Taux		
	Both sexes Les deux sexes	Male Masculin	Female Féminin	Both sexes Les deux sexes	Male Masculin	Female Féminin
AMERICA, NORTH - AMÉRIQUE DU NORD						
Saint Kitts and Nevis - Saint-Kitts-et-Nevis						
2001 (+C)						
65 - 69	19	9	10	...	...	...
70 - 74	29	17	12	...	...	...
75 - 79	63	31	32	...	...	...
80 - 84	56	25	31	...	...	...
85 +	76	33	43	...	...	...
Saint Lucia - Sainte-Lucie						
2005* (C)						
Total	1 107	625	482	6.7	7.8	5.7
0 - 4	53	30	23	3.9	♦4.4	♦3.3
0	46	28	18	...	...	...
1 - 4	7	2	5	...	...	...
5 - 9	2	1	1	...	...	...
10 - 14	7	4	3	♦0.1	♦0.1	♦0.1
15 - 19	14	12	2	♦0.4	♦0.5	♦0.3
20 - 24	19	15	4	♦0.8	♦1.4	♦0.2
25 - 29	24	18	6	♦1.2	♦1.9	♦0.5
30 - 34	33	21	12	♦1.8	♦2.7	♦0.9
35 - 39	25	19	6	2.6	♦3.5	♦1.9
40 - 44	40	30	10	♦2.1	♦3.3	♦1.0
45 - 49	38	28	10	3.6	♦5.6	♦1.8
50 - 54	49	25	24	4.4	♦6.5	♦2.3
55 - 59	42	23	19	7.6	♦7.6	♦7.5
60 - 64	82	52	30	8.4	♦9.6	♦7.3
65 - 69	103	63	40	20.1	27.5	♦13.7
70 - 74	88	52	36	28.8	37.5	21.1
75 - 79	114	72	42	29.2	36.6	22.6
80 +	361	154	207	58.7	79.4	40.5
80 - 84	154	70	84	127.0	129.4	125.3
85 +	207	84	123	...	...	...
Unknown - Inconnu	13	6	7	...	...	..
Saint Vincent and the Grenadines - Saint-Vincent-et-les Grenadines						
2003 (+C)						
Total	790	434	356	...	...	...
0	35	19	16	...	...	...
1 - 4	7	4	3	...	...	...
5 - 9	5	2	3	...	...	...
10 - 14	3	2	1	...	...	...
15 - 19	6	6	-	...	...	...
20 - 24	8	7	1	...	...	...
25 - 29	13	12	1	...	...	...
30 - 34	20	12	8	...	...	...
35 - 39	31	18	13	...	...	...
40 - 44	23	14	9	...	...	...
45 - 49	27	19	8	...	...	...
50 - 54	33	21	12	...	...	...
55 - 59	45	28	17	...	...	...
60 - 64	50	37	13	...	...	...
65 - 69	69	40	29	...	...	...
70 - 74	85	42	43	...	...	...
75 - 79	89	38	51	...	...	...
80 - 84	99	49	50	...	...	...
85 +	137	59	78	...	...	...
Unknown - Inconnu	5	5	-	...	...	..
Trinidad and Tobago - Trinité-et-Tobago						
2005 (C)						
Total	9 885	5 702	4 183	...	...	...
0	266	149	117	...	...	...
1 - 4	39	23	16	...	...	...
5 - 9	20	13	7	...	...	...
10 - 14	31	14	17	...	...	...
15 - 19	136	94	42	...	...	...
20 - 24	234	185	49	...	...	...
25 - 29	246	182	64	...	...	...
30 - 34	252	170	82	...	...	...

19. Deaths and death rates by age and sex: latest available year, 1998 - 2007
Décès et taux de mortalité selon l'âge et le sexe: dernière année disponible, 1998 - 2007 (continued - suite)

Continent, country or area, date, code and age (in years) / Continent, pays ou zone, date, code et âge (en années)	Number - Nombre			Rate - Taux		
	Both sexes Les deux sexes	Male Masculin	Female Féminin	Both sexes Les deux sexes	Male Masculin	Female Féminin
AMERICA, NORTH - AMÉRIQUE DU NORD						
Trinidad and Tobago - Trinité-et-Tobago						
2005 (C)						
35 - 39	258	161	97	...	...	...
40 - 44	434	284	150	...	...	...
45 - 49	479	306	173	...	...	...
50 - 54	540	345	195	...	...	...
55 - 59	712	452	260	...	...	...
60 - 64	812	482	330	...	...	...
65 - 69	949	568	381	...	...	...
70 - 74	927	515	412	...	...	...
75 - 79	1 057	572	485	...	...	...
80 - 84	1 043	552	491	...	...	...
85 +	1 445	631	814	...	...	...
Unknown - Inconnu	5	4	1	..	..	...
Turks and Caicos Islands - Îles Turques et Caïques						
2005 (C)						
Total	53	32	21	...	...	...
0	1	1	-	...	...	...
1 - 4	-	-	-	...	...	...
5 - 9	-	-	-	...	...	...
10 - 14	1	1	-	...	...	...
15 - 19	1	1	-	...	...	...
20 - 24	-	-	-	...	...	...
25 - 29	2	2	-	...	...	...
30 - 34	8	5	3	...	...	...
35 - 39	3	2	1	...	...	...
40 - 44	3	1	2	...	...	...
45 - 49	1	1	-	...	...	...
50 - 54	2	-	2	...	...	...
55 - 59	2	2	-	...	...	...
60 - 64	2	2	-	...	...	...
65 - 69	-	-	-	...	...	...
70 - 74	3	3	-	...	...	...
75 - 79	6	1	5	...	...	...
80 - 84	5	3	2	...	...	...
85 +	11	5	6	...	...	...
Unknown - Inconnu	2	2	-	..	..	..
United States of America - États-Unis d'Amérique						
2005 (C)						
Total	2 448 017	1 207 675	1 240 342	8.3	8.3	8.2
0	28 440	16 018	12 422	6.9	7.6	6.2
1 - 4	4 756	2 765	1 991	0.3	0.3	0.3
5 - 9	2 837	1 556	1 281	0.1	0.2	0.1
10 - 14	3 765	2 297	1 468	0.2	0.2	0.1
15 - 19	13 703	9 886	3 817	0.7	0.9	0.4
20 - 24	20 531	15 623	4 908	1.0	1.4	0.5
25 - 29	19 568	14 242	5 326	1.0	1.4	0.5
30 - 34	22 357	15 041	7 316	1.1	1.5	0.7
35 - 39	31 420	20 011	11 409	1.5	1.9	1.1
40 - 44	53 365	33 298	20 067	2.3	2.9	1.7
45 - 49	79 383	49 279	30 104	3.5	4.4	2.6
50 - 54	104 147	65 193	38 954	5.2	6.7	3.8
55 - 59	127 478	77 988	49 490	7.3	9.3	5.5
60 - 64	147 823	87 441	60 382	11.4	14.1	8.9
65 - 69	172 236	98 412	73 824	17.0	20.8	13.6
70 - 74	226 119	124 395	101 724	26.6	32.7	21.6
75 - 79	307 888	159 114	148 774	41.5	51.0	34.6
80 - 84	378 777	176 121	202 656	67.1	81.5	58.2
85 +	703 169	238 796	464 373	138.0	148.9	133.0
Unknown - Inconnu	255	199	56	..	..	..
United States Virgin Islands - Îles Vierges américaines						
2007 (C)						
Total	727	424	303	...	...	...
0	12	6	6	...	...	...
1 - 4	2	2	-	...	...	...
5 - 9	-	-	-	...	...	...

19. Deaths and death rates by age and sex: latest available year, 1998 - 2007
Décès et taux de mortalité selon l'âge et le sexe: dernière année disponible, 1998 - 2007 (continued - suite)

Continent, country or area, date, code and age (in years) / Continent, pays ou zone, date, code et âge (en années)	Number - Nombre			Rate - Taux		
	Both sexes Les deux sexes	Male Masculin	Female Féminin	Both sexes Les deux sexes	Male Masculin	Female Féminin
AMERICA, NORTH - AMÉRIQUE DU NORD						
United States Virgin Islands - Îles Vierges américaines						
2007 (C)						
10 - 14	2	1	1			
15 - 19	9	8	1	...	...	...
20 - 24	16	15	1	...	...	...
25 - 29	20	14	6	...	...	...
30 - 34	16	10	6	...	...	...
35 - 39	•16	13	3	...	...	...
40 - 44	33	21	12	...	...	...
45 - 49	26	13	13	...	...	...
50 - 54	50	34	16	...	...	...
55 - 59	51	29	22	...	...	...
60 - 64	79	55	24	...	...	...
65 - 69	50	36	14	...	...	...
70 - 74	68	43	25	...	...	...
75 +	273	120	153	...	...	...
Unknown - Inconnu	4	4	-	..	..	..
AMERICA, SOUTH - AMÉRIQUE DU SUD						
Argentina - Argentine						
2007 (C)						
Total	315 852	165 959[5]	149 698[5]	8.0	8.6	7.5
0 - 4	10 912	6 088[5]	4 808[5]	3.3	3.6	2.9
0	9 300	5 221[5]	4 063[5]	...	...	...
1 - 4	1 612	867[5]	745[5]	...	...	...
5 - 9	804	452[5]	351[5]	0.2	0.3	0.2
10 - 14	1 107	644[5]	462[5]	0.3	0.4	0.3
15 - 19	2 551	1 808[5]	742[5]	0.7	1.0	0.4
20 - 24	3 088	2 282[5]	802[5]	0.9	1.4	0.5
25 - 29	3 333	2 363[5]	965[5]	1.0	1.4	0.6
30 - 34	3 387	2 269[5]	1 118[5]	1.1	1.5	0.8
35 - 39	4 004	2 582[5]	1 420[5]	1.6	2.1	1.1
40 - 44	5 322	3 311[5]	2 007[5]	2.3	2.9	1.7
45 - 49	7 924	4 973[5]	2 950[5]	3.7	4.7	2.7
50 - 54	12 152	7 804[5]	4 344[5]	6.0	8.0	4.1
55 - 59	17 006	11 044[5]	5 954[5]	9.5	12.9	6.3
60 - 64	21 982	14 265[5]	7 708[5]	14.5	20.1	9.6
65 - 69	26 979	17 049[5]	9 920[5]	21.5	30.1	14.4
70 - 74	33 266	19 952[5]	13 299[5]	31.8	45.0	22.1
75 - 79	43 162	23 065[5]	20 082[5]	52.0	71.0	39.8
80 +	118 105	45 540	72 531	137.1	161.3	125.2
80 - 84	46 604	21 764[5]	24 828[5]	...	...	...
85 +	71 501	23 776[5]	47 703[5]	...	...	...
Unknown - Inconnu	768	468[5]	235[5]	..	..	..
Brazil - Brésil[12]						
2007 (U)						
Total	1 036 079	598 166	437 913			
0	35 159	19 951	15 208	...	...	...
1 - 4	7 186	3 947	3 239	...	...	...
5 - 9	4 542	2 645	1 897	...	...	...
10 - 14	5 572	3 431	2 141	...	...	...
15 - 19	18 095	14 359	3 736	...	...	...
20 - 24	26 296	21 526	4 770	...	...	...
25 - 29	27 346	21 199	6 147	...	...	...
30 - 34	27 294	20 142	7 152	...	...	...
35 - 39	31 265	22 018	9 247	...	...	...
40 - 44	40 110	26 944	13 166	...	...	...
45 - 49	50 306	32 803	17 503	...	...	...
50 - 54	60 247	38 873	21 374	...	...	...
55 - 59	69 181	43 148	26 033	...	...	...
60 - 64	76 713	46 482	30 231	...	...	...
65 - 69	89 618	52 885	36 733	...	...	...
70 - 74	101 623	56 914	44 709	...	...	...

Continent, country or area, date, code and age (in years) / Continent, pays ou zone, date, code et âge (en années)	Number - Nombre			Rate - Taux		
	Both sexes Les deux sexes	Male Masculin	Female Féminin	Both sexes Les deux sexes	Male Masculin	Female Féminin
AMERICA, SOUTH - AMÉRIQUE DU SUD						
Brazil - Brésil[12]						
2007 (U)						
75 - 79	111 836	58 632	53 204	...	...	...
80 - 84	104 056	50 253	53 803	...	...	...
85 - 89	77 879	33 895	43 984	...	...	...
90 - 94	46 099	17 593	28 506	...	...	...
95 - 99	17 248	5 970	11 278	...	...	...
100 +	4 193	1 247	2 946	...	...	...
Unknown - Inconnu	4 215	3 309	906	..	..	...
Chile - Chili						
2006 (C)						
Total	85 639	45 987	39 652	5.2	5.7	4.8
0	1 839	1 019	820	7.5	8.1	6.8
1 - 4	347	205	142	0.3	0.4	0.3
5 - 9	219	131	88	0.2	0.2	0.1
10 - 14	303	175	128	0.2	0.2	0.2
15 - 19	702	512	190	0.5	0.7	0.3
20 - 24	939	737	202	0.7	1.1	0.3
25 - 29	1 008	777	231	0.8	1.3	0.4
30 - 34	1 287	941	346	1.0	1.5	0.6
35 - 39	1 558	1 110	448	1.3	1.8	0.7
40 - 44	2 306	1 566	740	1.8	2.5	1.2
45 - 49	2 882	1 794	1 088	2.6	3.2	1.9
50 - 54	3 608	2 284	1 324	4.0	5.2	2.9
55 - 59	4 643	2 891	1 752	6.4	8.2	4.7
60 - 64	6 143	3 762	2 381	10.3	13.3	7.6
65 - 69	7 598	4 495	3 103	16.7	21.5	12.6
70 - 74	9 231	5 367	3 864	25.9	34.4	19.3
75 - 79	11 949	6 386	5 563	45.2	58.8	35.8
80 +	29 077	11 835	17 242	109.4	124.6	101.0
80 - 84	11 154	5 352	5 802	...	...	...
85 - 89	9 293	3 842	5 451	...	...	...
90 - 94	6 099	1 997	4 102	...	...	...
95 - 99	2 131	567	1 564	...	...	...
100 +	400	77	323	...	...	...
Colombia - Colombie						
2006 (U)						
Total	192 814	111 276[5]	81 507[5]	...	...	...
0	11 049	6 255[5]	4 791[5]	...	...	...
1 - 4	2 429	1 298[5]	1 131[5]	...	...	...
5 - 9	1 321	774[5]	546[5]	...	...	...
10 - 14	1 426	851[5]	575[5]	...	...	...
15 - 19	4 438	3 302[5]	1 134[5]	...	...	...
20 - 24	6 572	5 398[5]	1 172[5]	...	...	...
25 - 29	6 915	5 612[5]	1 302[5]	...	...	...
30 - 34	5 853	4 662[5]	1 190[5]	...	...	...
35 - 39	6 017	4 319[5]	1 695[5]	...	...	...
40 - 44	6 327	4 238[5]	2 088[5]	...	...	...
45 - 49	7 345	4 634[5]	2 710[5]	...	...	...
50 - 54	8 466	5 078[5]	3 388[5]	...	...	...
55 - 59	9 706	5 769[5]	3 936[5]	...	...	...
60 - 64	11 326	6 466[5]	4 859[5]	...	...	...
65 - 69	15 042	8 519[5]	6 522[5]	...	...	...
70 - 74	18 286	9 808[5]	8 477[5]	...	...	...
75 - 79	21 754	11 586[5]	10 168[5]	...	...	...
80 - 84	19 443	9 612[5]	9 831[5]	...	...	...
85 +	28 025	12 235[5]	15 790[5]	...	...	...
Unknown - Inconnu	1 074	860[5]	202[5]	..	...	...
Ecuador - Équateur[13]						
2007 (U)						
Total	58 016	33 103	24 913	...	...	...
0	3 529	2 027	1 502	...	...	...
1 - 4	1 278	692	586	...	...	...
5 - 9	596	356	240	...	...	...
10 - 14	647	385	262	...	...	...
15 - 19	1 230	814	416	...	...	...

Continent, country or area, date, code and age (in years) Continent, pays ou zone, date, code et âge (en années)	Number - Nombre			Rate - Taux		
	Both sexes Les deux sexes	Male Masculin	Female Féminin	Both sexes Les deux sexes	Male Masculin	Female Féminin
AMERICA, SOUTH - AMÉRIQUE DU SUD						
Ecuador - Équateur[13]						
2007 (U)						
20 - 24	1 919	1 487	432	...	...	...
25 - 29	2 029	1 511	518	...	...	...
30 - 34	1 747	1 282	465	...	...	...
35 - 39	1 745	1 175	570	...	...	...
40 - 44	1 929	1 262	667	...	...	...
45 - 49	2 273	1 437	836	...	...	...
50 - 54	2 558	1 536	1 022	...	...	...
55 - 59	3 035	1 826	1 209	...	...	...
60 - 64	3 298	1 935	1 363	...	...	...
65 - 69	3 769	2 141	1 628	...	...	...
70 - 74	4 674	2 520	2 154	...	...	...
75 - 79	5 572	3 017	2 555	...	...	...
80 - 84	5 651	2 956	2 695	...	...	...
85 - 89	4 965	2 431	2 534	...	...	...
90 - 94	3 530	1 519	2 011	...	...	...
95 +	1 947	732	1 215	...	...	...
Unknown - Inconnu	95	62	33	...	...	...
French Guiana - Guyane française[6]						
2007 (C)						
Total	690	405	285	...	...	...
0	77	39	38	...	...	...
1 - 4	18	11	7	...	...	...
5 - 9	9	4	5	...	...	...
10 - 14	8	5	3	...	...	...
15 - 19	13	10	3	...	...	...
20 - 24	14	12	2	...	...	...
25 - 29	16	11	5	...	...	...
30 - 34	23	15	8	...	...	...
35 - 39	28	21	7	...	...	...
40 - 44	41	24	17	...	...	...
45 - 49	48	35	13	...	...	...
50 - 54	26	16	10	...	...	...
55 - 59	32	24	8	...	...	...
60 - 64	33	25	8	...	...	...
65 - 69	48	24	24	...	...	...
70 - 74	46	29	17	...	...	...
75 - 79	62	32	30	...	...	...
80 - 84	57	26	31	...	...	...
85 - 89	50	27	23	...	...	...
90 - 94	28	12	16	...	...	...
95 - 99	10	3	7	...	...	...
100 +	3	-	3	...	...	...
Guyana[7]						
2003 (+C)						
Total	4 986	2 898	2 088	...	...	...
0	290	157	133	...	...	...
1 - 4	72	40	32	...	...	...
5 - 9	33	21	12	...	...	...
10 - 14	43	24	19	...	...	...
15 - 19	64	39	25	...	...	...
20 - 24	148	97	51	...	...	...
25 - 29	175	120	55	...	...	...
30 - 34	263	169	94	...	...	...
35 - 39	274	188	86	...	...	...
40 - 44	277	195	82	...	...	...
45 - 49	305	197	108	...	...	...
50 - 54	338	207	131	...	...	...
55 - 59	339	212	127	...	...	...
60 - 64	377	228	149	...	...	...
65 - 69	401	226	175	...	...	...
70 - 74	418	214	204	...	...	...
75 - 79	441	224	217	...	...	...
80 - 84	291	145	146	...	...	...
85 - 89	220	97	123	...	...	...
90 - 94	104	39	65	...	...	...

Continent, country or area, date, code and age (in years) Continent, pays ou zone, date, code et âge (en années)	Number - Nombre			Rate - Taux		
	Both sexes Les deux sexes	Male Masculin	Female Féminin	Both sexes Les deux sexes	Male Masculin	Female Féminin
AMERICA, SOUTH - AMÉRIQUE DU SUD						
Guyana[7]						
2003 (+C)						
95 - 99	36	12	24	...	...	...
100 + ...	77	47	30	...	...	...
Paraguay						
2006 (U)						
Total.........................	19 298	10 544[5]	8 709[5]	...	...	...
0	549	318[5]	229[5]	...	...	...
1 - 4	235	123[5]	112[5]	...	...	...
5 - 9	154	89[5]	65[5]	...	...	...
10 - 14	161	93[5]	67[5]	...	...	...
15 - 19	403	275[5]	128[5]	...	...	...
20 - 24	493	380[5]	112[5]	...	...	...
25 - 29	472	336[5]	135[5]	...	...	...
30 - 34	438	292[5]	145[5]	...	...	...
35 - 39	519	328[5]	191[5]	...	...	...
40 - 44	678	403[5]	275[5]	...	...	...
45 - 49	829	489[5]	336[5]	...	...	...
50 - 54	976	583[5]	393[5]	...	...	...
55 - 59	1 190	689[5]	499[5]	...	...	...
60 - 64	1 283	739[5]	542[5]	...	...	...
65 - 69	1 479	821[5]	655[5]	...	...	...
70 - 74	1 737	957[5]	775[5]	...	...	...
75 - 79	2 187	1 188[5]	994[5]	...	...	...
80 - 84	2 040	993[5]	1 040[5]	...	...	...
85 + ...	3 256	1 330[5]	1 921[5]	...	...	...
Unknown - Inconnu	219	118[6]	95[5]	..	..	...
Peru - Pérou[14]						
2006 (+U)						
Total.........................	82 620	44 503	38 117	...	...	...
0 - 4	7 556	4 199	3 357	...	...	...
5 - 9	743	425	318	...	...	...
10 - 14	811	450	361	...	...	...
15 - 19	1 373	804	569	...	...	...
20 - 24	1 816	1 156	660	...	...	...
25 - 29	1 949	1 283	666	...	...	...
30 - 34	2 028	1 300	728	...	...	...
35 - 39	2 335	1 469	866	...	...	...
40 - 44	2 673	1 561	1 112	...	...	...
45 - 49	3 144	1 772	1 372	...	...	...
50 - 54	3 553	1 965	1 588	...	...	...
55 - 59	4 084	2 309	1 775	...	...	...
60 - 64	4 858	2 695	2 163	...	...	...
65 - 69	6 047	3 358	2 689	...	...	...
70 - 74	7 574	4 151	3 423	...	...	...
75 - 79	8 589	4 594	3 995	...	...	...
80 + ...	23 487	11 012	12 475	...	...	...
Suriname						
2007 (C)						
Total.........................	3 374	1 864	1 510	6.6	7.2	6.0
0	134	72	62	13.7	14.7	12.7
1 - 4	42	21	21	1.0	♦1.0	♦1.1
5 - 9	16	9	7	♦0.3	♦0.3	♦0.3
10 - 14	19	10	9	♦0.4	♦0.4	♦0.4
15 - 19	48	26	22	1.0	♦1.1	♦1.0
20 - 24	71	45	26	1.6	2.0	♦1.2
25 - 29	96	51	45	2.3	2.4	2.2
30 - 34	107	62	45	2.7	3.1	2.3
35 - 39	127	89	38	3.4	4.7	2.1
40 - 44	148	96	52	4.4	5.7	3.2
45 - 49	192	116	76	6.6	7.9	5.3
50 - 54	178	111	67	7.4	9.3	5.6
55 - 59	204	122	82	10.7	13.2	8.4
60 - 64	242	142	100	16.1	19.6	12.8
65 - 69	289	165	124	25.2	30.4	20.5
70 - 74	407	226	181	47.7	56.8	39.8

Continent, country or area, date, code and age (in years) / Continent, pays ou zone, date, code et âge (en annèes)	Number - Nombre			Rate - Taux		
	Both sexes Les deux sexes	Male Masculin	Female Féminin	Both sexes Les deux sexes	Male Masculin	Female Féminin
AMERICA, SOUTH - AMÉRIQUE DU SUD						
Suriname						
2007 (C)						
75 - 79	373	204	169			
80 +	681	297	384	63.0	74.8	52.9
80 - 84	333	162	171	130.2	135.9	126.1
85 - 89	200	85	115	...	...	...
90 - 94	103	36	67	...	...	...
95 - 99	36	13	23	...	...	...
100 +	9	1	8	...	...	...
Unknown - Inconnu	-	-	-	...	...	...
Uruguay				..	..	..
2002 (C)						
Total	31 628	16 796[5]	14 819[5]			
0	708	401[5]	304[5]	9.6	10.5	8.7
1 - 4	104	69	35	14.0	15.4	12.3
5 - 9	63	31	32	0.5	0.6	0.3
10 - 14	67	42	25	0.2	0.2	0.2
15 - 19	182	139	43	0.2	0.3	♦0.2
20 - 24	249	199	50	0.7	1.0	0.3
25 - 29	260	196	64	1.0	1.5	0.4
30 - 34	301	200	101	1.1	1.6	0.5
35 - 39	339	218[5]	120[5]	1.4	1.8	0.9
40 - 44	494	273	221	1.6	2.1	1.1
45 - 49	754	467	287	2.4	2.7	2.1
50 - 54	1 108	724	384	4.0	5.1	2.9
55 - 59	1 501	990	511	6.5	8.8	4.3
60 - 64	2 095	1 422	673	9.9	13.8	6.4
65 - 69	2 842	1 818	1 024	15.0	22.0	9.0
70 - 74	3 938	2 395[5]	1 542[5]	22.0	31.8	14.3
75 +	16 534	7 149[5]	9 381[5]	33.3	47.7	22.7
Unknown - Inconnu	89	63[5]	22[5]	88.5	105.3	78.9
2007 (C)				..	..	..
Total	33 706	...	...			
0	572	...	...	10.1	...	...
1 - 4	83	...	...	11.9	...	...
5 - 9	50	...	...	0.4	...	...
10 - 14	76	...	...	0.2	...	...
15 - 19	185	...	...	0.3	...	...
20 - 24	224	...	...	0.7	...	...
25 - 29	267	...	...	0.9	...	...
30 - 34	301	...	...	1.1	...	...
35 - 39	358	...	...	1.3	...	...
40 - 44	454	...	...	1.7	...	...
45 - 49	679	...	...	2.2	...	...
50 - 54	1 080	...	...	3.3	...	...
55 - 59	1 468	...	...	5.9	...	...
60 - 64	2 058	...	...	9.0	...	...
65 - 69	2 689	...	...	14.6	...	...
70 - 74	3 656	...	...	21.1	...	...
75 - 79	4 953	...	...	32.6	...	...
80 - 84	5 324	...	...	51.6	...	...
85 - 89	4 690	...	...	86.1	...	...
90 +	4 122	...	...	141.7	...	...
Venezuela (Bolivarian Republic of) - Venezuela (République bolivarienne du)[15]				255.6	...	...
2002 (C)						
Total	105 388	64 917	40 471			
0	7 645	4 406	3 239	4.2	5.1	3.2
1 - 4	1 937	1 077	860	13.5	15.2	11.7
5 - 9	829	493	336	0.9	0.9	0.8
10 - 14	1 061	668	393	0.3	0.4	0.3
15 - 19	3 540	2 929	611	0.4	0.5	0.3
20 - 24	5 301	4 579	722	1.4	2.2	0.5
25 - 29	4 293	3 578	715	2.3	3.9	0.6
30 - 34	3 957	3 002	955	2.1	3.5	0.7
35 - 39	3 621	2 586	1 035	2.1	3.2	1.0
40 - 44	4 168	2 795	1 373	2.1	3.0	1.2
				2.8	3.7	1.8

Continent, country or area, date, code and age (in years) Continent, pays ou zone, date, code et âge (en années)	Number - Nombre			Rate - Taux		
	Both sexes Les deux sexes	Male Masculin	Female Féminin	Both sexes Les deux sexes	Male Masculin	Female Féminin

AMERICA, SOUTH - AMÉRIQUE DU SUD

Venezuela (Bolivarian Republic of) - Venezuela
(République bolivarienne du)[15]
2002 (C)

45 - 49	4 878	3 164	1 714	3.9	5.0	2.7
50 - 54	5 518	3 549	1 969	5.3	6.8	3.8
55 - 59	5 802	3 719	2 083	7.2	9.4	5.1
60 - 64	6 494	4 032	2 462	11.0	14.0	8.1
65 - 69	7 964	4 746	3 218	17.7	22.1	13.7
70 - 74	9 145	5 339	3 806	26.5	33.3	20.7
75 - 79	9 369	5 076	4 293	40.2	48.6	33.4
80 +	19 600	8 973	10 627	117.7	128.1	110.2
80 - 84	8 247	4 164	4 083	...	...	...
85 - 89	6 270	2 793	3 477	...	...	...
90 - 94	3 518	1 463	2 055	...	...	...
95 - 99	1 201	420	781	...	...	...
100 +	364	133	231	...	...	...
Unknown - Inconnu	266	206	60	..	..	..

ASIA - ASIE

Armenia - Arménie[16]
2007 (C)

Total	26 830	13 916	12 914	8.3	8.9	7.7
0 - 4	495	303	192	2.7	3.1	2.3
0	433	268	165	11.3	13.1	9.2
1 - 4	62	35	27	0.4	0.5	◆0.4
5 - 9	34	19	15	0.2	◆0.2	◆0.2
10 - 14	46	27	19	0.2	◆0.2	◆0.2
15 - 19	107	80	27	0.3	0.5	◆0.2
20 - 24	165	124	41	0.5	0.8	0.3
25 - 29	181	129	52	0.7	1.0	0.4
30 - 34	201	142	59	0.9	1.3	0.5
35 - 39	288	205	83	1.5	2.2	0.8
40 - 44	549	399	150	2.4	3.6	1.2
45 - 49	1 031	721	310	3.8	5.6	2.2
50 - 54	1 298	878	420	6.2	9.1	3.8
55 - 59	1 472	980	492	9.8	14.4	6.0
60 - 64	1 209	785	424	15.8	23.7	9.8
65 - 69	2 875	1 680	1 195	22.8	31.5	16.4
70 - 74	4 300	2 358	1 942	43.3	57.1	33.5
75 - 79	5 329	2 582	2 747	67.4	82.3	57.6
80 - 84	4 478	1 739	2 739	130.8	160.9	117.0
85 +	2 772	765	2 007	283.5	309.3	274.7
85 - 89	1 670	478	1 192	...	...	...
90 - 94	773	203	570	...	...	...
95 - 99	272	65	207	...	...	...
100 +	57	19	38	...	...	...

Azerbaijan - Azerbaïdjan[16]
2007 (+C)

Total	53 655	28 636	25 019	6.3	6.8	5.8
0 - 4	2 351	1 321	1 030	3.6	3.7	3.4
0	1 756	966	790	11.7	11.9	11.4
1 - 4	595	355	240	1.2	1.3	1.0
5 - 9	213	117	96	0.4	0.4	0.4
10 - 14	292	172	120	0.4	0.4	0.3
15 - 19	493	348	145	0.5	0.7	0.3
20 - 24	634	440	194	0.7	1.0	0.5
25 - 29	739	483	256	1.0	1.4	0.7
30 - 34	919	680	239	1.5	2.3	0.7
35 - 39	1 217	860	357	1.9	2.8	1.1
40 - 44	1 859	1 268	591	2.7	4.0	1.6
45 - 49	2 599	1 782	817	4.0	5.7	2.4
50 - 54	2 999	2 010	989	6.8	9.5	4.3
55 - 59	3 279	2 147	1 132	11.2	15.5	7.4
60 - 64	2 482	1 522	960	17.4	23.3	12.4
65 - 69	6 553	3 735	2 818	29.9	39.0	22.8

19. Deaths and death rates by age and sex: latest available year, 1998 - 2007
Décès et taux de mortalité selon l'âge et le sexe: dernière année disponible, 1998 - 2007 (continued - suite)

Continent, country or area, date, code and age (in years) / Continent, pays ou zone, date, code et âge (en années)	Number - Nombre			Rate - Taux		
	Both sexes Les deux sexes	Male Masculin	Female Féminin	Both sexes Les deux sexes	Male Masculin	Female Féminin
ASIA - ASIE						
Azerbaijan - Azerbaïdjan[16]						
2007 (+C)						
70 - 74	8 911	4 609	4 302	46.8	56.6	39.5
75 - 79	8 655	4 055	4 600	73.8	82.3	67.7
80 - 84	4 885	1 967	2 918	100.9	109.9	95.7
85 - 89	2 461	687	1 774	140.6	127.2	146.6
90 - 94	1 141	274	867	203.8	171.3	216.8
95 - 99	563	112	451	181.6	140.0	196.1
100 +	410	47	363	372.7	117.5	518.6
Bahrain - Bahreïn						
2007 (C)						
Total.	2 270	1 423	847	2.2	2.3	2.1
0 - 4	165	88	77	2.2	2.3	2.1
0	133	69	64	...	...	...
1 - 4	32	19	13	...	...	...
5 - 9	15	7	8	♦0.2	♦0.2	♦0.2
10 - 14	20	16	4	♦0.3	♦0.4	♦0.1
15 - 19	32	26	6	0.5	♦0.7	♦0.2
20 - 24	50	42	8	0.5	0.7	♦0.2
25 - 29	71	55	16	0.5	0.6	♦0.4
30 - 34	75	63	12	0.6	0.7	♦0.3
35 - 39	82	64	18	0.7	0.9	♦0.5
40 - 44	94	65	29	1.0	1.1	♦0.9
45 - 49	145	108	37	2.0	2.3	1.5
50 - 54	136	107	29	2.8	3.3	♦1.8
55 - 59	164	116	48	6.0	6.5	5.1
60 - 64	123	82	41	9.7	11.4	7.4
65 - 69	199	98	101	20.6	20.0	21.2
70 - 74	248	133	115	39.8	44.4	35.5
75 +	651	353	298	62.9	72.8	54.2
Bhutan - Bhoutan[17]						
2005 (I)						
Total.	4 498	2 390	2 108	7.1	7.2	7.0
0	503	270	233	40.8	44.3	37.5
1 - 4	269	143	126	5.4	5.6	5.1
5 - 9	139	85	54	2.0	2.4	1.5
10 - 14	88	46	42	1.1	1.2	1.1
15 - 19	126	65	61	1.7	1.7	1.6
20 - 24	123	65	58	1.7	1.6	1.9
25 - 29	133	74	59	2.3	2.4	2.3
30 - 34	145	79	66	3.4	3.4	3.4
35 - 39	182	107	75	4.7	5.1	4.3
40 - 44	174	95	79	5.8	5.9	5.7
45 - 49	250	129	121	9.0	8.7	9.5
50 - 54	204	113	91	9.3	9.6	8.9
55 - 59	239	126	113	14.6	14.4	14.8
60 - 64	291	145	146	20.0	19.2	20.8
65 - 69	331	163	168	29.1	27.2	31.3
70 - 74	368	188	180	42.1	41.8	42.4
75 +	933	497	436	96.8	102.7	90.8
Brunei Darussalam - Brunéi Darussalam						
2007 (+C)						
Total.	1 174	688	486	3.0	3.3	2.7
0 - 4	60	35	25	1.7	1.9	♦1.5
5 - 9	12	7	5	♦0.3	♦0.4	♦0.3
10 - 14	12	5	7	♦0.3	♦0.3	♦0.4
15 - 19	15	10	5	♦0.4	♦0.6	♦0.3
20 - 24	24	17	7	♦0.6	♦0.8	♦0.3
25 - 29	29	23	6	♦0.7	♦1.0	♦0.3
30 - 34	40	31	9	1.0	1.5	♦0.5
35 - 39	36	25	11	1.1	♦1.4	♦0.7
40 - 44	51	33	18	1.8	2.1	♦1.5
45 - 49	72	45	27	3.3	3.7	♦2.8
50 - 54	63	38	25	4.1	4.6	♦3.4
55 - 59	97	58	39	9.7	11.2	8.1
60 - 64	76	44	32	13.1	14.7	11.4

19. Deaths and death rates by age and sex: latest available year, 1998 - 2007
Décès et taux de mortalité selon l'âge et le sexe: dernière année disponible, 1998 - 2007 (continued - suite)

Continent, country or area, date, code and age (in years) / Continent, pays ou zone, date, code et âge (en années)	Number - Nombre			Rate - Taux		
	Both sexes Les deux sexes	Male Masculin	Female Féminin	Both sexes Les deux sexes	Male Masculin	Female Féminin
ASIA - ASIE						
Brunei Darussalam - Brunéi Darussalam						
2007 (+C)						
65 - 69	90	61	29	18.0	24.4	♦11.6
70 +	497	256	241	66.3	67.4	65.1
China - Chine[18]						
1999 (...)						
Total	7 420 000	4 140 000	3 280 000	...	...	...
0 - 4	474 000	237 000	237 000	...	...	...
5 - 9	40 000	22 000	18 000	...	...	...
10 - 14	33 000	20 000	13 000	...	...	...
15 - 19	72 000	38 000	34 000	...	...	...
20 - 24	104 000	59 000	45 000	...	...	...
25 - 29	165 000	87 000	78 000	...	...	...
30 - 34	180 000	112 000	68 000	...	...	...
35 - 39	147 000	93 000	54 000	...	...	...
40 - 44	229 000	150 000	79 000	...	...	...
45 - 49	306 000	199 000	107 000	...	...	...
50 - 54	286 000	177 000	109 000	...	...	...
55 - 59	414 000	242 000	172 000	...	...	...
60 - 64	673 000	432 000	241 000	...	...	...
65 - 69	906 000	540 000	366 000	...	...	...
70 - 74	1 028 000	594 000	434 000	...	...	...
75 - 79	947 000	528 000	419 000	...	...	...
80 - 84	799 000	381 000	418 000	...	...	...
85 - 89	423 000	174 000	249 000	...	...	...
90 +	193 000	54 000	139 000	...	...	...
China, Hong Kong SAR - Chine, Hong Kong RAS						
2006* (C)						
Total	37 457	20 983	16 474	5.5	6.4	4.6
0	118	65	53	2.8	2.8	2.7
1 - 4	36	22	14	0.2	♦0.3	♦0.2
5 - 9	32	20	12	0.1	♦0.1	♦0.1
10 - 14	46	25	21	0.2	0.2	♦0.1
15 - 19	68	42	26	0.3	0.4	0.1
20 - 24	124	88	36	0.4	0.7	0.2
25 - 29	215	149	66	0.5	0.7	0.4
30 - 34	277	160	117	0.7	1.0	0.5
35 - 39	412	238	174	1.1	1.4	0.8
40 - 44	714	431	283	1.6	2.0	1.2
45 - 49	1 043	653	390	2.8	3.7	2.0
50 - 54	1 503	965	538	4.2	5.6	2.7
55 - 59	1 770	1 210	560	7.3	9.9	4.4
60 - 64	1 771	1 261	510	11.3	15.4	6.9
65 - 69	2 742	1 932	810	19.8	26.8	13.1
70 - 74	4 530	3 009	1 521	33.1	44.1	23.8
75 - 79	5 916	3 627	2 289	56.3	76.0	43.3
80 - 84	6 345	3 407	2 938	108.0	129.1	98.3
85 +	9 795	3 679	6 116			
China, Macao SAR - Chine, Macao RAS						
2007 (C)						
Total	1 545	840	705	2.9	3.2	2.6
0 - 4	16	10	6	♦0.9	♦1.1	♦0.7
0	11	7	4	...	...	...
1 - 4	5	3	2	♦0.1	-	♦0.2
5 - 9	2	-	2	♦0.1		♦0.1
10 - 14	4	2	2	♦0.2	♦0.2	♦0.2
15 - 19	9	4	5	♦0.4	♦0.4	♦0.4
20 - 24	20	9	11	♦0.4	♦0.6	♦0.1
25 - 29	14	11	3	♦0.5	♦0.7	♦0.3
30 - 34	21	15	6	♦0.6	♦0.9	♦0.3
35 - 39	27	19	8	0.9	1.3	♦0.4
40 - 44	43	31	12	1.5	1.6	1.3
45 - 49	76	43	33	2.3	2.4	2.1
50 - 54	98	56	42	2.6	3.8	♦1.2
55 - 59	73	57	16	5.5	8.3	♦2.4
60 - 64	92	73	19	10.8	13.7	7.7
65 - 69	107	71	36			

19. Deaths and death rates by age and sex: latest available year, 1998 - 2007
Décès et taux de mortalité selon l'âge et le sexe: dernière année disponible, 1998 - 2007 (continued - suite)

Continent, country or area, date, code and age (in years) — Continent, pays ou zone, date, code et âge (en années)	Number - Nombre			Rate - Taux		
	Both sexes Les deux sexes	Male Masculin	Female Féminin	Both sexes Les deux sexes	Male Masculin	Female Féminin
ASIA - ASIE						
China, Macao SAR - Chine, Macao RAS						
2007 (C)						
70 - 74	140	89	51	15.1	21.7	9.8
75 +	803	350	453	45.1	50.7	41.2
75 - 79	222	115	107	...	...	...
80 - 84	242	119	123	...	...	...
85 +	339	116	223	...	...	...
Cyprus - Chypre[19]						
2007 (C)						
Total	5 391	2 821	2 570	6.9	7.3	6.5
0 - 4	36	18	18	0.9	♦0.8	♦0.9
0	32	17	15	3.7	♦3.8	♦3.6
1 - 4	4	1	3	♦0.1	♦0.1	♦0.2
5 - 9	11	6	5	♦0.3	♦0.3	♦0.2
10 - 14	11	4	7	♦0.2	♦0.1	♦0.3
15 - 19	22	15	7	♦0.4	♦0.5	♦0.3
20 - 24	54	42	12	0.8	1.3	♦0.4
25 - 29	32	28	4	0.5	♦0.8	♦0.1
30 - 34	38	28	10	0.6	♦1.0	♦0.3
35 - 39	46	36	10	0.8	1.3	♦0.4
40 - 44	69	44	25	1.2	1.6	♦0.9
45 - 49	85	56	29	1.5	2.0	♦1.0
50 - 54	159	109	50	3.2	4.4	2.0
55 - 59	194	139	55	4.2	6.1	2.3
60 - 64	243	157	86	6.5	8.6	4.4
65 - 69	397	256	141	12.4	16.6	8.6
70 - 74	557	326	231	22.5	28.4	17.4
75 - 79	747	385	362	40.2	47.3	34.6
80 - 84	1 000	468	532	81.9	90.7	75.5
85 +	1 649	684	965	172.2	181.5	166.2
85 - 89	871	380	491	...	...	...
90 - 94	556	227	329	...	...	...
95 - 99	197	74	123	...	...	...
100 +	25	3	22	...	...	...
Unknown - Inconnu	41	20	21	..	..	..
Georgia - Géorgie[16]						
2007 (C)						
Total	41 178	22 091	19 087	9.4	10.6	8.3
0 - 4	712	393	319	3.0	3.2	2.9
0	656	372	284	...	...	...
1 - 4	56	21	35	...	...	...
5 - 9	44	24	20	...	...	...
10 - 14	67	36	31	0.2	♦0.2	♦0.2
15 - 19	143	86	57	0.2	0.2	0.2
20 - 24	274	183	91	0.4	0.5	0.3
25 - 29	348	257	91	0.8	1.0	0.5
30 - 34	447	340	107	1.1	1.6	0.6
35 - 39	655	488	167	1.4	2.2	0.7
40 - 44	1 040	775	265	2.2	3.4	1.1
45 - 49	1 461	1 087	374	3.3	5.3	1.6
50 - 54	1 808	1 338	470	4.4	7.0	2.1
55 - 59	1 990	1 384	606	6.5	10.4	3.1
60 - 64	1 813	1 197	616	8.2	12.6	4.6
65 - 69	5 454	3 367	2 087	12.6	18.8	7.7
70 - 74	5 919	3 187	2 732	24.5	36.7	16.0
75 - 79	7 631	3 774	3 857	33.6	44.2	26.2
80 - 84	6 272	2 591	3 681	56.4	72.6	46.2
85 +	5 066	1 559	3 507	86.0	109.3	74.8
85 - 89	3 136	1 009	2 127	140.3	202.5	123.5
90 - 94	1 383	407	976	...	...	...
95 - 99	425	122	303	...	...	...
100 +	122	21	101	...	...	...
Unknown - Inconnu	34	25	9	..	..	..
Israel - Israël[20]						
2007 (C)						
Total	39 836	19 752[5]	20 083[5]	5.5	5.6	5.5
0	591	318[5]	272[5]	4.0	4.2	3.7

Continent, country or area, date, code and age (in years)	Number - Nombre			Rate - Taux		
Continent, pays ou zone, date, code et âge (en années)	Both sexes Les deux sexes	Male Masculin	Female Féminin	Both sexes Les deux sexes	Male Masculin	Female Féminin

ASIA - ASIE

Israel - Israël[20]
2007 (C)

	149	83	66	0.3	0.3	0.2
1 - 4	86	44	42	0.1	0.1	0.1
5 - 9	83	50	33	0.1	0.2	0.1
10 - 14	195	145	50	0.3	0.5	0.2
15 - 19	255	196	59	0.4	0.7	0.2
20 - 24	228	172	56	0.4	0.6	0.2
25 - 29	280	196	84	0.5	0.7	0.3
30 - 34	366	228	138	0.8	1.0	0.6
35 - 39	465	299	166	1.2	1.5	0.8
40 - 44	746	478	268	2.0	2.6	1.4
45 - 49	1 142	700	442	3.1	3.9	2.3
50 - 54	1 769	1 072	697	5.0	6.4	3.8
55 - 59	1 870	1 127	743	7.5	9.4	5.7
60 - 64	2 576	1 541	1 035	12.9	16.9	9.6
65 - 69	3 892	2 187	1 705	22.0	28.0	17.3
70 - 74	5 504	2 793	2 711	38.7	46.9	32.8
75 - 79	7 380	3 192	4 188	67.4	75.6	62.2
80 - 84	6 196	2 684	3 512	115.7	123.1	110.6
85 - 89	3 994	1 499	2 495	208.0	215.6	203.7
90 - 94	2 069	748	1 321	431.0	398.7	451.8
95 +	1 756	639	1 117	...	...	...
95 - 99	313	109	204	...	...	...
100 +				...	...	...

Japan - Japon[21]
2007 (C)

Total	1 108 334	592 784 (C)	515 550	8.7	9.5	7.9
0 - 4	3 809	2 083	1 726	0.7	0.7	0.6
0	2 828	1 534	1 294	...	...	...
1 - 4	981	549	432	...	...	...
5 - 9	552	314	238	0.1	0.1	0.1
10 - 14	534	325	209	0.1	0.1	0.1
15 - 19	1 599	1 087	512	0.3	0.3	0.2
20 - 24	3 049	2 091	958	0.4	0.6	0.3
25 - 29	3 641	2 446	1 195	0.5	0.6	0.3
30 - 34	5 410	3 634	1 776	0.6	0.8	0.4
35 - 39	7 679	5 036	2 643	0.8	1.1	0.6
40 - 44	10 064	6 699	3 365	1.2	1.6	0.8
45 - 49	14 966	9 915	5 051	1.9	2.6	1.3
50 - 54	24 562	16 363	8 199	3.0	4.0	2.0
55 - 59	49 777	34 316	15 461	4.7	6.5	2.9
60 - 64	58 505	40 891	17 614	7.0	10.1	4.1
65 - 69	80 094	55 026	25 068	10.3	14.8	6.2
70 - 74	116 667	77 495	39 172	16.9	24.4	10.5
75 - 79	159 772	100 145	59 627	28.9	42.0	19.0
80 - 84	188 314	102 136	86 178	49.3	70.9	36.2
85 +	378 819	132 353	246 466	116.9	149.2	104.7
85 - 89	173 407	72 030	101 377	...	...	...
90 - 94	134 751	44 147	90 604	...	...	...
95 - 99	58 983	14 222	44 761	...	...	...
100 +	11 678	1 954	9 724	...	...	...
Unknown - Inconnu	521	429	92	...		

Kazakhstan[16]
2007 (C)

Total	158 297	90 416	67 881	10.2	12.1	8.4
0	4 646	2 744	1 902	15.1	17.3	12.7
1 - 4	1 119	602	517	1.1	1.1	1.0
5 - 9	497	299	198	0.5	0.5	0.4
10 - 14	672	428	244	0.5	0.7	0.4
15 - 19	1 757	1 219	538	1.1	1.6	0.7
20 - 24	3 195	2 444	751	2.1	3.2	1.0
25 - 29	4 484	3 504	980	3.5	5.5	1.6
30 - 34	5 513	4 190	1 323	4.7	7.3	2.2
35 - 39	6 013	4 539	1 474	5.6	8.6	2.7
40 - 44	7 737	5 720	2 017	7.3	11.2	3.6
45 - 49	10 302	7 478	2 824	9.5	14.7	4.9
50 - 54	11 527	8 148	3 379	13.5	21.0	7.3

Continent, country or area, date, code and age (in years) / Continent, pays ou zone, date, code et âge (en années)	Number - Nombre			Rate - Taux		
	Both sexes Les deux sexes	Male Masculin	Female Féminin	Both sexes Les deux sexes	Male Masculin	Female Féminin
ASIA - ASIE						
Kazakhstan[16]						
2007 (C)						
55 - 59	12 376	8 359	4 017	18.3	28.2	10.6
60 - 64	8 862	5 667	3 195	26.0	39.8	16.1
65 - 69	18 136	10 665	7 471	36.8	55.8	24.7
70 - 74	16 362	8 647	7 715	51.9	73.5	39.1
75 - 79	18 123	7 955	10 168	81.1	109.2	67.5
80 - 84	14 488	4 543	9 945	117.0	139.7	108.9
85 - 89	6 842	1 690	5 152	185.2	200.8	180.6
90 - 94	3 367	679	2 688	311.5	323.5	308.6
95 - 99	1 157	196	961	451.8	287.8	511.2
100 +	347	44	303	458.4	143.8	671.8
Unknown - Inconnu	775	656	119	..	..	..
Kuwait - Koweït						
2007 (C)						
Total	5 293	3 355	1 938	2.2	2.3	2.0
0 - 4	533	290	243	2.3	2.4	2.1
0	449	242	207	...	...	...
1 - 4	84	48	36	...	...	...
5 - 9	62	36	26	0.3	0.3	◆0.3
10 - 14	64	40	24	0.4	0.4	◆0.3
15 - 19	95	73	22	0.6	0.9	◆0.3
20 - 24	171	140	31	0.8	1.1	0.3
25 - 29	236	197	39	0.8	1.0	0.3
30 - 34	227	174	53	0.8	0.9	0.5
35 - 39	265	193	72	1.0	1.1	0.8
40 - 44	284	210	74	1.5	1.7	1.1
45 - 49	314	237	77	2.2	2.6	1.6
50 - 54	355	274	81	4.0	4.7	2.6
55 - 59	311	203	108	5.9	6.1	5.5
60 - 64	391	245	146	12.9	13.9	11.5
65 - 69	408	229	179	21.9	22.2	21.6
70 - 74	467	248	219	42.8	43.3	42.2
75 - 79	392	204	188	67.8	70.0	65.6
80 +	551	270	281	124.4	126.7	122.3
80 - 84	275	135	140	...	...	...
85 - 89	135	67	68	...	...	...
90 - 94	89	44	45	...	...	...
95 +	52	24	28	...	...	...
Unknown - Inconnu	167	92	75	..	..	..
Kyrgyzstan - Kirghizstan						
2007 (C)						
Total	38 180	21 465	16 715	7.2	8.2	6.3
0	3 771	2 142	1 629	21.1	17.7	28.2
1 - 4	548	279	269	1.3	1.3	1.3
5 - 9	167	97	70	0.3	0.4	0.3
10 - 14	198	125	73	0.4	0.4	0.3
15 - 19	375	243	132	0.6	0.8	0.5
20 - 24	573	386	187	1.1	1.5	0.7
25 - 29	748	526	222	1.7	2.4	1.0
30 - 34	1 060	774	286	2.8	4.0	1.5
35 - 39	1 303	948	355	3.7	5.5	2.0
40 - 44	1 656	1 189	467	5.2	7.6	2.9
45 - 49	2 404	1 735	669	7.9	11.8	4.3
50 - 54	2 390	1 682	708	11.0	16.2	6.2
55 - 59	2 521	1 678	843	16.5	23.3	10.4
60 - 64	1 645	1 062	583	23.3	33.0	15.2
65 - 69	3 559	2 110	1 449	37.6	51.4	27.0
70 - 74	4 018	2 141	1 877	54.2	70.4	42.9
75 - 79	4 737	2 214	2 523	79.5	97.2	68.5
80 - 84	3 454	1 319	2 135	106.3	114.2	101.8
85 - 89	1 716	503	1 213	152.2	161.7	148.6
90 - 94	763	188	575	207.7	232.7	200.6
95 - 99	310	56	254	152.0	97.2	173.6
100 +	207	23	184	418.2	◆125.7	589.7
Unknown - Inconnu	57	45	12	..	..	..

Continent, country or area, date, code and age (in years) / Continent, pays ou zone, date, code et âge (en années)	Number - Nombre			Rate - Taux		
	Both sexes Les deux sexes	Male Masculin	Female Féminin	Both sexes Les deux sexes	Male Masculin	Female Féminin
ASIA - ASIE						
Malaysia - Malaisie						
2006 (C)						
Total........	115 084	66 210	48 874	4.3	4.9	3.7
0 - 4........	3 652	2 093	1 559	1.2	1.3	1.0
0........	2 877	1 648	1 229	...	...	...
1 - 4........	775	445	330	...	...	...
5 - 9........	682	377	305	0.2	0.3	0.2
10 - 14........	807	523	284	0.3	0.4	0.2
15 - 19........	1 782	1 321	461	0.7	1.0	0.4
20 - 24........	2 262	1 728	534	0.9	1.4	0.4
25 - 29........	2 305	1 775	530	1.1	1.6	0.5
30 - 34........	2 680	2 013	667	1.4	2.0	0.7
35 - 39........	3 219	2 312	907	1.7	2.5	1.0
40 - 44........	4 222	2 876	1 346	2.5	3.3	1.6
45 - 49........	5 739	3 735	2 004	3.9	4.9	2.8
50 - 54........	7 198	4 563	2 635	5.9	7.2	4.4
55 - 59........	8 635	5 455	3 180	9.7	11.9	7.3
60 - 64........	9 722	6 063	3 659	15.3	18.6	11.8
65 - 69........	12 545	7 402	5 143	26.5	32.1	21.2
70 - 74........	13 493	7 419	6 074	42.5	50.6	35.6
75 +........	36 141	16 555	19 586	100.6	104.8	97.2
75 - 79........	13 813	6 934	6 879	...	...	...
80 - 84........	10 810	4 881	5 929	...	...	...
85 - 89........	7 127	2 995	4 132	...	...	...
90 - 94........	3 072	1 245	1 827	...	...	...
95 +........	1 319	500	819	...	...	...
Maldives						
2007 (C)						
Total........	1 119	686	433	3.7	4.4	2.9
0........	66	47	19	11.5	15.9	♦6.8
1 - 4........	10	5	5	♦0.5	♦0.5	♦0.5
5 - 9........	9	5	4	♦0.3	♦0.3	♦0.3
10 - 14........	13	7	6	♦0.4	♦0.4	♦0.3
15 - 19........	11	6	5	♦0.3	♦0.3	♦0.3
20 - 24........	19	15	4	♦0.5	♦0.8	♦0.2
25 - 29........	15	12	3	♦0.6	♦0.9	♦0.2
30 - 34........	13	6	7	♦0.6	♦0.6	♦0.6
35 - 39........	14	11	3	♦0.7	♦1.2	♦0.3
40 - 44........	25	15	10	♦1.5	♦1.8	♦1.2
45 - 49........	29	19	10	♦2.0	♦2.6	♦1.4
50 - 54........	35	17	18	3.9	♦3.6	♦4.2
55 - 59........	33	17	16	5.4	♦5.3	♦5.5
60 - 64........	81	44	37	14.5	15.4	13.6
65 - 69........	146	92	54	25.5	30.5	19.9
70 - 74........	188	118	70	41.9	47.7	34.8
75 - 79........	174	107	67	70.5	72.1	68.0
80 +........	238	143	95	128.1	129.1	126.7
80 - 84........	123	66	57	...	...	...
85 - 89........	65	46	19	...	...	...
90 - 94........	28	17	11	...	...	...
95 - 99........	11	7	4	...	...	...
100 +........	11	7	4	...	...	...
Mongolia - Mongolie						
2007 (C)						
Total........	16 259	9 876	6 383	6.2	7.7	4.8
0........	994	547	447	20.3	22.0	18.6
1 - 4........	285	151	134	1.6	1.7	1.5
5 - 9........	122	74	48	0.5	0.6	0.4
10 - 14........	99	61	38	0.4	0.4	0.3
15 - 19........	194	142	52	0.6	0.9	0.3
20 - 24........	401	310	91	1.5	2.4	0.7
25 - 29........	455	340	115	2.0	3.1	1.0
30 - 34........	598	456	142	2.8	4.4	1.3
35 - 39........	813	605	208	4.2	6.5	2.1
40 - 44........	1 105	804	301	6.3	9.5	3.3
45 - 49........	1 347	946	401	9.0	13.1	5.1
50 - 54........	1 352	930	422	13.0	18.6	7.8

19. Deaths and death rates by age and sex: latest available year, 1998 - 2007
Décès et taux de mortalité selon l'âge et le sexe: dernière année disponible, 1998 - 2007 (continued - suite)

Continent, country or area, date, code and age (in years) / Continent, pays ou zone, date, code et âge (en années)	Number - Nombre			Rate - Taux		
	Both sexes Les deux sexes	Male Masculin	Female Féminin	Both sexes Les deux sexes	Male Masculin	Female Féminin
ASIA - ASIE						
Mongolia - Mongolie						
2007 (C)						
55 - 59	1 199	784	415	17.3	23.9	11.4
60 - 64	1 251	759	492	24.1	31.5	17.7
65 - 69	1 504	878	626	34.4	43.0	26.8
70 +	4 540	2 089	2 451	70.3	79.5	64.0
70 - 74	1 400	749	651	...	...	...
75 - 79	1 279	605	674	...	...	...
80 - 84	925	417	508	...	...	...
85 - 89	577	215	362	...	...	...
90 - 94	251	73	178	...	...	...
95 - 99	91	27	64	...	...	...
100 +	17	3	14	...	...	...
Myanmar						
2005 (U)						
Total	242 549	...	...			
0	38 872	...	...			
1 - 4	20 358	...	...			
5 - 9	10 488	...	...			
10 - 14	7 865	...	...			
15 - 19	6 726	...	...			
20 - 24	6 689	...	...			
25 - 29	7 016	...	...			
30 - 34	6 774	...	...			
35 - 39	7 402	...	...			
40 - 44	7 484	...	...			
45 - 49	7 984	...	...			
50 - 54	9 365	...	...			
55 - 59	10 458	...	...			
60 - 64	11 391	...	...			
65 - 69	23 252	...	...			
70 - 74	21 817	...	...			
75 - 79	16 011	...	...			
80 - 84	12 520	...	...			
85 +	9 786	...	...			
Unknown - Inconnu	291	...	...	...	..	..
Nepal - Népal[22]						
2001 (I)						
Total	106 789	59 544	47 245			
0	13 037	6 956	6 081	4.7	5.2	4.2
1 - 4	9 790	5 590	4 200	26.3	27.5	25.1
5 - 9	3 320	1 726	1 594	4.3	4.9	3.8
10 - 14	2 304	1 332	972	1.0	1.1	1.0
15 - 19	2 523	1 293	1 230	0.8	0.9	0.7
20 - 24	2 747	1 449	1 298	1.1	1.1	1.0
25 - 29	2 688	1 429	1 259	1.4	1.5	1.2
30 - 34	2 474	1 303	1 172	1.6	1.7	1.4
35 - 39	2 839	1 594	1 244	1.7	1.8	1.5
40 - 44	2 970	1 828	1 142	2.2	2.4	1.9
45 - 49	3 553	2 027	1 526	2.7	3.4	2.1
50 - 54	4 662	2 771	1 891	3.8	4.3	3.4
55 - 59	6 115	3 612	2 503	6.1	7.1	5.1
60 - 64	8 337	4 710	3 626	10.2	11.3	8.8
65 - 69	8 667	4 764	3 903	16.0	18.0	14.0
70 - 74	9 606	5 512	4 093	22.4	24.3	20.4
75 - 79	8 113	4 657	3 456	35.1	38.9	31.0
80 +	13 042	6 990	6 052	48.9	56.6	41.4
				100.6	111.8	90.1
Occupied Palestinian Territory - Territoire palestinien occupé						
2007 (U)						
Total	9 887	5 697	4 190			
0	794	420	374	...	...	...
1 - 4	299	165	134	...	...	...
5 - 9	143	71	72	...	...	...
10 - 14	134	101	33	...	...	...
15 - 19	263	223	40	...	...	...
20 - 24	410	361	49	...	...	...

19. Deaths and death rates by age and sex: latest available year, 1998 - 2007
Décès et taux de mortalité selon l'âge et le sexe: dernière année disponible, 1998 - 2007 (continued - suite)

Continent, country or area, date, code and age (in years) / Continent, pays ou zone, date, code et âge (en années)	Number - Nombre			Rate - Taux		
	Both sexes Les deux sexes	Male Masculin	Female Féminin	Both sexes Les deux sexes	Male Masculin	Female Féminin
ASIA - ASIE						
Occupied Palestinian Territory - Territoire palestinien occupé						
2007 (U)	254	207	47	...	...	...
25 - 29	229	178	51	...	...	...
30 - 34	193	129	64	...	...	...
35 - 39	264	173	91	...	...	...
40 - 44	293	204	89	...	...	...
45 - 49	397	253	144	...	...	...
50 - 54	534	341	193	...	...	...
55 - 59	728	410	318	...	...	...
60 - 64	751	377	374	...	...	...
65 - 69	1 031	534	497	...	...	...
70 - 74	1 069	509	560	...	...	...
75 - 79	937	464	473	...	...	...
80 - 84	617	290	327	...	...	...
85 - 89	317	154	163	...	...	...
90 - 94	117	69	48	...	...	...
95 - 99	113	64	49	...	...	...
100 +						
Oman[23]						
2007 (U)						
Total	6 449	4 071	2 378	...	...	...
0	304	162	142	...	...	...
1 - 4	117	57	60	...	...	...
5 - 9	69	36	33	...	...	...
10 - 14	66	48	18	...	...	...
15 - 19	127	102	25	...	...	...
20 - 24	234	191	43	...	...	...
25 - 29	204	169	35	...	...	...
30 - 34	187	147	40	...	...	...
35 - 39	196	156	40	...	...	...
40 - 44	190	151	39	...	...	...
45 - 49	291	229	62	...	...	...
50 - 54	327	241	86	...	...	...
55 - 59	372	257	115	...	...	...
60 +	2 590	1 604	986	...	...	...
Unknown - Inconnu	1 175	521	654	..	..	..
Pakistan[24]						
2005 (I)						
Total	1 019 467	579 377	440 090	7.1	7.8	6.3
0 - 4	368 059	211 759	156 300	19.4	21.9	16.8
5 - 9	23 661	12 863	10 798	1.1	1.1	1.0
10 - 14	15 408	8 412	6 996	0.8	0.8	0.8
15 - 19	16 574	7 309	9 266	1.0	0.8	1.2
20 - 24	23 454	10 197	13 257	1.7	1.5	2.0
25 - 29	19 050	9 934	9 116	1.9	2.0	1.8
30 - 34	16 415	8 425	7 990	2.0	2.2	1.9
35 - 39	20 240	10 672	9 568	2.6	2.7	2.4
40 - 44	24 539	14 051	10 488	3.8	4.3	3.2
45 - 49	28 193	17 196	10 997	4.7	5.6	3.8
50 - 54	45 835	23 314	22 521	10.5	10.2	10.9
55 - 59	45 765	27 898	17 867	13.3	15.1	11.2
60 - 64	65 863	40 859	25 003	23.7	27.3	19.5
65 - 69	53 933	26 352	27 581	27.4	24.2	31.4
70 - 74	66 763	37 156	29 607	49.1	48.5	50.0
75 - 79	48 494	24 009	24 486	74.2	64.7	86.7
80 - 84	44 377	21 462	22 915	97.2	84.2	113.5
85 +	92 843	67 508	25 334	294.4	351.9	205.0
Philippines						
2005 (C)						
Total	426 054	250 102	175 952	5.1	5.9	4.2
0 - 4	30 825	17 758	13 067	3.2	3.6	2.8
0	21 674	12 752	8 922	...	...	...
1 - 4	9 151	5 006	4 145	...	...	...
5 - 9	5 230	2 961	2 269	0.6	0.6	0.5
10 - 14	4 790	2 816	1 974	0.5	0.6	0.4
15 - 19	7 102	4 623	2 479	0.8	1.0	0.6

19. Deaths and death rates by age and sex: latest available year, 1998 - 2007
Décès et taux de mortalité selon l'âge et le sexe: dernière année disponible, 1998 - 2007 (continued - suite)

Continent, country or area, date, code and age (in years) Continent, pays ou zone, date, code et âge (en années)	Number - Nombre			Rate - Taux		
	Both sexes Les deux sexes	Male Masculin	Female Féminin	Both sexes Les deux sexes	Male Masculin	Female Féminin
ASIA - ASIE						
Philippines						
2005 (C)						
20 - 24	10 120	7 044	3 076	1.3	1.8	0.8
25 - 29	11 862	8 258	3 604	1.7	2.3	1.0
30 - 34	12 669	8 681	3 988	2.0	2.8	1.3
35 - 39	16 153	10 877	5 276	2.9	3.9	1.9
40 - 44	18 717	12 601	6 116	3.9	5.3	2.6
45 - 49	23 528	15 693	7 835	5.9	7.8	3.9
50 - 54	27 815	18 641	9 174	8.5	11.4	5.6
55 - 59	31 534	21 198	10 336	12.1	16.3	7.8
60 - 64	33 221	21 324	11 897	16.8	22.1	11.7
65 - 69	38 251	23 465	14 786	26.0	33.3	19.3
70 - 74	38 815	22 189	16 626	38.0	46.7	30.4
75 - 79	37 864	19 858	18 006	56.3	66.6	48.1
80 + ...	77 558	32 115	45 443	137.7	138.1	137.4
80 - 84	33 418	15 312	18 106	...	...	...
85 - 89	24 701	9 904	14 797	...	...	...
90 - 94	13 747	4 893	8 854	...	...	...
95 - 99	5 103	1 718	3 385	...	...	...
100 + ...	589	288	301	...	...	...
Qatar						
2007 (C)						
Total	1 776	1 319	457	1.4	1.4	1.5
0	117	57	60	7.5	7.1	7.9
1 - 4	25	21	4	♦0.5	♦0.8	♦0.2
5 - 9	15	6	9	♦0.2	♦0.2	♦0.3
10 - 14	24	16	8	♦0.4	♦0.6	♦0.3
15 - 19	60	51	9	1.1	1.6	♦0.4
20 - 24	99	90	9	0.6	0.7	♦0.3
25 - 29	130	122	8	0.6	0.7	♦0.2
30 - 34	123	111	12	0.7	0.8	♦0.3
35 - 39	127	113	14	0.9	0.9	♦0.5
40 - 44	110	91	19	1.0	1.1	♦0.9
45 - 49	123	104	19	1.6	1.7	♦1.2
50 - 54	138	114	24	2.6	2.7	♦2.3
55 - 59	117	97	20	4.4	4.6	♦3.6
60 - 64	105	66	39	8.3	7.1	11.5
65 - 69	115	71	44	19.3	18.3	21.0
70 - 74	108	62	46	29.2	26.7	33.4
75 - 79	89	51	38	54.9	49.5	64.5
80 - 84	78	40	38	82.1	69.7	101.1
85 - 89	38	17	21	84.4	♦60.9	♦122.8
90 + ...	35	19	16	78.7	♦65.1	♦104.6
90 - 94	17	9	8	...	...	...
95 + ...	18	10	8	...	...	...
Republic of Korea - République de Corée[25]						
2006 (C)						
Total	243 934	134 724	109 210	...	...	...
0	1 709	959	750	...	...	...
1 - 4	547	294	253	...	...	...
5 - 9	499	290	209	...	...	...
10 - 14	516	330	186	...	...	...
15 - 19	957	643	314	...	...	...
20 - 24	1 493	945	548	...	...	...
25 - 29	2 097	1 380	717	...	...	...
30 - 34	2 826	1 839	987	...	...	...
35 - 39	4 624	3 142	1 482	...	...	...
40 - 44	7 259	5 272	1 987	...	...	...
45 - 49	11 513	8 606	2 907	...	...	...
50 - 54	12 714	9 456	3 258	...	...	...
55 - 59	13 936	10 290	3 646	...	...	...
60 - 64	17 627	12 561	5 066	...	...	...
65 - 69	25 938	17 508	8 430	...	...	...
70 - 74	31 036	18 538	12 498	...	...	...
75 - 79	33 742	16 558	17 184	...	...	...
80 - 84	34 368	14 108	20 260	...	...	...
85 - 89	24 481	8 297	16 184	...	...	...

19. Deaths and death rates by age and sex: latest available year, 1998 - 2007
Décès et taux de mortalité selon l'âge et le sexe: dernière année disponible, 1998 - 2007 (continued - suite)

Continent, country or area, date, code and age (in years) Continent, pays ou zone, date, code et âge (en années)	Number - Nombre			Rate - Taux		
	Both sexes Les deux sexes	Male Masculin	Female Féminin	Both sexes Les deux sexes	Male Masculin	Female Féminin
ASIA - ASIE						
Republic of Korea - République de Corée[25]						
2006 (C)						
90 - 94	12 083	2 901	9 182	...	...	...
95 +	3 952	802	3 150	...	...	...
Unknown - Inconnu	17	5	12	..	..	..
Saudi Arabia - Arabie saoudite						
2005 (...)						
Total	92 486	54 253	38 233	...	...	...
0 - 4	12 889	6 692	6 197	...	...	...
5 - 9	977	524	453	...	...	...
10 - 14	977	566	411	...	...	...
15 - 19	1 350	791	559	...	...	...
20 - 24	1 695	998	697	...	...	...
25 - 29	2 248	1 371	877	...	...	...
30 - 34	2 750	1 681	1 069	...	...	...
35 - 39	3 309	2 131	1 178	...	...	...
40 - 44	3 997	2 698	1 299	...	...	...
45 - 49	4 754	3 266	1 488	...	...	...
50 - 54	5 285	3 629	1 656	...	...	...
55 - 59	5 538	3 658	1 880	...	...	...
60 - 64	6 116	3 756	2 360	...	...	...
65 - 69	6 924	3 985	2 939	...	...	...
70 - 74	8 082	4 448	3 634	...	...	...
75 - 79	8 176	4 484	3 692	...	...	...
80 +	17 419	9 575	7 844	...	...	...
Singapore - Singapour						
2007 (+C)						
Total	17 140	9 537[5]	7 599[5]	4.8	5.4	4.2
0 - 4	118	72[5]	45[5]	0.6	0.7	0.5
0	94	60[5]	33[5]	...	...	...
1 - 4	24	12	12			
5 - 9	26	15	11	♦0.1	♦0.1	♦0.1
10 - 14	29	18	11	♦0.1	♦0.1	♦0.1
15 - 19	70	44	26	0.3	0.3	♦0.2
20 - 24	163	121	42	0.7	1.1	0.4
25 - 29	178	123	55	0.7	1.0	0.4
30 - 34	179	108	71	0.6	0.8	0.5
35 - 39	249	179	70	0.8	1.2	0.5
40 - 44	446	291	155	1.4	1.8	1.0
45 - 49	655	418	237	2.1	2.6	1.5
50 - 54	950	642	308	3.4	4.6	2.2
55 - 59	1 194	764	430	5.4	6.9	3.9
60 - 64	1 225	790	435	9.0	11.8	6.3
65 - 69	1 692	1 071	621	14.9	19.9	10.4
70 - 74	2 125	1 223	902	27.0	33.8	21.3
75 - 79	2 429	1 327	1 102	42.8	54.4	34.0
80 - 84	2 195	1 095	1 100	69.7	89.0	57.3
85 +	3 202	1 224	1 978	128.1	147.5	118.4
85 - 89	1 732	720	1 012	...	...	...
90 - 94	1 013	364	649	...	...	...
95 - 99	386	122	264	...	...	...
100 +	71	18	53	...	...	...
Unknown - Inconnu	15	12[5]	-[5]	..	..	..
Sri Lanka						
2002 (+C)						
Total	111 863	69 242	42 621	...	...	...
0	4 189	2 377	1 812	...	...	...
1 - 4	856	457	399	...	...	...
5 - 14	1 361	772	589	...	...	...
15 - 24	4 214	2 829	1 385	...	...	...
25 - 34	4 907	3 696	1 211	...	...	...
35 - 44	7 456	5 769	1 687	...	...	...
45 - 54	12 599	9 327	3 272	...	...	...
55 - 64	15 549	10 753	4 796	...	...	...
65 - 74	23 582	14 265	9 317	...	...	...
75 +	37 150	18 997	18 153	...	...	...

Continent, country or area, date, code and age (in years)	Number - Nombre			Rate - Taux		
Continent, pays ou zone, date, code et âge (en années)	Both sexes Les deux sexes	Male Masculin	Female Féminin	Both sexes Les deux sexes	Male Masculin	Female Féminin
ASIA - ASIE						
Tajikistan - Tadjikistan[16]						
2007 (U)						
Total..	30 332	16 481	13 851	...	...	...
0..	2 168	1 272	896	...	...	...
1 - 4...	672	366	306	...	...	...
5 - 9...	236	142	94	...	...	...
10 - 14.......................................	260	148	112	...	...	...
15 - 19.......................................	413	267	146	...	...	...
20 - 24.......................................	541	324	217	...	...	...
25 - 29.......................................	547	347	200	...	...	...
30 - 34.......................................	705	480	225	...	...	...
35 - 39.......................................	810	500	310	...	...	...
40 - 44.......................................	1 020	614	406	...	...	...
45 - 49.......................................	1 223	762	461	...	...	...
50 - 54.......................................	1 464	880	584	...	...	...
55 - 59.......................................	1 611	968	643	...	...	...
60 - 64.......................................	1 492	851	641	...	...	...
65 - 69.......................................	3 165	1 853	1 312	...	...	...
70 - 74.......................................	4 002	2 130	1 872	...	...	...
75 - 79.......................................	4 392	2 251	2 141	...	...	...
80 - 84.......................................	2 955	1 410	1 545	...	...	...
85 - 89.......................................	1 607	588	1 019	...	...	...
90 - 94.......................................	608	205	403	...	...	...
95 - 99.......................................	240	74	166	...	...	...
100 +...	201	49	152	...	...	...
Thailand - Thaïlande						
2007 (+U)						
Total..	393 255	222 170	171 085	...	...	...
0..	5 781	3 269	2 512	...	...	...
1 - 4...	7 984	4 544	3 440	...	...	...
5 - 9...	1 985	1 186	799	...	...	...
10 - 14.......................................	2 445	1 502	943	...	...	...
15 - 19.......................................	5 808	4 571	1 237	...	...	...
20 - 24.......................................	6 676	5 133	1 543	...	...	...
25 - 29.......................................	9 437	6 823	2 614	...	...	...
30 - 34.......................................	12 916	9 164	3 752	...	...	...
35 - 39.......................................	15 875	11 197	4 678	...	...	...
40 - 44.......................................	19 200	13 335	5 865	...	...	...
45 - 49.......................................	22 225	15 076	7 149	...	...	...
50 - 54.......................................	24 591	15 736	8 855	...	...	...
55 - 59.......................................	27 366	16 887	10 479	...	...	...
60 - 64.......................................	28 360	16 788	11 572	...	...	...
65 - 69.......................................	35 082	19 857	15 225	...	...	...
70 +..	172 665	80 134	92 531	...	...	...
Unknown - Inconnu.............................	640	237	403	..	..	...
United Arab Emirates - Émirats arabes unis						
2003 (...)						
Total..	6 002	4 305	1 697	...	(...)	...
0..	477	272	205	...	...	...
1 - 4...	132	74	58	...	...	...
5 - 9...	94	59	35	...	...	...
10 - 14.......................................	79	57	22	...	...	...
15 - 19.......................................	174	134	40	...	...	...
20 - 24.......................................	253	221	32	...	...	...
25 - 29.......................................	302	249	53	...	...	...
30 - 34.......................................	297	256	41	...	...	...
35 - 39.......................................	308	269	39	...	...	...
40 - 44.......................................	405	347	58	...	...	...
45 - 49.......................................	515	437	78	...	...	...
50 - 54.......................................	502	411	91	...	...	...
55 - 59.......................................	357	284	73	...	...	...
60 - 64.......................................	565	348	217	...	...	...
65 - 69.......................................	418	225	193	...	...	...
70 - 74.......................................	386	204	182	...	...	...
75 - 79.......................................	244	147	97	...	...	...
80 +..	378	209	169	...	...	...
Unknown - Inconnu.............................	116	102	14	..	..	..

19. Deaths and death rates by age and sex: latest available year, 1998 - 2007
Décès et taux de mortalité selon l'âge et le sexe: dernière année disponible, 1998 - 2007 (continued - suite)

Continent, country or area, date, code and age (in years) / Continent, pays ou zone, date, code et âge (en années)	Number - Nombre			Rate - Taux		
	Both sexes Les deux sexes	Male Masculin	Female Féminin	Both sexes Les deux sexes	Male Masculin	Female Féminin
ASIA - ASIE						
Uzbekistan - Ouzbékistan[16]						
2000 (C)						
Total	135 598	70 794	64 804	5.5	5.8	5.2
0	10 091	5 805	4 286	19.1	21.4	16.6
1 - 4	5 417	2 925	2 492	2.3	2.4	2.2
5 - 9	1 474	886	588	0.4	0.5	0.4
10 - 14	1 436	852	584	0.5	0.5	0.4
15 - 19	2 001	1 289	712	0.7	0.9	0.5
20 - 24	2 849	1 758	1 091	1.3	1.6	1.0
25 - 29	3 427	2 177	1 250	1.7	2.2	1.3
30 - 34	3 660	2 403	1 257	2.1	2.9	1.4
35 - 39	4 181	2 759	1 422	2.5	3.4	1.7
40 - 44	5 086	3 277	1 809	3.6	4.8	2.6
45 - 49	5 290	3 445	1 845	5.4	7.2	3.7
50 - 54	5 765	3 647	2 118	9.4	12.2	6.7
55 - 59	6 104	3 794	2 310	14.2	17.6	10.8
60 - 64	12 287	7 257	5 030	22.3	27.5	17.5
65 - 69	14 077	7 757	6 320	35.9	43.2	29.7
70 - 74	17 094	8 713	8 381	52.7	61.0	46.2
75 - 79	12 547	4 824	7 723	72.9	80.3	68.9
80 - 84	8 807	2 836	5 971	114.2	129.9	108.1
85 - 89	7 198	2 312	4 886	164.0	194.7	152.6
90 - 94	3 782	1 295	2 487	195.5	192.3	197.2
95 +	3 025	783	2 242	316.6	202.4	394.2
95 - 99	1 963	579	1 384	...	...	...
100 +	1 062	204	858	...	...	...
EUROPE						
Åland Islands - Îles d'Åland[26]						
2007 (C)						
Total	249	133	116	...	...	...
0	-	-	-	...	...	...
1 - 4	-	-	-	...	...	...
5 - 9	-	-	-	...	...	...
10 - 14	-	-	-	...	...	...
15 - 19	-	-	-	...	...	...
20 - 24	2	1	1	...	...	...
25 - 29	-	-	-	...	...	...
30 - 34	-	-	-	...	...	...
35 - 39	1	1	-	...	...	...
40 - 44	2	1	1	...	...	...
45 - 49	-	-	-	...	...	...
50 - 54	4	2	2	...	...	...
55 - 59	4	3	1	...	...	...
60 - 64	18	12	6	...	...	...
65 - 69	22	19	3	...	...	...
70 - 74	17	12	5	...	...	...
75 - 79	26	14	12	...	...	...
80 - 84	41	22	19	...	...	...
85 - 89	54	24	30	...	...	...
90 - 94	41	17	24	...	...	...
95 - 99	15	5	10	...	...	...
100 +	2	-	2	...	...	...
Albania - Albanie						
2004 (C)						
Total	17 749	9 950	7 799	5.7	6.4	5.0
0	336	181	155	6.9	7.2	6.6
1 - 4	237	132	105	1.2	1.2	1.1
5 - 9	164	108	56	0.6	0.7	0.4
10 - 14	140	86	54	0.5	0.5	0.4
15 - 19	157	106	51	0.5	0.7	0.3
20 - 24	219	147	72	0.8	1.2	0.5
25 - 29	181	140	41	0.8	1.3	0.4
30 - 34	225	159	66	1.1	1.6	0.6
35 - 39	244	160	84	1.2	1.6	0.8

Continent, country or area, date, code and age (in years) / Continent, pays ou zone, date, code et âge (en années)	Number - Nombre			Rate - Taux		
	Both sexes Les deux sexes	Male Masculin	Female Féminin	Both sexes Les deux sexes	Male Masculin	Female Féminin
EUROPE						
Albania - Albanie						
2004 (C)						
40 - 44	365	249	116	1.6	2.2	1.0
45 - 49	469	313	156	2.4	3.1	1.6
50 - 54	586	397	189	3.8	5.0	2.5
55 - 59	676	451	225	5.6	7.3	3.8
60 - 64	1 248	820	428	10.4	13.7	7.1
65 - 69	1 720	1 158	562	17.5	22.9	11.7
70 - 74	2 428	1 478	950	33.8	42.5	25.7
75 - 79	2 608	1 462	1 146	56.9	72.9	44.4
80 - 84	2 768	1 256	1 512	100.3	114.3	91.1
85 - 89	1 652	719	933	182.5	212.1	164.8
90 - 94	936	298	638	266.4	305.2	251.4
95 +	390	130	260	781.6	1070.0	688.7
95 - 99	300	103	197	...	...	...
100 +	90	27	63	...	...	...
2007 (C)						
Total	14 528	...	...	4.6	...	...
0 - 4	289	...	...	1.2	...	...
0	205	...	...	...	...	...
1 - 4	84	...	...	...	...	...
5 - 9	87	...	...	0.3	...	...
10 - 14	99	...	...	0.3	...	...
15 - 19	137	...	...	0.4	...	...
20 - 24	159	...	...	0.5	...	...
25 - 29	161	...	...	0.7	...	...
30 - 34	165	...	...	0.8	...	...
35 - 39	198	...	...	0.9	...	...
40 - 44	238	...	...	1.2	...	...
45 - 49	398	...	...	1.9	...	...
50 - 54	539	...	...	3.1	...	...
55 - 59	626	...	...	4.4	...	...
60 - 64	741	...	...	6.8	...	...
65 - 69	1 348	...	...	12.8	...	...
70 - 74	1 884	...	...	23.5	...	...
75 - 79	2 371	...	...	44.5	...	...
80 - 84	2 121	...	...	76.1	...	...
85 +	2 954	...	...	173.9	...	...
Unknown - Inconnu	13	...	...	..	..	..
Andorra - Andorre						
2007 (C)						
Total	230	140	90	...	...	...
0 - 4	3	-	3	...	...	...
0	2	-	2	...	...	...
1 - 4	1	-	1	...	...	...
5 - 9	1	1	-	...	...	...
10 - 14	-	-	-	...	...	...
15 - 19	1	1	-	...	...	...
20 - 24	1	1	-	...	...	...
25 - 29	6	5	1	...	...	...
30 - 34	6	5	1	...	...	...
35 - 39	6	5	1	...	...	...
40 - 44	4	4	-	...	...	...
45 - 49	9	7	2	...	...	...
50 - 54	3	2	1	...	...	...
55 - 59	15	11	4	...	...	...
60 - 64	17	9	8	...	...	...
65 - 69	15	9	6	...	...	...
70 - 74	26	21	5	...	...	...
75 - 79	23	14	9	...	...	...
80 - 84	34	19	15	...	...	...
85 - 89	35	17	18	...	...	...
90 - 94	19	8	11	...	...	...
95 - 99	6	1	5	...	...	...
100 +	-	-	-	...	...	...

19. Deaths and death rates by age and sex: latest available year, 1998 - 2007
Décès et taux de mortalité selon l'âge et le sexe: dernière année disponible, 1998 - 2007 (continued - suite)

Continent, country or area, date, code and age (in years) / Continent, pays ou zone, date, code et âge (en années)	Number - Nombre			Rate - Taux		
	Both sexes Les deux sexes	Male Masculin	Female Féminin	Both sexes Les deux sexes	Male Masculin	Female Féminin

EUROPE

Austria - Autriche
2007 (C)

Total	74 625	34 978	39 647	9.0	8.6	9.3
0 - 4	335	189	146	0.8	0.9	0.8
0	280	158	122	3.6	4.0	3.2
1 - 4	55	31	24	0.2	0.2	♦0.2
5 - 9	34	22	12	0.1	♦0.1	♦0.1
10 - 14	49	29	20	0.1	♦0.1	♦0.1
15 - 19	224	165	59	0.4	0.6	0.2
20 - 24	300	239	61	0.6	0.9	0.2
25 - 29	248	183	65	0.5	0.7	0.2
30 - 34	322	239	83	0.6	0.9	0.3
35 - 39	528	366	162	0.8	1.1	0.5
40 - 44	922	599	323	1.3	1.7	0.9
45 - 49	1 467	959	508	2.3	2.9	1.6
50 - 54	2 025	1 344	681	3.7	5.0	2.5
55 - 59	3 024	1 985	1 039	6.1	8.2	4.1
60 - 64	3 886	2 564	1 322	9.0	12.3	5.9
65 - 69	5 955	3 828	2 127	12.9	17.6	8.7
70 - 74	6 172	3 789	2 383	20.6	28.4	14.4
75 - 79	10 229	5 647	4 582	36.7	49.1	28.0
80 - 84	14 409	5 898	8 511	65.4	83.2	57.0
85 - 89	13 126	4 130	8 996	117.6	136.1	110.7
90 - 94	7 681	2 036	5 645	215.5	248.6	205.7
95 +	3 689	767	2 922	348.4	368.9	343.4
95 - 99	3 266	690	2 576	...	...	...
100 +	423	77	346	...	...	...

Belarus - Bélarus[16]
2007 (C)

Total	132 993	69 698	63 295	13.7	15.4	12.2
0 - 4	684	400	284	1.5	1.7	1.3
0	435	250	185	4.4	4.9	3.8
1 - 4	249	150	99	0.7	0.8	0.6
5 - 9	110	65	45	0.2	0.3	0.2
10 - 14	127	80	47	0.2	0.3	0.2
15 - 19	432	318	114	0.6	0.8	0.3
20 - 24	1 006	795	211	1.2	1.9	0.5
25 - 29	1 405	1 134	271	1.9	3.0	0.7
30 - 34	1 849	1 491	358	2.7	4.4	1.0
35 - 39	2 410	1 878	532	3.6	5.7	1.6
40 - 44	3 564	2 763	801	4.9	7.9	2.2
45 - 49	6 077	4 648	1 429	7.4	11.8	3.3
50 - 54	7 586	5 634	1 952	10.8	17.3	5.2
55 - 59	9 704	6 787	2 917	16.4	25.5	8.9
60 - 64	8 195	5 655	2 540	23.9	39.1	12.8
65 - 69	13 467	8 420	5 047	30.1	49.9	18.1
70 - 74	16 862	9 223	7 639	44.2	70.3	30.5
75 - 79	22 001	9 928	12 073	68.9	100.7	54.7
80 - 84	19 945	6 375	13 570	108.5	146.2	96.8
85 +	17 453	4 011	13 442	221.0	260.5	211.4
85 - 89	10 620	2 692	7 928	...	...	...
90 - 94	4 579	933	3 646	...	...	...
95 - 99	1 857	317	1 540	...	...	...
100 +	397	69	328	...	...	...
Unknown - Inconnu	116	93	23	..	..	..

Belgium - Belgique[27]
2007 (C)

Total	100 658	49 804	50 854	...	...	...
0 - 4	593	349	244	...	...	...
0	487	287	200	...	...	...
1 - 4	106	62	44	...	...	...
5 - 9	53	29	24	...	...	...
10 - 14	83	47	36	...	...	...
15 - 19	248	172	76	...	...	...
20 - 24	378	288	90	...	...	...
25 - 29	385	279	106	...	...	...
30 - 34	520	360	160	...	...	...

518

19. Deaths and death rates by age and sex: latest available year, 1998 - 2007
Décès et taux de mortalité selon l'âge et le sexe: dernière année disponible, 1998 - 2007 (continued - suite)

Continent, country or area, date, code and age (in years) / Continent, pays ou zone, date, code et âge (en années)	Number - Nombre			Rate - Taux		
	Both sexes Les deux sexes	Male Masculin	Female Féminin	Both sexes Les deux sexes	Male Masculin	Female Féminin
EUROPE						
Belgium - Belgique[27]						
2007 (C)						
35 - 39	759	479	280			
40 - 44	1 238	773	465	...	...	...
45 - 49	2 022	1 238	784	...	...	...
50 - 54	3 104	1 938	1 166	...	...	...
55 - 59	4 179	2 691	1 488	...	...	...
60 - 64	5 283	3 425	1 858	...	...	...
65 - 69	6 392	4 119	2 273	...	...	...
70 - 74	9 880	5 962	3 918	...	...	...
75 - 79	15 164	8 441	6 723	...	...	...
80 - 84	19 367	9 228	10 139	...	...	...
85 - 89	16 682	6 380	10 302	...	...	...
90 - 94	9 861	2 740	7 121	...	...	...
95 - 99	3 791	767	3 024	...	...	...
100 +	676	99	577	...	...	...
Bosnia and Herzegovina - Bosnie-Herzégovine						
2007 (C)						
Total	35 044	18 154	16 890			
0 - 4	268	150	118	...	...	...
0	231	132	99	...	...	...
1 - 4	37	18	19	...	...	...
5 - 9	43	21	22	...	...	...
10 - 14	29	17	12	...	...	...
15 - 19	101	75	26	...	...	...
20 - 24	149	108	41	...	...	...
25 - 29	178	135	43	...	...	...
30 - 34	209	139	70	...	...	...
35 - 39	285	198	87	...	...	...
40 - 44	538	345	193	...	...	...
45 - 49	1 012	683	329	...	...	...
50 - 54	1 762	1 196	566	...	...	...
55 - 59	2 098	1 401	697	...	...	...
60 - 64	2 437	1 522	915	...	...	...
65 - 69	4 588	2 674	1 914	...	...	...
70 - 74	6 389	3 451	2 938	...	...	...
75 - 79	6 937	3 249	3 688	...	...	...
80 - 84	4 838	1 774	3 064	...	...	...
85 - 89	2 186	707	1 479	...	...	...
90 - 94	747	226	521	...	...	...
95 - 99	187	57	130	...	...	...
100 +	25	8	17	...	...	...
Unknown - Inconnu	38	18	20	..	..	..
Bulgaria - Bulgarie						
2007 (C)						
Total	113 004	59 823	53 181	14.8	16.1	13.5
0 - 4	829	464	365	2.4	2.6	2.2
0	690	388	302	9.7	10.6	8.8
1 - 4	139	76	63	0.5	0.5	0.5
5 - 9	79	44	35	0.2	0.3	0.2
10 - 14	97	52	45	0.3	0.3	0.3
15 - 19	268	187	81	0.6	0.8	0.3
20 - 24	417	311	106	0.8	1.1	0.4
25 - 29	507	369	138	0.9	1.3	0.5
30 - 34	653	459	194	1.1	1.6	0.7
35 - 39	887	589	298	1.6	2.1	1.1
40 - 44	1 428	981	447	2.8	3.9	1.8
45 - 49	2 594	1 832	762	4.9	6.9	2.8
50 - 54	4 412	3 156	1 256	8.1	11.9	4.5
55 - 59	6 765	4 762	2 003	12.3	18.3	6.9
60 - 64	8 284	5 648	2 636	17.6	26.2	10.3
65 - 69	10 048	6 343	3 705	26.0	37.3	17.1
70 - 74	15 725	8 852	6 873	41.7	55.8	31.5
75 - 79	19 944	9 701	10 243	68.7	83.1	59.0
80 - 84	21 999	9 272	12 727	118.9	134.4	109.7
85 - 89	12 579	4 854	7 725	186.6	203.9	177.1
90 - 94	4 258	1 558	2 700	303.4	332.0	289.0

Continent, country or area, date, code and age (in years) / Continent, pays ou zone, date, code et âge (en années)	Number - Nombre			Rate - Taux		
	Both sexes Les deux sexes	Male Masculin	Female Féminin	Both sexes Les deux sexes	Male Masculin	Female Féminin
EUROPE						
Bulgaria - Bulgarie						
2007 (C)						
95 - 99	1 122	364	758	382.8	376.0	386.1
100 + ...	109	25	84	387.9	◆290.7	430.8
Croatia - Croatie						
2007 (C)						
Total...........................	52 367	26 300	26 067	11.8	12.3	11.3
0 - 4.............................	269	136	133	1.3	1.3	1.3
0.................................	234	114	120	5.7	5.4	6.1
1 - 4.............................	35	22	13	0.2	◆0.3	◆0.2
5 - 9.............................	33	16	17	0.1	◆0.1	◆0.2
10 - 14...........................	32	20	12	0.1	◆0.2	◆0.1
15 - 19...........................	130	100	30	0.5	0.7	◆0.2
20 - 24...........................	207	167	40	0.7	1.1	0.3
25 - 29...........................	208	160	48	0.7	1.0	0.3
30 - 34...........................	249	187	62	0.8	1.2	0.4
35 - 39...........................	332	234	98	1.1	1.6	0.7
40 - 44...........................	575	418	157	1.8	2.6	1.0
45 - 49...........................	1 140	794	346	3.5	4.8	2.1
50 - 54...........................	2 060	1 480	580	6.1	8.8	3.4
55 - 59...........................	2 673	1 900	773	9.0	13.1	5.1
60 - 64...........................	2 931	2 027	904	13.1	19.5	7.5
65 - 69...........................	4 936	3 201	1 735	20.8	30.5	13.1
70 - 74...........................	7 496	4 401	3 095	34.2	48.7	24.0
75 - 79...........................	9 997	4 972	5 025	60.4	80.7	48.4
80 - 84...........................	9 565	3 401	6 164	101.1	120.1	93.0
85 + ...	9 523	2 677	6 846	206.1	228.4	198.5
85 - 89...........................	6 235	1 820	4 415	...	...	...
90 - 94...........................	2 376	643	1 733	...	...	...
95 - 99...........................	816	194	622	...	...	...
100 + ...	96	20	76	...	...	...
Unknown - Inconnu	11	9	2	..	..	..
Czech Republic - République tchèque						
2007 (C)						
Total...........................	104 636	52 719	51 917	10.1	10.4	9.8
0 - 4.............................	443	267	176	0.9	1.0	0.7
0.................................	360	218	142	3.1	3.7	2.5
1 - 4.............................	83	49	34	0.2	0.2	0.2
5 - 9.............................	45	26	19	0.1	◆0.1	◆0.1
10 - 14...........................	73	46	27	0.1	0.2	◆0.1
15 - 19...........................	252	179	73	0.4	0.5	0.2
20 - 24...........................	423	353	70	0.6	1.0	0.2
25 - 29...........................	517	413	104	0.6	1.0	0.3
30 - 34...........................	634	484	150	0.7	1.0	0.3
35 - 39...........................	834	598	236	1.1	1.6	0.7
40 - 44...........................	1 284	842	442	1.8	2.3	1.3
45 - 49...........................	1 950	1 343	607	3.0	4.1	1.9
50 - 54...........................	4 063	2 810	1 253	5.4	7.5	3.3
55 - 59...........................	6 822	4 726	2 096	8.9	12.6	5.3
60 - 64...........................	8 913	6 002	2 911	13.0	18.6	8.0
65 - 69...........................	8 903	5 638	3 265	18.8	26.4	12.5
70 - 74...........................	11 361	6 575	4 786	31.3	43.2	22.7
75 - 79...........................	16 691	8 123	8 568	51.0	64.8	42.4
80 - 84...........................	19 788	7 820	11 968	88.5	106.4	79.7
85 - 89...........................	13 394	4 407	8 987	138.7	160.6	130.0
90 - 94...........................	6 103	1 633	4 470	278.8	309.5	269.1
95 - 99...........................	1 967	412	1 555	331.9	326.5	333.3
100 + ...	176	22	154	323.5	◆183.3	363.2
Denmark - Danemark[28]						
2007 (C)						
Total...........................	55 604	27 045	28 559	10.2	10.0	10.4
0 - 4.............................	308	179	129	0.9	1.1	0.8
0.................................	256	150	106	4.0	4.5	3.4
1 - 4.............................	52	29	23	0.2	◆0.2	◆0.2
5 - 9.............................	28	16	12	◆0.1	◆0.1	◆0.1
10 - 14...........................	38	22	16	0.1	◆0.1	◆0.1
15 - 19...........................	116	82	34	0.4	0.5	0.2

19. Deaths and death rates by age and sex: latest available year, 1998 - 2007
Décès et taux de mortalité selon l'âge et le sexe: dernière année disponible, 1998 - 2007 (continued - suite)

Continent, country or area, date, code and age (in years) / Continent, pays ou zone, date, code et âge (en années)	Number - Nombre			Rate - Taux		
	Both sexes Les deux sexes	Male Masculin	Female Féminin	Both sexes Les deux sexes	Male Masculin	Female Féminin
EUROPE						
Denmark - Danemark[28]						
2007 (C)						
20 - 24	135	105	30	0.5	0.7	◆0.2
25 - 29	169	116	53	0.5	0.7	0.3
30 - 34	228	163	65	0.6	0.9	0.4
35 - 39	357	239	118	0.9	1.2	0.6
40 - 44	698	458	240	1.6	2.1	1.1
45 - 49	1 084	661	423	2.9	3.5	2.3
50 - 54	1 811	1 140	671	5.0	6.3	3.7
55 - 59	2 583	1 584	999	7.2	8.8	5.6
60 - 64	4 008	2 419	1 589	10.8	13.1	8.5
65 - 69	4 292	2 554	1 738	16.5	20.2	13.0
70 - 74	5 617	3 148	2 469	27.9	33.5	23.0
75 - 79	7 298	3 879	3 419	46.4	56.5	38.6
80 - 84	9 169	4 318	4 851	77.4	94.1	66.8
85 - 89	9 190	3 585	5 605	129.4	155.3	116.9
90 - 94	5 902	1 815	4 087	210.7	249.5	197.2
95 - 99	2 229	516	1 713	326.5	384.5	312.4
100 +	344	46	298	481.1	460.0	484.6
Estonia - Estonie						
2007 (C)						
Total	17 409	8 985	8 424	13.0	14.5	11.6
0 - 4	97	54	43	1.4	1.5	1.3
0	79	42	37	5.2	5.3	5.0
1 - 4	18	12	6	◆0.3	◆0.4	◆0.2
5 - 9	11	7	4	◆0.2	◆0.2	◆0.1
10 - 14	17	9	8	◆0.3	◆0.3	◆0.2
15 - 19	53	42	11	0.5	0.8	◆0.2
20 - 24	161	129	32	1.5	2.4	0.6
25 - 29	185	157	28	1.9	3.2	◆0.6
30 - 34	160	124	36	1.7	2.7	0.8
35 - 39	216	172	44	2.3	3.8	0.9
40 - 44	334	259	75	3.8	6.1	1.6
45 - 49	616	453	163	6.4	10.0	3.2
50 - 54	859	627	232	9.4	15.0	4.6
55 - 59	1 156	835	321	13.5	22.2	6.7
60 - 64	1 141	801	340	17.9	30.0	9.2
65 - 69	1 877	1 239	638	25.7	43.7	14.3
70 - 74	2 097	1 184	913	35.5	56.3	24.0
75 - 79	2 673	1 295	1 378	53.7	82.4	40.5
80 - 84	2 697	873	1 824	88.0	115.7	78.9
85 - 89	1 676	440	1 236	141.8	178.2	132.2
90 - 94	962	207	755	234.2	265.7	226.9
95 - 99	350	50	300	301.7	241.5	314.8
100 +	43	4	39	242.9	◆133.3	265.3
Unknown - Inconnu	28	24	4	..	..	..
Finland - Finlande[29]						
2007 (C)						
Total	49 077	24 809	24 268	9.3	9.6	9.0
0 - 4	207	119	88	0.7	0.8	0.6
0	161	93	68	2.7	3.1	2.4
1 - 4	46	26	20	0.2	◆0.2	◆0.2
5 - 9	28	13	15	◆0.1	◆0.1	◆0.1
10 - 14	40	21	19	0.1	◆0.1	◆0.1
15 - 19	152	108	44	0.5	0.6	0.3
20 - 24	243	177	66	0.7	1.0	0.4
25 - 29	254	199	55	0.8	1.2	0.3
30 - 34	277	211	66	0.9	1.3	0.4
35 - 39	403	308	95	1.2	1.8	0.6
40 - 44	677	471	206	1.8	2.5	1.1
45 - 49	1 082	761	321	2.9	4.0	1.7
50 - 54	1 811	1 293	518	4.6	6.6	2.7
55 - 59	2 783	1 935	848	6.8	9.5	4.2
60 - 64	3 167	2 176	991	9.6	13.4	5.9
65 - 69	3 593	2 389	1 204	14.0	19.8	8.9
70 - 74	4 362	2 795	1 567	21.0	30.2	13.6
75 - 79	6 758	3 803	2 955	36.9	51.8	26.9

19. Deaths and death rates by age and sex: latest available year, 1998 - 2007
Décès et taux de mortalité selon l'âge et le sexe: dernière année disponible, 1998 - 2007 (continued - suite)

Continent, country or area, date, code and age (in years) / Continent, pays ou zone, date, code et âge (en années)	Number - Nombre			Rate - Taux		
	Both sexes Les deux sexes	Male Masculin	Female Féminin	Both sexes Les deux sexes	Male Masculin	Female Féminin
EUROPE						
Finland - Finlande[29]						
2007 (C)	8 447	3 866	4 581	65.5	89.1	53.5
80 - 84	7 797	2 533	5 264	117.5	143.6	108.1
85 - 89	5 033	1 236	3 797	209.1	239.5	200.8
90 - 94	1 751	364	1 387	338.2	404.4	324.3
95 - 99	212	31	181	488.5	534.5	481.4
100 +						
France[30]						
2005 (C)						
Total	527 533	270 634	256 899	8.6	9.1	8.2
0	2 775	1 583	1 192	3.6	4.0	3.2
1 - 4	601	332	269	0.2	0.2	0.2
5 - 9	368	215	153	0.1	0.1	0.1
10 - 14	408	245	163	0.1	0.1	0.1
15 - 19	1 507	1 087	420	0.4	0.5	0.2
20 - 24	2 312	1 751	561	0.6	0.9	0.3
25 - 29	2 251	1 663	588	0.6	0.9	0.3
30 - 34	3 321	2 354	967	0.8	1.1	0.5
35 - 39	4 889	3 259	1 630	1.1	1.5	0.8
40 - 44	7 938	5 270	2 668	1.8	2.4	1.2
45 - 49	13 144	8 877	4 267	3.1	4.3	2.0
50 - 54	18 997	13 092	5 905	4.6	6.4	2.8
55 - 59	25 402	17 800	7 602	6.3	9.0	3.7
60 - 64	23 431	16 139	7 292	8.7	12.2	5.3
65 - 69	32 278	21 745	10 533	12.6	18.1	7.8
70 - 74	49 531	31 666	17 865	19.8	28.7	12.8
75 - 79	70 064	40 332	29 732	32.6	45.9	23.3
80 - 84	96 969	48 064	48 905	58.0	78.9	46.1
85 - 89	64 217	26 104	38 113	99.9	128.7	86.7
90 - 94	72 170	21 985	50 185	186.3	227.3	172.6
95 - 99	29 671	6 365	23 306	298.8	339.4	289.3
100 +	5 289	706	4 583	316.0	224.7	337.1
Germany - Allemagne						
2007 (C)						
Total	827 155	391 139	436 016	10.1	9.7	10.4
0 - 4	3 205	1 819	1 386	0.9	1.0	0.8
0	2 656	1 518	1 138	3.9	4.4	3.4
1 - 4	549	301	248	0.2	0.2	0.2
5 - 9	350	220	130	0.1	0.1	0.1
10 - 14	391	223	168	0.1	0.1	0.1
15 - 19	1 415	990	425	0.3	0.4	0.2
20 - 24	2 029	1 502	527	0.4	0.6	0.2
25 - 29	2 196	1 575	621	0.4	0.6	0.3
30 - 34	2 576	1 755	821	0.5	0.7	0.4
35 - 39	4 961	3 257	1 704	0.8	1.0	0.6
40 - 44	9 845	6 532	3 313	1.4	1.8	0.9
45 - 49	16 518	10 929	5 589	2.5	3.2	1.7
50 - 54	23 450	15 458	7 992	4.1	5.4	2.8
55 - 59	31 926	20 947	10 979	6.2	8.1	4.2
60 - 64	39 940	26 427	13 513	9.3	12.6	6.2
65 - 69	74 110	48 438	25 672	13.7	18.8	9.1
70 - 74	90 551	56 001	34 550	22.1	29.9	15.5
75 - 79	119 356	65 826	53 530	39.1	51.6	30.1
80 - 84	145 990	59 920	86 070	67.0	84.4	58.6
85 - 89	133 112	42 054	91 058	117.1	139.7	109.0
90 - 94	83 921	19 961	63 960	220.1	235.6	215.7
95 +	41 244	7 275	33 969	243.7	157.2	276.3
95 - 99	36 180	6 605	29 575	...	...	...
100 +	5 064	670	4 394	...	...	...
Unknown - Inconnu	69	30	39	..	..	..
Greece - Grèce						
2007 (C)						
Total	109 895	57 366	52 529	9.8	10.3	9.3
0 - 4	474	266	208	0.9	1.0	0.8
0	397	221	176	3.5	3.8	3.3
1 - 4	77	45	32	0.2	0.2	0.2
5 - 9	62	36	26	0.1	0.1	♦0.1

19. Deaths and death rates by age and sex: latest available year, 1998 - 2007
Décès et taux de mortalité selon l'âge et le sexe: dernière année disponible, 1998 - 2007 (continued - suite)

Continent, country or area, date, code and age (in years) / Continent, pays ou zone, date, code et âge (en années)	Number - Nombre			Rate - Taux		
	Both sexes / Les deux sexes	Male / Masculin	Female / Féminin	Both sexes / Les deux sexes	Male / Masculin	Female / Féminin
EUROPE						
Greece - Grèce						
2007 (C)						
10 - 14	63	38	25	0.1	0.1	♦0.1
15 - 19	240	187	53	0.4	0.6	0.2
20 - 24	495	394	101	0.7	1.1	0.3
25 - 29	680	542	138	0.8	1.3	0.3
30 - 34	635	473	162	0.7	1.1	0.4
35 - 39	845	598	247	1.0	1.3	0.6
40 - 44	1 242	853	389	1.5	2.0	0.9
45 - 49	1 857	1 296	561	2.3	3.3	1.4
50 - 54	2 613	1 810	803	3.5	5.0	2.2
55 - 59	3 650	2 592	1 058	5.4	7.8	3.0
60 - 64	4 889	3 357	1 532	7.9	11.4	4.8
65 - 69	7 133	4 742	2 391	12.4	18.1	7.6
70 - 74	12 351	7 618	4 733	21.1	29.2	14.6
75 - 79	18 518	10 120	8 398	38.9	48.5	31.3
80 - 84	21 428	9 940	11 488	75.0	82.3	69.6
85 - 89	17 042	6 791	10 251	139.9	130.8	146.8
90 - 94	11 107	4 172	6 935	393.5	313.7	464.6
95 - 99	3 906	1 328	2 578	494.3	289.4	778.1
100 +	665	213	452	252.6	269.3	245.4
Guernsey - Guernesey						
2000 (C)						
Total	565	264	301	...	...	...
0	4	3	1	...	...	...
1 - 4	1	-	1	...	...	...
5 - 9	-	-	-	...	...	...
10 - 14	-		-	...	...	...
15 - 19	4	3	1	...	...	...
20 - 24	1	-	1	...	...	...
25 - 29	1	1	-	...	...	...
30 - 34	2	1	1	...	...	...
35 - 39	2	2		...	...	...
40 - 44	4	4	-	...	...	...
45 - 49	7	5	2	...	...	...
50 - 54	13	9	4	...	...	...
55 - 59	13	7	6	...	...	...
60 - 64	30	15	15	...	...	...
65 - 69	45	29	16	...	...	...
70 - 74	57	27	30	...	...	...
75 - 79	71	38	33	...	...	...
80 - 84	103	55	48	...	...	...
85 - 89	108	45	63	...	...	...
90 - 94	68	14	54	...	...	...
95 - 99	24	3	21	...	...	...
100 +	5	2	3	...	...	...
Unknown - Inconnu	2	1	1	..	..	..
Hungary - Hongrie						
2007 (C)						
Total	132 938	68 241	64 697	13.2	14.3	12.2
0 - 4	685	370	315	1.4	1.5	1.3
0	577	310	267	5.9	6.2	5.6
1 - 4	108	60	48	0.3	0.3	0.3
5 - 9	62	32	30	0.1	0.1	♦0.1
10 - 14	108	64	44	0.2	0.2	0.2
15 - 19	244	176	68	0.4	0.6	0.2
20 - 24	342	251	91	0.5	0.8	0.3
25 - 29	478	357	121	0.6	0.9	0.3
30 - 34	798	591	207	1.0	1.4	0.5
35 - 39	1 229	863	366	1.7	2.4	1.0
40 - 44	2 239	1 597	642	3.6	5.2	2.1
45 - 49	4 375	3 023	1 352	6.8	9.7	4.1
50 - 54	8 054	5 622	2 432	10.1	14.8	5.8
55 - 59	9 609	6 572	3 037	13.9	20.7	8.2
60 - 64	10 518	7 001	3 517	18.5	27.9	11.1
65 - 69	12 421	7 584	4 837	25.2	37.5	16.6
70 - 74	15 324	8 461	6 863	37.2	54.1	26.8

Continent, country or area, date, code and age (in years) / Continent, pays ou zone, date, code et âge (en années)	Number - Nombre			Rate - Taux		
	Both sexes Les deux sexes	Male Masculin	Female Féminin	Both sexes Les deux sexes	Male Masculin	Female Féminin
EUROPE						
Hungary - Hongrie						
2007 (C)						
75 - 79	20 072	9 693	10 379	58.8	80.6	47.0
80 - 84	22 072	8 598	13 474	97.3	122.0	86.2
85 - 89	15 032	4 919	10 113	146.6	168.8	137.8
90 +	9 266	2 459	6 807	241.3	234.0	244.0
90 - 94	6 665	1 850	4 815	...	...	...
95 - 99	2 380	568	1 812	...	...	...
100 +	221	41	180	...	...	...
Unknown - Inconnu	10	8	2	..	..	..
Iceland - Islande						
2007 (C)						
Total	1 943	1 002	941	6.2	6.3	6.2
0 - 4	15	9	6	♦0.7	♦0.8	♦0.6
0	9	7	2	♦2.0	♦3.0	♦0.9
1 - 4	6	2	4	♦0.3	♦0.2	♦0.5
5 - 9	2	1	1	♦0.1	♦0.1	♦0.1
10 - 14	2	2	-	♦0.1	♦0.2	-
15 - 19	4	4	-	♦0.2	♦0.3	-
20 - 24	15	12	3	♦0.7	♦1.1	♦0.3
25 - 29	11	9	2	♦0.5	♦0.7	♦0.2
30 - 34	11	6	5	♦0.5	♦0.5	♦0.5
35 - 39	15	10	5	♦0.7	♦0.9	♦0.5
40 - 44	26	17	9	♦1.1	♦1.4	♦0.8
45 - 49	35	23	12	1.6	♦2.0	♦1.1
50 - 54	52	35	17	2.6	3.3	♦1.8
55 - 59	75	40	35	4.3	4.5	4.2
60 - 64	98	56	42	7.2	8.1	6.3
65 - 69	105	55	50	10.9	11.6	10.2
70 - 74	187	110	77	21.6	26.9	16.9
75 - 79	299	152	147	37.9	42.0	34.4
80 - 84	357	192	165	66.0	84.5	52.6
85 - 89	337	152	185	112.8	132.6	100.5
90 - 94	213	91	122	201.3	260.7	172.1
95 - 99	70	20	50	283.4	♦333.3	267.4
100 +	14	6	8	♦518.5	♦1500.0	♦347.8
Ireland - Irlande						
2007* (+C)						
Total	28 050	14 299	13 751	6.4	6.6	6.3
0 - 4	277	153	124	0.9	0.9	0.8
0	221	123	98	...	...	...
1 - 4	56	30	26	...	...	...
5 - 9	24	15	9	♦0.1	♦0.1	♦0.1
10 - 14	44	22	22	0.2	♦0.2	0.3
15 - 19	138	95	43	0.5	0.7	0.3
20 - 24	215	170	45	0.6	1.0	0.3
25 - 34	486	349	137	0.6	0.9	0.4
35 - 44	686	453	233	1.1	1.4	0.7
45 - 54	1 437	871	566	2.7	3.2	2.1
55 - 64	2 919	1 842	1 077	6.9	8.7	5.2
65 - 74	4 923	2 949	1 974	18.6	22.9	14.5
75 - 84	8 936	4 586	4 350	56.6	69.6	47.3
85 +	7 965	2 794	5 171	155.9	176.5	146.7
85 - 94	7 031	2 587	4 444	...	...	...
95 +	934	207	727			
Isle of Man - Île de Man						
2004 (+C)						
Total	798	390	408	...	...	...
0	2	1	1	...	...	...
1 - 4	-	-	-	...	...	...
5 - 9	-	-	-	...	...	...
10 - 14	1	1	-	...	...	...
15 - 19	3	3	-	...	...	...
20 - 24	5	4	1	...	...	...
25 - 29	3	3	-	...	...	...
30 - 34	3	1	2	...	...	...
35 - 39	6	5	1	...	...	...

Continent, country or area, date, code and age (in years) / Continent, pays ou zone, date, code et âge (en années)	Number - Nombre			Rate - Taux		
	Both sexes Les deux sexes	Male Masculin	Female Féminin	Both sexes Les deux sexes	Male Masculin	Female Féminin
EUROPE						
Isle of Man - Île de Man						
2004 (+C)						
40 - 44	7	4	3	...	...	...
45 - 49	11	5	6	...	...	...
50 - 54	17	8	9	...	...	...
55 - 59	31	18	13	...	...	...
60 - 64	33	19	14	...	...	...
65 - 69	60	45	15	...	...	...
70 - 74	82	46	36	...	...	...
75 - 79	118	59	59	...	...	...
80 - 84	169	77	92	...	...	...
85 - 89	111	43	68	...	...	...
90 - 94	96	36	60	...	...	...
95 +	40	12	28	...	...	...
Italy - Italie						
2004 (C)						
Total	545 051	272 864	272 187	9.4	9.7	9.1
0	2 168	1 189	979	4.0	4.2	3.7
1 - 4	377	199	178	0.2	0.2	0.2
5 - 9	254	145	109	0.1	0.1	0.1
10 - 14	342	212	130	0.1	0.1	0.1
15 - 19	1 063	777	286	0.4	0.5	0.2
20 - 24	1 690	1 346	344	0.5	0.8	0.2
25 - 29	2 184	1 679	505	0.5	0.8	0.3
30 - 34	2 781	1 988	793	0.6	0.9	0.3
35 - 39	3 865	2 646	1 219	0.8	1.1	0.5
40 - 44	5 610	3 667	1 943	1.3	1.6	0.9
45 - 49	7 592	4 801	2 791	1.9	2.4	1.4
50 - 54	11 453	7 264	4 189	3.1	4.0	2.2
55 - 59	17 874	11 625	6 249	4.8	6.4	3.3
60 - 64	26 142	17 196	8 946	7.9	10.8	5.2
65 - 69	39 852	25 820	14 032	12.4	17.2	8.2
70 - 74	59 477	36 897	22 580	20.8	29.2	14.2
75 - 79	84 065	47 357	36 708	35.7	49.4	26.3
80 - 84	105 547	49 898	55 649	62.8	83.0	51.6
85 - 89	75 148	29 323	45 825	111.3	139.2	98.7
90 - 94	71 759	22 905	48 854	184.2	219.8	171.2
95 - 99	22 572	5 351	17 221	284.7	322.0	274.8
100 +	3 201	553	2 648	379.8	377.5	380.2
Unknown - Inconnu	35	26	9	..	..	..
Latvia - Lettonie						
2007 (C)						
Total	33 042	16 360	16 682	14.5	15.6	13.6
0 - 4	236	120	116	2.2	2.2	2.2
0	203	98	105	8.8	8.4	9.3
1 - 4	33	22	11	0.4	◆0.5	◆0.3
5 - 9	26	17	9	◆0.3	◆0.3	◆0.2
10 - 14	37	22	15	0.3	◆0.4	◆0.3
15 - 19	119	87	32	0.7	1.0	0.4
20 - 24	161	137	24	0.9	1.5	◆0.3
25 - 29	271	219	52	1.7	2.7	0.7
30 - 34	351	288	63	2.2	3.6	0.8
35 - 39	550	401	149	3.5	5.1	1.9
40 - 44	803	604	199	5.0	7.8	2.4
45 - 49	1 320	969	351	7.6	11.8	3.9
50 - 54	1 665	1 193	472	11.0	17.1	5.8
55 - 59	2 125	1 481	644	15.3	24.2	8.3
60 - 64	2 429	1 661	768	21.5	35.4	11.6
65 - 69	3 550	2 175	1 375	27.4	43.4	17.3
70 - 74	3 973	2 127	1 846	39.7	61.1	28.3
75 - 79	5 152	2 277	2 875	62.4	88.1	50.7
80 - 84	4 989	1 414	3 575	97.3	124.4	89.6
85 - 89	3 044	737	2 307	159.4	181.4	153.5
90 - 94	1 572	305	1 267	252.6	251.9	252.7
95 - 99	571	104	467	348.8	359.9	346.4
100 +	79	11	68	420.2	◆268.3	462.6
Unknown - Inconnu	19	11	8	..	..	..

Continent, country or area, date, code and age (in years) / Continent, pays ou zone, date, code et âge (en années)	Number - Nombre			Rate - Taux		
	Both sexes Les deux sexes	Male Masculin	Female Féminin	Both sexes Les deux sexes	Male Masculin	Female Féminin
EUROPE						
Liechtenstein						
2007* (C)						
Total	227	115	112	...	...	...
0 - 4	1	-	1	...	...	...
0	-	-	-	...	...	...
1 - 4	1	-	1	...	...	...
5 - 9	-	-	-	...	...	...
10 - 14				...	...	...
15 - 19	-	-	-	...	...	...
20 - 24	1	1		...	...	...
25 - 29	2	1	1	...	...	...
30 - 34	1	1	-	...	...	...
35 - 39	1	-	1	...	...	...
40 - 44	1	1	-	...	...	...
45 - 49	9	5	4	...	...	...
50 - 54	12	5	7	...	...	...
55 - 59	15	11	4	...	...	...
60 - 64	21	15	6	...	...	...
65 - 69	27	16	11	...	...	...
70 - 74	28	18	10	...	...	...
75 - 79	29	13	16	...	...	...
80 - 84	44	19	25	...	...	...
85 - 89	27	9	18	...	...	...
90 - 94	5	-	5	...	...	...
95 - 99	3	-	3	...	...	...
100 +						
Lithuania - Lituanie						
2007 (C)						
Total	45 624	24 683	20 941	13.5	15.7	11.6
0 - 4	229	120	109	1.5	1.5	1.5
0	190	96	94	6.0	6.0	6.1
1 - 4	39	24	15	0.3	♦0.4	♦0.3
5 - 9	42	25	17	0.3	♦0.3	♦0.2
10 - 14	69	40	29	0.3	0.4	♦0.3
15 - 19	216	171	45	0.8	1.3	0.3
20 - 24	340	293	47	1.3	2.1	0.4
25 - 29	449	363	86	2.0	3.1	0.8
30 - 34	602	489	113	2.7	4.3	1.0
35 - 39	1 000	781	219	4.0	6.4	1.7
40 - 44	1 433	1 109	324	5.6	8.9	2.5
45 - 49	2 218	1 679	539	8.4	13.4	3.9
50 - 54	2 464	1 822	642	11.6	18.6	5.6
55 - 59	3 072	2 184	888	16.2	26.1	8.4
60 - 64	3 453	2 377	1 076	21.4	35.4	11.5
65 - 69	4 402	2 888	1 514	26.9	45.1	15.2
70 - 74	5 274	2 990	2 284	36.8	57.9	24.9
75 - 79	6 486	3 090	3 396	56.1	81.8	43.7
80 - 84	6 622	2 304	4 318	93.7	125.4	82.6
85 - 89	4 101	1 165	2 936	154.3	182.4	145.5
90 - 94	2 121	522	1 599	270.2	283.8	266.0
95 - 99	853	213	640	422.9	378.3	440.2
100 +	178	58	120	485.0	483.3	485.8
Luxembourg						
2007 (C)						
Total	3 866	1 932	1 934	8.1	8.1	8.0
0 - 4	19	13	6	♦0.7	♦0.9	♦0.4
0	10	8	2	♦1.8	♦2.9	♦0.7
1 - 4	9	5	4	♦0.4	♦0.4	♦0.4
5 - 9	1	-	1	-	-	♦0.1
10 - 14	5	-	5	♦0.2		♦0.3
15 - 19	10	6	4	♦0.4	♦0.4	♦0.3
20 - 24	16	12	4	♦0.6	♦0.8	♦0.3
25 - 29	18	13	5	♦0.6	♦0.8	♦0.4
30 - 34	32	25	7	0.9	♦1.4	♦0.3
35 - 39	28	16	12	♦0.7	♦0.8	♦0.6
40 - 44	43	33	10	1.0	1.6	♦0.5
45 - 49	91	58	33	2.4	3.1	1.8

19. Deaths and death rates by age and sex: latest available year, 1998 - 2007
Décès et taux de mortalité selon l'âge et le sexe: dernière année disponible, 1998 - 2007 (continued - suite)

Continent, country or area, date, code and age (in years) / Continent, pays ou zone, date, code et âge (en années)	Number - Nombre			Rate - Taux		
	Both sexes Les deux sexes	Male Masculin	Female Féminin	Both sexes Les deux sexes	Male Masculin	Female Féminin
EUROPE						
Luxembourg						
2007 (C)						
50 - 54	124	79	45	3.8	4.8	2.8
55 - 59	165	106	59	5.9	7.4	4.4
60 - 64	218	138	80	9.8	12.3	7.2
65 - 69	306	181	125	15.9	20.0	12.4
70 - 74	397	255	142	23.8	33.6	15.6
75 - 79	627	343	284	41.3	53.0	32.6
80 - 84	674	313	361	69.6	95.9	56.2
85 - 89	557	190	367	121.6	151.2	110.4
90 - 94	355	109	246	211.2	321.5	183.3
95 +	180	42	138	717.1	6000.0	565.6
95 - 99	155	36	119	...	...	...
100 +	25	6	19	...	...	...
Malta - Malte						
2007 (C)						
Total	3 111	1 610	1 501	7.6	7.9	7.3
0 - 4	26	10	16	♦1.3	♦1.0	♦1.7
0	25	9	16	♦6.5	♦4.4	♦8.7
1 - 4	1	1	-	♦0.1	♦0.1	-
5 - 9	2	1	1	♦0.1	♦0.1	♦0.1
10 - 14	5	3	2	♦0.2	♦0.2	♦0.2
15 - 19	8	7	1	♦0.3	♦0.5	♦0.1
20 - 24	17	16	1	♦0.6	♦1.1	♦0.1
25 - 29	15	13	2	♦0.5	♦0.8	♦0.1
30 - 34	19	15	4	♦0.7	♦1.0	♦0.3
35 - 39	20	10	10	♦0.8	♦0.8	♦0.8
40 - 44	34	25	9	1.3	♦1.9	♦0.7
45 - 49	38	19	19	1.3	♦1.2	♦1.3
50 - 54	90	58	32	3.1	3.9	2.2
55 - 59	147	82	65	4.8	5.4	4.3
60 - 64	206	129	77	7.9	10.2	5.8
65 - 69	228	150	78	13.4	18.9	8.6
70 - 74	390	218	172	25.1	32.0	19.7
75 - 79	478	254	224	42.1	55.8	32.9
80 - 84	587	289	298	77.2	98.9	63.7
85 - 89	487	209	278	131.2	155.7	117.3
90 +	314	102	212	237.3	271.3	223.9
90 - 94	226	84	142	...	...	...
95 - 99	76	17	59	...	...	...
100 +	12	1	11	...	...	...
Montenegro - Monténégro						
2007 (C)						
Total	5 979	3 048	2 931	9.5	9.9	9.2
0 - 4	68	41	27	1.7	2.0	♦1.5
0	58	36	22	7.5	8.9	♦6.0
1 - 4	10	5	5	♦0.3	♦0.3	♦0.3
5 - 9	12	8	4	♦0.3	♦0.4	♦0.2
10 - 14	7	5	2	♦0.2	♦0.2	♦0.1
15 - 19	14	10	4	♦0.3	♦0.4	♦0.2
20 - 24	40	29	11	0.8	♦1.1	♦0.4
25 - 29	34	28	6	0.7	♦1.2	♦0.3
30 - 34	40	31	9	0.9	1.4	♦0.4
35 - 39	51	37	14	1.2	1.8	♦0.7
40 - 44	96	64	32	2.2	3.0	1.5
45 - 49	147	99	48	3.3	4.5	2.2
50 - 54	303	195	108	7.0	8.9	5.0
55 - 59	362	226	136	9.7	12.7	7.0
60 - 64	381	230	151	15.3	20.3	11.1
65 - 69	677	415	262	23.8	32.5	16.7
70 - 74	914	487	427	38.6	46.8	32.2
75 - 79	1 054	496	558	65.1	72.4	59.8
80 - 84	954	358	596	114.2	111.2	116.0
85 - 89	476	176	300	164.1	175.5	158.1
90 - 94	223	76	147	298.9	329.0	284.9
95 - 99	86	23	63	310.5	♦232.3	353.9
100 +	40	14	26	493.8	♦1076.9	♦382.4

19. Deaths and death rates by age and sex: latest available year, 1998 - 2007
Décès et taux de mortalité selon l'âge et le sexe: dernière année disponible, 1998 - 2007 (continued - suite)

Continent, country or area, date, code and age (in years) / Continent, pays ou zone, date, code et âge (en années)	Number - Nombre			Rate - Taux		
	Both sexes Les deux sexes	Male Masculin	Female Féminin	Both sexes Les deux sexes	Male Masculin	Female Féminin
EUROPE						
Netherlands - Pays-Bas[31]						
2007 (C)				8.1	8.0	8.3
Total	133 022	64 797	68 225	0.9	1.0	0.8
0 - 4	882	519	363	4.0	4.6	3.4
0	736	435	301	0.2	0.2	0.2
1 - 4	146	84	62	0.1	0.1	0.1
5 - 9	88	44	44	0.1	0.1	0.1
10 - 14	110	53	57	0.3	0.3	0.2
15 - 19	253	172	81	0.4	0.5	0.2
20 - 24	359	245	114	0.4	0.5	0.2
25 - 29	353	235	118	0.5	0.6	0.4
30 - 34	523	322	201	0.7	0.9	0.6
35 - 39	933	570	363	1.1	1.2	1.0
40 - 44	1 454	803	651	2.0	2.2	1.8
45 - 49	2 489	1 369	1 120	3.3	3.6	3.0
50 - 54	3 756	2 075	1 681	5.4	6.4	4.4
55 - 59	6 007	3 597	2 410	8.7	10.6	6.8
60 - 64	8 021	4 910	3 111	13.7	17.5	10.1
65 - 69	9 696	6 041	3 655	22.7	29.8	16.6
70 - 74	13 304	8 084	5 220	40.2	53.5	30.4
75 - 79	19 078	10 733	8 345	69.9	92.4	57.1
80 - 84	23 720	11 373	12 347	125.5	159.8	110.8
85 - 89	22 697	8 658	14 039	212.3	262.6	197.4
90 - 94	13 932	3 951	9 981	337.2	395.7	325.0
95 - 99	4 661	941	3 720	506.1	507.5	505.9
100 +	706	102	604			
Norway - Norvège[32]						
2007 (C)				8.9	8.6	9.2
Total	41 954	20 216	21 738	0.7	0.8	0.7
0 - 4	217	114	103	3.1	3.2	2.9
0	180	97	83	0.2	◆0.1	◆0.2
1 - 4	37	17	20	◆0.1	◆0.1	◆0.1
5 - 9	22	10	12	0.1	◆0.1	◆0.1
10 - 14	39	24	15	0.3	0.4	◆0.2
15 - 19	93	65	28	0.6	0.8	0.3
20 - 24	157	113	44	0.6	0.9	0.4
25 - 29	190	139	51	0.6	0.8	0.3
30 - 34	185	130	55	0.8	0.9	0.6
35 - 39	276	163	113	1.1	1.3	0.9
40 - 44	388	236	152	2.0	2.4	1.5
45 - 49	636	394	242	3.1	3.7	2.5
50 - 54	959	578	381	4.9	5.7	4.1
55 - 59	1 428	844	584	8.1	10.0	6.1
60 - 64	2 173	1 361	812	13.0	16.8	9.5
65 - 69	2 408	1 505	903	21.1	26.9	16.0
70 - 74	3 136	1 855	1 281	37.7	48.6	29.3
75 - 79	5 189	2 918	2 271	68.6	87.8	56.2
80 - 84	7 809	3 899	3 910	122.5	153.1	107.8
85 - 89	8 806	3 560	5 246	210.1	259.8	192.8
90 - 94	5 534	1 762	3 772	346.0	400.2	332.1
95 - 99	1 942	459	1 483	498.8	514.0	495.5
100 +	304	55	249	..	..	..
Unknown - Inconnu	63	32	31			
Poland - Pologne						
2007 (C)				9.9	11.0	8.9
Total	377 226	202 241	174 985	1.5	1.6	1.3
0 - 4	2 688	1 517	1 171	6.1	6.7	5.5
0	2 322	1 305	1 017	0.3	0.3	0.2
1 - 4	366	212	154	0.1	0.2	0.1
5 - 9	246	147	99	0.2	0.2	0.2
10 - 14	434	264	170	0.5	0.7	0.3
15 - 19	1 362	1 015	347	0.7	1.1	0.3
20 - 24	2 217	1 783	434	0.8	1.2	0.3
25 - 29	2 398	1 894	504	1.1	1.7	0.5
30 - 34	3 132	2 465	667	1.7	2.6	0.7
35 - 39	4 099	3 228	871	2.9	4.4	1.4
40 - 44	7 019	5 325	1 694			

19. Deaths and death rates by age and sex: latest available year, 1998 - 2007
Décès et taux de mortalité selon l'âge et le sexe: dernière année disponible, 1998 - 2007 (continued - suite)

Continent, country or area, date, code and age (in years) / Continent, pays ou zone, date, code et âge (en années)	Number - Nombre			Rate - Taux		
	Both sexes Les deux sexes	Male Masculin	Female Féminin	Both sexes Les deux sexes	Male Masculin	Female Féminin
EUROPE						
Poland - Pologne						
2007 (C)						
45 - 49	14 067	10 341	3 726	5.0	7.4	2.6
50 - 54	22 885	16 604	6 281	7.6	11.3	4.0
55 - 59	29 549	20 594	8 955	11.2	16.4	6.4
60 - 64	25 667	17 443	8 224	15.4	23.0	9.0
65 - 69	31 965	20 744	11 221	21.6	32.7	13.3
70 - 74	44 411	26 330	18 081	32.1	47.5	21.8
75 - 79	57 578	29 058	28 520	50.2	69.2	39.2
80 - 84	60 220	23 579	36 641	83.9	106.9	73.7
85 +	67 289	19 910	47 379	170.3	189.7	163.3
85 - 89	38 945	12 805	26 140	...	...	...
90 - 94	20 054	5 265	14 789	...	...	...
95 - 99	7 349	1 620	5 729	...	...	...
100 +	941	220	721	...	...	...
Portugal[11]						
2007 (C)						
Total	103 512	53 378	50 134	9.8	10.4	9.2
0 - 4	439	234	205	0.8	0.8	0.8
0	353	186	167	3.4	3.5	3.3
1 - 4	86	48	38	0.2	0.2	0.2
5 - 9	62	39	23	0.1	0.1	♦0.1
10 - 14	87	42	45	0.2	0.2	0.2
15 - 19	212	155	57	0.4	0.5	0.2
20 - 24	380	279	101	0.6	0.8	0.3
25 - 29	479	365	114	0.6	0.9	0.3
30 - 34	740	549	191	0.9	1.3	0.5
35 - 39	1 083	771	312	1.4	1.9	0.8
40 - 44	1 581	1 116	465	2.0	2.9	1.2
45 - 49	2 272	1 583	689	3.0	4.3	1.8
50 - 54	3 007	2 135	872	4.4	6.4	2.5
55 - 59	3 800	2 604	1 196	5.8	8.3	3.5
60 - 64	4 916	3 349	1 567	8.6	12.6	5.1
65 - 69	6 921	4 440	2 481	13.4	18.9	8.9
70 - 74	11 124	6 744	4 380	22.7	31.4	15.9
75 - 79	15 747	8 602	7 145	40.0	53.1	30.9
80 - 84	20 011	9 561	10 450	75.7	96.6	63.1
85 +	30 632	10 794	19 838	174.8	188.5	168.2
85 - 89	16 781	6 690	10 091	...	...	...
90 - 94	10 165	3 204	6 961	...	...	...
95 - 99	3 246	826	2 420	...	...	...
100 +	440	74	366	...	...	...
Unknown - Inconnu	19	16	3	..	..	..
Republic of Moldova - République de Moldova[33]						
2007 (C)						
Total	43 050	22 238	20 812	12.0	12.9	11.2
0 - 4	534	282	252	2.9	2.9	2.8
0	446	232	214	11.9	12.0	11.8
1 - 4	88	50	38	0.6	0.7	0.5
5 - 9	52	36	16	0.3	0.4	♦0.2
10 - 14	93	59	34	0.4	0.4	0.3
15 - 19	252	165	87	0.8	1.0	0.5
20 - 24	337	252	85	1.0	1.4	0.5
25 - 29	422	302	120	1.4	2.0	0.8
30 - 34	581	438	143	2.3	3.4	1.1
35 - 39	797	570	227	3.5	5.0	1.9
40 - 44	1 362	1 018	344	5.6	8.7	2.7
45 - 49	2 461	1 750	711	8.6	12.9	4.7
50 - 54	3 100	2 079	1 021	12.3	17.7	7.6
55 - 59	3 851	2 406	1 445	18.8	25.9	13.0
60 - 64	2 959	1 713	1 246	24.5	32.2	18.4
65 - 69	5 056	2 701	2 355	40.2	52.5	31.7
70 - 74	5 870	2 823	3 047	58.0	71.7	49.3
75 - 79	6 557	2 841	3 716	84.0	99.4	75.1
80 - 84	5 101	1 652	3 449	119.9	124.0	118.0
85 - 89	2 534	848	1 686	154.2	169.0	147.6
90 - 94	891	245	646	242.7	226.6	249.4

19. Deaths and death rates by age and sex: latest available year, 1998 - 2007
Décès et taux de mortalité selon l'âge et le sexe: dernière année disponible, 1998 - 2007 (continued - suite)

Continent, country or area, date, code and age (in years) / Continent, pays ou zone, date, code et âge (en années)	Number - Nombre			Rate - Taux		
	Both sexes Les deux sexes	Male Masculin	Female Féminin	Both sexes Les deux sexes	Male Masculin	Female Féminin
EUROPE						
Republic of Moldova - République de Moldova[33]						
2007 (C)						
95 - 99	210	56	154	235.2	237.3	234.4
100 +..	30	2	28	♦234.4	♦60.6	♦294.7
Romania - Roumanie						
2007 (C)						
Total..	251 965	133 405	118 560	11.7	12.7	10.7
0 - 4..	3 046	1 748	1 298	2.9	3.2	2.5
0..	2 574	1 476	1 098	12.1	13.5	10.6
1 - 4..	472	272	200	0.6	0.6	0.5
5 - 9..	327	193	134	0.3	0.3	0.3
10 - 14..	343	214	129	0.3	0.4	0.2
15 - 19..	906	609	297	0.6	0.8	0.4
20 - 24..	1 029	785	244	0.6	0.9	0.3
25 - 29..	1 243	915	328	0.7	1.0	0.4
30 - 34..	1 832	1 319	513	1.1	1.5	0.6
35 - 39..	3 295	2 363	932	1.7	2.4	1.0
40 - 44..	3 841	2 769	1 072	3.2	4.6	1.8
45 - 49..	7 602	5 395	2 207	5.5	7.8	3.1
50 - 54..	12 866	9 163	3 703	8.3	12.3	4.6
55 - 59..	15 958	10 971	4 987	11.7	17.0	7.0
60 - 64..	16 745	11 030	5 715	17.0	24.4	10.7
65 - 69..	25 386	15 475	9 911	25.3	35.4	17.5
70 - 74..	35 322	19 387	15 935	38.5	50.6	29.8
75 - 79..	43 293	20 839	22 454	62.7	75.6	54.1
80 - 84..	42 793	17 886	24 907	106.1	119.8	98.0
85 - 89..	22 821	7 951	14 870	166.4	174.9	162.2
90 - 94..	10 185	3 353	6 832	290.1	290.5	289.8
95 - 99..	2 843	951	1 892	311.1	292.2	321.5
100 +..	289	89	200	155.7	152.7	157.1
Russian Federation - Fédération de Russie[16]						
2007 (C)						
Total..	2 080 445	1 095 849	984 596	14.7	16.7	12.9
0 - 4..	18 447	10 713	7 734	2.5	2.8	2.1
0..	14 858	8 598	6 260	9.3	10.5	8.1
1 - 4..	3 589	2 115	1 474	0.6	0.7	0.5
5 - 9..	2 205	1 343	862	0.3	0.4	0.3
10 - 14..	2 739	1 775	964	0.4	0.5	0.3
15 - 19..	11 569	8 131	3 438	1.1	1.6	0.7
20 - 24..	26 109	20 448	5 661	2.0	3.2	0.9
25 - 29..	40 041	31 756	8 285	3.5	5.5	1.4
30 - 34..	48 663	38 056	10 607	4.6	7.3	2.0
35 - 39..	52 042	39 599	12 443	5.4	8.3	2.5
40 - 44..	72 232	54 809	17 423	7.4	11.6	3.4
45 - 49..	115 167	85 987	29 180	9.6	15.3	4.6
50 - 54..	143 461	104 165	39 296	13.1	21.0	6.6
55 - 59..	164 529	113 706	50 823	17.6	27.9	9.6
60 - 64..	110 734	73 512	37 222	22.6	36.4	12.9
65 - 69..	233 139	138 035	95 104	35.3	56.8	22.8
70 - 74..	237 077	122 153	114 924	45.6	68.6	33.6
75 - 79..	315 674	131 500	184 174	74.9	104.6	62.3
80 - 84..	262 997	72 833	190 164	105.0	124.5	99.0
85 - 89..	125 069	25 124	99 945	162.3	171.7	160.0
90 - 94..	66 609	10 672	55 937	296.8	276.0	301.2
95 - 99..	18 855	2 622	16 233	335.9	266.8	350.6
100 +..	2 263	257	2 006	121.8	87.2	128.3
Unknown - Inconnu..	10 824	8 653	2 171	..	..	..
San Marino - Saint-Marin						
2004 (+C)						
Total..	185	94	91	...	...	...
0..	1	1	-	...	...	...
1 - 14..	-	-	-	...	...	...
15 - 19..	2	2	-	...	...	...
20 - 24..	2	2	-	...	...	...
25 - 29..	-	-	-	...	...	...
30 - 34..	1	-	1	...	...	...
35 - 39..	-	-	-	...	...	...

19. Deaths and death rates by age and sex: latest available year, 1998 - 2007
Décès et taux de mortalité selon l'âge et le sexe: dernière année disponible, 1998 - 2007 (continued - suite)

Continent, country or area, date, code and age (in years) / Continent, pays ou zone, date, code et âge (en années)	Number - Nombre			Rate - Taux		
	Both sexes Les deux sexes	Male Masculin	Female Féminin	Both sexes Les deux sexes	Male Masculin	Female Féminin
EUROPE						
San Marino - Saint-Marin						
2004 (+C)						
40 - 44	3	-	3	...	...	...
45 - 49	2	-	2	...	...	...
50 - 54	7	5	2	...	...	...
55 - 59	9	6	3	...	...	...
60 - 64	8	6	2	...	...	...
65 - 69	12	7	5	...	...	...
70 - 74	14	9	5	...	...	...
75 - 79	22	13	9	...	...	...
80 - 84	35	16	19	...	...	...
85 - 89	34	16	18	...	...	...
90 - 94	27	7	20	...	...	...
95 - 99	5	4	1	...	...	...
100 +	1	-	1	...	...	...
Serbia - Serbie[34]						
2007 (+C)						
Total	102 805	52 257	50 548	13.9	14.6	13.3
0 - 4	563	336	227	1.5	1.8	1.3
0	484	288	196	7.0	8.1	5.9
1 - 4	79	48	31	0.3	0.3	0.2
5 - 9	55	30	25	0.2	◆0.2	◆0.1
10 - 14	66	41	25	0.2	0.2	◆0.1
15 - 19	195	148	47	0.4	0.6	0.2
20 - 24	366	288	78	0.7	1.1	0.3
25 - 29	426	329	97	0.8	1.3	0.4
30 - 34	481	357	124	0.9	1.4	0.5
35 - 39	649	438	211	1.4	1.8	0.9
40 - 44	1 137	730	407	2.4	3.1	1.7
45 - 49	2 231	1 496	735	4.3	5.8	2.8
50 - 54	4 391	2 969	1 422	7.4	10.1	4.7
55 - 59	6 303	4 162	2 141	11.4	15.6	7.5
60 - 64	6 351	3 983	2 368	17.2	23.2	12.0
65 - 69	10 445	6 180	4 265	26.8	35.2	19.9
70 - 74	16 746	8 943	7 803	44.1	54.3	36.4
75 - 79	21 322	9 943	11 379	74.7	84.7	67.8
80 - 84	18 682	7 359	11 323	123.1	131.6	118.1
85 - 89	8 968	3 277	5 691	170.7	174.4	168.7
90 - 94	2 455	873	1 582	298.0	300.6	296.6
95 - 99	832	314	518	244.5	257.2	237.4
100 +	77	23	54	90.1	◆80.1	95.1
Unknown - Inconnu	64	38	26	..	..	..
Slovakia - Slovaquie						
2007 (C)						
Total	53 856	28 226	25 630	10.0	10.8	9.2
0 - 4	409	228	181	1.5	1.7	1.4
0	334	189	145	6.2	6.8	5.5
1 - 4	75	39	36	0.4	0.4	0.4
5 - 9	59	29	30	0.2	◆0.2	◆0.2
10 - 14	57	35	22	0.2	0.2	◆0.1
15 - 19	162	116	46	0.4	0.6	0.2
20 - 24	259	201	58	0.6	0.9	0.3
25 - 29	289	216	73	0.6	0.9	0.3
30 - 34	424	316	108	0.9	1.4	0.5
35 - 39	579	416	163	1.6	2.2	0.9
40 - 44	1 026	731	295	2.7	3.9	1.6
45 - 49	1 830	1 310	520	4.7	6.8	2.7
50 - 54	2 859	2 107	752	7.1	10.7	3.6
55 - 59	3 872	2 728	1 144	11.1	16.4	6.2
60 - 64	4 013	2 769	1 244	16.1	24.9	9.0
65 - 69	4 848	3 035	1 813	23.9	35.7	15.4
70 - 74	6 045	3 377	2 668	36.4	52.4	26.3
75 - 79	8 447	4 016	4 431	61.6	82.8	50.0
80 - 84	9 390	3 657	5 733	105.5	130.4	94.1
85 - 89	5 954	2 010	3 944	162.7	185.0	153.3
90 - 94	2 441	703	1 738	257.9	264.6	255.3

19. Deaths and death rates by age and sex: latest available year, 1998 - 2007
Décès et taux de mortalité selon l'âge et le sexe: dernière année disponible, 1998 - 2007 (continued - suite)

Continent, country or area, date, code and age (in years) Continent, pays ou zone, date, code et âge (en années)	Number - Nombre			Rate - Taux		
	Both sexes Les deux sexes	Male Masculin	Female Féminin	Both sexes Les deux sexes	Male Masculin	Female Féminin
EUROPE						
Slovakia - Slovaquie						
2007 (C)						
95 - 99	795	206	589	247.3	223.4	256.9
100 +	98	20	78	147.8	♦78.7	190.7
Slovenia - Slovénie						
2007 (C)						
Total	18 584	9 473	9 111	9.2	9.5	8.9
0 - 4	73	37	36	0.8	0.8	0.8
0	55	27	28	2.8	♦2.7	♦2.9
1 - 4	18	10	8	♦0.2	♦0.3	♦0.2
5 - 9	10	4	6	♦0.1	♦0.1	♦0.1
10 - 14	14	5	9	♦0.1	♦0.1	♦0.2
15 - 19	51	34	17	0.4	0.6	♦0.3
20 - 24	108	88	20	0.8	1.2	♦0.3
25 - 29	113	95	18	0.7	1.2	♦0.2
30 - 34	118	92	26	0.8	1.2	♦0.4
35 - 39	154	118	36	1.1	1.6	0.5
40 - 44	279	204	75	1.8	2.5	1.0
45 - 49	475	338	137	3.1	4.3	1.8
50 - 54	794	564	230	5.0	6.9	3.0
55 - 59	1 043	736	307	7.6	10.5	4.5
60 - 64	1 145	810	335	11.2	16.5	6.3
65 - 69	1 585	1 065	520	16.2	23.7	9.9
70 - 74	2 252	1 359	893	26.2	37.7	17.9
75 - 79	3 054	1 606	1 448	43.6	62.3	32.7
80 - 84	3 238	1 220	2 018	72.6	96.9	63.0
85 - 89	2 266	658	1 608	123.5	149.4	115.4
90 - 94	1 246	336	910	229.8	289.2	213.7
95 - 99	513	100	413	339.3	359.7	334.7
100 +	53	4	49	355.7	♦181.8	385.8
Spain - Espagne						
2007 (C)						
Total	385 122	201 144	183 978	8.6	9.1	8.1
0 - 4	2 197	1 204	993	0.9	1.0	0.9
0	1 808	997	811	3.8	4.1	3.5
1 - 4	389	207	182	0.2	0.2	0.2
5 - 9	227	127	100	0.1	0.1	0.1
10 - 14	278	172	106	0.1	0.2	0.1
15 - 19	795	592	203	0.3	0.5	0.2
20 - 24	1 169	891	278	0.4	0.6	0.2
25 - 29	1 693	1 300	393	0.5	0.7	0.2
30 - 34	2 260	1 614	646	0.6	0.8	0.3
35 - 39	3 412	2 371	1 041	0.9	1.2	0.6
40 - 44	5 405	3 791	1 614	1.5	2.1	0.9
45 - 49	7 475	5 101	2 374	2.3	3.2	1.5
50 - 54	9 895	6 899	2 996	3.6	5.0	2.1
55 - 59	13 162	9 427	3 735	5.2	7.7	2.9
60 - 64	17 850	12 669	5 181	7.8	11.5	4.4
65 - 69	21 464	14 821	6 643	11.4	16.8	6.7
70 - 74	37 906	24 682	13 224	19.9	28.8	12.7
75 - 79	55 828	32 859	22 969	33.9	47.0	24.3
80 - 84	72 386	36 535	35 851	63.0	82.2	50.8
85 - 89	67 756	27 144	40 612	111.8	133.3	100.9
90 - 94	44 585	14 027	30 558	196.0	222.1	185.9
95 - 99	16 684	4 408	12 276	295.1	316.6	288.1
100 +	2 695	510	2 185	476.1	373.1	509.0
Sweden - Suède						
2007 (C)						
Total	91 729	43 970	47 759	10.0	9.7	10.4
0 - 4	336	177	159	0.6	0.7	0.6
0	268	148	120	2.5	2.7	2.3
1 - 4	68	29	39	0.2	♦0.1	0.2
5 - 9	41	20	21	0.1	♦0.1	♦0.1
10 - 14	45	29	16	0.1	♦0.1	♦0.1
15 - 19	204	141	63	0.3	0.4	0.2
20 - 24	261	196	65	0.5	0.7	0.2
25 - 29	275	210	65	0.5	0.7	0.2

19. Deaths and death rates by age and sex: latest available year, 1998 - 2007
Décès et taux de mortalité selon l'âge et le sexe: dernière année disponible, 1998 - 2007 (continued - suite)

Continent, country or area, date, code and age (in years) Continent, pays ou zone, date, code et âge (en années)	Number - Nombre			Rate - Taux		
	Both sexes Les deux sexes	Male Masculin	Female Féminin	Both sexes Les deux sexes	Male Masculin	Female Féminin
EUROPE						
Sweden - Suède						
2007 (C)						
30 - 34	285	193	92	0.5	0.6	0.3
35 - 39	426	260	166	0.7	0.8	0.5
40 - 44	702	441	261	1.1	1.3	0.8
45 - 49	1 054	640	414	1.8	2.1	1.4
50 - 54	1 735	1 077	658	3.0	3.7	2.3
55 - 59	2 858	1 741	1 117	4.7	5.7	3.7
60 - 64	4 723	2 925	1 798	7.7	9.5	5.9
65 - 69	5 589	3 367	2 222	12.6	15.4	9.9
70 - 74	7 052	4 147	2 905	20.1	25.1	15.6
75 - 79	11 125	6 103	5 022	35.9	45.0	28.9
80 - 84	16 706	8 399	8 307	66.2	82.8	55.1
85 - 89	19 646	8 195	11 451	121.2	144.3	108.7
90 - 94	13 135	4 417	8 718	215.4	256.9	199.1
95 - 99	4 819	1 164	3 655	347.9	392.5	335.7
100 +	712	128	584	497.0	576.6	482.4
Switzerland - Suisse						
2007 (C)						
Total	61 089	29 533	31 556	8.1	8.0	8.2
0 - 4	341	175	166	1.0	1.0	1.0
0	293	152	141	7.9	8.0	7.8
1 - 4	48	23	25	0.2	♦0.2	♦0.2
5 - 9	36	21	15	0.1	♦0.1	♦0.1
10 - 14	40	21	19	0.1	♦0.1	♦0.1
15 - 19	149	104	45	0.3	0.4	0.2
20 - 24	224	165	59	0.5	0.7	0.3
25 - 29	230	161	69	0.5	0.7	0.3
30 - 34	237	152	85	0.5	0.6	0.3
35 - 39	386	249	137	0.7	0.9	0.5
40 - 44	704	446	258	1.1	1.4	0.8
45 - 49	969	608	361	1.6	2.0	1.2
50 - 54	1 488	937	551	2.9	3.6	2.1
55 - 59	2 259	1 411	848	4.7	5.9	3.5
60 - 64	3 231	2 087	1 144	7.2	9.4	5.1
65 - 69	3 778	2 395	1 383	10.7	14.2	7.5
70 - 74	5 196	3 131	2 065	17.6	23.3	12.8
75 - 79	7 401	4 133	3 268	29.5	39.1	22.5
80 - 84	10 565	5 079	5 486	55.3	70.7	46.0
85 - 89	11 559	4 752	6 807	100.2	123.4	88.5
90 - 94	8 448	2 670	5 778	176.0	199.6	166.9
95 +	3 848	836	3 012	228.1	232.4	227.0
95 - 99	3 327	744	2 583	...	...	...
100 +	521	92	429	...	...	...
The Former Yugoslav Republic of Macedonia - L'ex-République yougoslave de Macédoine						
2007 (C)						
Total	19 594	10 344	9 250	9.6	10.1	9.1
0 - 4	263	141	122	2.3	2.4	2.2
0	234	128	106	10.4	11.1	9.8
1 - 4	29	13	16	♦0.3	♦0.3	♦0.4
5 - 9	20	9	11	♦0.2	♦0.1	♦0.2
10 - 14	26	18	8	♦0.2	♦0.2	♦0.1
15 - 19	58	38	20	0.4	0.5	♦0.3
20 - 24	103	74	29	0.6	0.9	♦0.4
25 - 29	107	77	30	0.7	0.9	♦0.4
30 - 34	114	89	25	0.7	1.1	♦0.3
35 - 39	152	87	65	1.0	1.2	0.9
40 - 44	278	185	93	1.9	2.4	1.3
45 - 49	501	314	187	3.5	4.3	2.6
50 - 54	838	528	310	6.0	7.5	4.5
55 - 59	1 218	795	423	10.1	13.5	6.8
60 - 64	1 371	857	514	15.3	20.0	11.0
65 - 69	2 095	1 202	893	26.1	31.9	21.0
70 - 74	3 239	1 774	1 465	45.5	54.8	37.8
75 - 79	3 538	1 725	1 813	77.5	88.0	69.6
80 - 84	3 184	1 351	1 833	134.8	140.2	131.0

19. Deaths and death rates by age and sex: latest available year, 1998 - 2007
Décès et taux de mortalité selon l'âge et le sexe: dernière année disponible, 1998 - 2007 (continued - suite)

Continent, country or area, date, code and age (in years) / Continent, pays ou zone, date, code et âge (en annèes)	Number - Nombre			Rate - Taux		
	Both sexes Les deux sexes	Male Masculin	Female Féminin	Both sexes Les deux sexes	Male Masculin	Female Féminin
EUROPE						
The Former Yugoslav Republic of Macedonia - L'ex-République yougoslave de Macédoine						
2007 (C)						
85 - 89	1 789	789	1 000	228.9	250.3	214.5
90 - 94	524	228	296	311.3	353.5	285.2
95 +	176	63	113	302.9	315.0	296.6
95 - 99	153	56	97	...	...	...
100 +	23	7	16	...	...	...
Ukraine[35]						
2007 (C)						
Total	762 877	393 275	369 602	16.4	18.3	14.8
0 - 4	6 313	3 664	2 649	3.0	3.4	2.6
0	5 188	3 039	2 149	11.4	13.0	9.7
1 - 4	1 125	625	500	0.7	0.7	0.6
5 - 9	708	454	254	0.4	0.4	0.3
10 - 14	789	522	267	0.3	0.4	0.2
15 - 19	2 722	1 965	757	0.8	1.1	0.5
20 - 24	5 979	4 671	1 308	1.5	2.4	0.7
25 - 29	9 399	7 245	2 154	2.7	4.2	1.3
30 - 34	14 247	10 889	3 358	4.3	6.6	2.0
35 - 39	17 445	13 118	4 327	5.6	8.5	2.7
40 - 44	24 460	18 666	5 794	7.4	11.8	3.4
45 - 49	36 383	27 405	8 978	9.9	16.0	4.6
50 - 54	43 987	32 064	11 923	13.4	21.7	6.6
55 - 59	53 731	37 001	16 730	18.2	28.7	10.1
60 - 64	45 326	29 707	15 619	24.6	39.6	14.3
65 - 69	92 361	54 573	37 788	32.0	49.4	21.2
70 - 74	89 976	47 262	42 714	51.3	73.6	38.4
75 - 79	119 569	51 407	68 162	73.7	98.9	61.8
80 - 84	110 510	33 417	77 093	118.2	146.7	109.0
85 - 89	55 137	12 761	42 376	186.9	201.7	182.9
90 - 94	25 102	4 758	20 344	266.8	281.2	263.7
95 - 99	7 407	1 302	6 105	508.6	526.9	504.9
100 +	546	77	469	309.9	303.1	311.0
Unknown - Inconnu	780	347	433	..	..	..
United Kingdom of Great Britain and Northern Ireland - Royaume-Uni de Grande-Bretagne et d'Irlande du Nord[36]						
2005* (C)						
Total	582 663	276 803	305 860	9.7	9.4	10.0
0	3 671	2 104	1 567	5.1	5.7	4.5
1 - 4	588	328	260	0.2	0.2	0.2
5 - 9	336	186	150	0.1	0.1	0.1
10 - 14	485	284	201	0.1	0.1	0.1
15 - 19	1 345	909	436	0.3	0.4	0.2
20 - 24	1 876	1 337	539	0.5	0.7	0.3
25 - 29	2 039	1 408	631	0.5	0.8	0.5
30 - 34	2 995	2 006	989	0.7	1.0	0.5
35 - 39	4 654	3 006	1 648	1.0	1.3	0.7
40 - 44	6 930	4 225	2 705	1.5	1.9	1.2
45 - 49	9 738	5 868	3 870	2.4	2.9	1.9
50 - 54	13 892	8 297	5 595	3.8	4.6	3.0
55 - 59	22 734	13 589	9 145	5.8	7.0	4.6
60 - 64	29 549	18 036	11 513	9.5	11.9	7.2
65 - 69	41 515	24 598	16 917	15.3	18.8	12.0
70 - 74	59 200	34 220	24 980	25.3	31.6	19.9
75 - 79	84 915	44 962	39 953	43.6	53.6	36.1
80 - 84	109 294	50 805	58 489	74.0	90.1	64.0
85 - 89	91 279	35 277	56 002	120.7	142.1	110.2
90 +	95 618	25 357	70 261	228.0	245.1	222.4
90 - 94	67 100	19 790	47 310	...	...	...
95 - 99	24 337	5 035	19 302	...	...	...
100 +	4 181	532	3 649	...	...	...
Unknown - Inconnu	10	1	9	..	..	..

Continent, country or area, date, code and age (in years)	Number - Nombre			Rate - Taux		
Continent, pays ou zone, date, code et âge (en années)	Both sexes Les deux sexes	Male Masculin	Female Féminin	Both sexes Les deux sexes	Male Masculin	Female Féminin

OCEANIA - OCÉANIE

American Samoa - Samoas américaines
2006 (C)

Total..	267	156	111			
0..	17	9	8	...	...	...
1 - 4..	7	3	4	...	...	...
5 - 9..	1	1	-	...	...	...
10 - 14..	5	2	3	...	...	...
15 - 19..	3	-	3	...	...	...
20 - 24..	5	4	1	...	...	...
25 - 29..	4	3	1	...	...	...
30 - 34..	5	5	-	...	...	...
35 - 39..	10	6	4	...	...	...
40 - 44..	9	4	5	...	...	...
45 - 49..	19	10	9	...	...	...
50 - 54..	18	11	7	...	...	...
55 - 59..	21	13	8	...	...	...
60 - 64..	23	15	8	...	...	...
65 - 69..	27	18	9	...	...	...
70 - 74..	31	22	9	...	...	...
75 - 79..	28	19	9	...	...	...
80 - 84..	13	6	7	...	...	...
85 +...	21	5	16	...	...	...

Australia - Australie
2007 (+C)

Total..	137 854	70 569	67 285			
0..	1 203	655	548	6.6	6.8	6.4
1 - 4..	225	142	83	4.4	4.7	4.1
5 - 9..	119	64	55	0.2	0.3	0.2
10 - 14..	162	88	74	0.1	0.1	0.1
15 - 19..	518	353	165	0.1	0.1	0.1
20 - 24..	782	575	207	0.4	0.5	0.2
25 - 29..	875	631	244	0.5	0.8	0.3
30 - 34..	1 053	712	341	0.6	0.9	0.3
35 - 39..	1 467	972	495	0.7	1.0	0.5
40 - 44..	1 882	1 152	730	0.9	1.2	0.6
45 - 49..	2 913	1 816	1 097	1.2	1.5	1.0
50 - 54..	3 965	2 438	1 527	1.9	2.4	1.4
55 - 59..	5 469	3 424	2 045	2.9	3.5	2.2
60 - 64..	7 350	4 566	2 784	4.3	5.4	3.2
65 - 69..	9 040	5 702	3 338	6.9	8.6	5.3
70 - 74..	11 716	7 094	4 622	11.2	14.3	8.2
75 - 79..	18 163	10 639	7 524	18.2	22.9	13.8
80 - 84..	24 128	12 503	11 625	33.0	42.0	25.3
85 - 89..	23 589	10 104	13 485	58.2	72.6	48.0
90 - 94..	16 196	5 257	10 939	102.4	122.2	91.3
95 - 99..	5 977	1 486	4 491	180.2	203.1	170.9
100 +...	1 051	187	864	274.1	301.8	266.0
Unknown - Inconnu.............................	11	9	2	..	..	..

Fiji - Fidji
2004 (+C)

Total..	5 628	3 150	2 478			
0..	316	180	136	...	...	...
1 - 4..	83	53	30	...	...	...
5 - 9..	47	27	20	...	...	...
10 - 14..	51	24	27	...	...	...
15 - 19..	100	61	39	...	...	...
20 - 24..	103	58	45	...	...	...
25 - 29..	116	71	45	...	...	...
30 - 34..	124	64	60	...	...	...
35 - 39..	140	89	51	...	...	...
40 - 44..	247	138	109	...	...	...
45 - 49..	371	232	139	...	...	...
50 - 54..	463	267	196	...	...	...
55 - 59..	527	321	206	...	...	...
60 - 64..	641	366	275	...	...	...
65 - 69..	569	323	246	...	...	...
70 - 74..	597	311	286	...	...	...

Continent, country or area, date, code and age (in years) / Continent, pays ou zone, date, code et âge (en années)	Number - Nombre			Rate - Taux		
	Both sexes Les deux sexes	Male Masculin	Female Féminin	Both sexes Les deux sexes	Male Masculin	Female Féminin
OCEANIA - OCÉANIE						
Fiji - Fidji						
2004 (+C)						
75 - 79	414	219	195	...	...	...
80 - 84	361	191	170	...	...	...
85 - 89	223	97	126	...	...	...
90 - 94	81	40	41	...	...	...
95 +	54	18	36	...	...	...
Guam[37]						
2004 (C)						
Total	691	426	265	...	...	...
0	42	25	17	...	...	...
1 - 4	4	1	3	...	...	...
5 - 9	3	3	-	...	...	...
10 - 14	5	3	2	...	...	...
15 - 19	13	9	4	...	...	...
20 - 24	16	12	4	...	...	...
25 - 29	12	7	5	...	...	...
30 - 34	20	16	4	...	...	...
35 - 39	19	17	2	...	...	...
40 - 44	39	30	9	...	...	...
45 - 49	37	24	13	...	...	...
50 - 54	52	40	12	...	...	...
55 - 59	60	36	24	...	...	...
60 - 64	56	29	27	...	...	...
65 - 69	59	32	27	...	...	...
70 - 74	65	40	25	...	...	...
75 - 79	77	47	30	...	...	...
80 - 84	53	31	22	...	...	...
85 +	59	24	35	...	...	...
Marshall Islands - Îles Marshall						
2006 (+U)						
Total	318	171	147	...	...	...
0	27	17	10	...	...	...
1 - 4	13	7	6	...	...	...
5 - 9	4	3	1	...	...	...
10 - 14	1	1	-	...	...	...
15 - 19	11	7	4	...	...	...
20 - 24	8	4	4	...	...	...
25 - 29	6	5	1	...	...	...
30 - 34	10	4	6	...	...	...
35 - 39	15	10	5	...	...	...
40 - 44	20	10	10	...	...	...
45 - 49	16	11	5	...	...	...
50 - 54	26	11	15	...	...	...
55 - 59	38	26	12	...	...	...
60 - 64	21	9	12	...	...	...
65 +	102	46	56	...	...	...
Micronesia (Federated States of) - Micronésie (États fédérés de)						
2003 (U)						
Total	427	...	...	...	...	...
0	21	...	...	...	...	...
1 - 4	20	...	...	...	...	...
5 - 9	8	...	...	...	...	...
10 - 14	4	...	...	...	...	...
15 - 19	14	...	...	...	...	...
20 - 24	8	...	...	...	...	...
25 - 29	13	...	...	...	...	...
30 - 34	6	...	...	...	...	...
35 - 39	10	...	...	...	...	...
40 - 44	19	...	...	...	...	...
45 - 49	21	...	...	...	...	...
50 - 54	47	...	...	...	...	...
55 - 59	33	...	...	...	...	...
60 - 64	32	...	...	...	...	...
65 - 69	50	...	...	...	...	...
70 +	121	...	...	...	...	...

Continent, country or area, date, code and age (in years) / Continent, pays ou zone, date, code et âge (en années)	Number - Nombre			Rate - Taux		
	Both sexes Les deux sexes	Male Masculin	Female Féminin	Both sexes Les deux sexes	Male Masculin	Female Féminin
OCEANIA - OCÉANIE						
New Caledonia - Nouvelle-Calédonie						
2007 (C)						
Total	1 207	749	458	5.0	6.2	3.8
0	25	15	10	♦5.9	♦6.9	♦4.9
1 - 4	11	9	2	♦0.7	♦1.1	♦0.3
5 - 9	5	4	1	♦0.2	♦0.3	♦0.1
10 - 14	8	6	2	♦0.4	♦0.5	♦0.2
15 - 19	21	15	6	♦1.0	♦1.4	♦0.6
20 - 24	25	23	2	♦1.3	♦2.4	♦0.2
25 - 29	20	16	4	♦1.2	♦1.9	♦0.5
30 - 34	29	20	9	♦1.5	♦2.1	♦0.9
35 - 39	26	17	9	♦1.4	♦1.8	♦0.9
40 - 44	38	26	12	2.2	♦3.0	♦1.4
45 - 49	64	47	17	4.4	6.5	♦2.3
50 - 54	61	40	21	5.1	6.5	♦3.6
55 - 59	78	59	19	7.3	10.5	♦3.8
60 - 64	97	72	25	11.7	16.4	♦6.4
65 - 69	120	87	33	19.0	27.8	10.3
70 - 74	127	73	54	29.8	35.7	24.3
75 - 79	146	87	59	50.3	69.1	35.9
80 - 84	120	61	59	73.6	90.4	61.8
85 - 89	104	47	57	137.9	165.5	121.3
90 - 94	52	20	32	134.7	♦151.5	126.0
95 +	30	5	25	♦211.3	♦128.2	♦242.7
New Zealand - Nouvelle-Zélande[11]						
2007 (+C)						
Total	28 522	14 275	14 247	6.7	6.9	6.6
0 - 4	400	216	184	1.4	1.4	1.3
0	317	174	143	...	...	...
1 - 4	83	42	41	...	...	...
5 - 9	37	24	13	0.1	♦0.2	♦0.1
10 - 14	55	29	26	0.2	♦0.2	♦0.2
15 - 19	185	119	66	0.6	0.7	0.4
20 - 24	204	148	56	0.7	1.0	0.4
25 - 29	160	117	43	0.6	0.9	0.3
30 - 34	225	144	81	0.8	1.1	0.6
35 - 39	338	205	133	1.1	1.4	0.8
40 - 44	463	253	210	1.5	1.6	1.3
45 - 49	649	409	240	2.1	2.7	1.5
50 - 54	873	521	352	3.2	3.9	2.6
55 - 59	1 225	705	520	5.0	5.9	4.2
60 - 64	1 535	916	619	7.8	9.4	6.2
65 - 69	2 086	1 203	883	12.8	15.2	10.5
70 - 74	2 655	1 575	1 080	21.7	27.0	16.9
75 - 79	3 753	2 152	1 601	36.0	44.7	28.5
80 - 84	4 739	2 445	2 294	62.6	77.8	51.8
85 - 89	4 590	1 835	2 755	111.2	129.9	101.4
90 +	4 350	1 259	3 091	221.1	236.7	215.4
90 - 94	3 065	963	2 102	...	...	...
95 - 99	1 078	257	821	...	...	...
100 +	207	39	168	...	...	...
Northern Mariana Islands - Îles Mariannes septentrionales						
2005 (U)						
Total	*188*	*107*	*81*	...	...	...
0	*5*	*1*	*4*	...	...	...
1 - 4	*4*	*3*	*1*	...	...	...
5 - 9	*-*	*-*	*-*	...	...	...
10 - 14	*3*	*2*	*1*	...	...	...
15 - 19	*1*	*-*	*1*	...	...	...
20 - 24	*3*	*2*	*1*	...	...	...
25 - 29	*10*	*3*	*7*	...	...	...
30 - 34	*11*	*9*	*2*	...	...	...
35 - 39	*7*	*4*	*3*	...	...	...
40 - 44	*11*	*6*	*5*	...	...	...
45 - 49	*7*	*6*	*1*	...	...	...
50 - 54	*17*	*13*	*4*	...	...	...

19. Deaths and death rates by age and sex: latest available year, 1998 - 2007
Décès et taux de mortalité selon l'âge et le sexe: dernière année disponible, 1998 - 2007 (continued - suite)

Continent, country or area, date, code and age (in years) / Continent, pays ou zone, date, code et âge (en années)	Number - Nombre			Rate - Taux		
	Both sexes Les deux sexes	Male Masculin	Female Féminin	Both sexes Les deux sexes	Male Masculin	Female Féminin
OCEANIA - OCÉANIE						
Northern Mariana Islands - Îles Mariannes septentrionales						
2005 (U)						
55 - 59	19	11	8	...	...	...
60 - 64	20	9	11	...	...	...
65 - 69	20	14	6	...	...	...
70 - 74	20	11	9	...	...	...
75 - 79	13	6	7	...	...	...
80 - 84	8	5	3	...	...	...
85 - 89	5	1	4	...	...	...
90 - 94	2	-	2	...	...	...
95 - 99	2	1	1	...	...	...
100 +	-	-	-	...	...	...
Palau - Palaos						
2003 (C)						
Total	136	79	57	...	...	...
0	3	1	2	...	...	...
1 - 14	5	4	1	...	...	...
15 - 24	7	4	3	...	...	...
25 - 44	17	12	5	...	...	...
45 - 64	33	29	4	...	...	...
65 +	71	29	42	...	...	...
2005 (C)						
Total	134	...	...	...	...	...
0	5	...	...	...	...	...
1 - 4	1	...	...	...	...	...
5 - 9	-	...	...	...	...	...
10 - 14	-	...	...	...	...	...
15 - 19	2	...	...	...	...	...
20 - 24	1	...	...	...	...	...
25 - 29	5	...	...	...	...	...
30 - 34	4	...	...	...	...	...
35 - 39	6	...	...	...	...	...
40 - 44	9	...	...	...	...	...
45 - 49	13	...	...	...	...	...
50 - 54	14	...	...	...	...	...
55 - 59	9	...	...	...	...	...
60 - 64	10	...	...	...	...	...
65 - 69	8	...	...	...	...	...
70 - 74	11	...	...	...	...	...
75 +	36	...	...	...	...	...
Pitcairn						
2007 (C)						
Total	1	...	...	...	...	...
0	-	...	...	...	...	...
1 - 4	-	...	...	...	...	...
5 - 9	-	...	...	...	...	...
10 - 14	-	...	...	...	...	...
15 - 19	-	...	...	...	...	...
20 - 24	-	...	...	...	...	...
25 - 29	-	...	...	...	...	...
30 - 34	-	...	...	...	...	...
35 - 39	-	...	...	...	...	...
40 - 44	-	...	...	...	...	...
45 - 49	-	...	...	...	...	...
50 - 54	-	...	...	...	...	...
55 - 59	-	...	...	...	...	...
60 - 64	-	...	...	...	...	...
65 - 69	-	...	...	...	...	...
70 - 74	-	...	...	...	...	...
75 - 79	1	...	...	...	...	...
80 - 84	-	...	...	...	...	...
85 - 89	-	...	...	...	...	...
90 +	-	...	...	...	...	...

Continent, country or area, date, code and age (in years) / Continent, pays ou zone, date, code et âge (en années)	Number - Nombre			Rate - Taux		
	Both sexes Les deux sexes	Male Masculin	Female Féminin	Both sexes Les deux sexes	Male Masculin	Female Féminin
OCEANIA - OCÉANIE						
Tonga[38]						
2006 (I)						
Total	709	402	307	...	...	...
0	53	32	21	...	...	...
1 - 4	8	6	3	...	...	...
5 - 9	10	5	4	...	...	...
10 - 14	7	4	4	...	...	...
15 - 19	12	8	3	...	...	...
20 - 24	11	9	2	...	...	...
25 - 29	7	5	2	...	...	...
30 - 34	12	9	4	...	...	...
35 - 39	12	7	5	...	...	...
40 - 44	19	11	8	...	...	...
45 - 49	29	18	11	...	...	...
50 - 54	29	16	13	...	...	...
55 - 59	37	23	15	...	...	...
60 - 64	53	33	20	...	...	...
65 - 69	49	28	21	...	...	...
70 - 74	70	38	32	...	...	...
75 - 79	95	54	41	...	...	...
80 +	193	95	98	...	...	...
Tuvalu						
2005 (U)						
Total	59	33	26	...	...	...
0	6	5	1	...	...	...
1 - 4	2	1	1	...	...	...
5 - 9	-	-	-	...	...	...
10 - 14	-	-	-	...	...	...
15 - 19	-	-	-	...	...	...
20 - 24	1	1	-	...	...	...
25 - 29	-	-	-	...	...	...
30 - 34	1	1	-	...	...	...
35 - 39	2	2	-	...	...	...
40 - 44	2	2	-	...	...	...
45 - 49	3	3	-	...	...	...
50 - 54	6	3	3	...	...	...
55 - 59	4	3	1	...	...	...
60 - 64	7	2	5	...	...	...
65 - 69	6	2	4	...	...	...
70 - 74	1	-	1	...	...	...
75 - 79	8	4	4	...	...	...
80 - 84	8	3	5	...	...	...
85 - 89	2	1	1	...	...	...
Wallis and Futuna Islands - Îles Wallis et Futuna						
2006 (C)						
Total	77	31	46	...	...	...
0	-	-	-	...	...	...
1 - 4	1	-	1	...	...	...
5 - 9	-	-	-	...	...	...
10 - 14	2	2	-	...	...	...
15 - 19	2	2	-	...	...	...
20 - 24	1	1	-	...	...	...
25 - 29	1	-	1	...	...	...
30 - 34	-	-	-	...	...	...
35 - 39	4	2	2	...	...	...
40 - 44	-	-	-	...	...	...
45 - 49	-	-	-	...	...	...
50 - 54	2	1	1	...	...	...
55 - 59	13	5	8	...	...	...
60 - 64	11	2	9	...	...	...
65 - 69	8	3	5	...	...	...
70 - 74	11	4	7	...	...	...
75 - 79	7	3	4	...	...	...
80 - 84	10	4	6	...	...	...
85 - 89	4	2	2	...	...	...
90 - 94	-	-	-	...	...	...
95 +				...	...	...

FOOTNOTES - NOTES

◆ Rates based on 30 or fewer deaths. - Taux basés sur 30 décès ou moins.

Italics: estimates which are less reliable. - Italiques: estimations moins sûres.

* Provisional. - Données provisoires.

'Code' indicates the source of data, as follows:
C - Civil registration, estimated over 90% complete
U - Civil registration, estimated less than 90% complete
I - Other source, estimated reliable
+ - Data tabulated by date of registration rather than occurence.
... - Information not available

Le 'Code' indique la source des données, comme suit:
C - Registres de l'état civil considérés complets à 90 p. 100 au moins.
U - Registres de l'état civil qui ne sont pas considérés complets à 90 p. 100 au moins.
I - Autre source, considérée pas douteuses.
+ - Données exploitées selon la date de l'enregistrement et non la date de l'événement.
... - Information pas disponible.

[1] Excluding live-born infants who died before their birth was registered. Data refer to Algerian population only. - Non compris les enfants nés vivants décédés avant l'enregistrement de leur naissance. Les données ne concernent que la population algérienne.

[2] Data refer to the twelve months preceding the census in August. - Les données se rapportent aux douze mois précédant le recensement d'août.

[3] Based on the results of the population census. - D'après le résultats du recensement de la population.

[4] Data refer to January-August only. - Le chiffre correspond à la période allant de janvier à août.

[5] Figures for male and female do not add up to the total, since they do not include the category "Unknown". - La somme des chiffres indiqués pour les sexes masculin et féminin n'est pas égale au total parce qu'elle n'inclut pas la catégorie " inconnue ".

[6] Excluding live-born infants who died before their birth was registered. - Non compris les enfants nés vivants décédés avant l'enregistrement de leur naissance.

[7] Source: World Health Organization. - Source : Organisation mondiale de la santé.

[8] Including Canadian residents temporarily in the United States, but excluding United States residents temporarily in Canada. - Y compris les résidents canadiens se trouvant temporairement aux Etats-Unis, mais ne comprenant pas les résidents des Etats-Unis se trouvant temporairement au Canada.

[9] Resident deaths outside the islands are excluded if they are not buried in the islands. - Les décès de résidents hors des îles ne sont pas compris s'ils ne sont pas inhumés dans les îles.

[10] Data have been adjusted for undercoverage of infant deaths and sudden and violent deaths. - Ajusté pour la sous-estimation de la mortalité infantile, du nombre de morts soudaines et de morts violentes.

[11] Data refer to resident population only. - Pour la population résidante seulement.

[12] Excluding Indian jungle population. Data as reported by national statistical authorities; they may differ from data presented in other tables. - Non compris les Indiens de la jungle. Les données comme elles ont été déclarées par l'institut national de la statistique; elles peuvent être différentes de celles présentées dans d'autres tableaux.

[13] Excluding nomadic Indian tribes. - Non compris les tribus d'Indiens nomades.

[14] Data refer to registered events only. - Les données ne concernent que les événements enregistrés.

[15] Excluding Indian jungle population. - Non compris les Indiens de la jungle.

[16] Excluding infants born alive of less than 28 weeks' gestation, of less than 1 000 grams in weight and 35 centimeters in length, who die within seven days of birth. - Non compris les enfants nés vivants après moins de 28 semaines de gestations, pesant moins de 1 000 grammes, mesurant moins de 35 centimètres et décédés dans les sept jours qui ont suivi leur naissance.

[17] Data refer to the twelve months preceding the census in May. - Les données se rapportent aux douze mois précédant le recensement de mai.

[18] For statistical purposes, the data for China do not include those for the Hong Kong Special Administrative Region (Hong Kong SAR), Macao Special Administrative Region (Macao SAR) and Taiwan province of China. - Pour la présentation des statistiques, les données pour la Chine ne comprennent pas la Région Administrative Spéciale de Hong Kong (Hong Kong RAS), la Région Administrative Spéciale de Macao (Macao RAS) et Taïwan province de Chine.

[19] Data refer to government controlled areas. - Les données se rapportent aux zones contrôlées par le Gouvernement.

[20] Including data for East Jerusalem and Israeli residents in certain other territories under occupation by Israeli military forces since June 1967. - Y compris les données pour Jérusalem-Est et les résidents israéliens dans certains autres territoires occupés depuis 1967 par les forces armées israéliennes.

[21] Data refer to Japanese nationals in Japan only. - Les données se raportent aux nationaux japonais au Japon seulement.

[22] Data refer to the twelve months preceding the census in June. - Les données se rapportent aux douze mois précédant le recensement de juin.

[23] Data from Births and Deaths Notification System (Ministry of Health institutions and all other health care providers). - Les données proviennent du système de notification des naissances et des décès (établissements du Ministère de la santé et tous autres prestataires de soins de santé).

[24] Excluding data for the Pakistan-held part of Jammu and Kashmir, the final status of which has not yet been determined. Based on the results of the Pakistan Demographic Survey (PDS 2005). - Non compris les données concernant la partie du Jammu et Cachemire occupée par le Pakistan dont le statut définitif n'a pas été déterminé. Données extraites de l'enquête démographique effectuée par le Pakistan en 2005.

[25] Excluding alien armed forces, civilian aliens employed by armed forces, and foreign diplomatic personnel and their dependants. Including nationals outside the country. - Non compris les militaires étrangers, les civils étrangers employés par les forces armées ni le personnel diplomatique étranger et les membres de leur famille les accompagnant. Y compris les nationaux hors du pays.

[26] Also included in Finland. - Comprise aussi dans Finlande.

[27] Including armed forces stationed outside the country, but excluding alien armed forces stationed in the area. - Y compris les militaires nationaux hors du pays, mais non compris les militaires étrangers en garnison sur le territoire.

[28] Excluding Faeroe Islands and Greenland shown separately, if available. - Non compris les Iles Féroé et le Gröenland, qui font l'objet de rubriques distinctes, si disponible.

[29] Including nationals temporarily outside the country. Including Aland Islands. - Y compris les nationaux se trouvant temporairement hors du pays. Y compris les Îles d'Åland.

[30] Excluding Overseas Departments, namely, French Guiana, Guadeloupe, Martinique and Reunion, shown separately, if available. Including armed forces stationed outside the country. - Non compris les départements d'outre mer, c'est-à-dire la Guyane française, la Guadeloupe, la Martinique et la Réunion, qui font l'objet de rubriques distinctes, si disponible. Y compris les militaires nationaux hors du pays.

[31] Including residents outside the country if listed in a Netherlands population register. - Y compris les résidents hors du pays, s'ils sont inscrits sur un registre de population néerlandais.

[32] Including residents temporarily outside the country. Excluding Svalbard and Jan Mayen Island shown separately, if available. - Y compris les résidents se trouvant temporairement hors du pays. Non compris Svalbard et Jan Mayen qui font l'objet de rubriques distinctes, si disponible.

[33] Excluding infants born alive of less than 28 weeks' gestation, of less than 1 000 grams in weight and 35 centimeters in length, who die within seven days of birth. Excluding Transnistria and the municipality of Bender. - Non compris les enfants nés vivants après moins de 28 semaines de gestations, pesant moins de 1 000 grammes, mesurant moins de 35 centimètres et décédés dans les sept jours qui ont suivi leur naissance. Les données ne tiennent pas compte de l'information sur la Transnistria et la municipalité de Bender.

[34] Excluding data for Kosovo and Metohia. - Sans les données pour le Kosovo et Metohie.

[35] Excluding infants born living with birth weight of less than 500grams (or if birth weight is unknown - with length of less than 25 centimeters, or with gestation period of less than 22 weeks). - Non compris les données concernant les nouveau-nés pesant moins de 500 grammes (si le pods est inconnu — mesurant moins de 25 centimètres ou après moins de 22 semaines de gestations).

[36] Excluding Channel Islands (Guernsey and Jersey) and Isle of Man, shown separately, if available. - Non compris les îles Anglo-Normandes (Guernesey et Jersey) et l'île de Man, qui font l'objet de rubriques distinctes, si disponible.

[37] Including United States military personnel, their dependants and contract employees. - Y compris les militaires des Etats-Unis, les membres de leur famille les accompagnant et les agents contractuels des Etats-Unis.

[38] Estimate based on results of the population census. - Estimation fondeé sur les résultats du recensement de la population.

Table 20

Table 20 presents expectation of life at specified ages for each sex for the latest available year between 1998 and 2007.

Description of variables: Expectation of life, e_x is defined as the average number of years of life remaining to persons who have reached age x if they continue to be subject to the mortality conditions of the period indicated in the table.

Male and female expectations are shown separately for selected ages beginning at birth and proceeding with ages 5, 10, 15, 20, 25, 30, 35, 40, 45, 50, 55, 60, 65, 70, 75, 85, 90, 95 and 100 years.

The table shows life expectancy derived from an abridged or full life table as reported by the country or area. If data from both an abridged and a full life table are available, the data derived from an abridged life table are shown.

Data are shown with one decimal regardless of the number of digits provided in the original computation.

Life table computation: From the demographic point of view, a life table is regarded as a theoretical model of a population that is continuously replenished by births and depleted by deaths. The model gives a complete picture of the mortality experience of a population based on the assumption that the theoretical cohort is subject, throughout its existence, to the age-specific mortality rates observed at a particular time. Thus, levels of mortality prevailing at the time a life table is constructed are assumed to remain unchanged into the future until all members of the cohort have died.

Reliability of data: The values shown in this table come from official life tables. It is assumed that, if necessary, the basic data (population and deaths classified by age and sex) have been adjusted for deficiencies before their use in constructing the life tables.

Limitations: Expectation-of-life values are subject to the same qualifications as have been set forth for population statistics in general and death statistics in particular, as discussed in sections 3 and 4, respectively, of the Technical Notes. They must be interpreted strictly using the underlying assumption that surviving cohorts are subjected to the same age-specific mortality rates of the period to which the life table refers.

Earlier data: Expectation of life at specified ages for each sex has been shown in previous issues of the *Demographic Yearbook*. Data included in this table update the series covering a period of years as follows:

Issue	Years Covered
Historical Supplement CD, 1997	1948 – 1997
Special Issue on Population Ageing and the Situation of Elderly Persons, 1991	1950 – 1990
Historical Supplement, 1979	1948 – 1977
1st issue, 1948	1896 – 1947

Tableau 20

Le tableau 20 présente les espérances de vie à des âges déterminés, pour chaque sexe, qui correspondent à la dernière année pour laquelle on dispose de données.

Description des variables : L'espérance de vie, e_x, se définit comme le nombre moyen d'années restant à vivre aux hommes et aux femmes qui ont atteint l'âge x, à supposer qu'ils continuent de connaître les mêmes conditions de mortalité observées pendant la période sur laquelle porte le tableau.

Les chiffres sont présentés séparément pour chaque sexe à partir de la naissance et pour les âges suivants : 5,10, 15, 20, 25, 30, 35, 40, 45, 50, 55, 60, 65, 70, 75, 80, 85, 90, 95 et 100 ans.

Dans le tableau figurent les espérances de vie calculées selon les tables de mortalité abrégées ou complètes communiquées par les pays et les zones. Si les données provenant des tables de mortalité abrégées et complètes sont disponibles, les données présentées sont celles dérivées de la table abrégée.

Les données sont arrondies à la première décimale, indépendamment du nombre de décimales qui figurent dans le calcul initial.

Calcul des tables de mortalité : du point de vue démographique, les tables de mortalité sont considérées comme des modèles théoriques représentant une population constamment reconstituée par les naissances et réduite par les décès. Ces modèles donnent un aperçu complet de la mortalité d'une population et reposent sur l'hypothèse que chaque cohorte théoriquement distinguée connaît, pendant toute son existence, le taux de mortalité par âge observé à un moment donné. Les mortalités correspondant à l'époque à laquelle sont calculées les tables de mortalité sont ainsi censées demeurer inchangées dans l'avenir jusqu'au décès de tous les membres de la cohorte.

Fiabilité des donnés : étant donné que les chiffres figurant dans ce tableau proviennent de tables officielles de mortalité, elles sont toutes présumées sûres. En ce qui concerne les chiffres extraits de tables officielles de mortalité, on part du principe que les données de base (effectif de la population et nombre de décès selon l'âge et le sexe) ont été ajustées, en tant que de besoin, avant de servir à l'établissement de la table de mortalité.

Insuffisance des données : les espérances de vie appellent les mêmes réserves que celles qui ont été formulées à propos des statistiques de la population en général et des statistiques de mortalité en particulier (voir les sections 3 et 4 des Notes techniques). Lorsque l'on interprète les données, il ne faut jamais perdre de vue que, par hypothèse, les cohortes de survivants sont soumises, pour chaque âge, aux conditions de mortalité de la période visée par la table de mortalité.

Données publiées antérieurement : les espérances de vie à des âges déterminés pour chaque sexe figuraient déjà dans des éditions antérieures de *l'Annuaire démographique*. Les données présentées dans le tableau 22 actualisent les données qui portaient sur les périodes suivantes :

Éditions	Années considérées
Supplément historique (CD-ROM), 1997	1948 – 1997
Édition spéciale sur le vieillissement de la population et la situation des personnes âgées, 1991	1950 – 1990
Supplément rétrospectif, 1979	1948 – 1977
1e édition, 1948	1896 – 1947

20. Expectation of life at specified ages for each sex: latest available year, 1998 - 2007
Espérance de vie à un âge donné pour chaque sexe: dernière année disponible, 1998 - 2007

Continent, country or area and date / Continent, pays ou zone et date	At birth - A la naissance	5	10	15	20	25	30	35	40	45	50	55	60	65	70	75	80	85	90	95	100
AFRICA - AFRIQUE																					
Algeria - Algérie[1] 2002																					
Male - Hommes	72.5	70.6	65.8	61.0	56.3	51.6	46.9	42.2	37.6	33.0	28.5	24.1	19.9	16.1	12.4	9.0	5.9	...	...	...	...
Female - Femmes	74.2	72.1	67.3	62.5	57.7	52.9	48.1	43.3	38.6	34.0	29.5	25.1	20.7	16.6	12.8	9.3	6.1	...	...	...	...
Botswana[2] 1999																					
Male - Hommes	65.7	...	...	...	...	...	...	...	...	...	...	...	...	...	...	...	...	...	...	...	...
Female - Femmes	69.0	...	...	...	...	...	...	...	...	...	...	...	...	...	...	...	...	...	...	...	...
Burkina Faso 2006																					
Male - Hommes	55.8	...	...	...	...	...	...	...	...	...	...	...	...	...	...	...	...	...	...	...	...
Female - Femmes	57.5	...	...	...	...	...	...	...	...	...	...	...	...	...	...	...	...	...	...	...	...
Djibouti 1998																					
Male - Hommes	49.0	...	...	...	...	...	...	...	...	...	...	...	...	...	...	...	...	...	...	...	...
Female - Femmes	52.0	...	...	...	...	...	...	...	...	...	...	...	...	...	...	...	...	...	...	...	...
Egypt - Égypte 2001																					
Male - Hommes	65.6	64.7	59.9	55.1	50.4	45.6	40.9	36.2	31.6	27.2	22.9	18.9	15.4	12.1	9.2	6.8	5.2	4.0	...		
Female - Femmes	67.4	66.8	62.0	57.2	52.3	47.5	42.7	37.9	33.1	28.4	23.9	19.5	15.5	11.7	8.6	5.7	4.0	2.8	...		
2003																					
Male - Hommes	67.9	...	...	...	...	...	...	...	...	...	...	...	...	...	...	...	...	...	...	...	...
Female - Femmes	72.3	...	...	...	...	...	...	...	...	...	...	...	...	...	...	...	...	...	...	...	...
Kenya 1989 - 1999																					
Male - Hommes	52.9	54.8	51.1	46.6	42.3	38.3	34.5	21.0	27.7	24.4	21.0	17.7	14.5	11.6	8.9	6.7	5.0	3.8	3.1	2.5	...
Female - Femmes	60.4	63.0	59.0	54.3	49.9	45.9	42.2	38.6	34.8	30.9	27.0	23.1	19.3	15.6	12.2	9.2	6.7	4.8	3.6	2.5	...
Lesotho 2001																					
Male - Hommes	48.7	...	...	...	...	...	...	...	...	...	...	...	...	...	...	...	...	...	...	...	...
Female - Femmes	56.3	...	...	...	...	...	...	...	...	...	...	...	...	...	...	...	...	...	...	...	...
Malawi[2] 2007																					
Male - Hommes	45.7	...	...	...	...	...	...	...	...	...	...	...	...	...	...	...	...	...	...	...	...
Female - Femmes	48.3	...	...	...	...	...	...	...	...	...	...	...	...	...	...	...	...	...	...	...	...
Mauritius - Maurice 2006																					
Male - Hommes	69.1	65.3	60.4	55.4	50.6	45.9	41.2	36.6	32.2	27.9	23.8	20.0	16.4	13.3	10.5	8.1	6.2	4.2	...	...	...
Female - Femmes	75.9	72.0	67.0	62.1	57.2	52.4	47.5	42.7	38.0	33.3	28.8	24.5	20.5	16.8	13.4	10.4	7.8	5.6	...	...	...
Namibia - Namibie 2001																					
Male - Hommes	47.6	54.0	50.1	45.8	41.7	38.0	34.2	30.5	26.8	23.2	19.8	16.6	13.5	10.8	8.4	6.4	4.9	...	...	...	...
Female - Femmes	50.2	56.1	52.2	48.1	44.1	40.3	36.6	32.9	29.2	25.5	21.8	18.3	14.9	12.0	9.3	7.0	5.3	...	...	...	...
Réunion 2006																					
Male - Hommes	73.2	...	...	...	54.0	...	...	...	35.5	...	...	...	19.0	...	...	9.3					
Female - Femmes	80.9	...	...	...	61.6	...	...	...	42.1	...	...	...	23.9	...	...	12.3					
Saint Helena ex. dep. - Sainte-Hélène sans dép. 1998 - 2007																					
Male - Hommes	70.8	66.9	62.2	...	52.4	...	42.7	...	33.5	...	25.1	...	16.9	...	10.1	...	6.4	...	...	...	...
Female - Femmes	77.3	72.6	67.9	...	58.2	...	48.7	...	39.0	...	29.6	...	21.2	...	13.9	...	7.2	...	...	...	...
Seychelles 2007																					
Male - Hommes	68.9	65.0	60.2	55.3	50.5	45.9	41.6	37.0	32.7	28.7	24.4	20.9	17.1	14.1	11.0	9.0	7.4	...	...	...	...
Female - Femmes	77.7	73.3	68.5	63.5	58.5	53.7	48.9	44.3	39.5	35.3	31.0	26.4	22.2	18.5	15.1	12.1	9.2	...	...	...	...
South Africa - Afrique du Sud 2004																					
Male - Hommes	49.9	...	...	...	...	...	...	...	...	...	...	...	...	...	...	...	...	...	...	...	...
Female - Femmes	52.9	...	...	...	...	...	...	...	...	...	...	...	...	...	...	...	...	...	...	...	...
Tunisia - Tunisie 2007																					
Male - Hommes	72.3	...	...	...	...	...	...	...	...	...	...	...	...	...	...	...	...	...	...	...	...
Female - Femmes	76.2	...	...	...	...	...	...	...	...	...	...	...	...	...	...	...	...	...	...	...	...

Continent, country or area and date / Continent, pays ou zone et date	At birth - A la naissance	5	10	15	20	25	30	35	40	45	50	55	60	65	70	75	80	85	90	95	100
AFRICA - AFRIQUE																					
Zimbabwe																					
2001 - 2002																					
Male - Hommes	42.7	43.3	39.1	34.7	30.0	25.8	22.6	20.6	20.0	19.3	18.3	16.7	14.8	12.5	9.8	6.8	4.0	...	...	...	...
Female - Femmes	45.9	46.0	41.6	37.0	32.5	28.9	26.7	25.7	25.2	25.0	23.2	20.6	17.7	14.5	11.2	7.6	4.5	...	...	...	...
AMERICA, NORTH - AMÉRIQUE DU NORD																					
Anguilla																					
2000 - 2002																					
Male - Hommes	76.5	72.1	67.1	62.1	57.3	53.1	48.4	43.7	39.4	34.7	30.2	25.4	21.1	16.5	12.7	10.0	8.0	6.9	...	...	...
Female - Femmes	81.1	76.4	71.4	66.4	61.4	57.1	52.7	47.7	42.7	38.3	33.5	28.7	24.0	19.4	15.3	10.8	8.3	7.6	...	...	...
Aruba																					
2000																					
Male - Hommes	70.0	65.4	60.5	55.6	50.9	46.7	42.3	37.7	33.0	28.5	24.2	20.1	16.3	13.1	10.4	8.1	5.7	3.9	4.0	3.2	...
Female - Femmes	76.0	71.9	67.0	62.0	57.2	52.5	47.7	43.0	38.3	33.6	28.9	24.4	20.5	16.7	13.1	10.4	7.5	5.5	4.7	3.6	...
Bahamas																					
1999 - 2001																					
Male - Hommes	69.9	...	...	...	...	...	...	...	...	...	...	...	...	...	...	...	...	...	...	...	...
Female - Femmes	76.4	...	...	...	...	...	...	...	...	...	...	...	...	...	...	...	...	...	...	...	...
British Virgin Islands - Îles Vierges britanniques																					
2004																					
Male - Hommes	69.9	...	...	...	...	...	...	...	...	...	...	...	...	...	...	...	...	...	...	...	...
Female - Femmes	78.5	...	...	...	...	...	...	...	...	...	...	...	...	...	...	...	...	...	...	...	...
Canada																					
2004																					
Male - Hommes	77.8	73.3	68.3	63.4	58.6	53.8	49.0	44.2	39.5	34.8	30.2	25.8	21.6	17.7	14.1	10.9	8.1	5.9	4.3	...	...
Female - Femmes	82.6	78.0	73.1	68.1	63.2	58.3	53.4	48.5	43.6	38.8	34.2	29.6	25.2	21.0	17.0	13.3	10.0	7.2	5.1	...	...
Cayman Islands - Îles Caïmanes[3]																					
2006																					
Male - Hommes	76.3	72.1	67.1	62.1	57.7	53.3	48.9	44.0	39.3	34.5	29.8	25.3	20.8	17.1	13.6	10.2	8.2	6.4	3.3	5.3	2.5
Female - Femmes	83.8	79.8	74.8	69.8	65.1	60.1	55.2	50.2	45.3	40.4	35.7	30.9	26.1	21.9	17.5	13.9	10.4	6.9	7.0	3.1	2.5
Costa Rica																					
2007																					
Male - Hommes	76.8	72.7	67.8	62.8	58.1	53.4	48.7	44.1	39.5	34.9	30.4	26.1	22.0	18.1	14.5	11.2	8.5	6.3	4.6	3.5	11.7
Female - Femmes	81.7	77.7	72.8	67.8	62.9	58.1	53.2	48.3	43.5	38.7	34.1	29.5	25.0	20.8	16.9	13.2	10.1	7.4	5.7	4.8	5.7
Cuba																					
2005 - 2007																					
Male - Hommes	76.0	71.6	66.7	61.8	56.9	52.1	47.4	42.6	37.9	33.4	29.0	24.8	20.8	17.1	13.7	10.8	8.2	6.2	4.7	3.6	1.8
Female - Femmes	80.0	75.5	70.6	65.6	60.7	55.9	51.0	46.1	41.3	36.6	32.0	27.6	23.4	19.4	15.6	12.3	9.3	6.9	5.1	3.7	1.9
Dominican Republic - République dominicaine																					
2005 - 2010																					
Male - Hommes	69.2	66.8	62.0	57.2	52.6	48.3	44.1	39.9	35.7	31.6	27.6	23.7	20.1	16.8	13.9	11.3	9.3	...	...	...	...
Female - Femmes	75.5	72.6	67.8	62.9	58.1	53.3	48.7	44.2	39.6	35.2	30.9	26.7	22.7	19.0	15.6	12.7	10.3	...	...	...	...
El Salvador[4]																					
2000 - 2005																					
Male - Hommes	67.7	65.3	60.6	55.8	51.2	46.8	42.5	38.4	34.2	30.2	26.2	22.4	18.7	15.2	12.0	9.1	6.8	...	...	...	...
Female - Femmes	73.7	71.1	66.3	61.5	56.8	52.2	47.6	43.1	38.6	34.2	29.9	25.7	21.7	17.9	14.4	11.1	8.4	...	...	...	...
Greenland - Groenland																					
2003 - 2007																					
Male - Hommes	66.3	62.5	57.7	52.9	48.9	45.2	40.8	36.3	32.1	27.8	23.4	19.1	15.4	11.8	9.1	7.0	5.1	3.5	5.0	...	...
Female - Femmes	71.3	67.2	62.4	57.7	53.0	48.4	43.6	39.2	34.5	29.9	25.5	21.4	17.6	14.0	11.0	8.8	6.8	5.7	5.8	...	...
Guadeloupe																					
2002																					
Male - Hommes	74.6	70.2	65.3	60.5	55.7	51.2	46.8	42.2	37.7	33.2	29.0	24.8	20.9	17.3	13.8	10.6	7.9	5.1	2.0	0.5	...
Female - Femmes	81.5	77.0	72.1	67.1	62.1	57.3	52.4	47.6	42.9	38.2	33.5	28.8	24.4	20.3	16.4	12.7	9.0	5.7	2.3	0.5	...

20. Expectation of life at specified ages for each sex: latest available year, 1998 - 2007
Espérance de vie à un âge donné pour chaque sexe: dernière année disponible, 1998 - 2007 (continued - suite)

Continent, country or area and date / Continent, pays ou zone et date	At birth - A la naissance	5	10	15	20	25	30	35	40	45	50	55	60	65	70	75	80	85	90	95	100
AMERICA, NORTH - AMÉRIQUE DU NORD																					
Guatemala 1995 - 2000																					
Male - Hommes	61.4	60.6	56.0	51.2	46.8	42.7	38.8	34.9	31.2	27.4	23.7	20.1	16.8	13.6	10.7	8.2	6.1	...	...	...	...
Female - Femmes	67.2	66.2	62.6	56.9	52.3	47.7	43.3	38.9	34.6	30.4	26.3	22.3	18.6	15.2	12.0	9.2	6.9	...	...	...	...
Jamaica - Jamaïque 2006																					
Male - Hommes	69.7	67.0	62.2	57.3	52.6	47.9	43.2	38.5	33.8	29.3	24.9	20.8	17.0	13.5	10.5	8.0	6.0	4.5	3.4	2.7	...
Female - Femmes	75.2	71.6	66.6	61.7	56.8	52.0	47.1	42.3	37.6	32.9	28.3	23.9	19.7	15.9	12.5	9.5	7.1	5.2	3.8	2.8	...
Martinique 2007																					
Male - Hommes	76.5	72.4	67.5	62.6	57.8	53.3	48.7	44.1	39.5	34.9	30.3	26.1	21.8	17.6	14.1	10.7	7.7	5.2	3.7	1.8	...
Female - Femmes	82.9	78.5	73.6	68.6	63.7	58.8	54.0	49.2	44.4	39.6	34.8	30.1	25.6	21.2	17.1	13.4	10.0	7.1	4.6	1.9	...
Mexico - Mexique 2007																					
Male - Hommes	72.6	69.1	64.2	59.3	54.5	49.9	45.4	40.8	36.4	32.0	27.9	23.9	20.2	16.8	13.7	11.0	8.7	6.6	4.9	3.5	2.6
Female - Femmes	77.4	73.7	68.7	63.8	58.9	54.1	49.2	44.4	39.7	35.0	30.5	26.2	22.1	18.2	14.8	11.7	9.0	6.8	4.9	3.5	2.6
Netherlands Antilles - Antilles néerlandaises 2003 - 2007																					
Male - Hommes	72.0	68.0	63.1	58.2	53.6	49.3	44.8	40.2	35.6	31.1	26.7	22.6	18.7	15.2	12.1	9.4	7.2	5.5	4.3	3.9	5.1
Female - Femmes	79.3	75.1	70.2	65.3	60.4	55.5	50.6	45.8	41.0	36.3	31.7	27.3	23.1	19.0	15.3	12.0	9.1	6.5	4.6	3.4	1.6
Nicaragua 2005 - 2010																					
Male - Hommes	63.4	47.9	44.2	40.5	36.5	32.5	28.6	24.9	21.3	17.7	14.6	11.6	9.0	6.5	...	...	...	...	...	...	...
Female - Femmes	68.9	52.1	47.6	43.0	38.5	34.1	29.8	25.7	21.9	18.1	14.9	11.8	9.3	6.9	...	...	...	...	...	...	...
Panama[5] 2000																					
Male - Hommes	72.2	69.2	64.4	59.5	54.8	50.2	45.7	41.0	36.4	31.9	27.5	23.3	19.3	15.6	12.4	9.5	7.1	...	...	...	...
Female - Femmes	76.8	73.7	68.9	64.0	59.2	54.3	49.5	44.8	40.1	35.4	30.9	26.5	22.2	18.1	14.3	10.9	7.9	...	...	...	...
Puerto Rico - Porto Rico 2004 - 2006																					
Male - Hommes	74.1	69.8	64.9	59.9	55.2	50.9	46.5	42.0	37.6	33.3	29.1	25.1	21.3	17.7	14.4	11.3	8.7	6.5	4.8	3.4	2.3
Female - Femmes	81.5	77.2	72.3	67.3	62.4	57.5	52.7	47.9	43.1	38.4	33.8	29.3	24.9	20.8	16.9	13.3	10.1	7.4	5.2	3.7	3.1
Saint Kitts and Nevis - Saint-Kitts-et-Nevis 1998																					
Male - Hommes	68.2	65.0	60.1	55.3	50.5	45.8	41.1	36.5	32.7	28.5	24.3	20.6	16.6	13.3	11.0	9.1	6.6	4.7	3.4	2.2	0.4
Female - Femmes	70.7	67.5	62.5	57.6	52.7	48.0	43.4	38.8	34.4	29.8	25.4	21.3	17.6	14.3	11.3	8.9	6.3	4.6	3.3	2.2	0.4
Saint Lucia - Sainte-Lucie 2005																					
Male - Hommes	69.9	66.4	61.5	56.6	52.0	47.4	43.1	38.6	34.3	30.1	25.9	21.7	17.9	14.7	11.8	9.0	7.2	5.2	...	...	...
Female - Femmes	75.7	72.2	67.3	62.4	57.5	52.6	47.8	43.2	38.4	33.8	29.2	25.0	20.8	17.2	13.8	10.4	7.7	4.8	...	...	...
Saint Vincent and the Grenadines - Saint-Vincent-et-les Grenadines 2001																					
Male - Hommes	66.9	63.9	59.2	54.3	49.6	45.1	40.7	36.5	32.3	28.2	24.1	19.9	16.2	12.8	9.7	7.3	4.3	4.1	...	...	...
Female - Femmes	72.9	69.3	64.5	59.5	54.7	49.8	45.2	40.7	36.1	31.7	27.3	23.0	19.0	14.6	10.8	7.3	4.1	3.6	...	...	...
Trinidad and Tobago - Trinité-et-Tobago 2000																					
Male - Hommes	68.3	65.2	60.3	55.5	50.7	46.1	41.7	37.3	33.1	29.0	24.9	21.2	17.9	14.7	12.0	9.7	7.8	...	...	...	...
Female - Femmes	73.7	70.2	65.3	60.4	55.6	50.9	46.2	41.7	37.1	32.7	28.4	24.4	20.7	17.4	14.4	11.7	9.6	...	...	...	...
Turks and Caicos Islands - Îles Turques et Caïques 2001																					
Male - Hommes	79.0	75.3	70.3	65.3	60.3	55.8	50.8	46.0	41.2	37.1	33.0	28.4	24.3	20.8	17.5	12.5	7.5	4.1	...	...	...
Female - Femmes	77.4	72.5	67.5	62.5	57.5	52.9	48.2	43.4	38.6	33.8	29.6	25.0	20.0	17.0	13.2	11.7	10.3	8.8	...	...	...

20. Expectation of life at specified ages for each sex: latest available year, 1998 - 2007
Espérance de vie à un âge donné pour chaque sexe: dernière année disponible, 1998 - 2007 (continued - suite)

Continent, country or area and date / Continent, pays ou zone et date	At birth - A la naissance	5	10	15	20	25	30	35	40	45	50	55	60	65	70	75	80	85	90	95	100
AMERICA, NORTH - AMÉRIQUE DU NORD																					
United States of America - États-Unis d'Amérique																					
2005																					
Male - Hommes	74.9	70.5	65.6	60.6	55.9	51.3	46.6	42.0	37.3	32.8	28.5	24.4	20.4	16.8	13.3	10.2	7.7	5.6	4.0	2.8	2.0
Female - Femmes	79.9	75.5	70.6	65.6	60.7	55.9	51.0	46.2	41.4	36.8	32.2	27.8	23.5	19.5	15.6	12.1	9.1	6.6	4.7	3.2	2.2
AMERICA, SOUTH - AMÉRIQUE DU SUD																					
Argentina - Argentine																					
2000 - 2001																					
Male - Hommes	70.0	66.6	61.7	56.8	52.1	47.4	42.8	38.2	33.7	29.3	25.0	21.1	17.4	14.1	11.1	8.6	6.5	4.9	3.7	2.9	...
Female - Femmes	77.5	73.9	69.0	64.1	59.2	54.4	49.5	44.7	40.0	35.4	30.9	26.5	22.3	18.4	14.7	11.3	8.4	6.2	4.6	3.5	...
2006 - 2010																					
Male - Hommes	72.5	...	...	...	...	...	...	...	...	...	...	...	...	...	...	...	...	...	...	...	...
Female - Femmes	80.0	...	...	...	...	...	...	...	...	...	...	...	...	...	...	...	...	...	...	...	...
Bolivia (Plurinational State of) - Bolivie (État plurinational de)																					
1995 - 2000																					
Male - Hommes	59.8	60.8	56.7	52.2	48.0	43.7	39.5	35.3	31.2	27.1	23.2	19.5	15.9	12.7	9.8	7.5	5.9	...	...	...	...
Female - Femmes	63.2	63.8	59.7	55.2	50.8	46.5	42.1	37.8	33.6	29.4	25.3	21.4	17.6	14.0	10.8	8.3	6.5	...	...	...	...
Brazil - Brésil[5]																					
2007																					
Male - Hommes	68.8	66.1	61.2	56.4	51.8	47.5	43.2	38.9	34.6	30.5	26.6	22.8	19.3	16.1	13.3	10.8	8.9	...	...	...	...
Female - Femmes	76.4	73.3	68.4	63.4	58.6	53.8	49.0	44.3	39.6	35.1	30.7	26.5	22.5	18.8	15.4	12.4	9.9	...	...	...	...
Chile - Chili																					
2005 - 2010																					
Male - Hommes	75.5	71.2	66.3	61.4	56.6	51.9	47.2	42.5	37.9	33.3	28.9	24.7	20.7	17.0	13.7	10.8	8.3	...	...	...	...
Female - Femmes	81.5	77.2	72.2	67.3	62.4	57.5	52.6	47.7	42.9	38.1	33.4	28.9	24.5	20.4	16.5	13.0	9.9	...	...	...	...
Colombia - Colombie[6]																					
2005 - 2010																					
Male - Hommes	70.7	67.7	62.9	58.0	53.5	49.4	45.2	40.9	36.5	32.2	27.8	23.7	19.7	16.0	12.7	9.8	7.4	...	...	...	...
Female - Femmes	77.5	74.1	69.2	64.3	59.5	54.7	49.9	45.1	40.4	35.7	31.2	26.7	22.5	18.5	14.8	11.5	8.6	...	...	...	...
Ecuador - Équateur[7]																					
2005 - 2010																					
Male - Hommes	72.1	69.3	64.5	59.7	55.2	50.9	46.6	42.3	38.1	33.8	29.7	25.7	21.7	18.0	14.6	11.3	8.2	...	...	...	...
Female - Femmes	78.0	74.8	69.9	65.1	60.4	55.6	50.9	46.2	41.6	37.0	32.6	28.2	24.1	20.0	16.1	12.5	9.1	...	...	...	...
French Guiana - Guyane française																					
2007																					
Male - Hommes	75.1	71.3	66.4	61.5	56.8	52.2	47.7	43.1	38.7	34.3	30.3	25.7	21.5	17.5	13.8	10.5	8.2	5.7	3.6	2.1	...
Female - Femmes	80.8	77.0	72.1	67.2	62.3	57.4	52.6	47.8	43.0	38.5	33.9	29.2	24.5	19.9	16.6	12.7	10.2	7.8	5.1	2.2	...
Paraguay																					
2000 - 2005																					
Male - Hommes	68.6	...	...	...	...	...	...	...	...	...	...	...	...	...	...	...	...	...	...	...	...
Female - Femmes	73.1	...	...	...	...	...	...	...	...	...	...	...	...	...	...	...	...	...	...	...	...
Peru - Pérou[5]																					
1995 - 2000																					
Male - Hommes	65.9	65.9	61.4	56.6	52.0	47.4	42.9	38.5	34.1	29.8	25.7	21.7	18.1	14.7	11.7	9.2	7.0	...	...	...	...
Female - Femmes	70.9	70.2	65.6	60.7	55.9	51.2	46.5	41.9	37.3	32.9	28.5	24.3	20.3	16.5	13.3	10.4	7.8	...	...	...	...
Suriname[8]																					
2006																					
Male - Hommes	68.0	60.4	55.5	50.6	46.0	41.5	37.0	32.8	28.6	24.6	20.7	16.9	13.5	10.5	8.1	7.1	6.5	...	...	...	...
Female - Femmes	73.7	66.0	61.1	56.2	51.5	46.8	42.3	37.7	33.2	28.8	24.5	20.3	16.4	12.9	9.9	8.0	8.5	...	...	...	...
Uruguay																					
2006																					
Male - Hommes	72.1	68.5	63.6	58.7	53.8	49.1	44.4	39.7	35.0	30.5	26.0	21.9	18.1	14.7	11.7	9.0	6.7	4.8	3.4	2.7	...
Female - Femmes	79.5	75.7	70.8	65.8	60.9	56.1	51.2	46.3	41.6	36.8	32.3	27.8	23.6	19.4	15.5	11.9	8.8	6.3	4.4	3.1	...
2007																					
Male - Hommes	72.3	...	...	...	...	...	...	...	...	...	...	...	...	...	...	...	...	...	...	...	...
Female - Femmes	79.6	...	...	...	...	...	...	...	...	...	...	...	...	...	...	...	...	...	...	...	...

20. Expectation of life at specified ages for each sex: latest available year, 1998 - 2007
Espérance de vie à un âge donné pour chaque sexe: dernière année disponible, 1998 - 2007 (continued - suite)

Continent, country or area and date / Continent, pays ou zone et date	At birth - A la naissance	5	10	15	20	25	30	35	40	45	50	55	60	65	70	75	80	85	90	95	100
AMERICA, SOUTH - AMÉRIQUE DU SUD																					
Venezuela (Bolivarian Republic of) - Venezuela (République bolivarienne du)																					
1995 - 2000																					
Male - Hommes	68.6	66.6	61.8	56.9	52.3	47.8	43.3	38.8	34.3	29.9	25.6	21.6	17.9	14.5	11.4	8.6	5.9	...	...	...	...
Female - Femmes	74.5	72.1	67.2	62.3	57.5	52.6	47.8	43.1	38.4	33.7	29.2	24.9	20.8	16.9	13.3	9.9	6.9	...	...	...	...
2002																					
Male - Hommes	70.8	...	...	...	...	...	...	...	...	...	...	...	...	...	...	...	...	...	...	...	...
Female - Femmes	76.6	...	...	...	...	...	...	...	...	...	...	...	...	...	...	...	...	...	...	...	...
ASIA - ASIE																					
Afghanistan[5]																					
2002																					
Male - Hommes	43.0	...	...	...	...	...	...	...	...	...	...	...	...	...	...	...	...	...	...	...	...
Female - Femmes	43.0	...	...	...	...	...	...	...	...	...	...	...	...	...	...	...	...	...	...	...	...
Armenia - Arménie																					
2006 - 2007																					
Male - Hommes	70.2	66.3	61.4	56.4	51.6	46.8	42.0	37.3	32.7	28.3	24.1	20.1	16.4	13.1	10.3	7.8	5.7	3.9	2.6	1.6	0.7
Female - Femmes	76.6	72.5	67.6	62.7	57.7	52.8	47.9	43.0	38.2	33.5	28.8	24.3	20.0	15.9	12.4	9.2	6.4	4.1	2.7	1.8	0.7
Azerbaijan - Azerbaïdjan																					
2007																					
Male - Hommes	69.7	65.9	61.0	56.1	51.3	46.6	41.9	37.3	32.8	28.4	24.2	20.2	16.6	13.4	11.1	9.0	7.4	6.0	4.2	2.3	0.9
Female - Femmes	75.1	71.2	66.3	61.4	56.5	51.7	46.8	42.0	37.2	32.5	27.9	23.4	19.2	15.2	11.8	8.9	6.6	4.2	3.6	2.2	0.8
Bahrain - Bahreïn																					
2001																					
Male - Hommes	73.2	...	64.4	59.5	54.7	49.9	45.2	40.4	35.6	30.9	26.4	22.0	17.8	14.1	11.3	9.5	...	...	...	...	...
Female - Femmes	76.2	...	67.1	62.1	57.2	52.3	47.4	42.5	37.7	32.9	28.2	23.7	19.6	15.9	12.9	10.9	...	...	...	...	...
2005																					
Male - Hommes	73.1	...	...	...	...	...	...	...	...	...	...	...	...	...	...	...	...	...	...	...	...
Female - Femmes	77.3	...	...	...	...	...	...	...	...	...	...	...	...	...	...	...	...	...	...	...	...
Bangladesh																					
2007																					
Male - Hommes	65.4	...	...	...	...	...	...	...	...	...	...	...	...	...	...	...	...	...	...	...	...
Female - Femmes	67.9	...	...	...	...	...	...	...	...	...	...	...	...	...	...	...	...	...	...	...	...
Bhutan - Bhoutan																					
2005																					
Male - Hommes	65.7	...	...	...	...	...	...	...	...	...	...	...	...	...	...	...	...	...	...	...	...
Female - Femmes	66.9	...	...	...	...	...	...	...	...	...	...	...	...	...	...	...	...	...	...	...	...
Brunei Darussalam - Brunéi Darussalam																					
2007																					
Male - Hommes	75.2	...	...	...	...	...	...	...	...	...	...	...	...	...	...	...	...	...	...	...	...
Female - Femmes	77.8	...	...	...	...	...	...	...	...	...	...	...	...	...	...	...	...	...	...	...	...
China - Chine[9]																					
2000																					
Male - Hommes	69.6	...	...	...	...	...	...	...	...	...	...	...	...	...	...	...	...	...	...	...	...
Female - Femmes	73.3	...	...	...	...	...	...	...	...	...	...	...	...	...	...	...	...	...	...	...	...
China, Hong Kong SAR - Chine, Hong Kong RAS																					
2005																					
Male - Hommes	78.8	74.0	69.1	64.1	59.2	54.3	49.4	44.6	39.9	35.1	30.5	26.0	21.7	17.7	14.1	10.8	8.1	6.0	4.3	3.1	2.1
Female - Femmes	84.6	79.8	74.8	69.9	64.9	60.0	55.1	50.2	45.3	40.5	35.7	31.0	26.4	21.9	17.7	13.8	10.4	7.6	5.4	3.7	2.6
2006																					
Male - Hommes	79.4	...	...	...	...	...	...	...	...	...	...	...	...	...	...	...	...	...	...	...	...
Female - Femmes	85.5	...	...	...	...	...	...	...	...	...	...	...	...	...	...	...	...	...	...	...	...
China, Macao SAR - Chine, Macao RAS																					
2002 - 2005																					
Male - Hommes	77.6	73.1	68.2	63.2	58.3	53.5	48.8	44.1	39.4	34.7	30.2	25.7	21.3	17.1	13.2	9.8	7.1	4.7	2.8	1.5	1.3
Female - Femmes	82.3	77.7	72.7	67.8	62.8	57.9	53.0	48.1	43.3	38.5	33.7	28.9	24.2	19.7	15.2	11.2	8.1	5.7	3.7	2.3	2.7

20. Expectation of life at specified ages for each sex: latest available year, 1998 - 2007
Espérance de vie à un âge donné pour chaque sexe: dernière année disponible, 1998 - 2007 (continued - suite)

Continent, country or area and date / Continent, pays ou zone et date	At birth - A la naissance	5	10	15	20	25	30	35	40	45	50	55	60	65	70	75	80	85	90	95	100
ASIA - ASIE																					
Cyprus - Chypre[10]																					
2004 - 2005																					
Male - Hommes	77.0	72.4	67.5	62.5	57.8	53.0	48.3	43.6	38.8	34.1	29.5	25.0	20.7	16.7	13.1	9.7	6.9	4.8	3.3	2.3	...
Female - Femmes	81.7	77.0	72.1	67.2	62.2	57.3	52.4	47.6	42.7	37.8	33.1	28.3	23.8	19.3	15.2	11.3	8.1	5.6	4.5	3.4	...
Georgia - Géorgie																					
2007																					
Male - Hommes	70.5	66.6	61.6	56.7	51.8	47.1	42.4	37.9	33.5	29.3	25.3	21.5	17.7	14.2	11.6	8.9	6.7	4.9	...	...	...
Female - Femmes	79.4	75.5	70.6	65.7	60.8	55.9	51.1	46.2	41.5	36.8	32.1	27.6	23.2	19.0	15.4	12.2	9.7	8.1	...	...	...
India - Inde[11]																					
2002 - 2006																					
Male - Hommes	62.6	63.8	59.3	54.6	49.9	45.4	40.9	36.5	32.2	28.0	24.0	20.2	16.7	13.6	10.9	...	...	...	...	...	...
Female - Femmes	64.2	67.4	62.9	58.2	53.7	49.2	44.8	40.2	35.7	31.3	26.9	22.7	18.9	15.4	12.4		...	...	...	...	...
Iran (Islamic Republic of) - Iran (République islamique d')																					
2006																					
Male - Hommes	71.1	...	...	...	...	...	...	...	...	...	...	...	...	...	...	...	...	...	...	...	...
Female - Femmes	73.1	...	...	...	...	...	...	...	...	...	...	...	...	...	...	...	...	...	...	...	...
Israel - Israël[12]																					
2007																					
Male - Hommes	78.8	74.2	69.2	64.3	59.4	54.6	49.8	45.0	40.2	35.5	30.9	26.5	22.2	18.2	14.5	11.3	8.7	6.5	...	...	...
Female - Femmes	82.5	77.9	72.9	67.9	63.0	58.1	53.1	48.2	43.3	38.5	33.8	29.1	24.6	20.3	16.1	12.3	9.1	6.5	...	...	...
Japan - Japon[13]																					
2007																					
Male - Hommes	79.2	74.5	69.5	64.6	59.7	54.8	50.0	45.2	40.4	35.7	31.2	26.7	22.5	18.6	14.8	11.4	8.5	6.2	4.4	3.2	2.3
Female - Femmes	86.0	81.3	76.3	71.3	66.4	61.5	56.6	51.7	46.8	42.0	37.3	32.6	28.1	23.6	19.3	15.2	11.4	8.2	5.7	4.0	2.8
Jordan - Jordanie[14]																					
2007																					
Male - Hommes	71.6	...	...	...	...	...	...	...	...	...	...	...	...	...	...	...	...	...	...	...	...
Female - Femmes	74.4	...	...	...	...	...	...	...	...	...	...	...	...	...	...	...	...	...	...	...	...
Kazakhstan																					
2007																					
Male - Hommes	60.7	57.0	52.1	47.3	42.6	38.3	34.3	30.5	26.7	23.1	19.6	16.5	13.7	11.2	9.0	7.1	5.5	4.2	3.1	2.3	1.7
Female - Femmes	72.6	68.8	63.9	59.0	54.2	49.5	44.8	40.3	35.8	31.4	27.1	23.1	19.2	15.6	12.3	9.5	7.0	5.1	3.6	2.5	1.8
Kyrgyzstan - Kirghizstan																					
2007																					
Male - Hommes	63.7	61.2	56.3	51.4	46.6	41.9	37.4	33.1	29.0	25.0	21.4	18.0	14.9	12.2	10.0	8.2	6.9	5.5	4.7	5.6	2.7
Female - Femmes	72.3	69.6	64.7	59.7	54.9	50.1	45.3	40.6	36.0	31.5	27.1	22.9	19.0	15.3	12.1	9.5	7.3	5.7	4.6	3.9	1.7
Lao People's Democratic Republic - République démocratique populaire lao[15]																					
2005																					
Male - Hommes	55.0	...	...	...	...	...	...	...	...	...	...	...	...	...	...	...	...	...	...	...	...
Female - Femmes	63.0	...	...	...	...	...	...	...	...	...	...	...	...	...	...	...	...	...	...	...	...
Malaysia - Malaisie																					
2006																					
Male - Hommes	71.5	67.0	62.0	57.2	52.4	47.8	43.1	38.6	34.0	29.5	25.2	21.1	17.2	13.7	10.7	8.0	5.8	...	...	...	...
Female - Femmes	76.2	71.6	66.7	61.8	56.9	52.0	47.1	42.3	37.5	32.8	28.2	23.8	19.6	15.6	12.1	9.0	6.6	...	...	...	...
Maldives																					
2005																					
Male - Hommes	71.7	68.0	63.2	58.3	53.5	48.6	43.7	38.9	34.1	29.4	24.7	20.2	16.2	12.7	9.1	6.4	...	...	...	...	...
Female - Femmes	72.7	69.0	64.1	59.2	54.3	49.4	44.5	39.6	34.8	30.1	25.3	20.9	16.5	12.8	8.9	6.0	...	...	...	...	...
Mongolia - Mongolie																					
1998 - 2007																					
Male - Hommes	63.1	61.3	56.5	51.6	46.9	42.3	38.0	33.7	29.7	25.9	22.4	19.2	16.1	13.7	12.0	...	...	...	...	...	...
Female - Femmes	70.2	68.9	64.0	59.1	54.2	49.5	44.8	40.2	35.7	31.3	27.2	23.3	19.7	16.7	14.3	...	...	...	...	...	...
1999 - 2008																					
Male - Hommes	63.7	...	...	...	...	...	...	...	...	...	...	...	...	...	...	...	...	...	...	...	...
Female - Femmes	71.0	...	...	...	...	...	...	...	...	...	...	...	...	...	...	...	...	...	...	...	...
Myanmar[16]																					
2005																					
Male - Hommes	62.5	65.2	60.7	56.0	51.2	46.5	41.8	37.1	32.6	28.2	23.9	20.0	16.5	13.4	10.7	8.6	6.8	5.4	...	...	...
Female - Femmes	66.6	68.5	63.9	59.1	54.3	49.5	44.7	40.0	35.4	30.8	26.3	22.1	18.1	14.6	11.5	8.9	6.8	5.2	...	...	...

20. Expectation of life at specified ages for each sex: latest available year, 1998 - 2007
Espérance de vie à un âge donné pour chaque sexe: dernière année disponible, 1998 - 2007 (continued - suite)

Continent, country or area and date / Continent, pays ou zone et date	At birth - A la naissance	5	10	15	20	25	30	35	40	45	50	55	60	65	70	75	80	85	90	95	100
ASIA - ASIE																					
Nepal - Népal 2006																					
Male - Hommes	62.9	...	...	...	...	...	...	...	...	...	...	...	...	...	...	...	...	...	...	...	...
Female - Femmes	63.7	...	...	...	...	...	...	...	...	...	...	...	...	...	...	...	...	...	...	...	...
Occupied Palestinian Territory - Territoire palestinien occupé 2001																					
Male - Hommes	70.5	67.5	62.7	57.8	53.1	48.4	43.6	38.9	34.2	29.6	25.2	21.1	17.2	13.8	10.7	8.1	6.1	...	...	...	...
Female - Femmes	73.6	70.3	65.5	60.5	55.7	50.9	46.1	41.3	36.6	32.0	27.5	23.2	19.0	15.2	11.7	8.8	6.4	...	...	...	...
2007																					
Male - Hommes	70.0	...	...	...	...	...	...	...	...	...	...	...	...	...	...	...	...	...	...	...	...
Female - Femmes	72.6	...	...	...	...	...	...	...	...	...	...	...	...	...	...	...	...	...	...	...	...
Oman 2006																					
Male - Hommes	73.2	...	...	...	...	...	...	...	...	...	...	...	...	...	...	...	...	...	...	...	...
Female - Femmes	75.4	...	...	...	...	...	...	...	...	...	...	...	...	...	...	...	...	...	...	...	...
Pakistan[17] 2003[18]																					
Male - Hommes	64.7	66.6	61.9	57.1	52.4	47.7	43.1	38.6	34.1	29.7	25.6	21.8	18.5	15.4	11.9	...	...				
Female - Femmes	65.6	67.2	62.4	57.4	52.6	48.0	43.5	38.9	34.4	30.0	25.7	21.8	18.5	15.4	12.9	...	...				
2005[19]																					
Male - Hommes	64.0	...	...	...	...	...	...	...	...	...	...	...	...	...	...	...	...	...	...	...	...
Female - Femmes	65.0	...	...	...	...	...	...	...	...	...	...	...	...	...	...	...	...	...	...	...	...
Qatar 2007																					
Male - Hommes	81.0	76.9	72.0	67.2	62.7	57.9	53.1	48.3	43.5	38.7	34.0	29.4	25.1	20.9	17.6	14.8	12.5	...	...	...	
Female - Femmes	79.2	74.9	70.0	65.1	60.2	55.3	50.4	45.5	40.6	35.7	30.9	26.3	21.7	17.9	14.6	11.7	9.1	...	...	...	
Republic of Korea - République de Corée 2006																					
Male - Hommes	75.7	71.2	66.3	61.3	56.4	51.6	46.7	41.9	37.2	32.6	28.2	24.0	19.9	16.1	12.6	9.6	7.1	5.3	4.0	3.2	2.7
Female - Femmes	82.4	77.8	72.8	67.9	63.0	58.0	53.2	48.3	43.4	38.6	33.9	29.2	24.6	20.1	15.9	12.0	8.7	6.2	4.5	3.4	2.8
2007																					
Male - Hommes	76.1	...	...	...	...	...	...	...	...	...	...	...	...	...	...	...	...	...	...	...	...
Female - Femmes	82.7	...	...	...	...	...	...	...	...	...	...	...	...	...	...	...	...	...	...	...	...
Singapore - Singapour 2007																					
Male - Hommes	78.1	73.3	68.4	63.4	58.5	53.7	48.8	43.9	39.1	34.4	29.8	25.4	21.1	17.2	13.7	10.6	8.1	6.0	4.3	3.1	2.1
Female - Femmes	82.9	78.1	73.1	68.2	63.2	58.3	53.4	48.4	43.6	38.7	34.0	29.4	24.9	20.6	16.5	13.0	9.9	7.2	5.1	3.6	2.5
Tajikistan - Tadjikistan 2005																					
Male - Hommes	68.1	67.0	62.1	57.3	52.4	47.6	42.9	38.3	33.8	29.4	25.0	21.0	17.3	14.1	11.5	9.5	7.4	...	...	...	
Female - Femmes	73.2	71.7	66.8	61.9	57.0	52.2	47.4	42.6	37.9	33.2	28.8	24.4	20.6	17.1	14.2	12.0	10.2	...	...	...	
Thailand - Thaïlande 2005 - 2006																					
Male - Hommes	69.9	...	...	...	...	...	...	...	...	...	...	...	...	...	...	...	...	...	...	...	...
Female - Femmes	77.6	...	...	...	...	...	...	...	...	...	...	...	...	...	...	...	...	...	...	...	...
Turkey - Turquie[20] 2006																					
Male - Hommes	69.1	...	...	...	...	...	...	...	...	...	...	...	...	...	...	...	...	...	...	...	...
Female - Femmes	74.0	...	...	...	...	...	...	...	...	...	...	...	...	...	...	...	...	...	...	...	...
United Arab Emirates - Émirats arabes unis 2006																					
Male - Hommes	76.7	72.5	67.6	62.7	57.9	53.1	48.3	43.5	38.7	33.9	29.3	24.8	20.7	16.9	13.8	11.3	10.2	...	...	...	
Female - Femmes	78.8	74.5	69.5	64.6	59.7	54.8	49.8	44.9	40.0	35.2	30.4	25.8	21.6	18.0	15.4	14.0	14.5	...	...	...	
Yemen - Yémen 2004																					
Male - Hommes	60.2	...	...	...	...	...	...	...	...	...	...	...	...	...	...	...	...	...	...	...	...
Female - Femmes	62.0	...	...	...	...	...	...	...	...	...	...	...	...	...	...	...	...	...	...	...	...

Continent, country or area and date / Continent, pays ou zone et date	At birth - A la naissance	5	10	15	20	25	30	35	40	45	50	55	60	65	70	75	80	85	90	95	100

EUROPE

Åland Islands - Îles d'Åland[21]
2005
| Male - Hommes | 78.8 | 74.3 | 69.3 | 64.7 | 59.7 | 54.7 | 49.7 | 45.0 | 40.0 | 35.8 | 31.0 | 26.1 | 21.5 | 17.1 | 13.5 | 10.6 | 7.3 | 6.0 | 4.5 | 2.8 | 0.0 |
| Female - Femmes | 81.1 | 77.2 | 72.2 | 67.2 | 62.2 | 57.2 | 52.6 | 48.0 | 43.0 | 38.2 | 33.9 | 29.3 | 24.7 | 20.6 | 16.7 | 13.1 | 10.2 | 7.2 | 4.9 | 3.1 | 2.2 |

Albania - Albanie
2004
| Male - Hommes | 72.5 | 69.5 | 64.8 | 59.9 | 55.1 | 50.4 | 45.8 | 41.1 | 36.4 | 31.8 | 27.3 | 22.9 | 18.6 | 14.8 | 11.3 | 8.4 | 6.0 | 3.8 | ... | ... | ... |
| Female - Femmes | 77.3 | 74.4 | 69.5 | 64.7 | 59.8 | 54.9 | 50.0 | 45.2 | 40.3 | 35.5 | 30.8 | 26.1 | 21.6 | 17.3 | 13.2 | 9.6 | 6.4 | 3.8 | ... | ... | ... |

Austria - Autriche
2006
| Male - Hommes | 75.5 | 72.5 | 67.6 | 62.6 | 57.8 | 53.0 | 48.2 | 43.4 | 38.6 | 33.9 | 29.4 | 25.1 | 21.0 | 17.2 | 13.6 | 10.4 | 7.6 | 5.3 | 3.7 | 2.7 | ... |
| Female - Femmes | 81.5 | 78.0 | 73.0 | 68.1 | 63.2 | 58.2 | 53.3 | 48.4 | 43.5 | 38.7 | 34.0 | 29.4 | 24.9 | 20.6 | 16.4 | 12.5 | 9.0 | 6.2 | 4.2 | 3.0 | ... |

Belarus - Bélarus
2007
| Male - Hommes | 64.5 | 60.1 | 55.2 | 50.2 | 45.5 | 40.9 | 36.5 | 32.2 | 28.1 | 24.2 | 20.5 | 17.2 | 14.2 | 11.7 | 9.5 | 7.5 | 5.7 | 4.2 | 3.0 | 2.1 | 1.4 |
| Female - Femmes | 76.2 | 71.6 | 66.7 | 61.8 | 56.9 | 52.0 | 47.2 | 42.4 | 37.8 | 33.2 | 28.7 | 24.4 | 20.4 | 16.6 | 13.0 | 9.8 | 7.1 | 5.1 | 3.5 | 2.4 | 1.5 |

Belgium - Belgique
2006
| Male - Hommes | 77.0 | 71.4 | 66.5 | 61.5 | 56.7 | 51.9 | 47.1 | 42.4 | 37.7 | 33.1 | 28.6 | 24.3 | 20.3 | 16.5 | 12.9 | 9.7 | 7.1 | 5.0 | 3.4 | 2.5 | ... |
| Female - Femmes | 82.7 | 77.0 | 72.1 | 67.1 | 62.2 | 57.3 | 52.4 | 47.5 | 42.6 | 37.9 | 33.2 | 28.7 | 24.3 | 20.1 | 16.0 | 12.1 | 8.8 | 6.1 | 4.1 | 2.8 | ... |

Bosnia and Herzegovina - Bosnie-Herzégovine
2003
| Male - Hommes | 71.3 | ... | ... | ... | ... | ... | ... | ... | ... | ... | ... | ... | ... | ... | ... | ... | ... | ... | ... | ... | ... |
| Female - Femmes | 76.7 | ... | ... | ... | ... | ... | ... | ... | ... | ... | ... | ... | ... | ... | ... | ... | ... | ... | ... | ... | ... |

Bulgaria - Bulgarie
2005 - 2007
| Male - Hommes | 69.2 | 65.1 | 60.2 | 55.3 | 50.5 | 45.7 | 41.0 | 36.3 | 31.7 | 27.3 | 23.2 | 19.5 | 16.2 | 13.1 | 10.4 | 7.9 | 5.9 | 4.4 | 3.4 | 2.5 | 0.5 |
| Female - Femmes | 76.3 | 72.2 | 67.3 | 62.4 | 57.5 | 52.6 | 47.7 | 42.9 | 38.1 | 33.4 | 28.9 | 24.5 | 20.3 | 16.2 | 12.5 | 9.2 | 6.6 | 4.7 | 3.4 | 2.4 | 0.5 |

Czech Republic - République tchèque
2007
| Male - Hommes | 73.7 | 69.0 | 64.0 | 59.1 | 54.3 | 49.5 | 44.7 | 40.0 | 35.3 | 30.6 | 26.2 | 22.1 | 18.4 | 15.0 | 11.8 | 9.0 | 6.6 | 4.6 | 3.1 | 2.1 | 1.3 |
| Female - Femmes | 79.9 | 75.2 | 70.2 | 65.2 | 60.3 | 55.4 | 50.4 | 45.5 | 40.7 | 35.9 | 31.2 | 26.7 | 22.3 | 18.2 | 14.2 | 10.6 | 7.5 | 4.9 | 3.0 | 1.8 | 1.0 |

Denmark - Danemark[22]
2006 - 2007
| Male - Hommes | 75.9 | 71.4 | 66.4 | 61.5 | 56.6 | 51.8 | 47.0 | 42.2 | 37.4 | 32.8 | 28.3 | 24.1 | 20.1 | 16.3 | 12.8 | 9.8 | 7.2 | 5.1 | 3.6 | 2.5 | 2.0 |
| Female - Femmes | 80.5 | 75.8 | 70.9 | 65.9 | 61.0 | 56.0 | 51.1 | 46.2 | 41.3 | 36.5 | 31.9 | 27.5 | 23.2 | 19.1 | 15.2 | 11.8 | 8.8 | 6.3 | 4.3 | 3.0 | 2.1 |

Estonia - Estonie
2006
| Male - Hommes | 67.4 | 62.8 | 57.9 | 53.0 | 48.3 | 43.7 | 39.2 | 34.8 | 30.4 | 26.2 | 22.4 | 19.0 | 15.9 | 13.2 | 10.6 | 8.3 | 6.3 | 4.5 | ... | ... | ... |
| Female - Femmes | 78.5 | 73.9 | 68.9 | 64.0 | 59.1 | 54.2 | 49.4 | 44.5 | 39.8 | 35.1 | 30.5 | 26.2 | 22.1 | 18.3 | 14.4 | 10.9 | 7.9 | 5.6 | ... | ... | ... |

Finland - Finlande[23]
2007
| Male - Hommes | 75.8 | 71.1 | 66.2 | 61.2 | 56.4 | 51.7 | 47.0 | 42.3 | 37.6 | 33.1 | 28.7 | 24.6 | 20.6 | 16.9 | 13.4 | 10.2 | 7.5 | 5.3 | 3.7 | 2.4 | 2.1 |
| Female - Femmes | 82.9 | 78.1 | 73.1 | 68.2 | 63.3 | 58.4 | 53.5 | 48.6 | 43.7 | 39.0 | 34.3 | 29.7 | 25.3 | 21.0 | 16.8 | 12.8 | 9.3 | 6.3 | 4.2 | 2.8 | 1.6 |

France[24]
2006
| Male - Hommes | 77.2 | 72.6 | 67.7 | 62.7 | 57.9 | 53.1 | 48.3 | 43.5 | 38.8 | 34.3 | 29.9 | 25.8 | 21.9 | 18.1 | 14.5 | 11.2 | 8.3 | 6.0 | 4.3 | 3.6 | 5.8 |
| Female - Femmes | 84.2 | 79.5 | 74.5 | 69.6 | 64.6 | 59.7 | 54.8 | 49.9 | 45.1 | 40.3 | 35.7 | 31.2 | 26.7 | 22.4 | 18.1 | 14.1 | 10.5 | 7.4 | 5.0 | 3.6 | 3.3 |

Germany - Allemagne
2005 - 2007
| Male - Hommes | 76.9 | 72.3 | 67.3 | 62.4 | 57.5 | 52.7 | 47.8 | 43.0 | 38.2 | 33.5 | 29.1 | 24.8 | 20.7 | 16.9 | 13.4 | 10.2 | 7.6 | 5.4 | 3.7 | 2.7 | 1.9 |
| Female - Femmes | 82.3 | 77.6 | 72.6 | 67.7 | 62.7 | 57.8 | 52.9 | 47.9 | 43.1 | 38.3 | 33.6 | 29.0 | 24.6 | 20.3 | 16.2 | 12.3 | 8.9 | 6.2 | 4.1 | 2.9 | 2.1 |

Gibraltar
2001
| Male - Hommes | 78.5 | 73.5 | 68.5 | 63.5 | 58.5 | 53.5 | ... | 43.5 | ... | 33.9 | ... | 25.8 | ... | 17.9 | ... | 11.3 | ... | ... | ... | ... | ... |
| Female - Femmes | 83.3 | 79.5 | 75.0 | 70.0 | 65.0 | 60.0 | ... | 50.3 | ... | 40.3 | ... | 30.3 | ... | 20.6 | ... | 13.7 | ... | ... | ... | ... | ... |

Greece - Grèce
2007
| Male - Hommes | 77.0 | 72.4 | 67.4 | 62.5 | 57.6 | 52.9 | 48.3 | 43.5 | 38.8 | 34.2 | 29.7 | 25.4 | 21.3 | 17.4 | 13.8 | 10.6 | 7.9 | 5.9 | 4.5 | 3.3 | 2.4 |
| Female - Femmes | 82.0 | 77.3 | 72.4 | 67.4 | 62.5 | 57.5 | 52.6 | 47.7 | 42.9 | 38.1 | 33.3 | 28.7 | 24.1 | 19.6 | 15.3 | 11.4 | 8.0 | 5.7 | 4.2 | 3.0 | 2.1 |

20. Expectation of life at specified ages for each sex: latest available year, 1998 - 2007
Espérance de vie à un âge donné pour chaque sexe: dernière année disponible, 1998 - 2007 (continued - suite)

Continent, country or area and date / Continent, pays ou zone et date	At birth - A la naissance	5	10	15	20	25	30	35	40	45	50	55	60	65	70	75	80	85	90	95	100
EUROPE																					
Hungary - Hongrie 2007																					
Male - Hommes	69.2	64.7	59.7	54.8	49.9	45.1	40.3	35.6	31.0	26.7	22.9	19.5	16.3	13.4	10.6	8.2	6.1	4.1	2.6	1.5	0.6
Female - Femmes	77.3	72.9	67.9	63.0	58.0	53.1	48.2	43.3	38.5	33.9	29.5	25.3	21.2	17.3	13.6	10.2	7.2	4.7	2.8	1.6	0.6
Iceland - Islande 2006 - 2007																					
Male - Hommes	79.4	74.6	69.7	64.7	59.9	55.1	50.4	45.5	40.7	35.9	31.3	26.8	22.4	18.3	14.4	11.0	7.8	5.4	3.5	2.4	1.5
Female - Femmes	82.9	78.1	73.1	68.1	63.2	58.3	53.4	48.5	43.6	38.7	33.9	29.3	24.9	20.6	16.6	12.8	9.6	6.7	4.6	3.3	1.5
Ireland - Irlande 2002																					
Male - Hommes	75.1	70.7	65.7	60.8	56.0	51.3	46.5	41.8	37.0	32.3	27.8	23.4	19.2	15.4	11.9	8.9	6.5	4.6	3.3	2.4	1.7
Female - Femmes	80.3	75.7	70.8	65.8	60.9	56.0	51.1	46.2	41.4	36.6	31.9	27.4	22.9	18.7	14.8	11.2	8.2	5.8	4.1	2.9	2.1
Italy - Italie 2005																					
Male - Hommes	78.1	73.5	68.5	63.5	58.7	53.9	49.1	44.3	39.5	34.8	30.2	25.7	21.4	17.5	13.7	10.5	7.7	5.4	3.8	2.7	1.9
Female - Femmes	83.7	79.0	74.0	69.1	64.1	59.2	54.3	49.3	44.5	39.6	34.9	30.2	25.7	21.3	17.1	13.1	9.6	6.7	4.5	3.0	2.1
Latvia - Lettonie 2007																					
Male - Hommes	65.8	61.4	56.6	51.7	46.9	42.2	37.8	33.4	29.2	25.2	21.6	18.3	15.3	12.8	10.3	8.1	6.3	4.8	3.6	2.7	...
Female - Femmes	76.5	72.3	67.3	62.4	57.5	52.6	47.8	42.9	38.3	33.8	29.4	25.1	21.1	17.2	13.5	10.2	7.4	5.2	3.6	2.8	...
Lithuania - Lituanie 2007																					
Male - Hommes	64.9	60.3	55.4	50.5	45.8	41.3	36.9	32.6	28.6	24.8	21.3	18.2	15.4	12.9	10.5	8.2	6.2	4.6	3.4	2.6	2.1
Female - Femmes	77.2	72.7	67.8	62.9	58.0	53.1	48.3	43.5	38.9	34.3	30.0	25.7	21.7	17.9	14.1	10.6	7.5	5.2	3.5	2.3	2.1
Luxembourg 2005 - 2007																					
Male - Hommes	77.6	72.9	67.9	63.0	58.0	53.3	48.5	43.7	39.0	34.3	29.8	25.4	21.3	17.6	14.1	10.9	8.1	5.7	3.7	0.4	...
Female - Femmes	82.7	78.0	73.0	68.1	63.1	58.2	53.4	48.5	43.6	38.9	34.2	29.6	25.2	20.9	16.9	13.1	9.7	6.8	4.5	2.2	...
Malta - Malte 2007																					
Male - Hommes	77.2	72.8	67.8	62.9	58.0	53.3	48.5	43.7	38.9	34.2	29.4	25.0	20.6	16.6	13.0	9.8	7.2	5.4	...	...	...
Female - Femmes	81.7	77.5	72.8	67.8	62.8	57.9	52.9	48.0	43.2	38.3	33.5	28.9	24.4	20.1	15.9	12.3	9.1	6.6	...	...	...
Netherlands - Pays-Bas 2007																					
Male - Hommes	78.0	73.4	68.5	63.5	58.6	53.7	48.9	44.0	39.2	34.4	29.8	25.3	21.0	17.0	13.3	10.0	7.3	5.1	3.5	2.5	...
Female - Femmes	82.3	77.6	72.7	67.7	62.8	57.8	52.9	48.0	43.1	38.3	33.7	29.1	24.7	20.5	16.4	12.6	9.2	6.4	4.4	3.0	...
Norway - Norvège[25] 2007																					
Male - Hommes	78.2	73.5	68.6	63.6	58.7	54.0	49.2	44.4	39.6	34.8	30.2	25.7	21.4	17.4	13.7	10.3	7.4	5.1	3.5	2.4	1.8
Female - Femmes	82.7	78.0	73.0	68.0	63.1	58.2	53.3	48.4	43.5	38.7	34.0	29.4	24.9	20.6	16.5	12.7	9.2	6.4	4.3	2.8	1.9
Poland - Pologne 2007																					
Male - Hommes	71.0	66.5	61.6	56.6	51.8	47.1	42.4	37.7	33.2	28.8	24.8	21.1	17.7	14.6	11.7	9.1	7.0	5.2	...	...	...
Female - Femmes	79.7	75.2	70.3	65.3	60.4	55.5	50.6	45.7	40.9	36.1	31.6	27.2	22.9	18.9	15.0	11.4	8.4	6.0	...	...	...
Portugal 2005 - 2007																					
Male - Hommes	75.2	70.5	65.6	60.6	55.8	51.0	46.3	41.6	37.0	32.5	28.2	24.0	20.0	16.1	12.5	9.2	6.4	4.0	2.5	1.6	1.0
Female - Femmes	81.6	76.9	71.9	67.0	62.0	57.1	52.2	47.3	42.5	37.7	33.1	28.4	23.9	19.5	15.3	11.3	7.8	4.9	3.0	1.8	1.1
Republic of Moldova - République de Moldova 2007																					
Male - Hommes	65.0	61.1	56.2	51.3	46.5	41.8	37.2	32.8	28.5	24.6	21.0	17.7	14.8	11.9	9.7	7.7	6.1	4.7	3.7	2.4	...
Female - Femmes	72.6	68.6	63.7	58.8	53.9	49.0	44.2	39.4	34.8	30.2	25.8	21.7	18.0	14.4	11.3	8.7	6.5	5.0	3.6	2.5	...
Romania - Roumanie 2005 - 2007																					
Male - Hommes	69.2	65.5	60.6	55.7	50.9	46.1	41.3	36.6	32.1	27.7	23.8	20.1	16.7	13.6	10.8	8.3	6.1	4.5	3.3	2.4	1.8
Female - Femmes	76.1	72.3	67.4	62.5	57.6	52.7	47.8	42.9	38.1	33.5	29.0	24.6	20.4	16.4	12.7	9.5	6.7	4.7	3.3	2.3	1.6
Russian Federation - Fédération de Russie 2007																					
Male - Hommes	61.4	57.2	52.3	47.4	42.8	38.4	34.5	30.7	26.9	23.3	19.9	16.9	14.1	11.7	9.5	7.5	6.0	4.8	3.6	2.9	1.4
Female - Femmes	73.9	69.7	64.7	59.8	55.0	50.3	45.6	41.0	36.5	32.1	27.8	23.6	19.7	16.0	12.4	9.4	6.8	4.9	3.4	2.5	1.8

Continent, country or area and date / Continent, pays ou zone et date	At birth - A la naissance	5	10	15	20	25	30	35	40	45	50	55	60	65	70	75	80	85	90	95	100
EUROPE																					
San Marino - Saint-Marin 2000																					
Male - Hommes	77.4	73.0	68.0	63.1	58.5	53.8	49.1	44.3	39.5	34.7	30.1	25.6	21.4	17.2	13.5	10.5	7.7	5.7	3.8	2.3	0.5
Female - Femmes	84.0	79.6	74.6	69.6	64.7	59.7	54.8	49.9	45.0	40.2	35.4	30.7	26.0	21.6	17.1	13.1	9.3	6.3	4.3	2.7	0.5
Serbia - Serbie 2007																					
Male - Hommes	70.7	66.4	61.4	56.5	51.6	46.9	42.2	37.5	32.8	28.3	24.0	20.2	16.6	13.3	10.4	8.0	5.9	4.2	...	...	...
Female - Femmes	76.2	71.7	66.7	61.8	56.8	51.9	47.0	42.1	37.3	32.6	28.0	23.6	19.4	15.5	11.8	8.7	6.3	4.4	...	...	...
Slovakia - Slovaquie 2007																					
Male - Hommes	70.5	66.1	61.1	56.2	51.4	46.6	41.8	37.0	32.4	28.0	23.9	20.1	16.6	13.4	10.6	8.0	5.9	4.1	2.8	1.8	0.7
Female - Femmes	78.1	73.6	68.7	63.7	58.8	53.9	49.0	44.1	39.3	34.6	30.0	25.5	21.2	17.1	13.2	9.7	6.8	4.4	2.7	1.6	0.7
Slovenia - Slovénie 2006 - 2007																					
Male - Hommes	75.0	70.3	65.3	60.4	55.5	50.8	46.1	41.4	36.6	32.1	27.8	23.7	19.9	16.4	13.1	10.1	7.7	5.7	3.9	2.8	1.0
Female - Femmes	82.3	77.6	72.6	67.7	62.8	57.9	52.9	48.0	43.1	38.3	33.6	29.1	24.7	20.4	16.3	12.5	9.1	6.5	4.5	3.2	1.0
Spain - Espagne 2004 - 2005																					
Male - Hommes	77.0	72.4	67.4	62.5	57.6	52.8	48.0	43.2	38.5	33.9	29.5	25.2	21.1	17.2	13.6	10.4	7.6	5.4	3.7	2.1	0.5
Female - Femmes	83.5	78.8	73.9	68.9	64.0	59.1	54.1	49.2	44.4	39.6	34.8	30.2	25.6	21.1	16.8	12.8	9.3	6.4	4.2	2.3	0.5
Sweden - Suède 2007																					
Male - Hommes	78.9	74.2	69.2	64.3	59.4	54.6	49.8	44.9	40.1	35.4	30.7	26.2	21.9	17.8	14.1	10.6	7.7	5.3	3.6	2.6	1.9
Female - Femmes	83.0	78.3	73.3	68.3	63.4	58.5	53.5	48.6	43.7	38.9	34.1	29.5	25.0	20.7	16.6	12.7	9.3	6.4	4.4	3.1	2.2
Switzerland - Suisse 2007																					
Male - Hommes	79.2	74.6	69.7	64.7	59.9	55.1	50.2	45.4	40.6	35.9	31.2	26.7	22.5	18.4	14.6	11.2	8.2	5.8	4.2	3.4	...
Female - Femmes	84.1	79.5	74.5	69.5	64.6	59.7	54.8	49.9	45.0	40.1	35.4	30.8	26.3	21.9	17.6	13.7	10.0	7.0	4.9	3.8	...
The Former Yugoslav Republic of Macedonia - L'ex-République yougoslave de Macédoine 2006																					
Male - Hommes	71.7	67.7	62.7	57.8	52.9	48.1	43.3	38.5	33.7	29.1	24.7	20.7	16.9	13.4	10.3	7.6	5.5	3.8	2.8	2.4	...
Female - Femmes	75.9	71.8	66.8	61.9	56.9	52.0	47.1	42.2	37.4	32.6	28.0	23.6	19.3	15.2	11.5	8.4	5.8	4.1	3.3	2.4	...
Ukraine 2006 - 2007																					
Male - Hommes	62.5	58.5	53.6	48.7	43.9	39.4	35.1	31.1	27.2	23.7	20.3	17.3	14.5	11.9	9.6	7.6	5.9	4.5	3.2	2.2	0.8
Female - Femmes	74.2	70.1	65.2	60.2	55.4	50.5	45.8	41.2	36.7	32.3	27.9	23.7	19.8	16.0	12.5	9.4	6.8	4.9	3.4	2.3	0.8
United Kingdom of Great Britain and Northern Ireland - Royaume-Uni de Grande-Bretagne et d'Irlande du Nord[26] 2000																					
Male - Hommes	75.3	70.9	65.9	61.0	56.1	51.4	46.6	41.9	37.1	32.5	27.9	23.6	19.5	15.7	12.3	9.4	7.0	5.0	3.7	2.7	2.0
Female - Femmes	80.1	75.6	70.6	65.7	60.8	55.9	51.0	46.1	41.2	36.5	31.8	27.3	23.0	18.8	15.0	11.5	8.6	6.1	4.3	3.0	2.2
OCEANIA - OCÉANIE																					
Australia - Australie 2005 - 2007																					
Male - Hommes	79.0	74.5	69.6	64.6	59.7	55.0	50.2	45.5	40.7	36.0	31.4	27.0	22.6	18.5	14.7	11.3	8.3	6.0	4.2	3.1	2.4
Female - Femmes	83.7	79.1	74.2	69.2	64.3	59.4	54.5	49.6	44.7	39.9	35.2	30.5	26.0	21.6	17.4	13.5	10.0	7.1	4.8	3.4	2.6
French Polynesia - Polynésie française 2006																					
Male - Hommes	73.0	68.9	63.9	59.0	54.3	49.5	45.0	40.4	35.8	31.2	26.8	22.6	18.7	15.1	11.9	8.9	6.5	3.9	...	...	...
Female - Femmes	76.9	72.5	67.6	62.6	57.8	52.9	48.1	43.4	38.7	34.1	29.8	25.4	21.1	17.1	13.6	10.2	7.3	5.5	...	...	...

20. Expectation of life at specified ages for each sex: latest available year, 1998 - 2007
Espérance de vie à un âge donné pour chaque sexe: dernière année disponible, 1998 - 2007 (continued - suite)

Continent, country or area and date / Continent, pays ou zone et date	At birth - A la naissance	5	10	15	20	25	30	35	40	45	50	55	60	65	70	75	80	85	90	95	100
OCEANIA - OCÉANIE																					
Guam 2004																					
Male - Hommes	75.1	...	...	...	...	...	...	...	...	...	...	...	...	...	...	...	...	...	...	...	...
Female - Femmes	81.3	...	...	...	...	...	...	...	...	...	...	...	...	...	...	...	...	...	...	...	...
Kiribati 2005																					
Male - Hommes	58.9	58.2	53.6	48.9	44.4	40.0	35.6	31.3	27.1	23.1	19.4	16.0	13.0	10.4	8.3	6.6	5.3	4.2	...	...	
Female - Femmes	63.1	62.6	57.9	53.1	48.6	44.1	39.7	35.4	31.2	27.1	23.2	19.5	16.1	13.1	10.4	8.1	6.2	4.7	...	...	
Marshall Islands - Îles Marshall 2004																					
Male - Hommes	67.0	...	...	...	...	...	...	...	...	...	...	...	...	...	...	...	...	...	...	...	...
Female - Femmes	70.6	...	...	...	...	...	...	...	...	...	...	...	...	...	...	...	...	...	...	...	...
Nauru 1997 - 2002																					
Male - Hommes	52.5	...	...	...	...	...	...	...	...	...	...	...	...	...	...	...	...	...	...	...	...
Female - Femmes	58.2	...	...	...	...	...	...	...	...	...	...	...	...	...	...	...	...	...	...	...	...
New Caledonia - Nouvelle-Calédonie 2007																					
Male - Hommes	71.8	67.7	62.8	57.9	53.4	48.9	44.4	39.8	35.2	30.7	26.6	...	18.5	...	12.0	...	7.0	...	...	...	
Female - Femmes	80.3	75.8	70.8	65.9	61.0	56.1	51.2	46.5	41.7	37.0	32.3	...	23.4	...	15.1	...	8.7	...	...	...	
New Zealand - Nouvelle-Zélande 2006 - 2008																					
Male - Hommes	78.2	73.8	68.8	63.9	59.1	54.4	49.6	44.9	40.1	35.5	30.9	26.4	22.1	18.1	14.3	11.0	8.1	5.8	4.2	...	...
Female - Femmes	82.2	77.7	72.7	67.8	62.9	58.0	53.1	48.2	43.4	38.7	33.9	29.4	24.9	20.7	16.6	12.9	9.5	6.7	4.5	...	...
Palau - Palaos 2000																					
Male - Hommes	66.6	...	...	...	...	...	...	...	...	...	...	...	...	...	...	...	...	...	...	...	...
Female - Femmes	74.5	...	...	...	...	...	...	...	...	...	...	...	...	...	...	...	...	...	...	...	...
Papua New Guinea - Papouasie-Nouvelle-Guinée 2000																					
Male - Hommes	53.7	54.1	50.2	45.7	41.6	37.7	33.7	29.8	25.9	22.1	18.5	15.0	11.9	9.2	6.9	5.0	3.6	2.6	1.7	0.6	...
Female - Femmes	54.8	54.7	50.8	46.3	42.1	38.1	34.1	30.1	26.2	22.3	18.6	15.2	12.0	9.2	6.8	5.0	3.6	2.5	1.6	0.6	...
Tonga 2006																					
Male - Hommes	67.3	64.1	59.3	54.5	49.9	45.4	40.7	36.2	31.6	27.2	23.4	19.4	15.9	13.0	9.4	6.3	4.0	...	...	...	
Female - Femmes	73.0	69.3	64.6	59.8	55.0	50.1	45.2	40.4	35.7	31.3	27.1	23.0	19.0	15.3	11.6	8.6	6.1	...	...	...	
Tuvalu 1997 - 2002																					
Male - Hommes	61.7	59.5	54.8	50.0	45.2	40.6	35.9	32.1	28.0	24.1	20.0	17.1	13.7	10.8	9.0	6.9	5.4	...	...	...	
Female - Femmes	65.1	62.6	57.7	53.7	50.0	45.3	40.9	36.6	32.2	28.1	23.8	20.3	16.9	13.2	10.6	7.9	6.4	...	...	...	
Vanuatu 1999																					
Male - Hommes	65.6	...	...	...	...	...	...	...	...	...	...	...	...	...	...	...	...	...	...	...	...
Female - Femmes	69.0	...	...	...	...	...	...	...	...	...	...	...	...	...	...	...	...	...	...	...	...

FOOTNOTES - NOTES

[1] Data refer to Algerian population only. - Les données ne concernent que la population algérienne.

[2] Data refer to national projections. - Les données se réfèrent aux projections nationales.

[3] Data are based on a small number of deaths and therefore vary from year to year. - Les données sont basées sur un nombre limité de décès et par conséquent varient d'année en année.

[4] Data refer to projections based on the 1992 population census. - Les données se réfèrent aux projections basées sur le recensement de la population de 1992.

[5] Excluding Indian jungle population. - Non compris les Indiens de la jungle.

[6] Data refer to projections based on the 2005 population census. - Les données se réfèrent aux projections basées sur le recensement de la population de 2005.

[7] Excluding nomadic Indian tribes. - Non compris les tribus d'Indiens nomades.

[8] Provisional - Données provisoires.

[9] Life expectancy in 2000 is calculated by the death data of 2000's Population Census, which modified by the mortality rates from the annual national sample surveys on population changes since 1990 . For statistical purposes, the data for China do not include those for the Hong Kong Special Administrative Region (Hong Kong SAR), Macao Special Administrative Region (Macao SAR) and Taiwan province of China. - L'espérance de vie en 2000 par est calculée en se fondant sur les données relatives aux décès issues du recensement de la population de 2000 modifiées par les taux de mortalité extraits des enquêtes nationales annuelles par sondage concernant l'évolution de la population depuis 1990. Pour la présentation des statistiques, les données pour la Chine ne comprennent pas la Région Administrative Spéciale de Hong Kong (Hong Kong RAS), la Région Administrative Spéciale de Macao (Macao RAS) et Taïwan province de Chine.

[10] Data refer to government controlled areas. - Les données se rapportent aux zones contrôlées par le Gouvernement.

[11] Including data for the Indian-held part of Jammu and Kashmir, the final status of which has not yet been determined. - Y compris les données pour la partie du Jammu et du Cachemire occupée par l'Inde dont le statut définitif n'a pas encore été déterminé.

[12] Including data for East Jerusalem and Israeli residents in certain other territories under occupation by Israeli military forces since June 1967. - Y compris les données pour Jérusalem-Est et les résidents israéliens dans certains autres territoires occupés depuis 1967 par les forces armées israéliennes.

[13] Data refer to Japanese nationals in Japan only. - Les données se raportent aux nationaux japonais au Japon seulement.

[14] Excluding data for Jordanian territory under occupation since June 1967 by Israeli military forces. Excluding foreigners, including registered Palestinian refugees. - Non compris les données pour le territoire jordanien occupé depuis juin 1967 par les forces armées israéliennes. Non compris les étrangers, mais y compris les réfugiés de Palestine enregistrés.

[15] Based on the results of the 2005 Population and Housing Census. - Données fondées sur les résultats du recensement de la population et de l'habitat de 2005.

[16] Data refer to urban areas only. - Données ne concernant que les zones urbaines.

[17] Excluding data for the Pakistan-held part of Jammu and Kashmir, the final status of which has not yet been determined. - Non compris les données concernant la partie du Jammu et Cachemire occupée par le Pakistan dont le statut définitif n'a pas été déterminé.

[18] Based on the results of the Pakistan Demographic Survey (PDS 2003). - Données extraites de l'enquête démographique effectuée par le Pakistan en 2003.

[19] Based on the results of the Pakistan Demographic Survey (PDS 2005). - Données extraites de l'enquête démographique effectuée par le Pakistan en 2005.

[20] Based on the results of the Population Demographic Survey. - D'après les résultats de la Population Demographic Survey.

[21] Also included in Finland. - Comprise aussi dans Finlande.

[22] Excluding Faeroe Islands and Greenland shown separately, if available. - Non compris les Iles Féroé et le Gröenland, qui font l'objet de rubriques distinctes, si disponible.

[23] Including Aland Islands. - Y compris les Îles d'Åland.

[24] Excluding Overseas Departments, namely, French Guiana, Guadeloupe, Martinique and Reunion, shown separately, if available. - Non compris les départements d'outre mer, c'est-à-dire la Guyane française, la Guadeloupe, la Martinique et la Réunion, qui font l'objet de rubriques distinctes, si disponible.

[25] Excluding Svalbard and Jan Mayen Island shown separately, if available. - Non compris Svalbard et Jan Mayen qui font l'objet de rubriques distinctes, si disponible.

[26] Excluding Channel Islands (Guernsey and Jersey) and Isle of Man, shown separately, if available. - Non compris les îles Anglo-Normandes (Guernesey et Jersey) et l'île de Man, qui font l'objet de rubriques distinctes, si disponible.

Table 21

Table 21 presents number of marriages and crude marriage rates by urban/rural residence for every year with available data between 2003 and 2007.

Description of variables: Marriage is defined as the act, ceremony or process by which the legal relationship of husband and wife is constituted. The legality of the union may be established by civil, religious or other means as recognized by the laws of each country[1].

Marriage statistics in this table, therefore, include both first marriages and remarriages after divorce, widowhood or annulment. They do not, unless otherwise noted, include resumption of marriage ties after legal separation. These statistics refer to the number of marriages performed, and not to the number of persons marrying.

Statistics shown are obtained from civil registers of marriage. Exceptions, such as data from church registers, are identified in footnotes.

The urban/rural classification of marriages is that provided by each country or area; it is presumed to be based on the national census definitions of urban population which have been set forth at the end of the technical notes for table 6.

For certain countries, there is a discrepancy between the total number of marriages shown in this table and those shown in subsequent tables for the same year. Usually this discrepancy arises because the total number of marriages occurring in a given year is revised although the remaining tabulations are not.

Rate computation: Crude marriage rates are the annual number of marriages per 1 000 mid-year population. Rates by urban/rural residence are the annual number of marriages, in the appropriate urban or rural category, per 1 000 corresponding mid-year population. Rates presented in this table have been limited to those for countries or areas having at least a total of 30 marriages in a given year. These rates are calculated by the Statistics Division of the United Nations based on the appropriate reference population (for example: total population, nationals only etc.) if known and available. If the reference population is not known or unavailable the total population is used to calculate the rates. Therefore, if the population that is used to calculate the rates is different from the correct reference population, the rates presented might under- or overstate the true situation in a country or area.

Reliability of data: Each country or area has been asked to indicate the estimated completeness of the number of marriages recorded in its civil register. These national assessments are indicated by the quality codes "C" and "U" that appear in the first column of this table.

"C" indicates that the data are estimated to be virtually complete, that is, representing at least 90 per cent of the marriages occurring each year, while "U" indicates that data are estimated to be incomplete, that is, representing less than 90 per cent of the marriages occurring each year. The code "..." indicates that no information was provided regarding completeness.

Data from civil registers which are reported as incomplete or of unknown completeness (coded "U" or "...") are considered unreliable. They appear in italics in this table; rates are not computed for these data.

These quality codes apply only to data from civil registers. For more information about the quality of vital statistics data in general, see section 4.2 of the Technical Notes.

Limitations: Statistics on marriages are subject to the same qualifications that have been set forth for vital statistics in general and marriage statistics in particular as discussed in section 4 of the Technical Notes.

The fact that marriage is a legal event, unlike birth and death that are biological events, has implications for international comparability of data. Marriage has been defined, for statistical purposes, in terms of the laws of individual countries or areas. These laws vary throughout the world. In addition, comparability is further limited because some countries or areas compile statistics only for civil marriages although religious marriages may also be legally recognized; in other countries or areas, the only available records are church registers and, therefore, the statistics may not reflect marriages that are civil marriages only.

Because in many countries or areas marriage is a civil legal contract which, to establish its legality, must be celebrated before a civil officer, it follows that for these countries or areas registration would tend to be almost automatic at the time of, or immediately following, the marriage ceremony. This factor should be kept in mind when considering the reliability of data, described above. For this reason the practice of tabulating data by date of registration does not generally pose serious problems of comparability as it does in the case of birth and death statistics.

As indicators of family formation, the statistics on the number of marriages presented in this table are bound to be deficient to the extent that they do not include either customary unions, which are not registered even though they are considered legal and binding under customary law, or consensual unions (also known as extra-legal or de facto unions). In general, lower marriage rates over a period of years are an indication of higher incidence of customary or consensual unions.

In addition, rates are affected also by the quality and limitations of the population estimates that are used in their computation. The problems of under-enumeration or over-enumeration and, to some extent, the differences in definition of total population have been discussed in section 3 of the Technical Notes dealing with population data in general, and specific information pertaining to individual countries or areas is given in the footnotes to table 3.

Strict correspondence between the numerator of the rate and the denominator is not always obtained; for example, marriages among civilian and military segments of the population may be related to civilian population. The effect of this may be to increase the rates, but, in most cases, this effect is negligible.

It should be emphasized that crude marriage rates like crude birth, death and divorce rates, may be seriously affected by the age-sex-marital structure of the population to which they relate. Crude marriage rates do, however, provide a simple measure of the level and changes in marriage.

The comparability of data by urban/rural residence is affected by the national definitions of urban and rural used in tabulating these data. It is assumed, in the absence of specific information to the contrary, that the definitions of urban and rural used in connection with the national population census were also used in the compilation of the vital statistics for each country or area. However, it cannot be excluded that, for a given country or area, different definitions of urban and rural are used for the vital statistics data and the population census data respectively. When known, the definitions of urban in national population censuses are presented at the end of the technical notes for table 6. As discussed in detail in the notes, these definitions vary considerably from one country or area to another.

In addition to problems of comparability, marriage rates classified by urban/rural residence are also subject to certain special types of bias. If, when calculating marriage rates, different definitions of urban are used in connection with the vital events and the population data, and if this results in a net difference between the numerator and denominator of the rate in the population at risk, then the marriage rates would be biased. Urban/rural differentials in marriage rates may also be affected by whether the vital events have been tabulated in terms of place of occurrence or place of usual residence. This problem is discussed in more detail in section 4.1.4.1 of the Technical Notes.

Earlier data: Marriages and crude marriage rates have been shown in each issue of the *Demographic Yearbook*. For more information on specific topics, and years for which data are reported, readers should consult the Historical Index.

NOTES

[1] *Principles and Recommendations for a Vital Statistics System Revision 2*, Sales No. E. 01.XVII.10, United Nations, New York, 2001

Tableau 21

Le tableau 21 présente des données sur les mariages et les taux bruts de nuptialité selon le lieu de résidence (zone urbaine ou rurale) pour les années où l'information est disponible entre 2003 et 2007.

Description des variables : le mariage désigne l'acte, la cérémonie ou la procédure qui établit un rapport légal entre mari et femme. L'union peut être rendue légale par une procédure civile ou religieuse, ou par toute autre procédure, conformément à la législation du pays[1].

Les statistiques de la nuptialité présentées dans ce tableau comprennent donc les premiers mariages et les remariages faisant suite à un divorce, un veuvage ou une annulation. Toutefois, sauf indication contraire, elles ne comprennent pas les unions reconstituées après une séparation légale. Ces statistiques se rapportent au nombre de mariages célébrés, non au nombre de personnes qui se marient.

Les statistiques présentées reposent sur l'enregistrement des mariages par les services de l'état civil. Les exceptions (données provenant des registres des églises, par exemple) font l'objet d'une note à la fin du tableau.

La classification des mariages selon le lieu de résidence (zone urbaine ou rurale) est celle qui a été communiquée par chaque pays ou zone ; on part du principe qu'elle repose sur les définitions de la population urbaine utilisées pour les recensements nationaux telles qu'elles sont reproduites à la fin des notes techniques se rapportant au tableau 6.

Pour quelques pays il y a une discordance entre le nombre total de mariages présenté dans ce tableau et ceux présentés après pour la même année. Habituellement ces différences apparaissent lorsque le nombre total des mariages pour une certaine année a été révisé alors que les autres tabulations ne l'ont pas été.

Calcul des taux : les taux bruts de nuptialité représentent le nombre annuel de mariages pour 1 000 habitants au milieu de l'année. Les taux selon le lieu de résidence (zone urbaine ou rurale) représentent le nombre annuel de mariages, classés selon la catégorie urbaine ou rurale appropriée, pour 1 000 habitants au milieu de l'année. Les taux du tableau 21 ne se rapportent qu'aux pays ou zones où l'on a enregistré un total d'au moins 30 mariages pendant une année donnée. Ces taux sont calculés par la division de statistique des Nations Unies sur la base de la population de référence adéquate (par exemple : population totale, nationaux seulement, etc.) si connue et disponible. Si la population de référence n'est pas connue ou n'est pas disponible, la population totale est utilisée pour calculer les taux. Par conséquent, si la population utilisée pour calculer les taux est différente de la population de référence adéquate, les taux présentés sont susceptibles de sous ou sur estimer la situation réelle d'un pays ou d'un territoire.

Fiabilité des données : il a été demandé à chaque pays ou zone d'indiquer le degré estimatif de complétude des données sur les mariages figurant dans ses registres d'état civil. Ces évaluations nationales sont signalées par les codes de qualité "C" et "U" qui apparaissent dans la deuxième colonne du tableau.

La lettre "C" indique que les données sont jugées à peu près complètes, c'est-à-dire qu'elles représentent au moins 90 p. 100 des mariages survenus chaque année ; la lettre "U" signale que les données sont jugées incomplètes, c'est-à-dire qu'elles représentent moins de 90 p. 100 des mariages survenus chaque année. Le code "..." indique qu'aucun renseignement n'a été communiqué quant à la complétude des données.

Les données issues des registres de l'état civil qui sont déclarées incomplètes ou dont le degré de complétude n'est pas connu (code "U" ou "...") sont jugées douteuses. Elles apparaissent en italique dans le tableau et les taux correspondants n'ont pas été calculés.

Les codes de qualité ne s'appliquent qu'aux données provenant des registres de l'état civil. Pour plus de précisions sur la qualité des données reposant sur les statistiques de l'état civil en général, voir la section 4.2 des Notes techniques.

NOTE

[1] *Principes et recommandations pour un système de statistiques de l'état civil, deuxième révision*, numéro de vente : F.01.XVII.10, publication des Nations Unies, New York, 2003.

Insuffisance des données : les statistiques relatives aux mariages appellent les mêmes réserves que celles qui ont été formulées à propos des statistiques de l'état civil en général et des statistiques concernant la nuptialité en particulier (voir la section 4 des Notes techniques).

Le fait que le mariage soit un acte juridique, à la différence de la naissance et du décès, qui sont des faits biologiques, a des répercussions sur la comparabilité internationale des données. Aux fins de la statistique, le mariage est défini par la législation de chaque pays ou zone. Cette législation varie d'un pays à l'autre. La comparabilité est limitée en outre du fait que certains pays ou zones ne réunissent des statistiques que pour les mariages civils, bien que les mariages religieux y soient également reconnus par la loi ; dans d'autres, les seuls relevés disponibles sont les registres des églises et, en conséquence, les statistiques peuvent ne pas rendre compte des mariages exclusivement civils.

Étant donné que, dans de nombreux pays ou zones, le mariage est un contrat juridique civil qui, pour être légal, doit être conclu devant un officier d'état civil, il s'ensuit que dans ces pays ou zones l'enregistrement se fait à peu près systématiquement au moment de la cérémonie ou immédiatement après. Il faut tenir compte de cet élément lorsque l'on évalue la fiabilité des données, dont il est question plus haut. C'est pourquoi la pratique consistant à exploiter les données selon la date de l'enregistrement ne pose généralement pas les graves problèmes de comparabilité auxquels on se heurte dans le cas des statistiques concernant les naissances et les décès.

Les statistiques relatives au nombre des mariages présentées dans ce tableau donnent une idée forcément trompeuse de la formation des familles, dans la mesure où elles ne tiennent compte ni des mariages coutumiers, qui ne sont pas enregistrés bien qu'ils soient considérés comme légaux et créateurs d'obligations en vertu du droit coutumier, ni des unions consensuelles (appelées également unions non légalisées ou unions de fait). En général, une diminution du taux de nuptialité pendant un certain nombre d'années indique une augmentation des mariages coutumiers ou des unions consensuelles.

L'exactitude des taux dépend également de la qualité et des insuffisances des estimations de population qui sont utilisées pour leur calcul. Le problème des erreurs par excès ou par défaut commises lors du dénombrement et, dans une certaine mesure, le problème de l'hétérogénéité des définitions de la population totale ont été examinés à la section 3 des Notes techniques relative à la population en général ; des indications concernant les différents pays ou zones sont données en note à la fin du tableau 3.

Il n'a pas toujours été possible d'obtenir une correspondance rigoureuse entre le numérateur et le dénominateur pour le calcul des taux. Par exemple, les mariages parmi la population civile et les militaires sont parfois rapportés à la population civile. Cela peut avoir pour effet d'accroître les taux, mais, dans la plupart des cas, il est probable que la différence sera négligeable.

Il faut souligner que les taux bruts de nuptialité, de même que les taux bruts de natalité, de mortalité et de divortialité, peuvent varier sensiblement selon la structure par âge et par sexe de la population à laquelle ils se rapportent. Les taux bruts de nuptialité offrent néanmoins un moyen simple de mesurer la fréquence et l'évolution des mariages.

La comparabilité des données selon le lieu de résidence (zone urbaine ou rurale) peut être limitée par les définitions nationales des termes « urbain » et « rural » utilisées pour le classement de ces données. En l'absence d'indications contraires, on a supposé que les mêmes définitions avaient servi pour le recensement national de la population et pour l'établissement des statistiques de l'état civil pour chaque pays ou zone. Toutefois, il n'est pas exclu que, pour une zone ou un pays donné, des définitions différentes aient été retenues. Les définitions du terme « urbain » utilisées pour les recensements nationaux de population ont été présentées à la fin des notes techniques du tableau 6 lorsqu'elles étaient connues. Comme on l'a précisé dans les notes techniques relatives au tableau 6, ces définitions varient considérablement d'un pays ou d'une zone à l'autre.

Outre les problèmes de comparabilité, les taux de nuptialité classés selon le lieu de résidence (zone urbaine ou rurale) sont également sujets à des distorsions particulières. Si l'on utilise des définitions différentes du terme « urbain » pour classer les faits d'état civil et les données relatives à la population lors du calcul des taux et qu'il en résulte une différence nette entre le numérateur et le dénominateur et le taux de la population exposée au risque, les taux de nuptialité s'en trouveront faussés. La différence entre ces taux pour les zones urbaines et rurales pourra aussi être faussée selon que les faits d'état civil auront été classés d'après le lieu où ils se sont produits ou d'après le lieu de résidence habituel. Ce problème est examiné plus en détail à la section 4.1.4.1 des Notes techniques.

Données publiées antérieurement : les différentes éditions de *l'Annuaire démographique* regroupent des données sur le nombre des mariages. Pour plus de précisions concernant les années et les sujets pour lesquels des données ont été publiées, se reporter à l'index historique.

21. Marriages and crude marriage rates, by urban/rural residence: 2003 - 2007
Mariages et taux bruts de nuptialité, selon la résidence, urbaine/rurale: 2003 - 2007

Continent, country or area, and urban/rural residence / Continent, pays ou zone et résidence, urbaine/rurale	Code[a]	Number - Nombre					Rate - Taux				
		2003	2004	2005	2006	2007	2003	2004	2005	2006	2007
AFRICA - AFRIQUE											
Algeria - Algérie[1]											
Total..................	...	240 463	267 633	279 548	295 295	325 485	...	...	...	...	...
Egypt - Égypte[2]											
Total..................	+...	537 092	550 709	522 751	522 887	614 848	...	...	...	...	...
Urban - Urbaine	+...	185 880	175 361	170 556	168 323	204 910	...	...	...	...	...
Rural - Rurale	+...	351 212	375 348	352 195	354 564	409 938	...	...	...	...	...
Mauritius - Maurice											
Total..................	+C	10 812	11 385	11 294	11 471	11 547	8.8	9.2	9.1	9.2	9.2
Urban - Urbaine	+C	3 298	3 422	3 551	3 468	3 483	6.4	6.6	6.8	6.6	6.6
Rural - Rurale	+C	7 514	7 963	7 743	8 003	8 064	10.7	11.2	10.8	11.0	11.0
Réunion											
Total..................	C	3 147	3 169	3 069	2 982	2 899	4.2	4.1	3.9	3.8	3.6
Saint Helena ex. dep. - Sainte-Hélène sans dép.											
Total..................	C	20	10	10	10	15	...	...	...	...	...
Seychelles[3]											
Total..................	+C	823	905	886	984	1 081	9.9	11.0	10.7	11.6	12.7
South Africa - Afrique du Sud											
Total..................	...	178 689	176 521	180 657	184 860	183 030	...	...	...	...	...
Tunisia - Tunisie											
Total..................	...	63 676	68 976	73 971	81 340	76 809	...	...	...	...	...
AMERICA, NORTH - AMÉRIQUE DU NORD											
Anguilla[4]											
Total..................	C	75	70	89	74	43	6.1	5.6	6.5	5.2	2.9
Aruba[5]											
Total..................	C	663	606	715	546	531	7.0	6.2	7.1	5.3	5.1
Bahamas											
Total..................	C	2 039	2 043	1 731	2 599	2 021	6.4	6.4	5.3	7.9	6.1
Bermuda - Bermudes											
Total..................	C	861	868	820	876	...	13.7	13.7	12.9	13.7	...
British Virgin Islands - Îles Vierges britanniques											
Total..................	C	475	426	...	...	...	22.3	19.6	...	...	...
Canada											
Total..................	C	147 391	148 585	148 439	149 792	*151 695	4.7	4.6	4.6	4.6	*4.6
Cayman Islands - Îles Caïmanes											
Total..................	+C	344	337	418	529	482	7.9	7.6	8.6	10.2	8.9
Costa Rica											
Total..................	C	24 448	25 370[6]	25 631[6]	26 575[6]	26 010[6]	6.0	6.1	6.0	6.1	5.9
Urban - Urbaine[6]	C	...	16 194	14 060	14 964	13 868	...	6.6	5.6	5.8	5.3
Rural - Rurale[6]	C	...	9 176	11 571	11 611	12 142	...	5.4	6.6	6.5	6.7
Cuba											
Total..................	C	54 739	50 878	51 831	56 377	56 781[7]	4.9	4.5	4.6	5.0	5.1
Urban - Urbaine	C	50 103	46 655	48 335	52 818	52 155[7]	5.9	5.5	5.7	6.2	6.2
Rural - Rurale	C	4 636	4 223	3 496	3 559	4 626[7]	1.7	1.5	1.3	1.3	1.7
Dominica - Dominique											
Total..................	+C	220	240	264	294	...	3.1	3.4	3.7	4.1	...
Dominican Republic - République dominicaine											
Total..................	+C	37 225	38 642	39 439	42 289	39 903	4.2	4.2	4.3	4.5	4.2
El Salvador											
Total..................	...	24 972	25 172	24 396	24 441	28 568[8]	...	...	...	...	...
Urban - Urbaine	...	20 836	20 828	20 449	20 659	24 698[8]	...	...	...	...	...
Rural - Rurale	...	4 136	4 344	3 947	3 782	3 870[8]	...	...	...	...	...
Guadeloupe											
Total..................	C	1 701	1 771	1 727	1 736	1 427	3.9	4.0	3.9	3.8	3.5
Guatemala											
Total..................	C	51 247	53 860	52 186	57 505	...	4.2	4.3	4.1	4.4	...
Jamaica - Jamaïque											
Total..................	C	22 476	21 670	25 937	23 181	22 854	8.6	8.2	9.8	8.7	8.5

21. Marriages and crude marriage rates, by urban/rural residence: 2003 - 2007
Mariages et taux bruts de nuptialité, selon la résidence, urbaine/rurale: 2003 - 2007 (continued - suite)

Continent, country or area, and urban/rural residence / Continent, pays ou zone et résidence, urbaine/rurale	Code[a]	Number - Nombre					Rate - Taux				
		2003	2004	2005	2006	2007	2003	2004	2005	2006	2007
AMERICA, NORTH - AMÉRIQUE DU NORD											
Martinique — Total	C	1 440	1 425	1 453	1 477	1 341	3.7	3.6	3.7	3.7	3.4
Urban - Urbaine[9]	C	1 215	1 195	1 186	...	1 122	...	...	...	...	...
Rural - Rurale[9]	C	126	124	141	...	137	...	...	...	...	...
Mexico - Mexique — Total	+C	584 142	600 563	595 713	586 978	595 209	5.7	5.8	5.7	5.6	5.6
Urban - Urbaine[10]	+C	436 825	447 840	446 557	445 475	450 665	5.7	5.7	5.6	5.5	5.5
Rural - Rurale[10]	+C	132 873	134 918	132 052	126 157	126 566	5.4	5.5	5.4	5.2	5.3
Netherlands Antilles - Antilles néerlandaises[11] — Total	C	748	710	901	1 104	...	4.2	4.0	4.9	5.8	...
Nicaragua — Total	+U	21 390	18 679	23 069	23 320	20 918	...	...	...	...	...
Panama — Total	C	10 310	10 290	*10 512	10 747	11 516	3.3	3.2	*3.3	3.3	3.4
Urban - Urbaine	C	8 622	8 617	*8 845	9 033	9 584	...	...	*4.3	4.3	...
Rural - Rurale	C	1 688	1 673	*1 667	1 714	1 932	...	...	*1.4	1.4	...
Puerto Rico - Porto Rico — Total	C	25 236	23 650	23 511	23 185	...	6.5	6.1	6.0	5.9	...
Saint Lucia - Sainte-Lucie — Total	C	540	*459	...	...	...	3.4	*2.8	...	...	...
Saint Vincent and the Grenadines - Saint-Vincent-et-les Grenadines — Total	+C	491	526	576	...	...	4.7	5.0	5.6	...	...
Trinidad and Tobago - Trinité-et-Tobago — Total	C	7 440	7 889	8 144	...	...	5.8	6.1	6.3	...	...
Turks and Caicos Islands - Îles Turques et Caïques — Total	C	491	499	489	636	468	19.5	18.1	16.0	19.2	13.4
United States of America - États-Unis d'Amérique — Total	C	2 245 000	2 279 000	2 249 000	2 193 000	2 205 000	7.7	7.8	7.6	7.3	7.3
United States Virgin Islands - Îles Vierges américaines — Total	C	4 006	3 910	...	...	...	36.7	35.8	...	...	...
AMERICA, SOUTH - AMÉRIQUE DU SUD											
Argentina - Argentine — Total	C	129 049	128 212	132 720	134 496	136 437	3.4	3.4	3.4	3.5	3.5
Bolivia (Plurinational State of) - Bolivie (État plurinational de) — Total	U	25 816	36 349	27 179	35 608	*18 072	...	...	...	...	...
Brazil - Brésil[12] — Total	U	748 981	806 968	835 846	889 828	916 006	...	...	...	...	...
Chile - Chili — Total	+C	56 659	53 403	53 842	58 155	...	3.6	3.3	3.3	3.5	...
Urban - Urbaine[13]	+C	51 265	50 181	48 603	52 001	...	3.7	3.6	3.4	3.6	...
Rural - Rurale[13]	+C	5 394	3 222	5 239	6 154	...	2.6	1.5	2.4	2.8	...
Ecuador - Équateur[14] — Total	U	65 393	63 299	66 612	74 036	76 154	...	...	...	...	...
French Guiana - Guyane française — Total	C	508	539	596	629	667	2.8	2.9	3.0	3.2	3.1
Paraguay — Total	U	17 717	17 763	19 826	19 476	...	...	...	...	...	...
Peru - Pérou — Total	+C	81 129	80 646	82 277	89 162	117 551	3.0	2.9	3.0	3.2	4.1
Suriname — Total	C	1 936	1 951	2 013	2 144	2 161	4.0	4.0	4.0	4.3	4.2

Continent, country or area, and urban/rural residence / Continent, pays ou zone et résidence, urbaine/rurale	Code[a]	Number - Nombre					Rate - Taux				
		2003	2004	2005	2006	2007	2003	2004	2005	2006	2007
AMERICA, SOUTH - AMÉRIQUE DU SUD											
Uruguay Total	C	14 147	13 123	13 075	12 415	12 771	4.3	4.0	4.0	3.7	3.8
Venezuela (Bolivarian Republic of) - Venezuela (République bolivarienne du)[12] Total	C	74 562	74 103	86 093	89 772	93 003	2.9	2.8	3.2	3.3	3.4
ASIA - ASIE											
Armenia - Arménie Total	C	15 463	16 975	16 624	16 887	18 145	4.8	5.3	5.2	5.2	5.6
Urban - Urbaine	C	10 174	11 164	10 975	11 139	12 058	4.9	5.4	5.3	5.4	5.8
Rural - Rurale	C	5 289	5 811	5 649	5 748	6 087	4.6	5.0	4.9	5.0	5.3
Azerbaijan - Azerbaïdjan Total	+C	56 091	62 177	71 643	79 443	81 758	6.8	7.5	8.5	9.4	9.5
Urban - Urbaine	+C	26 935	30 873	35 593	39 345	41 814	6.3	7.2	8.2	9.0	9.4
Rural - Rurale	+C	29 156	31 304	36 050	40 098	39 944	7.3	7.8	8.9	9.8	9.6
Bahrain - Bahreïn Total	...	5 373	4 929	4 669	4 717	4 950	...	...	...	...	...
Brunei Darussalam - Brunéi Darussalam Total	...	2 262	2 027	2 258	2 095	2 176	...	...	...	...	...
China - Chine[15] Total	+C	8 114 000	8 671 000	8 231 000	9 450 000	9 914 000	6.3	6.7	6.3	7.2	7.5
China, Hong Kong SAR - Chine, Hong Kong RAS Total	C	35 439	41 376	43 018	50 328	...	5.3	6.1	6.3	7.3	...
China, Macao SAR - Chine, Macao RAS Total	+C	1 309	1 737	1 734	2 100	2 047	3.0	3.8	3.7	4.2	3.9
Cyprus - Chypre[16] Total[5]	C	5 556	5 349	5 881	4 887	...	7.7	7.3	7.8	6.3	...
Urban - Urbaine	C	9 563	4 275	...	...	...	...	...	...	...	...
Rural - Rurale	C	1 247	1 074	...	...	...	...	...	...	...	...
Georgia - Géorgie Total	C	12 696	14 866	18 012	21 845	24 891	2.9	3.4	4.1	5.0	5.7
Urban - Urbaine	C	8 161	10 485	13 119	15 861	18 521	3.6	4.6	5.7	6.9	8.0
Rural - Rurale	C	4 535	4 381	4 893	5 984	6 370	2.2	2.1	2.4	2.9	3.1
Iran (Islamic Republic of) - Iran (République islamique d')[17] Total	C	681 034	723 976	787 671	778 023	841 107	10.1	10.6	11.4	11.0	11.8
Urban - Urbaine	C	522 160	527 337	558 424	556 658	602 309	11.6	11.5	11.9	...	12.2
Rural - Rurale	C	158 874	196 639	229 247	221 365	238 798	7.1	8.8	10.3	...	10.9
Iraq Total	U	...	262 554	...	305 284	268 638	...	...	...	...	...
Israel - Israël[18] Total	C	39 154	39 860	41 029	44 685	...	5.9	5.9	5.9	6.3	...
Japan - Japon[19] Total	+C	740 191	720 417	714 265	730 971	719 822	5.9	5.7	5.7	5.8	5.7
Urban - Urbaine	+C	617 978	606 934	627 290	666 236	659 390	...	...	...	...	...
Rural - Rurale	+C	122 213	113 483	86 975	64 735	60 432	...	...	...	...	...
Jordan - Jordanie[20] Total	+C	48 784	53 754	56 418	59 335	60 548	8.9	10.0	10.3	10.6	10.6
Kazakhstan Total	C	110 414	114 685	123 045	137 204	146 379	7.4	7.6	8.1	9.0	9.5
Urban - Urbaine	C	66 794	69 794	77 074	85 622	85 768	7.9	8.1	8.9	9.8	10.5
Rural - Rurale	C	43 620	44 891	45 971	51 582	60 611	6.8	7.0	7.1	7.9	8.3
Kuwait - Koweït Total	C	12 246	12 359	12 419	12 584	13 315	5.8	5.7	5.5	5.4	5.5
Kyrgyzstan - Kirghizstan Total	C	34 266	34 542	37 321	43 760	44 392	6.8	6.8	7.3	8.4	8.5
Urban - Urbaine	C	9 953	11 039	11 651	12 372	13 426	5.6	6.1	6.4	6.7	7.3
Rural - Rurale	C	24 313	23 503	25 670	31 388	30 966	7.5	7.2	7.7	9.4	9.1

21. Marriages and crude marriage rates, by urban/rural residence: 2003 - 2007
Mariages et taux bruts de nuptialité, selon la résidence, urbaine/rurale: 2003 - 2007 (continued - suite)

Continent, country or area, and urban/rural residence / Continent, pays ou zone et résidence, urbaine/rurale	Code[a]	Number - Nombre					Rate - Taux				
		2003	2004	2005	2006	2007	2003	2004	2005	2006	2007
ASIA - ASIE											
Lebanon - Liban											
Total	C	30 636	30 014	29 705	29 078	35 796	...	8.0	...	...	9.5
Maldives											
Total	...	3 088	3 400	4 932	5 556		...	...	...	...	...
Urban - Urbaine	...	1 376	1 626	2 123	2 514	...	...	...	...	...	...
Rural - Rurale	...	1 712	1 774	2 809	3 042	...	...	...	...	...	...
Mongolia - Mongolie											
Total	C	14 572	11 242	14 993	48 996[21]	40 965	5.9	4.5	5.9	19.0	15.7
Urban - Urbaine	C	8 374	6 195	8 242	31 529[21]	26 043	5.8	4.2	5.4	20.2	16.4
Rural - Rurale	C	6 198	5 047	6 751	17 467[21]	14 922	5.9	4.9	6.6	17.2	14.6
Occupied Palestinian Territory - Territoire palestinien occupé											
Total	C	26 267	27 634	28 876	28 233	32 685	7.9	8.1	8.2	7.8	8.8
Philippines											
Total	U	593 553	582 281	518 595	...	...	...	...	...	...	...
Qatar											
Total	C	2 550	2 649	2 734	3 019	3 206	3.6	3.5	3.1	2.9	2.6
Republic of Korea - République de Corée[22]											
Total[23]	+C	304 932	310 944	316 375	332 752	*345 592	6.3	6.4	6.5	6.8	*7.1
Urban - Urbaine	+C	243 564	244 654	246 987	262 298	...	6.3	6.3	6.3	6.6	...
Rural - Rurale	+C	53 145	53 914	55 029	58 383	...	5.4	5.5	5.7	6.2	...
Saudi Arabia - Arabie saoudite											
Total	...	111 063	105 066	119 294	...	...	...	...	...	...	...
Singapore - Singapour[24]											
Total	+C	21 962	22 189	22 992	23 706	23 966	5.3	5.3	5.4	5.4	5.2
Sri Lanka											
Total	+U	195 914	191 985	194 352	197 458	195 193	...	...	...	...	...
Syrian Arab Republic - République arabe syrienne[25]											
Total	+U	200 986	178 166	179 075	205 557	237 592	...	...	...	...	...
Tajikistan - Tadjikistan											
Total	+C	39 102	47 320	52 352	57 278	97 713	5.9	7.1	7.6	8.2	13.7
Urban - Urbaine	+C	13 059	14 043	14 747	15 952	25 893	7.5	7.9	8.2	8.7	13.8
Rural - Rurale	+C	26 043	33 277	37 605	41 326	71 820	5.4	6.7	7.5	8.0	13.6
Turkey - Turquie[26]											
Total	C	565 468	615 357	641 241	636 121	638 311	8.1	8.6	8.9	8.7	8.6
United Arab Emirates - Émirats arabes unis											
Total	...	12 277	12 794	...	...	...	...	...	...	...	...
Viet Nam											
Total	C	502 916	519 173	506 278	493 383	480 064	6.2	6.3	6.1	5.9	5.6
Urban - Urbaine	C	144 028	145 918	142 301	138 683	134 316	6.9	6.7	6.4	6.1	5.7
Rural - Rurale	C	358 888	373 255	363 977	354 700	345 748	6.0	6.2	6.0	5.8	5.6
EUROPE											
Åland Islands - Îles d'Åland[27]											
Total	C	110	136	112	116	116	4.2	5.1	4.2	4.3	4.3
Urban - Urbaine	C	45	53	51	46	43	4.2	5.0	4.7	4.3	4.0
Rural - Rurale	C	65	83	61	70	73	4.1	5.3	3.8	4.4	4.5
Albania - Albanie											
Total	C	27 342	20 949	21 795	21 332	22 371	8.8	6.7	6.9	6.8	7.1
Urban - Urbaine	C	11 785	9 679	...	...	...	8.6	6.9	...	...	...
Rural - Rurale	C	15 557	11 270	...	...	...	9.0	6.5	...	...	...
Andorra - Andorre											
Total	C	197	218	224	296	258	2.8	2.9	2.8	3.7	3.1
Austria - Autriche[28]											
Total	C	37 195	38 528	39 153	36 923	35 996	4.6	4.7	4.8	4.5	4.3
Belarus - Bélarus											
Total	C	69 905	60 265	73 333	78 979	90 444	7.1	6.1	7.5	8.1	9.3
Urban - Urbaine	C	57 028	49 001	60 114	64 965	74 894	8.1	6.9	8.5	9.2	10.6
Rural - Rurale	C	12 877	11 264	13 219	14 014	15 550	4.5	4.1	4.9	5.3	6.0

21. Marriages and crude marriage rates, by urban/rural residence: 2003 - 2007
Mariages et taux bruts de nuptialité, selon la résidence, urbaine/rurale: 2003 - 2007 (continued - suite)

Continent, country or area, and urban/rural residence / Continent, pays ou zone et résidence, urbaine/rurale	Code[a]	Number - Nombre					Rate - Taux				
		2003	2004	2005	2006	2007	2003	2004	2005	2006	2007
EUROPE											
Belgium - Belgique[29]											
Total	C	41 777	43 296	43 141	44 813	45 561	4.0	4.2	4.1	4.3	4.3
Urban - Urbaine	C	41 176	42 756	42 596	44 231	44 944	4.0	4.2	4.1	4.3	4.3
Rural - Rurale	C	601	540	545	582	617	4.0	3.6	3.6	3.8	4.0
Bosnia and Herzegovina - Bosnie-Herzégovine											
Total	C	20 733	22 252	21 698	21 501	23 494	5.4	5.8	5.6	5.6	...
Bulgaria - Bulgarie[30]											
Total	C	30 645	31 038	33 501	32 773	29 640	3.9	4.0	4.3	4.3	3.9
Urban - Urbaine	C	24 543	24 857	26 658	26 159	23 456	4.5	4.6	4.9	4.8	4.3
Rural - Rurale	C	6 102	6 181	6 843	6 614	6 184	2.6	2.6	3.0	2.9	2.8
Croatia - Croatie											
Total	C	22 337	22 700	22 138	22 092	23 140	5.0	5.1	5.0	5.0	5.2
Urban - Urbaine	C	12 375	12 713	12 326	12 396	12 784	...	...	...	...	...
Rural - Rurale	C	9 962	9 987	9 812	9 696	10 356	...	...	...	...	...
Czech Republic - République tchèque											
Total	C	48 943	51 447	51 829	52 860	57 157	4.8	5.0	5.1	5.1	5.5
Urban - Urbaine	C	37 134	38 999	39 392	40 010	43 175	4.9	5.2	5.2	5.3	5.7
Rural - Rurale	C	11 809	12 448	12 437	12 850	13 982	4.4	4.6	4.6	4.7	5.1
Denmark - Danemark[31]											
Total	C	35 041	37 711	36 148	36 452	36 576	6.5	7.0	6.7	6.7	6.7
Estonia - Estonie											
Total	C	5 699	6 009	6 121	6 954	7 022	4.2	4.5	4.5	5.2	5.2
Urban - Urbaine[32]	C	3 933	4 183	4 341	4 893	4 811	4.2	4.5	4.7	5.3	5.2
Rural - Rurale[32]	C	1 491	1 582	1 533	1 810	1 958	3.6	3.8	3.7	4.4	4.8
Faeroe Islands - Îles Féroé											
Total	C	236	247	252	288	251	4.9	5.1	5.2	6.0	5.2
Finland - Finlande[33]											
Total	C	25 815	29 342	29 283	28 236	29 497	5.0	5.6	5.6	5.4	5.6
Urban - Urbaine	C	18 534	20 957	20 961	20 049	21 453	5.7	6.5	6.4	6.0	6.3
Rural - Rurale	C	7 281	8 385	8 322	8 187	8 044	3.7	4.2	4.2	4.2	4.3
France[34]											
Total	C	275 963	271 598	276 303	267 260	267 194	4.6	4.5	4.5	4.4	4.3
Urban - Urbaine[35]	C	210 905	205 239	206 846	196 863	196 151	...	...	...	...	...
Rural - Rurale[35]	C	59 503	60 768	63 658	63 937	65 407	...	...	...	...	...
Germany - Allemagne											
Total	C	382 911	395 992	388 451	373 681	368 922	4.6	4.8	4.7	4.5	4.5
Gibraltar[36]											
Total	C	179	159	182	161	...	6.3	5.5	6.3	5.5	...
Greece - Grèce											
Total	C	61 081	51 377	61 043	57 802	61 377	5.5	4.6	5.5	5.2	5.5
Urban - Urbaine	C	...	...	43 099	40 536	43 010	...	...	...	...	...
Rural - Rurale	C	...	...	17 944	17 266	18 367	...	...	...	...	...
Hungary - Hongrie											
Total	C	45 398	43 791	44 234	44 528	40 842	4.5	4.3	4.4	4.4	4.1
Urban - Urbaine[37]	C	30 703[38]	29 682	30 759	31 842	29 047	4.7	4.5	4.6	4.7	4.3
Rural - Rurale[37]	C	13 702[38]	12 963	12 471	11 784	11 121	3.8	3.7	3.6	3.5	3.4
Iceland - Islande[5]											
Total	C	1 473	1 515	1 659	1 753	1 708	5.1	5.2	5.6	5.8	5.5
Urban - Urbaine	C	1 400	1 428	1 576	1 681	1 630	5.2	5.3	5.7	6.0	5.6
Rural - Rurale	C	73	87	83	72	78	3.4	4.0	4.0	3.2	3.5
Ireland - Irlande											
Total	+C	*20 302	*20 619	21 355	*21 841	22 544	*5.1	*5.1	5.2	*5.2	5.2
Isle of Man - Île de Man											
Total	C	413	340	404	...	...	5.3	4.4	5.1	...	...
Italy - Italie											
Total	C	264 097	248 969	247 740	245 992	*250 041	4.6	4.3	4.2	4.2	*4.2
Jersey											
Total	+C	632	616	635	607	586	7.2	7.0	7.2	6.8	6.5
Latvia - Lettonie											
Total	C	9 989	10 370	12 544	14 616	15 486	4.3	4.5	5.5	6.4	6.8
Urban - Urbaine	C	7 373	7 664	9 081	10 563	11 020	4.7	4.9	5.8	6.8	7.1
Rural - Rurale	C	2 616	2 706	3 463	4 053	4 466	3.5	3.6	4.7	5.5	6.1
Liechtenstein											
Total	C	149	164	187	151	*182	4.4	4.8	5.4	4.3	*5.2

Continent, country or area, and urban/rural residence — Continent, pays ou zone et résidence, urbaine/rurale	Code[a]	Number - Nombre					Rate - Taux				
		2003	2004	2005	2006	2007	2003	2004	2005	2006	2007
EUROPE											
Lithuania - Lituanie											
Total	C	16 975	19 130	19 938	21 246	23 065	4.9	5.6	5.8	6.3	6.8
Urban - Urbaine	C	12 066	13 239	14 156	14 598	15 905	5.2	5.8	6.2	6.4	7.1
Rural - Rurale	C	4 909	5 891	5 782	6 648	7 160	4.3	5.1	5.1	5.9	6.4
Luxembourg[5]											
Total	C	2 001	1 999	2 032	1 948	1 969	4.4	4.4	4.4	4.1	4.1
Malta - Malte											
Total	C	2 350	2 402	2 374	2 536	2 479	5.9	6.0	5.9	6.2	6.1
Urban - Urbaine	C	...	2 210	...	...	...	...	...	...	...	...
Rural - Rurale	C	...	192	...	...	...	...	...	...	...	...
Monaco											
Total	C	183	171	161	...	...	...	...	...	...	...
Montenegro - Monténégro											
Total	C	4 050	3 440	3 291	3 462	4 005	6.5	5.5	5.3	5.5	6.4
Urban - Urbaine	C	2 962	2 322	...	...	...	7.7	6.0	...	...	...
Rural - Rurale	C	1 088	1 118	...	...	...	4.6	4.8	...	...	...
Netherlands - Pays-Bas[39]											
Total	C	80 427	73 441	72 263	72 369	72 485	5.0	4.5	4.4	4.4	4.4
Urban - Urbaine[38]	C	45 295	42 102	41 555	41 783	42 532	4.3	3.9	3.9	3.9	3.9
Rural - Rurale[38]	C	26 897	24 698	24 276	24 270	24 584	4.7	4.4	4.4	4.4	4.4
Norway - Norvège[40]											
Total	C	22 361	22 354	22 392	21 721	23 471	4.9	4.9	4.8	4.7	5.0
Poland - Pologne											
Total	C	195 446	191 824	206 916	226 181	248 702	5.1	5.0	5.4	5.9	6.5
Urban - Urbaine	C	118 709	116 407	125 630	137 163	150 166	5.0	5.0	5.4	5.9	6.4
Rural - Rurale	C	76 737	75 417	81 286	89 018	98 536	5.2	5.1	5.5	6.0	6.7
Portugal											
Total	C	53 735	49 178	48 671	47 857	46 329	5.1	4.7	4.6	4.5	4.4
Republic of Moldova - République de Moldova											
Total	C	24 961	25 164	27 187	27 128	29 213	6.9	7.0	7.6	7.6	8.2
Urban - Urbaine	C	11 520	11 160	12 553	13 174	14 622	7.8	7.6	8.5	8.9	9.9
Rural - Rurale	C	13 441	14 004	14 634	13 954	14 591	6.3	6.6	6.9	6.6	6.9
Romania - Roumanie											
Total	C	133 953	143 304	141 832	146 637	189 240	6.2	6.6	6.6	6.8	8.8
Urban - Urbaine	C	81 483	90 179	92 651	96 605	104 445	7.0	7.6	7.8	8.1	8.8
Rural - Rurale	C	52 470	53 125	49 181	50 032	84 795	5.2	5.4	5.0	5.2	8.8
Russian Federation - Fédération de Russie											
Total	C	1 091 778	979 667	1 066 366	1 113 562	1 262 500	7.6	6.8	7.5	7.8	8.9
San Marino - Saint-Marin											
Total	C	200	207[41]	223[41]	216[41]	216[41]	6.9	7.0	7.2	6.9	6.8
Serbia - Serbie[42]											
Total	+C	41 914	42 030	38 846	39 756	41 083	5.6	5.6	5.2	5.4	5.6
Urban - Urbaine	+C	25 904	26 248	25 168	25 288	...	6.1	6.2	5.9	5.9	...
Rural - Rurale	+C	16 010	15 782	13 678	14 468	...	4.9	4.9	4.3	4.6	...
Slovakia - Slovaquie											
Total	C	26 002	27 885	26 149	25 939	27 437	4.8	5.2	4.9	4.8	5.1
Urban - Urbaine	C	15 068	15 986	15 180	15 022	15 994	5.0	5.3	5.1	5.0	5.4
Rural - Rurale	C	10 934	11 899	10 969	10 917	11 443	4.6	5.0	4.6	4.5	4.7
Slovenia - Slovénie											
Total	C	6 756	6 558	5 769	6 368	6 373	3.4	3.3	2.9	3.2	3.2
Urban - Urbaine	C	3 624	3 521	2 971	3 357	3 203	3.7	3.6	3.1	3.5	3.2
Rural - Rurale	C	3 132	3 037	2 798	3 011	3 170	3.2	3.1	2.8	3.0	3.1
Spain - Espagne											
Total	C	212 300	216 149	209 415[43]	211 818[43]	201 579	5.1	5.1	4.8	4.8	4.5
Sweden - Suède											
Total	C	39 041	43 088	44 381	45 551	47 898	4.4	4.8	4.9	5.0	5.2
Switzerland - Suisse											
Total	C	40 056	39 460	40 139	39 817	40 330	5.5	5.3	5.4	5.3	5.3
Urban - Urbaine	C	30 901	30 154	30 809	30 649	30 936	5.8	5.6	5.7	5.6	5.6
Rural - Rurale	C	9 155	9 306	9 330	9 168	9 394	4.7	4.7	4.7	4.6	4.7

Continent, country or area, and urban/rural residence / Continent, pays ou zone et résidence, urbaine/rurale	Code[a]	Number - Nombre					Rate - Taux				
		2003	2004	2005	2006	2007	2003	2004	2005	2006	2007
EUROPE											
The Former Yugoslav Republic of Macedonia - L'ex-République yougoslave de Macédoine											
Total	C	*14 402	*14 073	14 500	14 908	15 490	*7.1	*6.9	7.1	7.3	7.6
Urban - Urbaine	C	...	...	7 709	7 848	8 347	...	...	...	...	...
Rural - Rurale	C	...	...	6 791	7 060	7 143	...	...	...	...	...
Ukraine											
Total	C	370 966	278 225	332 143	354 959	416 427	7.8	5.9	7.1	7.6	8.9
Urban - Urbaine	C	277 014	209 369	252 889	270 504	317 641	8.7	...	...	...	10.0
Rural - Rurale	C	93 952	68 856	79 254	84 455	98 786	6.0	...	...	...	6.6
United Kingdom of Great Britain and Northern Ireland - Royaume-Uni de Grande-Bretagne et d'Irlande du Nord[44]											
Total	C	306 214	...	...	...	...	5.1	...	...	...	...
OCEANIA - OCÉANIE											
American Samoa - Samoas américaines											
Total	C	285	287	202	171	...	4.6	4.5	3.1	2.6	...
Australia - Australie											
Total	+C	106 394	110 958[45]	109 323	114 222	116 322	5.3	5.5	5.4	5.5	5.5
Cook Islands - Îles Cook[46]											
Total	+C	623	645	755	*707	*786	33.9	31.8	37.4	*34.0	*37.3
Fiji - Fidji											
Total	+C	7 440	7 076	...	...	...	9.1	8.6	...	...	...
French Polynesia - Polynésie française											
Total	C	1 053	1 105	1 061	1 124	1 152	4.3	4.4	4.2	4.4	4.4
Guam											
Total	C	1 334	1 561	...	...	...	8.0	9.4	...	...	...
New Caledonia - Nouvelle-Calédonie											
Total	C	873	847	940	927	884	3.9	3.7	4.0	3.9	3.6
Urban - Urbaine	C	594	...	...	...	596	...	...	...	...	...
Rural - Rurale	C	279	...	...	...	288	...	...	...	...	...
New Zealand - Nouvelle-Zélande											
Total	+C	21 419	21 006	20 470	21 423[6]	21 494[6]	5.3	5.1	5.0	5.1	5.1
Niue - Nioué											
Total	C	12	14	7	19	13	...	...	...	...	...
Tonga[47]											
Total	+C	697	*677	...	...	...	6.9	*6.6	...	...	...

FOOTNOTES - NOTES

Italics: data from civil registers which are incomplete or of unknown completeness. - Italiques: données incomplètes ou dont le degré d'exactitude n'est pas connu, provenant des registres de l'état civil.

* Provisional. - Données provisoires.

[a] 'Code' indicates the source of data, as follows:
  C - Civil registration, estimated over 90% complete
  U - Civil registration, estimated less than 90% complete
  | - Other source, estimated reliable
  + - Data tabulated by date of registration rather than occurence.
  ... - Information not available

Le 'Code' indique la source des données, comme suit:
  C - Registres de l'état civil considérés complets à 90 p. 100 au moins.
  U - Registres de l'état civil qui ne sont pas considérés complèts à 90 p. 100 au moins.
  | - Autre source, considérée pas douteuses.
  + - Données exploitées selon la date de l'enregistrement et non la date de l'événement.
  ... - Information pas disponible.

[1] Data refer to Algerian population only. - Les données ne concernent que la population algérienne.
[2] Including marriages resumed after 'revocable divorce' (among Moslem population), which approximates legal separation. - Y compris les unions reconstituées après un 'divorce révocable' (parmi la population musulmane), qui est à peu près l'équivalent d'une séparation légale.
[3] Including visitors. - Visiteurs compris.
[4] Excluding visitors. - Les données non compris des visiteurs.
[5] Data refer to resident population only. - Pour la population résidante seulement.
[6] Marriages registered in which the groom was resident. - Mariages enregistrés où le marié était un résident.

[7] Marriages registered in which the bride was resident. - Mariages enregistrés, la mariée étant résidente.

[8] Excluding marriages of brides that are non-residents. - En excluant les mariages dont la mariée n'est pas une résidente.

[9] In urban/rural distribution, some data is not available which is the reason for the difference with the total. - Dans la répartition urbain/rural, certaines données ne sont pas disponible d'où la différence entre le total et la somme de urbain, rural.

[10] The difference between 'Total' and the sum of urban and rural is due to the unknown place of residence of bride/wife. Urban and rural distribution refers to the usual residence of the bride/wife. - La différence entre le total et la somme des chiffres urbains et ruraux s'explique par le lieu de résidence inconnu des maris. La répartition urbain/rural se réfère au domicile habituel de la jeune mariée/de l'épouse.

[11] Number of marriages of which at least one person was resident of the Netherlands Antilles (marital tourism is excluded). - Nombre de couples mariés dont l'un des membres au moins résidait aux Antilles néerlandaises (le tourisme conjugal n'est pas pris en compte).

[12] Excluding Indian jungle population. - Non compris les Indiens de la jungle.

[13] Urban and rural distribution refers to the usual residence of the groom/husband. - La répartition urbain/rural se réfère au domicile habituel du jeune marié/de l'époux.

[14] Excluding nomadic Indian tribes. - Non compris les tribus d'Indiens nomades.

[15] For statistical purposes, the data for China do not include those for the Hong Kong Special Administrative Region (Hong Kong SAR), Macao Special Administrative Region (Macao SAR) and Taiwan province of China. - Pour la présentation des statistiques, les données pour la Chine ne comprennent pas la Région Administrative Spéciale de Hong Kong (Hong Kong RAS), la Région Administrative Spéciale de Macao (Macao RAS) et Taïwan province de Chine.

[16] Data refer to government controlled areas. - Les données se rapportent aux zones contrôlées par le Gouvernement.

[17] Data refer to the Iranian Year which begins on 21 March and ends on 20 March of the following year. - Les données concernent l'année iranienne, qui commence le 21 mars et se termine le 20 mars de l'année suivante.

[18] Including data for East Jerusalem and Israeli residents in certain other territories under occupation by Israeli military forces since June 1967. - Y compris les données pour Jérusalem-Est et les résidents israéliens dans certains autres territoires occupés depuis 1967 par les forces armées israéliennes.

[19] Data refer to Japanese nationals in Japan only. - Les données se raportent aux nationaux japonais au Japon seulement.

[20] Excluding data for Jordanian territory under occupation since June 1967 by Israeli military forces. Excluding foreigners, including registered Palestinian refugees. - Non compris les données pour le territoire jordanien occupé depuis juin 1967 par les forces armées israéliennes. Non compris les étrangers, mais y compris les réfugiés de Palestine enregistrés.

[21] Since 2006, the Government of Mongolia has started to implement " Newly married couple" programme that aims to promote marriage. - En 2006, le Gouvernement mongol a lancé le programme intitulé « jeunes mariés » qui vise à promouvoir le mariage.

[22] Excluding alien armed forces, civilian aliens employed by armed forces, and foreign diplomatic personnel and their dependants. - Non compris les militaires étrangers, les civils étrangers employés par les forces armées ni le personnel diplomatique étranger et les membres de leur famille les accompagnant.

[23] Including nationals outside the country. - Y compris les nationaux hors du pays.

[24] Excluding marriages previously officiated outside Singapore or under religious and customary rites. - Les figures excluent les mariages célébrés précédemment au dehors de Singapour ou sous les rites réligieuse ou accoutumés.

[25] Excluding nomad population. - Non compris les nomades.

[26] Data from MERNIS (Central Population Administrative System). - Données de MERNIS (Système central de données démographiques).

[27] Also included in Finland. - Comprise aussi dans Finlande.

[28] Excluding aliens temporarily in the area. - Non compris les étrangers se trouvant temporairement le territoire.

[29] Including armed forces stationed outside the country, but excluding alien armed forces in the area unless marriage performed by local foreign authority. - Y compris les militaires nationaux hors du pays et les militaires étrangers en garnison sur le territoire, sauf si le mariage a été célébré pour l'autorité locale.

[30] Including nationals outside the country, but excluding foreigners in the country. - Y compris les nationaux à l'étranger, mais non compris les étrangers sur le territoire.

[31] Excluding Faeroe Islands and Greenland shown separately, if available. - Non compris les Iles Féroé et le Gröenland, qui font l'objet de rubriques distinctes, si disponible.

[32] Urban and rural distribution of marriages and divorces is displayed by place of residence of groom/husband. The difference between 'Total' and the sum of urban and rural is due to the unknown place of residence of grooms/husbands and to grooms/husbands living outside country. - Les mariages et divorces sont classés par rapport à la résidence urbaine/rurale de l'époux. La somme des mariages et divorces par résidence urbaine/rurale est différente du 'total' car elle ne tient pas compte ni des résidences inconnues de l'époux ni des mariages et divorces d'époux vivant à l'étranger.

[33] Only marriages in which the bride was resident in Finland. Including Aland Islands. - Seulement mariages où l'épouse réside en Finlande. Y compris les Îles d'Åland.

[34] Including armed forces stationed outside the country. Excluding Overseas Departments, namely, French Guiana, Guadeloupe, Martinique and Reunion, shown separately, if available. - Y compris les militaires nationaux hors du pays. Non compris les départements d'outre mer, c'est-à-dire la Guyane française, la Guadeloupe, la Martinique et la Réunion, qui font l'objet de rubriques distinctes, si disponible.

[35] Data for urban and rural, excluding nationals outside the country. - Les données pour la résidence urbaine et rurale , non compris les nationaux hors du pays.

[36] Data refer to marriages where one or both partners are residents. - Les données se réfèrent aux mariages dont l'un des époux ou tous les deux sont des résidents.

[37] Total includes the data of foreigners, persons of unknown residence and homeless, but the categories urban and rural do not. - Total incluant les étrangers, les personnes de résidence inconnue et les sans-abri, ce qui n'est pas le cas pour les catégories urbaines et rurales.

[38] The difference between 'Total' and the sum of 'urban' and 'rural' is due to the cases of unknown place of residence or residence abroad. - La différence entre le 'Total' et la somme des données selon la résidence urbaine/rurale se rapporte à la situation ou on ignore la résidence ou si la résidence est à l'étranger.

[39] Including same sex marriages. Marriages of couples of which at least one partner is recorded in a Dutch municipal register, irrespective of the country where the marriage was performed. - Y compris les mariages entre personnes du même sexe. Mariages où un des conjoints au moins est inscrit dans un registre municipal néerlandais, quel que soit le pays où le mariage a été contracté.

[40] Only marriages in which the groom was resident in Norway. Excluding Svalbard and Jan Mayen Island shown separately, if available. - Seulement mariages où l'époux réside en Norvège. Non compris Svalbard et Jan Mayen qui font l'objet de rubriques distinctes, si disponible.

[41] Includes civil and religious marriages as well as not specified. - Y compris les mariages civils, religieux ou non précisés.

[42] Excluding data for Kosovo and Metohia. - Sans les données pour le Kosovo et Metohie.

[43] Including same sex marriages. - Y compris les mariages entre personnes du même sexe.

[44] Excluding Channel Islands (Guernsey and Jersey) and Isle of Man, shown separately, if available. - Non compris les îles Anglo-Normandes (Guernesey et Jersey) et l'île de Man, qui font l'objet de rubriques distinctes, si disponible.

[45] In 2004, marriage registrations were sampled for the states of New South Wales, Victoria, Queensland and South Australia, while the other states and territories were fully enumerated. - En 2004, on a procédé à des enquêtes par échantillonnage concernant les enregistrements de mariages dans les états de New South Wales, Victoria, Queenslands et South Australia et à un dénombrement complet dans les autres états et territoires.

[46] Excluding Niue, shown separately, which is part of Cook Islands, but because of remoteness is administered separately. - Non compris Nioué, qui fait l'objet d'une rubrique distincte et qui fait partie des îles Cook, mais qui, en raison de son éloignement, est administrée séparément.

[47] Data refer to the island of Tongatapu only. - Les données se réfèrent uniquement à l'île de Tongatapu.

Table 22

Table 22 presents the marriages cross-classified by age of groom and age of bride for the latest available year between 1998 and 2007.

Description of variables: Marriage is defined as the act, ceremony or process by which the legal relationship of husband and wife is constituted. The legality of the union may be established by civil, religious or other means as recognized by the laws of each country[1].

Marriage statistics in this table, therefore, include both first marriages and remarriages after divorce, widowhood or annulment. They do not, unless otherwise noted, include resumption of marriage ties after legal separation. These statistics refer to the number of marriages performed, and not to the number of persons marrying.

Age is defined as age at last birthday, that is, the difference between the date of birth and the date of the occurrence of the event, expressed in completed solar years. The age classification used for brides in this table is the following: under 20 years, 5-year age groups through 90-94, and 100 years and over, depending on the availability of data. Age classification for grooms is restricted to 5-year age groups from 15 to 64, and 65 years and over.

In an effort to provide interpretation of these statistics, countries or areas providing data on marriages by age of groom and bride have been requested to specify "the minimum legal age at which marriage can take place with and without parental consent". This information is presented in the table 22-1 below.

Reliability of data: Data from civil registers of marriages that are reported as incomplete (less than 90 per cent completeness) or of unknown completeness are considered unreliable and are set in *italics* rather than in roman type. Table 21 and the technical notes for that table provide more detailed information on the completeness of marriage registration. For more information about the quality of vital statistics data in general, see section 4.2 of the Technical Notes.

Limitations: Statistics on marriages by age of groom and age of bride are subject to the same qualifications as have been set forth for vital statistics in general and marriage statistics in particular as discussed in Section 4 of the Technical Notes.

The fact that marriage is a legal event, unlike birth and death that are biological events, has implications for international comparability of data. Marriage has been defined, for statistical purposes, in terms of the laws of individual countries or areas. These laws vary throughout the world. In addition, comparability is further limited because some countries or areas compile statistics only for civil marriages although religious marriages may also be legally recognized; in other countries or areas, the only available records are church registers and, therefore, the statistics may not reflect to marriages that are civil marriages only.

Because in many countries or areas marriage is a civil legal contract which, to establish its legality, must be celebrated before a civil officer, it follows that for these countries or areas registration would tend to be almost automatic at the time of, or immediately following, the marriage ceremony. This factor should be kept in mind when considering the reliability of data, described above. For this reason the practice of tabulating data by date of registration does not generally pose serious problems of comparability as it does in the case of birth and death statistics.

Because these statistics are classified according to age, they are subject to the limitations with respect to accuracy of age reporting similar to those already discussed in connection with Section 3.1.3 of the Technical Notes. It is probable that biases are less pronounced in marriage statistics, because information is obtained from the persons concerned and since marriage is a legal act, the participants are likely to give correct information. However, in some countries or areas, there appears to be a concentration of marriages at the legal minimum age for marriage and at the age at which valid marriage may be contracted without parental consent, indicating perhaps an overstatement in some cases to comply with the law.

Aside from the possibility of age misreporting, it should be noted that marriage patterns at younger ages, that is, for ages up to 24 years, are influenced to a large extent by laws regarding the minimum age for marriage

Factors that may influence age reporting, particularly at older ages include an inclination to understate the age of the bride in order that it may be equal to or less than that of the groom.

The absence of frequencies in the unknown age group does not necessarily indicate completely accurate reporting and tabulation of the age item. It is sometimes an indication that the unknowns have been eliminated by assigning ages to them before tabulation, or by proportionate distribution after tabulation.

Another age-reporting factor that must be kept in mind in using these data is the variation that may result from calculating age at marriage from year of birth rather than from day, month and year of birth. Information on this factor is given in footnotes when known.

Earlier data: Marriages by age of groom and age of bride have been shown for the latest available year in most issues of the *Demographic Yearbook*. Data cross-classified by age of groom and bride have been presented in previous issues featuring marriage and divorce statistics. For information on the specific topics and the years covered, readers should consult the Historical Index.

22-1 Minimum legal age at which marriage can take place

Country or area	With parental consent		Without parental consent	
	Groom	Bride	Groom	Bride
Africa				
Egypt	18	16	...	...
Mauritius	16	16	18	18
America, North				
Anguilla	...	...	18	18
Bahamas	..	..	..	..
Bermuda	16	16	18	18
Canada	16	16	16	16
Costa Rica	16	16	18	18
Cuba	14	14	16	16
El Salvador	15	14	15	14
Mexico	16	14	18	18
Panama	16	14	18	18
Puerto Rico	16	14	18	16
America, South				
Brazil	14	12	...	...
Chile	14	12	18	18
Ecuador	14	12	...	...
Uruguay	14	12	18	18
Venezuela (Bolivarian Republic of)	21	18	...	...
Asia				
Armenia	18	17	...	...
Azerbaijan	18	17	...	...
Bahrain	15	...	...	...
China, Hong Kong SAR	16	16	21	21

Country or area	With parental consent		Without parental consent	
	Groom	Bride	Groom	Bride
China, Macao SAR	16	16	18	18
Israel	…	17	…	17
Japan	18	16	20	20
Kazakhstan	16	16	18	17
Kyrgyzstan	18	18	18	18
Occupied Palestinian Territory	15.5	14.5	…	…
Philippines	18-20	18-20	21	21
Republic of Korea	18	16	20	20
Singapore	18	18	21	21
Tajikistan	17	17	16	16
Turkey	15	14	18	18
Uzbekistan	17	17	17	17
Europe				
Albania	18	16	…	…
Austria	18	16	18	16
Belarus	18	18	18	18
Belgium	17	15	18	18
Bosnia and Herzegovina	18	18	18	18
Bulgaria	16	16	18	18
Croatia	16	16	18	18
Czech Republic	16	16	18	18
Denmark	18	15	18	18
Estonia	15	15	18	18
Finland	Under 18 consent of Ministry of Justice necessary	Under 18, consent of Ministry of Justice necessary	18	18
France	16	14	18	18
Hungary	16	16	18	18
Iceland	18	18	18	18
Ireland	…	…	18	18
Italy	16	16	…	…
Latvia	16	16	18	18
Lithuania	15 (by judgment)	15 (by judgment)	18	18
Luxembourg	…	…	18	18

Country or area	With parental consent		Without parental consent	
	Groom	Bride	Groom	Bride
Malta	16	16	18	18
Montenegro	16	16	18	18
Netherlands	16	16	18	18
Norway	16	16	18	18
Poland	-	16	18	18
Portugal	16	16	18	18
Republic of Moldova	16	14	18	16
Romania	17	16	18	18
Russian Federation	16	16	18	18
Serbia	16	16	18	18
Slovakia	16	16	18	18
Slovenia	15	15	18	18
Spain	…	…	18	18
Sweden	18	18	18	18
Switzerland	…	…	18	18
The Former Yugoslav Republic of Macedonia	16	16	18	18
Ukraine	14	14	18	17
United Kingdom of Great Britain and Northern Ireland	16	16	18	18
Oceania				
Australia	16	16	18	16
New Zealand	16	16	16	16

NOTES

[1] *Principles and Recommendations for a Vital Statistics System Revision 2*, Sales No. 01.XVII.10, United Nations, New York, 2001

Tableau 22

Le tableau 22 présente des statistiques concernant les mariages classés selon l'âge de l'époux et selon l'âge de l'épouse pour les années où les données sont disponibles entre 1998 et 2007.

Description des variables : le mariage désigne l'acte, la cérémonie ou la procédure qui établit un rapport légal entre mari et femme. L'union peut être rendue légale par une procédure civile ou religieuse, ou par toute autre procédure, conformément à la législation du pays[1].

Les statistiques de la nuptialité présentées dans ce tableau comprennent donc les premiers mariages et les remariages faisant suite à un divorce, un veuvage ou une annulation. Toutefois, sauf indication contraire, elles ne comprennent pas les unions reconstituées après une séparation légale. Ces statistiques se rapportent au nombre de mariages célébrés, non au nombre de personnes qui se marient.

L'âge désigne l'âge au dernier anniversaire, c'est-à-dire la différence entre la date de naissance et la date de l'événement, exprimée en années solaires révolues. Le classement par âge pour l'épouse utilisé dans ce tableau comprend les groupes suivants : moins de 20 ans, groupes quinquennaux jusqu'à 90-94 ans, et 100 ans et plus, selon la disponibilité des données. Le classement par âge pour l'époux est quinquennal de 15 jusqu' à 65 ans et 65 ans et plus.

Dans un effort de fournir l'interprétation de ces statistiques, les pays ou les zones fournissant des données sur les mariages par l'âge de l'épouse et de par l'âge de l'époux ont été demandés d'indiquer "l'âge légal minimum avec auquel le mariage peut avoir lieu avec et sans consentement parental". Cette information est présentée dans le tableau 22-1 ci-dessous.

Fiabilité des données : les données sur les mariages issues des registres de l'état civil qui sont déclarées incomplètes (degré de complétude inférieur à 90 p. 100) ou dont le degré de complétude n'est pas connu sont jugées douteuses et apparaissent en italique et non en caractères romains. Le tableau 21 et les notes techniques s'y rapportant présentent des renseignements plus détaillés sur le degré de complétude de l'enregistrement des mariages. Pour plus de précisions sur la qualité des données reposant sur les statistiques de l'état civil en général, voir la section 4.2 des notes techniques.

Insuffisance des données : les statistiques des mariages selon l'âge de l'époux et selon l'âge de l'épouse appellent les mêmes réserves que celles formulées à propos des statistiques de l'état civil en général et des statistiques de la nuptialité en particulier (voir la section 4 des Notes techniques).

Le fait que le mariage soit un acte juridique, à la différence de la naissance et du décès, qui sont des faits biologiques, a des répercussions sur la comparabilité internationale des données. Aux fins de la statistique, le mariage est défini par la législation de chaque pays ou zone. Cette législation varie d'un pays à l'autre. La comparabilité est limitée en outre du fait que certains pays et zones ne réunissent des statistiques que pour les mariages civils, bien que les mariages religieux y soient également reconnus par la loi ; dans d'autres, les seuls relevés disponibles sont les registres des églises et, en conséquence, les statistiques peuvent ne pas rendre compte des mariages exclusivement civils.

Le mariage étant, dans de nombreux pays ou zones, un contrat juridique civil qui, pour être légal, doit être conclu devant un officier d'état civil, il s'ensuit que, dans ces pays ou zones, l'enregistrement se fait à peu près systématiquement au moment de la cérémonie ou immédiatement après. Il faut tenir compte de cet élément lorsque l'on évalue la fiabilité des données, dont il est question plus haut. C'est pourquoi la pratique consistant à exploiter les données selon la date de l'enregistrement ne pose généralement pas les graves problèmes de comparabilité auxquels on se heurte dans le cas des statistiques des naissances et des décès.

Étant donné que ces statistiques sont classées selon l'âge, elles appellent les mêmes réserves concernant l'exactitude des déclarations d'âge que celles dont il a déjà été question à la section 3.1.3 des Notes techniques. Il est probable que les statistiques de la nuptialité sont moins faussées par ce genre d'erreur, car les renseignements sont donnés par les intéressés eux-mêmes, et, comme le mariage est un acte juridique, il y a toutes chances que leurs déclarations soient exactes. Toutefois, dans certains pays ou zones, il semble y avoir une concentration de mariages à l'âge minimal légal de nubilité ainsi qu'à l'âge auquel le mariage peut être valablement contracté sans le consentement des parents, ce qui peut indiquer que certains déclarants se vieillissent pour se conformer à la loi.

Outre la possibilité d'erreurs dans les déclarations d'âge, il convient de noter que la législation fixant l'âge minimal de nubilité influe notablement sur les caractéristiques de la nuptialité pour les premiers âges, c'est-à-dire jusqu'à 24 ans.

Parmi les facteurs pouvant exercer une influence sur les déclarations d'âge, en particulier celles qui sont faites par des personnes plus âgées, il faut citer la tendance à diminuer l'âge de l'épouse de façon qu'il soit égal ou inférieur à celui de l'époux.

Si aucun nombre ne figure dans la rangée réservée aux âges inconnus, cela ne signifie pas nécessairement que les déclarations d'âge et l'exploitation des données par âge aient été tout à fait exactes. C'est parfois une indication que l'on a attribué un âge aux personnes d'âge inconnu avant l'exploitation des données ou qu'elles ont été réparties proportionnellement entre les différents groupes après cette opération.

Il importe de ne pas oublier non plus, lorsque l'on utilisera ces données, que l'on calcule parfois l'âge des conjoints au moment du mariage sur la base de l'année de naissance seulement et non d'après la date exacte (jour, mois et année) de naissance. Des renseignements à ce sujet sont donnés en note chaque fois que possible.

Donnés publiées antérieurement : on trouve dans la plupart des éditions de l'*Annuaire démographique* des statistiques concernant les mariages selon l'âge de l'époux et selon l'âge de l'épouse qui ont été établis à partir des données les plus récentes dont on disposait à l'époque. Des données croisant l'âge des époux ont été présentés dans des éditions antérieurs, plus particulièrement consacrées aux statistiques de la nuptialité et de la divortialité. Pour plus de précisions concernant les années et les sujets pour lesquels des données ont été publiées, se reporter à l'index historique.

22-1 L'âge légal minimum avec auquel le mariage peut avoir lieu

Pays ou zone	Avec consentement parental		Sans consentement parental	
	Epoux	Epouse	Epoux	Epouse
Afrique				
Egypte	18	16	…	…
Maurice	16	16	18	18
Amérique du Nord				
Anguilla	…	…	18	18
Bahamas	..	..	..	..
Bermudes	16	16	18	18
Canada	16	16	16	16
Costa Rica	16	16	18	18
Cuba	14	14	16	16
El Salvador	15	14	15	14
Mexique	16	14	18	18
Panama	16	14	18	18
Porto Rico	16	14	18	16
Amérique du Sud				
Brésil	14	12	…	…
Chili	14	12	18	18
Equateur	14	12	…	…
Uruguay	14	12	18	18

Pays ou zone	Avec consentement parental		Sans consentement parental	
	Epoux	Epouse	Epoux	Epouse
Venezuela (République bolivarienne du)	21	18	…	…
Asie				
Arménie	18	17	…	…
Azerbaïdjan	18	17	…	…
Bahreïn	15	…	…	…
Chine, Hong Kong RAS	16	16	21	21
Chine, Macao RAS	16	16	18	18
Israël	…	17	…	17
Japon	18	16	20	20
Kazakhstan	16	16	18	17
Kirghizistan	18	18	18	18
Ouzbékistan	17	17	17	17
Philippines	18-20	18-20	21	21
République de Corée	18	16	20	20
Singapour	18	18	21	21
Tadjikistan	17	17	16	16
Territoire palestinien occupé	15.5	14.5	…	…
Turquie	15	14	18	18
Europe				
Albanie	18	16	…	…
Autriche	18	16	18	16
Bélarus	18	18	18	18
Belgique	17	15	18	18
Bosnie-Herzégovine	18	18	18	18
Bulgarie	16	16	18	18
Croatie	16	16	18	18
Danemark	18	15	18	18
Espagne	…	…	18	18
Estonie	15	15	18	18
Fédération de Russie	16	16	18	18
Finlande	Agrément du Ministère de la justice requis de moins de 18	Agrément du Ministère de la justice requis de moins de 18	18	18
France	16	14	18	18

Pays ou zone	Avec consentement parental		Sans consentement parental	
	Epoux	Epouse	Epoux	Epouse
Hongrie	16	16	18	18
Irlande	…	…	18	18
Islande	18	18	18	18
Italie	16	16	…	…
L'ex-République yougoslave de Macédoine	16	16	18	18
Lettonie	16	16	18	18
Lituanie	15 (en vertu d'une décision de justice)	15 (en vertu d'une décision de justice)	18	18
Luxembourg	…	…	18	18
Malte	16	16	18	18
Monténégro	16	16	18	18
Norvège	16	16	18	18
Pays-Bas	16	16	18	18
Pologne	-	16, 17	18	18
Portugal	16	16	18	18
République de Moldova	16	14	18	16
République tchèque	16	16	18	18
Roumanie	17	16	18	18
Royaume-Uni de Grande-Bretagne et d'Irlande du Nord	16	16	18	18
Serbie	16	16	18	18
Slovaque	16	16	18	18
Slovénie	15	15	18	18
Suede	18	18	18	18
Suisse	…	…	18	18
Ukraine	14	14	18	17
Océanie				
Australie	16	16	18	16
Nouvelle-Zélande	16	16	16	16

NOTE

[1] *Principes et recommandations pour un système de statistiques de l'état civil, deuxième révision*, numéro de vente F.01.XVII.10, publication des Nations Unies, New York, 2003.

22. Marriages by age of groom and by age of bride: latest available year, 1998 - 2007
Mariages selon l'âge de l'époux et selon l'âge de l'épouse: dernière année disponible, 1998 - 2007

Continent, country or area, year, code and age of bride / Continent, pays ou zone, date, code et âge de l'épouse	Total	____ Age of groom - âge de l'époux ____ 15-19	20-24	25-29	30-34	35-39	40-44	45-49	50-54	55-59	60-64	65+	Unknown Inconnu
AFRICA - AFRIQUE													
Egypt - Égypte[1]													
2007 (+...)													
Total	614 848	12 595[d]	160 879	244 921	107 562	33 813	17 913	11 191	7 676	5 581	3 303	4 451	4 963
16 - 19	182 482	8 515[d]	76 193	73 124	19 674	3 170	908	362	200	140	52	69	75
20 - 24	265 767	3 265[d]	73 314	123 772	48 799	10 123	3 458	1 393	700	411	201	248	83
25 - 29	99 289	584[d]	9 047	41 752	28 366	10 308	4 372	2 145	1 206	679	366	422	42
30 - 34	30 349	104[d]	1 195	4 240	8 351	6 472	4 212	2 307	1 433	888	553	578	16
35 - 39	13 945	49[d]	491	1 020	1 468	2 686	2 821	2 054	1 253	951	532	614	6
40 - 44	8 142	15[d]	144	317	461	647	1 508	1 693	1 252	872	543	683	7
45 - 49	4 776	9[d]	118	186	182	259	431	913	1 010	752	374	540	2
50 - 54	2 248	2[d]	30	75	69	64	110	210	455	538	318	377	-
55 - 59	1 104	1[d]	21	40	23	16	23	48	98	269	220	345	-
60 - 64	480	1[d]	8	11	10	8	12	16	24	43	110	237	1
65 - 69	198	1[d]	4	15	4	2	1	2	6	9	10	143	-
70 - 74	94	3[d]	1	4	3	1	2	3	1	4	3	105	-
75 +	140	-[d]	5	13	3	1	2	3	1	4	3	64	-
Unknown - Inconnu	5 834	46[d]	308	352	149	55	50	40	37	25	15	26	4 731
Mauritius - Maurice													
2007 (+C)													
Total	11 547	151	1 592	4 047	2 424	1 285	866	514	303	203	84	74	4
0 - 14	69	2	9	24	14	9	6	2	2	-	1	-	1
15 - 19	1 396	104	565	584	126	9	3	2	-	1	-	2	1
20 - 24	3 309	27	773	1 761	599	101	31	10	3	2	3	2	-
25 - 29	3 098	11	197	1 401	958	346	131	33	13	3	1	4	1
30 - 34	1 485	3	22	202	553	416	186	70	20	7	1	1	1
35 - 39	871	3	14	45	129	282	232	111	36	13	4	7	-
40 - 44	603	-	1	11	29	73	192	156	82	39	13	7	-
45 - 49	390	-	1	3	8	34	61	108	91	57	19	8	-
50 - 54	161	-	3	1	-	1	3	5	44	46	18	17	-
55 - 59	75	-	-	1	-	-	3	-	2	34	20	10	-
60 - 64	23	-	-	-	-	-	-	-	2	4	3	7	-
65 - 69	18	-	-	2	-	-	-	-	-	-	1	7	-
70 - 74	8	-	-	-	-	-	-	-	-	-	1	-	1
75 +	1	-	-	-	-	-	-	-	-	-	1	-	-
Unknown - Inconnu	40	1	7	12	8	7	1	-	1	1	1	-	1
Réunion													
2007[2] (C)													
Total	3 149	15	338	787	681	514	306	185	150	62	57	54	...
0 - 14	1	1	-	-	-	-	-	-	-	-	-	-	...
15 - 19	91	8	45	26	7	2	2	1	-	-	-	-	...
20 - 24	679	4	235	296	99	28	13	3	-	1	-	-	...
25 - 29	858	2	42	391	264	117	30	7	4	1	-	-	...
30 - 34	584	-	12	52	232	185	56	29	10	4	2	2	...
35 - 39	384	-	3	16	55	134	106	38	28	2	1	1	...
40 - 44	234	-	-	4	16	34	77	49	28	13	9	4	...
45 - 49	144	-	1	1	7	11	18	34	40	18	10	4	...
50 - 54	94	-	-	1	1	3	4	19	30	12	12	12	...
55 - 59	39	-	-	-	-	-	3	10	7	11	8	-	...
60 - 64	16	-	-	-	-	-	2	2	1	8	3	-	...
65 - 69	16	-	-	-	-	-	-	1	1	4	10	-	...
70 - 74	7	-	-	-	-	-	-	-	-	-	7	-	...
75 +	2	-	-	-	-	-	-	-	-	-	2	-	...
Seychelles[3]													
2007 (+C)													
Total	1 081	4	65	185	262	216	164	94	47	44[i]	...	...	...
0 - 14	-									[i]	...	...	...
15 - 19	26	4	12	5	4	1				[i]	...	...	...
20 - 24	121	-	37	41	22	14	6	1	-	[i]	...	...	...
25 - 29	275	-	11	100	100	32	20	8	1	3[i]	...	...	...
30 - 34	261	-	2	30	97	79	36	6	6	5[i]	...	...	...
35 - 39	194	-	2	3	28	66	51	31	9	4[i]	...	...	...
40 - 44	85	-	-	2	6	16	28	23	8	2[i]	...	...	...
45 - 49	63	-	-	3	5	6	18	17	9	5[i]	...	...	...
50 - 54	37	-	1	1	-	2	5	7	10	11[i]	...	...	...
55 +	19	-	-	-	-	-	-	1	4	14[i]	...	...	...

22. Marriages by age of groom and by age of bride: latest available year, 1998 - 2007
Mariages selon l'âge de l'époux et selon l'âge de l'épouse: dernière année disponible, 1998 - 2007 (continued - suite)

Continent, country or area, year, code and age of bride / Continent, pays ou zone, date, code et âge de l'épouse	Total	Age of groom - âge de l'époux											Unknown Inconnu
		15-19	20-24	25-29	30-34	35-39	40-44	45-49	50-54	55-59	60-64	65+	

AFRICA - AFRIQUE

South Africa - Afrique du Sud
2007 (...)

Total	183 030	268	12 542	40 796	44 011	32 358	20 246	12 872	7 998	5 172	2 799	3 961	4
0 - 14	19	6	5	3	2	-	-	-	-	-	-	-	-
15 - 19	3 115	136	1 487	1 052	292	102	27	8	9	-	2	-	-
20 - 24	34 649	101	8 346	16 324	6 789	2 102	603	228	89	41	14	12	-
25 - 29	53 465	14	2 157	19 261	20 678	7 754	2 303	830	293	102	45	28	-
30 - 34	38 061	7	411	3 214	13 041	13 142	5 217	1 852	706	288	87	96	-
35 - 39	22 710	2	105	715	2 474	7 196	6 924	3 206	1 211	553	179	145	-
40 - 44	13 312	1	26	163	541	1 550	3 862	3 844	1 889	857	346	233	-
45 - 49	8 117	1	4	51	156	409	1 000	2 176	2 242	1 176	470	432	-
50 - 54	4 459	-	1	9	26	84	239	538	1 176	1 208	608	570	-
55 - 59	2 473	-	-	2	9	14	56	146	290	709	586	661	-
60 - 64	1 342	-	-	1	1	3	11	38	69	167	356	696	-
65 - 69	695	-	-	-	2	2	3	5	17	56	77	533	-
70 - 74	353	-	-	1	-	-	1	1	6	11	18	315	-
75 - 79	188	-	-	-	-	-	-	-	1	4	10	173	-
80 - 84	52	-	-	-	-	-	-	-	-	-	1	51	-
85 +	16	-	-	-	-	-	-	-	-	-	1	16	-
Unknown - Inconnu	4	-	-	-	-	-	-	-	-	-	-	-	4

Tunisia - Tunisie
1998 (...)

Total	56 081	-	5 960	18 259	19 332	6 628	2 162	961	507	1 798[i]	...	...	474
15 - 19	7 411	...	1 821	3 017	2 009	412	68	19	2	10[i]	...	...	53
20 - 24	21 217	...	2 879	8 629	7 286	1 744	328	92	41	70[i]	...	...	148
25 - 29	15 689	...	833	4 977	6 691	2 187	533	161	61	132[i]	...	...	114
30 - 34	6 496	...	233	1 048	2 471	1 463	586	250	108	276[i]	...	...	61
35 - 39	2 515	...	67	245	492	554	417	209	127	379[i]	...	...	25
40 - 44	1 159	...	28	89	109	151	163	150	88	372[i]	...	...	9
45 +	918	...	32	57	50	35	52	73	72	543[i]	...	...	4
Unknown - Inconnu	676	...	67	197	224	82	15	7	8	16[i]	...	...	60

2007 (...)

Total	76 809	200[a]	5 130	20 482	26 252	13 140	5 056	2 038	1 888[n]	...	1 716	...	907
15 - 19	6 114	...	...	...	...	...	...	...	...	...	...	...	...
20 - 24	23 270	...	...	...	...	...	...	...	...	...	...	...	...
25 - 29	25 494	...	...	...	...	...	...	...	...	...	...	...	...
30 - 34	11 582	...	...	...	...	...	...	...	...	...	...	...	...
35 - 39	4 694	...	...	...	...	...	...	...	...	...	...	...	...
40 - 44	2 497	...	...	...	...	...	...	...	...	...	...	...	...
45 - 49	1 247	...	...	...	...	...	...	...	...	...	...	...	...
50 +	792	...	...	...	...	...	...	...	...	...	...	...	...
Unknown - Inconnu	1 119	...	...	...	...	...	...	...	...	...	...	...	...

AMERICA, NORTH - AMÉRIQUE DU NORD

Anguilla[4]
2005 (C)

Total	89	...	...	...	...	...	...	...	...	...	...	...	...
18 - 23	16	...	...	...	...	...	...	...	...	...	...	...	...
24 - 29	21	...	...	...	...	...	...	...	...	...	...	...	...
30 - 35	27	...	...	...	...	...	...	...	...	...	...	...	...
36 - 41	8	...	...	...	...	...	...	...	...	...	...	...	...
42 - 47	9	...	...	...	...	...	...	...	...	...	...	...	...
48 - 53	3	...	...	...	...	...	...	...	...	...	...	...	...
54 - 58	2	...	...	...	...	...	...	...	...	...	...	...	...
59 - 64	2	...	...	...	...	...	...	...	...	...	...	...	...
65 +	1	...	...	...	...	...	...	...	...	...	...	...	...

Aruba[5]
2007 (C)

Total	532	27	71	93	97	63	55	45	21	17	4	2	37
0 - 14	-	-	-	-	-	-	-	-	-	-	-	-	-
15 - 19	7	3	3	-	-	-	-	-	-	-	-	-	-
20 - 24	53	16	17	7	5	3	-	-	-	-	-	-	1
25 - 29	94	4	29	39	15	1	1	-	-	-	-	-	5
30 - 34	89	2	12	27	25	12	6	1	-	-	-	-	4

Age of groom - âge de l'époux

Continent, country or area, year, code and age of bride / Continent, pays ou zone, date, code et âge de l'épouse	Total	15-19	20-24	25-29	30-34	35-39	40-44	45-49	50-54	55-59	60-64	65+	Unknown Inconnu
AMERICA, NORTH - AMÉRIQUE DU NORD													
Aruba[5]													
2007													
35 - 39	77	1	7	9	28	12	8	5	1	-	-	-	6
40 - 44	71	-	2	6	12	15	19	10	2	-	-	-	5
45 - 49	44	-	-	1	6	8	10	8	4	3	-	-	4
50 - 54	34	-	-	1	2	5	6	7	7	9	-	-	7
55 - 59	30	-	1	1	-	4	1	7	2	1	2	-	-
60 - 64	11	-	-	-	-	2	1	3	2	1	2	-	-
65 - 69	4	-	-	-	-	-	2	1	-	1	-	-	-
70 - 74	3	-	-	-	-	-	-	2	-	1	-	-	-
75 - 79	2	-	-	-	-	-	-	-	-	1	1	-	-
Unknown - Inconnu	13	1	-	2	4	1	-	4	-	1	-	-	-
Bahamas													
2007 (C)													
Total	2 021	8	211	461	467	305	228	138	89	53	60[j]	...	1
0 - 14	58	3	31	14	7	3	-	-	-	-	2[j]	...	
15 - 19	374	4	116	147	56	26	18	5	-	-	1[j]	...	
20 - 24	522	1	38	214	172	63	22	10	1	-	3[j]	...	
25 - 29	384	-	20	48	150	91	41	21	8	2	10[j]	...	
30 - 34	305	-	4	25	58	77	85	32	8	6	7[j]	...	
35 - 39	165	-	2	10	13	31	43	25	26	8	8[j]	...	
40 - 44	109	-	-	2	8	14	10	37	19	11	10[j]	...	
45 - 49	55	-	-	1	1	-	7	4	19	13	6[j]	...	
50 - 54	30	-	-	-	2	-	2	3	7	10	13[j]	...	
55 +	18	-	-	-	-	-	-	1	1	3	-[j]	...	
Unknown - Inconnu	1	-	-	-	-	-	-	-	-	-	-[j]	...	1
Belize													
1998 (+C)													
Total	1 374	97	443	332	198	99	62	41	25	21	43[j]	...	13
0 - 14	13	...	...	...	...	...	...	...	...	...	...	...	...
15 - 19	329	...	...	...	...	...	...	...	...	...	...	...	...
20 - 24	434	...	...	...	...	...	...	...	...	...	...	...	...
25 - 29	273	...	...	...	...	...	...	...	...	...	...	...	...
30 - 34	142	...	...	...	...	...	...	...	...	...	...	...	...
35 - 39	64	...	...	...	...	...	...	...	...	...	...	...	...
40 - 44	31	...	...	...	...	...	...	...	...	...	...	...	...
45 - 49	35	...	...	...	...	...	...	...	...	...	...	...	...
50 - 54	13	...	...	...	...	...	...	...	...	...	...	...	...
55 - 59	14	...	...	...	...	...	...	...	...	...	...	...	...
60 +	15	...	...	...	...	...	...	...	...	...	...	...	...
Unknown - Inconnu	11	...	...	...	...	...	...	...	...	...	...	...	...
Bermuda - Bermudes													
2003 (C)													
Total	861	-[a]	191[k]	...	386[l]	...	162[m]	...	91[n]	...	31[j]	...	...
0 - 19	9	-[a]	7[k]	...	1[l]	...	1[m]	...	-[n]	...	-[j]	...	...
20 - 29	256	-[a]	135[k]	...	105[l]	...	14[m]	...	2[n]	...	-[j]	...	...
30 - 39	380	-[a]	45[k]	...	246[l]	...	75[m]	...	14[n]	...	-[j]	...	...
40 - 49	152	-[a]	4[k]	...	33[l]	...	60[m]	...	49[n]	...	6[j]	...	...
50 - 59	52	-[a]	-[k]	...	1[l]	...	11[m]	...	26[n]	...	14[j]	...	...
60 +	12	-[a]	-[k]	...	-[l]	...	1[m]	...	-[n]	...	11[j]	...	...
Canada													
2002 (C)													
Total	146 738	919	19 421	43 355	30 788	18 266	11 497	7 711	5 667	3 686	2 101	3 246	81
15 - 19	3 504	544	2 047	644	189	45	24	6	1	1	1	-	2
20 - 24	31 526	324	13 344	13 341	3 313	815	241	82	37	6	5	-	16
25 - 29	45 377	39	3 381	23 768	12 896	3 740	1 064	302	103	41	15	-	19
30 - 34	25 579	9	489	4 529	10 739	6 334	2 367	730	253	80	21	15	13
35 - 39	14 675	2	112	814	2 775	4 970	3 387	1 608	660	225	78	37	7
40 - 44	9 526	-	37	189	644	1 683	2 864	2 190	1 180	506	151	78	4
45 - 49	6 827	1	6	55	170	515	1 169	1 892	1 620	885	329	183	2
50 - 54	4 349	-	4	9	50	122	298	691	1 292	1 027	508	346	2
55 - 59	2 372	-	-	1	7	31	61	167	405	669	520	509	2
60 - 64	1 254	-	-	-	-	3	13	32	86	183	324	610	3
65 - 69	807	-	-	-	-	2	5	5	23	52	113	606	1
70 - 74	481	-	-	-	2	2	1	2	5	3	25	440	1

Continent, country or area, year, code and age of bride / Continent, pays ou zone, date, code et âge de l'épouse	Total	15-19	20-24	25-29	30-34	35-39	40-44	45-49	50-54	55-59	60-64	65+	Unknown Inconnu
AMERICA, NORTH - AMÉRIQUE DU NORD													
Canada													
2002													
75 + ...	431	-	-	-	-	-	-	3	2	7	11	408	-
Unknown - Inconnu	30	-	1	5	3	4	3	1	-	1	-	3	9
Costa Rica													
2006 (C)													
Total....................	26 575	938	5 937	7 067	4 251	2 536	1 714	1 117	1 990ʰ	...	...	...	1 025
0 - 14....................	30	8	12	2	4	1	-	1	1ʰ	...	...	...	1
15 - 19....................	3 548	516	1 761	798	245	104	51	27	17ʰ	...	...	...	29
20 - 24....................	7 622	259	2 915	2 675	978	409	190	74	86ʰ	...	...	...	36
25 - 29....................	6 150	75	809	2 574	1 509	605	299	147	116ʰ	...	...	...	16
30 - 34....................	3 072	35	227	640	919	609	297	162	165ʰ	...	...	...	18
35 - 39....................	1 829	23	97	193	328	425	338	192	217ʰ	...	...	...	16
40 - 44....................	1 297	7	46	77	139	217	302	229	270ʰ	...	...	...	10
45 - 49....................	834	2	16	33	64	78	128	163	341ʰ	...	...	...	9
50 + ...	1 078	2	14	15	27	55	92	115	750ʰ	...	...	...	6
Unknown - Inconnu	1 115	11	40	60	38	33	17	7	27ʰ	...	...	...	882
Cuba													
2007 (C)													
Total....................	56 781	1 392	8 103	8 750	9 422	8 553	7 202	4 123	2 768	2 252	1 763	2 452	1
0 - 14....................	71	22	36	12	1	-	-	-	-	-	-	-	-
15 - 19....................	5 640	805	2 529	1 225	559	270	126	53	23	28	11	11	-
20 - 24....................	11 638	381	3 656	3 405	2 153	1 065	514	199	106	74	45	40	-
25 - 29....................	8 230	88	1 035	2 164	2 299	1 386	665	283	119	70	59	62	-
30 - 34....................	8 117	62	445	1 034	2 166	2 073	1 308	503	211	118	102	95	-
35 - 39....................	7 490	18	218	532	1 277	2 038	1 781	761	368	237	124	136	-
40 - 44....................	6 144	8	114	229	569	1 078	1 671	1 058	626	377	192	222	-
45 - 49....................	3 623	5	38	73	226	376	670	768	573	415	246	233	-
50 - 54....................	2 226	1	11	38	91	130	238	298	425	412	315	267	-
55 - 59....................	1 591	2	8	12	38	69	115	118	190	319	336	384	-
60 - 64....................	1 034	-	7	16	24	35	68	48	84	136	204	412	-
65 - 69....................	528	-	3	3	10	18	22	17	32	36	86	301	-
70 - 74....................	241	-	2	3	4	8	11	7	5	23	20	158	-
75 - 79....................	118	-	1	2	3	1	8	6	4	5	14	74	-
80 - 84....................	55	-	-	1	1	5	1	1	2	1	5	38	-
85 + ...	35	-	-	1	1	1	4	3	-	1	5	19	-
Unknown - Inconnu	-	-	-	-	-	-	4	3	-	1	4	19	1
Dominican Republic - République dominicaine													
2007 (+C)													
Total....................	39 903	419	4 933	9 192	7 262	5 536	4 241	2 763	1 869	1 213	771	949	754
0 - 14....................	14	5	4	2	-	2	1	-	-	-	-	-	-
15 - 19....................	2 188	153	910	607	230	118	91	42	14	9	4	3	7
20 - 24....................	8 255	151	2 307	3 118	1 382	637	310	160	81	45	35	14	14
25 - 29....................	9 758	62	1 042	3 661	2 501	1 202	638	297	167	93	50	32	13
30 - 34....................	6 712	23	362	1 083	1 877	1 616	872	438	199	114	56	63	9
35 - 39....................	4 585	12	169	408	760	1 165	1 011	534	236	148	70	66	6
40 - 44....................	3 117	3	64	147	289	474	795	615	371	174	108	74	3
45 - 49....................	1 961	2	21	73	105	194	291	419	425	205	106	116	4
50 - 54....................	1 194	2	9	23	49	62	136	161	244	243	120	142	3
55 - 59....................	624	1	8	12	18	20	45	57	88	122	122	129	2
60 - 64....................	299	-	1	2	6	6	16	19	18	29	66	136	-
65 - 69....................	144	1	2	-	3	1	4	3	8	11	22	89	-
70 - 74....................	72	-	1	2	1	4	3	1	3	3	3	51	-
75 - 79....................	21	-	-	-	-	-	1	-	-	-	2	17	1
80 - 84....................	13	2	3	-	4	-	-	-	-	-	1	3	-
85 + ...	11	-	3	-	2	-	1	-	-	1	-	4	-
Unknown - Inconnu	935	2	27	54	35	35	26	17	15	16	6	10	692
El Salvador													
2007 (...)													
Total....................	28 675	3 807	7 946	6 646	3 927	2 218	1 545	980	624	369	233	298	37
0 - 14....................	-	-	-	-	-	-	-	-	-	-	-	-	-
15 - 19....................	1 202	643	408	91	27	9	1	1	1	3	1	1	3
20 - 24....................	6 562	1 815	3 293	1 045	272	67	24	9	4	3	-	3	8
25 - 29....................	7 366	804	2 656	2 780	770	215	86	28	9	2	-	-	10
30 - 34....................	4 763	321	962	1 613	1 297	375	132	37	12	4	1	2	4
35 - 39....................	2 897	128	368	612	803	653	218	72	27	5	6	1	3

Continent, country or area, year, code and age of bride / Continent, pays ou zone, date, code et âge de l'épouse	Total	15-19	20-24	25-29	30-34	35-39	40-44	45-49	50-54	55-59	60-64	65+	Unknown Inconnu
AMERICA, NORTH - AMÉRIQUE DU NORD													
El Salvador													
2007													
40 - 44	1 812	44	130	251	391	427	389	124	38	11	6	1	-
45 - 49	1 296	17	69	121	182	225	337	239	73	20	1	8	1
50 - 54	878	17	32	77	88	106	153	200	147	34	15	7	2
55 - 59	669	11	13	25	44	55	96	140	143	99	27	16	-
60 - 64	475	3	5	11	25	47	50	63	85	92	64	30	-
65 + ...	736	1	7	16	25	38	59	67	85	96	112	229	1
Unknown - Inconnu	19	3	3	4	3	1	-	-	-	-	-	-	5
Grenada - Grenade													
2000 (+C)													
Total...................	616	2	44	132	149	112	70	50	18	14	13	11	1
15 - 19	18	2	8	4	3	1	-	-	-	-	-	-	-
20 - 24	89	-	23	43	15	7	-	1	-	-	-	-	-
25 - 29	163	-	10	60	58	21	10	3	1	-	-	-	-
30 - 34	122	-	2	18	52	33	14	3	-	-	-	-	-
35 - 39	93	-	-	5	13	33	26	14	1	-	1	-	-
40 - 44	58	-	-	2	7	12	15	11	6	4	-	1	-
45 - 49	38	-	1	-	1	3	3	13	8	4	3	2	-
50 - 54	13	-	-	-	-	1	2	3	2	3	1	1	-
55 - 59	9	-	-	-	-	1	-	1	-	3	3	1	-
60 - 64	8	-	-	-	-	-	-	1	-	-	4	3	-
65 + ...	4	-	-	-	-	-	-	-	-	-	1	3	-
Unknown - Inconnu	1	-	-	-	-	-	-	-	-	-	-	-	1
Guadeloupe													
2003 (C)													
Total...................	1 701	3	49	320	437	328	197	121	74	63	41	68	-
0 - 14	-	-	-	-	-	-	-	-	-	-	-	-	-
15 - 19	28	1	8	13	4	2	-	-	-	-	-	-	-
20 - 24	226	2	24	116	56	19	5	4	-	-	-	-	-
25 - 29	423	-	14	139	169	74	19	4	1	2	-	1	-
30 - 34	412	-	2	46	159	128	46	18	3	6	2	2	-
35 - 39	238	-	-	4	33	79	69	35	8	7	3	-	-
40 - 44	122	-	-	-	14	19	35	23	18	6	7	-	-
45 - 49	94	-	1	2	-	6	18	22	25	13	5	2	-
50 - 54	61	-	-	-	-	-	4	9	10	18	13	7	-
55 - 59	35	-	-	-	2	1	-	6	6	6	4	11	-
60 - 64	29	-	-	-	-	-	1	-	3	5	4	16	-
65 - 69	11	-	-	-	-	-	-	-	-	-	2	9	-
70 + ...	22	-	-	-	-	-	-	-	-	1	1	20	-
Guatemala													
2006 (C)													
Total...................	57 505	18 790	17 622	8 550	3 973	2 172	1 522	1 230	842	599	391	547	157
0 - 14	19	13	1	-	1	-	-	-	-	-	-	-	-
15 - 19	8 409	5 969	1 655	217	29	7	3	2	2	2	-	7	7
20 - 24	20 576	9 346	8 529	1 818	282	57	20	12	7	-	6	17	16
25 - 29	12 375	2 616	5 323	3 426	714	140	42	5	5	1	-	2	5
30 - 34	5 644	552	1 403	1 924	1 317	301	68	32	7	6	3	6	3
35 - 39	2 937	167	385	675	856	611	168	50	11	4	2	4	-
40 - 44	2 066	57	162	252	422	583	401	129	36	12	2	4	2
45 - 49	1 546	33	83	107	163	251	434	354	87	23	8	1	1
50 - 54	1 103	16	35	54	79	105	192	333	212	44	16	13	1
55 - 59	882	6	22	35	54	51	94	154	235	160	57	14	-
60 - 64	721	3	5	19	29	35	50	88	133	196	111	51	1
65 - 69	441	5	10	8	17	15	28	36	44	77	110	91	-
70 - 74	322	1	3	10	5	10	11	25	38	46	47	126	-
75 + ...	333	1	3	5	5	5	10	10	25	28	29	211	1
Unknown - Inconnu	131	5	3	-	-	1	1	-	-	-	-	-	120
Jamaica - Jamaïque													
2006 (C)													
Total...................	23 181	70	2 153	5 477	4 987	3 749	2 672	1 676	1 032	568	323	474	...
0 - 14	-	-	-	-	-	-	-	-	-	-	-	-	...
15 - 19	368	31	168	89	35	23	11	6	1	1	1	2	...
20 - 24	3 726	22	1 251	1 579	531	195	86	31	19	4	2	6	...
25 - 29	6 263	11	501	2 670	1 870	742	277	108	43	15	16	10	...
30 - 34	4 635	4	136	715	1 660	1 242	525	199	86	41	11	16	...
35 - 39	3 194	1	62	266	571	940	765	360	123	55	24	27	...

22. Marriages by age of groom and by age of bride: latest available year, 1998 - 2007
Mariages selon l'âge de l'époux et selon l'âge de l'épouse: dernière année disponible, 1998 - 2007 (continued - suite)

Continent, country or area, year, code and age of bride / Continent, pays ou zone, date, code et âge de l'épouse	Total	15-19	20-24	25-29	30-34	35-39	40-44	45-49	50-54	55-59	60-64	65+	Unknown Inconnu
AMERICA, NORTH - AMÉRIQUE DU NORD													
Jamaica - Jamaïque													
2006													
40 - 44	2 190	1	18	105	221	402	635	440	202	102	23	41	...
45 - 49	1 452	-	15	35	75	147	273	364	292	133	66	52	...
50 - 54	708	-	1	15	18	39	63	122	200	105	67	78	...
55 - 59	327	-	1	-	5	17	24	28	45	71	67	69	...
60 - 64	179	-	-	2	1	1	10	15	15	27	32	76	...
65 - 69	84	-	-	1	-	-	2	1	4	10	9	57	...
70 - 74	35	-	-	-	-	-	1	2	1	3	2	26	...
75 +	20	-	-	-	-	1	-	-	1	1	3	14	...
Martinique													
2007 (C)													
Total	1 341	55	217	273	243	173	146	84	53	31	24	42	...
0 - 14	-	-	-	-	-	-	-	-	-	-	-	-	...
15 - 19	19	11	4	3	1	-	-	-	-	-	-	-	...
20 - 24	128	35	63	20	4	4	1	1	-	-	-	-	...
25 - 29	297	8	108	123	38	12	3	3	2	-	-	-	...
30 - 34	284	1	25	99	97	42	11	6	3	-	-	-	...
35 - 39	185	-	13	16	65	54	26	6	4	1	-	-	...
40 - 44	155	-	4	7	24	49	47	19	3	-	1	1	...
45 - 49	117	-	-	1	11	9	45	29	15	5	1	1	...
50 - 54	63	-	-	-	4	2	3	10	15	14	15	-	...
55 - 59	32	-	-	-	-	1	-	5	7	12	4	3	...
60 - 64	20	-	-	-	-	-	1	1	3	5	8	2	...
65 - 69	19	-	-	-	-	-	-	-	3	5	6	5	...
70 - 74	11	-	-	-	-	-	-	-	-	1	2	8	...
75 - 79	9	-	-	-	-	-	-	-	-	-	-	9	...
80 - 84	-	-	-	-	-	-	-	-	-	-	-	-	...
85 +	2	-	-	-	-	-	-	-	1	-	-	1	...
Mexico - Mexique													
2006 (+C)													
Total	586 978	66 559	194 375	155 156	79 094	35 032	18 670	11 643	7 464	5 648	5 093	7 663	504
0 - 14	4 014	2 097	1 405	332	102	32	11	4	1	1	4	1	-
15 - 19	148 442	49 221	72 672	19 776	4 828	1 237	386	147	52	35	22	16	-
20 - 24	194 555	13 485	95 820	61 749	17 020	4 299	1 272	511	190	92	43	16	16
25 - 29	122 443	1 438	20 334	58 286	29 591	8 188	2 725	1 006	449	210	112	88	15
30 - 34	55 144	228	3 256	12 180	20 978	10 913	4 271	1 756	770	392	200	188	12
35 - 39	25 056	44	621	2 175	5 064	7 456	4 961	2 388	1 070	626	315	325	10
40 - 44	13 519	11	121	429	1 114	2 133	3 476	2 917	1 516	794	516	490	10
45 - 49	8 545	7	33	108	269	563	1 114	2 077	1 777	1 101	757	737	2
50 - 54	5 547	-	4	20	62	129	308	602	1 159	1 273	1 005	983	2
55 - 59	3 655	-	5	4	15	33	88	159	326	800	1 146	1 075	2
60 - 64	2 389	-	4	3	5	14	26	54	108	214	695	1 265	4
65 - 69	1 529	-	1	3	-	2	9	7	27	72	203	1 204	1
70 - 74	849	1	1	-	1	1	4	4	10	25	56	746	-
75 - 79	367	-	1	-	-	1	1	2	2	7	12	341	-
80 - 84	112	-	-	-	2	-	-	1	1	3	1	104	-
85 - 89	31	-	-	-	-	-	-	-	-	1	1	29	-
90 - 94	6	-	-	-	-	-	-	-	-	1	-	5	-
95 +	15	-	2	-	-	-	-	-	-	-	-	13	-
Unknown - Inconnu	760	27	95	91	43	30	18	8	6	2	5	5	430
Panama													
2007 (C)													
Total	11 516	603	2 465	2 948	1 925	1 221	1 371[m]	...	682[n]	...	285[j]	...	10
15 - 19	129	73	42	9	4	-	-[m]	...	-[n]	...	-[j]	...	-
20 - 24	1 520	290	843	271	74	23	13[m]	...	3[n]	...	3[j]	...	-
25 - 29	2 839	151	990	1 253	312	88	35[m]	...	3[n]	...	2[j]	...	5
30 - 34	2 226	53	346	836	731	200	54[m]	...	3[n]	...	-[j]	...	3
35 - 39	1 495	23	136	358	441	364	164[m]	...	6[n]	...	2[j]	...	1
40 - 49	1 641	10	81	174	282	409	587[m]	...	88[n]	...	9[j]	...	1
50 - 59	838	2	14	26	62	94	336[m]	...	269[n]	...	35[j]	...	-
60 - 69	625	1	11	16	15	36	142[m]	...	266[n]	...	137[j]	...	1
70 +	199	-	2	4	3	6	39[m]	...	44[n]	...	101[j]	...	-
Unknown - Inconnu	4	-	-	1	1	1	1[m]	...	-[n]	...	-[j]	...	-

Continent, country or area, year, code and age of bride / Continent, pays ou zone, date, code et âge de l'épouse	Age of groom - âge de l'époux												
	Total	15-19	20-24	25-29	30-34	35-39	40-44	45-49	50-54	55-59	60-64	65+	Unknown Inconnu

AMERICA, NORTH - AMÉRIQUE DU NORD

Puerto Rico - Porto Rico
2006 (C)

	Total	15-19	20-24	25-29	30-34	35-39	40-44	45-49	50-54	55-59	60-64	65+	Unknown Inconnu
Total	23 185	1 004	5 097	5 733	3 590	2 313	1 570	1 183	851	622	527	695	...
0 - 14	35	18	17	-	-	-	-	-	-	-	-	-	...
15 - 19	2 546	731	1 329	369	70	30	8	4	4	1	-	-	...
20 - 24	5 718	212	2 730	1 976	561	171	41	14	5	5	2	1	...
25 - 29	5 577	36	824	2 570	1 327	519	181	76	27	10	5	2	...
30 - 34	3 102	6	145	595	1 120	688	308	142	56	20	14	8	...
35 - 39	1 961	1	42	167	374	555	413	201	126	57	18	7	...
40 - 44	1 415	-	8	41	97	232	366	325	174	95	48	29	...
45 - 49	1 037	-	1	12	32	85	178	266	201	107	94	61	...
50 - 54	703	-	1	2	4	22	52	108	162	154	93	105	...
55 - 59	472	-	-	-	3	8	20	32	63	107	122	117	...
60 - 64	320	-	-	1	1	1	3	11	25	45	80	153	...
65 - 69	172	-	-	-	1	1	-	1	8	13	37	111	...
70 - 74	76	-	-	-	-	1	-	3	-	5	8	59	...
75 - 79	35	-	-	-	-	-	-	-	-	3	5	27	...
80 - 84	11	-	-	-	-	-	-	-	-	-	-	11	...
85 +	5	-	-	-	-	-	-	-	-	-	1	4	...

Saint Kitts and Nevis -
Saint-Kitts-et-Nevis
1998 (C)

	Total	15-19	20-24	25-29	30-34	35-39	40-44	45-49	50-54	55-59	60-64	65+	Unknown Inconnu
Total	315	3	28	72	62	57	36	21	19	6	2	4	5
15 - 19	5	1	1	2	1	-	-	-	-	-	-	-	-
20 - 24	44	1	16	21	2	2	1	-	1	-	-	-	-
25 - 29	84	-	9	33	23	10	6	3	-	-	-	-	-
30 - 34	76	-	1	14	22	25	8	4	1	1	-	-	-
35 - 39	47	1	-	2	10	14	10	5	2	1	1	-	1
40 - 44	28	-	1	-	2	3	8	6	8	-	-	-	-
45 - 49	13	-	-	1	1	3	3	4	1	-	-	-	-
50 - 54	8	-	-	1	2	-	-	2	1	1	1	-	-
55 - 59	3	-	-	-	-	-	-	-	1	2	-	-	-
60 - 64	-	-	-	-	-	-	-	-	-	-	-	-	-
65 +	3	-	-	-	-	-	-	-	-	-	-	3	-
Unknown - Inconnu	4	-	-	-	-	-	-	-	-	-	-	-	4

Saint Lucia - Sainte-Lucie
2003* (C)

	Total	15-19	20-24	25-29	30-34	35-39	40-44	45-49	50-54	55-59	60-64	65+	Unknown Inconnu
Total	489	1	31	114	103	95	61	34	18	9	8	15	...
0 - 14	-	-	-	-	-	-	-	-	-	-	-	-	...
15 - 19	8	-	6	2	-	-	-	-	-	-	-	-	...
20 - 24	84	1	17	41	17	7	1	-	-	-	-	-	...
25 - 29	128	-	8	41	47	23	4	3	1	-	1	-	...
30 - 34	102	-	-	23	30	30	11	5	2	1	-	-	...
35 - 39	71	-	-	4	6	26	22	8	5	-	-	-	...
40 - 44	41	-	-	2	1	7	16	10	2	2	1	-	...
45 - 49	23	-	-	1	-	2	3	7	5	2	-	3	...
50 - 54	13	-	-	-	2	-	3	1	2	1	3	1	...
55 - 59	8	-	-	-	-	-	-	-	1	1	2	4	...
60 - 64	4	-	-	-	-	-	-	-	-	1	1	2	...
65 +	7	-	-	-	-	-	1	-	-	1	-	5	...

Trinidad and Tobago -
Trinité-et-Tobago
2005 (C)

	Total	15-19	20-24	25-29	30-34	35-39	40-44	45-49	50-54	55-59	60-64	65+	Unknown Inconnu
Total	8 144	122	1 350	2 247	1 591	927	703	458	297	180	127	142	...
0 - 14	3	1	-	1	1	-	-	-	-	-	-	-	...
15 - 19	623	72	300	178	50	14	7	1	-	-	-	1	...
20 - 24	2 285	39	794	907	355	120	43	16	7	2	1	1	...
25 - 29	2 127	9	197	911	629	234	89	36	12	7	2	1	...
30 - 34	1 177	-	38	186	376	288	179	62	21	11	15	1	...
35 - 39	716	-	15	45	125	189	187	90	36	16	7	6	...
40 - 44	503	1	4	15	45	61	130	131	58	32	14	12	...
45 - 49	330	-	-	2	8	10	49	90	80	39	33	19	...
50 - 54	188	-	2	1	2	6	10	24	59	44	20	20	...
55 - 59	92	-	-	-	-	1	6	5	19	15	20	26	...
60 - 64	56	-	-	-	-	3	3	2	5	10	7	26	...
65 +	43	-	-	-	-	1	-	1	-	4	8	29	...
Unknown - Inconnu	1	-	-	1	-	-	-	-	-	-	-	-	...

22. Marriages by age of groom and by age of bride: latest available year, 1998 - 2007
Mariages selon l'âge de l'époux et selon l'âge de l'épouse: dernière année disponible, 1998 - 2007 (continued - suite)

Continent, country or area, year, code and age of bride / Continent, pays ou zone, date, code et âge de l'épouse	Total	Age of groom - âge de l'époux											Unknown Inconnu
		15-19	20-24	25-29	30-34	35-39	40-44	45-49	50-54	55-59	60-64	65+	

AMERICA, NORTH - AMÉRIQUE DU NORD

Turks and Caicos Islands - Îles Turques et Caïques
2005 (C)

Age of bride	Total	15-19	20-24	25-29	30-34	35-39	40-44	45-49	50-54	55-59	60-64	65+	Unknown
Total	489	-	19	88	149	95	69	34	20	6	7	1	1
0 - 14	-	-	-	-	-	-	-	-	-	-	-	-	-
15 - 19	3	-	1	1	1	-	-	-	-	-	-	-	-
20 - 24	40	-	12	18	8	1	1	-	-	-	-	-	-
25 - 29	120	-	4	45	48	14	5	2	1	-	1	-	-
30 - 34	142	-	2	19	69	31	13	5	3	-	1	-	-
35 - 39	103	-	-	5	18	37	28	9	5	1	-	-	-
40 - 44	37	-	-	-	1	9	15	7	2	1	1	1	-
45 - 49	31	-	-	-	4	3	5	7	7	4	1	1	-
50 - 54	8	-	-	-	-	-	2	2	2	-	1	-	-
55 - 59	3	-	-	-	-	-	-	1	-	-	2	-	-
60 - 64	1	-	-	-	-	-	-	-	-	-	2	-	-
65 +	-	-	-	-	-	-	-	-	1	-	-	-	-
Unknown - Inconnu	1	-	-	-	-	-	-	-	-	-	-	-	1
2006 (C)													
Total	636	-	29	131	144	137	97	56	25	7	6	4	-
0 - 14	-	...	...	...	...	...	...	...	...	...	...	...	...
15 - 19	1	...	...	...	...	...	...	...	...	...	...	...	...
20 - 24	61	...	...	...	...	...	...	...	...	...	...	...	...
25 - 29	167	...	...	...	...	...	...	...	...	...	...	...	...
30 - 34	167	...	...	...	...	...	...	...	...	...	...	...	...
35 - 39	135	...	...	...	...	...	...	...	...	...	...	...	...
40 - 44	61	...	...	...	...	...	...	...	...	...	...	...	...
45 - 49	24	...	...	...	...	...	...	...	...	...	...	...	...
50 - 54	12	...	...	...	...	...	...	...	...	...	...	...	...
55 - 59	6	...	...	...	...	...	...	...	...	...	...	...	...
60 - 64	1	...	...	...	...	...	...	...	...	...	...	...	...
65 +	1	...	...	...	...	...	...	...	...	...	...	...	...
Unknown - Inconnu	-	...	...	...	...	...	...	...	...	...	...	...	...

AMERICA, SOUTH - AMÉRIQUE DU SUD

Brazil - Brésil[6]
2007 (U)

Age of bride	Total	15-19	20-24	25-29	30-34	35-39	40-44	45-49	50-54	55-59	60-64	65+	Unknown
Total	916 006	32 735	225 618	272 818	158 053	84 312	49 495	30 310	19 931	14 186	9 665	18 036	830
0 - 14	610	181	282	90	32	10	6	2	1	2	-	-	-
15 - 19	141 083	20 503	75 900	32 904	8 326	2 271	728	243	97	47	22	34	1
20 - 24	267 050	9 329	105 514	105 261	32 226	9 382	3 194	1 185	446	241	99	167	2
25 - 29	231 881	2 014	33 559	99 740	61 694	21 518	7 753	3 026	1 311	560	324	379	3
30 - 34	118 690	452	7 497	25 806	38 389	25 540	11 453	4 992	2 213	1 133	536	674	3
35 - 39	62 620	150	2 012	6 495	12 072	16 193	12 455	6 216	3 275	1 766	910	1 075	1
40 - 44	37 794	62	578	1 778	3 632	6 368	8 626	7 088	4 201	2 402	1 336	1 722	1
45 - 49	23 214	20	142	502	1 159	2 064	3 458	4 702	4 171	2 897	1 634	2 465	-
50 - 54	14 656	12	61	141	342	672	1 225	1 913	2 666	2 771	1 949	2 902	2
55 - 59	8 401	5	26	46	92	198	405	622	1 038	1 587	1 543	2 838	1
60 - 64	4 454	2	19	20	38	60	109	190	335	527	839	2 315	-
65 +	4 703	5	20	27	43	34	81	129	177	252	471	3 463	-
Unknown - Inconnu	850	-	8	8	8	2	2	2	-	1	2	2	815

Chile - Chili
2006 (+C)

Age of bride	Total	15-19	20-24	25-29	30-34	35-39	40-44	45-49	50-54	55-59	60-64	65+	Unknown
Total	58 155	1 152	11 884	19 373	12 702	5 946	2 402	1 378	871	649	528	1 270	...
0 - 14	-	-	-	-	-	-	-	-	-	-	-	-	...
15 - 19	4 523	659	2 507	1 000	257	66	16	10	4	1	-	-	...
20 - 24	16 875	409	6 899	6 858	2 059	473	114	44	6	1	1	2	...
25 - 29	18 348	68	2 029	9 073	5 324	1 343	352	101	26	13	7	12	...
30 - 34	8 929	11	352	1 965	3 881	1 810	577	197	78	28	16	14	...
35 - 39	4 297	4	72	380	918	1 775	623	277	109	63	37	39	...
40 - 44	1 882	1	19	68	199	349	454	319	210	119	57	87	...
45 - 49	1 159	-	6	23	46	91	191	270	182	147	87	116	...
50 - 54	800	-	-	6	16	27	53	113	162	131	103	189	...
55 - 59	502	-	-	-	2	10	18	35	61	88	107	181	...
60 - 64	355	-	-	-	-	2	2	9	19	39	59	225	...
65 - 69	239	-	-	-	-	-	1	12	15	33	178		...

Continent, country or area, year, code and age of bride / Continent, pays ou zone, date, code et âge de l'épouse	Total	15-19	20-24	25-29	30-34	35-39	40-44	45-49	50-54	55-59	60-64	65+	Unknown Inconnu
AMERICA, SOUTH - AMÉRIQUE DU SUD													
Chile - Chili													
2006													
70 - 74	139	-	-	-	-	1	2	1	3	11	121		...
75 +	107	-	-	-	-	1	-	1	1	6	98		...
Ecuador - Équateur[7]													
2007 (U)													
Total	76 154	6 578	23 387	20 121	10 700	5 739	3 352	2 181	1 488	889	589	1 011	103
0 - 14	656	266	293	69	16	6	1	2	-	-	-	-	1
15 - 19	16 393	4 419	8 360	2 638	656	193	56	32	10	4	5	7	6
20 - 24	24 748	1 587	11 242	8 203	2 473	794	238	116	52	21	6	8	3
25 - 29	16 381	239	2 759	7 088	4 043	1 382	496	216	98	22	11	23	2
30 - 34	7 531	40	490	1 563	2 449	1 682	747	292	131	70	32	32	3
35 - 39	4 021	10	131	379	728	1 128	838	433	215	95	34	28	2
40 - 44	2 534	5	61	113	211	385	657	554	285	128	73	61	1
45 - 49	1 537	6	14	39	83	117	224	340	365	178	78	93	-
50 - 54	947	1	7	9	18	26	63	137	225	202	130	129	-
55 - 59	499	-	2	2	3	11	16	38	71	110	117	129	-
60 - 64	326	-	1	1	1	2	7	6	29	38	77	164	-
65 - 69	193	-	3	-	2	4	3	7	5	13	16	140	-
70 +	221	-	1	-	3	1	1	4	2	6	9	194	-
Unknown - Inconnu	167	5	23	17	14	8	5	4	-	2	1	3	85
French Guiana - Guyane française													
2007 (C)													
Total	667	5	48	123	150	108	79	47	48	26	17	16	...
15 - 19	30	-	10	13	4	-	1	1	-	1	-	-	...
20 - 24	93	3	22	33	15	8	7	-	1	2	1	1	...
25 - 29	151	1	5	51	57	17	7	5	2	6	-	-	...
30 - 34	135	1	8	16	41	35	18	7	7	2	-	-	...
35 - 39	98	-	3	6	20	27	20	11	2	6	2	1	...
40 - 44	62	-	-	4	7	10	15	10	9	2	3	2	...
45 - 49	55	-	-	-	3	5	9	10	16	4	5	3	...
50 - 54	23	-	-	-	2	4	2	3	6	2	2	2	...
55 - 59	13	-	-	-	1	2	-	-	3	1	2	4	...
60 - 64	2	-	-	-	-	-	-	-	1	-	-	1	...
65 - 69	4	-	-	-	-	-	-	-	1	-	2	1	...
70 - 74	1	-	-	-	-	-	-	-	-	-	-	1	...
75 - 79	-	-	-	-	-	-	-	-	-	-	-	-	...
80 - 84	-	-	-	-	-	-	-	-	-	-	-	-	...
85 +	-	-	-	-	-	-	-	-	-	-	-	-	...
Paraguay													
2006 (U)													
Total	19 476	598	5 663	6 145	3 147	1 597	875	525	308	184	137	278	19
0 - 14	17	3	9	3	1	-	-	-	1	-	-	-	-
15 - 19	4 009	374	2 061	1 076	319	112	42	13	3	4	1	4	-
20 - 24	6 625	168	2 731	2 553	788	258	68	25	22	5	-	7	-
25 - 29	4 464	43	682	1 975	1 101	413	140	53	28	16	5	8	-
30 - 34	1 845	8	123	398	632	372	176	69	25	17	11	13	1
35 - 39	974	2	37	88	194	275	191	118	38	15	6	9	1
40 - 44	607	-	9	29	72	106	166	115	45	24	22	18	1
45 - 49	375	-	5	12	26	36	63	82	72	30	19	30	-
50 - 54	210	-	1	3	6	18	17	37	41	28	21	37	1
55 - 59	140	-	-	1	4	2	4	8	25	30	29	37	-
60 - 64	79	-	1	-	-	3	3	2	7	12	14	37	-
65 - 69	54	-	-	1	2	1	2	2	-	1	6	39	-
70 - 74	27	-	-	1	-	1	-	-	-	2	1	22	-
75 +	22	-	1	-	-	-	2	-	-	-	1	17	1
Unknown - Inconnu	28	-	3	5	2	-	1	1	1	-	1	-	14
Suriname													
2002 (C)													
Total	2 005	23	421	542	367	208	142	101	65	136[i]	...	...	...
0 - 14	6	...	...	...	...	...	...	...	...	...	...	...	...
15 - 19	382	...	...	...	...	...	...	...	...	...	...	...	...
20 - 24	596	...	...	...	...	...	...	...	...	...	...	...	...
25 - 29	333	...	...	...	...	...	...	...	...	...	...	...	...
30 - 34	233	...	...	...	...	...	...	...	...	...	...	...	...
35 - 39	187	...	...	...	...	...	...	...	...	...	...	...	...

| Continent, country or area, year, code and age of bride / Continent, pays ou zone, date, code et âge de l'épouse | Total | Age of groom - âge de l'époux | | | | | | | | | | | |

Continent, pays ou zone, date, code et âge de l'épouse	Total	15-19	20-24	25-29	30-34	35-39	40-44	45-49	50-54	55-59	60-64	65+	Unknown Inconnu
AMERICA, SOUTH - AMÉRIQUE DU SUD													
Suriname													
2002													
40 - 44	113	...	...	...	...	...	...	...	...	...	...	...	...
45 - 49	72	...	...	...	...	...	...	...	...	...	...	...	...
50 - 54	36	...	...	...	...	...	...	...	...	...	...	...	...
55 +	47	...	...	...	...	...	...	...	...	...	...	...	...
Uruguay													
2002 (C)													
Total	14 073	453[a]	3 015	4 227	2 292	1 209	1 335[m]	...	1 542[h]	...	...	...	...
0 - 19	1 728	300[a]	978	342	78	15	9[m]	...	6[h]	...	...	...	...
20 - 24	3 618	111[a]	1 434	1 446	423	120	57[m]	...	27[h]	...	...	...	...
25 - 29	3 900	33[a]	468	1 890	930	366	177[m]	...	36[h]	...	...	...	...
30 - 34	1 890	3[a]	93	384	642	363	318[m]	...	87[h]	...	...	...	...
35 - 39	972	-[a]	33	111	141	234	309[m]	...	144[h]	...	...	...	...
40 - 49	1 011	6[a]	9	36	72	105	378[m]	...	405[h]	...	...	...	...
50 +	954	-[a]	-	18	6	6	87[m]	...	837[h]	...	...	...	...
Unknown - Inconnu	-	-[a]	-	-	-	-	-[m]	...	-[h]	...	...	...	...
Venezuela (Bolivarian Republic of) - Venezuela (République bolivarienne du)[6]													
2007 (C)													
Total	93 003	3 804	21 810	27 776	16 657	9 160	5 199	3 216	2 171	1 275	1 917[j]	...	...
0 - 14	562	180	230	85	43	8	4	1	1	3	7[j]	...	...
15 - 19	12 806	2 412	6 445	2 650	828	285	105	32	17	8	20[j]	...	...
20 - 24	27 006	898	10 802	10 070	3 341	1 159	427	164	64	19	59[j]	...	...
25 - 29	25 124	222	3 355	11 264	6 316	2 478	856	360	141	69	61[j]	...	...
30 - 34	12 459	43	676	2 732	4 310	2 516	1 195	508	270	95	112[j]	...	...
35 - 39	6 429	23	194	676	1 255	1 792	1 208	663	343	150	123[j]	...	...
40 - 44	3 618	7	60	175	371	615	919	718	394	189	170[j]	...	...
45 - 49	2 180	4	24	67	115	206	337	496	458	241	231[j]	...	...
50 - 54	1 263	4	7	24	35	67	107	178	309	266	265[j]	...	...
55 - 59	728	3	3	6	15	19	32	66	121	168	294[j]	...	...
60 +	828	8	14	27	28	15	9	30	53	67	575[j]	...	...
ASIA - ASIE													
Armenia - Arménie													
2007 (C)													
Total	18 145	101	4 576	7 313	3 409	1 238	553	347	210	137	261[j]	...	...
15 - 19	1 999	72	980	824	109	12	-	-	-	-	2[j]	...	...
20 - 24	9 408	26	3 309	4 507	1 355	175	18	7	1	1	9[j]	...	...
25 - 29	4 168	3	255	1 842	1 440	485	103	24	8	4	4[j]	...	...
30 - 34	1 316	-	16	107	446	410	242	74	13	4	4[j]	...	...
35 - 39	416	-	5	16	38	113	107	90	32	8	7[j]	...	...
40 - 44	225	-	1	-	9	27	45	74	38	15	16[j]	...	...
45 - 49	233	-	2	6	5	12	24	54	69	35	26[j]	...	...
50 - 54	177	-	1	2	2	9	22	45	42	52[j]		...	...
55 - 59	90	-	-	-	1	-	4	2	3	22	58[j]	...	...
60 +	113	-	7	9	4	2	1	-	1	6	83[j]	...	...
Azerbaijan - Azerbaïdjan													
2007 (+C)													
Total	81 758	1 041	24 886	31 467	13 753	5 637	2 269	1 137	580	333	655[j]	...	...
15 - 19	19 751	636	9 101	7 807	1 928	241	24	6	2	-	6[j]	...	...
20 - 24	37 268	347	13 736	16 208	5 539	1 193	179	35	14	10	7[j]	...	...
25 - 29	14 781	45	1 743	6 351	4 146	1 824	509	116	27	7	13[j]	...	...
30 - 34	5 165	10	210	842	1 667	1 443	647	242	66	14	24[j]	...	...
35 - 39	2 345	1	66	201	354	706	510	288	114	50	55[j]	...	...
40 - 44	1 285	1	16	36	91	189	309	274	152	93	124[j]	...	...
45 - 49	673	-	8	11	20	35	82	145	124	74	174[j]	...	...
50 - 54	284	1	2	5	4	2	5	23	70	50	122[j]	...	...
55 - 59	104	-	-	2	2	1	3	6	8	22	60[j]	...	...
60 +	102	-	4	4	2	3	1	2	3	13	70[j]	...	...

Continent, country or area, year, code and age of bride / Continent, pays ou zone, date, code et âge de l'épouse	Total	Age of groom - âge de l'époux											Unknown Inconnu
		15-19	20-24	25-29	30-34	35-39	40-44	45-49	50-54	55-59	60-64	65+	
ASIA - ASIE													
Bahrain - Bahreïn													
2006[2] (...)													
Total	4 338	51	1 421	1 675	572	247	160	88	123[h]	...	...	...	-
0 - 14	12	-	9	1	1	-	-	-	-[h]	...	...	...	-
15 - 19	857	40	511	257	33	9	1	4	2[h]	...	...	...	-
20 - 24	2 091	10	823	969	210	43	25	5	6[h]	...	...	...	-
25 - 29	848	1	68	392	232	78	42	17	18[h]	...	...	...	-
30 - 34	276	-	9	43	78	73	35	19	19[h]	...	...	...	-
35 - 39	134	-	1	11	15	30	34	20	23[h]	...	...	...	-
40 - 44	71	-	-	1	2	10	14	13	31[h]	...	...	...	-
45 - 49	31	-	-	1	1	4	5	7	13[h]	...	...	...	-
50 +	18	-	-	-	-	-	4	3	11[h]	...	...	...	-
Unknown - Inconnu	...	...	...	...	...	...	...	...	...	...	...	...	-
Brunei Darussalam - Brunéi Darussalam													
2004 (...)													
Total	2 027	45	414	701	478	191	99	47	21	12	6	12	...
0 - 14	10	...	...	...	...	...	...	...	...	...	...	...	...
15 - 19	227	...	...	...	...	...	...	...	...	...	...	...	...
20 - 24	635	...	...	...	...	...	...	...	...	...	...	...	...
25 - 29	626	...	...	...	...	...	...	...	...	...	...	...	...
30 - 34	308	...	...	...	...	...	...	...	...	...	...	...	...
35 - 39	118	...	...	...	...	...	...	...	...	...	...	...	...
40 - 44	53	...	...	...	...	...	...	...	...	...	...	...	...
45 - 49	28	...	...	...	...	...	...	...	...	...	...	...	...
50 - 54	16	...	...	...	...	...	...	...	...	...	...	...	...
55 - 59	5	...	...	...	...	...	...	...	...	...	...	...	...
60 - 64	1	...	...	...	...	...	...	...	...	...	...	...	...
65 - 69	-	...	...	...	...	...	...	...	...	...	...	...	...
70 +	-	...	...	...	...	...	...	...	...	...	...	...	...
China, Hong Kong SAR - Chine, Hong Kong RAS													
2005 (C)													
Total	43 018	220[b]	3 525	9 948	10 834	6 056	4 099	2 978	1 938	1 247	687	1 486	...
16 - 19	935	92[b]	420	232	107	38	23	11	6	2	1	3	...
20 - 24	8 114	106[b]	2 188	2 622	1 483	780	467	284	98	48	14	24	...
25 - 29	14 231	16[b]	648	5 583	4 439	1 636	891	556	232	133	37	60	...
30 - 34	10 208	1[b]	175	1 222	3 927	2 078	1 130	681	440	261	123	170	...
35 - 39	4 687	1[b]	57	192	645	1 113	894	630	440	271	157	287	...
40 - 44	2 492	2[b]	20	59	153	277	482	474	360	224	156	285	...
45 - 49	1 198	1[b]	14	21	55	94	148	238	233	145	77	172	...
50 - 54	612	1[b]	2	13	19	27	50	76	102	99	46	177	...
55 - 59	252	-[b]	1	3	5	10	11	21	21	42	43	95	...
60 - 64	113	-[b]	-	-	1	1	3	5	1	10	23	69	...
65 - 69	73	-[b]	-	1	-	1	-	-	2	7	7	55	...
70 - 74	64	-[b]	-	-	-	1	-	1	3	5	2	52	...
75 +	39	-[b]	-	-	-	-	-	1	-	-	1	37	...
China, Macao SAR - Chine, Macao RAS													
2007 (+C)													
Total	2 047	23	388	637	494	212	113	89	48	23	10	10	...
15 - 19	52	9	32	6	5	-	-	-	-	-	-	-	...
20 - 24	642	10	289	202	84	28	13	10	4	2	-	-	...
25 - 29	742	4	59	366	221	62	10	14	5	1	-	-	...
30 - 34	371	-	6	52	156	77	31	26	13	6	2	2	...
35 - 39	126	-	1	8	17	32	32	17	9	7	2	1	...
40 - 44	67	-	-	2	5	9	24	13	7	2	2	3	...
45 - 49	32	-	1	1	6	3	2	6	8	2	3	-	...
50 - 54	10	-	-	-	-	-	1	2	2	3	-	2	...
55 - 59	3	-	-	-	-	1	-	-	-	-	1	1	...
60 - 64	1	-	-	-	-	-	-	1	-	-	-	-	...
65 - 69	-	-	-	-	-	-	-	-	-	-	-	-	...
70 +	1	-	-	-	-	-	-	-	-	-	-	1	...

22. Marriages by age of groom and by age of bride: latest available year, 1998 - 2007
Mariages selon l'âge de l'époux et selon l'âge de l'épouse: dernière année disponible, 1998 - 2007 (continued - suite)

Continent, country or area, year, code and age of bride / Continent, pays ou zone, date, code et âge de l'épouse	Total	15-19	20-24	25-29	30-34	35-39	40-44	45-49	50-54	55-59	60-64	65+	Unknown Inconnu
ASIA - ASIE													
Cyprus - Chypre													
2006[8,9] (C)													
Total....................	4 887	13	645	1 813	1 117	559	302	151	97	70	41	76	3
15 - 19	131	7	84	31	7	2	-	-	-	-	-	-	-
20 - 24	1 302	4	449	627	145	42	23	7	4	1	-	-	-
25 - 29	1 931	-	83	985	573	178	71	21	10	7	1	2	-
30 - 34	838	2	21	134	319	214	93	29	15	4	2	5	-
35 - 39	313	-	5	24	50	91	60	42	16	7	11	7	-
40 - 44	155	-	3	10	14	23	36	23	18	14	5	9	-
45 - 49	107	-	-	2	6	9	17	24	15	13	8	13	-
50 - 54	54	-	-	-	3	-	1	3	15	14	4	14	-
55 - 59	31	-	-	-	-	-	1	2	4	8	8	8	-
60 - 64	13	-	-	-	-	-	-	-	-	1	2	10	-
65 - 69	6	-	-	-	-	-	-	-	-	1	-	5	-
70 - 74	2	-	-	-	-	-	-	-	-	-	-	2	-
75 - 79	1	-	-	-	-	-	-	-	-	-	-	1	-
80 + ...	-	-	-	-	-	-	-	-	-	-	-	-	-
Unknown - Inconnu	3	-	-	-	-	-	-	-	-	-	-	-	3
Georgia - Géorgie													
2007 (C)													
Total....................	24 891	896[b]	6 591	7 354	4 611	2 536	1 322	691	358	204	306[j]	...	22
16 - 19	4 035	...	...	...	...	...	...	...	...	...	...	...	...
20 - 24	9 786	...	...	...	...	...	...	...	...	...	...	...	...
25 - 29	5 572	...	...	...	...	...	...	...	...	...	...	...	...
30 - 34	2 733	...	...	...	...	...	...	...	...	...	...	...	...
35 - 39	1 278	...	...	...	...	...	...	...	...	...	...	...	...
40 - 44	647	...	...	...	...	...	...	...	...	...	...	...	...
45 - 49	403	...	...	...	...	...	...	...	...	...	...	...	...
50 - 54	219	...	...	...	...	...	...	...	...	...	...	...	...
55 - 59	91	...	...	...	...	...	...	...	...	...	...	...	...
60 + ...	122	...	...	...	...	...	...	...	...	...	...	...	...
Unknown - Inconnu	5	...	...	...	...	...	...	...	...	...	...	...	...
Israel - Israël[10]													
2006 (C)													
Total....................	44 685	1 472	10 943	17 090	8 966	2 720	1 041	569	378	281	165	295	765
15 - 19	7 033	1 083	3 623	1 732	350	41	7	1	-	1	-	1	194
20 - 24	16 127	356	6 611	6 776	1 750	273	53	6	2	1	1	4	294
25 - 29	13 482	7	526	7 597	4 157	806	168	52	17	7	3	3	139
30 - 34	4 712	2	39	785	2 301	1 047	295	118	33	10	3	4	75
35 - 39	1 432	1	12	63	284	447	337	145	56	25	15	10	37
40 - 44	575	-	4	6	25	59	136	141	96	40	27	29	12
45 - 49	340	-	-	2	3	9	18	78	103	63	25	33	6
50 - 54	211	-	-	1	-	5	5	13	56	82	25	22	2
55 - 59	155	-	-	-	2	-	1	2	7	40	41	57	5
60 - 64	74	-	-	-	-	-	-	-	2	5	17	49	1
65 - 69	38	-	-	-	-	-	-	-	-	1	1	36	-
70 - 74	25	-	-	-	-	-	-	-	-	-	-	25	-
75 + ...	22	-	2	-	3	-	2	-	-	-	-	15	-
Unknown - Inconnu	459	23	126	128	91	33	19	13	6	6	7	7	-
Japan - Japon[11]													
2007 (+C)													
Total....................	611 267	6 563	78 276	206 699	162 608	80 613	32 920	16 380	10 024	8 563	4 394	4 225	2
15 - 19	14 303	4 707	6 392	1 964	710	283	107	65	32	32	8	3	-
20 - 24	117 159	1 630	52 711	40 232	14 440	4 770	1 566	824	483	341	112	50	-
25 - 29	240 522	173	15 738	133 726	64 761	17 631	4 668	1 992	929	615	205	84	-
30 - 34	142 083	35	2 786	26 259	67 733	31 558	8 532	2 895	1 205	709	271	100	-
35 - 39	57 768	12	553	3 902	12 955	22 162	11 015	3 941	1 688	1 041	337	161	1
40 - 44	18 127	5	76	518	1 658	3 457	5 577	3 478	1 661	1 087	418	192	-
45 - 49	8 332	-	14	67	290	620	1 154	2 407	1 790	1 239	494	257	-
50 - 54	5 087	1	6	20	44	110	233	583	1 561	1 549	626	354	-
55 - 59	4 088	-	-	7	10	15	55	169	537	1 533	1 086	676	-
60 - 64	1 941	-	-	1	6	6	9	19	115	323	649	813	-
65 - 69	1 084	-	-	2	-	-	4	6	21	82	155	814	-
70 - 74	505	-	-	1	-	1	-	1	1	12	23	466	-
75 - 79	184	-	-	-	-	-	-	-	1	-	7	176	-
80 + ...	83	-	-	-	-	-	-	-	-	-	3	79	1
Unknown - Inconnu	1	-	-	-	1	-	-	-	-	-	-	-	-

22. Marriages by age of groom and by age of bride: latest available year, 1998 - 2007
Mariages selon l'âge de l'époux et selon l'âge de l'épouse: dernière année disponible, 1998 - 2007 (continued - suite)

Continent, country or area, year, code and age of bride / Continent, pays ou zone, date, code et âge de l'épouse	Total	Age of groom - âge de l'époux											
		15-19	20-24	25-29	30-34	35-39	40-44	45-49	50-54	55-59	60-64	65+	Unknown Inconnu
ASIA - ASIE													
Jordan - Jordanie[12]													
1999 (+C)													
Total	39 443	1 100ª	10 920	15 384	6 781	2 378	1 017	621	361	345	231	305	...
0 - 14	36	6ª	15	13	2	-	-	-	-	-	-	-	...
15 - 19	12 991	866ª	5 824	4 847	1 096	209	75	44	9	15	4	2	...
20 - 24	15 789	185ª	4 377	7 316	2 862	692	195	73	39	22	11	17	...
25 - 29	6 517	29ª	537	2 663	1 938	758	272	156	70	48	24	22	...
30 - 34	2 414	8ª	110	399	671	495	268	145	98	103	62	55	...
35 - 39	990	6ª	31	95	152	166	135	130	76	65	66	68	...
40 - 44	414	-ª	16	31	41	41	49	52	41	49	34	60	...
45 - 49	163	-ª	7	10	15	10	16	17	18	20	14	36	...
50 +	129	-ª	3	10	4	7	7	4	10	23	16	45	...
Kazakhstan													
2007 (C)													
Total	146 379	4 516ª	53 202	47 966	20 357	9 019	4 561	2 804	1 621	1 004	1 329ʲ	...	...
0 - 17	1 653	435ª	943	235	34	3	2	-	1	-	-ʲ	...	...
18 - 19	19 235	2 488ª	11 721	4 223	697	77	20	6	1	2	-ʲ	...	...
20 - 24	72 121	1 443ª	35 762	27 327	6 157	1 115	229	64	15	6	3ʲ	...	...
25 - 29	28 988	127ª	4 170	13 619	7 683	2 408	686	188	64	27	16ʲ	...	...
30 - 34	11 956	17ª	490	2 096	4 595	2 994	1 113	427	142	47	35ʲ	...	...
35 - 39	5 539	4ª	92	387	944	1 905	1 292	588	189	93	45ʲ	...	...
40 - 44	2 726	1ª	16	65	177	399	884	675	291	138	80ʲ	...	...
45 - 49	1 801	1ª	2	10	55	95	253	620	427	197	141ʲ	...	...
50 - 54	1 086	-ª	2	2	9	19	66	189	353	247	199ʲ	...	...
55 - 59	625	-ª	-	-	-	3	14	37	115	180	276ʲ	...	...
60 +	649	-ª	4	2	6	1	2	10	23	67	534ʲ	...	...
Kuwait - Koweït													
2007 (C)													
Total	13 315	545ª	4 376	3 577	1 572	824	546	339	183	114	49	60	1 130
0 - 14	65	22ª	25	4	1	2	1	-	-	-	-	-	10
15 - 19	3 146	404ª	1 713	582	89	21	15	9	7	4	1	1	300
20 - 24	5 224	94ª	2 226	1 735	447	91	41	20	9	3	3	4	551
25 - 29	2 401	15ª	250	941	604	250	120	54	19	8	6	4	130
30 - 34	983	3ª	32	150	280	221	128	65	37	18	1	2	46
35 - 39	578	1ª	11	46	69	151	121	75	41	14	13	8	28
40 - 44	332	-ª	10	21	22	51	74	60	28	29	6	17	14
45 - 49	142	-ª	5	9	10	10	25	33	23	16	3	3	5
50 - 54	77	-ª	-	-	3	8	1	11	12	12	12	11	7
55 - 59	27	-ª	1	1	-	-	5	2	3	7	-	8	-
60 +	8	-ª	-	-	-	-	1	1	-	1	3	2	-
Unknown - Inconnu	332	6ª	103	88	47	19	14	9	4	2	1	-	39
Kyrgyzstan - Kirghizstan													
2007 (C)													
Total	44 392	823	14 995	16 597	6 507	2 581	1 244	709	421	238	96	180	1
0 - 14	-	-	-	-	-	-	-	-	-	-	-	-	-
15 - 19	7 813	563	4 615	2 356	258	20	1	-	-	-	-	-	-
20 - 24	22 672	238	9 648	10 384	2 078	269	37	13	3	-	1	1	-
25 - 29	7 899	20	667	3 482	2 773	744	146	41	15	8	2	1	-
30 - 34	3 054	2	56	324	1 208	992	319	100	31	14	4	4	-
35 - 39	1 424	-	6	38	163	473	465	179	59	22	8	11	-
40 - 44	681	-	2	9	19	64	226	189	97	37	12	25	1
45 - 49	413	-	-	2	7	17	39	146	116	55	14	17	-
50 - 54	210	-	-	-	-	1	10	29	75	53	18	24	-
55 - 59	126	-	1	-	-	1	1	11	19	39	23	31	-
60 - 64	36	-	-	-	-	-	-	-	3	6	9	18	-
65 - 69	38	-	-	-	-	-	-	1	2	4	4	27	-
70 - 74	19	-	-	-	-	-	-	-	1	-	1	17	-
75 +	4	-	-	-	-	-	-	-	-	-	-	4	-
Unknown - Inconnu	3	-	-	-	2	1	-	-	-	-	-	-	-
Mongolia - Mongolie													
2007 (C)													
Total	40 965	770ᵈ	12 660	14 965	9 191	2 322	662	306	89ʰ	...	...	...	...
18 - 19	2 257	...	...	...	...	...	...	...	...	...	...	...	...
20 - 24	15 180	...	...	...	...	...	...	...	...	...	...	...	...
25 - 29	13 836	...	...	...	...	...	...	...	...	...	...	...	...

22. Marriages by age of groom and by age of bride: latest available year, 1998 - 2007
Mariages selon l'âge de l'époux et selon l'âge de l'épouse: dernière année disponible, 1998 - 2007 (continued - suite)

Age of groom - âge de l'époux

Continent, country or area, year, code and age of bride / Continent, pays ou zone, date, code et âge de l'épouse	Total	15-19	20-24	25-29	30-34	35-39	40-44	45-49	50-54	55-59	60-64	65+	Unknown Inconnu
ASIA - ASIE													
Mongolia - Mongolie													
2007													
30 - 34	7 057	...	...	...	...	...	...	...	...	...	...	...	...
35 - 39	1 864	...	...	...	...	...	...	...	...	...	...	...	...
40 - 44	526	...	...	...	...	...	...	...	...	...	...	...	...
45 - 49	203	...	...	...	...	...	...	...	...	...	...	...	...
50 +	42	...	...	...	...	...	...	...	...	...	...	...	...
Occupied Palestinian Territory - Territoire palestinien occupé													
2007 (C)													
Total	32 685	2 509	13 066	11 108	3 150	1 028	615	362	244	211	391[j]	...	...
0 - 14	742	177	412	145	6	1	-	-	-	-	-[j]	...	...
15 - 19	16 434	2 127	8 561	4 883	724	95	28	7	5	1	3[j]	...	...
20 - 24	10 787	186	3 761	4 812	1 470	338	130	42	20	13	15[j]	...	...
25 - 29	2 886	16	293	1 157	695	367	168	95	49	27	19[j]	...	...
30 - 34	964	2	26	90	199	168	180	101	80	55	63[j]	...	...
35 - 39	499	1	8	16	48	46	83	74	45	54	124[j]	...	...
40 - 44	239	-	5	3	8	9	22	26	34	37	95[j]	...	...
45 - 49	93	-	-	2	-	4	3	14	8	17	45[j]	...	...
50 - 54	30	-	-	-	-	1	3	3	5	-	18[j]	...	...
55 - 59	5	-	-	-	-	-	-	-	2	-	3[j]	...	...
60 +	6	-	-	-	-	-	-	-	-	-	6[j]	...	...
Philippines													
2005 (U)													
Total	518 595	15 786[a]	155 408	175 647	84 140	38 494	19 390	11 559	18 116[h]	...	...	...	
0 - 19	69 335	8 859[a]	38 036	16 221	4 164	1 217	412	198	227[h]	...	...	...	55
20 - 24	200 210	6 074[a]	91 009	72 056	20 075	6 202	2 294	1 116	1 381[h]	...	...	...	1
25 - 29	141 944	685[a]	22 143	69 985	32 333	9 985	3 440	1 582	1 782[h]	...	...	...	3
30 - 34	55 228	114[a]	3 177	13 566	20 436	10 665	3 996	1 677	1 594[h]	...	...	...	9
35 - 39	24 969	32[a]	746	2 939	5 323	7 459	4 576	2 111	1 779[h]	...	...	...	3
40 - 44	12 353	12[a]	196	634	1 323	2 181	3 331	2 384	2 289[h]	...	...	...	4
45 - 49	6 726	6[a]	45	153	333	613	980	2 384	2 289[h]	...	...	...	3
50 +	7 736	3[a]	42	77	144	165	358	1 819	2 775[h]	...	...	...	2
Unknown - Inconnu	94	1[a]	14	16	9	7	3	669	6 278[h]	...	...	...	30
Qatar													
2007 (C)													
Total	3 206	47[a]	843	1 186	610	245	114	87	42	13	8	11	-
0 - 14	-	-[a]	-	-	-	-	-	-	-	-	-	-	-
15 - 19	485	31[a]	262	159	25	7	1	-	-	-	-	-	-
20 - 24	1 357	14[a]	476	615	193	42	10	5	1	-	-	-	-
25 - 29	775	-[a]	91	333	225	76	25	12	8	1	-	1	-
30 - 34	347	2[a]	10	62	129	74	33	23	9	3	2	2	-
35 - 39	133	-[a]	3	12	26	30	24	26	10	2	-	-	-
40 - 44	61	-[a]	1	3	8	12	15	11	6	2	-	-	-
45 - 49	34	-[a]	-	1	3	3	6	11	6	1	1	3	-
50 - 54	14	-[a]	-	1	1	1	-	3	2	3	2	4	-
55 - 59	-	-[a]	-	-	1	1	1	-	2	4	3	-	2
60 +	-	-[a]	-	-	-	-	-	-	-	-	-	-	-
Unknown - Inconnu	-	-[a]	-	-	-	-	-	-	-	-	-	-	-
Republic of Korea - République de Corée[13]													
2006 (+C)													
Total	332 752	1 039	15 051	115 521	111 895	40 095	19 512	13 479	7 582	4 429	2 247	1 901	-
0 - 14	15	9	4	1	1	-	-	-	-	-	-	-	-
15 - 19	7 763	778	1 172	919	1 336	2 116	1 020	301	90	17	9	4	-
20 - 24	49 498	219	10 274	22 412	10 119	3 799	1 785	674	144	52	15	5	-
25 - 29	158 852	28	3 262	84 468	60 921	7 433	1 701	691	233	87	19	9	-
30 - 34	62 702	3	281	7 065	35 571	14 912	3 075	1 179	391	170	45	10	-
35 - 39	22 858	1	48	550	3 369	9 367	5 712	2 486	924	290	87	24	-
40 - 44	13 671	1	8	78	477	1 928	4 543	4 103	1 598	648	199	88	-
45 - 49	9 477	-	1	25	88	459	1 385	3 279	2 547	1 117	409	167	-
50 - 54	4 633	-	1	3	11	70	256	668	1 389	1 375	602	258	-
55 - 59	1 809	-	-	-	1	10	32	88	230	556	550	342	-
60 - 64	877	-	-	-	1	1	3	9	32	98	273	460	-

22. Marriages by age of groom and by age of bride: latest available year, 1998 - 2007
Mariages selon l'âge de l'époux et selon l'âge de l'épouse: dernière année disponible, 1998 - 2007 (continued - suite)

Continent, country or area, year, code and age of bride / Continent, pays ou zone, date, code et âge de l'épouse	Total	15-19	20-24	25-29	30-34	35-39	40-44	45-49	50-54	55-59	60-64	65+	Unknown Inconnu
ASIA - ASIE													
Republic of Korea - République de Corée[13]													
2006													
65 - 69	396	-	-	-	-	-	-	1	4	18	38	335	-
70 - 74	147	-	-	-	-	-	-	-	-	1	1	145	-
75 +	54	-	-	-	-	-	-	-	-	-	-	54	-
Unknown - Inconnu	-	-	-	-	-	-	-	-	-	-	-	-	-
Singapore - Singapour[14]													
2007 (+C)													
Total	23 966	116	1 899	8 468	6 398	3 040	1 771	1 078	610	347	239[j]	...	...
0 - 14	-	-	-	-	-	-	-	-	-	-	[j]	...	...
15 - 19	643	91	253	140	46	38	34	20	12	6	3[j]	...	...
20 - 24	4 791	19	1 209	2 154	731	351	187	88	23	21	8[j]	...	...
25 - 29	10 528	5	359	5 371	3 215	921	377	180	62	31	7[j]	...	...
30 - 34	4 680	1	58	668	2 016	1 066	457	249	105	37	23[j]	...	...
35 - 39	1 825	-	14	104	326	526	419	218	135	57	26[j]	...	...
40 - 44	819	-	3	22	52	114	232	180	110	65	41[j]	...	...
45 - 49	399	-	3	7	9	20	51	101	106	62	40[j]	...	...
50 - 54	186	-	-	2	2	4	14	31	47	49	37[j]	...	...
55 - 59	62	-	-	-	1	-	-	9	8	15	29[j]	...	...
60 +	33	-	-	-	-	-	-	2	2	4	25[j]	...	...
Sri Lanka													
2001 (+U)													
Total	190 988	...	...	...	...	...	...	...	...	...	...	...	...
0 - 15	105	...	...	...	...	...	...	...	...	...	...	...	...
16 - 20	55 866	...	...	...	...	...	...	...	...	...	...	...	...
21 - 25	69 157	...	...	...	...	...	...	...	...	...	...	...	...
26 - 30	39 582	...	...	...	...	...	...	...	...	...	...	...	...
31 - 35	14 594	...	...	...	...	...	...	...	...	...	...	...	...
36 - 40	6 359	...	...	...	...	...	...	...	...	...	...	...	...
41 - 45	2 754	...	...	...	...	...	...	...	...	...	...	...	...
46 - 50	1 369	...	...	...	...	...	...	...	...	...	...	...	...
51 - 55	683	...	...	...	...	...	...	...	...	...	...	...	...
56 - 60	278	...	...	...	...	...	...	...	...	...	...	...	...
61 - 65	130	...	...	...	...	...	...	...	...	...	...	...	...
66 - 70	68	...	...	...	...	...	...	...	...	...	...	...	...
71 - 75	32	...	...	...	...	...	...	...	...	...	...	...	...
76 +	11	...	...	...	...	...	...	...	...	...	...	...	...
2003 (+U)													
Total	195 914	53 273[a]	61 991	47 776	18 480	7 595	3 589	3 210[g]	...	...	...	...	...
16 - 20	11 664	...	...	...	...	...	...	...	...	...	...	...	...
21 - 24	49 940	...	...	...	...	...	...	...	...	...	...	...	...
25 - 29	68 808	...	...	...	...	...	...	...	...	...	...	...	...
30 - 34	38 981	...	...	...	...	...	...	...	...	...	...	...	...
35 - 39	14 096	...	...	...	...	...	...	...	...	...	...	...	...
40 - 44	6 137	...	...	...	...	...	...	...	...	...	...	...	...
45 +	6 288	...	...	...	...	...	...	...	...	...	...	...	...
Tajikistan - Tadjikistan													
2007 (+C)													
Total	97 713	3 707	43 027	31 972	11 506	4 349	1 449	660	334	186	144	284	95
15 - 19	30 705	2 801	20 030	7 296	494	44	9	5	-	-	1	-	25
20 - 24	44 654	809	21 966	18 157	3 154	420	89	19	5	-	1	-	34
25 - 29	14 643	91	898	6 083	5 676	1 407	327	91	43	14	3	3	7
30 - 34	5 091	3	87	341	2 014	1 794	433	190	96	52	35	37	9
35 - 39	1 641	-	4	47	129	612	428	185	72	47	36	79	2
40 - 44	534	-	-	3	15	55	143	117	67	28	36	68	2
45 - 49	178	-	-	-	2	5	16	48	33	17	18	38	1
50 - 54	63	-	-	-	-	-	4	14	20	5	20	-	-
55 - 59	27	-	-	-	-	1	1	-	4	6	4	11	-
60 - 64	13	-	-	-	-	-	-	-	-	1	5	7	-
65 - 69	10	-	-	-	-	-	-	-	-	1	-	9	-
70 - 74	5	-	-	-	-	-	-	-	-	-	-	5	-
75 +	5	-	-	-	-	-	-	-	-	-	-	5	-
Unknown - Inconnu	144	3	42	45	22	11	3	1	-	-	-	2	15

Continent, country or area, year, code and age of bride / Continent, pays ou zone, date, code et âge de l'épouse	Total	Age of groom - âge de l'époux											
		15-19	20-24	25-29	30-34	35-39	40-44	45-49	50-54	55-59	60-64	65+	Unknown Inconnu
ASIA - ASIE													
Turkey - Turquie[15]													
2007 (C)													
Total	638 311	164 087	250 828	143 251	43 311	16 672	9 155	4 806	3 018	1 581	794	808	...
15 - 19	18 315	12 669	4 652	821	145	20	5	1	1	-	-	1	...
20 - 24	198 418	79 505	96 462	19 777	2 251	351	50	1	1	-	-	1	...
25 - 29	269 688	61 896	118 677	76 392	10 802	1 535	306	17	3	2	-	-	...
30 - 34	87 497	8 667	25 654	33 924	15 437	3 090	610	61	12	5	2	-	...
35 - 39	27 697	1 039	4 031	8 450	8 424	4 447	1 069	91	16	5	2	1	...
40 - 44	13 066	204	873	2 357	3 516	3 504	2 079	196	29	10	1	1	...
45 - 49	7 628	50	258	851	1 384	1 761	2 003	433	72	20	5	3	...
50 - 54	5 374	27	114	362	680	890	1 293	1 025	251	35	9	1	...
55 - 59	3 684	11	60	131	330	497	744	1 175	665	141	25	2	...
60 - 64	2 427	11	17	75	159	275	434	727	719	356	85	24	...
65 - 69	1 997	5	16	56	107	160	288	408	466	362	167	53	...
70 - 74	1 440	2	8	31	53	91	170	198	356	284	198	187	...
75 +	1 080	1	6	24	23	51	104	134	258	211	174	244	...
Uzbekistan - Ouzbékistan													
2000 (C)													
Total	168 908	8 783[a]	102 113	41 332	8 139	3 369	1 911	1 118	684	454	1 005[j]	...	...
0 - 17	9 606	1 762[a]	6 732	1 032	69	8	3	-	-	-	-[j]	...	...
18 - 19	52 422	5 687[a]	38 985	7 320	361	55	7	1	1	2	3[j]	...	...
20 - 24	84 289	1 299[a]	54 562	25 189	2 631	416	144	30	3	5	10[j]	...	...
25 - 29	13 386	34[a]	1 669	7 135	3 129	944	305	103	32	8	27[j]	...	...
30 - 34	4 351	1[a]	147	558	1 659	1 124	467	207	93	32	63[j]	...	...
35 - 39	2 103	-[a]	14	85	238	675	528	257	130	98	78[j]	...	...
40 - 44	1 134	-[a]	1	13	41	122	343	261	152	82	119[j]	...	...
45 - 49	626	-[a]	-	-	9	22	94	193	122	70	116[j]	...	...
50 - 54	440	-[a]	-	-	2	3	17	59	129	91	139[j]	...	...
55 - 59	194	-[a]	-	-	-	-	2	7	18	37	130[j]	...	...
60 +	354	-[a]	-	-	-	-	1	-	4	29	320[j]	...	...
Unknown - Inconnu	3	-[a]	3	-	-	-	-	-	-	-	-[j]	...	...
EUROPE													
Åland Islands - Îles d'Åland[16]													
2007 (C)													
Total	116	...	...	...	...	...	...	...	...	...	...	...	...
0 - 14		...	...	...	...	...	...	...	...	...	...	...	...
15 - 19	1	...	...	...	...	...	...	...	...	...	...	...	...
20 - 24	10	...	...	...	...	...	...	...	...	...	...	...	...
25 - 29	33	...	...	...	...	...	...	...	...	...	...	...	...
30 - 34	25	...	...	...	...	...	...	...	...	...	...	...	...
35 - 39	20	...	...	...	...	...	...	...	...	...	...	...	...
40 - 44	12	...	...	...	...	...	...	...	...	...	...	...	...
45 - 49	4	...	...	...	...	...	...	...	...	...	...	...	...
50 - 54	4	...	...	...	...	...	...	...	...	...	...	...	...
55 - 59	4	...	...	...	...	...	...	...	...	...	...	...	...
60 - 64	3	...	...	...	...	...	...	...	...	...	...	...	...
65 +	-	...	...	...	...	...	...	...	...	...	...	...	...
Unknown - Inconnu	-	...	...	...	...	...	...	...	...	...	...	...	...
Albania - Albanie													
2007 (C)													
Total	22 371	257[a]	4 716	10 147	4 648	1 540	509	272	282[h]	...	...	...	...
0 - 19	6 383	...	...	...	...	...	...	...	...	...	...	...	...
20 - 24	10 194	...	...	...	...	...	...	...	...	...	...	...	...
25 - 29	3 833	...	...	...	...	...	...	...	...	...	...	...	...
30 - 34	1 103	...	...	...	...	...	...	...	...	...	...	...	...
35 - 39	476	...	...	...	...	...	...	...	...	...	...	...	...
40 - 44	212	...	...	...	...	...	...	...	...	...	...	...	...
45 - 49	110	...	...	...	...	...	...	...	...	...	...	...	...
50 +	60	...	...	...	...	...	...	...	...	...	...	...	...
Austria - Autriche[17]													
2007 (C)													
Total	35 996	272	2 931	7 803	8 594	6 283	3 960	2 450	1 460	1 021	673	549	...
0 - 14	-	-	-	-	-	-	-	-	-	-	-	-	...

22. Marriages by age of groom and by age of bride: latest available year, 1998 - 2007
Mariages selon l'âge de l'époux et selon l'âge de l'épouse: dernière année disponible, 1998 - 2007 (continued - suite)

Continent, country or area, year, code and age of bride — Continent, pays ou zone, date, code et âge de l'épouse	Total	\<15-19\> Age of groom - âge de l'époux 15-19	20-24	25-29	30-34	35-39	40-44	45-49	50-54	55-59	60-64	65+	Unknown Inconnu
EUROPE													
Austria - Autriche[17]													
2007													
15 - 19	974	158	526	209	51	18	8	3	-	-	-	1	...
20 - 24	5 598	84	1 735	2 455	854	287	107	42	15	10	6	3	...
25 - 29	10 025	13	506	4 075	3 622	1 189	394	134	55	20	15	2	...
30 - 34	7 537	12	96	811	3 080	2 270	828	271	103	39	21	6	...
35 - 39	4 747	1	39	188	736	1 737	1 205	520	179	89	39	14	...
40 - 44	3 092	3	19	46	187	556	947	713	343	161	77	40	...
45 - 49	1 968	-	9	15	48	176	347	540	414	236	127	56	...
50 - 54	1 069	1	1	3	14	43	88	163	247	255	144	110	...
55 - 59	537	-	-	1	2	4	25	51	72	146	139	97	...
60 - 64	275	-	-	-	-	3	7	10	21	51	79	104	...
65 - 69	131	-	-	-	-	-	3	3	7	12	24	82	...
70 - 74	21	-	-	-	-	-	1	1	3	1	1	15	...
75 - 79	17	-	-	-	-	-	-	-	1	1	1	15	...
80 - 84	3	-	-	-	-	-	-	-	-	-	1	2	...
85 - 89	2	-	-	-	-	-	-	-	-	-	-	2	...
90 - 94	-												...
95 - 99	-												...
100 +	-												...
Belarus - Bélarus													
2007 (C)													
Total	90 444	10 175[a]	42 034	18 111	7 778	4 262	2 698	2 299	1 468	815	804[j]	...	...
0 - 17	97	73[a]	23	1	-	-	-	-	-	-	-	...	...
18 - 19	2 175	1 189[a]	846	103	27	8	1	-	-	-	1[j]	...	...
20 - 24	34 764	6 748[a]	23 502	3 865	528	92	19	7	2	1	1[j]	...	...
25 - 29	26 393	1 868[a]	13 979	8 204	1 820	412	85	20	4	3	4[j]	...	...
30 - 34	10 387	246[a]	2 765	3 792	2 446	855	214	56	6	8	4[j]	...	...
35 - 39	5 697	37[a]	643	1 416	1 682	1 269	427	169	42	18	3[j]	...	...
40 - 44	3 666	9[a]	179	468	781	903	814	373	118	70	13[j]	...	...
45 - 49	2 935	5[a]	64	180	325	454	728	828	268	148	34[j]	...	...
50 - 54	1 894	-[a]	23	55	118	186	279	532	519	309	75[j]	...	...
55 - 59	1 164	-[a]	8	21	29	64	92	233	333	176	257[j]	...	...
60 +	1 272	-[a]	2	6	22	19	39	81	176	257	670[j]	...	...
Belgium - Belgique[18]													
2007 (C)													
Total	45 561	160	4 181	13 190	9 203	5 973	4 310	3 244	2 303	1 379	853	765	-
0 - 14	-												-
15 - 19	984	76	498	282	84	23	12	6	2	-	-	-	-
20 - 24	8 506	58	2 637	4 167	1 046	368	130	58	25	12	2	3	-
25 - 29	14 181	15	827	7 213	4 137	1 265	426	185	65	31	10	7	-
30 - 34	7 262	4	127	1 069	2 768	1 923	805	343	141	50	20	12	-
35 - 39	4 965	6	50	284	782	1 530	1 234	623	287	101	47	21	-
40 - 44	3 632	1	22	102	230	566	1 059	887	452	205	65	43	-
45 - 49	2 742	-	13	41	110	221	465	745	635	290	157	65	-
50 - 54	1 661	-	5	18	27	55	140	275	461	357	194	129	-
55 - 59	937	-	2	11	15	19	29	103	182	251	182	143	-
60 - 64	424	-	-	3	4	2	8	17	45	65	134	146	-
65 - 69	137	-	-	-	-	1	1	1	3	13	24	94	-
70 - 74	77	-	-	-	-	-	1	1	4	4	11	56	-
75 - 79	42	-	-	-	-	-	-	-	1	-	5	36	-
80 - 84	8	-	-	-	-	-	-	-	-	-	1	7	-
85 - 89	3	-	-	-	-	-	-	-	-	-	-	3	-
90 - 94	-												-
95 - 99	-												-
100 +	-												-
Unknown - Inconnu	-												-
Bosnia and Herzegovina - Bosnie-Herzégovine													
2006 (C)													
Total	21 501	338	5 256	7 569	3 944	1 806	999	532	363	239	132	318	5
15 - 19	2 982	216	1 708	860	156	22	16	3	1	-	-	-	1
20 - 24	8 215	105	2 988	3 784	1 027	227	58	15	5	2	2	2	1
25 - 29	5 477	13	493	2 554	1 727	486	147	39	9	5	4	-	-
30 - 34	2 223	1	49	299	833	620	283	83	40	9	4	2	-
35 - 39	1 005	1	6	43	153	332	290	106	38	27	5	4	-

22. Marriages by age of groom and by age of bride: latest available year, 1998 - 2007
Mariages selon l'âge de l'époux et selon l'âge de l'épouse: dernière année disponible, 1998 - 2007 (continued - suite)

Continent, country or area, year, code and age of bride
Continent, pays ou zone, date, code et âge de l'épouse

Age of bride	Total	— Age of groom - âge de l'époux											Unknown Inconnu
		15-19	20-24	25-29	30-34	35-39	40-44	45-49	50-54	55-59	60-64	65+	

EUROPE

Bosnia and Herzegovina - Bosnie-Herzégovine
2006

Age of bride	Total	15-19	20-24	25-29	30-34	35-39	40-44	45-49	50-54	55-59	60-64	65+	Unknown
40 - 44	589	1	6	13	29	87	142	154	82	39	14	21	
45 - 49	378	-	-	7	8	20	43	87	85	54	31	43	1
50 - 54	296	-	-	-	1	7	15	32	86	65	33	57	
55 - 59	139	-	-	2	-	1	4	10	11	27	29	55	
60 - 64	69	-	-	-	1	-	1	1	3	7	9	47	
65 - 69	53	-	-	-	1	-	1	1	3	7	9	45	
70 - 74	27	-	-	-	1	-	-	-	2	3	2	25	
75 +	14	-	-	-	-	-	-	-	-	-	2	12	
Unknown - Inconnu	34	1	6	7	8	4	-	2	1	1	2	14	2

Bulgaria - Bulgarie[19]
2007 (C)

Age of bride	Total	15-19	20-24	25-29	30-34	35-39	40-44	45-49	50-54	55-59	60-64	65+	Unknown
Total	29 640	286	4 936	11 275	7 265	2 805	1 154	705	452	309	213	240	...
0 - 14	-												...
15 - 19	2 288	202	1 175	706	172	22	8	2	1	-	-	-	...
20 - 24	10 059	74	2 992	4 917	1 688	290	61	24	6	3	3	1	...
25 - 29	9 767	7	670	4 754	3 242	812	177	66	23	12	3	1	...
30 - 34	4 282	3	89	778	1 822	1 033	320	139	59	29	8	2	...
35 - 39	1 497	-	7	95	277	504	331	171	63	29	13	7	...
40 - 44	694	-	3	20	53	112	182	151	107	33	19	14	...
45 - 49	436	-	-	4	7	25	62	116	104	73	26	19	...
50 - 54	267	-	-	1	4	6	12	32	68	78	37	29	...
55 - 59	175	-	-	-	-	1	1	3	19	43	66	42	...
60 - 64	92	-	-	-	-	-	-	1	1	9	26	55	...
65 - 69	45	-	-	-	-	-	-	-	1	1	9	34	...
70 - 74	18	-	-	-	-	-	-	-	-	-	1	17	...
75 - 79	18	-	-	-	-	-	-	-	-	-	1	17	...
80 +	2	-	-	-	-	-	-	-	-	-	-	2	...

Croatia - Croatie
2007 (C)

Age of bride	Total	15-19	20-24	25-29	30-34	35-39	40-44	45-49	50-54	55-59	60-64	65+	Unknown
Total	23 140	208	4 016	8 838	5 365	2 074	944	561	351	257	149	371	6
0 - 14	-												
15 - 19	1 578	139	921	409	86	19	1	2	-	1	-	-	-
20 - 24	7 283	59	2 439	3 546	973	201	40	12	6	4	-	1	2
25 - 29	8 138	9	597	4 172	2 564	597	128	51	12	5	1	2	2
30 - 34	3 335	1	53	641	1 475	766	266	89	29	11	2	2	-
35 - 39	1 169	-	5	61	227	379	287	140	45	15	5	5	1
40 - 44	543	-	-	5	32	81	149	143	79	28	13	13	-
45 - 49	372	-	-	3	5	25	52	85	90	52	26	34	-
50 - 54	317	-	1	-	3	5	25	52	85	90	52	4	-
55 - 59	212	-	-	-	3	4	19	29	66	76	45	74	-
60 - 64	73	-	-	-	-	1	1	10	21	14	10	16	-
65 - 69	68	-	-	-	-	-	-	1	10	14	48	-	-
70 - 74	29	-	-	-	-	-	-	1	1	4	62	-	-
75 - 79	11	-	-	-	-	-	-	-	1	10	-	-	-
80 - 84	5	-	-	-	-	-	-	-	-	5	-	-	1
85 +	1	-	-	-	-	-	-	-	-	-	1	-	-
Unknown - Inconnu	6	-	-	1	-	1	1	-	1	-	1	-	2

Czech Republic - République tchèque
2007 (C)

Age of bride	Total	15-19	20-24	25-29	30-34	35-39	40-44	45-49	50-54	55-59	60-64	65+	Unknown
Total	57 157	185	4 676	19 179	16 332	6 266	3 603	2 222	1 914	1 386	801	593	...
0 - 14	-												...
15 - 19	1 063	81	487	304	127	37	18	5	2	2	-	-	...
20 - 24	11 211	74	2 823	5 463	2 160	480	138	39	23	8	1	2	...
25 - 29	22 324	23	1 076	10 756	7 854	1 739	565	205	70	24	5	7	...
30 - 34	11 239	4	236	2 197	4 969	2 296	949	338	169	56	20	5	...
35 - 39	4 130	2	37	365	917	1 181	907	395	204	75	40	7	...
40 - 44	2 516	-	13	75	222	367	666	553	382	156	61	21	...
45 - 49	1 731	1	2	13	66	117	232	427	462	266	106	39	...
50 - 54	1 477	-	1	4	17	37	98	197	461	387	197	78	...
55 - 59	834	-	-	2	-	11	26	51	108	308	203	125	...
60 - 64	402	-	-	-	-	-	4	10	32	88	134	134	...
65 - 69	126	-	-	-	-	-	-	2	1	12	26	85	...
70 - 74	57	-	-	-	-	-	-	-	-	2	5	50	...

22. Marriages by age of groom and by age of bride: latest available year, 1998 - 2007
Mariages selon l'âge de l'époux et selon l'âge de l'épouse: dernière année disponible, 1998 - 2007 (continued - suite)

Continent, country or area, year, code and age of bride / Continent, pays ou zone, date, code et âge de l'épouse	Total	15-19	20-24	25-29	30-34	35-39	40-44	45-49	50-54	55-59	60-64	65+	Unknown Inconnu
EUROPE													
Czech Republic - République tchèque													
2007													
75 - 79	33	-	1	-	-	1	-	-	-	2	3	26	...
80 - 84	12	-	-	-	-	-	-	-	-	-	-	12	...
85 - 89	1	-	-	-	-	-	-	-	-	-	-	1	...
90 +	1	-	-	-	-	-	-	-	-	-	-	1	...
Denmark - Danemark[20]													
2007 (C)													
Total	36 576	40	1 169	6 620	9 658	6 306	4 435	2 693	2 036	1 380	1 034	665	540
0 - 14	-	-	-	-	-	-	-	-	-	-	-	-	-
15 - 19	213	23	109	47	9	4	2	-	1	-	-	-	18
20 - 24	2 644	16	731	1 213	402	95	46	10	6	3	-	-	122
25 - 29	9 133	-	219	4 044	3 516	819	256	82	35	18	7	2	135
30 - 34	9 066	-	34	950	4 464	2 493	737	206	53	18	11	2	98
35 - 39	4 940	-	9	159	821	1 945	1 335	392	132	55	17	10	65
40 - 44	3 613	-	2	33	159	626	1 373	838	369	126	46	9	32
45 - 49	2 220	-	2	3	28	97	392	693	590	253	107	26	29
50 - 54	1 645	-	-	1	10	28	99	247	556	431	193	58	22
55 - 59	925	-	1	-	-	4	25	56	162	298	278	94	7
60 - 64	566	-	-	-	-	1	2	16	42	85	250	161	9
65 - 69	239	-	-	-	-	-	-	-	11	21	55	150	2
70 - 74	111	-	-	-	-	1	-	2	1	2	14	91	1
75 - 79	41	-	-	-	-	-	-	-	-	1	2	37	1
80 - 84	7	-	-	-	-	-	-	-	-	1	-	6	-
85 - 89	4	-	-	-	-	-	-	-	-	-	-	4	-
90 +	1	-	-	-	-	-	-	-	-	-	-	1	-
Unknown - Inconnu	1 208	1	62	170	249	193	168	151	78	68	54	14	
Estonia - Estonie													
2007 (C)													
Total	7 022	82	1 121	1 968	1 485	924	531	363	263	135	69	81	...
0 - 14	-	-	-	-	-	-	-	-	-	-	-	-	...
15 - 19	367	54	193	88	26	5	1	-	-	-	-	-	...
20 - 24	1 851	21	698	774	246	82	21	7	1	1	-	-	...
25 - 29	1 942	4	186	847	590	211	70	23	5	4	2	-	...
30 - 34	1 187	3	30	200	450	314	128	35	21	5	-	1	...
35 - 39	662	-	12	47	127	227	147	65	29	8	-	-	...
40 - 44	367	-	2	9	36	59	102	97	48	8	4	2	...
45 - 49	286	-	-	3	6	20	50	92	70	30	10	5	...
50 - 54	178	-	-	-	4	5	12	32	62	35	21	7	...
55 - 59	107	-	-	-	-	1	-	11	23	32	17	23	...
60 - 64	33	-	-	-	-	-	-	-	3	12	7	11	...
65 - 69	29	-	-	-	-	-	-	1	1	-	6	21	...
70 - 74	9	-	-	-	-	-	-	-	-	-	2	7	...
75 - 79	3	-	-	-	-	-	-	-	-	-	-	3	...
80 +	1	-	-	-	-	-	-	-	-	-	-	1	...
Finland - Finlande[21,22]													
2007 (C)													
Total	29 497	259	2 860	7 788	6 684	3 932	2 599	2 282	1 336	918	483	356	-
0 - 14	-	-	-	-	-	-	-	-	-	-	-	-	-
15 - 19	703	172	398	100	19	9	4	-	-	1	-	-	-
20 - 24	4 688	71	1 863	2 070	505	117	38	14	8	1	-	1	-
25 - 29	8 900	13	483	4 545	2 900	660	203	68	16	9	3	-	-
30 - 34	5 641	2	75	869	2 574	1 473	416	170	43	14	2	3	-
35 - 39	3 092	1	19	133	512	1 126	798	368	103	26	2	4	-
40 - 44	2 256	-	12	51	137	384	716	632	218	84	17	5	-
45 - 49	2 018	-	7	15	24	130	331	770	436	221	69	15	-
50 - 54	1 003	-	2	4	10	24	75	176	340	247	91	34	-
55 - 59	658	-	-	1	3	7	15	69	131	230	146	56	-
60 - 64	326	-	1	-	-	2	3	15	36	69	114	86	-
65 - 69	135	-	-	-	-	-	-	-	5	12	32	86	-
70 - 74	42	-	-	-	-	-	-	-	-	3	4	35	-
75 - 79	28	-	-	-	-	-	-	-	-	1	2	25	-
80 - 84	4	-	-	-	-	-	-	-	-	-	-	4	-
85 +	3	-	-	-	-	-	-	-	-	-	1	2	-
Unknown - Inconnu	-	-	-	-	-	-	-	-	-	-	-	-	-

22. Marriages by age of groom and by age of bride: latest available year, 1998 - 2007
Mariages selon l'âge de l'époux et selon l'âge de l'épouse: dernière année disponible, 1998 - 2007 (continued - suite)

Continent, pays ou zone, date, code et âge de l'épouse	Total	Age of groom - âge de l'époux											
	Total	15-19	20-24	25-29	30-34	35-39	40-44	45-49	50-54	55-59	60-64	65+	Unknown Inconnu
EUROPE													
France[23,24]													
2007 (C)													
Total	267 194	279	15 823	72 689	64 543	39 583	24 639	17 160	13 009	9 189	5 395	4 885	-
0 - 14	1	-	-	-	1	-	-	-	-	-	-	-	-
15 - 19	2 465	111	1 126	814	316	64	17	7	6	-	3	1	-
20 - 24	36 387	129	10 251	18 521	5 356	1 467	420	138	57	27	17	4	-
25 - 29	85 835	24	3 662	44 646	27 339	7 132	1 896	666	261	129	55	25	-
30 - 34	52 686	8	529	6 904	24 113	13 822	4 572	1 685	663	242	110	38	-
35 - 39	32 179	4	149	1 269	5 454	11 941	7 681	1 685	663	242	110	95	-
40 - 44	20 906	2	66	329	1 323	3 624	6 537	3 367	1 390	624	205	208	-
45 - 49	14 521	-	19	131	429	1 086	2 440	4 839	2 473	1 100	405	320	-
50 - 54	10 478	-	9	39	154	337	815	1 749	3 504	1 782	767	601	-
55 - 59	6 328	-	2	28	34	83	199	517	1 200	1 965	1 398	902	-
60 - 64	3 123	-	3	3	12	16	50	116	287	624	932	1 080	-
65 - 69	1 200	-	-	-	5	7	10	19	52	144	216	747	-
70 - 74	602	1	4	2	1	2	2	9	22	51	61	447	-
75 - 79	296	-	1	-	-	2	-	2	7	15	12	257	-
80 - 84	136	-	1	1	5	-	-	3	4	4	4	114	-
85 - 89	43	1	-	-	-	-	-	-	-	-	4	38	-
90 - 94	8	-	-	-	-	-	-	-	-	-	-	8	-
95 +	-	-	-	-	-	-	-	-	-	-	-	-	-
Unknown - Inconnu	-	-	-	-	-	-	-	-	-	-	-	-	-
Germany - Allemagne													
2007 (C)													
Total	368 922	7 164	57 609	104 614	71 339	46 659	31 383	22 249	13 839	7 267	3 549	3 250	...
0 - 14													...
15 - 19	1 412	728	575	78	15	10	6	-	-	-	-	-	...
20 - 24	28 127	3 946	18 370	4 817	723	170	60	28	8	4	1	-	...
25 - 29	82 003	1 755	26 015	44 425	7 899	1 375	360	120	45	7	2	-	...
30 - 34	81 838	451	8 401	36 293	28 814	6 172	1 270	321	89	20	5	2	...
35 - 39	63 591	159	2 765	13 307	22 446	18 053	5 088	1 354	326	74	13	6	...
40 - 44	42 117	71	942	3 938	7 914	13 117	10 822	3 933	1 094	234	41	11	...
45 - 49	26 685	36	351	1 164	2 337	4 993	7 805	6 898	2 381	561	121	38	...
50 - 54	17 326	13	121	347	745	1 714	3 532	5 334	3 970	1 192	265	93	...
55 - 59	11 480	3	49	139	289	641	1 496	2 576	3 325	2 201	574	187	...
60 - 64	6 634	2	14	71	95	262	578	1 053	1 560	1 601	978	420	...
65 - 69	4 351	-	5	27	38	110	250	448	713	901	941	918	...
70 - 74	1 811	-	1	6	13	23	83	125	194	292	373	701	...
75 +	1 547	-	-	2	11	19	33	59	134	180	235	874	...
Greece - Grèce													
2007 (C)													
Total	61 377	1	319	3 197	16 569	20 506	10 802	4 644	2 228	1 218	722	1 168	...
0 - 14	64	-	44	13	5	1	-	-	-	-	-	-	...
15 - 19	1 543	-	206	631	497	153	39	10	3	2	1	-	...
20 - 24	9 351	-	49	1 772	4 426	2 244	648	150	35	16	10	1	...
25 - 29	23 477	-	13	623	9 203	9 451	3 153	741	191	59	16	10	...
30 - 34	15 970	-	4	118	2 072	7 252	4 387	1 445	475	133	50	34	...
35 - 39	5 941	-	3	29	281	1 187	2 028	1 434	595	231	89	64	...
40 - 44	2 303	-	-	7	55	169	410	635	517	280	128	102	...
45 - 49	1 322	-	-	4	22	38	99	182	297	292	188	200	...
50 - 54	723	-	-	-	7	5	27	34	90	152	153	255	...
55 - 59	359	-	-	-	1	5	8	9	17	36	66	217	...
60 - 64	192	-	-	-	-	1	3	3	5	14	18	148	...
65 - 69	76	-	-	-	-	1	3	1	2	2	2	69	...
70 - 74	32	-	-	-	-	-	1	2	2	1	-	31	...
75 - 79	16	-	-	-	-	-	-	-	-	1	-	15	...
80 - 84	6	-	-	-	-	-	-	-	-	-	-	6	...
85 - 89	2	1	-	-	-	-	1	-	-	-	-	-	...
90 - 94	-	-	-	-	-	-	-	-	-	-	-	1	...
95 - 99													...
100 +													...
Unknown - Inconnu													...
Hungary - Hongrie													
2007 (C)													
Total	40 842	328	3 597	13 911	12 108	4 545	2 040	1 263	1 239	804	528	...	-
0 - 14	-	-	-	-	-	-	-	-	-	-	-	...	-
15 - 19	1 365	232	645	321	125	25	8	8	1	-	-	...	-

22. Marriages by age of groom and by age of bride: latest available year, 1998 - 2007
Mariages selon l'âge de l'époux et selon l'âge de l'épouse: dernière année disponible, 1998 - 2007 (continued - suite)

Age of groom - âge de l'époux

Continent, country or area, year, code and age of bride / Continent, pays ou zone, date, code et âge de l'épouse	Total	15-19	20-24	25-29	30-34	35-39	40-44	45-49	50-54	55-59	60-64	65+	Unknown Inconnu
EUROPE													
Hungary - Hongrie													
2007													
20 - 24	8 194	66	1 895	4 068	1 702	330	72	38	12	7	1	...	-
25 - 29	15 483	22	797	7 397	5 509	1 269	297	103	59	21	3	...	-
30 - 34	8 666	3	201	1 810	3 936	1 751	564	211	112	60	11	...	-
35 - 39	2 887	4	48	258	674	864	533	251	155	59	27	...	-
40 - 44	1 354	1	7	46	127	217	369	268	199	69	30	...	-
45 - 49	990	-	3	10	23	63	135	233	301	131	54	...	-
50 - 54	962	-	-	1	11	21	52	115	293	257	131	...	-
55 - 59	551	-	-	-	-	3	8	23	80	155	173	...	-
60 - 64	242	-	1	-	1	2	2	9	23	38	75	...	-
65 - 69	94	-	-	-	-	-	-	2	4	5	18	...	-
70 - 74	27	-	-	-	-	-	-	-	-	2	3	...	-
75 - 79	24	-	-	-	-	-	2	-	-	2	-	...	-
80 - 84	2	-	-	-	-	-	-	-	-	-	-	...	-
85 - 89	1	-	-	-	-	-	-	-	-	-	-	...	-
Unknown - Inconnu	-	-	-	-	-	-	-	-	-	-	-	...	-
Iceland - Islande[5]													
2007 (C)													
Total	1 708	2	86	391	415	303	209	124	76	50	27	22	3
0 - 14	-	-	-	-	-	-	-	-	-	-	-	-	-
15 - 19	7	2	2	2	1	-	-	-	-	-	-	-	-
20 - 24	196	-	60	95	25	10	4	-	-	-	-	-	2
25 - 29	487	-	15	241	172	39	10	6	2	1	-	-	-
30 - 34	395	-	7	45	175	121	32	12	2	1	-	-	-
35 - 39	242	-	1	7	32	93	73	16	12	5	-	-	-
40 - 44	174	-	-	1	8	33	71	44	12	5	-	-	-
45 - 49	94	-	1	-	1	6	17	35	25	4	3	2	-
50 - 54	48	-	-	-	1	-	1	7	15	17	3	3	1
55 - 59	37	-	-	-	-	1	-	2	4	17	9	4	-
60 - 64	22	-	-	-	-	-	1	-	2	4	7	8	-
65 - 69	3	-	-	-	-	-	-	-	-	-	-	3	-
70 - 74	3	-	-	-	-	-	-	-	-	-	-	3	-
75 - 79	-	-	-	-	-	-	-	-	-	-	-	-	-
80 - 84	-	-	-	-	-	-	-	-	-	-	-	-	-
85 - 89	-	-	-	-	-	-	-	-	-	-	-	-	-
90 - 94	-	-	-	-	-	-	-	-	-	-	-	-	-
95 - 99	-	-	-	-	-	-	-	-	-	-	-	-	-
100 +	-	-	-	-	-	-	-	-	-	-	-	-	-
Unknown - Inconnu	-	-	-	-	-	-	-	-	-	-	-	-	-
Ireland - Irlande													
2005 (+C)													
Total	21 355	116	1 025	6 475	7 903	3 145	1 289	598	358	209	120	112	5
0 - 14	-	-	-	-	-	-	-	-	-	-	1	-	-
15 - 19	246	78	103	43	13	6	2	-	-	1	1	-	-
20 - 24	2 052	31	551	981	372	83	21	9	2	1	1	-	1
25 - 29	8 481	3	293	4 165	3 155	679	138	33	8	5	2	1	-
30 - 34	6 733	3	58	1 093	3 681	1 391	361	98	32	9	2	1	4
35 - 39	2 208	1	14	150	585	785	438	151	64	14	3	3	-
40 - 44	780	-	5	21	67	154	242	145	81	39	20	6	-
45 - 49	404	-	1	13	21	36	68	111	82	44	16	12	-
50 - 54	223	-	-	5	1	8	15	43	65	40	33	13	-
55 - 59	120	-	-	-	1	1	2	6	19	40	28	23	-
60 - 64	58	-	-	-	1	-	-	1	5	17	11	23	-
65 - 69	21	-	-	-	-	-	1	1	-	-	3	16	-
70 - 74	9	-	-	-	-	-	-	1	1	-	-	9	-
75 - 79	5	-	-	-	-	-	-	-	-	-	-	5	-
80 - 84	1	-	-	-	-	-	-	-	-	-	-	-	-
85 - 89	1	-	-	-	-	-	-	-	-	-	1	-	-
90 - 94	1	-	-	-	-	-	-	-	-	-	1	-	-
95 +	-	-	-	-	-	-	-	-	-	-	-	-	-
Unknown - Inconnu	13	-	-	4	6	2	1	-	-	-	-	-	-
Isle of Man - Île de Man													
2005 (C)													
Total	404	6	42	72	87	63	51	26	22	17	10	8	...
0 - 14	-	...	...	...	...	...	...	...	...	...	...	...	...
15 - 19	5	...	...	...	...	...	...	...	...	...	...	...	...

22. Marriages by age of groom and by age of bride: latest available year, 1998 - 2007
Mariages selon l'âge de l'époux et selon l'âge de l'épouse: dernière année disponible, 1998 - 2007 (continued - suite)

Continent, country or area, year, code and age of bride / Continent, pays ou zone, date, code et âge de l'épouse	Total	15-19	20-24	25-29	30-34	35-39	40-44	45-49	50-54	55-59	60-64	65+	Unknown Inconnu
EUROPE													
Isle of Man - Île de Man													
2005													
20 - 24	65	...	...	...	...	...	...	...	...	...	...	...	...
25 - 29	98	...	...	...	...	...	...	...	...	...	...	...	...
30 - 34	79	...	...	...	...	...	...	...	...	...	...	...	...
35 - 39	61	...	...	...	...	...	...	...	...	...	...	...	...
40 - 44	40	...	...	...	...	...	...	...	...	...	...	...	...
45 - 49	26	...	...	...	...	...	...	...	...	...	...	...	...
50 - 54	16	...	...	...	...	...	...	...	...	...	...	...	...
55 - 59	5	...	...	...	...	...	...	...	...	...	...	...	...
60 - 64	7	...	...	...	...	...	...	...	...	...	...	...	...
65 - 69	1	...	...	...	...	...	...	...	...	...	...	...	...
70 - 74	-	...	...	...	...	...	...	...	...	...	...	...	...
75 - 79	1	...	...	...	...	...	...	...	...	...	...	...	...
Italy - Italie													
2006 (C)													
Total	245 992	664	13 469	62 272	84 775	42 659	18 548	8 917	5 289	3 896	2 262	3 241	...
0 - 14	-												...
15 - 19	4 735	382	2 563	1 281	359	101	29	11	3	3	1	2	...
20 - 24	35 528	218	7 845	17 714	7 318	1 652	449	175	73	47	21	16	...
25 - 29	85 441	49	2 382	33 916	36 857	9 131	2 063	562	242	138	49	52	...
30 - 34	68 223	11	483	7 929	33 580	18 599	5 197	1 479	509	238	117	81	...
35 - 39	27 570	2	125	1 094	5 594	10 510	6 166	2 351	947	460	178	143	...
40 - 44	11 788	2	40	208	846	2 216	3 486	2 440	1 266	726	299	259	...
45 - 49	5 698	-	19	78	140	338	904	1 320	1 174	840	443	442	...
50 - 54	3 438	-	10	32	43	76	205	442	738	801	492	599	...
55 - 59	1 864	-	1	8	19	15	36	114	262	483	389	537	...
60 - 64	937	-	1	3	12	6	10	15	63	123	213	491	...
65 - 69	486	-	-	4	3	11	3	5	7	29	53	371	...
70 - 74	190	-	-	5	2	3	3	5	7	29	53	158	...
75 - 79	65	-	-	-	2	1	-	3	4	8	7	61	...
80 - 84	23	-	-	-	-	-	-	-	1	-	-	22	...
85 +	6	-	-	-	-	-	-	-	-	-	-	6	...
Latvia - Lettonie													
2007 (C)													
Total	15 486	153	3 058	4 575	2 864	1 600	1 080	763	530	332	201	330	-
0 - 14	-												-
15 - 19	701	86	421	145	42	6	-	1	-	-	-	-	-
20 - 24	4 666	61	1 984	1 896	535	119	46	15	5	2	1	2	-
25 - 29	4 188	4	513	1 964	1 128	357	145	53	16	6	-	2	-
30 - 34	2 219	-	103	434	770	527	219	114	38	9	3	2	-
35 - 39	1 277	1	29	103	274	386	269	128	63	16	5	3	-
40 - 44	823	-	4	22	78	143	242	177	108	29	11	9	-
45 - 49	609	-	3	7	28	51	111	184	115	64	31	15	-
50 - 54	434	1	1	3	8	9	37	76	135	93	39	32	-
55 - 59	226	-	-	1	-	1	7	11	41	70	47	48	-
60 - 64	147	-	-	-	1	1	4	1	8	29	35	68	-
65 - 69	106	-	-	-	-	-	-	2	1	10	18	75	-
70 - 74	54	-	-	-	-	-	-	-	-	3	6	45	-
75 - 79	26	-	-	-	-	-	-	-	-	-	4	22	-
80 - 84	10	-	-	-	-	-	-	-	-	1	-	9	-
85 +	-	-	-	-	-	-	-	-	-	-	-	-	-
Unknown - Inconnu	-												-
Liechtenstein													
2007* (C)													
Total	182	-	11	44	48	30	21	10	6	7	4	1	-
Lithuania - Lituanie													
2007 (C)													
Total	23 065	377	5 380	8 060	3 825	2 049	1 135	836	518	351	215	319	-
0 - 14	4	1	2	-	1	-	-	-	-	-	-	-	-
15 - 19	1 509	219	926	294	54	13	2	-	1	-	-	-	-
20 - 24	8 367	137	3 592	3 578	816	166	43	23	7	5	-	-	-
25 - 29	6 656	15	746	3 472	1 611	558	166	56	18	9	3	2	-
30 - 34	2 670	4	89	554	949	670	255	92	38	12	6	1	-
35 - 39	1 404	1	21	122	280	421	305	161	55	23	12	3	-
40 - 44	861	-	1	35	87	163	227	190	90	43	12	13	-
45 - 49	659	-	2	5	22	42	103	212	148	83	24	18	-

22. Marriages by age of groom and by age of bride: latest available year, 1998 - 2007
Mariages selon l'âge de l'époux et selon l'âge de l'épouse: dernière année disponible, 1998 - 2007 (continued - suite)

Continent, country or area, year, code and age of bride / Continent, pays ou zone, date, code et âge de l'épouse	Total	Age of groom - âge de l'époux											Unknown Inconnu
		15-19	20-24	25-29	30-34	35-39	40-44	45-49	50-54	55-59	60-64	65+	
EUROPE													
Lithuania - Lituanie													
2007		-	1	-	3	15	30	81	118	84	55	37	-
50 - 54	424	-	1	-	1	1	2	16	34	74	56	45	-
55 - 59	229	-	-	-	1	1	1	5	7	17	32	69	-
60 - 64	132	-	-	-	1	-	1	-	2	1	11	68	-
65 - 69	83	-	-	-	-	-	-	-	-	-	4	39	-
70 - 74	43	-	-	-	-	-	-	-	-	-	-	24	-
75 - 79	24	-	-	-	-	-	-	-	-	-	-	-	-
80 +	-	-	-	-	-	-	-	-	-	-	-	-	-
Unknown - Inconnu	-	-	-	-	-	-	-	-	-	-	-	-	-
Luxembourg													
2007 (C)													
Total	1 969	5	115	454	519	331	197	167	98	42	24	17	-
0 - 14	-	-	-	-	-	-	1	-	-	-	1	-	-
15 - 19	19	3	9	3	2	-	3	4	-	-	-	-	-
20 - 24	250	2	78	107	42	14	19	13	10	1	1	-	-
25 - 29	622	-	18	258	234	68	51	20	6	1	1	-	-
30 - 34	459	-	6	70	188	116	62	36	20	4	2	1	-
35 - 39	265	-	2	10	40	88	41	38	15	6	3	1	-
40 - 44	148	-	2	4	6	32	38	38	27	8	4	-	-
45 - 49	108	-	-	2	3	10	16	38	17	10	8	2	-
50 - 54	57	-	-	-	3	2	3	12	17	10	2	6	-
55 - 59	29	-	-	-	1	1	1	6	3	2	2	3	-
60 - 64	7	-	-	-	-	-	-	-	-	2	-	2	-
65 - 69	2	-	-	-	-	-	-	-	-	1	-	1	-
70 - 74	2	-	-	-	-	-	-	-	-	-	-	1	-
75 - 79	1	-	-	-	-	-	-	-	-	-	-	-	-
80 - 84	-	-	-	-	-	-	-	-	-	-	-	-	-
85 - 89	-	-	-	-	-	-	-	-	-	-	-	-	-
90 - 94	-	-	-	-	-	-	-	-	-	-	-	-	-
95 - 99	-	-	-	-	-	-	-	-	-	-	-	-	-
100 +	-	-	-	-	-	-	-	-	-	-	-	-	-
Unknown - Inconnu	-	-	-	-	-	-	-	-	-	-	-	-	-
Malta - Malte													
2007 (C)													
Total	2 479	9	277	1 097	555	237	127	72	43	29	10	...	5
15 - 19	46	5	19	16	2	1	2	-	-	1	-	...	-
20 - 24	647	4	170	368	85	15	4	1	-	-	-	...	-
25 - 29	1 058	-	73	614	275	74	11	6	3	1	1	...	-
30 - 34	381	-	14	81	163	85	24	9	3	2	-	...	-
35 - 39	148	-	-	14	23	41	45	15	10	-	-	...	-
40 - 44	88	-	1	3	4	15	31	15	10	3	2	...	-
45 - 49	52	-	-	1	3	6	9	17	9	6	1	...	-
50 - 54	25	-	-	-	-	1	6	9	6	2	1	...	-
55 - 59	11	-	-	1	-	-	1	3	2	3	-	...	-
60 - 64	14	-	-	-	-	-	-	-	1	-	1	...	-
65 - 69	1	-	-	-	-	-	-	-	-	-	-	...	-
70 - 74	2	-	-	-	-	-	-	-	-	-	-	...	-
75 - 79	1	-	-	-	-	-	-	-	-	-	-	...	5
Unknown - Inconnu	5	-	-	-	-	-	-	-	-	-	-	...	5
Montenegro - Monténégro													
2007 (C)													
Total	4 005	53	653	1 391	959	468	227	104	56	37	14	43	-
0 - 14	-	...	...	...	...	...	...	...	...	...	...	...	...
15 - 19	429	...	...	...	...	...	...	...	...	...	...	...	...
20 - 24	1 339	...	...	...	...	...	...	...	...	...	...	...	...
25 - 29	1 289	...	...	...	...	...	...	...	...	...	...	...	...
30 - 34	549	...	...	...	...	...	...	...	...	...	...	...	...
35 - 39	208	...	...	...	...	...	...	...	...	...	...	...	...
40 - 44	82	...	...	...	...	...	...	...	...	...	...	...	...
45 - 49	51	...	...	...	...	...	...	...	...	...	...	...	...
50 - 54	26	...	...	...	...	...	...	...	...	...	...	...	...
55 - 59	19	...	...	...	...	...	...	...	...	...	...	...	...
60 - 64	5	...	...	...	...	...	...	...	...	...	...	...	...
65 +	8	...	...	...	...	...	...	...	...	...	...	...	...
Unknown - Inconnu	-	...	...	...	...	...	...	...	...	...	...	...	...

22. Marriages by age of groom and by age of bride: latest available year, 1998 - 2007
Mariages selon l'âge de l'époux et selon l'âge de l'épouse: dernière année disponible, 1998 - 2007 (continued - suite)

EUROPE

Continent, country or area, year, code and age of bride / Continent, pays ou zone, date, code et âge de l'épouse — Age of groom - âge de l'époux

Netherlands - Pays-Bas[25,26]
2007 (C)

Age of bride	Total	15-19	20-24	25-29	30-34	35-39	40-44	45-49	50-54	55-59	60-64	65+	Unknown Inconnu
Total	71 114	80	4 732	16 022	18 067	12 075	7 076	4 697	3 258	2 220	1 521	1 366	...
0 - 14	-	-	-	-	-	-	-	-	-	-	-	-	...
15 - 19	720	49	411	187	44	13	8	3	4	1	-	-	...
20 - 24	10 769	28	3 496	5 177	1 405	438	156	41	21	4	2	1	...
25 - 29	20 856	3	685	8 882	8 118	2 218	611	210	69	39	17	4	...
30 - 34	15 201	-	95	1 439	6 892	4 665	1 418	452	147	56	26	11	...
35 - 39	8 948	-	33	245	1 268	3 592	2 354	950	311	131	47	17	...
40 - 44	5 379	-	8	60	249	894	1 768	1 371	612	267	107	43	...
45 - 49	3 830	-	4	22	73	198	563	1 220	1 009	454	185	102	...
50 - 54	2 443	-	-	8	14	45	161	348	785	636	312	134	...
55 - 59	1 481	-	-	2	3	9	30	83	222	463	442	227	...
60 - 64	804	-	-	-	1	2	5	17	63	133	286	297	...
65 - 69	419	-	-	-	-	-	2	1	10	31	83	292	...
70 - 74	170	-	-	-	-	-	-	-	2	8	10	150	...
75 - 79	62	-	-	-	-	-	-	-	-	-	3	59	...
80 - 84	24	-	-	-	-	-	-	-	-	-	1	23	...
85 - 89	5	-	-	-	-	-	1	-	-	-	-	4	...
90 - 94	2	-	-	-	-	-	-	1	-	-	-	1	...
95 - 99	1	-	-	-	-	-	-	-	-	-	-	1	...
100 +	-	-	-	-	-	-	-	-	-	-	-	-	...

Norway - Norvège[27,28]
2007 (C)

Age of bride	Total	15-19	20-24	25-29	30-34	35-39	40-44	45-49	50-54	55-59	60-64	65+	Unknown Inconnu
Total	23 471	66	1 378	4 600	5 715	4 358	2 633	1 795	1 248	842	506	330	-
0 - 14	-	-	-	-	-	-	-	-	-	-	-	-	-
15 - 19	401	42	176	115	45	17	4	1	1	-	-	-	-
20 - 24	3 107	21	922	1 244	488	240	96	50	25	15	3	3	-
25 - 29	6 579	3	242	2 682	2 362	796	285	116	46	28	16	3	-
30 - 34	5 271	-	35	490	2 243	1 621	531	190	88	42	23	8	-
35 - 39	3 333	-	3	65	486	1 270	854	356	168	85	32	14	-
40 - 44	1 956	-	-	3	80	337	625	491	251	108	42	19	-
45 - 49	1 307	-	-	1	11	61	180	418	350	186	73	27	-
50 - 54	804	-	-	-	-	14	46	143	246	206	115	34	-
55 - 59	398	-	-	-	-	1	9	28	60	124	111	65	-
60 - 64	197	-	-	-	-	1	2	2	11	37	76	68	-
65 - 69	83	-	-	-	-	-	-	1	2	8	14	58	-
70 - 74	21	-	-	-	-	-	-	-	-	3	1	17	-
75 - 79	12	-	-	-	-	-	-	-	-	-	-	12	-
80 - 84	2	-	-	-	-	-	-	-	-	-	-	2	-
85 +	-	-	-	-	-	-	-	-	-	-	-	-	-
Unknown - Inconnu	-	-	-	-	-	-	-	-	-	-	-	-	-

Poland - Pologne
2007 (C)

Age of bride	Total	15-19	20-24	25-29	30-34	35-39	40-44	45-49	50-54	55-59	60-64	65+	Unknown Inconnu
Total	248 702	2 366	60 741	108 900	42 396	13 190	6 143	4 433	3 591	2 667	1 517	2 758	-
15 - 19	13 687	1 407	8 677	2 959	513	86	24	12	5	3	-	1	-
20 - 24	100 281	864	42 032	46 901	8 732	1 267	318	102	36	19	5	5	-
25 - 29	88 122	84	9 172	52 534	20 523	4 097	1 076	392	163	66	10	5	-
30 - 34	24 481	10	734	5 712	10 607	4 643	1 653	695	282	104	28	13	-
35 - 39	7 443	1	105	654	1 613	2 285	1 441	783	351	161	31	18	-
40 - 44	3 812	-	16	112	303	562	969	933	518	258	84	57	-
45 - 49	3 500	-	3	19	81	179	446	921	949	542	193	167	-
50 - 54	3 119	-	1	6	14	60	169	436	907	768	409	350	-
55 - 59	2 050	-	1	1	5	10	42	132	292	569	451	547	-
60 - 64	1 000	-	1	1	4	1	5	21	66	133	230	538	-
65 - 69	635	-	-	1	-	-	-	6	18	30	56	524	-
70 - 74	389	-	-	-	-	-	-	-	2	8	17	362	-
75 - 79	143	-	-	-	-	-	-	-	2	3	3	135	-
80 - 84	33	-	-	-	-	1	-	-	-	-	1	31	-
85 +	7	-	-	-	-	-	-	-	-	1	1	5	-
Unknown - Inconnu	-	-	-	-	-	-	-	-	-	-	2	5	-

Portugal
2007 (C)

Age of bride	Total	15-19	20-24	25-29	30-34	35-39	40-44	45-49	50-54	55-59	60-64	65+	Unknown Inconnu
Total	46 329	476	7 139	16 629	11 074	4 286	2 282	1 447	1 025	732	484	755	-
0 - 14	-	-	-	-	-	-	-	-	-	-	-	-	-
15 - 19	2 322	280	1 358	514	128	31	4	2	2	2	-	1	-
20 - 24	10 698	158	3 960	4 913	1 252	273	76	42	11	9	3	1	-

22. Marriages by age of groom and by age of bride: latest available year, 1998 - 2007
Mariages selon l'âge de l'époux et selon l'âge de l'épouse: dernière année disponible, 1998 - 2007 (continued - suite)

Continent, country or area, year, code and age of bride / Continent, pays ou zone, date, code et âge de l'épouse	Total	|—— Age of groom - âge de l'époux ——| 15-19	20-24	25-29	30-34	35-39	40-44	45-49	50-54	55-59	60-64	65+	Unknown Inconnu
EUROPE													
Portugal													
2007													
25 - 29	16 777	29	1 434	8 873	4 916	1 029	312	109	36	22	7	10	-
30 - 34	8 370	8	289	1 904	3 682	1 574	522	244	97	35	10	5	-
35 - 39	3 359	1	58	326	816	913	635	327	158	72	32	21	-
40 - 44	1 872	-	26	69	194	342	486	331	214	124	48	38	-
45 - 49	1 214	-	7	24	61	99	184	268	247	161	86	77	-
50 - 54	772	-	5	3	15	20	45	91	203	155	112	123	-
55 - 59	440	-	2	2	5	4	12	25	45	120	105	120	-
60 - 64	251	-	-	1	2	-	5	6	10	23	64	140	-
65 - 69	133	-	-	-	1	1	-	2	1	7	14	107	-
70 - 74	78	-	-	-	2	-	-	-	-	2	3	71	-
75 - 79	30	-	-	-	-	-	-	-	-	1	-	29	-
80 - 84	11	-	-	-	-	-	-	-	1	-	-	10	-
85 - 89	2	-	-	-	-	-	-	-	-	-	-	2	-
90 - 94	-	-	-	-	-	-	-	-	-	-	-	-	-
95 +	-	-	-	-	-	-	-	-	-	-	-	-	-
Unknown - Inconnu	-	-	-	-	-	-	-	-	-	-	-	-	-
Republic of Moldova - République de Moldova[29]													
2007 (C)													
Total	21 563	784	10 411	7 599	2 027	471	137	66	27	16	5	20	...
0 - 14	1	-	1	-	-	-	-	-	-	-	-	-	...
15 - 19	4 491	456	2 924	964	128	16	2	1	-	-	-	-	...
20 - 24	12 235	290	6 625	4 401	778	110	20	7	4	-	-	-	...
25 - 29	3 818	32	776	2 018	764	166	36	18	3	3	1	1	...
30 - 34	751	6	78	198	304	122	25	11	6	1	-	-	...
35 - 39	149	-	5	16	44	47	25	9	3	-	-	-	...
40 - 44	43	-	1	-	5	6	16	11	3	1	-	-	...
45 - 49	33	-	-	2	4	3	11	7	4	1	1	-	...
50 - 54	15	-	-	-	-	1	2	2	2	6	2	-	...
55 - 59	8	-	1	-	-	-	-	-	2	4	1	-	...
60 - 64	3	-	-	1	-	-	-	-	-	-	-	2	...
65 - 69	2	-	-	-	-	-	-	-	-	-	-	2	...
70 - 74	4	-	-	-	-	-	-	-	-	-	-	4	...
75 +	10	-	-	-	-	-	-	-	-	-	-	10	...
Romania - Roumanie													
2007 (C)													
Total	189 240	3 168	36 301	69 336	38 548	18 664	7 327	5 432	4 090	2 942	1 451	1 981	...
0 - 14	-	-	-	-	-	-	-	-	-	-	-	1	...
15 - 19	25 143	2 376	12 722	7 806	1 865	314	47	9	3	-	-	4	...
20 - 24	60 296	703	18 881	29 924	8 771	1 608	262	86	38	12	56	10	...
25 - 29	52 241	72	4 048	26 356	15 889	4 535	866	284	113	33	91	13	...
30 - 34	24 013	12	521	4 425	9 451	6 698	1 800	687	282	49	180	40	...
35 - 39	12 356	4	110	735	2 166	4 396	2 668	1 434	574	209	57	42	...
40 - 44	4 708	-	11	75	314	803	1 155	1 370	672	526	139	82	...
45 - 49	3 692	-	7	8	71	229	401	1 059	1 170	927	330	208	...
50 - 54	3 051	-	1	-	13	68	101	384	927	696	501	317	...
55 - 59	1 904	-	-	4	6	11	22	92	255	696	232	449	...
60 - 64	857	1	-	3	2	1	1	4	14	34	72	412	...
65 - 69	538	-	-	-	-	1	1	2	4	8	18	258	...
70 - 74	291	-	-	-	-	-	1	4	1	1	1	111	...
75 - 79	114	-	-	-	-	-	-	1	1	-	1	27	...
80 - 84	28	-	-	-	-	-	-	-	1	-	1	7	...
85 +	8	-	-	-	-	-	-	-	-	-	1	-	...
Russian Federation - Fédération de Russie													
2007 (C)													70
Total	1262500	...	...	...	...	275 288[e]	...	...	...	...	...	...	...
0 - 17	18 657	...	...	...	...	...	...	...	...	...	...	...	...
18 - 24	643 038	...	...	...	...	...	...	...	...	...	...	...	...
25 - 34	406 664	...	...	...	...	...	...	...	...	...	...	...	...
35 +	194 053	...	...	...	...	...	...	...	...	...	...	...	...
Unknown - Inconnu	88	...	...	...	...	...	...	...	...	...	...	...	...

22. Marriages by age of groom and by age of bride: latest available year, 1998 - 2007
Mariages selon l'âge de l'époux et selon l'âge de l'épouse: dernière année disponible, 1998 - 2007 (continued - suite)

Continent, country or area, year, code and age of bride — Continent, pays ou zone, date, code et âge de l'épouse	Total	Age of groom - âge de l'époux											Unknown Inconnu
		15-19	20-24	25-29	30-34	35-39	40-44	45-49	50-54	55-59	60-64	65+	

EUROPE

San Marino - Saint-Marin[30]
2004 (C)

Age of bride	Total	15-19	20-24	25-29	30-34	35-39	40-44	45-49	50-54	55-59	60-64	65+	Unknown
Total	207	-	9	56	59	30	14	7	3	8	2	2	17
0 - 14	-	-	-	-	-	-	-	-	-	-	-	-	-
15 - 19	-	-	-	-	-	-	-	-	-	-	-	-	-
20 - 24	16	-	4	4	1	-	2	-	-	-	-	-	-
25 - 29	63	-	1	28	20	4	-	2	-	1	-	-	4
30 - 34	37	-	-	3	13	13	4	-	1	1	-	-	8
35 - 39	11	-	-	-	2	2	4	-	-	-	-	-	4
40 - 44	5	-	-	-	1	-	2	1	-	2	1	-	1
45 - 49	4	-	-	-	-	-	1	1	-	2	-	-	-
50 - 54	2	-	-	-	-	1	1	-	1	1	-	-	-
55 - 59	1	-	-	-	-	-	-	-	1	-	-	1	-
60 +	-	-	-	-	-	-	-	-	1	-	-	-	-
Unknown - Inconnu	68	-	4	21	22	10	3	4	1	1	1	1	-

Serbia - Serbie[31]
2007 (+C)

Age of bride	Total	15-19	20-24	25-29	30-34	35-39	40-44	45-49	50-54	55-59	60-64	65+	Unknown
Total	41 083	442	6 622	14 067	9 738	3 990	1 971	1 276	883	745	384	855	110
0 - 14	-	-	-	-	-	-	-	-	-	-	-	-	-
15 - 19	3 496	292	1 768	1 111	256	47	9	6	-	1	-	-	5
20 - 24	12 390	127	3 906	5 866	1 950	396	85	23	-	1	1	-	5
25 - 29	12 586	15	771	5 904	4 324	1 127	282	89	9	6	1	7	14
30 - 34	6 209	3	118	982	2 732	1 469	569	200	24	19	5	10	16
35 - 39	2 226	1	21	105	338	721	542	296	73	32	12	8	11
40 - 44	1 203	-	4	21	67	144	321	320	122	46	13	18	3
45 - 49	914	-	1	9	14	42	113	215	158	96	27	44	1
50 - 54	810	-	-	3	10	11	26	88	223	140	74	81	2
55 - 59	498	-	-	3	-	5	8	26	204	227	93	146	2
60 - 64	189	-	-	1	2	3	2	5	50	148	90	167	1
65 - 69	182	-	-	1	1	1	2	5	6	14	44	111	1
70 - 74	73	-	-	-	1	-	2	-	5	9	20	143	-
75 +	61	-	-	1	3	2	2	1	1	1	1	69	-
Unknown - Inconnu	246	4	33	60	40	22	10	7	7	3	3	3	54

Slovakia - Slovaquie
2007 (C)

Age of bride	Total	15-19	20-24	25-29	30-34	35-39	40-44	45-49	50-54	55-59	60-64	65+	Unknown
Total	27 437	504	4 247	10 569	6 515	2 395	1 202	734	520	365	193	193	...
0 - 14	-	-	-	-	-	-	-	-	-	-	-	-	...
15 - 19	1 597	341	825	320	85	21	3	-	1	1	-	-	...
20 - 24	8 101	139	2 564	3 876	1 165	250	62	28	12	3	1	1	...
25 - 29	10 336	22	712	5 333	3 074	779	264	85	43	13	6	5	...
30 - 34	4 297	2	119	915	1 831	837	349	151	52	31	13	6	...
35 - 39	1 307	-	17	96	278	397	287	125	52	31	6	4	...
40 - 44	653	-	7	23	63	83	157	155	100	34	20	11	...
45 - 49	462	-	2	4	11	22	61	124	126	62	29	21	...
50 - 54	351	-	-	2	6	6	14	61	124	62	29	21	...
55 - 59	189	-	1	-	2	-	3	8	24	94	101	44	...
60 - 64	93	-	-	-	2	-	3	8	24	69	46	36	...
65 - 69	27	-	-	-	-	-	1	2	4	19	28	39	...
70 - 74	15	-	-	-	-	-	1	-	-	1	4	21	...
75 - 79	5	-	-	-	-	-	-	-	-	1	1	13	...
80 - 84	4	-	-	-	-	-	-	-	-	-	-	5	...
85 - 89	-	-	-	-	-	-	-	-	-	-	-	4	...
90 - 94	-	-	-	-	-	-	-	-	-	-	-	-	...
95 - 99	-	-	-	-	-	-	-	-	-	-	-	-	...
100 +	-	-	-	-	-	-	-	-	-	-	-	-	...

Slovenia - Slovénie
2007 (C)

Age of bride	Total	15-19	20-24	25-29	30-34	35-39	40-44	45-49	50-54	55-59	60-64	65+	Unknown
Total	6 372	27	484	2 208	1 926	752	383	211	159	101	39	82	-
0 - 14	-	-	-	-	-	-	-	-	-	-	-	-	-
15 - 19	117	12	54	44	4	1	-	2	-	-	-	-	-
20 - 24	1 128	11	276	576	205	41	12	5	1	1	-	-	-
25 - 29	2 659	3	119	1 331	934	191	57	15	5	3	1	-	-
30 - 34	1 399	1	27	220	670	316	104	35	15	8	1	2	-
35 - 39	453	-	3	29	93	152	99	45	22	8	1	1	-
40 - 44	243	-	4	7	15	34	85	50	22	15	6	5	-
45 - 49	160	-	1	-	2	15	17	46	34	31	9	5	-
50 - 54	95	-	-	-	2	2	6	15	25	27	9	9	-

22. Marriages by age of groom and by age of bride: latest available year, 1998 - 2007
Mariages selon l'âge de l'époux et selon l'âge de l'épouse: dernière année disponible, 1998 - 2007 (continued - suite)

Continent, country or area, year, code and age of bride
Continent, pays ou zone, date, code et âge de l'épouse

Age of groom - âge de l'époux

EUROPE

Slovenia - Slovénie — 2007

Age of bride	Total	15-19	20-24	25-29	30-34	35-39	40-44	45-49	50-54	55-59	60-64	65+	Unknown Inconnu
55 - 59	64	-	-	1	1	-	3	4	15	11	10	19	-
60 - 64	35	-	-	-	-	-	-	1	5	3	3	23	-
65 - 69	7	-	-	-	-	-	-	-	1	-	1	5	-
70 - 74	6	-	-	-	-	-	-	-	-	-	-	6	-
75 - 79	4	-	-	-	-	-	-	-	-	-	-	4	-
80 - 84	2	-	-	-	-	-	-	-	-	-	-	2	-
85 - 89	1	-	-	-	-	-	-	-	-	-	-	1	-
90 - 94	-	-	-	-	-	-	-	-	-	-	-	-	-
95 - 99	-	-	-	-	-	-	-	-	-	-	-	-	-
100 +	-	-	-	-	-	-	-	-	-	-	-	-	-
Unknown - Inconnu	-	-	-	-	-	-	-	-	-	-	-	-	-

Spain - Espagne — 2007 (C)

Age of bride	Total	15-19	20-24	25-29	30-34	35-39	40-44	45-49	50-54	55-59	60-64	65+	Unknown Inconnu
Total	201 579	472	9 990	62 769	69 047	29 408	12 748	6 900	4 271	2 582	3 392[j]	...	...
0 - 14	2	1	-	1	-	-	-	-	-	-	-	...	...
15 - 19	2 059	186	917	629	215	73	27	4	5	-	3[j]	...	...
20 - 24	22 696	184	5 330	11 736	3 820	1 017	347	146	66	26	24[j]	...	...
25 - 29	78 818	71	2 893	39 665	28 297	5 668	1 343	531	206	94	50[j]	...	...
30 - 34	57 651	23	612	9 105	30 622	12 292	3 190	1 058	439	189	121[j]	...	...
35 - 39	20 806	4	165	1 192	4 922	7 872	4 048	1 496	653	273	181[j]	...	...
40 - 44	9 303	3	48	284	870	1 868	2 702	1 840	928	441	319[j]	...	...
45 - 49	5 094	-	17	106	209	486	837	1 295	1 072	552	520[j]	...	...
50 - 54	2 701	-	7	26	73	102	199	401	663	581	649[j]	...	...
55 - 59	1 340	-	1	19	14	20	40	104	189	321	632[j]	...	...
60 +	1 109	-	-	6	5	10	15	25	50	105	893[j]	...	...

Sweden - Suède — 2007 (C)

Age of bride	Total	15-19	20-24	25-29	30-34	35-39	40-44	45-49	50-54	55-59	60-64	65+	Unknown Inconnu
Total	47 898	75	1 717	7 402	11 432	8 183	5 448	3 183	2 325	1 813	1 182	818	4 320
0 - 14	-	-	-	-	-	-	-	-	-	-	-	-	-
15 - 19	913	35	217	122	33	3	3	1	-	1	-	-	498
20 - 24	4 573	34	1 128	1 509	581	162	72	23	5	7	4	1	1 047
25 - 29	11 187	4	287	4 375	4 139	1 041	324	106	18	12	7	6	874
30 - 34	11 663	2	59	1 166	5 312	3 125	966	255	91	41	12	8	628
35 - 39	7 384	-	12	170	1 098	2 871	1 904	550	232	83	31	18	425
40 - 44	4 709	-	11	40	219	808	1 605	1 030	402	135	61	45	380
45 - 49	2 976	-	2	10	38	145	451	869	721	346	110	68	239
50 - 54	2 051	-	-	7	11	19	107	276	620	552	263	90	128
55 - 59	1 266	-	-	1	8	13	58	180	462	337	157	39	64
60 - 64	736	-	1	2	1	1	2	11	48	150	281	219	20
65 - 69	268	-	-	-	-	1	4	7	20	65	90	16	14
70 - 74	103	-	-	-	-	-	-	-	3	9	-	8	1
75 - 79	44	-	-	-	-	-	1	2	-	-	-	39	2
80 - 84	17	-	-	-	-	-	-	-	1	-	-	16	-
85 - 89	8	-	-	-	-	-	-	-	-	-	-	8	-
90 - 94	-	-	-	-	-	-	-	-	-	-	-	-	-
95 - 99	-	-	-	-	-	-	-	-	-	-	-	-	-
100 +	-	-	-	-	-	-	-	-	-	-	-	-	-

Switzerland - Suisse — 2007 (C)

Age of bride	Total	15-19	20-24	25-29	30-34	35-39	40-44	45-49	50-54	55-59	60-64	65+	Unknown Inconnu
Total	40 330	138	3 004	8 503	10 655	7 285	4 144	2 444	1 625	1 139	786	607	...
0 - 14	-	-	-	-	-	-	-	-	-	-	-	-	-
15 - 19	760	67	422	177	62	14	10	4	1	2	1	-	-
20 - 24	5 632	56	1 832	2 291	839	321	142	79	40	14	11	7	-
25 - 29	11 309	10	505	4 344	4 015	1 464	518	245	101	53	36	18	-
30 - 34	10 331	2	143	1 209	4 326	2 902	1 025	416	174	75	35	24	-
35 - 39	5 411	2	44	243	969	1 908	1 255	533	237	124	66	30	-
40 - 44	2 857	-	32	113	257	462	801	536	339	186	90	41	-
45 - 49	1 754	1	13	66	109	119	262	421	341	231	117	74	-
50 - 54	1 147	-	8	33	37	54	89	138	273	239	174	102	-
55 - 59	661	-	4	19	25	29	27	45	89	154	154	115	-
60 - 64	285	-	1	4	9	8	11	22	24	46	76	84	-
65 - 69	95	-	-	4	4	1	3	3	5	11	17	47	-
70 - 74	48	-	-	-	2	3	1	2	1	2	6	31	-
75 - 79	27	-	-	-	1	-	1	-	-	-	3	22	-
80 - 84	7	-	-	-	-	-	-	-	-	-	-	7	-

22. Marriages by age of groom and by age of bride: latest available year, 1998 - 2007
Mariages selon l'âge de l'époux et selon l'âge de l'épouse: dernière année disponible, 1998 - 2007 (continued - suite)

Continent, country or area, year, code and age of bride / Continent, pays ou zone, date, code et âge de l'épouse	Total	15-19	20-24	25-29	30-34	35-39	40-44	45-49	50-54	55-59	60-64	65+	Unknown Inconnu
EUROPE													
Switzerland - Suisse													
2007													
85 - 89	4	-	-	-	-	-	-	-	-	-	-	-	...
90 +	2	-	-	-	-	-	-	-	-	-	1	1	2
95 - 99	-	-	-	-	-	-	-	-	-	-	-	-	2
100 +	-	-	-	-	-	-	-	-	-	-	-	-	...
The Former Yugoslav Republic of Macedonia - L'ex-République yougoslave de Macédoine													
2007 (C)													
Total	15 490	423	4 221	5 901	2 814	1 067	500	242	137	70	43	72	...
0 - 14	-	-	-	-	-	-	-	-	-	-	-	-	...
15 - 19	2 485	298	1 453	614	97	18	3	1	1	-	-	-	...
20 - 24	6 099	119	2 408	2 765	682	103	16	5	-	1	-	-	...
25 - 29	4 320	4	317	2 249	1 328	321	77	17	5	-	1	-	...
30 - 34	1 415	1	30	235	600	354	131	48	12	4	-	1	...
35 - 39	560	-	9	23	79	219	150	54	13	9	1	3	...
40 - 44	280	-	3	6	11	36	150	54	13	9	1	3	...
45 - 49	169	-	-	4	9	36	98	63	37	9	7	10	...
50 - 54	91	1	1	5	5	11	22	47	38	19	9	10	...
55 - 59	42	-	-	-	5	3	1	7	26	17	12	13	...
60 - 64	16	-	-	-	3	1	2	-	3	10	10	13	...
65 - 69	6	-	-	-	-	1	-	-	1	1	2	11	...
70 - 74	3	-	-	-	-	-	-	-	1	-	1	4	...
75 +	4	-	-	-	-	-	-	-	-	-	-	3	4
Ukraine													
2007 (C)													
Total	416 427	13 341[a]	155 695	117 096	51 639	25 903	16 203	12 889	8 753	6 098	8 810[j]	...	...
0 - 15	400	123[a]	222	52	3	-	-	-	-	-	-[j]	...	...
16 - 19	66 461	8 148[a]	43 071	12 966	1 839	309	66	43	11	4	4[j]	...	...
20 - 24	181 603	4 471[a]	94 991	62 036	15 262	3 425	895	352	114	34	23[j]	...	...
25 - 29	77 543	500[a]	14 762	33 017	18 702	6 891	2 349	899	261	117	45[j]	...	...
30 - 34	34 355	78[a]	2 206	7 097	11 087	7 754	3 614	1 662	528	215	114[j]	...	...
35 - 39	18 142	17[a]	340	1 558	3 584	5 032	4 027	2 221	884	326	153[j]	...	...
40 - 44	11 588	4[a]	61	284	888	1 717	3 241	3 055	1 443	591	304[j]	...	...
45 - 49	10 086	-[a]	26	71	219	624	1 517	3 215	2 522	1 193	699[j]	...	...
50 - 54	6 691	-[a]	10	9	40	119	380	1 084	2 152	1 711	1 186[j]	...	...
55 - 59	4 456	-[a]	4	3	11	20	86	302	670	1 505	1 855[j]	...	...
60 +	5 102	-[a]	2	3	4	12	28	56	168	402	4 427[j]	...	...
United Kingdom of Great Britain and Northern Ireland - Royaume-Uni de Grande-Bretagne et d'Irlande du Nord[32]													
2002 (C)													
Total	293 021	2 023	28 666	74 858	72 592	44 189	25 558	15 910	11 891	8 055	4 324	4 955	-
0 - 14	-	-	-	-	-	-	-	-	-	-	-	-	-
15 - 19	7 505	1 100	3 628	1 771	687	191	77	31	9	7	2	2	-
20 - 24	51 478	659	16 996	21 406	8 351	2 659	909	283	128	54	19	2	-
25 - 29	82 892	167	5 757	37 256	26 710	8 790	2 792	826	351	154	55	19	14
30 - 34	62 279	57	1 525	10 717	26 222	14 924	5 598	1 960	794	335	154	55	34
35 - 39	35 978	27	519	2 725	7 698	11 770	7 452	3 328	1 483	622	335	95	52
40 - 44	21 019	9	169	709	2 178	4 131	5 582	4 120	2 436	1 102	622	252	102
45 - 49	13 232	3	51	205	547	1 245	2 231	3 469	2 927	1 439	1 102	385	198
50 - 54	8 955	1	13	45	154	366	698	1 439	2 927	2 565	1 688	556	310
55 - 59	4 903	-	5	14	36	90	182	698	1 439	2 565	2 151	937	586
60 - 64	2 366	-	-	8	7	13	22	91	350	925	1 408	1 076	817
65 - 69	1 251	-	1	2	-	8	9	22	91	210	406	659	950
70 - 74	662	-	-	1	-	2	9	10	48	97	215	861	-
75 - 79	328	-	-	-	-	2	5	2	12	20	49	569	-
80 - 84	128	-	1	-	-	-	1	-	1	9	17	300	-
85 - 89	44	-	-	-	-	-	1	1	1	5	119	-	-
90 - 94	1	-	-	-	-	-	-	1	1	2	41	-	-
Unknown - Inconnu	-	-	-	-	-	-	-	-	1	-	-	-	-

22. Marriages by age of groom and by age of bride: latest available year, 1998 - 2007
Mariages selon l'âge de l'époux et selon l'âge de l'épouse: dernière année disponible, 1998 - 2007 (continued - suite)

Continent, country or area, year, code and age of bride / Continent, pays ou zone, date, code et âge de l'épouse	Total	15-19	20-24	25-29	30-34	35-39	40-44	45-49	50-54	55-59	60-64	65+	Unknown Inconnu
OCEANIA - OCÉANIE													
Australia - Australie[33]													
2007 (+C)													
Total	116 322	546	13 729	33 839	26 849	15 335	8 568	6 084	4 310	3 206	1 870	1 986	...
0 - 14	-	-	-	-	-	-	-	-	-	-	-	-	...
15 - 19	2 092	303	1 109	470	135	37	19	9	6	-	3	3	...
20 - 24	23 286	194	9 588	9 808	2 558	750	210	96	43	24	8	7	...
25 - 29	37 172	39	2 518	19 036	11 014	3 196	824	315	126	67	25	12	...
30 - 34	23 045	5	393	3 756	10 116	5 696	1 899	717	270	128	40	26	...
35 - 39	12 149	4	85	624	2 470	4 195	2 639	1 244	512	225	109	41	...
40 - 44	6 513	3	21	109	429	1 062	1 905	1 600	790	371	160	66	...
45 - 49	5 004	-	10	24	90	302	818	1 461	1 217	704	239	140	...
50 - 54	3 228	-	5	10	28	70	206	496	996	827	380	211	...
55 - 59	1 869	-	-	3	8	20	32	114	270	629	496	297	...
60 - 64	1 000	-	-	-	-	5	10	23	68	189	303	401	...
65 - 69	524	-	-	-	-	-	4	7	11	34	82	385	...
70 - 74	249	-	-	-	-	3	-	3	-	3	23	218	...
75 - 79	136	-	-	-	-	-	-	-	-	3	3	129	...
80 - 84	45	-	-	-	-	-	-	-	-	-	-	43	...
85 +	10	-	-	-	-	-	-	-	-	-	-	9	...
Unknown - Inconnu	-	-	-	-	-	-	-	-	-	-	-	-	...
Fiji - Fidji													
2004 (+C)													
Total	7 076	125	2 060	2 429	1 113	522	334	217	125	74	40	37	...
0 - 14	-	...	...	...	...	...	...	...	...	...	...	...	...
15 - 19	1 176	...	...	...	...	...	...	...	...	...	...	...	...
20 - 24	2 990	...	...	...	...	...	...	...	...	...	...	...	...
25 - 29	1 438	...	...	...	...	...	...	...	...	...	...	...	...
30 - 34	656	...	...	...	...	...	...	...	...	...	...	...	...
35 - 39	367	...	...	...	...	...	...	...	...	...	...	...	...
40 - 44	204	...	...	...	...	...	...	...	...	...	...	...	...
45 - 49	128	...	...	...	...	...	...	...	...	...	...	...	...
50 - 54	62	...	...	...	...	...	...	...	...	...	...	...	...
55 - 59	35	...	...	...	...	...	...	...	...	...	...	...	...
60 - 64	13	...	...	...	...	...	...	...	...	...	...	...	...
65 +	7	...	...	...	...	...	...	...	...	...	...	...	...
Guam													
2003 (C)													
Total	1 334	41[a]	268	353	240	171	110	55	46	14	36[j]	...	...
0 - 19	96	23[a]	49	18	3	-	3	-	-	-	-[j]	...	...
20 - 24	334	14[a]	164	102	34	14	2	3	1	-	-[j]	...	...
25 - 29	374	2[a]	36	180	104	24	15	6	4	1	2[j]	...	...
30 - 34	230	1[a]	15	38	69	63	27	6	8	2	1[j]	...	...
35 - 39	140	1[a]	4	12	26	48	32	11	4	1	1[j]	...	...
40 - 44	74	-[a]	-	3	4	13	21	12	13	2	6[j]	...	...
45 - 49	42	-[a]	-	-	-	7	10	10	8	4	3[j]	...	...
50 - 54	23	-[a]	-	-	-	-	-	7	6	3	7[j]	...	...
55 - 59	10	-[a]	-	-	-	-	-	-	2	-	8[j]	...	...
60 - 69	8	-[a]	-	-	-	1	-	-	-	1	6[j]	...	...
70 +	3	-[a]	-	-	-	1	-	-	-	-	2[j]	...	...
New Caledonia - Nouvelle-Calédonie													
2007 (C)													
Total	884	...	...	179	208	159	179[m]	...	71[n]	...	43[j]		
0 - 24	134	...	...	52	31	5	7[m]	...	4[n]	...	-[j]		
25 - 29	222	...	...	102	76	21	14[m]	...	1[n]	...	-[j]		
30 - 34	185	...	...	18	79	56	22[m]	...	5[n]	...	4[j]		
35 - 39	132	...	...	6	15	53	47[m]	...	8[n]	...	2[j]		
40 - 49	160	...	...	1	7	24	82[m]	...	33[n]	...	13[j]		
50 - 59	38	...	...	-	-	-	7[m]	...	17[n]	...	14[j]		
60 +	13	...	...	-	-	-	-[m]	...	3[n]	...	10[j]		
New Zealand - Nouvelle-Zélande[34]													
2007 (+C)													
Total	21 494	210	2 625	5 434	4 620	2 991	1 880	1 353	891	639	392	...	-
15 - 19	512	130	272	76	27	2	2	-	2	-	-	...	-
20 - 24	3 949	63	1 766	1 528	416	112	41	14	8	1	-	...	-

22. Marriages by age of groom and by age of bride: latest available year, 1998 - 2007
Mariages selon l'âge de l'époux et selon l'âge de l'épouse: dernière année disponible, 1998 - 2007 (continued - suite)

Continent, country or area, year, code and age of bride / Continent, pays ou zone, date, code et âge de l'épouse	Total	Age of groom - âge de l'époux											
		15-19	20-24	25-29	30-34	35-39	40-44	45-49	50-54	55-59	60-64	65+	Unknown Inconnu
OCEANIA - OCÉANIE													
New Zealand - Nouvelle-Zélande[34]													
2007													
25 - 29	6 031	10	481	3 024	1 753	540	142	50	22	7	2	...	-
30 - 34	4 272	6	82	673	1 855	1 077	384	105	52	23	11	...	-
35 - 39	2 485	1	17	101	449	873	590	293	109	32	10	...	-
40 - 44	1 551	-	6	25	81	284	470	388	185	68	29	...	-
45 - 49	1 159	-	1	7	36	81	188	366	254	143	62	...	-
50 - 54	688	-	-	-	2	18	45	108	181	183	100	...	-
55 - 59	395	-	-	-	1	4	12	45	108	123	99	...	-
60 - 64	222	-	-	-	-	1	4	11	46	62	72	...	-
65 - 69	132	-	-	-	-	-	4	4	11	46	72	...	-
70 - 74	54	-	-	-	-	-	1	1	5	12	20	...	-
75 - 79	30	-	-	-	-	-	1	1	-	1	4	...	-
80 - 84	11	-	-	-	-	-	-	-	-	-	1	...	-
85 +	3	-	-	-	-	-	-	-	-	-	-	...	-
Samoa													
2001 (U)													
Total	*821*	*10*	*149*	*223*	*165*	*116*	*60*	*40*	*25*	*9*	*·12*	*8*	*4*
15 - 19	*71*	*...*	*...*	*...*	*...*	*...*	*...*	*...*	*...*	*...*	*...*	*...*	*...*
20 - 24	*285*	*...*	*...*	*...*	*...*	*...*	*...*	*...*	*...*	*...*	*...*	*...*	*...*
25 - 29	*177*	*...*	*...*	*...*	*...*	*...*	*...*	*...*	*...*	*...*	*...*	*...*	*...*
30 - 34	*114*	*...*	*...*	*...*	*...*	*...*	*...*	*...*	*...*	*...*	*...*	*...*	*...*
35 - 39	*83*	*...*	*...*	*...*	*...*	*...*	*...*	*...*	*...*	*...*	*...*	*...*	*...*
40 - 44	*39*	*...*	*...*	*...*	*...*	*...*	*...*	*...*	*...*	*...*	*...*	*...*	*...*
45 - 49	*23*	*...*	*...*	*...*	*...*	*...*	*...*	*...*	*...*	*...*	*...*	*...*	*...*
50 - 54	*12*	*...*	*...*	*...*	*...*	*...*	*...*	*...*	*...*	*...*	*...*	*...*	*...*
55 - 59	*11*	*...*	*...*	*...*	*...*	*...*	*...*	*...*	*...*	*...*	*...*	*...*	*...*
60 - 64	*1*	*...*	*...*	*...*	*...*	*...*	*...*	*...*	*...*	*...*	*...*	*...*	*...*
65 - 69	*2*	*...*	*...*	*...*	*...*	*...*	*...*	*...*	*...*	*...*	*...*	*...*	*...*
70 - 74	*-*	*...*	*...*	*...*	*...*	*...*	*...*	*...*	*...*	*...*	*...*	*...*	*...*
75 +	*-*	*...*	*...*	*...*	*...*	*...*	*...*	*...*	*...*	*...*	*...*	*...*	*...*
Unknown - Inconnu	*3*	*...*	*...*	*...*	*...*	*...*	*...*	*...*	*...*	*...*	*...*	*...*	*...*
Tonga[35]													
2004* (+C)													
Total	677	34	237	203	83	59	27	14	20[h]	...	...	...	-
0 - 14	-	...	...	...	...	...	...	...	...	...	...	...	-
15 - 19	107	...	...	...	...	...	...	...	...	...	...	...	...
20 - 24	262	...	...	...	...	...	...	...	...	...	...	...	...
25 - 29	161	...	...	...	...	...	...	...	...	...	...	...	...
30 - 34	76	...	...	...	...	...	...	...	...	...	...	...	...
35 - 39	44	...	...	...	...	...	...	...	...	...	...	...	...
40 - 44	17	...	...	...	...	...	...	...	...	...	...	...	...
45 - 49	6	...	...	...	...	...	...	...	...	...	...	...	...
50 +	4	...	...	...	...	...	...	...	...	...	...	...	...
Unknown - Inconnu	-	...	...	...	...	...	...	...	...	...	...	...	...

FOOTNOTES - NOTES

Italics: data from civil registers which are incomplete or of unknown completeness. - Italiques: données incomplètes ou dont le degré d'exactitude n'est pas connu, provenant des registres de l'état civil.

* Provisional. - Données provisoires.

'Code' indicates the source of data, as follows:
C - Civil registration, estimated over 90% complete
U - Civil registration, estimated less than 90% complete
| - Other source, estimated reliable
+ - Data tabulated by date of registration rather than occurence.
... - Information not available

Le 'Code' indique la source des données, comme suit:
C - Registres de l'état civil considérés complets à 90 p. 100 au moins.
U - Registres de l'état civil qui ne sont pas considérés complèts à 90 p. 100 au moins.

| - Autre source, considérée pas douteuses.
+ - Données exploitées selon la date de l'enregistrement et non la date de l'événement.
... - Information pas disponible.

[a] Refers to 0-19 years of age. - Données se raporten au groupe d'âges 0-19.
[b] Refers to 16-19 years of age. - Données se raporten au groupe d'âges 16-19.
[c] Refers to 17-19 years of age. - Données se raporten au groupe d'âges 17-19.
[d] Refers to 18-19 years of age. - Données se raporten au groupe d'âges 18-19.
[e] Refers to 35+ years of age. - Données se raporten au groupe d'âges 35+.
[f] Refers to 40+ years of age. - Données se raporten au groupe d'âges 40+.
[g] Refers to 45+ years of age. - Données se raporten au groupe d'âges 45+.
[h] Refers to 50+ years of age. - Données se raporten au groupe d'âges 50+.
[i] Refers to 55+ years of age. - Données se raporten au groupe d'âges 55+.
[j] Refers to 60+ years of age. - Données se raporten au groupe d'âges 60+.
[k] Refers to 20-29 years of age. - Données se raporten au groupe d'âges 20-29.
[l] Refers to 30-39 years of age. - Données se raporten au groupe d'âges 30-39.
[m] Refers to 40-49 years of age. - Données se raporten au groupe d'âges 40-49.
[n] Refers to 50-59 years of age. - Données se raporten au groupe d'âges 50-59.

1 Including marriages resumed after 'revocable divorce' (among Moslem population), which approximates legal separation. - Y compris les unions reconstituées après un 'divorce révocable' (parmi la population musulmane), qui est à peu près l'équivalent d'une séparation légale.

2 As reported by the country. Reasons for discrepancy with other tables not ascertained. - Données comme déclarées par le pays. On ne sait pas comment s'explique la divergence entre ces chiffres et les chiffres correspondants indiqués ailleurs.

3 Including visitors. - Visiteurs compris.

4 Excluding visitors. - Les données non compris des visiteurs.

5 Data refer to resident population only. - Pour la population résidante seulement.

6 Excluding Indian jungle population. - Non compris les Indiens de la jungle.

7 Excluding nomadic Indian tribes. - Non compris les tribus d'Indiens nomades.

8 Data refer to marriages of residents only. - Chiffres se rapportent exclusivement aux mariages de résidents.

9 Data refer to government controlled areas. - Les données se rapportent aux zones contrôlées par le Gouvernement.

10 Including data for East Jerusalem and Israeli residents in certain other territories under occupation by Israeli military forces since June 1967. - Y compris les données pour Jérusalem-Est et les résidents israéliens dans certains autres territoires occupés depuis 1967 par les forces armées israéliennes.

11 Data refer to Japanese nationals in Japan only; and to grooms and brides married for the first time whose marriages occurred and were registered in the same year. - Les données se raportent aux nationaux japonais au Japon seulement; et aux époux et épouses mariés pour la première fois, dont le mariage a été célébré et enregistré la même année.

12 Excluding data for Jordanian territory under occupation since June 1967 by Israeli military forces. Excluding foreigners, including registered Palestinian refugees. - Non compris les données pour le territoire jordanien occupé depuis juin 1967 par les forces armées israéliennes. Non compris les étrangers, mais y compris les réfugiés de Palestine enregistrés.

13 Excluding alien armed forces, civilian aliens employed by armed forces, and foreign diplomatic personnel and their dependants. - Non compris les militaires étrangers, les civils étrangers employés par les forces armées ni le personnel diplomatique étranger et les membres de leur famille les accompagnant.

14 Excluding marriages previously officiated outside Singapore or under religious and customary rites. - Les figures excluent les mariages célébrés précédemment au dehors de Singapour ou sous les rites réligieuse ou accoutumés.

15 Data from MERNIS (Central Population Administrative System). - Données de MERNIS (Système central de données démographiques).

16 Also included in Finland. - Comprise aussi dans Finlande.

17 Excluding aliens temporarily in the area. - Non compris les étrangers se trouvant temporairement le territoire.

18 Including armed forces stationed outside the country, but excluding alien armed forces in the area unless marriage performed by local foreign authority. - Y compris les militaires nationaux hors du pays et les militaires étrangers en garnison sur le territoire, sauf si le mariage a été célébré pour l'autorité locale.

19 Including nationals outside the country, but excluding foreigners in the country. - Y compris les nationaux à l'étranger, mais non compris les étrangers sur le territoire.

20 Excluding Faeroe Islands and Greenland shown separately, if available. - Non compris les Iles Féroé et le Gröenland, qui font l'objet de rubriques distinctes, si disponible.

21 Including Aland Islands. - Y compris les Îles d'Åland.

22 Only marriages in which the bride was resident in Finland. - Seulement mariages où l'épouse réside en Finlande.

23 Excluding Overseas Departments, namely, French Guiana, Guadeloupe, Martinique and Reunion, shown separately, if available. - Non compris les départements d'outre mer, c'est-à-dire la Guyane française, la Guadeloupe, la Martinique et la Réunion, qui font l'objet de rubriques distinctes, si disponible.

24 Including armed forces stationed outside the country. - Y compris les militaires nationaux hors du pays.

25 Marriages of couples of which at least one partner is recorded in a Dutch municipal register, irrespective of the country where the marriage was performed. - Mariages où un des conjoints au moins est inscrit dans un registre municipal néerlandais, quel que soit le pays où le mariage a été contracté.

26 Excluding same sex marriages. - À l'exclusion des mariages entre personnes du même sexe.

27 Excluding Svalbard and Jan Mayen Island shown separately, if available. - Non compris Svalbard et Jan Mayen qui font l'objet de rubriques distinctes, si disponible.

28 Only marriages in which the groom was resident in Norway. - Seulement mariages où l'époux réside en Norvège.

29 Data refer to first marriages only. - Données se rapportent aux premiers mariages seulement.

30 Includes civil and religious marriages as well as not specified. - Y compris les mariages civils, religieux ou non précisés.

31 Excluding data for Kosovo and Metohia. - Sans les données pour le Kosovo et Metohie.

32 Excluding Channel Islands (Guernsey and Jersey) and Isle of Man, shown separately, if available. - Non compris les îles Anglo-Normandes (Guernesey et Jersey) et l'île de Man, qui font l'objet de rubriques distinctes, si disponible.

33 Data for certain cells suppressed by national statistical office for confidentiality reasons. - Les données pour certaines cases ont été supprimées par le bureau national de statistiques pour des raisons de confidentialité.

34 Marriages registered in which the groom was resident. - Mariages enregistrés où le marié était un résident.

35 Data refer to the island of Tongatapu only. - Les données se réfèrent uniquement à l'île de Tongatapu.

Table 23

Table 23 presents number of divorces and crude divorce rates for as many years as possible between 2003 and 2007.

Description of variables: Divorce is defined as a final legal dissolution of a marriage, that is, that separation of husband and wife which confers on the parties the right to remarriage under civil, religious and/or other provisions, according to the laws of each country[1].

Unless otherwise noted, divorce statistics exclude legal separations that do not allow remarriage. These statistics refer to the number of divorces granted, and not to the number of persons divorcing.

Divorce statistics are obtained from court records and/or civil registers according to national practice. The actual compilation of these statistics may be the responsibility of the civil registrar, the national statistical office or other government offices.

The urban/rural classification of divorces is that provided by each country or area; it is presumed to be based on the national census definitions of urban population, which have been set forth at the end of the technical notes for table 6.

Rate computation: Crude divorce rates by urban/rural residence are the annual number of divorces per 1 000 mid-year population. Rates presented in this table have been limited to those countries or areas having at least a total of 30 divorces in a given year. These rates are calculated by the Statistics Division of the United Nations based on the appropriate reference population (for example: total population, nationals only etc.) if known and available. If the reference population is not known or unavailable the total population is used to calculate the rates. Therefore, if the population that is used to calculate the rates is different from the correct reference population, the rates presented might under- or overstate the true situation in a country or area.

Reliability of data: Each country or area has been asked to indicate the estimated completeness of the divorces recorded in its civil register. These national assessments are indicated by the quality codes "C" and "U" that appear in the first column of this table.

"C" indicates that the data are estimated to be virtually complete, that is, representing at least 90 per cent of the divorces that occur each year, while "U" indicates that data are estimated to be incomplete, that is, representing less than 90 per cent of the divorces occurring each year. The code "..." indicates that no information was provided regarding completeness.

Data from civil registers that are reported as incomplete or of unknown completeness (coded "U" or "...") are considered unreliable. They appear in *italics* in this table and the rates were not computed on data so coded. These quality codes apply only to data from civil registers. For more information about the quality of vital statistics data in general, see section 4.2 of the Technical Notes.

Limitations: Statistics on divorces are subject to the same qualifications as have been set forth for vital statistics in general and divorce statistics in particular as discussed in section 4 of the Technical Notes.

Divorce, like marriage, is a legal event, and this has implications for international comparability of data. Divorce has been defined, for statistical purposes, in terms of the laws of individual countries or areas. The laws pertaining to divorce vary considerably from one country or area to another. This variation in the legal provision for divorce also affects the incidence of divorce, which is relatively low in countries or areas where divorce decrees are difficult to obtain.

Since divorces are granted by courts and statistics on divorce refer to the actual divorce decree, effective as of the date of the decree, marked year-to-year fluctuations may reflect court delays and clearances rather than trends in the incidence of divorce. The comparability of divorce statistics may also be affected by tabulation procedures. In some countries or areas annulments and/or legal separations may be included. This practice is more common for countries or areas in which the number of divorces is small. Information on this practice is given in the footnotes when known.

Because the registration of a divorce in many countries or areas is the responsibility solely of the court or the authority which granted it, and since the registration recording such cases is part of the records of the court proceedings, it follows that divorces are likely to be registered soon after the decree is granted. For this reason the practice of tabulating data by date of registration does not generally pose serious problems of comparability as it does in the case of birth and death statistics.

As noted briefly above, the incidence of divorce is affected by the relative ease or difficulty of obtaining a divorce according to the laws of individual countries or areas. The incidence of divorce is also affected by the ability of individuals to meet financial and other costs of the court procedures. Connected with this aspect is the influence of certain religious faiths on the incidence of divorce. For all these reasons, divorce statistics are not strictly comparable as measures of family dissolution by legal means. Furthermore, family dissolution by other than legal means, such as separation, is not measured in statistics for divorce.

For certain countries or areas there is or was no legal provision for divorce in the sense used here, and therefore no data for these countries or areas appear in this table.

In addition, it should be noted that rates are affected also by the quality and limitations of the population estimates that are used in their computation. The problems of under-enumeration or over-enumeration, and to some extent, the differences in definition of total population, have been discussed in section 3 of the Technical Notes dealing with population data in general, and specific information pertaining to individual countries or areas is given in the footnotes to table 3.

As will be seen from the footnotes, strict correspondence between the numerator of the rate and the denominator is not always obtained; for example, divorces among civilian plus military segments of the population may be related to civilian population only. The effect of this may be to increase the rates but, in most cases, the effect is negligible.

As mentioned above, data for some countries or areas may include annulments and/or legal separations. This practice affects the comparability of the crude divorce rates. For example, inclusion of annulments in the numerator of the rates produces a negligible effect on the rates, but inclusion of legal separations may have a measurable effect on the level.

It should be emphasized that crude divorce rates like crude birth, death and marriage rates may be seriously affected by age-sex structure of the populations to which they relate. Like crude marriage rates, they are also affected by the existing distribution of the population by marital status. Nevertheless, crude divorce rates provide a simple measure of the level and changes in divorces.

The comparability of data by urban/rural residence is affected by the national definitions of urban and rural used in tabulating these data. It is assumed, in the absence of specific information to the contrary, that the definitions of urban and rural used in connection with the national population census were also used in the compilation of the vital statistics for each country or area. However, it cannot be excluded that, for a given country or area, different definitions of urban and rural are used for the vital statistics data and the population census data respectively. When known, the definitions of urban in national population censuses are presented at the end of the technical notes for table 6. As discussed in detail in the notes, these definitions vary considerably from one country or area to another.

In addition to problems of comparability, divorce rates classified by urban/rural residence are also subject to certain special types of bias. If, when calculating divorce rates, different definitions of urban are used in connection with the vital events and the population data, and if this results in a net difference between the numerator and denominator of the rate in the population at risk, then the divorce rates would be biased. Urban/rural differentials in divorce rates may also be affected by whether the vital events have been tabulated in terms of place of occurrence or place of usual residence. This problem is discussed in more detail in section 4.1.4.1. of the Technical Notes.

Earlier data: Divorces have been shown in previous issues of the Demographic Yearbook. The earliest data, which were for 1935, appeared in the 1951 issue. For more information on specific topics and years for which data are reported, readers should consult the Historical Index.

NOTES

[1] For definition, please see section 4.1.1 of the Technical Notes.

Tableau 23

Le tableau 23 présente des statistiques concernant les divorces et les taux bruts de divortialité pour le plus grand nombre d'années possible entre 2003 et 2007.

Description des variables : le divorce est la dissolution légale et définitive des liens du mariage, c'est-à-dire la séparation de l'époux et de l'épouse qui confère aux parties le droit de se remarier civilement ou religieusement, ou selon toute autre procédure, conformément à la législation du pays[1].

Sauf indication contraire, les statistiques de la divortialité n'englobent pas les séparations légales qui excluent un remariage. Ces statistiques se rapportent aux jugements de divorce prononcés, non aux personnes divorcées.

Les statistiques de la divortialité proviennent, selon la pratique suivie par chaque pays, des actes des tribunaux et/ou des registres de l'état civil. L'officier d'état civil, les services nationaux de statistique ou d'autres services gouvernementaux peuvent être chargés d'établir ces statistiques.

La classification des divorces selon le lieu de résidence (zone urbaine ou rurale) est celle qui a été communiquée par chaque pays ou zone ; on part du principe qu'elle repose sur les définitions de la population urbaine utilisées pour les recensements nationaux, qui sont reproduites à la fin des notes techniques du tableau 6.

Calcul des taux : les taux bruts de divortialité selon le lieu de résidence (zone urbaine ou rurale) représentent le nombre annuel de divorces enregistrés pour 1 000 habitants au milieu de l'année. Les taux du tableau 23 ne se rapportent qu'aux pays ou zones où l'on a enregistré un total d'au moins 30 divorces pendant une année donnée. Ces taux sont calculés par la division de statistique des Nations Unies sur la base de la population de référence adéquate (par exemple : population totale, nationaux seulement, etc.) si connue et disponible. Si la population de référence n'est pas connue ou n'est pas disponible, la population totale est utilisée pour calculer les taux. Par conséquent, si la population utilisée pour calculer les taux est différente de la population de référence adéquate, les taux présentés sont susceptibles de sous ou sur estimer la situation réelle d'un pays ou d'un territoire.

Fiabilité des données : il a été demandé à chaque pays ou zone d'indiquer le degré estimatif de complétude des données sur les divorces figurant dans ses registres d'état civil. Ces évaluations nationales sont désignées par les codes de qualité "C" et "U" qui apparaissent dans la deuxième colonne du tableau.

La lettre "C" indique que les données sont jugées à peu près complètes, c'est-à-dire qu'elles représentent au moins 90 p. 100 des divorces survenus chaque année ; la lettre "U" signale que les données sont jugées incomplètes, c'est-à-dire qu'elles représentent moins de 90 p. 100 des divorces survenus chaque année. Le code "..." indique qu'aucun renseignement n'a été communiqué quant à la complétude des données.

Les données issues des registres de l'état civil qui sont déclarées incomplètes ou dont le degré de complétude n'est pas connu (code "U" ou "...") sont jugées douteuses. Elles apparaissent en italique dans le tableau et les taux correspondants n'ont pas été calculés. Les codes de qualité ne s'appliquent qu'aux données extraites des registres de l'état civil. Pour plus de précisions sur la qualité des données reposant sur les statistiques de l'état civil en général, voir la section 4.2 des notes techniques.

Insuffisance des données : les statistiques des divorces appellent les mêmes réserves que celles formulées à propos des statistiques de l'état civil en général et des statistiques de divortialité en particulier (voir la section 4 des notes techniques).

Le divorce est, comme le mariage, un acte juridique, et ce fait influe sur la comparabilité internationale des données. Aux fins de la statistique, le divorce est défini par la législation de chaque pays ou zone. La législation sur le divorce varie considérablement d'un pays ou d'une zone à l'autre, ce qui influe aussi sur la fréquence des divorces, laquelle est relativement faible dans les pays ou zones où le jugement de divorce est difficile à obtenir.

Du fait que les divorces sont prononcés par les tribunaux et que les statistiques de la divortialité se rapportent aux jugements de divorce proprement dits, qui prennent effet à la date où ces jugements sont rendus, il se peut que des fluctuations annuelles accusées traduisent le rythme plus ou moins rapide auquel les affaires sont jugées plutôt que l'évolution de la fréquence des divorces. Les méthodes d'exploitation des données peuvent aussi influer sur la comparabilité des statistiques de la divortialité. Dans certains pays ou zones, ces statistiques peuvent comprendre les annulations et/ou les séparations légales. C'est notamment le cas dans les pays ou zones où les divorces sont peu nombreux. Lorsqu'ils sont connus, des renseignements à ce propos sont donnés en note à la fin du tableau.

Étant donné que dans de nombreux pays ou zones, le tribunal ou l'autorité qui a prononcé le divorce est seul habilité à enregistrer cet acte, et, comme l'acte d'enregistrement figure alors sur les registres du tribunal, l'enregistrement suit généralement de peu le jugement. C'est pourquoi la pratique consistant à exploiter les données selon la date de l'enregistrement ne pose généralement pas les graves problèmes de comparabilité auxquels on se heurte dans le cas des statistiques des naissances et des décès.

Comme on l'a brièvement mentionné ci-dessus, la fréquence des divorces est fonction notamment de la facilité relative avec laquelle la législation de chaque pays ou zone permet d'obtenir le divorce. Elle dépend également de la capacité des intéressés à supporter les frais de procédure. Il faut aussi citer l'influence de certaines religions sur la fréquence des divorces. Pour toutes ces raisons, les statistiques de divortialité ne sont pas rigoureusement comparables et ne permettent pas de mesurer exactement la fréquence des dissolutions légales des mariages. De plus, elles ne rendent pas compte des cas de dissolution extrajudiciaire du mariage, comme la séparation.

Dans certains pays ou zones, il n'existe ou il n'existait pas de législation sur le divorce selon l'acception retenue aux fins du tableau 23, si bien que l'on ne dispose pas de données les concernant.

De surcroît, il convient de noter que l'exactitude des taux dépend également de la qualité et des insuffisances des estimations de population qui sont utilisées pour leur calcul. Le problème des erreurs par excès ou par défaut commises lors du dénombrement et, dans une certaine mesure, le problème de l'hétérogénéité des définitions de la population totale ont été examinés à la section 3 des notes techniques, relative à la population en général ; des explications concernant les différents pays ou zones sont données en note à la fin du tableau 3.

Comme on le verra dans les notes, il n'a pas toujours été possible d'obtenir une correspondance rigoureuse entre le numérateur et le dénominateur pour le calcul des taux. Par exemple, les divorces parmi la population civile et les militaires sont parfois rapportés à la population civile seulement. Cela peut avoir pour effet d'accroître les taux, mais, dans la plupart des cas, il est probable que la différence sera négligeable.

Comme indiqué plus haut, les données concernant certains pays ou zones peuvent comprendre les annulations et/ou les séparations légales. Cette pratique influe sur la comparabilité des taux bruts de divortialité. Par exemple, l'inclusion des annulations dans le numérateur a une influence négligeable, mais l'inclusion des séparations légales peut avoir un effet appréciable.

Il faut souligner que les taux bruts de divortialité, de même que les taux bruts de natalité, de mortalité et de nuptialité, peuvent varier sensiblement selon la structure par âge et par sexe. Comme les taux bruts de nuptialité, ils peuvent également varier en raison de la répartition de la population selon l'état matrimonial. Les taux bruts de divortialité offrent néanmoins un moyen simple de mesurer la fréquence et l'évolution des divorces.

La comparabilité des données selon le lieu de résidence (zone urbaine ou rurale) peut être limitée par les définitions nationales des termes « urbain » et « rural » utilisées pour la mise en tableaux de ces données. En l'absence d'indications contraires, on a supposé que les mêmes définitions avaient servi pour le recensement national de la population et pour l'établissement des statistiques de l'état civil pour chaque pays ou zone. Toutefois, il n'est pas exclu que, pour une zone ou un pays donné, des définitions différentes aient été retenues. Les définitions du terme « urbain » utilisées pour les recensements nationaux de population ont été présentées à la fin des notes techniques du tableau 6 lorsqu'elles étaient connues. Comme on l'a précisé dans les notes techniques relatives au tableau 6, ces définitions varient considérablement d'un pays ou d'une zone à l'autre.

Outre les problèmes de comparabilité, les taux de divortialité classés selon le lieu de résidence (zone urbaine ou rurale) sont également sujets à des distorsions particulières. Si l'on utilise des définitions différentes du terme « urbain » pour classer les faits d'état civil et les données relatives à la population lors du calcul des taux et qu'il en résulte une différence nette entre le numérateur et le dénominateur pour le taux de la population exposée au risque, les taux de divortialité s'en trouveront faussés. La différence entre ces taux pour les zones urbaines et rurales pourra aussi être faussée selon que les faits d'état civil auront été classés d'après le lieu de l'événement ou d'après le lieu de résidence habituel. Ce problème est examiné plus en détail à la section 4.1.4.1 des notes techniques.

Données publiées antérieurement : des statistiques concernant les divorces ont déjà été présentées dans des éditions antérieures de l'*Annuaire démographique*. Les plus anciennes, qui portaient sur 1935, ont été publiées dans l'édition de 1951. Pour plus de précisions concernant les années et les sujets pour lesquels des données ont été publiées, se reporter à l'index historique.

NOTE

[1] Pour la définition, voir la section 4.1.1 des Notes techniques.

23. Divorces and crude divorce rates by urban/rural residence: 2003 - 2007
Divorces et taux bruts de divortialité selon la résidence, urbaine/rurale: 2003 - 2007

Continent, country or area, and urban/rural residence / Continent, pays ou zone et résidence, urbaine/rurale	Code[a]	Number - Nombre					Rate - Taux				
		2003	2004	2005	2006	2007	2003	2004	2005	2006	2007
AFRICA - AFRIQUE											
Egypt - Égypte[1]											
Total	U	69 867	64 496	65 047	65 461	77 878	...	...	...	...	...
Urban - Urbaine	U	35 442	31 360	32 791	33 603	42 595	...	...	...	...	...
Rural - Rurale	U	34 425	33 136	32 256	31 858	35 283	...	...	...	...	...
Mauritius - Maurice											
Total	+C	1 190	1 162	1 133	1 379	1 302	1.0	0.9	0.9	1.1	1.0
Réunion											
Total	C	1 194	1 516	1 499	1 553	...	1.6	2.0	1.9	2.0	...
Saint Helena ex. dep. - Sainte-Hélène sans dép.											
Total	C	12	8	8	4	10	...	...	...	...	...
Seychelles											
Total	+C	126	171	140	142	...	1.5	2.1	1.7	1.7	...
South Africa - Afrique du Sud											
Total	...	31 566	31 768	32 484	31 270	29 639	...	...	...	...	...
Tunisia - Tunisie											
Total	...	10 212	10 062	11 576	11 711	12 557	...	...	...	...	...
AMERICA, NORTH - AMÉRIQUE DU NORD											
Anguilla											
Total	+C	9	19	22	19	12	...	...	...	...	...
Aruba											
Total	C	480	484	444	529	417	5.0	5.0	4.4	5.1	4.0
Bahamas											
Total	C	324	657	360	296	*105	1.0	2.0	1.1	0.9	*0.3
Bermuda - Bermudes											
Total	C	207	185	213	179	...	3.3	2.9	3.4	2.8	...
British Virgin Islands - Îles Vierges britanniques											
Total	C	77	60	...	...	...	3.6	2.8	...	...	...
Canada											
Total	C	70 828	69 644	...	...	...	2.2	2.2	...	...	...
Cayman Islands - Îles Caïmanes											
Total	+C	...	...	145	158	162	...	...	3.0	3.0	3.0
Costa Rica											
Total	C	9 442	9 467	9 887	9 098	10 926	2.3	2.3	2.3	2.1	2.5
Cuba											
Total	C	33 851	35 594	34 359	35 837	34 559	3.0	3.2	3.1	3.2	3.1
Urban - Urbaine	C	31 130	33 017	32 251	33 739	32 217	3.7	3.9	3.8	4.0	3.8
Rural - Rurale	C	2 721	2 577	2 108	2 098	2 342	1.0	0.9	0.8	0.8	0.8
Dominica - Dominique											
Total	+C	55	75	70	89	...	0.8	1.1	1.0	1.3	...
Dominican Republic - République dominicaine											
Total	+C	14 618	17 691	16 649	18 071	16 705	1.6	1.9	1.8	1.9	1.8
El Salvador[2]											
Total	...	4 121	4 625	4 963	5 576	6 138	...	...	...	...	...
Urban - Urbaine[3]	...	3 993	4 415	4 722	5 369	5 940	...	...	...	...	...
Rural - Rurale[3]	...	128	210	241	207	198	...	...	...	...	...
Guatemala											
Total	C	967	1 888	2 888	1 917	...	0.1	0.2	0.2	0.1	...
Jamaica - Jamaïque											
Total	C	1 600	1 739	1 806	1 768	1 140	0.6	0.7	0.7	0.7	0.4
Mexico - Mexique											
Total	+C	64 248	67 575	70 184	72 396	77 255	0.6	0.7	0.7	0.7	0.7
Urban - Urbaine[4]	+C	55 272	58 689	61 926	62 997	67 851	0.7	0.7	0.8	0.8	0.8
Rural - Rurale[4]	+C	2 908	2 907	2 964	3 458	3 238	0.1	0.1	0.1	0.1	0.1
Netherlands Antilles - Antilles néerlandaises											
Total	C	540	513	534	491	...	3.1	2.9	2.9	2.6	...
Nicaragua											
Total	+U	3 170	2 779	3 916	5 839	3 474	...	...	...	...	...

23. Divorces and crude divorce rates by urban/rural residence: 2003 - 2007
Divorces et taux bruts de divortialité selon la résidence, urbaine/rurale: 2003 - 2007 (continued - suite)

Continent, country or area, and urban/rural residence / Continent, pays ou zone et résidence, urbaine/rurale	Code[a]	Number - Nombre					Rate - Taux				
		2003	2004	2005	2006	2007	2003	2004	2005	2006	2007
AMERICA, NORTH - AMÉRIQUE DU NORD											
Panama											
Total	C	*2 732	2 652	2 758	2 866	2 893	*0.9	0.8	0.9	0.9	0.9
Puerto Rico - Porto Rico											
Total	C	14 225	15 197	15 816	14 826	...	3.7	3.9	4.0	3.8	...
Saint Lucia - Sainte-Lucie											
Total	C	113	*114	...	...	...	0.7	*0.7	...	...	...
Saint Vincent and the Grenadines - Saint-Vincent-et-les Grenadines											
Total	+C	93	85	92	...	...	0.9	0.8	0.9	...	...
Trinidad and Tobago - Trinité-et-Tobago											
Total	C	1 611	1 852	2 785	...	...	1.3	1.4	2.2	...	...
Turks and Caicos Islands - Îles Turques et Caïques											
Total	C	9	16	24	22	...	...	...	...	...	...
United States Virgin Islands - Îles Vierges américaines											
Total	C	425	...	...	...	...	3.9	...	...	...	...
AMERICA, SOUTH - AMÉRIQUE DU SUD											
Brazil - Brésil[5]											
Total	...	135 564	130 527	153 839	164 974	180 455	...	...	...	...	...
Chile - Chili[6]											
Total	C	...	...	...	4 091	...	...	...	...	0.2	...
Ecuador - Équateur[7]											
Total	U	10 912	11 251	11 725	13 981	14 942	...	...	...	...	...
Suriname											
Total	C	629	607[8]	724[9]	663[9]	645[9]	1.3	1.2	1.5	1.3	1.3
Uruguay											
Total	+C	*14 003	*14 300	...	...	...	*4.2	*4.3	...	...	...
Venezuela (Bolivarian Republic of) - Venezuela (République bolivarienne du)[5]											
Total	...	20 077	21 260	21 451	24 481	28 823	...	...	...	...	...
ASIA - ASIE											
Armenia - Arménie											
Total	C	1 820	1 968	2 466	2 797	2 931	0.6	0.6	0.8	0.9	0.9
Urban - Urbaine	C	1 536	1 658	2 019	2 235	2 316	0.7	0.8	1.0	1.1	1.1
Rural - Rurale	C	284	310	447	562	615	0.2	0.3	0.4	0.5	0.5
Azerbaijan - Azerbaïdjan											
Total	+C	6 671	6 914	8 895	7 817	8 340	0.8	0.8	1.1	0.9	1.0
Urban - Urbaine	+C	5 555	5 606	6 864	5 841	6 093	1.3	1.3	1.6	1.3	1.4
Rural - Rurale	+C	1 116	1 308	2 031	1 976	2 247	0.3	0.3	0.5	0.5	0.5
Bahrain - Bahreïn											
Total	...	923	1 030	1 051	1 141	1 196	...	...	...	...	...
Brunei Darussalam - Brunéi Darussalam											
Total	...	349	392	...	...	...	...	...	...	...	...
Cambodia - Cambodge											
Total	...	...	158 011	...	...	...	...	...	...	...	...
Urban - Urbaine	...	...	24 778	...	...	...	...	...	...	...	...
Rural - Rurale	...	...	133 233	...	...	...	...	...	...	...	...
China - Chine[10]											
Total	+C	1 331 000	1 665 000	1 785 000	1 893 000	2 098 000	1.0	1.3	1.4	1.4	1.6

23. Divorces and crude divorce rates by urban/rural residence: 2003 - 2007
Divorces et taux bruts de divortialité selon la résidence, urbaine/rurale: 2003 - 2007 (continued - suite)

Continent, country or area, and urban/rural residence / Continent, pays ou zone et résidence, urbaine/rurale	Code[a]	Number - Nombre					Rate - Taux				
		2003	2004	2005	2006	2007	2003	2004	2005	2006	2007
ASIA - ASIE											
China, Hong Kong SAR - Chine, Hong Kong RAS											
Total	...	13 829	15 604	14 873	17 424	...	...	...	...	...	...
China, Macao SAR - Chine, Macao RAS											
Total	C	440	475	573	592	...	1.0	1.0	1.2	1.2	...
Cyprus - Chypre[11]											
Total	C	1 472	1 614	1 514	1 753	1 648	2.0	2.2	2.0	2.3	2.1
Urban - Urbaine[12]	C	1 162	1 293	1 208	1 424		...	...	...	...	...
Rural - Rurale[12]	C	267	258	254	268		...	...	...	...	...
Georgia - Géorgie											
Total	C	1 825	1 793	1 928	2 060	2 325	0.4	0.4	0.4	0.5	0.5
Urban - Urbaine	C	1 802	1 787	1 906	1 987	2 239	0.8	0.8	0.8	0.9	1.0
Rural - Rurale	C	23	6	22	73	86	...	...	...	0.0	0.0
Iran (Islamic Republic of) - Iran (République islamique d')[13]											
Total	C	72 359	73 882	84 243	94 040	99 852	1.1	1.1	1.2	1.3	1.4
Urban - Urbaine	C	64 213	63 406	70 024	78 801	84 120	1.4	1.4	1.5	...	1.7
Rural - Rurale	C	8 146	10 476	14 219	15 239	15 732	0.4	0.5	0.6	...	0.7
Israel - Israël[14]											
Total	C	10 689	11 185	11 030	13 439	...	1.6	1.6	1.6	1.9	...
Japan - Japon[15]											
Total	+C	283 854	270 804	261 917	257 475	254 832	2.2	2.1	2.1	2.0	2.0
Urban - Urbaine	+C	234 304	224 699	227 275	232 234	231 106	...	...	...	...	...
Rural - Rurale	+C	49 550	46 105	34 642	25 241	23 726	...	...	...	...	...
Jordan - Jordanie[16]											
Total	+C	9 022	9 791	10 231	11 413	11 793	1.6	1.8	1.9	2.0	2.1
Kazakhstan											
Total	C	31 717	31 492	32 377	35 834	36 107	2.1	2.1	2.1	2.3	2.3
Urban - Urbaine	C	26 451	26 288	26 973	29 533	28 011	3.1	3.1	3.1	3.4	3.4
Rural - Rurale	C	5 266	5 204	5 404	6 301	8 096	0.8	0.8	0.8	1.0	1.1
Kuwait - Koweït											
Total	C	3 998	4 899	4 538	4 239	4 945	1.9	2.3	2.0	1.8	2.1
Kyrgyzstan - Kirghizstan											
Total	C	5 367	5 311	6 097	6 870	7 371	1.1	1.0	1.2	1.3	1.4
Urban - Urbaine	C	3 280	3 441	3 543	3 947	4 113	1.8	1.9	1.9	2.1	2.2
Rural - Rurale	C	2 087	1 870	2 554	2 923	3 258	0.6	0.6	0.8	0.9	1.0
Lebanon - Liban											
Total	+C	4 328	4 372	4 746	4 388	5 859	...	1.2	...	...	1.6
Maldives											
Total	...	1 135	1 161	1 757	2 177	...	...	...	...	...	...
Urban - Urbaine	...	530	589	935	1 068	...	...	...	...	...	...
Rural - Rurale	...	605	572	822	1 109	...	...	...	...	...	...
Mongolia - Mongolie											
Total	C	884	1 098	1 622	1 448	1 757	0.4	0.4	0.6	0.6	0.7
Urban - Urbaine	C	813	1 032	1 508	1 310	1 590	0.6	0.7	1.0	0.8	1.0
Rural - Rurale	C	71	66	114	138	167	0.1	0.1	0.1	0.1	0.2
Occupied Palestinian Territory - Territoire palestinien occupé											
Total	C	3 909	3 961	4 211	3 756	4 043	1.2	1.2	1.2	1.0	1.1
Qatar											
Total	C	790	787	643	826	997	1.1	1.0	0.7	0.8	0.8
Republic of Korea - République de Corée[17]											
Total[18]	+C	167 096	139 365	128 468	125 032	*124 590	3.5	2.9	2.6	2.6	*2.6
Urban - Urbaine	+C	135 753	111 582	102 668	99 201	...	3.5	2.9	2.6	2.5	...
Rural - Rurale	+C	28 921	25 069	23 060	22 578	...	2.9	2.6	2.4	2.4	...
Saudi Arabia - Arabie saoudite											
Total	...	24 435	24 318	24 862	...	...	...	...	...	...	...
Singapore - Singapour											
Total	+C	6 293	6 047	6 569	6 649	6 812	1.5	1.5	1.5	1.5	1.5
Syrian Arab Republic - République arabe syrienne[19]											
Total	U	17 558	17 336	17 821	19 984	19 506	...	...	...	...	...

23. Divorces and crude divorce rates by urban/rural residence: 2003 - 2007
Divorces et taux bruts de divortialité selon la résidence, urbaine/rurale: 2003 - 2007 (continued - suite)

Continent, country or area, and urban/rural residence / Continent, pays ou zone et résidence, urbaine/rurale	Code[a]	Number - Nombre					Rate - Taux				
		2003	2004	2005	2006	2007	2003	2004	2005	2006	2007
ASIA - ASIE											
Tajikistan - Tadjikistan											
Total	+C	2 383	2 587	2 885	3 018	4 752	0.4	0.4	0.4	0.4	0.7
Urban - Urbaine	+C	2 112	2 202	2 135	1 664	2 514	1.2	1.2	1.2	0.9	1.3
Rural - Rurale	+C	271	385	750	1 354	2 238	0.1	0.1	0.1	0.3	0.4
Turkey - Turquie[20]											
Total	C	92 637	91 022	95 895	93 489	94 219	1.3	1.3	1.3	1.3	1.3
United Arab Emirates - Émirats arabes unis											
Total	...	3 243	3 577	...	...	...	...	...	...	...	...
Viet Nam											
Total	C	19 972	20 124	18 724	17 324	17 946	0.2	0.2	0.2	0.2	0.2
Urban - Urbaine	C	7 896	8 351	7 100	5 848	6 419	0.4	0.4	0.3	0.3	0.3
Rural - Rurale	C	12 076	11 773	11 624	11 476	11 527	0.2	0.2	0.2	0.2	0.2
Yemen - Yémen											
Total	...	104	...	...	...	...	...	...	...	...	...
EUROPE											
Åland Islands - Îles d'Åland[21]											
Total	C	56	53	41	63	60	2.1	2.0	1.5	2.3	2.2
Urban - Urbaine	C	24	25	19	32	32	...	...	...	3.0	2.9
Rural - Rurale	C	32	28	22	31	28	2.0	...	...	1.9	...
Albania - Albanie											
Total	C	3 634	2 968	3 929	4 075	3 305	1.2	0.9	1.3	1.3	1.0
Austria - Autriche[22]											
Total	C	19 066	19 590	19 453	20 336	20 516	2.3	2.4	2.4	2.5	2.5
Belarus - Bélarus											
Total	C	31 679	29 133	30 531	31 814	36 146	3.2	3.0	3.1	3.3	3.7
Urban - Urbaine	C	26 453	24 597	25 810	26 928	31 315	3.8	3.5	3.7	3.8	4.4
Rural - Rurale	C	5 226	4 536	4 721	4 886	4 831	1.8	1.6	1.7	1.8	1.9
Belgium - Belgique[23]											
Total	C	31 355	31 405	30 840	29 189	30 081	3.0	3.0	2.9	2.8	2.8
Urban - Urbaine	C	31 026	31 091	30 542	28 881	29 751	3.0	3.0	3.0	2.8	2.8
Rural - Rurale	C	329	314	298	308	330	2.2	2.1	2.0	2.0	2.2
Bosnia and Herzegovina - Bosnie-Herzégovine											
Total	C	1 918	1 523	1 763	1 659	1 826	0.5	0.4	0.5	0.4	...
Bulgaria - Bulgarie[24]											
Total	C	12 000	14 657	14 663	14 815	16 347	1.5	1.9	1.9	1.9	2.1
Urban - Urbaine	C	9 973	11 803	11 801	12 153	13 672	1.8	2.2	2.2	2.2	2.5
Rural - Rurale	C	2 027	2 854	2 862	2 662	2 675	0.9	1.2	1.2	1.2	1.2
Croatia - Croatie											
Total	C	4 934	4 985	4 883	4 651	4 785	1.1	1.1	1.1	1.0	1.1
Urban - Urbaine	C	3 553	3 509	3 533	3 371	3 375	...	...	...	...	...
Rural - Rurale	C	1 381	1 476	1 350	1 280	1 410	...	...	...	...	...
Czech Republic - République tchèque											
Total	C	32 824	33 060	31 288	31 415	31 129	3.2	3.2	3.1	3.1	3.0
Urban - Urbaine	C	26 569	26 841	25 233	25 214	24 627	3.5	3.6	3.3	3.3	3.2
Rural - Rurale	C	6 255	6 219	6 055	6 201	6 502	2.3	2.3	2.3	2.3	2.4
Denmark - Danemark[25]											
Total	C	15 763	15 774	15 300	14 343	14 066	2.9	2.9	2.8	2.6	2.6
Estonia - Estonie											
Total	C	3 973	4 158	4 054	3 811	3 809	2.9	3.1	3.0	2.8	2.8
Urban - Urbaine[26]	C	2 865	2 997	2 882	2 676	2 653	3.1	3.2	3.1	2.9	2.8
Rural - Rurale[26]	C	970	1 016	1 056	1 058	1 072	2.3	2.5	2.6	2.6	2.6
Faeroe Islands - Îles Féroé											
Total	C	57	48	67	61	62	1.2	1.0	1.4	1.3	1.3
Finland - Finlande[27]											
Total	C	13 475	13 234	13 383	13 255	13 224	2.6	2.5	2.6	2.5	2.5
Urban - Urbaine	C	9 613	9 344	9 451	9 396	9 558	3.0	2.9	2.9	2.8	2.8
Rural - Rurale	C	3 862	3 890	3 932	3 859	3 666	2.0	2.0	2.0	2.0	2.0
France[28]											
Total	C	125 175	131 335	152 020	135 910	...	2.1	2.2	2.5	2.2	...

Continent, country or area, and urban/rural residence / Continent, pays ou zone et résidence, urbaine/rurale	Code[a]	Number - Nombre					Rate - Taux				
		2003	2004	2005	2006	2007	2003	2004	2005	2006	2007
EUROPE											
Germany - Allemagne											
Total	C	213 975	213 691	201 693	190 928	187 072	2.6	2.6	2.4	2.3	2.3
Gibraltar											
Total	C	159	119	97	121	...	5.6	4.1	3.4	4.2	...
Greece - Grèce											
Total	C	12 033	12 307	13 494	13 218	...	1.1	1.1	1.2	1.2	...
Hungary - Hongrie											
Total	C	25 040	24 633	24 795	24 866	25 156	2.5	2.4	2.5	2.5	2.5
Urban - Urbaine[29]	C	18 135	17 567	17 685	17 910	18 278	2.8	2.7	2.7	2.7	2.7
Rural - Rurale[29]	C	6 770	6 850	6 863	6 728	6 755	1.9	1.9	2.0	2.0	2.0
Iceland - Islande[2]											
Total	C	531	560	564	516	515	1.8	1.9	1.9	1.7	1.7
Urban - Urbaine	C	508	524	531[30]	493	493	1.9	1.9	1.9	1.7	1.7
Rural - Rurale	C	23	36	32[30]	23	22	...	1.7	1.5	...	...
Ireland - Irlande											
Total	+C	2 970	3 347	3 411	...	...	0.7	0.8	0.8	...	...
Total[31]	C	...	...	...	3 466	3 684	...	...	...	0.8	0.8
Isle of Man - Île de Man											
Total	+C	338	...	...	...	...	4.4	...	...	...	...
Italy - Italie											
Total	C	43 856	45 097	47 036	49 534	...	0.8	0.8	0.8	0.8	...
Latvia - Lettonie											
Total	C	4 828	5 271	6 341	7 249	7 403	2.1	2.3	2.8	3.2	3.3
Urban - Urbaine	C	3 774	4 117	4 870	5 545	5 535	2.4	2.6	3.1	3.6	3.6
Rural - Rurale	C	1 054	1 154	1 471	1 704	1 868	1.4	1.6	2.0	2.3	2.6
Liechtenstein											
Total	C	84	101	94	81	*97	2.5	2.9	2.7	2.3	*2.7
Lithuania - Lituanie											
Total	C	10 599	10 997	11 097	11 202	11 336	3.1	3.2	3.3	3.3	3.4
Urban - Urbaine	C	8 377	8 106	8 105	7 946	8 044	3.6	3.5	3.6	3.5	3.6
Rural - Rurale	C	2 222	2 891	2 992	3 256	3 292	1.9	2.5	2.6	2.9	2.9
Luxembourg											
Total	C	1 026	1 055	1 046	1 182	1 106	2.3	2.3	2.2	2.5	2.3
Monaco											
Total	C	73	82	69	...	...	...	...	...	...	...
Montenegro - Monténégro											
Total	C	494	505	499	470	453	0.8	0.8	0.8	0.8	0.7
Urban - Urbaine	C	408	422	...	...	...	1.1	1.1	...	...	...
Rural - Rurale	C	86	83	...	...	...	0.4	0.4	...	...	...
Netherlands - Pays-Bas											
Total	C	31 479	31 098[33]	31 905	31 734	31 983	1.9	1.9	2.0	1.9	2.0
Urban - Urbaine[32]	C	22 700	21 614[33]	22 312	22 019	22 008	2.2	2.0	2.1	2.0	2.0
Rural - Rurale[32]	C	8 245	8 929[33]	9 074	9 195	9 457	1.5	1.6	1.6	1.7	1.7
Norway - Norvège[34]											
Total	C	10 757	11 045	11 040	10 598	10 280	2.4	2.4	2.4	2.3	2.2
Poland - Pologne[35]											
Total	C	48 632	56 332	67 578	71 912	66 586	1.3	1.5	1.8	1.9	1.7
Urban - Urbaine	C	40 876	45 954	53 611	57 915	53 210	1.7	2.0	2.3	2.5	2.3
Rural - Rurale	C	7 669	10 288	13 846	13 807	12 968	0.5	0.7	0.9	0.9	0.9
Portugal											
Total	C	22 818	23 348	22 853	23 935	*25 255	2.2	2.2	2.2	2.3	*2.4
Republic of Moldova - République de Moldova											
Total	C	14 672	14 918	14 521	12 594	13 923	4.1	4.1	4.0	3.5	3.9
Urban - Urbaine	C	10 565	11 015	10 816	9 652	11 003	7.1	7.5	7.3	6.5	7.4
Rural - Rurale	C	4 107	3 903	3 705	2 942	2 920	1.9	1.8	1.7	1.4	1.4
Romania - Roumanie											
Total	C	33 073	35 225	33 193	32 672	36 308	1.5	1.6	1.5	1.5	1.7
Urban - Urbaine	C	23 542	25 134	23 709	23 338	26 066	2.0	2.1	2.0	2.0	2.2
Rural - Rurale	C	9 531	10 091	9 484	9 334	10 242	0.9	1.0	1.0	1.0	1.1
Russian Federation - Fédération de Russie											
Total	C	798 824	635 835	604 942	640 837	685 910	5.5	4.4	4.2	4.5	4.8
San Marino - Saint-Marin											
Total	+C	45	62	61	...	...	1.6	2.1	2.0	...	...

Continent, country or area, and urban/rural residence / Continent, pays ou zone et résidence, urbaine/rurale	Co-de[a]	Number - Nombre					Rate - Taux				
		2003	2004	2005	2006	2007	2003	2004	2005	2006	2007
EUROPE											
Serbia - Serbie[36]											
Total.	+C	7 938	8 845	7 661	8 204	8 622	1.1	1.2	1.0	1.1	
Urban - Urbaine	+C	5 342	6 032	5 282	5 707	...	1.3	1.4	1.2	1.3	1.2
Rural - Rurale	+C	2 596	2 813	2 379	2 497	...	0.8	0.9	0.7	0.8	...
Slovakia - Slovaquie											...
Total.	C	10 716	10 889	11 553	12 716	12 174	2.0	2.0	2.1	2.4	2.3
Urban - Urbaine	C	7 720	7 700	8 209	8 926	8 378	2.6	2.6	2.7	3.0	2.8
Rural - Rurale	C	2 996	3 189	3 344	3 790	3 796	1.3	1.3	1.4	1.6	1.6
Slovenia - Slovénie											
Total.	C	2 461	2 411	2 647	2 334	2 617	1.2	1.2	1.3	1.2	1.3
Urban - Urbaine	C	1 533	1 442	1 623	1 379	1 473	1.6	1.5	1.7	1.4	1.5
Rural - Rurale	C	928	969	1 024	955	1 144	0.9	1.0	1.0	1.0	1.1
Spain - Espagne											
Total.	C	45 448	50 974	72 848	...	125 777	1.1	1.2	1.7	...	2.8
Sweden - Suède											
Total.		21 130	20 106	20 000	20 295	20 669	2.4	2.2	2.2	2.2	2.3
Switzerland - Suisse											
Total.	C	16 799	17 949	21 332	20 981	19 882	2.3	2.4	2.9	2.8	2.6
Urban - Urbaine	C	13 189	14 080	16 811	16 466	15 572	2.5	2.6	3.1	3.0	2.8
Rural - Rurale	C	3 610	3 869	4 521	4 515	4 310	1.8	2.0	2.3	2.3	2.1
The Former Yugoslav Republic of Macedonia - L'ex-République yougoslave de Macédoine											
Total.	C	1 405	1 645	1 552	1 475	1 417	0.7	0.8	0.8	0.7	0.7
Urban - Urbaine	C	...	...	1 009	...	848	...	...	...	...	...
Rural - Rurale	C	...	...	543	...	569	...	...	...	...	...
Ukraine											
Total.	C	177 183	173 163	183 455	179 123	178 364	3.7	3.7	3.9	3.8	3.8
Urban - Urbaine	C	138 053	134 372	141 971	138 993	138 630	4.3	...	...	...	4.4
Rural - Rurale	C	39 130	38 791	41 484	40 130	39 734	2.5	...	...	...	2.7
United Kingdom of Great Britain and Northern Ireland - Royaume-Uni de Grande-Bretagne et d'Irlande du Nord[37]											
Total.	C	166 536	167 138	155 052	...	*144 220	2.8	2.8	2.6	...	*2.4
OCEANIA - OCÉANIE											
Australia - Australie											
Total.	C	53 145	52 747	52 399	51 375	47 963	2.7	2.6	2.6	2.5	2.3
Guam											
Total.	C	883	1 975	...	...	...	5.3	11.9	...	...	...
New Caledonia - Nouvelle-Calédonie[38]											
Total.	C	246	247	341	...	...	1.1	1.1	1.5	...	...
Urban - Urbaine	C	139	...	...	...	...	...	...	...	...	...
Rural - Rurale	C	25	...	...	...	...	...	...	...	...	...
New Zealand - Nouvelle-Zélande											
Total.	+C	10 491	10 609	9 972	10 065	9 650	2.6	2.6	2.4	2.4	2.3
Northern Mariana Islands - Îles Mariannes septentrionales[39]											
Total.	U	...	...	*158*	*183*	*160*	...	...	...	...	...
Samoa											
Total.	U	*34*	*38*	*44*	...	...	...	...	...	...	...
Tonga											
Total.	+C	103	*110	...	...	...	1.0	*1.1	...	...	...

FOOTNOTES - NOTES

Italics: data from civil registers which are incomplete or of unknown completeness. - Italiques: données incomplètes ou dont le degré d'exactitude n'est pas connu, provenant des registres de l'état civil.

* Provisional. - Données provisoires.

Table 24

Table 24 presents the number of divorces according to the duration of marriage and the percentage distribution for the latest available year between 1998 and 2007.

Description of variables: Divorces are the final legal dissolutions of a marriage, which confer on the parties the right to remarry as defined by the laws of each country or area. Unless otherwise noted, divorce statistics exclude legal separations which do not allow remarriage. These statistics refer to the number of divorces granted, and not to the number of persons divorcing.

Duration of marriage is defined as the interval of time between the day, month and year of marriage and the day, month and year of divorce in completed years. It will be noted that this definition refers to the "legal" duration rather than the "effective" duration, it having been calculated until the day, month and year of the actual divorce decree rather than until the separation date or the date when the couple ceased to live as man and wife.

The duration of marriage classification used in this table to the extent possible, is the following: under one year, single years of duration through 9 years, 10-14 years, 15-19 years, 20 years and over and duration unknown, when appropriate.

Reliability of data: Data from civil registers of divorces which are reported as incomplete (less than 90 per cent completeness) or of unknown completeness are considered unreliable and are set in italics rather than in roman type. For more information about the quality of vital statistics data in general, see section 4.2 of the Technical Notes.

Limitations: Statistics on divorces by duration of marriage are subject to the same qualifications which have been set forth for vital statistics in general and divorce statistics in particular as discussed in Section 4 of the Technical Notes.

Earlier data: Divorces by duration by marriage, cross-classified by age of husband and by age of wife have been shown previously in issues of the Demographic Yearbook featuring marriage and divorce. For information on years covered, readers should consult the Historical Index.

Tableau 24

Le tableau 24 indique le nombre de divorces selon la durée du mariage et la répartition des pourcentages, pour la dernière année disponible entre 1998 et 2007.

Description des variables : le divorce est la dissolution définitive des liens du mariage qui confère aux parties le droit de se remarier, telle qu'elle est définie par la législation de chaque pays ou zone. Sauf indication contraire, les statistiques de la divortialité n'englobent pas les séparations légales qui excluent le remariage. Ces statistiques se rapportent aux jugements de divorce prononcés, non aux personnes divorcées.

La durée du mariage correspond à l'intervalle du temps qui s'est écoulé entre la date exacte (jour, mois et année) du mariage et la date exacte (jour, mois et année) du divorce exprimé en années révolues. On notera que cette définition est celle de la durée "légale" du mariage et non de sa durée "effective", puisque la durée est calculée jusqu'à la date (jour, mois et année) du jugement de divorce et non jusqu'à la date de la séparation ou la date à laquelle le couple a cessé de vivre comme mari et femme.

Le classement selon la durée du mariage utilisé dans ce tableau dans la mesure du possible comprend les catégories suivantes : moins d'un an, une catégorie par an jusqu'à 9 ans inclus, 10-14 ans, 15-19 ans, 20 ans et plus et, le cas échéant, une catégorie pour la durée du mariage inconnue.

Fiabilité des données : les données sur les divorces provenant des registres de l'état civil qui sont déclarées incomplètes (degré de complétude inférieur à 90 pour cent) ou dont le degré de complétude n'est pas connu, sont jugées douteuses et apparaissent en italique et non en caractères romains. Pour plus de précisions sur la qualité des données reposant sur les statistiques de l'état civil en general, voir la section 4.2 des Notes techniques.

Insuffisance des données : les statistiques des divorces selon la durée du mariage, appellent toutes les réserves qui ont été formulées à propos des statistiques de l'état civil en general et des statistiques des divorces en particulier (voir les explications figurant à la section 4 des Notes techniques).

Données publiées antérieurement : les statistiques des divorces selon la durée du mariage, classées selon l'âge de l'époux, d'une part, et selon l'âge de l'épouse, d'autre part, ont été présentées dans des éditions antérieures de l'Annuaire démographique qui avaient comme sujet spécial la nuptialité et la divortialité. Pour plus de précisions concernant les années pour lesquelles ces données ont été publiées, on se reportera à l'index historique.

24. Divorces and percentage distribution by duration of marriage, latest available year: 1998 - 2007
Divorces et répartition des pourcentages selon la durée du mariage, dernière année disponible: 1998 - 2007

Continent, country or area, year, code and duration of marriage (in years) / Continent, pays ou zone, année, code et durée du mariage (en années)	Number of divorces / Nombre de divorces	Per cent / Pour cent
AFRICA - AFRIQUE		
Egypt - Égypte		
2007 (U)		
Total....	77 878	100.0
Less than 1 - Moins de 1....	12 332	15.8
1....	9 995	12.8
2....	7 246	9.3
3....	4 863	6.2
4....	3 827	4.9
5....	2 531	3.2
6....	2 581	3.3
7....	2 204	2.8
8....	1 565	2.0
9....	1 284	1.6
10 - 14....	4 817	6.2
15 - 19....	2 628	3.4
20 +....	4 376	5.6
Not stated - Inconnu....	17 629	22.6
Mauritius - Maurice		
2007 (+C)		
Total....	1 302	100.0
Less than 1 - Moins de 1....	-	0.0
1....	27	2.1
2....	62	4.8
3....	88	6.8
4....	76	5.8
5....	69	5.3
6....	97	7.5
7....	77	5.9
8....	79	6.1
9....	69	5.3
10 - 14....	290	22.3
15 - 19....	195	15.0
20 +....	173	13.3
Not stated - Inconnu....	-	0.0
South Africa - Afrique du Sud		
2007 (...)		
Total....	29 639	100.0
Less than 1 - Moins de 1....	200	0.7
1....	999	3.4
2....	1 530	5.2
3....	1 712	5.8
4....	1 789	6.0
5....	1 809	6.1
6....	1 649	5.6
7....	1 620	5.5
8....	1 527	5.2
9....	1 396	4.7
10 - 14....	5 633	19.0
15 - 19....	3 762	12.7
20 +....	4 514	15.2
Not stated - Inconnu....	1 499	5.1
AMERICA, NORTH - AMÉRIQUE DU NORD		
Aruba		
2007 (C)		
Total....	417	100.0
Less than 1 - Moins de 1....	-	0.0
1....	12	2.9
2....	30	7.2
3....	15	3.6
4....	18	4.3
5....	42	10.1
6....	26	6.2
7....	13	3.1
8....	12	2.9

Continent, country or area, year, code and duration of marriage (in years) / Continent, pays ou zone, année, code et durée du mariage (en années)	Number of divorces / Nombre de divorces	Per cent / Pour cent
AMERICA, NORTH - AMÉRIQUE DU NORD		
Aruba		
2007 (C)		
9....	25	6.0
10 - 14....	84	20.1
15 - 19....	61	14.6
20 +....	55	13.2
Not stated - Inconnu....	24	5.8
Bahamas		
2000 (C)		
Total....	503	100.0
Less than 1 - Moins de 1....	-	0.0
1....	2	0.4
2....	12	2.4
3....	26	5.2
4....	12	2.4
5....	28	5.6
6....	29	5.8
7....	30	6.0
8....	34	6.8
9....	31	6.2
10 - 14....	121	24.1
15 - 19....	55	10.9
20 +....	123	24.5
Not stated - Inconnu....	-	0.0
Bermuda - Bermudes[1]		
2002 (C)		
Total....	230	100.0
Less than 5 - Moins de 5....	64	27.8
5 - 9....	60	26.1
10 - 14....	43	18.7
15 - 19....	29	12.6
20 +....	29	12.6
Not stated - Inconnu....	5	2.2
Canada		
2004 (C)		
Total....	69 644	100.0
Less than 1 - Moins de 1....	149	0.2
1....	1 360	2.0
2....	3 298	4.7
3....	4 166	6.0
4....	3 757	5.4
5....	3 587	5.2
6....	3 312	4.8
7....	3 076	4.4
8....	3 040	4.4
9....	2 744	3.9
10 - 14....	12 312	17.7
15 - 19....	9 816	14.1
20 +....	19 024	27.3
Not stated - Inconnu....	3	0.0
Cuba		
2007 (C)		
Total....	34 559	100.0
Less than 1 - Moins de 1....	2 747	7.9
1....	2 675	7.7
2....	2 465	7.1
3....	2 186	6.3
4....	1 929	5.6
5....	1 670	4.8
6....	1 404	4.1
7....	1 325	3.8
8....	1 314	3.8
9....	1 201	3.5
10 - 14....	6 559	19.0
15 - 19....	4 282	12.4
20 +....	4 767	13.8
Not stated - Inconnu....	35	0.1

24. Divorces and percentage distribution by duration of marriage, latest available year: 1998 - 2007
Divorces et répartition des pourcentages selon la durée du mariage, dernière année disponible: 1998 - 2007 (continued - suite)

Continent, country or area, year, code and duration of marriage (in years) Continent, pays ou zone, année, code et durée du mariage (en années)	Number of divorces Nombre de divorces	Per cent Pour cent	Continent, country or area, year, code and duration of marriage (in years) Continent, pays ou zone, année, code et durée du mariage (en années)	Number of divorces Nombre de divorces	Per cent Pour cent
AMERICA, NORTH - AMÉRIQUE DU NORD			**AMERICA, NORTH - AMÉRIQUE DU NORD**		
El Salvador[2]			Saint Lucia - Sainte-Lucie[1]		
2007 (...)			2002 (C)		
Total..........................	6 335	100.0	9..................................	-	0.0
Less than 1 - Moins de 1....................	294	4.6	10 - 14	12	30.0
1..	261	4.1	15 - 19	8	20.0
2..	212	3.3	20 +.................................	8	20.0
3..	234	3.7	Not stated - Inconnu....................	-	0.0
4..	259	4.1	Trinidad and Tobago - Trinité-et-Tobago		
5..	332	5.2	2005 (C)		
6..	329	5.2	Total..................................	2 785	100.0
7..	361	5.7	Less than 1 - Moins de 1	-	0.0
8..	290	4.6	1....................................	40	1.4
9..	294	4.6	2....................................	77	2.8
10 - 14	1 291	20.4	3....................................	80	2.9
15 - 19	853	13.5	4....................................	92	3.3
20 +....................................	1 325	20.9	5....................................	142	5.1
Not stated - Inconnu......................	-	0.0	6....................................	149	5.4
Jamaica - Jamaïque[3]			7....................................	120	4.3
2007 (C)			8....................................	144	5.2
Total..................................	1 140	100.0	9....................................	111	4.0
Less than 1 - Moins de 1	-	0.0	10 - 14	572	20.5
1..	1	0.1	15 - 19	417	15.0
2..	3	0.3	20 +.................................	838	30.1
3..	22	1.9	Not stated - Inconnu....................	3	0.1
4..	42	3.7	Turks and Caicos Islands - Îles Turques et Caïques		
5..	53	4.6	2005 (C)		
6..	62	5.4	Total.................................	24	100.0
7..	89	7.8	Less than 1 - Moins de 1	-	0.0
8..	96	8.4	1....................................	-	0.0
9..	75	6.6	2....................................	-	0.0
10 - 14	294	25.8	3....................................	-	0.0
15 - 19	160	14.0	4....................................	2	8.3
20 +....................................	242	21.2	5....................................	3	12.5
Mexico - Mexique[4]			6....................................	3	12.5
2006 (+C)			7....................................	2	8.3
Total..................................	72 396	100.0	8....................................	4	16.7
Less than 1 - Moins de 1	244	0.3	9....................................	1	4.2
1..	5 053	7.0	10 - 14	5	20.8
2..	4 479	6.2	15 - 19	2	8.3
3..	4 413	6.1	20 +.................................	2	8.3
4..	4 301	5.9	Not stated - Inconnu....................	-	0.0
5..	4 215	5.8			
6..	3 912	5.4			
7..	3 749	5.2	**AMERICA, SOUTH - AMÉRIQUE DU SUD**		
8..	3 323	4.6			
9..	2 938	4.1	Brazil - Brésil[5]		
10 - 14	12 446	17.2	2007 (...)		
15 - 19	8 888	12.3	Total	180 455	100.0
20 +....................................	14 292	19.7	Less than 3 - Moins de 3	3 982	2.2
Not stated - Inconnu	143	0.2	3....................................	5 946	3.3
Panama			4....................................	6 825	3.8
2007 (C)			5....................................	6 944	3.8
Total..................................	2 893	100.0	6....................................	7 416	4.1
Less than 5 - Moins de 5..................	486	16.8	7....................................	7 675	4.3
5 - 9..................................	582	20.1	8....................................	6 789	3.8
10 - 14	585	20.2	9....................................	6 546	3.6
15 - 19	393	13.6	10 - 14	29 298	16.2
20 +....................................	847	29.3	15 - 19	26 121	14.5
Not stated - Inconnu......................	-	0.0	20 +.................................	71 931	39.9
Saint Lucia - Sainte-Lucie[1]			Not stated - Inconnu....................	982	0.5
2002 (C)			Chile - Chili[6]		
Total..................................	40	100.0	2006 (C)		
Less than 5 - Moins de 5..................	2	5.0	Total.................................	4 091	100.0
5......................................	4	10.0	Less than 1 - Moins de 1	106	2.6
6......................................	2	5.0	1....................................	107	2.6
7......................................	2	5.0	2....................................	181	4.4
8......................................	2	5.0			

24. Divorces and percentage distribution by duration of marriage, latest available year: 1998 - 2007
Divorces et répartition des pourcentages selon la durée du mariage, dernière année disponible: 1998 - 2007 (continued - suite)

Continent, country or area, year, code and duration of marriage (in years) / Continent, pays ou zone, année, code et durée du mariage (en années)	Number of divorces / Nombre de divorces	Per cent / Pour cent
AMERICA, SOUTH - AMÉRIQUE DU SUD		
Chile - Chili[6]		
2006 (C)		
3	116	2.8
4	118	2.9
5	150	3.7
6	139	3.4
7	113	2.8
8	134	3.3
9	107	2.6
10 - 14	663	16.2
15 - 19	443	10.8
20 +	1 294	31.6
Not stated - Inconnu	420	10.3
Ecuador - Équateur[7]		
2007 (U)		
Total	14 942	100.0
Less than 1 - Moins de 1	128	0.9
1	451	3.0
2	501	3.4
3	585	3.9
4	632	4.2
5	688	4.6
6	775	5.2
7	765	5.1
8	721	4.8
9	698	4.7
10 - 14	3 092	20.7
15 - 19	2 244	15.0
20 +	3 662	24.5
Suriname[8]		
2005 (C)		
Total	724	100.0
Less than 1 - Moins de 1	17	2.3
1 - 3	73	10.1
4 - 6	119	16.4
7 - 9	113	15.6
10 - 12	99	13.7
13 - 15	63	8.7
16 - 18	62	8.6
19 - 21	54	7.5
22 - 24	34	4.7
25 +	90	12.4
Not stated - Inconnu	-	0.0
Uruguay		
2002 (+C)		
Total	6 761	100.0
Less than 1 - Moins de 1	48	0.7
1	113	1.7
2	198	2.9
3	252	3.7
4	284	4.2
5	331	4.9
6	354	5.2
7	360	5.3
8	316	4.7
9	284	4.2
10 - 14	1 265	18.7
15 - 19	1 006	14.9
20 +	1 950	28.8
Venezuela (Bolivarian Republic of) - Venezuela (République bolivarienne du)[5]		
2007 (...)		
Total	28 823	100.0
Less than 1 - Moins de 1	79	0.3
1 - 4	1 917	6.7
5 - 9	7 930	27.5
10 - 14	6 954	24.1
AMERICA, SOUTH - AMÉRIQUE DU SUD		
Venezuela (Bolivarian Republic of) - Venezuela (République bolivarienne du)[5]		
2007 (...)		
15 - 19	5 262	18.3
20 +	6 595	22.9
Not stated - Inconnu	86	0.3
ASIA - ASIE		
Armenia - Arménie		
2007 (C)		
Total	2 931	100.0
Less than 1 - Moins de 1	69	2.4
1	165	5.6
2	103	3.5
3	97	3.3
4	98	3.3
5 - 9	409	14.0
10 - 14	535	18.3
15 - 19	566	19.3
20 +	889	30.3
Azerbaijan - Azerbaïdjan		
2007 (+C)		
Total	8 340	100.0
Less than 1 - Moins de 1	237	2.8
1	580	7.0
2	615	7.4
3	569	6.8
4	486	5.8
5	342	4.1
6	357	4.3
7	309	3.7
8	304	3.6
9	313	3.8
10 - 14	1 483	17.8
15 - 19	1 456	17.5
20 +	1 289	15.5
Bahrain - Bahreïn		
2006 (...)		
Total	1 141	100.0
Less than 1 - Moins de 1	233	20.4
1 - 2	247	21.6
3 - 4	120	10.5
5 - 6	89	7.8
7 - 9	73	6.4
10 - 14	82	7.2
15 - 19	44	3.9
20 +	59	5.2
Not stated - Inconnu	194	17.0
Brunei Darussalam - Brunéi Darussalam		
2004 (...)		
Total	392	100.0
Less than 1 - Moins de 1	4	1.0
1	9	2.3
2	19	4.8
3	21	5.4
4	26	6.6
5	36	9.2
6	23	5.9
7	25	6.4
8	18	4.6
9	21	5.4
10 - 14	94	24.0
15 - 19	39	9.9
20 +	54	13.8
Not stated - Inconnu	3	0.8

24. Divorces and percentage distribution by duration of marriage, latest available year: 1998 - 2007
Divorces et répartition des pourcentages selon la durée du mariage, dernière année disponible: 1998 - 2007 (continued - suite)

Continent, country or area, year, code and duration of marriage (in years) / Continent, pays ou zone, année, code et durée du mariage (en années)	Number of divorces / Nombre de divorces	Per cent / Pour cent
ASIA - ASIE		
China, Macao SAR - Chine, Macao RAS		
2006 (C)		
Total............	592	100.0
Less than 5 - Moins de 5.................	86	14.5
5 - 9..............	160	27.0
10 - 14............	145	24.5
15 - 19............	80	13.5
20 +..............	120	20.3
Not stated - Inconnu..............	1	0.2
Cyprus - Chypre[9]		
2007 (C)		
Total............	1 648	100.0
Less than 1 - Moins de 1.................	36	2.2
1..............	127	7.7
2..............	124	7.5
3..............	129	7.8
4..............	100	6.1
5..............	112	6.8
6..............	86	5.2
7..............	70	4.2
8..............	82	5.0
9..............	76	4.6
10 - 14............	253	15.4
15 - 19............	174	10.6
20 +..............	279	16.9
Georgia - Géorgie		
2007 (C)		
Total............	2 325	100.0
Less than 1 - Moins de 1.................	404	17.4
1..............	82	3.5
2..............	88	3.8
3..............	75	3.2
4..............	65	2.8
5 - 9..............	352	15.1
10 - 14............	405	17.4
15 - 19............	339	14.6
20 +..............	489	21.0
Not stated - Inconnu..............	26	1.1
Israel - Israël[10]		
2006 (C)		
Total............	13 439	100.0
Less than 1 - Moins de 1.................	477	3.5
1..............	658	4.9
2..............	710	5.3
3..............	689	5.1
4..............	539	4.0
5..............	546	4.1
6..............	545	4.1
7..............	471	3.5
8..............	452	3.4
9..............	442	3.3
10 - 14............	1 650	12.3
15 - 19............	1 260	9.4
20 +..............	2 692	20.0
Not stated - Inconnu..............	2 308	17.2
Japan - Japon[11]		
2007 (+C)		
Total............	254 832	100.0
Less than 1 - Moins de 1.................	17 206	6.8
1..............	19 617	7.7
2..............	18 162	7.1
3..............	16 572	6.5
4..............	15 050	5.9
5 - 9..............	56 335	22.1
10 - 14............	33 693	13.2
15 - 19............	24 166	9.5

Continent, country or area, year, code and duration of marriage (in years) / Continent, pays ou zone, année, code et durée du mariage (en années)	Number of divorces / Nombre de divorces	Per cent / Pour cent
ASIA - ASIE		
Japan - Japon[11]		
2007 (+C)		
20 +..............	40 353	15.8
Not stated - Inconnu..............	13 678	5.4
Kazakhstan		
2007 (C)		
Total............	36 107	100.0
Less than 1 - Moins de 1.................	1 291	3.6
1..............	2 161	6.0
2..............	2 386	6.6
3..............	2 353	6.5
4..............	2 277	6.3
5 - 9..............	8 187	22.7
10 - 14............	6 538	18.1
15 - 19............	5 117	14.2
20 +..............	5 789	16.0
Not stated - Inconnu..............	8	0.0
Kuwait - Koweït		
2007 (C)		
Total............	4 945	100.0
Less than 1 - Moins de 1.................	1 393	28.2
1..............	762	15.4
2..............	432	8.7
3..............	355	7.2
4..............	246	5.0
5 - 9..............	800	16.2
10 - 14............	356	7.2
15 - 19............	237	4.8
20 +..............	364	7.4
Kyrgyzstan - Kirghizstan		
2007 (C)		
Total............	7 371	100.0
Less than 1 - Moins de 1.................	398	5.4
1..............	357	4.8
2..............	400	5.4
3..............	390	5.3
4..............	386	5.2
5..............	358	4.9
6..............	353	4.8
7..............	316	4.3
8..............	272	3.7
9..............	260	3.5
10 - 14............	1 259	17.1
15 - 19............	1 331	18.1
20 +..............	1 291	17.5
Not stated - Inconnu..............	-	0.0
Mongolia - Mongolie		
2007 (C)		
Total............	1 757	100.0
Less than 1 - Moins de 1.................	48	2.7
1 - 3..............	143	8.1
4 - 6..............	279	15.9
7 - 9..............	387	22.0
10 - 14............	412	23.4
15 - 19............	351	20.0
20 +..............	137	7.8
Occupied Palestinian Territory - Territoire palestinien occupé		
2007 (C)		
Total............	4 043	100.0
Less than 1 - Moins de 1.................	1 792	44.3
1..............	660	16.3
2..............	320	7.9
3..............	228	5.6
4..............	139	3.4
5..............	107	2.6
6..............	104	2.6
7..............	82	2.0

Continent, country or area, year, code and duration of marriage (in years) / Continent, pays ou zone, année, code et durée du mariage (en années)	Number of divorces / Nombre de divorces	Per cent / Pour cent
ASIA - ASIE		
Occupied Palestinian Territory - Territoire palestinien occupé		
2007 (C)		
8	50	1.2
9	62	1.5
10 - 14	191	4.7
15 - 19	139	3.4
20 +	169	4.2
Not stated - Inconnu	1	0.0
Qatar		
2007 (C)		
Total	997	100.0
Less than 1 - Moins de 1	368	36.9
1	92	9.2
2	72	7.2
3	79	7.9
4	56	5.6
5 - 9	155	15.5
10 - 14	72	7.2
15 - 19	38	3.8
20 +	63	6.3
Not stated - Inconnu	2	0.2
Republic of Korea - République de Corée[12]		
2006 (+C)		
Total	125 032	100.0
Less than 1 - Moins de 1	6 897	5.5
1	7 062	5.6
2	6 592	5.3
3	6 350	5.1
4	6 242	5.0
5	6 086	4.9
6	5 806	4.6
7	5 248	4.2
8	5 126	4.1
9	5 101	4.1
10 - 14	22 466	18.0
15 - 19	18 082	14.5
20 +	23 974	19.2
Singapore - Singapour		
2007 (+C)		
Total	6 812	100.0
Less than 5 - Moins de 5	1 236	18.1
5 - 9	2 345	34.4
10 - 14	1 234	18.1
15 - 19	766	11.2
20 +	1 231	18.1
Tajikistan - Tadjikistan		
2007 (+C)		
Total	4 752	100.0
Less than 1 - Moins de 1	328	6.9
1	340	7.2
2	326	6.9
3	336	7.1
4	258	5.4
5	212	4.5
6	216	4.5
7	168	3.5
8	171	3.6
9	160	3.4
10 - 14	909	19.1
15 - 19	619	13.0
20 +	520	10.9
Not stated - Inconnu	191	4.0
Turkey - Turquie[13]		
2007 (C)		
Total	94 219	100.0
Less than 1 - Moins de 1	3 779	4.0
1	9 231	9.8

Continent, country or area, year, code and duration of marriage (in years) / Continent, pays ou zone, année, code et durée du mariage (en années)	Number of divorces / Nombre de divorces	Per cent / Pour cent
ASIA - ASIE		
Turkey - Turquie[13]		
2007 (C)		
2	7 687	8.2
3	6 984	7.4
4	6 214	6.6
5	5 525	5.9
6	5 137	5.5
7	4 495	4.8
8	3 895	4.1
9	3 778	4.0
10 - 14	14 198	15.1
15 - 19	9 564	10.2
20 +	13 732	14.6
EUROPE		
Austria - Autriche[14]		
2007 (C)		
Total	20 516	100.0
Less than 1 - Moins de 1	296	1.4
1	1 179	5.7
2	1 881	9.2
3	1 814	8.8
4	1 351	6.6
5	1 083	5.3
6	895	4.4
7	830	4.0
8	758	3.7
9	712	3.5
10 - 14	3 183	15.5
15 - 19	2 668	13.0
20 +	3 866	18.8
Belarus - Bélarus		
2007 (C)		
Total	36 146	100.0
Less than 1 - Moins de 1	1 033	2.9
1	2 243	6.2
2	2 340	6.5
3	2 541	7.0
4	2 503	6.9
5 - 9	10 185	28.2
10 - 14	5 762	15.9
15 - 19	4 160	11.5
20 +	5 379	14.9
Bosnia and Herzegovina - Bosnie-Herzégovine		
2007 (C)		
Total	1 826	100.0
Less than 1 - Moins de 1	86	4.7
1	138	7.6
2	157	8.6
3	126	6.9
4	135	7.4
5	104	5.7
6	95	5.2
7	80	4.4
8	53	2.9
9	56	3.1
10 - 14	219	12.0
15 - 19	175	9.6
20 +	307	16.8
Not stated - Inconnu	95	5.2
Bulgaria - Bulgarie[15]		
2007 (C)		
Total	16 347	100.0
Less than 1 - Moins de 1	210	1.3

24. Divorces and percentage distribution by duration of marriage, latest available year: 1998 - 2007
Divorces et répartition des pourcentages selon la durée du mariage, dernière année disponible: 1998 - 2007 (continued - suite)

Continent, country or area, year, code and duration of marriage (in years) / Continent, pays ou zone, année, code et durée du mariage (en années)	Number of divorces / Nombre de divorces	Per cent / Pour cent
EUROPE		
Bulgaria - Bulgarie[15]		
2007 (C)		
1	488	3.0
2	593	3.6
3	688	4.2
4	627	3.8
5	676	4.1
6	661	4.0
7	682	4.2
8	658	4.0
9	622	3.8
10 - 14	2 983	18.2
15 - 19	3 070	18.8
20 +	4 389	26.8
Croatia - Croatie		
2007 (C)		
Total	4 785	100.0
Less than 1 - Moins de 1	97	2.0
1	171	3.6
2	206	4.3
3	227	4.7
4	239	5.0
5	273	5.7
6	225	4.7
7	224	4.7
8	180	3.8
9	179	3.7
10 - 14	770	16.1
15 - 19	632	13.2
20 +	1 362	28.5
Czech Republic - République tchèque		
2007 (C)		
Total	31 129	100.0
Less than 1 - Moins de 1	274	0.9
1	1 089	3.5
2	1 481	4.8
3	1 358	4.4
4	1 418	4.6
5	1 460	4.7
6	1 473	4.7
7	1 344	4.3
8	1 278	4.1
9	1 196	3.8
10 - 14	5 375	17.3
15 - 19	5 430	17.4
20 +	7 697	24.7
Not stated - Inconnu	256	0.8
Denmark - Danemark[16]		
2007 (C)		
Total	14 066	100.0
Less than 1 - Moins de 1	142	1.0
1	486	3.5
2	724	5.1
3	846	6.0
4	780	5.5
5	866	6.2
6	984	7.0
7	852	6.1
8	747	5.3
9	631	4.5
10 - 14	2 686	19.1
15 - 19	1 759	12.5
20 +	2 348	16.7
Not stated - Inconnu	215	1.5
Estonia - Estonie		
2007 (C)		
Total	3 809	100.0
Less than 1 - Moins de 1	96	2.5

Continent, country or area, year, code and duration of marriage (in years) / Continent, pays ou zone, année, code et durée du mariage (en années)	Number of divorces / Nombre de divorces	Per cent / Pour cent
EUROPE		
Estonia - Estonie		
2007 (C)		
1	243	6.4
2	244	6.4
3	224	5.9
4	219	5.7
5	190	5.0
6	154	4.0
7	134	3.5
8	111	2.9
9	116	3.0
10 - 14	523	13.7
15 - 19	557	14.6
20 +	998	26.2
Finland - Finlande[17]		
2007 (C)		
Total	13 224	100.0
Less than 1 - Moins de 1	132	1.0
1	741	5.6
2	917	6.9
3	889	6.7
4	775	5.9
5	704	5.3
6	631	4.8
7	575	4.3
8	514	3.9
9	431	3.3
10 - 14	1 979	15.0
15 - 19	1 619	12.2
20 +	2 808	21.2
Not stated - Inconnu	509	3.8
France[18]		
2003 (C)		
Total	125 175	100.0
Less than 1 - Moins de 1	8	0.0
1	994	0.8
2	4 571	3.7
3	7 067	5.6
4	6 873	5.5
5	6 697	5.4
6	6 395	5.1
7	5 886	4.7
8	5 210	4.2
9	4 939	3.9
10 - 14	22 342	17.8
15 - 19	16 280	13.0
20 +	37 913	30.3
Germany - Allemagne		
2007 (C)		
Total	187 072	100.0
Less than 1 - Moins de 1	55	0.0
1	1 051	0.6
2	4 324	2.3
3	7 575	4.0
4	9 707	5.2
5	11 656	6.2
6	11 145	6.0
7	10 893	5.8
8	10 028	5.4
9	8 611	4.6
10 - 14	35 338	18.9
15 - 19	30 349	16.2
20 +	46 340	24.8
Greece - Grèce		
2005 (C)		
Total	13 494	100.0
Less than 1 - Moins de 1	2	0.0
1	38	0.3

Continent, country or area, year, code and duration of marriage (in years) / Continent, pays ou zone, année, code et durée du mariage (en années)	Number of divorces / Nombre de divorces	Per cent / Pour cent
EUROPE		
Greece - Grèce		
2005 (C)		
2	724	5.4
3	739	5.5
4	688	5.1
5	624	4.6
6	802	5.9
7	669	5.0
8	673	5.0
9	502	3.7
10 - 14	2 633	19.5
15 - 19	1 964	14.6
20 +	3 206	23.8
Not stated - Inconnu	230	1.7
Hungary - Hongrie[8]		
2007 (C)		
Total	25 160	100.0
Less than 1 - Moins de 1	324	1.3
1	907	3.6
2	1 112	4.4
3	1 263	5.0
4	1 231	4.9
5	1 273	5.1
6	1 129	4.5
7	1 094	4.3
8	992	3.9
9	917	3.6
10 - 14	4 554	18.1
15 - 19	4 097	16.3
20 +	6 267	24.9
Iceland - Islande[2]		
2007 (C)		
Total	515	100.0
Less than 1 - Moins de 1	10	1.9
1	22	4.3
2	31	6.0
3	32	6.2
4	47	9.1
5	36	7.0
6	34	6.6
7	19	3.7
8	21	4.1
9	23	4.5
10 - 14	69	13.4
15 - 19	58	11.3
20 +	112	21.7
Italy - Italie		
2005 (C)		
Total	47 036	100.0
Less than 1 - Moins de 1	5	0.0
1	13	0.0
2	37	0.1
3	260	0.6
4	1 098	2.3
5	1 888	4.0
6	2 288	4.9
7	2 272	4.8
8	2 492	5.3
9	2 547	5.4
10 - 14	9 020	19.2
15 - 19	8 803	18.7
20 +	16 313	34.7
Latvia - Lettonie		
2007 (C)		
Total	7 403	100.0
Less than 1 - Moins de 1	29	0.4
1	226	3.1
2	293	4.0
EUROPE		
Latvia - Lettonie		
2007 (C)		
3	336	4.5
4	362	4.9
5	376	5.1
6	328	4.4
7	316	4.3
8	271	3.7
9	268	3.6
10 - 14	1 257	17.0
15 - 19	1 447	19.5
20 +	1 894	25.6
Liechtenstein		
2007* (C)		
Total	97	100.0
Less than 1 - Moins de 1	-	0.0
1	5	5.2
2	9	9.3
3	7	7.2
4	2	2.1
5	9	9.3
6	5	5.2
7	6	6.2
8	7	7.2
9	4	4.1
10 - 14	10	10.3
15 - 19	13	13.4
20 +	20	20.6
Lithuania - Lituanie		
2007 (C)		
Total	11 336	100.0
Less than 1 - Moins de 1	114	1.0
1	419	3.7
2	573	5.1
3	636	5.6
4	514	4.5
5	474	4.2
6	451	4.0
7	413	3.6
8	453	4.0
9	421	3.7
10 - 14	2 042	18.0
15 - 19	2 098	18.5
20 +	2 728	24.1
Luxembourg		
2007 (C)		
Total	1 106	100.0
Less than 1 - Moins de 1	9	0.8
1	12	1.1
2	33	3.0
3	74	6.7
4	55	5.0
5	72	6.5
6	68	6.1
7	56	5.1
8	70	6.3
9	47	4.2
10 - 14	221	20.0
15 - 19	169	15.3
20 +	220	19.9
Montenegro - Monténégro		
2007 (C)		
Total	453	100.0
Less than 1 - Moins de 1	16	3.5
1	38	8.4
2	46	10.2
3	41	9.1
4	33	7.3

24. Divorces and percentage distribution by duration of marriage, latest available year: 1998 - 2007
Divorces et répartition des pourcentages selon la durée du mariage, dernière année disponible: 1998 - 2007 (continued - suite)

Continent, country or area, year, code and duration of marriage (in years) / Continent, pays ou zone, année, code et durée du mariage (en années)	Number of divorces / Nombre de divorces	Per cent / Pour cent
EUROPE		
Montenegro - Monténégro		
2007 (C)		
5	25	5.5
6	24	5.3
7	24	5.3
8	18	4.0
9	14	3.1
10 - 14	59	13.0
15 - 19	49	10.8
20 +	66	14.6
Netherlands - Pays-Bas		
2007 (C)		
Total	31 983	100.0
Less than 1 - Moins de 1	306	1.0
1	952	3.0
2	1 251	3.9
3	1 501	4.7
4	1 788	5.6
5	1 734	5.4
6	1 622	5.1
7	1 662	5.2
8	1 396	4.4
9	1 304	4.1
10 - 14	5 566	17.4
15 - 19	4 912	15.4
20 +	7 989	25.0
Norway - Norvège[19]		
2007 (C)		
Total	10 280	100.0
Less than 1 - Moins de 1	7	0.1
1	206	2.0
2	439	4.3
3	542	5.3
4	686	6.7
5	733	7.1
6	675	6.6
7	611	5.9
8	463	4.5
9	458	4.5
10 - 14	1 559	15.2
15 - 19	1 186	11.5
20 +	2 440	23.7
Not stated - Inconnu	275	2.7
Poland - Pologne		
2007 (C)		
Total	66 586	100.0
Less than 1 - Moins de 1	376	0.6
1	1 901	2.9
2	2 629	3.9
3	3 129	4.7
4	3 191	4.8
5	3 305	5.0
6	3 293	4.9
7	3 334	5.0
8	3 106	4.7
9	2 782	4.2
10 - 14	11 616	17.4
15 - 19	10 318	15.5
20 +	17 606	26.4
Portugal		
2007* (C)		
Total	25 255	100.0
Less than 1 - Moins de 1	713	2.8
1	863	3.4
2	968	3.8
3	1 142	4.5
4	1 254	5.0
5	1 194	4.7
EUROPE		
Portugal		
2007* (C)		
6	1 199	4.7
7	1 254	5.0
8	1 126	4.5
9	988	3.9
10 - 14	4 292	17.0
15 - 19	3 509	13.9
20 +	6 753	26.7
Republic of Moldova - République de Moldova		
2006 (C)		
Total	12 594	100.0
Less than 1 - Moins de 1	588	4.7
1	842	6.7
2	880	7.0
3	701	5.6
4	596	4.7
5	601	4.8
6	592	4.7
7	541	4.3
8	450	3.6
9	388	3.1
10 - 14	2 302	18.3
15 - 19	1 634	13.0
20 +	2 479	19.7
Not stated - Inconnu	-	0.0
Romania - Roumanie		
2007 (C)		
Total	36 308	100.0
Less than 1 - Moins de 1	960	2.6
1	2 294	6.3
2	2 269	6.2
3	2 172	6.0
4	2 060	5.7
5	1 865	5.1
6	1 711	4.7
7	1 685	4.6
8	1 602	4.4
9	1 511	4.2
10 - 14	6 220	17.1
15 - 19	5 155	14.2
20 +	6 804	18.7
San Marino - Saint-Marin		
2004 (+C)		
Total	62	100.0
Less than 1 - Moins de 1	1	1.6
1 - 3	14	22.6
4 - 6	8	12.9
7 - 9	8	12.9
10 - 19	18	29.0
20 +	13	21.0
Serbia - Serbie[20]		
2007 (+C)		
Total	8 622	100.0
Less than 1 - Moins de 1	375	4.3
1	505	5.9
2	568	6.6
3	457	5.3
4	443	5.1
5	437	5.1
6	457	5.3
7	376	4.4
8	310	3.6
9	304	3.5
10 - 14	1 408	16.3
15 - 19	1 173	13.6
20 +	1 809	21.0

24. Divorces and percentage distribution by duration of marriage, latest available year: 1998 - 2007
Divorces et répartition des pourcentages selon la durée du mariage, dernière année disponible: 1998 - 2007 (continued - suite)

Continent, country or area, year, code and duration of marriage (in years) / Continent, pays ou zone, année, code et durée du mariage (en années)	Number of divorces / Nombre de divorces	Per cent / Pour cent
EUROPE		
Slovakia - Slovaquie		
2007 (C)		
Total	12 174	100.0
Less than 1 - Moins de 1	60	0.5
1	257	2.1
2	429	3.5
3	537	4.4
4	525	4.3
5	503	4.1
6	479	3.9
7	534	4.4
8	504	4.1
9	505	4.1
10 - 14	2 319	19.0
15 - 19	2 180	17.9
20 +	3 342	27.5
Slovenia - Slovénie		
2007 (C)		
Total	2 617	100.0
Less than 1 - Moins de 1	30	1.1
1	69	2.6
2	111	4.2
3	99	3.8
4	101	3.9
5	115	4.4
6	102	3.9
7	103	3.9
8	78	3.0
9	89	3.4
10 - 14	417	15.9
15 - 19	405	15.5
20 +	898	34.3
Spain - Espagne		
2007 (C)		
Total	125 777	100.0
Less than 1 - Moins de 1	1 338	1.1
1	3 583	2.8
2	4 815	3.8
3	5 621	4.5
4	5 782	4.6
5	5 413	4.3
6	5 778	4.6
7	5 784	4.6
8	5 265	4.2
9	5 010	4.0
10 - 14	21 254	16.9
15 - 19	19 103	15.2
20 +	37 031	29.4
Sweden - Suède		
2007 (C)		
Total	20 669	100.0
Less than 1 - Moins de 1	389	1.9
1	1 073	5.2
2	1 402	6.8
3	1 636	7.9
4	1 588	7.7
5	1 348	6.5
6	1 095	5.3
7	903	4.4
8	735	3.6
9	645	3.1
10 - 14	2 832	13.7
15 - 19	3 151	15.2
20 +	3 718	18.0
Not stated - Inconnu	154	0.7

Continent, country or area, year, code and duration of marriage (in years) / Continent, pays ou zone, année, code et durée du mariage (en années)	Number of divorces / Nombre de divorces	Per cent / Pour cent
EUROPE		
Switzerland - Suisse		
2007 (C)		
Total	19 882	100.0
Less than 1 - Moins de 1	67	0.3
1	342	1.7
2	573	2.9
3	801	4.0
4	798	4.0
5	1 066	5.4
6	1 365	6.9
7	1 268	6.4
8	960	4.8
9	849	4.3
10 - 14	3 607	18.1
15 - 19	3 152	15.9
20 +	5 034	25.3
The Former Yugoslav Republic of Macedonia - L'ex-République yougoslave de Macédoine		
2007 (C)		
Total	1 417	100.0
Less than 1 - Moins de 1	108	7.6
1	162	11.4
2	127	9.0
3	124	8.8
4	104	7.3
5	112	7.9
6	62	4.4
7	72	5.1
8	61	4.3
9	43	3.0
10 - 14	160	11.3
15 - 19	115	8.1
20 +	167	11.8
Ukraine		
2007 (C)		
Total	178 364	100.0
Less than 1 - Moins de 1	5 706	3.2
1	10 431	5.8
2	11 623	6.5
3	12 294	6.9
4	11 385	6.4
5 - 9	42 147	23.6
10 - 14	30 633	17.2
15 - 19	22 510	12.6
20 +	31 635	17.7
United Kingdom of Great Britain and Northern Ireland - Royaume-Uni de Grande-Bretagne et d'Irlande du Nord[21]		
2003 (C)		
Total	166 735	100.0
Less than 1 - Moins de 1	55	0.0
1	3 352	2.0
2	7 211	4.3
3	8 723	5.2
4	9 440	5.7
5	9 562	5.7
6	9 313	5.6
7	8 821	5.3
8	8 292	5.0
9	7 570	4.5
10 - 14	32 564	19.5
15 - 19	23 119	13.9
20 +	38 713	23.2
Not stated - Inconnu	-	0.0

24. Divorces and percentage distribution by duration of marriage, latest available year: 1998 - 2007
Divorces et répartition des pourcentages selon la durée du mariage, dernière année disponible: 1998 - 2007 (continued - suite)

Continent, country or area, year, code and duration of marriage (in years) / Continent, pays ou zone, année, code et durée du mariage (en années)	Number of divorces / Nombre de divorces	Per cent / Pour cent
OCEANIA - OCÉANIE		
Australia - Australie[22]		
2007 (C)		
Total	47 963	100.0
Less than 1 - Moins de 1	-	0.0
1	-	0.0
2	1 962	4.1
3	2 537	5.3
4	2 732	5.7
5	2 752	5.7
6	2 532	5.3
7	2 421	5.0
8	2 101	4.4
9	1 903	4.0
10 - 14	8 288	17.3
15 - 19	6 545	13.6
20 +	13 672	28.5
Not stated - Inconnu	-	0.0
New Caledonia - Nouvelle-Calédonie[23]		
2005 (C)		
Total	341	100.0
Less than 1 - Moins de 1	1	0.3
1	6	1.8
2	6	1.8
3	12	3.5
4	16	4.7
5	17	5.0
6	23	6.7
7	21	6.2
8	18	5.3
9	27	7.9
10 - 14	66	19.4
15 - 19	53	15.5
20 +	75	22.0
New Zealand - Nouvelle-Zélande		
2007 (+C)		
Total	9 650	100.0
Less than 3 - Moins de 3	226	2.3
3	446	4.6
4	585	6.1
5	518	5.4
6	529	5.5
7	465	4.8
8	455	4.7
9	398	4.1

Continent, country or area, year, code and duration of marriage (in years) / Continent, pays ou zone, année, code et durée du mariage (en années)	Number of divorces / Nombre de divorces	Per cent / Pour cent
OCEANIA - OCÉANIE		
New Zealand - Nouvelle-Zélande		
2007 (+C)		
10 - 14	1 727	17.9
15 - 19	1 410	14.6
20 +	2 891	30.0
Northern Mariana Islands - Îles Mariannes septentrionales[24]		
2007 (U)		
Total	160	100.0
Less than 1 - Moins de 1	2	1.3
1	3	1.9
2	5	3.1
3	9	5.6
4	4	2.5
5	14	8.8
6	11	6.9
7	9	5.6
8	6	3.8
9	8	5.0
10 - 14	34	21.3
15 - 19	20	12.5
20 +	35	21.9
Samoa		
2005* (U)		
Total	44	100.0
Less than 1 - Moins de 1	-	0.0
1	1	2.3
2	1	2.3
3	3	6.8
4	2	4.5
5	2	4.5
6	4	9.1
7	3	6.8
8	3	6.8
9	-	0.0
10 - 14	10	22.7
15 - 19	9	20.5
20 +	6	13.6

FOOTNOTES - NOTES

Italics: estimates which are less reliable. - Italiques: estimations moins sûres.

* Provisional. - Données provisoires.

a 'Code' indicates the source of data, as follows:
C - Civil registration, estimated over 90% complete
U - Civil registration, estimated less than 90% complete
| - Other source, estimated reliable
+ - Data tabulated by date of registration rather than occurence.
... - Information not available

Le 'Code' indique la source des données, comme suit:
C - Registres de l'état civil considérés complets à 90 p. 100 au moins.
U - Registres de l'état civil qui ne sont pas considérés complets à 90 p. 100 au moins.
| - Autre source, considérée pas douteuses.
+ - Données exploitées selon la date de l'enregistrement et non la date de l'événement.

... - Information non disponible.

[1] Unrevised data. - Les données n'ont pas été révisées.
[2] Data refer to resident population only. - Pour la population résidante seulement.
[3] Because of rounding, totals are not in all cases the sum of the parts. - Les chiffres étant arrondis, les totaux ne correspondent pas toujours rigoureusement à la somme des chiffres partiels.
[4] Duration of marriage is defined as time occurred between date of the wedding celebration and date of the presentation of the demand for divorce. - Durée du mariage définie comme le temps écoulé entre la célébration du mariage et la date de la présentation de la demande de divorce.
[5] Excluding Indian jungle population. - Non compris les Indiens de la jungle.
[6] A new divorce law took effect from October 2005. - Une nouvelle loi sur le divorce est entrée en vigueur en octobre 2005.
[7] Excluding nomadic Indian tribes. - Non compris les tribus d'Indiens nomades.
[8] Including annulments. - Y compris les annulations.
[9] Data refer to government controlled areas. - Les données se rapportent aux zones contrôlées par le Gouvernement.
[10] Including data for East Jerusalem and Israeli residents in certain other territories under occupation by Israeli military forces since June 1967. - Y

compris les données pour Jérusalem-Est et les résidents israéliens dans certains autres territoires occupés depuis 1967 par les forces armées israéliennes.

[11] Data refer to Japanese nationals in Japan only. Data refer to the period from the time of wedding or cohabitation was started, to the time at termination of cohabitation. - Les données se raportent aux nationaux japonais au Japon seulement. Les données se rapportent à la période allant du début à la fin du mariage ou de la cohabitation.

[12] Excluding alien armed forces, civilian aliens employed by armed forces, and foreign diplomatic personnel and their dependants. - Non compris les militaires étrangers, les civils étrangers employés par les forces armées ni le personnel diplomatique étranger et les membres de leur famille les accompagnant.

[13] Data from MERNIS (Central Population Administrative System). - Données de MERNIS (Système central de données démographiques).

[14] Excluding aliens temporarily in the area. - Non compris les étrangers se trouvant temporairement le territoire.

[15] Including nationals outside the country, but excluding foreigners in the country. - Y compris les nationaux à l'étranger, mais non compris les étrangers sur le territoire.

[16] Excluding Faeroe Islands and Greenland shown separately, if available. - Non compris les Îles Féroé et le Gröenland, qui font l'objet de rubriques distinctes, si disponible.

[17] Including nationals temporarily outside the country. Including Aland Islands. - Y compris les nationaux se trouvant temporairement hors du pays. Y compris les Îles d'Åland.

[18] Excluding Overseas Departments, namely, French Guiana, Guadeloupe, Martinique and Reunion, shown separately, if available. - Non compris les départements d'outre mer, c'est-à-dire la Guyane française, la Guadeloupe, la Martinique et la Réunion, qui font l'objet de rubriques distinctes, si disponible.

[19] Excluding Svalbard and Jan Mayen Island shown separately, if available. Data refer to male residents of Norway only. - Non compris Svalbard et Jan Mayen qui font l'objet de rubriques distinctes, si disponible. Ces données ne concernent que les hommes habitant en Norvège.

[20] Excluding data for Kosovo and Metohia. - Sans les données pour le Kosovo et Metohie.

[21] Excluding Channel Islands (Guernsey and Jersey) and Isle of Man, shown separately, if available. - Non compris les îles Anglo-Normandes (Guernesey et Jersey) et l'île de Man, qui font l'objet de rubriques distinctes, si disponible.

[22] Data for certain cells suppressed by national statistical office for confidentiality reasons. - Les données pour certaines cases ont été supprimées par le bureau national de statistiques pour des raisons de confidentialité.

[23] Based on place of residence at marriage not at divorce. - Les divorces sont comptés en fonction du lieu de résidence au mariage, et non pas au divorce.

[24] Data refer to the islands of Saipan, Tinian and Rota only. - Les données se réfèrent uniquement aux îles de Saipan, Tinian et Rota.

Table 25

Table 25 presents the number of divorces by number of dependent children and the percentage distribution for the latest available year between 1998 and 2007.

Description of variables: Divorces are the final legal dissolutions of a marriage, which confer on the parties the right to remarry as defined by the laws of each country or area. Unless otherwise noted, divorce statistics exclude legal separations which do not allow remarriage. These statistics refer to the number of divorces granted, and not to the number of persons divorcing.

The number of dependent children of divorced persons is defined as the total number of living children under 18 years of age who are dependent on either of the parties to a divorce at the time the petition for divorce is filed. This should include children of any previous marriage.

The classification for the number of dependent children used in this table is the following: 0, 1, 2, 3, 4, 5, 6, 7 and over and number unknown. The aggregate number of dependent children is also shown as reported.

Reliability of data: Data from civil registers of divorces which are reported as incomplete (less than 90 per cent completeness) or of unknown completeness are considered unreliable and are set in italics rather than in roman type. For more information about the quality of vital statistics data in general, see section 4.2 of the Technical Notes.

Limitations: Statistics on divorces by number of dependent children are subject to the same qualifications which have been set forth for vital statistics in general and divorce statistics in particular as discussed in Section 4 of the Technical Notes.

Earlier data: Divorces by number of dependent children have been shown previously in issues of the Demographic Yearbook featuring marriage and divorce statistics. For information on years covered, readers should consult the Historical Index.

Tableau 25

Le tableau 25 indique le nombre de divorces selon le nombre d'enfants à charge et la répartition des pourcentages, pour la dernière année disponible entre 1998 et 2007.

Description des variables : le divorce est la dissolution définitive des liens du mariage qui confère aux parties le droit de se remarier, telle qu'elle est définie par la législation de chaque pays ou zone. Sauf indication contraire, les statistiques de la divortialité n'englobent pas les séparations légales qui excluent le remariage. Ces statistiques se rapportent aux jugements de divorce prononcés, non aux personnes divorcées.

Le nombre d'enfants à la charge de personnes divorcées comprend le nombre total d'enfants vivants âgés de moins de 18 ans qui sont à la charge de l'un ou de l'autre des parents au moment du dépôt de la demande en divorce. Les enfants nés de tout mariage précédent doivent figurer dans ce total.

Le classement utilisé pour le nombre d'enfants à charge dans ce tableau comprend les catégories suivantes : 0, 1, 2, 3, 4, 5, 6, 7 et plus et, le cas échéant, une catégorie pour le nombre d'enfants à charge inconnue. Le nombre total d'enfants à change est aussi présenté comme rapporté.

Fiabilité des données : les données sur les divorces provenant des registres de l'état civil qui sont déclarées incomplètes (degré de complétude inférieur à 90 pour cent) ou dont le degré de complétude n'est pas connu, sont jugées douteuses et apparaissent en italique et non en caractères romains. Pour plus de précisions sur la qualité des données reposant sur les statistiques de l'état civil en general, voir la section 4.2 des Notes techniques.

Insuffisance des données : les statistiques des divorces selon le nombre d'enfants à charge, appellent toutes les réserves qui ont été formulées à propos des statistiques de l'état civil en general et des statistiques des divorces en particulier (voir les explications figurant à la section 4 des Notes techniques).

Données publiées antérieurement : les statistiques des divorces selon le nombre d'enfants à charge, ont été présentées dans des éditions antérieures de l'Annuaire démographique qui avaient comme sujet spécial la nuptialité et la divortialité. Pour plus de précisions concernant les années pour lesquelles ces données ont été publiées, on se reportera à l'index historique.

25. Divorces and percentage distribution by number of dependent children, latest available year: 1998 - 2007
Divorces et répartition des pourcentages selon le nombre d'enfants à charge, dernière année disponible: 1998 - 2007

Continent, country or area, year, code and number of dependent children / Continent, pays ou zone, année, code et nombre d'enfants à charge	Number of divorces / Nombre de divorces	Per cent / Pour cent	Continent, country or area, year, code and number of dependent children / Continent, pays ou zone, année, code et nombre d'enfants à charge	Number of divorces / Nombre de divorces	Per cent / Pour cent
AFRICA - AFRIQUE			**AMERICA, NORTH - AMÉRIQUE DU NORD**		
Egypt - Égypte			Cuba		
2007 (U)			2007 (C)		
Total	77 878	100.0	Total	34 559	100.0
0	58 345	74.9	0	22 509	65.1
1	8 056	10.3	1	7 669	22.2
2	5 474	7.0	2	2 173	6.3
3	3 475	4.5	3	110	0.3
4	1 505	1.9	4	9	0.0
5 +	1 023	1.3	5	1	0.0
Mauritius - Maurice			6	4	0.0
2007 (+C)			7 +	3	0.0
Total	1 302	100.0	Not stated - Inconnu	2 081	6.0
0	454	34.9	Aggregate number of dependent children -		
1	392	30.1	Nombre total d'enfants à charge	12 440	..
2	312	24.0	El Salvador[1]		
3	98	7.5	2007 (...)		
4	33	2.5	Total	6 335	100.0
5	8	0.6	0	1 934	30.5
6	5	0.4	1	1 230	19.4
7 +	-	0.0	2	835	13.2
Not stated - Inconnu	-	0.0	3	329	5.2
Aggregate number of dependent children -			4	70	1.1
Nombre total d'enfants à charge	1 512	..	5 +	29	0.5
South Africa - Afrique du Sud			Not stated - Inconnu	1 908	30.1
2007 (...)			Jamaica - Jamaïque		
Total	29 639	100.0	2007 (C)		
0	12 721	42.9	Total	1 140	100.0
1	7 991	27.0	0	641	56.2
2	6 695	22.6	1	284	24.9
3	1 837	6.2	2	162	14.2
4	297	1.0	3	42	3.7
5	50	0.2	4	10	0.9
6	15	0.1	5	1	0.1
7 +	7	0.0	6 +	-	0.0
Not stated - Inconnu	26	0.1	Aggregate number of dependent children -		
Aggregate number of dependent children -			Nombre total d'enfants à charge	779	..
Nombre total d'enfants à charge	28 480	..	Mexico - Mexique		
			2007 (+C)		
			Total	77 255	100.0
AMERICA, NORTH - AMÉRIQUE DU NORD			0	18 804	24.3
			1	22 059	28.6
Bahamas			2	15 996	20.7
2000 (C)			3	5 770	7.5
Total	503	100.0	4	1 095	1.4
0	172	34.2	5	178	0.2
1	133	26.4	6	34	0.0
2	110	21.9	7 +	11	0.0
3	61	12.1	Not stated - Inconnu	1 394	1.8
4	16	3.2	Aggregate number of dependent children -		
5	5	1.0	Nombre total d'enfants à charge	76 923	..
6	1	0.2	Panama		
7 +	5	1.0	2007 (C)		
Not stated - Inconnu	-	0.0	Total	2 893	100.0
Canada			0	632	21.8
2000 (C)			1	672	23.2
Total	71 144	100.0	2	355	12.3
0	50 309	70.7	3	113	3.9
1	8 182	11.5	4 +	70	2.4
2	9 198	12.9	Not stated - Inconnu	1 051	36.3
3	2 556	3.6	Saint Lucia - Sainte-Lucie[2]		
4	550	0.8	2002 (C)		
5 +	114	0.2	Total	40	100.0
Not stated - Inconnu	235	0.3	0	14	35.0
Aggregate number of dependent children -			1	8	20.0
Nombre total d'enfants à charge	37 016	..	2	8	20.0
			3	4	10.0
			4	4	10.0

25. Divorces and percentage distribution by number of dependent children, latest available year: 1998 - 2007
Divorces et répartition des pourcentages selon le nombre d'enfants à charge, dernière année disponible: 1998 - 2007
(continued - suite)

Continent, country or area, year, code and number of dependent children Continent, pays ou zone, année, code et nombre d'enfants à charge	Number of divorces Nombre de divorces	Per cent Pour cent
AMERICA, NORTH - AMÉRIQUE DU NORD		
Saint Lucia - Sainte-Lucie[2]		
2002 (C)		
5	2	5.0
Aggregate number of dependent children - Nombre total d'enfants à charge	62	..
Trinidad and Tobago - Trinité-et-Tobago		
2004 (C)		
Total	1 852	100.0
0	680	36.7
1	444	24.0
2	359	19.4
3	163	8.8
4	66	3.6
5	19	1.0
6	7	0.4
7 +	6	0.3
Not stated - Inconnu	108	5.8
Turks and Caicos Islands - Îles Turques et Caïques		
2006 (C)		
Total	22	100.0
0	5	22.7
1	4	18.2
2	8	36.4
3	4	18.2
4	-	0.0
5	-	0.0
6	-	0.0
7 +	1	4.5
AMERICA, SOUTH - AMÉRIQUE DU SUD		
Brazil - Brésil[3]		
2007 (...)		
Total	74 880	100.0
1	43 159	57.6
2	23 783	31.8
3	6 318	8.4
4	1 167	1.6
5	286	0.4
6	82	0.1
7 +	85	0.1
Aggregate number of dependent children - Nombre total d'enfants à charge	117 365	..
Ecuador - Équateur[4]		
2007 (U)		
Total	14 942	100.0
0	13 893	93.0
1	528	3.5
2	327	2.2
3	136	0.9
4	41	0.3
5	10	0.1
6	3	0.0
7 +	4	0.0
Venezuela (Bolivarian Republic of) - Venezuela (République bolivarienne du)[5]		
2007 (...)		
Total	28 823	100.0
0	10 545	36.6
1	10 592	36.7
2	5 814	20.2
3	1 561	5.4
4	245	0.9
5	51	0.2
6 +	15	0.1

Continent, country or area, year, code and number of dependent children Continent, pays ou zone, année, code et nombre d'enfants à charge	Number of divorces Nombre de divorces	Per cent Pour cent
ASIA - ASIE		
Armenia - Arménie		
2007 (C)		
Total	2 931	100.0
0	2 071	70.7
1	392	13.4
2 +	468	16.0
Azerbaijan - Azerbaïdjan		
2007 (+C)		
Total	8 340	100.0
0	5 273	63.2
1	1 462	17.5
2 +	1 605	19.2
Bahrain - Bahreïn		
2006 (...)		
Total	1 141	100.0
0	835	73.2
1 - 2	121	10.6
3 - 4	41	3.6
5 - 6	8	0.7
7 - 8	1	0.1
9 +	2	0.2
Not stated - Inconnu	133	11.7
Brunei Darussalam - Brunéi Darussalam		
2004 (...)		
Total	393	100.0
0	70	17.8
1	87	22.1
2	69	17.6
3	58	14.8
4	54	13.7
5	21	5.3
6	12	3.1
7 +	17	4.3
Not stated - Inconnu	5	1.3
Aggregate number of dependent children - Nombre total d'enfants à charge	911	..
China, Macao SAR - Chine, Macao RAS		
2006 (C)		
Total	592	100.0
0	183	30.9
1	207	35.0
2	103	17.4
3	17	2.9
4	1	0.2
5	-	0.0
6	1	0.2
7 +	-	0.0
Aggregate number of dependent children - Nombre total d'enfants à charge	474	..
Cyprus - Chypre[6]		
2006 (C)		
Total	1 753	100.0
0	897	51.2
1	472	26.9
2	306	17.5
3	50	2.9
4	20	1.1
5 +	8	0.5
Not stated - Inconnu	-	0.0
Aggregate number of dependent children - Nombre total d'enfants à charge	1 356	..
Georgia - Géorgie		
2007 (C)		
Total	2 325	100.0
0	1 437	61.8
1	559	24.0
2	300	12.9
3 +	29	1.2

25. Divorces and percentage distribution by number of dependent children, latest available year: 1998 - 2007
Divorces et répartition des pourcentages selon le nombre d'enfants à charge, dernière année disponible: 1998 - 2007
(continued - suite)

Continent, country or area, year, code and number of dependent children	Number of divorces	Per cent
Continent, pays ou zone, année, code et nombre d'enfants à charge	Nombre de divorces	Pour cent

ASIA - ASIE

Japan - Japon[7]
2007 (+C)

Total	254 832	100.0
0	110 074	43.2
1	68 022	26.7
2	56 761	22.3
3	16 660	6.5
4	2 662	1.0
5	479	0.2
6	132	0.1
7 +	42	0.0
Aggregate number of dependent children - Nombre total d'enfants à charge	245 685	..

Kazakhstan
2007 (C)

Total	36 107	100.0
0	14 575	40.4
1	14 544	40.3
2 +	6 988	19.4

Kyrgyzstan - Kirghizstan
2007 (C)

Total	7 371	100.0
0	3 669	49.8
1	2 109	28.6
2	1 162	15.8
3	328	4.4
4	84	1.1
5	16	0.2
6	3	0.0
7 +	-	0.0
Not stated - Inconnu	-	0.0
Aggregate number of dependent children - Nombre total d'enfants à charge	5 851	..

Republic of Korea - République de Corée[8]
2006 (+C)

Total	125 032	100.0
0	48 457	38.8
1	33 456	26.8
2	36 967	29.6
3	5 059	4.0
4	392	0.3
5	37	0.0
6	3	0.0
7 +	1	0.0
Not stated - Inconnu	660	0.5
Aggregate number of dependent children - Nombre total d'enfants à charge	124 345	..

Singapore - Singapour
2007 (+C)

Total	6 812	100.0
0	3 217	47.2
1	1 820	26.7
2	1 276	18.7
3	394	5.8
4 +	105	1.5

Tajikistan - Tadjikistan
2007 (+C)

Total	4 752	100.0
0	2 464	51.9
1	994	20.9
2	850	17.9
3	307	6.5
4	100	2.1
5	25	0.5
6	7	0.1
7 +	5	0.1
Aggregate number of dependent children - Nombre total d'enfants à charge	3 226	..

Continent, country or area, year, code and number of dependent children	Number of divorces	Per cent
Continent, pays ou zone, année, code et nombre d'enfants à charge	Nombre de divorces	Pour cent

ASIA - ASIE

Turkey - Turquie
2003 (U)

Total	50 108	100.0
0	21 805	43.5
1	11 695	23.3
2	9 764	19.5
3	3 912	7.8
4	1 606	3.2
5	722	1.4
6	350	0.7
7 +	254	0.5
Aggregate number of dependent children - Nombre total d'enfants à charge	45 977	..

EUROPE

Albania - Albanie
2002 (C)

Total	3 494	100.0
0	1 394	39.9
1	982	28.1
2	803	23.0
3	210	6.0
4	105	3.0
Not stated - Inconnu	-	0.0

Austria - Autriche[9]
2007 (C)

Total	20 516	100.0
0	8 725	42.5
1	4 822	23.5
2	5 193	25.3
3	1 366	6.7
4	324	1.6
5	86	0.4

Belarus - Bélarus
2007 (C)

Total	36 146	100.0
0	14 520	40.2
1	17 076	47.2
2 +	4 550	12.6

Belgium - Belgique[10]
2007 (C)

Total	30 081	100.0
0	2 761	9.2
1	2 873	9.6
2	2 303	7.7
3	710	2.4
4	158	0.5
5	33	0.1
6	9	0.0
7 +	4	0.0
Not stated - Inconnu	21 230	70.6
Aggregate number of dependent children - Nombre total d'enfants à charge	10 489	..

Bosnia and Herzegovina - Bosnie-Herzégovine
2006 (C)

Total	1 659	100.0
0	939	56.6
1	348	21.0
2	220	13.3
3	47	2.8
4	7	0.4
5 +	3	0.2

25. Divorces and percentage distribution by number of dependent children, latest available year: 1998 - 2007
Divorces et répartition des pourcentages selon le nombre d'enfants à charge, dernière année disponible: 1998 - 2007
(continued - suite)

Continent, country or area, year, code and number of dependent children / Continent, pays ou zone, année, code et nombre d'enfants à charge	Number of divorces / Nombre de divorces	Per cent / Pour cent
EUROPE		
Bosnia and Herzegovina - Bosnie-Herzégovine		
2006 (C)		
Not stated - Inconnu	95	5.7
Aggregate number of dependent children - Nombre total d'enfants à charge	1 216	..
Bulgaria - Bulgarie[11]		
2007 (C)		
Total	16 347	100.0
0	7 842	48.0
1	6 386	39.1
2	1 963	12.0
3	113	0.7
4	31	0.2
5	5	0.0
6	3	0.0
7 +	4	0.0
Not stated - Inconnu	-	0.0
Croatia - Croatie[12]		
2007 (C)		
Total	4 785	100.0
0	1 999	41.8
1	1 556	32.5
2	995	20.8
3	186	3.9
4	35	0.7
5	12	0.3
6	2	0.0
7 +	-	0.0
Not stated - Inconnu	-	0.0
Aggregate number of dependent children - Nombre total d'enfants à charge	4 316	..
Czech Republic - République tchèque		
2007 (C)		
Total	31 129	100.0
0	12 721	40.9
1	10 345	33.2
2	7 189	23.1
3	726	2.3
4	114	0.4
5	21	0.1
6	9	0.0
7 +	4	0.0
Not stated - Inconnu	-	0.0
Aggregate number of dependent children - Nombre total d'enfants à charge	27 546	..
Estonia - Estonie		
2007 (C)		
Total	3 809	100.0
0	1 805	47.4
1	1 316	34.5
2	570	15.0
3	94	2.5
4	14	0.4
5	9	0.2
6	-	0.0
7 +	1	0.0
Not stated - Inconnu	-	0.0
Aggregate number of dependent children - Nombre total d'enfants à charge	2 846	..
Finland - Finlande[13]		
2007 (C)		
Total	13 224	100.0
0	4 835	36.6
1	2 919	22.1
2	3 452	26.1
3	1 455	11.0

Continent, country or area, year, code and number of dependent children / Continent, pays ou zone, année, code et nombre d'enfants à charge	Number of divorces / Nombre de divorces	Per cent / Pour cent
EUROPE		
Finland - Finlande[13]		
2007 (C)		
4	419	3.2
5	99	0.7
6	29	0.2
7 +	16	0.1
Aggregate number of dependent children - Nombre total d'enfants à charge	16 662	..
France[14]		
2006 (C)		
Total	135 910	100.0
0	57 948	42.6
1	33 178	24.4
2	32 071	23.6
3	10 035	7.4
4 +	2 678	2.0
Germany - Allemagne		
2007 (C)		
Total	187 072	100.0
0	95 372	51.0
1	49 298	26.4
2	33 828	18.1
3	6 863	3.7
4 +	1 711	0.9
Aggregate number of dependent children - Nombre total d'enfants à charge	144 981	..
Greece - Grèce		
2005 (C)		
Total	13 494	100.0
0	4 009	29.7
1	3 702	27.4
2	3 691	27.4
3	689	5.1
4	149	1.1
5	30	0.2
6	12	0.1
7 +	7	0.1
Not stated - Inconnu	1 205	8.9
Aggregate number of dependent children - Nombre total d'enfants à charge	14 024	..
Hungary - Hongrie[15]		
2007 (C)		
Total	25 160	100.0
0	9 929	39.5
1	8 248	32.8
2	5 232	20.8
3	1 396	5.5
4	248	1.0
5	68	0.3
6	22	0.1
7 +	17	0.1
Not stated - Inconnu	-	0.0
Aggregate number of dependent children - Nombre total d'enfants à charge	24 487	..
Iceland - Islande[1]		
2007 (C)		
Total	515	100.0
0	205	39.8
1	121	23.5
2	129	25.0
3	54	10.5
4	6	1.2
5 +	-	0.0
Not stated - Inconnu	-	0.0

25. Divorces and percentage distribution by number of dependent children, latest available year: 1998 - 2007
Divorces et répartition des pourcentages selon le nombre d'enfants à charge, dernière année disponible: 1998 - 2007
(continued - suite)

Continent, country or area, year, code and number of dependent children / Continent, pays ou zone, année, code et nombre d'enfants à charge	Number of divorces / Nombre de divorces	Per cent / Pour cent
EUROPE		
Italy - Italie		
2006 (C)		
Total.....................	49 534	100.0
0.........................	31 168	62.9
1.........................	13 284	26.8
2.........................	4 627	9.3
3.........................	420	0.8
4 +.......................	35	0.1
Aggregate number of dependent children - Nombre total d'enfants à charge	23 940	..
Latvia - Lettonie		
2007 (C)		
Total.....................	7 403	100.0
0.........................	3 095	41.8
1.........................	3 063	41.4
2.........................	1 043	14.1
3.........................	153	2.1
4.........................	36	0.5
5.........................	6	0.1
6.........................	4	0.1
7 +.......................	3	0.0
Not stated - Inconnu	-	0.0
Aggregate number of dependent children - Nombre total d'enfants à charge	5 829	..
Lithuania - Lituanie		
2007 (C)		
Total.....................	11 336	100.0
0.........................	4 230	37.3
1.........................	4 753	41.9
2.........................	1 959	17.3
3.........................	295	2.6
4.........................	56	0.5
5.........................	25	0.2
6.........................	6	0.1
7 +.......................	12	0.1
Not stated - Inconnu	-	0.0
Aggregate number of dependent children - Nombre total d'enfants à charge	10 045	..
Luxembourg		
2007 (C)		
Total.....................	1 106	100.0
0.........................	372	33.6
1.........................	281	25.4
2.........................	325	29.4
3.........................	113	10.2
4.........................	12	1.1
5.........................	2	0.2
6.........................	1	0.1
7 +.......................	-	0.0
Not stated - Inconnu	-	0.0
Aggregate number of dependent children - Nombre total d'enfants à charge	1 334	..
Montenegro - Monténégro		
2004 (C)		
Total.....................	505	100.0
0.........................	213	42.2
1.........................	137	27.1
2.........................	110	21.8
3.........................	33	6.5
4.........................	10	2.0
5.........................	2	0.4
6 +.......................	-	0.0
Not stated - Inconnu	-	0.0
Aggregate number of dependent children - Nombre total d'enfants à charge	506	..

Continent, country or area, year, code and number of dependent children / Continent, pays ou zone, année, code et nombre d'enfants à charge	Number of divorces / Nombre de divorces	Per cent / Pour cent
EUROPE		
Netherlands - Pays-Bas		
2007 (C)		
Total.....................	31 983	100.0
0.........................	14 001	43.8
1.........................	6 481	20.3
2.........................	8 559	26.8
3.........................	2 373	7.4
4.........................	472	1.5
5.........................	71	0.2
6.........................	20	0.1
7 +.......................	6	0.0
Norway - Norvège[16]		
2007 (C)		
Total.....................	10 280	100.0
0.........................	4 506	43.8
1.........................	2 398	23.3
2.........................	2 448	23.8
3.........................	785	7.6
4.........................	120	1.2
5.........................	19	0.2
6.........................	3	0.0
7 +.......................	1	0.0
Not stated - Inconnu	-	0.0
Aggregate number of dependent children - Nombre total d'enfants à charge	10 249	..
Poland - Pologne		
2007 (C)		
Total.....................	66 586	100.0
0.........................	25 791	38.7
1.........................	26 166	39.3
2.........................	11 684	17.5
3.........................	2 273	3.4
4 +.......................	672	1.0
Not stated - Inconnu	-	0.0
Portugal		
2003 (C)		
Total	22 617	100.0
0.........................	6 661	29.5
1.........................	8 942	39.5
2.........................	5 621	24.9
3.........................	1 084	4.8
4.........................	221	1.0
5.........................	46	0.2
6.........................	23	0.1
7 +.......................	19	0.1
Aggregate number of dependent children - Nombre total d'enfants à charge	18 851	..
Republic of Moldova - République de Moldova		
2007 (C)		
Total	13 923	100.0
0.........................	9 258	66.5
1.........................	3 226	23.2
2.........................	1 245	8.9
3.........................	157	1.1
4.........................	32	0.2
5.........................	3	0.0
6.........................	2	0.0
7 +.......................		
Aggregate number of dependent children - Nombre total d'enfants à charge	6 345	..
Romania - Roumanie		
2007 (C)		
Total	36 308	100.0
0.........................	18 929	52.1
1.........................	12 825	35.3
2.........................	3 851	10.6
3.........................	524	1.4

25. Divorces and percentage distribution by number of dependent children, latest available year: 1998 - 2007
Divorces et répartition des pourcentages selon le nombre d'enfants à charge, dernière année disponible: 1998 - 2007
(continued - suite)

Continent, country or area, year, code and number of dependent children / Continent, pays ou zone, année, code et nombre d'enfants à charge	Number of divorces / Nombre de divorces	Per cent / Pour cent
EUROPE		
Romania - Roumanie		
2007 (C)		
4	122	0.3
5	33	0.1
6	15	0.0
7 +	9	0.0
Serbia - Serbie[17]		
2006 (+C)		
Total	8 204	100.0
0	3 497	42.6
1	2 504	30.5
2	1 800	21.9
3	268	3.3
4	40	0.5
5	6	0.1
6	4	0.0
7 +	-	0.0
Not stated - Inconnu	85	1.0
Slovakia - Slovaquie		
2007 (C)		
Total	12 174	100.0
0	4 180	34.3
1	4 684	38.5
2	2 738	22.5
3	466	3.8
4	85	0.7
5	18	0.1
6	1	0.0
7 +	2	0.0
Aggregate number of dependent children - Nombre total d'enfants à charge	7 994	..
Slovenia - Slovénie		
2007 (C)		
Total	2 617	100.0
0	1 269	48.5
1	706	27.0
2	576	22.0
3	61	2.3
4	4	0.2
5	1	0.0
6 +	-	0.0
Not stated - Inconnu	-	0.0
Aggregate number of dependent children - Nombre total d'enfants à charge	2 062	..
Spain - Espagne		
2005 (C)		
Total	72 848	100.0
0	32 718	44.9
1	23 194	31.8
2	10 993	15.1
3	1 323	1.8
4	113	0.2
5	20	0.0
6	10	0.0
7 +	23	0.0
Not stated - Inconnu	4 454	6.1
Aggregate number of dependent children - Nombre total d'enfants à charge	35 676	..
Sweden - Suède		
2007 (C)		
Total	20 669	100.0
0	8 821	42.7
1	4 836	23.4
2	4 724	22.9
3	1 605	7.8
4	363	1.8
5	111	0.5
6	34	0.2

Continent, country or area, year, code and number of dependent children / Continent, pays ou zone, année, code et nombre d'enfants à charge	Number of divorces / Nombre de divorces	Per cent / Pour cent
EUROPE		
Sweden - Suède		
2007 (C)		
7 +	20	0.1
Not stated - Inconnu	155	0.7
Aggregate number of dependent children - Nombre total d'enfants à charge	21 459	..
Switzerland - Suisse		
2007 (C)		
Total	19 882	100.0
0	10 922	54.9
1	4 328	21.8
2	3 720	18.7
3	780	3.9
4	119	0.6
5	11	0.1
6 +	2	0.0
Aggregate number of dependent children - Nombre total d'enfants à charge	14 651	..
The Former Yugoslav Republic of Macedonia - L'ex-République yougoslave de Macédoine		
2007 (C)		
Total	1 417	100.0
0	846	59.7
1	268	18.9
2	219	15.5
3	67	4.7
4	15	1.1
5	2	0.1
6 +	-	0.0
Not stated - Inconnu	-	0.0
Ukraine		
2007 (C)		
Total	178 364	100.0
0	76 213	42.7
1	83 229	46.7
2	16 872	9.5
3 +	2 050	1.1
Aggregate number of dependent children - Nombre total d'enfants à charge	123 817	..
United Kingdom of Great Britain and Northern Ireland - Royaume-Uni de Grande-Bretagne et d'Irlande du Nord[18]		
2003 (C)		
Total	153 490	100.0
0	49 173	32.0
1	33 588	21.9
2	35 355	23.0
3	11 265	7.3
4	2 821	1.8
5	780	0.5
6 +	-	0.0
Not stated - Inconnu	-	0.0
Aggregate number of dependent children - Nombre total d'enfants à charge	153 527	..
OCEANIA - OCÉANIE		
Australia - Australie		
2007 (C)		
Total	47 963	100.0
0	24 317	50.7
1	8 887	18.5
2	10 148	21.2
3	3 519	7.3
4	897	1.9
5	148	0.3

25. Divorces and percentage distribution by number of dependent children, latest available year: 1998 - 2007
Divorces et répartition des pourcentages selon le nombre d'enfants à charge, dernière année disponible: 1998 - 2007
(continued - suite)

Continent, country or area, year, code and number of dependent children Continent, pays ou zone, année, code et nombre d'enfants à charge	Number of divorces Nombre de divorces	Per cent Pour cent	Continent, country or area, year, code and number of dependent children Continent, pays ou zone, année, code et nombre d'enfants à charge	Number of divorces Nombre de divorces	Per cent Pour cent
OCEANIA - OCÉANIE			**OCEANIA - OCÉANIE**		
Australia - Australie			Northern Mariana Islands - Îles Mariannes		
2007 (C)			septentrionales[20]		
6	31	0.1	2007 (U)		
7 + ...	16	0.0	Total	160	100.0
Not stated - Inconnu	-	0.0	0	78	48.8
Aggregate number of dependent children -			1	40	25.0
Nombre total d'enfants à charge	44 371	..	2	23	14.4
New Zealand - Nouvelle-Zélande[19]			3	13	8.1
2007 (+C)			4	6	3.8
Total.......................................	9 650	100.0	5 + ...	-	0.0
0	5 332	55.3			
1	1 734	18.0			
2	1 859	19.3			
3	570	5.9			
4	124	1.3			
5	22	0.2			
6	7	0.1			
7 + ...	2	0.0			
Aggregate number of dependent children -					
Nombre total d'enfants à charge	7 824	..			

FOOTNOTES - NOTES

Italics: estimates which are less reliable. - Italiques: estimations moins sûres.

* Provisional. - Données provisoires.

a 'Code' indicates the source of data, as follows:
C - Civil registration, estimated over 90% complete
U - Civil registration, estimated less than 90% complete
| - Other source, estimated reliable
+ - Data tabulated by date of registration rather than occurence.
... - Information not available

Le 'Code' indique la source des données, comme suit:
C - Registres de l'état civil considérés complets à 90 p. 100 au moins.
U - Registres de l'état civil qui ne sont pas considérés complets à 90 p. 100 au moins.
| - Autre source, considérée pas douteuses.
+ - Données exploitées selon la date de l'enregistrement et non la date de l'événement.
... - Information non disponible.

[1] Data refer to resident population only. - Pour la population résidante seulement.
[2] Unrevised data. - Les données n'ont pas été révisées.
[3] Excluding Indian jungle population. Data as reported by national statistical authorities; they may differ from data presented in other tables. - Non compris les Indiens de la jungle. Les données comme elles ont été déclarées par l'institut national de la statistique; elles peuvent être différentes de celles présentées dans d'autres tableaux.
[4] Excluding nomadic Indian tribes. - Non compris les tribus d'Indiens nomades.
[5] Excluding Indian jungle population. - Non compris les Indiens de la jungle.
[6] Data refer to government controlled areas. - Les données se rapportent aux zones contrôlées par le Gouvernement.
[7] Data refer to Japanese nationals in Japan only. - Les données se raportent aux nationaux japonais au Japon seulement.
[8] Excluding alien armed forces, civilian aliens employed by armed forces, and foreign diplomatic personnel and their dependants. Dependent children are children under 20 years of age in Korea. - Non compris les militaires étrangers, les civils étrangers employés par les forces armées ni le personnel diplomatique étranger et les membres de leur famille les accompagnant. On entend par enfants à charge en Corée les enfants de moins de 20 ans.

[9] Excluding aliens temporarily in the area. - Non compris les étrangers se trouvant temporairement le territoire.
[10] Including divorces among armed forces stationed outside the country and alien armed forces in the area. - Y compris les divorces de militaires nationaux hors du pays et les militaires étrangers en garnison sur le territoire.
[11] Including nationals outside the country, but excluding foreigners in the country. - Y compris les nationaux à l'étranger, mais non compris les étrangers sur le territoire.
[12] Data refer to dependent children born in this marriage regardless of their age. - Les données se rapportent aux enfants dépendants nés du mariage quel que soit leur âge.
[13] Including nationals temporarily outside the country. Including Aland Islands. - Y compris les nationaux se trouvant temporairement hors du pays. Y compris les Îles d'Åland.
[14] Excluding Overseas Departments, namely, French Guiana, Guadeloupe, Martinique and Reunion, shown separately, if available. - Non compris les départements d'outre mer, c'est-à-dire la Guyane française, la Guadeloupe, la Martinique et la Réunion, qui font l'objet de rubriques distinctes, si disponible.
[15] Including annulments. - Y compris les annulations.
[16] Excluding Svalbard and Jan Mayen Island shown separately, if available. Data refer to male residents of Norway only. - Non compris Svalbard et Jan Mayen qui font l'objet de rubriques distinctes, si disponible. Ces données ne concernent que les hommes habitant en Norvège.
[17] Excluding data for Kosovo and Metohia. - Sans les données pour le Kosovo et Metohie.
[18] Excluding Channel Islands (Guernsey and Jersey) and Isle of Man, shown separately, if available. Data as reported by national statistical authorities; they may differ from data presented in other tables. - Non compris les îles Anglo-Normandes (Guernesey et Jersey) et l'île de Man, qui font l'objet de rubriques distinctes, si disponible. Les données comme elles ont été déclarées par l'institut national de la statistique; elles peuvent être différentes de celles présentées dans d'autres tableaux.
[19] Data refer to children under 17 years of age. - Les données concernent les enfants âgés de moins de 17 ans.
[20] Data refer to the islands of Saipan, Tinian and Rota only. - Les données se réfèrent uniquement aux îles de Saipan, Tinian et Rota.

Annex I: Annual mid-year population, United Nations estimates: 1998 - 2007
Annexe I: Population au milieu de l'année, estimations des Nations Unies : 1998 - 2007

Continent and country or area / Continent et pays ou zone	Population estimates (in thousands) - Estimations de population (en milliers)[1]									
	1998	1999	2000	2001	2002	2003	2004	2005	2006	2007

AFRICA - AFRIQUE

	1998	1999	2000	2001	2002	2003	2004	2005	2006	2007
Algeria - Algérie	29 646	30 072	30 506	30 954	31 414	31 885	32 366	32 855	33 351	33 858
Angola	13 547	13 896	14 280	14 704	15 164	15 647	16 135	16 618	17 089	17 555
Benin - Bénin	6 266	6 455	6 659	6 879	7 113	7 358	7 611	7 868	8 128	8 393
Botswana	1 660	1 693	1 723	1 749	1 772	1 794	1 815	1 839	1 865	1 892
Burkina Faso	11 008	11 330	11 676	12 046	12 438	12 853	13 290	13 747	14 225	14 721
Burundi	6 312	6 377	6 473	6 604	6 767	6 956	7 162	7 378	7 603	7 838
Cameroon - Cameroun	15 133	15 496	15 865	16 242	16 626	17 018	17 417	17 823	18 238	18 660
Cape Verde - Cap-Vert	423	431	439	447	455	462	470	477	485	492
Central African Republic - République centrafricaine	3 587	3 668	3 746	3 820	3 890	3 959	4 029	4 101	4 178	4 257
Chad - Tchad	7 848	8 116	8 402	8 708	9 032	9 366	9 697	10 019	10 326	10 623
Comoros - Comores	528	540	552	564	577	589	603	616	631	646
Congo	2 928	2 978	3 036	3 103	3 180	3 261	3 341	3 417	3 486	3 551
Côte d'Ivoire	16 400	16 851	17 281	17 688	18 075	18 453	18 839	19 245	19 673	20 123
Democratic Republic of the Congo - République démocratique du Congo	48 419	49 550	50 829	52 284	53 885	55 591	57 337	59 077	60 800	62 523
Djibouti	686	709	730	747	763	777	791	805	820	834
Egypt - Égypte	67 573	68 860	70 174	71 518	72 894	74 296	75 718	77 154	78 602	80 061
Equatorial Guinea - Guinée équatoriale	498	513	529	545	560	576	592	609	625	642
Eritrea - Érythrée	3 419	3 530	3 657	3 802	3 963	4 134	4 307	4 473	4 631	4 781
Ethiopia - Éthiopie	62 089	63 788	65 515	67 272	69 059	70 881	72 746	74 661	76 628	78 646
Gabon	1 176	1 205	1 233	1 261	1 289	1 316	1 343	1 369	1 396	1 422
Gambia - Gambie	1 213	1 257	1 302	1 347	1 391	1 436	1 481	1 526	1 571	1 616
Ghana	18 610	19 067	19 529	19 999	20 475	20 955	21 435	21 915	22 393	22 871
Guinea - Guinée	8 060	8 222	8 384	8 545	8 706	8 870	9 041	9 221	9 412	9 615
Guinea-Bissau - Guinée-Bissau	1 247	1 259	1 304	1 335	1 369	1 403	1 438	1 473	1 507	1 541
Kenya	29 844	30 633	31 441	32 269	33 119	33 992	34 890	35 817	36 772	37 755
Lesotho	1 825	1 859	1 889	1 915	1 937	1 958	1 977	1 995	2 014	2 032
Liberia - Libéria	2 439	2 648	2 824	2 958	3 057	3 138	3 225	3 334	3 471	3 627
Libyan Arab Jamahiriya - Jamahiriya arabe libyenne	5 134	5 239	5 346	5 457	5 569	5 685	5 803	5 923	6 045	6 169
Madagascar	14 386	14 827	15 275	15 730	16 190	16 657	17 131	17 614	18 105	18 604
Malawi	11 076	11 458	11 831	12 194	12 553	12 912	13 277	13 654	14 043	14 439
Mali	10 104	10 305	10 523	10 759	11 011	11 277	11 552	11 833	12 118	12 409
Mauritania - Mauritanie	2 463	2 532	2 604	2 677	2 753	2 830	2 908	2 985	3 062	3 139
Mauritius - Maurice[2]	1 169	1 182	1 195	1 207	1 219	1 231	1 242	1 252	1 262	1 271
Mayotte	138	143	149	154	159	164	169	174	179	184
Morocco - Maroc	28 109	28 475	28 827	29 166	29 495	29 821	30 152	30 495	30 853	31 224
Mozambique	17 329	17 778	18 249	18 746	19 259	19 784	20 311	20 834	21 353	21 869
Namibia - Namibie	1 744	1 785	1 824	1 862	1 898	1 935	1 971	2 009	2 048	2 089
Niger	10 304	10 662	11 031	11 408	11 797	12 203	12 636	13 102	13 604	14 140
Nigeria - Nigéria	118 899	121 836	124 842	127 918	131 061	134 270	137 544	140 879	144 273	147 722
Réunion	700	712	724	736	748	761	773	784	795	806
Rwanda	6 801	7 443	7 958	8 310	8 539	8 685	8 820	8 992	9 210	9 455
Sao Tome and Principe - Sao Tomé-et-Principe	135	138	140	143	145	148	150	153	155	158
Senegal - Sénégal	9 390	9 643	9 902	10 165	10 433	10 707	10 989	11 281	11 583	11 893
Sierra Leone	4 053	4 125	4 228	4 368	4 540	4 733	4 926	5 107	5 271	5 420
Somalia - Somalie	6 979	7 189	7 394	7 591	7 785	7 975	8 164	8 354	8 544	8 733
South Africa - Afrique du Sud	43 562	44 215	44 872	45 536	46 197	46 849	47 477	48 073	48 639	49 173
Sudan - Soudan	33 298	34 112	34 904	35 667	36 407	37 142	37 900	38 698	39 545	40 432
Swaziland	1 041	1 062	1 080	1 092	1 101	1 108	1 115	1 124	1 137	1 151
Togo	4 909	5 082	5 247	5 404	5 553	5 698	5 843	5 992	6 145	6 300
Tunisia - Tunisie	9 264	9 360	9 452	9 539	9 623	9 706	9 790	9 878	9 971	10 069
Uganda - Ouganda	22 975	23 687	24 433	25 216	26 035	26 890	27 779	28 699	29 652	30 638
United Republic of Tanzania - République Unie de Tanzanie	32 453	33 275	34 131	35 026	35 958	36 930	37 945	39 007	40 117	41 276
Western Sahara - Sahara occidental	286	298	315	337	362	389	416	440	462	480
Zambia - Zambie	9 925	10 200	10 467	10 724	10 972	11 219	11 472	11 738	12 019	12 314
Zimbabwe	12 248	12 370	12 455	12 502	12 518	12 510	12 492	12 475	12 459	12 449

AMERICA, NORTH - AMÉRIQUE DU NORD

	1998	1999	2000	2001	2002	2003	2004	2005	2006	2007
Aruba	87	89	91	93	95	97	99	101	103	104
Bahamas	296	300	305	309	313	317	321	325	330	334
Barbados - Barbade	254	252	252	251	251	252	253	253	254	255
Belize	239	245	252	258	264	270	276	282	288	295
Canada	30 124	30 398	30 687	30 993	31 315	31 646	31 979	32 307	32 628	32 945
Costa Rica	3 750	3 842	3 931	4 017	4 100	4 180	4 256	4 328	4 396	4 459
Cuba	11 028	11 058	11 087	11 114	11 139	11 161	11 180	11 193	11 201	11 204

Continent and country or area Continent et pays ou zone	Population estimates (in thousands) - Estimations de population (en milliers)[1]									
	1998	1999	2000	2001	2002	2003	2004	2005	2006	2007
AMERICA, NORTH - AMÉRIQUE DU NORD										
Dominican Republic - République dominicaine	8 550	8 690	8 830	8 970	9 111	9 252	9 393	9 533	9 674	9 814
El Salvador............	5 879	5 914	5 945	5 973	5 996	6 017	6 037	6 059	6 082	6 107
Grenada - Grenade............	101	101	101	101	102	102	102	103	103	103
Guadeloupe............	418	424	429	435	441	446	451	456	459	462
Guatemala	10 716	10 968	11 231	11 506	11 793	12 091	12 397	12 710	13 029	13 354
Haiti - Haïti	8 334	8 492	8 648	8 802	8 954	9 105	9 257	9 410	9 564	9 720
Honduras	5 975	6 102	6 230	6 359	6 490	6 622	6 756	6 893	7 032	7 174
Jamaica - Jamaïque............	2 527	2 547	2 568	2 589	2 610	2 631	2 650	2 668	2 683	2 696
Martinique............	379	382	385	388	391	393	396	398	400	402
Mexico - Mexique	96 571	98 103	99 531	100 840	102 042	103 165	104 251	105 330	106 411	107 487
Netherlands Antilles - Antilles néerlandaises	184	182	181	180	181	182	184	186	189	192
Nicaragua	4 937	5 021	5 101	5 177	5 249	5 318	5 386	5 455	5 525	5 595
Panama............	2 838	2 895	2 951	3 007	3 063	3 119	3 176	3 232	3 288	3 343
Puerto Rico - Porto Rico............	3 777	3 798	3 819	3 839	3 858	3 877	3 895	3 913	3 930	3 948
Saint Lucia - Sainte-Lucie............	153	155	157	159	160	162	164	165	167	169
Saint Vincent and the Grenadines - Saint-Vincent-et-les Grenadines............	108	108	108	108	108	108	109	109	109	109
Trinidad and Tobago - Trinité-et-Tobago............	1 284	1 290	1 295	1 300	1 305	1 309	1 314	1 318	1 323	1 328
United States of America - États-Unis d'Amérique	281 083	284 529	287 842	290 995	294 009	296 928	299 821	302 741	305 697	308 674
United States Virgin Islands - Îles Vierges américaines	108	108	109	109	109	109	110	110	110	110
AMERICA, SOUTH - AMÉRIQUE DU SUD										
Argentina - Argentine	36 111	36 535	36 939	37 318	37 676	38 023	38 372	38 732	39 105	39 490
Bolivia (Plurinational State of) - Bolivie (État plurinational de)............	7 981	8 148	8 317	8 489	8 662	8 835	9 009	9 182	9 354	9 524
Brazil - Brésil............	169 162	171 675	174 174	176 659	179 123	181 537	183 864	186 075	188 158	190 120
Chile - Chili............	15 039	15 231	15 419	15 602	15 780	15 955	16 127	16 297	16 467	16 636
Colombia - Colombie	38 447	39 111	39 773	40 432	41 087	41 741	42 395	43 049	43 704	44 359
Ecuador - Équateur............	11 974	12 145	12 310	12 470	12 624	12 773	12 919	13 063	13 203	13 342
French Guiana - Guyane française............	153	159	165	172	180	187	195	202	208	214
Guyana	757	756	756	757	759	761	763	764	764	764
Paraguay	5 131	5 240	5 350	5 461	5 571	5 682	5 793	5 904	6 015	6 127
Peru - Pérou	25 202	25 608	26 004	26 390	26 765	27 131	27 487	27 836	28 176	28 508
Suriname	454	461	467	474	481	487	494	500	505	510
Uruguay............	3 292	3 309	3 321	3 327	3 328	3 326	3 324	3 325	3 330	3 339
Venezuela (Bolivarian Republic of) - Venezuela (République bolivarienne du)............	23 483	23 945	24 408	24 871	25 334	25 797	26 261	26 726	27 191	27 656
ASIA - ASIE										
Afghanistan	19 666	20 041	20 536	21 175	21 923	22 755	23 627	24 507	25 390	26 290
Armenia - Arménie	3 109	3 090	3 076	3 065	3 061	3 060	3 062	3 065	3 068	3 072
Azerbaijan - Azerbaïdjan	8 003	8 062	8 121	8 182	8 242	8 306	8 376	8 453	8 538	8 632
Bahrain - Bahreïn	621	636	650	665	680	696	712	728	744	760
Bangladesh	135 692	138 235	140 767	143 289	145 797	148 281	150 726	153 122	155 463	157 753
Bhutan - Bhoutan............	530	545	561	578	597	616	634	650	664	676
Brunei Darussalam - Brunéi Darussalam............	318	326	333	341	348	356	363	370	377	385
Cambodia - Cambodge	12 251	12 512	12 760	12 994	13 217	13 432	13 647	13 866	14 092	14 324
China - Chine[3]	1 245 993	1 256 729	1 266 954	1 276 684	1 285 984	1 294 940	1 303 667	1 312 253	1 320 724	1 329 090
China, Hong Kong SAR - Chine, Hong Kong RAS[4]	6 510	6 594	6 667	6 727	6 775	6 814	6 849	6 883	6 916	6 948
China, Macao SAR - Chine, Macao RAS[5]	428	434	441	448	457	466	476	488	500	513
Cyprus - Chypre............	765	776	787	797	807	817	827	836	845	854
Democratic People's Republic of Korea - République populaire démocratique de Corée............	22 465	22 672	22 859	23 025	23 172	23 302	23 420	23 529	23 632	23 728
Georgia - Géorgie	4 862	4 804	4 745	4 686	4 629	4 573	4 519	4 465	4 411	4 358
India - Inde	1 006 996	1 024 799	1 042 590	1 060 371	1 078 111	1 095 767	1 113 283	1 130 618	1 147 746	1 164 670
Indonesia - Indonésie............	199 760	202 513	205 280	208 064	210 858	213 656	216 443	219 210	221 954	224 670
Iran (Islamic Republic of) - Iran (République islamique d') .	65 120	66 038	66 903	67 712	68 480	69 227	69 982	70 765	71 585	72 437
Iraq	23 144	23 901	24 652	25 398	26 137	26 862	27 564	28 238	28 876	29 486
Israel - Israël	5 821	5 954	6 084	6 211	6 334	6 454	6 573	6 692	6 811	6 932
Japan - Japon	126 286	126 500	126 706	126 907	127 097	127 263	127 384	127 449	127 451	127 396
Jordan - Jordanie............	4 657	4 749	4 853	4 973	5 103	5 245	5 400	5 566	5 747	5 941
Kazakhstan	15 259	15 077	14 957	14 909	14 927	14 997	15 092	15 194	15 298	15 408
Kuwait - Koweït	1 966	2 103	2 228	2 339	2 439	2 531	2 617	2 700	2 779	2 851
Kyrgyzstan - Kirghizstan	4 807	4 885	4 955	5 015	5 068	5 117	5 167	5 221	5 282	5 346

Continent and country or area / Continent et pays ou zone	Population estimates (in thousands) - Estimations de population (en milliers)[1]									
	1998	1999	2000	2001	2002	2003	2004	2005	2006	2007
ASIA - ASIE										
Lao People's Democratic Republic - République démocratique populaire lao	5 177	5 294	5 403	5 505	5 599	5 690	5 783	5 880	5 983	6 092
Lebanon - Liban	3 673	3 720	3 772	3 833	3 899	3 965	4 028	4 082	4 126	4 162
Malaysia - Malaisie	22 216	22 754	23 274	23 771	24 250	24 715	25 174	25 633	26 095	26 556
Maldives	263	268	272	276	280	284	288	292	297	301
Mongolia - Mongolie	2 332	2 360	2 389	2 419	2 451	2 484	2 517	2 550	2 581	2 611
Myanmar	45 614	46 141	46 610	47 014	47 363	47 681	48 000	48 345	48 723	49 129
Nepal - Népal	23 294	23 863	24 432	24 998	25 563	26 123	26 676	27 222	27 758	28 287
Occupied Palestinian Territory - Territoire palestinien occupé	2 927	3 036	3 149	3 266	3 387	3 510	3 636	3 762	3 889	4 017
Oman	2 318	2 361	2 402	2 443	2 484	2 526	2 570	2 618	2 670	2 726
Pakistan	140 849	144 516	148 132	151 682	155 194	158 694	162 224	165 816	169 470	173 178
Philippines	74 587	76 138	77 689	79 239	80 789	82 344	83 911	85 496	87 099	88 718
Qatar	568	590	617	648	685	732	797	885	1 001	1 138
Republic of Korea - République de Corée	45 755	46 110	46 429	46 707	46 948	47 164	47 366	47 566	47 766	47 962
Saudi Arabia - Arabie saoudite	19 718	20 260	20 808	21 363	21 927	22 496	23 059	23 613	24 153	24 680
Singapore - Singapour	3 828	3 933	4 018	4 080	4 121	4 154	4 199	4 267	4 364	4 485
Sri Lanka	18 559	18 656	18 767	18 896	19 040	19 197	19 362	19 531	19 704	19 882
Syrian Arab Republic - République arabe syrienne	15 702	16 091	16 511	16 961	17 438	17 952	18 512	19 121	19 789	20 504
Tajikistan - Tadjikistan	6 021	6 099	6 173	6 243	6 311	6 379	6 453	6 536	6 627	6 727
Thailand - Thaïlande	61 399	61 824	62 347	62 991	63 734	64 553	65 279	65 946	66 507	66 979
Timor-Leste	820	811	815	835	867	908	951	992	1 029	1 064
Turkey - Turquie	64 396	65 442	66 460	67 444	68 398	69 329	70 250	71 169	72 088	73 004
Turkmenistan - Turkménistan	4 387	4 442	4 502	4 566	4 634	4 704	4 774	4 843	4 911	4 977
United Arab Emirates - Émirats arabes unis	2 895	3 065	3 238	3 414	3 591	3 766	3 933	4 089	4 233	4 364
Uzbekistan - Ouzbékistan	24 091	24 439	24 776	25 102	25 417	25 724	26 024	26 320	26 611	26 900
Viet Nam	76 461	77 563	78 663	79 765	80 863	81 952	83 024	84 074	85 101	86 108
Yemen - Yémen	17 150	17 659	18 182	18 722	19 275	19 843	20 426	21 024	21 638	22 269
EUROPE										
Albania - Albanie	3 076	3 070	3 068	3 069	3 076	3 087	3 099	3 111	3 122	3 132
Austria - Autriche	7 976	7 985	8 005	8 039	8 084	8 135	8 186	8 232	8 272	8 307
Belarus - Bélarus	10 153	10 103	10 054	10 005	9 957	9 910	9 863	9 816	9 770	9 724
Belgium - Belgique	10 144	10 165	10 193	10 227	10 268	10 313	10 362	10 415	10 471	10 531
Bosnia and Herzegovina - Bosnie-Herzégovine	3 480	3 601	3 694	3 748	3 776	3 783	3 782	3 781	3 781	3 778
Bulgaria - Bulgarie	8 130	8 067	8 006	7 948	7 893	7 840	7 789	7 739	7 690	7 641
Croatia - Croatie	4 583	4 540	4 505	4 482	4 466	4 457	4 450	4 443	4 436	4 429
Czech Republic - République tchèque	10 267	10 245	10 224	10 206	10 190	10 180	10 180	10 195	10 225	10 268
Denmark - Danemark	5 294	5 315	5 335	5 354	5 371	5 387	5 402	5 417	5 431	5 445
Estonia - Estonie	1 389	1 379	1 370	1 363	1 357	1 353	1 349	1 347	1 345	1 343
Finland - Finlande	5 151	5 162	5 173	5 186	5 199	5 212	5 228	5 244	5 263	5 283
France	58 610	58 847	59 128	59 459	59 832	60 230	60 630	61 013	61 373	61 714
Germany - Allemagne	82 002	82 030	82 075	82 146	82 232	82 319	82 383	82 409	82 393	82 343
Greece - Grèce	10 863	10 905	10 942	10 974	11 000	11 021	11 042	11 064	11 087	11 112
Hungary - Hongrie	10 271	10 243	10 215	10 187	10 158	10 130	10 103	10 078	10 054	10 032
Iceland - Islande	276	278	281	283	286	288	291	296	301	308
Ireland - Irlande	3 706	3 750	3 804	3 868	3 941	4 020	4 103	4 187	4 271	4 355
Italy - Italie	57 036	57 030	57 116	57 306	57 586	57 927	58 291	58 645	58 982	59 305
Latvia - Lettonie	2 413	2 393	2 374	2 355	2 337	2 321	2 306	2 292	2 280	2 269
Lithuania - Lituanie	3 550	3 524	3 501	3 482	3 467	3 454	3 438	3 416	3 389	3 356
Luxembourg	426	431	437	442	448	453	459	464	470	475
Malta - Malte	385	387	389	392	394	397	400	403	405	406
Montenegro - Monténégro	653	659	661	650	650	640	631	625	621	621
Netherlands - Pays-Bas	15 735	15 826	15 915	16 001	16 084	16 164	16 241	16 316	16 389	16 460
Norway - Norvège	4 433	4 458	4 484	4 511	4 538	4 567	4 599	4 635	4 676	4 720
Poland - Pologne	38 540	38 487	38 433	38 381	38 331	38 284	38 239	38 198	38 163	38 132
Portugal	10 131	10 175	10 226	10 286	10 352	10 421	10 487	10 547	10 598	10 641
Republic of Moldova - République de Moldova	4 217	4 162	4 100	4 033	3 961	3 888	3 820	3 759	3 709	3 667
Romania - Roumanie	22 345	22 242	22 138	22 033	21 930	21 829	21 731	21 635	21 541	21 450
Russian Federation - Fédération de Russie	147 648	147 205	146 670	146 042	145 339	144 598	143 864	143 170	142 530	141 941
Serbia - Serbie	10 228	10 185	10 134	10 077	10 013	9 950	9 896	9 856	9 835	9 832
Slovakia - Slovaquie	5 374	5 376	5 379	5 380	5 381	5 382	5 383	5 386	5 389	5 394
Slovenia - Slovénie	1 979	1 982	1 985	1 988	1 991	1 994	1 997	2 001	2 005	2 010
Spain - Espagne	39 730	39 943	40 264	40 708	41 257	41 869	42 485	43 060	43 579	44 051
Sweden - Suède	8 847	8 848	8 860	8 886	8 924	8 970	9 018	9 066	9 113	9 159
Switzerland - Suisse	7 127	7 151	7 184	7 228	7 281	7 338	7 393	7 441	7 480	7 513

Annex I: Annual mid-year population, United Nations estimates: 1998 - 2007
Annexe I: Population au milieu de l'année, estimations des Nations Unies : 1998 - 2007 (continued - suite)

Continent and country or area Continent et pays ou zone	Population estimates (in thousands) - Estimations de population (en milliers)[1]									
	1998	1999	2000	2001	2002	2003	2004	2005	2006	2007

EUROPE

	1998	1999	2000	2001	2002	2003	2004	2005	2006	2007
The Former Yugoslav Republic of Macedonia - L'ex-République yougoslave de Macédoine	1 994	2 004	2 012	2 018	2 024	2 028	2 032	2 035	2 038	2 040
Ukraine	49 821	49 336	48 870	48 436	48 029	47 647	47 285	46 936	46 603	46 289
United Kingdom of Great Britain and Northern Ireland - Royaume-Uni de Grande-Bretagne et d'Irlande du Nord	58 522	58 703	58 907	59 138	59 392	59 667	59 958	60 261	60 575	60 899

OCEANIA - OCÉANIE

	1998	1999	2000	2001	2002	2003	2004	2005	2006	2007
Australia - Australie[6]	18 730	18 946	19 171	19 407	19 653	19 904	20 153	20 395	20 628	20 854
Fiji - Fidji	790	796	802	807	813	818	823	828	833	839
French Polynesia - Polynésie française	228	232	236	240	244	248	252	255	259	262
Guam	151	153	155	158	160	163	166	169	171	173
Micronesia (Federated States of) - Micronésie (États fédérés de)	108	107	107	107	108	108	109	109	110	110
New Caledonia - Nouvelle-Calédonie	207	211	215	219	223	227	231	235	239	243
New Zealand - Nouvelle-Zélande	3 798	3 830	3 868	3 912	3 962	4 013	4 064	4 111	4 153	4 193
Papua New Guinea - Papouasie-Nouvelle-Guinée	5 107	5 246	5 388	5 530	5 675	5 821	5 969	6 118	6 270	6 423
Samoa	174	175	177	178	178	179	179	179	179	179
Solomon Islands - Îles Salomon	393	404	416	427	438	450	462	474	486	498
Tonga	98	98	99	99	100	100	101	102	102	103
Vanuatu	182	186	190	194	199	205	211	216	222	228

FOOTNOTES - NOTES

1 For 1998-2007 all data refer to annual interpolated estimates of mid-year population. All estimates are produced by the United Nations, Department of Economic and Social Affairs, Population Division (2009) and published in World Population Prospects: The 2008 Revision.CD-ROM Edition - Extended Dataset in Excel and ASCII formats. - Les données pour 1998-2007 sont des estimations de population au milieu de l'année interpolée. Toutes ces données sont produites par Les Nations Unies, Département des Affaires Sociales et Économiques, Division de Population (2009)et ont été publiées dans World Population Prospects: The 2008 Revision. CD-ROM Edition - Extended Dataset in Excel and ASCII formats.

2 Including Agalega, Rodrigues and Saint Brandon. - Y compris Agalega, Rodrigues et Saint Brandon.

3 For statistical purposes, the data for China do not include Hong Kong and Macao Special Administrative Regions (SAR) of China. - A des fins statistiques, les données pour la Chine ne comprennent pas les Régions Administratives Spéciales (SAR) de Hong Kong et Macao.

4 As of 1 July 1997, Hong Kong became a Special Administrative Region(SAR) of China. - A partir du 1 juillet 1997, Hong Kong est devenue une Région Administrative Spéciale (SAR) de la Chine.

5 As of 20 December 1999, Macao became a Special Administrative Region (SAR) of China. - A partir du 20 décembre 1999, Macao est devenue une Région Administrative Spéciale (SAR) de la Chine.

6 Including Christmas Island, Cocos (Keeling) Islands and Norfolk Island. - Y compris Christmas Island, Cocos (Keeling) Islands et Norfolk Island.

Annex II: Vital statistics summary, United Nations medium variant projections: 2005-2010
Annexe II: Aperçu des statistiques de l'état civil, variante moyenne, projections des Nations Unies : 2005-2010

Continent and country or area Continent et pays ou zone	Crude birth rate - Taux bruts de natalité[1]	Crude death rate - Taux bruts de mortalité[1]	Infant mortality rate - Décès d'enfants de moins d'un an[1]	Expectation of life at birth - Espérance de vie à la naissance[1]		Total fertility rate - Indice synthétique de fécondité[1]	Natural increase - Accroissement naturel[1]
				Male - Masculin	Female - Féminin		
AFRICA - AFRIQUE							
Algeria - Algérie	20.8	4.9	31.1	70.9	73.7	2.38	1.586
Angola	42.9	17.1	117.5	44.9	48.8	5.78	2.578
Benin - Bénin	39.6	9.3	84.9	60.1	62.3	5.48	3.030
Botswana	24.7	11.7	36.2	54.6	54.8	2.89	1.294
Burkina Faso	47.8	13.1	80.1	51.6	54.2	5.94	3.468
Burundi	34.6	14.0	98.3	48.8	51.7	4.65	2.057
Cameroon - Cameroun	37.1	14.3	86.9	50.4	51.5	4.66	2.280
Cape Verde - Cap-Vert	24.3	5.0	25.8	68.3	73.6	2.76	1.925
Central African Republic - République centrafricaine	35.6	17.1	105.5	45.4	48.4	4.84	1.856
Chad - Tchad	45.8	16.8	129.9	47.4	50.0	6.19	2.903
Comoros - Comores	32.7	6.8	48.4	63.0	67.4	3.99	2.596
Congo	34.7	12.9	79.3	52.6	54.5	4.41	2.185
Côte d'Ivoire	35.1	10.9	86.8	56.0	58.6	4.64	2.421
Democratic Republic of the Congo - République démocratique du Congo	45.1	17.2	116.8	45.9	49.0	6.07	2.789
Djibouti	28.7	11.1	85.0	53.9	56.7	3.94	1.760
Egypt - Égypte	24.8	5.9	34.8	68.3	71.8	2.88	1.895
Equatorial Guinea - Guinée équatoriale	38.0	15.1	99.6	48.9	51.3	5.35	2.290
Eritrea - Érythrée	37.3	8.6	54.3	57.0	61.6	4.68	2.870
Ethiopia - Éthiopie	38.6	12.0	79.1	53.6	56.5	5.38	2.659
Gabon	27.5	9.8	51.1	59.0	61.7	3.35	1.770
Gambia - Gambie	37.0	11.4	76.5	54.2	57.4	5.09	2.559
Ghana	32.5	11.2	73.4	55.6	57.4	4.30	2.135
Guinea - Guinée	39.9	11.2	98.4	55.6	59.6	5.45	2.871
Guinea-Bissau - Guinée-Bissau	41.4	17.4	114.0	46.1	49.2	5.72	2.398
Kenya	39.0	11.7	63.9	53.7	54.5	4.95	2.731
Lesotho	29.1	16.9	69.6	44.5	45.8	3.37	1.226
Liberia - Libéria	38.6	10.6	95.1	56.7	59.4	5.14	2.795
Libyan Arab Jamahiriya - Jamahiriya arabe libyenne	23.4	4.1	18.0	71.7	76.9	2.72	1.933
Madagascar	36.2	9.3	65.2	58.5	61.8	4.77	2.687
Malawi	40.5	12.4	83.7	51.8	53.8	5.59	2.804
Mali	42.8	15.9	106.4	47.6	49.0	5.48	2.690
Mauritania - Mauritanie	33.8	10.5	72.8	54.7	58.5	4.52	2.333
Mauritius - Maurice[2]	14.1	7.2	14.6	68.5	75.8	1.77	0.694
Mayotte	25.4	2.9	6.9	72.1	80.2	3.15	2.248
Morocco - Maroc	20.5	5.8	30.6	69.0	73.4	2.37	1.470
Mozambique	39.5	16.1	90.1	46.9	48.7	5.11	2.343
Namibia - Namibie	27.8	8.5	35.0	60.3	62.3	3.40	1.933
Niger	54.1	15.2	88.2	50.3	52.0	7.14	3.887
Nigeria - Nigéria	40.1	16.5	109.4	47.3	48.3	5.31	2.364
Réunion	18.6	5.5	6.7	72.3	80.5	2.43	1.307
Rwanda	41.0	14.7	99.6	48.1	51.6	5.43	2.636
Sao Tome and Principe - Sao Tomé-et-Principe	32.4	7.5	72.3	63.6	67.4	3.85	2.487
Senegal - Sénégal	38.8	11.0	58.4	53.9	57.0	5.04	2.782
Sierra Leone	40.4	16.0	104.3	46.1	48.7	5.22	2.444
Somalia - Somalie	44.2	15.9	109.6	48.2	51.0	6.40	2.833
South Africa - Afrique du Sud	22.1	15.1	49.1	49.9	53.2	2.55	0.697
Sudan - Soudan	31.6	10.3	69.1	56.5	59.5	4.22	2.129
Swaziland	30.0	15.7	65.7	46.3	45.2	3.57	1.435
Togo	33.1	8.2	71.4	60.7	64.2	4.30	2.484
Tunisia - Tunisie	16.1	5.9	19.8	71.9	76.0	1.86	1.018
Uganda - Ouganda	46.3	12.9	74.0	51.8	53.0	6.38	3.348
United Republic of Tanzania - République Unie de Tanzanie	41.6	11.5	64.8	54.6	56.2	5.57	3.013
Western Sahara - Sahara occidental	23.3	5.8	44.2	64.3	68.1	2.69	1.751
Zambia - Zambie	43.2	17.5	94.6	44.6	45.6	5.87	2.566
Zimbabwe	30.0	16.2	57.7	43.4	44.3	3.47	1.383
AMERICA, NORTH - AMÉRIQUE DU NORD							
Aruba	11.8	7.3	15.5	72.1	77.4	1.73	0.449
Bahamas	16.9	6.0	9.0	70.6	76.2	2.02	1.087
Barbados - Barbade	11.2	7.7	10.1	74.2	79.8	1.52	0.357
Belize	24.9	3.7	16.7	74.4	78.2	2.93	2.126
Canada	10.6	7.4	4.8	78.3	82.9	1.56	0.321
Costa Rica	16.6	4.1	9.9	76.5	81.3	1.96	1.255
Cuba	10.5	6.8	5.1	76.7	80.8	1.50	0.366

Continent and country or area / Continent et pays ou zone	Crude birth rate - Taux bruts de natalité[1]	Crude death rate - Taux bruts de mortalité[1]	Infant mortality rate - Décès d'enfants de moins d'un an[1]	Expectation of life at birth - Espérance de vie à la naissance[1]		Total fertility rate - Indice synthétique de fécondité[1]	Natural increase - Accroissement naturel[1]
				Male - Masculin	Female - Féminin		
AMERICA, NORTH - AMÉRIQUE DU NORD							
Dominican Republic - République dominicaine	22.7	5.9	29.6	69.8	75.3	2.67	1.684
El Salvador.................	20.4	6.8	21.5	66.5	76.0	2.34	1.355
Grenada - Grenade.................	19.4	6.2	13.4	73.7	76.8	2.30	1.323
Guadeloupe.................	14.5	7.9	6.8	76.0	82.2	2.11	0.657
Guatemala	33.3	5.7	30.1	66.7	73.8	4.15	2.757
Haiti - Haïti.................	27.9	9.1	62.4	59.5	63.0	3.54	1.874
Honduras.................	27.7	5.1	28.1	69.8	74.5	3.30	2.268
Jamaica - Jamaïque.................	19.5	7.4	23.3	68.5	75.2	2.40	1.202
Martinique.................	12.6	7.7	6.6	76.5	82.3	1.91	0.491
Mexico - Mexique	19.1	4.7	16.7	73.8	78.7	2.21	1.434
Netherlands Antilles - Antilles néerlandaises	13.4	7.4	12.8	72.7	79.4	1.97	0.602
Nicaragua	24.8	4.7	21.5	69.9	76.1	2.75	2.011
Panama	20.8	5.0	18.2	73.0	78.3	2.56	1.577
Puerto Rico - Porto Rico.................	13.2	7.8	7.2	74.7	82.7	1.82	0.538
Saint Lucia - Sainte-Lucie	18.0	6.6	12.6	71.9	75.6	2.04	1.149
Saint Vincent and the Grenadines - Saint-Vincent-et-les Grenadines	17.7	7.5	23.3	69.5	73.8	2.13	1.021
Trinidad and Tobago - Trinité-et-Tobago.................	14.8	8.0	26.0	65.8	73.0	1.63	0.682
United States of America - États-Unis d'Amérique	14.2	7.8	5.9	76.9	81.4	2.09	0.635
United States Virgin Islands - Îles Vierges américaines	13.5	6.9	9.1	75.9	82.0	2.14	0.660
AMERICA, SOUTH - AMÉRIQUE DU SUD							
Argentina - Argentine.................	17.4	7.8	13.4	71.6	79.1	2.25	0.959
Bolivia (Plurinational State of) - Bolivie (État plurinational de).................	27.3	7.6	45.6	63.4	67.7	3.50	1.975
Brazil - Brésil.................	16.4	6.4	23.5	68.7	76.0	1.90	1.004
Chile - Chili.................	15.0	5.4	7.2	75.5	81.6	1.94	0.965
Colombia - Colombie	20.6	5.5	19.1	69.2	76.7	2.45	1.509
Ecuador - Équateur.................	21.0	5.2	21.1	72.1	78.1	2.57	1.583
French Guiana - Guyane française.................	25.2	3.7	13.4	72.6	79.9	3.27	2.153
Guyana	18.0	8.2	42.4	64.1	69.9	2.33	0.986
Paraguay	24.8	5.6	32.0	69.7	73.9	3.08	1.926
Peru - Pérou	21.3	5.4	21.2	70.5	75.9	2.59	1.594
Suriname	19.1	7.6	22.2	65.4	72.6	2.41	1.155
Uruguay.................	15.1	9.3	13.1	72.8	79.9	2.11	0.578
Venezuela (Bolivarian Republic of) - Venezuela (République bolivarienne du)	21.4	5.1	17.0	70.9	76.8	2.54	1.633
ASIA - ASIE							
Afghanistan	46.6	19.7	157.0	43.9	43.8	6.63	2.693
Armenia - Arménie	15.2	8.7	25.2	70.2	76.7	1.73	0.652
Azerbaijan - Azerbaïdjan	19.0	6.8	43.4	67.7	72.5	2.15	1.221
Bahrain - Bahreïn	18.2	2.6	9.9	74.3	77.5	2.29	1.552
Bangladesh	21.6	6.6	44.7	65.0	67.0	2.35	1.495
Bhutan - Bhoutan.................	21.5	7.2	44.5	64.1	67.7	2.67	1.432
Brunei Darussalam - Brunéi Darussalam.................	20.1	2.8	5.5	75.0	79.7	2.10	1.722
Cambodia - Cambodge	24.9	8.4	62.3	59.0	62.6	2.96	1.648
China - Chine[3]	13.5	7.0	22.9	71.3	74.8	1.76	0.654
Cyprus - Chypre.................	11.5	7.1	5.5	77.3	82.0	1.52	0.436
Democratic People's Republic of Korea - République populaire démocratique de Corée	13.8	9.9	48.0	65.1	69.3	1.86	0.388
Georgia - Géorgie	12.1	11.9	34.5	68.0	75.0	1.58	0.021
India - Inde.................	23.0	8.5	54.6	62.1	65.0	2.76	1.447
Indonesia - Indonésie.................	18.8	6.3	26.6	68.7	72.7	2.18	1.242
Iran (Islamic Republic of) - Iran (République islamique d') ..	18.9	5.7	29.1	70.0	72.7	1.83	1.319
Iraq	31.6	6.1	33.2	63.5	71.7	4.10	2.550
Israel - Israël	20.0	5.5	4.7	78.6	82.8	2.80	1.455
Japan - Japon	8.2	9.1	3.2	79.0	86.2	1.26	-0.094
Jordan - Jordanie.................	26.0	4.2	19.4	70.8	74.5	3.13	2.181
Kazakhstan	19.8	11.3	25.6	59.0	71.2	2.31	0.852
Kuwait - Koweït	17.9	1.9	9.1	76.0	79.9	2.18	1.605
Kyrgyzstan - Kirghizstan	22.4	7.4	37.3	64.1	71.6	2.56	1.500

Continent and country or area Continent et pays ou zone	Crude birth rate - Taux bruts de natalité[1]	Crude death rate - Taux bruts de mortalité[1]	Infant mortality rate - Décès d'enfants de moins d'un an[1]	Expectation of life at birth - Espérance de vie à la naissance[1]		Total fertility rate - Indice synthétique de fécondité[1]	Natural increase - Accroissement naturel[1]
				Male - Masculin	Female - Féminin		
ASIA - ASIE							
Lao People's Democratic Republic - République démocratique populaire lao	27.6	7.1	49.8	63.4	66.2	3.54	2.050
Lebanon - Liban	15.8	6.9	22.0	69.9	74.2	1.86	0.890
Malaysia - Malaisie	20.5	4.5	8.9	72.0	76.7	2.58	1.606
Maldives	18.8	4.6	24.0	69.8	72.9	2.06	1.419
Mongolia - Mongolie	19.0	6.7	42.1	63.2	69.8	2.02	1.229
Myanmar	20.7	9.9	75.4	59.0	63.4	2.31	1.072
Nepal - Népal	25.6	6.5	42.2	65.9	67.2	2.93	1.914
Occupied Palestinian Territory - Territoire palestinien occupé	35.9	3.7	17.5	71.8	75.0	5.09	3.218
Oman	22.1	2.7	12.3	74.2	77.5	3.08	1.935
Pakistan	30.2	7.0	63.9	66.0	66.7	4.00	2.322
Philippines	25.0	4.8	23.0	69.5	74.0	3.11	2.014
Qatar	12.2	2.0	8.3	74.9	76.9	2.43	1.016
Republic of Korea - République de Corée ...	9.5	5.5	4.4	75.9	82.5	1.21	0.401
Saudi Arabia - Arabie saoudite.........	23.6	3.6	18.8	70.9	75.3	3.16	1.992
Singapore - Singapour..................	8.2	5.1	3.0	77.9	82.8	1.26	0.306
Sri Lanka.............................	18.3	6.5	15.9	70.2	77.8	2.33	1.181
Syrian Arab Republic - République arabe syrienne	28.2	3.4	16.0	72.3	76.1	3.28	2.482
Tajikistan - Tadjikistan	28.1	6.4	60.2	64.1	69.4	3.45	2.172
Thailand - Thaïlande	14.6	8.9	6.8	65.7	72.0	1.81	0.564
Timor-Leste	40.2	8.8	66.7	60.0	61.7	6.52	3.136
Turkey - Turquie......................	18.4	6.0	27.5	69.4	74.3	2.13	1.247
Turkmenistan - Turkménistan	22.0	7.7	50.5	60.6	68.9	2.49	1.430
United Arab Emirates - Émirats arabes unis	14.0	1.5	9.7	76.6	78.8	1.94	1.251
Uzbekistan - Ouzbékistan	20.4	6.5	48.0	64.6	70.9	2.29	1.385
Viet Nam..............................	17.3	5.4	19.5	72.3	76.2	2.08	1.191
Yemen - Yémen	37.1	7.4	58.6	61.1	64.4	5.30	2.974
EUROPE							
Albania - Albanie	14.7	6.2	16.1	73.4	79.7	1.87	0.850
Austria - Autriche	9.1	9.3	4.3	77.2	82.6	1.38	-0.011
Belarus - Bélarus.....................	10.0	14.7	9.3	63.2	75.3	1.27	-0.470
Belgium - Belgique	11.3	9.7	4.1	76.7	82.6	1.77	0.156
Bosnia and Herzegovina - Bosnie-Herzégovine	9.2	9.8	12.8	72.4	77.7	1.21	-0.061
Bulgaria - Bulgarie....................	9.6	14.6	11.8	69.7	76.8	1.40	-0.504
Croatia - Croatie.....................	9.6	11.5	6.2	72.8	79.5	1.42	-0.195
Czech Republic - République tchèque	10.6	10.8	3.8	73.4	79.5	1.40	-0.018
Denmark - Danemark....................	11.5	10.3	4.4	76.0	80.6	1.84	0.125
Estonia - Estonie	11.8	12.9	7.7	67.6	78.5	1.63	-0.110
Finland - Finlande	11.1	9.4	3.2	76.2	83.0	1.82	0.175
France	12.2	8.6	3.9	77.6	84.7	1.89	0.363
Germany - Allemagne	8.1	10.3	4.1	77.1	82.4	1.32	-0.219
Greece - Grèce........................	9.7	10.2	3.8	77.1	81.3	1.37	-0.054
Hungary - Hongrie.....................	9.9	13.4	6.8	69.2	77.4	1.35	-0.357
Iceland - Islande.....................	14.7	6.1	2.9	80.2	83.3	2.09	0.867
Ireland - Irlande	15.6	6.4	4.5	77.5	82.3	1.95	0.920
Italy - Italie	9.3	9.9	3.9	78.1	84.1	1.37	-0.066
Latvia - Lettonie	10.1	13.8	9.0	67.3	77.2	1.39	-0.368
Lithuania - Lituanie	9.5	13.1	8.9	65.8	77.7	1.34	-0.365
Luxembourg............................	11.4	8.2	4.2	76.7	82.1	1.66	0.323
Malta - Malte	9.0	7.8	6.3	77.8	81.4	1.26	0.119
Montenegro - Monténégro	12.1	10.2	8.7	71.6	76.5	1.63	0.188
Netherlands - Pays-Bas	11.3	8.4	4.5	77.8	82.0	1.73	0.287
Norway - Norvège	12.3	8.7	3.5	78.3	82.8	1.89	0.357
Poland - Pologne	9.8	10.0	6.7	71.3	79.8	1.26	-0.021
Portugal..............................	9.9	10.1	4.2	75.4	81.9	1.38	-0.026
Republic of Moldova - République de Moldova	12.3	12.9	17.9	64.7	72.2	1.50	-0.065
Romania - Roumanie	10.0	12.3	14.6	69.1	76.2	1.32	-0.228
Russian Federation - Fédération de Russie	10.8	15.1	11.9	60.3	73.1	1.36	-0.430
Serbia - Serbie	11.6	11.6	11.7	71.7	76.3	1.61	-
Slovakia - Slovaquie..................	10.2	10.0	6.9	70.7	78.5	1.27	0.021
Slovenia - Slovénie...................	9.6	9.5	3.7	74.6	81.9	1.35	0.017
Spain - Espagne	11.0	8.7	3.9	77.6	84.1	1.42	0.229
Sweden - Suède	11.7	10.1	3.1	78.7	83.0	1.86	0.166
Switzerland - Suisse..................	9.7	8.3	4.1	79.3	84.1	1.45	0.142

Annex II: Vital statistics summary, United Nations medium variant projections: 2005-2010
Annexe II: Aperçu des statistiques de l'état civil, variante moyenne, projections des Nations Unies : 2005-2010 (continued - suite)

Continent and country or area / Continent et pays ou zone	Crude birth rate - Taux bruts de natalité[1]	Crude death rate - Taux bruts de mortalité[1]	Infant mortality rate - Décès d'enfants de moins d'un an[1]	Expectation of life at birth - Espérance de vie à la naissance[1]		Total fertility rate - Indice synthétique de fécondité[1]	Natural increase - Accroissement naturel[1]
				Male - Masculin	Female - Féminin		
EUROPE							
The Former Yugoslav Republic of Macedonia - L'ex-République yougoslave de Macédoine	10.9	9.1	14.8	71.8	76.6	1.44	0.177
Ukraine	9.9	16.0	12.4	62.8	73.8	1.31	-0.616
United Kingdom of Great Britain and Northern Ireland - Royaume-Uni de Grande-Bretagne et d'Irlande du Nord ..	12.2	9.9	4.8	77.2	81.6	1.84	0.226
OCEANIA - OCÉANIE							
Australia - Australie[4]	12.7	6.9	4.5	79.1	83.8	1.83	0.589
Fiji - Fidji	21.1	6.6	19.5	66.6	71.1	2.75	1.451
French Polynesia - Polynésie française	18.1	5.1	7.9	72.0	76.9	2.20	1.294
Guam	18.5	5.5	9.0	73.3	77.9	2.53	1.299
Micronesia (Federated States of) - Micronésie (États fédérés de)	25.5	6.1	34.1	67.7	69.3	3.62	1.938
New Caledonia - Nouvelle-Calédonie	16.5	5.5	6.1	72.8	79.7	2.09	1.095
New Zealand - Nouvelle-Zélande	13.8	7.0	4.6	78.2	82.2	2.01	0.679
Papua New Guinea - Papouasie-Nouvelle-Guinée	31.7	8.0	50.8	58.8	63.2	4.10	2.368
Samoa	23.8	5.3	22.3	68.5	74.9	3.98	1.841
Solomon Islands - Îles Salomon	30.8	6.2	44.3	65.1	67.0	3.92	2.454
Tonga	28.2	6.1	21.8	69.1	74.7	4.04	2.208
Vanuatu	30.4	5.0	28.3	68.3	72.1	4.00	2.540

FOOTNOTES - NOTES

[1] All data are mid-year medium variant projections, produced by the United Nations, Department of Economic and Social Affairs, Population Division (2009) and published in World Population Prospects: The 2008 Revision. CD-ROM Edition - Extended Dataset in Excel and ASCII formats. - Toutes ces données sont des projections de la population au milieu de l'année de variante moyenne; elles sont produites par Les Nations Unies, Département des Affaires Sociales et Économiques, ont été publiées dans World Population Prospects: The 2008 Revision. CD-ROM Edition - Extended Dataset in Excel and ASCII formats.

[2] Including Agalega, Rodrigues and Saint Brandon. - Y compris Agalega, Rodrigues et Saint Brandon.

[3] For statistical purposes, the data for China do not include Hong Kong and Macao Special Administrative Regions (SAR) of China. - A des fins statistiques, les données pour la Chine ne comprennent pas les Régions Administratives Spéciales (SAR) de Hong Kong et Macao.

[4] Including Christmas Island, Cocos (Keeling) Islands and Norfolk Island. - Y compris Christmas Island, Cocos (Keeling) Islands et Norfolk Island.

Index
Historical index

Subject-matter	Year of issue	Time coverage	Subject-matter	Year of issue	Time coverage
				1976	1966-75
A					
Abortions, Legal	1971	Latest	**B**		
	1972	1964-72			
	1973	1965-73	**Bibliography**	1948	1930-48
	1974	1965-74		1949/50	1930-50
	1975	1965-74		1951-1952	1930-51[i]
	1976	1966-75		1953	1900-53
	1977	1967-76		1954	1900-54[i]
	1978	1968-77		1955	1900-55[i]
	1979	1969-78			
	1980	1971-79	**Births**	1948	1932-47
	1981	1972-80		1949/50	1934-49
	1982	1973-81		1951	1935-50
	1983	1974-82		1952	1936-51
	1984	1975-83		1953	1950-52
	1985	1976-84		1954	1938-53
	1986	1977-85		1955	1946-54
	1987	1978-86		1956	1947-55
	1988	1979-87		1957	1948-56
	1989	1980-88		1958	1948-57
	1990	1981-89		1959	1949-58
	1991	1982-90		1960	1950-59
	1992	1983-91		1961	1952-61
	1993	1984-92		1962	1953-62
	1994	1985-93		1963	1954-63
	1995	1986-94		1964	1960-64
	1996	1987-95		1965	1946-65
	1997	1988-96		1966	1957-66
	1998	1989-97		1967	1963-67
	1999	1990-98		1968	1964-68
	2000	1991-99		1969	1950-69
	2001	1993-01		1970	1966-70
	2002	1993-02		1971	1967-71
	2003	1994-03		1972	1968-72
	2004	1995-04		1973	1969-73
	2005	1996-05		1974	1970-74
	2006	1997-06		1975	1956-75
	2007	1998-07		1976	1972-76
				1977	1973-77
- by age of mother and number of previous live births of mother	1971-1975	Latest		1978	1974-78
	1977-1981	Latest		1978HS[ii]	1948-78
	1983-2007	Latest		1979	1975-79
				1980	1976-80
				1981	1962-81
				1982	1978-82
Ageing (see: Population)				1983	1979-83
Annulments	1958	1948-57		1984	1980-84
	1968	1958-67		1985	1981-85
	1976	1966-75		1986	1967-86
				1987	1983-87
				1988	1984-88
Annulment rates	1958	1948-57		1989	1985-89
	1968	1958-67		1990	1986-90

Subject-matter	Year of issue	Time coverage	Subject-matter	Year of issue	Time coverage
	1991	1987-91		1987-1991	Latest
	1992	1983-92		1992	1983-92
	1993	1989-93		1993-1997	Latest
	1994	1990-94		1997HS[iii] [3]	1948-96
	1995	1991-95		1998-99	Latest
	1996	1992-96		1999CD[iv]	1990-98
	1997	1993-97		2000-2007	Latest
	1997HS[iii]	1948-97			
	1998	1994-98	- by age of mother and birth order	1949/50	1936-47
	1999	1995-99		1954	Latest
	1999CD[iv]	1980-99		1959	1949-58
	2000	1996-00		1965	1955-64
	2001	1997-01		1969	1963-68
	2002	1998-02		1975	1966-74
	2003	1999-03		1981	1972-80
	2004	2000-04		1986	1977-85
	2005	2001-05		1999CD[iv]	1990-98
	2006	2002-06			
	2007	2003-07	- by age of mother and sex	1965-1968	Latest
				1969	1963-68
- by age of father	1949/50	1942-49		1970-1974	Latest
	1954	1936-53		1975	1966-74
	1959	1949-58		1976-1978	Latest
	1965	1955-64		1978HS[ii]	1948-77
	1969	1963-68		1979-1980	Latest
	1975	1966-74		1981	1972-80
	1981	1972-80		1982-1985	Latest
	1999CD[iv]	1990-98		1986	1977-85
	2007	latest		1987-1991	Latest
				1992	1983-92
- by age of mother	1948	1936-47		1993-1997	Latest
	1949/50	1936-49		1997HS[iii]	1948-96
	1954	1936-53		1998-99	Latest
	1955-1956	Latest		1999CD[iv]	1990-98
	1958	Latest		2000-2007	Latest
	1959	1949-58			
	1960-1964	Latest	- by age of mother and urban/rural residence (see: by urban/rural residence, below)		
	1965	1955-64			
	1966-1968	Latest			
	1969	1963-68			
	1970-1974	Latest			
	1975	1966-74	- by birth order	1948	1936-47
	1976-1978	Latest		1949/50	1936-49
	1978HS[ii]	1948-77		1954	1936-53
	1979-1980	Latest		1955	Latest
	1981	1972-80			
	1982-1985	Latest			
	1986	1977-85			

Index
Historical index
(See notes at end of index)

Subject-matter	Year of issue	Time coverage	Subject-matter	Year of issue	Time coverage
	1953	1936-52		2002	1998-02
	1954	1936-53		2003	1999-03
	1955	Latest		2004	2000-04
	1959	1949-58		2005	2001-05
	1965	1955-64		2006	2002-06
	1969	1963-68		2007	2003-07
	1975	1966-74			
	1981	1972-80	- by urban/rural residence and age of mother	1965	Latest
	1986	1977-85		1969	Latest
	1999CD[iv]	1990-98		1975	1966-74
				1976-1980	Latest
- by urban/rural residence	1965	Latest		1981	1972-80
	1967	Latest		1982-1985	Latest
	1968	1964-68		1986	1977-85
	1969	1964-68		1987-1991	Latest
	1970	1966-70		1992	1983-92
	1971	1967-71		1993-1997	Latest
	1972	1968-72		1997HS[iii]	1948-96
	1973	1969-73		1998-1999	Latest
	1974	1970-74		1999CD[iv]	1990-98
	1975	1956-75		2000-2006	Latest
	1976	1972-76			
	1977	1973-77	- estimated: for continents	1949/50	1947
	1978	1974-78		1956-1977	Latest
	1979	1975-79		1978-1979	1970-75
	1980	1976-80		1980-1983	1975-80
	1981	1962-81		1984-1986	1980-85
	1982	1978-82		1987-1992	1985-90
	1983	1979-83		1993-1997	1990-95
	1984	1980-84		1998-2000	1995-00
	1985	1981-85		2001-2005	2000-05
	1986	1967-86		2006-2007	2005-10
	1987	1983-87			
	1988	1984-88			
	1989	1985-89			
	1990	1986-90	for macro regions	1964-1977	Latest
	1991	1987-91		1978-1979	1970-75
	1992	1983-92		1980-1983	1975-80
	1993	1989-93		1984-1986	1980-85
	1994	1990-94		1987-1992	1985-90
	1995	1991-95		1993-1997	1990-95
	1996	1992-96		1998-2000	1995-00
	1997	1993-97		2001-2005	2000-05
	1998	1994-98		2006-2007	2005-10
	1999	1995-99			
	1999CD[iv]	1985-99	for regions	1949/1950	1947
	2000	1996-00		1956-1977	Latest
	2001	1997-01		1978-1979	1970-75

Index
Historical index
(See notes at end of index)

Subject-matter	Year of issue	Time coverage		Subject-matter	Year of issue	Time coverage
	1997HS[iii]	1948-96			1963	1954-63
					1964	1960-64
- ever born, by age of mother and urban/rural residence					1966	1947-66
					1967	1963-67
	1971	1962-71			1968	1964-68
	1973	1965-73			1969	1965-69
	1975	1965-74			1970	1966-70
	1981	1972-80			1971	1967-71
	1986	1977-85			1972	1968-72
	1997HS[iii]	1948-96			1973	1969-73
					1974	1965-74
- involved in divorces					1975	1971-75
	1958	1949-57			1976	1972-76
	1968	1958-67			1977	1973-77
	1976	1966-75			1978	1974-78
	1982	1972-81			1978HS[ii]	1948-78
	1990	1980-89			1979	1975-79
					1980	1971-80
- living, by age of mother					1981	1977-81
	1949/50	Latest			1982	1978-82
	1954	1930-53			1983	1979-83
	1955	1945-54			1984	1980-84
	1959	1949-58			1985	1976-85
	1963	1955-63			1986	1982-86
	1965	1955-65			1987	1983-87
	1968	1955-67			1988	1984-88
	1969	Latest			1989	1985-89
	1978HS[ii]	1948-77			1990	1986-90
	1997HS[iii]	1948-96			1991	1987-91
					1992	1983-92
- living, by age of mother and urban/rural residence					1993	1989-93
					1994	1990-94
	1971	1962-71			1995	1991-95
	1973	1965-73			1996	1987-96
	1975	1965-74			1997	1993-97
	1981	1972-80			1997HS[iii]	1948-97
	1986	1977-85			1998	1994-98
	1997HS[iii]	1948-96			1999	1995-99
					2000	1996-00
Cities (see: Population)					2001	1997-01
					2002	1998-02
D					2003	1999-03
					2004	2000-04
Deaths	1948	1932-47			2005	2001-05
	1949/50	1934-49			2006	2002-06
	1951	1935-50			2007	2003-07
	1952	1936-51				
	1953	1950-52				
	1954	1946-53				
	1955	1946-54		- by age and sex	1948	1936-47
	1956	1947-55			1951	1936-50
	1957	1940-56			1955-1956	Latest
	1958	1948-57			1957	1948-56
	1959	1949-58			1958-1960	Latest
	1960	1950-59			1961	1955-60
	1961	1952-61			1962-1965	Latest
	1962	1953-62				

Subject-matter	Year of issue	Time coverage	Subject-matter	Year of issue	Time coverage
	1966	1961-65		2006	2002-06
	1967-1973	Latest	- by cause, age and sex	1951	Latest
	1974	1965-73		1952	Latest
	1975-1979	Latest		1957	Latest
	1978HS[ii]	1948-77		1961	Latest
	1980	1971-79		1967	Latest
	1981-1984	Latest		1974	Latest
	1985	1976-84		1980	Latest
	1986-1991	Latest		1985	Latest
	1992	1983-92		1991PA[vii]	1960-90
	1993-1995	Latest		1996	Latest
	1996	1987-95	- by cause, age and sex and urban/rural residence	1967	Latest
	1997	Latest	- by cause and sex	1967	Latest
	1997HS[iii]	1948-96		1974	Latest
	1998-2007	Latest		1980	Latest
- by age and sex and urban/rural residence	1967-1973	Latest		1985	Latest
	1974	1965-73		1996	Latest
	1975-1979	Latest		2006	2002-06
	1980	1971-79	- by marital status, age and sex	1958	Latest
	1981-1984	Latest		1961	Latest
	1985	1976-84		1967	Latest
	1986-1991	Latest		1974	Latest
	1992	1983-92		1980	Latest
	1993-1995	Latest		1985	Latest
	1996	1987-95		1991PA[vii]	1950-90
	1997	Latest		1996	Latest
	1997HS[iii]	1948-96		2003	Latest
	1998-2006	Latest	- by month	1951	1946-50
- by cause	1951	1947-50		1967	1962-66
	1952	1947-51[vi]		1974	1965-73
	1953	Latest		1980	1971-79
	1954	1945-53		1985	1976-84
	1955-1956	Latest		2001	1985-00
	1957	1952-56		2005	2001-05
	1958-1960	Latest	- by occupation and age, males	1957	Latest
	1961	1955-60		1961	1957-60
	1962-1965	Latest		1967	1962-66
	1966	1960-65		1957	Latest
	1967-1973	Latest	- by type of certification and cause:		
	1974	1965-73	numbers	1957	Latest
	1975-1979	Latest		1974	1965-73
	1980	1971-79		1980	1971-79
	1981-1984	Latest		1985	1976-84
	1985	1976-84	percent	1957	Latest
	1986-1991	Latest		1961	1955-60
	1991PA[vii]	1960-90			
	1992-1995	Latest			
	1996	1987-95			
	1997-2000	Latest			
	2002	1995-02			
	2004	1995-04			

Subject-matter	Year of issue	Time coverage	Subject-matter	Year of issue	Time coverage
	1998	1994-98	- by cause	1951	1947-49
	1999	1995-99		1952	1947-51[vi]
	2000	1996-00		1953	1947-52
	2001	1997-01		1954	1945-53
	2002	1998-02		1955-1956	Latest
	2003	1999-03		1957	1952-56
	2004	2000-04		1958-1960	Latest
	2005	2001-05		1961	1955-60
	2006	2002-06		1962-1965	Latest
	2007	2003-07		1966	1960-65
				1967-1973	Latest
- by age and sex	1948	1935-47		1974	1965-73
	1949/50	1936-49		1975-1979	Latest
	1951	1936-50		1980	1971-79
	1952	1936-51		1981-1984	Latest
	1953	1940-52		1985	1976-84
	1954	1946-53		1986-1991	Latest
	1955-1956	Latest		1991PA[vii]	1960-90
	1957	1948-56		1992-1995	Latest
	1961	1952-60		1996	1987-95
	1966	1950-65		1997-2000	Latest
	1972	Latest		2002	1995-02
	1974	1965-73		2004	1995-04
	1975-1979	Latest		2006	2002-06
	1978HS[ii]	1948-77			
	1980	1971-79	- by cause, age and sex	1957	Latest
	1981-1984	Latest			
	1985	1976-84		1961	Latest
	1986-1991	Latest		1991PA[vii]	1960-90
	1991PA[vii]	1950-1990			
	1992	1983-1992	- by cause and sex	1967	Latest
	1993-1995	Latest		1974	Latest
	1996	1987-95		1980	Latest
	1997	Latest		1985	Latest
	1997HS[iii]	1948-96		1996	Latest
	1998-2007	Latest		2006	2002-06
- by age and sex and urban/rural residence	1967	Latest	- by marital status, age and sex	1961	Latest
	1972	Latest		1967	Latest
	1974	1965-73		1974	Latest
	1975-1979	Latest		1980	Latest
	1980	1971-79		1985	Latest
	1981-1984	Latest		1996	Latest
	1985	1976-84			
	1986-1991	Latest	- by occupation, age and sex	1957	Latest
	1991PA[vii]	1950-1990			
	1992	1983-1992	- by occupation and age, males	1961	Latest
	1993-1995	Latest		1967	Latest
	1996	1987-95	- by urban/rural residence	1967	Latest
	1997	Latest		1968	1964-68
	1997HS[iii]	1948-96		1969	1965-69
	1998-2007	Latest		1970	1966-70
				1971	1967-71

Subject-matter	Year of issue	Time coverage	Subject-matter	Year of issue	Time coverage
	1972	1968-72		1980-1983	1975-80
	1973	1969-73		1984-1986	1980-85
	1974	1965-74		1984-1986	1980-85
	1975	1971-75		1987-1992	1985-90
	1976	1972-76		1993-1997	1990-95
	1977	1973-77		1998-2000	1995-00
	1978	1974-78		2001-2005	2000-05
	1979	1975-79		2006-2007	2005-10
	1980	1971-80			
	1981	1977-81	for macro regions	1964-1977	Latest
	1982	1978-82		1978-1979	1970-75
	1983	1979-83		1980-1983	1975-80
	1984	1980-84		1984-1986	1980-85
	1985	1976-85		1987-1992	1985-90
	1986	1982-86		1993-1997	1990-95
	1987	1983-87		1998-2000	1995-00
	1988	1984-88		2001-2005	2000-05
	1989	1985-89		2006-2007	2005-10
	1990	1986-90			
	1991	1987-91	for regions	1949/50	1947
	1992	1983-92		1956-1977	Latest
	1993	1989-93		1978-1979	1970-75
	1994	1990-94		1980-1983	1975-80
	1995	1991-95		1984-1986	1980-85
	1996	1987-96		1987-1992	1985-90
	1997	1993-97		1993-1997	1990-95
	1998	1994-98		1998-2000	1995-00
	1999	1995-99		2001-2005	2000-05
	1987	1983-87		2006-2007	2005-10
	1988	1984-88			
	1989	1985-89	for the world	1949/50	1947
	1990	1986-90		1956-1977	Latest
	1991	1987-91		1978-1979	1970-75
	1992	1983-92		1980-1983	1975-80
	1993	1989-93		1984-1986	1980-85
	1994	1990-94		1987-1992	1985-90
	1995	1991-95		1993-1997	1990-95
	1996	1987-96		1998-2000	1995-00
	1997	1993-97		2001-2005	2000-05
	1998	1994-98		2006-2007	2005-10
	1999	1995-99			
	2000	1996-00	- of infants (see: Infant deaths)		
	2001	1997-01			
	2002	1998-02	**Density of population**:		
	2003	1999-03	- of continents	1949/50	1920-49
	2004	2000-04		1951-1999	Latest
	2005	2001-05		2000	2000
	2006	2002-06		2001	2001
	2007	2003-07		2002	2002
				2003	2003
- estimated for continents	1949/50	1947		2004	2004
	1956-1977	Latest		2005	2005
	1978-1979	1970-75		2006	2006

Subject-matter	Year of issue	Time coverage		Subject-matter	Year of issue	Time coverage
- by age of mother	1954	1936-53			1987	1982-86
	1959	1949-58			1988	1983-87
	1965	1955-64			1989	1984-88
	1969	1963-68			1990	1985-89
	1975	1966-74			1991	1986-90
	1981	1972-80			1992	1987-91
	1986	1977-85			1993	1988-92
- by age of mother and birth order	1954	Latest			1994	1989-93
	1959	1949-58			1995	1990-94
	1965	3-Latest			1996	1987-95
	1969	1963-68			1997	1992-96
	1975	1966-74			1998	1993-97
	1981	1972-80			1999	1994-98
	1986	1977-85			1999CD[iv]	1990-98
- by period of gestation	1957	1950-56			2000	1995-99
	1959	1949-58			2001	1997-01
	1961	1952-60			2002	1998-02
	1965	5-Latest			2003	1999-03
	1966	1956-65			2004	2000-04
	1967-1968	Latest			2005	2001-05
	1969	1963-68			2006	2002-06
	1974	1965-73			2007	2003-07
	1975	1966-74		- illegitimate	1961	1952-60
	1980	1971-79			1965	5-Latest
	1981	1972-80			1969	1963-68
	1985	1976-84			1975	1966-74
	1986	1977-85			1981	1972-80
	1996	1987-95			1986	1977-85
- by sex	1961	1952-60		- illegitimate, percent		
	1965	5 Latest			1961	1952-60
	1969	1963-68			1965	5-Latest
	1975	1966-74			1969	1963-68
	1981	1972-80			1975	1966-74
	1986	1977-85			1981	1972-80
- by urban/rural residence					1986	1977-85
	1971	1966-70		- legitimate	1959	1949-58
	1972	1967-71			1965	1955-64
	1973	1968-72			1969	1963-68
	1974	1965-73			1975	1966-74
	1975	1966-74			1981	1972-80
	1976	1971-75			1986	1977-85
	1977	1972-76		- legitimate by age of mother	1959	1949-58
	1978	1973-77			1965	1955-64
	1979	1974-78			1969	1963-68
	1980	1971-79			1975	1966-74
	1981	1972-80			1981	1972-80
	1982	1977-81			1986	1977-85
	1983	1978-82				
	1984	1979-83				
	1985	1975-84				
	1986	1977-85				

Index
Historical index
(See notes at end of index)

Subject-matter	Year of issue	Time coverage	Subject-matter	Year of issue	Time coverage
	1986-1991	Latest		1994	1990-94
	1992	1983-92		1995	1991-95
	1993-1995	Latest		1996	1987-96
	1996	1987-95		1997	1993-97
	1997-2004	Latest		1998	1994-98
	2005	1996-05		1999	1995-99
	2006	Latest		2000	1996-00
	2007	Latest		2001	1997-01
				2002	1998-02
- by age and sex and urban/rural residence				2003	1999-03
	1967-1973	Latest		2004	2000-04
	1974	1965-73		2005	2001-05
	1975-1979	Latest		2006	2002-06
	1980	1971-79		2007	2003-07
	1981-1984	Latest			
	1985	1976-84	Infant mortality rates..............	1948	1932-47
	1986-1991	Latest		1949/50	1932-49
	1992	1983-92		1951	1930-50
	1993-1995	Latest		1952	1920-34[v]
	1996	1987-95			1934-51
	1997-1999	Latest		1953	1920-39[v]
					1940-52
- by month	1967	1962-66		1954	1920-39[v]
	1974	1965-73			1946-53
	1980	1971-79		1955	1920-34[v]
	1985	1976-84			1946-54
				1956	1947-55
- by urban/rural residence	1967	Latest		1957	1948-56
	1968	1964-68		1958	1948-57
	1969	1965-69		1959	1949-58
	1970	1966-70		1960	1950-59
	1971	1967-71		1961	1945-59[v]
	1972	1968-72			1952-61
	1973	1969-73		1962	1945-54[v]
	1974	1965-74			1952-62
	1975	1971-75		1963	1945-59[v]
	1976	1972-76		1963	1954-63
	1977	1973-77		1964	1960-64
	1978	1974-78		1965	1961-65
	1979	1975-79		1966	1920-64[v]
	1980	1971-80			1951-66
	1981	1977-81		1967	1963-67
	1982	1978-82		1968	1964-68
	1983	1979-83		1969	1965-69
	1984	1980-84		1970	1966-70
	1985	1976-85		1971	1967-71
	1986	1982-86		1972	1968-72
	1987	1983-87		1973	1969-73
	1988	1984-88		1974	1965-74
	1989	1985-89		1975	1971-75
	1990	1986-90		1976	1972-76
	1991	1987-91		1977	1973-77
	1992	1983-92		1978	1974-78
	1993	1989-93		1978HS[ii]	1948-78

Index
Historical index
(See notes at end of index)

Subject-matter	Year of issue	Time coverage	Subject-matter	Year of issue	Time coverage
	1982	1972-81		1976	Latest
	1983-1986	Latest		1982	Latest
	1987	1975-86		1990	Latest
	1988-1989	Latest	and previous		
	1990	1980-1989	marital status		
	1990-1997	Latest	of bride	1949/50	Latest
	1998	1993-97		1958	1948-57
	1999	1994-98		1968	1958-67
	2000	1995-99		1976	1966-75
	2001	1997-01		1982	1972-81
	2002	1998-02		1990	1980-89
	2003	1999-03	-by urban/rural		
	2004	2000-04	residence	1968	Latest
	2005	2001-05		1969	1965-69
	2006-2007	Latest		1970	1966-70
				1971	1967-71
- by age of				1972	1968-72
groom				1973	1969-73
classified by age				1974	1970-74
of bride	1958	1948-57		1975	1971-75
	1968	Latest		1976	1957-76
	1976	Latest		1977	1973-77
	1982	Latest		1978	1974-78
	1990	Latest		1979	1975-79
	2006-2007	Latest		1980	1976-80
				1981	1977-81
- by age of groom	1958	1948-57		1982	1963-82
and previous				1983	1979-83
marital status				1984	1980-84
	1968	Latest		1985	1981-85
	1976	Latest		1986	1982-86
	1982	Latest		1987	1983-87
	1990	Latest		1988	1984-88
				1989	1985-89
- by month	1968	1963-67		1990	1971-90
				1991	1987-91
- by previous				1992	1988-92
marital status of				1993	1989-93
bride:				1994	1990-94
and age	1958	1946-57		1995	1991-95
	1968	Latest		1996	1992-96
	1976	Latest		1997	1993-97
	1982	Latest		1998	1994-98
	1990	Latest		1999	1995-99
and previous				2000	1996-00
marital status				2001	1997-01
of groom	1949/50	Latest		2002	1998-02
	1958	1948-57		2003	1999-03
	1968	1958-67		2004	2000-04
	1976	1966-75		2005	2001-05
	1982	1972-81		2006	2002-06
	1990	1980-89		2007	2003-07
- by previous					
marital status					
of groom:					
and age	1958	1946-57	**Marriage, first**		
	1968	Latest			

Subject-matter	Year of issue	Time coverage	Subject-matter	Year of issue	Time coverage
	1989	1975-88		1951	1936-50
by country or area of last				1957	1948-56
residence	1948	1945-47		1961	1952-60
	1949/50	1945-48		1963-1965	Latest
	1951	1948-50		1966	1961-65
	1952	1949-51		1967	1962-66
	1954	1950-53		2000-2004	Latest
	1957	1953-56			
	1959	1956-58	- by sex and urban/rural		
	1977	1958-76	residence	1968-1973	Latest
	1989	1975-88		1974	1965-73
	1948	1945-47		1975-1979	Latest
	1949/50	1945-48		1980	1971-79
				1981-1984	Latest
- refugees, by country or area of destination:				1985	1976-84
				1986-1991	Latest
repatriated by the International Refugee				1992	1983-92
				1993-1995	Latest
				1996	1987-95
Organization	1952	1947-51		1997	Latest
				1997HS[iii]	1948-96
resettled by the International Refugee				1998-1999	Latest
			Neo-natal mortality rates		
Organization	1952	1947-51	- by sex	1948	1936-47
				1951	1936-50
Mortality [see: Death(s), Death rates, infant deaths, infant mortality rates, Foetal death(s), Foetal death ratios, Life tables, Maternal deaths, Maternal mortality rates, Neo-natal deaths, Neo-natal mortality rates, Perinatal mortality, Post-neo-natal deaths, Post-neo-natal mortality rates]				1957	1948-56
				1961	1952-60
				1966	1956-65
				1967	1962-66
				2000-2004	Latest
			- by sex and urban/rural		
			residence	1971-1973	Latest
				1974	1965-73
				1975-1979	Latest
				1980	1971-79
				1981-1984	Latest
Natality (see: Births and Birthrates)				1985	1976-84
				1986-1991	Latest
Natural increase rates	1958-1978	Latest		1992	1983-92
	1978HS[ii]	1948-78		1993-1995	Latest
	1979-1997	Latest		1996	1987-95
	1998	1995-98		1997	Latest
	1999	1996-99		1997HS[iii]	1948-96
	2000	1995-00		1998-1999	Latest
	2001-2005	2000-05			
	2006-2007	2005-10	**Net reproduction rates** (see: Reproduction rates)		
Neo-natal mortality			**Nuptiality** (see: Marriages)		
- by sex	1948	1936-47			

Subject-matter	Year of issue	Time coverage	Subject-matter	Year of issue	Time coverage
by age and sex, per cent	1949/50	1930-48	by occupation, age and sex and urban/rural residence		
	1954	Latest		1973	1965-73[vi]
	1955	1945-54		1979	1970-79[vi]
	1956	1945-55		1984	1974-84
	1964	1955-64		1988	1980-88[vi]
	1972	1962-72		1994	1985-94
by age and sex, per cent and urban/rural residence			by occupation, status and sex		
	1973	1965-73[vi]		1956	1945-55
	1979	1970-79[vi]		1964	1955-64
	1984	1974-84		1972	1962-72
	1988	1980-88[vi]	by occupation, status and sex and urban/rural residence		
	1994	1985-94			
by industry, age and sex	1956	1945-55		1973	1965-73[vi]
	1964	1955-64		1979	1970-7vi[vi]
	1972	1962-72		1984	1974-84
by industry, age, sex and urban/rural residence				1988	1980-88[vi]
				1994	1985-94
	1973	1965-74[vi]	by sex	1948	Latest
	1979	1970-79[vi]		1949/50	1926-48
	1984	1974-84		1955	1945-54
	1988	1980-88[vi]		1956	1945-55
	1994	1985-94		1960	1920-60
by industry, status and sex				1963	1955-63
	1948	Latest		1964	1955-64
	1949/50	Latest		1970	1950-70
	1955	1945-54		1972	1962-72
	1964	1955-64		1973	1965-73[vi]
	1972	1962-72		1979	1970-79[vi]
by industry, status and sex and urban/rural residence				1984	1974-84
				1994	1985-94
	1973	1965-73[vi]	by status, age and sex		
	1979	1970-79[vi]		1956	1945-55
	1984	1974-84		1964	1955-64
	1988	1980-88[vi]		1972	1962-72
	1994	1985-94	by status, age and sex and urban/rural residence		
by living arrangements, age, sex and urban/rural residence					
	1987	1975-86		1973	1965-73[vi]
	1995	1985-95		1979	1970-79[vi]
by occupation, age and sex				1984	1974-84
				1988	1980-88[vi]
	1956	1945-55		1994	1985-94
	1964	1955-64	by status, industry and sex		
	1972	1962-72		1948	Latest

Subject-matter	Year of issue	Time coverage	Subject-matter	Year of issue	Time coverage
	1949/50	Latest	unemployed, by age and sex		
	1955	1945-54			
	1964	1955-64		1949/50	1946-49
	1972	1962-72	- economically inactive by sub-groups and sex		
by status, industry, and sex and urban/rural residence				1956	1945-54
				1964	1955-64
				1972	1962-72
	1973	1965-73[vi]		1973	1965-73[vi]
	1979	1970-79[vi]		1979	1970-79[vi]
	1984	1974-84		1984	1974-84[vi]
	1988	1980-88[vi]		1988	1980-88[vi]
	1994	1985-94		1994	1985-94
by status, occupation and sex			- Elderly		
			- by economic, socio-demographic and urban/rural		
	1956	1945-55		1991PA[vii]	1950-90
	1964	1955-64	-female:		
	1972	1962-72	by age and duration of marriage	1968	Latest
by status, occupation and sex and urban/rural residence			by number of children born alive and age		
	1973	1965-73[vi]		1949/50	Latest
	1979	1970-79[vi]		1954	1930-53
	1984	1974-84		1955	1945-54
	1988	1980-88[vi]		1959	1949-58
	1994	1985-94		1963	1955-63
female, by marital status and age				1965	1955-65
				1969	Latest
	1956	1945-55		1971	1962-71
	1964	1955-64		1973	1965-73[vi]
	1968	Latest		1975	1965-74
	1972	1962-72		1978HS[ii]	1948-77
female, by marital status and age and urban/rural residence				1981	1972-80
				1986	1977-85
				1997HS[iii]	1948-96
	1973	1965-73[vi]	by number of children living and age		
	1979	1970-79[vi]			
	1984	1974-84		1949/50	Latest
	1988	1980-88[vi]		1954	1930-53
	1994	1985-94		1955	1945-54
foreign-born by occupation, age and sex (see also: country of birth above)				1959	1949-58
				1963	1955-63
				1965	1955-65
	1984	1974-84		1968-1969	Latest
		1980-88		1971	1962-71
	1994	1985-94		1973	1965-73[vi]
foreign-born by occupation and sex (see also: country of birth above)				1975	1965-74
				1978HS[ii]	1948-77
	1977	Latest		1981	1972-80
				1986	1977-85
				1997HS[iii]	1948-96

Index
Historical index
(See notes at end of index)

Subject-matter	Year of issue	Time coverage		Subject-matter	Year of issue	Time coverage
	1960	1920-60			1949/50	1900-50
	1970	1950-70			1951	1900-51
- married female by percentage and duration of marriage	1968	Latest			1952	1850-1952
					1953	1850-1953
					1954	Latest
- never married proportion by sex, selected ages	1976	1966-75			1955	1850-1954
	1978HS[ii]	1948-77			1956-1961	Latest
	1982	1972-81			1962	1900-62
	1990	1980-89			1963	Latest
- not economically active	1972	1962-72			1964	1955-64
					1965-1978	Latest
					1978HS[ii]	1948-78
- not economically active by urban/rural residence	1973	1965-73[vi]			1979-1997	Latest
	1979	1970-79[vi]			1997HS[iii]	1948-97
	1984	1974-84			1998-2007	Latest
	1988	1980-88[vi]		estimated	1948	1932-47
	1994	1985-94			1949/50	1932-49
- of cities:					1951	1930-50
capital city	1952	Latest			1952	1920-51
	1955	1945-54			1953	1920-53
	1957	Latest			1954	1920-54
	1960	1939-61			1955	1920-55
	1962	1955-62			1956	1920-56
	1963	1955-63			1957	1940-57
	1964-1969	Latest			1958	1939-58
	1970	1950-70			1959	1940-59
	1971	1962-71			1960	1920-60
	1972	Latest			1961	1941-61
	1973	1965-73			1962	1942-62
	1974-2007	Latest			1963	1943-63
					1964	1955-64
of 100000+ inhabitants	1952	Latest			1965	1946-65
	1955	1945-54			1966	1947-66
	1957	Latest			1967	1958-67
	1960	1939-61			1968	1959-68
	1962	1955-62			1969	1960-69
	1963	1955-63			1970	1950-70
	1964-1969	Latest			1971	1962-71
	1970	1950-70			1972	1963-72
	1971	1962-71			1973	1964-73
	1972	Latest			1974	1965-74
	1973	1965-73			1975	1966-75
	1974-2007	Latest			1976	1967-76
- of continents (see: of macro regions, below)					1977	1968-77
- of countries or areas (totals):					1978	1969-78
enumerated	1948	1900-48			1978HS[ii]	1948-78
					1979	1970-79
					1980	1971-80
					1981	1972-81
					1982	1973-82
					1983	1974-83
					1984	1975-84
					1985	1976-85

Subject-matter	Year of issue	Time coverage
	1986	1977-86
	1987	1978-87
	1988	1979-88
	1989	1980-89
	1990	1981-90
	1991	1982-91
	1992	1983-92
	1993	1984-93
	1994	1985-94
	1995	1986-95
	1996	1987-96
	1997	1988-97
	1997HS[iii]	1948-97
	1998	1989-98
	1999	1990-99
	2000	1991-00
	2001	1992-01
	2002	1993-02
	2003	1994-03
	2004	1995-04
	2005	1996-05
	2006	1997-06
	2007	1998-07
- of major regions	1949/50	1920-49
	1951	1950
	1952	1920-51
	1953	1920-52
	1954	1920-53
	1955	1920-54
	1956	1920-55
	1957	1920-56
	1958	1920-57
	1959	1920-58
	1960	1920-59
	1961	1920-60
	1962	1920-61
	1963	1930-62
	1964	1930-63
	1965	1930-65
	1966	1930-66
	1967	1930-67
	1968	1930-68
	1969	1930-69
	1970	1950-70
	1971	1950-71
	1972	1950-72
	1973	1950-73
	1974	1950-74
	1975	1950-75
	1976	1950-76
	1977	1950-77
	1978	1950-78
	1979	1950-79

Subject-matter	Year of issue	Time coverage
	1980	1950-80
	1981	1950-81
	1982	1950-82
	1983	1950-83
	1984	1950-84
	1985	1950-85
	1986	1950-86
	1987	1950-87
	1988	1950-88
	1989	1950-89
	1990	1950-90
	1991	1950-91
	1992	1950-92
	1993	1950-93
	1994	1950-94
	1995	1950-95
	1996	1950-96
	1997	1950-97
	1998-1999	1950-00
	2000	1950-00
	2001	1950-01
	2002	1950-02
	2003	1950-03
	2004	1950-04
	2005	1950-05
	2006	1950-06
	2007	1950-07
- of regions	1949/50	1920-49
	1952	1920-51
	1953	1920-52
	1954	1920-53
	1955	1920-54
	1956	1920-55
	1957	1920-56
	1958	1920-57
	1959	1920-58
	1960	1920-59
	1961	1920-60
	1962	1920-61
	1963	1930-62
	1964	1930-63
	1965	1930-65
	1966	1930-66
	1967	1930-67
	1968	1930-68
	1969	1930-69
	1970	1950-70
	1971	1950-71
	1972	1950-72
	1973	1950-73
	1974	1950-74
	1975	1950-75
	1976	1950-76

Subject-matter	Year of issue	Time coverage	Subject-matter	Year of issue	Time coverage
	1977	1950-77		1973	1950-73
	1978	1950-78		1974	1950-74
	1979	1950-79		1975	1950-75
	1980	1950-80		1976	1950-76
	1981	1950-81		1977	1950-77
	1982	1950-82		1978	1950-78
	1983	1950-83		1979	1950-79
	1984	1950-84		1980	1950-80
	1985	1950-85		1981	1950-81
	1986	1950-86		1982	1950-82
	1987	1950-87		1983	1950-83
	1988	1950-88		1984	1950-84
	1989	1950-89		1985	1950-85
	1990	1950-90		1986	1950-86
	1991	1950-91		1987	1950-87
	1992	1950-92		1988	1950-88
	1993	1950-93		1989	1950-89
	1994	1950-94		1990	1950-90
	1995	1950-95		1991	1950-91
	1996	1950-96		1992	1950-92
	1997	1950-97		1993	1950-93
	1998-1999	1950-00		1994	1950-94
	2000	1950-00		1995	1950-95
	2001	1950-01		1996	1950-96
	2002	1950-02		1997	1950-97
	2003	1950-03		1998-1999	1950-00
	2004	1950-04		2000	1950-00
	2005	1950-05		2001	1950-01
	2006	1950-06		2002	1950-02
	2007	1950-07		2003	1950-03
				2004	1950-04
- of the world	1949/50	1920-49		2005	1950-05
	1951	1950		2006	1950-06
	1952	1920-51		2007	1950-07
	1953	1920-52			
	1954	1920-53	- rural residence (see: urban/rural residence, below)		
	1955	1920-54			
	1956	1920-55			
	1957	1920-56	- single, by age and sex (see also: by marital status, above):		
	1958	1920-57			
	1959	1920-58			
	1960	1920-59			
	1961	1920-60	numbers	1960	1920-60
	1962	1920-61		1970	1950-70
	1963	1930-62	percent	1949/50	1926-48
	1964	1930-63		1960	1920-60
	1965	1930-65		1970	1950-70
	1966	1930-66	- urban/rural residence		
	1967	1930-67		1968	1964-68
	1968	1930-68		1969	1965-69
	1969	1930-69		1970	1950-70
	1970	1950-70		1971	1962-71
	1971	1950-71		1972	1968-72
	1972	1950-72		1973	1965-73
				1974	1966-74

Subject-matter	Year of issue	Time coverage	Subject-matter	Year of issue	Time coverage
	1975	1967-75		1998-07	Latest
	1976	1967-76	by country or area of birth and sex		
	1977	1968-77		1971	1962-71
	1978	1969-78		1973	1965-73[vi]
	1979	1970-79	by country or area of birth and sex and age		
	1980	1971-80		1977	Latest
	1981	1972-81			
	1982	1973-82	by citizenship and sex		
	1983	1974-83		1971	1962-71
	1984	1975-84		1973	1965-73[vi]
	1985	1976-85	by citizenship and sex and age		
	1986	1977-86		1977	Latest
	1987	1978-87		1983	1974-83
	1988	1979-88		1989	1980-88
	1989	1980-89	by ethnic composition and sex		
	1990	1981-90		1971	Latest
	1991	1982-91		1973	1965-73[vi]
	1992	1983-92		1979	1970-79[vi]
	1993	1984-93		1983	1974-83
	1994	1985-94		1988	1980-88[vi]
	1995	1986-95		1993	1985-93
	1996	1987-96	by households, number and size (see also: Households)		
	1997	1988-97		1968	Latest
	1998	1989-98		1971	1962-71
	1999	1990-99		1973	1965-73[vi]
	2000	1991-00		1976	Latest
	2001	1992-01		1982	Latest
	2002	1993-02		1987	1975-86
	2003	1994-03		1990	1980-89
	2004	1995-04		1995	1985-95
	2005	1996-05	by language and sex	1971	1962-71
	2006	1997-06		1973	1965-73[vi]
	2007	1998-07		1979	1970-79[vi]
by age and sex:				1983	1974-83
enumerated	1963	1955-63		1988	1980-88[vi]
	1964	1955-64[vi]		1993	1985-93
	1967	Latest	by level of education, age and sex		
	1970	1950-70		1971	1962-71
	1971	1962-71		1973	1965-73[vi]
	1972	Latest		1979	1970-79[vi]
	1973	1965-73		1983	1974-83
	1974-1978	Latest		1988	1980-88[vi]
	1978HS[ii]	1948-77		1993	1985-93
	1979-1996	Latest	by literacy, age and sex		
	1979-1997	Latest		1971	1962-71
	1997HS[iii]	1948-96		1973	1965-73[vi]
	1998-2007	Latest		1979	1970-79[vi]
estimated	1963	Latest			
	1967	Latest			
	1970	1950-70			
	1971-1997	Latest			
	1997HS[iii]	1948-96			

R

Rates (see under following subject-matter headings: Annulments, Births, Deaths, Divorces, Fertility, Illiteracy, Infant Mortality, Intercensal, Life Tables, Literacy Marriages, Maternal mortality, Natural increase, Neo-natal mortality, Population growth, Post-neo-natal mortality, Reproduction)

Ratios (see under following subject matter headings: Births, Child-woman, Fertility, Foetal deaths, Perinatal mortality)

Subject-matter	Year of issue	Time coverage
Survivors (see: Life tables)		
T		
Text (see separate listing in Appendix to this Index)		
Topic of each Demographic Yearbook		
- Divorce (see: Marriage and Divorce, below)		
- General demography	1948	1900-48
	1953	1850-1953
- Historical Supplement	1978HS[ii]	1948-78
	1997HS[iii]	1948-97
- Marriage and Divorce	1958	1930-57
	1968	1920-68
	1976	1957-76
	1982	1963-82
	1990	1971-90
- Migration (international)	1977	1958-76
	1989	1975-88
- Mortality	1951	1905-50
	1957	1930-56
	1961	1945-61
	1966	1920-66
	1967	1900-67
	1974	1965-74
	1980	1971-80
	1985	1976-85
	1992	1983-92
	1996	1987-96
- Natality	1949/50	1932-49
	1954	1920-53
	1959	1920-58
	1965	1920-65
	1969	1925-69
	1975	1956-75
	1981	1962-81
	1986	1967-86
	1992	1983-92
	1999CD[iv]	1980-99
- Nuptiality (see: Marriage and Divorce, above)		

Subject-matter	Year of issue	Time coverage
- Population Ageing and the Situation of Elderly Persons	1991PA[vii]	1950-90
- Population Census:		
Economic characteristics	1956	1945-55
	1964	1955-64
	1972	1962-72
	1973	1965-73[vi]
	1979	1970-79[vi]
	1984	1974-84
	1988	1980-88[vi]
	1994	1985-94
Educational characteristics	1955	1945-54
	1956	1945-55
	1963	1955-63
	1964	1955-64[vi]
	1971	1962-71
	1973	1965-73[vi]
	1979	1970-79[vi]
	1983	1974-83
	1988	1980-88[vi]
	1993	1985-93
Ethnic characteristics	1956	1945-55
	1963	1955-63
	1964	1955-64[vi]
	1971	1962-71
	1973	1965-73[vi]
	1979	1970-79[vi]
	1983	1974-83
	1988	1980-88[vi]
	1993	1985-93
Fertility characteristics	1940/50	1900-50
	1954	1900-53
	1955	1945-54
	1959	1935-59
	1963	1955-63
	1965	1955-65
	1969	Latest
	1971	1962-71
	1973	1965-73[vi]
	1975	1965-75
	1981	1972-81
	1986	1977-86
	1992	1983-92
Geographic characteristics	1952	1900-51
	1955	1945-54
	1962	1955-62
	1964	1955-64[vi]
	1971	1962-71

APPENDIX

Special text of each Demographic Yearbook:

Divorce:

'Uses of Marriage and Divorce Statistics', 1958.

Marriage:

'Uses of Marriage and Divorce Statistics', 1958.

Households:

'Concepts and definitions of households, householder and institutional population', 1987.

Migration:

'Statistics of International Migration', 1977.

Mortality:

'Recent Mortality Trends', 1951.
'Development of Statistics of Causes of Death', 1951.
'Factors in Declining Mortality', 1957.
'Notes on Methods of Evaluating the Reliability of Conventional Mortality Statistics', 1961.
'Recent Trends of Mortality', 1966.
'Mortality Trends among Elderly Persons', 1991PA[vii].

Natality:

'Graphic Presentation of Trends in Fertility', 1959.
'Recent Trends in Birth Rates', 1965.
'Recent Changes in World Fertility', 1969.

Population

'World Population Trends, 1920-1949', 1949/50.
'Urban Trends and Characteristics', 1952.
'Background to the1950 Censuses of Population', 1955.
'The World Demographic Situation', 1956.
'How Well Do We Know the Present Size and Trend of the World's Population?', 1960.
'Notes on Availability of National Population Census Data and Methods of Estimating their Reliability', 1962.
'Availability and Adequacy of Selected Data Obtained from Population Censuses Taken 1955-1963', 1963.
'Availability of Selected Population Census Statistics: 1955-1964', 1964.
'Statistical Concepts and Definitions of Urban and Rural Population', 1967.
'Statistical Concepts and Definitions of Household', 1968.
'How Well Do We Know the Present Size and Trend of the World's Population?', 1970.
'United Nations Recommendations on Topics to be Investigated in a Population Census Compared with Country Practice in National Censuses taken 1965-1971', 1971.
'Statistical Definitions of Urban Population and their Use in Applied Demography', 1972.
'Dates of National Population and Housing Census carried out during the decade1965-1974', 1974.
'Dates of National Population and/or Housing Censuses taken or anticipated during the decade 1975-1984', 1979.
'Dates of National Population and/or Housing Censuses taken during the decade1965-1974 and taken or anticipated during the decade 1975-1984', 1983.
'Dates of National Population and/or Housing Censuses taken during the decade1975-1984 and taken or anticipated during the decade 1985-1994', 1988 and 1993.
'Statistics Concerning the Economically Active Population: An Overview', 1984.

'Disability', 1991PA[vii].
'Population Ageing', 1991PA[vii].
'Special Needs for the Study of Population Ageing and Elderly Persons', 1991PA[vii].

General Notes

This cumulative index covers the contents of each of the 59 issues of the Demographic Yearbook. 'Year of issue' stands for the particular issue in which the indicated subject-matter appears. Unless otherwise specified, 'Time coverage' designates the years for which annual statistics are shown in the Demographic Yearbook referred to in 'Year of issue' column. 'Latest' or '2-Latest' indicates that data are for latest available year(s) only.

---

[i] Only titles not available for preceding bibliography.

[ii] Historical Supplement to the 30th DYB published in a separate volume in year 1979.

[iii] Historical Supplement to the 49th DYB published in a separate volume (CD-ROM) in year 2000.

[iv] Supplement to the 51st DYB focusing on natality published in a separate volume (CD-ROM) in year 2002.

[v] Five-year average rates.

[vi] Only data not available for preceding issue.

[vii] Population ageing published in separate volume.

Index
Index historique (suite)
(Voir notes à la fin de l'index)

Index
Index historique (suite)
(Voir notes à la fin de l'index)

Sujet	Année de l'édition	Période considérée
	1954	1900-54 [iv]
	1955	1900-55 [iv]

C

Cause de décès (voir: Décès)

Chômeurs (voir: Population)

Composition ethnique (voir: Population)

Sujet	Année de l'édition	Période considérée
Décès	1948	1932-47
	1949/50	1934-49
	1951	1935-50
	1952	1936-51
	1953	1950-52
	1954	1946-53
	1955	1946-54
	1956	1947-55
	1957	1940-56
	1958	1948-57
	1959	1949-58
	1960	1950-59
	1961	1952-61
	1962	1953-62
	1963	1954-63
	1964	1960-64
	1965	1961-65
	1966	1947-66
	1967	1963-67
	1968	1964-68
	1969	1965-69
	1970	1966-70
	1971	1967-71
	1972	1968-72
	1973	1969-73
	1974	1965-74
	1975	1971-75
	1976	1972-76
	1977	1973-77
	1978	1974-78
	1978SR [i]	1948-78
	1979	1975-79
	1980	1971-80
	1981	1977-81
	1982	1978-82
	1983	1979-83
	1984	1980-84
	1985	1976-85
	1986	1982-86
	1987	1983-87
	1988	1984-88
	1989	1985-89
	1990	1986-90
	1991	1987-91
	1992	1983-92
	1993	1989-93
	1994	1990-94
	1995	1991-95
	1996	1987-96

Sujet	Année de l'édition	Période considérée
	1997	1993-97
	1997SR [ii]	1948-97
	1998	1994-98
	1999	1995-99
	2000	1996-00
	2001	1997-01
	2002	1998-02
	2003	1999-03
	2004	2000-04
	2005	2001-05
	2006	2002-06
	2007	2003-07
-d'enfants de moins d'un an (voir: Mortalité infantile)		
-selon l'âge et le sexe	1948	1936-47
	1951	1936-50
	1955-1956	Dernière
	1957	1948-56
	1958-1960	Dernière
	1961	1955-60
	1962-1965	Dernière
	1966	1961-65
	1967-1973	Dernière
	1974	1965-73
	1975-1979	Dernière
	1978 SR [i]	1948-77
	1980	1971-79
	1981-1984	Dernière
	1985	1976-84
	1986-1991	Dernière
	1992	1983-92
	1993-1995	Dernière
	1996	1987-95
	1997	Dernière
	1997SR [ii]	1948-96
	1998-2007	Dernière
-selon l'âge et le sexe et la résidence (urbaine/rurale)	1967-1973	Dernière
	1974	1965-73
	1975-1979	Dernière
	1980	1971-79
	1981-1984	Dernière
	1985	1976-84
	1986-1991	Dernière
	1992	1983-92
	1993-1995	Dernière
	1996	1987-95
	1997	Dernière
	1997SR [ii]	1948-96
	1998-2006	Dernière
-selon la cause	1951	1947-50
	1952	1947-51 [iii]
	1953	Dernière
	1954	1945-53
	1955-1956	Dernière
	1957	1952-56
	1958-1960	Dernière
	1961	1955-60
	1962-1965	Dernière

Index
Index historique (suite)
(Voir notes à la fin de l'index)

Index
Index historique (suite)
(Voir notes à la fin de l'index)

Sujet	Année de l'édition	Période considérée	Sujet	Année de l'édition	Période considérée
	1956	1947-55	-estimatifs:		
	1957	1930-56	pour les continents	1949/50	1947
	1958	1948-57		1956-1977	Dernière
	1959	1949-58		1978-1979	1970-75
	1960	1950-59		1980-1983	1975-80
	1961	1945-59 [vi]		1984-1986	1980-85
		1952-61		1987-1992	1985-90
	1962	1945-54 [vi]		1993-1997	1990-95
		1952-62		1998-2000	1995-00
	1963	1945-59 [vi]		2001-2005	2000-05
		1954-63		2006-2007	2005-10
	1964	1960-64			
	1965	1961-65	pour les grandes		
	1966	1920-64 [vi]	régions (continentales)	1964-1977	Dernière
		1951-66		1978-1979	1970-75
	1967	1963-67		1980-1983	1975-80
	1968	1964-68		1984-1986	1980-85
	1969	1965-69		1987-1992	1985-90
	1970	1966-70		1993-1997	1990-95
	1971	1967-71		1998-2000	1995-00
	1972	1968-72		2001-2005	2000-05
	1973	1969-73		2006-2007	2005-10
	1974	1965-74			
	1975	1971-75	pour les régions	1949/50	1947
	1976	1972-76		1956-1977	Dernière
	1977	1973-77		1978-1979	1970-75
	1978	1974-78		1980-1983	1975-80
	1978SR [i]	1948-78		1984-1986	1980-85
	1979	1975-79		1987-1992	1985-90
	1980	1971-80		1993-1997	1990-95
	1981	1977-81		1998-2000	1995-00
	1982	1978-82		2001-2005	2000-05
	1983	1979-83		2006-2007	2005-10
	1984	1980-84			
	1985	1976-85	pour l'ensemble du		
	1986	1982-86	monde	1949/50	1947
	1987	1983-87		1956-1977	Dernière
	1988	1984-88		1978-1979	1970-75
	1989	1985-89		1980-1983	1975-80
	1990	1986-90		1984-1986	1980-85
	1991	1987-91		1987-1992	1985-90
	1992	1983-92		1993-1997	1990-95
	1993	1989-93		1998-2000	1995-00
	1994	1990-94		2001-2005	2000-05
	1995	1991-95		2006-2007	2005-10
	1996	1987-96			
	1997	1993-97	-selon l'âge et le sexe	1948	1935-47
	1997SR [ii]	1948-97		1949/50	1936-49
	1998	1994-98		1951	1936-50
	1999	1995-99		1952	1936-51
	2000	1996-00		1953	1940-52
	2001	1997-01		1954	1946-53
	2002	1998-02		1955-1956	Dernière
	2003	1999-03		1957	1948-56
	2004	2000-04		1961	1952-60
	2005	2001-05		1966	1950-65
	2006	2002-06		1967	Dernière
	2007	2003-07		1972	Dernière
				1974	1965-73
-d'enfants de moins d'un an				1975-1978	Dernière
(voir: Mortalités infantile)				1978SR [i]	1948-77
				1979	Dernière

Index
Index historique (suite)
(Voir notes à la fin de l'index)

Index
Index historique (suite)
(Voir notes à la fin de l'index)

Sujet	Année de l'édition	Période considérée
	1952-2004	Dernière
	2005	2005
	2006	2006
	2007	2007
-du monde	1949/50	1920-49
	1952-2004	Dernière
	2005	2005
	2006	2006
	2007	2007
Dimension de la famille vivante:		
-selon l'âge des femmes (voir également: Enfants)	1949-1950	Dernière
	1954	1930-53
	1955	1945-54
	1959	1949-58
	1963	1955-63
	1965	1955-65
	1968	1955-67
	1969	Dernière
	1971	1962-71
	1973	1965-73 [iii]
	1975	1965-74
	1978SR [i]	1948-77
	1981	1972-80
	1986	1977-85
	1997SR [ii]	1948-96
Divorces.....................	1951	1935-50
	1952	1936-51
	1953	1950-52
	1954	1946-53
	1955	1946-54
	1956	1947-55
	1957	1948-56
	1958	1940-57
	1959	1949-58
	1960	1950-59
	1961	1952-61
	1962	1953-62
	1963	1954-63
	1964	1960-64
	1965	1961-65
	1966	1962-66
	1967	1963-67
	1968	1949-68
	1969	1965-69
	1970	1966-70
	1971	1967-71
	1972	1968-72
	1973	1969-73
	1974	1970-74
	1975	1971-75
	1976	1957-76
	1977	1973-77
	1962	1953-62
	1963	1954-63
	1964	1960-64
	1965	1961-65

Sujet	Année de l'édition	Période considérée
	1966	1962-66
	1967	1963-67
	1968	1949-68
	1969	1965-69
	1970	1966-70
	1971	1967-71
	1972	1968-72
	1973	1969-73
	1974	1970-74
	1975	1971-75
	1976	1957-76
	1977	1973-77
	1978	1974-78
	1979	1975-79
	1980	1976-80
	1981	1977-81
	1982	1963-82
	1983	1979-83
	1984	1980-84
	1985	1981-85
	1986	1982-86
	1987	1983-87
	1988	1984-88
	1989	1985-89
	1990	1971-90
	1991	1987-91
	1992	1988-92
	1993	1989-93
	1994	1990-94
	1995	1991-95
	1996	1992-96
	1997	1993-97
	1998	1994-98
	1999	1995-99
	2000	1996-00
	2001	1997-01
	2002	1998-02
	2003	1999-03
	2004	2000-04
	2005	2001-05
	2006	2002-06
	2007	2003-07
-selon l'âge de l'épouse	1968	1958-67
	1976	1966-75
	1982	1972-81
	1987	1975-86
	1990	1980-89
-selon l'âge de l'épouse, classés par âge de l'époux	1958	1946-57
	1968	Dernière
	1976	Dernière
	1982	Dernière
	1990	Dernière
-selon l'âge de l'époux	1968	1958-67
	1976	1966-75
	1982	1972-81
	1987	1975-86
	1990	1980-89
-selon la durée du mariage	1958	1948-57
	1968	1958-67
	1976	1966-75

Index
Index historique (suite)
(Voir notes à la fin de l'index)

Index
Index historique (suite)
(Voir notes à la fin de l'index)

Sujet	Année de l'édition	Période considérée
Emigrants (voir: Migration internationale)		
Enfants, nombre:		
-dont il est tenu compte dans les divorces	1958	1948-57
	1968	1958-67
	1976	1966-75
	1982	1972-81
	1990	1980-89
-mis au monde, selon l'âge de la mère	1949/50	Dernière
	1954	1930-53
	1955	1945-54
	1959	1949-58
	1963	1955-63
	1965	1955-65
	1969	Dernière
	1971	1962-71
	1973	1965-73 [iii]
	1975	1965-74
	1978SR [i]	1948-77
	1981	1972-80
	1986	1977-85
	1997SR [ii]	1948-96
-vivants, selon l'âge de la mère	1940/50	Dernière
	1954	1930-53
	1955	1945-54
	1959	1949-58
	1963	1955-63
	1965	1955-65
	1968	1955-67
	1969	Dernière
	1971	1962-71
	1973	1965-73 [iii]
	1975	1965-74
	1978SR [i]	1948-77
	1981	1972-80
	1986	1977-85
	1997SR [ii]	1948-96
Espérance de vie (voir: Mortalité, tables de)		
Etat matrimonial (voir la rubrique appropriée par sujet, p.ex., Décès, Population, etc.)		

F

Sujet	Année de l'édition	Période considérée
Fécondité, indice synthétique de	1987-1997	Dernière
	1997SR [ii]	1948-96
	1998	1995-98
	1999	1996-99
	1999CD [vii]	1980-99
Fécondité proportionnelle	1949/50	1900-50
	1954	1900-52
	1955	1945-54
	1959	1935-59

Sujet	Année de l'édition	Période considérée
	1963	1955-63
	1965	1955-65
	1969	Dernière
	1975	1966-74
	1978SR [i]	1948-77
	1981	1962-80
	1986	1967-85
	1997SR [ii]	1948-96
	1999CD [vii]	1980-99
Fécondité, taux global de	1948	1936-47
	1949/50	1936-49
	1951	1936-50
	1952	1936-50
	1953	1936-52
	1954	1936-53
	1955-1956	Dernière
	1959	1949-58
	1960-1964	Dernière
	1965	1955-64
	1966-1974	Dernière
	1975	1966-74
	1976-1978	Dernière
	1978SR [i]	1948-77
	1979-1980	Dernière
	1981	1962-80
	1982-1985	Dernière
	1986	1977-85
	1987-1991	Dernière
	1992	1983-92
	1993-1997	Dernière
	1997SR [ii]	1948-96
	1998-2004	Dernière
	2005	2001-05
	2006	2002-06
	2007	2003-07

I

Sujet	Année de l'édition	Période considérée
Illégitime (voir également: Naissances et morts fœtales tardives):		
-morts fœtales tardives	1961	1952-60
	1965	5-Dernières
	1969	1963-68
	1975	1966-74
	1981	1972-80
	1986	1977-85
-morts fœtales tardives, rapports de	1961	1952-60
	1965	5-Dernières
	1969	1963-68
	1975	1966-74
	1981	1972-80
	1986	1977-85
-naissances	1959	1949-58
	1965	1955-64
	1969	1963-68
	1975	1966-74
	1981	1972-80
	1986	1977-85
	1999CD [vii]	1990-98

Index
Index historique (suite)
(Voir notes à la fin de l'index)

Index
Index historique (suite)
(Voir notes à la fin de l'index)

Index
Index historique (suite)
(Voir notes à la fin de l'index)

Index
Index historique (suite)
(Voir notes à la fin de l'index)

Index
Index historique (suite)
(Voir notes à la fin de l'index)

Sujet	Année de l'édition	Période considérée	Sujet	Année de l'édition	Période considérée
	1954	1938-53		2007	2003-07
	1955	1946-54			
	1956	1947-55	-illégitimes	1961	1952-60
	1957	1948-56		1965	5-Dernières
	1958	1948-57	-légitimes	1959	1949-58
	1959	1920-54 [vi]		1965	1955-64
		1953-58		1969	1963-68
	1960	1950-59		1975	1966-74
	1961	1945-49 [vi]		1981	1972-80
		1952-60		1986	1977-85
	1962	1945-54 [vi]	-légitimes selon l'âge de la mère		
		1952-61		1959	1949-58
	1963	1945-59 [vi]		1965	1955-64
		1953-62		1969	1963-68
	1964	1959-63		1975	1966-74
	1965	1950-64 [vi]		1981	1972-80
		1955-64		1986	1977-85
	1966	1950-64 [vi]	-selon l'âge de la mère	1954	1936-53
		1956-65		1959	1949-58
	1967	1962-66		1965	1955-64
	1968	1963-67		1969	1963-68
	1969	1950-64 [vi]		1975	1966-74
	1969	1959-68		1981	1972-80
	1970	1965-69		1986	1977-85
	1971	1966-70		1999CD [vii]	1990-98
	1972	1967-71	-selon l'âge de la mère et le rang de naissance		
	1973	1968-72		1954	Dernière
	1974	1965-73		1959	1949-58
	1975	1966-74		1965	3-Dernières
	1976	1971-75		1969	1963-68
	1977	1972-76		1975	1966-74
	1978	1973-77		1981	1972-80
	1979	1974-78		1986	1977-85
	1980	1971-79		1999CD [vii]	1990-98
	1981	1972-80	-selon la période de gestation		
	1982	1977-81		1957	1950-56
	1983	1978-82		1959	1949-58
	1984	1979-83		1961	1952-60
	1985	1975-84		1965	5-Dernières
	1986	1977-85		1966	1956-65
	1987	1982-86		1967-1968	Dernière
	1988	1983-87		1969	1963-68
	1989	1984-88		1974	1965-73
	1964	1959-63		1975	1966-74
	1990	1985-89		1980	1971-79
	1991	1986-90		1981	1972-80
	1992	1987-91		1985	1976-84
	1993	1988-92		1986	1977-85
	1994	1989-93		1996	1987-95
	1995	1990-94	-selon la résidence (urbaine/rurale)		
	1996	1987-95		1971	1966-70
	1997	1992-96		1972	1967-71
	1998	1993-97		1973	1968-72
	1999	1994-98		1974	1965-73
	1999CD [vii]	1990-98		1975	1966-74
	2000	1995-99		1976	1971-75
	2001	1997-01		1977	1972-76
	2002	1998-02		1978	1973-77
	2003	1999-03		1979	1974-78
	2004	2000-04		1980	1971-79
	2005	2001-05		1981	1972-80
	2006	2002-06		1982	1977-81

Index
Index historique (suite)
(Voir notes à la fin de l'index)

Sujet	Année de l'édition	Période considérée	Sujet	Année de l'édition	Période considérée
	1983	1978-82		1983	1979-83
	1984	1979-83		1984	1980-84
	1985	1975-84		1985	1976-85
	1986	1977-85		1986	1982-86
	1987	1982-86		1987	1983-87
	1988	1983-87		1988	1984-88
	1989	1984-88		1989	1985-89
	1990	1985-89		1990	1986-90
	1991	1986-90		1991	1987-91
	1992	1987-91		1992	1983-92
	1993	1988-92		1993	1989-93
	1994	1989-93		1994	1990-94
	1995	1990-94		1995	1991-95
	1996	1987-95		1996	1987-96
	1997	1992-96		1997	1993-97
	1998	1993-97		1997SR [ii]	1948-97
	1999	1994-98		1998	1994-98
	1999CD [vii]	1990-98		1999	1995-99
	2000	1995-99		2000	1996-00
	2001	1997-01		2001	1997-01
	2002	1998-02		2002	1998-02
	2003	1999-03		2003	1999-03
	2004	2000-04		2004	2000-04
	2005	2001-05		2005	2001-05
	2006	2002-06		2006	2002-06
	2007	2003-07		2007	2003-07
Mortalité infantile (nombres)	1948	1932-47	-selon l'âge et le sexe	1948	1936-47
	1949/50	1934-49		1951	1936-49
	1951	1935-50		1957	1948-56
	1952	1936-51		1961	1952-60
	1953	1950-52		1962-1965	Dernière
	1954	1946-53		1966	1956-65
	1955	1946-54		1967-1973	Dernière
	1956	1947-55		1974	1965-73
	1957	1948-56		1975-1979	Dernière
	1958	1948-57		1980	1971-79
	1959	1949-58		1981-1984	Dernière
	1960	1950-59		1985	1976-84
	1961	1952-61		1986-1991	Dernière
	1962	1953-62		1992	1983-92
	1963	1954-63		1993-1995	Dernière
	1964	1960-64		1996	1987-95
	1965	1961-65		1997-2004	Dernière
	1966	1947-66		2005	1996-05
	1967	1963-67		2006	Dernière
	1968	1964-68		2007	Dernière
	1969	1965-69			
	1970	1966-70	-selon l'âge et le sexe et la		
	1971	1967-71	résidence (urbaine/rurale)	1968-1973	Dernière
	1972	1968-72		1974	1965-73
	1973	1969-73		1975-1979	Dernière
	1974	1965-74		1980	1971-79
	1975	1971-75		1981-1984	Dernière
	1976	1972-76		1985	1976-84
	1977	1973-77		1986-1991	Dernière
	1978	1974-78		1992	1983-92
	1978SR [i]	1948-78		1993-1995	Dernière
	1979	1975-79		1996	1987-95
	1980	1971-80		1998-1999	Dernière
	1981	1977-81	-selon la résidence	1967	Dernière
	1982	1978-82			

Index
Index historique (suite)
(Voir notes à la fin de l'index)

Sujet	Année de l'édition	Période considérée		Sujet	Année de l'édition	Période considérée
(urbaine/rurale)	1968	1964-68			1961	1945-59 [vi]
	1969	1965-69				1952-61
	1970	1966-70			1962	1945-59 [vi]
	1971	1967-71				1952-62
	1972	1968-72			1963	1945-59 [vi]
	1973	1969-73				1954-63
	1974	1965-74			1964	1960-64
	1975	1971-75			1965	1961-65
	1976	1972-76			1966	1920-64 [vi]
	1977	1973-77				1951-66
	1978	1974-78			1967	1963-67
	1979	1975-79			1968	1964-68
	1980	1971-80			1969	1965-69
	1981	1977-81			1970	1966-70
	1982	1978-82			1971	1967-71
	1983	1979-83			1972	1968-72
	1984	1980-84			1973	1969-73
	1985	1976-85			1974	1965-74
	1986	1982-86			1975	1971-75
	1987	1983-87			1976	1972-76
	1988	1984-88			1977	1973-77
	1989	1985-89			1978	1974-78
	1990	1986-90			1978SR [i]	1948-78
	1991	1987-91			1979	1975-79
	1992	1983-92			1980	1971-80
	1993	1989-93			1981	1977-81
	1994	1990-94			1982	1978-82
	1995	1991-95			1983	1979-83
	1996	1987-96			1984	1980-84
	1997	1993-97			1985	1976-85
	1998	1994-98			1986	1982-86
	1999	1995-99			1987	1983-87
	2000	1996-00			1988	1984-88
	2001	1997-01			1989	1985-89
	2002	1998-02			1990	1986-90
	2003	1999-03			1991	1987-91
	2004	2000-04			1992	1983-92
	2005	2001-05			1993	1989-93
	2006	2002-06			1994	1990-94
	2007	2003-07			1995	1991-95
-selon le mois	1967	1962-66			1996	1987-96
	1974	1965-73			1997	1993-97
	1980	1971-79			1997SR [ii]	1948-97
	1985	1976-84			1998	1994-98
					1999	1995-99
Mortalité infantile, taux de	1948	1932-47			2000	1996-00
	1949/50	1932-49			2001	1997-01
	1951	1930-50			2002	1998-02
	1952	1920-34 [vi]			2003	1999-03
		1934-51			2004	2000-04
	1953	1920-39 [vi]			2005	2001-05
		1940-52			2006	2002-06
	1954	1920-39 [vi]			2007	2003-07
		1946-53		-selon l'âge et le sexe	1948	1936-47
	1955	1920-34 [vi]			1951	1936-49
		1946-54			1957	1948-56
	1956	1947-55			1961	1952-60
	1957	1948-56			1966	1956-65
	1958	1948-57			1997-2007	Dernière
	1959	1949-58				
	1960	1950-59		-selon l'âge et le sexe et la	1971-1973	Dernière

Index
Index historique (suite)
(Voir notes à la fin de l'index)

Index
Index historique (suite)
(Voir notes à la fin de l'index)

Index
Index historique (suite)
(Voir notes à la fin de l'index)

Index
Index historique (suite)
(Voir notes à la fin de l'index)

Index
Index historique (suite)
(Voir notes à la fin de l'index)

Sujet	Année de l'édition	Période considérée
	2006-2007	2005-10
pour les grandes régions (continentales)	1964-1977	Dernière
	1978-1970	1970-75
	1980-1983	1975-80
	1984-1986	1980-85
	1987-1992	1985-90
	1993-1997	1990-95
	1998-2000	1995-00
	2001-2005	2000-05
	2006-2007	2005-10
pour les régions	1949/50	1947
	1956-1977	Dernière
	1978-1979	1970-75
	1980-1983	1975-80
	1984-1986	1980-85
	1987-1992	1985-90
	1993-1997	1990-95
	1998-2000	1995-00
	2001-2005	2000-05
	2006-2007	2005-10
pour l'ensemble du monde	1949/50	1947
	1956-1977	Dernière
	1978-1979	1970-75
	1980-1983	1975-80
	1984-1986	1980-85
	1987-1992	1985-90
	1993-1997	1990-95
	1998-2000	1995-00
	2001-2005	2000-05
	2006-2007	2005-10
-selon l'âge et le sexe	1948	1935-47
	1949/50	1936-49
	1951	1936-50
	1952	1936-51
	1953	1940-52
	1954	1946-53
	1955-1956	Dernière
	1957	1948-1956
	1961	1952-60
	1966	1950-65
	1978SR [i]	1948-77
	1998-2007	Dernière
-selon l'âge et le sexe et la résidence (urbaine/rurale)	1967	Dernière
	1972	Dernière
	1974	1965-73
	1975-1978	Dernière
	1979	Dernière
	1980	1971-79
	1981-1984	Dernière
	1985	1976-84
	1986-1991	Dernière
	1991 VP [v]	1950-90
	1992	1983-92

Sujet	Année de l'édition	Période considérée
	1993-1995	Dernière
	1996	1987-95
	1997	Dernière
	1997SR [ii]	1948-96
	1998-2007	Dernière
-selon la cause	1951	1947-49
	1952	1947-51 [iii]
	1953	1947-52
	1954	1945-53
	1955-1956	Dernière
	1957	1952-56
	1958-1960	Dernière
	1961	1955-60
	1962-1965	Dernière
	1966	1960-65
	1967-1973	Dernière
	1974	1965-73
	1975-1979	Dernière
	1980	1971-79
	1981-1984	Dernière
	1985	1976-84
	1986-1991	Dernière
	1991 VP [v]	1960-90
	1992-1995	Dernière
	1996	1987-95
	1997-2000	Dernière
	2002	1995-02
	2004	1995-04
	2006	2002-06
-selon la cause, l'âge et le sexe	1957	Dernière
	1961	Dernière
	1991 VP [v]	1960-90
-selon la cause et le sexe	1967	Dernière
	1974	Dernière
	1980	Dernière
	1985	Dernière
	1991 VP [v]	1960-90
	1996	Dernière
-selon l'état matrimonial, l'âge et le sexe	1961	Dernière
	1967	Dernière
	1974	Dernière
	1980	Dernière
	1985	Dernière
	1996	Dernière
	2003	Dernière
-selon la profession, l'âge et le sexe	1957	Dernière
-selon la profession et l'âge (sexe masculin)	1961	Dernière
	1967	Dernière
-selon la résidence (urbaine/rurale)	1967	Dernière
	1968	1964-68
	1969	1965-69
	1970	1966-70
	1971	1967-71
	1972	1968-72
	1973	1969-73

Index
Index historique (suite)
(Voir notes à la fin de l'index)

Index
Index historique (suite)
(Voir notes à la fin de l'index)

Index
Index historique (suite)
(Voir notes à la fin de l'index)

Index
Index historique (suite)
(Voir notes à la fin de l'index)

Index
Index historique (suite)
(Voir notes à la fin de l'index)

Index
Index historique (suite)
(Voir notes à la fin de l'index)

Index
Index historique (suite)
(Voir notes à la fin de l'index)

Index
Index historique (suite)
(Voir notes à la fin de l'index)

Index
Index historique (suite)
(Voir notes à la fin de l'index)

Index
Index historique (suite)
(Voir notes à la fin de l'index)

Index
Index historique (suite)
(Voir notes à la fin de l'index)

Index
Index historique (suite)
(Voir notes à la fin de l'index)

Index
Index historique (suite)
(Voir notes à la fin de l'index)

Index
Index historique (suite)
(Voir notes à la fin de l'index)

Index
Index historique (suite)
(Voir notes à la fin de l'index)

Index
Index historique (suite)
(Voir notes à la fin de l'index)

Index
Index historique (suite)
(Voir notes à la fin de l'index)

Sujet	Année de l'édition	Période considérée
	1976	1967-76
	1977	1968-77
	1978	1969-78
	1979	1970-79
	1980	1971-80
	1981	1972-81
	1982	1973-82
	1983	1974-83
	1984	1975-84
	1985	1976-85
	1986	1977-86
	1987	1978-87
	1988	1979-88
	1989	1980-89
	1990	1981-90
	1991	1982-91
	1992	1983-92
	1993	1984-93
	1994	1985-94
	1995	1986-95
	1996	1987-96
	1997	1988-97
	1998	1989-98
	1999	1990-99
	2000	1991-00
	2001	1992-01
	2002	1993-02
	2003	1994-03
	2004	1995-04
	2005	1996-05
	2006	1997-06
	2007	1998-07
féminine: selon le nombre total d'enfants nés vivants et l'âge	1971	1962-71
	1973	1965-73 [iii]
	1975	1965-74
	1978SR [i]	1948-77
	1981	1972-80
	1986	1977-85
	1997SR [ii]	1948-96
féminine: selon le nombre total d'enfants vivants et l'âge	1971	1962-71
	1973	1965-73 [iii]
	1975	1965-74
	1978SR [i]	1948-77
	1981	1972-80
	1986	1977-85
	1997SR [ii]	1948-96
fréquentant l'école selon l'âge et le sexe	1971	1962-71
	1973	1965-73 [iii]
	1979	1970-79 [iii]
	1983	1974-83
	1988	1980-88 [iii]
	1988	1980-88 [iii]
	1993	1985-93
par année d'âge et par sexe	1971	1962-71
	1973	1965-73 [iii]

Sujet	Année de l'édition	Période considérée
	1979	1970-79 [iii]
	1983	1974-83
	1993	1985-93
selon la situation familiale selon l'âge et le sexe:	1991 VP [v]	Dernière
dénombrée	1963	1955-63
	1964	1955-64 [iii]
	1967	Dernière
	1970	1950-70
	1971	1962-71
	1972	Dernière
	1973	1965-73
	1974-78	Dernière
	1978SR [i]	1948-77
	1979-91	Dernière
	1991VP [v]	1950-90
	1992-97	Dernière
	1997SR [ii]	1948-97
	1998-2007	Dernière
selon l'âge et le sexe: estimée	1963	Dernière
	1967	Dernière
	1970	1950-70
	1971-1997	Dernière
	1997SR [ii]	1948-97
	1998-05	Dernière
selon l'alphabétisme, l'âge et le sexe	1971	1962-71
	1973	1965-73 [iii]
	1979	1970-79 [iii]
	1983	1974-83
	1988	1980-88 [iii]
	1993	1985-93
selon la composition ethnique et le sexe	1971	1962-71
	1973	1965-73 [iii]
	1979	1970-79 [iii]
	1983	1974-83
	1988	1980-88 [iii]
	1993	1985-93
	1971	1962-71
selon l'état matrimonial, l'âge et le sexe	1971	1962-71
	1973	1965-73 [iii]
selon la langue et le sexe	1971	1962-71
	1973	1965-73 [iii]
	1979	1970-79 [iii]
	1983	1974-83
	1988	1980-88 [iii]
	1993	1985-93
selon la nationalité juridique et le sexe	1971	1962-71
	1973	1965-73 [iii]
selon la nationalité juridique et le sexe et l'âge	1977	Dernière
	1983	1974-83
	1989	1980-88
selon le niveau d'instruction, l'âge et le sexe	1971	1962-71
	1973	1965-73 [iii]

Index
Index historique (suite)
(Voir notes à la fin de l'index)

Index
Index historique (suite)
(Voir notes à la fin de l'index)

Index
Index historique (suite)
(Voir notes à la fin de l'index)

Index
Index historique (suite)
(Voir notes à la fin de l'index)

APPENDICE

Texte spécial de chaque Annuaire démographique

Divorce:

"Application des statistiques de la nuptialité et de la divortialité", 1958.

Mariage:

"Application des statistiques de la nuptialité et de la divortialité", 1958.

Ménages:

"Concepts et définitions des ménages, du chef de ménage et de la population des collectivités", 1987.

Migration:

"'Statistiques des migrations internationales",1977.

Mortalité:

"Tendances récentes de la mortalité", 1951.
"Développement des statistiques des causes de décès",1951.
"Les facteurs du fléchissement de la mortalité",1957.
"Notes sur les méthodes d'évaluation de la fiabilité des statistiques classiques de la mortalité",1961.
"Mortalité: Tendances récentes",1966.
"Tendances de la mortalité chez les personnes âgées",1991VP [v].

Natalité:

"Présentation graphiques des tendances de la fécondité",1959.

"Taux de natalité: Tendances récentes",1965.

Population:

"Tendances démo-graphiques mondiales,1920-1949",1949/50.
"Mouvements d'urbanisation et ses caractéristiques",1952.
"Les recensements de population de 1950",1955.
"Situation démographique mondiale",1956.
"Ce que nous savons de l'état et de l'évolution de la population mondiale",1960.
"Notes sur les statistiques disponibles des recensements nationaux de population et méthodes d'évaluation de leur exactitude",1962.
"Disponibilité et qualité de certaines données statistiques fondées sur les recensements de population effectués entre 1955 et 1963",1963.
"Disponibilité de certaines statistiques fondées sur les recensements de population: 1955-1964",1964.

"Définitions et concepts statistiques de la population urbaine et de la population rurale",1967.
"Application des statistiques de la nuptialité et de la divortialité",1958.
"Ce que nous savons de l'état et de l'évolution de la population mondiale",1970.
"Recommandations de l'Organisation des Nations Unies quant aux sujets sur lesquels doit porter un recensement de population, en regard de la pratique adoptée par les différents pays dans les recensements nationaux effectués de 1965 à 1971",1971.
"Les définitions statistiques de la population urbaine et leurs usages en démographie appliquée",1972.

"Evolution récente de la fécondité dans le monde",1969.
"Dates des recensements nationaux de la population et de l'habitation effectués au cours de la décennie

Index
Index historique (suite)
(Voir notes à la fin de l'index)

1965-1974", 1974.

"Dates des recensements nationaux de la population et de l'habitation effectués ou prévus, au cours de la décennie 1975-1984",1979.

"Dates des recensements nationaux de la population et/ou de l'habitation effectués au cours de la décennie 1965-1974 et effectués ou prévus au cours de la décennie1975-1984",1983.

"Définitions et concepts statistiques du ménage",1968.

"Dates des recensements nationaux de la population et/ou de l'habitation effectués au cours de la décennie 1975-1984 et effectués ou prévus au cours de la décennie1985-1994", 1988, 1993.

"Statistiques concernant la population active: un aperçu",1984.

"'Etude du vieillissement et de la situation des personnes âgées: Besoins particuliers",1991VP [v].

"Les incapacités", 1991VP [v].

"Le vieillissement", 1991VP [v].

Notes générales

Cet index alphabétique donne la liste des sujets traités dans chacune de 51 éditions de l'Annuaire démographique. La colonne "Année de l'édition" indique l'édition spécifique dans laquelle le sujet a été traité. Sauf indication contraire, la colonne "Période considérée" désigne les années pour lesquelles les statistiques annuelles apparaissant dans l'Annuaire démographique sont indiquées sous la colonne "Année de l'édition". La rubrique "Dernière" ou " 2-Dernières" indique que les données représentent la ou les dernières années disponibles seulement.

[i] Le Supplément rétrospectif du 30ème Annuaire Démographique fait l'objet d'un tirage spécial publié en 1979.

[ii] Le Supplément rétrospectif du 49ème Annuaire Démographique fait l'objet d'un tirage spécial (CD-ROM) publié en 2000

[iii] Données non disponibles dans l'édition précédente seulement.

[iv] Titres non disponibles dans la bibliographie précédente seulement.

[v] Taux moyens pour 5 ans.

[vi] Vieillissement de la population.

[vii] Le Supplément du 51 Annuaire Démographique, ayant comme suject la natalité, fait l'objet d'un tirage spécial (CD-ROM) publié en 2002.